The Palgrave Handbook of Economics and Language

The Palgrave Handbook of Economics and Language

Edited by

Victor Ginsburgh

and

Shlomo Weber

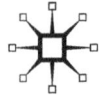
First published 2016 by
PALGRAVE MACMILLAN

Palgrave Macmillan in the UK is an imprint of Macmillan Publishers Limited,
registered in England, company number 785998, of Houndmills, Basingstoke,
Hampshire RG21 6XS.

Palgrave Macmillan in the US is a division of St Martin's Press LLC,
175 Fifth Avenue, New York, NY 10010.

Palgrave Macmillan is the global academic imprint of the above companies
and has companies and representatives throughout the world.

Palgrave® and Macmillan® are registered trademarks in the United States,
the United Kingdom, Europe and other countries.

ISBN 978–1–137–32504–4

This book is printed on paper suitable for recycling and made from fully
managed and sustained forest sources. Logging, pulping and manufacturing
processes are expected to conform to the environmental regulations of the
country of origin.

A catalogue record for this book is available from the British Library.

A catalog record for this book is available from the Library of Congress.

Contents

Part IV   Globalization and Minority Languages

20   English as a Global Language   583
Jacques Melitz

21   Challenges of Minority Languages   616
François Grin

22   Language Rights: A Welfare-Economics Approach   659
Bengt-Arne Wickström

23   A Game-Theoretic Analysis of Minority Language Use in Multilingual Societies   689
José-Ramón Uriarte

Figures and Tables

Figures

Tables

Contributors

Alícia Adserà is a research scholar and lecturer at the Woodrow Wilson School, Princeton University, and a faculty affiliate at the Office of Population Research. She is a research fellow at IZA and CreAM. Previously she was an associate professor at the University of Illinois, Chicago, and a research affiliate at the Population Research Center of the University of Chicago. Her interests are in economic demography, development and migration. She works on the role of economic conditions in fertility decisions as well as several migration topics such as returns to language, welfare drivers of migration flows and labour market progression. She is a recipient of fellowships from the University of Chicago-NICHD, the Alfred P. Sloan Foundation, the Government of Catalonia and the Bank of Spain. Her work has appeared in the *American Economic Review P&P*, *Economic Journal*, *Journal of Population Economics*, *Population Studies*, *Journal of Law, Economics and Organization* and *International Organization*, among others. She holds a PhD in economics from Boston University.

Efthymios Athanasiou is Assistant Professor of Economics at the New Economic School in Moscow, Russia. He holds a PhD in economics from the Centre for Operations Research and Econometrics (CORE) at the Université catholique de Louvain. Before his current appointment he was the Herb Simon Fellow in Scientific Philosophy at the Department of Philosophy, Carnegie Mellon University. His publication record includes papers in *Games and Economic Behavior*, *Social Choice Welfare* and *Mind*.

Wilhelm Barner-Rasmussen is Director of the Doctoral Programme and Head of Research Services at the Hanken School of Economics, Helsinki, Finland. He is also a research affiliate at the Department of Management and Organization at Hanken, as well as Adjunct Professor of International Business at Aalto University School of Business. Language in international management is a key theme of his research, an area within which he takes a particular interest in individual-level implications of variations in language skill. He has published on this topic in both practitioner-oriented and academic outlets including *Corporate Communications: An International Journal*, *Journal of International Business Studies*, *Journal of World Business* and *Management and Organization Review*. He has also co-organized a number of scholarly events on the theme of language, ranging from workshops for invited participants to tracks and symposia at leading international conferences such as the Academy of Management and EGOS.

Niall Bond is Reader in Languages and a researcher in intellectual history at the University of Lyons, a translator of books and articles and a conference interpreter.

Brandon de la Cuesta is a PhD candidate at Princeton University. His research focuses on electoral behaviour and corruption in Africa. His dissertation investigates the reputational effects of campaign strategies for voters. Additional research interests include the resource course and information-accountability interventions.

Klaus Desmet is the Altshuler Centennial Interdisciplinary Professor of Cities, Regions and Globalization at Southern Methodist University and a research fellow at the Centre for Economic Policy Research. He holds an MSc in business and engineering from the Université catholique de Louvain and a PhD in economics from Stanford University. He previously was a professor at Universidad Carlos III de Madrid. His research focuses on regional economics, international trade, economic growth and diversity. In 2010 he was awarded the August Lösch Prize, together with Esteban Rossi-Hansberg, for his contributions to regional science. His work has appeared in journals such as the *American Economic Review*, *Journal of Economic Theory* and *Journal of Development Economics*.

Peter H. Egger is Professor of Economics at the Department of Management, Technology and Economics, ETH Zurich, Switzerland. He is also a research coordinator of the Global Economy Area of CESifo, Munich, Germany; a fellow of the CEPR, London, UK; and an external research fellow of the Oxford Centre for Business Taxation at the Said Business School. Oxford University, the Norwegian Center of Taxation at the Norwegian School of Economics at Bergen, the Leverhulme Centre of Globalization and Economic Policy at University of Nottingham and the Federal Reserve Bank at Dallas. He is Editor-in-Chief of the *Review of International Economics* and serves on a number of boards of other international journals. He has published widely in international outlets with a general audience and with a specific orientation towards the fields of international economics, public economics, regional economics and econometrics.

Nigel Fabb is Professor of Literary Linguistics at the University of Strathclyde, UK. He holds a PhD in linguistics from MIT. He is the author of ten books on linguistics and literature, was editor of the *Journal of Linguistics* from 1997 to 2014, and from 2014 to 2017 holds a Leverhulme Major Research Fellowship to study the literary-linguistics and psychology of the sublime.

Victor Ginsburgh is Honorary Professor of Economics at the University of Brussels. He has written and edited several books and is the author of numerous papers in applied and theoretical economics, including industrial organization and general equilibrium analysis. His recent work includes economics of the arts (music, literature and the visual arts), wines and languages. His work has appeared in the *American Economic Review, Journal of Political Economy, Games and Economic Behavior, Journal of Economic Perspectives, Economic Journal, Journal of the European Economic Association, Empirical Studies of the Arts, Journal of Cultural Economics* and *Journal of Wine Economics.* His most recent books include *Handbook of the Economics of Art and Culture* (2006, 2013 with D. Throsby) and *How Many Languages Do We Need?* (2011, with S. Weber).

François Grin is Full Professor of Economics at the Faculty of Translation and Interpreting of the University of Geneva. His research focuses on language economics and language policy evaluation, with a strong interdisciplinary orientation. He is the author of numerous publications in these areas, including *The Economics of the Multilingual Workplace* (2010, with C. Sfreddo and F. Vaillancourt). He has worked as a consultant or advisor on language policy issues for national or regional authorities, as well as for international organizations. He has supervised several large-scale research projects on various aspects of language policy, and is currently the coordinator of the MIME (Mobility and Inclusion in Multilingual Europe) project financed by the European Commission.

Dietmar Harhoff is Director at the Max Planck Institute for Innovation and Competition. At the Ludwig-Maximilian-University Munich (LMU), where he was Director of the Institute for Innovation Research, Technology Management and Entrepreneurship (INNO-tec), he is Honorary Professor of Entrepreneurship and Innovation as well as Director of the LMU Entrepreneurship Center, and, in 2014, also took over the Research Center for Entrepreneurship and Innovation. His research focuses on issues in innovation and entrepreneurship, intellectual property and industrial economics. His research results have been published in a large number of books and journal articles. In addition to advising several public and private organizations, he is the Chairman of the Commission of Experts for Research and Innovation (EFI) of the German Federal Government and an elected member of the German Academy of Science and Engineering (acatech), the German National Academy of Sciences Leopoldina and the Royal Bavarian Academy of Sciences.

Johan Heilbron is a historical sociologist, trained at the University of Amsterdam and the EHESS in Paris, and currently Director of Research at the CNRS and a member of the Centre Européen de Sociologie et de Science

Politique (CESSP-CNRS-EHESS). He is also affiliated with the Erasmus Center for Economic Sociology (ECES) at Erasmus University in Rotterdam. His research concerns the development of the social sciences, economic organizations and institutions, and transnational exchange and cultural globalization. His publications include *The Rise of Social Theory* (1995), *The Rise of the Social Sciences and the Formation of Modernity* (co-edited, 2001), *Pour une histoire des sciences sociales: hommage à Pierre Bourdieu* (co-edited, 2004), *Wetenschappelijk onderzoek: dilemma's en verleidingen* (2005) and *French Sociology* (2015).

Karin Hoisl is Full Professor and holder of the Chair of Organization and Innovation at the University of Mannheim, Germany. Since November 2014 she has held a part-time professorship in the Economics and Management of Inventive Processes at Copenhagen Business School, Department of Innovation and Organizational Economics. Between March 2015 and September 2015 she held a Minerva Fast Track Position (W2) at the Max Planck Institute for Innovation and Competition. Between January 2011 and February 2015 she was Junior Professor of Invention Processes and Intellectual Property at LMU, Germany. She conducts empirical research in innovation, entrepreneurship and IP strategy. Her work has appeared in *Management Science, Organization Science, Strategic Management Journal* and *Research Policy*.

Nigel Holden has been a visiting research fellow at the Centre of International Business of Leeds University Business School since 2011, having held professorships at business schools in the UK, Denmark and Germany. A widely travelled management researcher, educator and keynote speaker, he has published extensively in a wide range of international management fields with special reference to cross-cultural management in the global knowledge economy, translation in international business, global talent management and business history. He is the senior consulting editor of the *Routledge Companion for Cross-Cultural Management* (2015).

Andrew John is Associate Professor of Economics at Melbourne Business School, University of Melbourne. He holds a PhD in economics from Yale University (1988). He has held academic appointments at Michigan State University, the University of Virginia and INSEAD. He has also held visiting appointments at the University of Michigan, the Helsinki School of Economics and Business Administration, and the University of Texas at Austin. His research interests, in addition to the economics of language, include coordination games, macroeconomic models with state-dependent pricing and consumer boycotts. His research has appeared in the *American Economic Review, Economic Journal, Journal of Marketing, Journal of Monetary Economics, Management Science, Quarterly Journal of Economics* and *Sloan Management Review*. He is also co-author of *Economics: Theory Through Applications* (2011, with Russell Cooper).

Denis V. Kadochnikov is an associate professor at the Faculty of Liberal Arts and Sciences of St Petersburg State University, Russia, and a senior research fellow of the International Centre for Social and Economic Research – Leontief Centre, Russia. His recent research focuses on various aspects of the political economy, economics of language and language policy, as well as the history of economic thought.

Mark Leikin is a professor in the Departments of Special Education and Learning Disabilities at the University of Haifa. He is the Director of the Research Laboratory for Neurocognitive Examination of Giftedness and editor of the journal *Issues in Special Education and Inclusion*. His research focuses on bilingual language acquisition and processing, language components in normal and abnormal reading processes, and neurocognition of general and mathematical giftedness.

Jacques Melitz is Professor Emeritus of Economics at Heriot-Watt University in Edinburgh and a visiting researcher at CREST, where he was for many years a regular member, and at CEPII. Both CREST and CEPII are in Paris. He has published widely on international macroeconomics, monetary economics, the history of thought and the economics of language, and has written a book on primitive money.

Juan D. Moreno-Ternero is an associate professor at the Department of Economics, University Pablo de Olavide, Seville, and a research associate at CORE, Université catholique de Louvain. He holds a PhD in economics from the University of Alicante and was a postdoctoral fellow at the Department of Political Science, Yale University, and at CORE, Université catholique de Louvain. His work has appeared in *Econometrica*, *Games and Economic Behavior*, *Social Choice and Welfare* and the *Journal of Health Economics*. He has acted as principal investigator of competitive research projects funded by the Spanish government since 2009. He has given more than 60 invited talks at universities worldwide, and contributed to more than 100 international conferences. He currently serves as associate editor of *Economic Theory*, *Mathematical Social Sciences* and the *Journal of the Spanish Economic Association*.

Ignacio Ortuño-Ortín is Professor of Economics at Universidad Carlos III de Madrid. He holds a PhD in economics from the University of California, Davis. His research interests focus on political economy, public economics, intergenerational social mobility and cultural diversity. His work has appeared in the

Journal of Public Economics, Journal of the European Economic Association, PlosOne and the *Journal of Development Economics*.

Mariola Pytliková is an assistant professor at CERGE-EI and a senior researcher at VŠB Technical University Ostrava. Previously she worked as a senior researcher at the Danish Institute of Governmental Research (KORA), and as an assistant professor and postdoctoral researcher at Aarhus University. She holds a PhD in economics from Aarhus University. She is a research fellow at IZA, CReAM and CELSI. She received the Kateřina Šmídková Award in 2015 and came second in the 2005 Young Economist competition from the Czech Economic Society. Her research interests are in the field of labour economics and industrial relations, in particular topics dealing with international migration and ethnic diversity, gender differentials and income inequality. Her work has appeared in the *Economic Journal, European Economic Review, Journal of Population Economics, European Journal of Population, Economics of Transition* and *Labor,* among others.

Gisèle Sapiro is Professor of Sociology at the École des hautes études en sciences sociales and is Research Director at the CNRS. Her interests include the sociology of intellectuals, of literature and of translation. She is the author of *La Guerre des écrivains, 1940–1953* (1999; translated as *The French Writers' War,* 2014), *La Responsabilité de l'écrivain. Littérature, droit et morale en France* (2011) and *La Sociologie de la littérature* (2014). She has also edited or co-edited *Pour une histoire des sciences sociales* (2004), *Pierre Bourdieu, sociologue* (2004), *Translatio. Le marché de la traduction en France à l'heure de la mondialisation* (2008), *Les Contradictions de la globalisation éditoriale* (2009), *L'Espace intellectuel en Europe* (2009), *Traduire la littérature et les sciences humaines: conditions et obstacles* (2012) and *Sciences humaines en traduction* (2014).

Andrew D. M. Smith is Lecturer in Language Studies at the University of Stirling. He holds a PhD in language evolution from the University of Edinburgh. His main research interests are in evolutionary and cognitive linguistics, focusing in particular on grammaticalization, the inferential sociocultural and cognitive bases of communication, metaphor, cultural evolution and word learning mechanisms. His most recent book is the edited collection *New Directions in Grammaticalization Research* (2015, with Graeme Trousdale and Richard Waltereit).

Selma K. Sonntag is a professor in the Department of Politics at Humboldt State University, California, and Chair of the Research Committee on the Politics of Language (RC50) of the International Political Science Association. She has published extensively in the field of language politics and comparative politics.

Her 2003 publication, *The Local Politics of Global English: Case Studies in Linguistic Globalization*, spawned a number of interventions and publications on the role of English in the international arena. Her 2015 volume, *State Traditions and Language Regimes*, co-edited with Linda Cardinal, contributes to the dialogue between applied linguistics and political science.

Enrico Spolaore is Professor of Economics at Tufts University and a research associate at the National Bureau of Economic Research. He holds a PhD in economics from Harvard University, and economics degrees from the University of Rome and the University of Siena. His main research interests are in political economy, economic growth and development, and international economics. His work has appeared in the *American Economic Review, Quarterly Journal of Economics, Review of Economic Studies, European Economic Review* and *Journal of Economic Growth*. He is also co-author of *The Size of Nations* (2003, with A. Alesina) and editor of the two-volume collection *Culture and Economic Growth* (2014).

Susanne Tietze is Professor of Management at Keele Management School, Keele University, UK. Her research focuses on the investigation of discursive practices in organizational settings, which have included themes of work–life balance, workplace flexibility, organizational change and communication processes. She has also researched the role of English as the dominant language of management knowledge and the use of languages in international work contexts. She is currently involved in a project that uses the conceptual lens of translation to explore multilingual communities and in particular the agency of translators and interpreters in collective sense-making processes. She has recently been co-editor of special issues about languages in international management for the *Journal of World Business* and *Journal of International Business Studies*.

Farid Toubal is Professor of Economics at Ecole Normale Supérieur of Cachan. He is also an associate professor at Paris School of Economics, Scientific Advisor at CEPII, the French research centre in international economics, a CESifo Research Network member (Munich, Germany) and a member of the steering committee of the research and policy laboratory of the French Public Investment Bank (BPIFrance le LAB). His work focuses on international economics, macroeconomics and cultural economics. With Jacques Melitz, he created a new public dataset on official, native and spoken languages across countries.

José-Ramón Uriarte is Professor of Economics at the University of the Basque Country. He is the Director of the Bilbao Laboratory of Experimental Analysis

(Bilbao LABEAN). His research interests are in minority language economics, modelling bounded rationality, experimental and behavioural economics. His work has appeared in *Advances in Complex Systems*, *Mathematical Social Sciences*, *Social Choice and Welfare*, *Journal of Risk and Uncertainty*, *Journal of Evolutionary Economics*, *JEBO*, *Review of Economic Design* and *Theory and Decisions*, among other journals.

Bruno van Pottelsberghe de la Potterie is Dean of the Solvay Brussels School of Economics and Management (SBS-EM) at the Université Libre de Bruxelles. He is Full Professor and, as holder of the Solvay S.A. Chair of Innovation, he teaches courses on the economics and management of innovation and intellectual property. He was Chief Economist of the European Patent Office (EPO) from 2005 to 2007. He has been advisor to the President and Rector of the ULB for technology transfer issues since 2004 and is a non-resident research fellow at Bruegel, a Brussels-based think tank, since 2007. His research focuses on patent systems, the valuation of patents and the role of IPRs. His work has appeared in *Research Policy*, *Journal of Public Economics* and *Industrial and Corporate Change*.

Charlotte Vandeput is a doctoral student at the International Centre for Innovation, Technology and Education Studies (iCite) of the Solvay Brussels School of Economics and Management, Université Libre de Bruxelles. Her research focuses on patent portfolio management and valuation.

Romain Wacziarg is Professor of Economics at the UCLA Anderson School of Management, and a research associate at the National Bureau of Economic Research. He holds a PhD from Harvard University, and was previously a professor at the Stanford Graduate School of Business. His research is concerned with the determinants of economic development, with a focus on institutional, cultural and demographic factors. His papers have appeared in the *American Economic Review*, *Quarterly Journal of Economics*, *Journal of Economic Growth*, *Journal of Development Economics*, *Journal of Public Economics* and *Journal of International Economics*.

Leonard Wantchekon is a professor in the Politics Department and associate faculty in the Economics Department, Princeton University. His research is broadly focused on political and economic development, particularly in Africa and his specific interests include topics such as democratization, clientelism and redistributive politics, resource curse and the long-term social impact of historical events. He is the author of numerous publications in leading academic journals and a member of the American Academy of Arts and Sciences and of the Executive Committee of the Council for International Teaching and Research at Princeton. He served as the Secretary of the American Political

Science Association (2008–09) and on the Ibrahim Index Technical Committee (2009–13). Finally, he is a core partner director at the Afrobarometer Network and the founder of the Africa School of Economics (ASE).

Shlomo Weber is Robert H. and Nancy Dedman Trustee Professor of Economics at Southern Methodist University, Dallas, and Leading Scientist at the Center for Study of Diversity and Social Interactions, New Economic School, Moscow. He holds a PhD from the Hebrew University of Jerusalem. He served as the Chairman of the Department of Economics at SMU, the Research Director of CORE at the Catholic University of Louvain, Belgium, and the Academic Director of the International School of Economics, Tbilisi, Georgia. He served as a member of the Executive Committee of the Board of Directors of GDN (Global Development Network) and of the International Advisory Board of EERC (Economic Education Research Consortium). His interests focus on documentation, measurement and impact of societal diversity and social interactions in heterogeneous societies. He is the co-author of *How Many Languages Do We Need? Economics of Linguistic Diversity* (2011, with Victor Ginsburgh). He also co-edited *The Oxford Handbook of the Russian Economy* (2013, with Michael Alexeev).

Bengt-Arne Wickström was Professor of Public Economics at Universität zu Berlin from 1992 until his retirement in 2013. He holds a PhD from the State University of New York at Stony Brook and held positions at Northwestern University, the Norwegian School of Economics and Business Administration (NHH), the University of Bergen, and Johannes-Kepler-Universität Linz. Since his retirement he has been Herder Professor at Andrássy-Universität Budapest. He has published in the field of public economics with special reference to public-choice theory, welfare economics and economic theories of justice. Lately, his work has been concentrated on various aspects of language economics.

Sue Wright is a research professor in the Centre for European and International Studies Research at the University of Portsmouth. She is the author of several books on the political context of language spread, including *Community and Communication* (2000) and *Language Policy and Language Planning* (2004). She is co-editor (with Helen Kelly Holmes) of the Palgrave book series *Language and Globalisation* and co-editor (with Ulrich Ammon and Jeroen Darquennes) of the journal *Sociolinguistica*.

Introduction

Victor Ginsburgh and Shlomo Weber

The origin of *economics of language* as a discipline is often credited to prominent economist Jacob Marschak (1965), whose interest in languages was
perhaps aided by his command of ten languages. Marshack was the first to
introduce explicitly the concept of costs and benefits into linguistic analysis. Some other early contributions (for example, Pool, 1972; Breton, 1978;
McManus et al., 1978; Grenier, 1984) notwithstanding, the impact of language
on social, political and economic outcomes was mainly the territory of linguists and sociolinguists, political scientists, anthropologists and psychologists.
Vaillancourt's (1982/1983) paper 'The Economics of Language and Language
Planning' contains 37 references of which more than half were concerned with
Quebec's linguistic problems. In his conclusion, he notes that '[t]he main goal
of this paper was to review the literature on the economics of language and of
language planning so as to provide the reader with an overview of its main findings. To the author's knowledge that literature, at least in English and French,
deals almost exclusively with the case of Quebec. If this is correct, then this
paper is a fairly complete survey of it.' Though this is probably not fully correct, it shows that the literature on language and economics was not quite
extensive, as is also evident from Lamberton's (2002) collection of existing
papers. In their important paper Selten and Pool (1991) quote 12 papers only,
of which seven are concerned with Quebec (six are written in French and one
in English).

This does not mean that economists were oblivious to the importance of linguistic diversity. Trade economists (Tinbergen, 1962) realized very early that
sharing a common language was conducive for expanding trade between countries. Labour economists interested in migration (Chiswick and Miller, 1992)
examined whether migration flows were influenced by common languages and
estimated the returns to learning the language of their target country. Business
economists analysed the challenges of multinational corporations in the face

1

of linguistic diversity (Marschan-Piekkari et al., 1999). Various policy-oriented economists addressed the impact of linguistic diversity in India, Nigeria and many other countries (Spolsky, 2003), as well as the importance of protecting minority languages (Grin, 1992).

The concept of linguistic diversity, introduced by linguists (Greenberg, 1956), geneticists (Cavalli-Sforza, 1997), ethnographers (*Atlas Narodov Mira*, 1964), sociologists (Lieberson, 1964, 1969) and political scientists (Fishman, 1968; Pool, 1972; Laitin, 1979, 1991), paved the way for a new strand of research outlined by Mauro (1995) and Easterly and Levine's (1997) path-breaking paper on the effects of ethnolinguistic diversity on corruption and growth in Africa. This was followed by of host of papers of the effects of languages on institutional settings and development, redistribution, regional and national development. An important aspect of this research agenda was to focus on standardizing linguistic use: that is, restricting the number of languages used for official purposes, in legal settings, educational institutions and the media.[1]

This *Handbook* brings together methodological, theoretical and empirical studies in the economics of language in a single framework of linguistic diversity that reflects the history and contemporary study of the topic. Linguistic diversity represents an important facet of culture and, given its ubiquity and centrality, human experience. The impact of linguistic diversity on economic outcomes and public policies has been noticed and examined not only by economists and other social scientists in the contemporary era (see the review by Guiso et al., 2006), but all the way back to John Mills and Karl Marx, who understood that cultural diversity is central to economic interaction (see also Lazear, 1999). Even before Mills and Marx, von Humboldt (1988 [1836]) emphasized the importance of language on culture. His ideas were further developed in the twentieth century by Sapir (1949) and Whorf (1956), whose contributions were synthesized as the 'Sapir-Whorf hypothesis': language and culture are interdependent, and perhaps the language people speak even influences some of their decisions and behaviour. Bretton (1976) confirmed this view: 'Language may be the most explosive issue universally and over time. This mainly because language alone, unlike all other concerns associated with nationalism and ethnocentrism, is so closely tied to the individual self.' This clearly indicates the emotional aspects of linguistic environments and the reluctance of peoples to be deprived from their native language, even if their leaders understand that today's globalized world may struggle to 'support' too many

---

[1] Note that, in this volume, the word 'standardization' is used in a sense that differs from the usual meaning of 'standardizing a language' by linguists which refers to the process of developing a standard for a given written and/or oral language, resulting in dictionaries, grammars and phonetics that are either accepted or imposed as a norm.

languages. A delicate balance in the space of monetary and psychological costs and benefits has to be found between efficiency and emotion.

* * *

We now provide the reader with a road-map through the different parts of the book. Each chapter guides readers to other chapters. The handbook is divided into four parts: (1) linguistic concepts; (2) languages and markets; (3) linguistic policies and economic development; and (4) globalization and minority languages.

* * *

Part I deals with a couple of linguistic concepts that economists and sociologists should be aware of. The first two chapters, written by linguists, overview the issues that could be useful to those who work in other disciplines (essentially, economists and sociolinguists). Chapter 1 offers Nigel Fabb's view (shared by most linguists in the tradition of Noam Chomsky and, more recently, Pinker, 1994) concerning the Sapir–Whorf hypothesis, which assumes that the structure of the language used by an individual (often as a native language) influences his or her way of thinking and behaving. Fabb carefully analyses the papers by Mavisakalyan (2011), Chen (2013) and others in the light of the essentials of linguistic theory, which is the starting point of his paper. Andrew D. M. Smith's Chapter 2 brings Fabb's 'static' aspects into dynamics to study how sounds, words, grammar and even the meaning of words change over time. This is the realm of historical linguistics, which provides the basic material used to construct linguistic trees that reconstruct old languages on the basis of existing ones and lead to one of the methods to evaluate distances between languages analysed in Chapter 5.

Chapter 3 by Andrew John also takes a dynamic framework and describes simple mathematical models that integrate economic behaviour and other factors to study how languages appear, survive or die, though he admits that 'the evolution of language is fundamentally a linguistic rather than an economic question'. The results obtained by John within a model in which languages may be born, grow and disappear, could mitigate the frightening prospect of linguistic and cultural loss. This is certainly what Claude Levi-Strauss had in mind in one of his last interviews in 2002:

> We may hope that at the very same time during which globalisation is taking place, somehow, in a secret way, new differences are appearing, that we cannot perceive but that will be understood by our heirs.[2]

---

[2] 'On peut se dire, en tout cas c'est un voeu pieux, qu'au moment où nous craignons une uniformisation universelle, en sous-main, sourdement, de nouvelles différences commencent à apparaître que nous ne pouvons même pas percevoir, mais que nos héritiers comprendront et qui, je l'espère, seront exploitées.'

And, indeed, *Ethnologue* lists 77 creole languages created by Dutch, English, French, Portuguese, Russian or Spanish colonization. They result from a blending (and simplified grammar, vocabulary and style) of the local and the colonizer's language and have become the mother tongues of many communities. In an interesting paper published by *Newsweek* on 7 March 2005, 'Not the Queen's English: Non-Native Speakers are Transforming the Global Language,' the author distinguishes more than fifty varieties of English, starting with BBC English and ending with Inuit and Athabascan English. So the evolution of languages continues, whatever the word (language, dialect or creole) used to describe them.

Chapter 4 by Mark Leikin brings us to a field born in the mid-1950s: neurolinguistics, at the same time as non-invasive research methods (such as electro-encephalography), and neuro-imaging techniques in three dimensions became available. This allowed neurolinguists to analyse *in situ* how language functions in the brain, and especially how the brain is able to process more than one language. Recent research also points out that there are large differences across individuals, and no unique model. The approach may also be crucial to understand why language is so deeply linked to emotions.

Chapter 5 by Victor Ginsburgh and Shlomo Weber provides an overview of various types of linguistic distances (lexicostatistical, cladistic – based on linguistic trees, communication, Levenshtein phonetic, and others) that are now utilized in the economics literature to help explain trade relations, migrations, translations and the acquisition of languages, studied in Part II of the volume in Chapters 9 (trade), 12 (migrations) and 14 (patenting). The authors also discuss distances between groups of people, and the construction of ethnolinguistic diversity indices which are studied in more depth in Chapter 15.

In Chapter 6, Enrico Spolaore and Romain Wacziarg focus on the interrelationships and correlations between linguistic, genetic and religious distances. They also introduce new measures of cultural distances based on differences in average answers to questions from the *World Values Survey*. Their theoretical model, shows that ancestral distances, measured by genetic distances, are positively correlated with linguistic, religious and cultural distances. They conclude by arguing that genetic distances, the study of which was started by Cavalli-Sforza (1997) and his colleagues, are a summary statistic for many other cultural traits that are transmitted from one generation to the next.

In Chapter 7 Efthymios Athanasiou, Juan D. Moreno-Ternero and Shlomo Weber examine how economic issues can have an impact on linguistic diversity and language acquisition, using the notion of communicative benefits introduced by Selten and Pool (1991). Network externalities (created by individual decisions to learn or to refrain from learning a non-native language on the basis of self-interest) are ignored, and can result in creating a situation that is often not a social optimum. The chapter examines remedies to raise economic efficiency by introducing various public policies, including cost subsidization of learning. Since inefficiencies can also result from the usage of too many languages, Athanasiou et al. use their theoretical model to analyse optimal choices of the set of official languages. Such measures of standardization result in 'disenfranchizing' large parts of the population of a country. This makes peaceful coexistence more difficult,[3] and, in the worst cases, leads to conflicts and civil wars.

Emotions created by languages are examined by Niall Bond and Victor Ginsburgh in Chapter 8 in the context of a literary journey in the works of several writers who were either deprived of or recanted their mother tongue, or who *voluntary had to* go back to it in their writings, in spite of painful memories of their native country. As Fernando Pessoa, one of the most heralded literary figures of the 20th century wrote: 'My homeland is my language.'[4] This is another argument for which economists should take into account some aspects of social life, in addition to economic efficiency.

*   *   *

Several chapters in Part II on languages and markets, namely Chapter 9 by Peter H. Egger and Farid Toubal on trade, Chapter 12 by Alícia Adserà and Mariola Pytliková on migrations, and Chapter 14 by Dieter Harhoff, Karin Hoist, Bruno van Pottelsberghe de la Potterie and Charlotte Vandeput on the international scope of patenting in Europe, explicitly include linguistic distances in the gravitational model, briefly described in Section 5.4 of Chapter 5. Common languages (or trade languages at the regional level) enhance international (or national) trade. This is so for Spanish in Latin America, Russian on the territory of the former Soviet Union and Eastern Europe, and English and French in Africa. However, the linguistic distance which used to be a dummy variable (0 for common language, 1 otherwise) in the original Tinbergen (1962) study now takes much more subtle forms and allows incorporating linguistic proximity between various languages. As pointed out by Egger and Toubal, this makes estimation procedures increasingly sophisticated. In their chapter on migrations, Adserà and Pytliková review the role of languages on the decision to migrate and on the necessity migrants feel to learn the language of the host country to be integrated, find better jobs and enjoy the wage premium offered by the knowledge of the language of the host country. Harhof et al. quantify the impact of (often ignored) translation costs on firms' decisions to validate a patent in a particular country after being granted by the European Patent

---

[3] This is also studied in Section 5.6 of Chapter 5, as well as in Chapters 16 to 19 where specific regional cases are analysed.

[4] 'Minha pátria é minha lengua.'

Office. In their analysis of the geographic scope of patent protection, Harhof et al. underline the crucial impact of translation costs.

The other three chapters of Part II take a more sociological or anthropological viewpoint. Chapter 10 by Nigel Holden looks at the nature and function of a common language in the Ancient Near Eastern and Mediterranean World. He argues that 'the merchants of the Ancient World, exactly like today's business practitioners, used language in their cross-cultural dealings'. He also argues that Latin, Greek or Babylonian, as well as Punic and Aramaic, were languages of administration, fully capable of sustaining international economic life in their respective eras of hegemony. Moreover, he points out that Latin, which held a special place as an administrative language at the time of the Roman Empire, sustained this capacity for centuries and became the liturgical language of the Roman Catholic Church and of the worldwide bureaucracy. This makes a strong case for Latin to be viewed as the founding language of modern management.

In Chapter 11, Nigel Holden, jointly with Susanne Tietze and Wilhelm Barner-Rasmussen, examines multinational corporations (MNCs) as multilingual arenas characterized by language complexity. Focusing on the multiple and fluid contexts of language use, the chapter reviews the language decisions and choices made in various MNC contexts and situations. They also offer the case study of a global healthcare MNC, Novo Nordisk, where multilingual and multi-specialist groups of corporate facilitators provided the linguistic and cultural glue to bond the dispersed companies through a new English language-based practice. The latter sustained strong Danish management and cultural values, while providing vocabulary and concepts to redefine and change governance practices across the company.

Chapter 13 by Johan Heilbron and Gisèle Sapiro combines economic and sociological considerations. Economic analysis is based on the aggregation of rationally calculating agents, and relates translations to the production of books in the source and destination languages, their characteristics, and also their linguistic and cultural distances. Sociologists, however, focus on the asymmetrical character of exchanges, and relate them to the unequal distribution of economic, political and cultural power and resources of language groups. Though most local bookshops in the world do stock books in local languages, this is declining as internet sellers, such as Amazon, inexorably lead to fewer and fewer independent shops. It should however be recognized that many more books are still produced in countries where English is important or even dominant, and this results in more translations from English into other languages than the other way around. English also remains, for the time being, a dominant literary language as authors from the British Commonwealth and from former British colonies often write in English, and this provides a much larger variety of situations than occurs in smaller and often one-country-confined languages.

* * *

Part III, devoted to linguistic policies and economic development, starts with Chapter 15 by Klaus Desmet, Ignacio Ortuño-Ortín and Romain Wacziarg, who argue that different types of linguistic cleavages matter for different economic outcomes. Whereas deep historical cleavages matter for determining a society's degree of redistribution, more shallow cleavages are instrumental in slowing down economic growth and development. They suggest that the degree of redistribution is determined by deeply rooted differences between linguistic groups who trust one another, whereas economic growth is impacted by coordination, collaboration and communication. More superficial linguistic differences have a negative impact on growth (Easterly and Levine, 1997) (even though Arcand and Grin, 2010, and Posner, 2004, reach a different conclusion). The recent burgeoning literature on linguistic (and ethnic) fractionalization shows that its impact is also negative on institutional efficiency and corruption (Mauro, 1995), quality of government (La Porta et al., 1999; Alesina et al., 2003), investment in public goods (Alesina et al., 1999) and political stability (Annett, 2001). Alesina and La Ferrara (2005) provide a survey of this literature. Desmet et al. show that linguistic diversity matters indeed, but deeply rooted differences are important to explain some economic outcomes, while shallow differences affect other outcomes, so that trying to erase superficial (and more recent) differences will not solve all the problems.

The importance of linguistic policies in multilingual societies, countries, unions and international organizations moved to the forefront of public debate in many countries and regions over the past century. Max Weber's (1910) rationalization theory suggests that adopting too many languages inevitably requires, whether explicitly or implicitly, some degree of standardization. Requirements of calculability, efficiency, predictability and control over uncertainties lead to bureaucratization and the creation of a common legal system and, hence, to a common language used for administrative purposes.

The economic advantages of standardization described in Part III represent only one part of the equation. The threat of survival and the feeling of disenfranchizement by those who face restrictions of their linguistic rights have to be taken into account. The contemporary era shows how oppression or suppression of languages or cultures lead to wars. It may be shocking and horrifying to think of the cost of linguistic policies in terms of human lives, but the failure to do so ignores the passion and violence generated by the defence of or attack upon one's own culture and language (see, for example, deVotta, 2004, on the Sri Lankan war). Respecting the 'will of the people' is a necessary condition for any sustainable success of long-range policies in a democratic setting but excluding parts of the population from the process of creation in our increasingly globalized and competitive environment simply does not make sense.

Such linguistic rationalization or standardization (or language planning) can be achieved through different means. One is merely choosing the language of the majority group (French in France, Han Chinese in China, Kuotsugo

Japanese in Japan). Another is to recognize a *lingua franca*, a language spoken by the majority of the population but that is not the mother tongue of a single large ethnic group in the country (Swahili in Tanzania, and more generally in East Africa, Bahasa in Indonesia, or even English in the United States). Chapters 16 to 19 describe some selected regional essays of standardization.

In Chapter 16, Sue Wright analyses the shift to a unique language in three European state nations (France, Spain and the United Kingdom). These changes were due to both economic and political reasons; they were faced with resistance and took quite some time to get implemented. French, for instance, was imposed on all French provinces in 1539 by King François I. In the early 1960s, a new (soft) fight for reviving regional languages started again in Provence and Brittany, and elsewhere too.

In Chapter 17, Selma K. Sonntag examines how standardization has been achieved in South Asia, including India with its ambitious but not very successful three-language policy promoted under Nehru; Sri Lanka, in which the policy resulted in a long and bloody civil war between two populations, the Sinhalese and the Tamil; Nepal, a country in which geography (and the population and linguistic diversity that it generated) impacted on economic development and political integration; and Pakistan, which imposed Urdu after its independence that followed from the British Raj in 1947.

Brandon de la Cuesta and Leonard Wantchekon (Chapter 18) consider linguistic policies that took (or did not take) place in sub-Saharan Africa, which has very large levels of ethnic and linguistic diversity in almost each country, and is still suffering from borders of countries imposed by international treaties during the 19th century, without taking into account the ethnic origins of the populations. Colonization made things worse, since in many cases the official language became the language of the colonizer, with the result that 'the majority of Africans are governed in a language that they do not understand, but few African states have given serious attention to linguistic policy' (Phillipson and Skutnabb-Kangas, 1995, cited by Spolsky, 2003, p. 182). As de la Cuesta and Wantchekon suggest, 'instituting the language of the largest ethnolinguistic group as the official language may further aggravate between-group tensions and competition'.

The last chapter in Part III is concerned with standardization in Russia. Denis V. Kadochnikov offers an extensive analysis of standardization policies that started during the 16th century and describes a large number of examples of how this became a struggle for political and economic control between central and local elites, as was the case in the rest of Europe.

* * *

The four chapters in Part IV deal with the apparent contradiction between promoting English to a global language while simultaneously sustaining the life and the rights of minority languages.

Chapter 20 by Jacques Melitz analyses whether English will fulfil the vows of those who push it to become the world's *lingua franca*. He shows that, indeed, this is already the case in some domains (science, international organizations, sports) but that it may not be so in other areas, including international trade. Melitz also shows that acquiring English does not seem to respond to different motives as can be the case for other languages, and that if trade flows with China, Brazil, and Spanish-speaking countries change, English may lose some ground.

The final chapters by François Grin, Bengt-Arne Wickström and José-Ramon Uriarte deal with various aspects concerned with the important issue of political and economic measures that can be taken to protect minority languages and limit the effects of disenfranchizing large or even small parts of populations in individual countries.

In Chapter 21 Grin builds a theoretical model of minority language and derives formal conditions needed for minority language protection and pro-motion measures to be effective. These conditions are transposed into a set of specific guidelines for a desired language policy. The chapter then shifts to a more general discussion of the value of aggregate linguistic diversity, of which minority languages constitute essential components.

In Chapter 22 Wickström discusses the distribution of language rights in multilingual settings and shows that the concavity of the cost structure in the number of beneficiaries generates a critical-mass criterion to determine an optimal rights structure. The analysis is further extended to more general settings, including the case where rights influence the status of a language and, subsequently, endogenous preferences for linguistic rights. The chapter also examines redistribution aspects of linguistic rights.

Finally, in Chapter 23, Uriarte studies bilingual democratic societies with one language spoken by every individual, and another spoken by the bilingual minority. While language rights are important, Uriarte argues that the survival of the minority language depends mainly on its actual use by bilinguals. This, in turn, is determined by linguistic conventions and social norms.

*   *   *

Most topics covered in the *Handbook* constitute rich sources for future research. Promising examples include the calculation of linguistic distances using statistical phonetics and functional data analysis (Hadjipantelis et al., 2012), the influence of common languages on bilateral (or multilateral) trades and the development of new (static as well as dynamic) and truly exogenous diversity indices. Recent studies on the economic impact of language on economic and ethical behaviour are very promising, and may give a new life to (a weakened form of) the Sapir–Whorf hypothesis.

More work is needed on the economics of language acquisition and the analysis of the future *linguae francae* of the world. Many of the forecasts made about the probable prevalence of English in the international press and television, as well as on the internet, do not seem to go in the expected direction: That is, the internet started as a 100 per cent endeavour in English but did not crowd out other languages, now representing some 60 to 70 per cent of the traffic. After all, in 1783, de Rivarol, a French writer and brilliant epigrammatist, celebrates French as the only language that can be universal, while 'English is dry and taciturn [and its] literature is not even worth a quick look'. This obviously did not convince de Candolle (1873), a prominent Swiss scientist (not a linguist), who only 90 years later wrote what follows:

> [O]ne has to think why some languages are preferred to others. During the 17th and 18th centuries, there existed good reasons why French succeeded Latin in Europe. At the time, French, a relatively simple and clear language, was spoken by a large proportion of educated people. It had the advantage of being close to Latin, which was well known. An Englishman or a German would know half of French if he knew Latin. A Spaniard or an Italian would know three quarters of it. A discussion or a paper written in French would have been understood by everybody. During the 19th century, civilization has extended to the north [of France] and the population has increased more there than in the south. The use of English tripled as a consequence of the United States. Science is more and more cultivated in Germany, England, Scandinavia, and Russia. The future predominance of the Anglo-American language is obvious.[5]

After all, can we call English the 1,000-words 'English' that became global and is, according to Crystal (1999), spoken by 1.5 billion people (and probably many more today)? Or will Globish kill Standard English?

---

[5] 'Il faut réfléchir aux causes qui font préférer une langue, et à celles qui en propagent l'emploi malgré les défauts qu'elle peut avoir. Aux XVIIe et XVIIIe siècles, il existait des motifs pour faire succéder le français au latin dans toute l'Europe. C'était une langue parlée par une grande proportion des hommes instruits de l'époque; une langue assez simple et fort claire. Elle avait l'avantage d'être voisine du latin, qu'on connaissait à merveille. Un Anglais, un Allemand avait tout naturellement appris la moitié du français en apprenant le latin. Un Espagnol, un Italien en savait d'avance les trois quarts. Si l'on soutenait une discussion en français, si l'on publiait dans cette langue, tout le monde comprenait. Dans le siècle actuel, la civilisation s'est beaucoup étendue au nord de la France et la population s'y est augmentée plus qu'au midi. L'emploi de la langue anglaise a triplé par le fait de l'Amérique. Les sciences sont de plus en plus cultivées en Allemagne, en Angleterre, dans les pays scandinaves et en Russie. [...] La prépondérance future de la langue anglo-américaine est évidente: elle sera imposée par le mouvement des populations dans les deux hémisphères.'

Research is also necessary on the economic impact of past standardization policies: What are the benefits in terms of efficiency, as well as the costs in terms of disenfranchizement? (See Ginsburgh et al., 2005.) Since some language standardization in a rapidly globalizing world becomes unavoidable (though not necessarily welfare improving), further research examining and simulating the consequences of standardization assumptions to ensure the feasibility of choices, including linguistic education of our descendants, is necessary. It may also be important to devise theoretically founded compensation schemes, as suggested by Ginsburgh and Weber (2011), to quell the complaints of those who feel disenfranchized or whose language is considered a minority language.

Acknowledgements

We had the good fortune to benefit from the continuous support and encouragements of many people at Palgrave Macmillan: Taiba Batool, Laura Pacey, Rachel Sangster, Gemma Shields, Ellie Shillito and Ania Wronski helped us at all stages, from the gestation to the birth of the manuscript. In the very last stage of the production of the book, Sunita Jayachandran seemed to be in front of her computer day and night, since, in spite of the time differences between the United States, Russia, Belgium and India we never had to wait for more than an hour to get answers to our many deep or shallow email questions. We are also particularly grateful to S. Weyers who chased the many (unavoidable) inconsistencies within and between the various chapters in their first, second, third and, sometimes, umpteenth version. At the New Economic School, Moscow, Aleksandra Davydova and Alyona Ovchinnikova helped with organizational matters at different stages.

Needless to say that we owe many thanks to the 33 contributors who were all (almost) on time, so that the book could be delivered to the publisher two weeks after the pre-set date of 1 June, 2015.

References

A. Alesina, R. Baqir and W. Easterly (1999) 'Public Goods and Ethnic Divisions', *Quarterly Journal of Economics*, 64, 1243–1284.

A. Alesina, A. Devleeschouwer, W. Easterly, S. Kurlat and R. Wacziarg (2003) 'Fractionalization', *Journal of Economic Growth*, 8, 155–194.

A. Alesina and E. La Ferrara (2005) 'Ethnic Diversity and Economic Performance', *Journal of Economic Literature*, 43, 762–800.

A. Annett (2001), 'Social Fractionalization, Political Instability, and the Size of the Government', *IMF Staff Papers*, 46, 561–592.

J.-L. Arcand and F. Grin (2010) 'Language in Economic Development: Is English Special and is Linguistic Fragmentation Bad?' In E. Erling and P. Seargeant (eds.) *English and Development* (Bristol: Multilingual Matters).

Atlas Narodov Mira (1964) (Miklucho-Maklai Ethnological Institute at the Department of Geodesy and Cartography of the State Geological Committee of the Soviet Union).

A. Breton (1978) *Bilingualism: An Economic Approach* (Montreal: C.D. Howe Institute).

H. Bretton (1976) 'Political Science, Language, and Politics' In W. O'Barr and J. O'Barr (eds.) *Language and Politics* (The Hague: Mouton).

L. Cavalli-Sforza (1997) 'Genes, Peoples and Languages', *Proceedings of the National Academy of Sciences of the USA*, 94, 7719–7724.

M. Chen (2013) 'The Effect of Language on Economic Behavior: Evidence from Savings Rates, Health Behaviors, and Retirement Assets', *The American Economic Review*, 103, 690–731.

B. Chiswick and P. Miller (1992) 'Language in the Immigrant Labor Market' In B. Chiswick (ed.) *Immigration, Language and Ethnicity: Canada and the United States* (Washington: American Enterprise Institute).

D. Crystal (1999) *A Dictionary of Language* (Chicago, IL: The University of Chicago Press).

A. de Candolle (1987 [1873]) *Histoire des sciences et des savants depuis deux siècles* (Paris: Fayard).

A. de Rivarol (2014 [1783]) *Discours sur l'universalité de la langue française* (Paris: Flammarion).

N. deVotta (2004) 'Ethnic Domination, Violence and Illiberal Democracy' In M. Alagappa, (ed.) *Civil Society and Political Change in Asia* (Stanford, CA: Stanford University Press).

W. Easterly and R. Levine (1997) 'Africa's Growth Tragedy: Policies and Ethnic Divisions', *The Quarterly Journal of Economics*, 112, 1203–1250.

J. Fishman (1968) 'Some Contrasts between Linguistically Homogeneous and Linguistically Heterogeneous Polities' In J. Fishman, C. Ferguson and J. Dasgupta (eds.) *Language Problems of Developing Nations* (New York: Wiley).

V. Ginsburgh, I. Ortuño-Ortin and S. Weber (2005) 'Disenfranchisement in Linguistically Diverse Societies. The Case of the European Union', *Journal of the European Economic Association*, 3, 946–964.

V. Ginsburgh and S. Weber (2011) *How Many Languages Do We Need? The Economics of Linguistic Diversity* (Princeton, NJ: Princeton University Press).

J. Greenberg (1956) 'The Measurement of Linguistic Diversity', *Language*, 32, 109–115.

G. Grenier (1984) 'The Effects of Language Characteristics on the Wages of Hispanic-American Males', *Journal of Human Resources*, 19, 35–52.

F. Grin (1992) 'Towards a Threshold Theory of Minority Language Survival', *Kyklos*, 45, 69–97.

L. Guiso, P. Sapienza and L. Zingales (2006) 'Does Culture Effect Economic Outcomes', *Journal of Economic Perspectives*, 20, 2–48.

P. Hadjipantelis, J. Aston and J. Evans (2012) 'Characterizing Fundamental Frequency in Mandarin: A Functional Principal Component Approach Utilizing Mixed Effect Models', *Journal of the Acoustical Society of America* 13, 4651–4664.

D. Laitin (1979) 'Language Choice and National Development: A Typology for Africa', *International Interactions*, 6, 291–321.

D. Laitin (1991) 'Language Choice Among Ghanaians', *Language Problems and Language Planning*, 15, 139–161.

D. Lamberton (ed.) (2002) *The Economics of Language* (Cheltenham, UK: Edward Elgar).

R. La Porta, F. Lopez de Silanes, A. Shleifer and R. Vishny (1999) 'The Quality of Government', *Journal of Law, Economics and Organization*, 15, 222–279.

E. Lazear (1999) 'Culture and Language', *Journal of Political Economy*, 107, 95–127.

S. Lieberson (1964) 'An Extension of Greenberg's Linguistic Diversity Measures', *Language* 40, 526–531.

S. Lieberson (1969) 'Measuring Population Diversity', *American Sociological Review*, 34, 850–862.

J. Marschak (1965) 'Economics of Language', *Behavioral Science*, 10, 135–140.

R. Marschan-Piekarri, D. Welch and L. Welch (1999) 'In the Shadow: The Impact of Language on the Structure, Power and Communication in the Multinational', *International Business Review*, 8, 421–440.

W. McManus, W. Gould and F. Welch (1978) 'Earnings of Hispanic Men: The Role of English Language Proficiency', *Journal of Labor Economics*, 1, 101–130.

P. Mauro (1995) 'Corruption and Growth', *The Quarterly Journal of Economics*, 110, 681–712.

A. Mavisakalyan (2011) 'Gender in Language and Gender in Employment', Working Paper, ANUCBE School of Economics.

R. Phillipson and T. Skutnabb-Kangas (1995) 'Language Rights in Postcolonial Africa' In R. Phillipson, M. Rannut and T. Skutnabb-Kangas (eds.) *Linguistic Human Rights: Overcoming Linguistic Discrimination* (Berlin and New York: Mouton De Gruyter).

S. Pinker (1994) *The Language Instinct* (New York: William Morrow).

J. Pool (1972) 'National Development and Language Diversity' In J. Fishman (ed.) *Advances in the Sociology of Language* (The Hague: Mouton).

D. Posner (2004) 'Measuring Ethnic Fractionalization in Africa', *American Journal of Political Science*, 48, 849–863.

E. Sapir (1949) *Selected Writings of Edward Sapir in Language, Culture, and Personality* (Berkeley, CA: University of California Press).

R. Selten and J. Pool (1991) 'The Distribution of Foreign Language Skills as a Game Equilibrium' In R. Selten (ed.) *Game Equilibrium Models*, vol. 4 (Berlin: Springer Verlag).

B. Spolsky (2003) *Language Policy* (Cambridge, UK: Cambridge University Press).

J. Tinbergen (1962) *Shaping the World Economy: Suggestions for an International Economic Policy* (New York: The Twentieth Century Fund).

F. Vaillancourt (1982/1983) 'The Economics of Language and Language Planning', *Language Problems and Language Planning*, 7, 162–178.

W. von Humboldt (1988, [1836]) *The Diversity of Human Language-Structure and Its Influence on the Mental Development of Mankind* (Cambridge, UK: Cambridge University Press).

M. Weber (1968, [1910]) *Economy and Society* (Berkeley, CA: University of California Press).

B. Whorf (1956) *Language, Thought and Reality: Selected Writings of Benjamin Lee Whorf* (Cambridge, MA: MIT Press).

Part I

Linguistic Diversity: Origins and Measurement

1
Linguistic Theory, Linguistic Diversity and Whorfian Economics

Nigel Fabb

1.1 Introduction

I begin this chapter by illustrating what theoretical linguists do and why generative linguistics in particular has argued that linguistic data is more abstract and more complex than at first appears. I then illustrate language diversity by comparing aspects of two languages, English and Ma'di, an East African language. Sections 1.2 and 1.3 focus on specific aspects of linguistic data, which are chosen to illustrate general points about linguistic theory and linguistic diversity. In Section 1.4, I briefly note several different theories of linguistic diversity which explore why languages vary and whether variation is limited by internal (psychological) or external (cultural) factors. In Section 1.5, I examine the 'Whorfian' hypothesis that linguistic form has a causal relation with thought and behaviour, summarize some of the relevant psycholinguistic work and then examine some articles by economists which claim causal relations between linguistic and social variation. Based in part on what I have said about linguistic theory and linguistic diversity, and in particular the abstractness of linguistic data, I will argue that the economists' claims cannot be sustained. In the final part of the chapter I discuss some ways in which stylistic variation within a language might affect thought.

1.2 Abstract linguistic form, and the rules and conditions which govern it

Linguistic theory is an attempt to understand the regularities and patterns which can be found in language. The fundamental discovery of modern linguistic theory is that a word or sentence can have a complex and multi-layered abstract structure; our knowledge of language is knowledge of that abstract linguistic form. These discoveries about language usually take as a starting point Noam Chomsky's (1957) *Syntactic Structures*, and in the first part of this section I outline some of the ideas presented in that book. I then illustrate the evidence for abstract linguistic form with a number of examples, because linguistics is always a matter of how specific problems are discovered and solved, and how these solutions fit into a larger theory of language.

1.2.1 Chomsky's *Syntactic Structures*

Modern linguistic theory begins with the publication of Noam Chomsky's 1957 book *Syntactic Structures* which was consolidated in his 1965 *Aspects of the Theory of Syntax*; in this section, I summarize some of the aspects of the early 'generative grammar' or 'generative linguistics' initiated by these books. Though no one still pursues this particular theoretical model, many of its findings remain true of theoretical linguistics. Chomsky begins by arguing for a distinction between two types of sentence: grammatical and ungrammatical. Ungrammatical sentences are combinations of words which are not accepted as sentences by native speakers, with the proviso that this is not a judgement based on meaning or social acceptability: that is, that speakers can make judgements of grammaticality based just on the form of a sentence. Chomsky proposes that a grammar of a language should be a device which generates all and only the grammatical sentences for that language. This type of grammar is identified with a psychological capacity, the human knowledge of language. The grammar of each language is a variation on principles of a 'universal grammar' which is innate and shared by all humans; the universal grammar offers 'switches' which are turned on in some specific combination to produce the grammar of a specific language.

Chomsky's goal is to establish what kind of grammar will generate the grammatical sentences of English (hence 'generative grammar'). He notes that English comprises an infinite number of different grammatical sentences which must be generated by a finite device; this is possible because the grammar allows recursion, where for example a sentence can contain a sentence repeatedly, without limit. A sentence is a sequence of words, but there is evidence that these words are grouped into constituents which are subject to generalizations. Thus the grammar does not just generate the sequence of words which makes up the sentence, but generates a structured sequence, organized into hierarchically arranged constituents (see Rizzi, 2013 for detailed discussion). For example, the sequence of words (in the title of each figure) in Figures 1.1, 1.2 and 1.3 are given a structure by the grammar shown schematically as a tree structure. As can be seen, the structures differ in whether they allow the pronoun and *John* to refer to the same person (note that the structures are simplified and schematic, and not a full linguistic structure for the sentences).

Note that *his* in Figure 1.1 can be interpreted as referring to John (but can also be interpreted as referring to someone else), while in Figure 1.2 *he* cannot be interpreted as John. This is not just a matter of which pronoun is used, because in Figure 1.3, *he* can be interpreted as John. This difference cannot

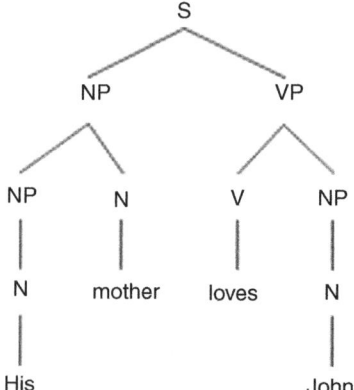

Figure 1.1 His mother loves John ('his' can be interpreted as 'John's')

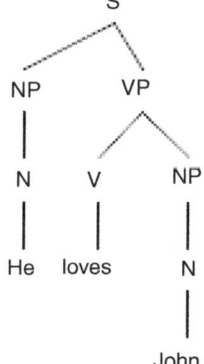

Figure 1.2 He loves John ('he' cannot be interpreted as 'John')

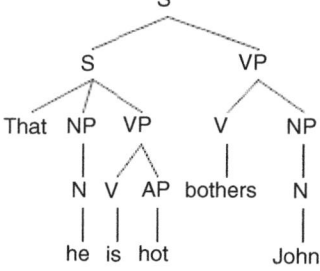

Figure 1.3 That he is hot bothers John ('he' can be interpreted as 'John')

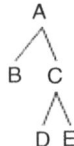

Figure 1.4   C-Command

be derived from the sequences directly, either from the sequences of words or from the number of words between the pronoun and the name. Instead, the difference is in how they are hierarchically related in the constituent structure as shown in the three figures. The explanation is based on a discovery made by theoretical linguists about the hierarchical relations between items in a tree, as I now explain.

A node in a tree dominates other nodes (i.e. all the nodes underneath it). The nodes immediately underneath a node (i.e. with no intervening nodes) are 'immediately dominated' by the node. So for example the topmost S dominates all the nodes in the tree, but immediately dominates only a noun phrase (NP) and a verb phrase (VP) in Figures 1.1 and 1.2 and a sentence (S) and a VP in Figure 1.3. The discovery about language is that there is a special kind of relation, called 'c-command', based on the relations of dominance (the nodes under a node) and immediate dominance (the nodes immediately under a node). Given a node X and a node Y which immediately dominates X, X c-commands all the nodes dominated by Y. Thus for example in Figure 1.4, B c-commands B, C, D and E, while E c-commands only D and E (the definition as given here means that a node always c-commands itself).

In Figure 1.1, the NP *his* does not c-command the NP *John*. But in Figure 1.2, the NP *he* does c-command the NP *him*. This is why co-reference is possible in one case but not the other. The rule for English (and most if not all other languages) is as follows:

A name cannot be c-commanded by a noun phrase (NP) which co-refers.

This rule is what prevents the pronoun in Figure 1.2 referring to the name: the pronoun c-commands the name because its NP is immediately dominated by the node S which dominates the name, and c-command prevents co-reference. In Figures 1.1 and 1.3, the NP which is the pronoun is buried deeper in the tree and so does not c-command the name; hence co-reference is possible. (At this point, I note again that this is a simplified account: the relevant structural relation is more complex than just 'c-command', here and elsewhere in the chapter, and has been subject to theoretical revision.) This example demonstrates two fundamental principles of linguistic theory, agreed by almost all linguists: that there is abstract form (in this case, the abstract constituent structure which holds of the words), and that linguistic principles refer to the abstract constituent structure.

Chomsky wants linguistic theory to formulate a grammar of a language which can explain aspects of the language, such as the co-reference possibilities described above. Another thing to explain is the ambiguity of the sequence of words *visiting relatives can be annoying*. This is ambiguous because there are two different constituent structures for the same sequence, one of which means that relatives are visiting (the subject is an NP referring to the relatives and can be restated as *relatives who visit*) and the other which means that relatives are being visited (the subject is a kind of clause referring to the visiting and can be restated as *to visit relatives*). To explain this fact demands that we accept some degree of abstractness, in the form of different constituent structures, and that the constituent structures can play a role in determining the meaning of the sequence of words.

A fundamental part of the *Syntactic Structures* theory is 'transformational rules' which relate different structured sequences to one another; because of the importance of these rules in this version of the theory it was called 'transformational generative grammar'. Thus the sequence *the man hit the ball* has the same truth conditions as *the ball was hit by the man*, and this can be achieved by a mechanism in the grammar (a transformational rule) which takes a structure and rearranges it: the phrase before and the phrase after the verb are changed in their locations in the constituent structure. Note that this rule affects multi-word constituents and not individual words, thus showing that knowledge of a sentence is knowledge not just of the sequence of words (audible on the surface) but knowledge of the structural relations between words. We have seen that there is an abstract level at which a constituent structure holds of strings of words. Transformational rules show that there must be more than one such level, such that a final string of words can be derived from distinct constituent structures at different levels, related by transformational rules. Chomsky concludes: 'to understand a sentence it is necessary (though of course not sufficient) to reconstruct its representation on each level'. There are multiple abstract representations on different abstract levels which underlie the surface sentence, and these abstract representations are claimed to be psychologically real. This has significant consequences for our understanding of what language and 'knowledge of language' are, with problematic consequences for Whorfian theories under which linguistic forms are caused by or cause extra-linguistic thought and behaviour.

Distinct 'levels' are hypothesized as domains within which certain types of representation exist, and rules map representations from one level to another: each sentence has a representation on all of these levels. One model of levels of representation, the 'government and binding theory' model (Chomsky, 1981), is shown in Figure 1.5.

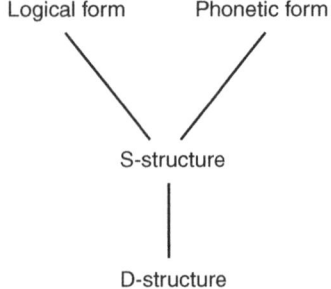

Figure 1.5   Government and binding theory

In this model, phrase structure rules build constituent structures at D-structure, and transformational rules produce derived constituent structures at S-structure. The constituent structures at S-structure are then subject to rules which produce representations of sentences, which at the level of phonetic form constitute speakable sentences; separately, the constituent structures at S-Structure are subject to rules which form representations of sentences at the level of logical form which can be interpreted as meaningful (e.g. using the language and form of predicate logic). As we will see shortly, two languages can have the same rule operating at different levels, leading to different surface forms (but with an underlying similarity). Much current generative linguistics follows the 'minimalist program' (Chomsky, 1995). It is a tenet of this approach that 'intermediate' levels of syntactic representation are dispensed with, but the distinction remains between how a sentence is represented for interpretation (its logical form) and how a sentence is represented for pronunciation (its phonetic form).

In the remainder of this section, I summarize three 'classic' examples (widely known and taught in introductory linguistics classes) of how generative linguistics has dealt with patterns and regularities in language. Generative linguistic theory stands or falls by its capacity to solve specific problems presented by a language and to fit the solutions into a model which can explain similar problems in any language.

1.2.2   Vowel shift in English

I begin by considering a problem presented by the sound patterns of English, which comes under the type of linguistics called 'phonology'. The English words *profane* and *profanity* are related: *profanity* is a noun produced by adding the suffix *-ity* to the adjective *profane*. However, when we inspect the sounds of the words we see that the second vowel in each is a different spoken vowel (the vowel spelled with an 'a'). This difference is called 'vowel shift' because one vowel has shifted into another (or more specifically, as we will see, an abstract underlying vowel has differently shifted into the two different surface forms). In all languages, distinct vowels can be differentiated by vowel 'height' (roughly, how high in the mouth the topmost part of the tongue is when the vowel is produced), and English has high, mid and low vowels. *Profane* has a long mid-vowel (more accurately a diphthong) phonetically represented as [ēy], and the phonetic representation of the word is [profēyn]. However, when the suffix is added, the word has a short low vowel [æ] as in [profænɪty]. This alternation is typical of the whole of the English vocabulary, where two versions of the same word alternate a long vowel at one height with a short vowel at a different height: the alternations are predictable and found throughout the vocabulary of English. We see it also in the changing vowels of *divine* and *divinity* (a contrast between low diphthong and high short vowel), and *serene* and *serenity* (a contrast between high diphthong and short mid-vowel). And it shows up also in the irregular verb forms, for example in the long high vowel of *meet* as opposed to the short mid-vowel of the past form *met*. Here we have a standard kind of problem for linguistic theory, similar to problems described in the previous section: two linguistic items are the same in one way and different in another, in a pattern which is characteristic of language as a whole.

The solution to this problem is at the core of *The Sound Pattern of English*, the 1968 book by Noam Chomsky and Morris Halle (Chomsky and Halle, 1968) which has the foundational role for phonology analogous to *Syntactic Structures* for syntax. They propose a universal theory (holding for all languages) of how sounds are organized in a language. In this theory, all words have an underlying form (the form in which they are stored in the mental lexicon), and the underlying form is subject to a fixed sequence of rules specified by the language, some of which leave the word unaffected and some of which change it, so that the surface form of the word can be different from the underlying form. For *profane* and *profanity*, they argue that the underlying form of the word is [profæn], a form which is then changed in different ways, depending on whether the suffix is added, to produce the two surface forms [profēyn] and [profæn+ity]. Note that the underlying vowel is different from both of the surface vowels (either in quality or in length). In Table 1.1, I show a simplified version of the sequence (omitting in this example other intervening rules which are part of English), which takes the word from its underlying form to its surface form.

The difference between dialects of English can sometimes be traced to a difference in whether or not the vowel shift rule applies; thus in the dialect of the south of England the word *house* has a low long diphthong [hāws] while the equivalent word in some Scottish dialects has a high long vowel [hūs] (hence the dialect spelling 'hoose'). Both dialects may have the same underlying form with a high back vowel [hūs] but the vowel shift rule changes the vowel only in the English dialect, and not in the Scottish dialect. The long vowels of southern standard English changed in quality over the early

Table 1.1   Profane and profanity

Underlying representations	profǣn	profǣn + ıty	Underlying vowel is long ǣ (same for unsuffixed and suffixed form)
Stress assignment	prof<u>ǣ</u>n	prof<u>ǣ</u>n + ıty	Stress is assigned (indicated by underlining)
Shortening rule	prof<u>ǣ</u>n	prof<u>ǣ</u>n + ıty	Antepenultimate vowel is shortened: affects 'profanity' only
Dipthongization rule	prof<u>ǣ</u>yn	prof<u>ǣ</u>n + ıty	Long vowels are diphthongized: affects 'profane' only
Vowel shift rule	prof<u>ē</u>yn	prof<u>ǣ</u>n + ıty	Stressed long vowels are altered in quality, e.g. [æ] moves up to become [e]: affects 'profane' only
Surface representations	prof<u>ē</u>yn	profǣnıty	Different surface vowels

modern period, so that there was a historical process of vowel shift; this historical process operated differently in different dialects, leading to differences between dialects. (This is how variation often emerges, starting by splitting dialects over time, ending with the dialects being identified as distinct languages.) Chomsky and Halle argue that the historical change can be understood as the introduction of the rule of vowel shift into the phonology of English. The historical change in long vowels (but not the related short vowels) partly explains why English spelling does not match surface sounds in a clear way: the use of the same written vowel 'a' in the spelling of *profane* and *profanity* reflects an earlier pronunciation of these words before the vowel shift rule was added, at a time when the two vowels were closer. The approach to phonology taken by Chomsky and Halle has been largely replaced by a different type of phonological theory called optimality theory. Optimality theory shows some theoretical continuity: there is an underlying form (the input) and a surface form (the output) and the relation between them is controlled by a set of ranked constraints (rather than rules); constraints are always violated, and the optimal matching of output to input involves the least-worst violation of constraints. What vowel shift shows is that the sounds of words in their underlying forms (as stored in the mental lexicon, before the operation of phonological rules) are not the same as the sounds of words as they are pronounced: a description of the surface sounds of the language does not represent every aspect of a speaker's knowledge of the language, a knowledge which is multi-layered.

1.2.3   Verb second in German

In this and the next section, I consider problems presented by sentence
structures and their interpretation, which comes under the study of 'syntax'.
In German, a finite verb is in second position in a main clause. Thus the finite
verb *kommt* ('comes') can be preceded by one constituent (which can consist
of one or more words). The constituent can be one of a number of different
types of syntactic entity, including as the subject (1) or an adverb (2) or indeed
a whole subordinate clause as in (4). The verb-second constraint is that in a
main clause the finite verb must be in second position, as the asterisk next to
(3) indicates in a sentence where the verb is final: an asterisk indicates that a
sentence is ungrammatical. The finite verb might be a main verb as in (1)–(2)
or an auxiliary verb as in (4).

> (1)   Er kommt morgen.
>   he comes tomorrow
> (2)   Morgen kommt er.
>   tomorrow comes he
> (3) * Er morgen kommt.
>   he tomorrow comes
> (4)   Dass er gestern gekommen ist habe ich gesagt.
>   [That he yesterday come is] have I said

In contrast, in subordinate clauses, the finite verb – here *komme* (conjunctive
'comes') – usually comes at the end, as (5) shows; the verb can no longer follow
the subject as (6) shows.

> (5)   Er sagte, dass er morgen komme.
>   He said, that he tomorrow comes.
> (6) * Er sagte, dass er komme morgen.
>   He said, that he comes tomorrow.

The location of a verb relative to its subject and object, and relative to other
aspects of a sentence, is one of the most widely noted syntactic differences
between languages. Thus in English the subject usually precedes the verb and
the verb precedes the object and English is called an SVO (subject-verb-object)
language, while in Japanese the verb usually comes at the end and Japanese is
called an SOV language. German is a mixed case – in main clauses it has verb
second (preceded by subject or object or some other item) while in subordinate clauses it appears to be SOV. There are two related approaches to these
matters taken by theoretical linguists. The first is that in a language with two
distinct orders, one or both of the orders are derived from some single underlying order: German underlyingly always has the verb in the same place in all

sentences and clauses, but a rule moves the verb to a different position. The alternative approach is more ambitious: it is that all languages have the verb in the same underlying position, and the differences between languages such as SVO and SOV, or verb second, are surface differences derived by rules. Questions of abstractness thus hold both within a language and more generally for all languages, with major consequences for how we understand variation, and how we interpret typologies of surface variation.

My goal here is to note briefly a single, very influential, argument about German which was first formulated by Hans den Besten in 1977 (Den Besten, 1983) and involves the grammatical sentence in (7).

> (7)   Er sagte, er komme morgen.
>   He said, he comes tomorrow.

This is a subordinate sentence in which one would expect to find the verb in final position as in (5), but now it is in second position and yet the sentence is grammatical. Den Besten argued that the crucial factor was not whether the sentence was main or subordinate, but instead related to the 'complementizer' of the sentence. The complementizer is an abstract component of a sentence's structure, which c-commands the rest of the sentence; in addition to providing a place where a word can move to, it also has a function of typing the sentence as a question, statement, etc. The complementizer position may or may not be filled by a word: it is an abstract form which is not necessarily audible in the spoken sentence. Den Besten argued that the complementizer position must be filled in German. If there is a word like *dass* (introducing a sentence as in (4), (5) or (6)) then this word fills the complementizer position. If that word is absent, as it is in most main sentences and in the subordinate sentence in (7), then the verb fills the complementizer position. If the verb does not fill the complementizer position, it is final in a German sentence. The position preceding the second-position verb is a position preceding the complementizer position, and any item can be moved up into it (e.g. the subject, object, adverb). This means incidentally that the subject which precedes the second position verb has also been moved to this position and is no longer 'in subject position'. Thus the hypothesis that there is a complementizer position (extensively supported by other theoretical work) and the possibility of moving a verb to fill it together explain the pattern of verb second in German.

Den Besten's was the first of a series of accounts of verb second which have now much elaborated on his account. The sequence of subject, verb, object and other items is dependent now on a significant amount of restructuring of underlying abstract structure. The rules which do the restructuring (the descendants of the transformational rules of *Syntactic Structures*) are manipulations of abstract structure which are found in all languages.

1.2.4 Long distance reflexives in Chinese

My third example of a problem identified by linguistic theory relates to a difference between English and Chinese, as illustrated in (8)–(9), from Cole et al. (1990).

(8) [s Zhangsan renwei [s Lisi zhidao [s Wangwu xihuan ziji]]]
     [s Zhangsan thinks [s Lisi knows [s Wangwu like self]]]
     'Zhangsan thinks that Lisi knows that Wangwu likes himself.' (ambiguous: Wangwu likes Wangwu, Wangwu likes Lisi, or Wangwu likes Zhangsan)
(9) [s John thinks [s Tom knows [s Bill likes himself]]] (unambiguous)

These two sentences are roughly word-for-word equivalents, consisting of a sentence which contains a sentence which contains a sentence, each with its own subject. A reflexive pronoun must in all languages find a co-referent, which is the NP which co-refers to it. The difference is that in the Chinese example (8), the reflexive pronoun *ziji* 'self' can have as its co-referent any of the three subjects (underlined), and so the overall sentence is ambiguous. In the English example (9) the reflexive pronoun *himself* can have as its co-referent only the subject of the sentence which contains it, *Bill*, and so the overall sentence is unambiguous. Chinese is said to have 'long distance reflexives', while English has only local reflexives; this is one of the characteristic ways in which languages can vary. I will however show that the 'long distance' describes how the reflexive is abstractly moved, not how it is interpreted.

As a general principle, a reflexive pronoun such as *ziji* or *himself* must be c-commanded by its co-referent (the NP which co-refers with the reflexive). Hence it is possible to say *Bill likes himself* but not *Himself likes Bill*, because the subject c-commands the object (as we saw earlier) but not vice versa. Reflexive pronouns in English must also find their co-referent within a local domain; they must be in the same sentence. This is why (9) has the interpretation that it does. Constituents thus function not only as ways of grouping words, but also as domains within which syntactic (and semantic) relationships are established; this is further evidence for the reality of syntactic constituent structure.

Why, then, does Chinese allow the reflexive apparently to find a co-referent in a different, higher sentence? The answer offered by Cole et al. is that it does not – instead, the reflexive is moved by a transformational rule into the higher sentence and thus finds its co-referent in the same sentence as it ends up in, after movement. Some types of movement have an effect on the pronounced order of words (as is the case for verb second in German, for example). But movement can also be covert, taking place in the abstract syntax without an effect on the phonological output, and Chinese has covert movement of this kind. The proposal is as follows (simplified). It depends on the existence of a covert piece of structure, similar in kind to the 'complementizer' position which we saw in the previous section, but this time between the subject and the verb, and which is called the 'Infl' position. Generative linguists think that all sentences in all languages have such a position (it has very significant indirect effects on the syntax of the sentence, including for example controlling whether a subject pronominal can be dropped, 'pro-drop', as discussed later in this chapter). This means that sentence (8) has a more elaborated structure, as shown in (10):

(10)   [$_S$ Zhangsan *Infl* renwei [$_S$ Lisi *Infl* zhidao [$_S$ Wangwu *Infl* xihuan ziji]]]

Now, in Chinese the reflexive pronoun must move to Infl in order to find a co-referent (as a rule specific to Chinese, not found in English); but once it moves to Infl it can move to any Infl. The three interpretations thus involve covert structures as in (11), (12) and (13).

(11)   [$_S$ Zhangsan *Infl* renwei [$_S$ Lisi *Infl* zhidao [$_S$ Wangwu **ziji-*Infl*** xihuan ___]]]
'Zhangsan thinks that Lisi knows that Wangwu likes Wangwu.'

(12)   [$_S$ Zhangsan *Infl* renwei [$_S$ Lisi **ziji-*Infl*** zhidao [$_S$ Wangwu *Infl* xihuan ___]]]
'Zhangsan thinks that Lisi knows that Wangwu likes Lisi.'

(13)   [$_S$ Zhangsan **ziji-*Infl*** renwei [$_S$ Lisi *Infl* zhidao [$_S$ Wangwu *Infl* xihuan ___]]]
'Zhangsan thinks that Lisi knows that Wangwu likes Zhangsan.'

Each of the interpretations thus has a different syntactic structure associated with it, thus using the syntax to disambiguate the string. This disambiguation takes place by a rule which moves a part of the sentence to another place, which has consequences for interpretation but no consequences for phonology; in terms of the structure of the grammar in Figure 1.5, the movement takes place between S-structure and logical form.

The difference between English and Chinese is that in Chinese the reflexive moves to Infl, and can move to any Infl; in English it does not. The principle remains true for both languages that a reflexive always finds its co-referent in the same sentence. This is a theoretical way of stating the variation, which is fundamentally different from a more surface-oriented way, which would say that in Chinese a reflexive can find its co-referent in a different clause. The justification for the approach presented here is that, as Cole et al. show, it fits both with general principles but also explains other aspects of Chinese. For example, in Chinese, the reflexive pronoun must take a subject as its antecedent not an object. In English it is possible to say *John told Mary about herself*, which is legitimate because the object *Mary* c-commands the reflexive pronoun *herself*. However, this is not possible in Chinese, because in Chinese the equivalent reflexive must move to Infl position before the co-reference is established, at which point it cannot be c-commanded by the object and so cannot find the object as a co-referent.

Linguistic theory tells us that variation can involve abstract structures which are not audible in the pronounced sentence, and can involve 'transformational' rules which transform one representation of a sentence into another. Certain principles and mechanisms are found in all languages: the structural relation of c-command, the Infl node, the principle that reflexives must find their antecedents in the same sentence. An account of something that varies between languages that can be considered genuinely explanatory must do more than just describe the variation. In this case the account provides a single underlying explanation for two apparently distinct phenomena (but which prove to co-vary across languages) – the ability of Chinese reflexives to find a co-referent outside their own clause and the restriction that the co-referent can only be a subject.

1.2.5   Summary: Linguistic problems and generative linguistic theory

In this section I have described three 'classic' linguistic problems and in each case have described one of the possible solutions to these problems. The three solutions all come from the 'generativist' approach to language, initiated by Chomsky. Other linguistic theories have offered other accounts of how to solve these problems. Almost all linguistic theories have certain things in common, and I conclude this section by noting two of them, since they are relevant to the questions of causal factors in linguistic variation which have been of interest to economists.

(i) A linguistic argument focuses on specific problems in the data and shows how their solution is part of a larger theory of language. New data is primarily of interest to the extent that it challenges or confirms an existing larger theory. Linguistic theories change and diverge; none of the accounts here correspond exactly to current accounts of the same problems and some current accounts are very different. This is all worth emphasizing because the underlying complexity of the problems can be lost in descriptive accounts of languages and typological overviews, both of which may be radical simplifications of the theoretical approach taken at any specific time.

(ii) Most linguistic theories are committed to the psychological reality of abstract linguistic form which is not audible in the spoken language. This can include constituent structure, rules and conditions, and perhaps most significantly the possibility that the heard ('surface') sequence and form of a word or sentence is not the same as its underlying form. Knowledge of a language is largely unconscious knowledge of all aspects of its form, including the underlying forms. This is important when assessing the extent to which knowledge of a language has 'Whorfian' effects on thought or behaviour, because these effects are almost always judged on the assumption that only surface form has psychological reality, an assumption which linguistic theory shows must be incorrect.

1.3   Linguistic diversity: An illustrative comparison between two languages

Ethnologue is a widely used database of languages, maintained by the Summer Institute of Linguistics organization which 'contains information on 7,106 known living languages', and is a subset – we do not know how small – of all the languages which have existed, which currently exist, and which will exist in the future. Information about a selection of these languages, and how they vary, has been extracted from grammars, articles and other sources, and organized in some major typological projects of which the largest and most diverse is probably the World Atlas of Language Structures (WALS). This has been used by some economists seeking typological correlations between linguistic forms and cultural values. In this section I illustrate linguistic diversity and discuss some of the gaps between a language and its representation in a database, by looking at specific differences between English and Ma'di, a language spoken mainly in South Sudan and northern Uganda. I am the co-author of the most substantial existing grammar of Ma'di (Blackings and Fabb, 2003), and this grammar is the source of most of the information about Ma'di in WALS.

When we call Ma'di or English 'a language' we are idealizing over a set of dialects which are considered to belong together, but which differ from one another: there are at least five for Ma'di, and there are very many for English. Ma'di is spoken in South Sudan and northern Uganda by around a quarter of a million Ma'di people, and by a diaspora population. It is not an official language; the official language of South Sudan is English (one of about 60 languages spoken in the country). Most Ma'dis will also speak at least one other language, including English, Swahili or Juba Arabic (a dialect of Arabic not necessarily understood in the north). Facts like these problematize language-to-nation correlations of the kinds made by some economists (and discussed later).

Languages have common ancestors, most of which have to be reconstructed based on familial resemblances. Ma'di is classified as belonging to the subfamily Central Sudanic of the genus Moru-Ma'di and the family Nilo-Saharan; in principle this might mean that Ma'di is one descendent of a hypothetical language which we could call proto-Nilo-Saharan. English is classified as belonging to the genus Germanic of the family Indo-European, and may be a descendent of a language which might be called proto-Indo-European. Note that though classified as in the genus Germanic, English has also been strongly influenced by French (in the genus Romance) and other European languages (because of its mixed history and the influence of French speakers in mediaeval Britain). There is no known ancestor connecting proto-Indo-European and proto-Nilo-Saharan, and perhaps there is indeed none. For a sceptical discussion of the possibility of ancient common ancestors for contemporary language families, see Nichols (2012).

In the remainder of this section I look at a selection of variations between languages, as manifested by differences between English and Ma'di, and begin with the sounds of languages. WALS is divided into chapters of which Chapter 1 (Maddieson, 2013) compares 'consonant inventories'; I refer to this as WALS-1. If we look at its inventory of consonants, we find that Ma'di has more consonants than English, mainly because the inventory of Ma'di includes complex consonants such as [kp]. For WALS, Ma'di would be classified as having a 'moderately large' inventory, compared to the English 'average'. The languages in WALS-1 vary in size between 6 and 122 consonants. Maddieson notes that theory influences any decision about how many consonants there are (as is true of every aspect of WALS). Ma'di has some types of consonants not found in English, with three implosive consonants including the [ɗ] of *màdî*, which is the name of the language ([ɗ] is orthographically written as apostrophe-d as in Ma'di). Implosives require the closure of the vocal tract followed by an intake of air (rather than the more usual expulsion of air), and are found mainly in this part of Africa according to WALS-7 (Maddieson, 2013). English has types of consonants not found in Ma'di including the dental non-sibilant fricative consonants [ð] and [θ] (the initial consonants of *this* and *thick* respectively); these are also quite rare cross-linguistically but unlike the implosives they belong to a rare consonant type which is scattered throughout the world's languages (WALS-19, Maddieson, 2013).

Now consider the inventory of vowels (WALS-2, Maddieson, 2013), where we find the reverse situation. English has a large vowel inventory, though the actual vowels (and the number of vowels) vary greatly between dialects; the inventory's size and variation are partly due to the complex relation between long and short vowels in the history of English. In contrast, Ma'di has an average vowel inventory of nine with no distinction between long and short. Ma'di (but not English) vowels are differentiated into those with 'advanced tongue root' and 'retracted tongue root' (differentiated by how far retracted the root of the tongue is, with no direct equivalent in English). In Ma'di, there is also an interesting rule in operation, which is that the vowel of an affix will (depending on other factors) take on the same advanced tongue root characteristic as the main word it is attached to. Thus for example the word [tū] means 'climb' and has an advanced tongue root vowel; if the prefix meaning 'repeatedly' is added to it the word is [ūtú], so that the vowel of the prefix is also advanced tongue root. If the same prefix is added to the word [zɔ̄] 'grow' to form the word [ūzɔ̄] we find that the vowel of the prefix is now retracted tongue root. A phonological rule is in operation here (just as we saw a phonological rule in Section 1.2, with the vowel shift). This is not just a variation in vowel inventory but a variation in the rules which apply within a word: Ma'di has a 'vowel harmony' process which harmonizes features of a vowel within a word. Various kinds of vowel harmony process are found throughout the world's languages (but not in English).

Consonants and vowels are combined into syllables, and languages can vary in the types of syllables they permit (WALS-12, Maddieson, 2013). Ma'di is classified as having a 'simple syllable structure' allowing only two types of syllable, either consonant plus vowel or just vowel. English allows both of these plus other types of syllable and has 'complex syllable structure'. Maddieson in WALS-12 notes that there is a correlation in the database between having simple syllables and having smaller consonant inventories (though this is not true for Ma'di), and raises the (unanswered) question of 'whether the association should be attributed to accidents of survival and spread of particular languages, or can be proposed as reflecting a design feature of language viewed as a whole'. This is typical of the problems which are presented by theoretical explanations for linguistic diversity.

Ma'di is a tone language (WALS-13, Maddieson, 2013), whereas English is not. In a tone language, the pitch or pitch contours on the syllables (i.e. its tone) are used to distinguish one word from another, such that a word has a specific tone pattern. Thus the Ma'di word *sá* with high tone means 'tail', the word *sā* with mid-tone means 'to plant or scour', and the word *sà* with low tone means 'to intervene and bring a fight to the end'; the consonant and vowel are the same in each word, only the tone varies. I now discuss three of the many complexities in the use of tone in Ma'di.

First, while in principle any type of syllable can carry any of the three tones, there are some restrictions: thus in a two-syllable word there are nine possible tonal sequences, but the sequence high-low is associated with words borrowed into the language from another language such as Arabic or English: all borrowed disyllables have this pattern, and all but two words in the language with this pattern are borrowed words. Longer borrowed words also have stereotyped tonal patterns. This illustrates that a language is not uniform in its properties: different types of vocabulary might be subject to different generalizations. A second aspect of tone in Ma'di is that some prefixes or suffixes are just 'floating tones' with no vowel or consonant involved. For example, the past and the non-past (present, future) forms of the verb are distinguished just by adding a low tone to the beginning of the non-past verb.

A third example involving tone demonstrates a case where tonally the spoken form of a word is not the same as its abstract form. Ma'di has a grammatical word *drʊ* meaning something like 'analogous to' which appears with one of two distinct tones, either high tone *drʊ́* or mid-tone *drʊ̄*. It has a mid-tone if it follows a word with a high tone, but if it follows a word with a mid- or low tone it has a high tone. Based on what we know about other languages, one possibility is that this is a 'contour' effect which requires contrast between adjacent linguistic elements, so that the tone on the word is different from the preceding tone. However, contour effects of this kind tend to be general within a language and not idiosyncratic to specific words, as is the case here. Blackings and Fabb (2003, p. 62) offer a different explanation, based on the difference between underlying and surface forms. We suggest that the word has the underlying form *HIGH-drʊ̄*, that is, that it has two tones, of which the first is an initial floating high tone (annotated *HIGH*) unattached to a vowel and the second is a mid-tone attached to the vowel [ʊ]. This is the form in which the word is stored in the mental lexicon, but it is never pronounced in this way. Instead, it is pronounced in one of two ways. If the word follows a high-toned vowel, its own initial floating high tone assimilates to the high tone of the preceding vowel, and the mid-tone remains on the word. If the word follows a non-high-toned vowel (i.e. mid or low) the high tone cannot assimilate to the preceding word and instead shifts rightwards to displace the mid-tone on the word, ending up on the vowel [ʊ]. Here again we see a phonological rule in operation which mediates between the abstract underlying form and the surface spoken form. This type of account localizes the effect on the word (so we would not expect it to show up on any other word) but it uses rules and other principles of structure which allow floating tones, assimilation of tones, and the possibility of a high tone displacing a mid-tone: these rules are seen more generally in other aspects of Ma'di, thus justifying their use here. The more generally explanatory an abstract explanation of this kind is, the better the explanation.

Morphology is the shape of a word such as the use of prefixes and suffixes. In Ma'di the past form of the verb is unmarked (it has no special morphology), while the non-past is marked (with special morphology) because it has a prefix (which is a floating low tone). In English the same past vs non-past distinction is made, but in contrast the non-past is unmarked (e.g. *jump*) while it is the past which is marked with a suffix (as in *jumped*). Another morphological difference between the languages relates to the marking of plurality on a noun; in English, most plural nouns have a suffix (or are irregular), while in Ma'di, most kinds of noun are morphologically the same in singular and plural with the exception of nouns of gender, age, kinship and occupation, which are marked for plural by changing the tonal pattern on the word. This restriction of plurality to human nouns is cross-linguistically quite common

(WALS-34, Haspelmath, 2013). However, (again unlike English) almost all Ma'di adjectives can be pluralized, where plural is indicated by changing the tone pattern on the adjective. Ma'di has no grammatical gender, in common with more than half the languages surveyed in WALS (WALS-30, 31, 32, Corbett, 2013); English has grammatical gender only in the pronouns, which WALS describes as cross-linguistically rare. Note that deterministic accounts of the relation between language and culture, which are particularly tempting when it comes to meanings relating to gender, would have to steer a careful path through the complexity of these differences, a complexity which is typical of all languages.

Languages can vary in their grammatical words. The English articles *a* and *the* come before the noun; the articles in Ma'di come after the noun. In English, an indefinite singular NP must usually have the indefinite article *a*, but in Ma'di, an equivalent NP can omit the article. There are several definite articles in Ma'di, one being a low tone suffix added to the noun which is used to indicate that the noun has a unique referent, another is the word *rɨ* which is used when the NP refers to something which has been earlier mentioned in the discourse (the closest equivalent to English *the*), and another word *nā* used when the referent has very recently been mentioned. The rules for which determiner to use, both in terms of meaning, and also in terms of syntactic context, are very complex in Ma'di. The complexity of the data around these articles in Ma'di is not reflected in WALS, which includes two specific classificatory points about Ma'di, one that (like English) the definite and demonstrative words are different, and the other that it is described as having 'no indefinite but definite article', which is partly true, but must be finessed. This demonstrates that the database necessarily under-represents the complexity of the data, a point which I have made repeatedly in this section and which has significant consequences for the final section of this chapter where I consider economists' uses of this and similar databases.

Pronouns are another class of grammatical words which have drawn the attention of economists, as we will see. Ma'di has distinct pronouns for first person singular and plural (like English *I* and *we*), but also has a third pronoun which can express either 'I and you' (inclusive first and second person) or 'someone' (indefinite third person). Ma'di has distinct pronouns for second person singular and plural (unlike English *you* which is used for both) but this is purely a distinction of number and does not express social relations (hence, unlike *tu* and *vous* in French). In the third person, unlike English, Ma'di tends to use the same pronouns for both, and plurality is instead marked by a distinct word *kɨˋ* or *pɨ̄* (the latter meaning 'and associates'). So the system of pronouns is different from the system in English, along many dimensions. This is further complicated by the fact that the realization of a pronoun depends on the function of the pronoun in the sentence (as in English, where *I* is the subject and *me* the object form); in Ma'di there are three distinct forms of the subject pronoun depending on whether it is the subject of an uninflected (past) verb, of an inflected (non-past) verb, or of a directive verb, and a further distinct form for object pronouns. The pronoun is sometimes realized as a distinct word (or two distinct words if one includes the plural marker), and sometimes as a prefix on the verb.

Any account of the pronominals of Ma'di must make theoretical assumptions, including assumptions about underlying forms which are not necessarily the same as those on the surface. Thus for example there are two forms of the first person singular pronoun preceding an uninflected (past) verb, one just a prefix *á* and one a longer form *má*. They do not differ significantly in meaning. In Blackings and Fabb (2003, p. 136) we suggest that the longer form is actually a sequence of two pronouns with the same meaning, the default first person pronoun *mā* (also used for object pronouns), preceding the prefix *á*, and both are merged and the high tone replaces the mid-tone (a process seen elsewhere, e.g. in *dŕí*, discussed above). As we will see later in this chapter, one influential economics article builds a theory by extracting very simplified differences from typological data about pronouns; my goal here is to show that such linguistic data may often be far from simple. The Ma'di system of pronouns is also relevant to the issue of how data is analysed and how it feeds into typological databases. What we identify as a third person pronoun *ká* has been analysed in other work on Ma'dı as an auxiliary verb; this is a very significant difference typologically, and both views cannot be right (but someone forming a database must make a choice between these incompatible alternatives, often silently).

Consider now tense and aspect. Tense is a modification of a verb to indicate the relative location of an event in time; in English the verb can have one of two tenses, either as in *ate* or *walked* which are past, or as in *eat* or *walk* which are non-past because they can be used for present or future. Futurity can also be expressed periphrastically by using a modal verb *will* or *shall*. As we will see in Section 1.5, differences in how tense works in a language are taken to be significant for economics by Chen (2013). Aspect is a modification of the verb to represent the internal temporal constituency of the event, with perfective aspect representing the event as a single unit, and imperfective aspect representing the event as internally granular, and interruptable. In English there is no clear grammaticalization of this distinction but imperfective is expressed periphrastically. A periphrastic expression of a meaning uses two or more words, and thus differs from a grammaticalized expression which uses one word (including its internal morphology). The periphrastic expression of imperfective in English uses the progressive form as in the sentence *I am eating*. If not progressive, an English verb is usually interpreted as perfective. Thus the sentence *I ate the sandwich when he entered the room* is best interpreted by treating the two verbs (perfectively) as representing single whole units and ordered one after another, while the sentence *I was eating the sandwich when he entered the room* is interpreted as the second (perfective) event coming in the middle of the first (imperfective) event. In Ma'di, tense and aspect are expressed not only by modification of the verb, but also by major differences in sentence structure. This is illustrated below. The primary distinction is between past and non-past, and the distinction of aspect between perfective and imperfective is parasitic on this (with complications, Blackings and Fabb, 2003, p. 172).

(14) ɔ́-ɲā gbándà
      he-eat cassava
      'he ate cassava' (past, and perfective)

(15) ká gbándà `-ɲā
      he cassava nonpast-eat
      'he is eating cassava' (or 'he eats cassava') (non-past, and imperfective)

The past verb carries no inflection, while the non-past verb has a prefix added to it which is a floating low tone. In addition, the past verb precedes its object (SVO order) while the non-past verb follows its object (SOV order). And the subject pronouns are different, with a prefix on the past verb and a separate pronominal on the non-past verb. However, when the sentence is negative, the 'past tense' version of the syntax and morphology is used for both past and non-past, and the tense distinction is instead expressed entirely by a choice between one of two negation words.

(16) ɔ́-ɲā gbándà kōrò
      he-eat cassava not (past)
      'he did not eat cassava'

(17) ɔ́-ɲā gbándà kō
      he-eat cassava not (non-past)
      'he does not eat cassava' (or 'he is not eating cassava', or 'he will not eat cassava')

I know of no published theoretical explanation of why these various differences – inflection of the verb, pronominal, and word order – all align, and why the differences disappear when the sentence is negated. I outline briefly a possible solution now, noting the relation between this problem and the problems around verb position and 'verb second' described in Section 1.2. I start by proposing that the two syntactic structures are underlyingly the same, that the underlying word order is SVO, and that tense is expressed abstractly at the right-hand end of the sentence. The specific rule is that when tense is non-past, some word which can express tense must be in this position. When a negation word occupies this position it picks up the non-past tense; if there is no negation then the non-past tense must be carried by something else and so the verb moves (rightwards past the object) to the tense position and picks up the tense as an inflection, thus producing the surface order. The subject pronoun would be realized as a separate word when no longer adjacent to the verb. This type of account hypothesizes abstract underlying word orders (and pronominal expression, etc.) which are not the same as those on the surface. It also introduces a theoretical claim which goes against one of the current cross-linguistic generalizations in generative linguistics, which is the 'final-over-final constraint' (Biberauer et al., 2007): this generalization predicts that a verb which precedes its object should not be moveable to a position which follows its sentence, as here. This means either that this explanation is incorrect or that the principle is incorrect, or that there is some other complicating factor: in this way, linguistic theory develops. Ma'di is classified by WALS as having no dominant word order (i.e. neither SVO or SOV), but a more abstract analysis which properly explains the patterns in the language might in fact find that it does have a dominant SVO word order with the other derived from it (Dryer, 2013 devotes a discussion in WALS-144 to Ma'di negation and word order, noting that only five described languages, all from the same area, show this pattern).

As a last example of a variation found in Ma'di, note that while (18) below is a grammatical sentence, (19) is not.

(18) ɔ̄-ɲā ádʒɨ̄nɨ̄
      he-eat yesterday
      'he ate yesterday'
(19) * ɔ̄-ɲā
      he-eat
      'he ate'

Sentence (19) is ungrammatical, as indicated by the asterisk preceding it. One of the important devices of theoretical linguistics which is not always reflected in descriptive grammars is the notion of ungrammaticality: speakers are able to distinguish between possible and impossible utterances in their language. My co-author Mairi Blackings and I visited a group of expatriate Ma'di speakers to discuss their intuitions of the language. They agreed that they could say (18) but not (19) and thought nothing of it; I have striking memories of their amusement when I pointed out that when they spoke English they had no such distinction between the two perfectly acceptable sentences *He ate yesterday* and *He ate*. They were surprised by this observation about the difference between two languages, both of which they spoke, and this neatly illustrates that judgements about grammaticality in a language are generally unconscious. No one taught them the fact about Ma'di that the uninflected ('past') verb cannot be the last word in a sentence; it must be followed by something else, which is here the word for 'yesterday' but could equally be other words. There is no published explanation for this and indeed it is not picked up in WALS and may perhaps be unique as a surface characteristic of a language. However, a theoretical linguist would ask whether it is the surface result of underlying patterns and rules which are found elsewhere but here producing a unique surface result due to the rules operating in a unique combination.

In this section I have indicated some of the ways in which English and Ma'di differ; my intention has been to show some of the complexity of the data presented by any language, many of which remain unexplained and demand theoretical linguistic study. We have seen that though these differences can be represented to some extent in the WALS project, it cannot really represent the complexity of the data or the possibility that the variation on the surface masks underlying similarities. As linguists, the authors of WALS are fully aware of this: it is an inevitable result of the simplifying process needed to produce the patterns in the 'big data'. However, this may not be recognized by non-linguists who draw on the simplified version in WALS, particularly in order to produce binarities which can be correlated with social or economic behaviour, as we will see in Section 1.5.

1.4 Theories of linguistic diversity

The forms of languages vary, but within limits: it is possible to imagine kinds of language which do not exist. Ma'di and English have certain forms in common, as demonstrated by the fact that they can be described by similar theoretical terminologies. When they vary from one another they vary in specific ways, such that they fit into bigger but still limited patterns of how languages can vary. In this section, I summarize different views on why languages have certain forms in common, and why they vary. I begin with the current version of generative linguistics, which is a very widely used linguistic theory. I then consider alternative accounts of linguistic form which argue that form is determined in part by external factors.

1.4.1 Chomsky, universal grammar, and the theory of principles and parameters

A form of the generative linguistic theory introduced by Chomsky in *Syntactic Structures* is the theory of 'principles and parameters'. This theory formulates a notion of universal grammar as a set of principles and parameters which govern how language is structured, and which is available as a cognitive capacity to all humans as a genetic inheritance. This is both a theory of linguistic form and a theory of the psychology of language. Rizzi (2013) offers an overview of the theory and introduces a collection of articles which discuss various aspects of it, including Cinque (2013) on typology. Like all theories of linguistic diversity, this remains a hypothesis, with many adherents but also with many competitors.

The psychological part of the theory proposes that all humans have an innate language faculty. This faculty enables the learning of language and hence determines what the possible forms of a language are. For this reason, all languages are predicted to conform to certain principles. Where there are variations between languages, some of these variations arise from determinate possibilities of variation which are set by the language faculty as 'parameters' which allow for one of various options to be selected. Thus for example, a parameter may provide options: the choice of a specific option in a parameter determines that an article precedes the noun (as in English) and the choice of a different option in the same parameter determines that an article follows the noun (as in Ma'di). The effects of parameter settings are likely to be indirect and interact with other parameters (i.e. my previous sentence oversimplifies: there is unlikely to be a parameter directly determining article position, but article position may be determined by the parameter setting interacting with other parameter settings, along with innate rules of the language system). Other parameters might be set to determine whether the language has 'verb second', whether it has an SOV or SVO order, whether it has long distance reflexives or not (but noting as for long distance reflexives that the parameters might be quite abstract, and have these as surface effects).

Parameter-setting is how a language is learned. When exposed to a language spoken around it, the child learns that language by making choices from the parameters, fixing a set of interacting variables to produce that specific language. Chomsky offers an argument of 'poverty of stimulus', that the data to which the child is exposed does not offer enough information on its own to enable the child to learn the language; instead the child must already 'know' certain aspects of the language and what its possible forms might be as part of his or her innate language faculty. The notion of universal grammar, which is the basis of the theory of principles and parameters, is a radical one: that all languages conform to certain basic principles, and that certain differences between them are based on the selection of specific pre-determined variants ('parameters').

1.4.2   Cultural evolution and linguistic diversity

Evans and Levinson (2009, p. 429) suggest that languages can in principle vary in any way at all, and that the forms of languages which currently exist do so as a combination of historical accident and other forces, but do not involve any language-specific faculty of the kind proposed by Chomsky: 'although there are significant recurrent patterns in organization, these are better explained as stable engineering solutions satisfying multiple design constraints, reflecting both cultural-historical factors and the constraints of human cognition'. They offer evidence for this claim by citing specific kinds of variation which they suggest cannot be reduced to underlying universals, though it should be noted that generativists who have responded to this article disagree with the linguistic evidence offered or its interpretation, and suggest that underlying universals can in fact be found. Evans and Levinson's proposal is that languages change and diverge in parallel with the changing and diverging cultures of their speakers. The reasons for similarities between languages are in part the same reason that there are similarities between cultures: languages and cultures have split apart over time, but there has not been enough time for major divergences to emerge. Another reason for similarities between languages is that there are external pressures, in part from general principles of cognition and in part from the environment, which limit variation. They take a slightly 'Whorfian' position here about causal relations between general cognition and language (Evans and Levinson, 2009, p. 436), citing earlier work by Levinson (2003) proposing that spatial cognition is causally related to the grammaticalization of spatial reference in a language (argued against by Li and Gleitman, 2002 and others, as noted in the next section). Evans and Levinson make a claim about the species-specificity of human language which is opposed, at a philosophical level, to that of Chomsky. Whereas Chomsky proposes that what distinguishes us as a species is that all of our languages are fundamentally alike, Evans and Levinson propose that we are distinguished as a species because our communication systems are fundamentally diverse.

1.4.3   Dediu and Ladd

Dediu and Ladd (2007) develop an account of the diversification of languages based on genetic discoveries by others, including Bruce Lahn's lab at the University of Chicago. They suggest that there is a correlation between the genetic difference and whether the populations differentiated genetically in these ways have a tone language or not. This is not an individual-level finding: in principle, any human (i.e. with any genetic make-up) can learn any human language (i.e. with any variety of linguistic form). However, Dediu and Ladd suggest that genetic factors can form a slight bias in what can be learned and how it is learned, and that over a population and over time, a collection of slight biases might lead to a population speaking a language with certain formal characteristics. They focus specifically on the learning of tone languages, and suggest that there is a genetic factor in some populations which makes a tone language easier for members of that population to learn. Ma'di, the language discussed earlier, is a tone language, and tone languages are quite common in certain areas of the world (e.g. Sub-Saharan Africa, South East Asia, Central America) and quite rare in others (e.g. Europe, North Africa, Australia). There are some languages (e.g. Japanese, Basque) with intermediate status, and dialects of a language can differ in whether they are tonal (Dediu and Ladd, 2007, p. 10945). They focus on two previously discovered alternative forms of genes (alleles), which are ASPM-D and MCPH-D, which emerged in some populations at an estimated 5.8 thousand years and 37 thousand years ago respectively: 'those areas of the world where the new alleles are relatively rare also tend to be the areas where tone languages are common' (ibid.). They propose that there is a causal relation between genetics and language, such that the genetic structure of a population can exert an influence on the language spoken. They propose that ASPM-D and MCPH-D have an effect on the brain areas involved in linguistic tone. This may produce a bias depending on whether one has these alleles, possibly by their making non-tone languages easier to learn. They note that there are many other contributing factors and that their findings do not support a racial or deterministic interpretation. The evolutionary suggestion is that, at some earlier stage, all languages may have been tone languages, but populations emerged with the new alleles which made it harder to learn tone languages, and so non-tone languages emerged. Dediu and Ladd's proposal has been widely discussed, because it offers a rare argument that genetic differences in human populations might be causally connected with language variation.

1.4.4   Linguistic theory and language diversity

Berwick et al. (2011, p. 3) suggest that there are four interacting factors which can determine why languages are different from one another. The first set of factors are innate and domain-specific (specific to language); these are the abstract elements of linguistic form as described for example by principles and parameters theory. Generative linguistics has always fundamentally concerned itself with these factors; opponents of this theory such as Evans and Levinson argue that these factors do not exist (i.e. that there is no innate language faculty). The second set of factors are innate and domain-general. These might include general aspects of perception, memory or other aspects of cognition which might have causal effects on the forms of language, and allow for or determine variations in languages; Dediu and Ladd's proposal belongs here, in addition to the very different 'Whorfian' proposals that language has a causal relation with thought. The third set of factors are external stimuli, including exposure to language: Evans and Levinson (2009) think that the cultural environment plays a major role in determining linguistic factors. The fourth set of factors involve natural laws including computational efficiency: it may be that language takes the forms it does, and varies within certain limits or in certain ways, for reasons of computational efficiency.

A proponent of principles and parameters theory might allow all four types of factor to contribute to the shape of any specific language; however, a crucial component of this theory is that innate factors play an important role in constraining the effects of the other factors, and limiting overall variation. Other theorists such as Evans and Levinson exclude the possibility of innate factors. The balance between external and internal factors, and between domain-specific (to language) and domain-general factors, is a matter of theoretical debate, based on the analysis of patterns and generalizations in the linguistic data (as shown in the previous two sections). It also depends on what one accepts as linguistic form. The key claim by Evans and Levinson is that surface linguistic forms are too diverse to be accommodated to universal principles as found in a faculty of language; the main response by generativists is that it is not at the level of surface forms but at the level of abstract forms (from which the surface is derived) that the underlying uniformities can be discovered. The debate around linguistic theory and language diversity is thus fundamentally a debate about whether there can be certain kinds of abstract linguistic form. This has relevance for the next section of this chapter, in which I explore the 'Whorfian' view that linguistic form has a causal relation with thought and behaviour, a view which has a following in the economics literature.

1.5　Whorfian psychology and economics: Causal relations between language and thought

In this section I explore proposals that specific linguistic forms have a correlation with thought, and the possibility in particular that language causes thought, such that the language one speaks leads one to think or behave in certain ways. If true, these claims might suggest that linguistic diversity might have a causal relation with cultural diversity. This approach requires a psychological mechanism by which language causes thought, and a mechanism of historical change by which languages and kinds of thought change over time such that the claimed psychological causation can create and sustain correlations between linguistic form and thought over time. This is called a 'Whorfian' approach to language and thought. Projects seeking causal relations along these lines have recently been pursued by economists, and I discuss some of their arguments here.

The notion that language has a causal relation with thought and behaviour is particularly associated with the writings of Edward Sapir (1884–1939) and Benjamin Lee Whorf (1897–1941), and is sometimes called the 'Sapir–Whorf hypothesis' though here I call it 'Whorfian'. Surveys of Whorfian ideas include the favourable account by Hill and Mannheim (1992), the account by Lucy (1997), and the hostile account by Gleitman and Papafragou (2005). Whorfianism has been of interest to psychologists and to economists, as well as others studying language and cognition in society, culture or business. Psychologists construct experiments to test whether language determines observable aspects of cognition. Both pro- and anti-Whorfian psycholinguistic findings exist, and there is no final agreement on this. Economists (and sociologists) propose causal relations between values for some linguistic variable derived from linguistic typology and values for social variables associated with the countries in which the languages are spoken; all the correlational studies which I discuss later in this section propose a causal link (possibly in the distant past) and so affirm a Whorfian hypothesis. If there is a causal link, this must be mediated through a causal relation between language and individual psychology, which is why it is relevant to consider the psycholinguistic evidence for Whorfianism.

Most theoretical linguists tend to be hostile to Whorfianism, whose early arguments, including Whorf's account of the expression of time in the American language Hopi, and claims about the vocabulary of colour relative to colour perception, did not survive fuller scrutiny of the data. However, there are many data-specific Whorfian arguments which claim that language causes thought, and each argument needs to be examined on its merits. Most of the rest of this section looks at specific arguments, and casts doubt in particular on those arguments which have been developed by economists. There are two fundamental bases from which theoretical linguists criticize Whorfian arguments. First, linguistic data is very complex; Whorfian arguments often extract binarities from simplified typological data which is a very attenuated version of the complexity of actual data. Second, what we know when we know a language may include very abstract representations, rather different from what we see on the surface. The idea which underlies much linguistic theory and particularly generative linguistics is that languages are much more alike abstractly than they are on the surface; hence there is not as much cognitively relevant linguistic variety as appears from the Whorfian adoption of surface typological variation. Gleitman and Papafragou (2005, p. 654) make this point when they say that 'much discussion about the relationship between language and thought has been colored by an underlying disagreement about the nature of language itself'.

I now discuss three sets of psychological experiments which test Whorfian ideas. Each of these involves an initial claim that Whorfianism is demonstrated, followed by one or more rebuttals. They indicate the potential fragility of Whorfian arguments.

(i) Bloom (1981) noted a difference between English and Chinese (Mandarin) in how they expressed counterfactuals (the statement of something which might but need not be the case). In English, the subjunctive form of the verb can be used, such as *were* in *If she were to come, she would be here by now*. In Chinese, counterfactuality is not expressed on the morphology of the verb, but is expressed pariphrastically (using the arrangement of words in the sentence), as e.g. 'if X then Y'. Bloom claimed that the direct expression of counterfactuality on the verb enabled monolingual English speakers to formulate better counterfactual interpretations of a story, as demonstrated by an experiment he conducted. However, Au (1983) showed that this effect could not be experimentally reproduced, argued that it was an artefact of how the experiment was constructed, and that different ways of setting up the experiment had results in which Chinese speakers were better at constructing counterfactuals, hence offering no evidence for Whorfianism.

(ii) In some languages, position is described allocentrically (relative to the person) and in others, deictically (e.g. relative to a compass point), so that in the latter type of language someone might say 'the spoon is to the north of the coffee cup'. Levinson (1996, 1997) describes experiments in which the spatial reasoning of subjects is affected by which of these types of language they speak, and this is cited as one of the functionalist arguments in Evans and Levinson (2009). However, Li and Gleitman (2002) and Li et al. (2011) argue against the validity of these experiments, on the basis of their own experiments and alternative explanations. They argue that the difference in experimental results comes from environmental and contextual factors impinging on the subjects, not from the differences in language. They say that 'ambient spatial circumstances' may be independently a factor both in the language used and in the spatial reasoning, but there is no independent causal relation between language and spatial reasoning. Thus Li et al. (2011, p. 51) claim that 'spatial reasoning is flexible and largely independent of the implied dictates of linguistic encoding'. They emphasize the experimental subject's reasoning about intentions and communication in the situation of being in an experiment, and suggest that this explains some of the effects reported by Levinson. Again, if these counter-arguments are right, this Whorfian argument fails.

(iii) A third argument relates to languages in which temporal sequence can be expressed vertically so that April is described as 'up' relative to May which is 'down'. Chinese (Mandarin) is such a language, while English is not. Boroditsky (2001, p. 18) conducted experiments which presented horizontal and vertical visual primes before asking for judgements about temporal sequence and concluded that 'Mandarin speakers relied on a "Mandarin" way of thinking about time even when they were thinking about English sentences. Mandarin speakers were more likely to think about time vertically when deciding whether "March comes *earlier* than April"'. It is important to note that Boroditsky shows that this effect can be altered very quickly by training English speakers to use vertical terms to talk about time, and then testing them, in which case their behaviours are similar to speakers of Mandarin. These proposed Whorfian effects of language are thus not deep-rooted in thought, but seem to be highly manipulable in the experimental situation. However, January and Kako (2007), Chen (2007) and Bender et al. (2010), all separately re-ran the experiments and were unable to reproduce the findings. Chen concludes that 'Chinese speakers do not conceptualize time differently than English speakers' (2007, p. 436). Again, there is no clear evidence for Whorfianism here.

These are three attempts to demonstrate Whorfian effects experimentally for three different aspects of a language. In each case, there are arguments for and arguments against. The debate continues, involving these and other aspects of linguistic form. The best conclusion for now is that there is no general agreement in psychology and psycholinguistics that specific forms of language cause specific forms of thought.

In the remainder of this section, I examine papers by economists which claim correlations between features of language and cultural values, and more specifically claim that language causes thought, or that thought (and perception) causes language to take on specific forms. Gay et al. (2013, p. 32) say:

> since grammatical features often force us to encode certain aspects of reality to the exclusion of other aspects, it follows that applying an evolutionary perspective to grammar formation could well reveal selective pressures to codify the most relevant or salient aspects of our ancestors' reality, including culture and past economic specialization.

I interpret this to mean that the cultural values of a group of people (ancestors) caused linguistic forms to come into existence, perhaps in a situation where the linguistic system offers alternatives, and selection of the chosen alternative is biased by cultural values. This is opposite from the causal direction explored by psycholinguists, and is of course very speculative as it involves unobservable past processes. However, it is probably true to say that most of the economics articles also assume that causation is in the other direction, that language causes cultural values; here a comparison with relevant psycholinguistic experiments is useful.

1.5.1 Grammatical gender and biological sex

In many languages, nouns are grouped into classes called 'genders', where class membership is manifested as agreement, where the features of one word affect or determine the features of an article or other word (Corbett, 1991). Thus for example in the West African language Fula, *ɲiiwa* 'elephant' belongs to a gender (along with other large animals and the word for 'field') which takes the article *ba*, i.e. *ɲiiwa ba* 'the elephant', while *dɛbbɔ* 'woman' belongs to a gender (along with other nouns including both male and female humans) which takes

the article *?a*. In this Fula linguistic classification, biological sex has little connection to the classification of nouns, but it is still called 'gender'. In other
languages, including those discussed here, there is a substantial correlation
between biological sex and gender, such that nouns for men may be classified
as in one gender, and nouns for women as in another gender.

Does grammatical gender have a causal influence on cognition? The main
focus of psychological research has been on how grammatical gender affects
thinking about non-sexed objects which have grammatical genders (such as
tables and chairs), in languages including Spanish and German. Boroditsky
et al. (2003) summarize experiments whose results suggest that the grammatical gender of (non-sexed) objects affects how people think about those objects.
These objects (without natural gender or sex) have conceptual gender associated with the grammatical gender assigned to them in a language: 'differences
in grammar, with no concomitant differences in culture, are enough to influence how people think about objects' (ibid., p. 72). They suggest that it is
because objects are grouped into categories by grammatical gender that other
similarities are assigned to them as a group. It is significant that this arises even
for an invented language with grammatical genders taught to English speakers, who immediately associate other gendered characteristics with the objects
(ibid., p. 71). As in Boroditsky (2001) cited above, Boroditsky et al. (2003) show
that it is possible to undo the influence of language on the subject very easily, suggesting that there is not a deep relation between one's language and
one's psychology. Accounts of many similar experiments have been published,
all involving the assignment (or not) of gendered characteristics to non-sexed
objects (e.g. Vigliocco et al., 2005; Cubelli et al., 2011; Boutonnet et al., 2012).
For example, Imai et al. (2014) examine German and suggest that biological sex-related properties are projected onto the articles which mark gender,
and that it is via this projection that the classificatory similarities between
items which share the same grammatical gender arise: grammatical gender does
not affect the conceptual representations or inferences about the associated
concepts. Bassetti (2014) suggests that grammatical gender effects on the non-
sexed objects are mitigated when a speaker knows two languages with different
gender assignments, which 'may increase awareness of the arbitrariness of language, thus reducing language-induced biases in mental representations of the
world'. This incidentally again suggests that any causal effect of grammatical
gender on cognition can be relatively easily interfered with, and so does not run
deep. The easy manipulation of Whorfian effects is an important lesson from
the experimental work which significantly problematizes the view expressed in
Whorfian economics that language deeply embeds cultural values.

Economists have used Boroditsky et al. (2003) as evidence for Whorfianism;
thus Santacreu-Vasut et al. (2014, p. 1) write that 'grammar, according to cognitive science research (Boroditsky et al., 2003), impacts a speaker's cognitive

framework and mental representation of social reality'. But Boroditsky et al. (2003, p. 76) actually conclude that it is premature to 'conclude that grammatical gender definitely does affect people's nonlinguistic representations'. Further, Boroditsky et al.'s article relates not to how grammatical gender affects social reality, but to whether grammatical gender affects the categorization and assigned properties of non-gendered objects. Thus there is no support from the cited psycholinguistic work for the economists' claims that grammatical gender has a causal relation with social thinking about men and women, claims which I now examine.

I begin with Mavisakalyan (2011), for whom 'gender systems in language promote gender inequalities'. This is demonstrated by choosing a set of languages which are identified as those spoken at home in a set of countries, and for each country identifying a majority language. The countries are assigned gender-based values. The languages are classified as 'strongly gendered' (gender marked in first and second persons), 'mildly gendered' (gender marked only in third person) and 'gender-neutral' (no gender marked in pronouns). Mavisakalyan says that the relative percentages of women in the labour force correlate with whether the majority language of the country is strongly gendered (there are 4.4 percentage point less women in the labour force than in gender-neutral languages), mildly gendered (there are 2.3 percentage point less women in the labour force than in gender-neutral languages), or gender neutral. I illustrate how this maps on to countries shortly.

Gay et al. (2013) differentiate five levels of gender intensity (GII = gender intensity index, from 0 to 4) which a language may fall into, with the highest gender-intensity language having a combination of the properties of (i) a sex-based gender system, (ii) with exactly two genders, (iii) in which only male entities are assigned male gender, and (iv) there is a gender distinction in first and/or second person pronouns. A language with all four properties is called a GII4 language. Lower gender intensities from GII3 to GII0 correlate with fewer of these gender properties. Spanish, Hebrew and Arabic are all classified as GII4. Gay et al. (2013, p. 41) write that

> at both the country and the individual level, women who speak in a language – or who live in countries with a dominant language – that marks gender more intensively are less likely to participate in economic and political life and more likely to face formal and informal barriers when seeking to access credit and land.

Santacreu-Vasut et al. (2013, 2014) repeat essentially the same argument as Gay et al., concluding that 'the average percentage of female presence on boards and committees is higher in countries with low gender marking than in those with high marking' (Santacreu-Vasut et al., 2014, p. 5).

Prewitt-Freilino et al. (2012) develop a similar argument (but in a different discipline, apparently not aware of the economists' arguments). They divide languages into three groups, of 'gendered', 'genderless' and 'natural'. Gendered languages have masculine and feminine gender assigned to nouns (sometimes other genders). Genderless languages have no grammatical gender in nouns or pronouns. Natural gender languages have grammatical gender only in pronouns. They find that 'countries that speak gendered languages evidence less gender equality than countries that speak natural gender or genderless languages', and 'countries that speak natural gender languages may be even more apt to exhibit gender equality – especially in the form of women's greater access to political empowerment – than in countries where gendered or genderless languages are spoken'.

These three research projects each find that a classification of languages (in terms of gender on pronouns) correlates with a classification of cultures (in terms of the position of women). In Table 1.2, I summarize the results for a selection of the languages they discuss, to illustrate how the same languages are differently ranked by different approaches. I have taken a subset of the discussed language which allows for comparison, and I have crudely aligned them as 'worst for women', 'best for women' and 'middling' (these terms are not used by the original articles).

Languages are sorted into kinds differently by the approaches of the different articles, as Table 1.2 shows. So, for example, while Spanish, Hebrew and Arabic are placed by all three articles in the most gendered category, English is sometimes least gendered and sometimes in the middle, while Hindi is most gendered for Prewitt-Freilino et al. (2012), has a gender intensity of 3 (out of a maximal 4) for Gay et al. (2013) but is least gendered for Mavisakalyan (2011); German and French similarly are sometimes grouped together and sometimes separated in how gendered they are, depending on criteria. It is not necessarily a problem that there is no consistent way of classifying how gendered a language is, since it is possible (in this type of argument) that different types of disadvantage for women correlate with different ways in which a language might be gendered, but it makes the arguments less grounded in objective linguistic reality. Recall also that there is no good evidence from psychology for any causal effects.

Before leaving this example, I want to note briefly the extent to which the typology ignores major differences between languages. Consider one component of Gay's gender intensity, which is whether first and second pronouns are gender marked; Hebrew and Spanish are said to have the same value, but this is so simplified as to be probably wrong. Hebrew gender marks all the first and second person pronouns. But European Spanish marks for gender only first and second person plural. The first person plural form which is used for a group of women is *nosotras* (sometimes informally used when the majority in

Table 1.2 Gender and language

Mavisakalyan (2011)

Worst for women	Strongly gendered	Arabic, Hebrew, Spanish
Middling	Mildly gendered	Chinese (Mandarin), Dutch, English, French, German, Greek, Italian, Lithuanian, Norwegian, Polish, Portuguese, Russian, Romanian, Swedish
Best for women	Gender-neutral	Azerbaijani, Chichewa, Estonian, Finnish, Hindi, Hungarian, Khmer, Malay, Mongolian (Khalkha), Thai, Turkish, Vietnamese

Gay et al. (2013)

Worst for women	GII4	Arabic, Hebrew, Spanish
	GII3	French, Hindi
Middling	GII2	German, Greek, Icelandic, Italian, Lithuanian, Portuguese Russian
	GII1	Chichewa, Dutch, English, Norwegian, Polish, Romanian, Swedish
Best for women	GII0	Azerbaijani, Khmer, Chinese (Mandarin), Estonian, Finnish, Hungarian, Indonesian, Korean, Malay, Mongolian (Khalkha), Thai, Turkish, Vietnamese

Prewitt-Freilino et al. (2012)

Worst for women	Gendered	Arabic, Dutch, French, German, Greek, Hebrew, Hindi, Irish, Italian, Korean, Portuguese, Polish, Romanian, Russian, Spanish, Tamil
Middling	Genderless	Azerbaijani, Chichewa, Chinese (Mandarin), Khmer, Estonian, Finnish, Hungarian, Indonesian, Malay, Lithuanian, Mongolian (Khalkha), Thai Turkish, Vietnamese
Best for women	Natural	English, Icelandic, Norwegian, Swedish

a meeting are women), while *nosotros* is meant to be used when all are men or in a mixed group. Second person plural, specifically in the 'familiar' form, when all are women is *vosotras* and *vosotros* when all are men; the 'non-familiar' form has *ustedes* for both genders. In South American Spanish, the gender distinction disappears in second person plural because *ustedes* is the only form used (for both familiar and non-familiar). Finally, *nosotros* and *nosotras* and *vosotros* and *vosotras* can probably be treated as compounds, sharing the same ungendered pronouns *nos* 'we' and *vos* 'you' combined with a gender-sensitive suffix *otros* and *otras* (Harley and Ritter, 2002). So gender may not be really marked at all on the pronouns in Spanish. In all these ways, gender is marked in a very different way from Hebrew (and less intensively), but this is lost entirely in the typological simplification; furthermore South American Spanish is less gendered than European Spanish.

1.5.2 Person and subject pronouns

Kashima and Kashima (1998, 2005) correlate aspects of the 'major language used in a country' with cultural dimensions associated with that country such as individualism and uncertainty avoidance. For example, they say that a language allows 'pronoun drop' if first and second person pronouns can be omitted in conversations, and say that Spanish, Italian and Greek allow pronoun drop, while English, French and German do not. Countries are divided into those whose major languages allow pronoun drop and those which do not, and individualism scores are assigned to those countries. They find that 'languages licensing pronoun drop are associated with lower levels of individualism than those that require the obligatory use of personal pronouns such as *I* or *you* as a subject of a sentence' (1998, p. 477). What reason is there to think that this correlation might arise from causation? Kashima and Kashima claim that the possibility of omission enables a speaker 'to manipulate the presence of the self and other in discourse' because omission of the first or second person subject reduces attention to the distinction between the self and the other, thus favouring a contextualized approach to the self and other rather than an individualistic one. This claim lacks psycholinguistic support.

Licht et al. (2007, p. 673) refer to the research reported in Kashima and Kashima (1998) and interpret it as follows: 'the license to drop pronouns, particularly to omit *I*, reduces the conceptual differentiation between person and context. It should therefore occur more frequently in societies whose cultures emphasize the contextualization of persons more and their uniqueness less'. Kashima and Kashima's argument is also used by Tabellini (2008) to argue that specific cultural values (e.g. that the individual is entitled to certain basic rights) will causally influence good government. He wants to show that certain values are embedded in a culture over a long time, and because language tends to change slowly, and is associated with a culture, he looks to language to provide long-lasting correlates of cultural values. He describes language as 'an instrument . . . correlated with the random evolution of ideas in the distant past' and that the grammatical rules are 'correlated with distant cultural traditions', thus explicitly taking on a Whorfian position. Tabellini (2008, p. 274) claims correlations are based on two values, as follows. First, languages in which the first person must be expressed by a pronoun positively correlate with indicators of generalized morality, 'trust' and 'respect' (leading to good government). The second value relates to T-V languages. These are languages which have differentiated second person pronouns; e.g. French has 'tu' and 'vous', differentiated both for singular vs plural but also differentiated for social relations. These T-V languages are claimed by Tabellini to correlate negatively with 'trust' and 'respect'. Thus for example, English has the two linguistic values which would make it a language correlating with trust and respect; Italian has neither. He concludes (2008, p. 278) that 'languages forbidding pronoun drop or that do not differentiate between T-V are associated with better government (the correlation here is mainly with the pronoun drop rule)'.

A linguist might make several objections to Kashima and Kashima's use of linguistic evidence, and here I list four. A first objection (which can be made for all the Whorfian economics articles) relates to whether the complexity of the data has been properly acknowledged. English – classified as a no-pronoun-drop language associated with individualism – actually does allow pronoun drop in various personal and public styles or registers, including newspaper headlines and diary writing (Haegeman and Ihsane, 2001). This problematizes the data underlying the study but also raises a question: if there is a causal relation between dropping the subject and non-individualism, does this mean that diaries express individualism less than other English genres? A second objection relates to how first and second person are expressed linguistically in English (no pronoun drop) vs Italian (pronoun drop). Both languages express first and second person; English does so only on the subject pronoun, while Italian does so on the verbal morphology and optionally also on the subject pronoun. It is not at all clear why one type of expression (on the verbal morphology as in Italian) should have a weaker causal effect than another (on a pronoun). In many Whorfian arguments, expression of a meaning as part of the verbal morphology is considered to have a greater causal effect than periphrastic expression, the opposite of what we have here. A third objection relates to how freely omittable a pronoun is; whether the subject person is expressed by a pronoun or not is often determined by syntactic or other contextual factors (this is true in Ma'di for example) such as discourse conditions or the need to focus the pronoun. These linguistic contextual factors can determine the choice of pronouns, so that choice is not free; this can over-ride the functional effects claimed by Kashima and Kashima.

A fourth objection comes from the very extensive theoretical linguistic work on the distinctions between what linguists call 'pro-drop' languages (those in which the subject pronoun can be omitted) and non-pro-drop languages. Pro-drop languages are diverse in kind (as Kashima and Kashima acknowledge); for example, in some such as Italian the verbal morphology provides information about the missing subject, while in others such as Chinese there is no relevant verbal morphology. Linguistic theorists seek to discover what underlying properties these languages have, which group them in certain ways: for example, most forms of English have no pro-drop and have a very small amount of partial verbal agreement with the subject, while Italian has pro-drop and uniformly full verbal agreement with the subject and Chinese has pro-drop and uniformly absent verbal agreement. Huang (1989) has argued that a pro-drop language must have uniform properties for agreement, either all present or all absent, hence grouping Italian and Chinese against English. In English the subject can be omitted only in a subordinate clause which has uniformly absent verbal morphology as in *I want [__ to leave]* where the subordinate verb 'leave' has a missing first person subject as marked by the line. Huang notes that the possibility of omitting the subject in a subordinate clause in English (uniformly without agreement) is analogous to omitting the subject in a main clause in Chinese (uniformly without agreement). Linguists also note that pro-drop is correlated with other properties in a language. Thus Romance languages like Italian which can omit the subject can also invert the subject as in the grammatical sentence *Ha mangiato Giovanni* ('Giovanni ate'); linguists seek a consistent explanation for this and for the possibility of a missing subject. In summary, linguists treat the possibility of having a missing subject as one piece in a complex puzzle, which is solved differently for the diverse ways in which it manifests in different languages, and which also is based on underlying similarities between languages. The simple typologies based on surface properties, which are the basis for Kashima and Kashima's paper, may not represent what people actually know when they know a language.

1.5.3 Tense

Chen (2013) proposes that 'languages with obligatory future-time reference lead their speakers to engage in less future-oriented behaviour', and that this is manifested in behaviours relating to savings and health. Chen divides languages into strong FTR ('future time reference') languages which are associated with this 'less future-oriented behaviour' and weak FTR languages. A strong FTR language such as English requires 'future events to be grammatically marked when making predictions', so that in English we must say *It will rain tomorrow*, grammatically marking the future with *will*, and we cannot say *It rains tomorrow*. A weak FTR language such as German allows *Morgen regnet es*, literally 'tomorrow rains it', with no grammatical marking of the future. Strong FTR languages (the ones which are 'worse' in how they affect economic planning) include Hebrew, French, Russian, Spanish, Korean, (European) Portuguese and English. Weak FTR languages (the ones which are 'better' in how they affect economic planning) are listed as: Norwegian, Danish, Swedish, Dutch, German, Finnish, Estonian, Chinese (Mandarin), Japanese and Brazilian Portuguese.

Chen is explicit about causation, which is good since it makes the mechanisms by which language affects thinking more open to analysis, but also reveals problems in the words which he chooses to describe the psychological processes. Thus Chen (2013, p. 695) says that 'language may affect future choices by changing how different future events feel', and in the next sentence says that using this language might 'lead weak-FTR speakers to perceive future events as less distant'. Though feeling and perception are different kinds of cognition, Chen has shifted from one to another. At various points in his article, Chen variously describes the kinds of cognition caused by linguistic forms as 'feeling' or having specific 'feels' (e.g. of vividness), 'perception' and 'distinguishing' (possibly related to perception), 'willingness (to behave)', 'belief', 'remembering' and 'making (some outcome) more attractive'. This terminological variety leaves psychological aspects of causation undefined.

The linguist Östen Dahl's theoretical and descriptive work on tense is a key source for Chen, and Dahl has responded negatively to a pre-publication version of Chen's article in a blog post (http://dlc.hypotheses.org/360, on 2013/03/09). I now summarize two of Dahl's objections.

(i) Chen uses a single criterion for deciding whether a grammar must distinguish 'prediction-based future time reference'. By this criterion, Finnish and Estonian have hardly any future marking connected to the verb and so for Chen are weak FTR languages, while Russian is treated as a strong FTR language. However, once a wider range of relevant grammatical facts are examined, the distinction into two types of language is not clear. Thus Finnish and Estonian mark the object of the verb differently in a sentence referring to the future (and thus might have been reanalysed as strong FTR). In Russian, perfective verbs have no special future form; rather, the present is normally interpreted as referring to the future, and this difference from other ways in which 'strong FTR' emerges in a language makes it less clear that Russian can be classified as 'strong FTR'. Many of the Whorfian economics articles identify some criterion for classifying languages into two kinds, here strong and weak FTR, but the complex ways in which languages differ work against such dichotomies, as they do here, where Dahl argues that there is a continuum, even when it comes to the specific matter of how weather predictions are expressed.

(ii) Chen distinguishes two types of language based on a single way of talking about the future, exemplified by whether the future must be used in weather forecasts. Dahl looks at a wider range of data which complicates this significantly (showing for example that future time reference is not fully grammaticalized in the Romance languages called strong FTR by Chen) and suggests that 'arguably, it should be the total set of patterns a language provides for speaking of the future that influences how we think of it rather than just the use of future tenses in prediction-based contexts'.

1.5.4 Whorfian linguistic economics

All the 'Whorfian economics' articles discussed here identify languages as having specific values for specific linguistic features, usually drawn from typological databases such as WALS. I now note some problems with using WALS in this way, drawing on criticisms by Dahl, and by Roberts and Winters (2012, 2013).

(i) Dahl (2013) says: 'when preparing the WALS map "The Future Tense" we decided to refrain from classifying futures in any other way than by whether they were expressed morphologically or not, since we found that the information in grammars was usually not sufficient for anything else'. Simplified data may be misused for correlations, concealing the true complexity of actual language data. In his co-authored article in WALS, he has this to say:

> Tense and aspect are notoriously difficult categories to describe adequately, and the treatment in grammars is often problematic, especially if one wants to use it for cross-linguistic comparison. As far as possible, we have tried to apply consistent criteria in classifying tense-aspect phenomena. For this reason, our interpretations sometimes differ from those found in grammars. The reader should thus not be surprised if a language is classified in an unexpected way.
>
> (Dahl and Velupillai, 2013)

(ii) Roberts and Winters (2012, 2013) offer a general discussion of the problems associated with using WALS or other large databases of linguistic features as the primary or sole source of evidence for formulating large-scale correlations of the kind seen in the economics articles. Their article more generally discusses, critically, the use of what they call nomothetic studies (statistical analyses of large-scale cross-cultural data). One of their concerns is that these databases are only as reliable as the sources – grammars and other descriptions – on which they are based, but these sources vary greatly in their reliability. This is because for some languages there is just one account by one analyst, and the reliability of the data depends on the analyst's skill, classificatory decisions and theoretical assumptions.

(iii) Dahl as well as Roberts and Winters note that cultural phenomena may be bundled with each other without any causal relation between them. Dahl notes for example that 'all the nine full member countries of the International Cricket Council also have left-hand driving', but there is no causal relation between these; instead, the countries have co-developed for historical reasons, resulting in their sharing certain features. Two historically related languages may similarly share some language-internal correlation between linguistic features, but for reasons of historical development rather than for any underlying principle. Some of the correlations between linguistic features and non-linguistic features similarly are 'bundles' which have co-developed historically but with no causal relation between them, and no general principle underlying the correlation.

In this section I have described various economics and psychology articles which propose that some aspects of linguistic form in a language can cause its speakers to think and behave in ways which are realized in the culture. There are two general reasons for being cautious about the conclusions drawn in these articles. First, there are concerns which theoretical and descriptive linguists might raise regarding the representations in these articles of the linguistic data, that its simplifications are no longer recognizable representations of the linguistic facts, and do not recognize the potential abstractness of the data. At a minimum, economists who wish to pursue causal arguments involving linguistic data might want to discuss them more extensively with theoretical linguists.

The second major problem relates to causation. Causation of this kind is necessarily difficult to demonstrate; there is no general background agreement amongst psycholinguists that specific Whorfian effects exist, and what evidence has been cited usually shows that Whorfian effects are very shallow and can be easily reversed experimentally. Whorfian economics thus needs to demonstrate a more rigorous theory of causation which is compatible with experimental work on language and thought (including the full range of evidence and counter-evidence), and which would support the correlations claimed.

1.6   Non-Whorfian proposals that language influences thought

Whorfian approaches to the causal influence of language on thought (or vice versa) are focused on the differences between languages and how those differences might cause differences in the way speakers of those languages think and behave. In this section I look at how a choice between options within a single language may have effects on how the speakers think. This is non-Whorfian because it does not involve claims that different languages have language-specific causal effects on thought or behaviour.

The British sociologist Basil Bernstein (1971) influentially argued that English is differentially accessed or used by different social classes, claiming that upper-middle-class children speak in an elaborated code (which he saw as a fuller use of the possibilities of the language) while working-class children speak in a restricted code (which he saw as an impoverished use of the possibilities of the language). Bernstein's work has been controversial (particularly amongst sociolinguists) but it has had significant influence in education, given the importance in educational theory of overcoming class-correlated disadvantage.

Stylistic choices might influence thought and behaviour. For example, a language may offer alternative ways of phrasing the same proposition (or asking the same question). A well-known account of this is Tversky and Kahneman's (1981) study of how two different ways of phrasing the same options in a question can lead to significantly different responses: they show that 'seemingly inconsequential changes in the formulation of choice problems caused significant shifts of preference' (1981, p. 457). The claim that stylistic choices can influence thought and behaviour is also important in critical discourse analysis, widely used in the social sciences while having little to do with the Whorfian question of whether the distinct forms of a language have the potential to influence thought. Critical discourse analysis is best understood as a methodology in social science; it has little relation to linguistic theory.

Psychological experiments have demonstrated that how a text is written can affect aspects of the psychology of the reader or hearer. These are on-line effects driven by stylistic choices within a single language, not Whorfian effects by which the language as a whole system shapes a culture's thinking. For example, Hasher et al. (1977, p. 111) showed that repetition of a statement 'increases a person's belief in the referential validity or truth of that statement'. This is a well-established finding which McGlone and Tofighbakhsh (2000) adapted to demonstrate experimentally that aphorisms which rhyme are judged to be truer than aphorisms which do not. In both cases, repetition (including rhyme as a type of repetition) increases the fluency of processing, and that fluent processing leads the hearer to attribute greater truth and even familiarity to the content of what is being processed (and they like it more). Psycholinguistic experiments have similarly shown weak effects on thought, judgement and behaviour which are determined by stylistic choices in a stimulus text. Here, we are in the domain of neuroeconomics, and it may be that relevant experiments might show stylistic effects on economically relevant decision making.

1.7 Conclusion

This chapter has illustrated some of the ways in which languages have diverse forms and has illustrated how linguistic diversity is explained by one of the dominant types of theoretical linguistics, generative linguistics. This discussion was the context for the part of the chapter in which I looked at a number of articles by economists and others, where the diverse forms of languages are said to have a causal connection with the diverse forms, particularly the values, of cultures. I have argued that it is premature to come to these conclusions. Languages vary in much more complex and detailed ways than is accommodated by the binary divisions favoured in the Whorfian articles. The Whorfian claim that language causes thought is not well established: it is still widely contested. And, finally, linguistic theory offers a vision of linguistic form which makes Whorfian causation less plausible in general, given the linguistic theoretical commitment to abstract form and how this explains linguistic variation. Any future work in Whorfian economics will need to take these considerations more fully into account.

Acknowledgements

Thanks to my editors, and to Mairi Blackings, Östen Dahl, Caroline Heycock, Bob Ladd, Joanna McPake, Seán Roberts, Gary Thoms, Stefano Versace and the Strathclyde Literary Linguistics group. I am responsible for any errors. Syntax trees were drawn with phpSyntaxTree.

References

T. Au (1983) 'Chinese and English Counterfactuals: The Sapir–Whorf Hypothesis Revisited', *Cognition*, 15, 155–187.

B. Bassetti (2014) 'Is Grammatical Gender Considered Arbitrary or Semantically Motivated? Evidence from Young Adult Monolinguals, Second Language Learners, and Early Bilinguals', *British Journal of Psychology*, 105, 273–294.

A. Bender, S. Beller and G. Bennardo (2010) 'Temporal Frames of Reference: Conceptual Analysis and Empirical Evidence from German, English, Mandarin Chinese, and Tongan', *Journal of Cognition and Culture*, 10, 283–307.

B. Bernstein (1971) *Class, Codes and Control. Volume 1: Theoretical Studies towards a Sociology of Language* (London: Routledge and Kegan Paul).

R. Berwick, P. Pietroski, B. Yankama and N. Chomsky (2011) 'Poverty of the Stimulus Revisited', *Cognitive Science*, 1–36.

H. den Besten (1983) 'On the Interaction of Root Transformations and Lexical Deletive Rules', revised version of a paper in *Studies in West Germanic Syntax, Dissertatie Tilburg*, 1989, 20, 14–100.

T. Biberauer, A. Holmberg and I. Roberts (2007) 'Disharmonic Word-order Systems and the Final-over-Final-Constraint (FOFC)' In A. Bisetto and F. Barbieri (eds) *Proceedings of XXXIII Incontro di Grammatica Generativa*. Available at http://amsacta.cib.unibo.it/archive/00002397/01/PROCEEDINGS_IGG.pdf

M. Blackings and N. Fabb (2003) *A Grammar of Ma'di* (Berlin: Mouton).

A. Bloom (1981) *The Linguistic Shaping of Thought: A Study in the Impact of Language on Thinking in China and the West* (Hillsdale: Erlbaum Associates).

L. Boroditsky (2001) 'Does Language Shape Thought? Mandarin and English Speakers' Conceptions of Time', *Cognitive Psychology*, 43, 1–22.

L. Boroditsky, L Schmidt and W. Phillips (2003) 'Sex, Syntax, and Semantics' In D. Gentner and S. Goldin-Meadow (eds) *Language in Mind: Advances in the Study of Language and Cognition* (Cambridge, MA: MIT Press).

B. Boutonnet, P. Athanasopoulos and G. Thierry (2012) 'Unconscious Effects of Grammatical Gender during Object Categorisation', *Brain Research*, 1479, 72–79.

J.-Y. Chen (2007) 'Do Chinese and English Speakers Think about Time Differently? Failure of Replicating Boroditsky (2001)', *Cognition*, 104, 427–436.

K. Chen (2013) 'The Effect of Language on Economic Behavior: Evidence from Savings Rates, Health Behaviors, and Retirement Assets', *The American Economic Review*, 103, 690–731.

N. Chomsky (1957) *Syntactic Structures* (The Hague: Mouton).

N. Chomsky (1965) *Aspects of the Theory of Syntax* (Cambridge, MA: MIT Press).

N. Chomsky (1981) *Lectures on Government and Binding* (Dordrecht: Foris).

N. Chomsky (1995) *The Minimalist Program* (Cambridge, MA: MIT Press).

N. Chomsky and M. Halle (1968) *The Sound Pattern of English* (New York: Harper & Row).

G. Cinque (2013) 'Cognition, Universal Grammar, and Typological Generalizations', *Lingua*, 130, 50–65.

P. Cole, G. Hermon and L-M. Sung (1990) 'Principles and Parameters of Long-Distance Reflexives', *Linguistic Inquiry*, 21, 1–22.

G. Corbett (1991) *Gender* (Cambridge: Cambridge University Press).

G. Corbett (2013) ' "30 Number of Genders", "31 Sex-based and Non-sex-based Gender Systems", "32 Systems of Gender Assignment" ' In M. Dryer and M. Haspelmath (eds) *The World Atlas of Language Structures Online* (Leipzig: Max Planck Institute for Evolutionary Anthropology).

R. Cubelli, D. Paolieri, L. Lotto and R. Job (2011) 'The Effect of Grammatical Gender on Object Categorization', *Journal of Experimental Psychology: Learning, Memory, and Cognition*, 37, 449–460.

Ö. Dahl and V. Velupillai (2013) 'Tense and Aspect' In Matthew S. Dryer and M. Haspelmath (eds) *The World Atlas of Language Structures Online* (Leipzig: Max Planck Institute for Evolutionary Anthropology). Available online at http://wals.info/chapter/s7 (Accessed on 2014-06-16).

D. Dediu and D. R. Ladd (2007) 'Linguistic Tone Is Related to the Population Frequency of the Adaptive Haplogroups of Two Brain Size Genes, ASPM and Microcephalin', *Proceedings of the National Academy of Sciences*, 104, 10944–10949.

M. Dryer (2013) '144 Position of Negative Morpheme with Respect to Subject, Object, and Verb' In M. Dryer and M. Haspelmath (eds) *The World Atlas of Language Structures Online* (Leipzig: Max Planck Institute for Evolutionary Anthropology).

N. Evans and S. Levinson (2009) 'The Myth of Language Universals: Language Diversity and its Importance for Cognitive Science', *Behavioral and Brain Sciences*, 32, 429–492.

V. Gay, E. Santacreu-Vasut and A. Shoham (2013) 'The Grammatical Origins of Gender Roles', BEHL Working Paper.

L. Gleitman and A. Papafragou (2005) 'Language and Thought' In K. Holyoak and R. Morrison (eds) *Cambridge Handbook of Thinking and Reasoning*, 633–662 (Cambridge: Cambridge University Press).

L. Haegeman and T. Ihsane (2001) 'Adult Null Subjects in the Non-pro-drop Languages: Two Diary Dialects', *Language Acquisition*, 9, 329–346.

H. Harley and E. Ritter (2002) 'Person and Number in Pronouns: A Feature-Geometric Analysis', *Language*, 78, 482–526.

L. Hasher, D. Goldstein and T. Toppino (1977) 'Frequency and the Conference of Referential Validity', *Journal of Verbal Learning and Verbal Behavior*, 16, 107–112.

M. Haspelmath (2013) '34 Occurrence of Nominal Plurality' In M. Dryer and M. Haspelmath (eds) *The World Atlas of Language Structures Online* (Leipzig: Max Planck Institute for Evolutionary Anthropology).

J. Hill and B. Mannheim (1992) 'Language and World View', *Annual Review of Anthropology*, 21, 381–406.

C-T. J. Huang (1989) 'Pro Drop in Chinese: A Generalized Control Approach' In O. Jaeggli and K. Safir (eds) *The Null Subject Parameter*, 185–214 (Dordrecht: D. Reidel).

M. Imai, L. Schalk, H. Saalbach and H. Okada (2014) 'All Giraffes Have Female-Specific Properties: Influence of Grammatical Gender on Deductive Reasoning about Sex-Specific Properties in German Speakers', *Cognitive Science*, 38, 514–536.

D. January and E. Kako (2007) 'Re-evaluating Evidence for Linguistic Relativity: Reply to Boroditsky (2001)', *Cognition*, 104, 417–426.

E. Kashima and Y. Kashima (1998) 'Culture and Language: The Case of Cultural Dimensions and Personal Pronoun Use', *Journal of Cross-Cultural Psychology*, 29, 461–487.

E. Kashima and Y. Kashima (2005) 'Erratum to Kashima and Kashima (1998) and Reiteration', *Journal of Cross-Cultural Psychology*, 36, 396–400.

S. Levinson (1996) 'Frames of Reference and Molyneux's Question: Crosslinguistic Evidence' In P. Bloom, M. Peterson, L. Nadel and M. Garrett (eds) *Language and Space*, 109–169 (Cambridge, MA: MIT Press).

S. Levinson (1997) 'From Outer to Inner Space: Linguistic Categories and Non-linguistic Thinking' In J. Nuyts and E. Pederson (eds) *Language and Conceptualization*, 13–45 (Cambridge: Cambridge University Press).

S. Levinson (2003) *Space in Language and Cognition: Explorations in Cognitive Diversity* (Cambridge: Cambridge University Press).

P. Li, L. Abarbanell, L. Gleitman and A. Papafragou (2011) 'Spatial Reasoning in Tenejapan Mayans', *Cognition*, 120, 33–53.

P. Li and L. Gleitman (2002) 'Turning the Tables: Language and Spatial Reasoning', *Cognition*, 83, 265–294.

A. Licht, C. Goldschmidt and S. Schwartz (2007) 'Culture Rules: The Foundations of the Rule of Law and other Norms of Governance', *Journal of Comparative Economics*, 35, 659–688.

J. Lucy (1997) 'Linguistic Relativity', *Annual Review of Anthropology*, 26, 291–312.

I. Maddieson (2013) '1 Consonant Inventories', '2 Vowel Quality Inventories', '7 Glottalized Consonants', '12 Syllable Structure', '13 Tone', '19 Presence of Uncommon Consonants' In M. Dryer and M. Haspelmath (eds) *The World Atlas of Language Structures Online*. (Leipzig: Max Planck Institute for Evolutionary Anthropology).

A. Mavisakalyan (2011) 'Gender in Language and Gender in Employment', ANUCBE School of Economics Working Paper.

M. McGlone and J. Tofighbakhsh (2000) 'Birds of a Feather Flock Conjointly (?): Rhyme as Reason in Aphorisms', *Psychological Science*, 11, 424–428.

J. Nichols (2012) 'Monogenesis or Polygenesis: A Single Ancestral Language for All Humanity?' In M. Tallerman and K. Gibson (eds) *The Oxford Handbook of Language Evolution* (Oxford: Oxford University Press).

J. Prewitt-Freilino, T. Caswell and E. Laakso (2012) 'The Gendering of Language: A Comparison of Gender Equality in Countries with Gendered, Natural Gender, and Genderless Languages', *Sex Roles*, 66, 268–281.

L. Rizzi (2013) 'Introduction: Core Computational Principles in Natural Language Syntax', *Lingua*, 130, 1–13.

S. Roberts and J. Winters (2012) 'Social Structure and Language Structure: The New Nomothetic Approach', *Psychology of Language and Communication*, 16, 89–112.

S. Roberts and J. Winters (2013) 'Linguistic Diversity and Traffic Accidents: Lessons from Statistical Studies of Cultural Traits', *PLOS1* August 14, 2013. DOI: 10.1371/journal.pone.0070902

E. Santacreu-Vasut, A. Shoham and V. Gay (2013) 'Do Female/Male Distinctions in Language Matter? Evidence from Gender Political Quotas', *Applied Economics Letters*, 20, 495–498.

E. Santacreu-Vasut, O. Shenkar and A. Shoham (2014) 'Linguistic Gender Marking and its International Business Ramifications', *Journal of International Business Studies*, 47, 1–9.

G. Tabellini (2008) 'Institutions and Culture', *Journal of the European Economic Association*, 6, 255–294.

A. Tversky, and D. Kahneman (1981) 'The Framing of Decisions and the Psychology of Choice', *Science*, 211, 453–458.

G. Vigliocco, D. Vinson, F. Paganelli and K. Dworzynski (2005) 'Grammatical Gender Effects on Cognition: Implication for Language Learning and Language Use', *Journal of Experimental Psychology: General*, 134, 501–520.

Websites

http://www.replicatedtypo.com. This is a blog on evolutionary linguistics, which has involved extensive critical discussion of correlations between social and linguistic factors, including some of the work in economics.

http://wals.info. The World Atlas of Language Structures (WALS). The largest database of typological linguistic information, freely available online.

http://sswl.railsplayground.net. Syntactic Structures of the World's Languages (SSWL): Another freely available online typological database, strongly influenced by generative linguistics.

http://www.ethnologue.com. A catalogue of over 7,000 languages of the world.

2
Dynamic Models of Language Evolution: The Linguistic Perspective

Andrew D. M. Smith

2.1 Introduction

Language is probably the key defining characteristic of humanity, an immensely powerful tool which provides its users with an infinitely expressive means of representing their complex thoughts and reflections, and of successfully communicating them to others. It is the foundation on which human societies have been built and the means through which humanity's unparalleled intellectual and technological achievements have been realized. Although we have a natural intuitive understanding of what a language is, the specification of a particular language is nevertheless remarkably difficult, if not impossible, to pin down precisely. All languages contain many separate yet integral systems which work interdependently to allow the expression of our thoughts and the interpretation of others' expressions: each has, for instance, a set of basic meaningless sounds (e.g. [e], [l], [s]) which can be combined to make different meaningful words and parts of words (e.g. *else, less, sell, -less*); these meaningful units can be combined to make complex words (e.g. *spinelessness, selling*), and the words themselves can then be combined in very many complex ways into phrases, clauses and an infinite number of meaningful sentences; finally each of these sentences can be interpreted in dramatically different ways, depending on the contexts in which it is uttered and on who is doing the interpretation. Languages can be analysed at any of these different levels, which make up many of the sub-fields of linguistics, and the primary job of linguistic theorists is to try to explain the rules which best explain these complex combinations. The hallmarks of human language, which distinguish it from less powerful communication systems used by animals, are frequently characterized in terms of lists of so-called *design features*, such as those itemized over half a century ago by Hockett (1960) and others. Language is unique in its *semanticity, productivity* and *mode of transmission*: it is a system spread through cultural learning which consists of relatively fixed mappings between form and meaning, yet can effortlessly accommodate infinite novelty of expression. Language gets its massive expressive power from its *duality of patterning* or *double articulation* (Martinet, 1949): linguistic utterances are assembled from small meaningful units (morphemes) combined according to a set of morphosyntactic rules, while the morphemes themselves are built from a second set of meaningless sounds (phonemes) using a different set of phonological rules. Linguistic knowledge is fundamentally *symbolic*, made up of an inventory of arbitrary associations between forms and meaning (de Saussure, 1916), which can be composed into complex signals whose meanings can be derived from the meanings of their component parts and the way these are combined (Krifka, 2001). Human language is also characterized by *recursion*, where forms can contain embedded components where the part and the whole share a syntactic category (Kinsella, 2009); this particular feature has famously been proposed as the core component of the putative innate faculty of language (Hauser et al., 2002). These (and perhaps other) design features effectively delimit the differences between human language on the one hand and animal communication systems on the other; yet they also underplay one of the most significant features of language, that it is characterized at every level by dynamism, massive diversity and constant change. Evans and Levinson (2009) point out that '[w]e are the only known species whose communication system varies fundamentally in both form and content' (Evans and Levinson, 2009, p. 431), and we are likewise the only known species whose communication system is not fixed, but on the contrary is constantly changing. Notably, all languages exist in two separate manifestations: internally, as relatively persistent (though changing) representations inside human brains, and externally, as ephemeral, transitory utterances which are produced and received by interlocutors; much recent work on the evolution of language focuses on how properties of language can be seen as adaptive to the need to alternate between these internal and external manifestations. In the remainder of this chapter I explore some of the ways in which linguistic diversity is realized, and some of the perspectives we have gained on understanding its dynamic nature: in Section 2.2, I describe diverse dimensions along which languages can vary; in Section 2.3, I investigate different approaches to language change on different timescales; in Section 2.4, I explore some of the formal models which have been used to explore the dynamic nature of language.

2.2 Language diversity

There are around 7,000 languages spoken in the world nowadays (Lewis, 2005); the precise tally is, perhaps surprisingly, impossible to calculate accurately, for two important reasons. Firstly, the criteria used to determine whether any system of linguistic expressions, or linguistic variety, should count as a different language from another system of linguistic expressions are not measured solely on objective linguistic terms, but are tied up with political decisions and aspirations which can draw different conclusions about the 'languagehood' of particular linguistic varieties. Linguistic criteria, for instance, are most frequently expressed in terms of the mutual intelligibility of varieties: can speakers of variety A understand speakers of variety B (and vice versa) based on their linguistic knowledge of their own variety? If they can, then the varieties can reasonably be considered to be dialects of the same language; if not, then they can be considered different languages. In the absence of major physical obstacles which reduce opportunities for people to mix with each other, of course, adjacent communities frequently speak mutually intelligible varieties, and sometimes such communities can form chains or dialect continua across very large areas, such as the unbroken chain of mutual intelligibility running from Portugal through Spain and France to the foot of Italy. In communities in areas around the political borders, however, people often consider that they speak different languages from their neighbours across the border (e.g. French or Italian), even though their varieties are linguistically almost identical. The opposite situation is also true, where political considerations can lead varieties which are *not* mutually intelligible to be widely considered dialects of a single language. Due to the historical and cultural unity of China, for instance, the major varieties of Sinitic languages there (e.g. Mandarin, Cantonese) are widely considered to be dialects (Goddard, 2005), yet they are linguistically as distinct from each other as the separate languages of Italian, French, Catalan, Spanish and Portuguese in Europe (Coulmas, 2013). Changes in political identities can have linguistic repercussions, too, as can be seen following the break-up of Yugoslavia in the 1990s, which led to the demise of the unified language formerly known as Serbo-Croat and the active building in the new countries of multiple distinct successor languages (Serbian, Croatian, Bosnian, Montenegrin), so that linguistic identities could better reflect the new and developing political situation (Greenberg, 2004).

Secondly, despite the heroic efforts of field linguists who devote their careers to describing, documenting and cataloguing languages across the world, surprisingly few languages are studied in great detail, and in fact many remain completely unknown. Those languages we do know are dying out dismayingly quickly; almost half the languages ever known to us have disappeared in the last 500 years (Nettle and Romaine, 2000), and estimates suggest that perhaps only a tenth of the languages spoken today will still be spoken at the end of the century (Krauss, 1992). This matters not just for the completeness of linguistic catalogues, but because languages are major repositories of the cultural knowledge of the communities which use them (Maffi, 2001), and the death of an undocumented language can mean the irrevocable loss of the traditional knowledge stored within its vocabulary and grammatical distinctions (Evans, 2010).

The pervasiveness of language diversity is regularly underestimated, however, and its significance underplayed. Below I will give a flavour of some of the countless ways in which languages vary, from their sounds to the way they assemble words, from their grammatical rules to the meanings they encode.

2.2.1   Sounds

One of the fundamental properties which gives language its expressive power is the *duality of patterning* described above (Martinet, 1949). All languages contain meaningless phonemes which can be used to build meaningful morphemes, but they differ widely in their number and type, in how the space of possible phonemes is divided up, and in the rules for combining the sounds together into larger units. I discuss each of these differences briefly below.

In terms of sound inventory size alone, some languages in Southern Africa differentiate up to 144 different phonemes,[1] while Rotokas, spoken in Papua New Guinea, manages with just 11. Some common sounds, such as the voiceless stops [p],[t],[k] or the nasals [m],[n], occur in the vast majority of languages across the world,[2] while other sounds have an extremely restricted geographical range, such as the labiodental flap [ⱱ] which is used only in particular areas of Central Africa. Whole groups of sounds are subject to similarly wide variation: while fricatives like [f],[v],[s],[z] form an important part of the sound inventory of the vast majority of human languages, they are not found at all in Australian aboriginal languages such as Dyirbal (Dixon, 1972), Kayardild (Round, 2009) and Yorta Yorta (Bowe and Morey, 1999). Click consonants (such as the *tut-tut* sound used to express disapproval by English speakers), on the other hand, are found as phonemes only in Khoisan and Bantu languages in southern and eastern Africa (Clements, 2000).

Even when languages do use the same sounds as each other, their phonological status within each language can be different. For all speakers of English, for instance, the sounds [s] and [ʃ] (the latter pronounced like 'sh') count as separate sounds, because they contrast with each other: changing from one sound to the other can produce a different word with a different meaning (e.g. sip-ship; gas-gash). Although Japanese speakers also use these sounds, however, they don't contrast in Japanese: instead they are predictable variants of the *same* sound, which is usually pronounced as [s], but is systematically pronounced as [ʃ] whenever it occurs before the vowel /i/, as for instance in the word *sushi* (Goddard, 2005). These contrastive distinctions are vitally important

---

[1] In many languages, the precise number of phonemes is a matter for debate, primarily because it can be unclear whether some complex articulatory combinations should count as one consonant or as a sequence of consonants (Zsiga, 2013).

[2] Although not without some striking exceptions such as Arabic, which lacks /p/, and Tahitian, which lacks /k/.

Table 2.1   Examples of tonal distinctions in Mandarin

Word	Pitch	Meaning
mā	high, level	mother
má	mid, rising	hemp
mǎ	low, falling then rising	horse
mà	high, falling	scold

to understanding and speaking a language, yet they are essentially arbitrary and can be extremely difficult to discern for non-native speakers: in Polish, for instance, there are two contrasting sounds [ɕ] and [ʂ] (e.g. [koɕ] 'mow' – [koʂ] 'basket'), which both sound extremely similar (roughly like 'sh') to English speakers who do not distinguish them.

All languages make use of changes in pitch, for instance to mark the boundaries of syntactic units, but again their status can vary quite remarkably: in English, we can raise the pitch at the end of a sentence to make a question out of a statement, but in languages like Mandarin, every word has a distinctive pitch associated with it, as can be seen in Table 2.1, which shows four different pronunciations of the sequence [ma], each with its own specific meaning. Languages like Mandarin in which pitch variations are used to distinguish different words are called *tone languages*, yet these also differ in the number of distinct tones they make use of, from simple tone languages like Shona which differentiate only two, to more complex ones which make many more distinctions (Ladefoged and Johnson, 2011).

Finally, the most notably diverse characteristics of sound systems concern the phonotactic rules which govern the combinations of sounds allowed in a language. Polynesian languages like Māori have extremely simple phonotactic rules, with all syllables consisting of a single optional consonant followed by a vowel, yielding words like *koko* 'shovel' or *kūao* 'young animal' (Harlow, 2007), while Caucasian languages like Georgian allow notoriously complex clusters of multiple initial consonants which appear almost unpronounceable to speakers of other languages, such as *prckvna* 'to peel' or *brdvna* 'to fight' (Butskhrikidze, 2002). Although all spoken languages have sound systems, therefore, the ways in which these are organized can be extremely variable, and the phonological distinctions which languages make appear to be arbitrarily fine (Pierrehumbert et al., 2000).

2.2.2   Words

Linguistic diversity is also particularly noticeable in morphology, the study of the minimally meaningful parts, or *morphemes*, from which words are made. Languages differ in terms of how much information each word contains, how their morphemes are combined into words, and how clearly defined the morphemes are within a word, each of which will be explored briefly in turn.

In an *isolating* language like Thai, illustrated in (2.1), almost every word contains just a single morpheme, while in a *synthetic* language like Swahili (2.2), words are considerably more complex, frequently containing multiple morphemes packaged together inside a single word. Most languages in fact lie somewhere between these extremes, and are characterized by a mixture of the two types of words. English, for instance, contains not only many monomorphemic words like *cat, build* or *good*, but also a considerable number of more complex multimorphemic words such *girl-ish-ly* or *over-pay-ment*.

(2.1)　Thai (Goddard, 2005, p. 3)

> *khǎw　dây　àan　nǎngsɨ̌ɨ*
> he/she　PAST　read　book
> 'he read a book'

(2.2)　Swahili

> *tu-li-mw-on-a*
> we-PAST-him-see-IND
> 'we saw him'

We can also classify morphemes into *roots*, which cannot be further broken down, and which normally contain the main content of the word's meaning, and *affixes* which are attached to the root and modify its meaning in some way. The English word *unhappiness*, for instance, contains the root *happy* and two affixes *un-* and *-ness* which add additional semantic content to the core meaning.[3] The order of roots and morphemes is extremely variable, although a detailed analysis of the inflectional morphology of almost 1,000 different languages (Dryer, 2013b) shows that while languages vary across the spectrum from those which make exclusive use of suffixes (e.g. Central Yup'ik) to those which make almost exclusive use of prefixes (e.g. Kihunde), there is a clear cross-linguistic inclination towards suffixing.[4] This has been attributed to processing constraints: although both kinds of affix arise originally from distinct words which have fused with adjoining words, Hall (1988) shows that suffixes

---

[3] Affixes are usually written with hyphens to denote that they cannot occur on their own, and must instead be attached either before the root (prefixes) on after the root (suffixes).

[4] Almost half (49 per cent) of the languages with inflectional morphology were classified as predominantly suffixing, with a further 15 per cent showing a 'moderate preference for suffixes'; only 7 per cent were classified as predominantly prefixing, with 11 per cent showing a moderate preference and the remaining 18 per cent having approximately equal levels of suffixing and prefixing.

are likely to be preferentially understood by hearers because they allow easier and quicker identification of the content words. In addition to the use of prefixes and suffixes, however, some languages also show even more complex morphological patterns, where morphemes are more tightly intermeshed with each other: affixes can be placed either inside roots (e.g. Tagalog *bili* 'buy', *b-um-ili* 'bought'; *sulat* 'break', *s-in-ulat* 'was broken'), surrounding them (e.g German *kauf-en* 'buy', *ge-kauf-t* 'bought'), or intermeshed in more complex ways. Semitic languages like Arabic and Hebrew, for example, use template morphology based on roots, typically made up of three consonants, into which vowels and other consonants are inserted in different ways to derive specific meanings. The Arabic root *ktb* 'write', for instance, yields both specific forms of the verb such as *katab* 'he wrote' and *biyiktib* 'he is writing' and separate words such as *kitaab* 'book', *kaatib* 'writer' and *maktaba* 'library', along with many others.

The third dimension along which we find considerable morphological diversity is the level of fusion within the forms, or how clearly distinguishable the individual morphemes are. In *agglutinating* languages, the boundaries between the morphemes are sharply defined, as can be seen in the Swahili example (2.2) above and by the Hungarian example (2.3), where a single word *barátságosabban* is built up from a series of clearly visible suffixes added in sequence to the root *barát* 'friend'. By contrast, in *fusional* forms such as the Latin adjective *bon-us* 'good', the shape of the individual morphemes is not clear; the grammatical information specifying the gender (masculine), number (singular) and case (nominative) of the adjective is all conflated into a single suffix *-us* which cannot be separated into distinct morphemes.

(2.3)   Hungarian (Siptár and Törkenczy, 2000, p. 26)

barát-ság-os-abb-an
friend-ship-ADJ-COMP-IND
'in a more friendly manner'

2.2.3   Grammar

On the grammatical level, too, individual languages show an enormous range of diversity, from the order in which words are assembled into sentences to the syntactic categories and patterns of agreement which are obligatorily expressed in a language, only a few of which can be mentioned here.

Word order is the most famous and widely cited typological feature of languages, and indeed the development of the whole field of linguistic typology can reasonably be traced back to Greenberg's famous paper on the basic word order in declarative sentences across languages (Greenberg, 1963). The three main elements of a sentence – subject (S), object (O) and verb (V) – are found in all six logically possible orders in different languages, although there is a notable preponderance of the two orders SOV and SVO, which together make up 89 per cent of the languages which have a dominant word order in Dryer's (2013a) cross-linguistic survey of almost 1,400 different languages.[5] In English, of course, word order is used to indicate which role (e.g. the doer of the activity, the person to whom the activity is done) that each noun phrase is playing in the sentence and is thus relatively fixed. Many other languages, however, use a very different grammatical means, known as case marking, in which morpho-logical affixes or function words accompany the noun phrases and/or the verb to mark these roles. In (2.4) we can see that each noun phrase in Japanese must be followed by a special functional postposition (here *ga, ni, o*) which provides crucial information about the relationship between the noun phrase and the verb *ageta*: the nominative marker *ga* follows the subject, the accusative marker *o* follows the direct object, and the dative marker *ni* follows the indirect object or beneficiary. In Swahili (2.5), by contrast, agreement prefixes (here *a-, -ki-*) are added to different parts of the verb complex, to specify and classify both the subject and object of the verb.[6]

(2.4)   Japanese

> *sensei*   *ga*   *gakusei*   *ni*   *hon*   *o*   *ageta*
> teacher   NOM   student   DAT   book   ACC   give.PAST
> 'the teacher gave the book to the student.'

(2.5)   Swahili

> *mtu*   *a-li-ki-on-a*   *kifaru*
> person   SUBJ.1-PAST.OBJ.7-see-IND   rhinoceros
> 'the person saw the rhinoceros.'

Case marking itself can also be realized in an assortment of ways. Both (2.4) and (2.5) illustrate sentences containing transitive verbs with two distinct arguments, a subject *A* and an object *P*, which are identified through different case and/or agreement markers, nominative markers for the subject and accusative markers for the object. In other sentences, however, the verb is intransitive, with just one logical argument *S* (e.g. 'the boy smiled.'); in (2.6) we can see that Swahili marks this argument with the same subject marker (a-) that it uses for the subject of the transitive sentence in (2.5), i.e. the markings for *A* and *S* are

---

[5] VSO accounts for 8 per cent of languages, while the other three logically possible orders are all extremely rare: VOS is found by Dryer in 25 languages, OVS in 11, and OSV in just four.
[6] The numbers in the Swahili glosses (2.5) and (2.6) refer to the class of the noun (roughly equivalent to gender in European languages) with which the prefix is agreeing.

identical, or $A = S$. In other languages, by contrast, the subject of an intransitive sentence is treated in the same way as the *object* of a transitive sentence, i.e. $P = S$. In the Basque examples in (2.7) and (2.8), for instance, both S and P appear in the absolutive case with no case marking, while the subject of the transitive sentence A has its own special ergative suffix *-k*.

(2.6) Swahili

> *mtu*   *a-li-lal-a*
> person   SUBJ.1-PAST-sleep-IND
> 'the person slept.'

(2.7) Basque (Trask, 1996, p. 151)

> *gizona   heldu zen*
> man.ABS   arrived
> 'the man arrived.'

(2.8) Basque (Trask, 1996, p. 151)

> *gizona-k   neska   ikusi zuen*
> man.ERG   girl.ABS   saw
> 'the man saw the girl.'

To complicate things further, many languages use both the Swahili-style nominative-accusative system and the Basque-style ergative-absolutive system to mark their arguments, and they even differ in the circumstances when each system is used. In languages like Lakhota and Guaraní, for instance, the marking of the transitive subject A may depend on a number of different semantic features such as the degree of voluntary control the subject is considered to have over the activity being performed, or whether the sentence is considered to be an event or a state of affairs (Mithun, 1991). In the Australian language Dyirbal, the marking is determined by the semantic referent of the subject, with participants in the speech act (I and you) using the ergative-absolutive system, but other participants (third person pronouns, nouns) using the nominative-accusative system. In Georgian, however, the determining factor is the tense of the sentence: the ergative-absolutive is used in the past but the nominative-accusative is used in the present (Song, 2001).

2.2.4 Meaning

Linguists have also begun to document the enormous diversity in which meaning is conceptualized and encoded in languages. Space prohibits a full exploration of this vast area, but to give some idea of the scale of cross-linguistic semantic variation, I will concentrate on a fundamental and relatively well-defined part of meaning structure, the conceptualizing of spatial relationships between objects.

In a major work exploring how spatial distinctions are expressed in around a dozen languages, Levinson and Wilkins (2006) found surprisingly profound diversity in the conceptualization and linguistic encoding of topological relations, motion and frames of reference, yet also that this diversity appears nevertheless to be constrained by underlying abstract dimensions of apparently universal relevance. Languages like English encode basic locative constructions, or responses to a question like 'Where is the X?', using a noun phrase to represent the figure, or focus of the scene, a form of the verb to be, and a prepositional phrase to represent the (back)ground of the scene, as shown in (2.9). Other languages, however, structure their basic locative constructions in very different ways, using case marking or spatial nouns instead of prepositions,[7] using multiple different locative verbs (e.g. equivalents of 'stand', 'sit', 'lie', 'hang') depending on the shape or function of the figure, even using no verbs at all, or using highly specific dispositional predicates which precisely orientate the figure and ground (Brown, 2006).

(2.9)   *the apple   is   in the bowl*
        NP   BE PP
        figure   *ground*
        'the apple is in the bowl.'

After a detailed investigation of the kinds of scenes which can be described using a language's *basic locative construction* (BLC), Levinson and Wilkins (2006) propose a topological space hierarchy in which all languages in their sample encode core scenes like 'cup on table' and 'ball under chair' using their BLC, but only some encode adhesion ('stamp on letter') in this way, fewer encode scenes in which the ground or the figure is pierced ('arrow in apple', 'apple on skewer') and fewer still encode scenes in which the ground is a human or other animate being ('ring on finger'). Looking at adpositions alone, the same eight scenes are encoded using between zero and seven different lexical items in the sample languages, with a wide range of distinctions being made (e.g. both Dutch and Yélî Dnye require seven adpositions, but while Dutch encodes different types of surface contact ('stamp on letter', 'cup on table') identically, Yélî Dnye conflates adhesion ('stamp on letter', 'ring on finger') under the same adposition. They conclude that abstract concepts like 'contact' and 'horizontal support' are more

---

[7] Or rather adpositions, a cover term encompassing both prepositions which occur before their arguments as in English, and postpositions which occur after their arguments in languages like Japanese.

likely candidates for universality than are concepts like IN and ON, contrary to conclusions which had been drawn after perusal of European languages alone (Levinson and Wilkins, 2006, pp. 519–520).

Famously, Talmy (2000) presented evidence of a major split between ways in which simple motion events are linguistically encoded, which can be seen even in relatively closely related languages such as English and French. In English (2.10), motion events are commonly expressed using verbs which describe the *manner* in which the motion takes place (e.g. slither, crawl, slide) and prepositional phrases describing its direction or path, while in French (2.11) the same concepts are expressed using verbs specifying the *direction* of the movement (e.g. enter, climb, descend) and an optional participle describing its manner (Israel, 2014).

(2.10) *the children*   *jumped*   *down the stairs*
                               manner   **direction**

(2.11) French (Israel, 2014, p. 173)

        les écoliers   *ont*   *descendu*   *l'escalier*   *en sautant*
        the schoolchildren AUX go.down.PST the staircase jumping
                               direction   **manner**
        'the schoolchildren jumped down the stairs'

Spatial frames of references are required to describe the relationship between figure and ground when they are separated in space, and Levinson and Wilkins (2006) also show that there are three systems used in natural languages which differ in what they use as the frame of reference within which the figure can be located: the *intrinsic* system uses a particular facet of the ground (e.g. 'in front of'), the *relative* or egocentric system uses the observer's own body (e.g. 'to the left of'), and the *absolute* system uses a set of conventionalized fixed points (e.g. 'south of'), with languages varying in which of these systems they employ most frequently. Australian languages such as Guugu Yimithirr (Levinson, 1997) and Warrwa (McGregor, 2006) are fascinating because they use an absolute frame of reference based on the cardinal compass directions almost exclusively, even for small-scale descriptions like the 'fork lies to the south' (Foley, 1997) and for body parts 'my north arm' (McGregor, 2006). Speakers of such languages are therefore always aware of the absolute position of objects, and their descriptions of items in books or on screens consequently change depending on the orientation of the pictures (Deutscher, 2010). Compass directions are not the only foundation of absolute frames of reference, however, with other systems being based on the prevailing ecological topography of the area in which the community lives: Jaminjung's frame of reference is based on the main river-drainage system (upstream-downstream) (Schultze-Berndt,

2006) and Tzeltal's is based on the direction of the main mountain range (uphill-downhill) (Brown, 2001, 2006), while Yélî Dnye's is based on the prevailing winds and on the topography of their island (central/mountainwards – peripheral/seawards) (Levinson, 2006).

This section has given a flavour of the range of ways in which linguistic diversity is manifested in the world's languages. In the next section, I focus on linguistic dynamism, its source and some of the timescales over which it can profitably be investigated.

2.3   Language change

Despite the fervently expressed desires of many commentators on language, who can regularly be found bemoaning aspects of the putative degeneration of modern language in the columns of newspapers around the world, all living languages are in an unceasing and indeed unavoidable state of flux. They change in countless different ways, from the very conspicuous and deliberate coining of new vocabulary to reflect changes in the artefacts and cultural concepts we want to refer to (e.g. selfie, vaping) to more obscure and unintentional cases of reanalysis, where the internal structure of a construction is understood in a different way from that which was originally intended (e.g. the original structure of the word *hamburg-er* was reanalysed as *ham-burger*, leading to novel coinages like *cheese-burger*) (Trask, 1996). Some changes in pronunciation can be understood straightforwardly in terms of a general tendency to reduce the effort required for articulation, by reducing the amount of movement required within the mouth (e.g. the pronunciation of words like *better* with a glottal stop instead of [t]), or by pronouncing sounds which occur close together more like one another (e.g. the pronunciation of words like *input* as *im-put*, with the nasal being articulated in the same part of the mouth as the following consonant).

The terms *language change* and *language evolution* are both wide-ranging and frequently overlapping in their denotation: sometimes synonymous, yet also often set in opposition to each other, both are frequently used to refer to wildly different notions on diverse timescales, from specific changes in the way a particular word is used at a particular point in time, to the biological evolution of particular cognitive capacities which have allowed us to learn and use language. In the following sections I will distinguish in turn three different aspects of language change which models have successfully been used to explore: the ubiquity of linguistic variation, the ultimate source of the constant state of flux in which language exists and an inevitable consequence of the way human communication works; the identification of historical relationships between languages and their classification into metaphorical family trees; and interactions between biological and cultural evolution from which language initially emerged.

2.3.1 Variation

People speak differently from the way in which their parents speak, and differently again from the way in which their children speak, even while they consider themselves (and are considered by others) to be speakers of the same language. Even within the same generation variation in people's pronunciation of certain sounds or in their usage of particular words and constructions gives other people crucial information about their identity: where they come from, their socio-economic status and ambitions, the groups of people they spend time with, and much more.

The systematic study of linguistic variation was originally spearheaded by sociolinguists such as Labov (1972) and Trudgill (1972), who introduced the idea of a formal linguistic *variable* which can be realized as multiple different variants in different contexts. Labov's (1972) pioneering work was focussed on the isolated island of Martha's Vineyard in Massachusetts, where islanders often used particularly idiosyncratic pronunciations of certain diphthongs. He found correlations between the extent to which these pronunciations were used and social variables such as age, occupation and geography, and showed that the idiosyncratic pronunciations were being used as a linguistic *marker* of the speaker's identity, in particular their commitment towards wanting to remain on the island, in the context of a collapsing fishing-based local economy and improvements in travel which had led both to large growth in the number of casual visitors to the island and to increasing opportunities for islanders to move to the mainland for work. At the same time, Trudgill (1972) was one of the first to quantify not only the striking connections between social class and the use of prestige variants, but also to show how the speech context itself also plays an important role, demonstrating that all speakers use fewer overtly prestigious forms as the context becomes increasingly informal. He also showed systematic differences between men's and women's speech which have been echoed in many subsequent studies: men consistently use more vernacular forms and women use more standard forms. Many explanations for these differences have been suggested, from claims that women are more aware of the social consequences of the way they speak, to suggestions that the increased use of vernacular forms by men (particularly working-class men) is an expression of their masculinity (Holmes, 2013). Frequently, however, variation is better explained in terms of social network properties, with denser social networks where everyone knows each other tending to inhibit linguistic change and looser social networks being more receptive to innovation. As Milroy put it in his famous study of working-class communities in Belfast, 'the closer an individual's network ties are with his local community, the closer his language approximates to localized vernacular norms' (Milroy, 1980, p. 175). Interestingly, Milroy also found more complex interactions between gender and social networks too, showing that as young women rather than men came to be chief breadwinners in the face of recession and the loss of traditional heavy industry which had been strongly male-dominated, their social networks became closer than in earlier generations, and their language reflected what had previously been considered markers of masculine speech.

The inevitability of variation in language stems from the fact that language is fundamentally a social interactional phenomenon (Croft, 2000) between people who belong to different, though potentially overlapping, social communities and have different individual experiences. Social communities are internally cohesive and externally distinctive collections of people who have come together because they have shared practices, beliefs or knowledge which are lacked by non-members of the community (Trousdale, 2010). We each belong to multiple interactive communities and sub-communities defined by our work, family, friends and recreational activities, in which we negotiate and express facets of our identity. Bolinger highlights that 'there is no limit to the number of ways in which human beings league themselves together for self-identification, security, gain, amusement, worship, or any of the other purposes that are held in common; consequently there is no limit to the number and variety of speech communities that are to be found in society' (Bolinger, 1975, p. 333). Our decisions about language use are a crucial part of this identity creation and maintenance, both within and outwith these communities. Moore (2004), for instance, shows how particular aspects of grammatical variation (e.g. using non-standard 'I were', 'he were') became used increasingly frequently by members of an emerging group of 'townie' girls in a school in north-west England, as they sought to signal their group identity as different from other established groups of girls at the school. In many multilingual societies, indeed, there are clear demarcation lines between different domains in which different languages are used, often with an official, prestigious language being used in more formal and religious contexts, and vernacular languages being used in informal contexts with friends, in the market and at home (Holmes, 2013). In truth, though, monolingual societies also display similar kinds of linguistic division between domains of use, albeit that they are more subtle because they are expressed through the use of different varieties of the *same* language rather than through different languages. The individuality and variability of our complex social networks and of our experiences within them are reflected in the individuality and variability of our linguistic repertoires, both in the ephemeral external linguistic behaviour we produce, and in the longer-lasting internal linguistic representations stored within our brains.

The process of linguistic communication itself is also inherently variable. Communication has often been thought of as a simple deterministic computational process in which the speaker's thoughts are encoded into an utterance, conveyed to the hearer, and then decoded back into meanings; assuming that both parties have the same encoding/decoding algorithms, then communication is successful (Shannon, 1948). Much work in the philosophy of language and in what is now known as pragmatics (Grice, 1975), however, showed that such a model cannot account for the nuances and detail of real-life communication, where the same utterance can be interpreted in radically different ways depending on the context in which it occurs (and, indeed, where different utterances can be interpreted identically). Communication is therefore not a simple encoding–decoding process, nor is it, even if we relax the assumption that interlocutors have the same algorithms, a process of 'reverse engineering' through which the hearer reassembles the speaker's meaning (Mufwene, 2002; Brighton et al., 2005), but rather it is a system based on the complementary and cooperative processes of ostension and inference (Sperber and Wilson, 1995; Scott-Phillips, 2014; Smith and Höfler, 2015), which relies crucially on the interlocutors being able to recognize and exploit their mutual common ground (Clark, 1996). Common ground is both wide-ranging and multi-faceted, including not only the interlocutors' fundamental shared recognition of each other as a potential conversation partner, but also a shared understanding of each other's intentions and of the joint goal of their conversation (Tomasello et al., 2005). It encompasses an understanding of relevant material from the communicative context, as well as shared attitudes, shared beliefs and shared conventions. These conventions, crucially for linguistic communication, include knowledge of the conventional (and of course arbitrary) meanings of particular words and constructions. Much common ground derives, of course, from the shared communities to which people belong, the distinctive behaviours and specialized vocabulary they share, but indeed every pair of interlocutors also has their own interpersonal common ground derived from their previous shared experiences together, and from the things one person knows their interlocutor knows about.

Common ground allows people to communicate successfully by providing a backdrop against which both ostension and inference can take place. The speaker[8] can act out an appropriate ostensive act, one whose deliberate and atypical nature both marks it as being intended as a communicative and encourages the hearer to interpret it in an opportune way. Having identified the signal as communicative, by its ostensive nature, the hearer then uses the evidence contained within the speaker's signal and the broader communicative context to inferentially construct a relevant meaning which makes sense of the signal. This process of meaning construction is not deterministic at all; rather it is inexact, ambiguous and underspecified, based on creative processes of inference and conceptual blending (Fauconnier and Turner, 2002; Höfler and

---

[8] Communication is not only spoken, of course, but I use the terms speaker and hearer in a general sense to indicate the person performing the communicative act and the person to whom the act is addressed.

Smith, 2009) which are inherently unstable and equivocal. Moreover, the individual nature of our cognitive representations means that, no matter how much common ground interlocutors share, there will inevitably be some (however minor) variation between their understandings of the same communicative episode and therefore between their internal linguistic representations; it is this variation which leads inexorably to the ubiquitous variation which pervades language (Smith and Höfler, 2015).

2.3.2 History

The fundamental goals of historical linguistics are to identify historical relationships between languages, particularly in cases where there is no corroborating written evidence, to describe the histories of languages and groups of languages, and, ultimately, to develop a comprehensive theory of language change (Harrison, 2005). When a language is spread over a reasonably large geographical area, the changes it undergoes will inevitably be different from area to area, yielding different dialects of the language; eventually (particularly when travel between dialect groups is difficult, as in pre-modern times), these dialects therefore tend to separate into different, mutually unintelligible languages. Languages which were once dialects of the same language (e.g. French and Spanish were originally dialects of Latin), but have diverged in this way, are said to belong to the same *language family*. This genealogical analogy is very widespread in historical linguistic terminology, so languages in the same family are said to be 'genetically' related to each other and to their 'common ancestor' language, and language families and higher groupings such as language 'phyla' are conventionally illustrated by linguistic 'family trees', but it is important to note that this terminology merely reflects an extended metaphor, and does *not* imply any true biological connection (although see Sections 2.4.2 and 2.4.3 for further discussion of work seeking to draw connections between genetic and linguistic features).

The establishment of such 'genetic' relationships among languages can be acknowledged when a particular feature the languages share is unlikely to have arisen independently or been borrowed between them, and can therefore best be explained in terms of the feature's 'inheritance' from a common ancestor language. In order to reduce the possibility of independent identical innovation in the languages under investigation, both natural resemblances (e.g. onomatopoeia like 'cuckoo') and chance resemblances (e.g. in the unrelated languages Hawai'ian and Greek, the word for honey is *meli* (Trask, 1996)) must be excluded from the analysis. This is primarily done by finding frequent and *systematic* correspondences between lexical items in the languages, through the painstaking technique of the *comparative method*, the 'gold standard' (McMahon and McMahon, 2005) of historical analysis. Table 2.2, for example, shows a small part of a system of regular correspondences in the initial consonants of

Table 2.2 Correspondences in West Germanic

English	Dutch	German	Meaning
path	pad	Pfad	'path'
pepper	peper	Pfeffer	'pepper'
plough	ploeg	Pflug	'plough'
pipe	pijp	Pfeife	'pipe'
plant	plant	Pflanze	'plant'

words in English, Dutch and German: in every row of the table (and in many more examples not shown), the words have the same meaning, and there is a systematic relationship in their form where initial [p] in English corresponds to [p] in Dutch and to [pf] in German.

The systematicity and predictability of these correspondences, therefore, is regarded as convincing evidence that we are dealing not with chance resemblances, but instead that the languages all belong to the same language family (West Germanic), and that they are all culturally descended from a common ancestor language or proto-language (proto-Germanic), possibly spoken roughly around the same time as Latin, but for which we have no confirmatory written records. The words in these correspondence sets are taken to be modified reflexes of a single item in the original proto-language, or *cognates*. Through a process of comparative reconstruction, which uses these correspondences to posit sounds in the ancestor language that could plausibly have developed into the sounds in the descendant languages, the words in the proto-language can be reconstructed with some degree of confidence. For example, for the correspondence set shown in Table 2.2, we would reconstruct an original sound *p,[9] which later became the affricate /pf/ in German but remained the same in English and Dutch, on the grounds that a change from /p/ to /pf/ is more frequent cross-linguistically and consequently more natural than the converse. The comparative method has been used to identify many language families and reconstruct putative proto-languages across the world; one of its greatest achievements was indeed the identification that many reconstructed proto-languages in Europe and North India were themselves related to each other, and thus that they were all descended from the same ancestor language, which we now know as Proto-Indo-European (Trask, 1996).

It is important to note, however, that such conclusions of descent from a common ancestor rests on some key assumptions. Most fundamentally, the comparison of lexical items across languages depends on the universal property

---

[9] The preceding asterisk here signifies that the form is not attested, but reconstructed using the comparative method.

of human language we saw in Section 2.1, that linguistic signs are intrinsically *arbitrary* (de Saussure, 1916), so the connection between words and their meanings is not motivated by any perceptual similarity but merely determined by cultural convention. Systematic similarities between languages are therefore indicative of shared linguistic ancestry because they would otherwise be surprising and unexpected. The arbitrariness of lexical items thus makes them much more suitable for the comparative method than other linguistic items such as syntactic constructions, where relationships between form and meaning are much more motivated and thus much more likely to recur across languages which are not related to each other.

Secondly, the Neogrammarian axiom of the comparative method is that sound change is assumed to be *regular* in each daughter language, and affects all items with the relevant sound in the relevant context (e.g. the initial *p in Table 2.2) simultaneously and with the same result. In fact, due to the ubiquity of variation in language that we have already seen in Section 2.3.1, and particularly the discovery that sound changes actually proceed through a language a few words at a time, through a process of lexical diffusion (Chen and Wang, 1975), we know that this axiom is not warranted, at least in its strongest form. Over the long timescales usually under consideration by historical linguists, however, the result of a sound change progressing through lexical diffusion is 'virtually indistinguishable' (McMahon and McMahon, 2005) from a change occurring universally and simultaneously, and the axiom can thus be recast as an approximation which holds sufficiently for the comparative method to remain valid.

Thirdly, and more problematically, however, the construction of language family trees must necessarily exclude contact-induced changes, or borrowings, which can cause spurious correspondences between unrelated languages and potentially undermine the comparative method (McMahon and McMahon, 2003). Borrowings need to be excluded from consideration before comparisons are undertaken, but it is unfortunately not always a trivial task to identify them: whenever linguistically diverse cultures come into contact with each other, a degree of multilingualism always ensues, which in turn facilitates the propagation of linguistic features from one group to the other. Contact-induced change is usually motivated by social factors like prestige, power and trade relationships described in Section 2.3.1, which can have wide-ranging effects on different linguistic systems. Although lexical items are usually thought to be the area most susceptible to borrowing (Sankoff, 2004), phonological, morphological and grammatical structures can also be borrowed in the right circumstances (Heine and Kuteva, 2005, 2006). The most common approach to weeding out borrowings from an analysis is to focus on basic and (near-) universal vocabulary items (e.g. kinship terms like *mother, father*, body parts like *head, eye*, and universal natural phenomena like *river, sun*) which are putatively 'less subject to replacement than other kinds of vocabulary' (Campbell, 2004, p. 178), and these are the basis for many of the phylogenetic models discussed in Section 2.4.2.

Finally, the evidence on which the comparative method depends is inevitably eroded by the same language change over time that it seeks to exploit to find the historical relationships. The more time that has passed since an ancestor language was spoken, the less evidence of shared ancestry will remain in its descendants, and thus the more problematic that ancestry will be to prove. Importantly, the rate of linguistic change is variable to such an extent that it is all but impossible to date linguistic changes without independent physical evidence such as written inscriptions of some sort (McMahon and McMahon, 2000).

These issues clearly show that the comparative method is certainly not a panacea for historical linguists, but it nevertheless remains an extremely useful tool which can shed considerable light on relationships between languages, as long as careful consideration is given to the data to which it is applied, and every effort is made to exclude inappropriate data to minimize the potential problems. Unfortunately, the necessary decisions on such data exclusions often require the prospective analyst to have a very considerable level of knowledge of the languages to be compared, and this high barrier to the valid use of the comparative method has led to the development of other superficially attractive but fundamentally flawed classificatory techniques such as *mass comparison* (often now called multilateral comparison) (Greenberg, 1987; Ruhlen, 1991, 1994). This contentious and highly controversial method has been severely criticized (Campbell, 1988; McMahon and McMahon, 1995) due to its methodology, which deliberately short-circuits the painstaking rigour of the comparative method in favour of collecting basic vocabulary items from a massive range of different languages, tabulating them and simultaneously comparing them to 'automatically' identify language groupings by noting the patterns which will inevitably be found. The twin requirements of frequent systematic correspondences to control against accidental similarity and of the comparative reconstruction of ancestral forms through regular and plausible sound change are both cast aside in favour of undefined criteria for determining matches in both form and meaning, which serve to render the technique of mass comparison devoid of scientific validity and its conclusions indistinguishable from chance (Campbell, 2004). As Aitchison (1996, p. 172) puts it: '[c]hance resemblances are easy to find among different languages if only vague likenesses among shortish words are selected.' Most breathtakingly, in response to complaints that much of the primary data used in the initial applications of mass comparison was strewn with errors, it has even been claimed with hopeless optimism that inaccurate or incomplete data supposedly has 'merely a randomising effect' (Greenberg, 1987, p. 29) on mass comparison and does not impact on its reliability.

Mass comparison's extremely liberal acceptance of any evidence in favour of languages being related, no matter how vague or tenuous, makes it a methodology which is 'very good at finding patterns, but no good at all at telling us whether those patterns mean anything' (McMahon and McMahon, 2005, p. 22). The key issue is that mass comparison conflates the process of hypothesis generation with that of hypothesis testing: although historical linguists have indeed always begun with observing resemblances between languages and wondering whether they might be related, this is far from assuming that an occasional resemblance actually proves that a historical relationship existed. Ostensibly comprehensive hierarchical linguistic classifications have been produced through the application of mass comparison (Ruhlen, 1994), though they contain extremely contentious language families such as Amerind ('[this] classification and its attendant methods must be rejected' (Campbell, 1988, p. 610)) and Indo-Pacific ('This idea lacks any substance' (Dixon, 1997, p. 35)), and even more controversial groupings of language families into macrofamilies such as Eurasiatic, finally culminating in the wildly speculative and unfounded 'last common ancestor' of all existing languages, Proto-World, angrily condemned as 'at best a hopeless waste of time' (Campbell and Poser, 2008, p. 393).

Although mass comparison has effectively no linguistic validity, it is nevertheless not without appeal outside the field of historical linguistics, precisely because of the illusory linguistic classifications it can produce in areas where historical linguists acknowledge that the data is no longer robust enough for the comparative method to work. One of the most famous uses that such classifications have found is in the comparison of genetic and linguistic trees (Cavalli-Sforza et al., 1988) discussed in Section 2.4.2, which sought to reconstruct human phylogeny by finding correlations between trees built from measures of genetic diversity between human populations and pseudo-historical linguistic trees based on mass comparison (Greenberg, 1987).

2.3.3 Evolution

The primary aim of evolutionary linguistics, on the other hand, is to explain the transition to language, how our unique communication system emerged from a non-linguistic system. Historically, the predominant view of language has been as an autonomous module within the brain, a *language organ* containing the universal structures which form the basis for all human languages (Chomsky, 1965). This view has been traditionally underpinned by the argument from the 'poverty of the stimulus', the claim that the linguistic evidence to which children are exposed is not sufficient to acquire the grammar they end up with (Chomsky, 1980) (although see Pullum and Scholz (2002) for a detailed empirical assessment which found no convincing support for the claim). An evolutionary account of this nativist view of language was developed by Pinker and Bloom (1990), based on the assumption that the language organ evolved biologically though natural selection for language learning, and making use of the *Baldwin effect*, through which traits which are originally acquired through learning can become encoded genetically, when learning changes the evolutionary environment so that genes which encode the learnt behaviour explicitly are selected for (Deacon, 1997). Although the Baldwin effect has been demonstrated in some evolutionary models where genotype and phenotype are directly connected (Turkel, 2002), it is not found in more biologically plausible scenarios (Yamauchi, 2001), and the encoding of specific linguistic parameters as envisaged by Pinker and Bloom (1990) can only occur when the linguistic target is fixed (Munroe and Cangelosi, 2002). When language is changing even very slowly, selection actually works in favour of neutral genes rather than specialized genes which encode linguistic principles directly, effectively because biological evolution is not able to keep pace with a moving target (Chater and Christiansen, 2009; Chater et al., 2009).

As a result of this, attention in evolutionary linguistics has largely shifted to the *cultural* evolution of language as an explanatory mechanism, turning the problem on its head to suggest that the languages themselves have evolved in order to become more learnable by human brains, and thus persist over time among human populations, rather than our brains evolving to learn language (Christiansen and Chater, 2008). According to cultural accounts, the requirement for language to oscillate continually between its internal and external manifestation as it is learnt and used leads to the emergence of languages which have adapted to be learnable by humans (Kirby, 2000; Zuidema, 2003; Smith, 2008). The burden of evolutionary explanation thus shifts to identifying the minimal set of cognitive capacities which can support the sharing of inferable cultural conventions (Smith and Kirby, 2008); these capacities need not be specific to language at all, but could have evolved biologically for some other purpose; they may be universal pressures such as memory or processing constraints but they may only apply in particular circumstances (or niches) such as populations with small numbers (Nettle, 1999) or with a relatively high number of second-language learners (Lupyan and Dale, 2010), as we will see in Section 2.4.3.

Explanations of both the biological evolution of relevant cognitive capacities and the cultural evolution of language in dynamic populations of cognitively adapted individuals are required for a full explanation of the emergence and evolution of language, and it has become increasingly clear that the interaction between biology and culture, too, is likely to be vital: biology provides cognitive adaptations which influence how we interact with each other, while these cultural interactions can cause qualitative structural changes to language itself. One profitable way of conceptualizing this is to consider language as a complex adaptive system (Gell-Mann, 1994; Beckner et al., 2009), a system where the linguistic structure is a set of emergent properties derived from communicative interactions, without any system-wide central guidance or optimization (Hopper, 1987; Bybee, 2006). The very different evolutionary timescales involved, however, mean that we are probably dealing with at least three separate complex adaptive systems, which interact with each other in interesting yet complex ways (Kirby and Hurford, 2002).

2.4 Dynamic models of language

The utility of a formal model lies in the rigour with which it allows theoretical mechanisms to be tested and evaluated. A model is always a simplification of the real system and thus potentially inaccurate in some important detail, but the explicit specifications of the assumptions behind the model mean that the consequences of the design decisions which have been implemented can be clearly demonstrated. There is a continuum of complexity on which models can be placed, from those which deliberately ignore many details so that they can zoom in on some potentially crucial attributes of the system, to those which embrace the details in an attempt to be more realistic, yet in doing so produce models whose results require much more nuanced interpretation and are less likely to yield clear conclusions (Smith, 2011). Various types of formal models have been used over the last few decades to explore many dynamic aspects of language, from computational simulations and mathematical models to more recent experimental approaches. In this section I will look at how these different types of modelling have shed light on different aspects of language dynamics, from the general properties of language change through phylogenetic analysis of language history to computational and experimental models of the cultural evolution of language.

2.4.1 Models of language change

Mathematical models have frequently been used to explore the general dynamics of language change, using a variety of evolutionary frameworks. Exemplar models, for instance, use a very general framework in which (linguistic) categories are made up of sets of individual tokens which are grouped together by their shared labels and organized in terms of some measure of similarity. The individual tokens represent usage events: every time the category is used, a new token is added to the system. Exemplar models are thus very good models of linguistic variation: every category contains many different variants, and different speakers therefore have different representations of the categories, reflecting their different experiences. The same exemplar categories can also be seen to form a distribution from which individuals' production of linguistic variants is drawn, and indeed each production yields another exemplar to be added to the category. In an evolutionary model, some of these variants must be *selected* according to some criteria, so that they are differentially produced over other competing variants. Wedel (2006) uses a series of exemplar models like this to show in detail how genetic drift results in the random fixation (when the whole community uses the same variant) of variants by pruning variation, how small increases in selection bias can result in the inhibition of sound changes where they would eliminate a functional contrast like those described in Section 2.2.1 and, conversely, how contrast can be shifted across segments in cases of low functional contrast.

Baxter et al.'s (2009) framework focuses explicitly on the types of selection mechanisms which can work on variants of a linguistic variable. Their model, which is based on Hull's (1988) general analysis of selection in evolutionary systems as developed into Croft's (2000) theory of utterance selection, makes a crucial distinction between the replicators, the linguistic entities which are replicated, and the interactors, the language users whose interaction with each other causes the differential replication of the linguistic entities, yielding four qualitatively different selection mechanisms, dubbed *neutral evolution, neutral interactor selection, weighted interactor selection* and *replicator selection*. Neutral evolution is directly equivalent to the solely random process of genetic drift, which can, as Wedel (2006) showed, produce random fixations without any need for true selection at all. Their mechanisms of interactor selection naturally focus on how the structure of the networks and communities in which the speakers interact can have substantial impacts on the replication of variants: in neutral interactor selection, frequencies of interaction between speakers is the only relevant factor; in weighted interactor selection, certain interactors are preferred over others, due to different social valuations on them and the social groups they belong to, and so the variants they use are indirectly preferred. In the final mechanism, replicator selection, the linguistic variants *themselves* have different social valuations which lead directly to their differential replication. Baxter et al. (2009) used their framework to investigate a notable theory of new dialect formation in isolated colonial communities such as New Zealand after the arrival of British settlers (Trudgill, 2008), which held that sociolinguistic features like identity and prestige play no part, but that the new society effectively begins with a blank slate in which linguistic variants have no pre-existing social values attached to them, and so the adoption of new variants is driven solely by the frequency of interaction between interlocutors (i.e. neutral interactor selection). Their analysis showed that although the linguistic characteristics of New Zealand English were indeed consistent with change simply through accommodation to interlocutors and frequency of interaction, as Trudgill had suggested, it was inconceivable for this mechanism alone to have been able to produce the level of dialect homogeneity which was actually seen in New Zealand in the available timescale, and therefore that some differential social valuation of either the interlocutors (weighted interactor selection) or the variants they used (replicator selection) would have been required.

Blythe and Croft (2012) used the same evolutionary framework to investigate the general mechanisms of propagation in language change, or how a new linguistic variant is diffused through a community and becomes conventionalized so that it replaces the original convention. Such replacement events, in common with many natural processes, are characterized by a trajectory which follows an approximate sigmoid S-curve, progressing from a slow beginning through a phase of rapid acceleration and a slow approach to completion. In particular, they focus on a systematic exploration of Baxter et al.'s (2009) selection mechanisms to see which of them can yield the characteristic diffusion curve, finding that replicator selection is 'almost certainly an essential mechanism for language changes that follow an S-curve' (Blythe and Croft, 2012, p. 293). Interestingly, they find that the mere existence of any differential valuation of variants is enough: it is not required for the emergence of an S-curve for individuals in the community to give variants the same values, nor for those values to remain constant. Their hedging of replicator selection as almost certainly essential stems from their finding that although they did manage to simulate an appropriate trajectory with weighted interactor selection alone, this was only possible under rather implausible conditions where the population was increasing exponentially over time and each new group into the populations weighted their immediate predecessors highly. A similar finding was reported by Gong et al. (2012), using a slightly different kind of evolutionary model based on the Price equation for the description of evolutionary processes (Price, 1970) in combination with the Pólya urn model of dynamics from epidemiology, which confirmed that replicator selection (which they term 'variant prestige') is the key selective pressure which drives the adoption of new variants in a population.

A more specific dynamic model of language change is presented by Kandler et al. (2010), who are interested in modelling the process of language shift, where members of a multilingual speech community abandon their original language for another language, frequently because the new language is seen as more useful in achieving social mobility or in providing access to greater economic opportunities (McMahon, 1994). Kandler et al. (2010) focus in particular on the shift from Celtic languages to English in Britain and Ireland over the last couple of centuries, and intriguingly show that, although monolingual speakers of the language with lower prestige always disappear, the minority language itself can still persist in a bilingual community, as long as there are both sufficient bilingual speakers and sufficient pressure on monolinguals in the high-status language to become bilingual. Applying this to the current situation of Gaelic in Scotland, they suggest, perhaps optimistically, that around 860 English speakers need to become bilingual in Gaelic each year for the language to become stable. See also Chapters 21, 22 and 23 in this volume for further discussion of minority languages.

2.4.2   Models of language history

Very different kinds of evolutionary model are used in phylogenetic approaches to historical linguistics, which seek both to infer language histories and also to use linguistic history as evidence for hypotheses in other disciplines, such as human dispersal or human genetics.

The basic foundation of phylogenetic analysis is the cognate set, based on a list of words in various languages corresponding to a standardized universal list of meanings; the most widely used lists are the Swadesh vocabulary lists of 100 or 200 core items (Swadesh, 1952), who originally created much longer lists, but settled on the smaller sets after various exclusions were necessary, most notably because the meaning was not sufficiently culturally neutral (e.g. snow), because meaning differences were not reliably lexicalized across languages (e.g. leg/foot), or because items were not reliable independent of each other (e.g. wife/woman). The cultural neutrality of the Swadesh lists is problematic, and this has led to the creation of various, culturally specific, modified Swadesh-style lists for use in phylogenetic analysis for specific parts of the world, for instance for South-East Asia and the Andes. There are also issues about semantic ambiguities in the lists, which were originally defined using single English words without further explanation (e.g. should 'cloud' refer to white cumulus or to black rainclouds?); Kassian et al. (2010) have therefore developed a series of more detailed, disambiguating semantic specifications for the standard 100-item list to provide a helpful standard for list compilers, who need to enter a word into the list for each language which is being analysed. This step is crucial to any phylogenetic model, and requires the specification of well-defined criteria for inclusion. Swadesh (1952) originally suggested that items on the list should be common, as morphologically simple as possible, and single words rather than phrases. The massive cross-linguistic semantic variation and ambiguity we saw in Section 2.2, however, can lead to severe problems in deciding which forms should be included (McMahon and McMahon, 2005). Many languages, for instance, have unrelated near-synonyms (e.g. English small/little) which could both equally well be used for the same item, while for other languages there is no simple one-to-one mapping: they may have multiple specific words which together cover one meaning on the list (Navajo, for instance, has no single word for *water*, but instead separate words for *drinking water*, *rain water* and *stagnant water* (Campbell, 2004)), or they may have one single word which covers more than one item on the list (e.g. *bark* and *skin*). Assuming such problem can be satisfactorily overcome, a cognate coding matrix is then created from the completed list, coding all attested cognates (i.e. words which can be shown to derive from a common ancestor) for each meaning with the same state. It is clear, therefore, that phylogenetic models rely not only on the existence of a validated Swadesh-style list, but also on the reliable prior application of the comparative method to accurately identify the cognates and to successfully exclude as many borrowings as possible.

The simplest lexicostatistical models quantify the level of relatedness between languages simply by counting the number of cognate items across the list: the higher the percentage of cognate vocabulary items, the more closely related the languages are assumed to be. More sophisticated models focus not just on a simple distance measure between languages (see Chapter 5 by Ginsburg and Weber for a detailed account of how linguistic distances can be calculated), but on producing an evolutionarily plausible route by which related languages have derived from a common ancestor language, finding the best tree for the largest number of cognate items. The most straightforward of these methods uses an assumption of parsimony similar to that assumed in the comparative method: the best tree is simply the one which minimizes the number of evolutionary changes which are required to arrive at the observed data. Maximum parsimony models have been successfully used to analyse the internal history of the Bantu language family, by for instance Holden (2002). Maximum compatibility trees are similar to maximum parsimony trees, but require in addition that languages with the same state for a particular meaning are represented as a single group within the tree, therefore ruling out the independent (convergent, in biological terms) evolution of cognates in different lineages of languages; such a model has been used by Nakhleh et al. (2005) to analyse Indo-European. In both cases, the analysis frequently results in several possible best-scoring trees, and so consensus trees which amalgamate these together are often used in order to visualize the results: strict consensus trees include only those splits which are in every one of the best-scoring trees, while majority consensus trees contain those which occur in more than half of them.

Other models make explicit assumptions about a particular hypothesis of linguistic change, and then estimate the evolutionary history of the languages of language families based on that hypothesis. A maximum likelihood analysis tries to find a single tree and model parameters which maximize the probability of producing the observed data, while Bayesian methods (Pagel and Meade, 2004) produce a probability distinction over the set of trees, allowing the explicit representation of phylogenetic uncertainty. Gray and Atkinson (2003), for instance, used a Bayesian model to establish the relationship between the frequency of usage and the rate of lexical change in four separate Indo-European languages. Unfortunately, the space of possible trees is enormous and highly skewed towards trees with low likelihood values, and there is no existing algorithm which can guarantee that the best tree will be found in reasonable computing time (Schmidt and von Haeseler, 2009); the best way round this is to use Markov Chain Monte Carlo sampling to move through the space until a stationary distribution is reached, and then build a consensus tree from the trees within the stationary distribution.

One key issue with all such phylogenetic models, however, is their accuracy, which of course depends upon the encoding and analysis of the data. Problematically, because we know only incomplete information about the true history of most languages, it can be difficult to evaluate the different models, although this is done to some extent by calibrating them on well-established language families for which extremely strong written evidence or historical records exist. Another, more subtle, problem with family trees as a model of language history, as mentioned in Section 2.3.2, is that they force an idealized view of language change which deliberately ignores all kinds of borrowing or influence from unrelated languages, and is completely unable, for instance, to represent the formation of creole languages which have multiple parents. For languages with extensive borrowing, network models are needed in order to be able to represent these conflicting relationships by reticulated joins between branches. Holden and Gray (2006), for instance, used a network model to try to resolve some of the outstanding problems in Bantu history which had proved intractable to tree-based analysis, and found that while West Bantu scattered very quickly into a number of different branches, East Bantu was characterized by extensive borrowing early in its development. The complexity of network models, however, and in particular their sensitivity to changes in internal parameter settings, can make them extremely different to interpret (McMahon and McMahon, 2005).

Much effort in the past few decades has been expended on connecting evidence about language histories with evidence from other disciplines, in order to shed further light on aspects of human history, seeking to correlate linguistic family trees or models more generally with archaeological or genetic evidence. The earliest and most famous of these was Cavalli-Sforza et al.'s (1988) attempted reconstruction of human phylogeny by finding correlations between linguistic trees and trees of genetic diversity, which was based on the innovative and intuitively appealing idea that when populations split and merge, both their genes and their languages could have been affected by common processes. There are clear and seductive parallels not only between direct genetic and historical linguistic inheritance, but also between processes of diffusion such as gene exchange through marriage and language convergence through borrowing. Despite this, the work has met with a considerable degree of criticism from many different quarters, not only due to its reliance on many of the extremely contentious linguistic groupings described in Section 2.3.2 above, but also due to methodological shortcomings in the production of the genetic trees and apparent analytical sleights of hand. The genetic trees were in fact phenograms reflecting overall genetic similarity between populations, which were simply assumed to be equivalent to the phylogeny of the populations without any further evidence (Bateman et al., 1990). The individual population groupings used were also problematic, with a minority of them being explicitly defined on the basis of the language spoken in their community, calling into question the independence of the genetic and linguistic trees which is required for any correlations to be valuable (McMahon and McMahon, 2005). Most seriously of all, the 'remarkable correspondence' between the genetic and linguistic trees claimed by Cavalli-Sforza et al. (1988, p. 6002) appears under closer examination to be illusory and largely due to the way in which the trees were visually presented: almost half of the linguistic families are matched with just a single population, and thus have no effect on the congruence of the trees at all (McMahon and McMahon, 1995), most of the other linguistic families are in fact split across different genetic populations, and neither of the putative linguistic superphyla in the linguistic trees (Nostratic and Eurasiatic) corresponds to any population aggregate on the genetic tree (Bateman et al., 1990).

Less controversially, linguistic evidence from phylogenetic analysis has been used to evaluate competing archaelogical hypotheses about human history. Gray and Jordan (2000), for instance, used a maximum parsimony model to derive a tree of 77 Austronesian languages which they showed to be significantly congruent with another tree representing the 'express train' model of the human colonization of the Pacific, supporting the theory of colonization by an original population in Taiwan which spread through a series of migrations to Polynesia. A similar parsimony analysis was also used by Holden (2002) to reconstruct the family history of the Bantu languages, who showed that the resultant tree closely mirrored existing archaeological evidence about the spread of farming in sub-Saharan Africa in the Neolithic and Early Iron Age.

Phylogenetic models have also been used for the purposes of *glottochronology*, a technique originally developed through analogy with carbon dating to estimate the dates of events in language family trees, particularly language splits. As in radioactive decay, the method assumed a 'stable regularity' (Lees, 1953, p. 113) in the rate at which basic vocabulary items would be replaced by new words. By averaging results derived from control data based on pairs of languages which could be independently dated (e.g. Latin and Spanish; Old Norse and Modern Swedish) and for which cognacy judgements were carried out using the standard comparative method, Lees (1953) derived a value of 0.8048 ($\pm$ 0.0176) per millennium for this glottochronological constant. Dating language splits is inherently troublesome because they represent gradual processes rather than precise historical events, but more problematically, by analysing further pairs of languages, Bergslund and Vogt (1962) were able to show that the glottochronological constant was actually an illusion, with widely varying rates of language change depending on a range of different factors such as the relative isolation of the language community and their specific cultural practices;[10] additional work has since shown that languages tend to change more quickly in smaller communities (Nettle, 1999), and that the emergence of a distinct language itself is associated with rapid, punctuated bursts of change followed by much longer periods of slower changes as the new language diverges from its ancestor (Atkinson et al., 2008). More recent phylogenetic models have begun to take account of varying rates of change, again borrowing methods from biology (Drummond and Suchard, 2010) to incorporate both probabilistic variation across the whole tree (relaxed clock models) and a series of different rates for different regions of the tree (random local clock models). In a famous example of this, for instance, Gray and Atkinson (2003) used a maximum likelihood model with a relaxed clock and smoothed variation across the tree, which they used to estimate an emergence date for Indo-European at around 8,000–9,500 years ago, strongly consistent with an Anatolian origin for the language and its subsequent expansion in association with the spread of agriculture.

2.4.3 Models of language evolution

Early models of language evolution were dominated by simple computer simulations exploring the biological evolution of the critical period for language learning (Hurford, 1991) and of symbols themselves (Hurford, 1989). Proponents of cultural explanations of the evolution of language, on the other hand, have shown that language acquisition is underpinned by general learning strategies rather than a language organ, showing for instance that learners can extract sufficient information from the transitional probabilities between words to be able to make successful grammaticality judgements in complex sentences (Reali and Christiansen, 2005) and that distributional information of this sort can be integrated with probabilistic phonological cues to create accurate representations of lexical categories (Reali et al., 2003). Such simulations are typically agent-based models, involving a simulated population of individuals (agents) initially endowed with some specified cognitive capacities and then left to interact with each other and update their linguistic knowledge over thousands of interactions and perhaps over multiple generations of agents dying and being replaced. This kind of modelling has been used to explore a wide range of issues from the emergence of phonological structure and the duality of patterning described in Section 2.2 (de Boer, 2001; Oudeyer, 2006; Zuidema and de Boer, 2009) to the evolution of vocabulary (Smith, 2004) and

---

[10] They describe a word taboo in East Greenlandic, for instance, where the name of a dead person cannot be mentioned during a mourning period; as people's names are often words in the language, new words need to be deliberately (and frequently) created to replace the taboo items.

syntactic structure (Kirby, 2000). More recently, a whole research programme (Steels, 2011) has been developed on the implementation of agent-based *language game* models, which model the emergence of aspects of language through the interactive negotiation of coordinated behaviour between agents, not only general concepts like the development of shared lexicons (Steels, 1999; Smith, 2005; Steels and Belpaeme, 2005) and the design feature of compositionality (Vogt, 2005), but also more focused grammatical and morphological features such as the emergence of case systems (van Trijp, 2012) and agreement (Beuls and Steels, 2013) through processes of grammaticalization.

Probably the primary agent-based model, which has now outgrown its computational origins to be used frequently in both mathematical and experimental models as well, is the *iterated learning* model (Kirby and Hurford, 2002; Smith et al., 2003b), which allows explorations of how the structure of language evolves through its transmission over a diffusion chain, with agents learning language through observing the linguistic usage of other agents who learnt their language in the same way. Simple iterated learning models have been instrumental in demonstrating the importance of cultural evolution in the evolution of language, showing how random languages can be transformed into stable, syntactically complex languages simply by being learnt over generations through a so-called *transmission bottleneck*. This term refers to the fact that learners have to learn from only partial experience of the language, and so have not explicitly learnt how to express certain meanings. The transmission bottleneck forces learners to generalize from the data they have encountered to represent such unobserved meanings, and this pressure biases the language towards compositionality and systematicity, rather than the idiosyncrasy which can persist without the bottleneck (Kirby, 2001; Smith et al., 2003a).

In the last decade, a set of experimental techniques has become popular in work on the dynamics of language evolution. The iterated learning model itself was transferred to this paradigm in a celebrated language experiment in which an unstructured 'alien' language of random words, with no connection between meanings and forms, was taught to participants; the words produced for the meanings by this generation were then taught to the next generation of participants (Kirby et al., 2008). Over cumulative generations, the languages adapted so that they were easier to learn, essentially by tolerating massive ambiguity and using the same word for multiple meanings; as a result of this the language's expressive power was lost. A second experiment reintroduced expressivity into the language by the explicit exclusion of ambiguity, and this resulted in the languages adapting differently, still becoming increasingly learnable, but this time by developing compositionality so that aspects of meanings were systematically reflected in the words produced, so that expressivity too was maximized.

In another, graphically based experiment, the competing pressures of learnability and expressibility were explored differently: Garrod et al. (2007) asked participants to play a Pictionary-style game in which one person draws an ostensive representation of some meaning, and the other infers what the meaning is. When participants play this game repeatedly in pairs, they develop a communicative system which is extremely expressive but in which the signals become increasingly simple after repeated use; the participants no longer need to draw all the detail, but can simply provide shorthand simplified cues to the meanings which effectively reside in their shared common history of use (Caldwell and Smith, 2012). The cues themselves are idiosyncratic and arbitrary, showing clearly how common ground and shared experience can drive the 'drift to the arbitrary' (Tomasello, 2008); this makes languages more internally efficient, but at the expense of learnability. In a further experiment, Theisen et al. (2010) introduced a pressure for learnability by embedding the game in an iterated learning chain, with new generations learning from the drawings produced by the previous generation; in this case the drawings still became increasingly conventionalized and arbitrary, but also developed compositionality, making them more learnable to future generations. More recently, Kirby et al. (2015) use both computational simulations and laboratory experiments to show convincingly that linguistic structure emerges culturally, as a direct result of the interactions between the twin pressures of expressivity and learnability.

Experimental techniques have also been used to explore the emergence of signals themselves: in a pioneering use of this technique, Galantucci (2005) investigated the coordination and conventionalization of signalling systems in an artificial context where existing communication systems were rendered useless but with other novel communicative opportunities; participants learnt in many cases to exploit the opportunities and developed shared expressive communicative systems. This paradigm was pared back further by Scott-Phillips et al. (2009) to a situation where participants could only move in a strictly controlled fashion around a small grid, yet needed to communicate successfully in order to coordinate their behaviour. Despite this extremely challenging situation, participants were able to develop successful communication systems, if they were able to signal their communicative intent by moving *ostensively* in a distinctive manner contrary to their expectations.

The controversy over Cavalli-Sforza et al.'s (1988) work, described in Section 2.4.2, cast a long shadow over work comparing genetics and linguistics for a considerable period of time, but over the last few years it has become clear that genes can have potentially surprising effects on linguistic structures. Dediu and Ladd (2007) first demonstrated the existence of a fascinating relationship at the population level between the allele frequencies in the population of two genes involved in brain development and the likelihood of the languages being spoken in the population having the tonal contrasts described in Section 2.2.1. Intriguingly, the two genes in question, ASPM and Microcephalin, have both emerged relatively recently in human evolution and are spreading quickly across the world, suggesting that they are favoured by natural selection and therefore that the correlation reflects some kind of small cognitive bias whose effects on language structure only become detectable after many generations of cultural evolution, although Dediu and Ladd are careful not to speculate on the precise details of this bias. The significance of the relationship was demonstrated by taking advantage of new large genetic and linguistic databases (Haspelmath et al., 2005) to test many thousands of other possible relationships, showing that although there is generally no relationship between genetic markers and linguistic features, the relationship between these two genes and tonal languages remained very strong. Similar correlations have been noted before, notably between linguistic diversity and biodiversity (Nettle, 1999; Maffi, 2001), but increases in the availability and ease of use of such databases have led over recent years to considerable growth in correlational studies searching for relationships between combinations of linguistic variables and other cultural traits, although researchers must be careful to avoid simplistic uncontrolled data dredging over many different variables, which will inevitably uncover spurious relationships (Roberts and Winters, 2013). Interestingly, many correlational studies have found evidence, however, for the evolutionary adaptation of aspects of languages to particular ecological and social niches in their dynamic environment. Lupyan and Dale (2010), for instance, showed an inverse correlation between population size and morphological complexity, finding evidence in support of Wray and Grace's (2007) theory that exoteric (outward-facing) languages used in large, disparate communities (such as English and Swahili) face pressure to be more easily learnable by non-native speakers and to be easily used by people from different backgrounds with little non-linguistic common ground, while esoteric (inward-facing) languages in small communities (such as Tatar and Elfdalian) face contrasting pressures to become reliable social markers of community membership, and thus showed increases in morphological complexity and opacity to ensure that only people able to spend a great deal of effort would be able to use them. Sometimes, the niche is physiological, such as Everett's (2013) findings that the languages spoken in populations living at high altitudes have more ejective consonants, from which he hypothesizes that lower air pressure may make ejectives easier to articulate or that ejectives may mitigate the dehydrating effects of exhalation in drier climates. This line of inquiry has been extended more recently, with Everett et al. (2015) showing that extremely cold and dry regions constrain the emergence and spread of tonal languages, because the reduced air quality appears to compromise the fine control needed to maintain the tonal distinctions.

2.5 Conclusion

The question of what makes human language special has been long debated and analysed, with its expressive power in particular often regarded with a reverential sense of awe and wonder. This chapter has focused on one crucial characteristic of language: its dynamic nature, which marks it as unique and rather strange in comparison to other communication systems. All languages are in a state of constant flux, characterized by dynamic variation and massive diversity at all levels of analysis. In Section 2.2, I gave a detailed overview of some of the striking ways in which this diversity is manifested across different languages, looking at the sounds they use and the way these are organized, the ways in which words are created from their component parts and then assembled into full sentences, and the conceptualization of simple spatial relationships between objects.

In Section 2.3, I set out three of the main timescales on which research into language change and evolution is carried out. The fundamental basis of linguistic change is its pervasive cumulative variation, which is primarily caused by the complex social functions for which language is used, and the nature of language in use, in particular its constant oscillation between internal linguistic representations and external linguistic behaviour, mediated by the co-operative communicative processes of ostension and inference. This pervasive variation leads to the constant creation of new linguistic varieties, which over time and space develop into separate languages stemming from a common source; much early work in linguistics as a scientific discipline, in fact, was in the identification of relationships between modern languages and in inferring and describing their shared and separate histories in terms of family trees and networks. On a yet longer timescale, evolutionary linguistics is interested in the initial emergence of language from a pre-linguistic communication system, particularly in how interactions between biological and cultural evolution can provide explanations of this emergence by investigating language as a complex adaptive system with properties emerging from language use in a social context.

Formal models have proved over the last few decades to be extremely important in the exploration and systematical testing of many aspects of the dynamic nature of language. In Section 2.4, I presented a number of recent models in this vein, including evolutionary models of the propagation of linguistic variants, phylogenetic models of language family histories and their use in wider debates about human history, and formal and experimental models of cumulative cultural evolution showing the adaptive nature of language itself under pressures of learnability and expressivity. It is clear that both the scope and variety of models have increased enormously over recent years, with many different techniques being developed to explore an increasing range of linguistic characteristics; the increased availability of large datasets has led, for instance, to many comparative studies exploring correlations between specific linguistic characteristics and genetic or geographic information.

References

J. Aitchison (1996) *The Seeds of Speech: Language Origin and Evolution* (Cambridge: Cambridge University Press).

Q. Atkinson, A. Meade, C. Venditti, S. Greenhill, and M. Pagel (2008) 'Languages Evolve in Punctuational Bursts', *Science*, 319, 588.

R. Bateman, I. Goddard, R. O'Grady, V. Funk, R. Mooi, J. Krees, and P. Cannell (1990) 'Speaking of Forked Tongues: The Feasibility of Reconciling Human Phylogeny and the History of Language', *Current Anthropology*, 31, 1–24.

G. Baxter, R. Blythe, W. Croft, and A. McKane (2009) 'Modeling Language Change: An Evaluation of Trudgill's Theory of the Emergence of New Zealand English', *Language Variation and Change*, 21, 257–296.

C. Beckner, R. Blythe, J. Bybee, M. Christiansen, W. Croft, N. Ellis, J. Holland, J. Ke, D. Larsen-Freeman, and T. Schoenemann (2009) 'Language Is a Complex Adaptive System: Position Paper', *Language Learning*, 59, 1–26.

K. Bergslund and H. Vogt (1962) 'On the Validity of Glottochronology', *Current Anthropology*, 3, 115–153.

K. Beuls and L. Steels (2013) 'Agent-based Models of Strategies for the Emergence and Evolution of Grammatical Agreement', *PLoS One*, 8, 358960.

R. Blythe and W. Croft (2012) 'S-curves and the Mechanisms of Propagation in Language Change', *Language*, 88, 269–304.

D. Bolinger (1975) *Aspects of Language* (New York: Harcourt Brace Jovanovich).

H. Bowe and S. Morey (1999) *The Yorta Yorta (Bangerang) Language of the Murray Goulburn, Including Yabula Yabula* (Canberra: Pacific Linguistics).

H. Brighton, K. Smith, and S. Kirby (2005) 'Language as an Evolutionary System', *Physics of Life Reviews*, 2, 177–226.

P. Brown (2001) 'Learning to Talk about Motion UP and DOWN in Tzeltal: Is There a Language-Specific Bias for Verb Learning?' In M. Bowerman and S. Levinson (eds.) *Language Acquisition and Conceptual Development*, 512–543 (Cambridge: Cambridge University Press).

P. Brown (2006) 'A Sketch of the Grammar of Space in Tzeltal' In S. Levinson and D. Wilkins (eds.) *Grammars of Space: Explorations in Cognitive Diversity*, 230–272 (Cambridge: Cambridge University Press).

M. Butskhrikidze (2002) *The Consonant Phonotactics of Georgian* (Utrecht: Landelijke Onderzoekschool Taalwetenschap).

J. Bybee (2006) 'From Usage to Grammar: The Mind's Response to Repetition', *Language*, 82, 711–733.

C. Caldwell and K. Smith (2012) 'Cultural Evolution and Perpetuation of Arbitrary Communicative Conventions in Experimental Microsocieties', *PLoS One*, 7, e43807.

L. Campbell (1988) 'Review of: Language in the Americas, J. H. Greenberg', *Language*, 64, 591–615.

L. Campbell (2004) *Historical Linguistics* (Edinburgh: Edinburgh University Press).

L. Campbell and W. Poser (2008) *Language Classification: History and Method* (Cambridge: Cambridge University Press).

L. Cavalli-Sforza, P. Menozzi, A. Piazza, and J. Mountain (1988) 'Reconstruction of Human Evolution: Bringing Together Genetic, Archaeological and Linguistic Data', *Proceedings of the National Academy of Sciences of the United States of America*, 85, 6002–6006.

N. Chater and M. Christiansen (2009) 'Language Acquisition Meets Language Evolution', *Cognitive Science*, 34, 1–27.

N. Chater, F. Reali, and M. Christiansen (2009) 'Restrictions on Biological Adaptation in Language Evolution', *Proceedings of the National Academy of Sciences of the United States of America*, 106, 1015–1020.

M. Chen and W. Wang (1975) 'Sound Change: Actuation and Implementation', *Language*, 51, 255–281.

N. Chomsky (1965) *Aspects of the Theory of Syntax* (Cambridge, MA: MIT Press).

N. Chomsky (1980) *Rules and Representations* (London: Basil Blackwell).

M. Christiansen and N. Chater (2008) 'Language as Shaped by the Brain', *Behavioral and Brain Sciences*, 31, 489–508.

H. Clark (1996) *Using Language* (Cambridge: Cambridge University Press).

G. Clements (2000) 'Phonology' In B. Heine and D. Nurse (eds.) *African Languages: An Introduction*, 132–160 (Cambridge: Cambridge University Press).

F. Coulmas (2013) *Sociolinguistics: The Study of Speakers' Choices* (Cambridge: Cambridge University Press).

W. Croft (2000) *Explaining Language Change: An Evolutionary Approach* (Singapore: Longman).

B. de Boer (2001) *The Origins of Vowel Systems* (Oxford: Oxford University Press).

F. de Saussure (1916) *Cours de Linguistique Générale* (Paris: Payot).

T. Deacon (1997) *The Symbolic Species* (London: Penguin).

D. Dediu and R. Ladd (2007) 'Linguistic Tone Is Related to the Population Frequency of the Adaptive Haplogroups of Two Brain Size Genes, Aspm and Microcephalin', *Proceedings of the National Academy of Sciences of the United States of America*, 104, 10944–10949.

G. Deutscher (2010) *Through the Language Glass: How Words Colour Your World* (London: William Heinemann).

R. Dixon (1972) *The Dyirbal Language of North Queensland* (Cambridge: Cambridge University Press).

R. Dixon (1997) *The Rise and Fall of Languages* (Cambridge: Cambridge University Press).

A. Drummond and M. Suchard (2010) 'Bayesian Random Local Clocks, or One rate to Rule them all', *BioMed Central Biology*, 8, 114.

M. Dryer (2013a) 'Order of Subject, Object and Verb' In M. Dryer and M. Haspelmath (eds.) *The World Atlas of Linguistic Structures Online* (Leipzig: Max Planck Institute for Evolutionary Anthropology).

M. Dryer (2013b) 'Prefixing vs. Suffixing in Inflectional Morphology' In M. Dryer and M. Haspelmath (eds.) *The World Atlas of Linguistic Structures Online* (Leipzig: Max Planck Institute for Evolutionary Anthropology).

N. Evans (2010) *Dying Words: Endangered Languages and What They Have to Tell Us* (Singapore: Wiley-Blackwell).

N. Evans and S. Levinson (2009) 'The Myth of Language Universals: Language Diversity and Its Importance for Cognitive Science', *Behavioral and Brain Sciences*, 32, 429–492.

C. Everett (2013) 'Evidence for Direct Geographic Influences on Linguistic Sounds: The Case of Ejectives', *PLoS One*, 8, e65275.

C. Everett, D. Blasi, and S. Roberts (2015) 'Climate, Vocal Folds, and Tonal Languages: Connecting the Physiological and Geographic Dots', *Proceedings of the National Academy of Sciences*, 112, 1322–1327.

G. Fauconnier and M. Turner (2002) *The Way We Think: Conceptual Blending and the Mind's Hidden Complexities* (New York: Basic Books).

W. Foley (1997) *Anthropological Linguistics: An Introduction* (London: Blackwell).

B. Galantucci (2005) 'An Experimental Study of the Emergence of Human Communication Systems', *Cognitive Science*, 29, 737–767.

S. Garrod, N. Fay, J. Lee, J. Oberlander, and T. MacLeod (2007) 'Foundations of Representations: Where Might Graphical Symbol Systems Come From?', *Cognitive Science*, 31, 961–987.

M. Gell-Mann (1994) *The Quark and the Jaguar* (New York: Freeman).

C. Goddard (2005) *The Languages of East and Southeast Asia* (Oxford: Oxford University Press).

T. Gong, L. Shuai, M. Tamariz, and G. Jäger (2012) 'Studying Language Change Using Price Equation and Pólya-urn Dynamics', *PLoS One*, 7, e33171.

R. Gray and Q. Atkinson (2003) 'Language-tree Divergence Times Support the Anatolian Theory of Indo-European Origins', *Nature*, 426, 435–439.

R. Gray and F. Jordan (2000) 'Language Trees Support the Express-Train Sequence of Austronesian Expansion', *Nature*, 405, 1052–1055.

J. Greenberg (1963) 'Some Universals of Grammar with Particular Reference to the Order of Meaningful Elements' In J. Greenberg (ed.) *Universals of Language*, 2nd edition, 73–113 (Cambridge, MA: MIT Press).

J. Greenberg (1987) *Language in the Americas* (Stanford, CA: Stanford University Press).

R. Greenberg (2004) *Language and Identity in the Balkans: Serbo-Croatian and Its Disintegration* (Oxford: Oxford University Press).

P. Grice (1975) 'Logic and Conversation' In P. Cole and J. Morgan (eds.) *Syntax and Semantics*, volume 3, 41–58 (New York: Academic Press).

C. Hall (1988) 'Integrating Diachronic and Processing Principles in Explaining the Suffix Preference' In J. Hawkins (ed.) *Explaining Language Universals*, 321–349 (Oxford: Blackwell).

R. Harlow (2007) *Māori: A Linguistic Introduction* (Cambridge: Cambridge University Press).

S. Harrison (2005) 'On the Limits of the Comparative Method' In B. Joseph and R. Janda (eds.) *The Handbook of Historical Linguistics*, 213–243 (Oxford: Blackwell).

M. Haspelmath, M. Dryer, D. Gil, and B. Comrie (eds.) (2005) *The World Atlas of Linguistic Structures* (Oxford: Oxford University Press).

M. Hauser, N. Chomsky, and T. Fitch (2002) 'The Faculty of Language: What Is It, Who Has It and How Did It Evolve?', *Science*, 298, 1569–1579.

B. Heine and T. Kuteva (2005) *Language Contact and Grammatical Change* (Cambridge: Cambridge University Press).

B. Heine and T. Kuteva (2006) *The Changing Language of Europe* (Oxford: Oxford University Press).

C. Hockett (1960) 'The Origin of Speech', *Scientific American*, 203, 88–96.

S. Höfler and A. Smith (2009) 'The Pre-Linguistic Basis of Grammaticalisation: A Unified Approach to Metaphor and Reanalysis', *Studies in Language*, 33, 886–909.

C. Holden (2002) 'Bantu Language Trees Reflect the Spread of Farming Across sub-Saharan Africa: A Maximum-Parsimony Analysis', *Proceedings of the Royal Society B*, 269, 793–799.

C. Holden and R. Gray (2006) 'Rapid Radiation, Borrowing, and Dialect Continua in the Bantu Languages' In P. Forster and C. Renfrew (eds.) *Phylogenetic Methods and the Prehistory of Languages*, 19–31 (Cambridge: MacDonald Institute Press).

J. Holmes (2013) *An Introduction to Sociolinguistics*, 4th edition (Abingdon: Routledge).

P. Hopper (1987) 'Emergent Grammar', *Berkeley Linguistics Conference (BLS)*, 13, 139–157.

D. Hull (1988) *Science as a Process: An Evolutionary Account of the Social and Conceptual Development of Science* (Chicago: University of Chicago Press).

J. Hurford (1989) 'Biological Evolution of the Saussurean Sign as a Component of the Language Acquisition Device', *Lingua*, 77, 187–222.

J. Hurford (1991) 'The Evolution of Critical Period for Language Acquisition', *Cognition*, 40, 159–201.

M. Israel (2014) 'Semantics: How Language Makes Sense' In C. Genetti (ed.) *How Languages Work: An Introduction to Language and Linguistics*, 150–179 (Cambridge: Cambridge University Press).

A. Kandler, R. Unger, and J. Steele (2010) 'Language Shift, Bilingualism and the Future of Britain's Celtic Languages', *Philosophical Transactions of the Royal Society of London, Series B – Biological Sciences*, 365, 3855–3864.

A. Kassian, G. Starostin, A. Dybo, and V. Chernov (2010) 'The Swadesh Wordlist: An Attempt at Semantic Specification', *Journal of Language Relationship*, 4, 46–89.

A. Kinsella (2009) *Language Evolution and Syntactic Theory* (Cambridge: Cambridge University Press).

S. Kirby (2000) 'Syntax without Natural Selection: How Compositionality Emerges from Vocabulary in a Population of Learners' In C. Knight, M. Studdert-Kennedy and J. Hurford (eds.) *The Evolutionary Emergence of Language: Social Function and the Origins of Linguistic Form*, 303–323 (Cambridge: Cambridge University Press).

S. Kirby (2001) 'Spontaneous Evolution of Linguistic Structure: An Iterated Learning Model of the Emergence of Regularity and Irregularity', *IEEE Journal of Evolutionary Computation*, 5, 102–110.

S. Kirby and J. Hurford (2002) 'The Emergence of Linguistic Structure: An Overview of the Iterated Learning Model' In A. Cangelosi and D. Parisi (eds.) *Simulating the Evolution of Language*, 121–148 (London: Springer Verlag).

S. Kirby, H. Cornish, and K. Smith (2008) 'Cumulative Cultural Evolution in the Lab: An Experimental Approach to the Origins of Structure in Human Language', *Proceedings of the National Academy of Sciences*, 105, 10681–10686.

S. Kirby, M. Tamariz, H. Cornish, and K. Smith (2015) 'Compression and Communication in the Cultural Evolution of Linguistic Structure', *Cognition*, 141, 87–102.

M. Krauss (1992) 'The World's Languages in Crisis', *Language*, 68, 4–10.

M. Krifka (2001) 'Compositionality' In R. Wilson and F. Keil (eds.) *The MIT Encyclopedia of the Cognitive Sciences*, 152–153 (Cambridge, MA: MIT Press).

W. Labov (1972) *Sociolinguistic Patterns* (Philadelphia: University of Pennsylvania Press).

P. Ladefoged and K. Johnson (2011) *A Course in Phonetics*, 6th edition (London: Wadsworth).

R. Lees (1953) 'The Basis of Glottochronology', *Language*, 29, 113–127.

S. Levinson (1997) 'Language and Cognition: The Cognitive Consequences of Spatial Description in Guugu Yimithirr', *Journal of Linguistic Anthropology*, 7, 98–131.

S. Levinson (2006) 'The Language of Space in Yélî Dnye' In S. Levinson and D. Wilkins (eds.) *Grammars of Space: Explorations in Cognitive Diversity*, 157–205 (Cambridge: Cambridge University Press).

S. Levinson and D. Wilkins (eds.) (2006) *Grammars of Space: Explorations in Cognitive Diversity* (Cambridge: Cambridge University Press).

P. Lewis (ed.) (2005) *Ethnologue: Languages of the World* (Dallas: SIL International).

G. Lupyan and R. Dale (2010) 'Language Structure Is Partly Determined Bysocial Structure', *PLoS One*, 5, e8559.

L. Maffi (ed.) (2001) *On Biocultural Diversity: Linking Language, Knowledge and the Environment* (Washington: Smithsonian Institute Press).

A. Martinet (1949) 'La double articulation linguistique', *Travaux du Cercle Linguistic de Copenhague*, 5, 30–37.

W. McGregor (2006) 'Prolegomenon to a Warrwa Grammar of Space' In S. Levinson and D. Wilkins (eds.) *Grammars of Space: Explorations in Cognitive Diversity*, 115–156 (Cambridge: Cambridge University Press).

A. McMahon (1994) *Understanding Language Change* (Cambridge: Cambridge University Press).

A. McMahon and R. McMahon (1995) 'Linguistics, Genetics and Archaeology: Internal and External Evidence in the Amerind Controversy', *Transactions of the Philological Society*, 93, 125–225.

A. McMahon and R. McMahon (2000) 'Problems of Dating and Time Depth in Linguistics and Biology' In C. Renfrew, A. McMahon and L. Trask (eds.) *Time Depth in Historical Linguistics (2 vols.)*, 59–74 (Cambridge: McDonald Institute for Archaeological Research).

A. McMahon and R. McMahon (2003) 'Finding Families: Quantitative Methods in Language Classification', *Transactions of the Philological Society*, 101, 7–55.

A. McMahon and R. McMahon (2005) *Language Classification by Numbers* (Oxford: Oxford University Press).

J. Milroy (1980) *Language and Social Networks* (Oxford: Blackwell).

M. Mithun (1991) 'Active/Agentive Case Marking and Its Motivations', *Language*, 67, 510–546.

E. Moore (2004) 'Sociolinguistic Style: A Multidimensional Resource for Shared identity Creation', *Canadian Journal of Linguistics*, 49, 375–396.

S. Mufwene (2002) 'Competition and Selection in Language Evolution', *Selection*, 3, 45–56.

S. Munroe and A. Cangelosi (2002) 'Learning and the Evolution of Language: The Role of Cultural Variation and Learning Costs in the Baldwin Effect', *Artificial Life*, 8, 331–339.

L. Nakhleh, D. Ringe, and T. Warnow (2005) 'Perfect Phylogenetic Networks: A New Methodology for Reconstructing the Evolutionary History of Natural Languages', *Language*, 81, 382–420.

D. Nettle (1999) 'Is the Rate of Linguistic Change Constant?', *Lingua*, 108, 119–136.

D. Nettle and S. Romaine (2000) *Vanishing Voices: The Extinction of the World's Languages* (Oxford: Oxford University Press).

P.-Y. Oudeyer (2006) *The Self-Organization of Speech* (Oxford: Oxford University Press).

M. Pagel and A. Meade (2004) 'A Phylogenetic Mixture Model for Detecting Pattern-Heterogeneity in Gene Sequence of Character-State Data', *Systematic Biology*, 53, 571–581.

J. Pierrehumbert, M. Beckman, and R. Ladd (2000) 'Conceptual Foundations of Phonology as a Laboratory Science' In N. Burton-Roberts, P. Carr and G. Docherty (eds.) *Conceptual and Empirical Foundations of Phonology*, 273–303 (Cambridge: Cambridge University Press).

S. Pinker and P. Bloom (1990) 'Natural Language and Natural Selection', *Behavioral and Brain Sciences*, 13, 707–784.

G. Price (1970) 'Selection and Covariance', *Nature*, 227, 520–521.

G. Pullum and B. Scholz (2002) 'Empirical Assessment of Stimulus Poverty Arguments', *The Linguistic Review*, 19, 9–50.

F. Reali and M. Christiansen (2005) 'Uncovering the Richness of the Stimulus: Structure Dependence and Indirect Statistical Evidence', *Cognitive Science*, 29, 1007–1028.

F. Reali, M. Christiansen, and P. Monaghan (2003) 'Phonological and Distributional Cues in Syntax Acquisition: Scaling Up the Connectionist Approach to Multiple-Cue Integration' In R. Alterman and D. Kirsh (eds.) *Proceedings of the 25th Annual Conference of the Cognitive Science Society*, 970–975 (Boston: Lawrence Erlbaum Associates).

S. Roberts and J. Winters (2013) 'Linguistic Diversity and Traffic Accidents: Lessons from Statistical Studies of Cultural Traits', *PLoS One*, 8, e70902.

E. Round (2009) 'Kayardild Morphology, Phonology and Morphosyntax', Ph.D. thesis, Yale University.

M. Ruhlen (1991) *A Guide to the World's Languages* (London: Arnold).

M. Ruhlen (1994) *On the Origin of Languages: Studies in Linguistic Taxonomy* (Stanford, CA: Stanford University Press).

G. Sankoff (2004) 'Linguistic Outcomes of Language Contact' In J. Chambers, P. Trudgill and N. Schilling-Estes (eds.) *The Handbook of Language Variation and Change*, 638–668 (Oxford: Wiley).

H. Schmidt and A. von Haeseler (2009) 'Phylogenetic Inference Using Maximum Likelihood Methods' In P. Lemey, M. Salemi and A. Vandamme (eds.) *The Phylogenetic Handbook: A Practical Approach to Phylogenetic Analysis and Hypothesis Testing*, 181–209 (Cambridge: Cambridge University Press).

E. Schultze-Berndt (2006) 'Sketch of a Jaminjung Grammar of Space' In S. Levinson and D. Wilkins (eds.) *Grammars of Space: Explorations in Cognitive Diversity*, 63–114 (Cambridge: Cambridge University Press).

T. Scott-Phillips (2014) *Speaking Our Minds: Why Human Communication Is Different, and How Language Evolved to Make It Special* (London: Palgrave MacMillan).

T. Scott-Phillips, S. Kirby, and G. Ritchie (2009) 'Signalling Signalhood and the Emergence of Communication', *Cognition*, 113, 226–233.

C. Shannon (1948) 'A Mathematical Theory of Communication', *Bell System Technical Journal*, 27, 379–423 and 623–656.

P. Siptár and M. Törkenczy (2000) *The Phonology of Hungarian* (Oxford: Oxford University Press).

A. Smith (2005) 'The Inferential Transmission of Language', *Adaptive Behavior*, 13, 311–324.

A. Smith (2008) 'Protolanguage Reconstructed', *Interaction Studies*, 9, 100–116.

A. Smith and S. Höfler (2015) 'The Pivotal Role of Metaphor in the Evolution of Human Language' In J. Díaz Vera (ed.) *Metaphor and Metonymy across Time and Cultures*, 123–139 (Berlin: Mouton de Gruyter).

K. Smith (2004) 'The Evolution of Vocabulary', *Journal of Theoretical Biology*, 228, 127–142.

K. Smith (2011) 'Why Formal Models Are Useful for Evolutionary Linguists' In K. Gibson and M. Tallerman (eds.) *Oxford Handbook of Language Evolution*, 581–588 (Oxford: Oxford University Press).

K. Smith and S. Kirby (2008) 'Cultural Evolution: Implications for Understanding the Human Language Faculty and Its Evolution', *Philosophical Transactions of the Royal Society of London, Series B – Biological Sciences*, 363, 3591–3603.

K. Smith, H. Brighton, and S. Kirby (2003a) 'Complex Systems in Language Evolution: The Cultural Emergence of Compositional Structure', *Advances in Complex Systems*, 6, 537–558.

K. Smith, S. Kirby, and H. Brighton (2003b) 'Iterated Learning: A Frame Work for the Emergence of Language', *Artificial Life*, 9, 371–386.

J.-J. Song (2001) *Linguistic Typology: Morphology and Syntax* (Harlow: Longman).

D. Sperber and D. Wilson (1995) *Relevance: Communication and Cognition* (Oxford: Blackwell).

L. Steels (1999) *The Talking Heads Experiment* (Antwerpen: Laboratorium), special pre-edition.

L. Steels (ed.) (2011) *Design Patterns in Fluid Construction Grammar* (Amsterdam: John Benjamins).

L. Steels and T. Belpaeme (2005) 'Coordinating Perceptually Grounded Categories through Language: A Case Study for Colour', *Behavioral and Brain Sciences*, 28, 469–529.

M. Swadesh (1952) 'Lexico-statistic Dating of Prehistoric Ethnic Contacts', *Proceedings of the American Philosophical Society*, 96, 453–463.

L. Talmy (2000) *Towards a Cognitive Semantics* (Cambridge, MA: MIT Press).

C. Theisen, J. Oberlander, and S. Kirby (2010) 'Systematicity and Arbitrariness in Novel Communication Systems', *Interaction Studies*, 11, 14–32.

M. Tomasello (2008) *Origins of Human Communication* (Harvard: MIT Press).

M. Tomasello, M. Carpenter, J. Call, T. Behne, and H. Moll (2005) 'Understanding and Sharing Intentions: The Origins of Cultural Cognition', *Behavioral and Brain Sciences*, 28, 675–735.

L. Trask (1996) *Historical Linguistics* (London: Arnold).

G. Trousdale (2010) *An Introduction to English Sociolinguistics* (Edinburgh: Edinburgh University Press).

P. Trudgill (1972) 'Sex, Covert Prestige, and Linguistic Change in the Urban British English of Norwich', *Language in Society*, 1, 179–196.

P. Trudgill (2008) 'Colonial Dialect Contact in the History of European Languages: On the Irrelevance of Identity to New-dialect Formation', *Language in Society*, 37, 241–280.

W. Turkel (2002) 'The Learning Guided Evolution of Natural Language' In E. Briscoe (ed.) *Linguistic Evolution through Language Acquisition: Formal and Computational Models*, 235–254 (Cambridge: Cambridge University Press).

R. van Trijp (2012) 'The Evolution of Case Systems for Marking Event Structure' In L. Steels (ed.) *Experiments in Cultural Language Evolution*, 169–206 (Oxford: John Benjamins).

P. Vogt (2005) 'The Emergence of Compositional Structures in Perceptually Grounded Language Games', *Artificial Intelligence*, 167, 206–242.

A. Wedel (2006) 'Exemplar Models, Evolution and Language Change', *The Linguistic Review*, 23, 247–274.

A. Wray and G. Grace (2007) 'The Consequences of Talking to Strangers: Evolutionary Corollaries of Socio-Cultural Influences on Linguistic Form', *Lingua*, 117, 543–578.

H. Yamauchi (2001) 'The Difficulty of the Baldwinian Account of Linguistic Innateness' In J. Kelemen and P. Sosík (eds.) *Advances in Artificial Life: Proceedings of the 6th European Conference on Artificial Life*, 391–400 (Heidelberg: Springer-Verlag).

E. Zsiga (2013) *The Sounds of Language: An Introduction to Phonetics and Phonology* (Oxford: Wiley-Blackwell).

W. Zuidema (2003) 'How the Poverty of the Stimulus Solves the Poverty of the Stimulus' In S. Becker, S. Thrun and K. Obermayer (eds.) *Advances in Neural Information Processing Systems 15 (Proceedings of NIPS '02)*, 51–58 (Cambridge, MA: MIT Press).

W. Zuidema and B. de Boer (2009) 'The Evolution of Combinatorial Phonology', *Journal of Phonetics*, 37, 125–144.

3
Dynamic Models of Language Evolution: The Economic Perspective

Andrew John

3.1 Introduction

The economics of language may not yet be a mainstream subfield of economics. It is, however, a vibrant area of study that has by now generated a substantial volume of research. The investigation of this topic is generally traced back to Marschak (1965), who appears to have been the first to bring economic concepts – such as costs and efficiency – to the study of language. Most of the chapters in this volume concern how language, broadly defined, influences economic variables; such research has demonstrated that there are benefits from incorporating linguistic variables and considerations into several different areas of traditional economic analysis. In this chapter I address the reverse question: how do economic analysis and economic reasoning provide insight into linguistic phenomena? More specifically, I consider how economics and economic models shed light on language *change*.

To be clear at the outset, the evolution of language is fundamentally a linguistic rather than an economic question. Understanding phonological variation, semantic drift, syntactic change and the like evidently lies in the realm of linguistic analysis and is well outside the domain of economics. (The linguistic perspective on language change is contained in Chapter 2 in this volume.) So the reader of this chapter could be forgiven for some scepticism about whether economists have a great deal to contribute to our understanding of language change. And indeed, economic models are for the most part silent on the questions of phonetics, phonology, morphology, syntax and semantics.[1] They are, however, relevant and useful in the domains of sociolinguistics

---

[1] That said, there is a branch of economics that attempts to model the fundamentals of language and communication in game-theoretic terms. In particular, Rubinstein (2000) and Glazer and Rubinstein (2006) have applied game theory to semantics and pragmatics. Briefly, these investigations have sought to explain the emergence of natural language

and historical linguistics, where the objects of study pertain more to language use and language communities rather than to the specific features of language themselves. In particular, economists have studied how economic forces and economic decisions influence language use, language learning and language transmission across time and geographical locations; they have also used modelling techniques from economics to provide insight into language evolution.

Discussion of the economic perspective on language change runs the risk both of being too narrow and of being too broad. To avoid being too narrow, I do not give great emphasis to disciplinary boundaries. Some of the papers I discuss are very clearly grounded in economics; others less so – for the chapter is concerned not just with economic models of language, but also with how they relate to approaches emerging from historical linguistics and computational linguistics. At the same time, the scope of the analysis must be delimited. Economic forces affect prosperity, politics and power, which in turn affect the emergence, disappearance and relative strength of languages and linguistic communities. With a little imagination, it would be possible to trace a link from just about any topic in economics to language use. Many of these channels of influence are real and important, yet have received little or no formal investigation in the economics-of-language literature. I leave such indirect links between economics and language, mediated by economic and political power, to one side.

3.2   How economic forces can influence language dynamics

There are three key ways in which economic reasoning and an understanding of economic forces can help explain dynamic linguistic phenomena.

First, the linkages from language to economics alluded to in the introduction often have some element of feedback to them. Research that is concerned with how linguistic variables affect economic decisions and outcomes often implicitly has reverse implications for changes in language use and the development of language communities. Such feedbacks have not, for the most part, been investigated very formally.

---

in game-theoretic terms, and to consider how notions of evolutionarily stable strategies might explain the emergence of words with understood meanings. In an abstract way, this research speaks to the emergence of communication, but perhaps has less to say about language evolution as linguists typically use the term. This line of research is in turn connected to work in computational linguistics that focuses on developing models of language evolution that are, in the terminology of Gong et al. (2014), 'rule-based'. See, for example, Steels (1999), Cucker et al. (2004) and Griffiths and Kalish (2007).

Second, many existing economic models of language and linguistic phenomena, though not explicitly dynamic, still make predictions about language use and language learning. Given that the use and acquisition of languages is a critical determinant of language change, these models can be dynamic in spirit, even if the formal modelling is static or contains only limited dynamics. The discussions in many of these papers strongly suggest that, even though the models are static, the authors are thinking about equilibrium as the steady state of a dynamic process.

Third, there are some explicitly dynamic models of language change. This research can be subdivided into papers that take a relatively short-run perspective (which in this context still may mean decades or generations) and papers that look at very long-run patterns of language change (over centuries or millennia).

3.3   Feedback mechanisms

As mentioned in the introduction, it is now clear from the literature that linguistic factors affect economic decisions in many ways. Many of those decisions can be expected to have positive feedback influences on language dynamics: relatively dominant languages are likely to influence economic choices in ways that further increase the dominance of those languages. Languages that are 'important' or of high value will tend to attract more speakers and thus become yet more important and more valuable. The following discussion of this phenomenon is brief and speculative, because these feedback mechanisms have not been widely explored in the literature.

Multinational corporations have to manage their internal language policies, most particularly the use of their home language in foreign subsidiaries. Their choices affect the extent to which English will continue its advance as the lingua franca of international business.[2] Thus corporate language management decisions are likely to be a significant factor in the spread of English (and other major languages) and the associated survival or decline of other language communities. Similar arguments apply to the decisions that companies make about offering products in multiple languages: such decisions, which of course respond to consumer preferences and market size, help to determine the languages that consumers are exposed to throughout the world.

Increases in the economic prosperity of a language community are likely to increase the importance and strength of the language spoken in that

---

[2] Anglemark and John (2012) use the Google books corpus to explore the rate at which English-language business terms are being adopted in other languages. For the six languages that they study, they find that English terms are making significant inroads in all languages except French, but that there is considerable variation across languages.

community. Therefore, any time that linguistic factors affect prosperity and growth, they are likely also to have indirect feedback effects on language use. For example, commonalities of language tend to be drivers of trade patterns, which in turn affect prosperity, knowledge transfer and economic growth. If a common language facilitates trade, it may therefore also lead to increased prosperity among speakers of that language, thus strengthening the language itself.

Similarly, there may be feedback from the inverse relationship between linguistic diversity and economic growth: countries that grow more slowly might be ones where smaller linguistic communities remain established and so linguistic diversity remains more entrenched. And Chen's (2013) finding that language characteristics affect saving and other forward-looking behaviour means, of course, that language characteristics can alter short- and long-run growth rates, again potentially influencing language use.

Finally, language communities that are prosperous will tend to attract high-quality human capital and become more prosperous still; similarly, the returns to speaking a language will typically be higher when the language is spoken in a prosperous economy, providing an incentive for individuals to invest in the acquisition of that language. Both effects increase the strength and influence of the language group.

3.4   Economic models of language learning and language use

Most of the literature in which economic reasoning is an *input* into linguistics focuses on the decision to learn languages or the decision to use languages; these choices determine the size and stability of language communities. A key idea, present in most of the models, is that language use exhibits substantial network externalities: the larger is a language community, the more valuable it is to be a member of that community.[3]

Network effects can be a very powerful source of increasing returns to scale. Indeed, it is the increasing returns from network effects that underlie the feedback mechanisms discussed in the previous subsection. Typically, network externalities also give rise to strategic complementarities: the greater the number of other people learning or using a language, the greater is the individual incentive to learn or use the language. Thus models built upon network

---

[3] This notion is at least implicit in many early economic discussions of language, such as Breton and Mieszkowski (1977), Hočevar (1983), Pool (1991), Vaillancourt (1991) and Laitin (1993), and was explicitly analysed by Selten and Pool (1991) and Church and King (1993). Other researchers to have built on this insight include John and Yi (1996), Breton (1999) and Dalmazzone (1999). The idea is discussed in more detail in Chapter 7 in this volume.

externalities contain strong forces that will tend to lead large and established languages to become larger and even more widely used, while driving smaller languages into disuse.

The well-established fact that a large number of the world's languages are disappearing is therefore all too easy to understand in the presence of network externalities. Indeed, as John and Yi (1996) argue, the phenomenon in greater need of explanation is perhaps not the extinction of languages, but instead their survival.

> Despite these extinctions, however, hundreds of languages and minority language communities continue to survive and flourish. The number of Spanish speakers in the United States has been increasing at least since 1950, and, as of 2000, has become the largest set of non-English speakers in U.S. history. French is still going strong in Canada, and Catalan is flourishing in Spain. Dozens of countries have multiple official languages and many other countries are to some extent multilingual. More generally, there are minority languages within a country, such as Spanish in the United States, and majority languages that are not global *linguae francae*, such as Korean in Korea, that are thriving.
>
> A more complete theory of language use, then, must be able to explain why languages and language communities continue to exist as well as why they disappear (John and Yi, 2001, p. 6).

John and Yi's suggested answer to this puzzle is that geography also matters. Local increasing returns in specific geographic areas may be strong enough to offset the global increasing returns from a single language, implying that a geographically isolated language community may be more likely to survive and thrive. They demonstrate this in a two-period model in which agents have a language endowment (monolingual in language A, monolingual in language B, or bilingual), and are also initially placed in one of two fixed physical locations.[4] Agents can choose to learn the other language, and then face an additional choice: they can remain in their original location or they can migrate to the other location.

There are strategic complementarities in both the learning and migration decisions, so it is not surprising that multiple equilibria emerge (Cooper and John, 1988). Depending on the production technology and the initial distribution of agents, there can be equilibria (i) where full assimilation takes place

---

[4] Language pedants (a club which the current author does not aspire to ever be admitted to) prefer the terms 'unilingual' or 'monoglot' on the grounds of etymological consistency, but 'monolingual' is the term with most currency.

(so one language falls into disuse), (ii) where different language communities coexist in a single location, and (iii) where language groups self-select to different locations. The presence of multiple locations makes it easier to preserve a minority language. Qualitatively similar results are found by Carida et al. (2013), who use a version of a Schelling segregation model in which individuals can migrate to different locations and have a preference for locating with those who speak the same language.

In John and Yi (1996) and Carida et al. (2013) languages can fall into complete disuse in equilibrium. These stark results are due in part to the fact that agents are homogeneous in terms of learning and migration costs.[5] Thus, in all these models, agents with the same endowment will make the same choice, which tends to drive the economies to corner solutions. Ginsburgh et al. (2007) and Gabszewicz et al. (2011), by contrast, have models in which learning costs have greater heterogeneity and in which multiple languages can therefore survive.[6]

Sperlich and Uriarte (2014) consider a situation where there is a majority language (A) spoken by all members of society and where, in addition, some speakers (bilinguals) can also speak their preferred minority language (B). There are no monolinguals in the minority language. Their paper suggests that the relative disuse of minority languages can be explained as a result of the choices that bilinguals must make when interacting with other agents in a Bayesian language use game. The strategic choice of bilinguals is whether to use the majority language or the minority language in a given new interaction. In equilibrium, bilinguals use a mixed strategy, sometimes choosing to hide their type, and sometimes choosing to reveal it; this turns out to be an evolutionarily stable strategy. Thus bilinguals can end up conversing in the majority language even if both would prefer to use the minority language.

Armstrong (2015) suggests that language acquisition can also serve a signalling function: in a world of asymmetric information, investment in learning a language is a (noisy) signal of overall ability. He adds such signalling effects into a two-language model with network externalities. The model generates a wage premium for bilingual speakers, reflecting both the true productive

---

[5] In Carida et al. (2013), these costs are zero (although success in learning and moving is probabilistic) and the 'tolerance' for other languages is identical for all agents, while in John and Yi (1996) the migration cost is zero and the learning cost, though endogenous (it is an opportunity cost of foregone production), is identical for all agents of a given type in a given location. A similar result holds in Church and King (1993), where learning costs are exogenous and constant for all agents.

[6] The earlier work of Selten and Pool (1991) also assumed heterogeneity in learning costs. However, their paper was primarily concerned with proving the existence of Nash equilibria in a very general setting with multiple languages, rather than more specific questions of language survival and language death.

benefits of bilingualism and the signalling benefits. While Armstrong focuses on the efficiency properties of the equilibrium, the relevant finding here is that signalling encourages bilingualism and thus increases the likelihood of survival of a minority language.

To summarize, network externalities are, almost by definition, a critical ingredient of most models of language use. Such externalities, and the associated strategic complementarities, provide strong incentives for each individual agent to use (and, if necessary, learn) the language spoken by the majority of other people in the population. The dynamic implication is that network externalities are a force that can drive languages to extinction. But there are countervailing factors that may help minority languages survive, including heterogeneous learning costs, a preference for using the minority language, signalling, and geographical separation. See also Chapters 21–23 in this volume.

3.5   Dynamic economic models of language use

The papers discussed in the previous subsection consider the learning and use of languages, and so do speak to some degree about changes in language communities. But because those models are essentially static, they have a limited ability to shed light on questions of language survival and language death – which are long-run dynamic processes. There are, in fact, very few true dynamic economic models of language evolution. I now turn to this branch of the literature.

3.5.1   Models of language extinction and language survival

Dynamic models of language evolution, like static models, are greatly concerned with the question of whether network effects and increasing returns necessarily force small languages into extinction. The results of static models are suggestive, but the question is dynamic and ultimately requires answering in frameworks that incorporate dynamic forces.

The first model of language evolution that is recognizable both as grounded in economics and as fully dynamic is probably that of Grin (1992). The framework of his paper is an economic model first and foremost because there is an optimizing decision – specifically, agents make a choice about language *use*. In Grin's model, there are two languages, and an agent can choose to conduct some economic activities in each language. The agent has utilities defined over these activities, and a time budget constraint.

Grin also introduces a language 'vitality' variable, which captures the 'perceived level of minority language health'. Greater vitality makes a language more productive in use. Focusing on the minority language, Grin derives a (static) demand curve for use of the language that depends upon the vitality of the language. He then posits a first-order difference equation that links vitality at date $t+1$ to usage of the language at date t, which depends in turn upon both the number of speakers and the vitality at t. At the same time, he supposes that the change in the number of speakers of the language is proportional to the lagged change in vitality. He characterizes the steady states in which vitality is constant – and thus (by his second dynamic assumption) the number of speakers of the minority language is also constant – and derives a condition for survival of the minority language.

The key insight of Grin's work is a formal demonstration that when a minority language has utility in use, it is possible for it to survive, even in the presence of network effects. However, the conditions for language survival can be stringent, requiring the minority language to be inherently more desirable in use than the majority language. The paper contains extensive analysis of the conditions for minority language survival as well as of the ways in which public policy could play a role in preserving such languages.

John and Yi (2001) provide a dynamic model of language change that is an extension of their two-period model discussed in the previous subsection. Whereas Grin's focus is primarily on steady states, John and Yi pay more attention to transitional dynamics. Agents are either monolingual in one of two languages, or bilingual. Endogenous transition probabilities govern the evolution of these language groups across generations. Specifically, each agent has one child, whose language ability depends (i) on the language of the parent, (ii) on the 'ambient language' (an endogenous variable that depends on the relative numbers of monolinguals of each language), and (iii) on an exogenous parameter intended to capture public policy, language status, relative prevalence of the two languages in media, and so on. The exogenous parameter thus captures some of the same ideas that underlie Grin's vitality variable, although it is not derived from individual preferences.

Not surprisingly, monolingualism (in either language) is, under weak assumptions, an absorbing state. Once almost everyone else speaks just one language, the remaining agents will gravitate towards speaking that language as well. The more interesting question is whether there can also be locally stable interior steady states, consistent with long-term survival of minority languages. John and Yi show that there can be a stable interior steady state if the transition probabilities are relatively insensitive to the ambient language. However, they also show that the symmetric interior steady state is unstable under fairly weak assumptions. The transition paths in the model qualitatively mimic patterns of language decline that are observed in the data, such as the decline of Welsh and the typical three-generation pattern of immigrant language assimilation.

When John and Yi combine these intergenerational dynamics with learning and locational choices (modelled in the same ways as in their 1996 paper) they find as before that agents may optimally choose to locate in ways that make minority languages self-sustaining. Patriarca and Leppänen (2004) likewise show that survival of multiple languages is possible when the languages are (endogenously) concentrated in different geographical areas.

The dynamic processes in John and Yi's setting are largely mechanistic, and it is natural to ask how the preservation of minority languages can be influenced by parental choices or by public policy. Bisin and Verdier's (2000) model of the intergenerational transmission of cultural traits is a useful starting point for this discussion. Their paper is concerned with religious and ethnic traits rather than language, which means that it does not have a direct analogue of bilingualism; more generally (as they explicitly acknowledge) language may not be a particularly good example of the kinds of traits they consider. The paper is nevertheless significant for language research because it presents a sophisticated theory of how parents' preferences cause traits to be transmitted through time, including how those preferences affect marriage decisions and socialization efforts by parents.

The dynamics of the Bisin–Verdier model contrast with those of John and Yi (2001). The Bisin–Verdier environment has at least one interior stable steady state. By contrast, the corner solutions of cultural homogeneity are *not* stable steady states because, in the vicinity of such points, minorities self-segregate more fully in the marriage market and invest more in socialization of their children. This reinforces the sense that Bisin and Verdier's model is probably not directly applicable to language: while it certainly is plausible that minority language speakers work harder on teaching their children the minority language, it seems unlikely that such effects would be sufficient to preserve an almost defunct language. But language models have yet to incorporate such a rich theory of intergenerational transmission, so adapting the Bisin–Verdier framework to intergenerational language change would be a significant addition to the literature.

Tamura (2001), building on Tamura (1997), does explicitly include parental decisions about children's language traits. He develops an overlapping generations model in which there are two groups of agents who are geographically separated and who do not speak a common language. Parents invest in the human capital of their children, and make a specific decision about whether to raise their children as bilingual or monolingual. Bilinguals serve as translators who (imperfectly) facilitate joint production across the two regions. Because of an agglomeration externality (increasing returns to scale), this raises overall output.

In equilibrium, parents are indifferent between raising monolingual or bilingual children. Bilinguals take longer to educate, so have lower human capital, but – because of their bilingual status – earn a higher return per unit of human capital. In equilibrium, these effects are exactly offsetting, which determines the size of the bilingual population. Thus Tamura's model shows how a group of bilingual individuals can emerge from societies that are initially monolingual.[7]

Kennedy and King (2005) construct an overlapping-generations model in which the acquisition of language by children is determined by public policy. Again, agents can be monolingual in one of two separate languages, or bilingual. Agents live for three periods (as children, young adults and old adults). Each agent has one child: that child inherits the language(s) of their parent, but monolingual children may also become bilingual as a result of publicly funded education. The extent of such education – that is, the number of children provided with language education – is determined according to the preferences of the median voter. Young monolingual adults have an economic interest in the education of children because a higher proportion of bilinguals increases the productivity of those agents in the next period, when they are old adults.[8]

Starting from initial conditions with no bilinguals and equal numbers of monolinguals in each language, Kennedy and King show that (under certain assumptions on parameters) the median voter will vote in favour of some publicly funded education. Over time, the proportion of bilinguals in the economy therefore grows, up until the point where a majority of voters prefer zero education.

The symmetric case is a knife-edge, however. When the proportions of monolinguals differ, preferences over the optimal tax rate differ across groups. The larger group's preferences hold sway, with the result that there is less education than the smaller group would like. Kennedy and King show that, as a consequence, the smaller group shrinks in size relative to the larger group.

Clingingsmith's (2015) analysis begins with careful documentation of an empirical phenomenon. He shows that languages above a threshold size (35,000 speakers in his analysis) obey Gibrat's Law: there is independence of the size of a language and the growth rate in the number of speakers of that language. If the data exhibit this property, then it follows that the size distribution of (relatively large) languages is unchanging. He reconciles this with increasing returns from language use by positing that agents interact primarily with those who are geographically close.

---

[7] Choi (2002) presents a trade model in which – as in Tamura's model – some agents have an incentive to become bilingual. In Choi's model, however, goods also have a specific language dimension – firms must decide whether to offer goods in one or both languages. An assumption of persistent wage disparity means that workers in the low-wage country have an incentive to become bilingual, after which firms have an incentive to offer goods in the dominant language only. Thus the eventual equilibrium is monolingual.

[8] To simplify the solution of their model, Kennedy and King ignore the fact that the voting choices of young adults in one generation may influence the tax rate they will face in the next period, when they are old; this link comes about because their decisions affect the voting decisions of young adults in the next generation.

In Clingingsmith's model, individuals interact on a network and periodically choose which language to use. The choice of language is a coordination game – agents base their decision on their expectations of the languages that will be chosen by others with whom they are likely to interact – and in equilibrium all agents on the same connected component of the network will speak the same language. Clingingsmith then uses some results from network theory to argue that, under certain assumptions on the underlying graph, the size distribution of locally connected components in the network is consistent with the observed size distribution of languages.

Clingingsmith's explanation of the survival of multiple languages, even in the face of increasing returns, is that agents only care about the languages spoken on their own component of the network. The dynamics in the model concern agents' choices of which language to use on their component: the result that individuals on a given component all speak the same language is a statement about the steady-state equilibrium of a dynamic process. But the underlying distribution of locally connected components is not governed by a dynamic process, so there is no mechanism in the model whereby the set of languages can change over time across the locally connected components.

Abrams and Strogatz (2003) have an approach to language change that resembles that of John and Yi (2001). In their model, there are two languages, and agents are classified as speakers of either one language or the other. Their model is best understood as one of language use rather than language knowledge, because they do not treat bilingual speakers as a separate category. They assume, like John and Yi (2001), that there are transition probabilities that govern the switch of agents from speaking one language to speaking the other, and which are functions of the fraction of the population that speaks each language. If $a(t)$ is the fraction of the population speaking language A at time t, $1 - a(t)$ is the fraction of the population speaking language B, and $P(a(t), s)$ represents the probability that a speaker switches from language A to language B, then the dynamic evolution of $a(t)$ is given by the differential equation:

$$da/dt = (1 - a(t))P(a(t), s) - a(t)P(1 - a(t), 1 - s).$$

In this equation, s represents the relative status or prestige of language A, which plays a similar role to Grin's (1992) vitality variable and John and Yi's (2001) policy/status parameter. The key innovation of Abrams and Strogatz, relative to previous research, is that they take their equation to the data and show that, by varying the parameter s, they are able to fit the decline of four different language groups.

Abrams and Strogatz's model paints a pessimistic view of minority language survival: their model tends to a unique steady state where the minority language becomes extinct. Put differently, their model cannot deliver a stable interior steady state. It can perhaps be viewed as the simplest benchmark case – one where changes in the size of language communities is driven almost solely by the current size of those communities. But, as the (largely prior) work in the economics literature reveals, their model does not include several factors that may encourage minority language survival. Kennedy and King (2005), John and Yi (2001) and Tamura (2001) show that the inclusion of bilinguals allows for interior steady states where multiple languages survive.[9] Grin (1992) shows that a minority language may survive if it is deemed to have inherent value in use. And John and Yi (1996, 2001), Patriarca and Leppänen (2004) and Clingingsmith (2015) show that minority languages can survive when there are multiple locations.

Abrams and Strogatz's model is more naturally classified as a computational-linguistics or complex-systems model rather than an economic model. In fact, many of the subsequent papers in this literature have appeared in physics journals rather than linguistics journals. Gong et al. (2014), surveying the literature, distinguish between 'rule-based models', which encode particular linguistic behaviours in agent-based simulations, and 'equation-based models', which summarize linguistic changes by aggregate dynamic relationships. While rule-based models have little in common with economic approaches to language (though see the discussion of Rubinstein's work in note 1 to this chapter), the papers of Grin (1992) and of John and Yi (2001) are, like that of Abrams and Strogatz (2003), clearly examples of equation-based modelling.

The entire line of research in computational linguistics that followed Abrams and Strogatz (2003) appears to have developed independently from the research on language in the economics literature, and consequently there have been several examples of independent discovery of similar results. While many researchers in computational linguistics have built on the foundation of Abrams and Strogatz, none of the resulting papers appears to have significantly engaged with economic questions. Greater interdisciplinary understanding is surely something to be desired here.

3.5.2 The long-run growth and decline of languages

The dynamic models discussed so far were primarily designed to look at the survival and death of minority languages. Specific examples discussed in the literature include Québecois French in Canada, Welsh in Wales, Spanish in the United States, Malay in Singapore, and many others. But there is a bigger question that can also be asked about language evolution: what has led to the

---

[9] Later work by Minett and Wang (2008) introduced bilinguals into a version of the Abrams and Strogatz model and – as in John and Yi (2001) – found that stable interior equilibria were possible.

appearance and disappearance of languages over time frames that are measured in millennia rather than decades?

There is, not surprisingly, a large literature in historical linguistics investigating this question. Wang and Minett (2005) provide a useful overview, in which they discuss the competing hypotheses of a single origin of language versus the independent emergence of language in multiple locations. They consider language death, which they explain using the model of Abrams and Strogatz (2003); they also discuss the diffusion of language. That said, there is very little research that considers how economic forces may have contributed to long-run patterns of language change.

Nettle (1998) documents the patterns of linguistic diversity in the modern world and notes that this diversity is highly uneven. For example, he observes that: 'Eight hundred and sixty-two languages are spoken in Papua New Guinea. This is 13.2% of the global total, yet Papua New Guinea represents only 0.4% of the world's land area, and only 0.1% of the world's population lives there' (p. 357). Nettle's explanation of this variation in diversity is subtle, but two points deserve emphasis here. First, he notes that 'in the absence of positive interaction, people's languages diverge' (p. 359). Second, he observes that 'the spread of a language is rooted in an economic system' so that 'languages are rooted in networks of social bonds which have a real economic importance' (p. 361).

Nettle's explanation of linguistic diversity is, at heart, an economic theory. He argues that when climatic variables result in longer growing seasons, agents face less risk about access to food supplies. In such environments there is less need for risk sharing, so smaller language groups are sustainable, which implies in turn that we should expect to see greater linguistic diversity. He also provides empirical evidence that is supportive of this view.

Michalopoulos (2012) draws on the arguments of Nettle and others to further advance the argument that geographical variation can explain ethnolinguistic diversity. Specifically, his claim is that heterogeneity in land quality leads to linguistic diversity. The mechanism is that variation in land endowments gives rise to location-specific human capital, which in turn leads to less population mobility and more localized ethnicities. Michalopoulos supports this thesis with rich, careful and creative empirical work. Importantly, he finds the link between geography and ethnolinguistic diversity breaks down in regions where there have been substantial recent migrations.

Neither Nettle (1998) nor Michalopoulos (2012) provides a fully worked-out theory or model of the evolution of linguistic diversity. In other work, Nettle (1999) has addressed this question more directly, using a straightforward mathematical representation of the evolution of language stocks. The story is as follows. Suppose we begin with an unpopulated geographic area, and then introduce a new people and language. Nettle argues, first, that new languages will initially be produced easily as the population spreads through the virgin territory, but that the production of new languages declines over time as the area becomes more populated. Second, Nettle assumes a constant extinction rate for existing languages. These assumptions can be written in the form of a simple dynamic equation, which he parameterizes as:

$$S_{t+1} = 0.955S_t + A/t,$$

where S_t is the stock of languages at time t and A is a parameter.

Initially, S_t and t are small, which implies that the stock of languages is growing. However, the arrival of new languages will eventually be insufficient to offset the decay of existing stocks, and the number of languages will decline. The dynamics implied by this equation mimic a key 'stylized fact' of historical linguistics, namely that the number of languages in the world increased for much of human history, but is now decreasing.

Nettle's (1999) approach to linguistic diversity is certainly informed by economic notions of production, exchange and risk-sharing, but his theoretical specification for the evolution of language stocks is mechanistic.[10] John (2015) provides a theoretical model in which language development and economic activity interact, and thus provides a theory – albeit highly stylized – that integrates economic and linguistic forces in non-trivial ways.

Economic models of language use and language demise almost invariably take the notion of a language as a primitive concept or unit of analysis. Work in linguistics on language death likewise usually takes the set of languages as given.[11] John takes a different approach: his primitive concept is the communicative ability of pairs of agents. In the model, successive generations of agents live at fixed locations, and make decisions about production and exchange with some set of neighbours. The ability of neighbouring agents to exchange efficiently depends upon their ability to communicate; language, in other words, is an input into the productive technology of the economy.

In accordance with Nettle's observation cited earlier, the model assumes that there is a natural tendency for languages to drift apart, which John models as a natural decay in communicative ability. However, contact between agents,

---

[10] This is not intended as criticism. The equation is, in Nettle's own words, merely a simple heuristic model; moreover, it is a minor piece of his much more comprehensive study of linguistic diversity in its many different manifestations.

[11] Here I distinguish the work that specifically deals with language death from the vast linguistics literature on language *change*, which addresses how individual languages evolve, the formation of creoles and pidgin languages, and other similar topics. This latter work also speaks to language death when language change is so extreme that the original language effectively dies out; Latin is a good example.

brought about by exchange, counteracts this effect.[12] The model also has an endogenous growth mechanism: economic growth leads to reductions in transport costs, which in turn make it easier for agents to search for and interact with a larger group of neighbours.

The paper defines a 'language community' as a group of neighbouring agents who can communicate with each other, but not with others outside the group, and shows that such communities arise endogenously in the model. If it is reasonable to assume that members of a language community speak a common language, John's (2015) model therefore delivers the endogenous appearance and disappearance of languages.[13] More precisely, the model can deliver the stylized fact of an initial increase and subsequent decrease in the number of languages. In a primitive economy, agents only interact with close neighbours, and so their languages tend to diverge. This increase in linguistic diversity tends to slow economic growth. Even though economic growth is slow, it remains positive, and so transportation costs gradually decline. Lower costs of transportation induce agents to choose to interact with a larger set of people, which eventually reverses the increase in linguistic diversity. The improved communication in turn becomes an additional engine of growth.

The most striking feature of this model is therefore that it can deliver distinct, geographically separated language communities. Specifically, a version of the model with small amounts of random variation results in asymmetrical search by agents. This asymmetry amplifies minor linguistic differences because people see a greater gain from trading with those with whom they can communicate most easily. There is a strategic complementarity in search decisions: agents interact more with those who already speak a similar language, thus bringing those languages closer together, and less with those who speak a different language, thus pushing those languages apart. Distinct language communities arise and natural borders between languages emerge.

Figure 3.1 reproduces a figure from John's paper to illustrate this finding. It shows the outcome of a simulation with 100 agents located on a circle (so agents 1 and 100 are neighbours). The simulation was run for 1,750 periods, and the figure shows what happened between period 1,501 and period

---

[12] Nerbonne (2010) presents evidence that random contact between geographically dispersed individuals can account for about 25 per cent of observed linguistic variation.

[13] There are two reasons why, as a theoretical matter, this link is not immediate. First, language communities could be overlapping, making it difficult to say where one language (in the familiar sense of the word) ends, and another begins. Of course, this is also a feature of real-life language communities; it is not always easy to define the boundaries of a language. Second, members of a language community according to the definition given could, in principle, speak multiple languages (again, in the familiar sense of the word).

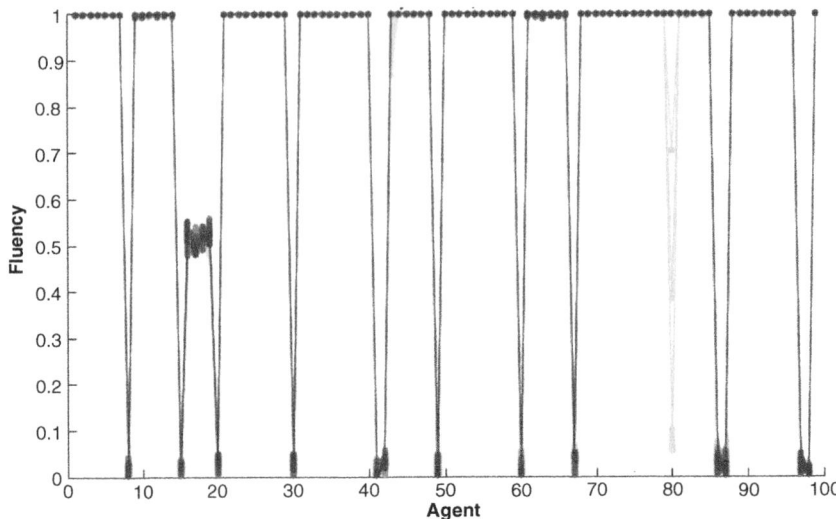

Figure 3.1   Endogenous formation of languages in the model of John (2015)

1,750. The horizontal axis represents geographical locations: that is, it represents the individual agents. The vertical axis shows the communicative ability of each pair of neighbouring agents: a value of zero indicates a complete inability to communicate, while a value of one represents perfect communication.

At time zero, the agents in the model share the same low level of communicative ability. But by date 1,750, nine sets of neighbouring points have emerged where all adjacent agents share a communicative ability equal to one. Such groups represent a language or, more precisely, a set of connected agents who can communicate perfectly. The gaps between these groups imply that those within a group have almost no ability to communicate with those outside the group. There is also a small group (agents 15–20) where the communicative ability of adjacent agents equals about 0.5. The members of this group trade among themselves, but are too few in number to sustain a high level of fluency. This group can be thought of as an endangered language with a small number of speakers.

Languages, after they emerge, are highly persistent but do not last forever. Reductions in transportation costs eventually make it worthwhile for agents to exchange with others even when their ability to communicate is low, and this eventually causes language groups to fuse together. In Figure 3.1, this can be seen in the neighbourhood of agent 80. Recall that the figure illustrates the changes in communicative ability between period 1,501 and 1,750. Over this time period, there was very little change – most of the language groups in place at the end of the period were also there at the start. But on each side of agent 80 there used to be two separate language groups, with a linguistic boundary (a point of low communicative ability) between them. Somewhere between time period 1,501 and 1,750, agents found it worthwhile to cross that boundary. As a result of the interaction between the two groups, the linguistic boundary disappeared and the two language groups fused into one. After this particular simulation is run for 4,000 periods, only five language communities remain.

Another notable feature of Figure 3.1 is that the language groups vary in size. Clingingsmith (2015) examined current languages in the world and found that the size distribution of large languages (those with more than 35,000 speakers) can be well described by a double Pareto distribution. Put more loosely, if languages are ranked according to their size, then a scatterplot of the log rank of languages against their log size is piecewise linear. In the John (2015) model, a qualitatively similar pattern emerges.

The work of Michalopoulos (2012), John (2015) and perhaps Nettle (1998) aside, the study of long-run language patterns has received almost no attention in the literature on economics and language. Yet, given that we know that language and economic activity are linked in significant and subtle ways, economic theorists and economic historians are well placed both to contribute to the literature on historical linguistics and to make clearer the links between economic development and the evolution of language groups. This is an exciting topic for future research.

3.6 Conclusion

The emerging literature that brings together economics and linguistics has by now clearly demonstrated that linguistic factors affect economic decisions. It has also suggested many ways in which economic forces can have an effect on language learning and language use. It is this two-way interaction that makes the economics of language such a rich area of study.

In particular, there are many microeconomic decisions that ultimately affect language outcomes, such as decisions about language learning, migration, language use, language usage within the firm, and so on. Such decisions both influence and are influenced by sociolinguistic patterns – the extent of linguistic diversity, the global reach of English, the place of minority languages, and perhaps even the role of the internet. These sociolinguistic patterns in turn affect macroeconomic outcomes, such as trade patterns and economic development and growth.

While economists and linguists are paying increasing attention to all of these topics, formal dynamic analyses of the evolution of languages and language groups are still relatively uncommon. It is even more striking that, though there is a substantial literature on economics and language, there are very few dynamic economic models of language change. Thus most of the dynamic models of language evolution that do exist have not taken explicit account of the economic forces that help determine language change. There is fertile ground for true interdisciplinary work that brings together sociolinguists, computational linguists and researchers in the economics of language.

Acknowledgements

All of my thinking about economics and language has been very heavily influenced by my collaboration – and more importantly my numerous wide-ranging conversations – with Kei-Mu Yi, Special Policy Advisor to the President, Federal Reserve Bank of Minneapolis. I would also like to thank Ian King and the editors of this volume for their helpful comments on this chapter.

References

D. Abrams and S. Strogatz (2003) 'Modelling the Dynamics of Language Death', *Nature*, 424, 24.

L. Anglemark and A. John (2012) 'The Differential Adoption of English Terms in International Business', Working Paper, Melbourne Business School.

A. Armstrong (2015) 'Equilibria and Efficiency in Bilingual Labour Markets', *Journal of Economic Behavior & Organization*, 112, 204–220.

A. Bisin and T. Verdier (2000) ' "Beyond the Melting Pot": Cultural Transmission, Marriage, and the Evolution of Ethnic and Religious Traits', *Quarterly Journal of Economics*, 115, 955–988.

A. Breton (1999) 'Une analyse économique de la langue', in A. Breton (ed.) *Economic Approaches to Language and Bilingualism*, 1–34 (Ottawa: Canadian Heritage).

A. Breton and P. Mieszkowski (1977) 'The Economics of Bilingualism', in W. Oates (ed.) *The Political Economy of Fiscal Federalism*, 261–273 (Lexington: Free Press).

I. Carida, F. Nemiña, J. Pinasco and P. Schiaffino (2013) 'Schelling-voter Model: An Application to Language Competition', *Chaos, Solitons & Fractals*, 56, 216–221.

K. Chen (2013) 'The Effect of Language on Economic Behavior: Evidence from Savings Rates, Health Behaviors, and Retirement Assets', *American Economic Review*, 103, 690–731.

E. Choi (2002) 'Trade and the Adoption of a Universal Language', *International Review of Economics and Finance*, 11, 265–275.

J. Church and I. King (1993) 'Bilingualism and Network Externalities', *Canadian Journal of Economics*, 26, 337–345.

D. Clingingsmith (2015) 'Are the World's Languages Consolidating? The Dynamics and Distribution of Language Populations', *The Economic Journal*, forthcoming.

R. Cooper and A. John (1988) 'Coordinating Coordination Failures in Keynesian Models', *Quarterly Journal of Economics*, 103, 441–463.

F. Cucker, S. Smale and D. Zhou (2004) 'Modeling Language Evolution', *Foundations of Computational Mathematics*, 4, 315–343.

S. Dalmazzone (1999) 'Economics of Language: A Network Externalities Approach' in A. Breton (ed.) *Exploring the Economics of Language* (Ottawa: Canadian Heritage), 63–87.

J. Gabszewicz, V. Ginsburgh and S. Weber (2011) 'Bilingualism and Communicative Benefits, *Annals of Economics and Statistics*, 101–102, 271–286.

V. Ginsburgh, I. Ortuño-Ortín and S. Weber (2007) 'Learning Foreign Languages: Theoretical and Empirical Implications of the Selten and Pool Model,' *Journal of Economic Behavior and Organization*, 64, 337–347.

J. Glazer and A. Rubinstein (2006) 'On the Pragmatics of Persuasion: A Game Theoretical Approach', *Theoretical Economics*, 1, 395–410.

T. Gong, L. Shuai and M. Zhang (2014) 'Modelling Language Evolution: Examples and Predictions', *Physics of Life Reviews*, 11, 280–302.

T. Griffiths and M. Kalish (2007) 'Language Evolution by Iterated Learning with Bayesian Agents', *Cognitive Science*, 31, 441–480.

F. Grin (1992) 'Towards a Threshold Theory of Minority Language Survival', *Kyklos*, 45, 69–97.

T. Hočevar (1983) 'Les aspects économiques de la dynamique fonctionnelle des langues', *Language Problems and Language Planning*, 7, 135–147.

A. John (2015) 'Linguistic Diversity in the Very Long Run', Melbourne Business School Working Paper.

A. John and K. Yi (1996) 'Language, Learning, and Location', Thomas Jefferson Center for Political Economy Discussion Paper 264, University of Virginia, reprinted as Federal Reserve Bank of New York Staff Report Number 26 (June 1997).

A. John and K. Yi (2001) 'Language and Location', unpublished MS.

P. Kennedy and I. King (2005) 'Dynamic Language Policy', unpublished MS.

D. Laitin (1993) 'The Game Theory of Language Regimes', *International Political Science Review*, 14, 227–239.

J. Marschak (1965) 'Economics of Language', *Behavioral Science,* 10, 135–40.

S. Michalopoulos (2012) 'The Origins of Ethnolinguistic Diversity', *American Economic Review*, 102, 1508–1539.

J. Minett and W. Wang (2008) 'Modelling Endangered Languages: The Effects of Bilingualism and Social Structure', *Lingua*, 118, 19–45.

J. Nerbonne (2010) 'Measuring the Diffusion of Linguistic Change', *Philosophical Transactions of the Royal Society B*, 365, 3821–3828.

D. Nettle (1998) 'Explaining Global Patterns of Linguistic Diversity', *Journal of Anthropological Archaeology*, 17, 354–374.

D. Nettle (1999) *Linguistic Diversity* (New York: Oxford University Press).

M. Patriarca and T. Leppänen (2004) 'Modeling Language Competition', *Physica A*, 338, 296–299.

J. Pool (1991) 'The World Language Problem', *Rationality and Society*, 3, 78–105.

A. Rubinstein (2000) *Economics and Language* (Cambridge: Cambridge University Press).

R. Selten and J. Pool (1991) 'The Distribution of Foreign Language Skills as a Game Equilibrium', in R. Selten (ed.) *Game Equilibrium Models, vol. 4, Social and Political Interaction* (Berlin: Springer), 64–87.

S. Sperlich and J. Uriarte (2014) 'The Economics of "Why Is It So Hard to Save a Threatened Language?"', Working Paper IL 77/14, University of the Basque Country.

L. Steels (1999) 'The Puzzle of Language Evolution,' *Kognitionswissenschaft*, 8, 4.

R. Tamura (1997) 'Language Homogeneity and Income', Clemson University Working Paper.

R. Tamura (2001) 'Translators: Market Makers in Merging Markets', *Journal of Economic Dynamics and Control*, 25, 1775–1800.

F. Vaillancourt (1991) 'The Economics of Language: Theory, Empiricism, and Application to the Asian Pacific', *Journal of Asian Pacific Communication (Multilingual Matters)*, 2, 29–44.

W. Wang and J. Minett (2005) 'The Invasion of Language: Emergence, Change and Death', *Trends in Ecology and Evolution*, 20, 263–269.

4
What Do We Learn from Neurolinguistics?

Mark Leikin

4.1 Introduction

Neurolinguistics is a relatively new and very promising scientific discipline that emerged in the mid-20th century and has been actively developing during the last five decades. Generally speaking, its main scope is to investigate relationships between the human brain and language. This topic is highly relevant from both a theoretical (including philosophical issues) and a practical (including clinical implications and modelling in computer science) point of view. The results of neurolinguistics studies have been published in numerous scientific journals including *Neuroscience, Neuropsychology, Neurophysiology, The International Journal of Neurolinguistics, Brain and Language* and *Brain and Cognition*.

This chapter contains a number of sections dealing with the main issues analysed in neurolinguistics. Section 4.2 presents a brief review of the history of neurolinguistics as a scientific discipline as well as a discussion of the terms and definitions used in the field. The other four sections (Sections 4.3–4.6) review such central topics of neurolinguistics as brain and language, the evolution of brain and language relationships, the development of brain and language relationships in childhood, and the neurolinguistics of bilingualism.

4.2 Terms, definitions and research areas

It seems logical to start with a simple yet critical question: What is neurolinguistics? At first glance the term 'neurolinguistics' (from the Greek νεῦρον – nerve, and the Latin *lingua* – language), similar to other terms that originate from a comparable word-formation model combining Greek and Latin roots (e.g. neuropsychology or psycholinguistics), appears to be transparent and comprehensible, even without one's being familiar with the scientific field it represents. However, both the term and the research area known as 'neurolinguistics' are not as simple as they appear to be.

While there are many definitions, all of them ultimately boil down to the notion that this is a scientific discipline that deals with the brain mechanisms underlying the human language faculty. That is, the science of neurolinguistics investigates how the human brain generates correct utterances in spoken and written form and how it understands such utterances. From these considerations neurolinguistics is positioned as a specific division of neuropsychology – a broader scientific discipline which investigates 'the relationship between ... the brain, and ... mental functions such as language, memory, and perception' (AHD, 2012). However, historically neuropsychology developed in the 19th century from research dedicated to the study of the relationship between brain damage and language disorders. The issues related to language pathology and language processing constituted preliminary (from the timeline viewpoint) and central (from the conceptual viewpoint) topics in the scientific field called neuropsychology (Head, 1926; Critchley, 1970; Caplan, 1987). Even so, the term 'neuropsychology' has existed for more than 100 years, while neurolinguistics is considered to be a relatively new term and a novel research area.

There is a claim (Ingram, 2007) that the term 'neurolinguistics' was introduced into scientific use in the early 1970s by Harry A. Whitaker (Whitaker, 1971), editor of the four-volume *Studies in Neurolinguistics* (1976–1979) (e.g. Whitaker and Whitaker, 1976) and founder of the *Journal of Neurolinguistics* in 1985. It is important to reiterate, however, that the study of the nervous organization of the language function began much earlier than when the term 'neurolinguistics' and, corresponding to this term, a strongly defined research field appeared for the first time.

Over a rather long period these studies focused on language pathology and, first and foremost, on the study of aphasia. Aphasia is generally defined as a disorder of the language function that occurs mostly due to local lesions in the relevant brain structures (Luria, 1966; Goodglass and Kaplan, 1972; Caplan, 1987). Such lesions are primarily caused by stroke (or cerebral vascular accident) and brain injury. As a result of aphasia, the patient loses, in whole or in part, the ability to use language for expression (speech and writing) and/or for understanding (auditory and reading comprehension). The history of research on aphasia began in the 19th century, when Broca for the first time described brain damage, localized in the so-called Brodmann's 44th area or Broca's centre[1]), the consequence of which was the loss of ability to express thoughts by means of speech. The publication in 1861 of the well-known paper by Broca (see Head, 1926) became a reference point for the history of neuropsychology as well as for aphasiology, which can now be considered to be part of clinical neurolinguistics (Caplan, 1987). The question of whether language pathology is

---

[1] A Brodmann area is a region of the brain (or cerebral) cortex defined by its structure and organization of cells. These areas were first described by the German researcher K. Brodmann, who worked in the late 19th and early 20th centuries, and after whom they are named (Brodmann's maps).

the exclusive interest of neurolinguistics remains open. Some scholars consider neurolinguistics to be a specific scientific domain dealing with the brain mechanisms of language pathologies, such as the language impairments expressed in aphasias and Alzheimer's disease (Critchley, 1970; Ingram, 2007). Other researchers prefer the broader interpretation of the term distinguishing clinical neurolinguistics as a special scientific field within a broader academic discipline known also as neurolinguistics (Luria, 1976; Caplan, 1987; Ahlsén, 2006).

Note, however, that the definition of neurolinguistics as a clinical discipline seems to derive from some sort of misunderstanding related to research methods and available experimental techniques and instruments. For a considerably long period of history, the main scientific methods for brain research consisted of post-mortem autopsy and comparison of symptoms observed in a patient with more or less localized brain damage, which were characteristic of military injuries (Head, 1926; Luria, 1947). However, the research interests of scholars who studied aphasia, for example, were never limited by matters of pathology only. *Ab ovo* neurolinguists wished to shed light on the brain organization of the language function (Head, 1926; Luria, 1947, 1948; Jackson, 1958/1869). That is, language disorders served as a window through which researchers attempted to observe details of the extremely complex mechanism underlying verbal ability (Goodglass and Quadfasel, 1954; Luria, 1966; Jakobson, 1971). Accordingly, there is nothing surprising in the fact that the first models of brain organization for language faculty that appeared in the 19th century were created by researchers in the field of vascular and traumatic aphasia (see, for example, Wernicke-Lichtheim-Geschwind's model of language; Poeppel and Hickok, 2004; or later models proposed by Goldstein, 1948; Jakobson, 1971; and Luria, 1966).

The situation changed fundamentally when neuropsychology and neurolinguistics enjoyed new non-invasive research methods and techniques such as EEG/ERP,[2] PET,[3] fMRI[4] and MEG.[5] These tools differ in their technical

---

[2] Electroencephalography (EEG) is the recording of electrical activity of the brain by a number of electrodes placed along the scalp. Event-related brain potential (ERP) is a derivative of the EEG technique that refers to averaged EEG responses being time-locked to the presentation of different types of stimulus (including such complex stimuli as words and sentences).

[3] Positron emission tomography (PET) is a functional neuroimaging technique (within nuclear medicine) that produces a three-dimensional image of functional processes in the brain.

[4] Functional magnetic resonance imaging (fMRI) is a functional procedure using magnetic resonance imaging technology that measures brain activity by detecting associated changes in blood flow.

[5] Magnetic encephalography (MEG) is a functional neuroimaging technique for mapping brain activity by recording magnetic fields produced by electrical currents occurring naturally in the brain.

characteristics as well as in their research capabilities. However, all of them facilitate the measurement of dynamic activity in the brain during performance of different cognitive tasks, including language-related tasks. Consequently, the development of the above mentioned techniques enabled a reformulation of the aims and objectives of neurolinguistics as a modern scientific discipline. Accordingly, determining the scope of the research interests of neurolinguistics, as well as defining its major aims and objectives, may be carried out on the basis of analysis of the subjects of some current studies that are positioned within neurolinguistics proper. In these studies a wide spectrum of language-related issues are discussed, including: language acquisition and development in relation to pre- and post-natal development of the nervous system, especially brain development; brain mechanisms of language production and comprehension; the nervous mechanism underlying spoken and written language functioning; second language acquisition and bilingual language processing; neurophysiological mechanisms of developmental (e.g. specific language impairments and dyslexia) and acquired (e.g. aphasias) language pathologies (Caplan, 1987; Locke, 1997; Paradis, 2004; Ahlsén, 2006; Van Lancker Sidtis, 2006; Abutalebi and Green, 2007; Ingram, 2007; Ardila, 2010; Malaia and Wilbur, 2010; Nergis, 2011; Jasinska and Petitto, 2013). It is obvious that such a wide range of research interests requires the use of data from various fields of science and especially from psychology (primarily cognitive and developmental psychology) and linguistics (especially psycholinguistics).

Thus, neurolinguistics may be defined as a subdivision of psychological science, located at the interface of psychology, neuroscience and linguistics which studies the brain mechanisms of different aspects and types of language behaviour. In accordance with specific scientific and practical goals, neurolinguistics may be subdivided into several specific sub-domains such as developmental neurolinguistics (Locke, 1997; Brauer, Anwander and Friederici, 2013), clinical neurolinguistics and aphasiology (Critchley, 1970; Caplan, 1987; Ingram, 2007; Ardila, 2010), neurolinguistics of bilingualism (Paradis, 2004; Abutalebi and Green, 2007; Fabbro, 2013; Jasinska and Petitto, 2013), historical or evolutionary neurolinguistics (phylogenetic or evolutionary aspects of language function development) (Arbib 2005; Berwick et al., 2013; Brambilla and Marini, 2014; Corballis, 2014), and the neurolinguistics of written language (Beaton, 2004; Graves et al., 2014).

Now that we are better able to answer the introductory question – What is neurolinguistics? – we can move on to the actual topic of this chapter: What do we learn from neurolinguistics? Note, however, that because this question is both very interesting and vast in scope, we will limit our discussion to only a few issues representing the development of modern neurolinguistics.

4.3 Brain and language

We have already established that essentially neurolinguistics aims to explore how the brain comprehends and produces language. This requires combining data and models from neuroanatomy and neurophysiology (how the brain is structured and how it functions) with data and models from linguistics and psycholinguistics (how language is structured and how it functions). Accordingly, we can see a well-known formula, which gave its name to one of the finest scientific journals in the field of neurolinguistics: *Brain and Language*.

Certainly, ideas and theories about the human brain as a specific 'body' and centre of the nervous system have changed over time, keeping pace with progress in research technologies, as well as with developments of new scientific disciplines, such as neuroanatomy and neurosurgery, genetics and neurophysiology. Scientific theories explaining the phenomena of human language and verbal communication have developed, too. In particular, already at the beginning of the 20th century, it was clear that research in the field of language cannot be limited merely to studying the language system. Such an approach (studying the 'language facts' or *parole*, according to Ferdinand de Saussure) could lead only to the creation of a static model of language as the system of language knowledge (i.e. *langue*; de Saussure, 2011), which was considered to be completely insufficient (see Head, 1926; Ingram, 2007; Vygotsky, 2012). Accordingly, various aspects of language behaviour have also become the objects of intensive research, including speech generation processes, speech comprehension and language acquisition in childhood. These changes in approach to studying the relationship between brain and language have turned neurolinguistics into an interdisciplinary study of language processing in the brain.

Scientific ideas in the field of neurolinguistics have come a long way in their development. It begins since the earlier localism and associationism theories, which assumed, respectively, that different higher (cognitive) functions are localized in different centres of the brain, mostly in the cortex, or that these functions are dependent on the connections between the above mentioned centres (see Caplan, 1987 and Ingram, 2007 for details). Further neurolinguistics developed through the model of dynamic localization of functions providing dynamic cooperation of different brain mechanisms located in different parts of the brain (Luria, 1966; Jakobson, 1971; Goodglass and Kaplan, 1972) to modern theories and models such as the theory of neural multifunctionality or the neural network model (Ahlsén, 2006; Ingram, 2007; Friederici and Gierhan, 2013; Cahana-Amitay and Albert, 2014).

We cannot, however, consider in detail both the historical background and the contemporary theories on brain mechanisms underlying the language faculty. So we will limit ourselves here to presenting a few main theses of modern neurolinguistics based on converging evidence from studies of brain damage, functional brain imaging and longitudinal studies of language development and language in ageing.

First, language processing is supported by different regions located in separate parts of the brain. In this case the term 'language processing' refers to all sets of psycholinguistic processes related to language production and comprehension (in spoken and written language), on all levels of linguistic representation (phonological, morphological, lexical, etc.) and in all fields of language use (automatic speech, naming or narrative production). Note also that the previously mentioned 'brain regions' are mostly located in the cerebral cortex (Broca's centre, Wernicke's centre, Angular Gurus, etc.), though some of them are found in the subcortical brain areas, for example, in the thalamus and the basal ganglia (Crosson, 1985; Johnson and Ojemann, 2000; Hebb and Ojemann, 2013). In most cases and, surprisingly, even for left-handers, the left brain hemisphere is dominant for language; that is, it is more language oriented than the right hemisphere. Even so, the processing of some important linguistic functions, such as humour comprehension or understanding of speech prosody, are associated solely with the right brain hemisphere (Iaccino, 1993; Ahlsén, 2006; Ingram, 2007).

Second, the numerous brain centres representing aggregates of all the interconnected neurons form a so-called neural network. A crucial precondition for these regions to function as a network is the transfer of information between them. This is guaranteed by several pathways linking different centres located in different parts of the brain; for example by dorsal and ventral pathways connecting relevant prefrontal and temporal language regions (Friederici and Gierhan, 2013).

Intensive studies during the last three decades show that the realization of various linguistic functions appears in space (meaning in a complex spatial system composed by the language-related mechanisms participating in function-processing) and in time. For example, Price (2010) demonstrates that an attempt to understand an unclear phrase (incomprehensible sentence) causes increased activation in a complete set of brain regions, including four inferior frontal regions, the posterior planum temporale and the ventral supramarginal gyrus. These effects are explained by the need for reliance on prior knowledge of semantic associations, word sequences and articulation that predict the content of the sentence. Thus, practically any use of language seems to require employing various processing resources and sources of information, that is, an activation of a variety depending on a specific goal of neural networks. Moreover, it is suggested (Cahana-Amitay and Albert, 2014) that non-linguistic functions also be incorporated into language models. Such an approach (see the theory of neural multifunctionality) assumes that in language processing there are various interactions among neural networks subserving cognitive (e.g. working-memory, attention and cognitive control), affective and praxis functions with neural networks specialized for linguistic functions such as phonetic segmentation, lexical retrieval and sentence comprehension.

Note in this regard that even at the very beginning of neurolinguistic research it was suggested that human brain organization enabling language use is the result of both phylogenetic (in the course of human evolution) and ontogenetic (in the course of a child's maturation) development. These issues will be discussed in the two following sections.

4.4   Evolution of brain and language relationships

Evolutionary neurolinguistics addresses various sources of information, which include palaeoanthropology (first of all, data on evolutionary changes in the size and shape of the cranium, and accordingly on size, weight and configuration of the human brain) and palaeohistory, comparative and historical linguistics, genetics, neuroanatomy and neurophysiology. Although evolutionary neurolinguistics is a relatively new field of neurolinguistics, its value is great, both from the practical and theoretical, especially philosophical, points of view.

In the literature on the evolution of brain mechanisms that provide the language faculty, there is a common view that language started to develop only when the human brain developed sufficiently from both the structural and functional points of view. Compared to other high cognitive functions, human language appears to be a relatively recent evolutionary acquisition. In fact, this seemingly happened anywhere between 50,000 and 80,000 years ago when our human ancestors left Africa (Tattersall, 2010; Berwick et al., 2013). In this regard researchers mainly emphasize two vitally important circumstances. First, animals, including primates, do not demonstrate anything even remotely similar to the human language faculty or human language.[6] That is, they did not develop language in the course of evolution, and they cannot 'learn' or 'acquire' human language in the course of their ontogenetic development, even in the optimal conditions created by researchers.

Second, although there are some individual differences in the ability to acquire and use language, no firmly established group differences have been found. Accordingly, the human language faculty seems to have emerged

---

[6] Here we can point out the capacity of human language (or verbal communication) 'to tell' about an event occurring 'not here and now' which distinguishes it from any other communication system (i.e. different types of non-verbal communication). Another important characteristic of human language that may also be unique is the ability to construct numerous language units at the highest level (word and sentence level) by using several units of the lowest level (e.g. morphemes and phonemes).

'suddenly' on the evolutionary timeline and has not evolved since (Berwick et al., 2013; Brambilla and Marini, 2014).

It seems most likely, however, that changes in the brain structure occurred gradually, in accordance with progress in language structure and language communication and the emergence of new requirements for speech, including anatomical changes in the human vocal chords and in the articulation apparatus, and spoken language comprehension. On the other hand, the human capacity for language may have evolved on the back of a relatively high development of human intelligence and other cognitive functions. This improved language ability was the answer to changing living conditions, including the development of social relationships (Ahlsén, 2006; Berwick et al., 2013; see also Vygotsky, 2012).

During the millennia following the emergence of language, human languages underwent considerable changes, which have ultimately become manifest in the present language variety (different languages, dialects, registers, etc.). Nevertheless, individual differences in the organization of brain mechanisms underlying the language function are not associated with distinctions in the linguistic structure of different languages. That is, use of language of various types, sometimes even in the course of several thousand years, caused no noticeable anatomical changes in the brain. Anatomical distinctions in brain mechanisms for the language faculty certainly do exist, but they belong either to gender differences or to individual differences only. As for ethnic, cultural and lingual (that is, differences in linguistic characteristics of language) distinctions, their influence is found only at the functional level (Chen et al., 2009). Thus, modern human language has a fixed 'neural architecture', which has not changed for a long period of time. Note, however, that this is true only for spoken language; written language has no such evolutionary-developed brain mechanisms. The most ancient alphabets appeared only about 5,000 years ago (Sampson, 1985), and special parallel brain mechanisms for processing written information simply did not manage to develop in such a short (from the evolutionary point of view) period of time (Beaton, 2004).

4.5   Development of brain and language relationships in childhood

Results of numerous studies (Chiron et al., 1997; Locke, 1997; Locke and Bogin, 2006; Friedrichi and Friederici, 2010; Brown and Jernigan, 2012; Bishop, 2013; Brauer et al., 2013) show that the above-mentioned complex system of brain mechanisms underlying the human language faculty appears not immediately at birth but is formed and developed during the long period of early childhood from birth to approximately age 6–7 or even much later. Brain maturation and structural development in early childhood have a very dramatic character. The brain not only increases in weight, anywhere from 400 to 1,400 grams, but also significantly changes structurally. During the development of the central nervous system, specific speech and language mechanisms are formed in various parts of the brain (i.e. in the cerebral cortex of both brain hemispheres and in various subcortical areas) and the number of connections both within these language-related centres and between them increases substantially. Brain structures become more complex and neural networks are formed. Additionally, the processes of brain maturation and development as well as those of language acquisition are influenced by both genetic and non-genetic factors (Bishop, 2013).

The role of genetic factors in language acquisition is extremely significant. Note in this regard that there are only two language-related facts. First, a language or verbal communication system seems to belong uniquely to the human race; it is acquired solely by human infants and is supported solely by a human brain. Second, the left brain hemisphere is dominant for language among the vast majority of people, including a great part of left-handers. However, the lateralization of cognitive functions – and language functions represent a very complicated and relatively long process – may also be influenced by non-genetic factors (Bishop, 2013).

Another important characteristic of language progress is the important or even critical role of language stimuli (the influence of external factors, in this case the language medium) in this process. The quantity and quality of such stimuli are critical for the timely development of brain mechanisms for the language faculty (Locke, 1997; Locke and Bogin, 2006). In this case, formation of the main language-related brain mechanisms must be completed by age six, approximately (Locke and Bogin, 2006; Kuhl, 2010). This is the so-called critical period for language acquisition,[7] which is accompanied by a significant structural growth of the brain and its morphological changes, with increases in the relevant cortical areas (Broca's area). Note in this context that anatomical and physiological development from infancy to young adulthood is continuous in nature and is simultaneously reflected by regular changes in language ability. However, the pre-school years can be regarded as critical and especially vital for progress in language ability both from the anatomical, including structural brain characteristics, and functional points of view.

---

[7] The critical period is considered to be when development of the brain (brain plasticity effect) enables acquiring a definite (in this case language) cognitive function. At the end of this period, language acquisition becomes impossible, though development of already acquired basic skills and core language knowledge is possible.

4.6   The neurolinguistics of bilingualism

The issue of bilingual[8] language acquisition (i.e. simultaneous or relatively successive learning of two different languages in early childhood) is usually considered separately from ordinary monolingual language acquisition (Ahlsen, 2006; Bialystok, 2009; Fabbro, 2013; Jasinska and Petitto, 2013). Generally, studies on bilingualism (Baker, 2001; Bialystok, 2009; Montrul, 2009) show that there are two main characteristics of such language acquisition and development. First, obviously bilingual infants need to acquire much more information than their monolingual peers because they learn two different linguistic codes simultaneously, that is two sets of grammatical, phonological or even pragmatic rules. The situation becomes even more complicated due to the fact that these children learn two languages in the context of reduced exposure to each of them. The second characteristic of bilingual language acquisition is the need to sort and properly compute the information for each acquired language; that is, the necessity to distinguish between two linguistic codes and to switch from one to the other depending on the demands in a given concrete situation. Even so, from the neurolinguistic perspective, bilinguals seem to learn two languages simply as 'one language', and their bilingual experience does not shape the brain differently, as compared to monolinguals, from the anatomical point of view (Paradis, 2004; Abutalebi and Green, 2007; Fabbro, 2013). However, the issue of structural and functional differences between monolingual and bilingual brains is treated differently in the literature (Abutalebi and Green, 2007; Leikin et al., 2012; Jasinska and Petitto, 2013; Li et al., 2014).

Several studies have suggested distinct non-overlapping cortical representations of the two languages in bilingual subjects (Paradis and Goldblum, 1989; Paradis, 2004). In addition, different electrophysiological patterns have been observed in first language processing of bilinguals and monolinguals (Donald et al., 1986; Abutalebi and Green, 2007; Leikin, 2008; Leikin and Ritvas, 2012). However, a number of other studies have found evidence for overlapping cortical representations in bilinguals (Sarfarazi and Sedgwick, 1996; Ullman, 2001; Paradis, 2004; Abutalebi and Green, 2007; Fabbro, 2013). Empirical findings (using fMRI and other neuroimaging tools) of the locations of activation sources for the two languages have also been contradictory (Illes et al., 1999; Wartenburger et al., 2003; Briellman et al., 2004; Leikin et al., 2012; Fabbro, 2013). Behavioural studies of bilingual language processing have yielded mixed results as well: some have suggested a separate activation of first and second language (Gerard and Scarborough, 1989) and others indicate that both languages are simultaneously activated (Dijkstra, 2001).

---

[8] Hereafter the term 'bilingual' is used in the wider sense of the word and refers to people who know more than one language.

Thus, neurolinguistic studies related to bilingualism have yielded contradictory findings resulting in controversy on the subject of brain organization and functioning in bilingualism. These controversies have been explained by differences in methodologies and mainly in subject populations: age, age of second language acquisition and type of bilingualism (Grosjean, 1998; Leikin et al., 2012; Jasinska and Petitto, 2013). There have been further suggestions to distinguish between different bilingual processing styles for phonetic and syntactic information, on the one hand, and for lexical-semantic information on the other (Marian et al., 2003; Leikin, 2008).

Summarizing the above mentioned facts, it can be concluded that between monolingual and bilingual brains there are essential distinctions in language processing. Differences have also been found between first and second language processing as well as between processing of various languages, such as English vs Chinese or Hebrew vs Russian. Additionally, processing differences related to such factors as proficiency in both languages, age of acquisition and type of bilingualism (balanced vs non-balanced) seem to influence brain activation in various linguistic tasks. Thus, generally speaking, it may be suggested that multiple language experiences may result in adaptive changes of the brain both in functional and structural (neural networks) planes (Li et al., 2014).

Another interesting but scantly studied issue is the relationship between bilingualism and the development of cognitive abilities. Research conducted in the last decade has shown that bilingualism has a strong influence not only on the development of language ability and linguistic skills but on cognitive development as well (Bialystok, 2009; Kroll et al., 2012). The advantages of bilingualism have been reported across a variety of domains, including a wide range of executive functions (e.g. in inhibition, cognitive flexibility and updating of working memory – see Hommel et al., 2011; Kroll et al., 2012), problem-solving (Bialystok, 2009; Adesope et al., 2010) and creativity, mostly expressed in divergent thinking or cognitive flexibility (Ricciardelli, 1992; Simonton, 2008; Adi-Japha et al., 2010; Kharkhurin, 2010, 2012; Hommel et al., 2011; Leikin, 2013). It has also been found that the performance of balanced bilingual individuals is better than that of their non-balanced peers (Cummins, 1976, 2000; Meisel, 2008; Leikin, 2013). Data from neurophysiological studies seem to confirm the existence of the influence of bilingual experience on the development of some cognitive (not linguistic) functions (Abutalebi and Green, 2007; Fabbro, 2013; Jasinska and Petitto, 2013). These considerations bring us back to the well-known hypothesis (Jasinska and Petitto, 2013; Li et al., 2014) asserting that the brain has an extraordinary ability to change functionally and structurally in response to environmental stimuli, cognitive demands or behavioural experience (the so-called 'neuroplasticity effect'). In this case, bilingualism seems to represent all three sources of change.

4.7   Conclusion

In summing up this brief review of the current state of neurolinguistics, note that we have only touched on a few central issues. Certainly the choice of these issues is of a somewhat subjective nature. Nevertheless, compared with 'brain and language' or 'developmental neurolinguistics', topics such as 'clinical neurolinguistics', 'neurolinguistics of reading and writing' and 'neurolinguistics of gender differences' seem to be overly specific. Discussion of these topics would make the review presented here much more complicated, requiring vast amounts of data from a great number of scientific domains (each of which, in turn, demands a detailed explanation). Note that the development of the above-mentioned scientific areas, alone, has led to an incredible expansion of our knowledge about the nervous basis of the language faculty, its development in childhood, changes in ageing and the nature of the damage found in various types of language impairments, including developmental disorders such as Specific Language Impairment, acquired disorders such as vascular aphasia and language impairments deriving from different degenerative disorders. Besides the development of various subdomains of neurolinguistics, this has led to a greater understanding of the importance of individual differences both in the language faculty and in its nervous substrate. The subject of individual differences has become central to modern neurolinguistics. Results of research in this area show that despite features common to the entire human race, language acquisition and development in childhood as well as language use throughout one's life possess distinct individual features. There are considerable differences between males and females (in favour of the latter), between monolinguals and bilinguals, between people who know how to read and write and illiterates. The differences related to other factors (e.g. cognitive or learning styles) have been noted too. Development of the neurolinguistics of individual differences seems to be a very promising field of research from the perspective of modern neurolinguistics, in particular, mostly because of the dramatic development in the technological and methodological foundations of neurolinguistics research.

References

J. Abutalebi and D. Green (2007) 'Bilingual Language Production: The Neurocognition of Language Representation and Control', *Journal of Neurolinguistics*, 20, 242–275.

O. Adesope, T. Lavin, T. Thompson and C. Ungerleider (2010) 'A Systematic Review and Meta-analysis of the Cognitive Correlates of Bilingualism', *Review of Educational Research*, 80, 207–245.

E. Adi-Japha, J. Berberich-Artzi and A. Libnawi (2010) 'Cognitive Flexibility in Drawings of Bilingual Children', *Child Development*, 81, 1356–1366.

AHD (2012) *The American Heritage Dictionary of the English Language*, Fifth Edition (Boston: Houghton Mifflin Harcourt).

E. Ahlsén (2006) *Introduction to Neurolinguistics* (Philadelphia: John Benjamins Publishing Company).

M. Arbib (2005) 'From Monkey-like Action Recognition to Human Language: An Evolutionary Framework for Neurolinguistics', *Brain and Behavioral Sciences*, 28, 105–124.

A. Ardila (2010) 'A Proposed Reinterpretation and Reclassification of Aphasic Syndromes', *Aphasiology*, 24, 363–394.

C. Baker (2001) *Foundations of Bilingual Education and Bilingualism* (Clevedon: Multilingual Matters).

A. Beaton (2004) *Dyslexia, Reading, and the Brain* (Hove and New York: Psychology Press).

R. Berwick, A. Friederici, N. Chomsky and J. Bolhuis (2013) 'Evolution, Brain, and the Nature of Language', *Trends in Cognitive Science*, 17, 89–98.

E. Bialystok (2009) 'Bilingualism: The Good, the Bad, and the Indifferent', *Bilingualism: Language and Cognition*, 12, 3–11.

D. Bishop (2013) 'Cerebral Asymmetry and Language Development: Cause, Correlate, or Consequence?', *Science*, 340, 6138.

P. Brambilla and A. Marini (eds) (2014) *Brain Evolution, Language and Psychopathology in Schizophrenia* (New York: Routledge).

J. Brauer, A. Anwander and A. Friederici (2013) 'Neuroanatomical Prerequisites for Language Functions in the Maturing Brain', *Cerebral Cortex*, 21, 459–466.

R. Briellman, M. Saling, A. Connell, A. Waites, D. Abbott and G. Jackson (2004) 'A High-field Functional MRI Study of Quadrilingual Subjects', *Brain and Language*, 89, 531–542.

T. Brown and T. Jernigan (2012) 'Brain Development during the Preschool Years', *Neuropsychological Review*, 22, 313–333.

D. Cahana-Amitay and M. Albert (2014) 'Brain and Language: Evidence for Neural Multifunctionality', *Behavioural Neurology*, ID 260381, http://dx.doi.org/10.1155/2014/260381

D. Caplan (1987) *Neurolinguistics and Linguistic Aphasiology* (Cambridge: Cambridge University Press).

C. Chen, G. Xue, L. Mei1, C. Chen and Q. Dong (2009) 'Cultural Neurolinguistics', *Progress in Brain Research*, 178, 159–171.

C. Chiron, I. Jambaque, R. Nabbout, R. Lounes, A. Syrota and O. Dulac (1997) 'The Right Brain Hemisphere Is Dominant in Human Infants', *Brain*, 120, 1057–1065.

M. Corballis (2014) 'Left Brain, Right Brain: Facts and Fantasies', *PLOS, Biology*, 12, DOI: 10.1371.

M. Critchley (1970) *Aphasiology and Other Aspects of Language* (London: Edward Arnold).

B. Crosson (1985) 'Subcortical Functions in Language: A Working Model', *Brain & Language*, 25(2), 257–292.

J. Cummins (1976) 'The Influence of Bilingualism on Cognitive Growth: A Synthesis of Research Findings and Explanatory Hypotheses', *Working Papers on Bilingualism*, 9, 1–44.

J. Cummins (2000) *Language, Power, and Pedagogy: Bilingual Children in the Crossfire* (Clevedon: Multilingual Matters).

F. de Saussure (2011) *Course in General Linguistics* (New York: Columbia University Press).

T. Dijkstra (2001) 'What We Know about Bilingual Word Recognition: A Review of Studies and Models', Plenary Address at the International Symposium on Bilingualism, Bristol.

M. Donald, R. Meuter and S. Ardal (1986) 'Event-related Brain Potentials in the First and Second Languages of Bilinguals', *Society of Neuroscience Abstracts*, 12, 721.

F. Fabbro (2013) *The Neurolinguistics of Bilingualism: An Introduction* (New York: Taylor & Francis Group).

M. Friedrichi and A. Friederici (2010) 'Maturing Brain Mechanisms and Developing Behavioral Language Skills', *Brain & Language*, 114, 66–71.

A. Friederici and S. Gierhan (2013) 'The Language Network', *Current Opinion in Neurobiology*, 23, 250–254.

L. Gerard and D. Scarborough (1989) 'Language-specific Lexical Access of Homographs by Bilinguals', *Journal of Experimental Psychology: Learning, Memory, and Cognition*, 15, 305–315.

K. Goldstein (1948) *Language and Language Disturbances* (New York: Grune & Stratton).

H. Goodglass and E. Kaplan (1972) *The Assessment of Aphasia and Related Disorders* (Philadelphia: Lea & Febiger).

H. Goodglass and F. Quadfasel (1954) 'Language Laterality in Left-handed Aphasics', *Brain*, 77, 521–548.

W. Graves, J. Binder, R. Desai and C. Humphries (2014) 'Anatomy Is Strategy: Skilled Reading Differences Associated with Structural Connectivity Differences in the Reading Network', *Brain and Language*, 133, 1–13.

F. Grosjean (1998) 'Studying Bilinguals: Methodological and Conceptual Issues', *Bilingualism: Language and Cognition*, 1, 131–149.

H. Head (1926) *Aphasia and Kindred Disorders of Speech* (Cambridge: Cambridge University Press).

A. Hebb and G. Ojemann (2013) 'The Thalamus and Language Revisited', *Brain and Language*, 126, 99–108.

B. Hommel, L. Colzato, R. Fischer and L. Christoffels (2011) 'Bilingualism and Creativity: Benefits in Convergent Thinking Come with Losses in Divergent Thinking', *Frontiers in Psychology*, 2, 1–5.

J. Iaccino (1993) *Left Brain-right Brain Differences: Inquiries, Evidence, and New Approaches* (New York: Psychology Press).

J. Illes, W. Francis, J. Desmond, J. Gabrieli, G. Glover, R. Poldrack and A. Wagner (1999) 'Convergent Cortical Representation of Semantic Processing in Bilinguals', *Brain and Language*, 70, 347–363.

J. Ingram (2007) *Neurolinguistics: An Introduction to Spoken Language Processing and Disorders* (Cambridge: Cambridge University Press).

J. Jackson (1958/1869) *Selected Writings*, vol. 2. (New York: Basic Books).

R. Jakobson (1971) *Studies on Child Language and Aphasia* (The Hague: Mouton and Co).

K. Jasinska and L. Petitto (2013) 'How Age of Bilingual Exposure Can Change the Neural Systems for Language in the Developing Brain: A Functional near Infrared Spectroscopy Investigation of Syntactic Processing in Monolingual and Bilingual Children', *Developmental Cognitive Neuroscience*, 6, 87–101.

M. Johnson and G. Ojemann (2000) 'The Role of the Human Thalamus in Language and Memory: Evidence from Electrophysiological Studies', *Brain and Cognition*, 42, 218–230.

A. Kharkhurin (2010) 'Bilingual Verbal and Nonverbal Creative Behavior', *International Journal of Bilingualism*, 14, 211–226.

A. Kharkhurin (2012) *Multilingualism and Creativity* (Bristol: Multilingual Materials).

J. Kroll, P. Dussias, C. Bogulski and J. Valdes-Kroff (2012) 'Juggling Two Languages in One Mind: What Bilinguals Tell Us about Language Processing and its Consequences for Cognition', *The Psychology of Learning and Motivation*, 56, 229–262.

P. Kuhl (2010) 'Brain Mechanisms in Early Language Acquisition', *Neuron*, 67, 713–727.

M. Leikin (2008) 'Syntactic Processing in Two Languages by Native and Bilingual Adult Readers: An ERP Study', *Journal of Neurolinguistics*, 21, 349–373.

M. Leikin (2013) 'The Effect of Bilingualism on Creativity: Developmental and Educational Perspectives', *International Journal of Bilingualism*, 6, 1–17.

M. Leikin and E. Ritvas (2012) 'Syntactic Processing in Three Languages by Native and Bilingual Adult Readers: An ERP Study', in M. Leikin, M. Schwartz and Y. Tobin (eds) *Current Issues in Bilingualism* (pp. 241–262) (New York: Springer Publishers).

M. Leikin, M. Schwartz and Y. Tobin (2012) 'Current Issues in Bilingualism: A Complex Approach to a Multidimensional Phenomenon', in M. Leikin, M. Schwartz and Y. Tobin (eds) *Current Issues in Bilingualism* (pp. 1–20) (New York: Springer Publishers).

P. Li, J. Legault and K. Litcofsky (2014) 'Neuroplasticity as a Function of Second Language Learning: Anatomical Changes in the Human Brain', *Cortex*, 58, 301–324.

J. Locke (1997) 'A Theory of Neurolinguistic Development', *Brain and Language*, 58, 265–326.

J. L. Locke and B. Bogin (2006). 'Language and Life History: A New Perspective on the Development and Evolution of Human Language', *Behavioral and Brain Sciences*, 29, 259–279.

A. Luria (1947) *Traumatic Aphasia* (Moscow: AMN USSR).

A. Luria (1948) *Restoration of Brain Functions after Trauma* (Moscow: AMN USSR).

A. Luria (1966) *Higher Cortical Functions in Man* (New York: Basic Books).

A. Luria (1976) *Basic Problems of Neurolinguistics* (The Hague: Mouton Publishers).

E. Malaia and R. Wilbur (2010) 'Sign Languages: Contribution to Neurolinguistics from Cross-Modal Research', *Lingua*, 120, 2704–2706.

V. Marian, M. Spivey and J. Hirsch (2003) 'Shared and Separate Systems in Bilingual Language Processing: Converging Evidence from Eye Tracking and Brain Imaging', *Brain and Language*, 86, 70–82.

J. Meisel (2008) 'Child Second Language Acquisition or Successive First Language Acquisition?', in B. Haznedar and E. Gavruseva (eds) *Current Trends in Child Second Language Acquisition* (pp. 55–80) (Amsterdam: Benjamins).

S. Montrul (2009) 'What Can Early Bilinguals Tell Us?', *Studies in Second Language Acquisition*, 31, 225–257.

A. Nergis (2011) 'To What Extent Does Neurolinguistics Embody EFL Teaching Methods?', *Procedia Social and Behavioral Sciences*, 15, 143–147.

M. Paradis (2004) *A Neurolinguistic Theory of Bilingualism* (Amsterdam and Philadelphia: John Benjamins Publishing Company).

M. Paradis and M. Goldblum (1989) 'Selective Crossed Aphasia in a Trilingual Aphasic Patient Followed by Reciprocal Antagonism', *Brain and Language*, 36, 62–75.

D. Poeppel and G. Hickok (2004) 'Towards a New Functional Anatomy of Language', *Cognition*, 92, 1–12.

C. J. Price (2010). 'The Anatomy Of Language: A Review of 100 fMRI Studies Published in 2009', *Annals of the New York Academy of Sciences*, 1191(1), 62–88.

L. Ricciardelli (1992) 'Bilingualism and Cognitive Development: A Review of Past and Recent Findings', *Journal of Creative Behavior*, 26, 242–254.

G. Sampson (1985) *Writing Systems: A Linguistic Introduction* (Stanford, CA: Stanford University Press).

M. Sarfarazi and E. Sedgwick (1996) 'Event Related Potentials (ERP) as a Function of Language Processing in Bilinguals', *Electroencephalography and Clinical Neurophysiology*, 99, 347.

D. Simonton (2008) 'Bilingualism and Creativity', in J. Altarriba and R. Heredia (eds) *An Introduction to Bilingualism: Principles and Processes* (Mahwah, NJ: Lawrence Erlbaum).

I. Tattersall (2010) 'Human Evolution and Cognition', *Theory in Biosciences*, 129, 193–201.

M. Ullman (2001) 'The Neural Basis of Lexicon and Grammar in First and Second Language: The Declarative/Procedural Model', *Bilingualism: Language and Cognition*, 4, 105–122.

D. Van Lancker Sidtis (2006) 'Does Functional Neuroimaging Solve the Questions of Neurolinguistics?', *Brain and Language*, 98, 276–290.

L. Vygotsky (2012) *Thought and Language* (Cambridge, MA: MIT Press).

I. Wartenburger, H. Heekeren, J. Abutalebi, S. Cappa, A. Villringer and D. Perani (2003) 'Early Setting of Grammatical Processing in the Bilingual Brain', *Neuron*, 37, 159–170.

H. A. Whitaker (1971) *On the Representation of Language in the Human Brain* (Edmonton: Linguistic Research).

H. Whitaker and H. A. Whitaker (eds) (1976) *Studies in Neurolinguistics: Vol. 1 (Perspectives in Neurolinguistics and Psycholinguistics)* (New York: Academic Press).

5
Linguistic Distances and Ethnolinguistic Fractionalization and Disenfranchisement Indices

Victor Ginsburgh and Shlomo Weber

5.1 Introduction

Ruhlen (1994) reconstructed 27 words of the very first language. Some linguists raised eyebrows about the words themselves, but not so much about the idea that all our languages descend from one, or a very small number of, language(s).[1] Today, most linguists think that the diversity of languages is the result of the migration 'out of Africa' of *Homo sapiens* over the last 50,000 to 100,000 years (Michalopoulos, 2012; Ashraf and Galor, 2013). If this is so, languages can be represented in the form of a tree similar to genealogical trees, starting with a root representing the *first* language, or ancestor, and followed by branches and twigs for descendants. This implies of course that languages are related by their vocabulary, syntax, phonology, etc. in the same way as children are related to their parents and more distant ancestors by some of their genes. Genetic differences are relatively easy to trace and DNA analyses have become common, for instance, in the case of disputed parenthood. It is, however, more difficult to 'count' the (dis)similarities between languages, since many characteristics, and not only vocabularies, are involved.

Linguistic, genetic and cultural aspects of a society or a nation are thus often correlated, since all three are closely linked to nature, but also to learning and history, that is, nurture. One can therefore wonder when it is appropriate to choose one or the other in representing proximity of individuals or groups to which they belong. In some cases, one of the measures is obvious. This is so

Parts of this chapter are based on Ginsburgh and Weber (2011, chapters 3 and 4). The authors are grateful to N. Fabb, J. Melitz and S. Weyers for many useful comments. S. Weber also wishes to acknowledge the support of the Ministry of Education and Science of the Russian Federation, grant No. 14.U04.31.0002, administered through the NES CSDSI.
[1] See Nichols (2012).

when describing the difficulty in acquiring a foreign language, though even here, there may be other types of proximities at work between, say, a Swedish- and a Danish-speaking individual than the mere proximity between the two languages. Otherwise, there is no obvious answer to the question of proper definition of linguistic diversity, and certainly no theory to invoke.

The chapter is organized as follows. Section 5.2 focuses on the reasons for which distances between languages are important, since they allow by-passing the difficult separation between, and definitions of, what is called *language* and what is called *dialect, creole, pidgin* and *trade language*. Section 5.3 surveys the various types of linguistic distances that are available and how they are computed. In Section 5.4, we introduce important applications in which linguistic distances as such play a role in explaining various economic outcomes: bilateral trade flows, migrations, language acquisition and the problem of translations. This discussion will be short since the volume contains special chapters dealing with each of these topics. In Section 5.5, we extend our discussion to linguistic distances between groups of people (countries or regions). In Section 5.6, we analyse how linguistic distances can be introduced into fractionalization (or diversity) and disenfranchisement indices to account for the proximity between groups, regions and countries. Chapter 2 in this volume should be read in conjunction with Sections 5.2 and 5.3.

5.2 Languages, dialects and trade languages

Before turning to the measurement issue discussed later in this chapter, it is use-ful to know how many languages exist, how many will be left to our heirs, and what distinguishes a language from a dialect. The 2009 edition of *Ethnologue*[2] lists 6,909 languages that are currently spoken in the world. Whether this num-ber is large or small, given the world population, is open for discussion, and so is the number itself, since it results from a rather subjective count. As *Ethnologue* (2009, p. 9) notes, 'every language is characterized by variation within the speech community that uses it. Those varieties are more or less divergent and are often referred to as dialects, which may be distinct enough to be considered separate languages or sufficiently similar' to be called dialects. Moreover, 'not all scholars share the same set of criteria for distinguishing a language from a dialect'. The criteria used by *Ethnologue* (2009, p. 9) to arrive at their count

---

[2] *Ethnologue. Languages of the World* is a comprehensive catalogue of the world's living languages. The project started in 1951. The last 1,250-pages-thick 2009 edition is a mine of information on languages, where they are spoken and the number of speakers in each country. If not otherwise mentioned, this is the information that is used in our book. See also *Ethnologue*'s website www.ethnologue.com/ which contains updated information.

'make it clear that the identification of a "language" is not solely within the realm of linguistics'.

A couple of examples are useful. *Ethnologue* lists 57 Zapotec languages in Mexico. Some of those, such as Zapotec (San Augustin Mixtepec), count less than 100 first-language speakers. The largest, Zapotec (Isthmus), has 85,000 speakers. In contrast, *Ethnologue* also lists five dialects in the Flemish part of Belgium (Antwerps, Brabants, Limburgs, Oostvlaams and Westvlaams) that are certainly all spoken by more than 100 people, and though they are considered variants of Dutch, can probably not be understood by a Netherlander from Amsterdam. Is Québéquois close to French? This can be questioned since on French TV, it happens that French Canadian series are subtitled in ... French.

There is not much known about what really happened between the birth of the first language and the large number of languages that exist today, nor on the pace at which some languages were born, while others died. Most of what we know was reconstructed by linguists on the basis of languages that exist today or extinct languages about which we have written documents, such as ancient Greek or Latin. Obviously, there are languages that have disappeared, or are no longer spoken as first languages. Latin is one such case, but there are certainly many others that we ignore. Hebrew that was no longer spoken as a first language is now Israel's official language.

Slavery and exploration, followed by colonization, had the effect of killing languages at a fast rate. So do, nowadays, mass tourism and globalization. To mitigate the frightening prospect of linguistic and cultural loss, there is 'good news' as new languages and cultures are also being born. This is certainly what Claude Levi-Strauss would have thought, when he said in one of his last interviews in 2002:

> On peut se dire, en tout cas c'est un voeu pieux, qu'au moment où nous craignons une uniformisation universelle, en sous-main, sourdement, de nouvelles différences commencent à apparaître que nous ne pouvons même pas percevoir, mais que nos héritiers comprendront et qui, je l'espère, seront exploitées.[3]

This is close to what Kibbee (2003, p. 51) writes about language renewal and new languages being born: '[a] language is a behaviour, not a physical characteristic. If two languages are in contact, then they influence each other. If a dog lives in the same house as a bird it does not grow wings, nor does the bird sprout paws'.

---

[3] We may hope that at the very same time during which globalization is taking place, somehow, in a secret way, new differences are appearing, that we cannot perceive but that will be understood by our heirs.

Pidgins and *creoles* have indeed grown and made communication easier. *Ethnologue* (2009, p. 29) lists 77 creole languages that were created by Dutch, English, French, Portuguese, Russian or Spanish colonization. They result from a blending (and simplified grammar, vocabulary and style) of the local and the colonizer's language and have become the mother tongues of many communities. Some examples are Papiamentu (in the Netherlands Antilles), Virgin Islands Creole English (Virgin Islands), Saint Lucian Creole French (Sainte Lucie), Korlai Creole Portuguese (India) or Aleut Mednyj (Russian Federation).[4] In an interesting paper published by *Newsweek* on 7 March 2005, 'Not the Queen's English: Non-native speakers are transforming the global language', the author distinguishes more than 50 varieties, including British English (BBC English, English English, Scottish English, Scots, Norn, Welsh English, Ulster Scots, Hiberno-English, Irish English), American English (Network Standard, Northern, Midland, Southern, Black English Vernacular, Gullah, Appalachian, Indian English) and Canadian English (Quebec English, Frenglish, Newfoundland English, Athabascan English, Inuit English), not to speak of Spanglish used by a growing community in the United States.

'Old' languages enrich each other and create exciting new blends that obviously share some or many characteristics with their predecessors.[5] It would obviously be politically incorrect to claim that newcomers to the linguistic scene, such as the many Creoles or Spanglish, are inferior to those that we speak, including our one-thousand-words English. The same is true for cultural, ethnic and religious traits, as is shown in the papers by Bisin and Verdier (2000, 2014), who describe the theoretical processes that can give birth to what we observe in terms of cultural mixtures. Sushis were 'exported' to the United States, changed there to embrace local tastes better, and are now 'reimported' as such by Japan.

It is also worth pointing out that many linguistically diverse countries or regions consisting of several (often recently) defined countries have endogenously generated their 'trade language'. This is so for a couple of important languages in Nigeria (which otherwise has over 520 living languages) as well as for Swahili, a Bantou language that was contaminated by Arabic (during the slave trade) and Portuguese (with the trading posts established after 1488, when Bartolomeu Dias reached the Cape of Good Hope and entered the Indian Ocean), as well as English (in the former British colonies where it is used) which spread on the East Coast of Africa.

How can we decide whether an idiom (language, dialect, variety, etc.) is different from another, and does this matter? Theoretically, one could take into

---

[4] Some historical linguists have even suggested that English is a creole. See Singh (2005).
[5] See the very entertaining book on this issue by McWorther (2001).

account distances between every pair of languages, including dialects[6] and the unimaginably large number of varieties and decide on a threshold which would distinguish a 'language' from small variations consisting of a few words, expressions or ways to pronounce them. This would of course be a daunting project, but some theoretical and empirical basics exist and are discussed in what follows.

5.3   Distances between languages

Languages can be distant from each other in many different ways. *Vocabulary* is often thought of being the main reason, and indeed, though English and German are part of the Indo-European family and belong to the same branch of so-called Germanic languages, the English word *moon* is related to but differs from *Mond* in German. And they both differ strongly from *lune* in French, though French is also an Indo-European language, but belongs to the branch referred to as Romance languages. Words differ, but even *moon* and *Mond* have different genders: the first is neutral, the second is masculine and *lune* is feminine.

The pronunciation and spelling of *moon* is close to *Mond*. The final *e* in *lune* is mute, while the *a* in the Italian or Spanish *luna* is not. Diphthongs, that is, sounds composed of two vowels joined to form one sound, as in *sound*, also add to the difficulty of a language. But the French student of English will wonder why the *ou* in *south* is not pronounced like the one in *tour*. Therefore, pronunciation also contributes to the distance between languages. *Phonetics* and *phonology* study how we use lips, tongue, teeth and vocal chords to produce the various sounds (phonemes) in each language. Both the production and perception of phonemes differ across languages. Each language has phonemes that may prove difficult to acquire by non-native speakers. It seems easier for a native speaker of a language that contains a large number of phonemes to learn a language with less phonemes, since for her both the production and perception of sounds are more developed.[7]

Syntax, the 'way in which linguistic elements (as words) are put together to form constituents as phrases or clauses',[8] illustrates another difference between languages. *I would like to observe the moon* translates into *Ich möchte (gerne) den Mond beobachten*. While the word *observe* is located in the middle of the English sentence, its translation *beobachten* ends the German sentence. It is quite difficult to grasp quickly the meaning of *fünfundzwanzig* euros when the German taxi driver tells you how much you ought to pay for the ride: the meaning is

---

[6] This was undertaken for German dialects in a recent paper by Falck et al. (2009).

[7] See Ladefoged and Maddieson (1996) for an extensive discussion.

[8] *Merriam-Webster Dictionary*, www.merriam-webster.com/dictionary/syntax.

twenty-five but it is spelled out *five and twenty* in German (as well as in other Germanic languages, such as Dutch or Danish).

Grammar is of course another worry. For instance, while German has declinations, only very few of them remain in English such as the so-called possessive genitive in *the moon's last quarter*. None of the declinations that exist in Latin were inherited in contemporary (spoken) French, and a French student who did not have to learn Latin or Greek (or German) at school will hardly know the meaning of the word 'declination'.

These are just a few examples to illustrate that computing the distance between two languages is a stiff challenge, and this is even without going into the fundamental issue of whether languages have a common structure.[9]

The comparative method used in *historical linguistics* aims at reconstructing 'common ancestry, and descent through time with gradual divergence from [a] common source' (McMahon and McMahon, 2005, p. 3), and is not interested in the intercommunication of people who speak different languages today.[10] It consists of two parts: 'the demonstration of linguistic relatedness, and the reconstruction of a hypothetical common ancestral system' (ibid., p. 5). It uses morphological resemblances, lexical items, syntax and sound correspondences, and identifies groups and subgroups of languages according to their similarity. The final result consists of a linguistic tree, with a root (the Ur-language or common ancestor) and branches which in turn grow into sub-branches, until one reaches final twigs, each of which corresponds to a unique language. Examples of such trees in different forms, including the old image representing a real tree, can be found by searching on the internet for the terms 'language tree images'.[11]

The result is comparable to what biologists (with the aid of scientists from other disciplines such as palaeontologists) adopt to construct biological and evolutionary trees. This is often called *cladistics*, a term that comes from the Greek root κλαδøς (klados) for branch. To generate a tree, the method starts with a table which lists several animal or vegetal species as well as characteristics describing the various species supposed to have a common ancestor. Trees (also called cladograms) are then constructed using the information given by the descriptive characteristics, and the one considered the 'best' is identified. Implicitly, cladistics also utilizes weights to generate the resulting tree, and therefore shares some of the issues outlined above.

The comparative method can be made looser (mass comparison) or tighter by using a unique characteristic of a language, its lexicon (which leads to lexicostatistics), but can also accommodate median situations.

---

[9] On the fights that this controversy still generates, see Harris (1993) and Baker (2001).
[10] We will come back to this point later.
[11] See Nakhleh et al. (2005) for a description and an example of the construction of the Indo-European language tree.

Mass comparison was used by Greenberg (1987) to classify native American languages. It is, claim McMahon and McMahon (2005, pp. 19, 22),

> so straightforward and non-technical that in the eyes of many historical linguists it scarcely qualifies as a method at all. As Wright (1991, pp. 55, 58) puts it 'First, forget all this stuff about rules of phonological correspondences. Second, forget all this stuff about reconstructing proto-languages. Third, write down words from a lot of different languages, look at them, and wait for similarities to leap out... Greenberg doesn't spell out criteria for deciding when two words correspond closely enough to qualify as a match. Greenberg himself may not need such pedantry; his intuitive sense for linguistic affinity is the subject of some renown. But other linguists may. And science is supposed to be a game anyone can play'.

which implies that what Greenberg did can neither be repeated nor tested.

Lexicostatistical methods are based on one dimension only: the similarities and supposed common roots of words in the vocabularies (the lexicon) of various languages. Languages can be related or similar, and these similarities can be explained by three mechanisms only. First, there may be words that look common for accidental reasons. This is so for onomatopoeic words. Second, languages may also borrow words from other languages belonging to another branch: English, for example, contains some 30 per cent of its lexicon borrowed from French after the Norman conquest in 1066 (and nowadays, French as well contains many English words). Third, two languages may descend from a common, older language.[12] This is the case for French, Italian, Spanish and Portuguese, which belong to the same branch, and have Latin as their ancestor.

Lexical distances are built on so-called *cognate* words, occurring in languages with a historical chain linking them via an earlier language, thus ignoring not only borrowings[13] and accidental similarities, but also syntax and grammar.

---

[12] Dyen et al. (1992) give the very poetic example of the word *flower* which is borrowed from the French *fleur*, while quite surprisingly, *blossom* and *fleur* descend from the same ancestral word.

[13] Ignoring borrowed words may rule out some factors that influence the closeness of two languages. The case of English and French is a good example. According to Janson (2002, pp. 157–158), 'around 90 per cent of the words in an English dictionary are of French, Latin or Greek origin'. This however does not make English closer to French, since 'if one counts words in a text or in a recording of speech [in English], the proportion of Germanic words is much higher, for they are the most frequent ones, while most of the loans that figure in a dictionary are learned, rare items'. The French linguist Hagège (2009, pp. 647–670) adds that English is particularly difficult to learn. He probably had in mind French speakers, but his remarks seem to be more general.

The reason is that linguists became (and still are) interested in constructing language trees, as well as estimating dates at which one language separated from another (glottochronology[14]).

Since it would be a formidable task to compare long lists of words for each couple of languages, linguists are forced to rely on a small selection of carefully chosen words, a so-called 'list of meanings'. Swadesh (1952) eventually introduced some rigour (Kessler, 2001, p. 31) in the choice of meanings that one can assume to be basic enough to exist in all languages and cultures (such as animal, bad, bite, black, child, die, eat, eye, hunt, numbers from *one* to *five*),[15] on which deductions can be based.[16] The list we are interested in consists of 200 basic meanings, which Swadesh later trimmed to 100. Both lists are still in use nowadays. See also Section 2.4.2 in Chapter 2, in this volume.

We examine in some detail the types of techniques used to compute linguistic distances which eventually are used to construct trees: (i) lexicostatistical distances; (ii) Levenshtein distances; (iii) distances based on linguistic trees; (iv) other methods.

5.3.1 Lexicostatistical distances

Dyen et al. (1992) used Swadesh's basic list of meanings to classify 84 Indo-European speech varieties. The conjecture that Aryan languages spoken in parts of India and European languages may have a common ancestor had already been made by William Jones, in 1786. See Gamkrelidze and Ivanov (1990), and also Ruhlen (1991), for a general overview. They describe the lexicostatistical method as consisting of four phases:

(a) Collecting for each of the meanings in Swadesh's list the words used in each speech variety under consideration.
(b) Making cognate decisions on each word in the lists for each pair of speech varieties, that is, deciding whether they have a common ancestral word, or not, or whether no clear-cut decision can be made; this phase is performed by linguists who know the language family.[17]

---

[14] The premises on which glottochronoly is based – in particular that the probability of a word losing its original meaning stays constant over time – are being questioned, and this area of research has fallen into some disrepute. See, however, Gray and Atkinson (2003), Searls (2003) and McMahon and McMahon (2005, pp. 177–204) for a recent revival of the concept.
[15] Note that Swadesh's list has been slightly changed to accommodate Southeast Asian and Australian languages.
[16] See Kessler (2001, pp. 199–257) for the lists of meanings chosen by Swadesh.
[17] See Warnow (1997) for further technical details.

(c) Calculating the lexicostatistical percentages, i.e. the percentages of cognates shared by each pair of lists; these percentages lie between one (if all words are cognate; actually, the largest number of cognates found by Dyen et al. was 154, leading to a percentage of 0.770) and zero (if there is no cognate).
(d) Partitioning the word lists into family trees; this is performed using one of the many existing clustering algorithms.

Table 5.1 gives an example of a list of words for the basic meanings of numbers one to five (which are part of Swadesh's 200 meanings) in 15 languages. This is essentially what is done in Step (a), usually for a much larger list of meanings and languages. In this table, the first four groups are Indo-European languages, which are themselves subdivided into Germanic, Romance, Celtic and Slavic subgroups. The two last consist of Hungarian, a language spoken in Europe, but that belongs to the Uralic and not to the Indo-European family and Swahili, one of the many Bantu languages spoken in Africa.

Steps (a) and (d) need no comments, though step (a) is not only time consuming, but difficult since the right choice has to be made among possible synonyms. We describe what is done in steps (b) and (c).

Table 5.1 Words for numbers 1 to 5 in some Indo-European languages, Hungarian and Swahili

	1	2	3	4	5
Danish	en	to	tre	fire	fem
Dutch	een	twee	drie	vier	vijf
English	one	two	three	four	five
German	eins	zwei	drei	vier	fünf
Swedish	en	två	tre	fyra	fem
French	un	deux	trois	quatre	cinq
Italian	uno	due	tre	quattro	cinque
Portuguese	um	dois	três	quatro	cinco
Spanish	uno	dos	tres	cuatro	cinco
Breton	unan	daou (m)	tri (m)	pevar (m)	pemp
Welsh	un	dau (m)	tri (m)	pedwar (m)	pump
Russian	odin	dva	tri	chetyre	piat'
Polish	jeden	dwa	trzy	czetry	pieć
Hungarian	egy	kettö	három	négy	ött
Swahili	moja	mbili	tatu	nne	tano

(m) is for masculine.

Step (b) is devoted to comparing words for every pair of languages.[18] This looks of course simple in Table 5.1, where languages are already grouped into families. The words in the first five languages (Danish, Dutch, English, German, Swedish) are all cognates, as the pairwise comparisons show. They all belong to the family of Germanic languages. The same can be verified for the next four languages (French, Italian, Portuguese, Spanish), which belong to the Romance family. The third group (Celtic) also has all five numbers that are cognate. But more importantly, the first three numbers in all three families can be seen to be cognates as well (and indeed, Germanic, Romance and Celtic language families are part of the larger family of Indo-European languages). Cognation decisions are less obvious and need more linguistic knowledge for the numbers four and five. Next come Slavic languages, which are very clearly related to each other and for which one also sees a relation of digits two and three with the previous groups, but this is less so for the other numbers. The words in the last two languages, Hungarian and Swahili, have little in common with those of the four families of Indo-European languages, but may nevertheless have a faraway ancestor (or Ur-language).[19] In general, cognate decisions need trained linguists,[20] as the following example, borrowed from Warnow (1997, p. 6586), shows. The Spanish word *mucho* has the same meaning as the English *much* and is obviously phonetically very similar. Sound change rules do, however, indicate that they *do not* come from a common ancestral word: *mucho* is derived from the Latin *multum* meaning *much*, while *much* is derived from the Old English *micel* meaning *big*.

Step (c) is easy once cognate decisions are made. It consists in counting the number of cognates for each pair of languages, and dividing it by the total number of meanings. If the only meanings to be compared were our five numbers, then the distances between each pair of the five Germanic languages would all be equal to 5/5. The same would be true for the pairwise distances within the two other families. Things get a little more difficult across the three families, since the words for digits four and five (compare the English *four* with the French *quatre* or the Brythonic *pedwar*) are certainly further apart. Assume

---

[18] It is not always possible to make a clear distinction between cognate and non-cognate; therefore, linguists usually add a third group of 'ambiguous decisions'.

[19] See Ruhlen (1994) for a deep but also entertaining exposition. He makes the reader construct the cognates and guess which languages belong to the same family. The book reads like a very good crime story, in which the detective is not looking for a criminal, but for the very first language.

[20] Though there are now efforts and experiments to computerize lexicostatistics. See McMahon and McMahon (2005, pp. 68–88).

that, as linguists, we decided to classify them as non-cognate. Then, the distance between, say English and French, would be 3/5. Finally, in our example the distance between any Indo-European language and Hungarian or Swahili would be equal to 0/5.

To present these percentages in the form of distances that economists are used to, the numbers given in Table 5.2 are equal to one minus the percentage of cognates. They concern the distances between 25 European languages[21] and the six European languages that are most spoken in the European Union: two are Germanic (English and German), three are Romance (French, Italian

Table 5.2   Distances between selected Indo-European languages (value times 1,000)

	English	French	German	Italian	Spanish	Polish
Albanian	883	878	870	877	883	871
Bulgarian	772	791	769	769	782	369
Catalan	777	286	764	236	270	784
Czech	759	769	741	753	760	234
Danish	407	759	293	737	750	749
Dutch	392	756	162	740	742	769
English	0	764	422	753	760	761
French	764	0	756	197	291	781
German	422	756	0	735	747	781
Greek	838	843	812	822	833	837
Icelandic	454	772	409	755	763	758
Italian	753	197	735	0	212	764
Latvian	803	793	800	782	794	668
Lithuanian	784	779	776	758	770	639
Norwegian	452	770	367	754	761	762
Polish	761	781	754	764	772	0
Portuguese	760	291	753	227	126	776
Romanian	773	421	751	340	406	784
Russian	758	778	755	761	769	266
Serbo-Croatian	766	772	764	755	768	320
Slovak	750	765	742	749	756	222
Slovene	751	782	733	760	772	367
Spanish	760	291	747	212	0	772
Swedish	411	756	305	741	747	763
Ukrainian	777	781	759	774	782	198

Source: Dyen et al. (1992, pp. 102–117).

---

[21] Basque, Estonian, Finnish, Hungarian and Turkish (spoken in Cyprus) are excluded, since they do not belong to the Indo-European family. The distances with Indo-European languages are set to 1 as an approximation.

and Spanish) and the last is Slavic (Polish). It is easy to check that Danish, Dutch, English, German, Icelandic, Norwegian and Swedish are related. So are the Romance languages Catalan, French, Italian, Portuguese, Romanian and Spanish, and the Slavic ones, Bulgarian, Czech, Russian, Serbo-Croatian, Slovak, Slovene, Ukrainian, Latvian and, to some extent, Lithuanian. Albanian and Greek are distant from any language belonging to the three previous families.

5.3.2   Levenshtein distances

In step (b) described in Section 5.3.1, knowledgeable linguists judge words (meanings) between two languages as being cognate (distance equal to zero), not cognate (distance equal to one) or ambiguous (and thus eliminated from the count). In step (c), the number of cognate words is computed and divided by the total number of words (minus the doubtful ones). The resulting number is considered to represent the distance between the two languages subject to the comparison. Levenshtein (1966) suggests an algorithm that enables measuring the distance between strings, for example those formed by words. The idea is to convert the word of one language into the word of the other one by inserting, deleting or substituting alphabetic (and phonetic, see below) characters; the minimal number of such transformations, divided by the maximum number of characters between the two words, is the Levenshtein – also called *edit* – distance between the two words.

As an example, let us consider the word *night*, one of those in Swadesh's 100 words list. The word is spelled *Nacht* in German and *notte* in Italian. A linguist would probably classify the words as cognate between all three languages. The Levenshtein distance between the English and the German words is two, since one needs to substitute *a* to *i* and *c* to *g*. The distance between English and Italian is four (substitute *o* for *i* and *t* for *g*; delete *h*; insert the final *e*). It so happens that the three words have the same number of characters. So the distance between the English and the German words is 2/5 while the one between the English and the Italian words is 4/5.[22] This is in accordance with our intuition: English and German are Germanic languages, while Italian is a Romance language, but all three are Indo-European.

The distance between two languages is now simply the average of the distances over all the meanings that are compared, and linguistic trees can be computed using clustering algorithms.

Computing Levenshtein distances is easy to program on a computer. This allows computing distances for a large number of languages, a tedious task in the case of lexicostatistical distances, which need decisions made by linguists.

---

[22] If the number of characters is not the same, one divides by the largest number of characters.

It may however lead to problems since obvious non-cognate words may be considered cognate by the computer. A nice example is the small Levenshtein distance of 1/6 between *kitten* and *mitten* which only needs the substitution of the first character in *kitten* by an *m*, though the words have little to do with each other. It is however less likely with Swadesh's 100 list, which compares words that have the same meaning in *different* languages.

5.3.3 Levenshtein phonetic distances

It should, however, be quite obvious that the similarities of characters in words is insufficient if these are spelled differently in the various languages that are analysed. This is especially true for vowels and diphthongs. Take for example the meaning *fire*, which is written *Feuer* in German. If the Levenshtein method discussed above is used, the distance is 3/5. But Levenshtein's method is usually performed by taking into account phonetic similarities by transcribing the words into their phonetic equivalents, using existing or especially tailored phonetic alphabets.[23] Phonetically the words *fire* and *Feuer* differ only through the English *i* and the German diphthong *eu* (which in English sounds like the /oi/ in the word *boiling*). The phonetic distance would be smaller, since the remainder of the two words is (roughly) pronounced in the same way. Another totally different phonetic approach based on speech sound will be discussed in Section 5.3.6.

5.3.4 Cladistic distances

An alternative way of computing linguistic distances is to utilize linguistic tree diagrams, based on world classifications of languages such as *Ethnologue* and compute cladistic distances. These have two advantages over lexicostatistical distances: they account for various aspects that characterize languages, such as lexicon, syntax, phonology, grammar, and are available for almost all languages in the world. As will be seen, however, they are less precise than lexical distances.

Fearon and Laitin (1999), Laitin (2000) and Fearon (2003) who suggested this approach[24] use the distances between linguistic tree branches as a proxy for distances between linguistic groups. In the original Fearon and Laitin (1999) index, the score takes the level of the first branch at which the languages break off from each other for every pair of languages. The higher the number, the higher the similarity of languages. The approach was later followed by many researchers.

---

[23] See Sections 5.3.4 and 5.3.6.
[24] According to McMahon and McMahon (2005, p. 125), a similar method had been suggested some years earlier by Poloni et al. (1997).

We use the (simplified) Indo-European language tree of Table 5.3 to calculate such distances for some languages.[25] Czech and Hungarian come from structurally unrelated linguistic families: Czech is an Indo-European language, while Hungarian belongs to the Uralic family. Therefore, the two languages share no common branches and break off on the first branch: their score is 1. Czech and

Table 5.3   Simplified Indo-European language tree

0. Ur-language
  1. Eurasiatic
    2. Uralic-Yukaghirc
      ...**Hungarian**
    2. Indo-European
      3. Germanic
      3. Italic
        4. Romance
          5. Italo-Western
            6. Italo-Dalmatian
              7. Italian
      3. Slavic
        4. East
          5. Belarusan
          5. Russian
          5. Ukrainian
        4. West
          5. Czech-Slovak
            6. Czech
            6. Slovak
          5. Lechitic
            6. Polish
      3. Albanian
      3. Armenian
      3. Baltic
      3. Celtic
      3. Greek
      3. Indo-Iranian
  ...

Note: Details are given for the languages used in the text only (Hungarian, Italian, Russian, Czech, Slovak and Polish, in bold) to illustrate the calculation of distances.
Source: The upper part of the tree in the first part of the table is based on Greenberg (2000, pp. 279–281). The tree for Indo-European languages is constructed using *Ethnologue*'s website, starting with the root at www.ethnologue.com/subgroups/indo-european, and then following the various branches.

---

[25] Though Indo-European languages were among the first to be discussed and represented under the form of a tree, this is now so for all the world's languages. For other families, see http://linguistic.org/multitree and click on 'Go to the MultiTree Browser'.

Italian share one common level since they are both Indo-European, but separate immediately after that, making their score equal to 2. Czech and Russian share two classifications: they are both Indo-European and Slavic, and break off on the third branch, as Russian belongs to the Eastern branch of the Slavic group, while Czech is part of the Western branch. Thus, their score is 3. Czech and Polish share three common levels: in addition to being Indo-European and Slavic, both belong to the Western branch of the Slavic group, and their score is 4. Finally, Czech and Slovak belong to the Czech-Slovak sub-branch of the Western branch of the Slavic group, which sets their score at 5. In order to produce linguistic distances the similarity measure r_{ij} between languages i and j is first normalized to fit the interval $[0, 1]$. For a break on the first branch, $r = 0$, for a break on the second branch, $r = 0.2$, for a break on the third branch, $r = 0.4$, for a break on the fourth branch, $r = 0.6$, for a break on the fifth branch, $r = 0.8$, and for identical languages, $r = 1$ (Laitin, 2000, p. 148). The linguistic distance d is then simply equal to $d = 1 - r$.

Fearon (2003) produces a dataset for 822 ethnic groups in 160 countries. However, he points out that an early break-off between two languages in such a tree generates a higher degree of dissimilarity than later break-offs. Therefore, the resemblance function r_{ij} should increase at a lower rate for larger values of distance. To sustain this feature, in his derivation Fearon utilizes the square root of linguistic distances, rather than distances themselves.[26]

5.3.5 Phonetic distances

There also exist methods that use *phonetic* similarities. One group of such methods, which carries the name of *dialectometry*, computes distances between the elements of a word in two different languages, often using the Levenshtein distance. This approach was pioneered by Goebl (1982) and Kessler (1995) for Irish dialects, and by Nerbonne and Heeringa (1997) for Dutch dialects. See Nerbonne and Heeringa (1997).

According to McMahon and McMahon (2005, pp. 212–214), the technique may work for dialects, but it would 'compromise the method if it were extended to comparisons between languages or across considerable spans of time, since it would then be more likely that changes in the order of segments [within words] would have taken place'. They give the example of the words *bridde* and *friste* in Middle English, which become *bird* and *first* in Modern English. There are other similar issues that would make the use of Levenshtein distances inappropriate. They suggest adaptations that can be found in Heggarty et al. (2005). See also McMahon and McMahon (2005, pp. 214–239).

---

[26] A variant of Fearon's formalization is used by Desmet et al. (2009).

A different approach of phonetics is considered by the Functional Phylogenies Group, in which linguists, phoneticians, statisticians, mathematicians, palaeontologists and an engineer in aeronautics work together and analyse phonetic sound properties 'that include pulse, intensity, sound wave components, spectrum, and/or duration of the examined sound segment, as well as fundamental frequency, [which is what the] listener identifies as pitch, and relates to how fast the vocal folds of the speaker vibrate during speech' (Hadjipantelis et al., 2012, p. 4652) as well as speech sound evolution. Speech sounds are treated as (continuous) functions (instead of discrete points) that are studied using statistical methods (such as principal components, Aston et al., 2010, and regression models). The group hopes to construct cladistic trees. Aston et al. (2012) give an example of how the meaning of the number 100 in Latin (centum) later separated between Italian (cento), on the one hand, and Spanish and French, on the other. Then the second branch consisting of Spanish and French split into Spanish (cien) and French (cent).

5.3.6   Adding typology to lexicostatistics: The ASJP project

A group of linguists associated with the Automated Similarity Judgment Program (ASJP)[27] combines lexicostatistics (using a subset of 40 words from Swadesh's 100 words list) with 85 phonological, grammatical and lexical structures described in Dryer and Haspelmath's (2013) *World Atlas of Language Structures* (WALS). ASJP transcribes the meanings using 41 different symbols (seven vowels and 34 consonants). It relies on Levenshtein distances.

5.3.7   Distances based on learning scores

The approaches described so far all belong to historical linguistics: they are not much interested in throwing light on current intercommunication between populations today. But they have served many other purposes, and their connection with genetics, migration patterns and archeology are of particular importance.[28] On the contrary, and as we shall see in Section 5.4, economists are interested in today's world and to what makes trades, migrations or translations easier.

Given the difficulty or the relative arbitrariness of representing the distance between two languages by a unique encompassing number or giving weights to different characteristics of languages and aggregate them (as is done in the ASJP project), the 'best' method (which takes into account all characteristics, as well as borrowed words) would be to follow the speed of the progress made by

---

[27] See http://email.eva.mpg.de/ wichmann/ASJPHomePage.htm for the aims of the programme, the database and a list of publications.
[28] See Cavalli-Sforza (1997, 2000), Cavalli-Sforza and Cavalli-Sforza (1995), Cavalli-Sforza et al. (1994), Renfrew (1987) and Michalopoulos (2012) among many others.

people who learn languages, and measure their proficiency in some objective way and at different moments during and at the end of their learning period. Such a measure was established by Hart-Gonzalez and Lindemann (1993) using a sample of native Americans who were taught a variety of languages. Chiswick and Miller (2007a) suggested that this measure could be positively correlated with the difficulty of inter-comprehension, and used the scores as distances between American English and some other languages spoken by immigrants. The scores vary between 1 for difficult (Japanese and Korean) to 3 for easy (Afrikaans, Norwegian, Romanian, Swedish).[29] Table 5.4 contains the full set of scores, some of which look quite surprising.[30]

If such distances were available for a large number of language pairs (and measured according to the same criteria), they would certainly be a very good alternative to the distances discussed in Sections 5.3.1 to 5.3.6 for three reasons at least. First, they encompass most of the difficulties encountered in acquiring a language. Second, scores would not necessarily be symmetric (as is the case for all other methods), since learning language A for a native speaker of B may be more difficult than learning B for a native speaker of A. Finally, borrowed words would also find their place, in possibly easing the learning of the other language. To our knowledge, this is the only set of consistent data on learning, and one can hardly imagine the amount of money, time and effort it would

Table 5.4 Scores of foreign students learning English

Score	Language of origin
3.00	Afrikaans, Norwegian, Romanian, Swedish
2.75	Dutch, Malay, Swahili
2.50	French, Italian, Portuguese
2.25	Danish, German, Spanish, Russian
2.00	Amharic, Bulgarian, Cambodian, Czech, Dari, Farsi, Finnish, Hebrew, Hungarian, Indonesian, Mongolian, Polish, Serbo-Croatian, Tagalog, Thai, Turkish
1.75	Bengali, Burmese, Greek, Hindi, Nepali, Sinhala
1.50	Arabic, Lao, Mandarin, Vietnamese
1.25	Cantonese
1.00	Japanese, Korean

Source: Chiswick and Miller (2007a, p. 578).

---

[29] This distance is used in two papers by Chiswick and Miller (2007b, Chapter 1), as well as by Hutchinson (2003) and Ku and Zussman (2010).

[30] Swahili, a Bantu language essentially used in Eastern Africa, is closer (that is, easier to learn) for an American than German or French. One can, therefore, wonder whether scores are calculated 'all other things being equal', and on a sufficient number of observations.

take to set up a coordinated project that would use this method, even if it were implemented only for the 2,450 combinations of the world's 50 most important languages.

5.3.8 Problems in using distances

The distance between British and American English is close to zero, if not zero, whatever the method used to measure it. This of course can raise eyebrows. There is a large (and ever increasing) number of meanings that are represented by different words in the United States and Great Britain, and it gets even worse with languages such as 'Spanglish' in the United States, 'Konglish' (spoken by an older generation in South Korea), or 'Globish' everywhere.

The phenomenon is obviously not limited to English. There are quite substantial differences between the German spoken in Germany and in Austria and there even exist Austrian-German dictionaries.[31]

The main problem is of course due to words borrowed in one language from other languages, which are often not accounted for as reported above, but nevertheless facilitate somewhat reading and learning, even if other dimensions such as grammar or pronunciation are different. Still, as we shall see now, 'historical' distances appear to significantly affect economic outcomes, and, even if they have defects, seem to be a good approximation of the differences between contemporary tongues.

A further restriction is symmetry, which implies that the degree of difficulty experienced by a Spaniard to learn Portuguese is the same as the one experienced by a Portuguese to learn Spanish. This is probably true as far as vocabulary is concerned. However, given that Portuguese phonetics are richer than Spanish phonetics, it may be easier for a Portuguese to learn Spanish than the other way round.

5.4 The effects of linguistic distances on economic outcomes

The linguistic distances discussed in the previous section have important applications and economists have shown that they significantly matter in many fields, such as international (and even national) trade, migrations, translations of literary books and language acquisition.[32]

Several applications using inter-country linguistic differences (trade, migrations, translations) are based on what is known as the 'gravity model', whose

---

[31] See, e.g., www.dictionaryquotes.com/quotations-subject/454/Language.php for a partial, but by no means exhaustive, list of more than 250 meanings represented by different words in Austria and Germany.

[32] Intra-country differences and fractionalization aspects of linguistic diversity are examined in Sections 5.5 and 5.6.

name comes from its analogy with Newton's 1687 Law of Universal Gravitation which postulates that any two objects in the universe exert gravitational attraction on each other with a force, denoted f_{AB}, that is proportional to the product of their masses, m_A and m_B, and inversely proportional to (the square of) the distance d_{AB} that separates the two objects. Distance thus has a negative effect on the attraction force.

Hägerstrand was probably the first (in 1957) to transpose this law and apply it to migrational flows in Sweden.[33]

But it was Tinbergen (1962) who made the model known by suggesting that it could be applied to study international trade flows between various countries. Now, the force f_{AB} represents the volume of exports from country A to country B, m_A and m_B are GDPs and d_{AB} is the geographic distance usually between the capitals of the two countries A and B. Distances can be more generally thought of as costs and impediments to trade and migration.

The gravitational equation became very popular, and fitted the data very well. In addition to trade and migrations, it was also used to explain the flows of translations of patents and literature.[34] Details on using distances are discussed in this volume: Chapter 9 for trade, Chapter 12 for migrations,[35] Chapter 14 for translations of patents and Chapter 20 for learning languages. Chapter 13 alludes to distances[36] in their discussion of translations of literary works.

5.5 Linguistic distances between groups

The linguistic distance between two distinct population groups, such as countries, is different from the distance between languages, independently of where they are spoken.

A simple approach is to consider the distance as a dichotomous variable which takes the value 0 if the same language is used 'extensively' in both countries (as is the case between Austria and Germany), and 1 otherwise.[37]

An alternative is to estimate the likelihood that citizens in two countries can speak a common language as reflected by Greenberg's (1956) H index of communication in a multilingual society. Actually, Greenberg rediscovered an index that had already been proposed a long time ago by Gini (1912/1955),

---

[33] According to Kerswill (2006, p. 4), who himself quotes it from a book by Lewis (1984).

[34] There are applications of the gravitational equation in other fields, e.g. explanations of flows of money laundering (Walker, 2000).

[35] Adserà and Pytliková (2015) construct a new linguistic proximity measure, based on information from *Ethnologue*. The measure takes into account how many levels of the linguistic family tree the languages of both the destination and the source countries share.

[36] Used by Ginsburgh et al. (2011).

[37] This 'rough' approach can be refined. See, e.g., Melitz (2008), who replaces the notion of 'extensive' by 'widely spoken' if at least 20 per cent of the population know the language.

but was the first to use it in the context of linguistic diversity. This estimate is determined by the probability that two members of the population chosen at random will have at least one language in common.

In order to illustrate the derivation of the index, consider a two-country case, say Germany and France. The communication distance between Germany and France is defined as the probability that a randomly chosen pair of French and German citizens speak no common language and are unable to communicate. Assume that all French and German citizens speak the language of their country, but in addition, 20 per cent of Frenchmen speak German and 25 per cent of Germans speak French; no other language is spoken. A French and German citizen will be unable to communicate only if they are both unilingual. Since 80 per cent of Frenchmen and 75 per cent of Germans are unilingual, the probability that they cannot understand each other is equal to $0.80 \times 0.75 = 0.60$.

The situation is more complicated if some Germans and Frenchmen can also communicate in, say, English. Now the French population consists of four groups: 70 per cent are unilingual, 15 per cent speak French and German, 10 per cent speak French and English, and 5 per cent speak all three languages; in Germany 60 per cent are unilingual, 15 per cent speak German and French, 15 per cent speak German and English, and 10 per cent speak all three languages. For communication between a Frenchman and a German to fail, we need at least one of them to be unilingual. Indeed, if both speak at least two languages, they will share a common language. Thus, 70 per cent of unilingual Frenchmen cannot communicate with 75 per cent of Germans (those who do not speak French). However, we need also to account for a possible interaction between 60 per cent of unilingual Germans and 10 per cent of Frenchmen who speak French and English, which is not covered by the previous case. The total percentage of those pairs of French and German citizens unable to communicate is therefore $0.70 \times 0.75 + 0.60 \times 0.10 = 0.585$.

A variant of such an index in a multi-country setting, the so-called Direct Communication Index, is obtained by adding the products of the respective percentages of speakers over all relevant languages. See Melitz (2008).

Lieberson (1964, 1969) used Greenberg's approach to evaluate the degree of communication between distinct linguistic communities. He calculated distances between three large East Coast Canadian cities, Toronto, Montreal and Ottawa. Such distances are also used in international trade and migration models.

5.6   Fractionalization and disenfranchisement indices

While the H index discussed above is based on the communication structure of a diverse society, most studies on societal diversity in economics and other disciplines focus on identification and measurement of diversity. We will distinguish two main types of indices: *fractionalization* and *disenfranchisement* indices.

Fractionalization indices, based on a partition of the society into distinct (ethno)linguistic groups, allow conducting cross-country or cross-regional comparisons and examining differences in various economic and political systems, institutions and outcomes influenced by linguistic diversity.

Disenfranchisement indices are related to the notion of linguistic disenfranchisement caused by government policies. A society (country) may have to or wish to 'standardize', that is, reduce the multilingualism that prevails and choose a set of official languages that will be used for administrative, legal and educational purposes, and 'discard' other languages that are also spoken in the country. To analyse in a rigorous way the potential impact of such policies that unavoidably create 'disenfranchised communities' requires a quantitative evaluation of disenfranchisement.

Note that there exists another important difference between fractionalization and disenfranchisement indices. In the first case, we examine and test the role of linguistic fractionalization in explaining various empirical phenomena. In the second case, we derive implications of disenfranchisement indices themselves, whose interest depends entirely upon the faith we place in the indices to judge which languages should be maintained, if one considers reducing the number of 'official' languages in a country or a region.

In evaluating both linguistic fractionalization and disenfranchisement, one has to recognize that there are distinctive languages that identify the members of a given society. The presence of different attributes generates a partition of this society into *groups* distinguished by their linguistic characteristics. For simplicity, we assume that each group speaks its own native language only. This assumption is obviously somewhat restrictive. As Laitin (2000, p. 143) points out: 'people have multiple ethnic heritages, and they can call upon different elements of those heritages at different times. Similarly, many people throughout the world have complex linguistic repertoires, and can communicate quite effectively across a range of apparently diverse cultural zones'. Meanwhile, some groups speak languages that are close (say, Venetian and Italian), other groups do not (Turkish and Greek). Therefore, distances also matter and should be taken into account when measuring diversity.

The most widely used dataset of worldwide ethnolinguistic fractionalization was constructed by a group of about 70 Soviet ethnographers from the Miklukho-Maklai Research Institute in Moscow, which was part of the Department of Geodesy and Cartography at the USSR State Geological Committee (Atlas Narodov Mira, 1964). Their country-by-country construction, widely known as ELF (Ethnolingistic Fractionalization), is based mainly on linguistic and historic origins of various groups. The findings of this remarkable and impressive project were introduced into the Western literature by Rustow (1967) and Taylor and Hudson (1972). The ELF dataset was expanded by Alesina et al. (2003), who disentangle the linguistic and ethnic aspects of fractionalization and construct separate datasets determined by linguistic, ethnic and religious affiliation. While the linguistic variable is calculated entirely on the basis of data from the 2001 edition of the *Encyclopedia Britannica*, the construction of the ethnic dataset necessitated using additional data from the CIA World Fact Book (2000), as well as Levinsohn (1998) and the Minority Rights Group International (1998). In summary, the impressive Alesina et al. datasets cover some 200 countries, 1,055 major linguistic groups and 650 ethnic groups. Alesina and Zhuravskaya (2008) went a step further and, using census data, extended the previous datasets to cover about 100 countries on a sub-national (regional) level. Desmet et al. (2009) construct an alternative dataset using cladistic distances based on *Ethnologue*'s trees.

5.6.1 Distance-weighted fractionalization indices

Formulation

Assume that the society consists of K distinct groups, where $s_1, \ldots, s_K$ represent the shares of the groups in the total population. Obviously, $\sum_{k=1}^{K} s_k = 1$. Denote by $d(k, l)$ the linguistic distance between groups k and l ($0 \le d(k, l) \le 1$), where $d(k, l)$ can be any of the types of distances discussed earlier in this chapter.

In his seminal paper Greenberg (1956) proposes a diversity index B that measures the average linguistic distance between two randomly chosen members of the society:[38]

$$B = \sum_{k=1}^{K} \sum_{l=1}^{K} s_k s_l d(k, l).$$

Desmet et al. (2009) suggest a variant in societies with a dominant group called 'centre'. In evaluating the total degree of diversity in such a centre-dominated society, their peripheral index PI takes into account the distances between the centre and peripheral groups only, but not those between peripheral groups themselves. The functional form of PI is similar to B, except that the distance between every pair of peripheral groups is zero. Thus, in a society with a central group whose population share is s_c, the PI index is written:

$$PI = s_c \sum_{k=1}^{K} s_k d(k, c).$$

This index is further refined by Akchurina et al. (2014) for the purpose of cross-country analysis. The term s_c is replaced by $DOM(c)$ in order to account

---

[38] See also Nei and Li (1979), Rao (1982), Ricotta and Szeidl (2006), Desmet et al. (2009) and Bossert et al. (2011).

for the influence and dominance of the centre with respect to peripheral groups that depend on their relative size and distribution of the population across different groups. This asymmetric treatment of groups is in line with Posner (2004) who argues that an appropriate index of diversity should distinguish groups on the basis of their involvement in political decisions (not all groups are equally involved or interested in all decisions: a rearrangement of higher education in Flanders is of no concern in French-speaking Belgium).

The majority of empirical and theoretical studies of diversity use a dichotomous distance between groups, where $d(k, l) = 1$ for any two distinct groups, and zero otherwise. It is easy to see that the B-index turns into a simpler expression called A-index by Greenberg:[39]

$$A = \sum_{k=1}^{K} \sum_{l=1}^{K} s_k s_l,$$

for all $k \neq l$. Given that $(\sum_{k=1}^{K} s_k)^2 = 1$, this index can (and is often) also be written:

$$A = 1 - \sum_{k=1}^{K} s_k^2.$$

Note that this index had already been introduced 100 years ago by Gini (1912) and that the expression $\sum_{k=1}^{K} s_k^2$ is the celebrated Hirschmann-Herfin-dahl Index (HHI) defined for an industry with K firms, where s_k stands for the market share of firm k.[40]

More than 30 years later, scholars across various disciplines almost simultaneously (and independently) addressed the issue of measuring diversity in their own field of research, re-establishing either the A-index itself or some closely related forms. In his one-page article Simpson (1949) produced what is now known as the Gini-Simpson index of biodiversity. A seminal contribution by Shannon (1948) also describes a diversity index, entropy, which influenced a large volume of research in information theory and statistics. It is given by the following expression:

$$E = - \sum_{k=1}^{K} s_k \log s_k.$$

---

[39] This index is often called ELF, which is somewhat misleading. What is usually called an ELF index in the literature is, in fact, the A-index applied to the so-called Ethno-Linguistic Fractionalization Soviet Atlas Narodov Mira (1964) dataset.

[40] HHI can be viewed as an indicator of the industry 'degree of monopolization' and is widely applied in competition and anti-trust law.

Both A and E represent special cases of the more general Hill (1973) diversity index:

$$HI = \left(\sum_{k=1}^{K} s_k^a\right)^{\frac{1}{1-a}}.$$

It can indeed be verified that for $a = 2$, the Hill index is equivalent to (has the same properties as) the A-index, though it has a slightly different form, while in the limit for $a = 1$, HI boils down to E.

Even though the A-index is the most often used 'size-based' diversity index in empirical studies, it is by no means exclusive. Fishman (1968) and Pool (1972) estimate linguistic homogeneity (the inverse of diversity) as the percentage of native speakers of the most widespread language in the country. Nettle (2000) uses the ratio between the number of languages spoken and total population. Gunnemark (1991) suggests computing the share (or the number) of members of each linguistic group for whom the language spoken at home is not the official or the country's most widely used language.

Applications

The indices described in the previous section are used in equations that explain the effect of fractionalization on economic or sociological outcomes y such as growth, redistribution, public good provision or corruption. The equation reads:

$$y = \gamma IND + \sum_k \xi_k z_k + \epsilon,$$

where γ and the ξ_k are parameters to be estimated, $z_k, k = 1, 2, \ldots, m$ are exogenous control variables, ϵ is an error term, and IND represents one of the indices described above. The parameter of interest is of course γ, since its sign indicates whether fractionalization has a *causal* positive or negative effect on y. Causality imposes, among other things, that IND is exogenous, which has often been disputed.

This follows Greenberg's (1956, p. 109) suggestion that such measures should be used to compare dissimilar geographical areas, and correlate (the term 'correlate' does not imply causality) the degree of linguistic diversity with political, economic, geographical, historical and other non-linguistic factors.

The program was first picked up by political scientists. Hibbs (1973) appeals to ethnolinguistic diversity in his study of mass political violence. The so-called Fishman-Pool hypothesis based on the works by Fishman (1968), Pool (1972) and Nettle (2000) (see also Chapter 17 in this volume) asserts that linguistic diversity has an impact on economic activities. Nettle (2000) points out that the index used by Fishman and Pool (the share of speakers of the most widespread language) does not fully account for the extent of multilingualism.

Alternatively, using Nettle's index (number of languages divided by the entire population) may lead to puzzling conclusions. Consider, for example, the impact of the break-up of the Soviet Union on linguistic diversity in Russia. The much smaller population of the Russian Federation speaks roughly the same number of languages as the one spoken in the former USSR. This results in a dramatic increase of the index, despite the fact that the relative share of the dominant group of Russian speakers in the Federation is much larger than in the USSR. The A and B indices discussed above avoid such problems.

Most papers (essentially written by economists) support the conclusion that linguistic fragmentation has a negative impact on economic development. Mauro (1995) argues that ethnic and linguistic fractionalization reduces institutional efficiency and increases the level of corruption generated by the lobbying activities of multiple groups. Easterly and Levine (1997), who coined the 'Africa's growth tragedy' expression, highlight the negative impact of diversity on economic growth. Alesina et al. (2003) and La Porta et al. (1999) claim that ethnic and linguistic fragmentation reduce the quality of governments. According to Alesina et al. (1999), ethnically fragmented communities run larger deficits and exhibit lower spending shares on basic public goods, including education. Annett (2001) points out that ethnic fractionalization leads to political instability and excessive government consumption that may, in turn, have a negative impact on growth. Alesina et al. (2012) show that the combination of linguistic diversity and economic inequality could be a cause of regional under-development.

While most papers summarized above use the A-index (with dichotomous linguistic distances), there are also several authors who have introduced one or the other linguistic distances described in Section 5.3. Their results are described in Chapters 6 and 15 in this volume. Introducing non-dichotomous linguistic distances, that is using B-type indices, seems to have a much stronger explanatory power, as shown by Desmet et al. (2009) in their study of the influence of ethnolinguistic diversity on redistribution within a country. Desmet et al. (2009) also incorporate linguistic distances in *polarization* indices introduced by Esteban and Ray (1994) to account for alienation between inter-group attitudes. The range of applications of polarization that relies on linguistic proximity of various groups is yet to be explored.[41]

But there are also examples where diversity could be a driving force for progress. Florida (2002) and Florida and Gates (2001) show that metropolitan regions with a higher degree of diversity in terms of education, cultural background, sexual orientation and country of origin correlate positively with

---

[41] Castaneda-Dower et al. (2014) extend the idea to dynamic polarization indices to study the link between polarization and the severity of the protracted conflict in Sri Lanka.

a higher level of economic development. Lian and O'Neal (1997) and Collier (2001) argue that more fractionalized societies could, under some conditions, perform in a better way than more homogeneous ones. A more diversified environment attracts creative individuals, ventures, businesses and capital. The success of Silicon Valley in the late 1990s is often attributed to the background of scientists, engineers and entrepreneurs who flocked to California from all corners of the world, including India, China, Taiwan and Israel: Saxenian (1999) points out that more than 30 per cent of businesses in Silicon Valley had an Asian-born co-founder. Diversity did not prevent and, in fact, even reinforced the commonality of worker's purpose and goals. Ottaviano and Peri (2005) investigate whether and how linguistic diversity affects wages rates in US cities and find that richer diversity is systematically associated with higher hourly wages.[42]

Linguistic diversity is thus treated as an exogenous variable determined by the static linguistic fabric of society and leaves aside the endogeneity issue created by previous changes of diversity over time and the effect this has on the estimation of parameter γ.

5.6.2 Distance-weighted disenfranchisement indices

Formulation

We now turn to measuring the degree of disenfranchisement (Ginsburgh and Weber, 2005) that voluntary restrictions of the number of languages may generate in a society.

Consider a multi-lingual society in which every member is characterized by his or her linguistic repertoire, represented by the languages he or she speaks. Assume that the society faces the problem of selecting a subset of languages (that will be called *core* languages in what follows) to be used in official documents, for communication between institutions and citizens, debates in official bodies, etc. Such restrictions may have a major negative impact on the wellbeing of some members by limiting their access to laws, rules and regulations and cause emotional pain and distress (see also Chapter 8 in this volume).

This makes us turn to the construction of disenfranchisement indices. We calculate disenfranchisement using two approaches. The first considers that individuals are attached to their native language only, which indeed eases their ability to read, write and communicate with others. They suffer if their native language is not included in the core set as it may also affect their sense of national pride and negatively impact on their involvement in the social, political and economic life of the society in which they live. The other alternative

---

[42] The innovative and creative aspect of diversity is also studied in theoretical papers by Lazear (1999).

assumes that multilingual citizens also care for languages that are part of their linguistic repertoire, and not only for their native language.

In order to compute disenfranchisement indices, and similarly to what is done for fractionalization indices, we need to identify:

(a) the functional form of the index;
(b) data on language proficiency (both native and acquired) of individuals in a given country, or group of countries;
(c) distances between languages.

Point (a) poses the challenging question to which theory has not yet provided a satisfactory answer: how should one aggregate individual feelings of disenfranchisement into a collective index? For simplicity, we use a linear aggregation mechanism by simply adding individual evaluations of disenfranchisement. If the sizes of linguistic communities are very unequal, one probably needs to make an adjustment for the differences by using a formulation close to the Penrose (1946) Law which introduces a discount factor for the weight of larger communities. As for (b) the data are usually provided by surveys or census information. Point (c) is discussed in Section 5.3.

Suppose that the set of core languages C is a subset of the entire linguistic menu of the country consisting of K languages. For every language k denote by $d(k, C)$ the minimal distance between language $k \in K$ and the languages in C. That is,

$$d(k, C) = \min_{l \in C} d(k, l),$$

where $d(k, l)$ is the linguistic distance between languages k and l. This leads us to the first disenfranchisement index:

$$DIS_B^n(C) = \sum_{k=1}^{K} s_k d(k, C),$$

where s_k is as before the share of the population that speaks language k. The index represents the average distance between native languages of all individuals and the set of core languages. This interpretation is similar to the one of Greenberg's index B, which explains the use of subscript B in the notation. Superscript n stands for native languages.

Instead of $d(k, C)$, one can also consider a dichotomous distance measure, in which case $d(k, C)$ is equal to zero if k is included in set C of core languages, and equal to one otherwise. This leads to a simplified version of the previous index:

$$DIS_A^n(C) = \sum_{k \notin C} s_k,$$

where summation is taken over all linguistic groups whose native language is not included in C. Again, subscript A is used since the formulation is close to Greenberg's A-index.

We now move to the other alternative that takes account of the entire linguistic repertoires instead of native languages only. Here we can no longer rely on the notion of linguistic groups identified by their unique native language since individuals with the same native language may speak different non-native languages. We thus need to identify the set of languages that every individual i speaks and partition each of the K linguistic groups into clusters of individuals with identical linguistic repertoires. As in our earlier discussion in Section 5.5 on communication distances with two languages, French and German, the group of French speakers can be divided into two clusters, unilingual French speakers and bilingual speakers of French and German. German speakers are divided into two clusters as well. Thus, in total, a society with two languages would consist of three clusters: unilingual French and unilingual German speakers, and all bilingual fellows.[43]

Denote the collection of all clusters in the society by Q, where for each cluster $q \in Q$, q identifies the set of languages spoken by the members of that cluster. We now need to define the distance between all linguistic clusters q and the set of core languages C by finding the shortest linguistic distance among all possible pairs of languages, when one language is in q and another is in C:

$$d(q, C) = \min_{k \in q, l \in C} d(k, l).$$

This leads to two additional disenfranchisement indices that are related to all languages spoken by individuals and not only to native ones. The first is:

$$DIS_B^a(C) = \sum_{q \in Q} s_q d(q, C),$$

where s_q denotes the population share of cluster q and superscript a stands for *all* languages and not only native ones and replaces superscript n used in the first index. $DIS_B^a(C)$ represents the average societal linguistic distance between the set of language spoken in the society and the set of core languages.

---

[43] If English is added, the population of French speakers can be divided into four clusters: unilingual French, bilingual French and German (who do not speak English), bilingual French and English (who do not speak German), and trilingual French, German and English speakers. A similar partition applies to German speakers, and in total there will exist six clusters: unilingual French and unilingual German speakers, bilingual French and German, bilingual French and English, bilingual German and English, and all trilingual speakers.

The second is a simplified version that obtains if we choose dichotomous distances. Here the distance $d(q, C)$ is equal to zero if there is at least one common language between the linguistic repertoire of the cluster q and the set C of core languages, and one if this intersection is empty, so that:

$$DIS_A^a (C) = \sum_q s_q,$$

where the summation is all over those clusters that have no common language with the set of core languages C.

Applications

These indices can be used to judge the impact on disenfranchisement of various choices of core (or official) languages. Fidrmuc et al. (2007) applied them to the case example of the European Union with its 23 (without Croatian) official languages that are supposed to be given equal treatment. Reality, in the Parliament as elsewhere, however, is different, as described by Wright (2007, 2009). It is therefore unavoidable that at some point the EU will have to consider (or admit that it decided to implement) a certain degree of linguistic standardization.

Fidrmuc et al. (2007) formulate a procedure for selecting subsets of languages among all eligible official languages in order to minimize the EU-wide disenfranchisement index, which measures the share of citizens (in the EU as a whole, but also in each member country) who would be unable to communicate under a particular restricted set of languages.[44] Data are based on a survey carried out in 2005 for all EU countries (Special Eurobarometer 243, 2006), including Bulgaria and Romania, that were candidates but not yet member states.

Using index $DIS_A^n(C)$, where each set C consists of a unique language for the seven most spoken languages in the EU results in showing that though English is, as expected, the most widely spoken language, it would nevertheless disenfranchise 62.6 per cent of EU citizens if it were the only core language; moreover, it would disenfranchise more than 50 per cent of the populations in 20 out of the 27 member states. Any other language (German, French, Italian, Spanish, Polish or Dutch) would do worse, both in the EU as a whole, and in most individual countries.

They also address the question of whether a subset of official languages could do better. The procedure used selects the sequence of subsets that minimize

---

[44] In their definition of disenfranchisement, a citizen is considered disenfranchised in a language (a) if he does not speak it (that is, if he does not cite it among the languages that he 'knows') or (b) if, when asked how proficient he is in a language that he 'knows', he responds that his knowledge is only basic.

disenfranchisement in the EU as a whole, for every given number of languages. Let m take the values $1, 2, 3, \ldots, 23$. Then, for every m, denote by T_m the subset of the 23 languages that minimizes the disenfranchisement index over all sets with m languages, ending up with a set T_m for every m between 1 and 23.

The results of these computations use index $DIS_A^a(C)$ where the sequence of sets C increases by one additional language at each step. The optimal one language set is English. For two languages, the optimal set contains English and German, and so on.

English is clearly the first language in any sequence as it is spoken well or very well by one-third of the EU population. German and French are in close race for the second position; German, with a 49.3 per cent disenfranchisement index, fares slightly better than French with 50.6 per cent one. The bundle of three languages leads to a disenfranchisement index of 37.8 per cent. Italian, Spanish or Polish would each make almost the same contribution to reducing disenfranchisement further. Spanish, in turn, performs only marginally better than Polish. With the six largest languages included, 16 per cent of the EU population would still remain disenfranchised. Adding Romanian brings the residual disenfranchisement index further down to 13 per cent. Of course, important differences across countries remain. The most dramatic case is Hungary, where only 16 per cent of the population can speak one of the first seven languages. Not surprisingly, Hungarian becomes the eighth language in the sequence. This also has a positive impact on Slovakia whose disenfranchisement index declines from 70 to 57 per cent. Portuguese is the ninth language, followed by Czech and Greek tied in tenth position.

Fidrmuc et al. (2007) also calculate a sequence of optimal sets based on the disenfranchisement indices of the youngest generation (15 to 29 years old) only. They show that German which was second to enter would be replaced by French. This is essentially due to the fact that among the younger generation in Germany and in Austria, 60 per cent of the population knows English, so that German becomes less necessary. Beyond the first three languages, the sequence is essentially the same as before. With ten languages, the disenfranchisement index that would prevail is 3.9 per cent. This percentage is even likely to decrease further as more and more children in upper secondary education study languages (essentially English, but to some extent, also French and German).

Table 5.5 reports results using index $DIS_B^a(C)$ (with lexicostatistical distances). In the single-language (English-only) scenario, accounting for linguistic proximity of other languages reduces the EU-wide disenfranchisement considerably, from 62.6 to 43.1 per cent. French which now comes in as second reduces disenfranchisement in all Romance-language countries, bringing the EU-wide index to 24 per cent. Polish enters as third. These are deviations with respect to the two sequences discussed earlier: French and Polish are ahead of German, which

Table 5.5 Disenfranchisement distance-adjusted indices in the EU: Optimal sequence of subsets of core languages

Number	1	2	3	4	5	6	7	8a	8b	9	10a	10b	10c
Languages	EN	FR	PL	GE	IT	HU	SP	GR	RO	GR& RO	CZ	FI	BG
Austria	23	23	23	0	0	0	0	0	0	0	0	0	0
Belgium	33	8	8	3	3	3	3	3	3	3	3	3	3
Bulgaria	64	62	29	28	28	28	28	28	28	28	20	33	2
Cyprus	41	40	40	39	39	39	39	0	39	0	0	0	0
Czech R.	59	58	19	16	16	15	15	15	15	15	0	14	14
Denmark	14	14	13	9	9	9	9	9	9	9	9	9	9
Estonia	60	60	35	34	34	28	28	28	28	28	15	11	15
Finland	65	65	65	64	64	45	45	45	45	45	45	0	45
France	60	0	0	0	0	0	0	0	0	0	0	0	0
Germany	26	26	24	0	0	0	0	0	0	0	0	0	0
Greece	55	54	53	50	50	50	50	0	50	0	0	0	0
Hungary	88	87	86	84	84	0	0	0	0	0	0	0	0
Ireland	1	1	1	1	1	1	1	1	1	1	1	1	1
Italy	57	15	15	14	1	1	1	1	1	1	1	1	1
Latvia	65	64	27	27	27	27	27	27	27	27	8	8	8
Lituania	64	64	27	26	26	26	26	26	26	26	13	13	13
Luxemburg	28	3	3	0	0	0	0	0	0	0	0	0	0
Malta	31	31	31	31	30	30	30	30	30	30	30	30	30
Netherlands	9	9	9	3	3	3	3	3	3	3	3	3	3
Poland	61	60	1	1	1	1	1	1	0	0	0	0	0
Portugal	64	24	24	24	18	18	10	10	10	10	10	10	10
Romania	66	35	35	34	28	26	25	25	1	1	1	1	1
Slovak R.	59	59	19	17	17	13	13	13	13	13	3	10	10
Slovenia	41	39	20	17	16	16	16	16	16	16	15	16	16
Spain	64	22	22	22	18	18	1	1	1	1	1	1	1
Sweden	14	14	14	10	10	10	10	10	10	10	10	10	10
UK	1	1	1	1	1	1	1	1	1	1	1	1	1
EU		43.1	24.0	16.6	11.4	9.0	6.9	5.2	4.0	4.1	2.9	2.1	2.1	2.1

Notes: One language is added to the previous ones in each column. In columns 8a, and 8b, two languages result in the same percentage reduction in disenfranchisement. In column 9, they are both added to the set. In columns 10a, 10b and 10c, three languages compete for the tenth place. Languages are abbreviated as follows: Bulgarian (BG), Czech (CZ), English (EN), French (FR), German (GE), Greek (GR), Finnish (FI), Hungarian (HU), Italian (IT), Spanish (SP), Polish (PL) and Romanian (RO).
Source: Fidrmuc et al. (2007).

is linguistically close to English. German and Italian, followed by Hungarian and Spanish. Finally, Greek ties with Romanian for the eighth position. Nine core languages would thus be sufficient to decrease (the distance-adjusted) disenfranchisement to 2.9 per cent.

Ginsburgh et al. (2005) take the examination of this issue a step further (though they used an older survey taken at a time when Poland was not yet a member of the EU). They look at optimal sets of official languages, which are determined by two parameters. One is the society's sensitivity towards language disenfranchisement of its members. The other is the degree of comprehensiveness of its *language regime*, which can take any intermediate form between the following two polar cases. Under *full interpretation* all documents and discussions in meetings are translated into all languages, whereas under *minimal interpretation*, all documents are translated into one core language. In practice, the language regime is chosen somewhere between these two extremes. The society's objective is, as above, to find a set of languages that minimizes a weighted sum of total EU disenfranchisement and costs. The weight attached to total disenfranchisement represents society's 'sensitivity' towards the linguistic concerns of its citizens. If the sensitivity parameter is high, then society cares about disenfranchisement of its citizens, and will implement a large number of (maybe even all) core languages. If sensitivity is low and cost considerations become more important, the society would shrink the set of core languages. They run simulations with different values of the weights given to the two parameters. These simulations show that it could be unwise to select English as the unique working language, not only because it is not always optimal, but also because it is optimal only for very small values of the weight which represents sensitivity to disenfranchisement. The best choice of three languages is English, French and German, though Italian could be a very reasonable substitute for French.[45] Spanish is obviously not a good choice within the Union if no account is taken of Mexico and Latin America, and its growing importance in the south and the west of the United States. The authors argue that it might be reasonable for the EU to adopt four working languages, three (English, French and German) for general use, while Spanish would be added for its importance in the rest of the world.[46]

The sequences of sets which minimize the EU's global index of disenfranchisement can be used to simulate the political feasibility of linguistic reforms and have the European Council (or the Parliament) casting votes on their preferred set.[47]

References

A. Adserà and M. Pytliková (2015) 'The Role of Languages in Shaping International Migration', *Economic Journal*, forthcoming.

D. Akchurina, D. Davydov, D. Krutikov, A. Khazanov and S. Weber (2014) 'Measurement of Diversity: Theory and Socio-Economic Applications', unpublished manuscript.

---

[45] The 2004 enlargement to countries of the former Eastern Bloc has improved the situation of German with respect to French.

[46] See also Pool (1996) for a different approach to the problem.

[47] See Fidrmuc et al. (2009).

A. Alesina, R. Baqir and W. Easterly (1999) 'Public Goods and Ethnic Divisions', *Quarterly Journal of Economics*, 114, 1243–1284.

A. Alesina, A. Devleeschouwer, W. Easterly, S. Kurlat and R. Wacziarg (2003) 'Fractionalization', *Journal of Economic Growth*, 8, 155–194.

A. Alesina, S. Michalopoulos and E. Papaioannou (2012) 'Ethnic Inequality', NBER Working Paper 18512.

A. Alesina and E. Zhuravskaya (2008) 'Segregation and the Quality of Government in a Cross-Section of Countries', NBER Working Paper 14316.

A. Annett (2001) 'Social Fractionalization, Political Instability, and the Size of the Government', *IMF Staff Papers*, 46, 561–592.

Q. Ashraf and O. Galor (2013) 'The "Out of Africa" Hypothesis, Human Genetic Diversity, and Comparative Economic Development', *American Economic Review*, 103, 1–46.

J. Aston, D. Buck, J. Coleman, C. Cotter, N. Jones, V. Macaulay, N. MacLeod, J. Moriarty and A. Nevins (2012) 'Phylogenetic Inference for Function-Valued Traits: Speech Sound Evolution', *Trends in Ecology and Evolution*, 2, 160–166.

J. Aston, J.-M. Chiou and J. Evans (2010) 'Linguistic Pitch Analysis Using Functional Principal Component Mixed Effect Models', *Journal of the Royal Statistical Society, Series C*, 59, 297–317.

Atlas Narodov Mira (1964) The Miklucho-Maklai Ethnological Institute at the Department of Geodesy and Cartography of the State Geological Committee of the Soviet Union.

M. Baker (2001) *The Atoms of Language* (Oshkosh, WI: Basic Books).

A. Bisin and T. Verdier (2000) 'Beyond the Melting Pot: Cultural Transmission, Marriage and the Evolution of Ethnic and Religious Traits', *Quarterly Journal of Economics*, 115, 955–988.

A. Bisin and T. Verdier (2014) 'Trade and Cultural Diversity' In V. Ginsburgh and D. Throsby (eds) *Handbooks in Economics: Art and Culture* (Amsterdam: Elsevier).

W. Bossert, C. d'Ambrosio and E. La Ferrara (2011) 'A Generalized Index of Fractionalization', *Economica*, 78, 723–750.

P. Castaneda-Dower, V. Ginsburgh and S. Weber (2014) 'Colonial Legacy, Polarization and Linguistic Disenfranchisement: The Case of the Sri Lankan War', manuscript.

L. Cavalli-Sforza (1997) 'Genes, Peoples and Languages', *Proceedings of the National Academy of Sciences of the USA*, 94, 7719–7724.

L. Cavalli-Sforza (2000) *Genes, Peoples, and Languages* (Berkeley, CA: University of California Press).

L. Cavalli-Sforza and F. Cavalli-Sforza (1995) *The Great Human Diasporas: The History of Diversity and Evolution* (Cambridge, MA: Perseus Books).

L. Cavalli-Sforza, P. Menozzi and A. Piazza (1994) *The History and Geography of Human Genes* (Princeton, NJ: Princeton University Press) (abridged edition).

B. Chiswick and P. Miller (2007a) 'Linguistic Distance: A Quantitative Measure of the Distance between English and other Languages' In B.Chiswick and P.Miller (eds) *The Economics of Language, International Analyses* (London and New York: Routledge).

B. Chiswick and P. Miller (2007b) *The Economics of Language, International Analyses* (London and New York: Routledge).

CIAWorld Fact Book (2000) available at www.cia.gov/news-information/pressreleases-statements/press-release-archive-2001/pr09182001.html

P. Collier (2001) 'Implications of Ethnic Diversity', *Economic Policy*, 16, 129–155.

K. Desmet, I. Ortuno-Ortín and R. Wacziarg (2009) 'The Political Economy of Ethnolinguistic Cleavages', NBER Working Paper 15360.

K. Desmet, I. Ortuno-Ortín and S.Weber (2009) 'Linguistic Diversity and Redistribution', *Journal of the European Economic Association*, 7, 1291–1318.

M. Dryer and M. Haspelmath (eds) (2013) *The World Atlas of Language Structures Online* (Leipzig: Max Planck Institute for Evolutionary Anthropology) (available online at http://wals.info, accessed on 27 July 2014.)

I. Dyen, J. Kruskal and P. Black (1992) 'An Indo-European Classification: A Lexicostatistical Experiment', *Transactions of the American Philosophical Society*, 82/5.

W. Easterly and R. Levine (1997) 'Africa's Growth Tragedy: Policies and Ethnic Divisions', *Quarterly Journal of Economics*, 112, 1203–1250.

J. Esteban and D. Ray (1994) 'On the Measurement of Polarization', *Econometrica*, 62, 819–851.

Ethnologue (2009) *Languages of the World*, M. Paul Lewis (ed.) (Dallas, TX: SIL International).

O. Falck, S. Heblich, A. Lameli and J. Södekum (2009) 'Dialects, Cultural Identity, and Economic Exchange', IZA Working Paper 4743.

J. Fearon (2003) 'Ethnic and Cultural Diversity by Country', *Journal of Economic Growth*, 8, 195–222.

J. Fearon and D. Laitin (1999) 'Weak States, Rough Terrain, and Large Ethnic Violence Since 1945', Paper Presented at the Annual Meetings of the American Political Science Association, Atlanta, GA.

J. Fidrmuc, V. Ginsburgh and S. Weber (2007) 'Ever Closer Union or Babylonian Discord? The Official-Language Problem in the European Union', CEPR Discussion Paper 6367.

J. Fidrmuc, V. Ginsburgh and S. Weber (2009) 'Voting on the Choice of Core Languages in the European Union', *European Journal of Political Economy*, 25, 56–62.

J. Fishman (1968) 'Some Contrasts between Linguistically Homogeneous and Linguistically Heterogeneous Polities' In J. Fishman, C. Ferguson and J. Dasgupta (eds) *Language Problems of Developing Nations* (New York: Wiley).

R. Florida (2002) *The Rise of the Creative Class: And How It's Transforming Work, Leisure, Community, and Everyday Life* (New York: Perseus Book Group).

R. Florida and G. Gates (2001) 'Technology and Tolerance: The Importance of Diversity to High-Tech Growth', Brookings Institute Discussion Paper.

T. Gamkrelidze and V. Ivanov (1990) 'The Early History of Indo-European Languages', *Scientific American*, March, 82–89.

C. Gini (1912/1955) 'Variabilità e mutabilità', Studi Economico-Giuridici della R. Universita di Cagliari, 3, 3–159. Reprinted in E. Pizetti and T. Salvemini (eds) *Memorie di metodologica statistica* (Roma: Libraria Eredi Virilio Vechi).

V. Ginsburgh, I. Ortuno-Ortin and S. Weber (2005) 'Disenfranchisement in Linguistically Diverse Societies. The Case of the European Union', *Journal of the European Economic Association*, 3, 946–964.

V. Ginsburgh and S. Weber (2005) 'Language Disenfranchisement in the European Union', *Journal of Common Market Studies*, 43, 273–286.

V. Ginsburgh and S. Weber (2011) *How Many Languages Do We Need? The Economics of Linguistic Diversity* (Princeton, NJ: Princeton University Press).

V. Ginsburgh, S. Weber and S. Weyers (2011) 'The Economics of Literary Translation: A Simple Theory and Evidence', *Poetics*, 39, 228–246.

H. Goebl (1982) 'Dialektometrie, Prinzipen und Methoden des Einsatzes der Numerischen Taxonomie im Bereich der Dialektgeographie' *Denkschriften der Österreichischen Akademie der Wissenschaften, philosophisch-historische Klasse*, 157, 1–123 (Wien: Verlag der Österreichischen Akademie der Wissenschaften).

R. Gray and Q. Atkinson (2003) 'Language-Tree Divergence Times Support the Anatolian Theory of Indo-European Origin', *Nature*, 426, 435–439.

J. Greenberg (1956) 'The Measurement of Linguistic Diversity', *Language*, 32, 109–115.

J. Greenberg (1987) *Language in the Americas* (Stanford, CA: Stanford University Press).

J. Greenberg (2000) *Indo-European and Its Closest Relatives* (Stanford, CA: Stanford University Press).

E. Gunnemark (1991) *Countries, Peoples, and Their Languages: The Linguistic Handbook* (Gothenburg, Sweden: Lanstryckeriet).

P. Hadjipantelis, J. Aston and J. Evans (2012) 'Characterizing Fundamental Frequency in Mandarin: A Functional Principal Component Approach Utilizing Mixed Effect Models', *Journal of the Acoustical Society of America*, 13, 4651–4664.

C. Hagège (2009) *Dictionnaire amoureux des langues* (Paris: Plon and Odile Jacob).

R. Harris (1993) *The Linguistic Wars* (Oxford: Oxford University Press).

L. Hart-Gonzalez and S. Lindemann (1993) 'Expected Achievement in Speaking Proficiency', Foreign Service Institute, U.S. Department of State: School of Language Studies.

P. Heggarty, A. McMahon and R. McMahon (2005) 'From Phonetic Similarity to Dialect Classification: A Principled Approach' In N. Delbecque, D. Geeraerts and J. van der Auwera (eds) *Perspectives in Variation: Sociolinguistic, Historical, Comparative* (Amsterdam: Mouton de Gruyter).

D. Hibbs (1973) *Mass Political Violence: A Cross-National Causal Analysis* (New York, NY: Wiley).

M. Hill (1973) 'Diversity and Evenness: A Unifying Notation and Its Consequences', *Ecology*, 54, 427–432.

W. Hutchinson (2003) 'Linguistic Distance as Determinant of Bilateral Trade', Working Paper 01-W30R, Department of Economics, Vanderbilt University.

T. Janson (2002) *Speak: A Short Story of Languages* (Oxford: Oxford University Press).

P. Kerswill (2006) 'Migration and Language' In K. Mattheier, U. Ammon and P. Trudgill (eds) *Sociolinguistics: An International Handbook of the Science of Language and Society* (Berlin: De Gruyter).

B. Kessler (1995) 'Computational Dialectology in Irish Gaelic' In *Proceedings of the 7th Conference of the European Chapter of the Association for Computational Linguistics* (Dublin: European Chapter of the Association for Computational Linguistics).

B. Kessler (2001) *The Significance of Word Lists* (Stanford, CA: Center for the Study of Language and Information).

D. Kibbee (2003) 'Language Policy and Linguistic Theory' In J. Maurais and M. Morris (eds) *Languages in a Globalising World* (Cambridge: Cambridge University Press).

H. Ku and A. Zussman (2010) 'The Role of English in International Trade', *Journal of Economic Behavior & Organization*, 75, 250–260.

P. Ladefoged and I. Maddieson (1996) *The Sounds of the World's Languages* (Oxford: Blackwell).

D. Laitin (2000) 'What Is a Language Community?', *American Journal of Political Science*, 44, 142–155.

R. La Porta, F. Lopez de Silanes, A. Shleifer and R. Vishny (1999) 'The Quality of Government', *Journal of Law, Economics and Organization*, 15, 222–279.

E. Lazear (1999) 'Globalization and the Market for Team-Mates', *Economic Journal*, 109, 15–40.

V. Levenshtein (1966) 'Binary Codes Capable of Correcting Deletions, Insertions, and Reversals', *Cybernetics and Control Theory*, 10, 707–710.

D. Levinsohn (1998) *Ethnic Groups Worldwide: A Ready Reference Handbook* (Phoenix: Oryx Press).

G. Lewis (1984) *Human Migration: A Geographical Perspective* (London: Croom Helm).

B. Lian and J. O'Neal (1997) 'Cultural Diversity and Economic Development: A Cross-National Study of 98 Countries, 1960–1985', *Economic Development and Cultural Change*, 46, 61–77.

S. Lieberson (1964) 'An Extension of Greenberg's Linguistic Diversity Measures', *Language*, 40, 526–531.

S. Lieberson (1969) 'Measuring Population Diversity', *American Sociological Review*, 34, 850–862.

P. Mauro (1995) 'Corruption and Growth', *The Quarterly Journal of Economics*, 110, 681–712.

A. McMahon and R. McMahon (2005) *Language Classification by Numbers* (Oxford: Oxford University Press).

J. McWorther (2001) *The Power of Babel* (New York, NY: Perennial Harper).

J. Melitz (2008) 'Language and Foreign Trade', *European Economic Review*, 52, 667–699.

S. Michalopoulos (2012) 'The Origins of Linguistic Diversity', *American Economic Review*, 102, 1508–1539.

Minority Rights Group International (1998) *World Directory of Minorities* (London: Minority Rights Group International).

L. Nakhleh, T. Warnow, D. Ringe and S. Evans (2005) 'A Comparison of Phylogenetic Reconstruction Methods of an Indo-European Dataset', *Transactions of the Philological Society*, 103, 171–192.

M. Nei and W.-H. Li (1979) 'Mathematical Model for Studying Genetic Variation in Terms of Restriction Endonucleases', *Proceedings of the US National Academy of Sciences*, 76, 5269–5273.

J. Nerbonne and W. Heeringa (1997) 'Measuring Dialect Difference Phonetically' In J. Coleman (ed.) *Workshop on Computational Phonology* (Madrid: Special Interest Group of the Association for Computational Linguistics).

D. Nettle (2000) 'Linguistic Fragmentation and the Wealth of Nations: The Fishman-Pool Hypothesis Reexamined', *Economic Development and Cultural Change*, 48, 335–348.

J. Nichols (2012) 'Monogenesis or Polygenesis: A Single Ancestral Language for all Humanity' In M. Tallerman and K. Gibson (eds) *The Oxford Handbook of Language Evolution* (Oxford: Oxford University Press).

G. Ottaviano and G. Peri (2005) 'Cities and Cultures', *Journal of Urban Economics*, 58, 304–337.

L. Penrose (1946) 'The Elementary Statistics of Majority Voting', *Journal of the Royal Statistical Society*, 109, 53–57.

E. Poloni, O. Semino, G. Passarino, S. Santachiara-Benerecetti, I. Dupanloup, A. Langaney and L. Excoffier (1997) 'Human Genetic Affinities for Y-Chromosome P49a,f: TaqI haplotypes Show Strong Correspondences with Linguistics', *American Journal of Human Genetics*, 61, 1015–1035.

J. Pool (1972) 'National Development and Language Diversity' In J. Fishman (ed.) *Advances in the Sociology of Language* (The Hague: Mouton).

J. Pool (1996) 'Optimal Language Regimes for the European Union', *International Journal of the Sociology of Languages*, 121, 159–179.

D. Posner (2004) 'Measuring Ethnic Fractionalization in Africa', *American Journal of Political Science*, 48, 849–863.

C. Rao (1982) 'Diversity and Dissimilarity Coefficients: A Unified Approach', *Theoretical Population Biology*, 21, 24–43.

C. Renfrew (1987) *Archeology and Language* (London: Jonathan Cape).

C. Ricotta and L. Szeidl (2006) 'Towards a Unified Approach to Diversity Measures: Bridging the Gap between the Shannon Diversity and Rao's Quadratic Entropy', *Theoretical Population Biology*, 70, 237–243.

M. Ruhlen (1991) *A Guide to World's Languages. Classification* (London: Edward Arnold).

M. Ruhlen (1994) *The Origin of Language* (New York: John Wiley and Sons).

D. Rustow (1967) *A World of Nations: Problems of Political Modernization* (Washington, DC: Brookings Institution).

A. Saxenian (1999) *Silicon Valley's New Immigrant Entrepreneurs* (San Francisco, CA: Public Policy Institute of California).

D. Searls (2003) 'Linguistics: Trees of Life and Language', *Nature*, 426, 391–392.

C. Shannon (1948) 'A Mathematical Theory of Communication', *Bell Systems Technical Journal*, 27, 379–423 and 623–656.

E. Simpson (1949) 'Measurement of Diversity', *Nature*, 163, 688.

I. Singh (2005) *The History of English* (London: Hodder Arnold Publications).

Special Eurobarometer 243 (2006) *Europeans and Their Languages* (Brussels: European Commission).

M. Swadesh (1952) 'Lexico-statistic Dating of Prehistoric Ethnic Contacts', *Proceedings of the American Philosophical Society*, 96, 121–137.

C. Taylor and M. Hudson (1972) *World Handbook of Social and Political Indicators* (Ann Arbor, MI: ICSPR).

J. Tinbergen (1962) *Shaping the World Economy: Suggestions for an International Economic Policy* (New York: The Twentieth Century Fund).

J. Walker (2000) 'Money Laundering: Quantifying International Patterns', *Australian Social Monitor*, 2, 139–147.

T. Warnow (1997) 'Mathematical Approaches to Comparative Linguistics', *Proceedings of the National Academy of Sciences of the USA*, 94, 6585–6590.

R. Wright (1991), 'Quest for the Mother Tongue', *Atlantic Monthly*, April, 36–68.

S. Wright (2007) 'English in the European Parliament: MEPs and Their Language Repertories', *Sociolinguistica*, 21, 151–165.

S. Wright (2009) 'The Elephant in the Room: Language Issues in the European Union', *European Journal of Language Policy*, 1, 93–119.

6
Ancestry, Language and Culture

Enrico Spolaore and Romain Wacziarg

6.1 Introduction

Populations that share a more recent common ancestry exchange goods, capital, innovations and technologies more intensively, but they also tend to fight more with each other.[1] Why does ancestral distance matter for these outcomes? In this chapter, we argue that when populations split apart and diverge over the long span of history their cultural traits also diverge. These cultural traits include language and religion but also a broader set of norms, values and attitudes that are transmitted intergenerationally and therefore display persistence over long stretches of time. In turn, these traits introduce barriers to interactions and communication between societies, in proportion to how far they have drifted from each other.

While the rate at which languages, religions and values diverge from each other over time varies across specific traits, we hypothesize and document a significant positive relationship between long-term relatedness between populations, measured by genetic distance, and a wide array of measures of cultural differences. In doing so, we provide support for the argument that the effect of genealogical relatedness on economic and political outcomes captures at least in part the effects of cultural distance. In sum, genetic relatedness is a summary measure for a wide array of cultural traits transmitted vertically across generations. These differences in vertically transmitted traits introduce horizontal barriers to human interactions.

We begin our chapter with a general discussion of measures of ancestral distance. We focus on genetic distance, a measure that has been used in a

---

[1] For recent references on technological transmission, see Spolaore and Wacziarg (2009, 2012, 2013). On interstate wars, see Spolaore and Wacziarg (2015). On trade and financial flows, the literature documenting links with linguistic and cultural distance is vast. Salient references include Melitz (2008), Melitz and Toubal (2012), Guiso et al. (2009) and Chapter 9 in this volume.

recent emerging literature on the deep roots of economic development. This measure captures how distant human societies are in terms of the frequency of neutral genes among them. It constitutes a molecular clock that allows us to characterize the degree of relatedness between human populations in terms of the number of generations that separate them from a common ancestor population. We next turn to measures of cultural differences. We consider three classes of such measures. The first is linguistic distance. Since these measures are described in great detail elsewhere in this volume, we keep our discussion brief.[2] The second class of measures is religious distance. We adopt an approach based on religious trees to characterize the distance between major world religions, and use these distances to calculate the religious distance between countries. Third, in the newest part of this chapter, we define and compute a series of measures of differences in values, norms and attitudes between countries, based on the World Values Survey (WVS). We show that these classes of measures are positively correlated between each other, yet the correlations among them are not large. This motivates the quest for a summary measure of cultural differences.

We next argue that genetic distance is such a summary measure. We start with a simple model linking genetic distance to cultural distance, providing a conceptual foundation for studying the relationship between relatedness and cultural distance. The model shows that if cultural traits are transmitted from parents to children with variation, then a greater ancestral distance between populations should on average be related with greater cultural distance. This relationship holds in expectations and not necessarily in each specific case (it is possible for two genealogically distant populations to end up with similar cultural traits), but our framework predicts a positive relationship between genetic distance and cultural distance. We next investigate empirically the links between genetic distance and the aforementioned metrics of cultural distance, shedding some light on their complex interrelationships. We find that genetic distance is positively correlated with linguistic and religious distance as well as with differences in values and attitudes across countries, and is therefore a plausible measure of the average distance between countries along these various dimensions jointly.

This chapter contributes to a growing empirical literature on the relationships between ancestry, language and culture over time and space. This literature has expanded in recent years to include not only work by anthropologists, linguists and population geneticists (such as, for instance, the classic contribution by Cavalli-Sforza et al., 1994), but also those of economists and other social scientists interested in the effects of such long-term variables on current economic, political and social outcomes (for general discussions, see for example Spolaore

---

[2] For instance, see Chapter 5 in this volume.

and Wacziarg, 2013, and chapters 3 and 4 in Ginsburgh and Weber, 2011). Economic studies using measures of genetic and cultural distances between populations to shed light on economic and political outcomes include our own work on the diffusion of development and innovations (Spolaore and Wacziarg, 2009, 2012, 2013), international wars (Spolaore and Wacziarg, 2015) and the fertility transition (Spolaore and Wacziarg, 2014). Other studies using related approaches include Guiso et al.'s (2009) investigation of cultural barriers to trade between European countries, Bai and Kung's (2011) study of Chinese relatedness, cross-strait relations and income differences, Gorodnichenko and Roland's (2011) investigation of the relation between culture and institutions, and Desmet et al.'s (2011) analysis of the relations between genetic and cultural distances and the stability of political borders in Europe.

This chapter is especially close to a section in the article by Desmet et al. (2011), where these authors provide an empirical analysis of the relationship between genetic distance and measures of cultural distance, using the World Values Survey. In particular, Desmet et al. (2011) find that European populations that are genetically closer give more similar answers to a broad set of 430 questions about norms, values and cultural characteristics included in the 2005 World Values Survey (WVS) sections on perceptions of life, family, religion and morals. They also find that the correlation between genetic distance and differences in cultural values remains positive and significant after controlling for linguistic and geographic distances. Our results here are consistent with their findings, but we use different empirical methods, a broader set of questions from all waves of the WVS, additional distances in linguistic and religious space, and a worldwide rather than European sample.

More broadly, this chapter is also connected to the evolutionary literature on cultural transmission of traits and preferences and the coevolution of genes and culture (e.g. Cavalli-Sforza and Feldman, 1981; Boyd and Richerson, 1985; Richerson and Boyd, 2004; Bell et al., 2009; and in economics Bisin and Verdier, 2000, 2001, 2010; Seabright, 2010; Bowles and Gintis, 2011), and to the growing empirical literature on the effects of specific genetic traits, measured at the molecular level, on economic, cultural and social outcomes.[3] However, as already mentioned, in our analysis we do not focus on the direct effects of inter-generationally transmitted traits subject to selection, but on general measures of ancestry based on neutral genes, which tend to change randomly over time and capture long-term relatedness across populations. Finally, our work is connected to a different but related set of contributions focusing on the economic and political effects of genetic and cultural diversity not between populations,

---

[3] For overviews and critical discussions, see for instance Beauchamp et al. (2011) and Benjamin et al. (2012).

but within populations and societies (Ashraf and Galor, 2013a, 2013b; Arbatli et al., 2013, Desmet et al., 2014).

This chapter is organized as follows. Section 6.2 addresses the measurement of ancestry using genetic distance. Section 6.3 discusses the constructions of each of our three classes of distances: linguistic, religious and values/norms/attitudes. Section 6.4 presents a simple theoretical framework linking genetic distance and distance in cultural traits. Section 6.5 reports patterns of correlations, both simple and partial, between genetic distance and cultural distance. Section 6.6 concludes.

6.2   Ancestry

6.2.1   Ancestry, relatedness and genetic markers

Who is related to whom? The biological foundation of relatedness is ancestry: two individuals are biologically related when one is the ancestor of the other, or both have common ancestors. Siblings are more closely related than first cousins because they have more recent common ancestors: their parents, rather than their grandparents. It is well known that genetic information can shed light on relatedness and common ancestry at the individual level. People inherit their DNA from their parents, and contemporary DNA testing can assess paternity and maternity with great accuracy. By the same token, genetic information can help reconstruct the relations between individuals and groups who share common ancestors much farther in the past.

From a long-term perspective, all humans are relatively close cousins, as we all descend from a small number of members of the species *Homo sapiens*, originating in Africa over 100,000 years ago. As humans moved to different regions and continents, they separated into different populations. Genetic information about current populations allows us to infer the relations among them and the overall history of humankind. Typically, people all over the world tend to share the same set of gene variants (alleles), but with different frequencies across different populations. Historically, this was first noticed with respect to blood groups. The four main blood groups are A, B, AB and O, and are the same across different populations. These observable groups (phenotypes) are the outcome of genetic transmission, involving three different variants (alleles) of the same gene: A, B, and O. Each individual receives one allele from each parent. For instance, A-group people may be so because they have received two copies of allele A (homozygotes) or because they have received a copy of allele A and one of allele O (heterozygotes). In contrast, O-group people can only be homozygotes (two O alleles), and AB-group people can only have an A from a parent and a B from the other parent.

By observing ABO blood groups, it is possible to infer the distribution of different alleles (A, B and O) in a given population. The frequencies of such alleles vary across populations. For example, one of the earliest studies of blood group differences across ethnic groups, conducted at the beginning of the 20th century and cited in Cavalli-Sforza et al. (1994, p. 18), found that the proportions of A and B alleles among the English were 46.4 per cent and 10.2 per cent respectively, were 45.6 per cent and 14.2 per cent among the French, while these proportions were 44.6 per cent and 25.2 per cent among the Turks and 30.7 per cent and 28.2 per cent among the Malagasy. It is reasonable to assume that these gene frequencies have varied mostly randomly over time, as an effect of *genetic drift*, the random changes in allele frequency from one generation to the next due to the finite sampling of which specific individuals and alleles end up contributing to the next generation. Under random drift, it is unlikely that the French and the English have ended up with similar distributions of those alleles just out of chance, and more likely that their distributions are similar because they share recent common ancestors. That is, they used to be part of the same population in relatively recent times. In contrast, the English and the Turks are likely to share common ancestors farther in the past, and the English and the Malagasys even farther down the generations.

Genetic information about ABO blood groups alone would be insufficient to determine the relationships among different populations. More information can be obtained by considering a larger range of *genetic markers*, that is, genes that change across individuals, and are therefore useful for studying their ancestry and relatedness. Blood groups belong to a larger set of classic genetic markers, which also include other blood-group systems (such as the RH and MN blood groups), variants of immunoglobulin (GM, KM, AM, etc.), variants of human lymphocyte antigens (HLA) and so on.

By considering a large number of classic genetic markers, pioneers in this area of human genetics, such as Cavalli-Sforza and his collaborators (e.g. see Cavalli-Sforza and Edwards, 1964; Cavalli-Sforza et al., 1994) were able to measure global genetic differences across populations, and to use such measures to infer how different populations have separated from each other over time and space. More recently, the great advances in DNA sequencing have allowed the direct study of *polymorphisms* (that is, genetic information that differs across individuals) at the molecular level. In particular, human genetic differences can now be studied directly by looking at instances of *single nucleotide polymorphism* or SNP (pronounced snip), a sequence variation in which a single DNA nucleotide – A, T, C or G – in the genome differs across individuals (e.g. Rosenberg et al., 2002; Seldin et al., 2006; Tian et al., 2009; Ralph and Coop, 2013).[4]

---

[4] A *haplogroup* is a group of similar haplotypes (collection of specific alleles) that share a common ancestor having the same SNP mutation. Among the most commonly studied

6.2.2 Genetic distance between human populations

Definition of F_{ST}

In order to capture global differences in gene frequencies between populations, geneticists have devised summary measures, called *genetic distances*. One of the most widely used measures of genetic distance, first suggested by Sewall Wright (1951), is called F_{ST}. In general, it can be defined as:

$$F_{ST} = \frac{V_p}{\bar{p}(1-\bar{p})}, \tag{1}$$

where V_p is the variance between gene frequencies across populations, and $\bar{p}$ their average gene frequencies.

For example, consider two populations (*a* and *b*) of equal size, and one *biallelic* gene, i.e. a gene that can take only two forms: allele 1 and allele 2. Let p_a and $q_a = 1 - p_a$ be the gene frequency of allele 1 and allele 2, respectively, in population *a*.[5] By the same token, p_b and $q_b = 1 - p_b$ are the gene frequency of allele 1 and allele 2, respectively, in population *b*. Without loss of generality, assume $p_a \geq p_b$ and define:

$$p_a \equiv \bar{p} + \sigma, \tag{2}$$

$$p_b = \bar{p} \quad \sigma, \tag{3}$$

where $\sigma \geq 0$. Then, we have:

$$F_{ST} = \frac{V_p}{\bar{p}(1-\bar{p})} = \frac{(p_a - \bar{p})^2 + (p_b - \bar{p})^2}{2\bar{p}(1-\bar{p})} = \frac{\sigma^2}{\bar{p}(1-\bar{p})}. \tag{4}$$

In general, $0 \leq F_{ST} \leq 1$. In particular, $F_{ST} = 0$ when the frequencies of the alleles are identical across populations ($\sigma = 0$), and $F_{ST} = 1$ when one population has only one allele and the other population has only the other allele – that is, when $\sigma = \bar{p}$. In that case, we say that the gene has reached *fixation* in each of the two populations – that is, there is no *heterozygosity* within each population.

---

human haplogroups are those passed only down the matrilineal line in the mitochondrial DNA (mtDNA) and those passed only in the patrilineal line in the Y-chromosome. While the analysis of the distribution of these specific haplogroups across populations is extremely informative to study the history of human evolution and human migrations, measures of overall genetic distance and relatedness between populations require the study of the whole genome. The measures of genetic distance that we discuss and use in the rest of this chapter capture this more comprehensive notion of relatedness between populations.

[5] Note that since $p_a + q_a = 1$ we also have $(p_a + q_a)^2 = p_a^2 + q_a^2 + 2p_a q_a = 1$.

In fact, F_{ST} is part of a broader class of measures called *fixation indices*, and can be reinterpreted in terms of a comparison between heterozygosity within each population and heterozygosity in the *sum* of the two populations.[6] The probability that two randomly selected alleles at the given locus are *identical* within the population (homozygosity) is $p_a^2 + q_a^2$, and the probability that they are different (heterozygosity) is:

$$h_a = 1 - \left(p_a^2 + q_a^2\right) = 2p_a q_a.$$ (5)

By the same token, heterozygosity in population b is:

$$h_b = 1 - \left(p_b^2 + q_b^2\right) = 2p_b q_b.$$ (6)

The average gene frequencies of allele 1 and 2 in the two populations are, respectively:

$$\bar{p} = \frac{p_a + p_b}{2},$$ (7)

and:

$$\bar{q} = \frac{q_a + q_b}{2} = 1 - \bar{p}.$$ (8)

Heterozygosity in the *sum* of the two populations is:

$$h = 1 - \left(\bar{p}^2 + \bar{q}^2\right) = 2\bar{p}\bar{q}.$$ (9)

Average heterozygosity is measured by:

$$h_m = \frac{h_a + h_b}{2}.$$ (10)

F_{ST} measures the variation in the gene frequencies of populations by comparing h and h_m:

$$F_{ST} = 1 - \frac{h_m}{h} = 1 - \frac{p_a q_a + p_b q_b}{2\bar{p}\bar{q}} = \frac{1}{4}\frac{(p_a - p_b)^2}{\bar{p}(1 - \bar{p})} = \frac{\sigma^2}{\bar{p}(1 - \bar{p})}.$$ (11)

In sum, if the two populations have identical allele frequencies ($p_a = p_b$), F_{ST} is zero. On the other hand, if the two populations are completely different at the

---

[6] More generally, the study of genetic distance between populations is part of the broader study of human genetic variation and diversity between and within populations. Interesting discussions of the economic effects of genetic diversity *within* populations and of the relationship between genetic and cultural diversity and fragmentation are provided in Ashraf and Galor (2013a, 2013b).

given locus ($p_a = 1$ and $p_b = 0$, or $p_a = 0$ and $p_b = 1$), F_{ST} takes value 1. In general, the higher the variation in the allele frequencies across the two populations, the higher is their F_{ST} distance. The formula can be extended to account for L alleles, S populations, different population sizes, and to adjust for sampling bias. The details of these generalizations are provided in Cavalli-Sforza et al. (1994, pp. 26–27).

Genetic distance and separation time

F_{ST} genetic distance has a very useful interpretation in terms of *separation time*, defined as the time since two populations shared their last common ancestors – that is, since they were the same population. Consider two populations whose ancestors were part of the same population t generations ago: t is the separation time between the two populations. Assume, for simplicity, that both populations have the same effective population size N.[7] Assume also that allele frequencies change over time only as the result of random genetic drift. Then it can be shown that:[8]

$$F_{ST} = 1 - e^{-\frac{t}{2N}}.$$ (12)

For a small F_{ST}, we can approximate it with $-\ln(1 - F_{ST})$, which implies that:

$$F_{ST} \simeq \frac{t}{2N}.$$ (13)

This means that the genetic distance between two cousin populations is roughly proportional to the time since the ancestors of the two populations split and formed separate populations. In this respect, we can therefore interpret genetic distance as a measure of the time since two populations shared a common ancestry.

Empirical estimates of genetic distance

In their landmark study *The History and Geography of Human Genes*, Cavalli-Sforza, Menozzi and Piazza (1994) provide some of the most detailed and comprehensive estimates of genetic distances between human populations, within and across continents. Their initial database contains 76,676 gene frequencies, corresponding to 6,633 samples in different locations. By culling and

---

[7] Effective population size only includes active breeders and is generally smaller than actual census size. More precisely, effective population size is the number of breeding individuals that would produce the actual sampling variance, or rate of inbreeding, if they bred in a way consistent with a series of idealized benchmark assumptions (e.g. see Falconer and Mackay, 1996, chapter 4, or Hamilton, 2009, chapter 3).

[8] See Cavalli-Sforza et al. (1994, p. 30 and references).

pooling such samples, they restrict their analysis to 491 populations. They focus on 'aboriginal populations that were at their present location at the end of the 15th century when the great European migrations began' (Cavalli-Sforza et al., 1994, p. 24). When studying genetic difference at the world level, the number is reduced to 42 representative populations, aggregating subpopulations characterized by a high level of genetic similarity. For these 42 populations, Cavalli-Sforza and coauthors report bilateral distances computed from 120 alleles.

Among this set of 42 world populations, the greatest genetic distance observed is between Mbuti Pygmies and Papua New Guineans, where the F_{ST} distance is 0.4573, while the smallest genetic distance (0.0021) is between the Danish and the English. When considering more disaggregated data for 26 European populations, the smallest genetic distance (0.0009) is between the Dutch and the Danes, and the largest (0.0667) is between the Lapps and the Sardinians. The mean genetic distance among the 861 available pairs in the world population is 0.1338. Figure 6.1 is a phylogenetic tree, constructed from genetic distance data, that visually shows how different human populations have split apart over time. The phylogenetic tree is constructed to maximize the correlation between Euclidian distances to common nodes (measured along the branches) and F_{ST} genetic distance computed from allele frequencies. Hence, the tree is a simplified summary of (but not a substitute for) the matrix of F_{ST} genetic distances between populations. Cavalli-Sforza et al. (1994) also calculated estimates of Nei's distance, which is a different measure of genetic distance between populations. While F_{ST} and Nei's distance have different analytical definitions and theoretical properties, they capture the same basic relationships, and their correlation is 93.9 per cent. Therefore, in the rest of this chapter we only use F_{ST} measures.

Cavalli-Sforza et al. (1994) provide genetic distance data at the population level, not at the country level. Therefore, economists and other social scientists interested in studying country-level data need to match populations to countries. In Spolaore and Wacziarg (2009), we did so using ethnic composition data by country from Alesina et al. (2003), who list 1,120 country-ethnic group categories. We matched ethnic group labels with population labels in Appendices 2 and 3 in Cavalli-Sforza et al. (1994). For instance, according to Alesina et al. (2003), India is composed of 72 per cent of 'Indo-Aryans' and 25 per cent 'Dravidians'. These groups were matched, respectively, to 'Indians' and 'Dravidians' (S.E. Indians) in Cavalli-Sforza et al. (1994). Another example is Italy, where the ethnic groups labelled 'Italians' and 'Rhaetians' (95.4 per cent of Italy's population) in Alesina et al. (2003) were matched to the genetic category 'Italian' in Cavalli-Sforza et al. (1994), and the 'Sardinians' ethnic group (2.7 per cent of Italy's population) was matched to the 'Sardinian' genetic group.

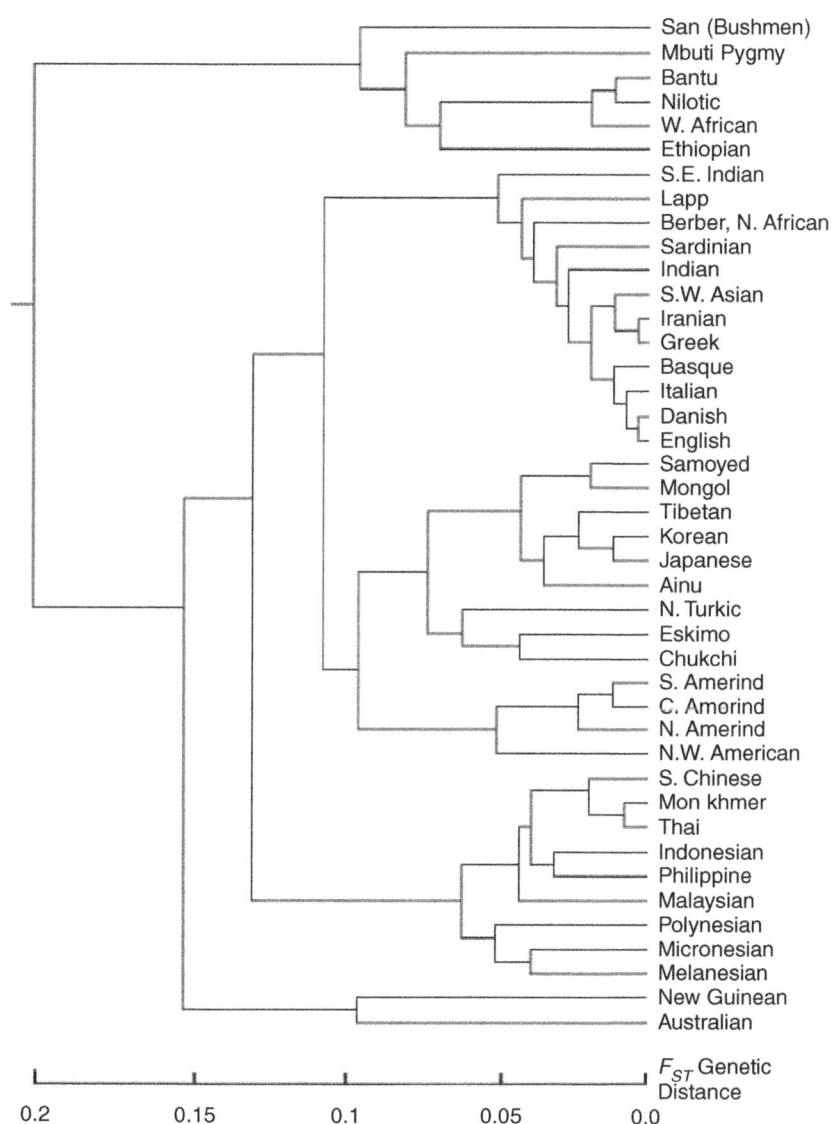

Figure 6.1 Genetic distance among 42 populations
Source: Cavalli-Sforza et al. (1994).

Using these matching rules, we constructed two measures of F_{ST} genetic distance between countries.[9] The first was the distance between the plurality ethnic groups of each country in a pair, i.e. the groups with the largest shares of each country's population. For instance, the plurality genetic distance between India and Italy is the genetic distance between the Indian genetic group and the Italian genetic group ($F_{ST} = 0.026$). This resulted in a dataset of 21,321 pairs of countries (207 underlying countries and dependencies) with available genetic distance data.[10] The second was a measure of weighted genetic distance. Many countries, such as the United States or Australia, are made up of sub-populations that are genetically distant, and for which both genetic distance data and data on the shares of each genetic group are available. Assume that country 1 contains populations $i = 1, \ldots, I$ and country 2 contains populations $j = 1, \ldots, J$ and denote by s_{1i} the share of population i in country 1 (similarly for country 2) and d_{ij} the genetic distance between populations i and j. The weighted F_{ST} genetic distance between countries 1 and 2 is then:

$$F_{ST}^W = \sum_{i=1}^{I} \sum_{j=1}^{J} \left(s_{1i} \times s_{2j} \times d_{ij} \right). \tag{14}$$

The interpretation of this measure is straightforward: it represents the expected genetic distance between two randomly selected individuals, one from each country.[11] Weighted genetic distance is very highly correlated with genetic distance based on dominant groups: the correlation is 93 per cent. In the rest of this chapter we will mostly use weighted F_{ST} distance, which is a more precise

---

[9] We also constructed genetic distance for populations as they were in 1500, based again on data from Cavalli-Sforza et al. (1994). For this variable, for instance, the United States is matched to the North Amerindian population. This measure of genetic distance in 1500 can either be used as an instrument for contemporary genetic distance (Spolaore and Wacziarg, 2009), or as an independent variable in applications that seek to explain pre-industrial economic outcomes (Spolaore and Wacziarg, 2013). However, we do not make use of this variable in this chapter, since we focus on the contemporary relationship between ancestry and culture.

[10] For 27 countries, the data on group shares was missing from Alesina et al.'s (2003) database, but a match to genetic groups based on plurality groups was possible through information from the *Encyclopedia Britannica*. Thus, our weighted measure of genetic distance covers 16,110 pairs, or 180 countries, whereas for the plurality match we have data on 21,321 pairs from 207 countries.

[11] Therefore, the weighted measure is not to be interpreted as F_{ST} genetic distance between the *whole* population of a country (say, all Australians) and the *whole* population of another country (say, all Americans), as if each country were formed by one randomly mating population (a *deme*). Instead, to each pair of individuals in each country is assigned their respective ancestrally inherited distance – that is, the distance corresponding to their respective ancestral groups – which may vary across individuals within each country when these countries are formed of different genetic groups.

measure of expected genetic distance between countries. Table 6.1 presents summary statistics for F_{ST} and F_{ST}^W.

6.3 Culture

To capture cultural distance we adopt a three-pronged approach. We first focus on a salient dimension of culture, language, likely to be strongly related with genetic distance because language, like genes, is transmitted from parents to children within populations, and because linguistic differentiation, like genetic differentiation, results over time from horizontal separation between populations. Religion is another salient characteristic of human societies, also transmitted intergenerationally with variations. Finally, in the most novel part of this chapter we use answers to the World Values Survey to construct broader metrics of distance in values, norms and attitudes. Jointly, these three classes of measures are referred to as *memetic distance*, by analogy with genetic distance, using a distinction between culturally transmitted traits (*memes*) and genetically transmitted traits (*genes*) that goes back to Dawkins (1976). We describe in turn the methods by which each of these measures was constructed, and provide descriptions of these variables, before turning to their interrelationships.

6.3.1 Linguistic distance

To capture linguistic distance, we employ two methods, one based on *language trees*, and the other based on *lexicostatistics*. These are arguably the most widely used in the social sciences, but there exist other types of measures of linguistic distance, discussed in Chapter 5 in this volume.

The classification of languages into trees is based on a methodology borrowed from *cladistics*. Linguists group languages into families based on perceived similarities between them.[12] For instance, in one commonly used classification of languages, from *Ethnologue*, French is classified as 'Indo-European – Italic – Romance – Italo-Western – Western – Gallo-Iberian – Gallo-Romance – Gallo-Rhaetian – Oil – Français'. Similarly, Italian is classified as 'Indo-European – Italic – Romance – Italo-Western – Italo-Dalmatian'. This can serve as the basis for characterizing the linguistic distance between French and Italian, because Italian shares four nodes with French. Variation in the number of common nodes corresponds to variation in linguistic distance. French and Italian, for instance, share no common nodes with non-Indo-European languages, and are therefore at a higher linguistic distance from them than they are with each other.

---

[12] For a further discussion of linguistic trees, see Chapters 15 and 5 in this volume.

Table 6.1 Simple summary statistics for measures of ancestral, linguistic and cultural distances

Variable	No. of pairs	No. of countries	Mean	Std. Dev.	Min	Max
Genetic distance						
F_{ST} distance, weighted	16,110	180	0.115	0.070	0.000	0.355
F_{ST} distance, plurality	21,321	207	0.117	0.081	0.000	0.338
Linguistic distance						
Tree-based linguistic distance, weighted	12,246	157	0.970	0.100	0.000	1.000
Tree-based linguistic distance, plurality	12,246	157	0.965	0.137	0.000	1.000
Cognate-based linguistic distance, weighted	1,953	63	0.599	0.268	0.000	0.918
Cognate-based linguistic distance, plurality	3,570	85	0.636	0.284	0.000	0.920
Religious distance						
Religious distance, weighted, Fearon	12,246	157	0.853	0.144	0.089	1.000
Religious distance, plurality, Fearon	12,246	157	0.786	0.313	0.000	1.000
Religious distance, weighted, WCD	19,306	197	0.747	0.163	0.127	0.997
Religious distance, plurality, WCD	19,306	197	0.628	0.358	0.000	1.000
Cultural distance based on the World Values Survey						
Overall cultural distance measure	2,701	74	0.000	33.015	−89.818	118.294
Category A: perceptions of life	2,701	74	0.000	12.110	−35.146	46.542
Category C: work	2,701	74	0.000	7.460	−14.102	37.550
Category D: family	2,701	74	0.000	3.436	−7.749	18.479
Category E: politics and society	2,701	74	0.000	11.872	−28.001	45.561
Category F: religion and morale	2,701	74	0.000	6.962	−13.140	26.975
Category G: national identity	2,701	74	0.000	1.967	−4.544	7.345
All binary questions	2,701	74	0.000	14.049	−36.103	57.345
All non-binary questions	2,701	74	0.000	21.911	−58.630	62.481

We use data from Fearon (2003), who assembled data on the prevalence of different languages for a large set of countries in the world from a variety of sources, and used the linguistic trees provided in *Ethnologue* to capture the distance between these languages. As we did with genetic distance, we compute two different measures: the number of common nodes between the two plurality languages of each country in a pair, *CN*, and the expected or weighted number of common nodes, CN^W. The latter exploits the fact that countries can be linguistically heterogeneous, and consists of computing the expected number of common linguistic nodes between two randomly chosen individuals, one from each country. More formally, for each country in a pair:

$$CN^W = \sum_{i=1}^{I} \sum_{j=1}^{J} \left(s_{1i} \times s_{2j} \times c_{ij} \right), \tag{15}$$

where s_{ki} is the share of linguistic group i in country k and c_{ij} is the number of common nodes between languages i and j.[13] Both *CN* and CN^W range from 0 to 15. From the two measures of linguistic proximity, following Fearon (2003) we use the following transformation to obtain corresponding measures of linguistic distance ranging from 0 to 1:

$$TLD = \sqrt{\frac{15 - CN}{15}}. \tag{16}$$

Here *TLD* refers to tree-based linguistic distance and we similarly define the weighted measures TLD^W by replacing *CN* with CN^W in Equation (16). The main advantage of this approach is that distances can be computed for a wide range of countries: we have 12,246 observations for *TLD* and TLD^W, from 157 underlying countries (Table 6.1 provides summary statistics). The drawback of tree-based measures is that linguistic distance is calculated on a discrete number of common nodes, which could be an imperfect measure of separation times between languages. A single split between two languages that occurred a long time ago would result in the same measure of distance than a more recent single split, but the languages in the first case may in fact be more distant than in the second. Similarly, numerous recent splits may result in two languages sharing few nodes, while a smaller number of very distant linguistic subdivisions could make distant languages seem close. This drawback justifies looking at an alternative measure.

---

[13] CN^W is, in fact, the *B*-index of Greenberg (1956), applied here to measuring the expected distance between two individuals chosen from each country in a pair, rather from within a single society. See Chapter 5 in this volume for further details on Greenberg's *B*-index.

This second measure of linguistic distance is based on lexicostatistics, the branch of quantitative linguistics classifying language groups based on whether words used to convey some common meanings – such as 'mother' or 'table' – are *cognate*, i.e. stem from the same ancestor word. Two languages with many cognate words are linguistically closer than those with non-cognate words. For instance, the words 'tavola' in Italian and 'table' in French both stem from the common Latin term 'tabula'. They are therefore cognate. Replicating this over a large number of meanings, the percentage of cognate words is a measure of linguistic proximity. We rely on data from Dyen et al. (1992), who use 200 underlying meanings. In the same way as before, we compute two measures of the percentage of cognate words: the percentage of cognate words between the plurality languages spoken in each country in a pair, *CLD*, and the weighted percentage, CLD^W, which represents the expected percentage of cognate words between two individuals randomly chosen from each country in a pair.[14] Once again, Table 6.1 provides summary statistics, showing that *CLD* and CLD^W vary between 0 and 0.92, with the sample mean equal to roughly 0.6.

The big advantage of the lexicostatistical approach is that it approximates linguistic differences in a more continuous way than the cladistic approach.[15] The most widely used source of lexicostatistical distance data in the social sciences is Dyen et al. (1992), which we use here. This particular source only covers Indo-European languages, and therefore metrics of linguistic distance are only available for country pairs where these languages are spoken. However, new data from the Automated Similarity Judgment Program (ASJP), combining lexicostatistical methods with measures of phonological, grammatical and lexical similarity between languages, covers a wider set of languages (Chapter 5 in this volume provides further references and details on this recent database). While we do not use this data here, its recent development opens new avenues for studying the effect of linguistic distance on socioeconomic outcomes since it consists of continuous metrics of linguistic similarity available for a broad set of languages.

The tree-based and cognate-based measures of linguistic distance, in the limited sample of Indo-European speaking countries for which the two sets of

---

[14] In cases of pairs composed of countries, like India, where Indo-European languages are spoken by a plurality, but non-Indo-European languages are spoken by a large minority, *CLD* may be available but not CLD^W. Indeed we have 63 underlying countries (1,953 pairs) for CLD^W and 85 countries (3,570 pairs) for *CLD*.

[15] Under the assumption that linguistic drift is constant across languages, i.e. that the rate of linguistic innovation over time is similar across languages, lexicostatistical distance can be argued to be correlated with separation times between languages. This insight gave rise to the field of *glottochronology*, the attempt to infer the dates of separation of population based on linguistic similarities between them. The assumption of common linguistic drift has been heavily debated.

measures are available, are relatively highly correlated. The correlation between the two weighted measures is 0.82, while the correlation between the plurality measures is 0.78.

6.3.2   Religious distance

To capture religious distance between countries, we adopt an approach analogous to the tree-based linguistic distance. We consider trees that describe the relationship between world religions. One such tree is from Mecham et al. (2006), displayed in Figure 6.2, and another is from the World Christian Database (2007, henceforth WCD), displayed in Figure 6.3. We make use of both in the empirical work that follows.

The trees consist of grouping religions into broad categories. For instance, 'Near-Eastern Monotheistic Religions' is one broad category common to both trees we use. These broad categories are further divided into finer classifications. For instance Near Eastern monotheistic religions are subdivided into Christianity, Islam and Judaism. These are further refined into yet greater levels of disaggregation. The number of common nodes between religions is a metric of religious proximity. For instance Lutherans are closer in religious space to Baptists than they are to the Greek Orthodox.

In the Mecham, Fearon and Laitin dataset there can be up to five common nodes between religions, while the WCD data is less finely disaggregated, so there can be up to three common nodes only.[16] Each source provides data on the frequency of each religion in each country, so distances between religions can be mapped to religious distance between countries. As before, we calculate the number of common nodes between the plurality religions of each country in a pair, as well as the expected number of common nodes (following a formula analogous to Equation (15)). Finally, to obtain measures of religious distance, we implement a transformation analogous to that in Equation (16). Summary statistics for the four resulting metrics are displayed in Table 6.1.

6.3.3   Cultural distance based on the World Values Survey

Answers to questions from social surveys can be used as indicators of a respondent's cultural norms, values and attitudes. By analogy with genetics, questions correspond to *gene loci* while the specific answers given are the *alleles*. Differences across populations in the answer shares to a specific question can be used to calculate the cultural distance between countries on that specific question. Finally, aggregating over questions allows the computation of indices of cultural distance in values, norms and attitudes space.

---

[16] Due to its finer level of disaggregation the Fearon, Mecham and Laitin classification and data is preferred. However, for the sake of completeness, we present results pertaining to both datasets below.

```
1.0  Asia-born Religion
     1.1  South Asian Religions
          1.11  Hinduism
     1.2  Far Eastern Religions
          1.21  Taoism
          1.22  Buddhism
                1.221  Therevada
                1.222  Cao Dai
                1.223  Hoa Hao
2.0  Near Eastern Monotheistic Religion
     2.1  Christianity
          2.11  Western Catholicism
                2.111  Roman Catholic
                2.112  Protestant
                       2.1121  Anglican
                       2.1122  Lutheran
                       2.1123  Presbyterian
                       2.1124  Methodist
                       2.1125  Baptist
                       2.1126  Calvinist
                       2.1127  Kimbanguist
                       2.1128  Church of Ireland
          2.12  Eastern Orthodox
                2.121  Greek Orthodox
                2.122  Russian Orthodox
                       2.1221  Old Believers
                2.123  Ukranian Orthodox
                       2.1231  Russian Patriarchy
                       2.1232  Kiev Patriarchy
                2.124  Albanian Orthodox
                2.125  Armenian Orthodox
                2.126  Bulgarian Orthodox
                2.127  Georgian Orthodox
                2.128  Macedonian Orthodox
                2.129  Romanian Orthodox
     2.2  Islam
          2.21  Sunni Islam
                2.211  Shaf'i Sunni
          2.22  Shi'I Islam
                2.221  Ibadi Shi'i
                2.222  Alevi Shi'i
                2.223  Zaydi Shi'i
          2.23  Druze
     2.3  Judaism
3.0  Traditional
4.0  Other
5.0  Assorted
6.0  None
```

Figure 6.2 Mecham, Fearon and Laitin religious tree
Source: Mecham et al. (2006).

1.0   Asia-born Religion
    1.1   South Asian Religions
        1.11   Jains
        1.12   Hindus
        1.13   Sikhs
        1.14   Zoroastrians
    1.2   Far Eastern Religions
        1.21   Confucianists
        1.22   Shintoists
        1.23   Taoists
        1.24   Buddhists
        1.25   Chinese Universists
2.0   Near Eastern Monotheistic Religion
    2.1   Christians
        2.11   Anglicans
        2.12   Independents
        2.13   Marginals
        2.14   Orthodox
        2.15   Protestants
        2.16   Roman Catholics
        2.17   Disaffiliated/Unaffiliated Christians
        2.18   Doubly-Affiliated Christians
    2.2   Muslims
    2.3   Jews
3.0   Ethnoreligionists
4.0   Spiritists
5.0   Bha'is
6.0   Doubly Professing
7.0   Other Religionists
8.0   Nonreligionists/Atheist
    8.1   Nonreligionists
    8.2   Atheist

Figure 6.3   World Christian Database religious tree
Source: World Christian Database (2007).

There are three major challenges when computing these indices. The first challenge is the choice of questions. Rather than choosing questions arbitrarily, which would be open to criticism, we consider the set of *all* values-related questions appearing in the World Values Survey 1981–2010 Integrated Questionnaire, i.e. those listed by the WVS as categories A through G.[17] All 740 questions can be considered when computing distances question by question. When calculating summary indices of cultural distance that aggregate across questions, however, it is important to have a sample that is balanced across country pairs, i.e. to have the same number of questions for each pair. Some of

---

[17] These categories are as follows: Category A: perceptions of life; Category B: environment; Category C: work; Category D: family; Category E: politics and society; Category F: religion and morale; Category G: national identity. Additional categories, S, X and Y, are not considered here since they relate either to the demographic characteristics of the respondent or characteristics of the survey (wave, year, etc.).

the questions were only asked in a subset of countries, sometimes a small sub-set. There is a trade-off between maintaining a large set of questions, in which case the number of country pairs shrinks, or maintaining a broad sample of country pairs, in which case the set of questions is reduced. In what follows we chose to do the latter, to maximize the representativeness of the sample of countries. This led to keeping 98 questions out of the original set. Data availability is the only concern that governs which questions remain. Yet since the remaining questions are those that were asked in the broadest set of countries, they constitute the core questions of the WVS. Focusing on these questions, that were asked in at least one wave of the WVS in 74 countries, we are left with distances computed for 2,701 pairs.[18]

The second challenge is the choice of a functional form for computing distances for each question. There are many possible choices, but we focus on the simplest one, which is to calculate the Euclidian distance. In further empirical work that is available upon request, we used Manhattan and F_{ST} cultural distances instead of Euclidian distance, finding results that are very similar to those reported here.[19] Consider countries 1 and 2 and question i from the WVS, which admits answers $j = 1, \ldots, J$. Some questions are binary ($J = 2$) and others admit more than two answers ($J > 2$).[20] Let s_{ij}^c denote the share of respondents in country $c \in \{1, 2\}$ giving answer j to question i. Then for binary questions, cultural distance CD_i^{12} between countries 1 and 2 is simply:

$$CD_i^{12} = \left| s_{i1}^1 - s_{i1}^2 \right|,\tag{17}$$

while for non-binary questions:

$$CD_i^{12} = \sqrt{\sum_{j=1}^{J} \left(s_{ij}^1 - s_{ij}^2 \right)^2}.\tag{18}$$

---

[18] We also implemented different choices in terms of the mix of country pairs and questions, increasing the number of questions at the cost of losing some country pairs. This led to no appreciable change in the results that follow. These results are available upon request.

[19] Desmet et al. (2011) used the F_{ST} functional form to calculate cultural distance based on answers from the World Values Survey for a sample of European countries, and explored the relationship between the resulting matrix of cultural distance and F_{ST} genetic distance in Europe, finding as we do a strong association between the two.

[20] We call these non-binary. Non-binary questions are further divided into those that admit an ordering on a scale (e.g. happiness on a scale from 1 to 10), and those that do not (e.g. do you prefer option 1, option 2 or option 3?). This distinction is not relevant here. For an in-depth discussion of question types in the WVS, see Desmet et al. (2014).

The third challenge is to aggregate question-specific distances in order to obtain summary measures of cultural distance. To create summary indices we first standardize the question-specific distances to have a mean of zero and a standard error equal to one. This ensures equal weighting of questions in every summary index. We next simply sum the question-specific indices, to compute several indices of cultural distance. We first sum across all 98 questions, to obtain an overall index. Next, we sum question-specific distances for each of the six categories of questions, as specified by the WVS.[21] Finally, we created an index for the whole group of binary questions and another one for the whole group of non-binary questions.

Summary statistics for these nine indices appear at the bottom of Table 6.1. By construction each index has mean zero and is available for all 2,701 pairs.[22]

6.4   Ancestry and culture: A simple conceptual framework

As we discussed in Section 6.2, genetic distance measures relatedness between populations and is roughly proportional to the time since two populations shared the same ancestors, that is, since they were the same population. Over time, ancestors transmit a large number of traits to their descendants, not only biologically (through DNA), but also culturally. This transmission takes place with variation and change over time. Therefore, on average, populations that are more closely related will have had less time to diverge from each other on a large set of culturally transmitted traits, such as language, religion, traditions, habits and values. This process establishes a close connection between ancestry, measured by genetic distance, and culturally transmitted traits: genetic distance and memetic distance should be positively correlated. A stylized formal model, adapted from Spolaore and Wacziarg (2009, 2012), can illustrate this relationship in a simplified and concise way.

For simplicity, we consider three populations, $i = 1, 2, 3$, living at the present time. Population 1 and population 2 descend from the same last common ancestor population, which lived one period ago. In contrast, population 3 only shares common ancestors with populations 1 and 2 going further in time, back to two periods ago. That is, population 3 is less closely related with populations 1 and 2 than these are with each other. Using the analogy discussed in

---

[21] Category B, questions relating to the environment, is dropped as no question from this category was asked in all of the 74 countries. Category A features 32 questions, category C features 14 questions, category D features 7 questions, category E features 30 questions, category F features 12 questions and category G features three questions. There were 35 binary questions and 63 non-binary questions.

[22] However one country, Puerto Rico, drops out in our regression analysis due to missing data on genetic distance, leaving us with 2,628 observations in the regressions of Section 6.5.

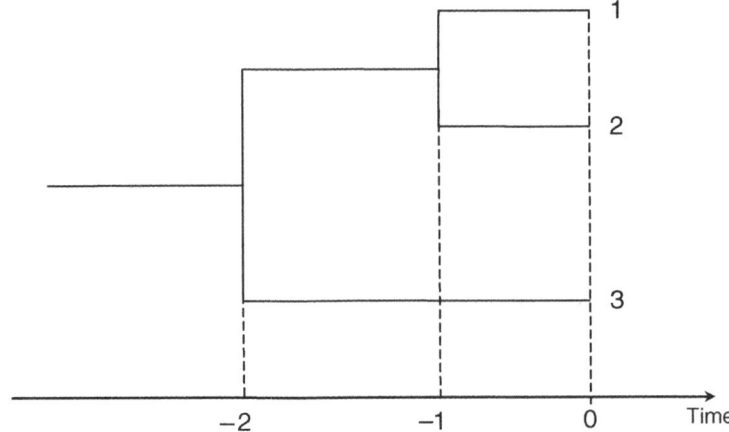

Figure 6.4   Population tree

Section 6.2, we can say that populations 1 and 2 are like siblings, while population 3 is a more distant cousin. The phylogenetic tree of the three populations is illustrated in Figure 6.4.

Building on the results described in Section 6.2.2, we can approximate the genetic distance $d_g(i,j)$ between population i and population j as the time since they were one population. Therefore, genetic distance $d_g(1,2)$ between population 1 and population 2 is smaller than genetic distance between population 1 and population 3, and also smaller than genetic distance between population 2 and population 3:

$$d_g(1,2)=F<d_g(1,3)=d_g(2,3)=F'. \tag{19}$$

How far in cultural traits are these populations from each other? While, in general, their cultural divergence may depend on complex processes of transmission across generations of a large set of cultural traits, it is useful to focus on the simplest possible mechanism of cultural transmission with variation, whereby culture is captured by just one trait (or *meme*), which we assume can be represented as a point on the real line. In each period t, a population i has cultural traits $c_i(t)$ that are inherited with variation from its ancestor population, which had traits $c_i(t-1)$, according to:

$$c_i(t)=c_i(t-1)+\varepsilon_i(t), \tag{20}$$

where $\varepsilon_i(t)$ measures random variation between time $t-1$ and time t. We assume the simplest possible mechanism for variation: cultural change as a random walk. That is, $\varepsilon_i(t)=\varepsilon>0$ with probability $1/2$ and $\varepsilon_i(t)=-\varepsilon<0$ with probability $1/2$. In addition, we assume that such shocks are independent across different populations ($\varepsilon_i(t)$ is independent of $\varepsilon_j(t)$ for $j\neq i$).

Let $d_c(i, j) \equiv |c_j - c_i|$ denote the distance in cultural traits between population i and population j. The expected memetic distance between population 1 and population 2, which share their last common ancestors only one period ago, is denoted by $E[d_c(1, 2)]$, and given by:[23]

$$E[d_c(1, 2)] = \varepsilon. \tag{21}$$

All variation between populations 1 and 2 is given by cultural change that took place between one period ago and now. In contrast, expected memetic distance between population 1 and population 3, and between population 2 and population 3, comes from shocks that took place both between one period ago and now, and between two periods ago and one period ago. On average, such shocks are associated with a larger distance in culturally transmitted traits:[24]

$$E[d_c(1, 3)] = E[d_c(2, 3)] = \frac{3\varepsilon}{2} > \varepsilon = E[d_c(1, 2)]. \tag{22}$$

Therefore, on average a larger genetic distance is associated with greater distance in cultural traits. This relation is not deterministic. Some pairs of populations that are more distant cousins may end up with more similar cultural traits than two more closely related populations, but that outcome is less likely to be observed than the opposite. Therefore, genetic distance and distance in culturally transmitted traits, such as language, religion and values, are expected to be positively correlated.

6.5 Ancestry and culture: Empirical evidence

In this section we conduct an empirical exploration of the relationship between genetic distance and our various measures of memetic distance to test the hypothesis that longer separation times are in fact positively related with differences in language, religion and norms, values and attitudes.

6.5.1 Genetic distance and linguistic distance

Measures of linguistic and genetic distances should be positively correlated. Cavalli-Sforza et al. (1994, pp. 98–105) observed that there is usually little genetic admixture between linguistic groups. Languages are generally transmitted intergenerationally. Thus, phylogenetic trees and linguistic trees tend to resemble each other. At the same time, we should not expect a perfect relationship, for several reasons. Firstly, as already mentioned, linguistic data based on trees feature a discrete number of nodes, whereas genetic distance

---

[23] For the derivation, see the Appendix.
[24] The derivation of this result, and of a generalization, is provided in the Appendix.

based on a large number of alleles, as is the case for the index we use is a continuous measure of separation times. Second, the functional forms for measures of genetic distance (F_{ST}) and linguistic distance (a nonlinear transformation of the number of different nodes, or the percentage of non-cognate words, depending on the measure) are different. Third, successful groups conquering the territories of distinct linguistic groups can impose their language without necessarily imposing their genes. Such was the case, for instance, with the Magyar conquest of Hungary: the resulting language was of the Uralic family, but the Magyar genetic admixture was so limited that the Hungarians are genetically very close to other Slavic populations, such as the Poles. An even more stark example comes from the population movements that followed the discovery of the New World, in particular the slave trade: the current descendants of former slaves do not speak the original West African languages of their ancestors. Similarly, the current inhabitants of the United States predominantly speak English, whereas their ancestors came from a diverse set of linguistic groups. Thus, modern migrations served to break the link between genetic and linguistic distance.

In Table 6.2, Panel A explores the basic correlations. We find that our various measures of linguistic distance are highly correlated among themselves. For instance, the correlation between weighted *TLD* and weighted *CLD* is 0.82. Weighted *TLD* is also positively correlated with weighted genetic distance, with a correlation equal to 0.22. However, *CLD* is not strongly correlated with genetic distance, in all likelihood because the sample is limited to Indo-European speaking countries, which tend to also be genetically close: there is not enough variation in the data to detect a significant correlation.

Table 6.3 presents regressions of our various measures of linguistic distance on genetic distance, with or without controls for a wide range of measures of geographic separation – including geodesic distance, the absolute difference in longitudes and latitudes, etc. Indeed one concern is that genetic distance merely reflects geographic proximity, and that genetic and linguistic distance are positively correlated simply because the relationship goes through geographic distance. We find that this is not the case, and that genetic distance is significantly related to tree-based measures of linguistic distance (*TLD*). In fact, the standardized beta coefficient on F_{ST} genetic distance, reported in the last line of Table 6.2, suggests that a 1 s.d. increase in genetic distance is associated with a 0.15–0.22 s.d. increase in linguistic distance, depending on the measure and specification.[25] For the cognate-based measures (*CLD*), the relationship is negative, but not robustly significant statistically.

---

[25] It is well known that the standardized beta is equal to the correlation coefficient for the univariate case. This can be verified by comparing the standardized betas in columns (1) and (3) to the corresponding ones in Table 6.2, Panel A.

Table 6.2   Simple correlations between linguistic, religious and genetic distances

Panel A: Linguistic distance

	Weighted *TLD*	Plurality *TLD*	Weighted *CLD*	Plurality *CLD*	Weighted F_{ST}
Plurality *TLD*	0.926*	1			
	(12,246)	(12,246)			
Weighted *CLD*	0.817*	0.798*	1		
	(1,035)	(1,035)	(1,953)		
Plurality *CLD*	0.740*	0.776*	0.979*	1	
	(2,145)	(2,145)	(1,953)	(3570)	
Weighted F_{ST}	0.220*	0.195*	−0.034	−0.058*	1
	(11,476)	(11,476)	(1,378)	(2,701)	(16,110)
Plurality F_{ST}	0.232*	0.210*	0.011	−0.031	0.939*
	(12,246)	(12,246)	(1,953)	(3,570)	(16,110)

Panel B: Religious distance

	Weighted *F-RD*	Plurality *F-RD*	Weighted *WCD-RD*	Plurality *WCD-RD*	Weighted F_{ST}
Plurality *F-RD*	0.839*	1			
	(12,246)	(12,246)			
Weighted *WCD-RD*	0.784*	0.622*	1		
	(11,325)	(11,325)	(19,306)		
Plurality *WCD-RD*	0.698*	0.640*	0.819*	1	
	(11,325)	(11,325)	(19,306)	(19,306)	
Weighted F_{ST}	0.181*	0.121*	0.091*	0.064*	1
	(11,476)	(11,476)	(15,400)	(15,400)	(16,110)
Plurality F_{ST}	0.168*	0.114*	0.056*	0.034*	0.939*
	(12,246)	(12,246)	(19,306)	(19,306)	(16,110)

Notes: Number of observations in parentheses; * denotes 5% significance.

As mentioned already, the population movements that followed the discovery of the New World were important factors breaking the link between genetic and linguistic distance. To investigate this issue, Table 6.4 isolates the sample consisting of Old World countries. This excludes any country pair containing a country from the Americas or Oceania. We find much larger correlations than in Table 6.3. For instance, the standardized betas on weighted *TLD* now range between 0.29 and 0.41. Moreover, the correlations between genetic distance and *CLD* turn positive, and significant in the univariate cases. These results show there exists a strong correlation between genetic and linguistic distance for country pairs least likely to have experienced language replacement over the course of the last 500 years.

Table 6.3 Linguistic distance and contemporary genetic distance, full sample

	(1) Weighted TLD	(2) Weighted TLD	(3) Plurality TLD	(4) Plurality TLD	(5) Weighted CLD	(6) Weighted CLD	(7) Plurality CLD	(8) Plurality CLD
Weighted F_{ST}	0.320 (24.12)***				-0.173 (1.27)	-0.260 (1.65)*	-0.325 (3.03)***	-0.643 (5.73)***
Genetic distance		0.242 (16.54)***	0.385 (21.24)***	0.284 (14.14)***				
Geodesic distance (1,000s of km)		-0.001 (2.03)**		-0.002 (1.73)*		-0.018 (2.56)**		-0.010 (2.72)***
Absolute difference in longitudes		0.030 (5.09)***		0.037 (4.59)***		0.214 (3.87)***		0.197 (6.70)***
Absolute difference in latitudes		0.001 (0.23)		0.000 (0.03)		-0.012 (0.19)		-0.059 (1.68)*
1 for contiguity		-0.087 (14.15)***		-0.122 (14.44)***		-0.131 (3.14)***		-0.215 (7.10)***
=1 if either country is landlocked		0.011 (5.60)***		0.013 (4.88)***		0.047 (2.54)**		0.046 (3.94)***
=1 if either country is an island		0.010 (4.12)***		0.010 (3.06)***		0.052 (3.08)***		0.071 (6.04)***
=1 if pair shares at least one sea or ocean		-0.059 (18.07)***		-0.071 (15.85)***		-0.176 (9.61)***		-0.160 (10.59)***
Constant	0.935 (536.89)***	0.937 (371.07)***	0.922 (388.29)***	0.925 (267.22)***	0.624 (48.97)***	0.646 (34.36)***	0.672 (68.14)***	0.648 (45.15)***
Adjusted R^2	0.05	0.12	0.04	0.10	0.00	0.14	0.00	0.17
N	11,476	11,476	11,476	11,476	1,378	1,378	2,701	2,701
Standardized beta	0.220	0.166	0.195	0.143	-0.034	-0.051	-0.058	-0.115

Notes: OLS regressions, dependent variable displayed in the second row. t-statistics in parentheses in the second row; * significant at 10%; ** significant at 5%; *** significant at 1%. TLD = Tree-based linguistic distance; CLD = Cognate-based linguistic distance (Indo-European languages only).

Table 6.4 Linguistic distance and contemporary genetic distance, Old World

	(1) Weighted TLD	(2) Weighted TLD	(3) Plurality TLD	(4) Plurality TLD	(5) Weighted CLD	(6) Weighted CLD	(7) Plurality CLD	(8) Plurality CLD
Weighted F_{ST} Genetic distance	0.293	0.255	0.344	0.300	0.771	0.399	1.334	0.423
	(39.25)***	(24.25)***	(30.44)***	(18.51)***	(2.59)**	(1.05)	(5.39)***	(1.48)
Geodesic distance (1,000s of km)		−0.004		−0.006		−0.011		0.036
		(7.23)***		(6.41)***		(0.45)		(5.09)***
Absolute difference in longitudes		0.037		0.050		0.232		−0.031
		(9.26)***		(8.12)***		(1.40)		(0.73)
Absolute difference in latitudes		0.038		0.049		0.241		−0.278
		(7.73)***		(6.56)***		(1.02)		(3.27)***
1 for contiguity		−0.073		−0.097		−0.173		−0.203
		(22.77)***		(19.77)***		(4.74)***		(7.27)***
=1 if either country is landlocked		−0.005		−0.003		0.006		−0.012
		(4.77)***		(1.85)*		(0.30)		(0.87)
=1 if either country is an island		0.004		0.004		−0.116		−0.009
		(2.68)***		(1.78)*		(3.24)***		(0.44)
=1 if pair shares at least one sea or ocean		−0.021		−0.020		−0.035		−0.051
		(9.95)***		(6.14)***		(1.21)		(2.15)**
Constant	0.948	0.955	0.941	0.948	0.681	0.667	0.694	0.687
	(957.57)***	(650.87)***	(628.54)***	(419.09)***	(52.95)***	(32.85)***	(65.49)***	(45.66)***
Adjusted R^2	0.17	0.26	0.11	0.18	0.02	0.16	0.03	0.20
N	7,626	7,626	7,626	7,626	351	351	780	780
Standardized beta	0.410	0.357	0.329	0.288	0.137	0.071	0.190	0.060

Notes: OLS regressions, dependent variable displayed in the second row. *t*-statistics in parentheses; *significant at 10%; **significant at 5%; ***significant at 1%. TLD = Tree-based linguistic distance; CLD = Cognate-based linguistic distance (Indo-European languages only).

6.5.2   Genetic distance and religious distance

Like language, religious beliefs tend to be transmitted intergenerationally, leading us to expect a positive correlation between religious distance and genetic distance. However, several factors may limit the extent to which religious distance correlates with genealogical distance. First, while they may find their sources in ancient religious beliefs, several major world religions appeared relatively recently. For instance, one of the oldest monotheistic religions, Judaism, appeared only 3,500 years ago. Second, in line with the first observation, the rate of drift of religious beliefs is likely to be much faster than that of genes, so that populations that are genetically similar often espouse different religious beliefs. In fact, two recent religious innovations, Christianity and Islam, occurred among closely related populations in the Middle East. Third, religious beliefs are transmitted horizontally through conquests and conversions, perhaps to a faster extent than even languages, as it is easier to change one's religion than one's language. Thus, the emergence and horizontal diffusion of new religions is likely to weaken the link between religious distance and genetic distance perhaps to a greater extent than for linguistic distance. Fourth, the aforementioned functional form differences between metrics of linguistic and genetic distance apply with the same force to measures of religious distance.

Despite these caveats, we do find that religious distance is positively correlated with genetic distance. The first piece of evidence is presented in Panel B of Table 6.2. There we see, for instance, that weighted religious distance based on the Mecham, Fearon and Laitin religious tree ($F - RD$) bears a 0.18 correlation with weighted genetic distance. Correlations are smaller using measures based on the World Christian Database tree ($WCD - RD$), which are less finely disaggregated. We also find substantial positive correlations among our various measures of religious distance, but these correlations are not sufficiently high to justify looking at only one measure.

Tables 6.5 and 6.6 present regression evidence, again with or without controls for geographic distance for each of the four measures of religious distance. In all but one of the specifications, genetic distance comes out with a positive statistically significant coefficient. The standardized magnitude of the effect of genetic distance is generally smaller than for linguistic distance, in line with the observation above. Yet, in particular for $F - RD$, we find standardized effects comprised between 8.3 and 18.1 per cent, again consistent with our model of cultural drift. Moreover, unlike for language, we do not find a particular tendency for the effect to be more pronounced among Old World countries (Table 6.6).

Table 6.5 Religious distance and genetic distance, full sample

	(1) Weighted FRD	(2) Weighted FRD	(3) Plurality FRD	(4) Plurality FRD	(5) Weighted WCD-RD	(6) Weighted WCD-RD	(7) Plurality WCD-RD	(8) Plurality WCD-RD
Weighted F_{ST}	0.376 (19.70)***							
Genetic distance		0.307 (14.38)***	0.542 (13.10)***	0.373 (8.01)***	0.208 (11.29)***	0.085 (4.14)***	0.329 (7.95)***	0.010 (0.21)
Geodesic distance (1,000s of km)		−0.002 (1.85)*		−0.003 (1.24)		−0.002 (2.43)*		0.008 (3.48)***
Absolute difference in longitudes		0.042 (4.85)***		0.072 (3.85)***		0.077 (9.33)***		0.033 (1.76)*
Absolute difference in latitudes		−0.024 (2.54)**		0.009 (0.44)		−0.023 (2.75)***		−0.100 (5.19)***
1 for contiguity		−0.081 (8.87)***		−0.208 (10.41)***		−0.095 (9.60)***		−0.203 (9.03)***
=1 if either country is landlocked		0.002 (0.83)		−0.025 (3.96)***		0.014 (5.00)***		−0.017 (2.67)***
=1 if either country is an island		0.038 (10.56)***		0.075 (9.52)***		−0.016 (5.43)***		0.016 (2.42)**
=1 if pair shares at least one sea or ocean		−0.069 (14.37)***		−0.120 (11.53)***		−0.052 (11.93)***		−0.102 (10.44)***
Constant	0.809 (318.81)***	0.813 (217.33)***	0.725 (131.71)***	0.732 (89.83)***	0.735 (294.46)***	0.730 (195.12)***	0.604 (107.71)***	0.601 (70.93)***
Adjusted R^2	0.03	0.09	0.01	0.06	0.01	0.07	0.00	0.04
Number of pairs	11,476	11,476	11,476	11,476	15,400	15,225	15,400	15,225
Standardized effect	0.181	0.148	0.121	0.083	0.091	0.037	0.064	0.002

Notes: OLS regressions, dependent variable displayed in the second row. *t*-statistics in parentheses; *significant at 10%; **significant at 5%; ***significant at 1%. *FRD* = Fearon, Meecham and Laitin religious distance; *WCD-RD* = World Christian Database religious distance.

Table 6.6 Religious distance and genetic distance, Old World

	(1) Weighted FRD	(2) Weighted FRD	(3) Plurality FRD	(4) Plurality FRD	(5) Weighted WCD-RD	(6) Weighted WCD-RD	(7) Plurality WCD-RD	(8) Plurality WCD-RD
Weighted F_{ST}	0.363	0.058						
	(19.29)***	(2.13)**						
Genetic distance			0.525	0.005	0.360	−0.018	0.494	−0.293
			(11.93)***	(0.08)	(16.44)***	(0.59)	(9.76)***	(4.02)***
Geodesic distance (1,000s of km)		−0.003		−0.008		−0.003		0.006
		(2.14)**		(2.41)**		(1.71)*		(1.59)
Absolute difference in longitudes		0.112		0.180		0.197		0.219
		(10.81)***		(7.34)***		(16.63)***		(7.75)***
Absolute difference in latitudes		0.135		0.289		0.104		0.190
		(10.96)***		(9.90)***		(7.52)***		(5.78)***
1 for contiguity		−0.052		−0.184		−0.066		−0.171
		(6.25)***		(9.24)***		(6.46)***		(7.05)***
=1 if either country is landlocked		0.000		−0.031		0.022		0.001
		(0.04)		(4.37)***		(6.39)***		(0.12)
=1 if either country is an island		0.020		0.058		0.002		0.060
		(4.92)***		(5.98)***		(0.62)		(6.18)***
=1 if pair shares at least one sea or ocean		−0.031		−0.044		0.008		0.015
		(5.50)***		(3.37)***		(1.21)		(0.98)
Constant	0.830	0.800	0.758	0.726	0.743	0.681	0.620	0.522
	(326.57)***	(210.25)***	(127.48)***	(80.43)***	(251.17)***	(155.53)***	(90.64)***	(49.88)***
Adjusted R^2	0.05	0.13	0.02	0.08	0.03	0.16	0.01	0.08
Number of pairs	7,626	7,626	7,626	7,626	8,778	8,646	8,778	8,646
Standardized beta	0.216	0.034	0.135	0.001	0.173	−0.009	0.104	−0.061

Notes: OLS regressions, dependent variable displayed in the second row. t-statistics in parentheses; *significant at 10%; **significant at 5%; ***significant at 1%. FRD = Fearon, Meecham and Laitin religious distance; WCD-RD = World Christian Database religious distance.

6.5.3 Genetic distance and cultural distance

Our final exploration concerns the relationship between genetic distance and distance in norms, values and attitudes. We start with an analysis of the relationship between genetic distance and question-specific distances, for all available questions from the WVS. Under the null hypothesis of no relationship between genetic and cultural distances, we would expect 5 per cent of the correlations to be significant (2.5 per cent positive and significant), and the distribution of correlations to be centred around zero. Figure 6.5 presents a histogram of sample correlations between bilateral distance for each question, and weighted genetic distance, for the full set of 740 questions.[26] The mode of the distribution is well to the right of zero, with a mean of about 10 per cent. Of the correlations 71.6 per cent were positive. In 53.1 per cent of the cases the correlation with genetic distance is both positive and significant, far in excess of what we would expect under the null. A substantial subset of the questions feature correlations that are quite large – for 22.4 per cent of the questions, the correlations are in excess of 0.20 and statistically significant at the 5 per cent level.[27]

These simple correlations could confound the effects of geographic distance with those of genetic distance. To address this issue, we ran regressions, for each question, of WVS distance on genetic and geodesic distance. Figure 6.6 presents a histogram of the standardized beta coefficient on genetic distance, representing the effect of a 1 s.d. change in genetic distance as a share of a standard deviation in the dependent variable. Of the standardized betas 66.9 per cent are positive, and 47.2 per cent are both positive and significant at the 5 per cent level. We also find a number of large effects, with 20 per cent of the standardized betas greater than 0.20.[28] Controlling for geodesic distance does not modify the conclusion reached earlier.

While these results are informative, they conflate questions on very different subjects, and of different types (binary versus non-binary). So we now turn to the relationship between our nine indices of cultural distance, and genetic distance. The analysis is now limited to the 98 questions available for 74 countries. Table 6.7 presents simple correlations. Genetic distance bears a correlation of 0.27 with our summary measure of cultural distance. The last line of the

---

[26] The underlying sample varies across questions, which could introduce some bias. However, the results are not different when we focus on the set of 98 questions for which we have a balanced sample of 2,701 country pairs.

[27] For the restricted set of 98 questions covering a balanced set of countries, 63.3 per cent of the correlations were positive and significant, and 75.5 per cent of them were positive.

[28] For the restricted set of 98 questions, 67.3 per cent of the standardized beta coefficients on genetic distance were positive, and 53.1 per cent of the effects were positive and significant at the 5 per cent level.

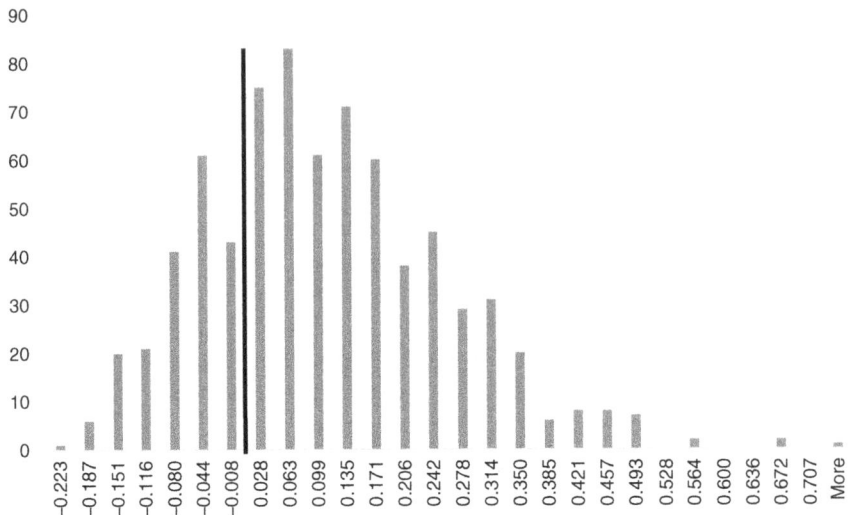

Figure 6.5 Distribution of correlations between cultural and genetic distances (740 questions)

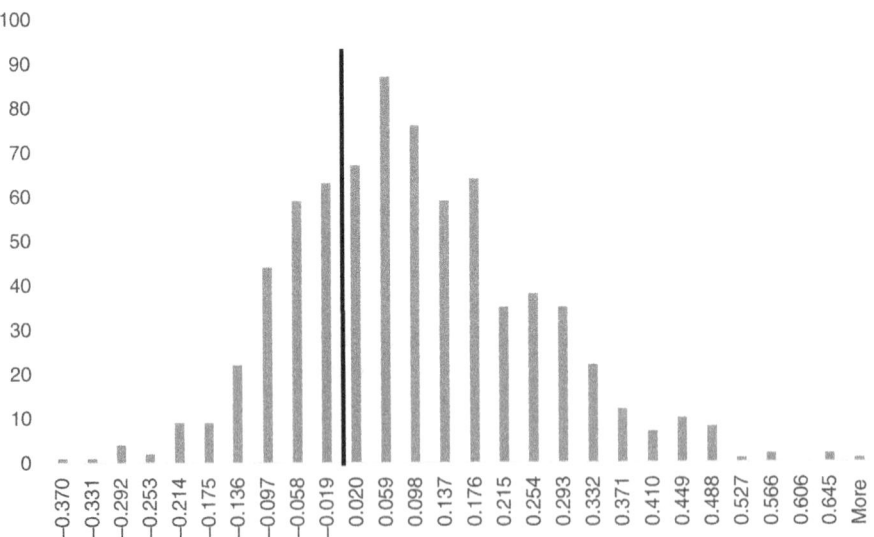

Figure 6.6 Distribution of beta coefficients on genetic distance (740 questions, with geodesic distance control)

Table 6.7 Correlations between genetic distance and cultural distance measures

	CD, all questions	CD, cat. A	CD, cat. C	CD, cat. D	CD, cat. E	CD, cat. F	CD, cat. G	CD, binary questions	CD, non-binary questions
CD, category A	0.879*	1							
CD, category C	0.644*	0.481*	1						
CD, category D	0.619*	0.528*	0.373*	1					
CD, category E	0.802*	0.598*	0.284*	0.392*	1				
CD, category F	0.728*	0.544*	0.394*	0.398*	0.476*	1			
CD, category G	0.431*	0.315*	0.306*	0.203*	0.298*	0.275*	1		
CD, binary questions	0.870*	0.837*	0.816*	0.584*	0.515*	0.544*	0.305*	1	
CD, non-binary questions	0.949*	0.787*	0.448*	0.559*	0.878*	0.749*	0.453*	0.670*	1
Weighted F_{ST} gen. dist.	0.269*	0.245*	0.074*	0.028	0.299*	0.216*	0.130*	0.147*	0.312*

Notes: Correlations based on 2,628 observations; * denotes 5% significance. Key for WVS question categories: Category A: Perceptions of Life; Category C: Work; Category D: Family; Category E: Politics and Society; Category F: Religion and Morale; Category G: National Identity.

table shows that genetic distance is positively and significantly correlated with eight of our nine measures of cultural distance based on the WVS. The only category for which this is not the case is category D, pertaining to questions about family. Among the other categories, the correlation with genetic distance varies between 7.4 per cent (questions on work) and 29.9 per cent (questions on politics and society).

In Tables 6.8 and 6.9 we turn to regression analysis, following the same format as earlier: for each index we present a univariate regression and one that controls for geographic barriers. Table 6.8 focuses on the aggregate index covering all 98 questions, and then the indices for binary and non-binary questions. We find a large, statistically significant positive relationship between genetic distance and cultural distance. In the specification with controls (column 2), the standardized effect of genetic distance is 25.5 per cent. While the effect remains positive and significant for both binary and non-binary questions, it is largest for the latter – with a standardized effect of 30.2 per cent. Interestingly, the inclusion of geographic distance controls serves to weaken the effect of genetic distance only a little bit.

Table 6.9, finally, breaks things down by question category. In the bottom panel, with geographic controls, we see positive and significant effects of genetic distance on cultural distance for all but category D (Family). The largest effects, quantitatively, are for categories A (Perceptions of Life), E (Politics and Society) and F (Religion and Morale). Future work should seek to delve more deeply into the characteristics of questions most closely associated with ancestral distance.

6.6   Conclusion

What does genetic distance measure? In this chapter we have argued that genetic distance is a summary measure for differences in a wide range of inter-generationally transmitted human traits. We focused on language, religion and values, finding empirical evidence of a positive correlation between genetic distance and linguistic, religious and cultural distances. It is important to note that genetic distance is not strongly correlated with only a small and specific subset of differences in cultural traits. On the contrary, genetic distance tends to be broadly and significantly correlated with a vast range of differences in cultural traits. Thus, while specific correlations with individual sets of traits are typically moderate in magnitude, there is an overall relation between ancestry and culture, consistent with a conceptual framework in which a broad range of cultural traits are transmitted with variation across generations over time. Genetic distance is a useful summary measure capturing differences in this broad range of cultural traits.

Table 6.8   Cultural distance and genetic distance

	(1) Total	(2) Total	(3) Binary	(4) Binary	(5) Non-binary	(6) Non-binary
F_{ST} genetic distance, weighted, current match	143.891 (14.33)***	138.547 (12.24)***	33.291 (7.60)***	29.873 (6.02)***	110.600 (16.82)***	108.675 (14.65)***
Geodesic distance, 1,000s of km		-1.088 (2.18)**		-0.334 (1.52)		-0.754 (2.30)**
Absolute difference in longitudes		0.072 (2.00)**		0.019 (1.21)		0.053 (2.24)**
Absolute difference in latitudes		0.108 (2.16)**		0.037 (1.67)*		0.071 (2.17)**
1 for contiguity		-34.347 (9.92)***		-13.900 (9.16)***		-20.447 (9.00)***
Number of landlocked countries in the pair		-8.833 (7.35)***		-4.027 (7.65)***		-4.806 (6.10)***
Number of island countries in the pair		-3.325 (2.12)**		-2.704 (3.93)***		-0.622 (0.60)
1 if pair shares at least one sea or ocean		-12.034 (5.23)***		-2.999 (2.98)***		-9.034 (5.99)***
Constant	-10.570 (10.88)***	-3.688 (2.50)**	-2.368 (5.58)***	0.702 (1.09)	-8.202 (12.88)***	-4.390 (4.54)***
Adjusted R^2	0.07	0.14	0.02	0.08	0.10	0.16
No. observations	2,628	2,513	2,628	2,513	2,628	2,513
Standardized beta	0.269	0.255	0.147	0.130	0.312	0.302

Notes: Dependent variable: cultural distance, based on Euclidian distance metric. *t*-statistics in parentheses; *significant at 10%; **significant at 5%; ***significant at 1%. The sample includes 73 countries (2,628 country pairs) and the total index of cultural distance is based on 98 WVS questions.

Future research should seek to improve on this evidence. Recent progress in the measurement of linguistic differences, using systematic quantitative methods, will allow for a more precise evaluation of the effects of linguistic distance on political economy outcomes. Similarly, improvements in the gathering of genetic data should lead to improvements in our ability to detect effects of ancestral distance on cultural distance and in turn on political economy outcomes. As more genetic data on more finely defined populations become available, more granular analyses of the relationship between genetic and cultural distance will become possible. Third, alternative datasets on values, norms and attitudes also exist, either regionally or worldwide, and could be used to complement our analysis.

Research seeking to quantify human barriers to socioeconomic interactions across populations is in its infancy. With this chapter we have sought to clarify what observable traits are captured by ancestral distance, but much remains to be done.

Table 6.9   Cultural distance and genetic distance (by question category)

	(1) Category A	(2) Category C	(3) Category D	(4) Category E	(5) Category F	(6) Category G
Univariate specification						
F_{ST} genetic distance,	47.613	8.947	1.555	57.536	24.133	4.106
weighted	(12.92)***	(3.82)***	(1.43)	(16.06)***	(11.32)***	(6.71)***
R^2	0.06	0.01	0.00	0.09	0.05	0.02
Standardized beta	0.244	0.074	0.028	0.299	0.216	0.130
Multivariate specification						
F_{ST} genetic distance,	47.591	7.010	1.468	55.279	24.836	2.363
Weighted	(11.55)***	(2.62)***	(1.20)	(13.59)***	(10.09)***	(3.39)***
Adjusted R^2	0.14	0.05	0.08	0.14	0.08	0.04
Standardized beta	0.241	0.058	0.026	0.284	0.218	0.075

Notes: t-statistics in parentheses; *significant at 10%; **significant at 5%; ***significant at 1%. The univariate specification is based on 2,628 observations (country pairs). The multivariate specification is based on 2,513 observations. All specifications include an intercept. Key for WVS question categories: Category A: Perceptions of Life; Category C: Work; Category D: Family; Category E: Politics and Society; Category F: Religion and Morale; Category G: National Identity. The multivariate specification includes the following geographic controls: geodesic distance, absolute difference in longitudes, absolute difference in latitudes, dummy for contiguity, number of landlocked countries in the pair, number of island countries in the pair, dummy = 1 if pair shares at least one sea or ocean.

Appendix: Derivations of the results in Section 6.4

First, we show that $E[d_c(1,2)] = \varepsilon$. The result is immediate. With probability 1/4 both populations experience a positive shock ε, and with probability 1/4 both populations experience a negative shock $-\varepsilon$. Hence, with probability 1/2, their vertical distance is zero. With probability 1/2 one population experiences a positive shock ε and the other a negative shock $-\varepsilon$, implying a cultural distance equal to $|\varepsilon - (-\varepsilon)| = 2\varepsilon$. On average, the expected cultural distance is

$$E[d_c(1,2)] = \frac{1}{2}0 + \frac{1}{2}2\varepsilon = \varepsilon. \tag{23}$$

Second, we show that

$$E[d_c(1,3)] = E[d_c(2,3)] = \frac{3\varepsilon}{2} > \varepsilon = E[d_c(1,2)]. \tag{24}$$

In fact, this is a special instance of the more general case in which the shock between today and a period ago is given by $\varepsilon > 0$ with probability 1/2 and $-\varepsilon$ with probability 1/2, while the shock to cultural traits between two periods ago and one period ago is $\varepsilon' > 0$ with probability 1/2 and ε' with probability 1/2. In Section 6.4, we show the result for the special case $\varepsilon = \varepsilon'$.

In general, with probability 1/4 population 1's ancestor populations and population 2's ancestor populations experienced identical shocks both between two periods ago and one period ago, and between one period ago and now. That is, with probability $1/4$ we have $d_v(1,3) = 0$. By the same token, with probability $1/4$ the two populations experienced identical shocks between two periods ago and one period ago, but different shocks between one period ago and now, implying $d_c(1,3) = 2\varepsilon$, and with probability $1/4$ identical shocks between one period ago and now, but different shocks between two periods ago and one period ago, implying $d_c(1,3) = 2\varepsilon'$. With probability $1/8$, one population lineage has experienced two positive shocks $(\varepsilon' + \varepsilon)$ while the other has experienced two negative shocks $(-\varepsilon' - \varepsilon)$, therefore leading to a distance equal to $2\varepsilon' + 2\varepsilon$. Finally, with probability $1/8$ one population lineage has experienced a positive shock ε' and a negative shock $-\varepsilon$ while the other population lineage has experienced $-\varepsilon'$ and ε. In this latest case, we have $d_c(1,3) = |2\varepsilon - 2\varepsilon'|$. In sum, expected cultural distance is given by

$$E[d_c(1,3)] = \frac{1}{4}2\varepsilon' + \frac{1}{4}2\varepsilon + \frac{1}{8}(2\varepsilon' + 2\varepsilon) + \frac{1}{8}|2\varepsilon - 2\varepsilon'|,$$

which is equal to $\varepsilon + \dfrac{\varepsilon'}{2}$ if $\varepsilon \geq \varepsilon'$ and equal to $\varepsilon' + \dfrac{\varepsilon}{2}$ if $\varepsilon \leq \varepsilon'$, or, equivalently

$$E[d_c(1,3)] = \max\left\{\frac{\varepsilon'}{2} + \varepsilon, \varepsilon' + \frac{\varepsilon}{2}\right\}. \tag{25}$$

The same expected cultural distance holds between populations 2 and 3.

In the special case $\varepsilon = \varepsilon'$, condition (25) simplifies to $E[d_c(1,3)] = E[d_c(2,3)] = 3\varepsilon/2$, the result shown in Section 6.4.

Acknowledgements

We thank Shekhar Mittal for excellent research assistance, and Klaus Desmet, Victor Ginsburgh, Paola Giuliano and Shlomo Weber for helpful comments. All errors are our own.

References

Q. Ashraf and O. Galor (2013a) 'The "Out of Africa" Hypothesis, Human Genetic Diversity, and Comparative Economic Development', *American Economic Review*, 103, 1–46.

Q. Ashraf and O. Galor (2013b) 'Genetic Diversity and the Origins of Cultural Fragmentation', *American Economic Review Papers and Proceedings*, 103, 528–533.

A. Alesina, A. Devleeschauwer, W. Easterly, S. Kurlat and R. Wacziarg (2003) 'Fractionalization', *Journal of Economic Growth*, 8, 55–194.

E. Arbatli, Q. Ashraf and O. Galor (2013) 'The Nature of Civil Conflict', Working Paper, Brown University.

Y. Bai and J. Kung (2011) 'Genetic Distance and Income Difference: Evidence from Changes in China's Cross-Strait Relations', *Economics Letters*, 110, 255–258.

J. Beauchamp, D. Cesarini, M. Johannesson, M. van der Loos, P. Koellinger, P. Groenen, J. Fowler, J. Rosenquist, A. Thurik and N. Christakis (2011) 'Molecular Genetics and Economics', *Journal of Economic Perspectives*, 25, 57–82.

A. Bell, P. Richerson and R. McElreath (2009) 'Culture Rather than Genes Provides Greater Scope for the Evolution of Large-Scale Human Prosociality', *Proceedings of the National Academy of Sciences of the United States*, 106, 17671–17674.

D. Benjamin, D. Cesarini, M. van der Loos, C. Dawes, P. Koellinger, P. Magnusson, C. Chabris, D. Conley, D. Laibson, M. Johannesson and P. Vissche (2012) 'The Genetic Architecture of Economic and Political Preferences', *Proceedings of National Academy of Sciences of the United States*, 109, 8026–8031.

A. Bisin and T. Verdier (2000) 'Beyond the Melting Pot: Cultural Transmission, Marriage, and the Evolution of Ethnic and Religious Traits', *Quarterly Journal of Economics*, 115, 955–988.

A. Bisin and T. Verdier (2001) 'The Economics of Cultural Transmission and the Evolution of Preferences', *Journal of Economic Theory*, 97, 298–319.

A. Bisin and T. Verdier (2010) 'The Economics of Cultural Transmission and Socialization', NBER Working Paper 16512.

S. Bowles and H. Gintis (2011) *A Cooperative Species: Human Reciprocity and Its Evolution* (Princeton: Princeton University Press).

R. Boyd and P. Richerson (1985) *Culture and the Evolutionary Process* (Chicago: University of Chicago Press).

L. Cavalli-Sforza and A. Edwards (1964) 'Analysis of Human Evolution', *Proceedings of the 11th International Congress Genetics*, 2, 923–933.

L. Cavalli-Sforza and M. Feldman (1981) *Cultural Transmission and Evolution: A Quantitative Approach* (Princeton: Princeton University Press).

L. Cavalli-Sforza, P. Menozzi and A. Piazza (1994) *The History and Geography of Human Genes* (Princeton: Princeton University Press).

R. Dawkins (1976) *The Selfish Gene* (Oxford: Oxford University Press).

K. Desmet, I. Ortuño-Ortín and R. Wacziarg (2014) 'Culture, Ethnicity and Diversity', Working Paper, UCLA.

K. Desmet, M. Le Breton, I. Ortuño-Ortín and S. Weber (2011) 'The Stability and Breakup of Nations: A Quantitative Analysis', *Journal of Economic Growth*, 16, 183–213.

I. Dyen, J. Kruskal and P. Black (1992) 'An Indoeuropean Classification: A Lexicostatistical Experiment', *Transactions of the American Philosophical Society*, 82, 1–132.

D. Falconer and T. Mackay (1996) *Introduction to Quantitative Genetics* (Harlow: Pearson Education Limited).

J. Fearon (2003) 'Ethnic and Cultural Diversity by Country', *Journal of Economic Growth*, 8, 195–222.

V. Ginsburgh and S. Weber (2011) *How Many Languages Do We Need? The Economics of Linguistic Diversity* (Princeton: Princeton University Press).

Y. Gorodnichenko and G. Roland (2011) 'Culture, Institutions and the Wealth of Nations', Working Paper, UC Berkeley.

J. Greenberg (1956) 'The Measurement of Linguistic Diversity', *Language*, 32, 109–115.

L. Guiso, P. Sapienza and L. Zingales (2009) 'Cultural Biases in Economic Exchange', *Quarterly Journal of Economics*, 124, 1095–1131.

M. Hamilton (2009) *Population Genetics* (Chichester: Wiley-Blackwell).

R. Mecham, J. Fearon and D. Laitin (2006) 'Religious Classification and Data on Shares of Major World Religions', Manuscript, Stanford University.

J. Melitz (2008) 'Language and Foreign Trade', *European Economic Review*, 52, 667–699.

J. Melitz and F. Toubal (2012) 'Native Language, Spoken Language, Translation and Trade', CEPR Discussion Paper 8994.

P. Ralph and G. Coop (2013) 'The Geography of Recent Genetic Ancestry Across Europe', *PLoS Biology*, 11(5), see http://journals.plos.org/plosbiology/article?id=10.1371/journal.pbio.1001555

P. Richerson and R. Boyd (2004) *Not by Genes Alone: How Culture Transformed Human Evolution* (Chicago: University of Chicago Press).

N. Rosenberg, J. Pritchard, J. Weber, H. Cann, K. Kidd, L. Zhivotovsky and M. Feldman (2002) 'Genetic Structure of Human Populations', *Science*, 298, 2381–2385.

P. Seabright (2010) *The Company of Strangers: A Natural History of Economic Life* (Princeton: Princeton University Press).

M. Seldin, R. Shigeta, P. Villoslada, C. Selmi, J. Tuomilehto, G. Silva, J. Belmont, L. Klareskog and P. Gregersen (2006) 'European Population Substructure: Clustering of Northern and Southern Populations', *PLoS Genetics*, 2(9).

E. Spolaore and R. Wacziarg (2009) 'The Diffusion of Development', *Quarterly Journal of Economics*, 124, 469–529.

E. Spolaore and R. Wacziarg (2012) 'Long-Term Barriers to the International Diffusion of Innovations' In J. Frankel and C. Pissarides (eds) *NBER International Seminar on Macroeconomics 2011*, pp. 11–46 (Chicago: University of Chicago Press).

E. Spolaore and R. Wacziarg (2013) 'How Deep Are the Roots of Economic Development?', *Journal of Economic Literature*, 51, 325–369.

E. Spolaore and R. Wacziarg (2014) 'Fertility and Modernity', Forthcoming, *Review of Economics and Statistics*.

E. Spolaore and R. Wacziarg (2015) 'War and Relatedness', Working Paper, UCLA and Tufts University.

C. Tian, R. Kosoy, R. Nassir, A. Lee, P. Villoslada, L. Klareskog, L. Hammarström, H.-J. Garchon, A. Pulver, M. Ransom, P. Gregersen and M. Seldin (2009) 'European Population Genetic Substructure: Further Definition of Ancestry Informative Markers for Distinguishing among Diverse European Ethnic Groups', *Molecular Medicine*, 15, 371–383.

World Christian Database (2007) http://www.worldchristiandatabase.org/wcd/

S. Wright (1951) 'The Genetical Structure of Populations', *Annals of Eugenics,* 15, 323–354.

7
Language Learning and Communicative Benefits

Efthymios Athanasiou, Juan D. Moreno-Ternero and
Shlomo Weber

7.1 Introduction

Most economic contributions in this handbook deal with the way languages and linguistic diversity affect economic outcomes. The reverse direction, that is, how economic issues can have an impact on linguistic diversity and the evolution and acquisition of languages, is explored to a lesser degree, with the exception of Chapter 3 on language evolution (as well as, and to some extent, Chapters 16 to 19 on linguistic standardization in this volume). One can immediately point out that linguistic diversity and, more specifically, an equal distribution of linguistic skills in multi-lingual societies offers both individual and societal opportunities and challenges. Indeed, there are economic and cultural incentives to acquire languages in addition to one's mother tongue. It may be beneficial for an individual to acquire languages spoken by important trade partners of his or her own country. If there existed a universal and dominant *lingua franca* spoken by everybody, the incentives of learning foreign languages in our increasingly globalized society would not be that strong. Even though de Swaan (2001) claims that 'globalization proceeds in English', many commercial and trade negotiations in China, India, Latin America and other parts of the world are conducted in other languages than English. China's and India's populations are much larger than that of all English speaking countries combined, and one can wonder why a Chinese businessman would learn English, as he has direct access to 1.5 billion potential domestic customers. The same applies to individuals in English-speaking countries. However, the improving English-language skills in China, and the ever-rising demand for studying Chinese in the US and Africa, imply that language acquisition is enhanced by trade, as Ginsburgh et al. (2014) show.

Additional examples of economic benefits from learning other languages include their direct impact on earnings. Job opportunities are more often open to applicants whose linguistic repertoire includes several languages. In their study of European labour markets, Ginsburgh and Prieto (2011) show that while the foreign language wage premium is almost non-existent in the UK and quite low in the Netherlands, where the majority of the population is conversant in English, the premium is substantial in Austria, Finland, France, Germany, Greece, Italy, Portugal and Spain.[1] Another example is the importance of languages in making immigration decisions. Once in the new country, the migrant will have to learn, or at least polish his knowledge of the local language to get a job, and thus face a learning decision. The importance of linguistic skills for migrants' labour markets is confirmed by the literature on patterns of language acquisition by immigrants in traditional immigration targets such as Australia, Canada, Germany, Israel, the United Kingdom and the United States (see Chapter 12 in this volume and Chiswick and Miller, 2014). Learning foreign languages also has non-economic effects, such as being immersed into a different culture and gaining unfiltered access to its history, arts and literature in the original language, which is considered worthwhile by some individuals.

Individuals must evaluate economic benefits of learning other languages and weigh them against the cost of acquisition, which may include tuition fees charged by schools and payments to private teachers, as well as the opportunity cost of time committed to classes and homework. In order to evaluate those benefits, we use the general concept of *communicative benefits* introduced in Selten and Pool's (1991) seminal paper, which subsumes both private monetary rewards as well as the cultural and social *pure communicative* benefits of being exposed to and gaining access of other cultures. The communicative benefits of an individual are assumed to be positively correlated with the number of others with whom he or she can communicate by using one of the languages he or she speaks. Naturally, a larger number of people with whom one can communicate raises the attractiveness of learning other languages.

The chapter is organized as follows. By relying on Selten and Pool's concept of communicative benefits, we describe and characterize the language acquisition Nash equilibrium that emerges in societies with multiple linguistic groups. We then proceed with an analysis of the efficiency, which is itself divided into several parts. First, we examine the efficiency properties of the equilibrium and discuss public policies, including cost subsidies which may be necessary to enhance efficiency. We also discuss the options of a social planner and other aspects of social beneficial communication patterns within the society and of socially optimal language acquisition mechanisms. We finally expand the analysis to include the possibility of selecting official languages to increase efficiency and communication within a society.

---

[1] See also Chiswick and Miller (2007), MacManus et al. (1978), Vaillancourt and Lacroix (1985), and Ginsburgh and Weber (2011).

7.2   Communicative benefits

Suppose that society N, which consists of a finite[2] set of individuals, is partitioned in two linguistic groups, N^E and N^F, the populations of which will be denoted by n_E and n_F, respectively. Each citizen speaks the native language of his or her group, E or F, and nobody speaks the language of the other group.

An individual i may choose to learn the other language or not. Parameter $a_i \in \{0, 1\}$ captures his or her decision. We write $a_i = 1$ to denote that i speaks the other language and $a_i = 0$ to denote that he or she does not. Thus, the vector $a_N \in \{0, 1\}^n$ provides a pattern of language acquisition, or, in simpler terms, determines whether each individual $i \in N$ learns the foreign language or not.

The linguistic composition of the society and the patterns of linguistic acquisition (which can be obtained by a random drawing of individuals of both societies) determine the communicative benefits introduced by Selten and Pool (1991).[3] In Figure 7.1 a set of five individuals is divided in two-language groups, $N^E = \{1, 2, 3\}$ and $N^F = \{4, 5\}$. Nodes represent individuals. An arrow stemming from a node and pointing to a set of nodes denotes the fact that the individual who is represented by that node speaks the other language. This simple picture represents both initial conditions and the prevailing pattern of communication. In our case, only individual 1 learns the other language. This means that only one member of N^E will be able to communicate with each member of N^F while each member of N^F may communicate with 1, and 1 only, among the members of N^E.

In broad terms, the communicative benefit assigns a utility value to the partition $\{N^E, N^F\}$ and patterns of language acquisition a_N, and conveys the

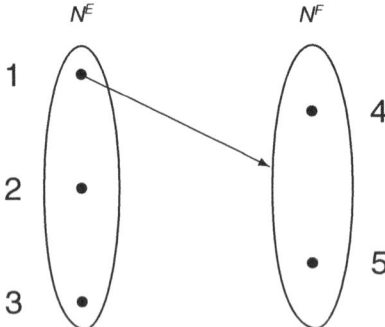

Figure 7.1   An example: Individual 1, whose native language is E, learns language F

---

[2] The finiteness of the set of individuals is not essential. In fact, some models surveyed in this chapter are derived for societies with an infinite number of individuals.

[3] The game-theoretical Selten-Pool model is, in fact, much more general than the variant presented here.

individual disposition over situations that can be fully described by pictures that bear the characteristics of the one in Figure 7.1.

Let $\theta_i^j \in \mathbb{R}_+$ be the value that each individual $i \in N^E$ derives from being able to communicate with individual j who belongs to the other group. Let $\theta_i = (\theta_i^1, \ldots, \theta_i^{n_F}) \in \mathbb{R}_+^{n_F}$. In this setting, let $g : \mathbb{R}_+ \to \mathbb{R}_+$ be an increasing function. For each $i \in N^E$ and each $a_N \in \{0, 1\}^n$, the communicative benefit of i is given by:

$$V_i(a_N) = g\left(\sum_{j \in N^F} \theta_i^j \min\{1, a_i + a_j\}\right).$$

Similarly, for every $j \in N^F$ and each $a_N \in \{0, 1\}^n$, the communicative benefit of j is given by:

$$V_j(a_N) = g\left(\sum_{i \in N^E} \theta_j^i \min\{1, a_j + a_i\}\right).$$

This formulation accommodates two manifest features of the communicative benefit. Individuals care with whom they communicate. The benefit of communication increases with the number of individuals one is able to communicate with. Each link between two individuals generated by the pattern of language acquisition is evaluated separately by the individual to reflect the fact that the possibility of communicating varies across the individuals of the other group. However, for each individual, these agent-specific benefits are summed in order to reflect that the incidence of communication has value in itself. Hence, an individual may be driven to learn the other language either by some key individuals in the other group that is of particular significance, or by the mere size of the other group. The communicative benefit does not incorporate a utility valuation of the initial conditions, that is the partition of individuals into language groups. Admittedly, this carries value, too. However, the communicative benefit focuses on the evaluation of the pattern of language acquisition and is influenced by the effect of the initial conditions only in so far as they affect the final outcome.

The role of the min operator is to ensure that communication between two individuals via more than one language does not have a bearing on the communicative benefit. Indeed, the value of $\min\{1, a_i + a_j\}$ is 1 if at least one of the individuals i and j learns the language of the other group, and zero if both refrain from learning. This formulation treats language as a means to an end, rather than an end in itself. Hence, it captures some of the factors (but not all) that drive people to learn foreign languages. The preferences underlying the expression above are effectively defined over the opportunities that language acquisition presents to the individual and their corresponding value. They are not defined over languages themselves.

To complete the specification of the utility function, we need to address the issue of the cost that learning entails. For each $\lambda \in \{E, F\}$, let the cost of learning language λ be $c_\lambda \geq 0$. There is no a priori reason for having $c_E = c_F$. A key factor that underlies the cost of learning an other language is the linguistic distance between native and target language (see Chapter 5 in this volume). However, this does not necessarily imply that, other things being equal, the cost of learning Spanish if one speaks Portuguese natively is the same as the cost of learning Portuguese for a native Spanish speaker. But individual aptitude has an undisputed influence on the cost. For each $i \in N^E$, let $s_i \in [0, 1]$ be a parameter that captures i's facility to learn foreign languages. The cost for i of learning language λ can then be captured by the expression $s_i c_\lambda$. Having $s_i = 0$ may reflect a situation where an individual is brought up into a bilingual environment or can learn another language in his or her sleep. Hence, this modelling choice allows for some form of native bilingualism. Utility is thus given by the expression:

$$U_i(a_N) = g\left(\sum_{j \in N^F} \theta_i^j \min\{1, a_i + a_j\}\right) - a_i s_i c_F,$$

for each $i \in N^E$. Similarly, for each $j \in N^F$, the net communicative benefit is:

$$U_j(a_N) = g\left(\sum_{j \in N^E} \theta_j^i \min\{1, a_j + a_i\}\right) - a_j s_j c_E.$$

Selten and Pool (1991) show that under those (and, in fact, more general) conditions there exists a linguistic Nash equilibrium for this game. Additional conditions have to be imposed to characterize the equilibrium. Church and King (1993) construct a simplified model, where for all pairs of individuals the value of pairwise communication benefit θ_i^j is independent of i and j and is simply set to one. Moreover, the cost of learning is the same across individuals and language groups. The utility function for an individual $i \in N^E$ boils down to:

$$U_i(a_N) = g\left(\sum_{j \in N^F} \min\{1, a_i + a_j\}\right) - a_i c.$$

Under these simplifying assumptions the value of the cost parameter becomes the determining factor in the model and all members of the same group exhibit identical behaviour in equilibrium, yielding the existence of corner solutions only. Church and King demonstrate that equilibria depend on the value of the cost parameter c. If c is high then no group learns the language of the other; if c is low enough, then everybody learns the language of the other community (which results in an efficiency loss for any $c > 0$). The most interesting is the intermediate case in which only the members of a smaller community learn the other language, while the members of a larger one refrain from doing so.

The reason is quite obvious: the number of members of the other group justifies language acquisition for a smaller community but not for a larger one.

Church and King's model has been extended by Ginsburgh et al. (2007) for the case of multiple (more than two) linguistic communities. They show that a unique linguistic equilibrium arises if the function g in the expression for the communicative benefits exhibits super-modularity and individuals share the same preferences for communication. A further extension of this model to the case with heterogeneous learning aptitudes in each region (or country) has been analysed by Gabszewicz et al. (2011). They consider the following linear functional form of communication benefits for each member $i \in N^E$ and $j \in N^F$, respectively:

$$U_i(a_N) = \sum_{j \in N^F} \theta_i^j \min\{1, a_i + a_j\} - a_i s_i c_F,$$

$$U_j(a_N) = \sum_{j \in N^E} \theta_j^j \min\{1, a_j + a_i\} - a_j s_j c_E,$$

where both values s_i and s_j are distributed uniformly over the interval $[0, 1]$.

The assumption that individuals in the same community face different learning costs enriches the set of equilibrium outcomes, since in equilibrium, some (yet not all) individuals in a given language group may opt to learn the other language, which leads to the existence of interior equilibria, though some may be unstable. The size of each language group along with the profile of learning costs fully determines which equilibrium outcome will prevail. They also describe a range of comparative statics results that evaluate how the share of learners depends on the different parameters. In particular, the number of learners declines if the cost of learning the other language rises. The fact that the number of learners in the community is positively correlated with the learning costs of their own language is probably less obvious. Indeed, the effect is indirect: the increase of the learning costs of language E reduces the number of learners in F. Thus, the acquisition of F becomes more attractive for members of E, as by learning of F they gain access to a larger group of unilingual members of F. Also, an increase in the population of a group makes its language more attractive to acquire.

The model we use as the backdrop for the discussion can be readily extended to accommodate more than two languages and two groups. It must be conceded that doing so would result in some additional insights. Notwithstanding, we opted to maintain the exposition as unencumbered and accessible as possible. The two language model is rich enough to accommodate the basic conceptual and analytical challenges that need to be addressed.

This model was taken to data by Ginsburgh et al. (2007, 2014). As reported in Chapter 20 in this volume, the second paper estimates an equation that relates learning decisions of 13 of the most important world languages by citizens who live in some 190 countries and find that learning is influenced positively by trade, which exhibits a special form of communicative benefits.

7.3 Efficiency

As all papers above recognize, an inherent component of the communicative benefit is that it induces a network externality. Let us assume that individuals only care about the amount of communication they may achieve, although their general disposition towards communication may vary. Let us also assume that all individuals have the same ability to learn the foreign language. For each $i \in N^E$, each $j \in N^F$ and each $a_N \in \{0, 1\}^n$, the expression for the individual utility of i thus reduces to:

$$U_i(a_N) = \theta_i \sum_{j \in N^F} \min\{1, a_i + a_j\} - a_i c_F,$$

and

$$U_j(a_N) = \theta_j \sum_{i \in N^E} \min\{1, a_j + a_i\} - a_j c_E.$$

Consider the following example. Let $N^E = \{1, 2\}$, $N^F = \{3, 4, 5\}$ and $\theta_N = [(1, 1)(0, 0, 0)]$. In words, individuals 1 and 2 attach a value of 1 to the possibility of communicating with an individual outside their language group, while individuals 3, 4 and 5 do not care about communication. For some arbitrarily small $\epsilon > 0$, let $c_E = n_F + \epsilon$ and $c_F = \epsilon$. Each individual's pure strategy is simply a decision on whether to learn the foreign language or not. For each $a_N \in \{0, 1\}^n$ and each $i \in N^E$,

$$\text{if } a_i = 1 \text{ then } v_i(a_N) = \theta_i \sum_{j \in N^F} \min\{1, 1 + a_j\} - c_F = -\epsilon.$$

Therefore, each individual in N^E has a dominant strategy not to learn. The same applies to individuals in the group N^F.

In contrast, the linguistic assignment that maximizes the sum of utilities is $a_N^* = [(0, 0)(1, 1, 1)]$. That is, in the optimum, all individuals whose native tongue is F learn language E, while no one in group E learns the other language. If this pattern of communication were to prevail, all individuals would be communicating with each other. For efficiency to come about though, a mode of sharing the benefits of communication needs to be established.

Communication externalities may also take the form of mis-coordination. Consider the following example. Let $N^E = \{1, 2\}$, $N^F = \{3, 4\}$ and $\theta_N = [(1, 1)(1, 0)]$. For some arbitrarily small $\epsilon > 0$, let $c_E = c_F = 1 + \epsilon$. There exist two Nash equilibria:

$a_N^* = [(1,1)(0,0)]$ and $a_N^{**} = [(1,0)(1,0)]$. Only the first among the two corresponds to the optimal social outcome.

Externalities are inherent in the nature of communication. Consequently, the pattern of communication that emerges in groups of individuals that act on their self-interest often fails to achieve the social optimum.

7.3.1 Efficiency of equilibria

Let us first examine the case of identical learning cost c studied in Church and King (1993). If the social planner cannot discriminate between different communities and individuals, we can still examine whether the equilibrium satisfies *constrained efficiency*.

Note that if there exist two Nash equilibria where one of the groups learns the language of the other, only one could be efficient. A smaller community should engage in learning, while the larger one should not do so. Suppose, for the sake of presentation, that the population n_E is larger than n_F. Then, we have three possible outcomes, which depend on the value of c:

(i) the costs are high so that no learning occurs in equilibrium, which is also a constrained-efficient outcome;
(ii) the costs are low so that the situation where only community F studies the language of E is both an equilibrium and a constrained-efficient outcome;
(iii) in the intermediate cost range the learning of the language of E by community F is efficient, whereas no learning emerges as a Nash equilibrium.

The divergence between the efficient and equilibrium outcomes is rooted in network externalities. When an individual makes a language acquisition choice, she does not take into account that her potential learning of the other language allows others to communicate with her and to raise the total level of societal communicative benefits.

One of the possible remedies for reducing the gap between efficiency and equilibrium is the subsidization of learning costs across the society. By offering tuition reductions (in the case of schools) the government could shrink the range of cost values that yield the 'no learning' equilibrium and expand the range where equilibrium and efficiency requirements produce the same outcome: community F learns the language of E.

The same subsidization policy could be applied in the case of a heterogeneous distribution of learning aptitudes. As Gabszewicz et al. (2011) point out, in the interior equilibrium where only a part of individuals in each community learns the other language, the number of learners is suboptimal and insufficient. The reason is exactly the one mentioned above. In presence of network externalities, best response considerations do not take into account the impact of learning choices of an individual on members of the other community. The latter group would obviously benefit if the other group learns. In the absence of a direct mechanism to enforce learning, cost subsidization policies could be a step in the right direction.

7.3.2   The planner's problem

The purpose of this section is to explore the scope of public intervention in the process of language acquisition. We discuss the reasons that legitimize public policy, the constraints that incentives place on its design, and the various objectives it should strive to accomplish.

A benevolent planner aims at bringing about desirable social outcomes. He operates under constraints. Principal among them is the necessity to accommodate individual incentives. The planner's problem allows for more possibilities if individuals have quasi-linear preferences. We will assume that this is the case. Hence, allowing for the possibility of an individual transfer $t_i \in \mathbb{R}$, the final utility of each agent $i \in N$, at assignment $a_N \in \{0, 1\}^N$, becomes

$$u_i(a_N, t_i) = v_i(a_N) + t_i.$$

The problem the planner faces amounts to associating a linguistic assignment coupled with a profile of transfers with each possible economy $e = ((\theta_{NE}, \theta_{NF}); (c_E, c_F))$ in the domain $\{0, 1\}^n \times \mathbb{R}^2_+$. A mechanism is a function

$$\varphi : \{0, 1\}^n \times \mathbb{R}^2_+ \rightarrow \{0, 1\}^n \times \mathbb{R}^n_+.$$

A mechanism can be construed as the planner's prescription. It assigns an outcome to each contingency that may arise. Hence, $\varphi(e) = (a_N, (t_1, \ldots, t_n))$, while the individual bundle prescribed to $i \in N$ by φ is denoted by $\varphi_i(e) = (a_i, t_i)$.

7.3.3   Efficient assignments

The main reason for studying the planner's problem stems from the fact that decentralized outcomes are generically inefficient. It is therefore legitimate to wonder whether public intervention may bring about a welfare improvement or even ensure the implementation of efficient outcomes. A linguistic assignment is *efficient* if it maximizes the sum of net communication benefits.

Depending on the particular list of initial parameters at hand, we need to solve the following optimization problem $P(e)$:

$$\max_{a_N \in \{0,1\}^n} \left[\sum_{i \in N^E} \left(\theta_i (\sum_{j \in N^F} \min\{1, a_i + a_j\}) - a_i c_F \right) \right.$$
$$\left. + \sum_{j \in N^F} \left(\theta_j (\sum_{i \in N^E} \min\{1, a_i + a_j\}) - a_j c_E \right) \right].$$

For each $e \in \{0, 1\}^n \times \mathbb{R}_+^2$, let $\Sigma(e)$ be the set of assignments that solve $P(e)$. This is a discrete optimization problem. Athanasiou et al. (2015) provide an algorithm that produces for each $e \in \mathcal{E}$, one $a_N \in \Sigma(e)$. For each $e \in \mathcal{E}$, there are at most $2^{|N|}$ candidate solutions. As the set of candidate solutions is finite, $\Sigma(e) \neq \emptyset$ for each $e \in \mathcal{E}$.

A naive algorithm that solves $P(e)$ enumerates all the candidate solutions. Athanasiou et al. (forthcoming) propose an algorithm that runs in polynomial time, that is, it enables a computer to solve the problem quickly, far more so compared to the naive algorithm. However, this depends on the assumption of two-language groups. For an arbitrary number of language groups their algorithm becomes more cumbersome.

Efficient linguistic assignments take various forms depending on the economy. Generically, optimality does not involve all members of a language group to learn. What is more, at an efficient assignment people from either language group may learn. These are not eccentric possibilities. On the contrary, they are prevalent as long as the number of individuals in both groups remains finite. Quite naturally, in large populations, one-sided learning prevails.

These possibilities already allude to the fact that the implementation exercise is involved. A mechanism satisfies efficiency if it always selects an efficient linguistic assignment:

Assignment efficiency: For each $e \in \mathcal{E}$, if $(a_N, t_N) = \varphi(e)$ then $a_N \in \Sigma(e)$.

7.3.4 Implementing efficient linguistic outcomes

A natural question that can be raised is whether a mechanism φ that satisfies *assignment efficiency* may also accommodate incentives.

A mechanism can be manipulated in three distinct ways. First, the individual may misreport relevant information she holds private. In particular, she may lie about her disposition towards communication. Second, the individual may choose not to conform to the prescriptions of the mechanism. Third, the individual may refuse to participate. A mechanism is effectively implementable if it is impervious to these forms of manipulation.

First, under all possible circumstances, the mechanism should induce all individuals to reveal their willingness to communicate truthfully independently of whether others choose to do so. This property, called *strategy-proofness*, facilitates the implementation exercise in a fundamental way. The planner does not need to know the exact type of each individual, nor the distribution of types across the population:

Strategy-proofness: For each $e \in \mathcal{E}$, $i \in N$ and $\theta'_i \in \mathbb{R}_+$, $u_i(\varphi_i(\theta_N, c_E, c_F); \theta_i) \geq u_i(\varphi_i(\theta'_i, \theta_{N \setminus \{i\}}, c_E, c_F); \theta_i)$.

Second, the mechanism should ensure compliance by all individuals involved. There are two ways in which an individual may exhibit non-compliance. First, he may choose to ignore a prescription to learn. Second, he may learn despite being prescribed not to (he may be 'home-schooled'). Between the two, the latter is significantly more costly to ward against. However, neither of the two possibilities transpires if the mechanism is efficient. If an individual finds it profitable to unilaterally deviate from the linguistic assignment bearing the full cost of his or her action, then the assignment cannot be optimal. Therefore, *assignment efficiency* bears also an incentive justification. It facilitates compliance and reduces the cost of implementation.

Finally, participation to the mechanism needs to be voluntary. The mechanism should refrain from coercion. This is a minimal legitimacy requirement:

Individual rationality: For each $e \in \mathcal{E}$ and $i \in N$, $u_i(\varphi_i(e); \theta_i) \geq 0$.

Unfortunately, any mechanism that complies with these three properties runs a deficit. This deficit can be construed as a measure of the cost that communication externalities place on society. This result can be traced back to Green and Laffont (1979). Athanasiou et al. (forthcoming) provide a proof that is context specific. Moreover, building on results by Krishna and Perry (1997), they show that the phenomenon is quite prevalent by providing a set of sufficient conditions for a deficit to ensue.

Proposition 1 *If a mechanism* φ *satisfies* strategy-proofness, assignment efficiency *and* individual rationality, *then there exists* $e \in \{0, 1\}^n \times \mathbb{R}_+^2$ *such that* $\varphi(e) = (a_N, (t_1, \ldots, t_n))$ *and* $\sum_{i \in N} t_i > 0$.

Thus the cost of implementation takes the form of a loss in welfare that can be readily expressed in pecuniary form. The deficit is a direct consequence of communication externalities. In its intensity it captures the barriers that policy faces and may explain the circumstances that impede patterns of language acquisition that enable communication among all.

7.4 Efficient choices of official languages

Another policy instrument that can be used to raise the level of communicative benefit within a multilingual society is the introduction of a relatively small number of official languages,[4] used in education, courts and the media (see Pool, 1991). The knowledge of common languages enhances economic cooperation and cross-regional economic links. It also enhances economic efficiency

---

[4] There are 11 official languages in South Africa, and 24 in the European Union.

and often leads to strengthening national cohesiveness. However, there is another side to the choice of official languages. A person whose native language is not accepted as an official language can feel *disenfranchised* (Ginsburgh and Weber, 2011). As Pool (1991, p. 495) points out, 'those whose languages are not official spend years learning others' languages and may still communicate with difficulty, compete unequally for employment and participation, and suffer from minority or peripheral status'.

Thus, in order to consider introducing official languages as an efficiency-enhancing device that raises the level of communicative benefits, one has to carefully examine their selection. The purpose of this section is to place the choice of official language on fair and attractive foundations, by focusing on commonality of agents and mitigating the negative aspects of the possibly unavoidable restriction of the number of such languages. It is worth pointing out that the model may apply to establish conventions for the choice of a unique or a small number of language(s) in a conversation involving a group of multinational agents.[5] In this sense it enriches the setting of Section 7.2. to account for the existence of a larger number of languages.

Let $M = \{1, 2, \ldots, m\}$ be the set of all languages spoken in society N. If individual $i \in N$ speaks language $l \in M$, we write $a_{il} = 1$. Otherwise, we write $a_{il} = 0$.[6] As before, we assume that there is no distinction between speaking a language well or not, or between native and non-native languages. Let $A = (a_{il})_{(i,l) \in N \times M}$ denote the resulting matrix with entries 0 or 1 that hence summarizes the multilingual reality of society N. Let $\mathcal{A}$ denote the set of such matrices.

A rule $R : \mathcal{A} \to M$ is a mapping selecting a given language $l \in M$ for each matrix A. That is, we assume from the outset that rules only yield *unary* sets. In order to address the subsequent issue of tie breaks, which arises from this assumption, we assume the existence of a given (exogenous) strict ordering $\succ$ among languages. We refer to $\succ$ as the *tie-breaking* rule.

The first obvious rules that come to mind are the so-called dictatorial ones. A *language dictatorship* would always select a given language, whereas an *agent dictatorship* would always select the language spoken by a given agent, provided the tie-breaking rule introduced above holds.[7] Dictatorial rules would be in conflict with standard formalizations of the principle of impartiality, which refers to the fact that ethically irrelevant information is excluded from the evaluation process. More precisely, agent dictatorships would violate the axiom of *anonymity*, which says that the identity of agents should not matter and

---

[5] See Chapter 11 in this volume.

[6] Note that in presence of two languages only, as in Section 7.2, the notation a_i is sufficient to indicate whether individual i speaks another language. In the multilingual setting we need to specify whether individual i speaks language l, which necessitates the double index notation.

[7] Note that the tie-breaking rule could be considered in itself as language dictatorship.

the choice of an official language should not depend on who speaks it. Language dictatorships, on the other hand, would violate the natural counterpart axiom of anonymity, *neutrality*, which says that the name of languages should not matter either. Neutrality expresses a symmetric treatment of languages. There are compelling reasons in our setting to endorse a symmetric treatment of agents (as formalized by the axiom of anonymity), but not necessarily of languages. For instance, one might want to provide a slight advantage to the language identified in the status quo. Somewhat related, one might want to break hypothetical ties in a precise way, given our assumption of unary images of rules, i.e. that there exists a unique official language. For these reasons, we shall define *weak neutrality* as the property of neutrality, when restricted to the case in which there are no ties to break. Language dictatorships will also violate this axiom and, hence, we shall discard them from our analysis.

Another axiom with normative appeal in this context is *monotonicity*, which establishes the fact that if a language is selected, it would also be selected after one agent, who did not speak it before, learns it, *ceteris paribus*.

As stated below, the three previous axioms point towards a rule. This is the so-called *minimal disenfranchisement rule* (MD), which selects a language excluding (disenfranchising) the lowest possible number of agents.[8] Formally,

MD: For each $A \in \mathcal{A}$, let

$$A^m = \arg\max \left\{ \sum_{i \in N} a_{il} : l \in M \right\}.$$

Then, $MD(A) = l^*$, where $l^* \in A^m$ is such that $l^* \succ l$ for each $l \in A^m \setminus \{l^*\}$.

In words, *MD* is the rule selecting the language with a highest number of speakers (*score*). If several languages have the same score, we resort to the given (exogenous) strict ordering among languages mentioned above, as a tie-breaking norm.[9] Moreno-Ternero and Weber (2015) prove the following results:

Proposition 2 *The minimal disenfranchisement rule satisfies anonymity, weak neutrality and monotonicity.*

It is worth mentioning that the minimal disenfranchisement rule also selects in this context the language that maximizes communication benefits described in the previous section, that is, the number of pairs of agents that can communicate using a given language.

---

[8] The term is inspired by the notion described by Ginsburgh et al. (2005).

[9] Note that $\sum_{i \in N} a_{il}$ yields the number of agents speaking language l, i.e. the 1 entries in the *l*th column of A. Obviously, $n - \sum_{i \in N} a_{il}$ yields the number of agents not speaking (disenfranchised by) language l, i.e. the 0 entries in the *l*th column of A.

The (benchmark) model just described could be considered as a model of collective choice under dichotomous preferences. The contrast between our model and the seminal work on the topic by Bogomolnaia et al. (2005) is that we consider a specific tie-breaking norm to obtain deterministic rules, whereas they endorse a probabilistic approach and consider lotteries/time sharing.[10] More precisely, the alternative to our *MD* rule in Bogomolnaia et al. (2005) is the so-called utilitarian mechanism, defined as the uniform lottery over the subset of outcomes liked (languages spoken, in our model) by the largest number of agents. Such a mechanism is anonymous, neutral, strategy-proof and ex ante efficient (although it is not characterized by such a combination of properties). Somewhat related, our *MD* rule is a specific instance of approval voting (Brams and Fishburn, 1978), with the proviso that only one alternative is selected (based on our tie-breaking norm). If no specific cardinality is imposed on the definition of a social choice function, then approval voting is characterized in this context by anonymity, neutrality, strategy-proofness and strict monotonicity (Vorsatz, 2007).

The problem of the choice of official languages becomes more complex when one extends the benchmark model presented before in either of several plausible directions. One plausible extension (that we shall not consider here) is the one in which a distinction between speaking a language well or not (or between native and non-native languages) is made. Another plausible extension is to analyse the case in which several official languages are allowed. In what follows, we consider the case of two official languages.

Let M^2 be the set of pairs of different languages in M. Now, a rule $R: \mathcal{A} \to M^2$ selects for each matrix A a pair of languages $\{l, q\} \in M$. We shall call those rules *pair rules*, although we might refer to them simply as rules if there is no possible confusion.

A natural starting point is to propose pair rules that extend to this setting the minimal disenfranchisement rule highlighted above. Two plausible options arise. The first consists of selecting the pair of languages such that the number of agents speaking none of them is as low as possible. The second consists of selecting the pair of languages with the highest individual scores. The former option also suggests a somewhat dual rule, which would select the pair of languages such that the number of agents speaking both of them is as large as possible. As a matter of fact, the three rules just outlined could be seen as members of a general family of *pair-scoring rules*. In order to introduce this formally, we need some additional notation. Let $f: \{0, 1\}^2 \to \mathbb{R}$ be a non-decreasing and symmetric function, i.e. $f(0, 0) \leq f(1, 0) = f(0, 1) \leq f(1, 1)$. Let $\mathcal{F}$ denote the set of such functions.

---

[10] See also Bogomolnaia and Moulin (2004).

D^f: For each $f \in \mathcal{F}$, $A \in \mathcal{A}$, and $\{l, m\} \in M^2$, let

$$\rho_f(l, m) = \sum_{i \in N} f\{a_{il}, a_{im}\},$$

and

$$A^{\rho_f} = \arg\max \left\{ \rho_f(l, m) : \{l, m\} \in M^2, l \succ m \right\}.$$

Then, $D^f(A) = \{l^*, m^*\}$, where $(l^*, m^*) \in A^{\rho_f}$ is such that either $l^* \succ l$ for each $(l, m) \in A^{\rho_f} \setminus \{(l^*, m^*)\}$, or $m^* \succ m$ for each $(l^*, m) \in A^{\rho_f} \setminus \{(l^*, m^*)\}$.

Each rule of the family selects the two languages with a highest score, according to the corresponding function f (with ties broken via $\succ$). Note that if $f(\cdot, \cdot) \equiv \max(\cdot, \cdot)$ then $D^f \equiv D^{\max}$ is the first rule suggested above. Similarly, if $f(\cdot, \cdot) \equiv \sum(\cdot, \cdot)$ then $D^f \equiv D^{sum}$ is the second rule suggested above. Finally, if $f(\cdot, \cdot) \equiv \min(\cdot, \cdot)$ then $D^f \equiv D^{\min}$ is the third rule suggested above.

We now introduce another pair rule, inspired by the notion of communicative benefits.

D^{SP}: For each $A \in \mathcal{A}$, and $\{l, m\} \in M^2$, let

$$\rho_{SP}(l, m) = |\left\{(i, j) \in N^2 : \text{there exists } \lambda \in \{l, m\} \text{ such that } a_{i\lambda} = a_{j\lambda} = 1\right\}|,$$

and

$$A^{\rho_{SP}} = \arg\max \left\{ \rho_{SP}(l, m) : \{l, m\} \in M^2, l \succ m \right\}.$$

Then, $D^{SP} = \{l^*, m^*\}$, where $(l^*, m^*) \in A^{\rho_{SP}}$ is such that either $l^* \succ l$ for each $(l, m) \in A^{\rho_{SP}} \setminus \{(l^*, m^*)\}$, or $m^* \succ m$ for each $(l^*, m) \in A^{\rho_{SP}} \setminus \{(l^*, m^*)\}$.

In words, D^{SP} selects the pair of languages guaranteeing the highest number of pairs of agents that can communicate thanks to a language in the pair.

The following example shows that D^{SP} is not equivalent to any of the three other focal rules presented above.[11] Consider the following matrix A:

$$A = \begin{pmatrix} 0 & 1 & 1 \\ 0 & 1 & 1 \\ 1 & 0 & 1 \\ 1 & 0 & 0 \\ 0 & 1 & 1 \end{pmatrix}.$$

The example conveys a group of five agents and three possible languages $\{1, 2, 3\}$, with the tie-breaking rule $1 \succ 2 \succ 3$. Three agents speak languages 2 and 3, whereas one agent speaks languages 1 and 3, and another agent

---

[11] As a matter of fact, D^{SP} is not a pair-scoring rule.

only speaks language 1. It is straightforward to see that the pair of languages $\{1,3\}$ maximizes the number of pairs of agents that are able to communicate, i.e. $D^{SP}(A) = \{1,3\}$. On the other hand, all agents speak at least one language within the pair $\{1,2\}$. Thus, $D^{\max}(A) = \{1,2\}$. Finally, the pair of languages $\{2,3\}$ encompasses the two languages with the highest individual scores. It also has the highest number of agents speaking both languages within the pair, i.e. $D^{sum}(A) = \{2,3\} = D^{\min}(A)$.

All the rules presented above satisfy the extensions to this setting of the three axioms presented above for the case of the choice of a unique official language. The following axioms allow us to distinguish among those rules.

First, we consider the axiom of *consistency*, stating that the (pair) rule always selects as a member of the pair the language selected by *MD* for the same problem. In other words, the rule consistently extends *MD* to the setting of pairs of languages.[12] It is straightforward to show that D^{sum} and D^{SP} obey consistency. The following examples show that neither $D^{\max}$ nor $D^{\min}$ does so.

$$
A^1 = \begin{pmatrix} 1 & 1 & 0 \\ 1 & 1 & 0 \\ 1 & 0 & 1 \\ 1 & 0 & 1 \\ 0 & 0 & 1 \\ 0 & 1 & 0 \end{pmatrix} \qquad
A^2 = \begin{pmatrix} 1 & 0 & 0 \\ 1 & 0 & 0 \\ 1 & 0 & 0 \\ 1 & 0 & 0 \\ 0 & 1 & 1 \\ 0 & 1 & 1 \\ 0 & 1 & 1 \end{pmatrix}.
$$

The example given in A^1 conveys a group of six agents and three possible languages $\{1,2,3\}$, with the tie-breaking rule $1 \succ 2 \succ 3$. Two agents speak languages 1 and 2. Two other agents speak languages 1 and 3. One agent speaks only language 2 and the last one speaks only language 3. Thus, language 1 minimizes disenfranchisement. However, all agents speak at least one language within the pair $\{2,3\}$. Thus, $D^{\max}(A^1) = \{2,3\}$.

The example in A^2 conveys a group of seven agents and three possible languages $\{1,2,3\}$, with the tie-breaking rule $1 \succ 2 \succ 3$. Four agents only speak language 1, whereas three agents speak languages 2 and 3. Thus, language 1 minimizes disenfranchisement. However, the pair $\{2,3\}$ has the highest number of agents speaking both languages within the pair. Thus, $D^{\min}(A^2) = \{2,3\}$.

The next axiom, *no redundancy*, states that if an agent speaks one of the two selected languages, the knowledge of the second does affect the selection of the pair. It is straightforward to show that $D^{\max}$ obeys no redundancy. The following example shows that neither D^{sum} nor $D^{\min}$ does so. The example in A^3 conveys a

---

[12] The axiom is inspired by a notion that has played a fundamental role in axiomatic work, and for which normative underpins have been provided (see Thomson, 2012).

group of six agents and three possible languages $\{1, 2, 3\}$, with the tie-breaking rule $1 \succ 2 \succ 3$. Two agents speak languages 1 and 2. Another agent speaks languages 1 and 3. One agent only speaks language 1, whereas two agents only speak language 3.

$$A^3 = \begin{pmatrix} 1 & 1 & 0 \\ 1 & 1 & 0 \\ 1 & 0 & 0 \\ 1 & 0 & 1 \\ 0 & 0 & 1 \\ 0 & 0 & 1 \end{pmatrix}.$$

Here, the pair $\{1, 3\}$ encompasses the two languages with the highest individual score, i.e. $D^{sum}(A^3) = \{1, 3\}$. However, consider a new example $\hat{A}^3$, with the only change that the agent who spoke languages 1 and 3 in A^3 only speaks language 1 now. Then, by virtue of the tie-breaking rule, the pair $\{1, 2\}$ would now encompass the two languages with the highest individual score, i.e. $D^{sum}(\hat{A}^3) = \{1, 2\}$.

Suppose now that the tie-breaking rule for the example in A^3 is $1 \succ 3 \succ 2$. The pair $\{1, 2\}$ has the highest number of agents speaking both of the languages within the pair (2), i.e. $D^{min}(A^3) = \{1, 2\}$. However, consider a new example $\bar{A}^3$, with the only change that one of the agents who spoke languages 1 and 2 in A^3 only speaks language 1. Then, by virtue of the new tie-breaking rule, the pair $\{1, 3\}$ would now have the highest number of agents speaking both languages within the pair (1), i.e. $D^{min}(\bar{A}^3) = \{1, 3\}$.

Similarly, the example modelled by A, introduced above, shows that D^{SP} also violates no redundancy. As mentioned above, $D^{SP}(A) = \{1, 3\}$. Now, consider a new example $\bar{A}$, with the only change that one of the agents who spoke languages 2 and 3 in A only speaks language 2. Here three pair of agents who were able to communicate with the pair of languages $\{1, 3\}$ can no longer communicate. Thus, the pair of languages $\{1, 2\}$ becomes more prominent, i.e. $D^{SP}(\bar{A}) = \{1, 2\}$.

7.5   Conclusion

In this chapter we have focussed on a relatively unexplored topic dealing with the economic incentives of learning foreign languages. We have used the Selten-Pool notion of communicative benefits to establish equilibrium patterns of language acquisition, and describe theoretical and empirical findings in this relatively new field of research. It is important to point out the reason for which equilibrium outcomes often fail the efficiency (and even the constrained efficiency) test. The problem lies in the network externality: in making his or her language acquisition decision, an individual does not take into account how his or her own decision affects the level of communicative benefits of others. We then discussed possible public policies that can reduce the gap between equilibrium and desired efficiency. Our analysis of efficiency leads us to identify the requirements that guarantee socially beneficial communication patterns and optimal language acquisition mechanisms within a society.

We also analysed how to raise the level of communicative benefits (and economic efficiency) by examining optimal choices of sets of official languages that facilitate economic cooperation, cultural exchange and enhanced trade relationship with a country and with other trading partners. However, the selection of official languages is a delicate and often difficult task which, according to Pool (1991), is due to the divisive, symbolic and contentious nature of language conflict, the inherent incompatibilities between language communities, the reluctance of the majority group to concede linguistic rights to minorities, and the power of civil servants to protect their linguistic privileges. The chapter therefore lays down fair and sound principles that may help to overcome such difficulties.

It is worth pointing out that most of the issues described here are relatively new. They therefore require further research, both theoretical and empirical, to address the patterns of language acquisition emerging in our rapidly changing economic and social environment. The tools described here could also be useful in examining the benefits and costs of linguistic policies in several countries in Europe, South and North America, and Africa.

Acknowledgements

We wish to thank Jorge Alcalde-Unzu and Marc Vorsatz for an illuminating conversation on the intricacies of approval voting. Athanasiou and Weber wish to acknowledge the support of the Ministry of Education and Science of the Russian Federation, grant No. 14.U04.31.0002, administered through the NES Center for the Study of Diversity and Social Interactions. Moreno-Ternero also acknowledges financial support from the Spanish Ministry of Science and Innovation (ECO2011-22919).

References

E. Athanasiou, S. Dey and G. Valletta (2015) 'Groves Mechanisms and Communication Externalities', *Review of Economic Design*.

A. Bogomolnaia and H. Moulin (2004) 'Random Matching under Dichotomous Preferences', *Econometrica*, 72, 257–279.

A. Bogomolnaia, H. Moulin and R. Stong (2005) 'Collective Choice under Dichotomous Preferences', *Journal of Economic Theory*, 122, 165–184.

S. Brams and P. Fishburn (1978) 'Approval Voting', *American Political Science Review*, 72, 831–847.

B. Chiswick and P. Miller (2007) *The Economics of Language, International Analyses* (London and New York: Routledge).

B. Chiswick and P. Miller (2014) 'International Migration and Economics of Language', IZA Discussion paper 7880.

J. Church and I. King (1993) 'Bilingualism and Network Externalities', *Canadian Journal of Economics*, 26, 337–345.

A. de Swaan (2001) *Words of the World* (Cambridge: Polity Press).

J. Gabszewicz, V. Ginsburgh and S. Weber (2011) 'Bilingualism and Communicative Benefits', *Annals of Economics and Statistics*, 101–102, 271–286.

V. Ginsburgh, J. Melitz and F. Toubal (2014) 'Foreign Language Learning: An Econometric Analysis', CEPR Discussion Paper 9091.

V. Ginsburgh, I. Ortuno-Ortin and S. Weber (2005) 'Language Disenfranchisement in Linguistically Diverse Societies: The Case of the European Union', *Journal of the European Economic Association*, 3, 946–965.

V. Ginsburgh, I. Ortuno-Ortin and S. Weber (2007) 'Learning Foreign Languages: Theoretical and Empirical Implications of the Selten and Pool Model', *Journal of Economic Behavior and Organizations*, 64, 337–347.

V. Ginsburgh and J. Prieto (2011) 'Returns to Foreign Languages of Native Workers in the European Union', *Industrial and Labor Relations*, 64, 599–618.

V. Ginsburgh and S. Weber (2011) *How Many Languages Do We Need? The Economics of Linguistic Diversity* (Princeton: Princeton University Press).

J. Green and J. Laffont (1979) *Incentives in Public Decision Making* (Amsterdam: North-Holland).

V. Krishna and M. Perry (1997) 'Efficient Mechanism Design', Manuscript, Pennsylvania State University.

W. MacManus, W. Gould and F. Welsch (1978) 'Earnings of Hispanic Men: The Role of English language Proficiency', *Journal of Labor Economics*, 1, 101–130.

J. Moreno-Ternero and S. Weber (2015) 'An Axiomatic Approach to the Choice of Official Languages', Manuscript.

J. Pool (1991) 'The Official Language Problem', *American Political Science Review*, 85, 495–514.

R. Selten and J. Pool (1991) 'The Distribution of Foreign Language Skills as a Game Equilibrium' In R. Selten (ed.) *Game Equilibrium Models*, Vol. 4 (Berlin: Springer-Verlag).

W. Thomson (2012) 'On the Axiomatics of Resource Allocation: Interpreting the Consistency Principle', *Economics and Philosophy*, 28, 385–421.

F. Vaillancourt and R. Lacroix (1985) 'Revenus et langue au Québec', http://www.cslf.gouv.qc.ca/publications/PubD120/D120-6

M. Vorsatz (2007) 'Approval Voting on Dichotomous Preferences', *Social Choice and Welfare*, 28, 127–141.

8
Language and Emotion

Niall Bond and Victor Ginsburgh

8.1 Introduction

In this chapter we explore language and emotion from the vantage of an intellectual historian and conference interpreter – with three active working languages (in order of acquisition, English, German and French) and a smattering of other Romance languages – and the vantage of a multilingual economist who was raised in his early years in German (and some Swahili) and went on to work in English and French. We focus primarily on the emotional implications of thinking and expressing oneself in more than one language. Reflection on the effect that knowledge of more than one language may have on the emotions leads to the recognition that possessing several languages can offer and impose occasions to perceive of and describe emotional states with a different precision and more varied nuances of meaning than knowing a single language. Thought processes that are conveyed by languages are triggered by and trigger emotions. The ultimate values to which the most rational thought processes are subjected are irrational and often emotional. As researchers and thinkers, we are called upon to write and think in languages and linguistic cultures with differing rules as to what is of interest, what can be said and what should be censored. Where might the abilities and handicaps of a polyglot with regard to emotion lie? One of the first human experiences is that passions, concupiscent and irascible, as Thomas Hobbes expressed it, are socially regulated. And when one moves from one community to another, one realizes that the regulations of

N. Bond translated the quotes from French and German writers into English. The English translations appear in the main text, the original French or German are relegated to footnotes. V. Ginsburgh is grateful to S. Weber who invited him to write with him on language and emotions; this unfortunately has not (yet) happened. He is also grateful to S. Weyers for many discussions on language and culture, including the many comments on this chapter and, in particular, for having introduced him to Julian Green, as well as to R. Kast, a Frenchman born in Algeria, who still considers himself an Algerian.

such emotions are not identical. France, Germany, the United Kingdom and the United States are culturally all relatively close. And yet moves between their cultural universes and between the cultural empires that lie within them involve confrontations with a divergence of values and emotional conflicts the resolution of which may lie in the acceptance of a juxtaposition of contradictory feelings.

After a first discussion of the very notion of emotions (Section 8.2) described by sociologists, philosophers and psychologists, we will turn to some of those who moved voluntary or were sometimes forced to move from one language (usually their mother tongue) to the language of their adoption (or of a colonized country) as well as to those who exiled themselves, but kept writing in their mother tongue. We cannot know or guess the emotions of such people, and therefore we have had to rely on what they wrote about their switch (or refusal to switch) to another language than their native tongue. These people are essentially writers and poets, and their thoughts are discussed in Sections 8.3 to 8.7. Section 8.8 will briefly conclude our voyage into literature and poetry.

8.2   Emotions and the polyglot

Ferdinand Tönnies's (1887) *Gemeinschaft und Gesellschaft*, with its considerations of the foundation of communities, linguistic and other, was groundbreaking for the modern social sciences, offering value-laden commentary on language as a primary bond in communities and on polyglots.[1] For Tönnies, language does not spring forth from hostility but from 'familiarity, interiority and love' – and in particular the 'deep understanding between a mother and a child' allows the 'mother tongue' to grow with the greatest ease and liveliness. Tönnies writes that even expressions of hostility in one's mother tongue may harbour friendship and unity issuing from a unity of consanguinity, a proximity of blood and a mixture of blood which allows the possibility of a community of human wills to be expressed the most directly through geographic and ensuing intellectual proximity. In Tönnies's intellectual universe, language is rift with emotion and is an original expression of the *Wesenwille* (essential will) of the speaker. Yet for Tönnies, with the polyglot, more is less, and rather remarkably so. For we know that Tönnies was himself a remarkable polyglot, having been versed in Ancient Greek and Latin to a level that allowed him to write a doctoral dissertation in Latin. He corresponded with Bertrand Russell in English, with Émile Durkheim in French and with Harald Hoffding in Danish. Yet his depiction of the polyglot is the condemnation of the rootless, as emerges in his discussion of the encounter between traders and sedentary cultures. Trade is seen as alien and execrable in sedentary cultures, and the trader is

---

[1] On Tönnies, see also Bond (2013).

typical of the educated – homeless, a traveller, with some knowledge of foreign customs and arts, bearing no love or piety for those of any particular country, with a command of several languages, with the gift of the gab and double tongued, capable of adapting to any surroundings while never losing sight of his aims, capable of changing character and mentality (beliefs or opinions) as though they were yesterday's fashion. The multilingual trader is the very opposite of the peasant who is tied to the soil or of the solid craftsman and burgher, whose horizons are more restricted. Tönnies seems to be suggesting that the ability to choose between languages reduces both emotional loyalties to language and the emotiveness of any given language. And yet while he does seem to put his finger upon a specific human type, and there are no doubt traders of the sort he describes, he ignores the significant number of human beings who do not reduce themselves to a common denominator among the languages at their disposal. Polyglots are occasionally suspected of putting profit over community. In his lecture 'On the Various Methods of Translation', presented on 14 June 1813 to the Königlichen Akademie der Wissenschaften (Royal Academy of the Sciences), Schleiermacher (1977) made a somewhat disdainful reference to 'mere interpreting', which strips language of all aspects that cannot be reduced to callous cash payment. But contrary to such suspicions, many educated polyglots draw from the intellectual and emotional wealth that the plurality of languages affords to enrich their emotional lives and those of others. The differences in languages and the expressions of things perceived or felt allow them to achieve a heightened awareness – Tönnies uses the expression, *Bewusstheit*. Through such hybridity, individuals may make a contribution to the languages in which they operate.

Multilingualism creates links to a plurality of communities, each of which is subject to a plurality of orders. 'When in Rome, do as the Romans do' does not necessarily imply 'think as the Romans think' or 'feel as the Romans feel'. The transferring of feelings through words across cultures can trigger alienation but also trigger recognition. The work undertaken on the history of emotions by Ute Frevert (2013) at the Max Planck Institute, it should be remembered, had as one of its starting points the notion of *Ehrgefühl* or feeling of honour, which for many (generally male) speakers stood for a complexity of genuinely perceived or merely displayed emotions and obscured other emotions which rose to the surface once the overriding notion of a feeling of honour had declined and emotiveness was unburdened of the connoted opprobrium of self-indulgence or the effeminate. Historians such as Peter Gay (1985), author of *Freud for Historians*, and sociologists such as Theodor W. Adorno et al. (1950) in *The Authoritarian Personality* also emphasize the importance of self-censorship in society. Bearers of 'deviant desires' or emotions were described in English as 'unspeakables', for instance in connection with Oscar Wilde, and the history of language and emotions has been a history of the non-expression or the very circumspect expression of emotions. Yet English, the language of the 'stiff upper lip' and the repressed for some, is also perceived of as a language of liberation through the absorption of the foreign to which it has lent itself as the creole language of a maritime global power which is a bearer of a universalist creed of liberation.

The acquisition of new languages can be seen as the opening up of new markets of feelings through hitherto unknown linguistic means of expressions, and through hitherto unconceived of individuals who use other languages to express feelings that may be recognized. The multilingual realize more than others that expressions of emotions of a particular sort may be frowned upon or be verbally impossible in one linguistic culture and applauded in another, and are more sceptical of 'universals'. They may, as Tönnies suggests, adopt strategies in compartmentalized existences, preferring conceptualization in English for irreverence, German for metaphysical speculation or French for expressions of sensual pleasures less appreciated in cultures in which enjoyment is prepared in factories and not by artisans.[2] But these are sweeping generalizations. Language preferences, experience suggests, are themselves the product of experience and imply a continuation of conversations in languages commenced in linguistic communities of two or more, even in such instances in which the second or the Other is oneself. Such linguistic promiscuity need not imply a lessening of loyalties, but may involve a diversification of feelings of loyalties.

Feelings have tended to be regarded as intruders into the locus of rational control, whether physical, economic, military, etc., as is evidenced in the earliest mention of emotions in scientific discourse. Ute Frevert regards this suspicion of emotions inter alia as a result of the seduction of emotions by National Socialism. It can be said that functionalism involved the wholesale repression of the ultimate irrationality and emotiveness of ultimate values, even when those ultimate values consist in the repression of emotional values. The desire to grasp emotions scientifically goes back several centuries. When, in his *The Expression of Emotions in Man and Animals*, still under the notable influence of phrenology, Charles Darwin (1872) writes that the young and the old of widely different races, both with man and animals, express the same state of mind by the same movements, he is assuming something that behaviourists later ruled out: that we can establish and thus compare states of mind. When Charles Bell (1824) wrote in *Anatomy and Philosophy of Expression* that 'expression is to the passions as language is to thought', he had created

---

[2] Or 'I speak Spanish to God, Italian to women, French to men and German to my horse', a quote attributed to Charles V.

a strict divide between passions or feelings on the one hand, and thought on the other, so as to prevent the intrusion of the feelings into the domain of rationality. Darwin's observation that 'the force of language is much aided by the expressive movements of the face and body' suggests that language and concomitant expressions of will are subjected to some higher purposive rationality lodged in the human mind. Such assumptions might have been abandoned with the reception of Arthur Schopenhauer's (1818/1859) *Die Welt als Wille und Vorstellung*, which only penetrated the English-speaking world with its first translation in the 1880s. Darwin's aim to argue the universality of expressions of emotions seems to stand in contradiction to the crux of evolutionism, which is that human beings change. The very language of Darwin invites reflection on the lexical fields which he seeks to delimit in a universal way: as an example, the term 'helplessness', to be found in Chapter 11 of his *The Expression of Emotions in Man and Animals*, can be translated into French as *impuissance*. The quest for a universal catalogue of physical gestures for the expression of emotions seems ill directed not only between cultures but diachronically, if we consider performance aspects of facial gesticulations among recent generations in France for example. Darwinians believed that passions subsided with increasingly dispassionate generations of human subjects, an assumption that remains to be validated: dispassionate behaviour may have been envisaged as a compliance with the social conventions of civility of the day according to the tenets of the Church of England or Empire. Such civilities have yielded to other channellings of thoughts and feelings. The passions and emotions of human beings are pointed in different directions and one distinct pointer appears to be languages.

That emotions do not have universal markers has emerged in the study of links between emotions and mentalities in an awareness of the necessary subjectivity of historians. This preoccupation was taken up by Alain Corbin (2000), a historian of forms of sensitivity, from his interest in the developments of the olfactory sense with its relations to the emotional. This interest in emotions as contingent and culturally trained may itself be related to values foregrounded in parts of French academia but not globally. That there should be a history of emotions that may to an extent transcend cultural and linguistic boundaries in no way precludes differences in the way peoples of different linguistic cultures may allow themselves consciously to feel and express those feelings in words, many of which defy translation.

The plurality of languages that Tönnies describes as lying in the culturally disloyal service of a mentality necessarily subjugated to capitalism and hence a form of servitude even amongst society's apparently dominating class in reality opens up a freedom of choice, not just of nouns, adjectives, verbs, adverbs and syntax, but more importantly of conversational partners and communicative recipients with their greater or lesser openness towards expressions of emotions, the full range of their determinations and possible transgressions of norms which are applied to channelling emotions. There are equally linguistic cultures, sometimes related to confessional cultures, which are more conducive to the acceptance of transgression and the abdication of our actions to our senses than others, some of which may go so far as to celebrate the compulsively transgressive and the abandonment of control.

The order of acquisition of languages has not been shown to determine either the elaborateness of codes mastered in the languages, inclusive of emotional registers, or the intensity of emotions felt when a language that was acquired more or less late is the vehicle of the expression of those emotions. A mother tongue will not necessarily be the language in which thoughts are clearest and emotions the most powerful. Emotiveness in exchanges is affected not only by the permissiveness of emotional codes and by the lexical wealth which allows for the expression of feelings, but equally by grammar and syntax, as the German–French philosopher, Heinz Wismann (2012), argues in his essay, *Penser entre les langues*. The French language, he argues, offers a sort of 'connivance' or complicity inasmuch as speakers in a conversation take the liberty of interrupting others' sentences and finishing them as though the syntax extended an invitation to fusion. He argues that this is precluded in German because of the syntactical necessity to finish the sentence with a verb, the key element. Wismann stresses that what is of interest is how subjects convey intended meaning (*vouloir dire*) through grammar (p. 18).

Changing languages for the purpose of honing our capacity of judgement is akin to exile. For Wismann, the very deployment of intellectual acuity is invariably accompanied by a form of exile (p. 43). He defines intellectual acuity, the readiness to engage in a criticism which places all convictions founded upon tradition or authority, as a mental process intended to lead elsewhere than back to a sedentary mindset. This intellectual habitus is akin to what is described in Yiddish as that of a '*Luftmensch*' (Wismann, p. 45). Wismann sums up the feeling as being between two things – being at home while not being at home, being confident while lacking in assurance – which is less a posture of indecision than the refusal of allowing oneself to be fully absorbed by a single position. However, moving from one community or perfectly delimited linguistic universe to another is difficult and painful, for belonging to a community is deeply tied to a need for not merely material but also symbolic solidarity which gives the feeling of having a home; *freischwebende Intelligenz* was defined by Alfred Weber as a cosmopolitan outlook before the term was taken on by Karl Mannheim (1929) to suggest that there was an intelligentsia without economic ideological references in his work on ideology and utopia. This sense of exile is the subject of Norman Manea's (2012) *The Fifth Impossibility: Essays on Exile and Language*.

8.3   Choosing languages within language communities

While Walter Benjamin (1923) has assumed that genuine literature has no target since it is born of a need of expression independent of the community in which the work emerges, we are of the opinion that linguistic expressions emerge in communities. Thus, the freest floating intelligences are tied up in an intricate web of other subjects whose linguistic expressions influence them. Language is social action in the Weberian inasmuch as it is oriented around the action of others. The absence of receptors of communication is an improbable assumption when speakers or writers set forth to publish something. Publishing, linguistic expression towards a community, involves myriad aspects of attitude towards the codes, the norms and the means offered by a language. This is explicit, for instance, in Ngugi wa Thiong'o's decision to 'decolonize the mind', moving from English to his native language, writing the first modern novel in Gikuyu in 1980, *Caitaani mutharaba-Ini* (*Devil on the Cross*), on prison-issued toilet paper.

Here, the decision to forswear English is related to the repudiation of the most global linguistic vehicle and its concomitant ideological assumptions, notwithstanding the cultural assimilation into the global system that English may imply when the author taught at Yale University and New York University. A very different attitude is evidenced by the Japanese author, Akira Mizubayashi (2011), who moved to Montpellier in 1973 at the age of 20 and cultivated a literary French as far off as Tokyo, publishing a French language work, *Une langue venue d'ailleurs* (*A Language which Has Come from Elsewhere*). At the same time, French was a language that was not imposed by colonial forces, but offered as a foreign realm of freedom and nuance.

The emotional potential of a newly acquired language contrasts with the loss incurred when one forgets a language or recognizes the alienation that arises when one is confronted with stark changes in the language. Linguistic forgetfulness is the subject of Daniel Heller-Roazen's (2008) *Echolalias*, which concerns the forgetting of a language by an individual or the disappearance of a language altogether. The extreme individual case is aphasia, i.e. the loss or impairment of the power to use words as symbols or ideas that results from a brain lesion. Yet aphasia does not necessarily imply the inability either to conceptualize or to feel, as is shown through speech recovery.

The suggestion that language is more than a means of communicating was emphasized at the very beginning of the 19th century by Wilhelm von Humboldt (1988 [1836]). It was later emphasized by anthropologist Franz Boas (1940), linguists Edward Sapir (1949) and Benjamin Whorf (1956), and came to be known as the Sapir–Whorf hypothesis: language and culture are interdependent, and the structure of the language that one uses (often as native language) influences the way of thinking and behaving. The consequences, summarized by Kramsch (1998, p. 12), are that, despite the possibility of translating from one language to another, 'there will always be an incommensurable residue of untranslatable culture associated with the linguistic structures of any given language'.

This bold hypothesis (language and culture are interdependent, and the structure of the language that one uses, often as native language, influences our way of thinking and behaving) was rejected by the scientific community, since it would have led to the 'relativity' of scientific discoveries; but it was also rejected by linguists themselves.[3] Nowadays, a weaker hypothesis is thought to hold, namely that 'there are cultural differences in the semantic associations evoked by seemingly common concepts. The way a given language encodes experience semantically, makes aspects of that experience not exclusively accessible, but just more salient for the users of that language' (Kramsch, 1998, p. 13). In short, language reflects cultural preoccupations and acts as a constraint on the way we think, and culture is expressed through the use of the language (Kramsch, 1998, p. 14). Language is thus not only a means of communication, but also a carrier of culture and of emotions.

Why does the human being have such an intimate relation with its language? What is it that makes the famous Portuguese writer Fernando Pessoa write that 'my homeland is my language' or contemporary French linguist Claude Hagège claim that 'languages are the flags of dominated people' or that '[the] fight for French is a fight of the mind'? Why does political scientist Henry Bretton (1976) suggest that 'fear of being deprived of communicating skills seems to raise political passion to a fever pitch'? Here are also two sentences attributed to Nelson Mandela: 'If you talk to a man in a language he understands, that goes to his head. If you talk to him in his language, that goes to his heart', which echoes Ngugi wa Thiong'o's (1986, p. 17) 'learning, for a colonial child, became a cerebral activity and not an emotionally felt experience'. And why is it that, in Western movies, things usually move from left to right, while, in Iranian movies, they often go from right to left, following the way Persian is written (Carrière and Eco, 2009, p. 47)?

Stumbling or tumbling over several languages has happened to many people, but we will turn to writers and poets who have narrated their emotions and have (often beautifully) expressed their despair as they decided, or were forced, to move to a language other than their mother tongue, as well as to some who explicitly made the decision *not* to write in their mother tongue. This happened to writers who lived through colonial times and were taught in the language of the colonizer,[4] as well as to many of those who had to flee for their lives from

---

[3] See Chapter 1 in this volume.

[4] 'One of the most humiliating experiences was to be caught speaking Gikuyu in the vicinity of the school. The culprit was given corporal punishment – three to five strokes

dictatorships. But there are also some who migrated voluntarily and decided to adopt (or not to adopt) the language of the country in which they landed.

The reasons why a writer switches from his mother tongue to another language, or refuses to change while in exile, or would like to have been born in another language, are very diverse, but are in most cases linked to very deep and contradictory emotions. Instead of commenting on what they felt, we have preferred to leave the writers to express themselves (see Sections 8.4–8.7).

In his introduction to *D'autres langues que la mienne*, Michel Zink (2014, pp. 8–19) suggests that writing in a language other than one's native language has been common to almost all civilizations since writing existed. He gives some examples. Lucian of Samosata (2nd century BC), who refers to himself as Assyrian and 'barbarian' (Harmon, 1913), decided to write in Attic Greek. Most literary writings from the Middle Ages were in Latin, 'the language of nobody', notes Zink.[5] Dante Alighieri (1265–1321) and Petrarch (1304–1374) started to write in a language that was later called Italian.

Shakespeare wrote about himself in his sonnets but they were not about linguistic emotions. We may, however, surmise that he expressed his emotions in his plays. In *Richard II*, the king exiles Thomas Mowbray to Venice (where he dies shortly after he was exiled). He does not lament the loss of land or status but rather the inability to speak his native language:[6]

> A heavy sentence, my most sovereign liege,
> . . .
> Have I deserved at your Highness' hands.
> The language I have learn'd these forty years,
> My native English, now I must forego;
> And now my tongue's use is to me no more
> . . .
> Within my mouth you engaol'd my tongue,
> Doubly portcullis'd with my teeth and lips;
> And dull, unfeeling, barren ignorance
> Is made my gaoler to attend me.
> . . .
> I am too old to fawn upon a nurse,
> Too far in years to be a pupil now.
> What is thy sentence, then but speechless death,
> Which robs my tongue from breathing native breath?

---

of the cane on bare buttocks – or was made to carry a metal plate around the neck with inscriptions such as I AM STUPID OR I AM A DONKEY' (Ngugi wa Thiong'o, 1986, p. 11).
[5] See also Bourgain (2014).
[6] See Ginsburgh and Weber (2011, pp. 22–23).

Though Richard's decision was driven neither by anti-imperialism, nor by considerations of linguistic policy, Thomas Mowbray's plight is not an isolated episode. Language policies often tend to alienate groups of individuals whose cultural, societal and historical values and sensibilities are perceived to be threatened by what Ginsburgh and Weber (2011) call 'linguistic disenfranchisement', when linguistic rights are restricted or even denied. Not always, though.

8.4　'Colonized' writers

In his book *Decolonizing the Mind* (published in 1986 but written in 1981), Ngugi wa Thiong'o, a Kenyan writer, makes it clear why language is an essential expression of culture (pp. 3–5, 9):

> The biggest weapon wielded and actually daily unleashed by imperialism against that collective defiance is the cultural bomb. The effect of a cultural bomb is to annihilate a people's belief in their names, in their languages, in their environment, in their heritage of struggle, in their unity, in their capacities and ultimately in themselves. It makes them see their past as one wasteland of non-achievement and it makes them want to distance themselves from that wasteland. It makes them want to identify with that which is the furthest removed from themselves; for instance, with other peoples' languages rather than their own.

> The choice of language and the use to which language is put is central to a people's definition of themselves in relation to the entire universe. Hence language has always been at the heart of two contending social forces in the Africa of the twentieth century.

> Berlin in 1884 saw the division of Africa into the different languages of the European powers. African countries, as colonies and even today as neo-colonies, came to be defined and to define themselves in terms of the languages of Europe: English-speaking, French-speaking or Portuguese-speaking African countries. [W]riters also came to be defined and to define themselves in terms of the languages of imposition. Even at their most radical and pro-African position in their sentiments and articulation of problems they still took it as axiomatic that the renaissance of African cultures lay in the language of Europe.

> Language carries culture, and culture carries, particularly through orature and literature, the entire body of values by which we come to perceive ourselves and our place in the world ... Language is thus inseparable from ourselves as a community of human beings with a specific form and character, a specific history, a specific relationship to the world.

And indeed, Ngugi wa Thiong'o knows this from his own experience. In 1977, he stopped writing plays, novels and short stories in English and turned to Gikuyu and Kiswahili, two languages used in Kenya, the country where he was born.[7] *Decolonizing the Mind*, published in 1986 and from which the long quote that precedes is taken, was the last text he wrote in English, his farewell bid to English for any of his writings, including explanatory prose.

A similar view was expressed by David Mandessi Diop,[8] a politician and literary writer born in France to a Senegalese father and a Cameroonian mother:

> The African creator, deprived of the use of his language and cut off from his people, might turn out to be only the representative of a literary trend (and that not necessarily the least gratuitous) of the conquering nation. His words, having become a perfect illustration of the assimilationist policy through imagination and style, will doubtless rouse the warm applause of a certain group of critics. In fact, these praises will go mostly to colonialism, when it can no longer keep its subjects in slavery, transforms them into docile intellectuals patterned after Western literary fashions which, besides, is another more subtle form of bastardization.

It would be easy to suggest that Ngugi's, and to some extent, also Diop's behaviour are fuelled by strong political and so-called 'anti-imperialistic' views generated by colonialism. The Nigerian writer Obiajunwa Wali (1963, p. 14) uses instead a linguistic argument to convince Africans to write in their native language:

> If linguistic science devotes so much energy and attention to African languages in spite of their tribal and limited scope, why should imaginative literature which in fact has more chances of enriching the people's culture, consider it impossible to adventure in this direction? There is practically no use being made of [African languages] in creative writing, simply because we are all busy fighting over the commonplaces of European literature.

But Martinique-born Marxist Frantz Fanon, who so influenced many 'liberation movements' wrote his most famous book, *Les damnés de la terre* (1961), in French.[9] The resolute anti-colonialist, Aimé Césaire, who declared he belonged to the race of the oppressed and co-founded the négritude movement in French literature, also wrote in French.

---

[7] Kiswahili is the lingua franca in almost all countries of east Africa.

[8] 'A Contribution to the Debate on National Poetry' (1956), quoted by Ogede (1998, p. 130).

[9] The English translation, *The Wretched of the Earth*, was published in 1963 by Grove Weidenfeld.

Many African novelists and poets kept writing in English or in French, and adamantly defended their right to do so. Here is what Nigerian novelist Chinua Achebe (1964) has to say:

> Is it right that a man should abandon his mother tongue for someone else's? It looks like a dreadful betrayal and produces a guilty feeling. But for me there is no other choice. I have been given the language and I intend to use it.

In a review of Achebe's *Morning Yet on Creation Day*, Innes (1976, p. 244) notes that 'in some cases Achebe's readiness to ignore the existence of [those who criticize his use of English], his acceptance of Senghor's rather simplistic opposition between the African and European aesthetic, weakens the impact of his essays'.

This brings us to writers born in former French colonies or territories. Léopold Sedar Senghor, a Senegalese poet (and politician), took a diametrically opposed position:

> What does using French represent for me as a black author? The question deserves to be answered all the more since we are addressing the Poet here, and I have defined the languages of black Africa as poetic languages. As a response, I shall take up the argument of factuality. I think in French; I express myself better in French than in my mother tongue.[10]

He is even more explicit in the postface to his poems *Ethiopiques* (1956):

> French is one of those great organs in which you can pull all the stops, creating every possible effect, from the most suave sweetness to the ferocity of the storm. It can alternate or simultaneously be the flute, the oboe, the trumpet, the tam tam and even the canon. And French has given us its words for the abstract – which are so rare in our mother tongues – in which tears become gems. Our words bear the aura of sap and blood; words in French shed the rays of a thousand lights, like diamonds. Rockets which set alight our night.[11]

He was the first African to be elected to the Académie Française.

---

[10] *Que représente pour moi, écrivain noir, l'usage du français? La question mérite d'autant plus réponse qu'on s'adresse, ici, au Poète et que j'ai défini les langues négro-africaines 'de langues poétiques.' En répondant, je reprendrai l'argument de fait. Je pense en français; je m'exprime mieux en français que dans ma langue maternelle* (Senghor, 1962, p. 842).

[11] *Le français, ce sont des grandes orgues qui se prêtent à tous les timbres, à tous les effets, des douceurs les plus suaves aux fulgurances de l'orage. Il est, tour à tour ou en même temps, flûte,*

But there may be worse. Nobel prize winner V. S. Naipaul, born in Trinidad, a grandchild of Indian immigrants who worked on sugar plantations, writes in English about the Islamic world, Latin America, Africa, India and the Caribbean. According to Edward Said (1986, p. 53):

> he *totally* ignore[s] a massive infusion of critical scholarship about those regions in favor of the tritest, cheapest and the easiest of colonial mythologies about wogs and darkies, myths that even Lord Cromer and Forster's Turtons and Burtons would have been embarrassed to trade in outside their private clubs.

In a discussion with O'Brien et al. (1996, p. 465), Said adds

> I'm simply saying that, on the basis of his being a Trinidadian, he [Naipaul] has had ascribed to him the credentials of a man who can serve as witness for the third world; and he is a very convenient witness. He is a third worlder denouncing his own people, not because they are victims of imperialism, but because they seem to have an innate flaw, which is that they are not whites.

8.5 Migrating writers

Migrating authors can be subdivided into two categories. There are those who cannot or do not wish to adopt the language of the country to which they migrate, such as Elias Canetti, Imre Kertesz and Norman Manea. There are also those who 'try to become more native than the natives themselves' (Nic Craith, 2012, p. 134), such as Aharon Appelfeld, Samuel Beckett, Joseph Conrad, Eugen Ionesco and many others. But there are also 'in betweens', like Nabokov or Julien (born Julian) Green, who, though they fell in love with their adoptive country, cannot make a clear-cut decision.

For reasons that are obvious, we shall distinguish between Jewish writers (Appelfeld, Hannah Arendt, Paul Celan, Imre Kertesz and Norman Manea) who were often forced to migrate from their country of birth after Hitler in Germany, or some other dictator in Eastern Europe came to power, and writers who migrated for other reasons (Samuel Beckett, Emil Cioran, Joseph Conrad, Eugène Ionesco, Milan Kundera and many others).

Aharon Appelfeld, born in 1932 in Jodova, at the time in Romania, now in Ukraine, emigrated to Palestine in 1946. Though he understood and probably

---

hautbois, trompette, tamtam et même canon. Et puis le français nous a fait don de ses mots abstraits – si rares dans nos langues maternelles –, où les larmes se font pierres précieuses. Chez nous, les mots sont naturellement nimbés d'un halo de sève et de sang; les mots du français rayonnent de mille feux, comme des diamants. Des fusées qui éclairent notre nuit.

spoke several other languages, his mother tongue is German, and according to Philip Roth (2001) who also interviewed him, his Jewish family was indeed fully assimilated and he treasured the German language he understood at the time he left Romania.

This is what he says in an interview by Parson in 1982:

> Knowing a lot of languages, but really not rooted in a language. My home language was German, but I'd spoken many other languages, of course. My grandparents, they'd spoken Yiddish. The maids in my home were Ukrainian, so I spoke Ukrainian. The regime was Romanian, so I picked up a bit of Romanian. And then I was in Russia and picked up Russian, then Italy and picked up some Italian. So I came with a bunch of words, different languages – but still very deeply disoriented. It's taken many years for me to get oriented – who I am, to whom I belong. This was a very deep effort.

At some point during the interview, Parson (1982) points out: 'you mentioned once that the German language repulsed you. How did you mean that – the sound of the language or what it stood for?'. And this is how he answered:

> You see, it would be not only a paradox, it would be tragic, to write in the language of the murderers. Just to think about it is enough to stop it. I suffered as a Jew and I was trying to find my roots. My family were Jews, the history and culture of the Jews – naturally it brought me to Hebrew.

Hannah Arendt (1994), a Jewish political theorist (who did not want to be called a philosopher) whose mother tongue was German, ceased to write in German, but reacts very differently:[12]

> I have always consciously refused to lose my mother tongue... I write in English [now], but I have never lost a feeling of distance from it.[13] There is a tremendous difference between your mother tongue and another language. For myself I can put it extremely simply: In German I know a rather large part of German poetry by heart; the poems are always somehow in the back of my mind... The German language is the essential thing that has remained and that I have consciously preserved... What is one to do? It wasn't the German language that went crazy... What is left? Only the mother tongue.

---

[12] Was bleibt? Es bleibt die Mutterprache. See https://www.youtube.com/watch?v=J9SyTEUi6Kw for her 1964 interview with Günter Gaus (Hannah Arendt im Gespräch mit Günter Gaus).

[13] After moving to the United States in 1941.

When, after World War II, she briefly returned to Germany, she felt 'indescribably happy that I could listen to German being spoken on the streets'.[14] Theodor Adorno who had exiled himself to Great Britain and the United States before World War II even made it more obvious by going back to Frankfurt University in 1949. And many other Jewish writers, such as Elias Canetti (born in Bulgaria), Imre Kertesz (born in Hungary) and Norman Manea (born in Romania), had to or decided to migrate, though their migration before or after the war was not easy or painless.

Nobel Prize winner Elias Canetti was born in Bulgaria in a Sephardic Jewish family and raised in Ladino, Bulgarian and English. His parents spoke German together, and though he was impressed by the language, he did not understand them:

> My parents spoke German when together, and I was not meant to understand any of it; they spoke Spanish to us children and all the relatives; all events of those first years took place in Spanish or Bulgarian.

> I had very good reason to feel excluded when my parents started talking together. They became lively and merry and I associated this transformation, which I noticed, with the sound of the German language, and asked what such and such meant. They laughed and told me that it was too early, and that those were things I would understand later. I believed that there were wonderful things that could only be expressed in this language.[15]

His father died when he was eight years old and his mother 'forced' him to learn German which made him terribly unhappy – 'I was terrified of being ridiculed by her and during the day, wherever I was, I repeated the sentences'[16] – as well as terribly happy:

> We spent three months in Lausanne, and sometimes I think that there was never so portentous a period in my life. It was in Lausanne, after all, that

---

[14] For an excellent analysis on Arendt's position on her German native language, see Cassin (2015, pp. 85–132).

[15] *Meine Eltern untereinander sprachen deutsch, wovon ich nichts verstehen dürfte. Zu uns Kindern und zu allen Verwandten sprachen sie spanisch ... Alle Ereignisse jener ersten Jahren spielten sich au spanisch oder bulgarisch ab* (Canetti, 1977, p. 19).

Ich hatte also guten Grund, mich ausgeschlossen zu fühlen, wenn die Eltern mit ihren Gesprächen anfingen. Sie würden überaus lebhaft und lustig dabei und ich verband diese Verwandlung, die ich wohl bemerkte, mit dem Klang der deutschen Sprache ... und fragte sie dann, was dies oder jenes bedeutete. Sie lachten und sagten, es sei zu früh für mich, das seien Dinge, die ich erst später verstehen könne ... Ich glaubte, dass es sich um wunderbare Dingen handeln müsse, die man nur in dieser Sprache könne (Canetti, 1977, p. 38).

[16] *Ich lebte nun in Schrecken vor ihrem Hohn und wiederholte mir untertags, wo immer ich war, die Sätze* (Canetti, 1977, p. 100).

through the influence of my mother I was born again into the German language and through the labours of this birth was born the passion that linked me to both, to the language and to my mother. Without both of these, which were basically one and the same, the further course of my life would have been meaningless and incomprehensible.[17]

I cannot explain why I did not resent my father for this. However, I no doubt cultivated a deep resentment against my mother, which only went away when she later taught me German herself, after his death.[18]

He became as Kramsch (2004) notes 'literally reborn in/into/German' to such an extent that:

Of the fairy tales I heard, I only remembered those about werewolves and vampires. I can remember all the details of them, but not in the language in which I heard them. I heard them in Bulgarian, but I know them in German; this mysterious transmission is perhaps the most remarkable thing I can tell about my youth, particularly as the linguistic fate of most children is different: [All of the events of my childhood] were later for the most part translated into German.[19]

However, in an interview with Friedrich Witz in 1968, he mentions that German 'was a belated mother tongue, implanted in true pain',[20] but all his books, including his four volume autobiography, were written in German.

Paul Celan (1920–1970), also born in Romania to a Jewish family, had to endure similar sufferings. He left his native country and eventually landed in

---

[17] *Wir verbrachten drei Monate in Lausanne, und manchmal denke ich, eine so folgenreiche Zeit hat es in meinem Leben nie wieder gegeben...Immerhin, in Lausanne,...wurde ich unter der Einwirkung meiner Mutter zur deutschen Sprache wiedergeboren und unter dem Krampf dieser Geburt entstand die Leidenschaft, die mich mit beidem verband, mit der Sprache und mit der Mutter. Ohne diese beiden, die im Grunde ein und dasselbe waren, wäre der weiter Lauf meines Leben sinnlos und unbegreiflich* (Canetti, 1977, p. 107).

[18] *Ich kann nicht erklären, warum ich dem Vater nicht eigentlich dafür grollte. Wohl aber bewahrte ich mich einen tiefen Groll gegen die Mutter und es verging erst, als sie mir Jahre später, nach seinem Tod, selber deutsch beibrachte* (Canetti, 1977, p. 39).

[19] *Von den Märchen, die ich hörte sind mir nur die über Werwölfe und Vampire in Erinnerung geblieben...Sie sind mir in allen Einzelheiten gegenwärtig, aber nicht in der Sprache, in der ich sie gehört habe. Ich habe sie auf bulgarisch gehört, aber ich kenne sie deutsch, diese geheimnisvolle Übertragung ist vielleicht das Merkwürdigste, was ich in meiner Jugend zu berichten habe, und da das sprachliche Schicksal der meisten Kinder andres verläuft* (Canetti, 1977, p. 18). *[Alle Eregnisse meiner Jugend] haben sich mir später zum größten Teil ins deutsche übersetzt* (Canetti, 1977, p. 19).

[20] *war eine spät und unter wahrhaftigen Schmerzen eingepflanzte Muttersprache* (Canetti, 2005, p. 195).

Paris after the war, but reacted in a fully different way than Appelfeld, and kept writing poetry in German, his native tongue: 'there is nothing in the world for which a poet will give up writing, not even when he is a Jew and the language of his poems is German' (Celan and Felstiner, 2001, p. 56). But, according to Jackson (2014, pp. 266–267), he used only once the word 'deutsch' in his published writings, and this was in a poem addressed to his mother who was a great admirer of German literature and taught him the language:

And can you tolerate, mother, as you once did, ach, at home,
the quiet, German, painful rhyme?[21]

Another Nobel Prize laureate, Imre Kertesz, born in Budapest, Hungary, deported to Auschwitz at age 14 and to Buchenwald, now lives in Berlin. He made his reason clear in an interview with the German newspaper *Welt Online* (6 November 2009),[22] when he announced that, as a natural inhabitant of a large city (*Großstädter*), he did not belong in the city of his birth, Budapest, which had been altogether Balkanized, but in Berlin.[23] Meanwhile, Kertesz keeps writing in his Hungarian mother tongue.

'In the beginning was the Word, the ancients told us. In the beginning for me, the word was Romanian.' This is how Norman Manea starts his essay 'The Exiled Language' (Manea, 2012, p. 253), though he also heard German, Yiddish, Ukrainian and Polish words. Born in Romania in 1936, he was deported to a camp in Transnistria at age five. When he came back to Romania in 1945, his parents arranged for him to be privately tutored in German. In the camp, he learned Yiddish and Ukrainian. He also studied some Hebrew, and in high school he learnt French and Russian, 'but none of the languages I had taken up ever became fully internalized. In the end, I feel at home in only one language' (Manea, 2012, p. 254).

---

[21] *Und duldest du, Mutter, wie einst, ach, daheim,*
 Den leisen, den deutschen, den schmerzlichen Reim?
[22] See http://www.welt.de/kultur/article5098828/In-Ungarn-haben-Antisemiten-das-Sag en.html (retrieved 3 March 2015).
[23] Welt Online: *Verehrter, lieber Herr Kertész, am 9. November werden Sie 80 Jahre alt, aber das schönste Geschenk zu diesem Geburtstag bekommen nicht Sie, sondern jemand anderes.*

Imre Kertész: *Ach ja? Wer denn?*
Welt Online: *Die Stadt Berlin! Weil Sie immer noch in ihren Mauern leben.*
Kertész: *Aber was reden Sie da – ich bin ein Berliner!*
Welt Online: *Komisch, irgendwo habe ich gelesen, Sie stammten aus Budapest...*
Kertész: *Lieber, Sie lesen zuviel. Lassen Sie mich Ihnen sagen: Ich bin ein Großstädter, bin es immer gewesen. Ein Großstädter gehört nicht nach Budapest. Die Stadt ist ja vollkommen balkanisiert. Ein Großstädter gehört nach Berlin!*

In 1986, he left what he calls the socialist 'penal colony' and

> boarded to Berlin knowing full well that I might have traded my tongue for a passport...My second exile (this time at age 50 instead of 5) gave expropriation and deligitimization new meaning. The honor of being expelled was inseparable from being silenced as a writer. Nonetheless, I did take my nomadic language with me, like a snail its house (Manea, 2012, pp. 257–258).

> [I knew] that the Romanian of Caragiale and Bacovia[24] was also that of Zelea Codreanu.[25] It is unfortunate and very disturbing when great writers and intellectuals become accomplices of the ideology and language of hatred; but, again, Romanian was for me also the language of love and friendship and literary apprenticeship, the language my parents and grandparents speak to me even though they are dead (Manea, 2012, p. 260).

The last paragraph of his essay starts in a way similar to the beginning:

> Not only in the beginning was the word. Before the final silence, we often end our existence with the Word. Chekhov spoke his last words *'Ich sterbe'* ('I am dying') not in the language of his life and works but in that of the land where he ended his earthly adventure. In the rare dreams in which I see my parents, they speak Romanian. And yet, I cannot foresee in which language I will take my leave of this world (Manea, 2012, pp. 272–273).

But like Canetti and Kertsz, and unlike Appelfeldt, Manea keeps writing in his Romanian mother tongue.

Samuel Beckett, the Irish writer and 1969 Nobel laureate, must have spoken excellent French since in 1940 he joined the French resistance as a courier. Speaking French even with a slight English or Irish accent would have quickly caused him trouble. And he started to write in French after World War II. His best-known work, *En attendant Godot* was published in 1952 in French; the English translation, *Waiting for Godot*, appeared only two years later. According to Jackson (2014, pp. 262–263), who met him once, he chose to switch to French, because

> he felt to have lost the necessary distance to keep writing in English: 'I did no longer master English', he said, 'it was English that mastered me or

---

[24] Caragiale (1852–1912) was a famous Romanian playwright, poet and short story writer of Greek origin. Bacovia (1881–1957) was a Romanian symbolist poet.
[25] Codreanu (1899–1938) was a far right politician, founder and leader of the Iron Guard, a nationalist and anti-Semitic organization.

spoke to me and to recover the distance, I opted for French. A few years later, during a trip to England, I understood that my English no longer was the same as the one spoken in the country, and I could restart writing in English. Now, texts come in one tongue or in the other, this is very mysterious.

Joseph Conrad (1857–1924), born in what is now Ukraine to Polish parents, wrote his novels and short stories in English. Eugène Ionesco (1909–1994) switched very quickly from one book, *Nu*, written in Romanian, while he was still in Romania, to French. Manea (2012, p. 267) suggests, however, that 'Eugen Ionescu [sic] claimed that he himself would probably have been a better writer in Romania than the more important one he became in France'. Milan Kundera born in Prague in 1929 switched from Czech to French after emigrating to France in 1975.

And authors continue to switch languages. On 19 September 2014, *Le Monde* published a long article on young authors who had switched from various languages to French. Ryoko Sekiguchi, born in Japan and whose first writings are in Japanese, has been living in Paris since 1997. She decided to write in French: 'I feel that in Japanese, I am not as natural, and even less funny than in French. Today, I realize that I became two different authors'. Anne Weber stated that 'I was born in Germany and arrived in France at age 18. My first three books were written in French, and I translated them into German. Now I inverted the order, probably because my fourth book was related to my father and my origins'.

Luba Jurgenson, born in Russia, said that 'writing in French is a happy experience, I do not have the impression that my tongue was cut. Being exiled is not necessarily as traumatic as what Manea experienced and wrote: "Giving me a passport cut my tongue"'.

Atiq Rahimi, born in Afghanistan, migrated to France at age 22. His first book was written in Farsi; he went back to Afghanistan in 2002 and stopped writing in Farsi after this visit.

8.6   Between languages: Nabokov, Green and Tabucchi

Nabokov was born in Russia at the turn of the 19th century. He grew up with Russian, English and French. His family moved to Berlin in 1922, then to France in 1937, and finally to the United States in 1940. His first novels were written in Russian. He turned to English in particular with *Lolita* (1959), which he translated into Russian, because he

imagined that in some distant future somebody might produce a Russian version of *Lolita* . . . I saw that every paragraph could lend itself to a hideous mistranslation, being pock-marked with pitfalls. In the hands of a harmful drudge, the Russian version of *Lolita* would be entirely degraded and botched by vulgar paraphrases or blunders. So I decided to translate it myself (Tofler, 1964).

The mere translations of Nabokov's (1959) first lines of *Lolita*, as well as what Nabokov writes about his own translation of the book written in English into his native Russian, are a good illustration of such situations. Here are these first lines of *Lolita*:

Lolita, light of my life, fire of my loins. My sin, my soul. Lo-lee-ta: the tip of the tongue taking a trip of three steps down the palate to tap, at three on the teeth. Lo. Lee. Ta.[26]

and their translation into French, in which the English rhythm and alliterations are missing:[27]

Lolita, lumière de ma vie, feu de mes reins. Mon péché, mon âme. Lo-li-ta: le bout de la langue fait trois petit bonds le long du palais pour venir, à trois, cogner contre les dents. Lo.Li.Ta.

The lines are of course perfectly translated and understandable, but are far from conveying Humbert Humbert's love for Lo and Nabokov's teasing look at Humbert that transpires in the English original version. The Russian translation by Nabokov himself goes as follows:

Lolita, svet moej zhizni, ogoní moih chresel. Greh moj, dusha moja. Lo-li-ta: konchik jazika sovershaet putí v tri shazhka vniz po nebu, chtoby na tretíem tolknutísja o zuby. Lo. Li. Ta.

---

[26] Here is what Nabokov said on the choice of the name Lolita:

For my nymphet I needed a diminutive with a lyrical tilt to it. One of the most limpid and luminous letters is 'L'. The suffix '-ita' has a lot of Latin tenderness, and this I required too. Hence: Lolita. However, it should not be pronounced as you and most Americans pronounce it: *Low-lee-ta*, with a heavy, clammy 'L' and a long 'o'. No, the first syllable should be as in 'lollipop', the 'L' liquid and delicate, the 'lee' not too sharp (Tofler, 1964).

[27] Translation by E.H. Kahane, Paris: Gallimard, 1959, approved by Nabokov, who was also fluent in French.

It is worth quoting what Nabokov wrote about his own translation of *Lolita* from English into Russian:[28]

> The history of this translation is the story of a disillusionment. Alas, that 'wondrous Russian tongue' that, it seemed to me, was waiting for me somewhere, was flowering like a faithful springtime behind a tightly locked gate, whose key I had held in safekeeping for so many years, proved to be nonexistent, and there is nothing behind the gate but charred stumps and a hopeless autumnal distance, and the key in my hand is more like a skeleton key. I console myself, first of all, with the thought that the fault for the clumsiness of the translation offered here lies not only with the translator's loss of touch with his native speech but also with the *spirit* (our italics) of the language.

Different languages express feelings and perceptions of feelings in a different way. To quote again from Nabokov's *Postscript* to his novel in Russian:

> Everything tenderly human, but also everything coarse and crude, juicy and bawdy, comes out no worse in Russian than in English; but the subtle reticence so peculiar to English, the poetry of thought, the instantaneous resonance between the most abstract concepts in Russian become clumsy, prolix and often repulsive in terms of style and rhythm.

Julian Green, born in Paris to American parents, wrote all his novels in French, with the exception of *Memories of Happy Days* (1942), written in the United States after leaving Paris as World War II started. Here is why (Green, 2004c, pp. 246–248, *passim*):

> In July 1940, I had the idea of writing a book on France as I knew her in my childhood and the early part of my youth... I began my book in French, of course, and I say 'of course' because up to that time I had practically never written in any other language than French. I wrote about twenty pages. At this point I put down my pen and wondered who was going to print my book and who was going to read it... For all those reasons, I decided to put aside the pages I had already written in French and to make a completely new start, in English.

And this is what happened to him (Green, 2004c, pp. 248–252, *passim*):

> This was, for me, something of an adventure... However, I set myself to work. I approached the English language as you might approach a person

---

[28] *Postscript to the Russian Edition of Lolita*, translated by Earl D. Sampson.

you know quite well and who, nevertheless, intimidates you a little...The best I could do, it seemed to me, was to use the very simplest words I could muster, the everyday words which my mother taught me as a child, and I really believe that I succeeded in saying what I wanted to say...Having written about two dozen pages, I summoned my courage and read what I had written. What struck me most, however, was how little these English sentences resembled the French sentences I had written on the same subject. Now, what I expected to read was a sort of unconscious translation from the French, or at least a very close equivalent, whereas what I saw might have been written by another hand than mine...I do not want to imply more than I mean. The subject was the same. The choice of details quite different. I did not say the same things in both languages, because, when writing in English, I had the feeling that in some obscure way I was not quite the same person...There is an Anglo-Saxon way of approaching a subject, just as there is a French way. The difference between the two is essential, although not easily defined. Also, the choice of words – I was about to say the choice of colors – varies considerably from one language to another. It has sometimes been denied, but I nevertheless think it true, that ideas are unconsciously suggested to us by words.[29]

This adventure, as he calls it, is described, almost in the same way, in two short stories published in Green (1985) in English *and* in French,[30] and reprinted in 2004 (Green, 2004a) where, interestingly, the author is Julian Green (with an A in Julian) and translated by Julien Green (with an E, the French spelling that he uses in his books written in French). But the 2004a volume appeared after he died in 1998.

Antonio Tabucchi (1943–2012), translator of Pessoa into Italian and teacher of the Portuguese language, wrote almost all his novels in Italian, with the exception of *Requiem* (1993) written in Portuguese. This is the 'note' that Tabucchi (1993, p. 9) put at the very beginning of the novel:

This story, which takes place on a Sunday in July in a Lisbon which is deserted and torrid is the Requiem that the character I call 'I' should have played throughout the book. If I were asked why this story was written in Portuguese I would answer that such a story could only be written in Portuguese, that was all...At any rate, I realized that I could not write a

---

[29] Note that even if Green had probably not thought of it, the last sentence is very Whorfian.

[30] *Le language et son double/The Language and its Shadow* was published in 1985. The page numbers are taken from Green (2004a) where Green (2004b) and Green (2004c) are included.

Requiem in my own language, but that I had to use another language, a place of affection and reflection.[31]

Requiem, he explains, has a dream as its origin. His father had died seven years earlier from cancer of the larynx. He had survived the operation for two and a half years, but could no longer speak. After the operation, Tabucchi would speak to his father who would respond by writing on a slate. But after some time, Tabucchi himself decided to use a slate as well, so that his father would not feel he was in a position of 'inferiority' (Tabucchi, 1993, pp. 153–185).

In the dream his father had appeared and was *speaking* to him in Portuguese (a language that he did not know) and they were both in Lisbon. When the dream came back to Tabucchi, he was sitting in a cafe in Paris and started scribbling in his notebook. The waiter asked him whether he was a writer, to which he answered yes. Then the same waiter asked him whether he was writing in Italian; to which he responded, 'in general I am an Italian novelist but this time I am writing in Portuguese' (Tabucchi, 1993, p. 174):

> The following year, when Feltrinelli decided to publish the novel, the problem of translating it into Italian arose, and I preferred not to do it myself – I had unconsciously crossed the river to arrive at another linguistic bank, and could not go in the opposite direction.[32]

It would be impossible to end this dedication of Tabucchi to his father without mentioning the following 'detail'. He called his father Pa', an apocope of 'papà' in the region where they were living. At the time Tabucchi started learning Portuguese, he told his father that in Portuguese the word *pá* (with an acute accent) was a sign of affability between two persons. This was the only Portuguese word that his father knew. And it became a habit to use it by both father and son when they were communicating with other people: the father would call his son *pá* and the son would call his father *pa'*:

> While others thought it was the same word, I knew that my father mentally put in an accent when he pronounced it, while he knew I was pronouncing

---

[31] *Cette histoire qui se déroule par un dimanche de juillet dans une Lisbonne déserte et torride, est le Requiem que le personnage que j'appelle 'Je' a dû jouer tout au long de ce livre. Si l'on me demandait pourquoi cette histoire a été écrite en portugais, je répondrais qu'une histoire pareille ne pouvait être écrite qu'en portugais, et voilà tout…En tout cas, je me suis rendu compte que je ne pouvais pas écrire un Requiem dans ma propre langue, mais qu'il me fallait user d'une langue différente, une langue qui soit un lieu d'affection et de réflexion* (Tabucchi, 1993, p. 9).
[32] *L'année suivante, quand l'éditeur Feltrinelli décida de publier le roman, le problème de la traducion en italien se posa, et je préférai ne pas m'en charger…J'avais traversé inconsciemment le fleuve pour rejoindre une autre rive linguistique, je ne pouvais pas faire le parcours inverse* (Tabucchi, 1993, p. 184).

it with an apostrophe – it was a differentiated use of a homophone: I called him father and he called me 'my boy'; who knows whether a novel written in a language which is not our own cannot be born of a tiny word reserved exclusively for us and belonging to no one else. A syllable may sometimes contain a universe.[33]

8.7 'Denying' the language in which they wrote: Kafka and Derrida

Both Franz Kafka and Jacques Derrida were born into Jewish families. What makes them close is that the first wrote in German, but longed for Yiddish that he did not know well, while Derrida wrote in French but was longing for Ladino, Hebrew and Berber.

At the time Franz Kafka started to write (circa 1900), only some 10 per cent of the Prague population was still speaking German; 40 per cent of those were Jews. Though his parents declared they were Czechs and spoke Czech, Franz claimed to speak German (which was of course the case) and was therefore considered German.[34]

Most commentators on Kafka's work cite two short pieces (Kafka, 1912, 1917) that, according to them, make it clear that he was attached to and would probably have preferred to write in Yiddish than in German. Though Kafka seems to put these words in his friend Jizchak Löwy's mouth, commentators usually think that this is how he would have described himself:

That transformed me. Before the beginning of the play I felt quite different than with 'them'.... And people spoke loudly and unabashedly in the mother tongue; I was not conspicuous with my long Kaftänchen and did not need to feel ashamed... Throughout the night I could not get to sleep, my heart told me that I should serve in the temple of Jewish art and become a Jewish actor.[35]

---

[33] *Celles-ci* [the other people] *croyaient qu'il s'agissait du même mot, mais moi, je savais que mon père, en le prononçant, y mettait mentalement un accent aigu, et lui savait que j'y mettais mentalement l'apostrophe de l'apocope. C'était une utilisation différenciée d'un mot homophone: je l'appellais 'papà' et lui il m'appelait 'garçon'. Qui sait si un roman écrit dans une langue qui n'est pas la nôtre ne peut pas naître d'un minuscule mot qui, lui, est exclusivement à nous, et n'appartient à personne d'autre. Une syllabe peut parfois contenir un univers* (Tabucchi, 1993, pp. 184–185).

[34] Le Rider (2014, p. 84).

[35] *Das hat mich ganz umgewandelt. Schon vor Beginn des Spiels habe ich mich ganz anders gefühlt als bei 'jenen'... Und man sprach laut und ungeniert in der Muttersprache, ich bin niemandem aufgefallen mit meinem langen Kaftänchen und musste mich gar nicht schämen... Die ganze Nacht habe ich vor Aufregung nicht geschlafen, das Herz sagte mir, daß auch ich einst im Tempel der jüdischen Kunst dienen, ein jüdischer Schauspieler werden soll* (Kafka, 1917).

He also gave an introductory talk to a presentation of Yiddish poems by the same Löwy, announcing that people understand more jargon (Yiddish) than they believe, and that they should cease to be afraid of Yiddish:

Yiddish has no grammars, and while amateurs of Yiddish try to write grammars, Yiddish continues to prevail restlessly, while the people do not allow grammar enthusiasts to take over the language. Yiddish consists solely of foreign words. If you have been seized by Yiddish with its Chassidic melody and the essence of the eastern European Jewish actor, you will no longer recognise your earlier peace of mind, you will be frightened not so much by the jargon, but by yourself.[36]

Le Rider (2014) also adds the following excerpt from a letter to Max Brod (Kafka, 1921) which makes it unclear whether Kafka could have considered German to be his mother tongue:

Most who began to write German wanted to get away from Jewishness, usually with the unclear approbation of the fathers (and this lack of clarity was what made us so indignant). They wanted this, but with their hind legs they were still on the ground of their fathers' Jewishness, and with their front legs they found no new ground. Their despair about this was their inspiration ... They lived between three impossibilities (which I only call linguistic impossibilities by coincidence, since it is simplest to call them that, though they could be called something quite different): the impossibility of not writing, the impossibility of writing German, the impossibility of writing different, and one might add a fourth impossibility, the impossibility of writing ... So it was an impossible literature in every respect, a gypsy literature, stolen by the German child from the crib and prepared in a hurried manner because someone had to dance on the wire. (But it wasn't even the German child, it was nothing, it was only said that someone was dancing.)[37]

---

[36] *Vor den ersten Versen der ostjüdischen Dichter möchte ich Ihnen, sehr geehrte Damen und Herren, noch sagen, wie viel mehr Jargon [Yiddish] Sie verstehen als Sie glauben. Ich habe nicht eigentlich Sorge um die Wirkung, die für jeden von Ihnen in des heutigen Abend vorbereitet ist, aber ich will, daß sie gleich frei werde, wenn sie es verdient. Dies kann aber nicht geschehen, solange manche unter Ihnen eine solche Angst von dem Jargon haben ... Er hat keine Grammatiken. Liebhaber versuchen Grammatiken zu schreiben aber der Jargon wird immerfort gesprochen; er kommt nicht zu Ruhe. Das Volk läßt ihn den Grammatikern nicht. Er besteht nur aus Fremdwörtern ... Wenn Sie aber einmal Jargon ergriffen hat – und Jargon ist alles, Wort, chassidische Melodie und das Wesen dieses ostjüdischen Schauspielers selbst – dann werden Sie Ihre frühere Ruhe nicht mehr wiedererkennen. Dann werden Sie die wahre Einheit des Jargon zu spüren bekommen, so stark, dass Sie sich fürchten werden, aber nicht mehr von dem Jargon, sondern vor sich.*

[37] *Weg vom Judentum, meist mit unklarer Zustimmung der Väter (diese Unklarheit war das Empörende), wollten die meisten, die deutsch zu schreiben anfingen, sie wollten es, aber mit den*

This is very close to the situation that Derrida (1930–2004) had to live with. He was born to a Jewish family in Algeria, and the language he *had* to speak was French. Here are some excerpts from the beautiful book he wrote in 1996:

> I only have one language, and it is not mine... For I could never call French, this language I am speaking to you, 'my mother tongue'.[38]

> In what language should one write memoires when there is no authorised mother tongue? How can I say a valid 'I remember' when you have to invent your language and your 'I', and invent them at the same time, beyond this wave of amnesia triggered by this dual prohibition?[39]

Derrida spent his youth in Algeria, a French territory (not a colony), where in 1942 the anti-Semitic Vichy laws were implemented. Despite the Décret Crémieux of 1870 which gave French citizenship to all Algerian Jews (but not to Muslim Arabs or Berbers), he was expelled in 1942 from his school following application of the Vichy laws. Many things were not allowed to him. Or they were hidden: his second forename Elie was given to him at his circumcision, but did not appear on his birth certificate:

> When people prohibit access to a language, one does not prohibit particular things, gestures or actions. One prohibits access to saying, in other words everything, a certain type of saying. But this is the fundamental prohibition, the absolute prohibition, the prohibition of diction and of saying. The prohibition I am talking about; the prohibition from which I talk, talk to myself and tell myself that it is not one prohibition among others... There is neither a natural border nor a legal limit. We had the choice, the formal right to learn or not to learn Arabic or Berber. Or Hebrew. At lycée at least – and

---

Hinterbeinchen klebten sie noch am Judentum des Vaters und mit den Vorderbeinchen fanden sie keinen neuen Boden. Die Verzweiflung darüber war ihre Inspiration... Sie lebten zwischen drei Unmöglichkeiten, (die ich nur zufällig sprachliche Unmöglichkeiten nenne, es ist das Einfachste, sie so zu nennen, sie könnten aber auch ganz anders genannt werden): der Unmöglichkeit, nicht zu schreiben, der Unmöglichkeit, deutsch zu schreiben, der Unmöglichkeit, anders zuschreiben, fast könnte man eine vierte Unmöglichkeit hinzufügen, die Unmöglichkeit zu schreiben... also war es eine von allen Seiten unmögliche Literatur, eine Zigeunerliteratur, die das deutsche Kind aus der Wiege gestohlen und in großer Eile irgendwie zugerichtet hatte, weil doch irgendjemand auf dem Seil tanzen muß. (Aber es war ja nicht einmal das deutsche Kind, es war nichts, man sagte bloß, es tanze jemand.) (Kafka, 1921).

[38] *Je n'ai qu'une langue, or ce n'est pas la mienne* (Derrida, 1996, p. 15)... *Car jamais je n'ai pu appeler le français, cette langue que je te parle, 'ma langue maternelle'* (Derrida, 1996, p. 61).

[39] *Dans quelle langue écrire des mémoires dès lors qu'il n'y a pas eu de langue maternelle autorisée? Comment dire un 'je me rappelle' qui vaille quand il faut inventer et sa langue et son je, les inventer en même temps, par delà ce déferlement d'amnésie qu'a déchaîné le double interdit?* (Derrida, 1996, p. 57).

Arabic rather than Berber. I do not recollect anyone learning Hebrew at lycée. The prohibition took place among other paths. More crafty, peaceful, silent and liberal paths.[40]

As for language, in the narrower sense, we could not even take recourse to a familiar substitute, to some inner idiom of the Jewish community, a sort of language of retreat which, like Yiddish, would have guaranteed an element of intimacy, the protection of being 'at home' as opposed to the language of the official culture … 'Ladino' was not practiced in the Algeria I knew, particularly in the big cities such as Algiers, in which the Jewish population was concentrated.[41]

8.8 Conclusion

Winter (2014, p. 4) suggests that 'emotions are a mechanism assisting us in decision making. They were shaped, and developed during our evolution in order to amplify our chances of survival'. His book is accordingly subtitled 'our emotions are more rational than we think'.

Leaving Austria, Germany or Eastern European countries in the second half of the 1930s or after World War II had started was obviously rational (in the economic sense, since the lives of most of those who left were at great risk) both for Jewish and other writers such as Thomas Mann, his brother Heinrich as well as his children Erika, Golo and Klaus, though they all kept writing in German in their newly chosen country. Some Jewish writers switched to another language (Aharon Appelfeld who emigrated to Israel and no longer wanted to speak German, Hannah Arendt who landed in the US but was still very much attached to her native language), while some did not give up their native language (Celan in German, Kertesz in Hungarian, Manea in Romanian).

---

[40] *Quand on interdit l'accès à une langue, on n'interdit aucune chose, aucun geste, aucun acte. On interdit l'accès au dire, voilà tout, à un certain dire. Mais c'est là justement l'interdit fondamental, l'interdiction absolue, l'interdiction de la diction et du dire. L'interdit dont je parle; l'interdit depuis lequel je dis, me dis et me le dis, ce n'est donc pas un interdit parmi d'autres…. Il n'y avait là ni frontière naturelle ni limite juridique. On avait le choix, on avait le droit formel d'apprendre ou de ne pas apprendre l'arabe ou le berbère. Ou l'hébreu…Au lycée du moins – et l'arabe plutôt que le berbère. Je ne me rappelle pas que personne ait jamais appris l'hébreu au lycée. L'interdit opérait donc selon d'autres voies. Plus rusées, pacifiques, silencieuses, libérales* (Derrida, 1996, pp. 58–59).

[41] *Quant à la langue, au sens étroit, nous ne pouvions même pas recourir à quelque substitut familier, à quelque idiome intérieur à la communauté juive, à une sorte de langue de retraite qui aurait assuré, comme le yiddish, un élément d'intimité, de protection d'un 'chez soi' contre la langue de la culture officielle…Le 'ladino' n'était pas pratiqué dans l'Algérie que j'ai connue, en particulier dans les grandes villes comme Alger, où la population juive se trouvait concentrée* (Derrida, 1996, pp. 90–91).

Canetti is a special case, since he voluntarily switched to German while he was young and wrote all his books in German afterwards. Joseph Conrad, Eugène Ionesco, Milan Kundera and, to some extent, Vladimir Nabokov stopped writing in their native language (Polish, Romanian, Czech, Russian) and started writing in the language of their country to which they decided, but were not forced, to migrate. Some African-born writers felt very strongly that French or English were so much more beautiful than their native language for voicing their emotions, though they were often open nationalists and expressed anti-imperialistic and anti-colonial opinions (Achebe, Diop, Fanon, Senghor). Kenyan-born Ngugi wa Thiong'o decided to discontinue writing in English and went back to his native language (Gikuyu) in his books. Finally, Kafka and Derrida, who were respectively raised in German and in French, both disliked and even rejected their native language, though they never could write in languages that they longed for (Kafka for Yiddish or Hebrew; Derrida for Hebrew, Ladino or Arabic) because they did not know them.

In the case of obviously emotion-driven decisions – to keep writing in one's native language even though those who spoke it could have murdered them had they stayed in 'their' country; or on the contrary to be an African or Martinique-born nationalist and adopt, sometimes with enthusiasm, the language of one's colonizers –, drawing conclusions from our analysis would look far-fetched. Of course, people differ, and Winter's results are 'averages' over groups of people, though they are sometimes also based on introspection and the reactions of a single person. He gives an example on pages 3–4 of his book where he thinks he was saved from 'plunging directly into the abyss below' (from a cliff in California, where a wedding party was taking place) by an emotion generated when he thought of his own wedding and family. This emotion made him make, at some later point, the rational decision 'to travel less often for the sake of improving my marriage'.

Most of the results in his book are based on 'games' (in the sense of game theory) played by several individuals, so that he was able to compute mean or median responses and test that they were, in some sense, 'statistically significant', in pointing to emotions that could be interpreted as being rational or leading to rational behaviour. It may well be that the group of people described in this chapter is either too small or too different from 'the average or median economic agent', hence the subject is still open to further research.

References

C. Achebe (1964) 'The African Writer and the English Language', in C. Achebe (ed.) (1975) *Morning Yet on Creation Day: Essays* (London: Heineman).

T. Adorno, E. Frenkel-Brunswik, D. Levinson and N. Sanford (1950) *The Authoritarian Personality* (New York: Harper and Row).

A. Arendt (1994) 'What Remains? The Language Remains: A Conversation with Günter Gaus', in H. Arendt (ed.) *Essays in Understanding, 1930–1954* (New York: Schocken Books).

C. Bell (1824) *Essays on the Anatomy and Philosophy of Expression* (London: John Murray).

W. Benjamin (1923) *Charles Baudelaire, Tableaux Parisiens. Deutsche Übertragung mit einem Vorwort über die Aufgabe des Übersetzers* (Heidelberg: Verlag von Richard Weißbach).

F. Boas (1940) *Race, Language and Culture* (Chicago, IL: University of Chicago Press).

N. Bond (2013) *Understanding Ferdinand Tönnies' Community and Society: Social Theory and Political Philosophy between Enlightened Liberal Individualism and Transfigured Community* (Berlin and London: Lit Verlag).

P. Bourgain (2014) 'La langue que l'on fait sienne', in M. Zink (ed.) *D'autres langues que la mienne* (Paris: Odile Jacob).

H. Bretton (1976) 'Political Science, Language, and Politics', in W. O'Barr and J. O'Barr (eds) *Language and Politics* (The Hague: Mouton).

E. Canetti (1977) *Die Gerettete Zunge. Geschichte einer Jugend* (München: Carl Hanser Verlag).

E. Canetti (2005) 'Gespräch mit Friedrich Witz', in E. Canetti(ed) *Aufsätze, Reden, Gespräche* (München, Wien: Hanser).

J.-C. Carrière and U. Eco (2009) *N'espérez pas vous débarrasser des livres* (Paris: Grasset & Fasquelle).

B. Cassin (2015) *La nostalgie. Quand donc est-on chez soi?* (Paris: Arthème Fayard/Pluriel).

P. Celan and J. Felstiner (2001) *Selected Poems and Prose of Paul Celan* (New York: W.W. Norton).

A. Corbin (2000) *Historien du sensible*, entretiens avec Gilles Heuré (Paris: La Découverte).

C. Darwin (1872) *The Expression of Emotions in Man and Animals* (London: John Murray).

J. Derrida (1996) *Le monolinguisme de l'autre ou la prothèse d'origine* (Paris: Galilée)

F. Fanon (1961) *Les damnés de la terre* (Paris: Editions Maspero).

U. Frevert (2013) *Vergängliche Gefühle* (Göttingen: Wallstein).

P. Gay (1985) *Freud for Historians* (New York and Oxford: Oxford University Press).

V. Ginsburgh and S. Weber (2011) *How Many Languages Do We Need? The Economics of Linguistic Diversity* (Princeton, NJ: Princeton University Press).

J. Green (1985) *Le language et son double/The Language and its Shadow* (Paris: Editions de la Différence).

J. Green, traduit par J. Green (2004a) *Le language et son double* (Paris: Fayard).

J. Green (2004b) 'An experiment in English', in J. Green, traduit par J. Green (ed.) *Le language et son double* (Paris: Fayard).

J. Green (2004c) 'My First Book in English', in J. Green, traduit par J. Green (ed.) *Le language et son double* (Paris: Fayard).

A. Harmon (1913) 'Lucian of Samosata: Introduction and Manuscripts', in A. Harmon(ed) *Lucian: Works* (Cambridge, MA: Harvard University Press).

D. Heller-Roazen (2008) *Echolalias: On the Forgetting of Language* (New York: Zone Books).

W. Humboldt, von (1988 [1836]) *The Diversity of Human Language–Structure and Its Influence on the Mental Development of Mankind* (Cambridge, UK: Cambridge University Press).

C. Innes (1976) 'Morning Yet on Creation Day: Essays by Chinua Achebe', *Research in African Literatures*, 7, 242–245.

J. Jackson (2014) 'Paroles d'étranger: A propos des poésies de Paul Celan et d'André Bouchet', in M. Zink (ed.) *D'autres langues que la mienne* (Paris: Odile Jacob).

F. Kafka (1912) 'Einleitungvortrag über Jargon' (retrieved November 2014 at http://www.kafka.org/index.php?jargon).

F. Kafka (1917) 'Vom jüdishen Theater', in F. Kafka *Das achte Oktavheft*, Kapitel 9, (retrieved November 2014 at http://gutenberg.spiegel.de/buch/die-acht-oktavhefte-164/9).

F. Kafka (1921) 'Brief an Max Brod' (available at http://homepage.univie.ac.at/werner.haas/1921/bk21-027.htm).

C. Kramsch (1998) *Language and Culture* (Oxford: Oxford University Press).

C. Kramsch (2004) 'The Multilingual Experience: Insights from Language Memoirs', *Transit*, 1, 1–12.

J. Le Rider (2014) 'Quelle est ma langue maternelle? Réflexions sur Fritz Mauthner, Franz Kafka et Elias Canetti', in M. Zink (ed.) *D'autres langues que la mienne* (Paris: Odile Jacob).

N. Manea (2012) 'The Exiled Language', in N. Manea, *The Fifth Impossibility: Essays on Exile and Language* (New Haven: Yale University Press).

K. Mannheim (1929) *Ideologie und Utopie* (Bonn: Friedrich Cohen).

A. Mizubayashi (2011) *Une langue venue d'ailleurs* (Paris: Gallimard).

V. Nabokov (1959) *Lolita* (Paris: Olympia Press).

Ngugi wa Thiong'o (1986) *Decolonizing the Mind: The Politics of Language in African Literature* (Oxford: James Currey).

M. Nic Craith (2012) *Narratives of Place, Belonging and Language* (Basingstoke: Palgrave Macmillan).

C. O'Brien, E. Said and J. Lukacs (1996) 'Intellectuals in the Post-Colonial World: Response and Discussion', in R. Boyers and P. Boyers (eds) *The New Salmagundi Reader* (Syracuse, NY: Syracuse University Press).

O. Ogede (1998) 'David Mandessi Diop', in P. Parekh and S. Jagne (eds) *Postcolonial African Writers* (Westport, CT: Greenwood Press).

A. Parson (1982) 'Interview: Aharon Appelfeld', *The Boston Review*, December.

P. Roth (2001) *Shop Talk: A Writer and His Colleagues and Their Work* (Boston: Houghton Mifflin).

E. Said (1986), 'Intellectuals and the Post-Colonial World', *Salmagundi*, 70/71, 44–64.

E. Sapir (1949) *Selected Writings of Edward Sapir in Language, Culture, and Personality* (Berkeley, CA: University of California Press).

F. Schleiermacher (1977) *Hermeneutik und Kritik: mit einem Anhang sprachphilosophischer Texte Schleiermachers* (Frankfurt a. M.: Suhrkamp).

A. Schopenhauer (1818/1859) *Die Welt als Wille und Vorstellung* (Leipzig: Brockhaus).

L. Senghor (1962) 'Le français, langue de culture', *Esprit*, Novembre, 837–844.

A. Tabucchi (1993) *Requiem* (Paris: Christian Bourgois).

A. Tofler (1964) 'Playboy Interview: Vladimir Nabokov', *Playboy*, January (retrieved November 2014 at http://longform.org/stories/playboy-interview-vladimir-nabokov).

F. Tönnies (1887) *Gemeinschaft und Gesellschaft* (Leipzig: Fuess's Verlag).

O. Wali (1963) 'The Dead End of African Literature', *Transition*, 10, 13–16.

B. Whorf (1956) *Language, Thought and Reality: Selected Writings of Benjamin Lee Whorf* (Cambridge, MA: MIT Press).

E. Winter (2014) *Feeling Smart: Why Our Emotions Are more Rational than We Think* (New York: PublicAffairs).

H. Wismann (2012) *Penser entre les langues* (Paris: Albin Michel).

M. Zink (2014) 'Ouverture. Quelle langue est mienne', in M. Zink (ed.) *D'autres langues que la mienne* (Paris: Odile Jacob).

Part II
Languages and Markets

9

Common Spoken Languages and International Trade

Peter H. Egger and Farid Toubal

9.1 Introduction

International trade economists are used to controlling for common languages in most studies on the determinants of bilateral trade. The usual measure of common language is a binary variable based on one or several common official languages. The use of this measure lies mainly in the difficulty of quantifying common language use more thoroughly. However, it is not obvious that a common official language adequately reflects the broader impact of language commonality on trade, including language-related ethnic ties and trust and the mere ability to communicate. For this reason, the impact of a binary common official language variable on bilateral trade might mismeasure the role of common languages on bilateral trade at large. In a recent study, Melitz and Toubal (2014) provide an important step toward the understanding of the impact of common languages on bilateral trade based on data on 42 common native and spoken languages in 195 countries. They find that the joint impact of different aspects of common languages is at least twice as large as the one of a common official language. Their findings, moreover, suggest that common *spoken* languages are particularly important, and the ease of communication plays a substantial role in explaining the role of common languages for bilateral trade.

In this chapter, we focus on the role of common *spoken* languages on bilateral trade. A spoken language is either acquired by non-native speakers or is innate. We therefore propose discerning the influence of common spoken *native* languages from that of common spoken *acquired* languages. This distinction is important, if one is interested in knowing whether the promotion of language learning has an impact on bilateral trade. An analysis of common languages on trade of that kind faces several challenges. For instance, the measurement of a spoken language itself is challenging, and measures thereof have to make judgements about what to consider (i.e. which languages, countries and time span). Also, an empirical analysis of the impact of common languages on trade faces the problem of circular causation: trade stimulates migration and vice versa; and trade stimulates the learning of useful languages and vice versa. We shall come back later to a discussion of the problem and its potential resolution. In terms of the effects on trade flows, one might be interested to know to what extent language commonality affects fixed (independent of volume) trade costs versus variable (*ad valorem*-type) trade costs, and to what extent it affects trade in complex, differentiated goods relative to trade in standard, homogeneous goods. The present chapter will allude to these and other topics.

The chapter proceeds from descriptive evidence in Section 9.2 to theoretical considerations in Section 9.3, to a survey of selected methodological issues and a presentation of novel empirical findings in Section 9.4. Section 9.5 concludes with a brief summary and an outline of potential future research questions.

9.2   Common native and spoken languages around the globe and their measures

A distinction between common native languages (CNLs) and common spoken languages (CSLs) is useful for various reasons. For instance, differences in CNLs across countries or regions cannot easily be changed by society or policymakers, and little can (and even should) be done to influence them. A CNL is a potential carrier of values and norms that may influence preferences (for goods from certain countries) as well as (information-related) costs to trade beyond CSLs. A CSL is the choice of individuals, and it can – and, eventually, should – be influenced by economic policy through the financing of language education and the provision of such education in schools and universities.

In what follows, we provide descriptive evidence on CNLs and CSLs by way of figures as well as tables. Since a native language is (with small exceptions) always also a spoken language, we will discern common spoken native languages (CSNLs) from common spoken acquired (i.e. non-native) languages (CSALs), and provide information on CSLs as a combined measure of the two. Let $L_{ij} \in \{CSNL_{ij}, CSAL_{ij}, CSL_{ij}\}$ measure the overlap between countries i and j in any one of the three concepts.

Table 9.1 reports correlation coefficients among the common language variables between all pairs of 195 countries including the diagonal of the correlation matrix (i.e. there are $38,025 = 195^2$ observations).[1] The unconditional correlations between *CSL* and *CSNL* on the one hand and *CSL* and *CSAL* on the other are strong and positive. As expected, there is a negative correlation

---

[1] The estimation makes use of 195×194 observations. The observations on the diagonal of the matrix are used to compute the general equilibrium welfare changes in Section 9.4.4.

Table 9.1 Correlation matrix

	$CSNL_{ij}$	$CSAL_{ij}$	CSL_{ij}
$CSNL_{ij}$	1.000		
$CSAL_{ij}$	−0.037	1.000	
CSL_{ij}	0.659	0.441	1.0000

between *CSNL* and *CSAL*, since the total number of potential speakers in a country is normalized to unity and fixed.

Define ℓ to be an individual element in the set of $\mathcal{L}$ languages spoken around the globe, and $s_{L\ell i}$ to be the share of the population speaking language ℓ in concept L and country i. Then, we may define a measure L_{0ij} of common language spokenness between countries i and j as follows:

$$L_{0ij} = \sum_{\ell \in \mathcal{L}} s_{L\ell i} s_{L\ell j}. \tag{1}$$

As pointed out in Melitz and Toubal (2014), L_{0ij} is not necessarily bounded from above by unity.[2] However, this can easily be adjusted to obtain $L_{ij} \in [0, 1]$. In what follows, we will report two types of measures:

$$L_i^d = L_{ii}; \qquad L_i^f = \frac{\sum_{j \neq i} L_{ij} POP_j}{\sum_{j \neq i} POP_j}, \tag{2}$$

where L_i^d is a measure of domestic language homogeneity in country i, and L_i^f is a measure of language homogeneity of country i with other countries (POP_j is the population of country j). A higher index implies a larger degree of homogeneity. We report some statistics concerning the variables in Table 9.2.

Table 9.2 Common languages measure: Summary statistics

Variable	Obs.	Mean	Std. Dev.
$CSNL_i^d$	195	0.435	0.390
$CSAL_i^d$	195	0.174	0.232
CSL_i^d	195	0.636	0.350
$CSNL_i^f$	37,830	0.031	0.138
$CSAL_i^f$	37,830	0.037	0.097
CSL_i^f	37,830	0.124	0.233

---

[2] This is due to the fact that a citizen may speak several languages.

As is obvious from Table 9.2, average language homogeneity is much higher within countries than between countries. This is particularly the case when comparing CSL_i^f and CSL_i^d, but also holds for the other measures.

Figures 9.1 to 9.3 display $CSNL_i^d$, $CSAL_i^d$ and CSL_i^d, while Figures 9.4 to 9.6 display $CSNL_i^f$, $CSAL_i^f$ and CSL_i^f, by way of maps. In these figures, darker grey colours refer to a higher value of language proximity (or overlap).[3]

$CSNL_i^d$ is highest in South America, in Europe and in Russia. There is a much higher degree of native language plurality in other countries. $CSAL_i^d$ is highest in northern and central Europe as well as in western Africa. The pattern of CSL_i^d in Figure 9.3 is largely coherent with the one of $CSNL_i^d$ in Figure 9.1. The Moran statistics in Figures 9.1 to 9.3 suggest a U-shaped pattern of spatial clustering across the levels of domestic country language proximity: countries with a very homogeneous domestic language portfolio tend to be close to each other (not necessarily speaking the same language, though) and ones which have a very dispersed domestic language portfolio also tend to be fairly strongly spatially clustered.

Inspection of the spatial patterns of $CSNL_i^f$, $CSAL_i^f$ and CSL_i^f, shown in Figures 9.4 to 9.6, suggests that the latter are largely different from those of $CSNL_i^d$, $CSAL_i^d$ and CSL_i^d for three fundamental reasons. First, some populations

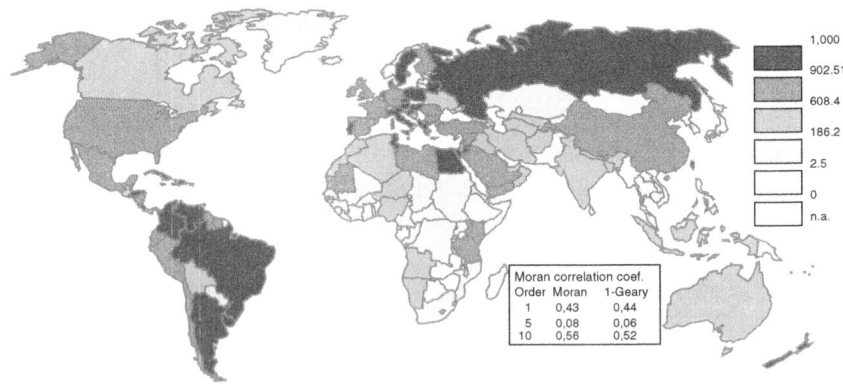

Figure 9.1 Common spoken native language ($CSNL_i^d$)

---

[3] The legends to the figures provide details about the quantitative meaning of the shades and about the Moran and the Geary statistics. The Moran statistic measures the degree of spatial correlation of the variable across countries. The statistic is bounded between minus and plus one, where a higher value refers to a greater degree of spatial clustering. The Geary index is another measure of spatial correlation. It is inversely related to the Moran statistic though more sensitive to local spatial correlation.

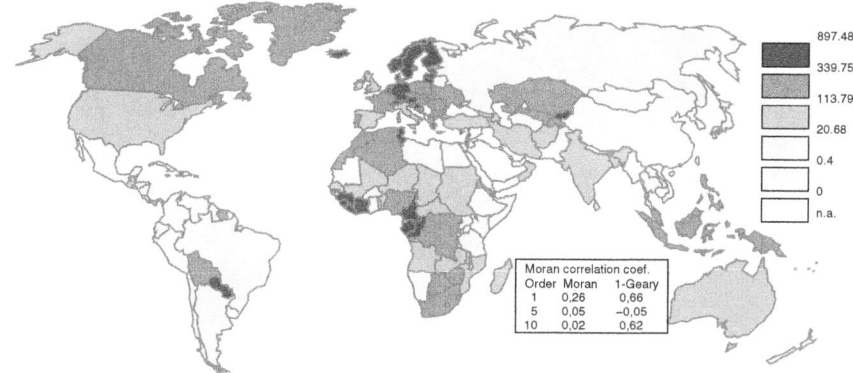

Figure 9.2   Common spoken acquired language ($CSAL_i^d$)

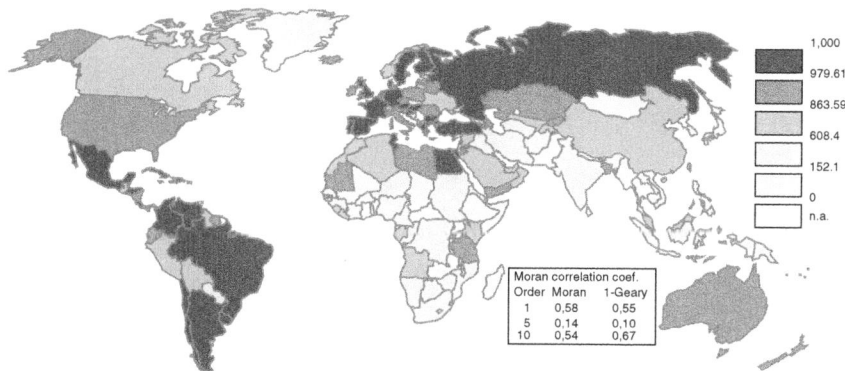

Figure 9.3   Common spoken language (CSL_i^d)

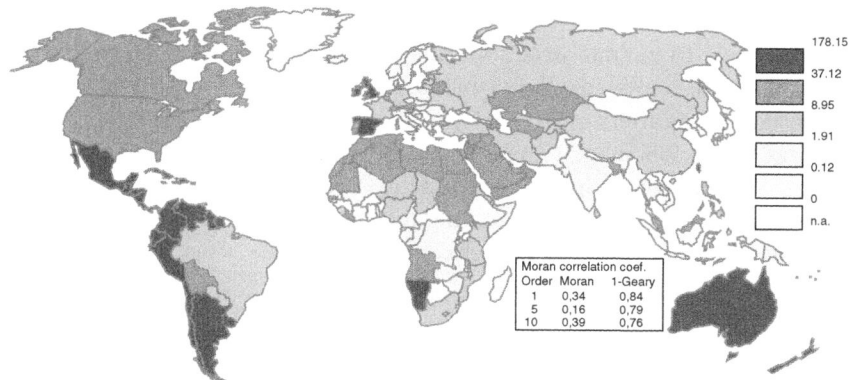

Figure 9.4   Common spoken native language ($CSNL_i^f$)

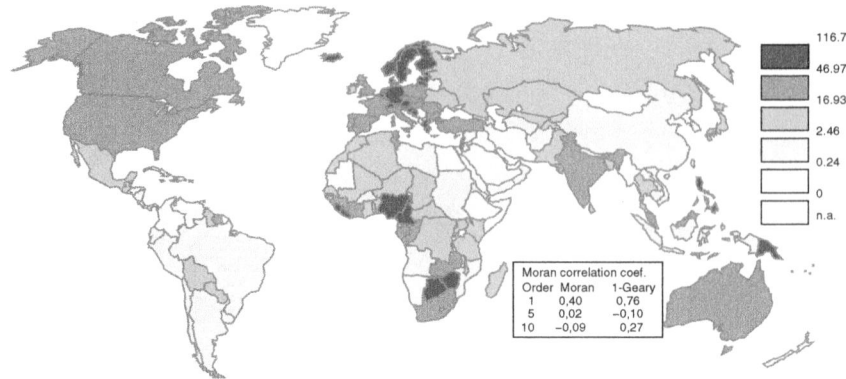

Figure 9.5   Common spoken acquired language $(CSAL_i^f)$

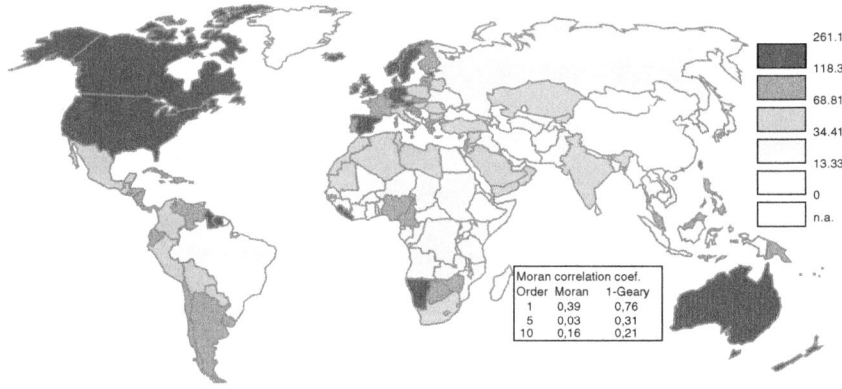

Figure 9.6   Common spoken language (CSL_i^f)

are more likely to migrate; second, some countries are more open to immigration; and, third, some languages (such as English) are more likely to be taught and learned than others.

Figures 9.4 to 9.6 suggest that, across all concepts $CSNL_i^f$, $CSAL_i^f$ and CSL_i^f, English, Scandinavian, Spanish (especially, European) and German-speaking countries are better connected to the average (population-weighted) foreign economy by way of CSLs than other countries.

9.3   A trade economist's stylized view on languages

9.3.1   A generic gravity equation of bilateral trade

Modern trade theory provides a sound foundation of the so-called gravity equation (see Anderson, 1979; Eaton and Kortum, 2002; Anderson and van

Wincoop, 2003, 2004; Helpman et al., 2008; Bergstrand et al., 2013). This equation formulates bilateral trade as an increasing function of economic country size and a decreasing function of trade frictions or facilitations between countries. It is one of the most successful empirical models in economics in terms of its fit of the data. We use the gravity model in our study to understand the role of language commonality for bilateral trade. For this, we largely follow Anderson and van Wincoop (2003) in the model set-up and specify bilateral imports of country i from country j, M_{ij}, as a multiplicative function of bilateral preferences and trade costs, t_{ij},[4] of exporter-specific multilateral preferences and trade costs, Π_i, of importer-specific multilateral preferences and trade costs, P_j, of exporter and importer GDP, $Y_i Y_j$, and of world GDP, Y. Using $1 - \sigma$ to refer to the partial effect or so-called elasticity of trade (with respect to trade costs), we may specify M_{ij} as

$$M_{ij} = \left(\frac{t_{ij}}{\Pi_i P_j} \right)^{1-\sigma} \frac{Y_i Y_j}{Y}. \tag{3}$$

Three issues are important to consider with the above model. First, the balance of payments (or resource constraint) implies that GDP is defined as $Y_i = \sum_{j=1}^{J} M_{ij} = \sum_{j=1}^{J} M_{ji}$, and $Y = \sum_{i=1}^{J} Y_i$. Second, multilateral preferences and trade costs are defined as $\Pi_i^{1-\sigma} = \sum_{j=1}^{J} (Y_j/Y)(t_{ij}/P_j)^{1-\sigma}$ for exporters and as $P_i^{1-\sigma} = \sum_{i=1}^{J} (Y_i/Y)(t_{ij}/\Pi_i)^{1-\sigma}$ for importers. Notice that these three constraints imply that the marginal effect of t_{ij} on M_{ij} differs from $1 - \sigma$ which corresponds to the direct or partial effect. The direct effect of a change in t_{ij} on M_{ij} is moderated by general equilibrium effects through $\frac{Y_i Y_j}{Y(\Pi_i P_j)^{1-\sigma}}$. Third, t_{ij} is a universal measure of *ad valorem* trade costs which depends on many things including language commonality.

For any country j, a measure of aggregate consumption – and aggregate utilitarian welfare – in such a model is the ratio of aggregate nominal expenditures Y_j in this country j and the consumer-price index, P_j:

$$U_j = \frac{Y_j}{P_j}. \tag{4}$$

Using superscript c to denote counterfactual levels of exogenous and endogenous variables and Δ for a change, the trade and welfare effects of some change in trade costs (such as language commonality) in percentage terms are

$$\Delta M_{ij} = 100 \frac{M_{ij}^c}{M_{ij}} - 100 = 100 \left(\frac{t_{ij}^c}{t_{ij}} \right)^{1-\sigma} \left(\frac{\Pi_i^c P_j^c}{\Pi_i P_j} \right)^{1-\sigma} \frac{Y_i Y_j}{Y_i^c Y_j^c} \frac{Y^c}{Y} - 100, \tag{5}$$

---

[4] We treat differences in consumer prices of goods from a given exporting country across importing countries as stemming either from trade frictions or from Armington (1969) preferences for goods from different countries.

$$\Delta U_j = 100\frac{U_j^c}{U_j} - 100 = 100\frac{Y_j^c}{Y_j}\frac{P_j}{P_j^c} - 100. \tag{6}$$

9.3.2   Trade costs and trade

We model bilateral preferences and trade frictions in a customary log-linear form, whereby

$$(1-\sigma)\ln t_{ij} = \text{language}_{ij}\lambda + \sum_{k=1}^{K} \beta_k \ln z_k, \tag{7}$$

where language$_{ij}$ is either a binary indicator variable equal to 1 if countries j and i have a common official language and zero otherwise, or it is a fractional spoken language overlap measure such as CSL_{ij}, $CSNL_{ij}$ or $CSAL_{ij}$. As mentioned earlier, CSL_{ij} is the probability that two randomly drawn people from two countries i and j understand one another in some common language. $CSNL_{ij}$ and $CSAL_{ij}$ are the probabilities that a randomly drawn pair of persons from two countries speak the same native or acquired language, respectively. By construction, all common language measures considered here are not only symmetric, but are also assumed to induce symmetric effects on bilateral imports (M_{ij}) and exports (M_{ji}).[5] $\ln z_k$ is the k_{th} measurable non-language factor determining $\ln t_{ij}$, λ is a scalar or a conformable row vector of parameters, and β_k are estimable parameters. The additional $\ln z_k$ terms are controls in order to discern the impact of language commonality from other determinants of bilateral trade.

We use bilateral distances and binary indicator variables measuring whether two countries have a common border as measurable trade costs, as well as three additional binary indicators that control for geography, such as when two countries are both islands, or they belong to the same continent, or they are both landlocked. Pre-World War II colonial history in the 20th century and earlier is also highly important. People in former colonies of an ex-colonizer often know the language of the ex-colonizer and, as a result, people in two ex-colonies of the same ex-colonizer will also tend to know the ex-colonizer's language. We therefore use binary indicator variables for common border, relations between ex-colonies and ex-colonizer, and relations between pairs of ex-colonies of the same ex-colonizer as additional control variables, basing ex-colonial relationships on the situation as of 1939, i.e. at the start of World War II.

In addition, we include further variables that have been used in the gravity literature on international trade more recently. The reason is that, to a certain

---

[5] Some recent work suggests that, to the extent that it reflects trust, language commonality may induce asymmetric effects in a pair of two countries (see Guiso et al., 2009 and Felbermayr and Toubal, 2010). We shall disregard this point, here.

Table 9.3 Summary statistics

Variable	Dimension	Mean	Std. dev.	N
Common spoken language	Fractional	0.124	0.233	37,830
Common spoken acquired language	Fractional	0.037	0.097	37,830
Common spoken native language	Fractional	0.031	0.138	37,830
Value of trade				
Total	Real-non-neg.	0.233	2.837	37,830
Total	Logarithm	7.709	3.757	22,387
Differentiated products	Real-non-neg.	0.155	2.198	37,830
Reference priced	Real-non-neg.	0.044	0.504	37,830
Homogeneous products	Real-non-neg.	0.034	0.478	37,830
Distance	Logarithm	8.802	0.783	37,830
Contiguity	Binary	0.014	0.116	37,830
Islands	Binary	0.060	0.237	37,830
Same continent	Binary	0.210	0.407	37,830
Landlocked	Binary	0.023	0.150	37,830
Ex-colonizer/colony	Binary	0.007	0.082	37,830
Common colonizer	Binary	0.121	0.326	37,830
Common religion	Fractional	0.146	0.210	37,830
Common legal systems	Binary	0.186	0.389	37,830
History of war	Real-non-neg.	0.003	0.042	37,830

extent, these variables measure common history and culture and their omission might lead to a biased estimate of the partial effect of language commonality on bilateral trade. These control variables are a binary indicator of common legal systems, a fractional variable for common religions and an indirect measure of trust such as history of wars between pairs of countries.

Most of the variables are taken and described in detail in Melitz and Toubal (2014). The dimension and summary statistics of the variables used in the estimation are given in Table 9.3.

9.3.3   Estimation strategies

For an empirical analysis of the impact of common language on trade, at least three issues should be considered. First, a large fraction of possible bilateral trade relations are equal to zero. This can be explained by the existence of fixed costs to bilateral trade (see Helpman et al., 2008). Fixed trade costs imply that trade will be positive only if profits cover at least fixed trade costs. This means that two margins of trade are interesting to consider when assessing the role of common languages and other elements in the trade-cost function: the extensive country (or country-pair) margin of bilateral trade – i.e. the probability of positive bilateral trade – and the intensive country (or country-pair) margin of bilateral trade – i.e. the level of positive volume of bilateral trade. Second, conditional on their determinants, bilateral trade flows are heteroskedastic: smaller bilateral trade flows exhibit a bigger variance than larger bilateral trade flows (see Egger and Nigai, 2014). Accordingly, log-transforming the exponentially multiplicatively determined bilateral trade flows does not only force us to eliminate the numerous zeros from the analysis but also leads to biased estimates (see Santos Silva and Tenreyro, 2006). Third, the structure of the model in Section 9.3.1 is such that bilateral trade depends multiplicatively not only on trade costs but also on exporter-specific and importer-specific factors, where the latter include Y_i, Y_j, P_i and P_j which are implicit functions of trade costs (and, by this token, of common language).

From an empirical standpoint, a joint treatment of zeros and heteroskedasticity in exponentially multiplicative gravity models of bilateral trade is possible in so-called two-part exponential-family models. With regard to zeros, Helpman et al. (2008) and Egger et al. (2011) propose using probit models. With regard to heteroskedasticity in positive bilateral trade data, Santos Silva and Tenreyro (2006) suggest using the Poisson pseudo-maximum-likelihood (PPML) estimator (See Head and Mayer, 2015 for a discussion of the estimation of the gravity equation). For a joint treatment of zeros and heteroskedasticity, Egger et al. (2011) suggest two-part PPML models, where the extensive country's (or country-pair's) margin of bilateral trade is estimated by probit and the intensive margin is estimated by PPML. A straightforward treatment of the country-specific factors in the models for either margin can be achieved by including fixed effects for each exporter and importer.

9.3.4   A smörgåsbord of econometric problems

Apart from the general estimation issues discussed in Subsection 9.3.3, a number of further econometric problems could be considered. These consist of the possible endogeneity of common language measures, the relatively time-invariant nature of common language measures in panel data models where country-pairs' trade flows are observed over several years, and the boundedness of language overlap measures. We provide possible remedies in what follows.

Endogeneity

One potential problem is the endogeneity of common language variables as determinants of bilateral trade. Endogeneity means that the stochastic process generating common language and the one generating bilateral trades are correlated. There are two fundamental sources of such stochastic interdependence: first, common languages could be mismeasured while bilateral trades depend on the true level of languages overlap; second, common languages and bilateral trades could be a function of joint factors (omitted or hard to measure) such as historical and cultural factors as well as of migrations (historically and contemporaneously). With bilateral trade as the outcome, primarily $CSAL_{ij}$ but even

$CSNL_{ij}$ may be endogenous (see Egger and Lassmann, 2013; Egger and Toubal, 2014; Ginsburgh et al., 2014; Melitz and Toubal, 2014). With endogenous language variables, one may adopt a control function approach, instrumental variable regressions or switching regressions. In any case, it is advisable to utilize some regressors among the covariates determining common language that do not explain bilateral trade.[6] In what follows, we focus on a somewhat more detailed description of instrumental variables for language commonality and the control function approach to remove the endogeneity bias in (log-)linear or exponential-family models of bilateral imports, M_{ij}.

Instrumental variables. Potential suitable instruments for common language variables are historical factors (e.g. information based on the movement of populations, genetic distance measures, past colonial relationships, linguistic proximity and possibly, other cultural communalities between countries). However, none of these instruments will be entirely satisfactory as the common spoken language variables reflect the integrated multidimensional process of learning languages and, apart from that, the aforementioned variables may affect trade indirectly through other cultural or historical factors than just common language. In most nonlinear models, the control function approach and the instrumental variable approach are equivalent, since the use of predicted endogenous variables from a first stage instead of the observed endogenous variables is not feasible, unlike in linear regression models.

Control function approach.   This approach is more general than maximum likelihood methods. The control function estimators first estimate the model of endogenous regressors as a function of instruments and then use the errors from this model as an additional regressor in the main model. With the fractional variables $CSNL_{ij}$ and $CSAL_{ij}$ no exact control function is available. However, one could estimate fractional models or fractional two-part models (to take account of the mass point at zero for these two variables) in a first stage, involving the set of explanatory variables $R_{CSNL,ij}$ and $R_{CSAL,ij}$ that may be identical or not. Then, one could take the linear predictions of these models, $\widehat{CSNL}^{*}_{ij} = R_{CSNL,ij}\hat{\beta}_{CSNL}$ and $\widehat{CSAL}_{ij} = R_{CSAL,ij}\hat{\beta}_{CSAL}$, respectively, and use them in, e.g., a polynomial (or even a non-parametric) form in the conditional expectation $\overline{M}_{ij}$ of M_{ij}. For instance, a model of bilateral imports, M_{ij}, with a quadratic control function involving both $CSNL_{ij}$ and $CSAL_{ij}$ is described as $E(M_{ij}|R_{M,ij}, CSNL_{ij}, CSAL_{ij}, \widehat{CSNL}^{*2}_{ij}, \widehat{CSAL}^{*2}_{ij}, \widehat{CSNL}^{*3}_{ij}, \widehat{CSAL}^{*3}_{ij})$, using again some suitable generalized linear model to specify the dispersion of M_{ij}.

---

[6] See Wooldridge (2002, ch. 18) for a general review of options to reduce the endogeneity bias and Egger et al. (2011) for an application of these approaches to international trade.

Time-invariance of common language variables

When using panel data (repeated cross-sections of country-pairs over time) on bilateral trade flows, the data are triple-indexed.[7] Using t to refer to time, even though economic theory does not necessarily call for it, it is advisable to rely on error assumptions that account for the repeated observation of ij, jt and it in a so-called three-way panel (see Baltagi et al., 2003). In almost all datasets, it will be the case that a model which assumes ij-indexed variables to be exogenous will be rejected (see Baltagi et al., 2003).[8] In fact, the endogeneity bias of many gravity models which rely on parameterizations of all ij-indexed bilateral trade costs is large and eventually leads to a huge bias in the structural estimates of trade costs (see Egger and Nigai, 2014). However, a problem with the inclusion of fixed ij-specific fixed effects is that parameters on time-invariant variables – such as $\{CSL_{ij}, CSNL_{ij}, CSAL_{ij}\}$ – cannot be estimated, since these variables are perfectly collinear with the ij-type fixed effects.

However, one could apply strategies to rely on parameterized country-pair fixed effects with random country-pair error components along the lines of Hausman and Taylor (1981) for log-linear gravity models and of Hahn and Meinecke (2005) for nonlinear models. Either approach would entertain the repeated observation of triple-indexed variables (such as applied bilateral tariff rates, preferential trade agreement membership and other covariates) in the various dimensions of the panel (ij, jt, it) to construct sets of instruments for ij-indexed variables from within the vector of regressors, $R_{X,ij}$, which excludes the common language variables.

Other-than-official language measures as censored variables

Notice that all fractional measures of CSLs, $\{CSL_{ij}, CSNL_{ij}, CSAL_{ij}\}$, whatever the effort put in their construction and data collection, are censored. The reason is that authors who collect data on spoken languages do (have to) impose cutoff levels on the fraction of speakers per language community to be taken into account in a country. Hence, there is censoring from below (or left-censoring) in econometric terms. One way of overcoming this issue would be to impute the data.

Let us briefly outline what could be done by using the example of CSLs, CSL_{ij}. Clearly, empirically CSL_{ij} is not only bounded from below but has a mass point at zero and is never unity in the data. One could transform CSL_{ij} to obtain

[7] Clearly, in principle, one should think even of cross-sectional bilateral trade data as panel data, due to their double-indexed nature (see Baltagi et al., forthcoming).
[8] This is not necessarily the case with jt-indexed and it-indexed variables, since those could remove the information in the triple-indexed disturbances through structural estimation and controlling for so-called multilateral resistance terms along the lines of Anderson and van Wincoop (2003).

a measure $\widetilde{csl}_{ij} = \ln \frac{CSL_{ij}}{1-CSL_{ij}}$. This strategy eliminates all data points for which $CSL_{ij} = 0$. The variable $\widetilde{csl}_{ij}$ could now be regressed on determinants $R_{CSL,ij}$ of CSL_{ij}, in a Tobit model with left-censoring, assuming normality about the disturbances. Such a strategy would be consistent with Schafer (1997); see also Schafer and Graham (2002). One could then compute the conditional expectations of that model for the censored data points plus repeatedly sampled disturbances from the normal distribution to obtain a sampled set of uncensored predictions $\widetilde{csl}_{ij}^{+}$. The latter could be used to obtain a sampled set of uncensored $\widehat{CSL}_{ij}^{+} = \frac{\exp(\widetilde{csl}_{ij}^{+})}{1+\exp(\widetilde{csl}_{ij}^{+})}$. Clearly, when using the latter in regressions, one would want to resample over both the imputation and the outcome stage (where the latter would be concerned with modelling M_{ij} and estimating the coefficient of CSL_{ij}).

9.4 Empirical results

9.4.1 Estimates of the magnitude of the direct effect of language on aggregate bilateral trade

The partial or so-called direct effects of languages reflect the coefficient estimates on language variables in linear regressions (or the marginal effects on language variables in nonlinear regressions). Such estimates ignore feedback effects on import flows from other price changes. We discuss the results of the estimation of general equilibrium effects of languages in Section 9.4.4.

In the first three columns of Table 9.4, we report the marginal effects of CSL, CSNL and CSAL on the probability of positive imports at the country-pair level.[9] The empirical specifications are estimated using a probit model. In columns 1 and 2, we introduce CSL and CSNL alternatively. The coefficients of both variables are positive, and they are statistically significant.

Since a native language is always also a spoken language, we distinguish the effect of CSNL from CSAL in column 3. The inclusion of CSAL does not affect the impact of CSNL on the extensive country margin of imports. CSAL is positive but statistically insignificant. However, we have to bear in mind that there is a certain degree of multicollinearity between CSNL and CSAL.

In the last three columns of Table 9.4, we examine the effect of CSLs on the value (or volume) of imports. This is commonly referred to as the intensive country or country-pair margin of bilateral imports. However, since we include zero as well as positive import flows in the PPML analysis, we should think of this analysis as a mixed treatment of extensive and intensive country-pair

---

[9] This is also referred to as the extensive country or country-pair margin of bilateral imports. The partial effects are evaluated at the sample means.

Table 9.4   Impact of common spoken languages on the margins of bilateral imports

	Probability of importing			Value of imports		
	(1)	(2)	(3)	(4)	(5)	(6)
CSL	0.125***			0.289*		
	(0.021)			(0.151)		
CSNL		0.168***	0.168***		0.457***	0.457***
		(0.034)	(0.034)		(0.170)	(0.170)
CSAL			0.007			0.034
			(0.048)			(0.309)
Distance (log)	−0.212***	−0.208***	−0.208***	−0.556***	−0.566***	−0.566***
	(0.008)	(0.008)	(0.008)	(0.042)	(0.041)	(0.041)
Contiguity	−0.061	−0.055	−0.055	0.528***	0.504***	0.503***
	(0.043)	(0.043)	(0.043)	(0.085)	(0.083)	(0.084)
Islands	0.065***	0.068***	0.068***	0.237**	0.219*	0.219*
	(0.019)	(0.019)	(0.019)	(0.120)	(0.123)	(0.123)
Continent	0.076***	0.080***	0.079***	0.443***	0.448***	0.447***
	(0.012)	(0.012)	(0.012)	(0.076)	(0.075)	(0.077)
Landlocked	0.001	0.004	0.004	0.269	0.300*	0.300*
	(0.023)	(0.023)	(0.023)	(0.170)	(0.157)	(0.157)
Ex colonizer/colony	0.073	0.093	0.093	0.356**	0.389**	0.389**
	(0.090)	(0.088)	(0.088)	(0.168)	(0.174)	(0.174)
Common colonizer	0.110***	0.119***	0.119***	0.173	0.187	0.187
	(0.012)	(0.012)	(0.012)	(0.114)	(0.115)	(0.115)
Common religion	0.077***	0.089***	0.089***	0.012	0.036	0.037
	(0.019)	(0.019)	(0.019)	(0.114)	(0.107)	(0.107)
Common legal systems	0.105***	0.099***	0.099***	0.240***	0.163**	0.162**
	(0.013)	(0.013)	(0.013)	(0.068)	(0.079)	(0.078)
History of war	−0.840***	−0.838***	−0.838***	−0.055	−0.020	−0.020
	(0.218)	(0.217)	(0.217)	(0.098)	(0.096)	(0.096)
Observations	37,056	37,056	37,056	37,830	37,830	37,830
R-squared				0.879	0.883	0.883
Reset Chi^2				11.64	10.78	10.31
Reset *p*-value				0.001	0.001	0.001

Notes: All regressions contain exporter and importer fixed effects. Robust standard errors in parentheses adjusted for clustering by country pair. ***significant at 1% level; **significant at 5% level; *significant at 10% level.

margins.[10] Notice that the number of observations in the Probit model in Table 9.4 is smaller than in the PPML model. The reason is that some of the extensive margin results are predicted perfectly (with probability zero or unity) which leads to a loss of those observations in the Probit model. In columns 4

---

[10] We present a cleaner intensive-margin analysis based on positive import flows in Table 9.5.

and 5, we find a positive impact of CSL and CSNL on bilateral trade. The effect of CSL is estimated with a lower degree of precision than the one of CSNL, though. In column 6, CSNL has a positive and significant effect on the value of bilateral imports. As before, the effect of CSAL is not statistically significantly different from zero.

The estimated coefficients picked up by the gravity variables have the expected signs. Contiguity and ex-colonialism induce a positive effect on bilateral import volume. They do not affect the probability of positive imports, though. Common colonizer, religion and history of war have a statistically significant effect only on the probability of positive bilateral imports.

In Table 9.5, we use alternative estimation strategies. Even when running PPML on the positive subsample only (as one would do in a two-part model as suggested in Egger et al., 2011),[11] the main results do not change.

Apparently, neither OLS nor a two-step Heckman-type model leads to the same conclusions. In both models – which use $m_{ij} = \ln(M_{ij})$ as the dependent variable – all parameters on the language variables are larger than in the PPML model of Table 9.4, and they are statistically significant. Clearly, one problem of these models is that they may be biased if the disturbances are heteroskedastic (see Santos Silva and Tenreyro, 2006; Egger and Staub, 2015). However, PPML as run here would be problematic if the assumptions in the Heckman-type model were met (i.e. the disturbances were identically and independently distributed and jointly normal between the extensive and intensive margin models).

9.4.2 Endogeneity issues

We use a control function approach to deal with the issue of endogeneity (see Section 9.3.4) and report the associated results in Table 9.6. With such an approach, the estimates of the common language variables on both the probability of positive bilateral imports and on the value of bilateral imports are larger than before.

The partial effects of CSLs on the extensive country-pair margin of bilateral imports are estimated with a high degree of precision in columns 1 to 3. In column 3, both CSNLs and CSALs are statistically significant. We note that, while the effect of CSALs seems to be slightly larger than the one of CSNLs, the difference between the coefficients is not statistically significant.

Turning to the impact of common spoken languages on the value of bilateral imports, we find a significant impact of CSLs. In columns 5 and 6, the coefficients on CSNLs are positive and statistically significant. Notice that they are estimated with a slightly lower degree of precision than in Table 9.4 (as is

---

[11] As said before, only such an analysis permits interpreting the respective results as to refer to the intensive country-pair margin only.

Table 9.5 Alternative estimation strategies: Value of imports

	OLS			Heckman (second stage)			PPML (positive values)		
	(1)	(2)	(3)	(4)	(5)	(6)	(7)	(8)	(9)
CSL	0.794*** (0.067)			0.894*** (0.075)			0.288* (0.150)		
CSNL		0.889*** (0.094)	0.875*** (0.094)		1.168*** (0.117)	1.162*** (0.117)		0.452*** (0.170)	0.451*** (0.169)
CSAL			0.643*** (0.169)			0.677*** (0.176)			0.035 (0.310)
Distance (log)	-1.441*** (0.027)	-1.430*** (0.028)	-1.433*** (0.028)	-1.429*** (0.027)	-1.406*** (0.027)	-1.408*** (0.027)	-0.548*** (0.042)	-0.558*** (0.042)	-0.558*** (0.041)
Contiguity	0.700*** (0.101)	0.753*** (0.101)	0.738*** (0.101)	0.657*** (0.097)	0.701*** (0.097)	0.682*** (0.097)	0.523*** (0.084)	0.499*** (0.083)	0.498*** (0.084)
Islands	0.343*** (0.083)	0.340*** (0.083)	0.345*** (0.083)	0.373*** (0.081)	0.375*** (0.081)	0.382*** (0.081)	0.237** (0.120)	0.219* (0.123)	0.219* (0.123)
Continent	-0.088** (0.043)	-0.051 (0.043)	-0.078* (0.044)	-0.097** (0.043)	-0.054 (0.043)	-0.082* (0.043)	0.448*** (0.076)	0.453*** (0.075)	0.452*** (0.076)
Landlocked	0.699*** (0.101)	0.703*** (0.101)	0.702*** (0.101)	0.716*** (0.104)	0.724*** (0.104)	0.725*** (0.104)	0.274 (0.169)	0.304* (0.157)	0.305* (0.157)
Ex-colonizer/colony	1.506*** (0.117)	1.585*** (0.118)	1.592*** (0.118)	1.416*** (0.134)	1.464*** (0.134)	1.468*** (0.134)	0.349** (0.168)	0.381** (0.174)	0.381** (0.174)
Common colonizer	0.846*** (0.056)	0.904*** (0.056)	0.880*** (0.057)	0.829*** (0.053)	0.892*** (0.053)	0.867*** (0.053)	0.167 (0.114)	0.182 (0.115)	0.181 (0.115)
Common religion	0.386*** (0.068)	0.468*** (0.068)	0.467*** (0.068)	0.381*** (0.071)	0.455*** (0.070)	0.454*** (0.070)	0.011 (0.114)	0.035 (0.107)	0.036 (0.107)
Common legal systems	0.282*** (0.046)	0.241*** (0.048)	0.247*** (0.048)	0.304*** (0.047)	0.246*** (0.048)	0.253*** (0.048)	0.237*** (0.068)	0.161** (0.079)	0.160** (0.078)
History of war	-0.364** (0.184)	-0.334* (0.180)	-0.336* (0.181)	-0.367 (0.242)	-0.325 (0.242)	-0.327 (0.242)	-0.052 (0.098)	-0.018 (0.096)	-0.018 (0.097)
Observations	22,387	22,387	22,387	37,830	37,830	37,830	22,387	22,387	22,387
R-squared	0.758	0.758	0.758				0.879	0.883	0.883
Reset Chi²							8.135	7.391	7.049
Reset p-value							0.00434	0.00655	0.00793

Notes: All regressions contain exporter and importer fixed effects. Robust standard errors in parentheses adjusted for clustering by country pair. ***significant at 1% level; **significant at 5% level; *significant at 10% level.

Table 9.6 Impact of common spoken languages on the margins of bilateral imports (control function approach)

	Probability of importing			Value of imports		
	(1)	(2)	(3)	(4)	(5)	(6)
CSL	0.246***			0.369*		
	(0.034)			(0.198)		
CSNL		0.343***	0.357***		0.760**	0.677**
		(0.118)	(0.118)		(0.314)	(0.292)
CSAL			0.551***			0.115
			(0.139)			(0.691)
Distance (log)	−0.210***	−0.205***	−0.206***	−0.577***	−0.560***	−0.564***
	(0.008)	(0.008)	(0.008)	(0.041)	(0.042)	(0.041)
Contiguity	−0.073*	−0.064	−0.071	0.499***	0.528***	0.526***
	(0.043)	(0.044)	(0.044)	(0.086)	(0.083)	(0.085)
Islands	0.047**	0.064***	0.065***	0.254**	0.203*	0.201*
	(0.020)	(0.019)	(0.019)	(0.120)	(0.122)	(0.122)
Continent	0.074***	0.080***	0.076***	0.430***	0.447***	0.450***
	(0.012)	(0.012)	(0.012)	(0.074)	(0.073)	(0.075)
Landlocked	0.004	0.004	0.003	0.214	0.312**	0.294*
	(0.023)	(0.023)	(0.023)	(0.178)	(0.156)	(0.160)
Ex-colonizer/colony	0.025	0.074	0.068	0.686***	0.440***	0.432**
	(0.092)	(0.088)	(0.090)	(0.153)	(0.168)	(0.169)
Common colonizer	0.099***	0.116***	0.107***	0.181	0.181	0.186
	(0.013)	(0.012)	(0.013)	(0.120)	(0.117)	(0.117)
Common religion	0.060***	0.082***	0.080***	0.198*	0.129	0.100
	(0.022)	(0.020)	(0.020)	(0.112)	(0.110)	(0.108)
Common legal	0.099***	0.095***	0.094***	0.228***	0.220***	0.217***
systems	(0.013)	(0.014)	(0.013)	(0.068)	(0.077)	(0.075)
History of war	−0.856***	−0.842***	−0.807***	−0.101	−0.027	−0.027
	(0.217)	(0.218)	(0.220)	(0.100)	(0.098)	(0.099)
Observations	37,056	37,056	37,056	37,830	37,830	37,830
R-squared				0.882	0.886	0.889
Reset Chi^2				9.853	11.23	9.627
Reset *p*-value				0.001	0.001	0.002

Notes: All regressions contain exporter and importer fixed effects. Robust standard errors in parentheses adjusted for clustering by country pair. ***significant at 1% level; **significant at 5% level; *significant at 10% level.

expected with instrumental-variables estimation). We find no significant direct impact of CSALs on imports in column 6.

Based on columns 3 and 6, we find that the acquisition of a CSAL matters directly for the probability of importing but does not influence the value of importing. This is consistent with CSALs to matter for fixed rather than for variable costs of importing.

9.4.3   Language effects on categories of goods traded

In this subsection, we use the sub-aggregates proposed by Rauch (1999) to examine the impact of the linguistic variables on homogeneous, listed and differentiated goods.[12] Homogeneous goods are traded on organized trading platforms. Listed goods are still standard enough to be traded on the basis of price lists without knowledge of the particular supplier. Differentiated goods are bought from a specific supplier. We expect linguistic influences to become progressively more important as we go from homogeneous to listed and to differentiated goods, since the degree of complexity of the goods and the required information for the customer rises. For the same reason, we expect ethnic ties and trust to be more important in that order.[13] In Section 9.4.2, we used the control function approach to deal with the problem of endogeneity. The results are presented in Tables 9.7 and 9.8.

Table 9.7 reports partial effects of the impact of CSLs on the probability of positive bilateral imports of the three types of commodities.

In column 1, we find a positive and significant impact of CSLs on bilateral trade of homogeneous goods. This suggests that spoken language is essential for conveying information and affects the fixed costs of importing. In column 2, we discern the effect of CSNLs from CSALs. While a CSNL does not influence the probability of importing homogeneous goods, a CSAL is highly significant. This is compatible with the idea that the role of a CSL on homogeneous imports is mostly driven by a CSAL, while owing little to personal affinities and trust.

Columns 3 and 4 show the effects for listed goods. The results are qualitatively similar to those for homogeneous goods. The partial effects are slightly larger, though. These results suggest that trust and ethnicity matter also for the probability of importing listed goods.

In the case of differentiated goods in columns 5 and 6, all three language variables are highly significant. A CSNL affects positively the probability of positive imports. This result confirms that linguistic influences become more important as we turn from the trade of simple to more complex goods.

The results concerning the impact of CSLs on the value of imports reported in Table 9.8 are less clear-cut. In the case of homogeneous goods, the coefficients of CSLs, CSNLs and CSALs are all insignificant. In the case of listed goods, the

---

[12] We report findings for Rauch's conservative aggregation scheme (which minimizes the number of goods that are classified as either traded on an organized exchange or reference priced). Our results remain qualitatively similar when using Rauch's conservative aggregation scheme.

[13] See Guiso et al. (2009), Felbermayr and Toubal (2010) and Felbermayr et al. (2011) for arguments along those lines.

Table 9.7 Impact of common spoken languages on the probability of imports (Rauch's decomposition)

	Probability of importing					
	Homogeneous goods		Listed goods		Differentiated goods	
	(1)	(2)	(3)	(4)	(5)	(6)
CSL	0.179***		0.218***		0.324***	
	(0.023)		(0.037)		(0.037)	
CSNL		0.117		0.151		0.485***
		(0.075)		(0.136)		(0.131)
CSAL		0.474***		0.708***		0.808***
		(0.097)		(0.165)		(0.157)
Distance (log)	−0.171***	−0.172***	−0.302***	−0.298***	−0.240***	−0.235***
	(0.006)	(0.006)	(0.010)	(0.010)	(0.009)	(0.009)
Contiguity	0.086***	0.082***	0.038	0.029	−0.021	−0.024
	(0.027)	(0.027)	(0.052)	(0.052)	(0.048)	(0.049)
Islands	0.041***	0.049***	0.066***	0.071***	0.047**	0.065***
	(0.015)	(0.015)	(0.023)	(0.023)	(0.023)	(0.022)
Continent	−0.008	−0.011	0.005	0.005	0.089***	0.090***
	(0.008)	(0.009)	(0.014)	(0.015)	(0.014)	(0.014)
Landlocked	0.053***	0.052***	0.052*	0.050*	0.037	0.035
	(0.017)	(0.017)	(0.029)	(0.028)	(0.026)	(0.026)
Ex-colonizer/colony	0.175***	0.201***	0.234***	0.248***	0.059	0.107
	(0.035)	(0.034)	(0.076)	(0.076)	(0.101)	(0.099)
Common colonizer	0.111***	0.111***	0.151***	0.150***	0.124***	0.130***
	(0.010)	(0.010)	(0.015)	(0.015)	(0.014)	(0.014)
Common religion	0.065***	0.073***	0.093***	0.092***	0.083***	0.099***
	(0.015)	(0.014)	(0.025)	(0.023)	(0.025)	(0.022)
Common legal systems	0.066***	0.065***	0.118***	0.102***	0.086***	0.078***
	(0.009)	(0.010)	(0.015)	(0.016)	(0.014)	(0.015)
History of war	−0.147	−0.125	−0.592***	−0.557***	−0.907***	−0.853***
	(0.113)	(0.114)	(0.196)	(0.196)	(0.233)	(0.234)
Observations	37,056	37,056	37,056	37,056	37,056	37,056

Notes: All regressions contain exporter and importer fixed effects. Robust standard errors in parentheses adjusted for clustering by country pair. ***significant at 1% level; **significant at 5% level; *significant at 10% level.

coefficients of CSLs and CSALs are significant, supporting the idea that the ease of communication matters more than the influence of ethnicity and trust for the imports. For differentiated goods, we do not find a significant impact of CSLs on the bilateral imports, but there is a significant impact of CSNLs on their value.

Table 9.8 Impact of common spoken languages on the value of bilateral imports (Rauch's decomposition)

	Value of imports					
	Homogeneous goods		Listed goods		Differentiated goods	
	(1)	(2)	(3)	(4)	(5)	(6)
CSL	−0.219		0.548***		0.276	
	(0.399)		(0.209)		(0.241)	
CSNL		−0.096		0.296		0.855***
		(0.832)		(0.343)		(0.304)
CSAL		−1.605		1.414**		−0.083
		(1.416)		(0.687)		(0.729)
Distance (log)	−0.878***	−0.864***	−0.610***	−0.615***	−0.543***	−0.536***
	(0.072)	(0.070)	(0.041)	(0.041)	(0.043)	(0.041)
Contiguity	0.328*	0.370**	0.340***	0.366***	0.438***	0.403***
	(0.170)	(0.165)	(0.089)	(0.093)	(0.083)	(0.082)
Islands	0.269	0.094	0.525***	0.426*	0.217*	0.199*
	(0.236)	(0.218)	(0.200)	(0.219)	(0.115)	(0.114)
Continent	0.363***	0.388***	0.478***	0.461***	0.398***	0.418***
	(0.128)	(0.133)	(0.074)	(0.075)	(0.074)	(0.072)
Landlocked	0.912***	0.974***	0.527**	0.592***	0.046	0.152
	(0.299)	(0.295)	(0.221)	(0.206)	(0.185)	(0.158)
Ex-colonizer/colony	1.052***	0.802***	0.845***	0.609***	0.749***	0.461***
	(0.279)	(0.228)	(0.194)	(0.222)	(0.176)	(0.177)
Common colonizer	−0.072	−0.097	0.374**	0.365**	0.184	0.214*
	(0.250)	(0.246)	(0.164)	(0.164)	(0.128)	(0.116)
Common religion	−0.291	−0.331*	0.378***	0.360**	0.383***	0.198*
	(0.223)	(0.196)	(0.143)	(0.157)	(0.116)	(0.119)
Common legal systems	0.515***	0.590***	0.136	0.099	0.155**	0.059
	(0.160)	(0.172)	(0.091)	(0.091)	(0.067)	(0.081)
History of war	0.375*	0.311	0.022	0.048	−0.217**	−0.093
	(0.210)	(0.205)	(0.126)	(0.131)	(0.105)	(0.103)
Observations	37,830	37,830	37,830	37,830	37,830	37,830
R-squared	0.676	0.887	0.916	0.681	0.893	0.916

Notes: All regressions contain exporter and importer fixed effects. Robust standard errors in parentheses adjusted for clustering by country pair. ***significant at 1% level; **significant at 5% level; *significant at 10% level.

9.4.4 General equilibrium and welfare effects on the intensive country margin of aggregate bilateral trade

Clearly, in view of the discussion in Sections 9.4.1 to 9.4.3, the point estimates reported in Tables 9.4 to 9.8 only reflect the partial effects of languages on bilateral imports. In general equilibrium, income and prices change in response to changes in transaction costs, and this leads to cross-country effects. To illustrate

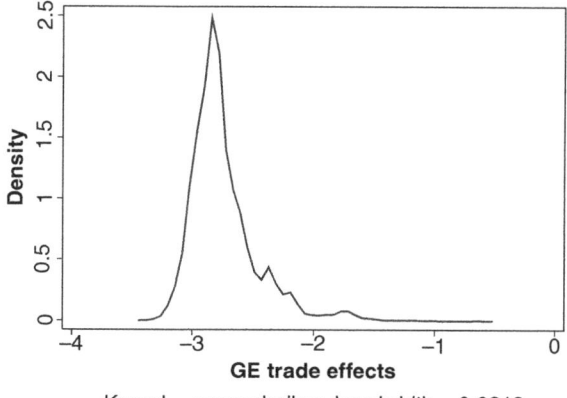

Kernel = epanechnikov, bandwidth = 0.0219

Figure 9.7 Total general-equilibrium-consistent responses of bilateral exports to a five-percentage-point increase in common spoken native and acquired languages across all country-pairs in 195 economies

this point, consider the point estimates for bilateral trade in the PPML model in columns 4 to 6 of Table 9.4, which includes both $CSNL_{ij}$ and $CSAL_{ij}$. For simplicity, let both $CSNL_{ij}$ and $CSAL_{ij}$ change by five percentage points so that the change of $t_{ij}^{1-\sigma}$ is $\exp(0.05(\lambda_{CSNL} + \lambda_{CSAL}))$. This induces a change of multilateral costs as well as of the incomes and the GDP shares of the importing country. Based on the theoretical gravity structure in Section 9.3, these changes are well defined.[14]

We examine the general equilibrium impact of a five-percentage-point increase in CSNLs and CSALs across all 195 country pairs. The findings are summarized in Figure 9.7, which shows the distribution of the estimated effects across countries on their bilateral trade. It turns out that the effect on trade tends to be negative, which may seem surprising, since this means that a convergence in CSLs reduces average bilateral trades by some 2.7 per cent. However, we should bear in mind that the corresponding effects are on nominal bilateral trade flows, and that changing $CSNL_{ij}$ and $CSAL_{ij}$ around the globe affects consumer prices, producer prices, as well as price indices for all countries. The corresponding results mean that average bilateral trades decline in terms of the prices of the numeraire country. Hence, what matters and can be interpreted is the relative change across countries (and country-pairs). Clearly, this does not mean that such a change leads to welfare losses. Using the same simulation exercise, we report in Table 9.9 the corresponding welfare changes in per cent.

---

[14] A model distinguishing explicitly between extensive and intensive margin effects would be somewhat more involved. General equilibrium comparative statics results in such models are analysed in Egger et al. (2011).

284

Table 9.9 Welfare changes due to a five-percentage-point increase in common spoken native and acquired languages across all country-pairs in 195 economies (changes in per cent)

Country	Welfare change	Country	Welfare change	Country	Welfare change	Country	Welfare change	Country	Welfare change
United States	0.16	Bel. & Lux.	0.75	Moldova	0.81	Togo	0.82	Tonga	0.87
Japan	0.21	Qatar	0.75	Uruguay	0.81	Burundi	0.82	Niue	0.87
United Kingdom	0.43	Iran	0.75	Angola	0.81	Nepal	0.83	Cook Isl.	0.87
Germany	0.45	Hungary	0.75	Armenia	0.81	Burkina Faso	0.83	Nauru	0.87
Italy	0.45	Chile	0.76	Sri Lanka	0.81	Somalia	0.83	Nicaragua	0.87
China	0.48	Nigeria	0.76	Tanzania	0.81	Seychelles	0.83	Tuvalu	0.87
Australia	0.53	Czech Rep.	0.77	Sudan	0.81	Cambodia	0.83	Netherlands Antilles	0.87
Singapore	0.54	Romania	0.77	Albania	0.81	Madagascar	0.83	Kiribati	0.87
Taiwan	0.54	Lebanon	0.77	Turkmenistan	0.81	Mali	0.83	Norfolk Isl.	0.88
Brazil	0.54	Bahrain	0.78	Kazakhstan	0.81	Laos	0.83	Aruba	0.88
Hong Kong	0.55	Slovakia	0.78	Uzbekistan	0.81	Ecuador	0.83	Micronesia	0.89
France	0.55	Bangladesh	0.78	Cameroon	0.81	Comoros	0.83	Pitcairn Isl.	0.89
Spain	0.57	Ukraine	0.78	Bosnia and Herzegovina	0.81	Iceland	0.83	Marshall Isl.	0.89
South Korea	0.62	Syria	0.79	Benin	0.81	Senegal	0.83	Suriname	0.89
India	0.63	Tunisia	0.79	Malta	0.81	Sao Tome and Principe	0.83	Falkland Isl.	0.89
South Africa	0.66	Belarus	0.79	Peru	0.81	Mauritania	0.84	Haiti	0.89
Turkey	0.66	Ireland	0.79	Georgia	0.81	Bhutan	0.84	Northern Mariana Isl.	0.89
Netherlands	0.66	Pakistan	0.79	Uganda	0.81	Guinea	0.84	Trinidad and Tobago	0.89
United Arab Emirates	0.68	Croatia	0.79	Brunei	0.82	Sierra Leone	0.84	Greenland	0.90

Country		Country		Country		Country		Country	
Israel	0.68	Cyprus	0.79	Ivory Coast	0.82	Gambia	0.84	St. Lucia	0.90
Greece	0.68	Colombia	0.79	Rep. of the Congo	0.82	New Caledonia	0.84	Palau	0.90
Sweden	0.69	Algeria	0.79	Vietnam	0.82	Gibraltar	0.84	Dominica	0.91
Indonesia	0.69	Jordan	0.79	Zimbabwe	0.82	Guinea-Bissau	0.84	Guyana	0.91
Russia	0.69	Morocco	0.79	Andorra	0.82	Cape Verde	0.84	Belize	0.91
Saudi Arabia	0.69	Bulgaria	0.79	Ghana	0.82	Liberia	0.84	Barbados	0.92
Mexico	0.70	Iraq	0.79	Gabon	0.82	El Salvador	0.85	St. Pierre and Miq.	0.92
New Zealand	0.70	Lithuania	0.79	Tajikistan	0.82	Paraguay	0.85	Cayman Isl.	0.92
Denmark	0.70	Venezuela	0.79	Zambia	0.82	Dominican Rep.	0.85	Jamaica	0.92
Portugal	0.71	Oman	0.80	Kyrgyzstan	0.82	Costa Rica	0.85	Grenada	0.92
Kuwait	0.72	Libya	0.80	Dem. Rep. of the Congo	0.82	Guatemala	0.85	Turks and Caicos Isl.	0.92
Argentina	0.72	Mauritius	0.80	Afghanistan	0.82	Bolivia	0.85	St. Vin. and the Gren.	0.93
Poland	0.72	Azerbaijan	0.80	Rwanda	0.82	Cuba	0.85	Antigua and Barbuda	0.93
Austria	0.72	Slovenia	0.80	Central African Rep.	0.82	Panama	0.85	Montserrat	0.93
Finland	0.73	Latvia	0.80	Chad	0.82	Papua New Guinea	0.85	St. Kitts and Nevis	0.93
Egypt	0.74	Estonia	0.80	Mozambique	0.82	Fiji	0.86	British Virgin Isl.	0.94
Switzerland	0.74	Philippines	0.80	Niger	0.82	Vanuatu	0.86	Anguilla	0.94
Malaysia	0.74	Kenya	0.80	Malawi	0.82	Solomon Isl.	0.86	Bahamas	0.94
Norway	0.74	Yemen	0.80	Eritrea	0.82	Honduras	0.86	Bermuda	0.96
Thailand	0.74	Macedonia	0.81	Djibouti	0.82	St. Helena	0.87	Canada	0.99

Table 9.10 Explaining welfare changes

	Welfare changes			
	(1)	(2)	(3)	(4)
GDP (log)	−0.045***	−0.054***	−0.054***	−0.053***
	(0.007)	(0.010)	(0.010)	(0.010)
Population (log)	0.007	0.014**	0.011*	0.010*
	(0.005)	(0.006)	(0.006)	(0.006)
Landlocked	0.002	0.004	0.004	0.002
	(0.011)	(0.012)	(0.013)	(0.012)
Literacy rate			−0.038	−0.009
			(0.035)	(0.033)
Linguistic diversity				0.052*
				(0.030)
America		0.096***	0.104***	0.115***
		(0.019)	(0.020)	(0.024)
Asia		0.008	0.018	0.019
		(0.021)	(0.022)	(0.021)
Europe		0.048	0.060*	0.063*
		(0.029)	(0.032)	(0.033)
Oceania		−0.037	−0.017	−0.020
		(0.026)	(0.026)	(0.025)
Observations	195	195	189	187
R-squared	0.517	0.601	0.610	0.612
Number of countries	195	195	189	187

Notes: Robust standard errors in parentheses. ***significant at 1% level; **significant at 5% level; *significant at 10% level.

A five-percentage-point increase in common spoken native and acquired language has a positive impact on welfare. The effect is heterogeneous across countries, though. To put the results into perspective, we regress the welfare changes on some economic and linguistic variables using PPML techniques.[15] The results are presented in Table 9.10.

We find larger welfare changes in countries with smaller GDPs. Population size has a positive impact on the magnitude of the welfare effects once we condition on the continent.[16]

In the last two columns, we examine the effects of linguistic diversity and literacy rates. Both variables are taken from Melitz (2008). While literacy rates do not affect welfare changes, we find a positive effect of linguistic diversity. The effect is, however, estimated with a low degree of confidence.

[15] OLS estimates lead to qualitatively similar results.

[16] Africa serves as the benchmark category. Relative to Africa, the changes in welfare are larger in America and similar in Europe.

9.5   Conclusion

The goal of this chapter is to provide a survey of issues related to CSLs and international trade. We have presented a host of topics ranging from measurement to descriptive statistics, from an interpretation of effects in international economic models to their estimation, and to novel empirical evidence of their effects on international trade flows and welfare. Future research on this matter might, among other things, progress along the following lines.

First of all, subnational and international language boundaries should be considered as discontinuities which are distinct from national borders. We know that only a minority of firms import from several 'foreign' (other than the location of the production or sales site) destinations and that these firms are unusually big and efficient. However, little is known as to how firms operating in single ethnicities and language zones compare with those that operate in multiple ethnicities and language zones. For France, Mayer and Ottaviano (2007) show that the percentage of firms which export to other French-speaking destinations is unusually large but also that the firms which exploit this linguistic advantage have lower average productivity than the remaining French exporting firms. In further work, it may prove important to distinguish between language commonality as an argument in fixed versus variable cost functions. If fixed costs are important, foreign sales across language barriers require more efficiency to be profitable than equally large foreign sales within a single language context.

Second, existing evidence on language commonality is focused mainly on aggregate findings. It may be necessary to use more disaggregated data – e.g. on a regional, firm-level or individual-level dimension – to reveal effects, in particular, of spoken acquired languages. Such results would be particularly useful to undertake cost–benefit analyses on foreign language training.

Third, it may be worth having more complete data on spoken languages. This would help to overcome some of the measurement problems addressed in the chapter.

Acknowledgements

In preparing this draft, the authors have benefitted from extensive discussions with Jacques Melitz.

References

J. Anderson (1979) 'A Theoretical Foundation for the Gravity Equation', *American Economic Review*, 69, 106–116.

J. Anderson and E. Van Wincoop (2003) 'Gravity with Gravitas: A Solution to the Border Puzzle', *American Economic Review*, 93, 170–192.

J. Anderson and E. Van Wincoop (2004) 'Trade Costs', *Journal of Economic Literature*, 42, 691–751.

P. Armington (1969) 'A Theory of Demand for Products Distinguished by Place of Production', *IMF Staff Papers*, 16, 159–178.

B. Baltagi, P. Egger and M. Pfaffermayr (2003) 'A Generalized Design for Bilateral Trade Flow Models', *Economics Letters*, 80, 391–397.

B. Baltagi, P. Egger and M. Pfaffermayr (forthcoming) 'Panel Data Gravity Models of International Trade', In B. Baltagi (ed.) *The Oxford Handbook of Panel Data* (Oxford: Oxford University Press).

J. Bergstrand, P. Egger and M. Larch (2013) 'Gravity Redux: Estimation of Gravity-Equation Coefficients, Elasticities of Substitution, and General Equilibrium Comparative Statics Under Asymmetric Bilateral Trade Costs', *Journal of International Economics*, 89, 110–121.

J. Eaton and S. Kortum (2002) 'Technology, Geography, and Trade', *Econometrica*, 70, 1741–1779.

P. Egger, M. Larch, K. Staub and R. Winkelmann (2011) 'The Trade Effects of Endogenous Preferential Trade Agreements', *American Economic Journal: Economic Policy*, 3, 113–143.

P. Egger and A. Lassmann (2013) 'The Causal Impact of Common Native Language On International Trade: Evidence from a Spatial Regression Discontinuity Design', CEPR Discussion Paper No. 9441.

P. Egger and S. Nigai (2014) 'Structural Gravity with Dummies Only', CEPR Discussion Paper No. 10427.

P. Egger and K. Staub (2015) 'GLM Estimation of Trade Gravity Models with Fixed Effects', *Empirical Economics*, forthcoming.

P. Egger and F. Toubal (2014) 'Consumer Welfare Gains from Speaking Common Languages', Mimeo.

G. Felbermayr, B. Jung and F. Toubal (2011) 'Ethnic Network, Information and International Trade: Revisiting the Evidence', *Annales d'Économie et de Statistique*, 97–98, 41–70.

G. Felbermayr and F. Toubal (2010) 'Cultural Proximity and Trade', *European Economic Review*, 54, 279–293.

V. Ginsburgh, J. Melitz and F. Toubal (2014) 'Foreign Language Learning: An Econometric Analysis', CESifo Working Paper No. 4923.

L. Guiso, P. Sapienza and L. Zingales (2009) 'Cultural Biases Affect Economic Exchange', *The Quarterly Journal of Economics*, 124, 1095–1131.

J. Hahn and J. Meinecke (2005) 'Time Invariant Regressor in Nonlinear Panel Model with Fixed Effects', *Econometric Theory*, 21, 455–469.

J. Hausman and W. Taylor (1981) 'Panel Data and Unobservable Individual Effects', *Econometrica*, 49, 1377–1398.

K. Head and T. Mayer (2015) 'Gravity Equations: Workhorse, Toolkit, and Cookbook', In E. Helpman, K. Rogoff and G. Gopinath (eds) *Handbook of International Economics* 4 (Amsterdam: Elsevier Science Publishers).

E. Helpman, M. Melitz and Y. Rubinstein (2008) 'Estimating Trade Flows: Trading Partners and Trading Volumes', *Quarterly Journal of Economics*, 123, 441–487.

T. Mayer and G. Ottaviano (2007) 'The Happy Few: The Internationalisation of European Firms: New Facts Based on Firm-Level Evidence', Bruegel Blueprint Series, Vol. III.

J. Melitz (2008) 'Language and Foreign Trade', *European Economic Review*, 52, 667–699.

J. Melitz and F. Toubal (2014) 'Native Language, Spoken Language, Translation and Trade', *Journal of International Economics*, 93, 351–363.

J. Rauch (1999) 'Networks Versus Markets in International Trade', *Journal of International Economics*, 48, 7–35.

J. Santos Silva and S. Tenreyro (2006) 'The Log of Gravity', *Review of Economics and Statistics*, 88, 641–658.

J. Schafer (1997) *Analysis of Incomplete Multivariate Data* (London: Chapman & Hall CRC).

J. Schafer and J. Graham (2002) 'Missing Data: Our View of the State of the Art', *Psychological Methods*, 7, 147–177.

J. Wooldridge (2002) *Econometric Analysis of Cross Section and Panel Data* (Cambridge, MA: The MIT Press).

10
Economic Exchange and Business Language in the Ancient World: An Exploratory Review

Nigel Holden

10.1 Introduction

There is a general consensus among scholars (e.g. Janssens et al., 2004; Peltokorpi, 2007; López-Duarte and Vidal-Suárez, 2010, p. 578; Holden and Michailova, 2014) that the issues of language as a central component of business communication are under-represented in the contemporary literature on international business. So to write a chapter on this theme with respect to the Ancient World is accordingly a novel enterprise and perhaps all the more so seeing that its businessmen have received 'scant attention' from 'lifelong classical scholars' (McNeill, 2011, p. xii), whilst business historians seldom venture beyond the 18th century (Vink, 2002, p. 220). This chapter is therefore breaking new ground at least from the general standpoint of management scholarship. Niall Ferguson, in his book *The Ascent of Money* (2008), writes: 'only understand the origins of an institution or instrument and you will find its present day role much easier to understand'. This chapter is written in complete agreement with that conviction.

The language of business in antiquity appears at first glance to be a rather unprepossessing topic. After all, the sheer pace, scope, self-enveloping intensity and boundary-defying capability of modern business connectivity all too readily persuade us there can be nothing of value, nothing of interest or relevance about the peculiarities of language usage in the Ancient World. It follows that my aim will be to rebut such a point of view. Indeed, the conviction guiding this chapter is that the business language of the Ancient World finds not merely distant, but often strikingly direct, correlates in countries and cultures right up to the present day. But not only that: discussion of the topic supplies an unusual prism through which to view the modern business world and human action in unexpectedly rewarding ways without the all-trammelling effects of the communication technologies. It gives us new perspectives on the central,

290

yet seldom posed, question at the very heart of business communication: what are the ends to which business people put language to attain their purposes?[1]

None of the great business empires of the Ancient World, although they differed dramatically in structure, *Weltanschauung* and relationships with their respective temporal, military and priestly authorities, could have sustained themselves without a fully functioning language of business: in other words, an occupational communication system with spoken and written modes, which was sensitive to context, capable of bearing specific terminology to describe business operations, and permitting articulate communication at various levels of interaction. After all one had to know how to speak to august patrons, to fractious suppliers, to fastidious customers, to unruly mule drivers, to exotic foreign business partners, barbarian or otherwise, and, last but not least, to the capricious gods.

We know with reasonable accuracy what particular languages were used in ancient commerce, including those which at different times served as lingua francas. At the same time deciphered and translated documents give us considerable insight into business organizations and practices. But it is of course impossible to know precisely *how* the merchants of the remote past used language in everyday speech. This chapter will attempt to convey a flavour of precisely that, though admittedly in an indirect way.

Our story covers the period from the invention of writing in the Ancient World around 5,000 years ago and will end – to give a date of convenience – at around AD 250, as this date represents 'the end of our juristic and epigraphic sources for the late Republican and early imperial period' (Aubert, private communication). The term 'Ancient World' will embrace (a) the Ancient Near East, including Mesopotamia, Ancient Egypt, Ancient Iran and some of the countries of the Levant (in short, more or less the region we associate today with the term 'Middle East'); and (b) that portion of classical antiquity which refers to Greece and Rome and their wider geographical extent and influence. This conception of course omits reference to two other great contemporary Asian civilizations, namely China and India, both of which had trading relationships with the various empires, kingdoms and city states of the Mediterranean and Near East.

Section 10.2 will set the scene with various language considerations. After that come the big themes: the context of trade in antiquity (Section 10.3), the written word (Section 10.4), the spoken language of business (Section 10.5), commercial terms in various languages (Section 10.6), the businessman as unsavoury personage in Greek and Latin literature (Section 10.7), and the special status of Latin (Section 10.8). But, before we begin properly, a caveat must

---

[1] N. Holden (1986). *The development of the concept of communication competence in relation to firms' interactions in overseas markets.* Manchester Business School, PhD thesis.

be introduced. The literature about ancient civilizations is enormous. To exemplify that, in his acclaimed history of Ancient Egypt, Wilkinson cites more than 600 works (some of them refer to items in French and German, which in turn are major languages of scholarship about antiquity). He covers nearly 3,000 years of history and 31 dynasties (excluding a further 300 years of Macedonian and Ptolemaic rule). And that is about but one of the great civilizations of antiquity. Accordingly, this chapter is written with a conscious sense of the vastness of the historical and indeed linguistic context. However, the topic of language in the Ancient World is so fascinating, so irresistible to write about.

10.2 Language considerations

In addressing matters of language, the necessarily explorative treatment will *not* be from a philological standpoint (the traditional way of discussing ancient languages), but from what linguists term a pragmatic perspective, whereby attention is directed to 'the study of language from the point of view of the user, especially of the choices he makes, the constraints he encounters in social interaction, and the effects his use of language has on the other participants in an act of communication' (Crystal, 1980, p. 278). Applying a necessarily cautious pragmatic approach to the speech and language behaviour of long since deceased social groups, of whom we do not have a shred of a recorded (i.e. audio-recorded) example, is of course a highly precarious enterprise, for which I can only use the modern business world (my normal territory of investigation) as a key point of reference.

I am, however, taking it as axiomatic that the occupational language behaviour of business people of the Ancient World was just as powerfully influenced by the exigencies and instrumentalities of the marketplace as it is for their contemporaries in today's global knowledge economy. Among these exigencies and instrumentalities, the quest for profit, which is discussed below, is the all-important independent variable concentrating all minds. I am also taking it as self-evident that the businessmen of antiquity hardly needed the Greek historian Herodotus (*c.*484–425 BC) to remind them that 'human prosperity never abides long in the same place' (Herodotus, 2003, p. 5).[2]

The international quest for profitable business would take them 'on pioneering explorations and new trade routes' (Roberts, 2011, p. 117) throughout the known world and far beyond to unconquered realms. But beyond that, their momentous travels required them to be, as we would say today, effective

---

[2] Cf what Karl Marx and Friedrich Engels wrote in *The Communist Manifesto*, published in 1848: 'the need of a constantly expanding market for its products chases the whole bourgeoisie over the whole surface of the globe. It must nestle everywhere, settle everywhere, establish connexions everywhere'.

intercultural communicators in their business dealings, and with all manner of strange fellows at that. They might actually speak the latter's language passably well, or use a serviceable lingua franca, or simply strain to convey bonhomie and trustworthiness in their own unintelligible tongue, and all the while listening to the babble of those strange fellows as if their utterances were actually scintillating.

As we shall see, the Ancient World was not short of words in various languages to describe all manner of commercial arrangements and the persons carrying them out. I am using the words trader, merchant and businessman more or less interchangeably, though they are not synonymous with each other, many having distinct connotations in their own languages. Generally speaking, unless it is clearly specified, it is to be assumed that the traders, merchants and businessmen are engaged in international – hence cross-cultural – commercial activities. I will avoid the word 'manager' altogether, as its modern connotations are about the day-to-day running of a business as opposed to doing business. Besides, a language like Latin had many words for various kinds of distinct business functionaries which could be translated by the portmanteau word 'manager'.

10.3   Context of trade and antiquity

From the vantage point of today's world with our iPads and iPhones, jet aircraft and global orientation, it is all too easy to scoff at 'the fastest mortal thing' at the time of Greek historian Herodotus (2003, p. 533) in the 5th century BC being a mere horse-borne messenger on the Royal Road of Persia; to deride the writing systems of the Near Eastern civilizations being by our standards incredibly cumbersome (but the same might be said of the modern Japanese writing system); and to mock traders and merchants, who (like military commanders) respectfully performed 'the hallowed practice' of 'watching the skies' (Goldsworthy, 2007, p. 210) for propitious signs for their enterprises.[3]

Yet in their own ways the trading systems and arrangements of the Assyrian, Phoenician, Greek and Roman business empires were sophisticated in areas we might not suspect such as international finance, cross-border investment, advertising and even knowledge management. Indeed, the activities of the business of the Ancient World prefigured the practices of modern business. In their study of business in antiquity Moore and Lewis (1999, pp. 43–67, 69–100, 225–267) describe the merchants of Phoenicia around 1100–850 BC as the 'first

---

[3] Aubert (1994, p. 21) refers to a source (Pliny the Elder) which describes how 'cloth dealers used to watch the sky on the night of 10 November and, on the basis of the position of certain stars, determine whether the winter would be cold or wet, setting the prices of coats and cloaks accordingly'.

industrial samurai', noting how that great American business format, the multi-national corporation, had its counterpart in Assyrian business practices about a thousand years earlier, and arguing that the Romans from 146 BC to AD 14 used family enterprises that had much in common with modern global virtual corporations. Not for nothing has the Eternal City been described as 'Rome, Inc.' (Bing, 2006).

As for money, that 'reliably valuable, divisible, and portable form of wealth' (Roberts, 2011, p. 21), it only began to make a big impact as coinage (as opposed to pre-coinage money such as bullion, hides, grain, slaves, wine and so forth) on the way business was conducted in Greece around the 6th century BC. Aubert (2014, pp. 1–2) notes that 'barter...was certainly not the preserve of the uncivilized' and that 'by the late Augustan period [late 1st century BC], the whole Mediterranean world and beyond must have been familiar with Graeco-Roman coinage and other forms of money'. It took many centuries for the Ancient World to evolve monetized economies. Yet, paradoxically the Mesopotamians had developed 'the first known financial instruments' more than 2,000 years earlier which 'anticipated modern methods of payment like checks, letters of credit, and negotiable bills of exchange' (Roberts, 2011, pp. 21–22).

But perhaps the most stunning ancient practice with a decidedly modern look is to be found in Rome, when 'by the early 2nd century BC slaves were capable of carrying out transactions on behalf of their master and of negotiating binding contracts' (Aubert, 1994, p. 3). In such cases slaves are best seen as extensions of their masters, though they could only conclude a contract up to the value of their own pocket money (*peculium*).[4] Trusted slaves were, to be modish about it, *empowered*.[5] Aubert (2006) supplies the reason for this paradox. Once slaves were 'free of aristocratic prejudice against non-agricultural work, a show of dynamism, creativity and discipline was their best bet for social promotion. Masters and slaves had a shared interest in the latter's success, so that the legal and social distance between them was less significant' (Aubert, 2014, p. 546). This perhaps partly explains why 'it is possible to speak of slaves having rights' ('*on peut parler d'un droit de l'esclavage*') (Aubert, 2012, p. 20).

Underpinning trade was the profit motive. Roberts (2011, p. 2) claims that 'the concept and possibility of selling at a profit first arose in Mesopotamia about 5,000 years ago', though it is fairly certain that traders and merchants of even earlier times grasped the importance of making a profit and, correspondingly, of avoiding a loss. One thing we can be certain about is that merchants

---

[4] I am indebted to Professor Elizabeth Meyer for this and comments on the nature of Roman contracts.

[5] For a thorough discussion of the term 'empowerment', see Collins (2000, pp. 213–249).

and traders quickly recognized that long-distance trade was more than just lucrative: it generated 'super-profits' (Braudel, 1983, p. 405). Indeed, it has been argued that 'distance did seem to matter less in ancient than it does in modern times, implying that autarky was not more, and perhaps even less sustainable five millennia ago' (Bossuyt et al., 2001, p. 381).

As they grew and became more acquisitive, the empires evolved into resource-seeking operations. Their merchants scoured the known world and even beyond for metals (not just gold and silver; there was demand for copper, lead and tin), timber, ivory, precious stones, sea-shells for dyes, and luxuries such as myrrh and exotic animals. All this entailed the creation of networks and market intelligence on a grand scale or, rather, as Moore and Lewis (1999, p. 187) perceptively put it, market accessibility intelligence. The momentous invention of writing, the introduction of coinage, the introduction of weights and measures, the emergence of contracts – all these innovations made the activity of business in the Ancient World increasingly sophisticated, whereby procedures were formalized and made central to the ambitions of each empire and their rulers.

There can be no doubt that the businessmen of the Ancient World were in the main redoubtable protagonists. Moore and Lewis (1999, p. 271) have no qualms about suggesting that 'their international business achievements were probably more impressive than those of modern business people'.

Moore and Lewis also argue that the major civilizations of the Ancient World exhibited capitalist behaviours, though they reveal marked differences. Table 10.1 shows their schematization of these behaviours.

Table 10.1 Forms of capitalism

Era or empire in economy	Approximate dates BC	Form of capitalism	State involvement
Assyrian	2000–1000	Temple/princely	High in concert with religion
Phoenician	1800–1000	Temple/naval/ trans-continental	High in concert with religion
Carthaginian	1000–200	Temple/naval/ trans-continental	Medium in concert with religion
Greek	1400–600	Entrepreneurial	Relatively low
Rome	700–AD 100	Entrepreneurial/ militarized family capitalism	Medium

Source: Moore and Lewis (1999), slightly modified.

From what we know about markets and business in today's world, we may surmise that business in the Ancient World was characterized by:[6]

(a) relationship-building processes, underpinned by exchange processes;
(b) sharing of *anything tangible or intangible* with perceived value as resources among the parties concerned;
(c) time and effort on key relationships across functions as well as vis-à-vis markets;
(d) the clustering of key relationships into (focal) networks, the all-important pathways to distant resources.

This characterization, based on modern notions of buying and selling in industrial markets, is worth moderating with a historian's view of business in the Ancient World. Though she is referring to Rome in the 1st century AD, Meyer (2004, p. 148) provides this picture, no doubt apposite for the entire period we are reviewing in this chapter: 'the world of business is a world of trust. It is also a world of risk, of speedy decisions, of people not always known to you, and of appearances': appearances – looking the part, projecting the right image – being crucial for 'establish[ing] that trust'.

Everything depended on trust, for which the Romans had the term *bona fides* ('good faith'). In Meyer's fortuitous juxtaposition of the two completely intermeshed worlds of risk and trust, we can form a clear idea of the special calculus of ancient business which concentrated the merchant's mind: how to minimize risk (which could literally take life-threatening forms) and to project that all-important air of trustworthiness. There was nothing that you could tell a merchant of those days about risk and the associated 'turbulent and volatile business environment', as the modern cliché has it. He knew too that in the end trust was something that had to be earned – often under duress – and this in the end was something that not even the most benevolent of gods could grant. In a word, he had to be resourceful beyond measure and possess a persuasive turn of phrase.

Then as now, merchants and traders needed to develop a range of competences for gathering market information, for managing supply lines and for cross-cultural communication. Therefore, just like today, they needed a combination of hard and soft skills relevant for each particular network and each particular relationship. But risk and danger were never far away: trade routes without military protection could be ambushed; cargoes could be lost through shipwreck; merchants and their retinue might be killed, imprisoned, ransomed or sold into slavery. For example, in 88 BC King Mithridates of Pontus in Anatolia delivered a 'calculated and devastating…blow' (Holland, 2003, p. 46)

---

[6] Based on Ford (1990, pp. 42–57).

against Roman settlements in Asia, massacring 'up to 150,000 Italian business people, their families and local companions' (Roberts, 2011, p. 167).[7]

But, if there was risk, there was also reward. We may advantageously quote the French historian, Fernand Braudel (1983, pp. 406, 400–401), whose authoritative descriptions of economic life in the early modern period apply to some extent to trading conditions in antiquity: 'distance alone in an age of difficult and irregular communications...created ordinary conditions for profiteering', whilst the truly successful merchants, 'although few in number, had acquired the keys to long-distance trade...they normally benefited from the acquiescence of state and society, and were thus able regularly, quite naturally and without any qualms, to bend the rules of the market economy'.

It was precisely because of their actual or perceived chicanery that the merchants of antiquity were subject to denigration and contempt, and nowhere more so than in Greece and Rome, as we shall see. An outcome of this, as Goldsworthy (2007, p. 28) notes, is that 'the activities of traders rarely feature other than peripherally in our ancient sources'. But he adds crucially that 'it is important not to underestimate their numbers or the scale of their operations. Such men profited greatly from Roman imperialism, even if it seems extremely unlikely that they had much influence on the decision-making processes that directed the Republic's foreign affairs' (Goldsworthy, 2007, pp. 28–29).

But if the general disparagement of merchants was especially pronounced in Greece and Rome, it was a less marked feature in Mesopotamia. For example, Phoenician merchants in Ugarit around 1500 BC were so 'respectable' that 'the most successful might join the elite chariot corps and were sometimes ennobled' (Roberts, 2011, p. 32). In Rome, exactly as in Great Britain at its imperial zenith in the 19th century, business people could emphatically not be 'trusted with the care of the nation's continuity' (Weiner, 1985, p. 70).

10.4 The written word

A discussion of language and business in the Ancient World must give due prominence to the momentous invention of writing, which 'certainly transformed international trade' (Wilkinson, 2011, p. 56). It is generally held that the 'technique of writing [was] developed by the Sumerians and Akkadians around 3000 BC, and...became for the succeeding 2,500 years thereafter the standard means of writing in the Mesopotamian civilization and the civilisations derived from it' (Pope, 1975, p. 182). The writing system was cuneiform with clay tablets as the medium. However, as MacGregor (2011, p. 77) points out, cuneiform in its earliest manifestations was 'not a writing system in the

---

[7] 'More than 80,000 Romans' according to the British classical scholar Lane Fox (2006, p. 346).

strict sense, but a kind of mnemonic'. In centuries to come writing would be committed to wooden tablets and the much more perishable papyri.[8]

Brosius (2006, p. 246) notes that 'the primary function...of the earliest cuneiform tablets was to record economic transactions of grain, livestock and textiles in the temple and palace economies, but this was extended to record the economic and legal affairs of private and business enterprises'. So it was that writing acted as 'a feedback loop in enabling and encouraging, through accuracy and accountability in economic transactions, the growth of ever more modes of exchange and redistribution' (Matthews, 1997, cited in Bossuyt et al., 2001).

In 1925 Hittite documents found in Kültepe-Kanesh, 'a well-planned Anatolian city with a vast business district' (Moore and Lewis, 1999, p. 41), 'were clearly of a mercantile nature. They spoke of contracts, partnerships, profits, consignment of orders and other transactions' (ibid., p. 39). These documents – business tablets, to be precise – would have been written around 2000 BC. The merchants of Asia – or to be precise their scribes – 'the first professionals' (Roberts, 2011, p. 26) – recorded their transactions on clay tablets which

> may be considered as the visible traces of the (otherwise invisible) trade links that existed between cities...The tens of thousands of texts written before and during the Akkadian empire and the third Ur dynasty are essentially records of transactions, contracts and inventories, established by scribes who may be considered as the bookkeepers of the temple or palace in each city (Bossuyt et al., 2001, p. 375).

It was 'the *idea* [*sic*] of writing which came to Egypt along with a raft of other Mesopotamian influences...the concept, but not the writing system itself', whereupon 'writing was swiftly embraced by Egypt's early rulers, who recognised its potential, not least for economic management' (Wilkinson, 2011, p. 55). The flash of genius lay in grasping that inscribed signs could be used to represent speech sounds. As in Mesopotamia, Egyptian merchants discovered the value of writing for recording their transactions. In Egypt's case 'contents, quantity, quality and provenance' (ibid.) could all be noted in the visually stunning hieroglyphs.

It would of course be many centuries before the cuneiform scripts, which came in a number of variations, and hieroglyphs revealed their long-held secrets, as cities, temple complexes and burial grounds of the Ancient Egypt and

---

[8] My colleague, Dr Roger Brock, tells me that lead was also used as a medium for inscribing contracts. Such items, dating to the 5th century BC, have been found bearing Greek and Etruscan scripts muddled up.

Asia began to be excavated. The decipherments, which surely 'deserve their reputation as the summit achievement of literary scholarship' (Pope, 1975, p. 191),
permitted 'the decoding of tens of thousands of clay tablets bearing mysterious writing in long-dead languages', thus creating a 'coherent story of the
first 2,000 years of mankind's civilisation' and vouchsafing 'a detailed description of its business practices' (Moore and Lewis, 1999, pp. 30–31). We therefore
have an amazingly rich account of trade and commerce in the Ancient World
well before the emergence of Greece and Rome. Indeed some of the very earliest tablets ever discovered record commercial transactions. They help to give
a detailed picture of economic life and trade relations as well as the status
of languages as bearers of commercial terms, some of which we will discuss
below.

It would, however, be quite wrong to give the impression that most traders
could read and write. For an absolute majority of them writing was 'a fairly
impenetrable code' (Aubert, private communication). However, we should not
exclude the possibility that the essentially illiterate traders acquired a smattering of writing and simplified and hence distorted signs into both a mnemonic
and private code to record confidential information.[9] This means that traders
and merchants would acquire so-called 'craftman's literacy', referring to an adequate competence in writing 'for specific ends' (Aubert, 2004). A good example
of this facility is indicated in the writing in Latin on wooden tablets found in
Britain.[10] Produced around AD 100, the writing is no more than 'tiny spidery
scrawls, which to the uninitiated were written in some unknown language'
(Birley, 1977, p. 135). One cannot exclude the possibility that the writer wrote
in a deliberately illegible way. If that is so, it is hard to imagine that this kind
of rough and ready cryptography had not been replicated throughout all the
business empires of the Ancient World.

> [Writing] was the work of a specialist who made his living by it. He was
> the 'scribe' who worked for commercial concerns and temples, making lists,
> drawing up formal documents and the like, and was also needed in the diplo-
> matic and political affairs of a nation in order to assist in foreign affairs and
> keeping the nation's life in order (Wright and Fuller, 1965, p. 40).

Accordingly scribes had to be 'learned' (Gurney, 1952, p. 126) and no doubt
discreet. Surely, their lives 'must have been very exciting' (MacGregor, 2011,

---

[9] Some years ago I visited the National Palace Museum in Taipei. There were displays
illustrating the evolution of Chinese writing. One showed how Chinese merchants deliberately simplified and distorted the characters to encrypt their confidential information.
[10] See Meyer (2004) for detailed discussion of the Roman tablet.

p. 79) in their work for and hobnobbing with the high and mighty. For traders and merchants, they would among other things prepare contracts.

By their nature contracts were formal in the sense that they were overwhelmingly issued by those in power – by the state in modern parlance – and were an affirmation of what was to be done or delivered. In the case of Rome, as Meyer (2004, pp. 59–63), an authority on Roman law, tells us, writing on tablets used 'archaic and archaizing language' and as such 'conveyed . . . authority'. It would all in all be seriously mistaken to suggest that contracts dominated business life in antiquity in ways remotely comparable to the modern era. As Aubert (private communication) has noted, 'in ancient Rome, writing was not crucial in the law of contract, contracts being mostly oral or consensual. Writing may twist our perception of trade because of the nature of the sources (orally conducted business leaves no trace)'.

The conclusion of all Roman-law scholars appears to be that the performance of the formal verbal utterance of stipulation was necessary for the formal contract. Under Roman law stipulation referred to the making of a contract in the form of a question and answer to render it legally valid. An issue for some scholars is whether a written document was also necessary or just merely useful. The legal sources only say that without a document it was difficult to prove the terms of a verbally agreed contract. In the case of informal contracts i.e. those that do not use the formal language of stipulation, these probably depended on writing and on occasional enforcement by the praetor, a senior magistrate. In other words, there was validity inhering in the nature of the act itself.

Either way we may deduce that in the Roman era commercial language began to develop into two mutually reinforcing and interpenetrating modes: the written language for confirming arrangements allowing for the performative role of speech acts; the spoken language for creating an atmosphere and informality among interlocutors (Baron, 2000, p. 21). The formality of commercial writing with its stilted expressions has been a hallmark of business language for centuries. Indeed, it was not so long ago in the UK that a businessman would conclude a letter with the mantra: 'I remain, Sir, your obedient servant', whilst we encounter in France today that splendid formulation '*Je vous prie d'agréer, Monsieur, l'assurance de mes salutations distinguées*'.

Before discussing the nature of spoken business language in the Ancient World, let us observe in passing one notable occurrence to do with written language. This concerns the development of advertising and branding. In Ancient Greece potters and vase-makers produced their items 'for tailored markets, promoted their brand-name wares, and even publicly ridiculed their competitors with negative advertising' (Moore and Lewis, 1999, p. 270) – that is more than 2,000 years before Pepsi so devastatingly mocked Coke ads. We might add that the Greeks also 'instituted trademark regulation' on their best wine, so that imports could 'not dilute the value of their own brand' (Roberts, 2011, p. 63).

One way this was done, for example, was by inscribing the names of magistrates on wine amphorae as a guarantee of authenticity. 'In Roman times', Moore and Lewis (1999, p. 270) continue, 'amphorae often carried stamps on their handles and were inscribed with the name of their shipper, their contents, and a date. As a modern brand does today, the shipper mark or brand could be used as a way of reducing the risk of purchase by providing a "guarantee" of the quality of a product'.

On this topic Aubert (private communication) draws attention to the fact that the stamped inscription on amphorae and other clay artefacts refers to their maker, not to the producer of its content. On amphorae, the content is identifiable through painted inscriptions added at a later stage. At all events both the Greeks and the Romans pioneered branding, whilst the Greeks can be credited with the creative use of commercial language.

10.5   The spoken language of business in the Ancient World

In the Ancient World the ever-expanding growth of international business led to the creation of markets on a vast scale. The market – that 'favoured terrain of supply and demand' (Braudel, 1983, p. 26) – is surely among mankind's earliest institutions, pre-dating by countless centuries the making of records vouch-safed by the invention of writing around 3,000 BC. As noted above, we cannot possibly know *how* merchants of the Ancient World spoke to each other. Yet, we are in a position to make an educated guess, regardless of whether we are concerned with merchants who used Akkadian, Greek and Latin or even a mish-mash of tongues. A notable clue is supplied by the eminent French sociologist Marcel Mauss, who made a study of the rituals of giving gifts as an accompaniment to economic exchange in archaic societies, that is to say in societies that existed prior to the invention of writing:

Mauss (180, p. 26) observes that

the importance of these gifts arises from the extraordinary competition which exists among members of an expedition. They seek out the best possible partner in the other tribe. For the cause is a great one; the association made establishes a kind of clan link between partners. To get your man you have to seduce and dazzle him, while paying proper regard to rank, you must get in before the others and make exchanges of the most valuable things . . . The underlying motives are competition, rivalry, show, and a desire for greatness and wealth.

Mauss (1980, p. 1) adds that 'the form usually taken is that of the gift generously offered: the accompanying behaviour is formal pretence and social deception, while the transaction itself is based on obligation and economic self-interest'.[11] So there we have it. From the earliest times the merchant is one, we may surmise, who does not necessarily engage in completely untrue utterances, yet who on occasion resorts to hyperbole, flattery and deliberate vagueness. As we have already noted, our merchant would have the facility of adjusting his speech level according to context. He might have even mastered 'the bureaucratic language of temple and palace transactions' (Moore and Lewis, 1999, p. 56). In addition we can posit that he would ensure that his language behaviour would convey what we call today 'cross-cultural sensitivity', though that expression must be understood in context; which brings us to Herodotus.

In his wonderful *Histories* Herodotus notes that it is natural for anyone to regard the beliefs and customs of one's own country as better than those of any other. 'That being so', he perceptively observes, 'it is unlikely that anyone but a madman would mock at such things' (Herodotus, 2003, p. 187) about other people's countries. In other words, no merchant would go to another country and offend its inhabitants by flaunting an ill-considered opinion about *their* gods. Besides, merchants were all too aware that in their mysterious way the gods gave 'heavenly sanction and earthly direction to their international investments and partnerships' (Moore and Lewis, 1999, p. 97). It was therefore best not to tempt fate.

Accordingly one respected other people's gods too. Besides, 'seeing that every nation had a different theology, it was difficult for at least some hard-headed merchants to still assert that his gods were superior to those of his customer' (ibid., p. 157). Thus, for all his dissembling and banter, the merchant of ancient times knew how to apply the supreme 'law' of cross-cultural communication: to handle others, even barbarians, with 'intelligence and tact'.[12] In cross-cultural contacts, therefore, it is even quite possible that merchants as a generally loquacious species knew when on occasion to keep their mouths shut. But it is equally possible that they enjoyed the banter even if it did not always lead to an actual business agreement. Centuries later Adam Smith would acknowledge this tendency with this perceptive observation: 'for people, who like talking, the exchange of words is indispensable – even if the exchange of objects does not follow' (cited in Braudel, 1983, p. 73).

In so far as we may rely on Mauss's commentary as a reliable pointer to the nature of spoken business discourse in antiquity, we may further surmise that in their interactions merchants used a language which has a striking resemblance to the modern languages of Japan and China, in which communication is as

---

[11] It should not be overlooked that an entire global industry, advertising, is based on social deception.

[12] The diplomat and Japanologist Sir Ernest Satow (1843–1929) wrote that handling relationships with the Japanese required 'the application of intelligence and tact'.

much directed towards 'the art of constructing and maintaining networks as a long-term investment' as securing the business at hand, whereby 'the accompanying language is...elaborate, circuitous and face-saving' (Holden and Glisby, 2010, p. 65). A key feature of the linguistic effects would no doubt be the liberal use of high-flown compliments, tried and trusted courtesies and (obsequious) flattery. Flattery has of course been an essential component of business discourse in every human tongue, ancient or modern: indeed for as long as there have been markets. No businessman in any era of history has ever seriously believed that 'flattery will get you nowhere'. Overall we may surmise that the cross-cultural business contacts in the Ancient World evolved on the basis of rough-and-ready oral translations or, more perceptively, on the basis of 'working misunderstandings' (Batteau, 2000, p. 733) among motley languages in interplay, whereby those translations in free-flowing cross-cultural exchanges were, exactly as in modern international business practice, 'spontaneous, *ad hoc* and improvised' (Holden and Michailova, 2014, p. 10).

I conclude this section with a linguistic curiosity of ancient business practice that has by no means died out in modern economies. Roberts (2011, p. 77) mentions that pedlars in Greece 'called out their wares with distinctive cries', each no doubt with its own prosodies and patter. Occupational language is therefore no new thing. Indeed, the cries of every 'financial pedlar' in any modern stock exchange or trading floor of any international bank bear witness to the persistence of 'sonic topographies' (Wilson, 1995, p. 2) for attracting attention and customers.

10.6   Commercial terms in various languages of the Ancient World

Tablets in cuneiform, once deciphered, provide us with commercial terms in everyday usage. For example, in Akkadian we find a word, *dam-gàr*, that refers to merchants who formed 'guild-like associations' (Moore and Lewis, 1999, p. 58). Note that it is referring to a particular class of merchant. The word *naruqqum* is 'essentially a capital fund invested by several merchants for a merchant active in foreign trade' (ibid., p. 67). This is a truly early reference to sophisticated financial practices, whilst the word *kârum*, which came to mean 'market' originally, denoted a harbour – an unmistakable allusion to substantial sea-borne trade. One of the earliest recorded words in Hittite is 'contract' (Watkins, 2008, p. 6). This suggests that merchants grasped the value of the written word to record and equally importantly *confirm* whatever had been agreed between buyers and sellers.

Phoenician makes a number of distinctions to do with merchants. The term *bidaluma* refers to 'lesser merchants' bound by feudal oath to merchant princes in contrast to *mrkm* (Ugarit) which refers to 'private or crown traders' (*bns mlk* meaning royal merchant) and *ubru* which refers to foreign merchants in Canaanite (Moore and Lewis, 1999, pp. 87–88). We also have the word *tappatu* which refers to partnerships that were 'a pyramidical form of partnership' (ibid.). These few words alone indicate that merchants and traders created a necessary vocabulary for their activities, relationships and organizational forms.

The language with arguably the greatest number of commercial terms is surely Latin. In part this is due to the sheer power and longevity of the Roman Empire and the scale of its international business operations. As Moore and Lewis (1999, p. 242) explain: 'the Roman Empire presided over the greatest era of trade and cross-border investment (both within and without its borders) in antiquity'. The sheer complexity of Rome's business operations required an occupational vocabulary to reflect not only its diversity, but also the roles of individuals as bankers, entrepreneurs, backers, overseers and owners. However, certain words began to suffer from semantic overload exactly in line with the modern usage of terms like 'manager', 'excellence' and 'globalisation' (Holden and Tansley, 2008). With respect to Latin, Aubert (1994, pp. 6–7) points out that the verbs *'emere'* (to buy) and *'vendere'* (to sell), 'when used in legal texts, could refer to a wider range of transactions than just purchase and sale', referring to 'various activities, such hiring or renting commodities, facilities, or services, or acting as guarantors' (ibid., p. 17), whilst the word *institor* designates a merchant, a retailer, or pedlar and 'ordinarily refers to a lower social stratum'. *Institores* could be 'engaged in seaborne as well as land based trade' (ibid., p. 17). As a suspicious individual in the eyes of respectable society, the *institor* leads a perpetually embattled existence. If he were to plead 'I am only trying to make an honest living', this would merely add to the derisive mirth of Rome's upper classes.

Indeed, the businessman was seen as a suspicious (if necessary) wheeler-dealer, who pursued his activities *nec otium* (literally without free time or without let-up in modern parlance). From this expression we derive the English word 'negotiate', whilst in modern French and Spanish we find the words *négoce* and *negocios*, both of which mean 'business'. There is even an attested diminutive form, *negotiolum* ('a little bit of business'), which is found in one of Cicero's famous letters to Atticus written around 50 BC. In a standard translated version of the letter Cicero (1968) lets his friend know that he has settled 'your little affairs' (*tua negotiola*), which turns out to refer to the settlement of a bill of exchange (*permutatio*). It is evident that the usage is somewhat jocular: just a little helpful favour for a very close friend performed by Rome's greatest rhetorical brain!

10.7   The businessman as unsavoury personage in Greek and Latin literature

The general contempt for the commercial classes is a notable theme in both Greek and Latin culture, as is richly attested in their respective literary output.

As for Greece, no lesser personage than Homer conveyed in *The Iliad* and *Odyssey* 'a very strong and negative view of commerce as an occupation. The noble ideal of that period was to gain from warfare or plunder, not by exchange' (Curtin, 1986, p. 75). The Romans were equally dismissive in their literary output, however much the spread and economic viability of the Empire depended on its merchants for what we should regard as special services: creating networks in territories *outside* its nominal boundaries, and for supplying military intelligence on tribes' disposition towards Rome (Goldsworthy, 2007, p. 404).

In a play by Aristophanes, called *The Knights*, a character rants about the utter vulgarities of the market place. He pillories an Athenian sausage vendor for possessing 'the attributes of a demagogue: a screeching, horrible voice, a perverse, cross-grained nature and the language of the market-place' (Moore and Lewis, 1999, p. 175).[13] There we have the characterization of the trader as a loud-mouth. How this picture of the raucous Athenian marketplace almost undermines Winckelmann's famous characterization of the art of Ancient Greece as 'noble simplicity and tranquil greatness' (*edler Einfalt, stille Grösse*)! In Rome it was no better, where several of the Republic's most distinguished literati – the poets Ovid and Horace, Plautus the playwright, the Stoic philosopher Seneca – all wrote disparagingly of business people. As Aubert (1994, p. 22) has pointed out: 'in the mind of upper class Roman writers, a shrewd businessman is not considered worthy of the same respectability as an astute and knowledgeable cultivator'.

But, human nature being what it is, you will surely find someone who relishes in the notoriety of being a vulgar outsider to respectable society, and we actually have a plausible example based on characterization presumably from precise observation. In his poem *Fasti* the Roman poet Ovid (43–17 AD) describes 'merchants entering the temple of Mercury and praying in a hypocritical voice to the god to overlook... past greed while granting... present and future business success' (cited by Moore and Lewis, 1999, p. 247). Here is one of them in action, incorrigibly admitting that he 'may have falsely invoked the name of Jupiter' in his business dealings: 'may tomorrow open the door for me for fresh perjuries, and may the gods above not care if I utter any! Only grant me profits. Grant me the joy of profit made, and see to it that I enjoy cheating the buyer'.

The name Mercury is linked etymologically with the root *merc-, which gives us Latin-derived words such as mercantile and merchant (see the entry under

---

[13] This rant finds an almost perfect echo in this damning of the British business classes in the mid-1800s. Here is the author and cultural critic, Matthew Arnold (1822–1888), scorning 'their way of life, their habits, their manners, *the very tones of their voices*' (added emphasis), cited in Weiner (1985, p. 37). In Tokugawa Japan (1600–1868) merchants 'might be killed with impunity by any samurai for mere disrespectful language' (Sansom, 1976, p. 472).

'Mercurius' in Hammond and Scullard, 1984, p. 673). Mercury is the god of merchants, but he was not quite as respectable as the other gods, being also known as 'a trickster and a thief' (Curtin, 1986, p. 6). The association would not be lost on any educated Greek or Roman. What these lines from *Fasti* also well convey is the way in which some merchants plainly thought invoking the gods or indeed 'watching the skies' was a waste of time.

Such 'antimercantile views' (ibid., p. 75) of the Greek and Roman elites far outlasted the Ancient World. They still exist in modern times. But, if the elites of Greece, Rome, Babylon or Persia 'deemed it beneath their dignity to dirty their hands with the practicalities of business', they did not have to worry, since 'there was no lack of willing proxies' (Butterworth and Laurence, 2006, p. 48) keen to supply their needs – and fads – from all over the known world at the right price. In fact, the Greeks left business to the capable Phoenicians, who incidentally were dubbed by Homer as 'greedy knaves' (Roberts, 2011, p. 37). But of course merchants and traders knew perfectly well that the ruling classes, then as now, would pay a ridiculous price for exotic luxuries, accessories and fashion items for themselves, their favourites and cronies.[14] Roman demand for exotica from India in the age of Augustus was said to be 'insatiable' (Keay, 2000, p. 122).

10.8   Latin: Not just a lingua franca

If Greek was the first language to give legal force to the structures of business and commercial arrangements, Latin extended the practice not only organically, but also internationally as well as across the centuries to the present day. As Goldsworthy (2007, p. 203) reminds us, 'Roman laws tended to be long and complex – one of Rome's most enduring legacies to the world is cumbersome legal prose'. This is the Latin that was used in contracts throughout the Roman Empire. But its geographical spread and authority make Latin unique among all the languages that served as lingua francas in the Ancient World. It had a property that we associate with the English today: hegemonic status (Tietze and Dick, 2013, p.122). Indeed, given that Rome in the 1st century AD dominated the economy of the known world, we may say that Latin was, as it were, the English of its day – the incontestable global language of its era. Neither Greek

---

[14] Surely this description with the elite's obsession with fashion would apply to the Ancient World as much as to 17th century Europe, when it was penned. Nicholas Barbon, a 17th-century writer of pamphlets in London noted: 'fashion or the alteration of dress' is a great promoter of trade, 'because it urges people to spend money on new clothes before the old ones are worn out: it is the life and soul of commerce: it...keeps the whole merchant body in movement: it is an invention which makes man live in perpetual springtime, without ever seeing the autumn of his clothes' (cited in Braudel, 1983, p. 312).

nor Akkadian can compare with Latin from this point of view. Indeed to regard Latin as a lingua franca on a par with others is to detract from its very greatness.

Latin also evolved many words for various kinds of actors that would be covered by the terms manager and agent, but these translations need to be appreciated against the background of forms of Roman business organization. An analogy might be with the term 'Soviet manager', an expression that only makes sense if understood in the Soviet context. Various Latin words can broadly speaking be translated by the word manager in English: *magister, socii, negotiator, institor, manceps, publicanus*, words which taken together represent considerable diversity of business arrangements in Rome. Even the unlikely looking word *actor* (which of course is etymologically connected to the English word 'agent') meant in one specific context 'business manager' (Aubert, 1994, p. 350), that context being the Roman bath. All in all, Latin can be well described as a commercial language of great vigour.

10.9 Conclusion

Our 3,000 year survey for a single chapter has perforce been highly selective. Historical scholarship about antiquity is, as we noted earlier, of massive proportions. Even so, in this chapter I have tried to create a special path against this truly daunting background and for reasons of space have not discussed relevant topics such as accounting systems, the handling of numbers (and fractions) in texts, coinage as well as weights and measures in antiquity, let alone the fascinating topic of Rome's business activities with India (Keay, 2000, pp. 121–123).

The modern branch of business history rarely ventures into the Ancient World. Yet this chapter has revealed how valuable the study of business practices in the Ancient World can be for understanding aspects of modern-day business. But in the light of the various impacts of globalization, modern communication technologies, the spread of business education as a worldwide industry, it is understandable that modern, sceptically minded business people and even professors of business may not like to think that antiquity can conceivably be a store of key learning points.

Scholars of international business among others may say that there is no worthwhile knowledge or experience that the Assyrian trader cooped up in his home office chock-a-block with writing tablets can impart to managers guiding today's multinational corporations. However, that Assyrian may have a good working knowledge of two or three languages, which makes him immediately superior to the vast majority of the business executives of the US and UK.[15] But

---

[15] In a contribution about corporate languages, Brannen and Doz (2012) refer approvingly to the multilingual capabilities of the Phoenicians.

those sceptics may be amazed to find many of their cherished practices, preoccupations and fads – such as management of overseas subsidiaries, the creation of industrial clusters and notions of the knowledge-based economy – recognizably existed in antiquity. As for language behaviour, it has been possible to shed light on this from multiple perspectives.

We have been able to show very clearly the distinction in the roles of written and spoken language, to comment on the evolution of, and variation within, commercial terminology, to suggest that intercultural communication behaviour in the Ancient World must to some extent be predicated on respect for other people's gods, to draw parallels between antiquity and modern times in terms of the verbal abuse hurled at business people (a remarkable case of *plus ça change*), and even to redefine what we understand by the terms commercial language and lingua franca when applied to Latin. What emerges from our tentative exploration is evidence of a complex relationship not only between language and the practice of business, but also between the very structures of business and the designations to describe them.

From the point of view of modern management studies (and possibly of the general reader too), it is easy to regard Latin, Greek or Babylonian as well as Punic and Aramaic as commercial languages or lingua francas, but in reality they are better seen as languages of administration, fully capable of sustaining (among other things) *international* economic life in their respective eras of hegemony. To regard them as 'mere' languages in which business happened to be conducted is surely to miss the point, and no more so than in the case of Latin. Not only does Latin hold a special place as a language of administration at the time of the Roman Empire, it retained and developed this capacity for centuries to come as not just the liturgical language of the Roman Catholic Church, but also that of the worldwide bureaucracy that underpinned it. There is therefore even a strong case to be made for Latin to be viewed as the foundation language of modern management. It is simply jejune to grant this honour to American business English.[16]

We cannot but otherwise assume that the business people of antiquity engaged in 'prolonged haggling over what could be bought and sold, when and for how long' (Roberts, 2011, p. 370) before it came to agreement. There is little reason to doubt that the 'sonic topographies' of language in commercial contacts, negotiations *and* the Ancient World's equivalent of the business lunch were variously accommodating, evasive, high-flown and ever geared to the promotion of one's absolutely trustworthy self. In short, it would seem that for

---

[16] Cf. this observation of Hofstede in 1993, but still valid today: 'management as the word is presently used is an American invention'.

centuries the language behaviour among business people has been associated with histrionic effusion and ever preoccupied with impression management.

There really is nothing new under the sun.

Acknowledgements

I would like to express my deep gratitude to Jean-Jacques Aubert, Professor of Classical Philology and Ancient History at the University of Neuchâtel, for his very valuable comments on an earlier draft of this chapter and for answering my many questions so patiently and thoroughly. I am also indebted to Elizabeth Meyer, Professor of Greek and Roman History, University of Virginia, for handling my query concerning the role of speech and writing with respect to the enactment of Roman law and for providing many other helpful comments. I would also like to thank Dr Emma Stafford and Dr Roger Brock of the Department of Classics, University of Leeds, for guidance on the origins of early Greek writing and manifestations of branding in Ancient Greece, respectively.

References

J.-J. Aubert (1994) *Business Managers in Ancient Rome: A Social and Economic Study of Institores, 200 BC–AD 250* (Leiden: E. J. Brill).

J.-J. Aubert (2004) 'De l'Usage de l'écriture dans la gestion d'enterprise à l'époque romaine' In J. Andreau, J. France and S. Pittia (eds) *Mentalités et choix économiques des Romains: Scripta Antiqua 7* (Bordeaux: Ausonius Editions).

J.-J. Aubert (2006) 'Managers' In G. Shipley, J. Vanderspool, D. Mattingley and L. Foxhall (eds) *The Cambridge Dictionary of Classical Civilization* (Cambridge: Cambridge University Press).

J.-J. Aubert (2012) 'L'esclavage en droit romain ou l'impossible réification de l'homme', *Esclavage et Travail Forcé: Cahiers de la Recherche sur les Droits Fondamentaux*, 10, 19–25.

J-J Aubert (2014) 'For Swap or Sale? The Roman Law of Barter' In C. Apicella, M-L. Haack and F. Lerouxel (eds) *Les affaires de Monsieur Andreau: économie et société du monde romain* (Bordeaux: Ausonius Editions).

N. Baron (2000) *Alphabet to Email: How Written English Evolved and Where It's Heading* (London: Routledge).

A. Batteau (2000) 'Negations and Ambiguities in the Cultures of Organization', *American Anthropologist*, 102, 726–740.

S. Bing (2006) *Rome Inc.: The Rise and Fall of the First Multinational Corporation* (New York: W. W. Norton).

R. Birley (1977) *Vindolanda: A Roman Frontier Post on Hadrian's Wall* (London: Thames and Hudson).

A. Bossuyt, L. Broze and V. Ginsburgh (2001) 'On Invisible Trade Relations between Mesopotamian Cities during the Third Millennium BC', *The Professional Geographer*, 53, 374–383.

M. Brannen and Y. Doz (2012) 'The Languages of Strategic Agility: Trapped in Your Jargon or Lost in Translation', *California Management Review*, 54, 77–97.

F. Braudel (1983) *Civilization and Capitalism 15th–18th Century: The Wheels of Commerce* (London: Book Club Associates).

M. Brosius (2006) 'Cuneiform' In G. Shipley, J. Vanderspool, D. Mattingley and L. Foxhall (eds) *The Cambridge Dictionary of Classical Civilization* (Cambridge: Cambridge University Press), p. 246.

A. Butterworth and R. Laurence (2006) *Pompeii: The Living City* (London: Phoenix).

Cicero (1968) 'Letter to Atticus, 106' In D. R. Shackleton Bailey (ed.) *Cicero's Letters to Atticus* (Cambridge: Cambridge University Press), pp. 36–38.

D. Collins (2000) *Management Fads and Buzzwords: Critical-practical Perspectives* (London: Routledge).

D. Crystal (1980) *A First Dictionary of Linguistics and Phonetics* (London: André Deutsch).

P. Curtin (1986) *Cross-cultural Trade in World History* (Cambridge: Cambridge University Press).

N. Ferguson (2008) *The Ascent of Money: A Financial History of the World* (London: Penguin Books).

D. Ford (ed.) (1990) *Understanding Business Markets: Interaction, Relationships, Networks* (London: Academic Press).

A. Goldsworthy (2007) *Caesar: The Life of a Colossus* (London: Phoenix).

O. Gurney (1952) *The Hittites* (Harmondsworth, UK: Pelican Books).

N. Hammond and H. Scullard (eds) (1984) *The Oxford Classical Dictionary* (Oxford: Oxford University Press).

Herodotus (2003) *The Histories*, edited by J. Marcinola (London: Penguin Books).

G. Hofstede (1993) 'Cultural Constraints in Management Theories', *Academy of Management Executive*, 7, 81–94.

N. Holden and M. Glisby (2010) *Creating Knowledge Advantage: The Tacit Dimensions of International Competition and Cooperation* (Copenhagen: Copenhagen Business School Press).

N. Holden and S. Michailova (2014) 'A More Expansive Perspective on Translation in IB Research: Insights from the Russian Handbook of Knowledge Management', *Journal of International Business Studies*, 45, 906–918.

N. Holden and C. Tansley (2008) 'Management in Other Languages: How a Philological Approach Opens Up New Cross-cultural Vistas' In S. Tietze (ed.) *International Management and Language* (London: Routledge), 198–213.

T. Holland (2003) *Rubicon: The Triumph and Tragedy of the Roman Republic* (London: Little, Brown).

M. Janssens, J. Lambert and C. Steyaert (2004) 'Developing Language Strategies for International Companies: The Contribution of Translation Studies', *Journal of World Business*, 39, 414–430.

J. Keay (2000) *India: A History* (New York: Grove Press).

R. Lane Fox (2006) *The Classical World: An Epic History of Greece and Rome* (London: Penguin Books).

C. López-Duarte and M. Vidal-Suárez (2010) 'External Uncertainty and Entry Mode Choice: Cultural Distance, Political Risk and Language Diversity', *International Business Review*, 19, 575–588.

N. MacGregor (2011) *The History of the World in 100 Objects* (London: Penguin Books).

R. Matthews (1997) 'The Emergence of Writing in the Ancient Near East' In P. Talon, K. van Lerberghe and P. Akkermans (eds) *En Syrie, aux origines de l'écriture* (Brussels: Brepols).

M. Mauss (1980) *The Gift: Forms and Functions of Exchange in Archaic Societies* (London: Routledge & Kegan Paul).

W. McNeill (2011) 'Forward' In K. Roberts (ed.) *The Origins of Business, Money and Markets* (New York: Columbia University Press), pp. ix–xiii.

E. Meyer (2004) *Legitimacy and Law in the Roman World* (Cambridge: Cambridge University Press).

K. Moore and D. Lewis (1999) *Birth of the Multinational: 2,000 Years of Ancient Business History* (Copenhagen: Copenhagen Business School Press).

V. Peltokorpi (2007) 'Intercultural Communication Patterns and Tactics: Nordic Expatriates in Japan', *International Business Review*, 16, 68–82.

M. Pope (1975) *The Story of Decipherment: From Egyptian Hieroglyphic to Linear B* (London: Thames and Hudson).

K. Roberts (2011) *The Origins of Business, Money and Markets* (New York: Columbia University Press).

G. Sansom (1976) *Japan: A Short Cultural History* (Tokyo: Charles E. Tuttle).

S. Tietze and P. Dick (2013) 'The Victorious English Language: Hegemonic Practices in the Management Academy', *Journal of Management Inquiry*, 22, 122–134.

N. Vink (2002) 'Historical Perspective in Marketing Management, Explicating Experience', *Journal of Marketing Management*, 8 (3), 219–237.

C. Watkins (2008) 'Hittite' In R. Woodard (ed.) *The Ancient Languages of Asia Minor* (Cambridge: Cambridge University Press), pp. 6–30.

M. Weiner (1985) *English Culture and the Decline of the Industrial Spirit 1850–1980* (Harmondsworth, UK: Penguin Books).

T. Wilkinson (2011) *The Rise and Fall of Ancient Egypt: The History of a Civilisation from 3000 BC to Cleopatra* (London: Bloomsbury).

E. Wilson (1995) 'Plagues, Fairs and Street Cries: Sounding Society and Space in Early Modern London', *Modern Language Studies*, 25, 1–42.

G. Wright and R. Fuller (1965) *The Book of the Acts of God* (London: Pelican Books).

11
Language Use in Multinational Corporations: The Role of Special Languages and Corporate Idiolects

Susanne Tietze, Nigel Holden and Wilhelm Barner-Rasmussen

11.1 Introduction

In this chapter we argue that multinational corporations (MNCs) can be understood from a language perspective; and in this we include national languages (e.g. English, Finnish, German, Japanese) as well as special languages (such as occupational vocabularies which we discuss fully below). We also take account of considerations of language as sociolects, which are context-specific applications of languages, where specialist discourses mingle with national languages in unique contexts-of-use. Together, these form the highly complex transnational business communication capital of MNCs. We bring a sense of order into this complexity through an attempt to develop a mental map of this language complexity in the MNC. Therefore, we draw on a metaphor by which we align the MNC to a metropolis, and we use in particular recent research located in Manchester, UK, where language diversity and its effects were studied. Thus, we propose that there exists a specific analogy between language usage and behaviour in cities and in MNCs. This at first glance unusual analogy will be exploited to create this mental map, whereby we attempt to capture myriad forms of languages and language use within the MNC, both in their local context and their international extension.

Our mental map will explore the nature of (a) 'special languages' (i.e. occupation-specific language forms) within the MNC according to their task, context and function; and (b) corporate sociolects (i.e. in-company language registers associated with specific tasks in given environments). We take it as axiomatic that national languages (including English), special languages and sociolects form the basis of transnational business communications. This attempt at language mapping can help scholars of language and the MNC not only to appreciate, but also to visualize the subtleties of relationships among the hierarchy, task specializations and the use of sociolects and special languages in their written and spoken modes.

In developing our line of argument, we will first provide an overview of the research that was conducted in the city of Manchester with a view to setting the metaphorical scene for the approach. We then proceed to present a detailed overview of the language-sensitive literature, which has emerged and is still developing in the field of international business. Here, we introduce important terminology such as language standardization, common corporate language, organizational and individual aspects in language use and choice, and the effects and consequences of such choices. This section also includes analytic commentary about the role and use of the dominant lingua franca of business, i.e. the English language. We then introduce the notions of special languages and sociolects, which together with national languages form the complex map on which English, languages, sociolects and special languages meet to form the transnational business communication capital of the MNC.

We add substance to the literature review and theoretical framework by providing an in-depth study of a particular MNC, Novo Nordisk, where multilingual and multi-specialist groups of corporate facilitators provided the linguistic and cultural glue to bond the dispersed MNC through a new (English) language-based practice, which encapsulated strong Danish management and cultural values, while providing vocabulary and concepts to redefine and change governance practices across the MNC.

In the discussion we align the various strands of the chapter by reflecting on the international business language-sensitive literature, its emphasis on national languages and its preoccupation with the English language in the light of our conceptual apparatus, which has been expanded to include sociolects and special languages. Only when these are understood in the light of each other can language-interested scholars move forward to appreciate and include processes of agency (as visible in language choice, for example) with other factors such as strategic direction and subsidiary location in the MNC.

11.2 Cities and the MNC

When we are talking about globally operating organizations that employ multicultural workforces often exceeding 200,000 people (in the case of Walmart the figure is two million), the mapping of these internal linguistic relationships would appear to be exceptionally daunting. But resolution is at hand when we consider that the number of employees working for MNCs equates to the population of sizeable cities, which very importantly possess, as we shall argue, MNC characteristics. Table 11.1 lists the number of employees of several well-known MNCs and cities with a roughly corresponding population.

Table 11.1   MNC workforces (1,000s) and comparably sized cities

MNC	Total workforce	Urban areas with a roughly corresponding population
Walmart (USA)	2,100 (800)	Vancouver (Canada)
VW (Germany)	501 (277)	Zaragoza (Spain)
Siemens (Germany)	360 (244)	Augsburg (Germany)
Nestlé (Switzerland)	328 (318)	Eindhoven (Netherlands)
GE (USA)	301 (170)	Murmansk (Russia)
Hutchison Whampoa (Hong Kong)	250 (206)	Arhus (Denmark)
Deutsche Telekom (Germany)	235 (113)	Dijon (France)
Fiat (Italy)	197 (134)	Santa Barbara (USA)
Sony (Japan)	168 (109)	St John's (Canada)
Anheuser-Busch (Belgium)	116 (108)	Cheltenham (UK)

Note: The figures in brackets indicate the number of foreign employees.
Sources: City data: Demographia World Urban Areas, 9th edition (2013), www.demographia.com/db-worldua.pdf (accessed 12 October 2013); company data: UNCTAD (2012).

The idea that cities 'possess unique characteristics that differentiate them from other units of "place" such as countries, regions or provinces' (McDonald, 2014) has received increased scholarly attention since the pioneering work of Jacobs (1969, 1984, 2000),[1] which characterized cities as distinctive economic entities. Cities not only provide cohesion 'as nodes for bringing together a diverse range of complex economic processes' (McDonald, 2014), but this very diversity, both economic and social, 'is packed into limited space, facilitates haphazard, serendipitous contact among people' (Jacobs, 1969, cited in Storper and Venables, 2004). We list below the characteristic features of cities, which equally apply to MNCs:

1. independence (high degree of autonomy);
2. resource-seeking (in other regions and countries) and wealth-creating;
3. permanence;
4. large population (to be numbered in tens of thousands);
5. encouragement of artisans and people with special skills;
6. magnet for foreigners, skilled and unskilled;
7. hub of international networks;
8. governance structure and hierarchy;
9. extensive use of relatively unskilled workers for jobs entailing high routine or low intellectual content.

---

[1] The importance of cities to economic, political, cultural and social development in antiquity is well established by historians (e.g. Moore and Lewis, 1999; Bossuyt et al., 2001; Roberts, 2011); see also Chapter 10 in this volume.

The attendant 'transactional structures and circumstances... necessitate close contact between persons', whilst giving rise to 'cross-fertilization between sectorally-specialized networks' (Storper and Venables, 2004). There is a resemblance here with the day-to-day workings of the MNC. Both contexts serve as clusters for all manner of occupations, promote mobility (both cities and MNCs have internal labour markets), facilitate socialization, and are cradles of complex intercultural communication behaviour.

It is also the case that large cities host scores of languages that are in permanent interplay, shaping and being shaped by 'complex economic processes', are indeed 'packed into limited space', facilitate all manner of random contact as well as sustaining networks which are in turn linked to occupations and all manner of shared activities such as education, sport and culture. The significant feature of languages in cities lies not in what might be called their philological constitution, but their usage to reflect the nature of association and communication among inhabitants according to social, educational, economic and occupational features. This suggests that there exists a specific analogy between language usage and behaviour in cities and MNCs.

11.2.1 Multilingual Manchester

Thanks to an ongoing web-based research project at the University of Manchester in the UK, we have access to remarkable data pertaining to the 153 languages identified in that city of half a million inhabitants (*Multlingual Manchester*, 2013). The findings of this project help us directly to establish a clear notional connection between the city and the MNCs as highly comparable zones of linguistic diversity and 'occupation-oriented' communication. Believed to be the largest of its kind in the world, the project has three aims:

1. to promote awareness of language diversity;
2. to identify and respond to language needs (such as foreign language learning, access to English courses and maintenance of heritage languages);
3. to document and inform about some of the smaller languages spoken in the city.

The project has produced a fact sheet on its findings (available at http://mlm. humanities.manchester.ac.uk/wp-content/uploads/2014/04/MLMFactsheet.pdf). Reports have been published on the following themes: policy, communities, neighbourhoods, business, schools and public services, families, and the media. The main findings, extracted from the fact sheet, are as follows:

1. Between 150 and 200 languages are spoken by long-term residents.
2. Forty per cent of young people are bilingual; close to 50 per cent of the adult population is estimated to be multilingual.

3. Close to 20 per cent of adult Manchester's population declared a language other than English to be their 'main language' in the 2011 census.
4. There are several large communities of speakers of various European, Asian and African languages, whilst knowledge of three European languages, namely Portuguese, French and Russian, is widespread, notably as a second language.
5. The city's languages are widely dispersed, but dense multilingual communities are to be found in particular locations in the centre as well as in the suburbs.
6. Manchester's commercial sector makes use of community languages to market products and services; commercial signage in Chinese, Urdu, Polish, Arabic and Bengali and other languages is common in the city's public spaces.
7. Language skills are often in demand on the Manchester job market.
8. Eighty per cent of Manchester residents whose first language is not English report that they speak English well or very well. Seventeen per cent – mostly elderly – report that they cannot speak English well, and 3 per cent (some 2,400) not at all.

11.2.2 From multilingual Manchester to the MNC

If we reflect on these findings and apply them to the MNC as a multilingual community in its own right, there are striking similarities:

1. several languages are spoken;
2. the main language is English, which is the lingua franca of (virtually) all non-native groups;
3. there is plenty of bilingualism;
4. apart from English, two or three other languages stand out as being widely known;
5. the linguistic distribution is uneven;
6. there is a demand for language skills.

When we present Manchester's sociolinguistic face like this, it follows that its many languages are more than an agglomeration of registers, patterns and occupational languages: a massive linguistic resource or, rather, in the formulation of Gerhards (2012, p. 3), 'transnational linguistic capital'.

The population of cities is never static. Hence, there is a perpetual shift in the representation and importance of languages at any given time. But there is an anomaly here, if we accept the data in Table 11.1 as being representative of MNCs in general. The proportion of foreign employees in some MNCs (for example, Nestlé, Fiat, Sony and Anheuser-Busch) would appear to be far higher than the foreign-born/ethnic proportion of the population of cities. If we take the case of London, one the world's most culturally diverse cities with a population of 8 million, where some 300 languages are spoken,[2] 45 per cent of the population is estimated to be white British.[3] In New York, a city very similar in size to London, there are around 3 million so-called foreign-born inhabitants or some 30 per cent.[4]

Likewise, a fictitious MNC in which the corporate language is English displays similar diversity. In its total geographical spread and in terms of the ethnic/linguistic composition of its international workforce, the number of languages spoken in the MNC can exceed 50 (in the EU there are 24 official and working languages only[5]). In the case of MNCs headquartered in countries where English is not the national language, a high proportion of the employees are bilingual, with English being their second language. The MNC hosts languages in locations such as subsidiaries that are akin to urban districts and communities when there will be a high usage of the local language *even if* English is the corporate language. Correspondingly, announcements on notice boards (for example, about staff social events) will often be in the local language. Issues of language identity, language usage in relation to domain as well as code-switching (the project has reports on all three topics) are extremely important in the MNC context with respect to HRM, international mobility of staff and talent management. There is, however, one area that the reports from Manchester do not cover and that concerns a major feature of linguistic reality of MNCs. This concerns the prevalence of so-called 'special languages'.

Special language is an accepted linguistic term that refers to a domain-specific sub-language with its own specialist terms. According to Sager et al. (1980, p. 69), 'special languages are semi-autonomous, complex semiotic systems based on and derived from a general [i.e. from a national] language; their use presupposes special education and is restricted to communication among specialists in the same or closely related fields'. In the case of a city like Manchester, with its four universities and widespread industries and business sectors, the number of special languages underpinning academic research and every kind of productive activity will run, literally, to thousands.

It follows that a special language is intimately linked to its domain of operation both as a physical location and its distribution throughout MNC networks of domain professionals. An MNC then will be a vast domain of special languages, covering arrays of functions such as marketing, human resources (HR), accounting and legal affairs, technical and scientific activities, production and

---

[2] http://www.all-languages.org.uk/news/features/languages_are_great_britain
[3] http://www.bbc.co.uk/news/uk-england-london-20680565
[4] http://www.nyc.gov/html/dcp/pdf/census/nny2013/nny_2013.pdf
[5] http://ec.europa.eu/languages/languages-of-europe/eu-languages_en.htm

logistics. If we are to develop a serviceable mental map of language within the MNC, it *must* accommodate the existence of special languages as well as be able to articulate the existence of national languages.

11.3   Research on language aspects of the MNC: A pragmatic perspective

When concerning oneself with the MNC as the unit of analysis, one considers languages, national, special or otherwise, as they are used by employees, managers, customers and suppliers of the MNC. In other words, such studies are located in the linguistic field called 'pragmatics', which is concerned with language in context from the user's point of view. We take pragmatics to be 'the study of language from the point of view of the user, especially of the choices he makes, the constraints he encounters in social interaction, and the effects his use of language has on the other participants in an act of communication' (Crystal, 1980, p. 278).

This approach represents a comparatively rare application of linguistics to a distinctive class of managed organization and as such meets a challenge raised by various contributors to the international business language-sensitive literature (e.g. Janssens et al., 2004; Usunier, 2011; Piekkari et al., 2013; Brannen et al., 2014). Therefore our literature review is located in 'pragmatics' as the empirical studies explore the language use and behaviours as displayed in and by MNCs from this perspective. We focus in particular on questions of language use in contexts, and the reasons for this use, as well as on individual and organizational choice and the effects these choices have. It is important to note that this body of emerging literature focuses almost exclusively on the role and use of national languages and their relationship with English as the dominant lingua franca. This field excludes considerations of sociolects and special languages. Therefore, following the literature review, we introduce a map of languages in the MNC which is more comprehensive as it allows us to locate both national languages, including English, as well as special languages in particular. This we supplement with a case study set in a Danish MNC in the next section.

11.3.1   National languages in the MNC

In the literature on language(s) in the context of MNCs, three interrelated questions have attracted a significant amount of research interest, namely: *which* language(s) is (are) used in particular contexts, *why*, and *with what consequences*.

For all three questions, existing research can be further grouped into two levels of analysis: organizational and individual. Perhaps mirroring a more general development in international management research, the primary tendency over time seems to have been from the organizational, or macro, level towards the individual, or micro, level. We will elaborate on this and other observations below.

We do not intended to downplay the importance of other themes or issues, such as the significant energy invested in establishing the legitimacy of language in international management as a distinct topic worthy of study in its own right (e.g. Piekkari and Zander, 2005; Welch et al., 2005; Brannen et al., 2014). Nor is our structure intended to deny that, within each of the three groupings outlined above, issues have emerged that have subsequently evolved into their own lines of inquiry. On the contrary, we hope that our account will serve to highlight and explain these developments.

A final caveat is that, since the late 1990s, the literature on language(s) in MNCs has burgeoned to the extent that a full review may already be out of reach. This is despite efforts in the form of journal special issues (*International Studies of Management & Organization*, 2005; *Journal of World Business*, 2011; *Journal of International Business Studies*, 2014) and a series of international workshops and conferences (Critical Management Studies, 2007; Workshop on Language in Multinational Management, 2009; European Group for Organizational Studies, 2010 and 2013; Academy of Management, 2011 and 2012) to entertain a dialogue involving all scholars in the area, irrespective of disciplinary or national boundaries. Thus, this review should not be seen as an effort to compile a comprehensive catalogue of language-related work, nor indeed a list of exemplary contributions.

11.3.2 Which language is used in a particular context?

In their landmark case study of Finnish multinational KONE, Marschan-Piekkari et al. (1999, p. 379) introduced the term 'language standardization', referring to top management efforts to establish a formally designated corporate language (common corporate language, CCL) and associated general rules and policies for internal and external communication in the MNC. However, their study also highlighted that even if formally instituted, the CCL is not necessarily the language actually used to interact within the firm. In KONE, other languages, notably Finnish (used by top management) and different regional languages (such as Spanish and German), were used in parallel with the official English.

This finding was followed up by other studies that documented the efforts to establish a CCL in different empirical contexts; problematized the notion of language standardization by pointing out that what is a 'common corporate language' may be ambiguous and contested or even deliberately expressed in a vague way; highlighted that different functions and hierarchical levels have different skills in the CCL; provided further evidence that it is often complemented by local languages and regional lingua francas.

Fredriksson et al. (2006) studied CCL in the context of the German MNC Siemens and identified a certain level of ambiguity concerning which one of two languages – German and English – held CCL status within the company. They also found discrepancies between company policy and employee practices with regard to language use. Even in parts of the company where English was recognized as the CCL, German was often used in parallel to it.

Bruntse (2003) in a study of Danish–Norwegian–Swedish airline SAS documented a rare explicit decision not to appoint formally any of the three 'home country' languages as the CCL so as not to tip the power balance in the company toward any of the three nations. Instead, an informal mix of the three closely related languages was used. It was known within the company as 'SASperanto'.

Barner-Rasmussen and Aarnio (2011) examined language use in Finnish subsidiaries of foreign MNCs. They found that, even in MNCs where English was formally established as the CCL and dominated communications with corporate parents and European sister units, communication with local partners mostly took place in the main local language (Finnish), while a regional language (Swedish) was used in 28 per cent of communications with sister units in the neighbouring Nordic countries. This is similar to the findings of the KONE case study, suggesting a widespread behavioural pattern.

Furthermore, subsidiary-level skills in the CCL varied significantly so that white-collar functions such as top management and marketing were considerably more fluent than were e.g. service departments. Heikkilä and Smale (2011) arrived at similar findings concerning skills in English related to human resource issues when a new e-HRM system operating in English was introduced.

Steyaert et al. (2011) studied language issues at the headquarters of two MNCs located in the French-speaking part of quadrilingual Switzerland. The major languages used in that context were the local language – French – and English, which in that context was labelled as a 'third language', being neither the local language nor any of Switzerland's other three national languages. However, in some situations several different languages were used at the same time, bringing to mind the observation of Charles (1998) that the term 'multilingual reality' is an apt description of many European business contexts. Steyaert and colleagues were also able to identify a total of six patterns that respondents used to navigate this multiplicity of languages; we will return to these later on.

Peltokorpi and Vaara (2012), in a study of 101 Japanese subsidiaries of foreign MNCs, found the local language to be the dominant one in all the studied units, despite corporate policies to the contrary in some cases. Even in cases where English had been formally designated as the common corporate language, its use was significantly restricted by the availability of local employees with a relevant mix of professional and language skills.

Harzing and Pudelko (2013) conducted a comparative study of MNCs from multiple geographical contexts and were able to moderate previous findings concerning the dominance of English as the predominant CCL globally. Pointing out the geographical biases of previous research, Harzing and Pudelko (2013, p. 94) found the use of English to be 'pervasive, except for MNCs from the Asian countries. In these countries the use of English as a corporate language is still very unusual, only 16 per cent of the companies have explicitly designated English as a corporate language'. Instead, Harzing and Pudelko found that half of the Asian MNCs in their sample did not have a CCL at all, and of those that did, 70 per cent used their HQ language.

All in all, this line of inquiry has conclusively demonstrated that English dominates as the CCL of multinationals globally, except for Asian ones; but that beneath the surface of the CCL, a plethora of local and regional languages are used. Several authors have explicitly arrived at the notion that MNCs are multilingual organizations (Barner-Rasmussen and Björkman, 2005; Fredriksson et al., 2006; Luo and Shenkar, 2006; Piekkari, 2008). This is despite the continuing spread of English – a global phenomenon (Crystal, 2003) that appears to be particularly strong in the context of international management (Tietze, 2004; Bargiela-Chiappini, 2006) – and the associated managerial harmonization efforts and organizational mechanisms devised to handle language multiplicity (see Harzing et al., 2011).

As the literature has developed, the notion of language management from the corporate apex (e.g. Luo and Shenkar, 2006) has met with increasing scepticism (see e.g. Janssens et al., 2004; Vaara et al., 2005). In the words of Steyaert et al. (2011, p. 271), 'there seems to be growing consensus that the adoption of a common corporate language is not the endpoint of a language policy but forms one of the possible anchor points around which to deal with multilingual complexity'. The insight that MNCs are polyglot and seem likely to remain so has drawn research attention to actual language practices within these organizations, that is, individual and group-level language skills and micro-level interactions.

Furthermore, it has been observed that this multilingual nature of the MNC is primarily enacted in the subsidiaries of the firm, which is where translation issues arising at the interface of the CCL and local languages are handled in practice (Barner-Rasmussen and Aarnio, 2011; Harzing et al., 2011; Steyaert et al., 2011; Peltokorpi and Vaara, 2012; Harzing and Pudelko, 2013). As Piekkari and Tietze (2011) have noted, 'translation is concomitant with the existence of multiple languages'.

11.3.3 Why is a particular language used in a particular context?

Existing empirical work on the question of why a particular language comes to be used in a particular context can again be subdivided into studies focusing on the organizational level or the individual level of analysis. In the former category, a significant line of inquiry has been the question of why an MNC chooses a particular corporate language. More specifically, since empirical work has found English to predominate as the CCL (with the recent exception of Asian MNCs mentioned above), interest has focused on (a) different interpretations of why MNCs choose English as their common corporate language, and (b) efforts to understand the rationale of those firms that have not chosen English.

One explanation of the strong position of English as a CCL has been that it is simply one aspect of its emergence as a global language (Crystal, 2003) and the trend toward 'Englishization' (Dor, 2004) across a range of human activities. Factors that researchers have identified as promoting the spread of English specifically in business life include the ICT revolution, the boom in international mergers and acquisitions, and the strong political and economic base for the English language offered by first the British Empire and then the USA (House, 2003). Tietze (2004) has added the emergence of professional management education, which traces its historical and intellectual roots to the US and is often delivered in English, notably in classroom contexts where there may not be a single native speaker.

Interviews with practitioners in Western MNCs have repeatedly yielded evidence suggesting that the adoption of English as the CCL is considered a necessary practical step to take once a firm reaches a certain level of internationalization, simply because it is the only language that can realistically be used by groups consisting of many different nationalities (see e.g. Harzing et al., 2011; Neeley et al., 2012). This practical argument has perhaps been especially common among interviewees at the level of corporate top management or representing corporate centres. In this discourse, alternative approaches to language management (e.g. multilingual approaches such as documented by Steyaert et al., 2011) tend to be considered as impractical considering the daily realities of the MNC and insensitive to the actual challenges of 'getting the job done'. This approach is well expressed by Neeley et al. (2012), who list competitive pressures, the globalization of tasks and resources, and the need to integrate acquired or merged firms across national boundaries as key reasons for adopting English as the CCL, and provides the names of several large MNCs that have chosen this route.

Another interpretation of the tendency to adopt English as the CCL is as a sign of mimetic isomorphism (DiMaggio and Powell, 1983). In this view, the practical pressures to adopt English as a CCL are further strengthened by legitimacy considerations, as firms that want to be perceived as international or global – whether in relation to employees or potential recruits (Piekkari, 2008; Piekkari and Tietze, 2012), or competitors and investors – conform to institutional pressures in favour of English (Barner-Rasmussen and Aarnio, 2011;

Harzing and Pudelko, 2013). In this view, adopting English as the official corporate language is partly done in order to project an international image and signal belonging to a group of 'international players' or 'advanced, modern and global' companies (Piekkari and Tietze, 2012) instead of being a parochial, regional actor.

It should be noted that these interpretations have mainly been based on empirical data from northern European multinationals from countries whose languages are not commonly spoken globally. In this context, the recent finding by Harzing and Pudelko (2013), that Asian MNCs are significantly more inclined than Nordic, European or American MNCs to use their HQ language as their CCL, is noteworthy. Combined with the theoretical discussion by Luo and Shenkar (2006), who propose that the HQ language is determined by MNC strategy, structure and transnationality, and subsidiary language by subsidiary organizational form, strategic role and expatriate deployment, it provides useful pointers for identifying some dynamics that govern the choice of CCL in multinational firms.

In Harzing and Pudelko's (2013) sample, half of the Asian MNCs did not have a formally designated CCL, and in most of those that did, the language in question was their HQ language. In other words, Asian MNCs frequently used Asian languages in their internal communication. Harzing and Pudelko interpreted this as a consequence of the fact that Asian HQ and subsidiaries in their sample often shared the same language, pre-empting the need for introducing some other corporate language. They also observed that the Asian languages in question (especially Chinese and Japanese) are widely spoken at least regionally, further decreasing the perceived need to resort to another language in order to conduct business internationally. However, Harzing and Pudelko also pointed out that this probably indicated that the firms in question did not have significant activities outside Asia, or at least did not prioritize these very highly.

In a different twist on the theme of a CCL other than English, a bank formed through a merger of a Finnish and a Swedish bank first chose Swedish as its corporate language, but then quickly changed it to English due to the resulting outcry in the Finnish part of the organization (Piekkari et al., 2005; Vaara et al., 2005). We will return to the individual-level drivers and consequences of this case later on; here we simply note that the choice of corporate language was initially approached by top management as a matter of rational decision-making that did not include emotional, political or power considerations.

This yields the conclusion that CCL choice is fundamentally a top management decision driven by inter-unit communication needs as perceived in the light of the firm's current market reach. Neither the European nor the Asian cases examined in previous research provide much evidence for employee involvement in determining the CCL, nor for a proactive approach where a CCL different from the HQ language would be introduced first and international expansion would occur only later on. Even in the case of Rakuten of Japan, whose quick and dramatic switch to English as the CCL has been viewed as an example of proactive language management (e.g. Maeda, 2010), this move was preceded by an international expansion spree (Neeley et al., 2012).

11.3.4   Individual reasons

Moving now to research at the individual, dyad and small group level on why a particular language (or languages) is (are) chosen in day-to-day work situations, we have already cited considerable evidence that top management *fiat* is not enough to explain individual-level language choice. Indeed it seems that the large amount of literature on official corporate language choice does not properly reflect the actual relevance of this language for daily communication in the MNC. Rather, the official corporate language is only one determinant among many actual language choices in specific communication situations. This insight has prompted a search for other, complementary, and perhaps more important, determinants.

Marschan-Piekkari et al. (1999) found that individuals who spoke the same language communicated more intensely between each other than across language boundaries, seemingly because communication was felt to be smoother and less complicated and the threshold of contacting a colleague in a sister or HQ unit was much lower when the communication could be carried out in a shared language. As part of the same pattern, Marschan-Piekkari et al. (1999) also found that individuals at subsidiary level who spoke the parent company language tended to leverage this capability in contacts with the HQ, and that HQ representatives tended to reciprocate, thus eschewing the CCL in favour of the shared language. The rationale was that communication quality and 'feel' were significantly improved when both parties were skilled in the common language.

Mäkelä et al. (2007) subsequently interpreted this through the theoretical lens of homophily, that is, the tendency to prefer to interact with similar others, and argued that linguistic closeness is one dimension of interpersonal similarity. Another way of understanding the reasons for choosing a language that the involved parties speak as well as possible is that language can be seen as a system of meanings that humans use to construct their realities (Tietze et al., 2003) and connect different socio-cultural, institutional and individual worlds (Tietze, 2008). The more aligned the systems of meaning of the communicating individuals are, the smaller the risk of misunderstandings and complications.

In the bank merger case documented by Vaara et al. (2005), Finnish organizational members' primary cause of protest when Swedish was introduced as the common language was that their weaker language skills compared to their

Swedish colleagues led them to be marginalized as professionals and weakened their position in the competition for internal resources and prestige. Swedish was also resented due to historical reasons which imbued the language with colonial connotations for some Finnish organizational members. The subsequent switch to English was welcomed because this was a foreign language for both parties, putting them on a more equal footing.

Steyaert et al. (2011) documented several practices of individual-level language choice, some of which are similar to those already reported in other contexts and some of which apparently are deeply embedded in a particular institutional environment, namely Switzerland with its four official languages. As already noted, the two practices that occurred the most frequently in their data were adaptation to the local language and employing a third language (English, which was perceived to be practical as a 'common platform to work from' while lacking the emotional baggage of the national languages). Other practices included: adapting to the language preferences of one's interlocutor (as a sign of politeness and a willingness to accommodate the preferences of the other), collectively and explicitly negotiating about the language to be used in a particular situation, using multiple languages simultaneously, and improvisation.

In a recent empirical study on Japanese data, Peltokorpi and Vaara (2012) found language practices in the subsidiaries they studied to be an outcome of both corporate language policies and key characteristics of the local context, specifically the limited availability of staff fluent in English. Concretely this implied that the local language was used to a greater or lesser extent in all the studied units, and that efforts to enforce English as the CCL were significantly limited by the availability of local employees with the relevant mix of professional and language skills. Thus, actual language policies and practices were formed in and through the interplay between HQ strategies and local responses to these.

In sum, the literature is rich with examples of individual-level language choice patterns, in non-arduous as well as arduous situations. The predominant impression of the reported empirical accounts is that most people simply opt for the language that offers as many as possible of the involved individuals the possibility to understand and participate in the work task at hand with a minimum of psychological and practical discomfort. We extend these findings by emphasizing that considerations of which natural language to use mingle with considerations of the task at hand (corporate sociolects) and which specialist knowledge these require (specialist vocabulary). In practice, this may entail actions such as:

1. adapting the language according to who is involved while occasionally excluding some participants or adapting to the (implicit or explicit)

preferences of powerful participants, which may not be in line with corporate language policies;

2. adhering to practices and institutional frameworks that are perceived as relevant and legitimate to the context, which sometimes entails protests against language policies that are not felt to fulfil these criteria;

3. translating, shifting between languages (code switching) or using multiple languages in parallel, or relying on colleagues who are able to do so.

11.3.5   What are the consequences of using a particular language in a particular context?

The patterns uncovered by Marschan-Piekkari et al. (1999) have been verified in subsequent studies and have been found to have significant consequences at both the organizational and individual level. At the organizational level, a primary and important consequence of the observed language patterns was that they gave rise to an informal 'shadow' organizational structure, based on language clusters, in the studied MNC. Mäkelä et al. (2007) provided further case study support for this finding. Also quantitative evidence has been found of language skills being positively related to both inter-unit communication intensity (Barner-Rasmussen and Björkman, 2005) and perceived levels of shared vision and trustworthiness between units (Barner-Rasmussen and Björkman, 2007).

These findings strongly suggest that language skills play a fundamental role in realizing the potential of 'transnational' (Bartlett and Ghoshal, 1987, 1989) or 'metanational' MNCs (Doz et al., 2001) to handle and leverage knowledge resources more successfully than other organizational forms (Brannen et al., 2014). Still, we agree with Harzing and Pudelko (2013) that the understanding of these dynamics so far remains relatively superficial.

Marschan-Piekkari et al. (1999) also observed individuals with relevant language skills ('language nodes') to be more involved in inter-unit communication than their formal position would have indicated, and to have better access to information. They documented terms such as 'Finnish mafia' being used in their Finland-based case firm to describe these patterns. By contrast, linguistically less skilled colleagues and even superiors tended to withdraw from the same communication relationships or delegate them to the 'language nodes', who thereby were given or actively assumed roles as 'bridge builders' (Marschan-Piekkari et al., 1999) or 'bridge individuals' (Feely and Harzing, 2003). Other authors have subsequently deepened the exploration of individual-level consequences of language skills or lack thereof, and this can be said to be a major strand of the current literature.

Individuals with appropriate language skills have been found to be more likely to take on formal or informal gatekeeper, liaison or translator positions in relation to linguistically less skilled colleagues, subordinates and superiors. This, in turn, enables the former to build networks and informal or even formal positions of power (SanAntonio, 1987; Holden and van Kortzfleisch, 2004; Vaara et al., 2005, Piekkari, 2008; Tietze, 2008, 2010). Mäkelä et al. (2010) also found individuals with appropriate language skills to be more likely to be labelled as 'high potentials', further boosting their career opportunities within the MNC.

The role of 'bridging' individuals' cultural skills in relation to their linguistic skills is currently a topic of active research. The issue is important because individuals with different backgrounds will perceive the social world differently and use different interpretive mechanisms. Hence, the transfer of meaning from one culture to another is not possible without understanding the cultural context (Brannen, 2004), which in turn requires linguistic competence since language is both a dimension of and a key to culture (Brannen 2004; Piekkari and Zander, 2005); as Henderson Kassis (2005) has shown, superficially sharing the same language (such as English as CCL in many cases) is not enough and may result in substantial misunderstandings and communication failures.

Indeed, Tietze (2010) has explicitly argued that successfully performing a 'bridging' role includes not only the ability to translate between languages, but also the ability to interpret between meaning systems, idioms and discourses. Harzing et al. (2011) empirically identified several categories of 'bridging' individuals, including persons with in-depth familiarity with the cultures and languages of both the groups they bridge between. Ribeiro (2007) studied Japanese translators in Brazilian firms and found that they also acted as buffers or mediators in cultural terms, filtering out or rephrasing culturally inappropriate messages and thus helping avert communication problems.

Building on these findings, Barner-Rasmussen et al. (2014) show empirically how language skills and cultural skills support each other, the most effective 'linchpins' in their study being individuals who score high on both dimensions. In the context of Finnish–Russian and Finnish–Chinese HQ–subsidiary relationships, they provide examples of individuals who, due to their personal cultural skills and, in particular, language skills, wield considerable power and influence independently of their formal position, enabling them to act as key 'linchpins' in inter-unit relationships.

The special position of linguistically skilled individuals inevitably has a downside for their linguistically less competent colleagues. A number of authors have documented the power of language to: exclude otherwise competent individuals from training opportunities or participation in joint development projects; hamper their career advancement (Marschan-Piekkari et al., 1999; Piekkari et al., 2005; Piekkari and Tietze, 2012); subject them to feelings of ostracism (Neeley et al., 2012); and distort power–authority relationships (Blazejewski, 2006; Harzing and Feely, 2008; Harzing and Pudelko, 2013).

Such patterns have been identified across numerous different language combinations and organizational contexts as reviewed above. Examples include: subsidiary employees lacking skills in the HQ language; expatriates lacking skills in the subsidiary language; senior subsidiary managers being less skilled than junior managers in a newly established CCL; subsidiary representatives being more skilled in the CCL than their colleagues at HQ; and one party in a merger being less skilled than the other in the new HQ language, or the CCL.

Thus, many of the consequences of language in international management are related to individuals and their position and career prospects within the MNC. As languages shift, some individuals with important experience may be marginalized, while others with relevant language skills may gain in visibility and power. In any particular organizational situation, individuals may decide to flee, fight or adapt to these dynamics as they try to strike a balance between the resources and capabilities accessible to them and the different, often conflicting, pressures and demands of the changing interplays of language. Steyaert et al. (2011) suggest the concept of 'linguistic landscape' or 'linguascape' to denote and explain different language choices in specific organizational contexts along the twin dimensions of space and time.

In sum, research located in MNCs has focused on the existence and relationship of natural languages, and specifically English, with reference to different contexts, situations and locations. There is little in this literature that concerns itself with the relationship between the content of language (i.e. special languages) and the context factors and tasks (corporate sociolects). In order to understand this relationship better, we now turn to some theoretical considerations and the major case study of a Danish MNC.

11.4　Special languages

According to Sager et al. (1980, pp. 63–64) 'special languages form mutually exclusive, though overlapping sets of sub-languages based on the division of knowledge of a speech community'. In an organization like an MNC the number of special languages could be enormous, covering various specialized functions such as marketing, HRM or finance, and technical and scientific as well as legal operations. The distinctive feature of a special language is its lexicon, which can be so specialized in a formal sense as well as in its connotations, which may be inscrutable to outsiders, and in its powers of reference. A key point about a special language is that it may be said to revolve around specialist terminology. Its character therefore has a certain formal quality. Furthermore the body of its specialist terms can in principle be directly translated into other languages. That is to say, unlike sociolects which we discuss below, special languages are not rooted in a social place in an organizational context, but in (professional) activities that need a discourse for the communication of specialist knowledge.

11.4.1 Sociolects

The term 'sociolect', which has its pedigree in sociolinguistics via dialectology (Halliday, 2007, p. 26), has already been briefly introduced. As we are going to apply it in a novel way (not to society, but to a specific organizational context), we need to add some preliminary words of explanation. As defined by the sociolinguist Trudgill (2003, p. 122), a sociolect is 'a variety or lect which is thought of as being related to it speakers' social background rather than geographical background'. The main distinction between a sociolect and dialect, which are frequently confused, concerns the settings they are created in. A dialect's main identifier is geography where a certain region uses specific phonological, morphosyntactic or lexical rules (Trudgill, 2003, p. 35). Agha (2007, p. 135) develops this concept by stating that 'the demographic dimensions marked by speech are matters of geographic provenance alone, such as speaker's birth locale, extended residence and the like'.

For our purposes the term 'sociolect' has advantages over 'dialect' in that the latter term directs attention to geographic rather than social and in particular organizational settings and calls to mind some kind of deviation from standard forms of national languages in terms of pronunciation as well as specific lexical and grammatical usages. The term 'sociolect' is plainly more suitable for the description of language behaviour in organizational contexts in which factors such as socio-economic status, ethnicity, age and gender (Labov, 2012, p. 122) as well as organizational position have a bearing on the character and domain of a given sociolect. Hence in this chapter we are speaking about *corporate sociolects*. So, for example, in the case of Novo Nordisk, which we discuss below, a male senior manager may use a particular form of Danish, clearly identifying him as educated in general, and indicative of the socio-economic status of a particular segments of Danish society. In addition, he may speak fluent English as well as having been socialized in his occupational specialist language of chemistry, his first disciplinary background before he became a senior manager. This might have included the completion of a Master of Business Administration programme, so that the full linguistic repertoire this manager brings to international encounters comprises several languages, several specialist languages as well as the corporate sociolects bearing in mind tasks, contexts and situational requirements.

In a large organization such as an MNC it is impossible to calculate the precise number of job-related sociolects in active use: no more than one could compute the number of languages spoken in any one city at a given time. There is, however, one cluster rather than one particular manifestation which gives identity to managers, whose style of language is sometimes disparagingly termed 'management speak'. These sociolects are much concerned with the reinforcement of identity, projection of authority, the exercise of power and taking and 'ownership' of decisions.

The boundary between sociolects and special languages are tricky to specify in the MNC context, not least because the boundary between a corporate sociolect and special language is not necessarily clear-cut. For example, in a marketing department of an MNC, there will be manifestations, and indeed overlapping, of the two language forms. The special language and terminology of marketing overlap with the sociolect of the marketing department as it emerged over time through the internal and external interactions, which may lead to the development of context-specific words, expressions and meanings.

Such a sociolect of marketing can be so specific to those people working in that particular context that it can only function in a meaningful way there. It is distinct from the occupational discourse of marketing with its function-specific terminology and schemes of reference, i.e. the special language of marketing, which is transferable between different units and is less context-bound. Suppose a member of our hypothetical MNC applies for a job with another company. In an interview he or she will talk about work experience in the special language of marketing. If he or she spoke about marketing sociolectally (as it were), this will be largely unintelligible to the interviewers, as context-specific information would overshadow the professionalized and more generalizable vocabulary and meanings of the specialist marketing language. Also, the special language can, in principle, have correlates in other languages. Thus, there is a French, a German and a Japanese special language of marketing, each of which is rooted in the governing concepts of the activity. In principle, then, special languages are translatable among (national) languages – corporate sociolects are either not or substantially less so – and in this sense have international extension. This would appear to be the reverse of corporate sociolects which are not just context-specific, but context-bound.

As we have dealt with directly relevant material regarding the use of national languages (including English), specialist languages and corporate sociolects, we now turn to a Danish health care MNC, Novo Nordisk. The material is based on two case studies published by Holden (2002) and Holden and Glisby (2010).

11.4.2   Novo Nordisk: The role of facilitators in a multilingual, multi-sociolect and multi-specialist MNC

Novo Nordisk, whose headquarters are located just to the north of Copenhagen, is one of the world's biggest biotechnology companies, being the world's second largest producer of insulin used in the treatment of diabetes, and the world's largest producer of industrial enzymes used in the food industry as well as for the production of detergents. The pharmaceutical business accounts for more than 75 per cent of Novo Nordisk's total worldwide sales, which, according to the current annual report, amounted to $14,300 million. Although it is one of the largest companies in Denmark, by world standards Novo Nordisk is small for a pharmaceutical company. Worldwide the company employs some 37,000 people and is represented by wholly owned operations in 76 countries. In seven countries it has manufacturing facilities. As such Novo Nordisk is one of Denmark's most internationalized companies. In Denmark it is perceived as a solid, if somewhat traditionally minded, company, but it would be mistaken to regard it as conservative. Being in the pharmaceutical business, Novo Nordisk is an ethically conscious company.

Both case studies feature a small team of internationally operating trouble-shooters, known as 'facilitators' in Novo Nordisk parlance, who visit company subsidiaries and affiliates acting as 'mediators of company philosophy and management precepts as well as (*ad hoc*) consultants' (Holden, 2002, p. 125). The case study below will describe the provenance and activities of the facilitators and discuss their language behaviour based on information gathered during structured interviews with them as professionals working in a peripatetic multicultural team. As we shall see, Novo Nordisk provides a fascinating picture of the interplay between a highly distinctive sociolect and arrays of special languages.

The first group of 14 facilitators was comprised of six Danes, two Britons, one Malaysian, one Japanese, two Americans, one South African and one Spaniard. Between them, they had nearly 200 years of combined experience working for Novo Nordisk, having worked in sales and marketing, production, logistics, regional management, IT, auditing and R&D management. The profile of the team as it was in 2010 has retained a similar balance of Danes/non-Danes, company responsibilities and international experience. But it is worth noting that one of the 2010 team was a female scientist, a Chinese national, who speaks fluent English and Danish. The facilitators characterize their work as comprising three main components: assess, assist and facilitate.

> Through on-site auditing/facilitating of departments, factories, and affiliates, the facilitators *assess* whether or not the company-wide minimum standard requirements or 'ground rules' are met. These are specified in the Novo Nordisk Way of Management, which comprises a vision, a charter and a set of company policies and precepts providing operational guidance on specific issues. They *assist* the unit in question in correcting identified non-conformity with these requirements. Through on-site identification of 'best practices' applied, they *facilitate* communication and sharing of these across the organization (Holden and Glisby, 2010, p. 186).

The total audit process, including the supply of feedback to the units, has become known as facilitation within Novo Nordisk. The on-site visits for each facilitation typically takes a week or less, but each duo's involvement (there are always two facilitators working together) is in fact longer, factoring in preparation time and follow-up activities. In summary, the facilitators:

1. obtain objective evidence through a fact-finding process;
2. provide objective, validated assessments and conclusions;
3. include recommendations for improvements, where appropriate;
4. agree on action plans with the unit or process managers;
5. follow up on the implementation of the action plan;
6. fulfil their responsibilities in a manner demonstrating integrity, objectivity and professional behaviour.

Working in ever-changing duos, the facilitators spend approximately half their professional lives engaged in facilitations all over the world. They are a redoubtable company resource. Their interactions with their colleagues in diverse cultural settings require each facilitator to possess and apply significant competences as cross-cultural communicators for conveying professional credibility and securing trust.

Although they see themselves as knowledge *sharers*, the facilitators' true contribution is as knowledge *creators*. First, they create new knowledge for the company on the basis of facilitation events. This knowledge can relate to best practice: important insights about any aspect of the company's business. It can be used to enhance decisions affecting processes, practices and people. The facilitators also create new knowledge about facilitation itself, and a good deal of that knowledge is tacit.

The facilitators' tacit knowledge is to be understood as multi-layered, comprising these facets:

1. general (i.e. about the company and the way it operates);
2. situation-specific (one might say here 'facilitation-specific');
3. relationship-specific;
4. network-specific (they know who has access to which resources and how they use them).

11.4.3   The Facilitators: National languages, special languages and sociolects

It is a central notion of the facilitator concept that the team's professional expertise covers a wide range of company functions, to which they bring pre-existing special languages based on their education and professional activities.

The 2010 group of facilitators drew on special languages associated with various scientific and engineering disciplines as well as domains such as law and business administration. All the facilitators master their respective special languages in English and in their native languages. Thus, where a facilitation is of a very technical nature, a facilitator will be selected in advance who has a direct or related competence.

Although at first glance it is possible to characterize the facilitators as a multilingual team based on their diverse native languages, it is also necessary to see them as 'a container' of special languages, as defined earlier in the chapter. It is the combination of their multiple national languages, their English competence and their multiple specialist languages which enables them to develop a rather unusual kind of *corporate sociolect*, which is articulated in English, but remains rooted in Danish managerial culture. This sociolect

1. evolves on the basis of the totality of activities undertaken by facilitators and on the way in which they interact – and have interacted – with (a) each other; (b) the units they have facilitated; and (c) the corporate management of Novo Nordisk;
2. is not a sociolect in the conventional sense as it has international extension and plays a vital role in enabling cross-border organizational learning;
3. evolves its own written forms.

This latter point calls for an explanation. When they were formed, the facilitators who were provided with their own suite of offices at corporate headquarters were viewed with great suspicion. They were seen as 'interfering enforcers', 'cultural watchdogs' and even 'the KGB of corporate management'. From the point of view of wary employees, it is easy to imagine that the facilitators were evolving an exclusive discourse as readily symbolized by their un-Danish accommodation (un-Danish in the sense that its physical detachment goes against the grain of Danish egalitarianism). Indeed they were creating what one might call 'a sociolect of facilitation', a form of company language which was being immediately designed for international use with the aim of creating closeness to employees in their own locations.

As they rapidly acquired experience of facilitation, they developed new understandings about handling different cultures (in the general sense of that expression), about specific situations which might require considerable tact or about particular challenges about communicating the Novo Nordisk 'Way of Management'. So it was that within two years of operation they had begun 'to write their own materials, including a charter of standards, procedures and guidelines' (Holden, 2002, p. 125). Seeing that every facilitation called for a written report, it follows that *the sociolect of facilitation* was modifying the company's understanding of, and discussions about, its international management processes. In short the facilitators had 'written their own script' (Holden, 2002, p. 122) and this script, largely developed for their convenience, became a general influence within the company as an international entity. Their sociolect was operating in effect as a cross-cultural instrument of professional interanimation. Importantly, however, this sociolect of facilitation cannot function in transnational contexts without engagement with the various special languages of the facilitators nor without the general language of Novo Nordisk and is held together through the unifying potential of the English language.

The case study then shows how the various special languages of the facilitators created a sociolect based on English, which in turn became *a new special language* within Novo Nordisk. However, this special language of facilitation should emphatically not be seen as a language of management. It is better described as a language of governance, which we tentatively define as a language which underpins rather than directs the system by which policies and decisions are enacted in an MNC. A remarkable feature of this sociolect-derived language of governance is that it has acquired international extension – even international authority – within Novo Nordisk.

If our analysis is correct, we can perhaps imagine Novo Nordisk in its own pragmatic space with the flows of various internal languages, national and organizational, helping to influence the lexical composition and usages associated with the sociolect of facilitation. As these flows are carriers of all kinds of knowledge, information, experiences and impressions of Novo Nordisk employees, so they are ever-changing, hence they *revitalize* the sociolect of facilitation. Another special feature of the pragmatic space is that it also constitutes a *zone of governance* which is independent of, yet runs parallel to, the formal language of management (English) in Novo Nordisk. As a language of governance, its special property is that the fact that it has evolved – through experience and not design – to reinforce the values associated with the Novo Nordisk Way of Management. In this respect the sociolect/special language of the facilitators is a truly striking form of 'transnational linguistic capital' (Gerhards, 2012, p. 13; see note 3 for the web reference), which can be transferred across MNC units and communities through the use of the English language.

We comment on the matter of code-switching, which in linguistics is associated both with bilingualism or the switching between a minority language and one of wider use, in order to show solidarity with a particular group (Crystal, 1997, pp. 364–365). In the contexts of multilingual organizations code-switching relates to situations when second language users revert to talking among themselves in their native language; this, in turn, can cause a feeling of irritation, and even exclusion and suspicion, amongst other language speakers. Once again the Novo Nordisk experience provides a rather different slant on this topic. We have to recall that the facilitators' sociolect frequently operates as a language of governance. In this guise its task is to pursue conformity to the Novo Nordisk Way of Management. It does not require employees at any level, in any location within the corporation, to switch any code per se, but it nevertheless requires them to perform acts of benign *Gleichschaltung* to ensure this all-important conformity.[6]

11.5 Discussion

Broadly speaking, the treatment of language in the international business literature confines itself to national and supranational languages, English of course falling into both categories and occupying its incontestable position as the principal language. Yet, while the language-sensitive international business literature is cognizant of the complexities that are created and expressed through the simultaneous existence of several national languages in an MNC, it has yet to engage with other linguistic approaches, such as we have attempted to capture in our discussion of corporate sociolects and special languages. In the context of MNC research, the focus of the field is on national languages, rather than on their functions as languages of business (i.e. for initiating and maintaining relationships with customers, market intermediaries and other external stakeholders) and how they are played out and inform the emergence of sociolects and special languages.

Our investigation into the sociolect of facilitation within Novo Nordisk raises various issues of interest in the context of the current international business literature. First, we should note that we know exactly when, where and how this sociolect arose: as a result of a corporate management initiative in May 1996 to create the facilitators, whose formal existence commenced on 1 January 1997. From that date their language began to take shape in their allocated suite of offices in the headquarters near Copenhagen.

This kind of insight provided by the case study is very unusual in the international business literature, which is invariably vague about the *growth* of corporate language forms of any description. In connection with this we have

---

[6] The German word *Gleichschaltung* has entered English as an accepted foreign term. It is a compound derived from the adjective *gleich*, meaning 'equal', and the verb *schalten*, meaning among other things 'to switch', 'operate', 'engage'. The term *Gleichschaltung* gained fashionability or notoriety during the Nazi period, when it came to mean 'force or bring into line'. *The Oxford Dictionary of English* (2006, p. 735) defines the word as 'the standardization of political, economic and social institutions as carried out in authoritarian states'. We have been careful to suggest that the facilitators engage in benign acts of *Gleichschaltung*. No doubt some readers will not take kindly to our use of this term. For a discussion about the relationship between *Gleichschaltung* and the German language in an industrial setting in the Nazi period, see Chapter 10 in this volume.

been able to study its evolution and notably its conversion from 'mere' sociolect to new corporate special language and as such a language of governance. There are grounds for calling the sociolect of facilitation what Brannen and Doz (2012, p. 80) term 'a contextually specific corporate language': except to these authors such a language 'is an artifact of how strategic thoughts are formulated as well as how they are communicated and discussed'. The language of governance developed by the facilitators is simply not an artefact. It is both organic and evolving; it also operates independently of Novo Nordisk's corporate management.

This analysis gives new possibilities for understanding the myth of the Tower of Babel when applied to MNCs. All analogies about the Tower of Babel take as their point of departure the fact that multilingualism in organizations is a source of major challenges, requiring practical solutions (Harzing et al., 2011). It is generally assumed that the languages in question are those of national or distinct ethnic cultures, though not by Tietze (2010), who sees the issue of multilingualism as bound up with the use of language and discourse to 'create an increasingly interconnected and globalized world'. In line with this perspective, our case study of Novo Nordisk as a small MNC makes it absolutely clear that a more productive Babel-based analogy with the MNC must embrace the notion of corporate sociolects and special languages, because it is these, in whatever national language they manifest themselves, which give any organization its unique sociolinguistic signature.

11.6   Conclusion

The notion of the city has provided us with an analogue for the linguistic mental mapping of the MNC. The on-going linguistic audit of Manchester was a very useful pivot for this purpose. We then applied the notions of sociolect and special language to the study of the internal communication systems of the Danish MNC, Novo Nordisk. Together with our review of language-based research, located in MNCs, it emerged that language complexity in an MNC is high as it is based on the use and existence of multiple languages which need to be understood in relation to the English language and the existence of special languages and company and context-specific sociolects, which together from the linguistic signature of an MNC. Research is yet to engage with these complexities and how languages/English, sociolects and special languages form a topology which remains emerging and changing.

We have provided a first attempt in investigating a case where a particular and special group of MNC employees, the facilitators, used language and special language skills to evolve their own sociolect as a powerful symbol of identity, used it in conjunction with arrays of special languages and even created a written language around the activity of facilitation.

By concentrating on sociolects and special languages alone, we were able to highlight many unusual language features within Novo Nordisk, which would appear to add new dimensions to Steyaert et al.'s (2011) concept of 'linguascapes' with its emphasis of discursive practices within the MNC. Furthermore, our analysis reinforced the conviction of Marschan-Piekkari et al. (1999) about the existence in MNCs of 'a shadow structure', lying behind the formal organization chart, based on language.

This treatment of the terms 'corporate sociolect' and 'special languages' has been purely exploratory in the quest to (partially) specify the linguistic mental map of Novo Nordisk. This mapping has seemingly unusual features owing to the special role of the facilitators, so no claim can be made as to generalizability of our findings and interpretations of them.

With reference to the English language as Novo Nordisk's adopted CCL, it is of course the language of many of its special languages. Second, it is also the foundation language of the corporate sociolect developed by the facilitators. While this sociolect does *not* have a foot in the Danish language whatsoever, it is very significantly rooted in Danish management culture. In its English guise this corporate sociolect is arguably the single most influential form of company language of Novo Nordisk as an international concern.

In other words, although Novo Nordisk has adopted English completely as its corporate language (the Danish language hardly featured in our description), a rather obvious (though misleading) conclusion is that English is the main and only language of communication within the company as an internationally distributed organization. This might appear to be the cardinal feature of language use within the company – however, this does not mean that the English language dominates over all meaning systems and communications – rather, it is the nexus of ties between English as a common bond and how it facilitates the emergence of a corporate sociolect of governance, which explains the permanence of this 'linguistic signature' from the conception of the facilitator group in the 1990s to the second decade of the 21st century.

The language-sensitive literature located in MNCs has concerned itself with the role of languages and English in the emergent formation of the MNC. Here, contributions have developed an understanding about the strategic alignment of languages, the effects of language choices and the existence of discursive linguascapes. We propose that the field of language-sensitive international business scholarship needs to align different 'takes on language' into a more comprehensive and appropriate approach to appreciate the complexities of linguistic topographies of MNCs. In this chapter we have attempted to do so by drawing on the notions of 'sociolects' and 'special languages' to provide vocabulary to appreciate the complexities where national languages meet with specialist languages, context-specific corporate expressions and vocabularies. Furthermore, the case study of Novo Nordisk has also shown that human agency is part of the linguistic signature of MNCs, where choices and decisions inform and create the pragmatic space where MNC relationships are expressed and created, strategies aligned and shaped.

References

B. Agha (2007) *Language and Social Relations* (Cambridge: Cambridge University Press).

F. Bargiela-Chiappini (2006) '(Whose) English(es) for Asian Business Discourse(s)?', *Journal of Asian Pacific Communication*, 16, 1–24.

W. Barner-Rasmussen and C. Aarnio (2011) 'Shifting the Faultlines of Language: A Quantitative Functional-level Exploration of Language Use in the MNC Subsidiaries', *Journal of World Business*, 46, 288–295.

W. Barner-Rasmussen and I. Björkman (2005) 'Surmounting Interunit Barriers: Factors Associated with Interunit Communication Intensity in the Multinational Corporation', *International Studies in Management and Organization*, 35, 28–46.

W. Barner-Rasmussen and I. Björkman (2007) 'Language Fluency, Socialization and Interunit Relationships in Chinese and Finnish Subsidiaries', *Management and Organization Review*, 3, 105–128.

W. Barner-Rasmussen, A. Ehrnrooth, A. Koveshnikova and K. Mäkelä (2014) 'Language and Cultural Skills as Determinants of Boundary Spanning within the MNC', *Journal of International Business Studies*, 45, 886–905.

A. Bartlett and S. Ghoshal (1987) Managing across Borders: New Organizational Responses', *Sloan Management Review*, 29, 47–57.

A. Bartlett and S. Ghoshal (1989) *Managing Across Borders: The Transnational Solutions* (Boston, NY: Harvard University Press).

S. Blazejewski (2006) 'Transferring Value-infused Organizational Practices in Multinational Companies: A Conflict Perspective' In M. Geppert and M. Mayer (eds) *Global, Local and National Practices in Multinational Companies* (Basingstoke: Palgrave), pp. 63–104.

A. Bossuyt, L. Broze and V. Ginsburgh (2001) 'On Invisible Trade Relations between Mesopotamian Cities during the Third Millennium BC', *The Professional Geographer*, 53, 374–383.

M. Brannen (2004) 'When Mickey Loses Face: Recontextualisation, Semantic Fit and the Semiotics of Foreignness', *Academy of Management Review*, 29, 593–616.

M. Brannen and Y. Doz (2012) 'The Languages of Strategic Agility: Trapped in Your Jargon or Lost in Translation', *California Management Review*, 54, 77–97.

M. Brannen, R. Piekkari and S. Tietze (2014) 'The Multifaceted Role of Language in International Business: Unpacking the Forms, Functions and Features of a Critical Challenge to MNC Theory and Performance', *Journal of International Business Studies*, 45, 495–507.

J. Bruntse (2003) *It's Scandinavian: dansk-svensk kommunikation i SAS* (Institute for Nordic Philology, Copenhagen University, Copenhagen).

M. Charles (1998) 'Europe: Oral Business Communication', *Business Communication Quarterly*, 61, 85–93.

D. Crystal (1980) *A First Dictionary of Linguistics and Phonetics* (London: André Deutsch).

D. Crystal (1997) *The Cambridge Encyclopedia of Language* (Cambridge: Cambridge University Press).

D. Crystal (2003) *English as a Global Language*, 2nd edn (Cambridge: Cambridge University Press).

P. DiMaggio and W. Powell (1983) 'The Iron Cage Revisited: Institutional Isomorphism and Collective Rationality in Organizational Fields', *American Sociological Review*, 48, 147–160.

D. Dor (2004) 'From Englishization to Imposed Multilingualism: Globalization, the Internet and the Political Economy of the Linguistic Code', *Public Culture*, 16, 97–118.

Y. Doz, J. Santos and P. Williamson (2001) *From Global to Metanational* (Boston: Harvard Business School Press).

A. Feely and A.-W. Harzing (2003) 'Language Management in Multinational Companies', *Cross Cultural Management*, 10, 37–52.

R. Fredriksson, W. Barner-Rasmussen and R. Piekkari (2006) 'The Multinational Corporation as a Multilingual Organization: The Notion of a Common Corporate Language', *Corporate Communication*, 11, 406–423.

J. Gerhards (2012) 'From Babel to Brussels: European Integration and the Importance of Transnational Linguistic Capital', Berlin Studies on the Sociology of Europe 28, available at www.polsoz.fu-berlin.de

M. Halliday (2007) *Language and Society* (London: Continuum).

A.-W. Harzing and A. Feely (2008) 'The Language Barrier and Its Implications for HR-Subsidiary Relationships', *Cross-cultural Management*, 15, 49–60.

A.-W. Harzing, K. Köster and U. Magner (2011) 'Babel in Business: The Language Barrier and Its Solutions in the HQ-subsidiary Relationship', *Journal of World Business*, 46, 296–304.

A.-W. Harzing and M. Pudelko (2013) 'Language Competencies, Policies and Practices in Multinational Corporations: A Comprehensive Review and Comparison of Anglophone, Asian, Continental European and Nordic MNCs', *Journal of World Business*, 48, 87–97.

J. Heikkilä and A. Smale (2011) 'The Effects of Language Standardization on the Acceptance and Use of e-HRM systems in Foreign Subsidiaries', *Journal of World Business*, 46, 305–313.

J. Henderson Kassis (2005) 'Language Diversity in International Management Teams', *International Studies of Management & Organization*, 35, 66–82.

N. Holden (2002) *Cross-cultural Management: A Knowledge Management Perspective* (Harlow, UK: Pearson Education).

N. Holden and M. Glisby (2010) 'Creating Knowledge Advantage: The Tacit Dimensions of International Competition and Cooperation' (Copenhagen: Copenhagen Business School).

N. Holden and H. van Kortzfleisch (2004) 'Why Cross-cultural Knowledge Transfer Is a Form of Translation in More Ways than You Think', *Knowledge and Process Management*, 11, 127–138.

J. House (2003) 'English as a Lingua Franca: A Threat to Multilingualism?', *Journal of Sociolinguistics*, 7, 556–578.

J. Jacobs (1969) *The Economy of Cities* (New York: Vintage).

J. Jacobs (1984) *Cities and the Wealth of Nations* (New York: Random House).

J. Jacobs (2000) *The Nature of Economics* (New York: Vintage).

M. Janssens, J. Lambert and C. Steyaert (2004) 'Developing Language Strategies for International Companies: The Contribution of Translation Studies', *Journal of World Business*, 39, 414–430.

W. Labov (2012) *Dialect Diversity in America: The Politics of Language Change* (Charlottesville: University of Virginia Press).

Y. Luo and O. Shenkar (2006) 'The Multinational Corporation as a Multilingual Community: Language and Organization in a Global Context', *Journal of International Business Studies*, 37, 321–339.

M. Maeda (2010) *Uniqlo, Rakuten Make Official Language English* (Japan Center for Economic Research, Tokyo: www.jcer.or.jp/eng/research/pdf/maeda20100715e.pdf).

R. Marschan-Piekkari, D. Welch and L. Welch (1999) 'In the Shadow: The Impact of Language on Structure, Power and Communication in the Multinational', *International Business Review*, 8, 421–440.

C. McDonald (2014) 'The Impact of Subnational Heterogeneity on Foreign Direct Investment Location Decisions and the Performance of Foreign Affiliates: The Case of Multinational Enterprises in China', unpublished PhD thesis, University of Leeds.

K. Mäkelä, I. Björkman and M. Ehrnrooth (2010) 'How Do MNCs Establish Their Talent Pools? Influences on Individuals' Likelihood of Being Labelled as Talent', *Journal of World Business*, 45, 134–142.

K. Mäkelä, H. Kalla and R. Piekkari (2007) 'Interpersonal Similarity as a Driver of Knowledge Sharing within Multinational Corporations', *International Business Review*, 16, 1–22.

K. Moore and D. Lewis (1999) *Birth of the Multinational: 2,000 Years of Ancient Business History* (Copenhagen: Copenhagen Business School Press).

Multilingual Manchester (2013) (Manchester: Communications and Marketing Division of the University of Manchester) http://mlm.humanities.manchester.ac.uk/wp-content/uploads/2014/04/MLMFactsheet.pdf

T. Neeley, P. Hinds and C. Cramton (2012) 'The (Un)Hidden Turmoil of Language in Global Collaboration', *Organizational Dynamics*, 413, 236–244.

V. Peltokorpi and E. Vaara (2012) 'Language Policies and Practices in Wholly Owned Foreign Subsidiaries: A Recontextualization Perspective', *Journal of International Business Studies*, 43, 808–833.

R. Piekkari (2008) 'Languages and Careers in Multinational Corporations' In S. Tietze (ed.) *International Management and Language* (London: Routledge), pp. 128–137.

R. Piekkari and S. Tietze (2011) 'A World of Languages: Implication for International Management Research and Practice', *Journal of World Business*, 46, 267–269.

R. Piekkari and S. Tietze (2012) 'Language and International Human Resource Management' In G. Stahl, I. Björkman and S. Morris (eds) *Handbook of Research in International Human Resource Management*, 2nd edn (Cheltenham, UK: Edward Elgar), pp. 549–565.

R. Piekkari, E. Vaara, J. Tienari and R. Säntti (2005) 'Integration or Disintegration? Human Resource Implications of the Common Corporate Language Decision in a Cross-Border Merger', *International Journal of Human Resource Management*, 16, 330–344.

R. Piekkari, D. Welch, L. Welch, J.-P. Peltonen and T. Vesa (2013) 'Translation Behavior: An Exploratory Study within a Service Multinationals', *International Business Review*, 22, 771–783.

R. Piekkari and L. Zander (2005) 'Language and Communication in International Management', *International Studies of Management & Organization*, 35, 3–9.

R. Ribeiro (2007) 'The Language Barrier as an Aid to Communication', *Social Studies of Science*, 37, 561–584.

K. Roberts (2011) *The Origins of Business, Money and Markets* (New York: Columbia University Press).

J. Sager, D. Dungworth and P. McDonald (1980) *English Special Languages: Principles and Practice in Science and Technology* (Wiesbaden: Oscar Brandstetter Verlag).

P. SanAntonio (1987) 'Social Mobility and Language Use in an American Company in Japan', *Journal of Language and Social Psychology*, 6, 191–200.

C. Steyaert, A. Ostendorp and C. Gaibrois (2011), 'Multilingual Organizations as Linguascapes: Negotiating the Position of English through Discursive Practices', *Journal of World Business*, 46, 270–278.

M. Storper and A. Venables (2004) 'Buzz: Face-to-face Contact and the Urban Economy', *Journal of Economic Geography*, 4, 351–370.

S. Tietze (2004) 'Spreading the Management Gospel – in English', *Language and Intercultural Communication*, 4, 176–189.

S. Tietze (2008) *International Management and Language* (London: Routledge).

S. Tietze (2010) 'International Managers as Translators', *European Journal of International Management*, 4, 184–199.

S. Tietze, L. Cohen and G. Musson (2003) *Understanding Organizations through Language* (London: Sage).

P. Trudgill (2003) *A Glossary of Sociolinguistics* (Oxford: Oxford University Press).

J.-C. Usunier (2011) 'Language as a Resource to Assess Cross-cultural Equivalence in Quantitative Management Research', *Journal of World Business*, 46, 314–319.

E. Vaara, J. Tienari, R. Piekkari and R. Säntti (2005) 'Language and the Circuits of Power in a Merging Multinational Corporation', *Journal of Management Studies*, 16, 333–347.

D. Welch, L. Welch and R. Piekkari (2005) 'Speaking in Tongues: The Importance of Language in International Management Processes', *International Studies of Management and Organization*, 35, 10–27.

12
Language and Migration

Alícia Adserà and Mariola Pytliková

12.1 Introduction

Language proficiency is extremely important for international migrants. Better language proficiency means easier assimilation in the host country and greater returns to human capital as well as better job opportunities and job matches, among other things. In addition language skills surely influence a number of non-economic outcomes such as social integration, the size of the migrant's social network, his or her political participation and civic engagement, as well as educational attainment, health outcomes and family life. Familiarity with the destination language helps to minimize migration costs (both the direct out-of-pocket expenses and the psychological costs of leaving the home country) and serves as an informational channel to learn about other determinants of migration.

Even though language proficiency is clearly important, many immigrants have poor host language skills and struggle to acquire them. Insights on the role of language in international migration, and into the underlying processes and factors that determine migrants' proficiency, are crucial for the successful design of policy measures that address the hurdles of language acquisition. In this chapter, we review the economics of language with a focus on international migration. Research in the area focuses on (1) the role of language in migration decisions, (2) the determinants of language proficiency among migrants, and (3) the effects of immigrants' linguistic skills and language acquisition on their labour market and socio-economic outcomes.

12.2 The role of language in migration decisions

Earlier literature on the determinants of migration is based on gravity models derived from Newton's law of gravity. The main hypothesis is that migration is associated with the sizes of population in origin and destination countries and inversely related to distances to destinations. The basic gravity model has been further modified to include a number of additional variables that are expected to influence the decision to migrate. The more recent literature on the determinants of migration flows generally employs a model of human capital investment to motivate its econometric specifications (as in Clark et al., 2007; Ortega and Peri, 2009, 2013; Grogger and Hanson, 2011; Adserà and Pytlikova, 2015). Potential migrants decide where to locate among a set of alternative destinations by searching the country with the highest expected net welfare. To do so they take into account their potential earnings and likelihood of employment in their destination as well as the costs they will have to bear to move to that location. The latter can include both a set of direct out-of-pocket expenditures and indirect costs such as psychological costs of leaving their country of birth, family and friends, as well as costs associated with the need to upgrade skills and behavioural norms at arrival to attain the economic benefits of the host country. Large differences between the culture and language of the source and destination countries may constitute barriers to migration.

12.2.1   Linguistic distances and migration flows

Better language proficiency is associated with easier assimilation in the host country and greater return of human capital from the source country, as well as better job matches, among other things. Language also serves as an informational channel to learn about other determinants of migration. For instance, knowing the destination language allows immigrants to acquire information about institutions such as formal labour market access and immigrants' rights (Palmer and Pytlikova, 2015), or to learn about natives' attitudes towards immigrants (Gorinas and Pytlikova, 2016). The significance of language for migration brings to mind the 'border' effect identified in trade models. In fact trade theorists such as Melitz and Toubal (2014) use a set of measures to estimate the impact of linguistic proximity in bilateral trade and find that a common language raises it by around 200 per cent.[1] The role of language on trade is reviewed in Chapter 9 in this volume.

As done by trade scholars, researchers on the determinants of migration typically estimate a gravity-type model that includes relative population sizes and distances to destinations. This basic macro-model is combined with variables that appear in the micro-human capital model to obtain an equation of the following form

$$\ln m_{ijt} = F(GDP_i, GDP_j, Unemp_i, Unemp_j, Stock_i, D_{ij}, X_{ijt}, \delta_i, \delta_j, \theta_t),$$

---

[1] See also Isphording and Otten (2013).

where the dependent variable m_{ijt} generally denotes gross flows of migrants from country i to country j divided by the population of the country of origin i at time t, though in some cases it is specified as either aggregate flows or change in stocks. Independent variables often include measures of income per capita in both origin (GDP_i) and destination (GDP_j), and, if available, unemployment rates ($Unemp$) in both countries as well as the stock of migrants ($Stock_i$) from each origin i who already live in a destination as a proxy for migrants' *diasporas*. In addition models often include origin (δ_i), destination (δ_j) (or pair-wise) fixed effects, time effects (θ_t) and a large set of controls X_{ijt} for physical distance, common border, common colonial past, genetic distance, political rights or institutions, etc. Finally, models include either an indicator for common language or a measure of the linguistic distance between origin and destination languages (D_{ij}).

Earlier findings on the role of language in determining migration flows are somewhat mixed. This is likely due to data restrictions and to the relative homogeneity of countries employed in some papers. More recent work that uses larger time spans and richer panel data, which are now available, and a broader set of linguistic distance unveils a stronger relationship. To discern if language constitutes a barrier to migration, the simplest specifications use an indicator of whether two countries share a common language. In a study of flows to the US from 81 source countries for the years 1971–1998, Clark et al. (2007) find that having English as the first official language increases flows from a source country. However, this finding is not robust to the introduction of the pre-existing number of immigrants from the same origin.

A set of later papers that employ panel datasets with varying numbers of origins, destinations and time periods, such as Pedersen et al. (2006, 2008), Grogger and Hanson (2011), Beine et al. (2011) and Ortega and Peri (2013, 2015), also find that sharing a common language increases migration flows. Surprisingly Mayda (2010) and Ortega and Peri (2009) do not. A likely explanation for this inconsistency is the size and composition of their sample of flows that includes only 14 OECD countries. A detailed summary of findings of the effect of language on international migration is presented in Table 12.1.

Most recent studies employ more sophisticated indices that aim to capture linguistic distances. Belot and Hatton (2012) use the number of common nodes in the encyclopedia of languages Ethnologue's linguistic tree that are shared between two languages to measure the importance of cultural differences in explaining the degree of educational selectivity of outmigration across source countries. They find a net positive effect of language on skill selectivity, indicating that a closer proximity between destination and origin languages facilitates the transferability of human capital.

Belot and Ederveen (2012) employ a linguistic lexical distance for Indo-European languages proposed by Dyen et al. (1992) that ranges from 0 to 1,000

Table 12.1 The role of language in the literature on determinants of migration

Paper	Countries studied	Time period	Form of language variable	Language affects the choice of destination?
Karemera et al. (2000)	Flows to US and Canada	1976–1986	English/English or French dummy	no
Pedersen et al. (2006)	Flows to 26 OECD countries from 129 countries	1990–2000	Common language dummy	yes
Clark et al. (2007)	Flows to US from 81 countries	1971–1998	English dummy	yes
Pedersen et al. (2008)	Flows to 22 OECD countries from 129 countries	1990–2000	Common language dummy	yes
Ortega and Peri (2009)	Flows to 14 OECD countries from 73 countries	1980–2005	Common language dummy	no
Keuntae and Cohen (2010)	Flows to 17 OECD countries from 230 countries	1950–2007	Common official language dummy	yes
Mayda (2010)	Flows to 14 OECD countries from 79 countries	1980–1995	Common language dummy	no
Beine et al. (2011)	Stocks in 30 OECD countries from 195 countries	1990 and 2000	Common language dummy	yes
Grogger and Hanson (2011)	Stocks in 15 high-income OECD countries	2000	Common language dummy	yes
Belot and Ederween (2012)	Flow to 22 OECD countries	1990–2003	Dyen lexicostat. distance	yes
Belot and Hatton (2012)	Stocks in 21 OECD countries from 70 countries	2000–2001	Ethnologue distance	yes
Beine and Salomone (2013)	Stocks in 30 OECD countries from 195 countries	1990 and 2000	Common language dummy	yes
Ortega and Peri (2013)	Flows to 15 OECD countries from 120 countries	1980–2006	Common language dummy	yes
Adserà and Pytliková (2015)	Flows to 30 OECD countries from 233 countries	1980–2010	Dyen, Ethnologue, and Levenshtein	yes
Gorinas and Pytliková (2016)	Flows to 30 OECD countries from all source countries	1980–2010	Ethnologue distance	yes
Kahanec et al. (2016)	Flows to 22 EU countries from 12 states that became members in 2004 and 2007		Ethnologue distance	yes
Ortega and Peri (2015)	Stocks in 194 countries from 194 countries	2010	Common language dummy	yes
Palmer and Pytliková (2015)	Flows to EU/EFTA from EU countries	2004–2010	Ethnologue distance	yes

Source: Chiswick and Miller (2014) and author's information.

and decreases with the similarity of words from each language for a sample of meanings. Belot and Ederveen show that cultural barriers explain patterns of migration flows within OECD countries better than economic opportunities do. Their results imply that a 1 s.d. decrease in linguistic distance raises migration flows by 56 per cent, an effect twice as large as that estimated for GDP per capita.

Adserà and Pytliková (2015) use the largest panel data to date of both migration flows and stocks for 30 OECD destinations and over 200 origins that span 1980–2010. They construct their own linguistic proximity measure, based on information from the encyclopedia of languages Ethnologue. The linguistic proximity index takes into account how many levels of the linguistic family tree the languages of both the destination and the source countries share. The index is calculated separately for the distance between first official languages, the minimum distance between any official language or the two most widely spoken languages in both countries and, finally, for the most widely spoken language in each country (which are not necessarily the official ones). For robustness, Adserà and Pytliková (2015) also employ two alternative measures of linguistic distance: the Dyen et al. (1992) and the Levenshtein (1966) distance based on phonetic dissimilarity and produced by the Max Planck Institute for Evolutionary Anthropology (see Dryer and Haspelmath, 2013). For more detail on linguistic distance measures, see the Ginsburgh and Weber chapter in this volume.

Compared to other traditional push and pull factors, the effect of linguistic proximity on migration flows as measured by the Ethnologue-base index is lower than that of ethnic networks or destination GDP per capita level, but much stronger than that of unemployment rates (Adserà and Pytliková, 2015). Emigration flows to a country with the same language as opposed to a country with a language that does not share any level in the linguistic tree are around 20 per cent higher.[2] As an example, emigration rates to France from Benin where French is the first official language should be around 18 per cent higher than those from Zambia's (whose language shares only one level of the tree with French) but only 6 per cent higher than those from Sao Tome (whose language shares up to four levels with French). A reason that may account for the relatively smaller impact of language found in Adserà and Pytliková (2015) compared with Belot and Ederveen (2012) is that the latter study is restricted to within-OECD migration, whereas the former employs a very comprehensive dataset with more heterogeneous source countries. A 1 s.d. decrease of linguistic proximity increases migration flows by roughly 0.02 s.d. only

---

[2] With Dyen et al. and Levenshtein linguistic distances, the implied increase in emigration rates to countries with similar language as opposed to linguistically distant countries ranges between 14 and 20 per cent (Adserà and Pytliková, 2015).

(a tenth of the impact of a similar change in GDP per capita but larger than for changes in unemployment). The implied size of the effect is similar when either the distance between the most commonly used language in each country or the minimum distance between any of the multiple official or widely spoken languages in both countries are used instead.

Adserà and Pytliková (2015) also show that linguistic proximity matters more for migration flows from source countries with better-educated populations, which is in line with results by Belot and Hatton (2012) who find a positive effect of language proximity on skill selectivity. A large need for skill transferability for highly skilled migrants may account for the findings. Beine and Salomone (2013) find that a common official language tends to raise the proportion of skilled migrants at the expense of less skilled ones, and this holds regardless of the gender of migrants.

Besides analysing the determinants of international migration flows, some papers focus on whether language plays a role in the choices of migrants within destinations. The location selection of migrants is particularly interesting in countries with distinct geographic, cultural or linguistic differences such as Quebec within Canada. The main papers on this topic focus on the US (Bauer et al., 2005) and Canada (McDonald, 2004; Hou, 2005).

12.2.2   English as a global language

A few languages (such as English, French or Spanish) have a prominent role in international transactions, television, the internet and the job market. As a result any individual is likely to be exposed to them regardless of his or her country of origin. Among them, English is currently the most global language, as discussed in Chapter 20 in this volume.

Countries whose major languages are among one of these 'widely-spoken' languages are bound to attract a larger flow of migrants than others. There are different forces that may account for these migration patterns. First, since schools often teach English as a second language in many source countries, immigrants are more likely to have some pre-migration basic knowledge of it and may prefer to move to English-speaking destinations to lower the costs associated with the transfer of their home skills to the receiving labour market. English is also widely available on the internet and the media, especially in countries where dubbing is not the norm. Second, foreign language proficiency is an important part of human capital in the labour market of the source country (see e.g. European Commission (2006) on language proficiency as an essential skill for finding a job in host countries). Toomet (2011) shows that, among Estonian workers, English proficiency increases wages by 15 per cent. Thus, learning and improving fluency in a global language in destination countries may be particularly attractive for temporary migrants who hope to use these skills when they return home.

The fact that English-speaking nations may attract an unusual share of migrants can account for the relatively weaker results of the relevance of a common language that some researchers find when the sample is restricted to English-speaking destinations, as discussed in the previous section. In order to analyse whether this regularity holds in a larger sample of countries and to understand better the distinctive role of English, Adserà and Pytliková (2015) estimate their models separately for English and non-English speaking destinations. They find that the estimated impact of linguistic proximity on migration flows is stronger for non-English than for English destinations when measuring linguistic distance with either the first official or the major language in origin and destination. Instead, when using any official language or the two most-widely spoken languages at either origin or destination, the influence of linguistic distance plays a significant role for all destination countries, though it still matters more for non-English countries. Since English and other colonial languages are often first, second or third official languages in many countries, the most generous index shortens the linguistic distance of these origins to English-speaking destinations. Overall, results imply that a likely higher pre-migration English proficiency of the average migrant reduces the importance of the actual linguistic distance between mother tongue and English and makes these destinations more attractive by decreasing costs.

12.2.3 Linguistic enclaves and migration flows

The migration literature shows that flows are larger towards destinations with a larger stock of individuals from the same origin (Munshi, 2003; Pedersen et al., 2006, 2008; Mayda, 2010; Beine et al., 2011; Belot and Ederveen, 2012; Adserà and Pytliková, 2015). Ethnic or linguistic communities that share a similar cultural background (such as 'Chinatown', 'Little Italy' or 'Germantown') result from migrants clustering in some geographic areas or neighbourhoods (Belot and Ederveen, 2012). In ethnic enclaves, and in general, in countries with large shares of individuals with similar ancestry, migrants find 'networks' (family members, friends and people of the same source country) that ease both their direct and psychological migration costs as well as the need to learn the local language. Through networks potential migrants receive information on the immigration country, on the likelihood of getting a job, on economic and social systems, immigration policy, people and culture (Bertrand et al., 2000; Munshi, 2003; Gorinas and Pytliková, 2016; Palmer and Pytliková, 2015). The community may also offer public services, language training and children's education provision better tailored to receive a newcomer and his or her family. Network effects also explain the persistence of migration flows (see Bauer et al., 2005; Clark et al., 2007; Adserà and Pytliková, 2015). Similarly, Pedersen et al. (2008), McKenzie and Rapoport (2010) and Beine et al. (2011) find that diasporas explain a large part of the variability and selection in migration flows.

The presence of large ethnic and linguistic communities in destination lowers the pressure to learn the local language immediately after arrival and decreases the relevance of the linguistic distance in migration decisions. Adserà and Pytliková (2015) find that linguistic proximity between a migrant's mother tongue and that of the destination country matters significantly less in the presence of a large share of individuals with a language similar (either the same or very close in terms of the Ethnologue linguistic tree) to that of the migrant in the destination country. Newcomers are able to live and work in a relatively closed community. These linguistic or cultural enclaves might constitute a mixed-blessing for migrants since they may slow down their (and most importantly, their children's) socio-economic assimilation to their new country of residence. Some immigrants even spend their whole lives working within these linguistic enclaves and do not learn the destination language (see Chiswick and Miller, 1995, 1996 for Australia, Israel and Canada; Boyd, 2009 for Canada; Dustmann and Fabri, 2003 for the UK; Beckhusen et al., 2013 for the US). However, as we discuss later, some papers show that the enclave may offer overall a positive balance even if the language fluency of migrants is poorer (Portes and Jensen, 1989; Edin et al., 2003; Damm, 2009).

12.2.4 Immigration and naturalization policies

The relevance of linguistic proximity in determining the direction and strength of migration flows is likely mediated by immigration policies that affect the selection of immigrants across destinations. Policies in countries such as Australia, Canada and New Zealand emphasize skills of candidates in their application decisions and award points for English language proficiency (and French in Canada), educational attainment and age at migration when issuing permanent resident visas.

In an attempt to measure the importance of such policies, Mayda (2010) investigates how changes in the strictness of entry requirements affect the size and direction of the flows to 14 OECD countries during the period 1980–1995. Stricter policies that require applicants to have high skills and some language knowledge (such as in Australia or Canada) may result in more positively selective pools of migrants and decrease the relevance of traditional pull and push factors (such as differences in income per capita) in explaining the extent of aggregate flows. Mayda's findings are mixed. Stricter immigration quotas seem to reduce the relevance of push factors but they do not affect much that of pull factors. As a result the role of cultural and most importantly linguistic differences may become more relevant. Belot and Hatton (2012) find that introducing a point system raises the share of high-skilled migrants by about 6 percentage points and probably results in an increase in fluency of newcomers in the local language. Belot and Ederveen (2012) find that language and religion explain migration patterns within the OECD, even though cultural distance (as measured by values and norms) does not.

Whether naturalization policies involve language-proficiency tests may also affect migration decisions. Migrants are likely to be concerned not only by obtaining permanent residency but also by acquiring full citizenship rights, particularly in countries where some forms of labour market access or welfare programmes are restricted to nationals. Adserà and Pytliková (2015) code the existence of both formal and informal language requirements for naturalization for 30 OECD destinations for the period 1980–2010. They find that migration flows to countries with stricter language requirements are smaller, but linguistic proximity between origin and destination remains an independent determinant of migration.

12.3   Language proficiency among migrants

Being able to communicate in the host country's language plays a key role in the successful integration into labour markets and society. Language proficiency among migrants can be determined by the *exposure* to the host language, *efficiency* in language acquisition and *economic incentives* to learn a new language. The three determinants of proficiency have been conceptualized in the literature as the three Es of language proficiency (Chiswick, 1991; Chiswick and Miller, 1995, 2014).

12.3.1   Exposure of immigrants to language learning

Immigrants can be exposed to the host country language both prior to or after migrating. Pre-migration exposure takes place through for example foreign language classes and courses at schools. Some countries open special language classes for workers who are still at home; this is the case for classes in Swedish held in Poland provided to Polish medical personnel, who express an interest to work in Sweden. People can also be exposed to foreign language through the media or the internet, special software and games designed to teach languages, TV and books. Yet, empirical research on this type of home country foreign language exposure is scarce, simply because the information is not readily available to researchers. Existing research in the area concentrates on the role of former colonies, multiple official languages and neighbouring countries (Chiswick and Miller, 2001; Isphording, 2014). For instance, people coming from former British or US colonies (such as India, Nigeria or the Philippines) or from countries where English is among the official or main-spoken languages (e.g. Australia or Canada) tend to be proficient in English.

Most existing research, however, relates to post-migration exposure to the destination language. We know from the literature that the time elapsed since immigration affects destination language acquisition positively. This 'time' effect shows that language proficiency increases steeply in the first post-migration years, and slows down later (Espenshade and Fu, 1997; Chiswick and Miller, 2001, 2007; Isphording and Otten, 2013, 2014). Obviously, the speed of language acquisition depends on how intensively the time following migration is used to learn.

Intensity of exposure is however hard to measure. Some studies use data on enrollment of migrants into formal language education (Cohen-Goldner and Eckstein, 2008, 2010 for Israel; Andersson and Nekby, 2012 for Sweden; Clausen et al., 2009 and Heinesen et al., 2013 for Denmark; Sarvimäki and Hämäläinen, 2015 for Finland). Others use the percentage of population speaking the same language as the migrant as a measure of exposure (Chiswick and Miller, 1995).

Finally, intensity of exposure can be influenced by a number of aspects. For instance, the incentives to learn the language can be lower for those who reside in ethnic or linguistic enclaves. Research in this area shows a negative relationship between destination language acquisition and the density of ethno-linguistic enclaves (see Chiswick and Miller, 1995, 1996 for Australia, Israel and Canada; Dustmann and Fabbri, 2003 for the UK; Boyd, 2009 for Canada; Beckhusen et al., 2013 for the US). Migrants with no intention to stay permanently (temporary migrants and commuters) tend to have less incentive to invest in a language, in particular a language which is rather unimportant in their home country's labour market (Dustmann, 1993, 1999; Chiswick and Miller, 2001, 2007, 2008; Isphording and Otten, 2013; Dustmann and Gorlach, 2015). In his later work, using survey information on immigrants' intended migration duration and instrumenting this variable with unforeseen events (e.g. family deaths in the home country), Dustmann (1999) shows that those with non-permanent intentions do indeed invest less in learning. Moreover migrants are aware of the fact that host country language skills may depreciate during the periods of leave from the country.

Language used by family or household members also affects the migrant's exposure. The effect of fluent family members, however, depends on the role they are playing. If they act as translators they reduce incentives for language acquisition; if they act as teachers, they improve the language skills of immigrants (Chiswick and Miller, 2005; Meng and Gregory, 2005). Marriage before migration also tends to be less effective with respect to language learning compared to marriage after migration (Dustmann, 1994; Chiswick and Miller, 2005, 2007; Chiswick and Houseworth, 2011). Children affect their parents' proficiency as they can serve as teachers (Chiswick, 1998; Chiswick and Miller, 2005, 2007, 2008).

12.3.2   Efficiency in language learning

It is not equally easy for all newcomers to learn the language of their host country. One of the key factors in efficiency of learning is the age at immigration.

Learning is easy for children and much more difficult at later age: existing studies consistently find a negative relationship between age of arrival and language acquisition. There is a long-standing debate among linguists on the age range within which language learning is almost effortless and after which it becomes much more difficult to become fluent and have no foreign accent (Chiswick and Miller, 2001, 2008; Mayberry et al., 2001; Isphording and Otten, 2013).

It is also easier for immigrants to acquire a language if their own native language is linguistically closer to that to be learned (Chiswick and Miller, 2001, 2005; Isphording, 2014; Isphording and Otten, 2014). Isphording (2014) shows that immigrants drop behind native speakers in their literacy score as the distance between the language of origin and destination (as measured by the Levenshtein index which takes into account phonetics) increases. Although this gap improves over time, it takes years to close down. Isphording (2014) argues that linguistic distance interacts with the effect of age at arrival: immigrants who moved after age 11 and come from linguistically distant countries are the most disadvantaged. Those who moved as small children face only very small 'distance' problems. But according to the study, adults face a much steeper learning curve (Isphording, 2014). This has important consequences since estimates show that there is a relationship between better reading and writing abilities and employment possibilities. The cause for not performing well in the host country may thus eventually be due to linguistic (and cultural) distance.

Education is one of the factors influencing efficiency in language acquisition. Several studies document the fact that highly educated immigrants tend to be more proficient in the host country language and tend to be faster in learning a new language (Dustmann, 1994; Chiswick, 1998; Isphording and Otten, 2013, 2014).

In addition to age at arrival and linguistic distance, there are a number of usually non-observables such as motivation, psychological factors and cognitive abilities that influence efficiency. These differ according to whether migrants move for economic reasons, family reasons or whether they are refugees. Family migrants and refugees tend to be less favourably selected in terms of abilities than economic migrants (Chiswick, 1999). Refugees, in particular, would probably not move under normal conditions or peace. The literature confirms that economic migrants are more proficient in the host country language than refugees, while family-based migrants are somewhere in-between (Chiswick and Miller, 2006, 2007).

12.3.3 Economic incentives

Language acquisition depends also on economic incentives such as higher earnings (which will be detailed in Section 12.4) or better job prospects. Acquisition is also positively affected by the expected duration of the stay (Dustmann, 1999; Chiswick and Miller, 2006, 2007, 2008; Isphording and Otten, 2014).

12.3.4 Language-based policies of integration of immigrants

Although language skills generally improve with the duration of residence in the host country (Chiswick and Miller, 1994, 1995), a formal integration policy in the form of language training may accelerate integration. It is, however, not straightforward to evaluate the effects of language training. A problem may arise if language skills are unobserved or measured with considerable error, since immigrants may self-select into language training based on their language proficiency, which may in turn cause a bias in the estimated effects of participation. A number of recent papers evaluate the effects of language courses on immigrants' language proficiency and labour market outcomes while addressing those potential selection processes. The majority of studies find a significant positive effect of training programmes on language proficiency and on labour market outcomes (see Cohen-Goldner and Eckstein, 2008, 2010 for Israel; Andersson and Nekby, 2012 for Sweden; Clausen et al., 2009 and Heinesen et al., 2013 for Denmark; Sarvimäki and Hämäläinen, 2015 for Finland). Sarvimäki and Hämäläinen (2015) find large positive effects on employment and earnings from a reform of immigrant integration programs that re-allocate resources from traditional Active Labour Market Programmes (ALMPs) towards a training specifically designed for immigrants, in particular more language training. The authors claim that the effects come not only from language skills per se, but also from the match between immigrants' pre-migration skills and language training, thus improving skill transferability of immigrants into the host country labour market.

12.4 Language and the returns to human capital

In economic theory, language proficiency and foreign language command is viewed as part of human capital, and in the same way as formal education, it is productive and thus rewarded in the labour market (see Chiswick, 2008; Chiswick and Miller, 2007, 2014 for a general overview). Language proficiency like other forms of human capital is tied inevitably to a given person, and is both beneficial and costly to acquire. The benefits of good language command show up through better economic outcomes such as higher earnings, better employment possibilities, and occupations matching migrants' education and skills, as well as increased efficiency in search for goods and services.

In addition, language skills influence a number of non-economic outcomes such as social integration and the size of the social network, civil and political participation and engagement, education, health and family life, such as intermarriage and parenting. Costs of language skill acquisition come up in the form of effort and time spent on learning, costs of classes, as well as indirect costs of foregone earnings while learning.

A large part of the literature on the relation between language and returns to human capital concerns immigrants because the command of the host country's language is fundamental for their integration. Numerous studies find that lack of destination language proficiency has a large detrimental impact on economic assimilation as measured by earnings and employment (see e.g. Dustmann, 1994; Chiswick and Miller, 1995, 1996, 2001, 2002; Kossoudji, 1988; Leslie and Lindley, 2001; Schaafsma and Sweetman, 2001; Dustmann and van Soest, 2002; Lindley, 2002; Dustmann and Fabbri, 2003; Bleakley and Chin, 2004; Rooth and Saarela, 2007). In the next subsection, we review some of the key references related to immigrant language proficiency and returns to human capital.

The effects of language proficiency on labour market outcomes, particularly on earnings, have received the largest attention in the literature. One of the reasons for focusing on earnings is the greater availability of data on wages, or income in general, than on other outcomes.

In analyses of language and earnings, some type of 'Mincerian wage equation' is used, where the natural logarithm of wage is regressed on a number of explanatory variables. The choice of variables often depends on available data (such as register-based longitudinal data, longitudinal household surveys, linked employer–employee data). The equation typically includes human capital variables (education, labour market experience and tenure), demographic and household characteristics (age, gender, ethnicity, parental background, children, marital status and other household characteristics) and a number of other controls such as employer and regional characteristics as well as variables capturing information about immigrants themselves (years since migration, destination language proficiency, characteristics of ethnic concentration in the region in which they live, as a proxy for ethno-linguistic enclaves and networks).

The main findings suggest that fluency in the host-country language can increase earnings of immigrants in a range of 5–35 per cent. Work in this area is surveyed in greater detail below.

12.4.1   Methodological problems

One of the main concerns that arise when trying to estimate the effect of language proficiency on earnings and other socio-economic outcomes is that proficiency itself might be affected by the outcomes, and therefore reverse causality may be an issue. Additionally, the fluency of an immigrant in the destination language is likely to be correlated with other unobserved factors that may also impact on earnings such as openness to new surroundings, exchanges with natives, extent of the migrant's networks, his or her ability or attitudes towards preserving the culture of his or her country of origin, among others. Finally, there might be a problem of measurement error stemming from self-reported language proficiency. Those errors could be either random or persistent over time, if individuals have the tendency consistently to over or under-report their true language skills (Dustmann and van Soest, 2001). As a result, ordinary least squares (OLS) estimates of the effect of proficiency of the destination language on earnings and other outcomes are likely to be biased and do not produce causal estimates. The problems of endogeneity of language proficiency, measurement errors and unobserved heterogeneity pose considerable challenges.

The literature has adopted different strategies to tackle the problems. Most empirical studies rely on an instrumental variable (IV) approach, in which a predicted language proficiency variable enters the Mincerian equation. A number of instruments have been used to address endogeneity issues (see Shields and Wheatley Price, 2002; Chiswick and Miller, 2014 for a summary on which we will rely). Some popular instruments are veteran status, foreign inter-marriage, children and minority languages concentration measures (e.g. in Chiswick and Miller, 1994; Chiswick, 1998), father's education (Dustmann and van Soest, 2002), language of the interview used in the survey (Shields and Wheatley, 2002) and age of arrival (Bleakley and Chin, 2004, 2010). The coefficients obtained by IV estimation are usually larger than those obtained by OLS, which suggests that the potential upward bias from reverse causality and unobserved heterogeneity overweighs the downward bias from misreporting (Dustmann and van Soest, 2002; Dustmann and Fabbri, 2003; Bleakley and Chin, 2004).

One of the most popular instrumental-variables strategy has focused on the sample of migrants who arrive at the destination country as children. A reason to focus on such individuals and on their age at immigration is that there seem to be critical ages at which people acquire certain particular skills, such as proficiency in the local language. An ample literature shows that fluency in the language of the destination decreases with age at immigration (Chiswick, 1991; Stevens, 1992, 1999; Espenshade and Fu, 1997; Massey and Espinosa, 1997; Akresh et al., 2007).

Bleakley and Chin (2004) show that outcomes of immigrants from non-English speaking countries systematically differ from those of other migrants only among those arriving after the *critical period* for language acquisition (11 years old). They use individual-level data from the US Census of 1990 to study how earnings of immigrants who arrived before age 18, and were 25–38 years old in 1990, were related to their age at arrival. Consistent with the existence of a critical period of language acquisition, they show that there are no significant differences in adult English proficiency among immigrants from English and non-English speaking countries who migrated very early in life. Moreover, while the relation between age at arrival and English proficiency is flat for migrants from English-speaking countries, proficiency decreases almost linearly with age at arrival for those from non-English speaking countries who arrived after that age. Bleakley and Chin (2004) provide an identification strategy for the causal impact of language proficiency on earnings by exploiting these differences between younger and older arrivals on English language skills to construct an instrumental variable for English proficiency. Age at migration on its own is likely to affect socio-economic outcomes of migrants through channels other than language (such as better networks or knowledge of local norms) and, as a result, it may fail the exclusion restriction as an instrumental variable. They use immigrants from English-speaking countries to control for the impact of age at migration, which is unrelated to English fluency.

Bleakley and Chin (2004) estimate a first stage equation by OLS for English proficiency ENG_{ija} for an individual i born in country j who arrived in the US at age a:

$$ENG_{ija} = \alpha_1 + \pi_1 k_{ija} + \gamma_{1j} + \delta_{1a} + X_{ija}\rho + \varepsilon_{ija}, \qquad (1)$$

where γ_{1j} is fixed country of birth effects, δ_{1a} is fixed age at arrival effects, and X_{ija} is a vector of exogenous explanatory variables which characterize immigrants (sex, race, age). Noting that the outcomes obtained by immigrants arriving from English and non-English speaking countries start to diverge after the age of arrival of 11, they use as instrument for language proficiency a variable constructed by interacting a, the age at arrival (beyond the critical age of 11) and where $I(j)$ takes the value one when the country of origin j is non-English speaking:

$$k_{ija} = \max(0, a - 11) \times I(j). \qquad (2)$$

Results point to a strong negative relationship between English proficiency and the instrument k_{ija} in (2). Using fitted values for English proficiency from (1), they estimate a second stage equation where the dependent variable is the annual wage rate:

$$\ln W_{ija} = \alpha + \beta ENG^*_{ija} + \gamma_j + \delta_a + X_{ija} + \eta_{ija}, \qquad (3)$$

where ENG^*_{ija} are the fitted values obtained from regression (1). The estimated impact of language proficiency on earnings is higher in IV than OLS estimates. They explain those somewhat surprising differences by arguing that even though OLS should be upward biased by ability, measurement errors in language skills are likely to be responsible for the downward bias of the OLS coefficient. Results are robust to different specifications and to the exclusion of migrants from Canada.

A key finding of the paper is that higher educational attainment appears to be the mechanism behind the effect of language on earnings. Overall, a one unit increase of English ability (a variable that ranges from 0 to 3) implies an increase of about 0.33 (log) wages in very basic models. In specifications that also include education as an exogenous variable, the estimated impact of proficiency decreases by a factor of 3 and then by a factor of 10 when returns to schooling are also accounted for in the model. Higher educational attainment seems to be responsible for about 90 per cent of the impact of language fluency on earnings. As we discuss later, the same mechanism may be at play in other socio-economic spheres of migrants' lives.

12.4.2 Language and migrants' earnings

The rich literature on the role of language proficiency on earnings covers a range of languages, countries and time periods. There is a consensus in the literature that language proficiency has a positive effect on earnings, although the size of the effect varies. In particular, research in this area suggests that fluency in the host-country language can increase earnings of immigrants in a range of 5–35 per cent (Chiswick and Miller, 2014 for a summary; Dustmann 1994; Chiswick and Miller, 1995, 1996, 2003; Dustmann and van Soest, 2001, 2002; Leslie and Lindley, 2001; Lindley, 2002; Bleakley and Chin, 2004, 2008; Rooth and Saarela, 2007). We now review a couple of key studies in different countries.

In the US, a number of studies have been conducted on returns to English. Chiswick and Miller (1995) are among the first to use an IV approach to account for potential endogeneity of language. They find that the language premium for male immigrants' earnings is larger than 20 per cent. By exploiting differences on adult English proficiency between immigrants from non-English speaking countries who arrive as young children versus others, Bleakley and Chin (2004, 2010) find that linguistic competence is a key variable to explain disparities in terms of educational attainment, earnings and social outcomes.

Dustmann (1994) analyses the effect of German language proficiency on earnings in Germany, using cross-sectional data of immigrants from the German Socio-Economical Panel survey. Applying OLS with a Heckman selection correction, he finds that there is a 7 per cent earnings premium for both men and women due to speaking proficiency, and 7 and 15 per cent for writing proficiency for men and women, respectively. Dustmann and van Soest (2002) exploit the same panel to address the potential endogeneity of language as well as potential misreporting errors. Using the father's education and leads and lags of language skills as an exogenous variation in their IV regressions, they find a 12–14 per cent earnings premium for those who speak fluent German.

Using UK cross-sectional data from Fourth National Survey on Ethnic Minorities (FNSEM) and Family and Working Lives Survey (FWLS) surveys, Dustmann and Fabbri (2003) evaluate effects of English language command on earnings and employment probabilities of immigrants in the UK. They use a propensity score estimator with ethnic minority concentrations and number of children as instruments to deal with unobserved heterogeneity and endogeneity. They show that the effect of English proficiency on earnings ranges between 10 and 36 per cent depending on the empirical method used. Miranda and Zhu (2013) study the language effects on the immigrant–native wage gap in the UK. Using the critical age-based instrument, they find a 23–25 per cent wage premium to speaking English as an additional language.

Adserà and Chiswick (2007) employ the European Community Household Panel (1994–2000) to study the earnings of immigrants by gender across Europe. Controlling for countries of destination, they find that the earnings of migrants whose mother tongue belongs to the same language group as that of the country of destination (Romance, English, Nordic or German/Dutch) are 11 and 14.5 per cent higher for women and men, compared to those coming from a different linguistic group. Results are fairly close if a dummy for common language is included. They also find that a large proportion of migrants move to European countries with similar languages since, other things being equal, adjustment costs are lower (Chiswick and Miller, 1995, 1998; Chiswick, 1998; Adserà and Pytliková, 2015).

For Israel, Chiswick (1998) uses an IV approach with age at arrival as instrument. He finds that using Hebrew as the primary language increases male immigrants' earnings by as much as 35 per cent.[3]

A recent study by Budría and Swedberg (2012) examines the effect of Spanish proficiency on earnings in Spain. Using a dummy variable for arrival in Spain before age ten as instrument, they find that Spanish proficiency raises wages by some 27 per cent. Di Paolo and Raymond (2012) find an 18 per cent premium to Catalan proficiency. In addition to the critical age instrument, they also use the following as alternative instruments: owing a library with more than 100 books at home, reading frequently, speaking Catalan at home, watching Catalan news and reading newspapers, and ethnic composition of regions.

Adserà and Ferrer (2014b) assess whether language plays a different role for immigrants and native-born in Canada. They combine large samples of four Canadian censuses (1991–2006), the linguistic proximity of the immigrant's mother tongue to English or French, and information of the occupational skills of the job the immigrant holds. They find that the wages of migrants whose mother tongues have little connection to English (or French) do not converge to similar levels as those whose languages are closer to English (or French). In addition their jobs tend to require more physical strength and lower analytical requirements than those of native speakers.

Finally, Yao and van Ours (2015) analyse the role of language played on labour market performance of immigrants in the Netherlands. They find

---

[3] Note that among later studies, age at arrival in host countries will become a commonly used instrument for language skills.

that women with low Dutch proficiency have 48 per cent lower wages than Dutch-proficient females with similar characteristics, whereas for males Dutch language skills seem to be less important. In fact, and contrary to all previous studies, the authors find no Dutch wage premium for male immigrants. They argue that this may be a consequence of the fact that many immigrants are fluent in English, which makes communication between natives and immigrants easier. Given that they had no information on English proficiency in their data, they could not dig deeper into this issue.

12.4.3   The premium of foreign language knowledge

A growing number of papers report significant returns to foreign language skills among natives in developed countries. Saiz and Zoido (2005) study the returns to foreign languages among US college graduates. Their results suggest a 2%–3% wage premium for college graduates who can speak a second language. Williams (2011) reports significant earnings premia for foreign language usage at work in 12 European countries. Ginsburgh and Prieto-Rodriguez (2011) confirm the substantial return to English proficiency in several European countries. Lang and Siniver (2009) show significantly important returns to English in Israel (as well as Hebrew among immigrants from Russia), although the return to English appears heterogeneous for different groups of workers. Sizable returns to English were found in Germany for both native Germans and immigrants; returns are particularly large for immigrants in part because they tend to work in the service sector which is linked to higher trade (Stöhr, 2015).

The return to foreign language proficiency has been analysed as well in a few other countries: Latvia and Estonia, South Africa, India and Turkey. Toomet (2011) finds that local languages do not pay off in Latvia and Estonia, while English proficiency produces a significant premium. Levinsohn (2007) and Casale and Posel (2011) report high returns to English in South Africa. So do Azam et al. (2013) for English in India. Di Paolo and Tansel (2015) find positive and significant returns to English and Russian in Turkey, which increase with the level of competence. Isphording (2013) detects high returns to English, German and French on the Spanish labour market. Thus, the evidence confirms that foreign language proficiency is a valuable asset both in developed and developing countries.

12.4.4   Language as a mediator of skill and knowledge transfer

As should be clear from the previous sections, numerous studies have shown that language plays a significant role in mediating the rate of return to formal education and labour market skills. Immigrants with a good command of the host country's language have much higher returns to human capital than those with poor language command. Thus learning the host country language is a key factor to acquiring educational and labour market skills.

Language is also an important mediator of knowledge transfer. A recent strand of literature focuses for instance on the effects of ethnic diversity on the host country's economy. In particular, ethnic diversity may bring substantial benefits in terms of firm innovation, productivity and exports (Parrotta et al., 2014a). Employees of different cultural backgrounds can provide diverse perspectives, valuable ideas and problem-solving abilities; they also facilitate achieving optimal creative solutions and stimulate innovation (Hong and Page, 2004). Employees of different ethnic backgrounds may stimulate firms to improve or develop new products sold abroad as they also possess knowledge about other markets and customers' tastes (Osborne, 2000; Kerr and Lincoln, 2010). However, ethnic diversity may also create communication barriers, reduce workforce cohesion and prevent cooperative participation in production activities, which in turn may hinder knowledge spillovers and exchange among employees and workers (Lazear, 1999). Thus, benefits of ethnically diverse workforces in firms can materialize best when the costs of cross-cultural dealings are minimized. Recent studies show that language skills play an important role in reducing communication barriers and create a bridge for knowledge transfer (Parrotta et al., 2014a,b).

12.4.5 The impact of language-based immigration policies

As noted before, migration policies are likely to affect the characteristics of newcomers to a country. To understand differences in human capital among Canadian migrants, Aydemir (2011) employs the Longitudinal Survey of Immigrants to Canada, which offers information on short-run labour market outcomes of migrants after arrival. The study focuses more on the effect of different visa types that signal the immigrant skills. Aydemir distinguishes two different types of migrants: skilled workers and those who arrive for family reunification reasons. He finds that immigrants under the skilled workers programme have much higher levels of educational attainment than family-reunited immigrants. Even spouses of main applicants under the skilled workers programme have more years of schooling than people under other immigration policy. Such positive educational selection is, however, not always accompanied by positive effects on labour outcomes such as labour force participation, employment and earnings. To analyse these effects, the author uses selection across visa categories. Results show that males under both immigration programmes have similar labour market results, but females from the skilled workers group enjoy a higher level of labour participation than those coming through family reunification. The author explains that this may be due to the fact that men are investing in local human capital in the beginning, and women temporarily enter the labour force to support the family. Therefore, in the short run, women earn more and enjoy a larger labour force participation and a lower unemployment rate. Cobb-Clark et al. (2005) find similar results.[4]

Another interesting outcome discussed by Aydemir (2011) is that schooling and experience have no or even a negative effect on the participation in the labour force and employment, and a small positive effect on earnings for men, but not for women. Regression estimates show that ability in speaking the local language has significant and positive effects on labour market outcomes, whereas linguistic skills in reading and writing have no effect. Overall, the author argues that in countries with point systems, in which education, experience and language abilities increase the likelihood of obtaining entry, labour market returns among new migrants are not significantly different in the short run than in countries without such point policies. Family class migrants can enjoy higher labour participation rates, as well as earnings, because they have probably much better access to local information than other migrants. They can use their family networks, while those who arrive as skilled workers are less likely to have access to a network during the first years after migration.

12.5   Language and migrants' socio-economic assimilation

As noted in the previous section, language proficiency is not only expected to affect earnings but also an array of other socio-economic outcomes such as fertility, health, marriage patterns and residential choice.

12.5.1   Fertility

The role of language in the fertility behaviour of migrants is perhaps the most widely studied in different contexts (especially in the US) and with different methods. Existing analyses find greater English fluency to be associated with lower fertility in the US (Sorenson, 1988; Swicegood et al., 1988; Bleakley and Chin, 2010) and Canada (Adserà and Ferrer, 2014a). Some early papers on the subject focus on Mexican immigrants in the US. Sorensen (1988) employs a set of new questions on language use and English proficiency introduced for the first time in the 1980 US Census. She studies fertility patterns of 40–44-year-old women in endogamous Mexican American and non-Hispanic white couples living in Texas, New Mexico and Arizona. Results show that the likelihood of having an additional child at any parity level decreases with English use at home by both the wife and the husband even after educational attainment and

---

[4] Adserà and Ferrer (2014c) show that recent women migrants to Canada do not drop out of the labour force after the first years but rather their participation continues to increase with the number of years spent in the country.

English proficiency of the couple is taken into account. Among non-Hispanic couples, the likelihood to transit to parity five or more is also higher among those with low English proficiency who do not speak English at home, even after controlling for educational attainment and place of birth.

In a closely related paper, Swicegood et al. (1988) study the impact of English proficiency on fertility outcomes among ever-married Mexican–American women aged 15–44 in the 5 per cent Public Use Microdata Sample from the 1980 US Census. They find that the total number of children ever born to a woman and the presence of children under three in the household decreases with English proficiency and that the impact of proficiency is larger among the most educated and younger women in the sample. Swicegood et al. (1988) note that those behavioural patterns seem to be more related to opportunity cost calculations than to cultural differences.

A problem with the use of language proficiency in econometric models is its potential endogeneity. Individuals with better language skills may have other unobservable characteristics closer to natives that are also related to other social outcomes. In addition, migrant selectivity may imply that the fertility plans of new immigrants may resemble more those of natives in the destination country than the fertility behaviour of their peers in the source country, even before they arrive at their new location. Certain migration policies in destination countries may bolster this selection process. In the 1990s, Canadian immigration policies, for example, targeted educated immigrants and instituted a point system that rewards knowledge of English or French. As a result, recent waves of Canadian immigrants are relatively more educated and closer to Canadian natives than elsewhere. Similar policies are also in place in Australia. Taking selectivity into account is always a data challenge since it is generally necessary to have information from both destination and source countries to ascertain the degree of selection. In her analysis of fertility among immigrants in the US, Kahn (1988) conducts one of the first attempts in the literature. She uses country-level information on fertility in source countries as well as characteristics of the immigrants themselves compared to those of their countries of origin to check whether they play a role in the fertility adaptation of migrants to US patterns. She finds that the fertility behaviour of those who are more assimilated (duration of the stay in the US, intermarriage or language proficiency) is closer to US norms than to source-country norms.

As explained when discussing the effect of language on earnings, restricting the analysis to migrants who arrived as children may address some of the endogeneity concerns since researchers can exploit differences in age at arrival that are associated with critical learning periods. In the case of fertility, if cultural norms regarding reproductive behaviour that are formed at a particular age (for instance, the onset of puberty) are difficult to adjust later in life (Ryder, 1973), age at migration can have an additional meaning. A mother tongue that is not one of the official languages at destination may make it difficult for a child to access local cultural cues through school and peers to form his or her fertility preferences.

Bleakley and Chin (2010) rely on the same instrument as in their earlier work to show that the outcomes of immigrants from non-English speaking countries systematically differ from those of other migrants only among those arriving after the critical period for language acquisition of nine years of age. Among other socio-economic outcomes, they study fertility patterns of migrants who arrived before age 15 and are currently between ages 25 and 55 in the 2000 US census. In their first stage regression they find a sizable effect of age at arrival on language proficiency among those arriving from a non-English speaking country. English proficiency (measured on a scale of 0 to 3) decreases by 0.1 for each arrival year after age nine. The second stage regression on fertility outcomes is fitted for all individuals in the sample as well as separately by gender. The number of children present in the household of immigrants with higher English fluency is smaller than for others, even though English-proficient women are not significantly more likely to be childless. Differences at the extensive margin also account for the lower number of children among more English-proficient men, though they disappear when the sample is restricted to married men. Single parenthood or out-of-wedlock births are not significantly associated with English proficiency. These findings are robust to controlling for the interaction between age at arrival with either the fertility rate or GDP per capita in their country of origin as well as to dropping either Canada or Mexico from the sample of migrants.

Though they do not use an IV strategy, Adserà and Ferrer (2014a) estimate the fertility of Canadian migrants who arrived before adulthood at different ages, relative to that of natives. They estimate these models separately for two groups of migrants depending on whether or not their mother tongue is an official language in their Canadian province of residence (either English or French). They find no sharp discontinuity around age nine, as do Bleakley and Chin (2010), but rather an increasing relative fertility for later arrival ages for both groups. Nonetheless fertility is lower among immigrants with English or French as their official mother tongue than among others for every age at arrival.

Even though they do not employ linguistic proficiency directly, a set of papers highlight cultural differences in explaining the diversity of fertility patterns across origins (Fernandez and Fogli, 2006; Georgiadis and Manning, 2011).

12.5.2   Other social outcomes

Most relevant studies on migrants' marriage literature include some indicator of language ability as a control in the regressions that estimate the probability of intermarriage. In general they find that higher proficiency in the language of the country of destination reduces the probability of endogamous marriages (Stevens and Swicegood, 1987 for the US; Meng and Gregory, 2005 for Australia, among others). Consistent with this finding, Duncan and Trejo (2007) show that Mexican Americans who intermarry tend to be more fluent in English (besides being more educated and enjoying larger earnings) than those who marry other Mexicans (both immigrants and US born). Bleakley and Chin (2010) show that the positive effect of language ability on the probability of marrying someone of the same ancestry is robust to endogeneity considerations and that spousal quality (in terms of education and earnings) increases with fluency. In addition they find that English proficiency decreases the probability of being married, both by decreasing the probability of ever having married and increasing the probability of being divorced (Bleakley and Chin, 2010). Results by Dávila and Mora (2001) are somewhat mixed. English proficiency decreases the probability of being married among women, but increases it for men.

Language proficiency is shown to affect health outcomes among immigrants. Clark and Isphording (2015) focus on the impact of language proficiency on the health of children who migrated to Australia. Using instrumental variable techniques similar to those of Bleakley and Chin (2004), they discover a large negative effect of English deficiency on physical health.

Finally a couple of papers study the influence of language ability on residential choice. Language is often considered the dependent variable, such as in Lazear (2007) who looks at the role of linguistic enclaves on proficiency. Otherwise the literature finds that individuals with poorer language skills tend to live in neighbourhoods with large shares of individuals from their country of origin (Funkhouser and Ramos, 1993 for Dominicans and Cubans in the US; Toussaint-Comeau and Rhine, 2004 for Mexicans in Chicago; Bleakley and Chin, 2010 across Public Use Microdata Areas in the US). Bertrand et al. (2000) use the density of linguistic enclaves to study whether it independently influences an individual's welfare participation by facilitating the transmission of knowledge and attitudes toward welfare in their community.

12.5.3 Second generation

Some researchers analyse the impact of language use at home and linguistic background of the parents to explain outcomes of the second generation (see for example, Grogger and Trejo, 2002; White and Glick, 2009). Leon (2003) employs ability to read/write with English fluency to estimate the impact of parental human capital on second-generation school enrolment in the 1910 and 1920 censuses. Bleakley and Chin (2008) use a similar instrumental variable strategy as in their other works to analyse whether the impact of the difference in linguistic proficiency of parents carries on to second-generation educational outcomes. They rely on the 2000 US Census to find that English proficiency by immigrant parents has a significant impact on their US-born children's proficiency while they are young, but it does not explain fluency differences later in life. Further, they find that parental English proficiency has a positive impact on pre-school attendance and that the poorer English proficiency at the time of school entry of children of less fluent immigrants increases their chances of dropping out of high school or being held back.

Using a comprehensive longitudinal dataset on immigrants and their children, Casey and Dustmann (2008) investigate the intergenerational transmission of language skills among immigrants, and the effect of language skills on the economic performance of second-generation immigrants. There is a positive association between parents' and children's fluency, conditional on parental and family characteristics. Parental fluency through the ultimate language proficiency of their children affects female labour market outcomes.

12.6   Conclusion

This chapter has provided a summary of research on the importance of language for immigrants in their decision to move and for their successful assimilation and integration in their host countries. We have also discussed research on factors which influence language learning and language proficiency.

We first reviewed the literature on determinants of migration with a special focus on language. Migrants take their language skills into consideration when deciding whether and where to migrate. Knowing the host country language or speaking a language that is closer to the host-country language means lower costs of migration and adaptation in comparison to moving to a country where the migrant must learn a distant language. Almost all empirical studies confirm that language and linguistic distances play an important role on migrants' decisions to migrate and on their choice of destination.

We also provided a summary of research on the determinants of language proficiency among migrants. It is very important to know which factors affect language acquisition, since being able to communicate is crucial to the successful integration into the host country's labour market and society. Research in this area focuses on pre- and post-migration exposure to the host country's language, and on efficiency and economic incentives to language acquisition.

Finally, we have provided an overview of the returns to language acquisition. Migrants with a good language command experience better economic outcomes such as higher earnings, larger employment probabilities and better occupational matches. In addition, the benefits of language acquisition show up in a number of non-economic outcomes such as social integration and size of social network, civil and political participation and engagement, education, health and family life. Yet, language learning also generates some costs such as effort and time spent on language learning, direct costs on language classes, as well as indirect costs of foregone earnings while learning. There are important policy implications that can be derived from the existing research on returns to language skills. Encouraging immigrants to invest in language acquisition and proficiency through, for instance, language classes and training programmes would make their assimilation easier, benefiting both immigrants and host economies. There is also some new research on the effect of language on other social outcomes, such as fertility, intermarriage and health. Although the area is rather under-researched, it still provides some important insights for policy-makers and migrants as well.

Acknowledgements

The authors would like to thank Ingo Isphording for his comments on an earlier version of the chapter. Pytliková's research was funded in part by the Operational Programme Education for Competitiveness (No. CZ.1.07/2.3.00/20.0296) by a Czech Science Foundation grant (No. GA15-23177S) and by an SGS Research grant (No. SP2015/120).

References

A. Adserà and B. Chiswick (2007) 'Are There Gender Differences in Immigrant Labor Market Outcomes Across European Countries?', *Journal of Population Economics*, 20, 495–526.

A. Adserà and A. Ferrer (2014a) 'Factors Influencing the Fertility Choices of Child Immigrants in Canada', *Population Studies*, 68, 65–79.

A. Adserà and A. Ferrer (2014b) 'The Effect of Linguistic Proximity on the Occupational Assimilation of Immigrant Men', CLSRN Working Paper 144.

A. Adserà and A. Ferrer (2014c) 'The Myth of Immigrant Women as Secondary Workers: Evidence from Canada', *American Economic Review*, 104, 360–364.

A. Adserà and M. Pytliková (2015) 'The Role of Languages in Shaping International Migration', *Economic Journal*, 586, 49–81.

R. Akresh, P. Verwimp and T. Bundervoet (2007) 'Civil War, Crop Failure, and Child Stunting in Rwanda', World Bank Policy Research Working Paper 4208.

J. Andersson and L. Nekby (2012) 'Intensive Coaching of New Immigrants: An Evaluation Based on Random Program Assignment', *Scandinavian Journal of Economics*, 114, 575–600.

A. Aydemir (2011) 'Immigrant Selection and Short-Term Labor Market Outcomes by Visa Category', *Journal of Population Economics*, 24, 451–475.

M. Azam, A. Chin and N. Prakash (2013) 'The Returns to English-language Skills in India', *Economic Development and Cultural Change*, 61, 335–367.

T. Bauer, G. Epstein and I. Gang (2005) 'Enclaves, Language, and the Location Choice of Migrants', *Journal of Population Economics*, 18, 649–662.

J. Beckhusen, F. Raymond, T. de Graaff, J. Poot and B. Waldorf (2013) 'Living and Working in Ethnic Enclaves: Language Proficiency of Immigrants in U.S. Metropolitan Areas', *Papers in Regional Science*, 92, 305–398.

M. Beine, F. Docquier and C. Ozden (2011) 'Diasporas', *Journal of Development Economics*, 95, 30–41.

M. Beine and S. Salomone (2013) 'Network Effect in International Migration: Does Education Matter more than Gender?', *Scandinavian Journal of Economics*, 115, 354–380.

M. Belot and S. Ederveen (2012) 'Cultural and Institutional Barriers in Migration between OECD Countries', *Journal of Population Economics*, 25, 1077–1105.

M. Belot and T. Hatton (2012) 'Skill Selection and Immigration in OECD countries', *Scandinavian Journal of Economic*, 114, 681–730.

M. Bertrand, M. Luttmer and S. Mullainathan (2000) 'Network Effects and Welfare Cultures', *The Quarterly Journal of Economics*, 115, 1019–1055.

H. Bleakley and A. Chin (2004) 'Language Skills and Earnings: Evidence from Childhood Immigrants', *Review of Economics and Statistics*, 84, 481–496.

H. Bleakley and A. Chin (2008) 'The Intergenerational Transmission of Language Human Capital among Immigrants', *Journal of Human Resources*, 43, 267–298.

H. Bleakley and A. Chin (2010) 'Age at Arrival, English Proficiency, and Social Assimilation among US Immigrants', *American Economic Journal: Applied Economics*, 2, 165–192.

M. Boyd (2009) 'Language at Work: The Impact of Linguistic Enclaves on Immigrant Economic Integration', Canadian Labour Market and Skills Researcher Network Working Paper No. 41.

S. Budría and P. Swedberg (2012) 'The Impact of Language Proficiency on Immigrants' Earnings in Spain', IZA Discussion Paper No. 6957.

D. Casale and D. Posel (2011) 'English Language Proficiency and Earnings in a Developing Country: The Case of South Africa', *The Journal of Socio-Economics*, 40, 385–393.

T. Casey and C. Dustmann (2008) 'Intergenerational Transmission of Language Capital and Economic Outcomes', *Journal of Human Resources*, 43, 299–324.

B. Chiswick (1991) 'Speaking, Reading and Earnings among Low-Skilled Immigrants', *Journal of Labor Economics*, 9, 149–170.

B. Chiswick (1998) 'Hebrew Language Usage: Determinants and Effects on Earnings Among Immigrants in Israel', *Journal of Population Economics*, 11(2), 253–271.

B. Chiswick (1999) 'Are Immigrants Favorably Self-Selected?', *American Economic Review*, 89, 181–185.

B. Chiswick (2008) 'The Economics of Language: An Introduction and Overview', IZA Working Paper 3568.

B. Chiswick and P. Miller (1994) 'The Complementarity of Language and Other Human Capital: Immigrant Earnings in Canada', *Economics of Education Review*, 22, 469–480.

B. Chiswick and P. Miller (1995) 'The Endogeneity Between Language and Earnings: International Analyses', *Journal of Labor Economics*, 13, 246–288.

B. Chiswick and P. Miller (1996) 'Ethnic Networks and Language Proficiency among Immigrants', *Journal of Population Economics*, 9, 19–35.

B. Chiswick and P. Miller (1998) 'English Language Fluency among Immigrants in the United States', *Research in Labor Economics*, 17, 151–200.

B. Chiswick and P. Miller (2001) 'A Model of Destination-Language Acquisition: Application to Male Immigrants in Canada', *Demography*, 38, 391–409.

B. Chiswick and P. Miller (2002) 'Immigrant Earnings: Language Skills, Linguistic Concentrations and the Business Cycle', *Journal of Population Economics*, 15, 31–57.

B. Chiswick and P. Miller (2005) 'Do Enclaves Matter in Immigrant Adjustment?', *City and Community*, 4, 5–35.

B. Chiswick and P. Miller (2006) 'Language Skills and Immigrant Adjustment: The Role of Immigration Policy' In D. Cobb-Clark, R. Henderson and Siew-Ean Khar (eds) *Public Policy and Immigrant Settlement* (Cheltenham: Edward Elgar), pp. 121–148.

B. Chiswick and P. Miller (2007) 'Computer Usage, Destination Language Proficiency and the Earnings of Natives and Immigrants', *Review of the Economics of the Household*, 5, 129–157.

B. Chiswick and P.W. Miller (2008) 'Why Is Payoff to Schooling Smaller for Immigrants?', *Labour Economics*, 15, 1317–1340.

B. Chiswick and C. Houseworth (2011) 'Ethnic Intermarriage among Immigrants: Human Capital and Assortative Mating', *Review of Economics of the Household*, 9, 149–180.

B. Chiswick and P. Miller (2014) 'International Migration and the Economics of Language' In B. Chiswick and P. Miller (eds) *Handbook on the Economics of International Migration* Volume 1A (Amsterdam: North-Holland), pp. 211–270.

X. Clark, T. Hatton and J. Williamson (2007) 'Explaining U.S. Immigration, 1971–1998', *The Review of Economics and Statistics*, 89, 359–373.

A. Clarke and I. Isphording (2015) 'Language Barriers in Immigrant Health Production', IZA Discussion Paper 8846.

J. Clausen, E. Heinesen, H. Hummelgaard, L. Husted and M. Rosholm (2009) 'The Effect of Integration Policies on the Time until Regular Employment of Newly Arrived Immigrants: Evidence from Denmark', *Labour Economics*, 16, 409–417.

D. Cobb-Clark, M. Connolly and C. Worswick (2005) 'Post-Migration Investments in Education and Job Search: A Family Perspective', *Journal of Population Economics*, 18, 663–690.

S. Cohen-Goldner and Z. Eckstein (2008) 'Labor Mobility of Immigrants: Training, Experience, Language and Opportunities', *International Economic Review*, 49, 837–872.

S. Cohen-Goldner and Z. Eckstein (2010) 'Estimating the Return to Training and Occupational Experience: The Case of Female Immigrants', *Journal of Econometrics*, 156, 86–105.

A. Damm (2009) 'Ethnic Enclaves and Immigrant Labor Market Outcomes: Quasi-Experimental Evidence', *Journal of Labor Economics*, 27, 281–314.

A. Dávila and M. Mora (2001) 'The Marital Status of Recent Mexican Immigrants in the United States in 1980 and 1990', *International Migration Review*, 35, 506–524.

A. Di Paolo and J.L. Raymond (2012) 'Language Knowledge and Earnings in Catalonia', *Journal of Applied Economics*, 15(1), 89–118.

A. Di Paolo and A. Tansel (2015) 'Returns to Foreign Language Skills in a Developing Country: The Case of Turkey', *The Journal of Development Studies*, 51, 407–421.

M. Dryer and M. Haspelmath (eds) (2013) *The World Atlas of Language Structures Online* (Leipzig: Max Planck Institute for Evolutionary Anthropology).

B. Duncan and S. Trejo (2007) 'Ethnic Identification, Intermarriage, and Unmeasured Progress by Mexican Americans' In G. Borjas (ed.) *Mexican Immigration to the United States* (Chicago, IL: University of Chicago Press) 229–267.

C. Dustmann (1993) 'Earnings Adjustment of Temporary Migrants', *Journal of Population Economics*, 6, 153–168.

C. Dustmann (1994) 'Speaking Fluency, Writing Fluency and Earnings of Migrants', *Journal of Population Economics*, 7, 133–156.

C. Dustmann (1999) 'Temporary Migration, Human Capital, and Language Fluency of Migrants', *Scandinavian Journal of Economics*, 10, 297–314.

C. Dustmann and F. Fabbri (2003) 'Language Proficiency and Labour Market Performance of Immigrants in the UK', *Economic Journal*, 113, 695–717.

C. Dustmann and J. Gorlach (2015) 'The Economics of Temporary Migrations', *Journal of Economic Literature*, forthcoming.

C. Dustmann and A. van Soest (2001) 'Language Fluency and Earnings: Estimation with Misclassified Language Indicators', *Review of Economics and Statistics*, 83, 663–674.

C. Dustmann and A. van Soest (2002) 'Language and the Earnings of Immigrants', *Industrial and Labor Relations Review*, 55, 473–492.

I. Dyen, J. Kruskal and P. Black (1992) 'An Indo-European Classification: A Lexicostatistical Experiment', *Transactions of the American Philosophical Society*, 82, iii–iv, 1–132.

P. Edin, P. Fredriksson and O. Åslund (2003) 'Ethnic Enclaves and the Economic Success of Immigrants: Evidence from a Natural Experiment', *Quarterly Journal of Economics*, 118, 329–357.

J. Espenshade and H. Fu (1997) 'An Analysis of English-language Proficiency among U.S. Immigrants', *American Sociological Review*, 62, 288–305.

European Commission (2006) 'Special Eurobarometer on "Europeans and their languages"', http://ec.europa.eu/public_opinion/archives/ebs/ebs_243_sum_en.pdf (accessed: 1 February 2012).

R. Fernandez and A. Fogli (2006) 'Fertility: The Role of Culture and Family Experience', *Journal of the European Economic Association*, 4, 552–561.

E. Funkhouser and F. Ramos (1993) 'The Choice of Migration Destination: Dominican and Cuban Americans to the Mainland United States and Puerto Rico', *International Migration Review*, 27, 537–556.

A. Georgiadis and A. Manning (2011) 'Change and Continuity among Minority Communities in Britain', *Journal of Population Economics*, 24, 541–568.

V. Ginsburgh and J. Prieto-Rodriguez (2011) 'Returns to Foreign Languages of Native Workers in the EU', *Industrial and Labor Relations Review*, 64, 599–618.

C. Gorinas and M. Pytliková (2016) 'Do Natives' Attitudes Influence International Migration?', *International Migration Review*, forthcoming.

J. Grogger and G. Hanson (2011) 'Income Maximization and the Selection and Sorting of International Migrants', *Journal of Development Economics*, 95, 42–57.

J. Grogger and S. Trejo (2002) 'Falling Behind or Moving Up? The Intergenerational Progress of California's Mexican-Origin Population', Public Policy Institute of California.

E. Heinesen, L. Husted and M. Rosholm (2013) 'The Effects of Active Labour Market Policies for Immigrants Receiving Social Assistance in Denmark', *IZA Journal of Migration*, doi:10.1186/2193-9039-2-15.

L. Hong and S. Page (2004) 'Groups of Diverse Problem Solvers Can Outperform Groups of High-Ability Problem Solvers', *Proceedings of the National Academy of Sciences*, 101, 16385–16389.

F. Hou (2005) 'The Initial Destinations and Redistribution of Canada's Major Immigrant Groups: Changes over the Past Two Decades', *Statistics Canada Research*, Catalogue No. 11F0019MIE-No. 254.

I. Isphording (2013) 'Returns to Local and Foreign Language Skills', *Labour*, 27, 443–461.

I. Isphording (2014) 'Disadvantages of Linguistic Origin: Evidence from Immigrant Literacy Scores', *Economics Letters*, 123, 236–239.

I. Isphording and S. Otten (2013) 'The Costs of Babylon: Linguistic Distance in Applied Economics', *Review of International Economics*, 21, 354–369.

I. Isphording and S. Otten (2014) 'Linguistic Barriers in the Destination Language Acquisition of Immigrants', *Journal of Economic Behavior and Organization*, 105, 30–50.

M. Kahanec, M. Pytliková and K. Zimmermann (2016) 'The Free Movement of Workers in an Enlarged European Union: Institutional Underpinnings of Economic Adjustment' (forthcoming) In M. Kahanec and K. Zimmermann (eds) *Labor Migration, EU Enlargement, and the Great Recession* (Berlin: Springer-Verlag), ISBN 978–3–662–45320–9.

J. Kahn (1988) 'Immigrant Selectivity and Fertility Adaptation in the United States', *Social Forces*, 67, 108–128.

W. Kerr and W. Lincoln (2010) 'The Supply Side of Innovations: H-1B Visa Reforms and U.S. Ethnic Invention', *Journal of Labor Economics*, 28, 473–508.

K. Keuntae and J. Cohen (2010) 'Determinants of International Migration Flows to and from Industrialized Countries: A Panel Data Approach Beyond Gravity', *International Migration Review*, 44, 899–932.

S. Kossoudji (1988) 'The Impact of English Language Ability on the Labor Market Opportunities of Asian and Hispanic Immigrant Men', *Journal of Labor Economics*, 6, 205–228.

K. Lang and E. Siniver (2009) 'The Return to English in a Non-English Speaking Country: Russian Immigrants and Native Israelis in Israel', *The B.E. Journal of Economic Analysis & Policy*, 9 (1), 1935–1682.

E. Lazear (1999) 'Globalisation and the Market for Team-Mates', *The Economic Journal*, 109, 15–40.

E. P. Lazear (2007) 'Mexican assimilation in the United States' In G. J. Borjas (ed.) *Mexican Immigration to the United States* (Chicago: University Press/NBER Cambridge, MA), pp. 107–122.

A. Leon (2003) 'Does Ethnic Capital Matter? Identifying Peer Effects in the Intergenerational Transmission of Ethnic Differentials', MIT Department of Economics, Manuscript.

D. Leslie and J. Lindley (2001) 'The Impact of Language Ability on Employment and Earnings of Britain's Ethnic Communities', *Economica*, 68, 587–606.

V. Levenshtein (1966) 'Binary Codes Capable of Correcting Deletions, Insertions, and Reversals', *Cybernetics and Control Theory*, 10, 707–710.

J. Levinsohn (2007) 'Globalization and the Returns to Speaking English in South Africa' In A. Harrison (ed.) *Globalization and Poverty* (Chicago, IL: University of Chicago Press), pp. 629–646.

J. Lindley (2002) 'The English Language Fluency and Earnings of Ethnic Minorities in Britain', *Scottish Journal of Political Economy*, 49, 467–487.

D. Massey and K. Espinosa (1997) 'What's Driving Mexico U.S. Migration? A Theoretical, Empirical, and Policy Analysis', *American Journal of Sociology*, 102, 939–999.

R. Mayberry, E. Lock and H. Kazmi (2001) 'Linguistic Ability and Early Language Exposure', *Nature*, 417, 38.

A. Mayda (2010) 'International Migration: A Panel Data Analysis of the Determinants of Bilateral Flows', *Journal of Population Economics*, 23, 1249–1274.

J. McDonald (2004) 'Toronto and Vancouver Bound: The Location Choice of New Canadian Immigrants', *Canadian Journal of Urban Research*, 13, 85–101.

D. McKenzie and H. Rapoport (2010) 'Self-selection Patterns in Mexico-U.S. Migration: The Role of Migration Networks', *The Review of Economics and Statistics*, 92, 811–821.

J. Melitz and F. Toubal (2014) 'Native Language, Spoken Language, Translation and Trade', *Journal of International Economics*, 93, 351–363.

X. Meng and R. Gregory (2005) 'Intermarriage and the Economic Assimilation of Immigrants', *Journal of Labor Economics*, 23, 135–175.

A. Miranda and Y. Zhu (2013) 'English Deficiency and the Native–Immigrant Wage Gap', *Economics Letters*, 118, 38–41.

K. Munshi (2003) 'Networks in the Modern Economy: Mexican Migrants in the US Labor Market', *The Quarterly Journal of Economics*, 118, 549–599.

F. Ortega and G. Peri (2009) 'The Causes and Effects of International Migrations: Evidence from OECD Countries 1980–2005', NBER Working Paper 14833.

F. Ortega and G. Peri (2013) 'The Effect of Income and Immigration Policies on International Migrations', *Migration Studies*, 1, 1–28.

F. Ortega and G. Peri (2015) 'Migration, Trade and Income', *Journal of International Economics*, forthcoming.

E. Osborne (2000) 'The Deceptively Simple Economics of Workplace Diversity', *Journal of Labor Research*, 21, 463–475.

J. Palmer and M. Pytliková (2015) 'Labor Market Laws and Intra-European Migration: The Role of the State in Shaping Destination Choices', *European Journal of Population*, 31, 127–153.

P. Parrotta, D. Pozzoli and M. Pytliková (2014a) 'Does Labour Diversity Affect Firm Productivity?', *European Economic Review*, 66, 144–179.

P. Parrotta, D. Pozzoli and M. Pytliková (2014b) 'The Nexus Between Labor Diversity and Firm's Innovation', *Journal of Population Economics*, 27, 303–364.

P. Pedersen, M. Pytliková and N. Smith (2006) 'Migration into OECD Countries, 1990–2000' In C. Parsons and T. Smeeding (eds) *Immigration and the Transformation of Europe* (Cambridge: Cambridge University Press), pp. 43–84.

P. Pedersen, M. Pytliková and N. Smith (2008) 'Selection and Network Effects: Migration Flows into OECD Countries, 1990–2000', *European Economic Review*, 52, 1160–1186.

A. Portes and L. Jensen (1989) 'The Enclave and the Entrants: Patterns of Ethnic Enterprise in Miami before and after Mariel', *American Sociological Review*, 54, 929–949.

D. Rooth and J. Saarela (2007) 'Native Language and Immigrant Labour Market Outcomes: An Alternative Approach to Measuring the Returns to Language Skills', *Journal of International Migration and Integration*, 8, 207–221.

Norman B. Ryder (1973) 'A Critique of the National Fertility Study', *Demography* 10, 495–506.

A. Saiz and E. Zoido (2005) 'Listening to What the World Says: Bilingualism and Earnings in the United States', *The Review of Economics and Statistics*, 87, 523–538.

M. Sarvimäki and K. Hämäläinen (2015) 'Integrating Immigrants: The Impact of Restructuring ALMP', *Journal of Labor Economics*, forthcoming.

J. Schaafsma and A. Sweetman (2001) 'Immigrant Earnings: Age at Immigration Matters' *Canadian Journal of Economics*, 34, 1066–1099.

M. Shields and S. Wheatley Price (2002) 'The English Language Fluency and Occupational Success of Ethnic Minority Immigrant Men Living in English Metropolitan Areas', *Journal of Population Economics*, 15, 137–160.

A. M. Sorenson (1988) 'The Fertility and Language Characteristics of Mexican-American and Non-Hispanic Husbands and Wives', *The Sociological Quarterly*, 29, 111–130.

G. Stevens (1992) 'The Social and Demographic Context of Language Use in the United States', *American Sociological Review*, 57, 171–785.

G. Stevens (1999) 'Age at Immigration and Second Language Proficiency among Foreign-Born Adults: Age at Immigration and Second Language Proficiency among Foreign-Born Adults', *Language in Society*, 28, 555–578.

G. Stevens and G. Swicegood (1987) 'The Linguistic Context of Ethnic Endogamy-Born Adults: Age at Immigration and Second Language Proficiency among Foreign-Born Adults', *American Sociological Association*, 2, 73–82.

T. Stöhr (2015) 'The Returns to Occupational Foreign Language Use: Evidence from Germany', *Labour Economics*, 32, 86–98.

G. Swicegood, F. Bean, E. Herphey Stephen and W. Opitz (1988) 'Language Usage and Fertility in the Mexican-Origin Population of the United States', *Demography*, 25, 17–33.

O. Toomet (2011) 'Learn English, Not the Local Language! Ethnic Russians in the Baltic States', *American Economic Review*, 101, 526–531.

M. Toussaint-Comeau and S. Rhine (2004) 'Tenure Choice with Location Selection: The Case of Hispanic Neighborhoods in Chicago', *Contemporary Economic Policy*, 22, 95–110.

M. White and J. Glick (2009) *Achieving Anew: How New Immigrants Do in American Schools, Jobs and Neighborhoods* (New York: Russel Sage Foundation).

D. Williams (2011) 'The Economic Returns to Multiple Language Usage in Western Europe', *International Journal of Manpower*, 32, 372–393.

Y. Yao and J. van Ours (2015) 'Language Skills and Labor Market Performance of Immigrants in the Netherlands', *Labour Economics*, 34, 76–85.

13

Translation: Economic and Sociological Perspectives

Johan Heilbron and Gisèle Sapiro

13.1 Introduction

Translating and interpreting, the process by which verbal utterances in one language are expressed in another, takes on a variety of forms and functions depending on the context in which it takes place. The translation of sacred texts has traditionally been a source of social concern and religious controversy. Negotiations between rulers and states have, just like international trade, routinely involved forms of translating. The international circulation of movies and television programmes is accompanied by dubbing and subtitling. Literary debates frequently engage with translations as well, either as models to be followed or as examples to be resisted. Since it is impossible to do justice to this variety of translation practices in a single chapter, we shall restrict ourselves to one major form of translation: the translation of books. Book translations leave public traces; in the modern era they imply a transfer of property rights, are registered, appear in book statistics, and are publicly evaluated and debated. As such they represent an observable and interrelated subset of translation practices, which has only recently begun to attract attention from social scientists.

Although the practice of translating has existed for centuries, scholarly work on translation long remained a peripheral activity that was almost exclusively restricted to scholars in literature and linguistics (Baker and Saldanha, 2008; Baker, 2009; Venuti, 2012). Focused on comparing translated texts with their source text or source language, literary scholars have been concerned with identifying deviations from the original, comparing translations among each other, and interpreting the differences for assessing the meaning of the translated work. Linguists have, in a sense, been concerned with the opposite issue. Their interest was less in subtle differences among translations or between translations and their original, than in the fundamental similarity of languages and the equivalence of their modes and repertoires of expression.

Although reflections on translation can be traced back a long time (Rener, 1989), it is only since the 1970s that 'translation studies' emerged as an academic field of its own. By advocating the establishment of a separate domain of research and teaching, its protagonists aimed to move beyond merely literary and linguistic concerns and to broaden the range of inquiry and specify the scope and structure of the field. Having experienced a rapid expansion since the 1970s, translation studies today is an established field with its own chairs, departments, textbooks, reference works, journals and professional associations (see Baker and Saldanha, 2008; Gambier and Doorslaer, 2011–2014; Berman and Porter, 2014).

Proposing the expression 'translation studies' to distinguish it from previous denominations (translatology, science of translation or *Uebersetzungswissenschaft*) the Amsterdam-based American translator James Holmes outlined what the new field should be about. In a widely circulated, programmatic paper of the early 1970s, 'The Name and Nature of Translation Studies' (1972, reprinted in Holmes, 1988), Holmes observed that translation scholars were dispersed over different disciplines (languages, linguistics), had no accepted name for their studies, and lacked a shared understanding of their field and common channels of communication. According to Holmes the field was best called 'translation studies' and it was to be divided in a 'pure' and an 'applied' branch. The pure branch consisted of a theoretical part, concerned with general or partial theories, and an empirical or descriptive part, concerned with studying the translation process, its products and their functions. The applied branch was concerned with training translators, translation aids and translation criticism.

The programme of translation studies that Holmes proposed initially developed mainly in small, multi-lingual countries like Belgium, the Netherlands and Israel. Of particular importance for the movement was the approach of Itamar Even-Zohar and Gideon Toury, who became the leading protagonists of the 'descriptive' branch of translation studies. Based at the University of Tel Aviv, their research programme emphasized the need to understand translations not so much in relation to the source text or source language, but within the context in which translations are actually produced and published, i.e. in the 'target' culture. Unlike the older approaches, the shift from source text to target culture stimulated research on historically varying 'translation norms' (Toury, 1995) and, more generally, on the socio-cultural status of translations within the literary and cultural system of the target culture (Even-Zohar, 1990).

While 'descriptive' translation studies raised new questions about the role of translations in target cultures, the movement tended to remain focused on texts and intertextual comparisons. The social conditions of translating did not receive systematic attention and economic aspects were largely ignored. Only since the 1990s have social scientists started to engage seriously with issues of translation.[1] The emerging interest in the social sciences was less a response to the expanding field of translation studies, as a reflection on the issues of 'globalization'. Since the fall of the Berlin Wall and the collapse of communism in Eastern Europe coincided with the rapid spread of new communication technologies (personal computers, the internet) and policies favouring deregulation and liberalization, international exchanges extended, intensified and accelerated. In virtually all sectors markets and industries were becoming more global, and political and cultural institutions were equally confronted with challenges to the power of national states. Processes of internationalization and globalization became central research topics in all of the social sciences, and in the cultural domain they attracted attention in particular of media specialists, sociologists and anthropologists (Crane, 2002; Hopper, 2007).

Interest in translation came especially from sociologists, whose work has prompted translation scholars to speak of a 'social' or 'sociological turn' in translation studies (Pym et al., 2006; Wolf and Fukari, 2007). There was less interest in other social sciences; in economics not more than a handful of papers exist (Hjorth-Andersen, 2001; Melitz, 2007; Ginsburgh et al., 2011). Parallel to the emerging interest for translation in the social sciences, translation scholars have themselves also become more interested in what the social sciences have to offer. Understanding translation practices in the target culture, they realized, implies paying attention to translators, both individually and as a social and professional group, to the functioning of the publishing industry and the book market, and to the process of reception (see Pym et al., 2008).

In this chapter we will briefly present some of the main questions, concepts and findings that have arisen in social science research on translation. For reasons of convenience, we distinguish the following levels:

1. Transnational or global translation flows; this level is concerned with international flows and the world market or world system of translations.
2. The production and circulation of translations focuses on the publishing industry and the economic, political and cultural dimensions of its functioning.
3. The selection, importing and reception of translations. Here, attention is given to issues of linguistic diversity, the role of cultural proximity and power relations, and the relative weight of economic or specifically cultural considerations in the decision-making process of publishers and readers.

---

[1] We restrict ourselves here to translations in the literal sense of the word, leaving aside the largely metaphorical uses of the term in approaches like the 'actor-network theory' of Michel Callon and Bruno Latour.

13.2 International translation flows and the global market of translations

Translations are goods which circulate across the borders of states and the boundaries of languages. State borders and language boundaries do not always coincide. Some languages have a merely local character within the political unit they are part of, whereas others, like the languages of colonial powers and empires, tend to have a much broader reach than that of nation-states. Translation markets therefore vary greatly in size and in the position they occupy in the international flows of translations.

National borders matter, because they imply specific taxes, prices and exchange rules. In cases of co-publication by publishers from different countries of the same linguistic area, they also shape the 'packaging' of the book (the cover and presentation may be different in the United States and in the United Kingdom) and sometimes the orthographic and typographic rules. National states have, in addition, shaped industry structures and linguistic boundaries. Peripheral zones of the book market developed their own publishing industry much later: the United States started only during the 18th century; the industry emerged in Spanish-speaking Latin American countries only during the 1930s, and Quebec started during the second half of the 20th century. Most colonial countries have been commercial outlets for industries located in colonizing countries, and in many French-speaking African countries the book market is still dominated by French conglomerates like Hachette.

Beyond state policies and national institutions, translation flows depend on the relations between languages and language groups. When texts travel beyond the boundaries of their linguistic area of origin, and in contrast to standardized industrial products or even cultural products like music, texts do not circulate in their original form; rather they are recreated in another language. It is thus a different product from the original that circulates and its production requires a considerable investment in time and often in monetary terms as well.

13.2.1 Comparing translation ratios

We now analyse three types of translation ratios: by book categories or book genres, by national book production across countries, and by source languages.

The first source of variation by genre is related to the fact that, in some book categories, translations are frequent and international exchanges are well developed, whereas for other genres translations play only a minor role. The holy books of the world's religions, which are carried by churches and international communities of believers, have been among the most widely translated texts in human history. In the modern era, 'fiction' in the broad sense of the term is generally the largest category of book publications with a high share of translations. In other categories translations are rare: national markets tend to be protected and depend strongly on state regulation and institutions of national governance (Heilbron, 1995). This is typically the case for schoolbooks, which represent a large part of the national book production as well, though the translation ratio is low. Some of the variation in the translation ratio by genre can be explained directly by historical changes in the book industry. The increasing share of children's books in national book production, for example, has been followed by a similar rise of youth books in international translation and some of their authors now rank among the 50 most translated authors in the world (Milo, 1984, pp. 110–111). The most recent example is J. K. Rowling's *Harry Potter* series, published between 1997 and 2013, which became worldwide bestsellers.

Translation ratios also vary across countries: they are small in large and dominant countries, and large in small and dependent countries. In the 1990s, translations represented around 3 per cent of the national book production in the US and the UK; 15–18 per cent in Germany and France; 25 per cent in Italy, Spain and the Netherlands; 35 and 45 per cent in Portugal and Greece (Ganne and Minon, 1992; Heilbron, 1999; Jurt, 1999). Although the vocabulary differs somewhat, sociologists have interpreted this variation between countries and languages as being rooted in unequal relations of power (Heilbron, 1995, 1999). Less powerful nations tend to have high levels of imports and depend on other nations, whereas powerful nations typically import less but export more.[2]

A third and related source of variation appears in the distribution of translations on the world market. The most widely used source for international translation statistics is the *Index Translationum*, a database put together by UNESCO. During the three decades that followed 1979, the *Index* collected more than two million titles.[3] Since the database relies on national statistics of UNESCO members, its reliability varies per country and the inter-country comparability raises serious problems. For some countries, the Netherlands for example, the data exhibit highly improbable yearly fluctuations; for other countries (France for instance), the data seem relatively close to national statistics (Heilbron, 1999; Bokobza and Sapiro, 2008). Comparability is another

---

[2] The most significant approaches are framed in terms of core–periphery structures or of dominance and dependency. Despite terminological differences these approaches may be seen as belonging to the same theoretical family, since they all stress unequal exchange and power relations. For core–periphery models of world systems theory, see Wallerstein (2004); for a field theoretical approach to domination and unequal exchange, see Bourdieu (1991, 1999).

[3] The *Index Translationum* was created in 1931 as an international bibliography of translations. It was part of the policy to stimulate international exchanges and improve international understanding. The more than two million references registered after 1979 are available online. They originate from 100 UNESCO member states (see www.unesco.org).

concern, since what is registered as a 'book' is not identical across countries. Some countries count annual reports of corporations, doctoral dissertations or governmental publications as books; this will inevitably lower their translation ratios since such 'books' are very seldom translated.

But in spite of the shortcomings and deficiencies of the *Index Translationum*, the database can be used with caution as providing some indication of the translation flows between languages and the structure of the world market for translations. The general pattern that emerges is unambiguously that of a hierarchical system with a clear-cut core–periphery structure. Some languages have a much larger share of the international market than others. In that sense they can be said to be more 'central', while others are more 'peripheral' (De Swaan, 1993, 2001; Heilbron, 1995, 1999, 2002). Translations are massively made from a very small number of languages. The top 20 source languages amount to nearly 96 per cent of the total of translations listed in the *Index* (Brisset and Aye, 2007). Among those 20, 16 are European languages, which account for 93 per cent of all the books listed in the *Index*.

More than half (55 per cent) of the books translated during the period 1979–2007 are from English (Brisset and Aye, 2007), which occupies the most central, even hyper-central, position. Well behind English three 'central' languages emerge: French, German and Russian, respectively representing 10, 9 and 5 per cent of the world market. Eighty per cent of all recorded translations are thus from four languages only (English, French, German and Russian). Languages such as Italian, Spanish and Swedish can be said to occupy a semi-central position with a share that varies between 1 and 3 per cent. All other languages, which have a share of less than 1 percent, can be considered as peripheral, despite the fact that some of them (Chinese, Arabic, Japanese, Portuguese) represent linguistic groups that are among the largest in terms of primary speakers. This means, incidentally, that the number of primary speakers is not decisive in determining the degree to which a language can be considered to be 'central' or 'peripheral'. Nor can the mere number of primary speakers explain the size of the book production in these languages, which depends on other factors such as literacy, state policies and level of economic development.

13.2.2 Core–periphery dynamics

This core–periphery structure, however, is not a static system that would exist in some state of equilibrium. It is, on the contrary, a dynamic constellation, marked by relatively slow changes in the long run as well as by more rapid short-term transformations. Historical examples illustrate both types of dynamics. In early modern Europe, Latin gradually lost its central position to national vernaculars, which were carried by the institutions of emerging nation-states (Wacquet, 2001). Among these vernaculars French, the language of the largest European court and the nobility, was adopted by the upper layers of society in many European countries thus obtaining a central position in early modern translation flows (Burke and Po-chia Hsia, 2009). Only in the course of the 19th century did English and German become major competitors of French (Heilbron, 1995). In the course of the 20th century English became the predominant language worldwide, and its share in translations increased steadily. In the Netherlands, for example, which is situated between Germany, England and France, translations from English almost continuously expanded, in particular after World War II: the share of translations from English increased from almost 40 per cent in 1946 to 75 per cent in 2000 (Heilbron, 1995, 2008). As a result of the growing interest in American literature, translations from English increased from 33 to 50 per cent of all translated books in France between 1920 and 1930 (Girou de Buzareingues, 1972, p. 268). They recently (1948–2002) account for two-thirds of literary translations into French. However, this average conceals important cyclical variations. After World War II, American fiction was widely introduced in France and the share of English reached 75 per cent in 1948 according to the *Index Translationum*. It represented 70 per cent in the following decade, then fell to 62 per cent between 1958 and 1967, increased to 68 per cent between 1968 and 1976, reaching a peak of 75 per cent again in 1975; another peak was reached in 1984 followed by a brutal decrease in 1986, but since then the growth has been steady from 600 books published in 1988, to 3,600 in 2002 (Sapiro, 2008, pp. 148–149, and forthcoming a).

As visible in Table 13.1, a brutal change can be observed for Russian after the collapse of communism in Eastern Europe. In the years preceding the fall of the Berlin wall (1985–1989) translations from Russian represented almost 11 per cent worldwide; they fell to a mere 3.3 per cent (1990–1994) and then to 1.5 per cent (1995–1999). After occupying a central position, comparable to that of French and German, Russian fell from a central to a semi-central position, comparable to that of Italian and Spanish. The language that benefitted most from the fall of Russian was not Chinese, Arabic or German, but English, which captured almost the entire share lost by Russian. The share of English as a source language for translations worldwide increased from 46 per cent (1985–1989) to 56 per cent (1990–1994) and to 61 per cent during the late 1990s.

Historical shifts in the flow of translations such as those implied by the decline of Latin, the rise of (supra) national languages like French, German and English, or the growth of English and the fall of Russian are processes for which various factors have to be taken into account. But before properly addressing the issue of explanatory factors, a few other empirical regularities need to be highlighted.

An important feature of translation flows is that the core–periphery structure roughly seems to correspond to the level of translations within each country or, more precisely, within each language group (Heilbron, 1999). As was

Table 13.1 Source languages of book translations worldwide, 1980–2009

	1980–84		1985–89		1990–94		1995–99		2000–04		2005–09	
	Number	%	Number	%	Number	%	Number	%	Number	%	Number	%
English	112,696	43.1	13,5067	45.7	190,008	56.0	246,301	61.1	290,241	59.7	265,459	59.3
French	28,533	10.9	32,851	11.1	38,907	11.5	36,135	9.0	43,709	9.0	36,979	8.3
German	22,703	8.7	25,255	8.6	30,993	9.1	38,521	9.6	44,511	9.2	38,738	8.7
Russian	31,133	11.9	31,528	10.7	11,284	3.3	5,998	1.5	7,874	1.6	8,505	1.9
Italian	7,707	2.9	8,703	2.9	9,736	2.9	11,677	2.9	15,116	3.1	14,357	3.2
Spanish	4,016	1.5	5,457	1.8	9,088	2.7	9,860	2.4	13,363	2.7	11,460	2.6
Swedish	5,106	2.0	5,253	1.8	6,029	1.8	6,601	1.6	8,130	1.7	7,478	1.7
Danish	3,051	1.2	2,663	0.9	3,100	0.9	3,564	0.9	4,216	0.9	3,932	0.9
Dutch	2,369	0.9	2,780	0.9	2,808	0.8	3,473	0.9	3,963	0.8	3,468	0.8
Czech	2,819	1.1	3,895	1.3	2,711	0.8	1,349	0.3	2,165	0.4	3,292	0.7
Polish	2,523	1.0	2,335	0.8	1,982	0.6	1,942	0.5	2,586	0.5	2,541	0.6
Japanese	1,168	0.4	1,748	0.6	2,067	0.6	4,154	1.0	8,726	1.8	10,898	2.4
Hungarian	3,062	1.2	2,899	1.0	1,460	0.4	1,020	0.3	924	0.2	1,077	0.2
Norwegian	1,510	0.6	1,550	0.5	1,939	0.6	2,616	0.6	3,266	0.7	2,972	0.7
Arabic	1,769	0.7	1,896	0.6	1,884	0.6	1,709	0.4	2,428	0.5	2,228	0.5
Portuguese	988	0.4	1,424	0.5	1,655	0.5	1,845	0.5	3,083	0.6	2,280	0.5
Hebrew	1,312	0.5	1,360	0.5	1,669	0.5	1,878	0.5	1,930	0.4	1,710	0.4
Chinese	2,714	1.0	1,777	0.6	1,859	0.5	2,161	0.5	2,417	0.5	2,536	0.6
Finnish	822	0.3	1,162	0.4	1,133	0.3	1,835	0.5	1,622	0.3	1,793	0.4
Catalonian	482	0.2	576	0.2	1,131	0.3	1,685	0.4	2,429	0.5	1,842	0.4
Subtotal	236,483	90.4	270,179	91.5	320,312	94.7	384,324	95.4	462,699	95.2	423,545	94.6
Other languages	25,147	9.6	25,083	8.5	17,933	5.3	18,586	4.6	23,317	4.8	24,028	5.4
Total	261,630	100.0	295,262	100.0	339,376	100.0	402,910	100.0	486,016	100.0	447,573	100.0

Source: Index Translationum.

indicated above, the more central the international position of a language is, the lower the translation rate *within* that language. There thus seems to be an inverse relationship between the international position of a language in the world market of translations, and the domestic translation ratio. A central position in international exchange implies that there are many translations *out* of this language (by definition), but this corresponds to relatively few translations *into* this language. And the other way around: there are few translations *from* peripheral languages (again by definition), though this generally implies many translations *into* these languages. While dominant countries 'export' their cultural products and translate little into their languages, dominated countries export little and import a substantial number of foreign books, principally by translation.

In the global translation economy, exchange is an asymmetrical process, and the 'globalization' of the 1990s increased rather than decreased these imbalances. The supremacy of English is more pronounced than it ever was, there is a slight decline in the position of central languages such as French and German, Russian has fallen considerably, and there are few indications from the *Index Translationum* that the proportion of translations from peripheral languages has improved much. In advanced economies, books are nowadays translated from more languages than 30 years ago, but the overall proportion of translations from peripheral languages has not clearly increased. Recent developments, therefore, seem to confirm the argument made by Melitz (2007) that 'if one language is sufficiently larger than others. . ., it will tend to crowd out the rest in translations'.

Distinguishing language groups by their degree of centrality not only implies that translations flow more from the core to the periphery than the other way around, but also that the communication between peripheral groups often passes via a more central language. Thus, the English translation of a Norwegian or Korean novel is quickly announced by its original publisher, who foresees that translation into a central language will be immediately followed by translations into several other languages. What is translated from one peripheral language into the other, therefore, often depends on what is translated from these peripheral languages into one of the central languages (Van Es and Heilbron, 2015). So the more central a language is in the world market of translations, the more it has the capacity to function as an intermediary or *vehicular language*, that is as a means of communication between language groups which are themselves peripheral or semi-peripheral.

Another feature that can be derived from the international position of languages and language groups is that the more central a language is, the more types of books are translated from this language. Book statistics in the Netherlands, for example, distinguish 33 book categories, ranging from 'religion' and 'law' to 'prose' and 'history'. Only translations from the most central language, English, are represented in all 33 categories. Translations from German are found in 28 categories, translations from French in 22 categories, and from Italian in 10 categories (Heilbron, 1995). In other words, centrality in international translation flows implies also variety. Since the small number of books translated from peripheral languages is generally concentrated in a very small number of categories, the opposite also holds true: book translations from peripheral languages lack the variety that increases with the degree of centrality.

The core–periphery structure of the international translations market has implications not only for the number and variety of translations, but also for the social status of translated books and translators, and the translation strategies that are prevalent. In the most central languages, there are relatively few translations, translators do not have a very high status, and translation norms tend to be derived from indigenous literary standards. In more peripheral language groups, translations are more important, they have a higher status, and 'foreignizing' strategies are more legitimate.[4]

13.2.3   Why is this so?

The uneven exchanges between language groups that form the basis of the varying share of languages in the international translation market have been explained in different ways. The most basic explanation has related the degree of centrality of languages to the number of books published in that language. The argument is simple and straightforward: since there are many more books published in English than in any other language, there are also many more books translated from English than from any other language (de Swaan, 2001, pp. 41–59; Pym and Chrupala, 2005; Ginsburgh et al., 2011). The size of the book production indeed explains a significant part of the varying degree of the centrality of languages. Larger publishing systems can sustain a more varied production, which is potentially of interest to smaller publishing systems with less variety, while at the same time it decreases the need for imports.

But despite the general validity of the argument, there is no mechanical relationship between the size of the book production in a certain country or language, and its share in the translation market. There are large and fast growing publishing systems from which little is translated (Chinese, Arabic, Portuguese). A factor that has been added for that reason is the linguistic and cultural proximity of languages (Ginsburgh et al., 2011). Linguistic and cultural proximity can be seen as the equivalent of transportation costs in international trade: if languages (and therefore cultures) are more similar, translation

---

[4] Domestication and foreignizing are opposite translation strategies; they are based on how much a translation assimilates a foreign text to the translating language and culture, and how much it rather signals the differences of that text (Venuti, 1998, 2008).

is easier and less costly. One may thus explain the low level of translations from Chinese into European languages by the linguistic and cultural distance between the two languages. Although this argument can indeed explain part of the variation observed, it does not explain why many more books are translated from European languages into Chinese than the other way around (see also Section 13.4).

Certain historical shifts, like the decline of French or the rise of English, do not seem to correlate directly with the changing size of the publishing industry either. The fall of translations from Russian after 1989 is more related to political changes than to a presumed change in the number of books published or in linguistic proximities. With the collapse of the Soviet Union, the politically and ideologically driven translations from Russian into the languages of its East European satellite states fell dramatically. Sociologists have therefore argued for a multidimensional approach, integrating other factors in the model.

Translation markets, according to the argument, are embedded in the power relations between nation states and language groups. These power relations are of three types – political, economic and cultural (see Section 13.3). In these relations, the means that are used in political, economic and cultural struggles are unequally distributed. Cultural exchanges are therefore unequal exchanges that express relations of power and domination. In accordance with such an analysis, translation flows should be situated in a transnational field characterized by the power relations among nation states, their languages and their literature.

Analysing the flows of translations in the light of power relations among language groups allows an understanding of certain historical shifts and changes. A major change, for example, was the rise of the American publishing industry that began challenging the dominant position of British and French firms; this more central role resulted from economic, political as well as cultural factors. Conversely, a country's loss of prestige or power and the resulting fall of the status of its language, have consequences on the level of translation activity as well. The relative decline of French as compared to English has typically been followed by a growth in the number of translations into French, from 10 per cent in the 1970s to close to 18 per cent in the 1990s. In the case of Russian the sharp drop in translations from Russian after 1989 was accompanied by a sharp rise in the number of foreign translations published into Russian. As already suggested, the growth of the national market cannot properly explain the variation in the translation ratios, and linguistic distances or proximities have remained stable in both cases.

13.3 Political, economic and cultural factors

Several factors – political, economic and cultural – may be distinguished in producing translations (Heilbron and Sapiro, 2007; Sapiro, 2014). In certain contexts, these factors enjoy a relative autonomy from one another, in others they are closely intertwined. For instance, in communist regimes, where there was no free market, the economic logic was highly embedded in the political one. The constraints on the production and circulation of symbolic goods and on international cultural exchanges vary as we move from contexts of high political control to contexts of market exchange (Sapiro, 2003). The mode of production and circulation of texts will depend on these different factors.

13.3.1 Political and ideological factors

Translations may serve political or ideological objectives; they can be a means to disseminate a doctrine or a vision of the world. Political parties and organizations have contributed to the international circulation of works such as those of Marx and Engels, through more or less organized networks. Lenin was the most translated author between 1955 and 1980 according to the *Index Translationum* (Venuti, 1998, p. 158). Many political and ideological movements have, in fact, had translation policies as part of their propaganda efforts.

In countries where the economic field is subordinated to the political field and where the institutions governing cultural production as well as the organization of intellectual professions are state-run, as in fascist or communist countries, the production and circulation of symbolic goods is highly politicized from the outset. The place and role of translations in such regimes has become a very active area of research (Billiani, 2007; Thomson-Wohlgemuth, 2009 on the German Democratic Republic; Rundle 2010 on Fascist Italy). During World War II and the German occupation of France, the Third Reich banned translations from French into German, except for a few writers who were active supporters of collaboration. At the same time the German Occupier forced French publishers to translate as many German authors as possible as part of their policy to break France's cultural hegemony (Loiseaux, 1995, pp. 110–111).

As this example illustrates, the translation policies implemented by nation states are usually part of a broader policy aiming at the promotion of their national culture and, for the dominant ones, at strengthening their hegemony or influence ('soft power'). One of the more specific factors explaining the dramatic fall of translations from Russian after 1989 is the end of the funding policy implemented by the Russian government to support translations from Russian into various dialects within the USSR, and into languages of areas under its hegemony (various East European languages but also others like Arabic). It must be stressed, however, that such a policy is not specific to authoritarian regimes. During the Cold War, for instance, both US government institutions and private foundations funded translations of liberal and democratic thinkers in the struggle against communism: the Congress for Cultural Freedom was funded by the CIA (Saunders, 1999). In 1952, the American State Department also encouraged the creation of a private, non-profit organization, Franklin

Publications, entrusted with promoting the translation of American works in various countries and languages of the Third World, especially in the Middle East. In the mid-1980s, the book office of the US embassy in Cairo launched a clear political translation programme for a selection of titles; this programme is still active today (Jacquemond, 2009, pp. 8–9). In countries like France, the Netherlands and Israel, literary works are supported as well, with no specific ideological objective but the promotion of the national culture abroad, or the improvement of the image of the country.

Conversely, state support for the translation of foreign works into local languages has often also served educational or scientific purposes to maintain a certain level or quality, or to catch up with the competition from a 'developmental' perspective, as exemplified by the case of Arab countries (Jacquemond, 2009). In such cases, political and cultural factors are intertwined. Economic factors may also be used to justify state intervention in favour of translations. In France, for instance, government support to export books translated from French is justified not only as a means to favour the radiance (*rayonnement*) of French culture worldwide and to exert soft power (*diplomatie d'influence*), but also to support the French publishing industry.

Ideological constraints have effects on circulation channels (illegal vs legal) as well as on reception, as illustrated by the case of imports and reception in France of literary works from Eastern European countries during the communist period (Popa, 2006, 2010). They may have effects on translation itself and on the practice of translating using censorship or self-censorship, and through their specific ideological orientation (the use of specific words with positive or negative connotations).

13.3.2 The logics of the market

Some translations are governed essentially by the logic of the market. In cases of extreme liberalization of the book market (for example in the US and the UK), cultural goods appear primarily as commercial products that must generate profits. This is best illustrated by producing standardized worldwide best-sellers. Several studies have shown that the publishing industry is more and more dominated by large business firms, which tend to impose criteria of commercial profitability and pay hardly any attention to literary and intellectual criteria (Bourdieu, 1999; Reynaud, 1999; Schalke and Gerlach, 1999; Schiffrin, 2000; Sapiro, 2009b; Thompson, 2010). This phenomenon is also observed in sectors that are in principle more protected, such as academic publishing, as is attested by the deep crisis-hitting university presses in the US and Great Britain (Thompson, 2005). But economists and sociologists differ in their understanding of the economic logic. Economists have framed the production of translations in terms of rationally calculating costs and benefits. Translation rights are acquired when expected benefits, monetary or other, outweigh costs.

Sociologists such as Bourdieu distinguish a variety of resources or forms of capital (in addition to economic, cultural, political and social capital) that agents are endowed with and which they mobilize in the various (sub) fields in which they are active. Bourdieu insisted that the mode of accumulation of these different forms of capital does not correspond to the logic of rationally calculated investment decisions. As in some other fields, publishing appeals much more to the 'practical sense' of its agents, who have been socialized in certain fields or sub-fields (and not in others), and who use their resources by relying on their 'feel for the game' and their dispositions rather than on their capacity for rational calculation (Bourdieu, 1990, 2005). Supply and demand are not simply given, but seen as social constructions that are initiated and maintained by specific groups. Non-market forces, notably state institutions, are involved in these construction processes (Smelser and Swedberg, 2005).

Between the extremes of political control and market exchange, one finds a series of possible configurations in which the relative importance of political and economic factors varies according to the degree of protection of the national market and the degree to which culture fulfils an ideological purpose. Historically, one observes an alternation between phases of strong regulation and of free exchange. Thus, the tight control of monarchical regimes that still prevailed in the 18th century was followed by a phase of liberalization in the early 19th century. The transnational circulation of symbolic goods, for the most part unregulated, underwent a major expansion. At the end of the 19th century, policies of market regulation were established to curb the effects of economic liberalism and to protect national markets. The 1886 Berne Convention for the Protection of Literary and Artistic Works, to which many countries adhered progressively, was the main tool of this international regulation.

As a result of the liberalization of exchanges and the unification of a world market for records, books and movies after World War II, political constraints have weakened as compared to economic constraints. Liberalization in the cultural domain accelerated after the GATT agreements of 1986, in the course of the Uruguay Round, which extended the liberalization of exchanges into service trades – and hence to immaterial or incorporeal goods and especially to cultural products (Jennar and Kalafatides, 2007). The fall of the Berlin Wall in 1989 reinforced the process. This extension challenged the principle of the 'cultural exception', that is to say, the status of exception granted to cultural goods, entitling them to be protected from purely mercantile mechanisms. This provoked a strong reaction in countries like France and led the European Parliament to adopt in 1993 a resolution rallying member states to the principle of 'cultural exceptionalism', which was replaced in 1999 by the notion of 'cultural diversity' under the aegis of UNESCO (Regourd, 2004; Bustamante, 2014).

13.3.3   Cultural factors

The patterns of production and circulation cannot be explained only by political and/or economic factors. As already suggested, specific cultural factors need to be taken into account as well. One should note that the practice of translation preceded the emergence of the book market and that it contributed to its development. Historically speaking, the first bestseller in translation was the Bible – the first printed text appeared in 1455 – and which is still the most translated text (around 400 full translations, with 2,300 partial ones). The wide diffusion of the sacred text in different languages was determined by religious factors as well as by the logics of the emerging market. But translations existed before the text was printed, despite the prohibition pronounced by the Jewish authorities which feared heretic appropriations after the destruction of the Second Temple. The Catholic Church, which had commissioned Jerome a retranslation of the Old Testament from the original Hebrew text (and not from the Greek translation), reaffirmed the superiority of this translation to any other during the Council of Trent. Translations in vernacular languages were not authorized, in order to control the versions that circulated and to reserve the reading of the sacred text to the clergymen altogether. Martin Luther's retranslation of the Bible (1532) was a religious and intellectual endeavour driven by the will to return to the source text rather than to subscribe to the Latin Vulgate; it became the main weapon of the Reformation against the Catholic Church. Thus translation was a major issue at stake in the struggles that constituted the religious field and it was instrumental in different schisms (between Catholicism and Protestantism, but also between various forms of both). Historically, translations also played a major role in the formation of publishing fields in national languages, which it helped to standardize, in many cases well before an indigenous production of texts in these languages developed (Even-Zohar, 1990, pp. 45–52).

In the modern era, cultural factors can be understood in the light of the relative autonomy that cultural fields (the artistic, literary and scientific field, as well as all other fields of cultural production) gradually – though not in a continuous linear process – gained with regard to the state and the market (Bourdieu, 1993, pp. 112–141). As a result of this process, the market of symbolic goods is a specific type of economy that has its own criteria of valuation. According to Bourdieu (1993, pp. 74–111, 1996, 2008), the book market is split between a pole of large-scale production, ruled by the logics of profitability in the short run, and a pole of small-scale production, where intellectual, literary or aesthetic logics prevail over purely economic considerations, and where the issue for a publisher is to accumulate symbolic capital, which can be converted into economic benefits in the long run (the publisher's 'backlist'), even at the price of taking financial risks. Because of the specific competition between firms or imprints and the symbolic capital at stake, Bourdieu defines this opposition as the main principle that structures the field of publishing.

This model can be used to describe the functioning of the market of translations, not only at the national, but also at the global level (Sapiro, 2008, 2010a). Whereas the making of global bestsellers illustrates the quest for profitability in the short run, along with the wide circulation of thrillers and romantic novels, a sizeable share of the import process of foreign literature and academic books in translation arises from the specific logics which prevail in the area of small-scale circulation, as witnessed by the modes of selection, often based on criteria of literary or intellectual value rather than on success with the public at large, and small print runs. The economist Jacques Melitz (2007, p. 193), who defines the literary works that survive as 'capital', acknowledges this long-term investment. These works are usually called 'classics' and are often defined by literary scholars as the 'canon'.

Using the *Index Translationum*, the historian Daniel Milo (1984) shows that, after World War II, the classical Graeco-Latin canon, which had been dominant on the world market of translations before the war, was replaced by European literary works in vernacular languages from the 19th century, which had become the new 'classics'. Considering translation as a symbolic stock exchange which measures the changing value of authors and works, he regards the number of translations of an author as an indicator of his or her value in different periods. He classifies writers according to their cultural legitimacy (assessed by their presence in encyclopaedias, secondary school teaching programmes and academic research, such as the number of PhD dissertations devoted to them) or non-legitimacy (which includes genres such as thrillers and youth literature). 'Legitimate authors' were divided into three groups: 20th century, 19th century and classical authors (encompassing all authors who have written before the 19th century). Authors like Aeschylus, Sophocles, Euripides, Horace, Plutarch, Seneca, Plautus and Tacitus, who were among the 60 most translated authors at the beginning of the 1930s, disappeared from this list after World War II; Plato was the only one who survived. They were ousted by Tolstoy, Dickens, Dostoyevsky and Balzac, to quote only the steadiest on the list of the 30 most translated writers. The second major evolution starts by the end of the 1950s: the number of 'non-legitimate authors' among the most translated writers increases significantly. Around the 1970s, authors of thrillers (such as Agatha Christie and Peter Cheyney) exceed the declining number of legitimate authors. This evolution indicates that market demand has overtaken educational and cultural hierarchies.

It should be noted that, because of increasing commercial constraints, the space of small-scale production most often relies on subsidies, both in publishing and translations. In France, a system of aids for translations into French was established at the end of the 1980s, in order to promote cultural diversity. This programme, implemented by the Centre national du livre (National Centre of the Book), which depends on the Ministry of Culture, indeed supported the translations of works from about 30 languages between 2003 and 2006, but 70 per cent of the funds were allocated to translations from English (a figure which is slightly higher than this language's share among all the books translated into French, and twice as large as its share among small-scale publishers). Conversely, a new subsidization programme aimed at helping translations of French literary and academic works into other languages was set up in 1990 by the Ministry of Foreign Affairs (the *'Programme d'aide à la publication'* or PAP), which completes the existing support for translation (from and into French) allocated by the French Ministry of Culture.

Such subsidies exist also in the Netherlands, Israel and other countries. They are triggered by cultural policies that attempt at incorporating certain cultural goods into the national heritage. Unlike in fascist or communist regimes, where cultural production was regulated in order to control ideological orientations, state intervention in liberal democracies is designed in principle to curb the effects of economic constraints in a market economy, in particular the risk of standardizing and homogenizing cultural productions aimed at the greatest number of consumers. This system of protection for so-called 'merit goods' was created as a result of pressures from authors, publishers and booksellers. Though the system varies across countries, it attests to the recognition by states of market failures and the symbolic legitimacy resulting from the process by which the field of cultural production gained autonomy. This recognition is institutionalized in some cases in a legislative framework, as in fixed book prices and the ban on book advertising on French television – though these laws are nowadays threatened by the WTO's extension of the principles of free trade to services.

The opposition between large-scale and small-scale production is useful for comparing national markets of translation. Despite legal differences between the French-speaking and English-speaking areas, one can see a structural parallel between state support and funding by philanthropic foundations to the non-profit publishing sector (Sapiro, 2010a). The opposition between large-scale and small-scale production partly overlaps with the distinction between the trade and the not-for-profit segments, and, within the trade sector, between large conglomerates and independent firms. Many small and independent trade publishers are located in between, and function more according to the logics of small-scale production. In a parallel way, there is a division of labour within large conglomerates between imprints producing what literary agents call 'commercial' products for the mass market (rack size), and imprints publishing 'upmarket' products with a smaller circulation. To assess how these different segments of the book market 'behave' with regard to translation, we have to look more closely at patterns of importation and reception.

13.4 Selection, import and reception patterns

Sociological approaches to markets have, as we briefly mentioned earlier, conceptualized supply and demand as social constructions, and processes of economic exchange as embedded in a variety of non-economic relations. Markets for cultural or symbolic goods, furthermore, have specific characteristics. In his approach of cultural production, Bourdieu highlighted the difference between small-scale firms, which produce goods by and for specialists, and large-scale firms, which produce for the public at large. Small-scale production depends, in particular, on how critics and other connoisseurs value the output; their judgement can result in consecration and canonization even in the absence of any short-term commercial success.

The French sociologist Lucien Karpik suggested a similar argument. In his view markets for cultural goods do not correspond to the assumptions of standard economics, because cultural goods are neither homogeneous nor differentiated as assumed in models of monopolistic competition. Literary books, songs and movies are 'singularities' that are primarily defined by their quality (Karpik, 2010). While economists tend to reduce the issue of quality to pricing, assuming that price differentials adequately reveal differences in valuation, in markets for singularities price competition is less important than quality competition. Singularities such as books or movies are multidimensional goods, defined by a combination of qualities (characters, story, style, plot). Since according to Karpik there is no objective way to measure these qualities, singularities are characterized by uncertainty.[5] In the absence of a common metric, there is no unanimity about quality judgements, and with a plurality of preferences, markets for singularities are complex institutions. Editors, publishers and consumers do not act on the basis of prices, maximizing profits or utility, but on the basis of judgements and qualitative criteria. Markets governed by prices need to be distinguished from markets governed by judgements. To make these judgements, agents use socially constructed devices such as reviews, expert reports, reputations, ratings, prizes, interpersonal networks and the like (see also English, 2005). These devices, which have to be credible in order to be trusted, allow both producers and consumers to be sufficiently informed for making reasonable choices. We now turn to three issues which characterize the market for translations: linguistic diversity, cultural proximity and power relations, and symbolic recognition.

---

[5] The absence of objective measures, however, is a matter of discussion; see Ginsburgh and Weyers (2014).

13.4.1   Linguistic diversity in translations

One of the issues, already raised, is linguistic diversity. Melitz (2007, p. 212) points out that the supremacy of English can crowd out other languages, a tendency which is a threat to the welfare of future generations:

> Authors writing in the dominant language will not have a better chance of publishing an original manuscript. Quite the contrary, those doing imaginative writing in other languages will face much softer conditions for publication than those writing in the major one. However, with respect to translation and therefore the prospect of reaching a world audience, those writing in the dominant language are privileged.

Far from simply reflecting the size of the market, Melitz observes that the dominance of English in the market of translations has actually increased in spite of the falling share of English language books worldwide. Against this line of reasoning, it has been argued that book production in English is still the largest in the world and culturally so diversified that this can explain why so much is translated from English into other languages, and relatively little from other languages into English (Ginsburgh et al., 2011).

This argument, however, often invoked by large companies as well, is disputed by small publishers and translators, who promote translation as a more 'authentic' expression of diversity (Sapiro, 2010a). In his opening speech to the 2009 session of the World Voices Festival of International Literature, launched in 2006 by the PEN American Center, its chair, Salman Rushdie, recorded that the festival was created 'out of the deep concern that, in the climate of those days, the conversation between the US and the rest of the world was breaking down'. He mentioned the low figures of translations in the US as evidence (see also Allen, 2007). The notion of 'authentic voices' from the world is opposed by the advocates of translation to the standardized products that large conglomerates sell under the label of globalization, as a small trade publisher argues in an interview with G. Sapiro (3 October 2008):

> Now you have more interest on the part of the big publishing houses in the world because they just want to have everything. It is a kind of aspect of globalization. It is not that they want to present to the American people, to American readers, authentic voices to explain what is really going on in these countries by people who really know, it is not that at all. It is kind of the opposite. It is just they will go wherever they have to go to get a sexy story or the same story with new exotic locations. It is really worse than I can even describe.

Moreover, books produced at the periphery of the anglophone area hardly circulate in its big cities as is the case in French-, Spanish- or Arabic-speaking areas:

one can hardly find a book published at the periphery in central big cities, apart maybe in very specialized bookstores; they are also much less (or even not) reviewed in the major newspapers and journals published in these cities. This is also the case at international book fairs, which reproduce the hierarchy between countries: publishers from the periphery occupy a marginal position in the most important ones (Sorà, 1998; Serry and Vincent, 2013).

This asymmetrical circulation within the anglophone world has consequences for the diversity of the books translated from English. Most of these are originally published in the US and in the UK. For instance, between 1997 and 2006, French publishers bought the translation rights for at least 4,000 titles from the US, 2,973 from the UK, 1,049 from Canada, 90 from Australia, 44 from India, 38 from Ireland, 26 from South Africa, 11 from New Zealand and two from Nigeria (according to the data gathered by the French National Union of Publishers, the Syndicat national de l'édition).

The situation was even worse in the past. Between 1948 and 1957, 70.8 per cent of the translations from English to French came from the US, and 29.2 per cent from the UK, according to the *Index Translationum*. At the time, as in the interwar period, the translation market was still concentrated in Europe. The US entered the game in the 1930s and became dominant after World War II. It was under the aegis of UNESCO, which launched a programme for supporting translations of works from non-Western cultures in the 1950s, that the geo-cultural border of the European translation market opened up to Latin American and Asian authors during the next decade (Sapiro, forthcoming a). The access of former colonized countries to political independence and the migratory trajectories of some authors from these countries also favoured the imports of their literary works to centres of the book market, either in translation or in the language of the colonizer. But they have for long occupied a marginal position – such as being 'ghettoized' into specific series such as '*Continent noir*' at Gallimard – and have been given very little attention by major literary journals (Ducournau, 2012). The incitement to globalization fostered this phenomenon in the 1990s, with the notion of 'world literature'. Some authors coming from the 'peripheries' won important literary prizes: in 1992, the Saint Lucia poet Derek Walcott was awarded the Nobel Prize, the Sri Lankan born Canadian novelist Michael Ondaatje received the Booker Prize, and the Caribbean writer Patrick Chamoiseau won the Prix Goncourt. Non-Western authors and artists started getting more attention in newspapers during this period (Berkers et al., 2011), and most of them are now published or exhibited by publishers or galleries located in central cities such as New York, London, Paris and Berlin (see Sapiro, 2010b and forthcoming b, for francophone writers translated in the US during this period; and Quemin, 2006, 2013 for the contemporary art market in general).

As discussed in Section 13.1, linguistic diversity is not randomly distributed on the global translation market. The number of translated languages varies across different categories of books and is much higher for literature. Even within this genre, diversity is not distributed evenly and novels are much more represented. The distinction between small-scale and large-scale production reveals variations in language diversity (Sapiro, 2008, 2010a). In France, large-scale production is almost entirely dominated by translations from English worldwide bestsellers, thrillers and romantic novels, but small-scale production is much more diversified. In the foreign literature series of prestigious literary French publishers, such as Gallimard's *'Du monde entier'*, the share of books translated from English is only one-third, and the number of languages represented reaches 30, the number of countries 40. This configuration also explains why the share of translation is so low in the Anglo-American world: there are virtually no translations from large-scale produced books, since the supply written in English is sufficient, and the prevailing criteria of profitability lead editors to avoid translation costs and time-consuming search procedures.

13.4.2 Cultural proximity and power relations

The logic underlying the selection of languages requires some explanation. As already mentioned, linguistic and cultural proximity has been proposed by Ginsburgh et al. (2011) as a factor facilitating translations, since both publishers and readers are assumed to look for easier and more accessible novels. Although it is a factor that has to be accounted for, it can be neutralized by other factors, and it does not do justice to the power relations between languages on the one hand, and to the diversity of functions that publishing and reading can fulfil on the other.

Cultural proximity can be counterbalanced by conflicting relations (think of Hebrew and Arabic) or reinforced by common political interests, as illustrated by the relation between Brazil and Argentina, which built their national identities through translations (Sorà, 2002, 2003). On the other hand, cultural distances can be bridged in cases of strategic alliances or bi-national agreements that include a clause on cultural exchanges and can favour the institutionalization of linguistic training in a country. For instance, teaching Hebrew in secondary schools in France was institutionalized in the 1970s with the creation of two competitive national exams to become a secondary school teacher (the CAPES in 1973 and the *agrégation* in 1977); this, in turn, enlarged the basis for recruiting translators from Hebrew and potential importers from this language. As a result (and some other factors), translations from Hebrew expanded in the 1980s (Sapiro, 2002 and forthcoming). Readers' motivations vary and range from education to entertainment, and from practical to aesthetic interests (Mauger and Poliak, 1998). For instance, tourism and the quest for exoticism or political interest for a country can foster cultural interest: the interest of Western publishers in the literary production of Eastern European countries was related to writers opposed to the communist regimes and decreased suddenly after the fall of the Berlin Wall in 1989 (Popa, 2010). The interest in Hebrew literature in France has been essentially motivated by political interest as well (Sapiro, 2002), though, and, contrary to the expectations of publishers, this interest did not come from the Jewish community only.

Cultural proximity between languages does not take into account migratory phenomena either; these may play a role in the circulation of works, depending on the socio-economic and cultural status of migrants (for instance, the North African immigration to France did not bring with it many translators and importers, as economic and cultural – as well as social – capital was lacking).

Proximity does not account for the asymmetries of exchanges between languages either. How can one explain, for example, the unequal exchanges between France and Germany? Whereas there are more books produced in Germany than in France (according to the *Index Translationum*, Germany published 93,124 books in 2009 and France 63,690 in 2010), the exchange ratio has always been favourable to French: there are more French books translated into German than German books into French.[6] Although the gap between the overall number of translations from German, Italian and Spanish into French and from French into these languages tends to decrease in the 1990s, the ratio remains favourable to French, despite the fact that, in 2008, Spain produced more books (86,300) than France (Sapiro, 2009a).

In fact, these asymmetries reflect much more the symbolic capital of languages. According to Casanova (2005), languages are endowed with an unequal amount of literary capital: dominant languages possess more of it, since both their historically accumulated reputation and prestige, and the number of texts written in these languages and universally regarded as important, have an effect. Dominated languages are those endowed with little literary capital and a low level of international recognition. This differential accumulation of symbolic capital, which may also vary between creative domains (in philosophy, for instance, German and French have had until recently a larger amount of symbolic capital than English), underlies the unequal power relations among national cultures; this obviously has consequences on the reception of cultural goods as well as on their functions and uses: for a national literary field 'under construction' the translation of a canonical work of classic literature may serve

---

[6] The ratio of the number of French titles for which translation rights were sold to German publishers vs the number of German titles the rights of which were acquired by French publishers was equal to 4.8 between 1996 and 2000 and to 3.8 between 2001 and 2005 in favour of French, according to the data collected by the French Syndicat national de l'édition.

to accumulate symbolic capital, whereas the translation of a text from a dominated literature into a dominant language constitutes a consecration for the author (Casanova, 2009).

13.4.3 Economic success and symbolic recognition

It is often assumed that when publishers acquire translation rights they are looking for best-selling books in other countries. But this assumption is too restrictive. Sales obviously are a criterion for acquiring translation rights, but while it is the main criterion for large-scale productions, it is never the only one for small-scale productions and it sometimes does not even play a significant role: when Chicago University Press decided to acquire the rights of the 15 volumes of Derrida's seminars before they were even published in French, it was not money that led them to their decision, but the symbolic capital represented by the author's name.

Publishing a translation might seem less risky for publishers, since the book has already gone through a selection and evaluation process, but the production costs are higher than for indigenous books, since translation rights need to be purchased and publishers have to pay for translation. As a matter of fact, the relative weights of these two factors may vary geographically and historically, and tend to be a function of the unequal power relations between countries, cultures and firms. For firms that occupy a dominant position in national or international publishing, for example, translations can be a means of appropriating and accumulating symbolic capital (Serry, 2002).

As interviews with editors, publishers and agents reveal, symbolic recognitions such as press reviews (which do not necessarily have a significant impact on sales) or literary prizes (which do influence sales, but also attest to recognition by peers) are taken into account in the decision-making process.[7] And though they admit being impressed by sales, publishers who were interviewed admit that success in one country does not guarantee the book will sell in another one. National book markets still have their specificity in the small-scale production market at least.

That sales is not a criterion in itself can be illustrated by two cases. Despite its large success in France (more than two million copies in the year after its publication by Gallimard in 2006), all American and British publishers turned down Muriel Barbery's *Elegance of the Hedgehog*, considering it 'too French' (Archives of the French Publishers Agency). The English rights were finally acquired by Europa Editions, a small company founded by the owners of the Italian Edizioni E/O to bring European literature to the Anglo-American market. The English translation published in 2008 became a huge bestseller. Jonathan

---

[7] Note that mass-market products are very seldom reviewed or awarded.

Littell's *The Kindly Ones*, also published in 2006 by Gallimard and awarded the Prix Goncourt, is a counter-example. The English rights were bought by HarperCollins, which paid roughly one million dollars, much more than what is usual for this kind of book; yet it did not sell as expected (Rich, 2009).

Such cases are quite common. Archival research and data provided by publishers show that up-market literary translations seldom sell 10,000 copies and, when they do, they are considered very successful. Most of them sell less than 4,000 copies in markets as large as the US or France. In the 1930s, the French publisher Gaston Gallimard decided to keep going translating Faulkner in spite of the 'indifference of the public' as he wrote in an unpublished letter (Gallimard Archives; Sapiro, forthcoming c). *Sanctuary*, released in French in 1933, sold 3,900 copies in 1938; *As I Lay Dying*, published in 1934, sold 1,008. Gallimard published four more translations of Faulkner's novels until 1939, the year in which he also released a translation of Margaret Mitchell's *Gone with the Wind*; sales reached 385,000 copies ten years after its publication, and 840,000 in 1961, thanks to the 1939 film adaptation. This duality is typical of symbolic goods. Publishers call it 'balancing' or 'equalization': short-sellers help finance long-sellers (economists call this cross-subsidization).

This policy of internal balancing has been undermined by the concentration of publishing firms into large conglomerates and the financialization of the industry. Shareholders increasingly contest policies of cross-subsidization and demand that each book or book series be profitable (Schiffrin, 2000), though this does not apply to small independent firms (for which the level of profitability is also much lower) and to non-profit publishers. During an interview, a small publisher specializing in Latin American literature defined her best-selling author as the 'sponsor' of the other more recent or less famous authors. She also mentioned a German writer whom she continues to publish though she loses money on him, because she trusts his literary value.[8] Even in large conglomerates, some imprints are dedicated to up-market literature, for which expectations are not as high in terms of sales as for mass-market products.

The agents involved in the decision process in the two types of firms are not identical. Professional agents and scouts rule large-scale production. Translators, authors and critics play a role in small-scale production. They are part of an international network and share information, advice and judgement, which are essential in legitimizing works and contribute significantly to the selection and production of books. Translators, for instance, are often consulted by publishers and regularly suggest works to be translated; this is extremely rare in large-scale production. A similar process operates on the reception side, where

---

[8] Interview with G. Sapiro, 27 August 2007.

individualized reviews, prizes and reputations, rather than sales, standardized narratives and advertising, shape the demand of readers.

13.5 Conclusion

Translation has for long been a topic reserved for literary scholars and linguists. As a distinct field 'translation studies' emerged during the 1970s, and it is only in the beginning of the 1990s that social scientists started to explore the issue. In our brief survey of the emerging social science research on translations (restricted to books), we have highlighted three levels of analysis.

The first level is concerned with describing and analysing the international flow of translations and the structure and dynamics of the global market. Most of this work, which is based on a single database, the *Index Translationum*, revolves around the following questions. How has the share of various source-languages evolved over time? How can the structure of the world market be conceptualized and explained? And are the consequences of the growing share of English increasing homogeneity or maintaining diversity? Economists and sociologists tend to have different interpretations. Economists relate translations to the production of books in the source and destination languages, to linguistic and cultural distances, and to characteristics of the source and destination languages, represented by fixed effects. Sociologists insist on the asymmetrical character of exchanges and relate them to the unequal distribution of economic, political and cultural resources of language groups.

The second level of analysis explores the different kinds of factors and dynamics which underlie the circulation of translations, distinguishing political, economic and cultural factors. Economists usually frame the production of translations in terms of rationally calculating costs and benefits, while sociologists like Bourdieu have distinguished a variety of forms of capital that agents are endowed with (in addition to economic, cultural, political and symbolic capital). Bourdieu insisted that the mode of accumulation of these different forms of capital relies much more on the 'practical sense' of its agents, who have been socialized in certain fields or sub-fields (and not in others). The publishing field itself consists of two sectors: large scale and restricted scale production. The former is governed by short-term economic motives, the latter by symbolic benefits and long-term perspectives. The large-scale production sector tends to translate from English and concentrates on best-sellers; the other sector is far more diversified.

The third level, concerned with the selection, imports and reception of translations, shows how power relations between languages, economic considerations, political stakes, symbolic capital as well as other cultural factors can help map and explain the heterogeneity of the supply of translations in terms of language diversity, selection of languages and of works. It starts with the observation that literary books are neither homogeneous products nor equivalent versions of a standard product. Instead they can be seen as 'singularities' for which a combination of qualities is more important than price. Markets for such types of goods depend, according to Karpik, on judgement rather than on calculation, and rely on a range of social devices (best-seller lists, rankings, book reviews, prizes, reputations) in selecting from a highly diversified supply. The way publishers and consumers use such devices depends on their position in the field of cultural production and in the social field at large. This brings us back to the difference between large-scale and restricted production, that is between a market governed by best-sellers, advertising and popular genres, and a specifically literary market in which reviews, reputations and prizes predominate.

References

E. Allen (2007) 'Translation, Globalization and English' In E. Allen (ed.) *To Be Translated or Not to Be. PEN/IRL Report on the International Situation of Literary Translation* (Barcelona: Institute Ramon Lull), pp. 17–33.

M. Baker (ed.) (2009) *Critical Readings in Translation Studies* (London/New York: Routledge).

M. Baker and G. Saldanha (eds) (2008) *The Routledge Encyclopedia of Translation Studies* (London/New York: Routledge).

P. Berkers, S. Janssen and M. Verboord (2011) 'Globalization and Ethnic Diversity in Western Newspaper Coverage of Literary Authors: Comparing Developments in France, Germany, the Netherlands, and the United States, 1955–2005', *American Behavioral Scientist*, 55, 624–641.

S. Berman and C. Porter (eds) (2014) *Companion to Translation Studies* (Oxford/Malden: Wiley-Blackwell).

F. Billiani (ed.) (2007) *Modes of Censorship and Translation: National Contexts and Diverse Media* (Manchester: St Jerome).

A. Bokobza and G. Sapiro (2008) 'L'analyse des flux de traduction et la construction des bases de données' In G. Sapiro (ed.) *Translatio. Le marché de la traduction en France à l'heure de la mondialisation* (Paris: CNRS Editions).

P. Bourdieu (1990) *The Logic of Practice* (Cambridge: Polity Press).

P. Bourdieu (1991) *Language and Symbolic Power* (Cambridge: Polity Press).

P. Bourdieu (1993) *The Field of Cultural Production: Essays on Art and Literature* (Cambridge UK: Polity Press).

P. Bourdieu (1996) *The Rules of Art* (Cambridge/Stanford: Polity Press-Stanford University Press).

P. Bourdieu (1999) 'The Social Conditions of the International Circulation of Ideas' In R. Shusterman (ed.) *Bourdieu: A Critical Reader* (Oxford/Malden: Wiley-Blackwell).

P. Bourdieu (2005) *The Social Structures of the Economy* (Cambridge: Polity Press).

P. Bourdieu (2008) 'A Conservative Revolution in Publishing', *Translation Studies*, 1, 123–153.

A. Brisset and B. Aye (2007) *Translation and Cultural Diversity: Report on World Translation Flows* (Paris: IATIS/UNESCO).

P. Burke and R. Po-chia Hsia (eds) (2009) *Cultural Translation in Early Modern Europe* (Cambridge: Cambridge University Press).

M. Bustamante (2014) 'L'UNESCO et la culture: construction d'une catégorie d'intervention internationale, du "développement culturel" à la "diversité culturelle" ', PhD dissertation, Ecole des Hautes Etudes en Sciences Sociales, Paris.

P. Casanova (2005) *The World Republic of Letters* (Cambridge, MA: Harvard University Press).

P. Casanova (2009) 'Translation as Unequal Exchange' In Mona Baker (ed.) *Critical Readings in Translation Studies* (London/New York: Routledge), pp. 285–303.

D. Crane (2002) 'Culture and Globalization: Theoretical Models and Emerging Trends' In D. Crane, N. Kawashima and K. Kawasaki (eds) *Global Culture: Media, Arts, Policy, and Globalization* (London/New York: Routledge).

De Swaan (1993) 'The Emergent World Language System', *International Political Science Review*, 14, 219–226.

De Swaan (2001) *Words of the World: The Global Language System* (Cambridge: Polity Press).

C. Ducournau (2012) 'Écrire, lire, élire l'Afrique. Les mécanismes de réception et de consécration d'écrivains contemporains issus de pays francophones d'Afrique subsaharienne', PhD dissertation, Ecole des Hautes Etudes en Sciences Sociales, Paris.

J. English (2005) *The Economy of Prestige: Prizes, Awards and the Circulation of Cultural Value* (Cambridge, MA: Harvard University Press).

I. Even-Zohar (1990) 'Polysystem Studies', *Poetics Today*, 11, 45–51.

Y. Gambier and L. van Doorslaer (eds) (2011–2014) *Handbook of Translation Studies* (Amsterdam/Philadelphia: John Benjamins Publishing Company).

V. Ganne and M. Minon (1992) 'Géographies de la traduction' In F. Barret-Ducrocq (ed.) *Traduire l'Europe* (Paris: Payot).

V. Ginsburgh and S. Weyers (2014) 'Évaluer l'art: propriétés ou conventions?', *La vie des idées*, 28 October, www.laviedesidees/Evaluer-l-Art-Proprietes-ou.html

V. Ginsburgh, S. Weber and S. Weyers (2011) 'The Economics of Literary Translation: Some Theory and Evidence', *Poetics: Journal of Empirical Research on Culture, the Media and the Art*, 39, 228–246.

C. Girou de Buzareingues (1972) 'La traduction en France' In J. Cain, R. Escarpit and H.-J. Martin (eds) *Le Livre français hier, aujourd'hui, demain* (Paris: Imprimerie nationale).

J. Heilbron (1995) 'Nederlandse vertalingen wereldwijd. Kleine landen en culturele mondialisering' In J. Heilbron, W. de Nooy and W. Tichelaar (eds) *Waarin een klein land. Nederlandse cultuur in internationaal verband* (Amsterdam: Prometheus).

J. Heilbron (1999) 'Towards a Sociology of Translation: Book Translations as a Cultural World System', *European Journal of Social Theory*, 2, 429–444.

J. Heilbron (2002) 'Echanges culturels transnationaux et mondialisation', *Regards sociologiques*, 22, 141–154.

J. Heilbron (2008) 'Responding to Globalization: The Development of Book Translations in France and the Netherlands' In A. Pym, M. Shlesinger and D. Simeoni (eds) *Beyond Descriptive Translation Studies: Investigations in Homage to Gideon Toury* (Amsterdam/Philadelphia: John Benjamins), pp. 187–197.

J. Heilbron and G. Sapiro (2007) 'Towards a Sociology of Translation: Current Issues and Future Prospects' In M. Wolf and A. Fukari (eds) *Constructing a Sociology of Translation* (Amsterdam/Philadelphia, John Benjamins), pp. 93–107.

C. Hjorth-Andersen (2001) 'A Model of Translations', *Journal of Cultural Economics*, 25, 203–217.

J. Holmes (1988) *Translated! Papers on Literary Translation and Translation Studies* (Amsterdam: Rodopi).

P. Hopper (2007) *Understanding Cultural Globalization* (Cambridge: Polity Press).

R. Jacquemond (2009) 'Translation Policies in the Arab World. Representations, Discourses, Realities', *The Translator*, 15, 1–21.

R. Jennar and L. Kalafatides (2007) *L'AGCS. Quand les Etats abdiquent face aux multinationales* (Paris: Raisons d'agir).

J. Jurt (1999) ' "L'intraduction" de la littérature française en Allemagne', *Actes de la recherche en sciences sociales*, 130, 86–89.

L. Karpik (2010) *Valuing the Unique: The Economics of Singularities* (Princeton: Princeton University Press).

G. Loiseaux (1995) *La littérature de la défaite et de la collaboration, d'après 'Phönix oder Asche?' de Bernhard Payr* (Paris: Fayard).

G. Mauger and C. Poliak (1998) 'Les usages sociaux de la lecture', *Actes de la recherche en sciences sociales*, 123, 3–24.

J. Melitz (2007) 'The Impact of English Dominance on Literature and Welfare', *Journal of Economic Behavior & Organization*, 64, 193–215.

D. Milo (1984) 'La bourse mondiale de la traduction: un baromètre culturel', *Annales*, 1, 92–115.

I. Popa (2006) 'Translation Channels: A Primer on Politicised Literary Transfer', *Target: International Review of Translation Studies*, 18, 205–228.

I. Popa (2010) *Traduire sous contraintes. Littérature et communisme* (Paris: CNRS Éditions).

A. Pym and G. Chrupala (2005) 'The Quantitative Analysis of Translation Flows in the Age of an International Language' In A. Branchadell and M. West (eds) *Less Translated Languages* (Amsterdam/Philadelphia: John Benjamins), pp. 27–38.

A. Pym, M. Shlesinger and Z. Jettmarova (eds) (2006) *Sociocultural Aspects of Translating and Interpreting* (Amsterdam/Philadelphia: John Benjamins).

A. Pym, M. Shlesinger and D. Simeoni (eds) (2008) *Beyond Descriptive Translation Studies: Investigations in Homage to Gideon Toury* (Amsterdam/Philadelphia: John Benjamins).

A. Quemin (2006) 'Globalization and Mixing in the Visual Arts: An Empirical Survey of "High Culture" and Globalization', *International Sociology*, 21, 522–550.

A. Quemin (2013) *Les stars de l'art contemporain* (Paris: CNRS Editions).

S. Regourd (ed.) (2004) *De l'exception à la diversité culturelle* (Paris: La documentation française).

F. Rener (1989) *Interpretatio: Language and Translation from Cicero to Tyler* (Amsterdam/Atlanta: Rodopi).

B. Reynaud (1999) 'L'emprise des groupes sur l'édition française au début des années 80', *Actes de la recherche en sciences sociales*, 130, 3–10.

M. Rich (2009) 'Publisher's Big Gamble on Divisive French Novel', *The New York Times*, 3 March.

C. Rundle (2010) *Publishing Translations in Fascist Italy* (Oxford: Peter Lang).

G. Sapiro (2002) 'L'importation de la littérature hébraïque en France. Entre communautarisme et universalisme', *Actes de la recherche en sciences sociales*, 144, 80–98.

G. Sapiro (2003) 'The Literary Field between the State and the Market', *Poetics: Journal of Empirical Research on Culture, the Media and the Arts*, 31, 441–461.

G. Sapiro (2008) 'Translation and the Field of Publishing: A Commentary on Pierre Bourdieu's "A Conservative Revolution in Publishing" from a Translation Perspective', *Translation Studies*, 1, 154–167.

G. Sapiro (2009a) 'L'Europe, centre du marché mondial de la traduction' In G. Sapiro (ed.) *L'Espace intellectuel en Europe 19ᵉ-20ᵉ siècle* (Paris: La Découverte), pp. 249–287.

G. Sapiro (ed.) (2009b) *Les Contradictions de la globalisation éditoriale* (Paris: Nouveau Monde).

G. Sapiro (2010a) 'Globalization and Cultural Diversity in the Book Market: The Case of Translations in the US and in France', *Poetics: Journal of Empirical Research on Culture, the Media and the Arts*, 38, 419–439.

G. Sapiro (2010b) 'French Literature in the World System of Translation' In C. McDonald and S. Suleiman (eds) *French Global: A New Approach to Literary History* (New York: Columbia University Press), pp. 298–319.

G. Sapiro (2014) 'The Sociology of Translation: A New Research Domain' In S. Berman and C. Porter (eds) *Companion to Translation Studies* (Oxford/Malden: Wiley-Blackwell), pp. 82–94.

G. Sapiro (2015a) 'Translation and Symbolic Capital in the Era of Globalization: French Literature in the United States', *Cultural Sociology*, 9(3), 320–346.

G. Sapiro (2015b) 'Strategies of Importation of Foreign Literature in France in the 20th Century: The Case of Gallimard, or the Making of an International Publisher' In S. Hegelsson and P. Vermeulen (eds) *Institutions of World Literature: Writing, Translation, Markets* (London: Routledge), pp. 143–159.

G. Sapiro (forthcoming a) 'L'essor des traductions en français au XXe siècle et la diversification des langues' In J.-Y. Masson and B. Banoun (eds) *Histoire des traductions en langue française* (Paris: Verdier).

G. Sapiro (forthcoming b) 'Translation and Identity: Social Trajectories of the Translators of Hebrew literature in French', *TTR: Traduction, Terminologie, Rédaction*, 27.

F. Saunders (1999), *Who Paid the Pied Piper? The CIA and the Cultural Cold War* (London: Granta Books).

C. Schalke and M. Gerlach (1999) 'Le paysage éditorial allemand', *Actes de la recherche en sciences sociales*, 130, 29–47.

A. Schiffrin (2000) *The Business of Books* (New York: Verso).

H. Serry (2002) 'Constituer un catalogue littéraire', *Actes de la recherche en sciences sociales*, 144, 70–79.

H. Serry and J. Vincent (2013) 'Penser le rôle des foires internationales dans la mondialisation de l'édition. L'exemple des éditeurs québécois à la Buchmesse de Francfort', *Le Mouvement Social*, 243, 105–116.

N. Smelser and R. Swedberg (eds) (2005) *Handbook of Economic Sociology* (Princeton: Princeton University Press).

G. Sorà (1998) 'Francfort: la foire d'empoigne', *Liber. Revue internationale des livres*, March, 2–3.

G. Sorà (2002) 'Un échange dénié. La traduction d'auteurs brésiliens en Argentine', *Actes de la recherche en sciences sociales*, 145, 61–70.

G. Sorà (2003) *Traducir el Brasil. Una antropologia de la circulacion internacional de ideas* (Buenos Aires: Libros del Zorzal).

J. Thompson (2005) *Books in the Digital Age: The Transformation of Academic and Higher Education Publishing in Britain and the United States* (Cambridge: Polity Press).

J. Thompson (2010) *Merchants of Culture: The Publishing Business in the Twenty-First Century* (Cambridge/Malden: Polity Press).

G. Thomson-Wohlgemuth (2009) *Translation under State Control: Books for Young People in the German Democratic Republic* (London/New York: Routledge).

G. Toury (1995) *Descriptive Translation Studies and Beyond* (Amsterdam: John Benjamins).

N. Van Es and J. Heilbron (2015) 'Fiction from the Periphery: How Dutch Writers Enter the Field of English-language Literature', *Cultural Sociology*, 9, 296–319.

L. Venuti (1998) *The Scandals of Translation: Towards an Ethics of Difference* (London: Routledge).

L. Venuti (2008) *The Translator's Invisibility: A History of Translation* (London/New York: Routledge) (first published 1995).

L. Venuti (ed.) (2012) *The Translation Studies Reader* (London/New York: Routledge).

F. Wacquet (2001) *Latin, Or the Empire of the Sign* (London: Verso).

I. Wallerstein (2004) *World-Systems Analysis* (Durham/London: Duke University Press).

M. Wolf and A. Fukari (eds) (2007) *Constructing a Sociology of Translation* (Amsterdam: John Benjamins).

14

Languages, Fees and the International Scope of Patenting

Dietmar Harhoff, Karin Hoisl, Bruno van Pottelsberghe de la Potterie and Charlotte Vandeput

14.1   Introduction

Recent developments in patenting activity are the subject of a growing litera-ture. Existing research contributes to a better understanding of the incentives that drive economic agents to rely on the patent system (e.g. Cohen et al., 2000; Arundel, 2001; Blind et al., 2006; Peeters and van Pottelsberghe, 2006; von Graevenitz et al., 2013) and on potential implications of their behaviour for the effectiveness of the patent system. Lately, a number of researchers have started to explore the design of the patent system itself, i.e. the role of fees and costs of patenting (Archontopoulos et al., 2007; Harhoff et al., 2009; de Rassenfosse and van Pottelsberghe, 2013), the duration of examination (Thomas, 2010; Harhoff, 2011), as well as patent office governance and management (Friebel et al., 2006).

Recent changes in the European patent system comprise the coming into force of the London Agreement in 2008,[1] the agreement of the EU Council to draft EU regulations regarding an EU Patent in 2011,[2] and the introduc-tion of new claim-based[3] fees at the European Patent Office (EPO) in 2008 and 2009.[4] Whereas the first two changes aimed at reducing the burden of costs for the applicants of European (EP) patents, the latter change aimed at increasing

---

[1] See www.epo.org/law-practice/legal-texts/london-agreement.html (accessed on 27 January 2012).
[2] See www.epo.org/law-practice/legislative-initiatives/eu-patent.html (accessed on 27 January 2012).
[3] Claims define the legal scope of a patent, they are used to describe the technological scope of a protection.
[4] See www.epo.org/service-support/updates/2008/20080305f/claims-fees.html (accessed on 27 January 2012).

patenting costs to reduce the complexity of applications. Even though many practitioners have argued that patent office fees account for only a small fraction of total patenting costs, they often represent marginal costs while attorney fees – which are assumed to make up for the major part of patenting costs – are largely sunk *ex ante*. First empirical evidence points to a considerable impact of fees. Archontopoulos et al. (2007), for instance, find that after an increase of the claim fee in the US in 2004,[5] the average number of claims per patent decreased from 28 to 23. De Rassenfosse and van Pottelsberghe (2012) summarize evidence from empirical studies indicating inelastic, though not small, reactions to fee changes ranging from −0.03 to −0.60.

With the exception of early work by Pakes (1986) and Schankerman and Pakes (1986) and empirical analyses by Lanjouw (1998) who analyse the impact of post-grant renewal fees and litigation costs, existing research has focused on pre-grant fees and costs. The objective of this chapter is to provide an in-depth analysis of the impact of post-grant costs and fees, i.e. translation costs and fees for validating an EP patent in different jurisdictions as well as for keeping it in force. The European patent system provides an excellent setting for understanding the drivers of international patenting strategies, since it imposes rather heterogeneous cost regimes on patent applicants. Once a patent is granted by the EPO, the applicant has the option, but not the obligation, to validate the patent in any of the countries for which patent protection was requested. At this point, the patent may have to be translated into a different language. Hence, these costs are marginal in the sense that at the point of decision-making all examination and application fees are sunk, the grant decision has been made, and the receipt of the national patent only depends on the costs considered here.

Translations into Nordic languages or Greek are, for instance, particularly expensive. First, because these languages are rare, i.e. the number of native speakers is small. Second, for Greek, since the distance between this language and English, German or French is particularly large, this increases the translations costs. Hence, linguistic distances may affect patenting decisions. More specifically, patents may not be validated in some countries due to high costs associated with a translation.

We provide estimates of the impact of post-grant fees and costs on patenting using a model of validation decisions as a function of translation costs and fees for validating and maintaining the patent. In the following, an empirical model of validation behaviour is tested with a unique dataset that includes all

---

[5] Up to 2004, the USPTO charged $18 for the 21st and each subsequent claim. From December 2004, it increased the claims fee to $50 for the 21st and each subsequent claim (Archontopoulos et al., 2007).

patents that were granted by the EPO in 2003.[6] Given our research design, our estimates are also informative about the determinants of the geographical scope of patenting. While the extension of international patent families is frequently used as an indicator of patent value (Putnam, 1996; Harhoff et al., 2003), its determinants have hardly been identified. Only a few studies have focused on the drivers of international patenting, e.g. Bosworth (1984), Eaton and Kortum (1996), Porter and Stern (2000) and Deng (2007). None of them have taken into account the role of translation costs. Our empirical results suggest that the size and the wealth of the origin and destination countries significantly affect the probability of observing a patent validation. These determinants reflect the benefits that a particular applicant from one country will enjoy from patenting in another European Patent Convention (EPC) country. The geographical distance between countries also plays an important role – costs of transportation are still present and limit the benefit of a patent, since the world is not 'completely flat' (Friedman, 2006). The costs of translating EPO-granted patents into different European languages and the level of validation and renewal fees affect the probability of patent validation negatively.

Our results provide potentially important policy implications. The patent system was originally designed to provide incentives to create innovation. Recently, firms increasingly have learned to use it strategically to gain advantage over their competitors. Our results show that fee changes are potentially important elements of patent office policies seeking to impact on applicant behaviour – higher fees will have a dampening effect on patent validations. This is even more important given that changes or adaptations to administrative rules of patent systems typically require lengthy processes, which have to take into account the views of different stakeholders. Conversely, changes in the level of fees can be introduced quickly in order to curb or encourage particular developments.

The chapter is structured as follows. In the next section, we discuss the institutional context of the European patent system and develop the hypotheses to be tested. Section 14.3 describes the dataset, the construction of the dependent and explanatory variables, the econometric framework and discusses the descriptive statistics. The results of the multivariate tests are presented and interpreted in Section 14.4.

14.2 Institutional background and hypotheses

The EPO grants patents for each of the signatory or accession states to the EPC. The EPC signed in Munich in 1973 is a contract constituting the European

---

[6] In another paper (Harhoff et al., 2009) we rely on a complementary approach, analysing the validation behaviour at the aggregate level of country-to-country patent flows.

Table 14.1 Members of the EPC as of October 2010

Date of entry into the EPC	Country	Date of entry into the EPC	Country
7 Oct 1977	Belgium, Germany, France, Luxembourg, the Netherlands, Switzerland, United Kingdom	1 Dec 2002	Slovenia
1 May 1978	Sweden	1 Jan 2003	Hungary
1 Dec 1978	Italy	1 Mar 2003	Romania
1 May 1979	Austria	1 Mar 2004	Poland
1 Apr 1980	Liechtenstein	1 Nov 2004	Iceland
1 Oct 1986	Greece, Spain	1 Dec 2004	Lithuania
1 Jan 1990	Denmark	1 Jul 2005	Latvia
1 Dec 1991	Monaco	1 Mar 2007	Malta
1 Jan 1992	Portugal	1 Jan 2008	Norway, Croatia
1 Aug 1992	Ireland	1 Jan 2009	Former Yugoslav Republic of Macedonia
1 Mar 1996	Finland	1 Jul 2009	San Marino
1 Apr 1998	Cyprus	1 May 2010	Albania
1 Nov 2000	Turkey	1 Oct 2010	Serbia
1 Jul 2002	Bulgaria, Czech Republic, Estonia, Slovakia		

Patent Organization and providing an independent legal system under which European patents are to be granted. The EPC came into force in 1977 and the EPO was founded in the very same year. On 1 June 1978, the first European patent application was filed with the EPO. Table 14.1 contains a list of today's 38 member states and the date of entry into the European system.

Applications may be filed directly at the EPO (as first filings) or be forwarded to the EPO within the priority year after having been filed as a priority application in a national patent office (NPO).[7] At the latest after one year (under the EPC[8]) or 31 months (under the Patent Cooperation Treaty[9] (PCT)), the application may be transferred to the EPO. Historically, the EPO examination

---

[7] Cf. Guellec and van Pottelsberghe (2007) and Stevnsborg and van Pottelsberghe (2007) for an in-depth description of the various filing routes which may lead to an application at the EPO.

[8] See www.epo.org/about-us/organisation/member-states.html (accessed on 8 September 2011).

[9] The Patent Cooperation Treaty was signed in Washington in 1970 and entered into force in 1978. By filing a patent application under the PCT, it is possible to obtain protection in up to 138 PCT contracting states (see www.wipo.int/pct/en/treaty/about.htm (accessed on 8 September 2011).

process has taken slightly more than four years (van Zeebroeck, 2007; Harhoff and Wagner, 2009).

The EPC states in which the applicant would like to receive patent protection have to be designated by the applicant. The designation is subject to the payment of a designation fee. The term for designating EPC member states expires six months after the European Patent Bulletin announces the publication of the search report (Article 79 (2) EPC). However, contracting states 'may be withdrawn at any time up to the grant of the European patent' (Article 97 (3) EPC).[10] Before July 1999, applicants were obliged to pay a designation fee for *each* designated contracting state (Article 2 (2), (3) Rules relating to Fees). In December 1998, the EPO amended its 'Rules relating to Fees'. Effective as of 1 July 1999 'designation fees being deemed paid for all contracting states upon payment of seven times the amount of this fee' (amended Article 2 (3) Rules relating to Fees).[11] Thus, with the payment of designation fees for seven countries, it became possible to designate all EPC countries.

The choice of the regional scope of patent protection is made by the applicant once the patent has been granted. At that time, the applicant must eventually have the patent translated into the official languages of these countries, and pay the validation fees as well as the renewal fees for each year of protection.[12] The set-up is, therefore, appropriate for assessing the sensitivity of applicants to marginal increases of fees and transaction costs.

In what follows, we take into account the extant analyses of firms' patenting behaviour in order to derive hypotheses regarding the potential determinants of the geographical scope chosen by firms. One of the early studies on the geographical scope of patent protection is provided by Slama (1981). The author investigates the determinants of international patent application flows at the country level using German patent application data between 1967 and 1978. Bosworth (1984) uses UK patent data from 1974 to assess the factors influencing the decision to transfer technology across borders. The two studies suggest that the GDP of both the applicant's and the target country are relevant for the validation decision. Once GDP is accounted for, Slama (1981) does not find any significant influence of the population of the destination and the source country on patent application flows between two countries.

---

[10] See www.epo.org/law-practice/legal-texts/epc.html (accessed on 8 September 2011).
[11] See www.epo.org/law-practice/legal-texts/archive/documentation/rules-relating-fees.html (accessed on 8 September 2011).
[12] This fragmentation of the European patent system has been criticized for years by the business sector, as it induces a high managerial complexity and is associated with relatively high cumulative fees and translation costs. Cf. van Pottelsberghe and François (2009) and van Pottelsberghe and Mejer (2010) for simulations of total patenting costs in the European patent system. International comparisons show that even after the London Agreement the costs of patenting are at least four times higher in Europe than in the US.

So far, little research has been done on the influence of costs and fees on the patenting behaviour of firms.[13] Pakes and Schankerman (1984) and Schankerman and Pakes (1986) have shown that renewal decisions are affected by the level of renewal fees. A few other studies have investigated the role of patent fees. For instance, de Rassenfosse and van Pottelsberghe (2013) show that priority filing fees at national patent offices have a negative and significant impact on the number of patent applications. However, the demand for first filings at national offices is determined by a rather complex set of factors. An alternative and potentially more telling experiment would be to analyse the patents already granted by one institution and then analyse in which countries they are then taken for validation. The present study pursues this approach and uses the validation phase following the EPO grant as the research setting.

The research design adopted in this chapter allows identifying the impact of post-grant fees and translation costs on the patenting behaviour of applicants. Post-grant fees (i.e. translation costs, validation fees and fees for maintaining patent protection for the years four to six after application at the EPO) are of particular importance for our analysis, since we assume that they drive the validation decision of applicants and consequently are important determinants of the scope of protection. Moreover, these costs are marginal in the sense that at the point of decision-making all examination and application fees are sunk, and the receipt of the national patent only depends on the costs considered here. We also take early renewal fees into account because they represent the expenses that an applicant has to pay when extending patent protection once the patent has been validated. We use the renewal fees requested by the national patent offices from years four to six after the application date at the EPO as a measure of these costs.

Assuming that applicants rationally decide about the regional scope of their patent portfolio, the following hypotheses relating to translation costs as well as validation and early renewal fees are put forward:

H.1: The probability of patent validation in an EPC country decreases with an increase in relevant translation costs.

H.2: The probability of patent validation in an EPC country decreases with an increase in the country-specific validation fees.

---

[13] de Rassenfosse and van Pottelsberghe (2007) investigate the role of priority filing fees at national patent offices and Harhoff et al. (2009) analyse the extent to which fees explain validation flows at the country level using a gravity model. de Rassenfosse and van Pottelsberghe (2012) provide time series evidence on the potential impact of cumulated fees at the United States Patent and Trademark Office (USPTO), the Japan Patent Office (JPO) and at the European Patent Office (EPO) on the demand for patents. All these studies obtain results that suggest that fees influence the patenting behaviour of applicants.

H.3: The probability of a patent validation in an EPC country decreases with
an increase in the country-specific early renewal fees.

14.3   Data and econometric modelling

In this chapter we use a novel dataset on validation decisions of applicants at
the EPO. The data comprise all patents granted by the EPO in 2003. Information on filing and grant dates, the country of origin of the priority filings, the
language of the official proceedings at the EPO and the technical classification
of the patent application (IPC classes) were extracted from the EPO's EPASYS
database as of 15 January 2006. Data on the lapse of patents into the public domain was obtained from the EPASYS database as of December 2006. The
data were supplemented with information on renewal payments, which were
received from the EPO post-grant system as of December 2006. The empirical
analysis relies on 53,904 patents granted in 2003 and validated in at least one
EPC member state. Granted patents, which had not been validated in any of
the EPC member states, were excluded from the dataset.[14]

14.3.1   The econometric model

The probability of observing a validation of a patent from applicant country
A in validation country B is modelled as a function of post-grant fees and costs
(costs for translation, validations and renewals). We assume that translation
costs increase with language distance and this effect is stronger for patents
in which many claims need to be translated. A number of control variables
describing the patent, the country of origin of the patent and the country for
which protection is sought are also added. Our probit equation thus takes the
form:[15]

$$\Pr(V_{AB}) = \Phi(\beta_0 + \beta_1 LD_{AB} + \beta_2 Claims + \beta_3 LD_{AB} \times Claims + \beta_4 VF_B + \beta_5 RF_B$$
$$+ \sum_k \gamma_k Controls)$$

where V_{AB} is a dummy variable (1,0) that indicates whether a patent from
applicant country A in validation country B was validated or not, LD_{AB} is the
linguistic distance between national languages A and B, *Claims* refers to the

---

[14] The number of patents granted by the EPO in 2003 was 59,992, but 6,088 (or 10 per
cent) were not included in the dataset because they had not been validated in any of the
EPC countries (the patent was withdrawn by the applicant after the decision to grant by
the EPO).

[15] A Wald test was employed to test if a log linear or a linear specification was more
appropriate. The results clearly showed that the logarithmic specification was superior.

(log of) the number of claims of the validated patent, VF_B and RF_B refer to the validation and renewal fees. Finally, *Controls* refers to other control variables.

National patents derived from an EPO grant from international patent families.[16] Validation decisions within a family are connected to the initial patent. To account for the correlational structure within a patent family, we use a cluster estimator for adjusting the variance-covariance matrix of our probit estimator (Wooldridge, 2002).

14.3.2   Description of the variables

Dependent variable

The dependent variable is patent validation. After being granted, an EP patent has to be validated in each state for which protection is sought, i.e. the patent has to be converted into a bundle of patents having the same legal status as patents granted through the national procedures.[17] In 2003, that is prior to the enforcement of the London Agreement in 2008, this required the filing of a translation of the patent specification, and the payment of national validation or publication fees within a specified term (Art. 65(1) EPC).[18] However, a validation was also possible without filing a translation in the event the language of the official proceedings at the EPO was (one of) the official language(s) of the validation country.[19] Furthermore, payment of a validation fee was in some countries, such as Switzerland and Belgium.

The patent validation variable is defined as a dummy variable, taking the value one if a patent (granted by the EPO) of applicant country A has been validated in country B, and zero otherwise.[20] We infer the validation status

---

[16] Families include all patents filed abroad from an initial filing in a national patent office.

[17] See www.epo.org/applying/european/validation.html (accessed on 8 September 2011).

[18] See www.epo.org/law-practice/legal-texts/epc.html (accessed on 8 September 2011). For a detailed description of the EP grant and validation procedure, see Harhoff et al. (2009).

[19] An EP patent application must be filed in one of the official languages of the EPO, i.e. English, German or French, the so-called procedural languages. Applications filed in other languages have to be translated into one of the three official languages within a term of three months. See www.epo.org/applying/ basics.html (accessed on 8 September 2011).

[20] The 20 applicant countries include Austria (AT), Australia (AU), Belgium (BE), Canada (CA), Switzerland (CH), Germany (DE), Denmark (DK), Spain (ES), Finland (FI), France (FR), United Kingdom (UK), Ireland (IE), Israel (IL), Italy (IT), Japan (JP), Korea (KR), the Netherlands (NL), Norway (NO), Sweden (SE) and the USA (US) (selection criteria: minimum of 100 patents granted in 2003). The 17 countries of validation include Austria (AT), Belgium (BE), Switzerland (CH), Cyprus (CY), Germany (DE), Denmark (DK), Spain (ES), Finland (FI), France (FR), United Kingdom (UK), Greece (GR), Ireland (IE), Luxembourg (LU), Monaco (MC), the Netherlands (NL), Portugal (PT) and Sweden (SE). Italy (IT) is not included due to the lack of information on validations in that country. Broad estimates by the EPO suggest that 30–40 per cent of the patents granted by the EPO are generally validated in Italy.

from our data, assuming that a patent has been validated in a given country if (i) renewal fees are paid for the patent to the national patent office of the country and/or (ii) the patent lapses in the given country. In cases where patents lapsed within one year after grant (in all validation countries), the patents were considered as lapsed *ab initio* and were removed from the dataset. This is equivalent to assuming that these patents had never been validated in any country.[21]

Explanatory and control variables

Linguistic distances. These distances are based on research carried out by Dyen et al. (1992) who computed distances between 95 Indo-European speech varieties. See Chapter 5 in this volume.

Validation fee. The variable corresponds to the fee a patent holder has to pay to validate a granted patent in a member state of the EPC. Information on validation fees was extracted from the 'Official Journal and the National Law Relating to the EPC'.[22] The validation fee may comprise a fixed component and a variable (i.e. a page-based) component. However, most of the countries only charge a fixed fee. Some countries do not charge validation fees at all (Belgium, Switzerland, Luxembourg, Monaco and the UK). For the countries which charge a page-based fee (Austria, Finland, Sweden, Denmark and Spain) the average number of pages per patent, provided by the EPO, was used to compute the average total validation fees.

Renewal fees. These fees have also been referred to as maintenance costs, i.e. costs to keep a patent valid for an additional year. With few exceptions, renewal fees increase with the year of renewal, but display considerable variation across countries. Renewal fees for the different years were again extracted from the 'Official Journal and the National Law Relating to the EPC'. Since we assume that the fees that have to be paid during the first years after grant matter most for the decision to validate a patent in a particular country, cumulative renewal fees for the years four to six from the date of filing of the application at the EPO are included in the regression. According to Harhoff and Wagner (2009), the average grant lag at the EPO amounts to about four years. Harhoff et al. (2009) show that during this three year period, 66.5 per cent of all the patents belonging to a given cohort are granted.

GDP per capita and population. Annual data on GDP in current prices (US dollars in billions) and the population of the different countries were obtained

---

[21] When the lapse and renewal data sources contained conflicting results (less than 1 per cent of the cases) information on patent lapses were preferred over renewal information. The decision to prefer information on patent lapses was suggested by an EPO expert.

[22] See www.epo.org/law-practice/legal-texts/epc.html (accessed on 8 September 2011).

from the World Economic Outlook Database as of September 2006.[23] GDP per capita is taken as a proxy for the wealth of a country. The population variable is used as a proxy for the market size of a country.

Physical distance between capital cities. The physical distance between the capital cities of the applicant and the validation country was provided by Kristian Skrede Gleditsch, Department of Government, University of Essex.[24]

EPC membership duration (validation country). The average number of years of EPC membership of the validation countries was obtained from the EPO.[25] The variable is included in the regression to test whether the duration of EPC membership reflects learning effects. As the transfer rate of domestic priority filings to the EPO increases with EPC membership (de Rassenfosse and van Pottelsberghe, 2007), one may expect that this duration also affects the probability that a patent is validated in a particular country.

Region of the applicant. Four dummy variables characterize the location of the applicants' home countries: US, Japan, other non-European country[26] and European country.[27] The latter forms the reference group. These regional dummies are used to account for unobserved heterogeneity between applicants from these country groups.

Number of claims at grant. To account for the size of a patent specification, the number of claims at the time of the grant is included in the regression. We treat the number of claims as a proxy for the overall number of pages that need to be translated, and thus as the scale factor in translation costs. Archontopoulos et al. (2007) show that there is a strong correlation between the number of pages included in a patent and the number of claims it contains.

Citations. It is likely that more relevant patents are validated in more EPC member states. We, therefore, include an additional variable accounting for the potential importance of the patent. In particular, we use the number of citations as a rough proxy for a patent's relevance (Gambardella et al., 2008). Since patents that are validated in many countries are more visible and may,

---

[23] See www.imf.org/external/pubs/ft/weo/2006/02/data/index.aspx (accessed on 8 September 2011).

Since Monaco was missing in this database, GDP data were supplemented with data extracted from the United Nations Statistics Division (see http://unstats.un.org/unsd/snaama/dnllist.asp (accessed on 8 September 2011)). GDP data for Monaco were estimated based on the assumption that the level of GDP per capita is proportional to that of Luxembourg.

[24] See http://privatewww.essex.ac.uk/~ksg/mindist.html (accessed on 8 September 2011).

[25] See www.epo.org/about-us/epo/member-states.html (accessed on 8 September 2011).

[26] Australia (AU), Canada (CA), Israël (IL), Korea (KR).

[27] Austria (AT), Belgium (BE), Switzerland (CH), Germany (DE), France (FR), United Kingdom (UK), Ireland (IE), the Netherlands (NL), Denmark (DK), Finland (FI), Norway (NO), Sweden (SE), Spain (ES) and Italy (IT).

therefore, also be more frequently cited by patent examiners, we use the number of citations a patent application received within three years after publication. The end of this time span will usually precede the grant of the patent so that we avoid endogeneity problems.

Patent portfolio (five years). The number of patents granted to the applicant(s) within five years before the grant of the focal patent is also used in the probit model. The 'portfolio size' variable accounts for the resources available to the applicants as well as to proxy their patenting experience.

Technical areas. Patent applications are classified according to 14 technical areas, known as 'joint clusters' (JCs), used by the EPO since 2004 to assign patent applications to examiners.[28] As there is some factual and empirical evidence (van Pottelsberghe and van Zeebroeck, 2008) showing that some technologies (i.e. biotechnology and organic chemistry) are traditionally subject to a large geographical scope of protection, whereas others are validated in a very limited number of countries, the assigned area of technology may well affect the observed geographical scope of protection within the EPC.

Technology position of validation vs applicant country. To control for the relative technology attractiveness of the validation country, we include a variable that accounts for the technology position of the validation country B compared to that of the applicant country A by dividing the number of patents in technology i of the validation country B by the number of patents in technology i of the applicant country A during the five years before the grant of the patents (i.e. 1998–2002):

$$Technology\ position_{i,BA} = \frac{Patents_{iB}}{Patents_{iA}}$$

where $i = 1, \ldots, 30$ refers to the technical area of the validated patent based on the classification proposed by the French Patent Institute and the ISI Institute of the Fraunhofer Gesellschaft (OECD, 1994). We expect that this measure will be positively associated with validation decisions, since a large production of patents in a particular technology in a potential target country is likely to indicate a large market for that technology in that country. Interviews with patent attorneys suggest for example that almost all patents applied for automotive technology target Germany as the designation because this country constitutes one of the largest markets for automotive product and process technology. That, of course, is driven by strong domestic demand for the product itself.

---

[28] EPO joint clusters: industrial chemistry, organic chemistry, polymers, biotechnology, telecommunications, audio/video/media, electronics, electricity/electrical machines, computers, measuring optics, handling/processing, vehicles/general technology, civil engineering/thermodynamics, human necessities. See Archontopoulos et al. (2007) for additional information about the assignment of the IPC classes to the EPO joint clusters.

Table 14.2 Validation fees and early renewal fees for the year 2003

Country	Validation fee (euros)		Renewal fee (euros)		
	Fixed	Page-based (pages free)	Year 4	Year 5	Year 6
Austria	116	25 (5)	94	101	138
Belgium	0	–	45	60	75
Switzerland	0	–	0	270	270
Cyprus	87	–	52	70	87
Germany	150	–	70	90	130
Denmark	148	11 (35)	148	169	189
Spain	245	10 (22)	25	48	71
Finland	85	10 (4)	125	140	165
France	35	–	25	25	135
United Kingdom	0	–	0	72	101
Greece	299	–	46	54	70
Ireland	35	–	90	114	134
Luxembourg	0	–	37	47	59
Monaco	0	–	31	50	70
The Netherlands	25	–	0	242	279
Portugal	91	–	41	53	59
Sweden	120	17 (8)	76	98	120

Source: Official Journal and the National Law Relating to the EPC; exchange rates: CA/D 1/03.

14.3.3 Descriptive statistics[29]

Table 14.2 displays the validation fees and the early renewal fees of the 17 EPC member states contained in our sample for the year 2003. Switzerland, Monaco, Belgium, Luxembourg and the UK request no validation fees. The remaining countries request a fixed fee varying between €25 (the Netherlands) and €299 (Greece). Only five countries (Austria, Denmark, Spain, Finland and Sweden) charge an additional page-based validation fee varying between €10 (Spain and Finland) and €25 (Austria) per page, once the number of pages exceeds a certain limit. The table also shows that all countries charge renewal fees (even if some countries only charge fees from year 5). The requested amount varies considerably between countries.

Figure 14.1 summarizes renewal and validation fees for patents granted in 2003, categorized by translation cost groups. It clearly appears that validating and keeping a patent in force for years 4 to 6 is more expensive in Nordic countries and in Greece, a consequence of the high translation costs. On the

---

[29] Additional descriptive statistics can be found in the working paper 'Languages, Fees and the International Scope of Patenting' available online at http://ssrn.com/abstract= 2602635.

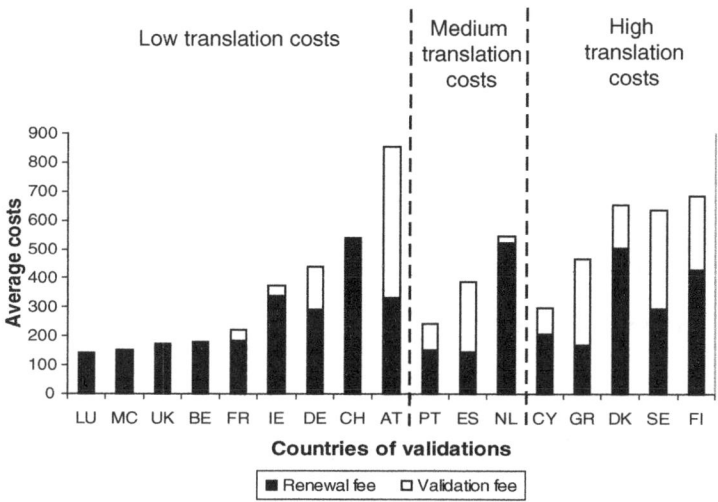

Figure 14.1 Average costs (validation and renewal fees) to validate a patent in a member state of the EPC and to keep it in force for years 4 to 6 (patents granted in 2003)
Note: Country abbreviations are provided in note 20.
Source: European Patent Office

other hand, translations into Dutch, Portuguese and Spanish are less expensive. German, English and French are the least expensive languages in terms of translation costs. Twenty-seven per cent of the observed validations had to be translated into an expensive language, 19 per cent into a less expensive language, and 28 per cent into one of the least expensive languages. Furthermore, validating and keeping a patent in force for years 4 to 6 is particularly expensive in Austria due to a high page-based validation fee (Austria charges a fee of €25 per page in excess of five pages).

14.4 Empirical implementation and results

Table 14.3 summarizes the results of four probit models.[30] Model 1 only contains the control variables. Model 2 adds the measure for translation costs, i.e.

---

[30] As a robustness check, we compared the determinants of validations over two grant years (2003 and 1995). To make a comparison of the two grant years reasonable, the two samples were built symmetrically with respect to potential validation countries. In particular, later entrants into the EPC (i.e. FI and CY) were excluded from the 2003 sample. Results are consistent with respect to the geographical context, languages, costs and fees. The only differences are that the wealth of the applicant country has a significantly negative effect on validations for the grant year 1995, whereas the effect is positive in 2003. A possible explanation of this difference may be that in recent years small applicant countries with a relatively low GDP per capita (e.g. ES, BE and AT) validated more countries per granted EP patent. Consistently, the distance between the capital cities of the applicant and the validation country has a negative impact. The coefficient decreases slightly from

Table 14.3 Patent validations for 2003 (marginal effects from robust probit regression)

	Model 1	Model 2	Model 3	Model 4
Fees and costs				
Linguistic distance		−0.175**	−0.109**	−0.159**
		[0.002]	[0.007]	[0.007]
Linguistic distance × claims at grant (log)			−0.028**	−0.015**
			[0.003]	[0.003]
Validation fees (log)				−0.023**
				[0.000]
Renewal fees for years 4–6 (log)				−0.191**
				[0.001]
Geographical context				
GDP per capita of applicant country (log)	0.161**	0.131**	0.130**	0.099**
	[0.015]	[0.015]	[0.015]	[0.015]
GDP per capita of validation country (log)	0.266**	0.194**	0.193**	0.373**
	[0.002]	[0.002]	[0.002]	[0.003]
Population of applicant country (log)	0.037**	0.037**	0.037**	0.033**
	[0.002]	[0.002]	[0.002]	[0.002]
Population of validation country (log)	0.116**	0.121**	0.121**	0.147**
	[0.001]	[0.001]	[0.001]	[0.001]
Costs of business in the target country				
Years of membership EPC of the applicant country (log)	0.041**	0.013**	0.013**	−0.056**
	[0.001]	[0.001]	[0.001]	[0.002]
Physical distance between capital cities (log)	−0.020**	−0.004*	−0.004*	−0.012**
	[0.002]	[0.002]	[0.002]	[0.002]
Technology position of validation vs applicant country (log)	0.151**	0.153**	0.153**	0.145**
	[0.003]	[0.003]	[0.003]	[0.003]
USA (dummy)	−0.070**	−0.091**	−0.090**	−0.066**
	[0.007]	[0.007]	[0.007]	[0.008]
Japan (dummy)	−0.094**	−0.121**	−0.121**	−0.106**
	[0.005]	[0.005]	[0.005]	[0.005]
Other non-Europe (dummy)	−0.067**	−0.108**	−0.108**	−0.098**
	[0.009]	[0.008]	[0.008]	[0.008]
Other patent characteristics				
Number of claims at grant (log)	0.015**	0.016**	0.029**	0.023**
	[0.002]	[0.002]	[0.002]	[0.002]
Citations (log)	0.028**	0.029**	0.029**	0.030**
	[0.002]	[0.002]	[0.002]	[0.002]
Number of granted patents (5 years) (log)	−0.011**	−0.011**	−0.011**	−0.012**
	[0.000]	[0.000]	[0.000]	[0.000]
Control variables (see details in Table 14.4)				
EPO industry clusters (Wald test); Reference group: vehicles/general	$Chi^2 (13) =$ 5,729.37	$Chi^2 (13) =$ 5,760.68	$Chi^2 (13) =$ 5,764.48	$Chi^2 (13) =$ 5,850.82
Technology (dummy)	$p = 0.000$	$p = 0.000$	$p = 0.000$	$p = 0.000$

Observations	862,549	862,549	862,549	862,549
Chi^2 (26)	62,209	72,091	72,018	78,048
Pseudo R^2	0.231	0.238	0.238	0.262
Log-likelihood	−397,111	−393,531	−393,461	−381,124

*Significantly different from 0 at 5 per cent level; **significantly different from 0 at 1 per cent level.
Notes: The dependent variable is 'validation of a patent' (which equals 1 if a patent from a country A has been validated in country B; 0 otherwise). Robust standard errors adjusted for intra-group EPO industry clusters in square brackets.

the linguistic distance. Model 3 adds the interaction between the linguistic distance and the number of claims which controls for the size of the patent application. This number is highly correlated with the number of pages. Finally Model 4 exhibits the full model, i.e. also including validation and renewal fees. Unless explicitly mentioned, we describe the results of Model 4.

The results reveal that an increase of the linguistic distance by 1 per cent decreases the probability of a validation by 15.9 per cent. This result confirms our hypothesis 1.

Model 4 also includes an interaction term 'linguistic distances × number of claims at grant' to account for the size of the validated patents. The effect of linguistic distances on the validation behaviour is still negative and significantly different from zero, and the number of claims has a positive impact. The interaction term is negative and significantly different from zero which suggests that larger patents are less likely to be validated in countries with high translation costs.

An increase of 1 per cent in the validation fees leads to a decrease in the validation probability of 2.3 per cent. Renewal fees reduce the probability of observing a validation in a country. A 1 per cent increase in the renewal fees would lead to a reduction in the probability of validation of about 19.1 per cent. Hence, hypotheses 2 and 3 are also confirmed by the data.

The control variables pick up the expected signs. Model 4 shows that wealth of the applicant and the validation country has a significant impact on the probability of observing a validation. In particular, an increase in the GDP per capita of the applicant country *A* by 1 per cent leads to an increase of the probability to observe a validation by 9.9 per cent. An increase in the GDP per capita of the target country *B* by 1 per cent raises the probability of observing a validation by 37.3 per cent. Both estimators are significantly different from zero at the 1 per cent level. Applicants from richer countries have on average more income at their disposal to file patents abroad. The wealth of the destination

---

1995 to 2003. Possibly, distances become less important over time, e.g. due to the internet and advancement of communication technologies. The complete results are available upon request.

country is assumed to attract more validations as demand conditions in the market are more attractive for firms.

The size of the applicant and of the validation countries – as measured by the number of inhabitants – also has a positive impact on the probability of a validation. Overall, the results in Table 14.3 show that the wealth and size of the validation countries generally have a higher effect than the same characteristics of the applicant countries.

The parameter associated with the age of EPC membership is negative and significantly different from zero: the longer the EPC experience of a country, the lower the likelihood of a validation in that country. As expected, the technology position of validation countries in relation to that of the application countries has a positive and significantly different from zero effect on the validation behaviour of the applicant country. The number of claims also shows a positive and significantly different from zero parameter: larger patents are filed in more countries. A possible explanation is that patent applicants and attorneys devote more efforts on promising filings, and that the number of claims, therefore, may reflect the patent's importance.

The variable capturing the physical distance between the applicant and the validation countries has a negative and significantly different from zero impact on the probability of a validation. Model 4 also shows the role of the geographical origin of the applicants. The probability of a validation is the lowest for the applicants originating from Japan and other non-European countries, and is the highest for applicants based in Europe. These results are in line with the findings of Guellec and van Pottelsberghe (2001) that large countries are less dependent on internationalization, since they already benefit from large domestic markets.

Model 4 further contains variables measuring the value of the applications (forward patent citations) and the portfolio size of the applicant, as proxied by the number of patents granted to the applicants during the five years preceding the grant of the underlying patents. Validations are more likely to occur for more valuable patent applications. In particular, a 1 per cent increase in the value of a patent, i.e. a higher number of three-year citations, increases the probability of a validation by 3 per cent. However, a 1 per cent larger five-year patent portfolio of the applicants decreases the likelihood of a validation by 1.2 per cent. In other words, patents of larger firms or of firms that hold more patents are characterized by a more focused geographical scope of protection. Firms with a larger patent portfolio are characterized by more selective market coverage.

EPO industry cluster dummies were used in all models as control variables. A Wald test conducted for each model reveals that the technical areas have a significant impact on the validation behaviour of applicants. The parameters associated with industry clusters, estimated in Model 4, are shown in

Table 14.4 Patent validations for 2003: Coefficients of the technical joint clusters in Model 4 (marginal effects from robust probit regression)

Industrial chemistry	0.108**
	[0.005]
Organic chemistry	0.314**
	[0.006]
Polymers	0.118**
	[0.005]
Biotechnology	0.346**
	[0.007]
Telecommunications	0.011
	[0.006]
Audio/video/media	0.025**
	[0.006]
Electronics	0.019**
	[0.005]
Electricity & electrical machines	0.019**
	[0.005]
Computers	0.018**
	[0.007]
Measuring optics	0.026**
	[0.005]
Handling & processing	0.076**
	[0.005]
Civil engineering/thermodynamics	0.024**
	[0.005]
Human necessities	0.082**
	[0.005]
Pseudo R^2	0.262

**significantly different from 0 at 1 per cent level.
Notes: The dependent variable is 'validation of a patent' (which equals 1 if a patent from a country *A* has been validated in country *B*; 0 otherwise). Reference group: vehicles & general technology.
Robust standard errors adjusted for intra-group correlation in square brackets.

Table 14.4. The findings are consistent with the scope-year index put forward in van Pottelsberghe and van Zeebroeck (2008): patents in biotechnology and organic chemistry are validated in more countries and enforced longer than the patents filed for other technologies.

14.5 Conclusion

The European patent system provides an interesting setting for the empirical analysis of patent systems. The variation in our data allows us to investigate to what extent patent applicants are influenced by fees and translation costs, as well as by physical distances between and market attractiveness of the validation country relative to the applicant country (represented by its size, its wealth or the technical position). We have analysed a particularly clear decision-making situation where fees and translation costs are the only remaining expenses that separate applicants from patent protection.

Overall, the world may have become more globalized, but it certainly has not become 'completely flat'. Physical distance still matters and so do linguistic and cultural distances. Our results regarding the impact of fees and translation costs provide important implications for patent policy-makers. Costs and fees turn out to be important determinants of applicant behaviour and may therefore be an important tool for policy changes. While rule changes in the patent system typically require long-lasting and complex decision-making processes, fee changes can be effective in the short run. Consequently, they should not be considered as instruments safeguarding the treasury of patent agencies – they can affect and steer applicant behaviour in a socially beneficial direction.

Language has always been a challenge for the European patent system, and especially for the setting up of the Unitary Patent (van Pottelsberghe, 2011, 2015). Translation requirements are the main reasons underlying Spain and Italy's drop out of the Unitary Patent project. So far, only 25 countries have ratified the convention. The latter would be validated in all member states after its grants by the EPO upon request of the patent owner. This could constitute a solution to the issue of high translation costs. The 'Translation Regulation' attached to the Unitary Patent indeed specifies that no further translation should be required after a transitional period of 12 years during which patents granted in German or French will need a translation into English and those granted in English will have to be translated into French and German (Council Regulation (EU) No. 1260/2012). The Unitary Patent could alleviate the cost of translation in the future, once decisions about the structure of the renewal fees as well as the setting up of the Unitary Patent Court have been made.

Acknowledgements

The authors thank Nicolas van Zeebroeck for developing the methodology for identifying validations and for constructing the dataset. The authors would like to thank the EPO for providing access to the patent renewal data used in this chapter and Bettina Reichl for extracting the fee data. Dietmar Harhoff acknowledges support by the Deutsche Forschungsgemeinschaft (DFG) within its SFB/TR 15 collaborative research programme (Project C2). Furthermore, the authors would like to thank Georg von Graevenitz, seminar audiences at KU Leuven, ZEW Mannheim, in particular, Alberto Galasso, and the Third EPIP Conference for helpful comments.

References

E. Archontopoulos, D. Guellec, N. Stevnsborg, B. van Pottelsberghe de la Potterie and N. van Zeebroeck (2007) 'When Small Is Beautiful: Measuring the Evolution and Consequences of the Voluminosity of Patent Applications at the EPO', *Information Economics and Policy*, 19, 103–132.

A. Arundel, (2001) 'The Relative Effectiveness of Patents and Secrecy for Appropriation', *Research Policy*, 30, 611–624.

K. Blind, J. Edler, R. Frietsch and U. Schmoch (2006) 'Motives to Patent: Empirical Evidence from Germany', *Research Policy*, 35, 655–672.

D. Bosworth (1984) 'Foreign Patent Flows to and from the United Kingdom', *Research Policy*, 13, 115–124.

W. Cohen, R. Nelson and J. Walsh (2000) 'Protecting Their Intellectual Assets: Appropriability Conditions and Why U.S. Manufacturing Firms Patent (Or Not)', NBER Working Paper No. 7552.

Council regulation (EU) No 1260/2012 of 17 December 2012 Implementing Enhanced Cooperation in the Area of the Creation of Unitary Patent Protection with regard to the Applicable Translation Arrangements (OJ L 361 31.12.2012 p.89).

Y. Deng (2007) 'Private Value of European Patents', *European Economic Review*, 51, 1785–1812.

G. de Rassenfosse and B. van Pottelsberghe de la Potterie (2007) 'Per un Pugno di Dollari: A First Look at the Price Elasticity of Patents', *Oxford Review of Economic Policy*, 23, 1–17.

G. de Rassenfosse and B. van Pottelsberghe de la Potterie (2012) 'On the Price Elasticity of Demand for Patents', *Oxford Bulletin of Economics and Statistics*, 75, 58–77.

G. de Rassenfosse and B. van Pottelsberghe de la Potterie (2013) 'The Role of Fees in Patent Systems: Theory and Evidence', *Journal of Economic Surveys*, 27, 696–716.

I. Dyen, J.B. Kruskal and P. Black (1992) 'An Indo-European Classification: A Lexicostatistical Experiment', *Transactions of the American Philosophical Society New Series*, 82, iii–132.

J. Eaton and S. Kortum (1996) 'Trade in Ideas Patenting and Productivity in the OECD', *Journal of International Economics*, 40, 251–278.

G. Friebel, A. Koch, D. Prady and P. Seabright (2006) 'Objectives and Incentives at the European Patent Office', study commissioned by the Staff Union of the European Patent Office (SUEPO), at http://idei.fr/doc/by/seabright/report_epo.pdf

T. Friedman (2006) *The World Is Flat: The Globalized World in the Twenty-First Century*, (London: Penguin Books).

A. Gambardella, D. Harhoff and B. Verspagen (2008) 'The Value of European Patents', *European Management Review*, 5, 69–84.

D. Guellec and B. van Pottelsberghe de la Potterie (2001) 'The Internationalization of Technology Analyzed with Patent Data', *Research Policy*, 30, 1253–1266.

D. Guellec and B. van Pottelsberghe de la Potterie (2007) *The Economics of the European Patent System* (Oxford: Oxford University Press).

D. Harhoff (2011) Deferred Patent Examination, Manuscript München, Germany: Ludwig-Maximilians-Universität München.

D. Harhoff, K. Hoisl, B. Reichl and B. van Pottelsberghe de la Potterie (2009) 'Patent Validation at the Country Level: The Role of Fees and Translation Costs', *Research Policy*, 38, 1423–1437.

D. Harhoff, F. Scherer and K. Vopel (2003) 'Citations, Family Size, Opposition and the Value of Patent Rights', *Research Policy*, 32, 1343–1363.

D. Harhoff and S. Wagner (2009) 'Modelling the Duration of Patent Examination at the European Patent Office', *Management Science*, 55, 1969–1984.

J. Lanjouw (1998) 'Patent Value in the Shadow of Infringement: Simulation Estimations of Patent Value', *Review of Economic Studies*, 65, 671–710.

OECD (1994) *Using Patent Data as Science and Technological Indicators: Patent Manual 1994*, Paris: OECD.

A. Pakes (1986) 'Patents as Options: Some Estimates of the Value of Holding European Patent Stocks', *Econometrica*, 54, 755–784.

A. Pakes and M. Schankerman (1984) 'The Rate of Obsolescence of Patents, Research Gestation Lags and the Private Rate of Return to Research Resources' In Z. Griliches (ed.) *R&D, Patents and Productivity* (pp. 73–88) (Chicago: University of Chicago Press).

C. Peeters and B. van Pottelsberghe de la Potterie (2006) 'Innovation Strategy and the Patenting Performances of Large Firms', *Journal of Evolutionary Economics*, 16, 109–135.

M. Porter and S. Stern (2000) 'Measuring the "Ideas" Production Function: Evidence from International Patent Output', NBER Working Paper No. 7891.

J. Putnam (1996) 'The Value of International Patent Rights', PhD thesis, Yale University.

M. Schankerman and A. Pakes (1986) 'Estimates of the Value of Patent Rights in European Countries During the Post 1950 Period', *Economic Journal*, 96, 1052–1076.

J. Slama (1981) 'Analysis by Means of a Gravitation Model of International Flows of Patent Applications in the Period 1967–1978', *World Patent Information*, 3, 2–8.

N. Stevnsborg and B. van Pottelsberghe de La Potterie (2007) 'Patenting Procedures and Filing Strategies' In D. Guellec and B. van Pottelsberghe de la Potterie (eds) *The Economics of the European Patent System* (Oxford: Oxford University Press).

J. Thomas (2010) *Deferred Examination of Patent Applications: Implications for Innovation Policy* (Washington, DC: Congressional Research Service Report 7–5700).

B. van Pottelsberghe de la Potterie (2011) 'Europe should Stop Taxing Innovation', *World Patent Information*, 33, 16–22.

B. van Pottelsberghe de la Potterie (2015) 'European Patent System', *Encyclopedia of Law and Economics* (New York: Springer Science+Business Media).

B. van Pottelsberghe de la Potterie and D. François (2009) 'The Cost Factor in Patent Systems', *Journal of Industry, Competition and Trade*, 9, 329–355.

B. van Pottelsberghe de la Potterie and M. Mejer (2010) 'The London Agreement and the Cost of Patenting in Europe', *European Journal of Law and Economics*, 29, 211–237.

B. van Pottelsberghe de la Potterie and N. van Zeebroeck (2008) 'A Brief History of Space and Time: The Scope-Year Index as a Patent Value Indicator Based on Families and Renewals', *Scientometrics*, 75, 319–338.

N. van Zeebroeck (2007) 'Patents Only Live Twice: A Patent Survival Analysis in Europe', Working Papers Centre Emile Bernheim 07–028.

G. Von Graevenitz, S. Wagner and D. Harhoff (2013) 'Incidence and Growth of Patent Thickets: The Impact of Technological Opportunities and Complexity', *Journal of Industrial Economics*, 61, 521–563.

J. Wooldridge (2002) *Introductory Econometrics: A Modern Approach* (Cincinnati, OH: South-Western College Publishing).

Part III

Linguistic Policies and Economic Development

15

Linguistic Cleavages and Economic Development

Klaus Desmet, Ignacio Ortuño-Ortín and Romain Wacziarg

15.1 Introduction

What is the effect of linguistic diversity on economic and political outcomes? Much of the recent literature on this topic investigates how linguistic cleavages affect civil conflict, redistribution, economic growth, public goods and governance.[1] Most of the cross-country evidence suggests that linguistic diversity has negative effects on these political economy outcomes. These findings may help explain why the US has a smaller welfare state than Europe, why some countries develop more slowly than others or why some African countries tend to have a higher incidence of civil conflict than others.

This chapter focuses on two important questions in this literature. The first question has to do with measurement, and in particular with defining the relevant linguistic groups used to measure linguistic fractionalization. For example, should we consider Flemish and Dutch to be two distinct groups? We will argue that the answer depends on the particular political economy outcome we are interested in: different linguistic cleavages matter for different outcomes. A second question has to do with the relationship between linguistic diversity and the level of development. In contrast to other political economy outcomes such as economic growth, less attention has been paid to the level of GDP and its relationship with linguistic fractionalization.

Diversity is usually measured by a fractionalization index that takes into account the number and the sizes of the different groups. One common

---

[1] Salient references include: (1) on civil conflict, Fearon and Laitin (2003), Montalvo and Reynal-Querol (2005) and Esteban et al. (2012); (2) on redistribution, Alesina et al. (2001), Alesina and Glaeser (2004), Desmet et al. (2009) and Dahlberg et al. (2012); (3) on economic growth, Easterly and Levine (1997) and Alesina et al. (2003); (4) on public goods and governance, La Porta et al. (1999), Alesina et al. (2003), Habyarimana et al. (2007). For more general surveys of this vast and expanding literature, see Alesina and La Ferrara (2005) and Stichnoth and Van der Straeten (2013).

criticism of this approach is that in many cases it is difficult to determine which dimension – language, ethnicity, religion, culture – defines the relevant groups (Laitin and Posner, 2001). Here we ask a related question, focusing exclusively on linguistic heterogeneity. Even when focusing only on language as the main dimension of heterogeneity, we are faced with the question of what constitutes the relevant linguistic classification. Almost everyone would consider Lombard and Piedmontese to be variants of Italian, rather than two distinct languages. In contrast, most would consider Hindi and German to be distinct language groups, despite both belonging to the Indo-European family. But of course there are many in-between situations where doubts may arise: are Galician and Spanish or Icelandic and Norwegian sufficiently different to classify them as distinct groups?

In trying to determine the relevant groups to construct measures of linguistic diversity, in Desmet et al. (2012) we argued that different cleavages may matter for different political economy outcomes. To make our point, we used a phylogenetic approach, based on information from language trees, to compute diversity measures at different levels of aggregation. At the highest level of aggregation, only the world's main language families, such as Indo-European and Nilo-Saharan, would define different groups, whereas at the lowest level of aggregation, even the different variants of Italian, such as Lombard and Venetian, would define different linguistic groups.

We used measures of linguistic diversity at different levels of aggregation to study the determinants of redistribution, conflict and growth. We found that for redistribution and conflict, diversity measures at high levels of aggregation matter most, whereas for economic growth, diversity measures at low levels of aggregation are more significant determinants. To interpret these results, we observed that linguistic trees give a historical dimension to the analysis. For instance it is estimated that the split between Indo-European languages and non-Indo-European languages happened about 8,700 years ago. In contrast, the split between Icelandic and Norwegian occurred only after the 12th century (Gray and Atkinson, 2003). Hence, these findings indicate that, for redistribution, coarse divisions, going back far in time, matter most. Solidarity and empathy may not overcome deep cleavages, but can more easily bridge shallow divisions. In contrast, fine divisions are enough to hinder a country's economic growth, an outcome for which coordination and communication between economic agents matters for the economy to operate efficiently.

In this chapter, we build on our earlier work, extending our results to an analysis of how linguistic diversity affects the level of development. The recent literature in macro-development has paid increasing attention to levels rather than growth, starting with Hall and Jones (1999) and Acemoglu et al. (2001). Yet the effect of ethnolinguistic diversity on levels of development has not been the subject of a lot of research. If our interpretation is correct, we should expect shallow cleavages also to suffice to impact negatively on a country's level of development. As noted by Parente and Prescott (1994), growth differences in income per capita across countries tend to be transitory, whereas level differences are not. Thus, the effect of linguistic diversity on growth could differ from its effect on income per capita levels. We find, in fact, that it does not. For per capita income levels, as for growth, heterogeneity measures based on finer linguistic distinctions matter more than those based on coarse ones. This finding constitutes a confirmation of our earlier interpretation, where coarse linguistic divisions created conflict and a lack of redistribution. In contrast, finer ones were sufficient to generate adverse effects on outcomes such as growth that require coordination and communication between heterogeneous groups.

The rest of the chapter is organized as follows. Section 15.2 explains the phylogenetic approach of using language trees to compute measures of diversity at different levels of aggregation. Section 15.3 illustrates the usefulness of this phylogenetic approach by briefly revisiting the main findings in Desmet et al. (2012), comparing the impact of linguistic diversity on redistribution and growth. Section 15.4 analyses the relationship between linguistic diversity and the level of development, and situates the new findings in the broader literature. Section 15.5 concludes by summarizing our economic interpretation of the empirical findings.

15.2   A phylogenetic approach to linguistic diversity

In this section we explain how to use language trees to compute measures of linguistic diversity, based on either coarse or fine divisions between languages. We then compute these different measures for 226 countries, and show that a country's measured linguistic diversity depends crucially on whether we take into account fine divisions between languages or not.

15.2.1   Linguistic trees

Linguistic trees show the genealogical relationships between languages.[2] Linguistic differentiation occurs because populations become separated from each other. For example, the fall of the Roman Empire with the subsequent segmentation of populations and linguistic drift divided Latin into the different Romance languages that we know today. The degree of relatedness between languages in linguistic trees therefore gives a rough measure of the time that has elapsed since the two languages became separated. For example, Gray and Atkinson (2003) estimate that for the Indo-European language group, the split between the languages that would later give rise to present-day Hindi and

---

[2] See Chapter 5 in this book for a further discussion of how language trees are constructed.

German occurred about 6,900 years ago, whereas the split between what would become Swedish and German goes back only 1,750 years. Correspondingly, Hindi and German are separated by more branches in linguistic trees than Swedish and German.

Although this does not imply that linguistic trees act as precise clocks that measure the separation times of populations, as genetic distance does, deeper linguistic cleavages do correspond to greater linguistic differences between populations. In fact, Cavalli-Sforza et al. (1988) argue that there is a relationship between the world's main language groups and the world's most important genetic clusters.[3] This is consistent with several studies on Europe that have shown a significant correlation between genetic and linguistic diversity (Sokal, 1988). In a more recent, broader study, covering 50 populations across all continents, Belle and Barbujani (2007) reach a related conclusion. They find that language differences have a detectable effect on DNA diversity, above and beyond the effects of geographic distance. Like genes, language is passed on from generation to generation.

Since linguistic trees capture the degree of relatedness between languages, they can be used to compute different measures of diversity. Some of these measures can be based on coarse divisions, going back far in time, while others also include more shallow, recent divisions between languages.

Before calculating these different indices, recall that the standard A-index measure of fractionalization captures the probability that two individuals chosen at random belong to different groups (Greenberg, 1956).[4] Formally, in a country with N groups, indexed by i, the A-index is:

$$A = 1 - \sum_{i=1}^{i=N} s_i^2, \tag{1}$$

where s_i is the population share of group i.

In much of the literature the different groups i are taken as exogenously given. Instead, here we exploit the genealogical relationships between languages to define groups at different levels of coarseness. This is illustrated in Figure 15.1, showing the genealogical relationships between the main languages spoken in Pakistan. At the most disaggregated level, each of those seven languages (Panjabi, Pashto, Sindhi, Seraiki, Urdu, Balochi and Brahui) are taken to be a different group. Using the population shares that appear below the

---

[3] For a further discussion and an empirical analysis of the relationship between genetic and linguistic distances between countries, see Chapter 6 in this volume.

[4] In the economics literature the Greenberg A-index is typically referred to as the ELF index. However, strictly speaking, the term ELF refers to the *Atlas Narodov Mira* dataset, and not to the fractionalization index itself. As elsewhere in this handbook, we therefore adopt the A-index terminology.

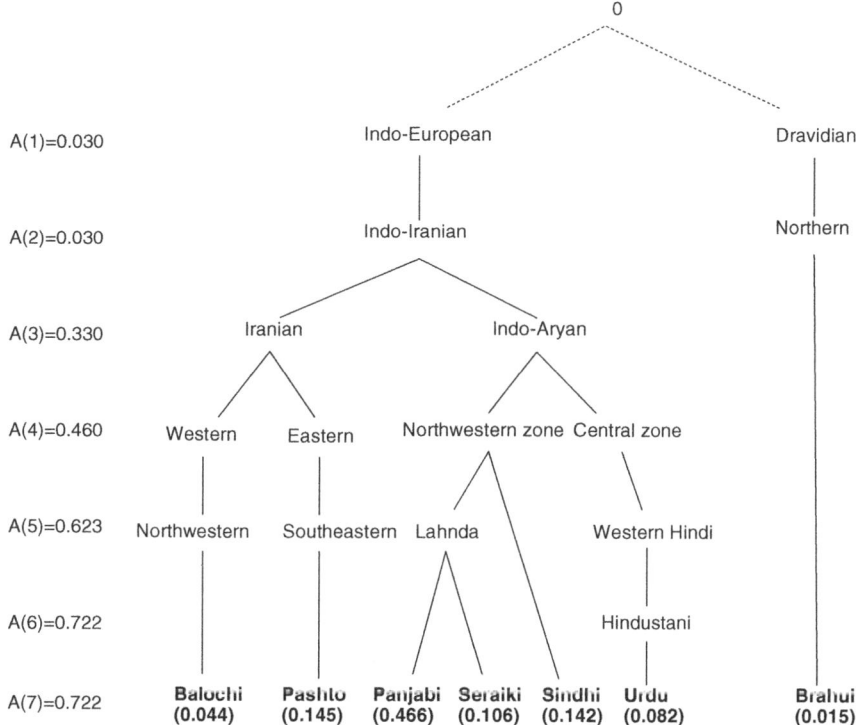

Figure 15.1 Phylogenetic tree of main languages spoken in Pakistan
Source: Desmet et al. (2012).

language names, this gives us an A-index of 0.722. That is, the probability that two randomly chosen Pakistani individuals speak different languages is 72.2 per cent. Because there are seven levels of aggregation in this language tree, we denote this measure of fractionalization as A(7).

As we go up the language tree, some languages become part of the same group. For example, when going up two levels, Panjabi, Seraiki and Sindhi all belong to the same group. Together, they now account for a 0.714 share of the population. At that level of aggregation, the other four languages continue to constitute different groups. The corresponding A-index, which we refer to as A(4), is now 0.460. That is, at aggregation level 4, the probability that two randomly chosen Pakistanis belong to a different group is only 46.0 per cent. Of course, by construction, the A-index decreases with the level of aggregation. At level 1, only two broad language families survive, Indo-European, accounting for 98.5 per cent of the population, and Dravidian, accounting for 1.5 per cent. Correspondingly, A(1) drops to 0.030, and by this account Pakistan no longer appears to be very linguistically diverse: when randomly choosing two Pakistanis, the probability that one speaks an Indo-European language and the other a Dravidian language is only 3 per cent. As already mentioned, diversity at higher levels of aggregation captures deeper cleavages than diversity at lower levels of aggregation.

One issue when computing these different A-indices is that in general not all languages are equidistant from the root. This can easily be seen in Figure 15.1. Although we have drawn all languages to be at the same distance from Proto-Human, in reality not all seven languages are removed by the same number of branches from the origin. While Urdu is seven branches away from the origin, Sindhi is six branches away, and Brahui is only three branches from the origin. To get around this issue, we move all languages down to the lowest level, thus making them equidistant from the origin. To be more precise, we are implicitly assuming that between Sindhi and the node called 'Northwestern zone' there are two intermediate languages, one at level 5 and another at level 6, that capture the evolution of 'Northwestern zone' into what today is Sindhi. The interested reader is referred to Desmet et al. (2012) for a more detailed discussion of different ways of completing a tree to ensure that all languages are equidistant from the origin. These different methods do not yield vastly different empirical results or indices.

15.2.2 Fractionalization at different levels of aggregation

Using data on the speakers of the 6,912 world languages in Ethnologue (2005), together with information on linguistic trees, we can compute for each country different A-indices at different levels of aggregation. The linguistic tree in Ethnologue has a maximum of 15 levels.[5] By positioning all present-day spoken languages at the same distance from the origin, we can compute for each country 15 A-indices, one for each level of disaggregation. More formally, for every level of disaggregation j, denote the partition of the country into $N(j)$ groups with population shares $s_{i(j)}$, where $i(j) = 1, 2, \ldots, N(j)$. We can then define a fractionalization index for any level of disaggregation j by

$$A(j) = 1 - \sum_{i(j)=1}^{N(j)} s_{i(j)}^2.$$ (2)

A country's relative level of diversity depends dramatically on the level of aggregation. To get a sense of how different things may look, Figure 15.2 shows maps of A(2) and A(15).[6] When computing A(2), French and German are allocated to different groups, but Spanish and French are not, whereas when computing A(15) all of the 6,912 languages recorded in the Ethnologue are

---

[5] See Barrett at al. (2001) for an alternative language classification with only seven levels.
[6] The complete dataset is available at http://faculty.smu.edu/kdesmet/

(a) Panel A: Linguistic fractionalization A(2)

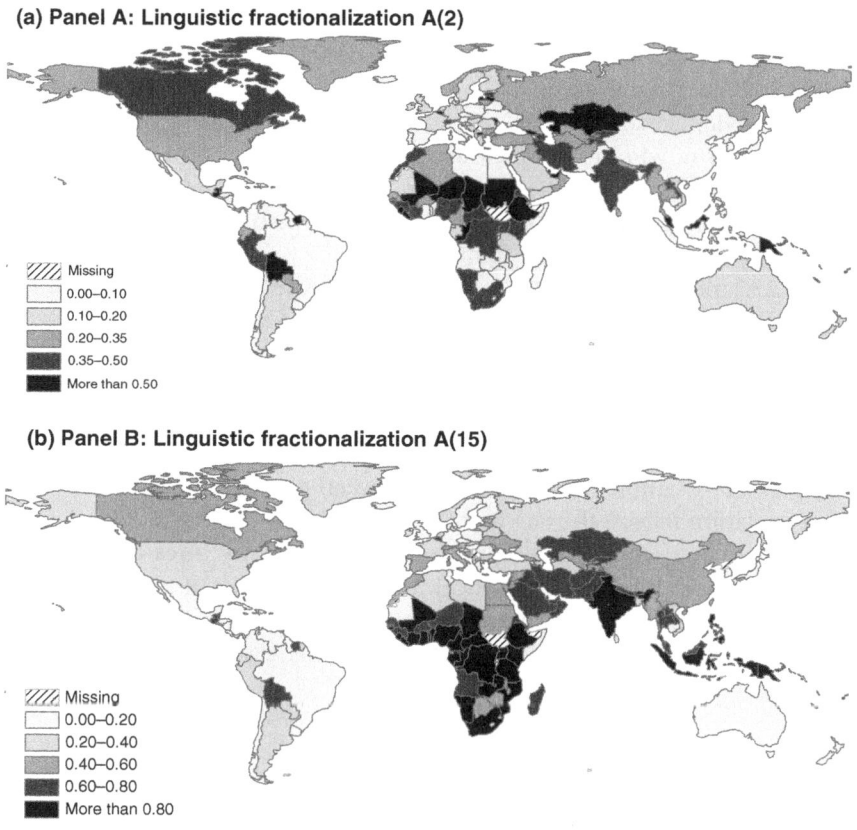

(b) Panel B: Linguistic fractionalization A(15)

Figure 15.2 Linguistic fractionalization at different levels of aggregation: A(2) and A(15)

allocated to different groups, even if they are very similar. The differences are striking. Many countries in central and southern Africa have very high levels of diversity at Level 15, but relatively low levels of diversity at Level 2. Mozambique is a good example. According to Ethnologue, the country has 43 languages, which explain why it ranks tenth out of 226 using A(15). However, 99.8 per cent of Mozambicans speak a language of the Niger-Congo group, explaining why the country drops to the 200th position when using A(2). As a result, Mozambique A(15) is 0.929 whereas A(2) is 0.004. Hence, depending on whether we consider deep cleavages or shallow cleavages, we would view Mozambique to be either a very diverse or a very homogeneous country.

In contrast, many countries in the Sahel region are highly diverse, independently of whether we look at A(2) or A(15). Chad, for example, ranks sixth when measuring diversity at Level 15, and is the most diverse country in our sample when measuring diversity at Level 2. In that country A(15) is 0.950 and

A(2) is 0.805. This is the case because in Chad about a third of the population speaks an Afro-Asiatic language, about half a Nilo-Saharan language and the rest a language of the Niger-Congo family. Many Latin American countries, such as Bolivia, Ecuador or Peru, also have relatively similar levels of diversity, independently of whether we measure diversity at Level 2 or Level 15. Most of the diversity in those countries derives from the division between Spanish and non-Spanish speakers, where most of the non-Spanish speakers do not pertain to the Indo-European language family.

Table 15.1 provides further information about the different A-indices. Panel A reports the summary statistics. As expected, the degree of diversity increases with the level of disaggregation. Panel B reports the correlations between the different measures. The correlation between A(1) and A(15) is only 0.526, indicating that these two measures are actually quite different. Of course, the correlations become much larger when we compare higher degrees of disaggregation. For example, the correlation between A(9) and A(15) is 0.943. This high correlation reflects the fact that the vast majority of languages are less than ten branches away from the origin. As a result, in nearly three-quarters of the countries A(9) and A(15) are identical. In only a handful of countries, mostly located in southern Africa, are the two measures substantially different. These countries include Gabon, South Africa, Zimbabwe, Uganda and Mozambique.

Table 15.1 Summary statistics: A-index

Panel A. Means and standard deviations*

Variable	Mean	Std. dev.	Min	Max
A(1)	0.156	0.18	0	0.647
A(3)	0.241	0.221	0	0.818
A(6)	0.328	0.272	0	0.941
A(9)	0.377	0.292	0	0.987
A(15)	0.412	0.308	0	0.99

*226 observations.

Panel B. Correlations*

	A(1)	A(3)	A(6)	A(9)	A(15)
A(1)	1				
A(3)	0.77	1			
A(6)	0.579	0.826	1		
A(9)	0.56	0.748	0.9	1	
A(15)	0.526	0.672	0.798	0.943	1

*226 observations.
Source: Desmet et al. (2012).

For this reason it is usually sufficient to focus on a subset of the 15 measures of linguistic heterogeneity, as we sometimes do in the empirical work below.

15.3 Linguistic diversity, redistribution and economic growth

In this section we summarize the most important insights of Desmet et al. (2012), where we let the data inform us which level is more relevant for the issue at hand. There are two reasons for this approach. First, it is not obvious which criterion one would use to choose the 'right' level of aggregation, so that any attempt would likely be somewhat arbitrary. In fact, the arbitrariness of linguistic classifications characterizes common practice in the literature. This is the problem we are trying to address. Second, and more important, depending on the issue at hand, a different level of aggregation may be more or less relevant. By discovering which diversity measure has more predictive power, we can learn something economically meaningful. For example, if we were to find that fractionalization based on deep cleavages is what matters for redistribution, then we would conclude that solidarity and empathy have to do with deep fault lines in society that go back far in time and are deeply engrained. If, instead, we were to find that even shallow divisions reduce people's willingness to redistribute, then our interpretation would be quite different.

The main finding is that the relevant linguistic cleavages vary dramatically across different political economy outcomes. In the case of civil conflict and redistribution, deep divisions seem to be more important, whereas in the case of growth even shallow divisions are enough to hamper economic performance. These results are obtained by regressing the outcome of interest on linguistic fractionalization at successively greater levels of linguistic disaggregation and a series of control variables that are often used for each dependent variable in the existing literature. The standardized beta on linguistic fractionalization is our summary measure of the magnitude of its effect on the outcome under scrutiny. It measures the effect of a 1 s.d. increase in fractionalization on the outcome of interest (expressed as a percentage of the standard deviation of that outcome). Figure 15.3 compares the standardized betas on fractionalization at different levels of aggregation for redistribution (Panel A) and economic growth (Panel B).

The figure in Panel A is based on an ordinary least squares (OLS) regression of transfers and subsidies as a share of GDP on fractionalization, with a number of standard controls.[7] The regression is run 15 times, once for each level of

---

[7] This regression corresponds to Table 4 in Desmet et al. (2012) and is based on 103 countries. The exact list of controls, in addition to the A-index at different levels of aggregation, is log GDP per capita, log population, a small island dummy, latitude, legal origin dummies and regional dummies.

434

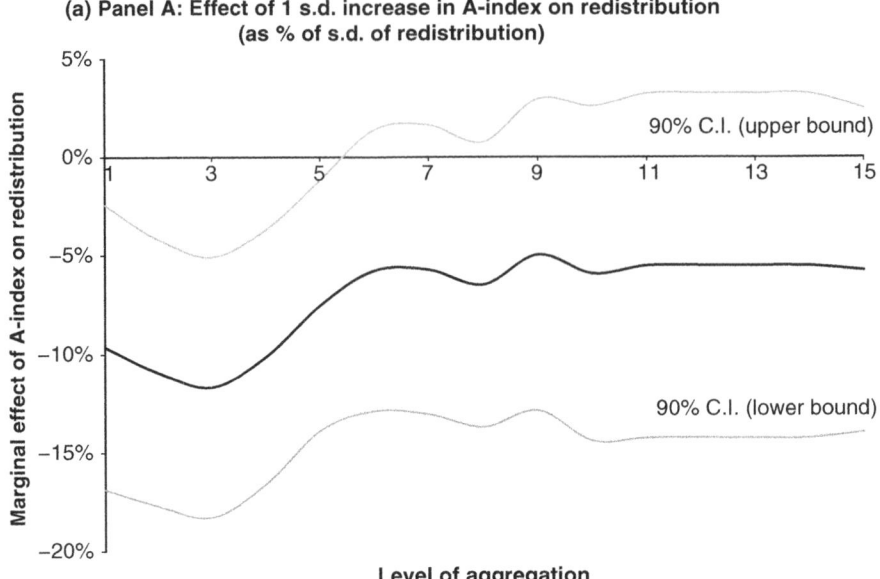

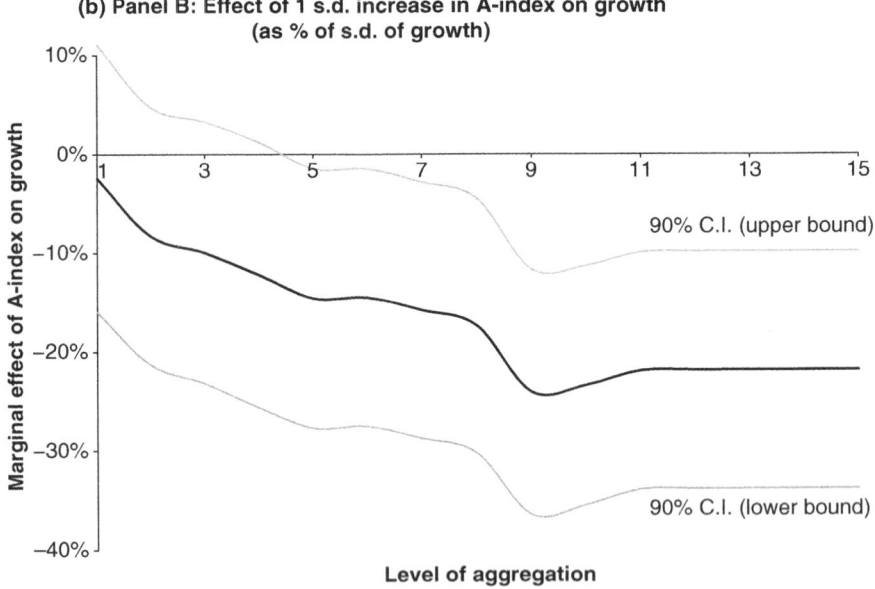

Figure 15.3 Effect of a 1 s.d. increase in the A-index
Source: Desmet et al. (2012).

aggregation, and Panel A then displays the standardized betas. As can be seen, the effect of a 1 s.d. increase in A(1) as a share of the standard deviation of redistribution is −9.6 per cent, and statistically significant at the 5 per cent level. Once we pass the A(5) bar, fractionalization no longer has a statistically significant effect on redistribution. Hence, social solidarity travels well across shallow cleavages, but ceases to do so when divisions are deep.

The results for growth are very different. The figure in Panel B is based on an OLS regression of growth in GDP per capita for the period 1970–2004 on fractionalization, with a number of standard controls.[8] Again, the regression is run 15 times, once for each level of aggregation. As shown in Panel B, the effect of fractionalization becomes more negative and statistically more significant at lower levels of aggregation. The standardized beta reaches a maximum of −24 per cent at A(9), and after that more or less stabilizes. This suggests that shallow divisions are enough to hinder economic growth, but does not imply that deep cleavages are unimportant. However, if we focus exclusively on deep cleavages, we miss the shallow divisions, which also matter.

We argue that civil war and redistribution are more driven by differences in 'preferences' (disagreements over policy or political control), whereas economic growth has more to do with the efficiency of 'technology' (inability to coordinate and communicate). Our results indicate that when it comes to issues involving conflicts between groups, as in the case of war or redistribution, the deeper linguistic fault lines matter most. In contrast, when it comes to economic growth, the efficiency of an economy depends on the ease of trade, communication, coordination and collaboration. Shallow linguistic differences between groups are enough to have a negative impact on economic growth.[9]

15.4 Linguistic diversity and economic development

In this section we explore which level of aggregation is more important for a country's *level* of development. This is of interest for several reasons. First, the relation between linguistic diversity and the level of economic development has been somewhat understudied. Much of the literature on linguistic diversity focuses on civil conflict, redistribution, economic growth, public goods and

---

[8] This regression corresponds to Table 6 in Desmet et al. (2012) and is based on a single cross-section of 100 countries. The exact list of controls is log initial GDP per capita, investment share of GDP, average years of schooling, growth of population, log population, interaction between openness and log population, openness, legal origin dummies and regional dummies.

[9] One could wonder why the effect of diversity on growth is maximized at A(9), rather than at A(15). However, as already mentioned, in nearly all countries A(9) and A(15) are identical, which also explains why in Panel B of Figure 15.3 the difference between A(9) and A(15) is minimal.

governance, with less attention being paid to the level of development. Notable exceptions are Fishman (1968), Pool (1972), and more recently, Nettle (2000) and Nettle et al. (2007).[10]

In this rather limited literature, there is a lack of consensus on the relation between linguistic diversity and GDP per capita. On the one hand, Pool (1972, p. 222) takes a negative view and goes as far as stating that 'a country that is linguistically highly heterogeneous is always undeveloped or semideveloped, and a country that is developed always has considerable language uniformity'. Pool's conclusions are based on the simple correlation between linguistic diversity and GDP per capita in a cross-section of countries, a notable weakness. However, other studies which do control for confounding variables, such as Nettle (2000), find a similar result.[11] On the other hand, Fishman (1991) takes a more positive (or neutral) view and claims that, when controlling for enough other explanatory variables, linguistic heterogeneity ceases to affect the level of economic development. Laitin and Ramachandran (2014) reach a similar conclusion: once they account for linguistic distance from the official language, diversity no longer influences GDP per capita. The lack of agreement in this literature is one of our motivations for revisiting the relation between linguistic diversity and the degree of development using our phylogenetic approach.

A second reason for our interest is that, as argued by Parente and Prescott (1994), long-run growth rates tend to converge across countries, but differences in the *level* of development are often quite persistent. Hence, to understand long-run relative differences across countries, it is more reasonable to look at levels, rather than growth rates. Of course, much of the empirical growth literature takes this into account by focusing on conditional convergence regressions. By controlling for initial GDP per capita, the other regressors can be interpreted as determinants of the steady-state differences in the levels of development. Here, instead, we look directly at the level of development. This has the additional advantage of getting around the issue of growth rates often being quite transitory, a problem pointed out by Easterly et al. (1993) and Hall and Jones (1999).

A third reason for investigating the effect of linguistic diversity on income levels is that if our earlier interpretation for the case of growth is correct, we would expect shallow divisions to hamper economic development as much as deep divisions. In that sense, we can interpret our analysis of economic

---

[10] For a discussion of some of this literature, see also the chapter by Sonntag in this book.
[11] One drawback is that these papers measure linguistic diversity as the share of the population who are speakers of the most widespread language, although Nettle (2000) also considers the number of languages per million of people and Nettle et al. (2007) consider an A-index of diversity.

development as constituting an additional test of our earlier interpretation of the effect of linguistic heterogeneity on growth.

To analyse the relation between fractionalization at different levels of aggregation and a country's level of development, we use the following standard econometric specification:

$$y = \delta A(j) + X\beta + \varepsilon, \tag{3}$$

where y is income per capita in the year 2000, $A(j)$ is the A-index at aggregation level j, X is a matrix of controls, and ε is an error term. All data come from Desmet et al. (2012), Ashraf and Galor (2013) and the references therein.

In Table 15.2 we start regressing a country's GDP per capita in 2000 on the A-index at different levels of aggregation, with a basic set of geographic controls (latitude, percentage of arable land, mean distance to nearest waterway) and regional dummies. Comparing the first four columns, the effect of linguistic fractionalization is always negative. The statistical significance is maximized at A(9). The last four columns also control for legal origins and religious composition. This does not change the results: the effect of linguistic fractionalization is negative, and its predictive power is strongest at aggregation level 9. As in the case of economic growth, this suggests that relatively shallow divisions are enough to hurt economic development. Since there are six more levels of disaggregation – going from A(10) to A(15) – one could argue that A(9) represents an intermediate level of linguistic cleavages. Recall, however, that the correlation between A(9) and A(15) is 0.94, and that the difference between both indices is due to only a handful of mostly southern African countries.

Figure 15.4 represents the standardized betas for all different levels of the A-index corresponding to columns (1) to (4) in Table 15.2. As can be seen, the negative effect of fractionalization on economic development is maximized, both economically and statistically, at A(9). An increase by 1 s.d. in A(9) lowers economic development by 16.7 per cent when expressed as a share of the standard deviation in GDP per capita. As expected, the effect is largely unchanged for levels A(10) through A(15). To further illustrate the effect of A(9) on economic development, Figure 15.5 shows a scatterplot of column (7) from Table 15.2. It takes log of GDP per capita, partialled out from all the control variables in column (7), and plots it against A(9), itself also partialled out from all the controls. The fitted line represents the negative partial relationship between A(9) and economic development.

It is important to mention here that our results cannot strictly be interpreted as causal. As suggested by Greenberg (1956), among others, causality may run the other way, with economic development reducing the degree of linguistic diversity.[12] In fact, the two variables might have co-evolved in a complex way.

---

[12] See also De Grauwe (2006), Alesina and Reich (2014) and Amano et al. (2014).

Table 15.2 Log income per capita in 2000 and A-index at different levels of aggregation

	(1) A(1)	(2) A(6)	(3) A(9)	(4) A(15)	(5) A(1)	(6) A(6)	(7) A(9)	(8) A(15)
A-index (different levels of aggregation)	−0.44 [−1.05]	−0.833*** [−3.25]	−0.931*** [−3.58]	−0.659** [−2.37]	−0.234 [−0.59]	−0.433* [−1.71]	−0.686*** [−2.76]	−0.490* [−1.88]
Log absolute latitude	0.161 [1.53]	0.145 [1.46]	0.116 [1.16]	0.129 [1.25]	0.192* [1.93]	0.190** [1.98]	0.167* [1.76]	0.173* [1.79]
Percentage of arable land	−0.020*** [−3.52]	−0.021*** [−3.86]	−0.021*** [−3.92]	−0.020*** [−3.74]	−0.018*** [−3.33]	−0.018*** [−3.36]	−0.018*** [−3.48]	−0.018*** [−3.47]
Mean distance to nearest waterway	−0.687*** [−4.06]	−0.700*** [−4.39]	−0.676*** [−4.26]	−0.698*** [−4.29]	−0.479*** [−2.94]	−0.486*** [−3.07]	−0.450*** [−2.88]	−0.467*** [−2.95]
Latin America and Caribbean	−0.520** [−2.21]	−0.702** [−2.98]	−0.759*** [−3.20]	−0.697*** [−2.84]	−0.984*** [−2.94]	−1.037*** [−3.07]	−1.130*** [−4.60]	−1.116*** [−4.42]
Sub-Saharan Africa	−1.618*** [−6.92]	−1.611*** [−7.28]	−1.530*** [−6.98]	−1.477*** [−6.50]	−1.694*** [−3.99]	−1.698*** [−4.22]	−1.668*** [−7.94]	−1.623*** [−7.58]
East and Southeast Asia	−0.702** [−2.47]	−0.715** [−2.60]	−0.699*** [−2.56]	−0.708** [−2.53]	−0.580** [−7.63]	−0.578** [−7.91]	−0.563** [−2.09]	−0.580** [−2.12]
French legal origin					−0.275 [−2.09]	−0.153 [−2.11]	−0.011 [−0.02]	−0.083 [−0.14]
German legal origin					0.562 [−0.48]	0.653 [−0.27]	0.722 [1.14]	0.682 [1.06]
Socialist legal origin					−0.443 [0.87]	−0.381 [1.01]	−0.304 [−0.54]	−0.333 [−0.59]
UK legal origin					−0.017 [−0.77]	0.077 [−0.67]	0.204 [0.39]	0.156 [0.29]
Share of Muslims					0 [−0.03]	0 [0.14]	−0.07 [0.39]	−0.18 [0.29]
Share of Roman Catholics					0.010*** [−0.10]	0.009*** [0.03]	0.009*** [−0.07]	0.010*** [−0.18]
Share of Protestants					0.010* [3.29]	0.010* [3.01]	0.010** [2.97]	0.010* [3.12]
Constant	9.157*** [21.03]	9.499*** [22.64]	9.651*** [22.52]	9.492*** [21.09]	8.825*** [12.46]	8.888*** [12.70]	8.982*** [13.03]	8.936*** [12.76]
Observations	152	152	152	152	150	150	150	150
R-squared	0.5078	0.5381	0.5447	0.5227	0.6295	0.6364	0.6484	0.6381

t-statistics in brackets.
***p<0.01, **p<0.05, *p<0.1.

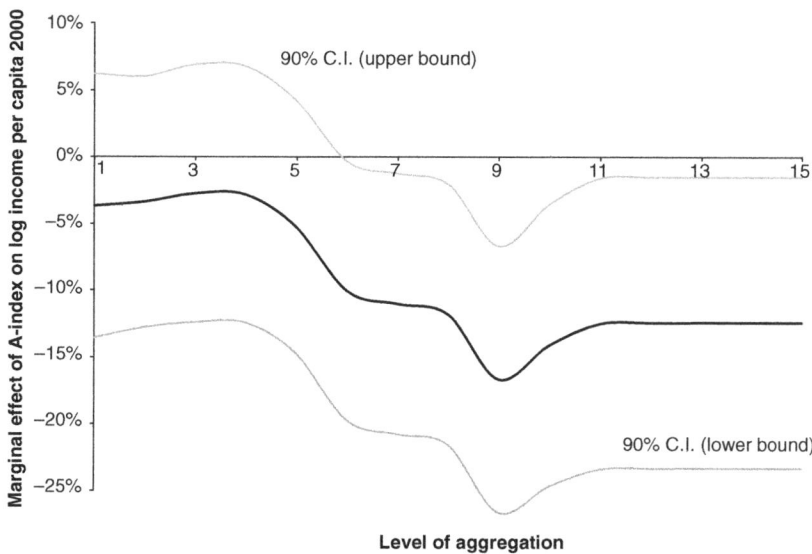

Figure 15.4   Effect of a 1 s.d. increase in the A-index on GDP per capita (expressed as % of s.d. in GDP per capita)

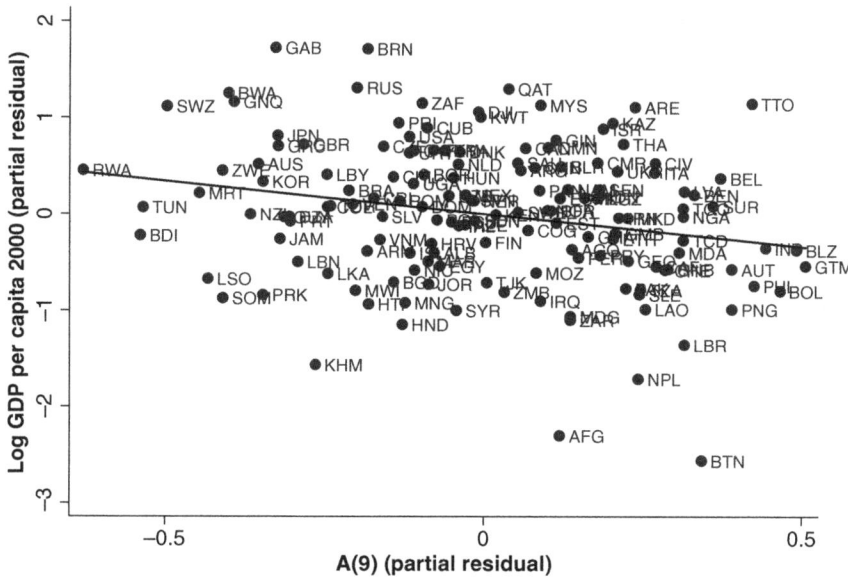

Figure 15.5   Conditional log GDP per capita vs A(9)

In order to provide a more convincing proof of causality, we would need data on linguistic diversity several generations ago. To the best of our knowledge, such data are not available for a large enough set of countries. Combined with the results on growth, however, where initial per capita income is controlled for on the right hand side, the level results are suggestive of an effect of linguistic diversity on growth.

Table 15.3 performs some further robustness checks. Hall and Jones (1999) argue that a country's level of development depends on its social infrastructure, which they define as policies favourable to productive activities and the accumulation of skills, rather than policies that promote rent-seeking, corruption and theft. In the first four columns of Table 15.3, we introduce the Hall and Jones (1999) measure of social infrastructure, which is a combination of government anti-diversion policies and the country's openness to free trade, as an additional control. Consistent with Hall and Jones (1999), social infrastructure has a positive effect on a country's level of development, but it does not change our basic insight. Although including social infrastructure somewhat weakens the statistical significance of linguistic fractionalization, A(9) continues to be significant at the 5 per cent level.

Spolaore and Wacziarg (2009) find that the genetic distance to the technology leader constitutes a barrier to the diffusion of development. They argue that more closely related societies learn more from each other, so that the flow of ideas, knowledge and technology between two populations is facilitated if they share a more recent common ancestor. In the last four columns of Table 15.3, we therefore control for the genetic distance from the US. As in Spolaore and Wacziarg (2009), we find that an increase of the genetic distance to the US lowers a country's income per capita. As for our variable of interest, the result is again unchanged: linguistic fractionalization continues to have a negative impact on a country's level of development, and its predictive power is maximized when the A-index is measured based on linguistic groups at Level 9.

In recent work, Ashraf and Galor (2013) have found that development bears a hump-shaped relation with genetic diversity. In their theory, diversity is good for innovation but bad for trust and coordination, so that there is an optimal level of diversity that maximizes development: on the one hand, higher diversity makes it harder to collaborate, which negatively affects efficiency and makes it harder for countries to operate at their production possibility frontier. On the other hand, higher diversity also implies more complementarities between people, making it more likely for countries to develop and adopt superior technologies, thus pushing out their production possibility frontier. Combining these two forces, they find that countries with intermediate levels of diversity perform best. Table 15.4 controls for genetic diversity and

Table 15.3 Log income per capita in 2000 and A-index at different levels of aggregation: Robustness

	(1) A(1)	(2) A(6)	(3) A(9)	(4) A(15)	(5) A(1)	(6) A(6)	(7) A(9)	(8) A(15)
A-index (different levels of aggregation)	0.046 [0.14]	-0.231 [-1.17]	-0.414** [-2.10]	-0.18 [-0.87]	-0.124 [-0.32]	-0.548** [-2.15]	-0.724*** [-2.94]	-0.451* [-1.75]
Log absolute latitude	0.159** [2.15]	0.147** [2.08]	0.133* [1.90]	0.145** [2.02]	0.133 [1.30]	0.104 [1.04]	0.089 [0.90]	0.11 [1.10]
Percentage of arable land	-0.014*** [-3.09]	-0.014*** [-3.18]	-0.015*** [-3.31]	-0.014*** [-3.22]	-0.018*** [-3.32]	-0.018*** [-3.47]	-0.018*** [-3.57]	-0.018*** [-3.50]
Mean distance to nearest waterway	-0.422** [-2.27]	-0.410** [-2.27]	-0.391** [-2.20]	-0.411** [-2.27]	-0.428** [-2.59]	-0.405** [-2.54]	-0.376** [-2.38]	-0.410** [-2.55]
Latin America and Caribbean	-0.410* [-1.85]	-0.442** [-1.99]	-0.528** [-2.36]	-0.473** [-2.03]	-0.895*** [-3.55]	-0.928*** [-3.74]	-1.027*** [-4.14]	-1.015*** [-3.94]
Sub-Saharan Africa	-1.189*** [-5.99]	-1.210*** [-6.25]	-1.202*** [-6.31]	-1.182*** [-6.08]	-1.238*** [-3.89]	-1.153*** [-3.74]	-1.153*** [-3.80]	-1.190*** [-3.85]
East and Southeast Asia	-0.462* [-1.92]	-0.428* [-1.78]	-0.391 [-1.65]	-0.437* [-1.81]	-0.288 [-0.91]	-0.211 [-0.68]	-0.22 [-0.72]	-0.292 [-0.94]
French legal origin	0.173 [0.39]	0.254 [0.58]	0.327 [0.75]	0.246 [0.55]	-0.112 [-0.19]	0.142 [0.24]	0.243 [0.41]	0.084 [0.14]
German legal origin	0.378 [0.79]	0.421 [0.88]	0.443 [0.94]	0.41 [0.86]	0.732 [1.11]	0.923 [1.41]	0.958 [1.49]	0.853 [1.30]
Socialist legal origin	0.382 [0.75]	0.425 [0.83]	0.428 [0.85]	0.41 [0.80]	-0.202 [-0.34]	0.001 [0.00]	0.036 [0.06]	-0.08 [-0.13]
UK legal origin	0.269 [0.67]	0.335 [0.84]	0.393 [1.00]	0.337 [0.84]	0.163 [0.29]	0.4 [0.71]	0.486 [0.88]	0.347 [0.61]
Share of Muslims	-0.004 [-1.60]	-0.004 [-1.42]	-0.004 [-1.54]	-0.004 [-1.62]	0 [-0.14]	0 [0.05]	0 [-0.10]	-0.001 [-0.20]
Share of Roman Catholics	0.002 [0.66]	0.001 [0.54]	0.001 [0.54]	0.002 [0.62]	0.010*** [3.36]	0.009*** [3.03]	0.009*** [3.03]	0.010*** [3.19]
Share of Protestants	0.003 [0.70]	0.003 [0.78]	0.004 [0.85]	0.003 [0.78]	0.013** [2.24]	0.014** [2.47]	0.014** [2.53]	0.013** [2.34]
Social infrastructure	2.042*** [5.57]	2.026*** [5.57]	1.971*** [5.48]	2.002*** [5.45]				
Genetic distance to the U.S.					-0.050* [-1.86]	-0.063** [-2.34]	-0.059** [-2.26]	-0.049* [-1.87]
Constant	7.719*** [12.44]	7.787*** [12.73]	7.900*** [13.04]	7.817*** [12.62]	9.052*** [12.77]	9.203*** [13.17]	9.258*** [13.45]	9.164*** [13.05]
Observations	112	112	112	112	148	148	148	148
R-squared	0.838	0.8403	0.8451	0.8393	0.6348	0.6469	0.6571	0.6428

t-statistics in brackets.
***$p<0.01$, **$p<0.05$, *$p<0.1$.

genetic diversity squared. It also allows for the timing of the Neolithic Revolution to affect today's level of development, a hypothesis advanced by Diamond (1997).[13] Our findings are consistent with those in Ashraf and Galor (2013). Turning to our variable of interest, the results are unchanged. A(9) continues to be statistically significant at the 5 per cent level.

Taken together, these results suggest that fine divisions are enough to negatively impact on a country's level of development. Even shallow cleavages can lead to inefficiencies. Markets become more segmented; trade and economic exchange encounter implicit barriers; and collaboration in productive activities becomes harder.

15.5 Conclusion

The depth of linguistic cleavages matters for political economy outcomes. Deep cleavages are associated with deleterious outcomes related to disagreements over the control of resources and common policies. For instance, measures of linguistic diversity based on deep cleavages, going back thousands of years, have a negative effect on civil conflict and redistribution. In contrast, more recent linguistic cleavages are sufficient to introduce barriers between populations, reducing their ability to communicate, interact and coordinate. These more superficial linguistic differences hinder growth and economic development by segmenting markets and limiting the scope for fruitful economic transactions.

Our explanation for these contrasting findings is based on drawing a distinction between the effects of linguistic cleavages on preferences (a demand-side explanation) versus their effect on technology (a supply-side explanation). Deep cleavages, because they originate earlier in history, are associated with starker differences in preferences, norms, values, attitudes and culture. In more recent work, Desmet et al. (2014) use data from the World Values Survey and show indeed that the degree of overlap between cultural values and ethnolinguistic identity is highly predictive of civil conflict. That is, countries where ethnicity helps predict cultural values and preferences are more likely to experience civil wars. This is entirely consistent with what we argue here, namely that deep cleavages – those most likely to be associated with deep cultural and preference differences between linguistic groups – are those most likely to generate conflict and low solidarity between groups.

---

[13] Note that genetic diversity and the timing of the Neolithic Revolution are 'ancestry adjusted', meaning that the result is based not on a country's geography, but on a country's ancestral population (Putterman and Weil, 2010). For example, the timing of the Neolithic Revolution for Australia is coded as closer to that of England due to the presence of a large population of English descent in Australia.

Table 15.4 Log income per capita in 2000, predicted genetic diversity and A-index at different levels of aggregation

	(1) A(1)	(2) A(6)	(3) A(9)	(4) A(15)
A-index	0.313	−0.392	−0.590**	−0.306
(different levels aggregation)	[0.78]	[−1.41]	[−2.17]	[−1.25]
Log absolute latitude	0.183	0.168	0.159	0.16
	[1.60]	[1.55]	[1.51]	[1.42]
Percentage of arable land	−0.021***	−0.022***	−0.022***	−0.022***
	[−3.88]	[−4.30]	[−4.50]	[−4.32]
Mean distance	−0.423*	−0.410*	−0.398*	−0.404*
to nearest waterway	[−1.76]	[−1.84]	[−1.83]	[−1.79]
Latin America and Caribbean	−0.967***	−1.048***	−1.136***	−1.077***
	[−3.90]	[−3.92]	[−3.95]	[−3.87]
Sub-Saharan Africa	−1.427***	−1.229***	−1.150***	−1.268***
	[−4.51]	[−3.92]	[−3.74]	[−4.09]
East and Southeast Asia	−0.522	−0.498	−0.434	−0.492
	[−1.31]	[−1.35]	[−1.18]	[−1.28]
French legal origin	−0.319	−0.139	−0.058	−0.168
	[−0.66]	[−0.29]	[−0.12]	[−0.35]
German legal origin	0.271	0.37	0.374	0.327
	[0.51]	[0.75]	[0.82]	[0.65]
Socialist legal origin	−0.593	−0.487	−0.484	−0.508
	[−1.18]	[−1.00]	[−1.04]	[−1.04]
UK legal origin	−0.161	0.016	0.086	0.002
	[−0.36]	[0.04]	[0.20]	[0.00]
Share of Muslims	−0.009***	−0.008***	−0.009***	−0.009***
	[−3.35]	[−3.13]	[−3.30]	[−3.43]
Share of Roman Catholics	0.005*	0.004	0.004	0.005
	[1.72]	[1.53]	[1.58]	[1.60]
Share of Protestants	0.005	0.007	0.007	0.006
	[0.76]	[1.13]	[1.24]	[1.05]
Predicted diversity	292.464***	259.711***	247.288***	257.583***
(ancestry adjusted)	[3.57]	[3.35]	[3.11]	[3.28]
Predicted diversity squared	−205.384***	−183.971***	−175.261***	−181.806***
(ancestry adjusted)	[−3.55]	[−3.35]	[−3.12]	[−3.27]
Neolithic Revolution timing	0.317	0.543**	0.578**	0.454**
(ancestry adjusted)	[1.26]	[2.17]	[2.55]	[2.00]
Constant	−97.279***	−86.708***	−82.528***	−85.474***
	[−3.40]	[−3.20]	[−2.97]	[−3.10]
Observations	144	144	144	144
R-squared	0.669	0.673	0.682	0.673

t-statistics in brackets.
***$p<0.01$, **$p<0.05$, *$p<0.1$.
Bootstrapped standard errors, accounting for the use of generated regressors, as in Ashraf and Galor (2013).

In contrast, more superficial linguistic differences, sufficient to limit intelligibility and communication between distinct groups, introduce transactions costs and barriers, i.e. technological hindrances. These differences may be insufficient to generate deep disagreements in terms of preferences and culture, but are sufficient to create limits to coordination, cooperation and transactions, segmenting markets and reducing the scope of economic interactions. Our finding, detailed in this chapter, that linguistic diversity measured at fine levels of disaggregation has a negative effect on growth and development is entirely consistent with this interpretation.

These findings shed some light on the mechanisms through which linguistic heterogeneity affects political economy outcomes, but much remains to be done. The precise mechanisms linking linguistic heterogeneity should be the subject of further research using a wide array of methodologies – not only cross-country comparative approaches but also more micro-economic and experimental approaches. Scholarly inquiry into these important questions is only in its infancy.

References

D. Acemoglu, S. Johnson and J. Robinson (2001) 'The Colonial Origins of Comparative Development', *American Economic Review*, 91, 1369–1401.

A. Alesina, A. Devleeschauwer, W. Easterly, S. Kurlat and R. Wacziarg (2003) 'Fractionalization', *Journal of Economic Growth*, 8, 155–194.

A. Alesina and E. Glaeser (2004) *Fighting Poverty in the U.S. and in Europe: A World of Difference* (New York: Oxford University Press).

A. Alesina, E. Glaeser and B. Sacerdote (2001) 'Why Doesn't the U.S. Have a European-style Welfare System?', *Brookings Papers on Economic Activity*, 2, 187–254.

A. Alesina and E. La Ferrara (2005) 'Ethnic Diversity and Economic Performance', *Journal of Economic Literature*, 43, 762–800.

A. Alesina and B. Reich (2014) 'Nation Building' NBER Working Paper No. 18839.

T. Amano, B. Sandel, H. Eager, E. Bulteau, J. Svenning, B. Dalsgaard, C. Rahbek, R. Davies and W. Sutherland (2014) 'Global Distribution and Drivers of Language Extinction Risk', *Proceedings of the Royal Society*, B 2014 281, 20141574.

Q. Ashraf and O. Galor (2013) 'The "Out of Africa" Hypothesis, Human Genetic Diversity, and Comparative Economic Development', *American Economic Review*, 103, 1–46.

D. Barrett, G. Kurian and T. Johnson (2001) *World Christian Encyclopedia; A Comparative Survey of Churches and Religions in the Modern World*, 2nd edn. (Oxford: Oxford University Press).

E. Belle and G. Barbujani (2007) 'Worldwide Analysis of Multiple Microsatellites: Language Diversity Has a Detectable Influence on DNA Diversity', *American Journal of Physical Anthropology*, 133, 1137–1146.

L. Cavalli-Sforza, A. Piazza, P. Menozzi and J. Mountain (1988) 'Reconstruction of Human Evolution: Bringing Together Genetic, Archaeological and Linguistic Data', *Proceedings of the National Academy of Sciences of the United States of America*, 85, 6002–6006.

M. Dahlberg, K. Edmark and H. Lundqvist (2012) 'Ethnic Diversity and Preferences for Redistribution', *Journal of Political Economy*, 120, 41–76.

P. De Grauwe (2006) 'Language Diversity and Economic Development', Manuscript, Katholieke Universiteit Leuven.

K. Desmet, I. Ortuño-Ortín and R. Wacziarg (2012) 'The Political Economy of Linguistic Cleavages', *Journal of Development Economics*, 97, 322–338.

K. Desmet, I. Ortuño-Ortín and R. Wacziarg (2014) 'Culture, Identity and Diversity' Working Paper, UCLA.

K. Desmet, I. Ortuño-Ortín and S. Weber (2009) 'Linguistic Diversity and Redistribution', *Journal of the European Economic Association*, 7, 1291–1318.

J. Diamond (1997) *Guns, Germs and Steel: The Fates of Human Societies* (New York: W.W. Norton).

W. Easterly, M. Kremer, L. Pritchett and L. Summers (1993) 'Good Policy or Good Luck? Country Growth Performance and Temporary Shocks', *Journal of Monetary Economics*, 32, 459–483.

W. Easterly and R. Levine (1997) 'Africa's Growth Tragedy: Policies and Ethnic Divisions', *Quarterly Journal of Economics*, 112, 1203–1250.

J. Esteban, L. Mayoral and D. Ray (2012) 'Ethnicity and Conflict: An Empirical Study', *American Economic Review*, 102, 1310–1342.

Ethnologue (2005) *Ethnologue: Languages of the World*, 15th edn (Dallas, TX: SIL International).

J. Fearon and D. Laitin (2003) 'Ethnicity, Insurgency, and Civil War', *American Political Science Review*, 97, 75–90.

J. Fishman (1968) 'Some Contrasts between Linguistically Homogeneous and Linguistically Heterogeneous Polities' In J. Fishman, C. Ferguson and J. Das Gupta (eds) *Language Problems of Developing Nations* (New York: Wiley), pp. 53–68.

J. Fishman (1991) 'An Inter-polity Perspective on the Relationships between Linguistic Heterogeneity, Civil Strife and Per Capita Gross National Product', *International Journal of Applied Linguistics*, 1, 5–18.

R. Gray and Q. Atkinson (2003) 'Language-tree Divergence Times Support the Anatolian Theory of Indo-European Origin', *Nature*, 426, 27 November, 435–439.

J. Greenberg (1956) 'The Measurement of Linguistic Diversity', *Language*, 32, 109–15.

J. Habyarimana, M. Humphreys, D. Posner and J. Weinstein (2007) 'Why Does Ethnic Diversity Undermine Public Goods Provision?', *American Political Science Review*, 101, 709–725.

R. Hall and C. Jones (1999) 'Why Do Some Countries Produce so much more Output Per Worker than Others?', *Quarterly Journal of Economics*, 114, 83–116.

R. La Porta, F. Lopez-de-Silanes, A. Shleifer and R. Vishny (1999) 'The Quality of Government', *Journal of Law, Economics, and Organization*, 15, 222–279.

D. Laitin and D. Posner (2001) 'The Implications of Constructivism for Constructing Ethnic Fractionalization Indices', *APSA-CP: The Comparative Politics Newsletter*, 12 13–17.

D. Laitin and R. Ramachandran (2014) 'Language Policy and Human Development', unpublished manuscript.

J. Montalvo and M. Reynal-Querol (2005) 'Ethnic Polarization, Potential Conflict and Civil War', *American Economic Review*, 95, 796–816.

D. Nettle (2000) 'Linguistic Fragmentation and the Wealth of Nations: The Fishman-Pool Hypothesis Reexamined', *Economic Development and Cultural Change*, 48, 335–348.

D. Nettle, J. Grace, M. Choisy, H. Cornell, J. Guégan and M. Hochberg (2007) 'Cultural Diversity, Economic Development and Societal Instability' *PlosOne*, DOI: 10.1371/journal.pone.0000929.

S. Parente and E. Prescott (1994) 'Barriers to Technology Adoption and Development', *Journal of Political Economy*, 102, 298–321.

J. Pool (1972) 'National Development and Language Diversity' In J. Fishman (ed.) *Advances in the Sociology of Language*, Volume II (The Hague: Mouton), pp. 213–230.

L. Putterman and D. Weil (2010) 'Post-1500 Population Flows and The Long-Run Determinants of Economic Growth and Inequality', *Quarterly Journal of Economics*, 125, 1624–1682.

R. Sokal (1988) 'Genetic, Geographic and Linguistic Distances in Europe', *Proceedings of the National Academy of Sciences of the United States of America*, 85, 1722–1726.

E. Spolaore and R. Wacziarg (2009) 'The Diffusion of Development', *Quarterly Journal of Economics*, 124, 469–529.

H. Stichnoth and K. Van der Straeten (2013) 'Ethnic Diversity, Public Spending, and Individual Support for the Welfare State: A Review of the Empirical Literature', *Journal of Economic Surveys*, 27, 364–389.

16
Language Choices: Political and Economic Factors in Three European States

Sue Wright

16.1 Introduction

Language has first and foremost an information-carrying function. Being able to express ideas in language allows human beings to remember the past, organize the present and plan the future. Language allows individuals to negotiate with each other, to cooperate and to live in groups. The utility of language is thus its fundamental attribute. However, the fact that this human skill has developed as *languages* rather than *language* has added another very important function: the use of a language variety within a group defines the parameters of the group; it includes as members all those who are speakers and excludes all those who cannot speak the language. Language thus has a role to play in the construction of political/social identity as communication takes place and social interaction cements relationships among members of the language community. This second function, the role of language in creating group identity, has been the major focus of sociolinguistics and applied linguistics. There has not been the same volume of literature on language and utility. In a rare book on language and economics, Grin and his co-authors criticize this deficiency, noting that the applied linguistics literature does not habitually concern itself with 'economic variables like productivity, costs and profits, and [that] the causal links through which they might be connected with linguistic variables such as workers' linguistic repertoires are never investigated' (Grin et al., 2010, p. 3).

They are right. Sociolinguists have not taken the economic aspects of language use into consideration systematically. However, when one looks closely at the processes of identity construction, it becomes clear that there is often a strong economic motivation that dovetails with the more relational aspects of identification and belonging. Pierre Bourdieu is one of the few scholars who have developed this idea and his work investigates the relationship of

447

language and market forces. In the creation of the community of national communication which is a constant in nation building,[1] Bourdieu notes how the conditions of a monopolistic market come into being:

> *C'est dans le processus de la constitution de l'Etat que se créent les conditions de la constitution d'un marché linguistique unifié et dominé par la langue officielle.* (It is only in the process of state building that we get the conditions necessary for a single linguistic market, dominated by the official language) (Bourdieu, 1982, p. 27).

He makes clear how knowledge and mastery of this language are used to define groups and protect advantage:

> *Les échanges linguistiques sont aussi les échanges de pouvoir symbolique où s'actualisent les rapports de force entre les locuteurs ou leurs groupes respectifs.* (Language interactions are also negotiations of symbolic power, in which the relative influence of speakers (or their respective groups) becomes apparent) (ibid., p. 14).

Using Bourdieu's insights on group identity and market forces, I want to investigate the relationship of language and identity and language and utility. My argument will be that the shift to a national language comes about through a complex mix of 'top down' policy pressure and 'bottom up' individual action. In the first section, I focus on three of the old state-nations of Europe – France, Spain and the UK – to examine how their populations moved to French, Castilian and English under the twin propulsions of political and economic pressure, and how these processes differed in the three contexts. In the second section I examine groups within these three states who took different positions on linguistic incorporation into the state-nation and discuss their reasons for doing so. What are the factors that influence language choice? Do these examples suggest that languages can be sustained where there is strong cultural identity? Or is it political and/or economic advantage which is the driving force in language choice? In the final section I consider social and geographical mobility and the role of elites in nation building. A comparison of groups on the periphery of the three states suggests that the relative permeability/impermeability of national elites has consequences for group formation and for language practices and language loyalty.

---

[1] There are many ways in which elites have promoted a national language for a national group; multilingual nation-states are relatively rare. For a discussion of this, see Wright (2004).

16.2 Nation building

The idea of the nation-state has two expressions in Europe. In the first, the boundaries of the state were set by dynastic expansion. The disparate groups that found themselves within the state boundaries fell under the nation-building pressures of state elites, as these latter attempted to weld the citizenry into a cohesive nation. This was the case in France, Spain and the UK. In the second, the elite of a cultural and linguistic group aimed to provide it with territory within which it would be the sole or dominant group. This was the case in German and Italian unification, as groups along the dialect continua were brought together under one umbrella. Other ethnic nation-states were set up at the end of World War I, as the victors upheld the right for national self-determination. In a fortuitous coincidence, the self-determination of nations could be presented as an ideal and at the same time provide a useful way of dismantling the defeated empires.

It is the first process that interests us here. France, Spain and the UK, the three nation-states that provide the case studies for this chapter, could be termed 'state-nations', since the state pre-dated the nation in all of them.

The process of state-nation building started in the early modern period, as dynasties wrested power from their feudal aristocracies, and established state bureaucracies for the administration of their lands. They stabilized their frontiers, and, following the doctrine of *cuius regio eius religio,* determined the religious affiliations of the populations within those frontiers. Law became the affair of the state rather than the church. A growing class of merchants and manufacturers provided an alternative tax base. At the beginning of the process there was thus the apparatus of a centralizing state but as yet no cohesive population; the subjects of the various monarchs were diverse in terms of culture and language, even if this linguistic diversity was only change along dialect continua.

16.2.1 Push and pull factors in France

The desire to make the state and the nation congruent grew slowly. First came the aim to make administration easier for the centre. As legal texts, e.g. contracts, began to be produced in the vernacular rather than in Latin, monarchs moved to ensure that the language variety used was their variety and no other. In the reign of François I of France, the edict of Villers-Cotterêts (1539) required those who interacted with the crown through the medium of the law courts or the bureaucracy to use French, the language variety of the court and king. However, this language law only concerned a small number. The monarch was content to deal with the elite in the provinces and to leave the peasants to their own linguistic devices. The great rural masses had no compelling reason to learn the language variety of the capital nor the opportunity to do so.

It was only with the 1789 revolution that the majority of the population came under top down pressure to move to French. The revolution changed the status of the French from subjects to citizens and, in the new context, where these citizens rather than the monarch embodied the sovereignty of the state, their political elite needed to communicate with them. The mass of people had to be informed about the new political organization and be convinced to support it. At first the revolutionaries took into account the fact that most of the population of 25 million with whom they were dealing were not French speakers (Grégoire, 1794). From January 1790 until July 1793 many laws and notices sent out to the provinces were translated into Alsatian, Basque, Breton, Catalan, Corsican, Flemish, Franco-Provençal, Occitan, etc. (Leclerc, 2007).[2] Then there was abrupt change. The costs and difficulties of translation had become apparent; war with the neighbouring states brought those speaking the languages of the periphery under suspicion;[3] civil war within the state caused certain language groups (e.g. Vendéens) to be viewed as traitors; the *Terreur* instilled a climate of suspicion where divergence and difference were not tolerated. The idea of the one and indivisible state took root, and linguistic homogeneity became a major aim.

It was not possible in the economic conditions of the First Republic, always on a war footing, to instigate the language learning necessary to bring about the shift to a single national language. A decree of the National Convention, passed on 27 January 1794, which called for a French speaking teacher in every commune where French was not the majority language came to nothing. After the French defeat at Sedan in 1870, however, the politicians of the Third Republic returned to the issue. The loss of Alsace-Lorraine to the Prussians triggered strong nationalist sentiment throughout France and paved the way for muscular nation building. This included free and obligatory elementary schooling for all, introduced by Jules Ferry in 1881 and 1882. This schooling inculcated republican values and patriotism and was the key means by which the knowledge and use of French spread in the country (Cerquiglini, n.d.; Evans and Godin, 2004).

The boys educated in the first decades of the Ferry school system were of course to be the soldiers in the trenches of World War I. What the classroom started, conscription and total war completed. The move to French was inevitable in the context of conflict. First the danger of not understanding one's comrade in the battle line imposed shift; second it became a patriotic

---

[2] On 14 January 1790, the député Bouchette's proposal to translate all the decrees of the Assemblée into the regional languages was accepted. Thirty Occitan speaking departments were the first group to stop the practice (www.languefrancaise.net/HLF/RF).

[3] Barère's famous report (1794) lambasts the speakers of languages other than French and accuses them of treachery and anti-revolutionary sentiments.

duty to use the language of the nation in a period of war (Baconnier et al., 1985).

The second set of pressures that brought linguistic unification were economic and stemmed from decisions made by individuals. Many shifted to French to improve their economic position and to be socially mobile. France was an early innovator in industrialization and from the 17th century onwards there were concentrations of manufacture which attracted those seeking a livelihood unconnected with the land. From the small workshops set up by Colbert in the reign of Louis XIV to the great industrial complexes of the Third Republic, new industries attracted families from the countryside. The sites of industrialization were linguistic melting pots where French became the lingua franca.

The workforce to staff industrialization was available. The French countryside experienced a demographic boom in the long 19th century (1789–1913) and from the late 18th century onwards there was constant migration from country to town, in part because of this overpopulation (Gachon, 1970). By 1851 a quarter of the French population lived in a town (Braudel, 1986).

The railway infrastructure, begun during the Second Empire, channelled the migration flows. Paris was the hub of the railway network and it was much easier, even if often much further, to get to the capital from the provinces than to get from one province to another or to cross the national border. Thus, for example, the southern French, some of whom had traditionally sought work in Catalonia or Piedmont in times of hardship on the land (Ferrater Mora, 1944/2012), now went north to Paris to seek work. Some areas, e.g. Auvergne orientale and Aveyron, experienced a substantial loss of population under the influence of the new transport (Gachon, 1970; Crozes and Magne, 1993). Those who made the journey north had to make a major language shift. Whereas migration to the nearby towns of the Mediterranean coast had only required accommodation to other varieties on the langues d'oc dialect continuum, the move to Paris and the industrial areas of the north brought the migrants into a French speaking environment (Nordman, 1998).

Industrialization changes the way that a society educates its young. In the setting of traditional agriculture, apprenticeship is an adequate way of passing unchanging information down the generations. But, as Gellner (1983) explained, industry needs its workforce to be literate and numerate so that workers dealing with machinery understand basic principles and can adapt and apply them as the manufacturing process develops. Since such generic education is a high cost undertaking with no immediate return, it usually becomes a state affair supported by taxes (Gellner, 1983). So one of the impetuses for a national education system is the need for an educated industrial workforce. As noted above, in the early 1880s the Ferry laws made schooling both free and obligatory for all. The requirements of industry dovetailed neatly into the nation-building project of the Third Republic (Weber, 1976).

The spread of French was guaranteed by the social mobility it conferred. Whereas in other states knowledge of the national language is often a necessary but not sufficient condition for social promotion, French-medium education actually did open the doors for aspiring young men from all parts of France.

Of course class and money still counted, but not entirely. Ambitious young Frenchmen had only to consider the different backgrounds and varied birthplaces of the presidents of their country (Table 16.1) to see that social and geographical origins were not insuperable blocks to preferment; males from all regions and classes could advance as long as they passed through the mill of cultural and linguistic unification.

By the mid-20th century France was French speaking.[4] The republican ideal of one language and one people on one territory had been widely accepted by the French population. The pressure of patriotic ideology and the requirements of self-interest coincided.

Table 16.1   The social and geographical origins of the presidents of the Third Republic

President	Dates of presidency	Place of birth	Date of birth	Father's profession
Louis-Adolphe Thiers	1871–1873	Marseilles	1797	Locksmith
Mac-Mahon	1873–1879	Autun	1808	Aristocrat
Jules Grévy	1879–1887	Jura	1807	Farmer
Marie-François-Sadi Carnot	1887–1894	Limoges	1837	Lawyer
Jean Casimir-Perier	1894–1895	Paris	1847	Politician
Félix Faure	1895–1899	Paris	1841	Artisan
Émile Loubet	1899–1906	Drôme	1838	Farmer
Armand Fallières	1906–1913	Lot-et Garonne	1841	Clerk of local court
Raymond Poincaré	1913–1920	Bar-le-Duc	1860	Top civil servant
Paul Deschanel	1920–1920	Brussels	1855	Writer and politician
Alexandre Millerand	1920–1924	Paris	1859	Shopkeeper
Gaston Doumergue	1924–1931	Gard	1863	Farmer
Paul Doumer	1931–1932	Aurillac	1857	Labourer
Albert Lebrun	1932–1940	Meurthe et Moselle	1871	Farmer

Source: Adapted from www.gouvernement.fr.

---

[4] Chanet (1988) argues that this is not clear cut, and that it was too difficult to suppress the local regional languages. My argument is slightly different. I argue that no one was fully monolingual in a regional language after the experience of the Republican school which touched everyone for a period of several years. Schooling was obligatory up to the age of 14 from 1936 and to 16 from 1959.

16.2.2 Push and pull factors in the United Kingdom

The pull factors in the UK are in some ways similar to those in France. The process of linguistic unification begins with legislation to require non English speaking subjects of the king to use English in interaction with the state. In the Act of Union of 1536, Henry VIII stipulated that he wanted English, the language of his court and capital, to be the sole language for those Welsh who had business with the state, and for those in the ruling class in Wales who wanted to take public office under the English crown.

This move to the monolingual state might have halted when James VI of Scotland inherited the English throne and became king of both countries in 1603. James VI and his court in Edinburgh spoke Scots, a language on the same West Germanic dialect continuum as English. However, when he assumed rule for the whole of Britain, he accommodated to his more numerous English speaking subjects by using their language, alongside Scots[5] and his writings in Scots were translated into English for them (Wormald, 1983). Scots persisted in the London court until the mid-17th century with letters from Charles I, James' son, attesting to its continued presence. Scots disappeared, however, as the power of the Stuart dynasty was checked.

When the Acts of Union were passed by the English and Scottish Parliaments in 1707 and the two countries merged into the United Kingdom of Great Britain, there was no language element in the Acts. It was taken for granted that the UK parliament, meeting in October 1707 for the first time, would use English. And this continued even as a German speaking monarch (George I) took the throne in 1714. The variety of English used in the capital continued to be the language of power and prestige.

How can we account for this, if the crown was not English speaking in this period? First of all the power of the king had been curtailed. From 1689 Britain had been governed under a system where the monarch ruled in conjunction with the two houses of parliament. The power and influence of the political elite increased as those of the now constitutional monarch decreased. From this date until the Great Reform Act of 1832 members of parliament were elected by a small upper-class minority of Protestant adult males, and politicians of both the Commons and Lords were men from the landed gentry. This political elite was English speaking, and therefore English remained the language of power.

Second, there was the effect of the Reformation and its influence on language practices. The English, Welsh and Scots had mostly become Protestant following the choices made by their monarchs in the course of the 16th

---

[5] This can be seen in collections of his letters. The language choice seems to depend on the background of his advisors in the matter as well as the audience/recipient. Cf. Centre for the Scots Leid (www.scotslanguage.com/RoyalScots/How_our_royal_language_was_lost).

century. For Protestants, Bible study in the vernacular is central to their religious observance. Bibles became more easily available after the introduction of printing to Europe, and literacy increased in all Protestant areas. Bible study in the vernacular had far-reaching consequences: as populations became familiar with the text, their language varieties converged. In the UK, the Bible in general use was a translation ordered by James VI/I and published in 1611. The language of the King James Bible was the language variety of London and the universities of Oxford and Cambridge, and this was the norm that spread.[6]

These high levels of literacy developing in tandem with vernacular print capitalism reinforced national consciousness. Anderson (1991) has argued that the novel provided readers with a constructed view of their national group and that the national press contributed to the imagined community of the nation. In the UK it was possible to organize the distribution of daily newspapers at an early stage. In 1830 there were 157 miles of railway track in the UK; by 1901 there were 30,385 miles of track. By the 1850s newspapers could be delivered to most major towns within 24 hours. The fast distribution of newspapers allowed citizens to read the same news texts within much the same time frame in all parts of the state and had a powerful effect both on sentiments of national cohesion and on the spread of standard English.

When compulsory state primary schooling was introduced through the Elementary Education Acts in the last two decades of the 19th century, the literacy rate in English was already high. The 1871 census[7] records 80.6 per cent for males and 73.2 per cent for women.

The push factors for linguistic change were, as in France, closely linked to the decisions that individuals and families took to leave the land and to move to towns and employment in industry. In the UK leaving the land was sometimes not a personal choice. There is a long history of land enclosure, and landlords evicted small farmers in several different periods to make way for more profitable ways of farming (Thirsk, 1984; Richards, 2013). The rural exodus came to a crescendo, however, in the 18th and 19th centuries as the mechanization of

---

[6] There were also translations of the Bible into Welsh and Lowlands Scots which had a standardizing effect in these two languages.

[7] Most children were already being schooled through English when primary education became obligatory: the Gaelic speaking Scots in the Highlands and Islands had come under pressure in 1616, when James VI/I sought to establish schools in every parish in the Highlands and eradicate Gaelic; the Irish had been exposed to English in the free national schools since 1831; the Welsh came under pressure to use English after an infamous report (1847) by three Welsh Anglicans (Lingen, Symons and Vaughan Johnson) ascribed Welsh economic problems to the widespread use of Welsh. Literacy had increased in the industrial areas of England where many industrialists (particularly Quakers) practised a paternalistic capitalism and provided schools for workers' children.

farming and the phenomenal growth of British manufacturing radically altered patterns of demand for workers. Between 1700 and 1890 the proportion of the British workforce in industry rose from 22 to 43 per cent. By 1850 only 22 per cent of the workforce remained in agriculture (Overton, 1996).

The industrial labour force, drawn from all parts of the UK, flocked to Manchester and the mill towns of the north, and to Birmingham and the metal towns of the Midlands. Cities and industrial conurbations were linguistic melting pots: speakers of different English dialects lost their specificities and Welsh, Scots and Gaelic speakers shifted to English. This could happen even in parts of the state where English was not the indigenous language. For example, the mining areas of south Wales became English speaking with the influx of miners from other parts of the UK (Lundén, 1979). And as the speakers of the other languages and dialects of the UK left their ancestral territories, the vitality of these languages and dialects was undermined.

Innovation and new technologies opened up space for social mobility in the UK. This was a safety valve in UK society because the aristocratic class practised rigorous social closure right up until World War II (Colley, 1992). However, in the burgeoning industries and commerce of the 18th and 19th centuries there were possibilities for those who were intelligent and enterprising, and an additional power group evolved. The knowledge flows, exchanges and networks among this new class of entrepreneurs and inventors (Tocqueville, 1828/1958; Bairoch, 1985) connected the industrial centres of the North and the Midlands. Standard English spread in written form with the proliferation of technical texts. Pronouncing dictionaries and elocution manuals proliferated, as the new elite began to consider that standard English was a class dialect that it would benefit them to acquire (Crowley, 1989).

By the beginning of the 20th century, the various linguistic groups of the UK had shifted to English, at the very least for their public life. By the end of the century, there were no monolinguals among the indigenous populations.[8]

16.2.3   A different scenario in Spain

Spanish nation-building came at a slightly later date compared to the other two state-nations described above. Admittedly Spain became a unified territory under the rule of one dynasty at the end of the 15th century when Isabella I of Castile married Ferdinand II of Aragon (1469). Hobsbawm (1990, p. 16) suggests that Spain is 'one of the earliest kingdoms to which it is not unrealistic to attach the label "nation-state"'. However, despite being under one ruler with

---

[8] With large-scale immigration into the UK in the second half of the 20th century, there are of course some older members of families who were not English speaking when they settled and did not ever acquire the language.

reasonably stable borders,[9] Spain continued to be ruled in the traditional feudal way. Ferdinand and Isabella did not leave a male heir and their crown passed to Charles from the House of Habsburg, who had also inherited vast territories outside Spain and who became the Holy Roman Emperor Charles V. He and his descendants governed their diverse and non-contiguous domains in the feudal manner, relying on local governors. The regions of Spain continued to be very autonomous with their own institutions, infrastructure, tax and legal systems, language and customs.

Charles was rarely in Spain. Primarily concerned with maintaining and aggrandizing his empire and with fighting the spread of Protestantism, he, and then later his son, ruled mostly from Antwerp and Brussels. Indeed Charles' apparent lack of commitment to the Spanish state sparked a rebellion early in his reign. The rebels in the Comuneros revolts in Castilian towns wanted the king to spend more time in Spain, to remove foreigners from positions of power at court, to adopt the customs of the Spanish kings, and call the Cortes[10] to meet every three years (Zagorin, 1982). This is an interesting contrast with France and England in this period. Whereas François I and Henry VIII sought to impose on their subjects a single state language in public affairs, in Spain it was the subjects who tried to put pressure on their king to speak Castilian.

The move to Castilian as the official language throughout the Spanish state came as part of the Nueva Planta decrees introduced by the Bourbon king, Philip V. These laws were in part an attempt by a French-born king to introduce policy in line with other European-centralizing monarchs and in part as a punishment for those territories which had fought against him in the War of the Spanish Succession (1705–1714) (Schrijver, 2006). The Catalans and the Valencians had supported his opponent and they were penalized by the abolition of their institutions, privileges and ancient charters. The laws of Castile now applied to the majority of the state, and there was no longer a distinction between Castilian and Aragonese with respect to rights and law. Most internal borders and customs were suppressed. Top civil servants and judges were appointed directly from Madrid, and Castilian became the sole language of government in Aragon, replacing Latin, Catalan and other Spanish languages.

However, the strength of the commitment to the Catholic Church in Spain was a brake on this nascent nation building. The close association of church and state had a long history. Pope Alexander VI had accorded Ferdinand and Isabella the title of Los Reyes Católicos for their victory in Grenada, which ended 700 years of Islamic rule on the Iberian peninsula, and for their defence

---

[9] The territory was defined and had stable borders from an early date. The border with Portugal was largely established in the 13th century and the northern borders were settled in the 17th century at the end of the Thirty Years War (Nordman, 1998).

[10] This body represented not only the nobility but also the church and the municipalities.

of Catholic dogma in their lands. Charles V had been at the forefront of the Counter-Reformation, leading the Catholic armies against Protestant rulers after 1517. Closely linked to the Vatican, the Spanish state continued to respect the Catholic Church as a source of law, in contrast to those states in the early modern period where law was beginning to be a national affair. The Inquisition remained a power in Spain until the 19th century. These close relations with the Church also blocked the development of a national education system. In contrast to the nation-states where education became a matter for the state in the 19th century, the Church remained the main provider of education in Spain until a late date. There was no universal state education until the Second Republic in Spain (i.e. the 1930s). Under the control of the Church, education did not play the nation building role it did in France and the UK. As Boyd (1997, p. 8) says, 'the quality and the extension of Spanish education at the end of the nineteenth century were dismal, and its contribution to the creation of a uniform national culture was nearly nil'. Church schools inhibited the spread of Castilian since the medium was usually the local language (Álvarez-Junco, 2000). The third way that the Catholic Church impeded nation building was in the more nebulous area of identity. National symbols took a long time to appear in Spain and it proved particularly difficult to 'invent tradition', as the Church had already seized such a large part of the festive calendar and secured many of the major civic spaces for monuments to its martyrs, saints and apostles (ibid.).

Thus the great mass of Spaniards were not invited into history in Nairn's (1977/2003) sense. The introduction of any kind of civic education was continually shelved as the Catholic Right feared that it might introduce liberal and secular ideas (Boyd, 1997). Álvarez-Junco (2000) believes that the rural populations of Andalusia and Castile continued to identify themselves as regional and confessional, rather than national, until well into the 20th century. Boyd (1997) claims that peasants maintained extremely local identities until the Second Republic, and a cohesive national community of communication was never fully accomplished.

Colonial empire, which had proved a major influence in British nation building and patriotism, was not so influential in the Spanish case. Being a colonial power brought immense wealth, and the possibility of sharing such economic success often encourages identification with a polity. This was undoubtedly so for those who benefited from the shipbuilding, voyaging, soldiering and trading associated with imperialism, and whose families prospered in the new territories, but until the Nueva Planta decrees, trade with the Americas was largely the preserve of the Castilians.[11]

---

[11] Of course, non-Castilians were not immune to the negative sides of colonial expansion. The circulation of gold and silver from the Americas triggered massive inflation in the 16th and 17th centuries, which meant many Spaniards did not experience the 'Golden Age' as a time of plenty with reasons to be pleased to be Spanish.

The loss of all the colonies on the South and Central American mainland in the early 19th century and the cession to the US of the Caribbean islands of Puerto Rico and Cuba in 1898 meant that an imperializing popular nationalism on the British model was impossible in turn of the century Spain (Romero Salvadó, 1999). Indeed, after the trauma of losing a war to the US in 1898 the colonial empire appeared to be the cause of the fracturing of whatever unity Madrid elites had achieved.

Catalonians in particular were starting to detach themselves from the post-colonial state. Without its empire, Spain became a less attractive political home for the Catalans (Romero Salvado, 1999). It was also less interesting economically. The Catalans had eventually shared in the economic opportunities of the Spanish empire and by the last decades of the 19th century, 60 per cent of their exported goods were sold to Cuba (Conversi, 1997). When they were no longer able to do so, the economic reasons for being part of Spain dwindled. Catalan nationalism grew. The commercial and industrial sectors in Barcelona had long been angry with their rulers whom they saw as aristocrats out of touch with economic reality and seemingly unable to protect their interests (Smith, 2014). So among the Catalan bourgeoisie there was a growing desire to sever links or, at least, weaken ties (Conversi, 1997).

We have seen that industrialization reinforced top-down nation building. As workers went to the cities, ancestral ties were broken and new patterns of association brought them into contact with their co-nationals from other regions. The cities were a cultural and linguistic melting pot that encouraged convergence. In Spain, Catalonia was the major industrializing area and a region that retained a strong regional cultural and linguistic identity. So internal migration, industrialization, urbanization and the development of mass politics were not necessarily encouraging convergence to the national language, Castilian, but to the language of the industrial growth area, Catalan (Rosés, 2003).[12] Education, from primary to higher, was relatively well developed in Catalonia. In other regions without a developing industrial sector, the aristocratic elites did not always see the utility of an educated workforce and indeed were fearful of it; and, without social mobility, there was no pressure from below, as peasants saw education as the loss of income from child labour rather than as an economic opportunity (Boyd, 1997).

In 19th and early 20th century Spain the national government was dominated by landed elites, with close ties to the Catholic Church, reliant for the production of parliamentary majorities on clientelism and patronage, and

---

[12] Catalonia had always been a *terra de pas* (Ferrater Mora, 1944/2012): an area for inward migration, attracting workers because of its industries and commerce. To many of these, as well as to some Catalan workers, Catalanism seemed an exclusive bourgeois nationalism, which rejected them. There was conflict between owners and workers, and under Alejandro Lerroux a proletarian anti-Catalanist party was formed.

dedicated to the exclusion of other interest groups or political creeds (Carr, 1980). The ruling class, a hereditary nobility with its focus on land as power, had little interest in industrial and commercial development, and had systematically fought the ideas of the Enlightenment (Wuthnow, 2009). Inevitably, this unbending system found itself under systematic attack from republicans and organized working-class movements of socialists and, after 1910, anarcho-syndicalists (Romero Salvadó, 1999). The divisions were geographical as well as class based; Catalan and Basque nationalists were central to the opposition to Madrid. The clash resulted in civil war (1936–1939).

The subsequent victory of the Right brought a military dictatorship to power, which practised extreme centralization. However, the Franco regime's policy to castilianize Spain was planned as punishment as much as, if not more than, nation building. There was little carrot, only stick in the Castilianization process. The dictatorship sought to suppress the other languages of Spain, and they disappeared from the public space in the mid-20th century. However, they took on a symbolic role and were maintained in private settings. In the Basque Country and Catalonia, knowledge and use of Basque and Catalan became a tool for maintaining identity and resisting the dictatorship.

16.3   Language, advantage and group membership

In these three scenarios of state-nation development there are thus some commonalities, but also some significant differences. Each state-nation had groups on the geographical periphery of their territory that governments and elites needed to incorporate if nation-building were to be successful. These groups were discrete communities of communication with a distinct history and culture and separate patterns of identity and loyalty. An analysis and comparison of how their members reacted to nation-building from the centre may give us an insight into the factors that were significant in the process, and how questions of economic motivation dovetail with the more relational aspects of identity and belonging. In the following case studies of cultural/linguistic groups from each of the three states (speakers on the Occitan dialect continuum from the south of France, Irish Gaelic speakers in the UK/Ireland, and Catalan speakers in Spain) the relative weight of economy and identity becomes clear, and the importance of social and geographical mobility is shown to play a major role in language loyalty.

16.3.1   The Félibrige: Maintenance of cultural and linguistic difference with no aims for devolution or independence

In 19th-century Europe the ideas of nationalism found fertile ground among the proto-elites of groups that could be presented as proto-nations. Throughout the continent, the new middle-class intelligentsia of nationalism was eager 'to invite the masses into history' (Nairn, 1977/2003, p. 328). These 'national awakenings' were framed in a Romantic paradigm, in which an ancient nation reconquers its culture, history and language.

If the elites in the south of France had wanted to reject the muscular nation-building of the French state and to make a case for an independent Midi, they could have done so. They could have followed the 'national awakening' route taken by so many proto-elites of proto-nations throughout Europe. They could have built a strong case for a claim to independent nationhood in the conventional ethno-nationalist way through reference to history and appeals to identity. All the traditional elements were to hand: a separate myth of origin (the legacy of the Roman empire rather than the Frankish); a separate culture (the literary and musical legacy of the troubadours); a distinct language (the 'oc' dialect continuum goes from Catalan in the west to Piedmontese in the east, and is linguistically distinguishable from other Romance dialect continua to the north and to the south); forcible incorporation into the French state (the crusade against the Albigensians in the 13th century); and a different political tradition (oligarchy within towns governed by consuls). However, in their vast majority they did not do so: the southern elite mostly consented to the melting pot version of nationalism on offer from Paris, submitted to the push-pull factors described above and accepted that French constituted the *marché linguistique* of which they were part.

The fact that a very successful language revivalist movement developed around Avignon in the latter half of the 19th century might seem to challenge this claim. However, the seven poets who founded the Félibrige[13] in 1854 were at no point a proto-elite for a new political unit. The movement was not part of the 19th century 'national awakenings'; it was quite different from the many national independence movements orchestrated by local elites that employed the renaissance of folk language and culture as a first step towards extracting their group from rule by distant masters.

In contrast to the many regional activists across Europe who had autonomy if not independence as their goal, the Félibres (members of the group) were only interested in the revitalization of the cultural and literary tradition of the south and explicitly rejected any nationalist political agenda. They exercised utmost caution in the political sense[14] and took care not to appear federalist.

---

[13] Joseph Roumanille, Frédéric Mistral, Théodore Aubanel, Anselme Mathieu, Jean Brunet, Paul Giéra and Alphonse Tavan.

[14] We can see an example of the care they took not to appear anti-French in Frédéric Mistral's decision to remove the term '*traitre*' (traitor) from his 1860 poem *Mireille* (Jourdanne, 1897). He had used the epithet to describe the troops of Simon de Montfort, the northern baron who had laid waste Languedoc in the crusade against the Albigensians in the 12th century. Mistral's self-censoring brings him into the mainstream republican

As their literary movement grew in size and importance, they wrote their refusal to engage politically into their statutes:[15]

Article 2: *Sont interdites dans les réunions félibréennes les discussions politiques ou religieuses.* (Discussion of politics or religion is expressly forbidden in Felibrige meetings) (Statuts du Félibrige, 1876).

The Félibres' main concern was literary, to produce heroic poetry written in the regional language, Provençal. One of the most famous works, Mistral's epic poem *Miréio*, was explicitly modelled on Dante and Virgil. At the same time the Félibres were influenced by the Romantic movement and much of their writing was self-consciously ethnographic and idealized the peasant condition. They celebrated an 'authentic' Provence, rural, untouched by modernity and devoutly Catholic (Dymond, 2012), although this was a world that was already undergoing change.

One aim of the Félibres was to win the peasants to a new and 'better' literature. Their intended audience is often given as the rural farm workers of Provence: *'car cantan que pèr vautre, o pastre e gènt di mas'* (Mistral, 1868, p. 2). However, it is highly unlikely that the rural speakers of Provençal were the main readership. Folk songs and stories circulated in the oral tradition among a largely illiterate audience[16], and the stories that pleased were racy and vulgar. There is little evidence to show that the high Romantic style of a poem such as *Mirèio* appealed to the home grown Provençal audience (Martel, 1988). Moreover, the linguistic decisions that the Félibres took reduced their chances of reaching a rural audience. They were not writing in the language spoken by the labourers in the vineyards or the fields, but in an idealized, 'purified' language of their own invention. Mistral has been widely attacked as 'cobbling together from ancient and contemporary sources an artificial language that erased local particularities' (Dymond, 2012, p. 139). But, as a contemporary historian of the movement noted, the Félibres had not set out to write in the language of the people. They always expected their readers to make the effort to understand and be 'elevated' by the literary forms they were using: *'On l'entend assez aisement à l'aide de la langue vulgaire, et qui voudra y mordre y morde'* (based on

---

tradition where it was/is the practice to ignore or play down the former conflicts of the people(s) on French territory.

[15] This continues to the present day as the official Félibrige website confirms: *'Les statuts du Félibrige (Art. 3) interdisent à notre mouvement tout soutien, toute prise de position, en faveur d'un parti politique quel qu'il soit'* (the constitution of the Felibrige does not allow the movement to support any political party nor to express a partisan opinion) (http://felibrige.org/).

[16] Indeed the tradition of the *conteur* is still alive in Provence. See, for example, the monthly meetings at Le Moulin des Contes, Place de l'Oustau Rou in Hyères, Var.

their knowledge of everyday language, people will follow easily enough and whoever wants to get to grips with [the texts] will make the effort) (Jourdanne, 1897/2000, p. 17).

The evidence suggests that this did not happen. When we consider the extent of literacy, who in the target group was literate and in what language, together with short print runs of 300, 500, at most 1,000 copies for the majority of their work (Martel, 2001), we have to conclude that the Félibres were not reaching large numbers of local people. The only Félibrige literature finding its way into peasant homes was their yearly almanac, the *Armana Prouvençau*, which provided a farming calendar, local recipes, folk remedies and traditional tales, alongside some of the shorter poems produced by the Félibres.

In contrast, the Félibres had international presence and recognition. They gained readers outside Provence, in Paris and abroad, and many titles had more success outside Provence than within. Mistral in particular provoked enthusiastic response across France and across Europe. His *Mirèio* was translated into a variety of languages including German, Italian, Spanish, Romanian, English and Bohemian. Gounod composed an opera in French based on the story of *Mirèio* in 1863. The Félibrige attracted intellectuals and artists to the Midi, as we can see from the records of those who attended the Fêtes latines (e.g. in Montpellier, 1878). The Nobel Prize for literature awarded to Mistral in 1904 confirms this international prestige.

The Nobel Prize was awarded in part for Mistral's most monumental work, *lou Tresor dóu Félibrige*, a 2,200 page Provençal–French dictionary with 80,000 entries. In this lexical work Mistral was setting out 'to make neo-Provençal a literary language conforming to fixed standards of purity' (Nobel, n.d.). On the other hand, the dictionary is not a tool for standardization. Each entry begins with the Provençal term and then comes equivalents in major varieties of the langue d'oc dialect continuum: Auvergnat, Gascon, Limousin and Languedocien. The dictionary is a recognition of dialect diversity and quite unlike the rigorous linguistic homogenization underpinning the 'national awakenings' in other parts of Europe, where one codified variety provided the standard for the whole group.[17] The Félibrige retained respect for variety along the dialect continuum and the founding members actively encouraged writers to set up local societies in other towns. There was pressure to use the

---

[17] However, despite their limited respect for dialect diversity, they still made enemies, with other groups accusing them of normative practice (Dymond, 2012). This was perhaps inevitable: the stunning literary success of Mistral was bound to foreground the cultural practices of the area around Avignon and Arles and the massive dictionary with its innovative orthography promoted Provençal in head position, with the other dialects as alternatives.

Mistralian orthographic principles but standardization was not high on the agenda.

This difference between the Provençaux and the other 'national awakenings' stemmed from the absence of a political project: no group was fighting to take control of the language for political ends; no proto-elite was seeking to standardize and spread a single proto-national language for a proto-national group. Rejecting political engagement the Félibres were not interested in standardization for the normal political reasons, the process of nation building where the codification and standardization of a single dialect is a first step towards linguistic homogeneity, and where the shift to the national standard is closely tied to patriotism and national loyalty. The desire within the movement was purely to maintain cultural heritage and develop a high culture literary tradition.

There was thus an interesting situation. A high status group with Europe-wide recognition of their literary production was encouraging Provençal as a language of high culture. A massive Provençal–French dictionary had been produced, using a new orthography. But the Félibrige, this group taking an intellectual lead, did not have the political objectives that, in other situations of language promotion, had ensured the successful spread of a language variety. In consequence, there were no clear economic advantages in following the Félibrige's linguistic lead. For the rural masses there was no evident advantage to shifting from the local variety of *oc* to Mistralian Provençal. So, for the few who were literate in one of the *langues d'oc*, Mistralien orthography was largely rejected, and is still a subject of dispute to this day (Blanchet, 2004). The Félibrige continues as a literary society, but as we witnessed in the centenary commemorations of Mistral's death, the movement is only of interest to a tiny cultured minority.

There is, however, one major legacy from the group – pluricentrism. The Félibrige's system of local organizations supporting local literary production in local varieties, and Mistral's practice within *Lou Tresor dóu Felibrige* of recognizing difference within the dialect continuum, led to the *'langue d'oc'* being considered multiple *'langues d'oc'* and to the term 'pluricentric' language. This has continued to the present day and is both a strength and a weakness. The weakness is, of course, that learning any one variety on the dialect continuum only gives the learner access to a limited number of speakers, since the differences among the varieties are significant.[18] Here we have, of course, one of the key problems of minority language maintenance. What variety on a dialect continuum is to be supported and promoted? Where one variety is

---

[18] There are six main dialect varieties (with sub-divisions within them): Auvergnat, Gascon, Languedocien, Limousin, Provençal and Vivaro-alpin.

chosen, codified, standardized, given status in the public space and taught in schools, then speakers of other varieties can become double minorities, non-native speakers of both the national and the regional standards.[19] On the other hand, if all varieties are given equal status, use of numerous varieties in the public space is unmanageable and these varieties are likely to be used only in the private domain, as the L (low) language in a diglossic situation.

In this pluricentrism we have an important lesson from the French Midi relevant to the economic–language relationship. It seems that the laudable desire to respect difference among varieties on a dialect continuum will undermine the profitability of learning a variety. When the putative learner asks 'with whom will I be able to interact?' the answer will be 'a relatively small number, and perhaps a few more if you make the effort to learn how to negotiate and accommodate across dialect boundaries'. As history has shown, this has not proved a very persuasive argument. The numbers of competent speakers of the *langues d'oc* have dropped decade by decade,[20] and one among the many reasons could well be the restricted nature of the linguistic market for any one dialect, or in Bourdieu's terms the failure of knowledge of a *langue d'oc* to confer '*un certain capital linguistique*' (1982, p. 60).

Thus this first language revivalist movement in the Midi brought some fame to an intellectual elite from the comfortable middle class or the old monarchist families. The Félibres were part of the wider Romantic movement, drawing on a folk heritage for their art, and gaining some recognition throughout Europe for their literary production. But they differed from most 19th-century linguistic activists by having no political aim. There was thus never the lure of the '*profit matériel*' (Bourdieu, 2001, p. 78) that results from the use of a language in the public space; there were no economic reasons to persuade speakers of the *langue(s) d'oc* to adopt the Félibres' variety. At the end of his life Mistral recognized that they had not touched the people in the way that he had hoped (Jourdanne, 1897). The Félibres provide one set of evidence that intellectual-led, literary-focused, language revivalism contributes only in the most marginal and weak way to regional language renaissance and maintenance.

16.3.2 The Catalans: Maintenance of cultural and linguistic difference to underpin political ambitions for devolution

In the early 19th century the conservative Romantic movement, the Renaixença, had inspired the Félibres. This group of Catalan poets, composers,

---

[19] For a discussion of this, see the debate in Strubell (1999), Hoffmann (1996) and Wright (2007).

[20] It is difficult to give reliable figures because there is no language question in the French national census. The available surveys are partial in both senses of the word.

historians and writers drew from an idealized past and portrayed an idealized present in their work, just as the Félibres were to do.

However, from the late 19th century, the linguistic and cultural movements in the two settings diverged. And, as we shall see, many of the dissimilarities stem from different economic and political factors. In the 1870s the Renaixença was eclipsed by the Modernista movement, again centred on Barcelona, but now looking outward and to an experimental future rather than inward and to a romanticized past. The new Catalanism was more encompassing, concerned not only with art and literature but also technical progress and urban regeneration. Inevitably as it developed in this way, the artistic movement branched into the political arena. As Conversi (1997, p. 23) records, 'through Modernism a new brand of intellectuals entered Catalanist politics' and a regional elite began to construct a new Catalan society and identity. In the fervour of experiment and innovation, Madrid seemed to be a dead hand that held back Catalan progress.

The context in which Catalonia had come to be part of the Spanish state was the feudal arrangement of dynastic marriage. In the 12th century Catalonia had been united with the kingdom of Aragon. From then until the 15th century the resulting polity had been a major Mediterranean maritime empire. It had been a marriage, that of Ferdinand of Aragon and Isabella of Castile mentioned above, that had created the kingdom of Spain. There was, therefore, no narrative of conquest to colour relations between the Castilians and the Catalans. There was, however, a long tradition of irritation in Barcelona, for what its inhabitants perceived as their second-class status. There was some foundation for this. First, the discovery of the Americas and the spread of the Spanish empire in South America had redirected maritime activity away from Barcelona to ports with better access to the Atlantic, and the Castilian monopoly on American trade angered Catalan merchants. Second, the Catalans' defeat in the War of the Spanish Succession had led to a loss of autonomy which rankled. Third, in the complexities of the Carlist wars, the conservative rural Catalans had stood against the monarchy and were again on the losing side. Thus many levels and categories of Catalan society had some historic reason to distance themselves from Madrid. The legacy of this past together with the weakness of national symbols and the absence of a national educational system (discussed above) combined to keep the Catalans from investing in the nation. However, the very strongest reason for their lack of enthusiasm for Madrid was economic. Catalonia was the most industrialized region in Spain and the Catalans reproached the Castilian ruling class for its general lack of interest in and understanding of their industrial and commercial concerns. The history of the early 20th century reveals how the Catalans increasingly felt that they would do better on their own without the repressive control of the Castilians or that, at the very least, they had the right to a more equal relationship.

By the turn of the 20th century, cultural, political and economic factors had thus come together to combine many Catalans in Solidaritat Catalana, a broad coalition party which called for greater autonomy for Catalonia. In the 1907 national elections the party had massive support, and for the following 16 years much power was devolved to the Catalans. In 1914, the Mancomunitat de Catalunya was set up, bringing the Catalan speaking regions under one administrative umbrella. Catalan which had been suppressed as a language of administration in the Nueva Planta decrees came back into the public space in the region.

In the first decade of the 20th century Modernisme had begun to give way to Noucentisme, a movement where there was increased interest in social reform as well as renewed vigour in the region's artistic life. Barcelona was a major European centre for artistic experiment, and some of the artists who had been working in Paris relocated to Barcelona during World War I. This context influenced Catalan nationalism and, as activists like Prat de la Riba started to articulate the ideology in works such as *La nacionalitat catalana* (1906), it was presented as outward looking and inclusive. Multilingual publications such as *Iberia* aided this openness (Arenas, 2012). This innovation and internationalism, together with an economic situation that was better in Catalonia than the rest of Spain, made early 20th-century Catalonia a place of optimism with a belief in progress and improvement.

In the Catalonian context, the Catalan language had market value and prestige which rivalled Castilian in many domains. The language was the vessel of Catalan identity; it was also the language of social and economic success. The Catalans undertook language planning in the classic fashion, described by Cooper (1989). As far as status planning was concerned, the Catalan language gained status and a role in the public space with the Mancomunitat from 1913 onwards. As far as corpus planning was concerned, the language was codified and standardized. Pompeu Fabra was the key figure in this, publishing *Normes ortogràfiques* in 1913, *Diccionari ortogràfic* in 1917, *Gramàtica catalana* in 1918 and *Diccionari General de la Llengua Catalana* in 1932. Among the Barcelona elite there was general acceptance that a language used in the public space needed an agreed standard. As far as acquisition planning was concerned, standard Catalan was promoted through its use in publishing, private schools and the Institut d'Estudis Catalans.

In 1923 there was a backlash against increasing decentralization. An army-led coup brought General Miguel Primo de Rivera to power. During his dictatorship, he rescinded all Catalan autonomy and banned the Catalan language and Catalan symbols. However, the role of the language as the symbol for Catalan identity seemed to be heightened by its repression; proscription of the language only confirmed language loyalty among a resentful population (Strubell, 1999).

The dictatorship lasted seven years and by 1931 Spain was a republic for the second time. With the victory of the socialist and nationalist party, Esquerra Republicana de Catalunya, in local elections, Catalonia moved to the Left and towards a republicanism that was tending to self-determination. In 1932 Catalonia gained a statute of autonomy and home rule institutions. However, Madrid blocked much of the Catalans' radical innovation and the Catalan middle class itself began to be fearful of the way Catalanism was developing as a revolutionary socialist movement.

In February 1936, the Catalans were prominent in the radical Popular Front that won the Spanish national elections. From February to July 1936 when General Franco led a military revolt against the government there was a period of intense social change. Increasingly, Catalans spearheaded the revolutionary movement. When the Franquists won the civil war in April 1939, repression was most brutal in those areas which had embraced both socialism and regionalism. The Catalan leaders were either killed or went into exile. There was a witch hunt against all expressions of Catalan identity, as Franco set out to restore a unitary and centralized state. A quarter of a million Catalans fled. Some of those who remained were executed. During the six month occupation of Barcelona, Catalan libraries were destroyed, cultural institutions disbanded, university staff purged, teachers sent to other parts of Spain. Speaking Catalan in public was punished and using it in the workplace could lead to dismissal.

However, Franco's suppression of Catalan autonomy and identity did not destroy Catalan language and culture, but once again drove them underground. In fact, after a dark period of mourning one can see that repression seems actually to have encouraged Catalan vitality and solidarity (Hoffmann, 1996; Strubell, 1999). Conversi (1997, p. 123) detects a spiral process: 'the state wanted to erase Catalan culture because it attributed a political meaning to it but culture itself increased its political meaning as a consequence of state repression'. Whenever there was the faintest chink in the dictatorship's armour, the language reappeared. In Catalonia the opposition to the regime was cultural resistance (in contrast to the armed struggle in the Basque region).

In 1975, Franco died. In 1978, a new constitution was approved which introduced a degree of regional devolution. Catalonia achieved an independent government (the Generalitat) and its own parliament and courts. Catalan was declared the *llengua propria* of Catalonia (own language), although Castilian shared its status of official language. As the language moved back into the public space, it became clear that four decades of repression had not eradicated Catalan language competence.

Since then, over the last four decades, there has been an intense programme of 'normalization', i.e. the government in Catalonia, the Generalitat, has conducted a muscular policy to (re)insert Catalan into the domains where Castilian Spanish had taken over. In consequence it has become difficult to live in

Catalonia without knowledge of Catalan. On a banal level it is needed for every-day actions such as buying tickets from the talking ticket-vending machines in Barcelona's metro system; on a more serious plane it is the language needed to use the education or health system. In many professions it is a prerequisite to know Catalan. Migrants who learn Catalan find jobs more quickly and are promoted more frequently (Alarcón and Garzón, 2011). A non-speaker is blocked from full participation in public life.[21] And although, as Spaniards, the Catalans are legally obliged by the terms of the constitution to know the national language, there are many whose patterns of association mean that they can get by very well without Castilian. As a result of this recalibration of language and power, the Spaniards from other parts of Spain who have moved to Catalonia can find themselves disadvantaged by their lack of Catalan competence. The restricted opportunities to use their national language has become a bone of contention and there is much anti-Catalan vitriol to be found – from the letters pages of national newspapers to internet blogs, chat and comments.

At the same time there is also a sharp anti-Spanish discourse in Catalan public debate. The political parties that favour independence from Spain have gained ground. And interestingly the old sense that, economically, links with Madrid are not to Catalonia's advantage resurface continually. The focus of present disaffection is economic as much as cultural and relates to the fiscal balance. Central government collects taxes from the Autonomous Communities and then disburses in investment and services. The Catalans are aggrieved that over a quarter of a century they have contributed an average of 19.5 per cent of central government revenues, but have only received an average of 14 per cent of government spending. Over this 25 year period their proportion of the population has averaged 16 per cent (Bosch et al., 2010). Catalans are comparatively prosperous in the Spanish context, and as such would be net payers in any national welfare system. However, Catalan discourse in the context of the national economic crisis shows how many do not see themselves as part of the national group. There is evidence of a strong belief that they finance co-nationals whom they see as corrupt and/or less hardworking (Sabogal, 2014).[22]

---

[21] The Catalans are civic nationalists. Jordi Pujol, president of Catalonia for 23 years, and the founder of Convergéncia Democrática de Catalunya, encapsulated this in his 1980 statement that 'Catalan is anyone who lives and works in Catalonia, and wants to be Catalan'.

[22] This stereotyping of their fellow nationals is fuelled by frequent scandals, but there is no evidence to position Catalonia in opposition to the rest of Spain. Jordi Pujol, the Catalan leader from 1989 to 2003, has just been disgraced after it emerged that he hid a personal fortune from the Spanish taxman for three decades (O'Leary, 2014).

On 11 September 2012, one-and-a-half million Catalans marched to demand self-determination. On 27 September 2012, the Catalan Parliament agreed that a referendum should be held on independence from Spain. The Spanish government then announced it would veto such a referendum. The leader of Catalonia's government and largest party, Arturo Mas, whose commitment is to a referendum and independence, is under increasing pressure from more extreme and impatient separatist groupings. The Spanish Prime Minister, Mariano Rajoy, is under very strong pressure from the Right in his Popular Party. From the right wing generally there has been a call for military intervention – e.g. Vidal-Quadras, MEP in the European Peoples' Party;[23] Francisco Alaman, colonel in the Spanish army (Mason, 2012). In October 2014, the regional government gave into pressure and cancelled the referendum which had been arranged for 9 November 2014. However, in 2015 the pro-independence parties forced a regional election which they billed as a substitute for the referendum. With a record turn-out of 77 per cent, the separatists won an absolute majority. At the time of writing in 2015 it is difficult to predict whether the Catalans will gain more autonomy (or independence) or whether there will be renewed pressure from the centre. Both scenarios have historical antecedents.

In the Catalan experience the power of *le marché linguistique* is evident. When a group is thriving economically and flourishing culturally, persuading both its members (as well as newcomers) to maintain (or acquire) the (regional/national) language is likely to be successful. Catalan has maintained value in Bourdieu's linguistic market sense. However, the Catalans also demonstrate that language loyalty is not just a function of economic utility. In times of oppression, repression and persecution, when it was personally disadvantageous to maintain their language, the Catalans clung to it as a marker of identity. When the language was forbidden, it went underground and constituted a form of resistance.

16.3.3   The Occitanists: Maintenance of linguistic difference overshadowed by the need for protection from the state

In the south-west of France language activists have been close to the Catalans throughout the 19th and 20th centuries, and often inspired by them. Their case, however, contrasts sharply with the Catalan experience and is also profoundly different from that of their neighbours to the east, the Provençaux.

---

[23] This was published on the website www.theparliamentmagazine.eu/latest-news/article/newsarticle/leading-mep-caught-up-in-catalan-independence-row, but has since been removed from the site.

The circumstances in which Languedoc came to be ruled from Paris contrast with the relatively peaceful assimilation of Provence.[24] Languedoc was conquered after a particularly violent war. From the early 19th century onward there was growing regional interest in the subject and a number of historians – minor figures like Quatresou de Parctelaine, Moulignier, Schmidt or Gouet or major figures like Sismondi, Guizot and Thierry – explored the issue. There were several aspects of the invasion that fired interest. It was significant that the invasion that led to the defeat of the south-west was not an ordinary struggle among feudal lords but a 'holy war'. Innocent III's call for a crusade against the Albigensian heresy gave the northerners who invaded the south a free hand. As the enemy had been designated infidel, there were no restraints on the conduct of the troops. The invasion was brutal even in the context of medieval warfare. The war could be shown as wiping out an exceptional civilization. The society into which the northern barons swept so destructively could be portrayed as superior in many ways to their own. Troubadour music and literature and sophisticated patterns of local self-government could be cited to position the Occitan lands at the forefront of European culture and politics. And when the historians reviewed the causes for the war, Albigensian beliefs and values seemed more prescient than heretical. The Albigensians could be assessed differently in the wake of the Protestant Reformation, the Enlightenment and the French revolution. In most histories, the Catholic Church with its Inquisition was shown to be the villain of the piece.

So, when the Félibrige movement spread to Languedoc in the late 1860s, it took a completely different form from the apolitical movement in Provence. There was an anti-Paris dimension to the linguistic and cultural revival, fuelled in part by a sense of historical injustice. And, in contrast to the Avignon group, many of the Languedocien regionalists were militantly socialist and republican. The group that formed around Auguste Fourès and Xavier de Ricard in Montpellier would thus become known as the Félibres rouges. From the start they set themselves up in competition with Mistral's group, launching a rival almanac, *l'Armanac de la Lauseta*.

In 1878 the Félibres rouges published three articles which can be seen as their manifesto (Martel, 2012). The first concerned a linguistic matter. Ricard attacked the way the founding Félibrige had sub-divided the Oc dialect continuum into dialects. He saw this as authoritarian top-down intrusion and argued that speakers themselves should decide their affiliations democratically and bottom up. The second took an even more polemical tone; Ricard accused the Provençaux of being reactionary. He again attacked them for their

---

[24] Provence was nominally part of the Holy Roman empire. The French king inherited and then incorporated it definitively into the French state in 1486.

linguistic presumption, criticizing the way they were pressing all meridional groups to use the Mistralian spelling reform. The third article proclaimed what the Montpellier group was offering – a republican revivalist movement in contrast to and in competition with the Catholic royalists of Avignon (Martel, 2012). This is the point at which the group adopted the term 'Occitan', which would define them. Ricard wrote:

> *Il me semble que pour le langage particulier du Midi, le nom occitanien serait le nom véritable, il ne serait pas si long que celui de langue d'oc, et embrasserait tous nos parlers (avec celui de la Catalogne) comme le nom d'Occitanie embrasserait toutes nos provinces. Mais de Provence et de provençal il n'en faut point parler hors du territoire de Provence.* (It seems to me that the name 'Occitan' should be adopted for the language of the Midi. It is not as unwieldy as 'langue d'oc', it would cover all varieties (including Catalan) and would bring in all our regions. We should not use the terms 'Provence' and 'Provençal' outside the actual territory of Provence) (Ricard, 1878, cited in Martel, 2012, p. 30).

Thus 'Occitan' came to denote the language(s) of the *oc* dialect continuum in the linguistic sense in much the same way as *langue(s) d'oc*, but it also connoted a political stance. Those who use the term Occitan are more likely to conceive the linguistic space as a cultural and linguistic whole. In addition they are likely to have a political project for that unity.[25]

The Occitanists were fired by developments in Catalonia but the economic, political and social context with which they had to work was significantly different from the situation across the state border. In the second half of the 19th century and the first decade of the 20th both industrial and agricultural workers in the Midi had experienced falling wages, redundancies and unemployment, with the result that many were in a state of abject poverty. The strikes by the weavers of Mazamet and Lodève in 1845, the miners of Aveyron in 1869 and 1886 and Carmaux in 1892, the dockers in Sète in 1905, the revolt of the agricultural workers in les Landes in 1906 and the labourers in the vineyards in 1907 were protests against an economic system which kept them at poverty levels. However, as Johnson (1995) suggests, the strikes and revolts were not just expressions of rage at profits which the workers were not sharing, but also manifestations of despair from those in industries in economic decline. Johnson sees the Midi as one of the first regions to suffer from post-industrialization, as its silks and woollen industries lost markets, coal production waned and the

---

[25] The division between radical Occitanists geographically situated in Languedoc and the conservative Félibrige east of the Rhone can be said to continue today (see Blanchet, 2004).

vineyards, already suffering from the devastation of phylloxera, faced competition from Algeria. In his view the disastrous economic situation in parts of the Midi forced the Left to look to the state for the welfare protection that could help the region survive.[26] This was not a time or a place where the south would have benefited from breaking away from Paris. If Johnson's analysis is correct, it explains in part why the Occitanists could not follow the Catalan model. The Catalans wanted to distance themselves from Madrid and take the lead in their own affairs; the Occitans needed Paris and its support.

The linguistic situation was thus quite different in the two adjacent regions and the reasons for the renaissance of Catalan as a language of the public space did not pertain for Occitan. In fact new ideologies in the Midi seemed to lead to the spread of French. The rural socialism and trade unionism that emerged from the economic and social transformation of the wine industry between 1850 and 1914 were movements anchored in national, if not international, socialist networks (Frader, 1991).

Tensions had been developing between owners and labourers in the vineyards, which were run as large capitalist enterprises. Strikes and revolts had proliferated in this industrial form of viticulture. The workers had joined trade unions and the French Socialist party had established a base among smallholders. Finally, in 1907 the pressure came to a head and a massive uprising of *vignerons* shook the entire south with huge demonstrations. However, this turned out to be a class rather than a regional revolt. The left-wing politicians supporting the *vignerons*, the revolutionary syndicalist trade union movement and the *vignerons'* leaders themselves were not always locals. And even when they were, they often positioned themselves as players in national networks and international alliances. They were intent on getting central government to act; there was little devolutionary regionalism in the protest. Some of the banners on the *vignerons'* marches might have read '*Volem viure al país*' but most were in French (Napo, 1971). *Le Tocsin*, the paper of the movement, was in French. And although Marcelin Albert, one of the leaders of the revolt, may have evoked the suffering of the south at the hands of the north in the Albigensian crusade, the speech in which he did so was in French (Napo, 1971).

The reasons for this are multiple: first, the addressees were their compatriots, the government and the French tax payers on whom they were calling for help; second, those who were educated and literate were so because of the French medium education system or the French medium workers' education associations; third, the thousands who marched in the demonstrations spoke different

---

[26] In Johnson's view this explains why 19th-century Occitanism had a relatively modest agenda: 'Proudhon's federalism and his glorification of the intelligent and independent artisanal worker and peasant combined with the song and story of Occitan tradition to create a quite palatable ideological mix' (Johnson, 1995, p. 249).

dialect varieties and it may well be that French served as a lingua franca for the dialects where mutual accommodation and inter-comprehension were difficult; fourth, and perhaps most importantly, the image of the state and the region in the French context was quite different from the Spanish. In the latter, the capital represented the dead hand of tradition and obscurantism and the region was the site of innovation and creativity. In the French Third Republic, a large body of opinion held the reverse view. Regionalism was obscurantist, illiberal and reactionary and the regional language could be a tool in the hands of traditionalists. It was a way for the Catholic church to keep peasants in a state of tutelage and away from new ideas. George Leygues in an attack on the clergy in the Chambre des Députés in 1902 voiced the opinion of many: *'dans certaines contrées on se méfie de la langue française parce qu'elle apporte avec elle comme un souffle moderne'* (in some provinces there is suspicion of French because it brings with it the wind of change) (Leygues, 1902 cited by Martel, 2007, p. 8).

The Occitanists were thus in a difficult position. Their enthusiasm was revitalized by the successes of Catalan nationalism/regionalism just across the border, but they could not whip up support among the majority of the southern French whose waning loyalty to Occitan and Occitanism seemed irreversible. Nonetheless a small group continued to try. Occitanist politico-cultural aims were expressed in publications such as *Oc* (founded in Toulouse in 1923 by the Gascon, Girard) and *Occitània* (founded by the Marseillais, Camproux). In 1931 the Societat d'Estudis Occitans was founded on the model of the Institut d'Estudis Catalans which had existed since 1907. The linguist, Louis Alibert, set out to reform the spelling of Occitan, following the approach that Pompeu Fabra had taken for Catalan.

The Occitanist ambition was to make this the standard for the Occitan speaking space. But this was impossible in the context of waning support for Occitan. Those who continued to maintain an Occitan dialect were the most conservative rural communities with little reason to move from their variety to a standard. They were already diglossic with standard French as the H (high) language and their dialect as the L (low). The introduction of standard written Occitan into the mix would have rendered them doubly diglossic, and most saw no reason to go down this route. There was no political context in which to impose a standard top down and the small group of Occitan militants could provide no economic pull factors to persuade speakers to shift. In contrast to Catalonia, where economic advantage and social mobility came through acquisition of standard Catalan and membership of Catalan speaking society, in 'Occitania' there was no advantage to the individual in choosing standard Occitan over dialect forms, nor indeed of choosing Occitan-medium networks over French. First, as we have seen, the southern French did not want to go it alone; they needed support from central government. Second, the centre was open to local elites. As Bourdieu explains, the French periphery did not need to break away to have access to political power. In the post-revolutionary world, acceptance of the national language, the national power structures and the national ethos would suffice to enter the networks of national power:

> *Les membres de ces bourgeoisies locales de curés, médecins ou professeurs, qui doivent leur position à la maitrise des instruments d'expression, ont tout à gagner à la politique linguistique de la Révolution: la promotion de la langue officielle au statut de langue nationale leur donne le monopole de fait de la politique et, plus généralement, de la communication avec le pouvoir central et ses représentants qui définira, sous toutes les républiques, les notables.* (The members of the provincial middle classes (the clergy, doctors, teachers) who owed their position to their ability to express themselves had everything to gain from the language policies of the French revolutionaries. When the official language was made the national language they gained political ascendancy locally and access to central power and its representatives. In all the Republics, this [linguistic power] defined the elites) (Bourdieu, 1982, p. 30).

Third, the industrialization[27] of farming and wider networks of distribution and a new habitus favoured French. A newly standardized Occitan language had no evident role to play in an economic and political setting where most of the local political and business elite was satisfied with the nation as primary locus of allegiance.

At the time of writing in 2015 little has changed. A small group of Occitanists persists and Occitan is taught to a small minority in private bilingual schools. In 2014 there were 3,278 children studying in these schools with 209 teachers (Confederacion Occitana de las escòlas laïcas calendretas, 2014). An equally small minority choose the language as a subject option in the state system. There are small university departments of Occitan, principally engaged in producing teachers of the language. It is interesting to note that educationalists do not use a standard Occitan but respect the diversity of the dialect continuum, following the Mistralian model. Course books and teacher training support the teaching of the language as plural and not standard.

---

[27] For example, the flower and vegetable growers of the Var had developed communitarian traditions and socialist sympathies in the late 19th century (Frader, 1991). The Var had a strong cooperative movement from the early 20th century onwards. These were outward looking communities engaged with wider socialist ideas, taking technological ideas from the wider world, and using the new transport infrastructure to send produce throughout the domestic market. In their language practices the farmers were pragmatic and while they continued to use Occitan for some social interaction there was no discernible resistance to using French in their communications with the wider world.

There is very little Occitan in the traditional media. The state TV channel, France 3, provides between six and 26 minutes of Occitan medium programmes per week, again in a variety of dialects. The introduction of TV via the internet allowed an increase in such Occitan-medium programmes. For example, CSA, broadcasting on the web as www.octele.com, started on 20 December 2013 and by early June 2014 had reached 15,000 homes; 30,000 videos had been watched in their entirety and 200,000 had been watched partially (private communication, 19 June 2014).

These and other small-scale initiatives show that Occitan has not disappeared, but the number involved in all these initiatives and activities is tiny. Moreover, it is now a minority of present Occitan speakers that has learnt the language as a first language at home and most are acquiring Occitan as a second language. Among the variety of reasons for doing this, there is little evidence of instrumental motivation.

16.3.4   The Irish: A successful fight for independence and relatively unsuccessful maintenance of linguistic difference

The fourth and last case study is Ireland. If we analyse the relations between Irish Gaelic and English speakers, we can see some resemblances to the other three examples, but there are also divergences. Ireland had been invaded by the English crown in the same kind of feudal invasion that had brought the south-west of France under the rule of the French king. However, the processes to redirect loyalty to the new central authorities which developed in France were blocked in the case of Ireland and the UK. Just as Madrid did not anchor the Catalans into the state-nation, London failed to give the Irish compelling reasons to stay within the state.

The early story of English and Irish relations is a classic feudal tale. Anglo-Norman barons first arrived in the 12th century, with a view to carving out estates for themselves in Ireland, divided at the time into a series of small kingdoms.[28] Anglo-Normans married into the local Gaelic aristocracies and much like the Norse invaders of the 9th and 10th centuries underwent Gaelicization. The kings in London, attempting from time to time to assert their feudal overlordship, fought against this. A law in 1360 banned those of Anglo-Norman descent from speaking Gaelic and the Statutes of Kilkenny in 1367 attempted to halt cultural assimilation. Both were clearly ineffectual as similar acts were passed in the 15th and 16th centuries.

---

[28] Their king, Henry II, fearful of the development of a rival Anglo-Norman kingdom intervened and backed by the pope claimed suzerainty over Ireland. The feudal hierarchy was always going to be hard to maintain, particularly as Henry II had to concentrate on keeping his Angevin empire on continental Europe intact.

In the 16th century the Tudors were dismantling the feudal system and Henry VIII was concerned to bring about 'a uniform commonwealth within the country' (Gillespie, 2005, p. 101). In his *Act for the English Order, Habit and Language* he ruled:

> That every person or persons, the Kings true subjects, inhabiting this land of Ireland... shall use and speake commonly the English tongue and language, and that every such person... having childe or children, shall endeavour themselves to cause and procure his said childe and children to use and speake the English tongue and language, and... shall bring up and keep his said childe and children in such places, where they shall or may have occasion to learn the English tongue, language, order, and condition (in Corcoran, 1916, p. 43).

On religion he commanded that the Irish should convert to Anglicanism. From his reign until the 18th century, successive waves of British Protestant settlers were sent to Ireland. In theory their role was to anglicize and convert the Irish Catholic population; in fact they blocked the process of integration, because a two tier system suited them better, protecting their economic and political ascendancy (Lustick, 1985).

Thus, rather than integrating the Irish into the British state, the settlements produced two distinct communities: on the one hand, the Catholics comprising the Old English, the former elite enduring from the Anglo-Norman conquests, and the Gaelic speaking Irish; on the other, the Protestants comprising the new Anglo-Irish elite, who were Anglican, and the Scots settlers mostly concentrated in Ulster, who were Presbyterian (Tanner, 2001). This was a divided country, with a Protestant ascendancy, where the old assimilatory processes of Gaelicization no longer applied, and where inclusive nation-building was not developing as in the rest of the UK. In the various British and continental (religious) wars of the 17th and 18th centuries, the two populations habitually supported opposing sides.

In the 18th century, the Catholic Irish found themselves in a situation of second-class citizenship; the *Laws for the Suppression of Popery* commonly known as the Penal Laws prevented them from political participation, limited their ownership of land, and blocked their right to organize education. Disaffected, the Catholics saw in the American and French revolutions a model for their own liberation. Aware of this and fearful of rebellion and Irish alliance with enemy states, the British government promised full emancipation for the Catholic majority.[29] This promise proved hard to fulfil because of the

---

[29] In 1801 an Act of Union joined Britain and Ireland. However, this was not a union in the sense of the 1707 Act which had fused the two Protestant states of England and

implacable resistance of the Anglo-Irish Protestant lobby (Lustick, 1985, p. 37). By the time the British government was persuaded, albeit reluctantly, to repeal the Penal Laws and concede some voting rights in 1829, the Catholics had become totally disenchanted, having seen much of their land taken over by Protestants from England, Scotland and Wales.[30]

Their bitterness grew in the Famine years (1846–1849). Central government not only failed to bring aid but could be seen to be a contributor to the situation through their economic and social policies. Throughout the 19th century, the desire to disengage from the UK grew. The Movement for Repeal of the Act of Union in the 1840s and the Home Rule movement (1874–1913) resulted finally in the independence struggle (1916–1921) and self-determination for southern Ireland.

The cultural and linguistic revivalist movement in Ireland that dovetailed with the growth of Irish nationalism from the middle of the 19th century followed the classic pattern of 'national awakenings' (Hutchinson, 1987). Writers and scholars used Gaelic language and literature to encourage a national consciousness, collecting and reviving folk tales and folk music. Linguists presented Irish Gaelic as a unified language with a long past. Historians and antiquarians contributed to building the national story and to telling the Irish who they were and how they differed from the rest of the UK. An Irish language press developed and in 1882 the Gaelic medium Journal, *Irisleabhar na Gaedhilge*, was published and became the first widely read bilingual Irish periodical. Gaelic was used in the Gaelic Athletic Association, created in 1884 to promote traditional sports. The Gaelic league was an umbrella organization for various societies and clubs promoting this cultural nationalism.

However, using the Gaelic language to underpin the independence movement proved more difficult than in many other national groups seeking self-determination since the shift to English in Ireland was well advanced by the beginning of the 20th century. As the editor of the *Roscommon Journal* in 1912 put it: 'local life has a notable tendency for matters English' (quoted in Wheatley, 2005, p. 62). Many of those attracted by the cultural revivalist message had little or no competence in Gaelic and needed to attend the numerous basic language classes provided under the aegis of the Gaelic League all over Ireland.

Scotland. The 1801 Act has to be seen as the incorporation of a Catholic population that the monarch and parts of the British government held to be dangerous in the context of the Napoleonic wars.

[30] A comprehensive survey of landowners in Ireland in the late 19th century (Hussey De Burgh, 1878) showed that the largest landowners were members of the British elite, mostly absentee landlords, and revealed how few Gaelic speaking Irish or Old English families were still landowners. The overwhelming majority of Catholics were tenant farmers or landless peasants on the estates of these Anglo-Irish Protestant families.

English had taken hold through education. Under the punitive Penal Laws, schooling had become the exclusive province of the Protestants, and the Act to Restrain Foreign Education (1695) instructed that 'no person whatsoever of the popish religion shall publickly or in private houses teach school, or instruct youth in learning' (Corcoran, 1916, p. 95). Thus, the long tradition of Irish literacy was broken. There was some resistance, and Catholic education went underground and Catholics were taught clandestinely in so-called Hedge Schools.[31]

These covert education arrangements petered out as the British parliament passed the Catholic Emancipation Act (1829) to repeal the Penal Laws, and the Education Act (1831) introduced free state education for Irish children. This schooling initiative which pre-dates free state education in the rest of the UK by four decades was clearly an attempt at nation building after the disastrous alienation of the Catholic population over the previous two centuries. There was respect for religious difference, with secular subjects taught under the aegis of the state and the churches supplementing this core with religious education, but there was no provision for language difference. The language in the schools was to be English and the British government kept close control of the curriculum (Ellis et al., 2007). The school system in Ireland began to anglicize the children who attended.

The immediate effect that English medium education had on the language patterns of the Gaelic speaking community is difficult to gauge since a much more potent reason for language shift arose in the 1840s. Much of the decline of Gaelic in 19th-century Ireland actually came from the physical loss of speakers in the Gaelic speaking areas (Gaeltacht). In the Famines of the 1840s there were perhaps as many as a million deaths. And the initial suffering caused by the crop failures was exacerbated by large-scale evictions from farms where rents could no longer be paid or where landlords moved to more profitable forms of agriculture. The ordeal of these experiences left the Gaelic speaking community traumatized and destroyed patterns of traditional life and broke cultural continuity.

The only self-help available was migration, and in the Famine decade 1.5 million left the west and centre of Ireland. In total more than 2.5 million Gaelic speakers were no longer living in the Gaeltacht. In this desperate situation,

---

[31] A Commission of Inquiry reported in 1826 that of the 550,000 pupils enrolled in all schools in Ireland, 403,000 were in Hedge Schools. The students in these schools were taught variously as there was, of course, no programme common to all and classes depended on the knowledge of the teachers. There is evidence that Irish Gaelic literacy and literature were a large part of the curriculum; Latin was included since many of the students hoped to enter the priesthood; English was taught, in part, as preparation for migration (Dowling, 1935/1968).

attitudes to English were complicated. On the one hand it was the language of the centre that had oppressed them and which was not helping them in their hour of need, but at the same time knowledge of the language provided some preparation for work in the US, Canada, Australia and England, which were the main destinations for migration. Irish Gaelic thus declined in Ireland because of the disappearance of viable communities where it was traditionally spoken. The actual loss of speakers in the Famines and the departure of those able to start again elsewhere depopulated the Gaeltacht.

It could also be argued that Irish Gaelic was not the only language available as a medium for the national movement. In some places the shift to English had taken place centuries before. In the area around Dublin, settled by the Vikings and then the heartland of the Anglo-Norman conquest in the 12th and 13th centuries, Irish Gaelic had long been eclipsed. In this area, known as the Pale, the Anglo-Norman elite did not undergo large-scale Gaelicization, and Dublin English developed with distinct features from an early period (Hickey, 2002). A number of Dublin-born writers had produced work that was influential throughout the English speaking world (e.g. Swift, Sheridan, Shaw and Wilde).

Among the English speaking Irish there was a parallel cultural revivalist movement, this time with English being used to rework Irish history, ancient literature and folk tradition. The *New Ireland Review*, founded in 1894; the New Irish Library, published by the London-based Fisher Unwin; the Irish Literary Theatre, founded in 1899 and to become the Abbey Theatre in 1904 – all contributed to a cultural revival centring on a Dublin elite, and in Hiberno-English. This provoked intense anger among those who wanted to break away and construct a new state in a new language with a new elite. Eoin MacNeill wrote: 'let them write for the "English-speaking world" or the "English-speaking race" if they will. But let them not vex our ears by calling their writings Irish and national' (cited in Tierney, 1980, p. 16). Patrick Pearse thought the Irish Literary Theatre should be 'strangled at birth' (ibid., p. 17). To have part of the national awakening hijacked by London publishers and English medium writers blocked fundamental change in the elite. However, those writing in English had immense effect on the political situation. Works such as Yeats' *Easter 1916* helped mobilize the population, turning a defeated uprising into 'heroic national myth' (Smith, 1990, p. 40).

When independence came in 1922, the Irish Republic was thus in an interesting linguistic position. Gaelic was no longer the first language of the majority of its citizens: rural emigration, English-medium schooling, and the long history of English as the language of power had reworked the linguistic map. It was possible to express Irish identity through English, since a distinct Hiberno-Irish variety had developed.[32] A rich literary tradition of Hiberno-English literature

---

[32] English in Ireland developed several forms: the language of Dublin, the heartland of early conquest in the 12th and 13th centuries was Anglo-Norman, with English as the

included work in the service of independence. In debates before the formulation of the constitution some Irish deputies argued the case that English should be a co-equal national language because it was the first language of the majority of Irish citizens.

However, the writers of the constitution of the independent Irish state made Gaelic the national language (and from this point in time the language is usually referred to simply as Irish). De Valera, the first elected president, was committed to a conservative society, rooted in traditional Catholic principles and rural values (Williams, 1967). The revival of the Irish language was part of this. The English version of Article 8 of Bunreacht na hÉireann, the Constitution of Ireland reads:

1. The Irish language as the national language is the first official language.
2. The English language is recognised as a second official language.

But, there were always going to be problems with making a long-minoritized language, spoken regularly only by a population of tens of thousands, the primary language in a state with millions of citizens with a different first language. The ruling elites had to deal with a number of linguistic contradictions and problems. On the one hand, there was a powerful and influential lobby supporting Irish. Hart (2003) notes the strong correlation between commitment to Irish and participation in the armed struggle for Irish independence. On the other, the institutions which the new state was taking over functioned in English and the civil servants who had run them mostly continued to do so under the new regime. The government permitted the descendants of the Protestant ascendancy to stay and encouraged them to take part in building the nation. There was thus cultural capital associated with both English and Irish in the new state.

Clearly there had to be a concerted effort to give Irish economic as well as symbolic value if the vision of an Irish speaking Ireland was to become reality. All children had Irish classes and language qualifications acted as gatekeepers to a number of educational pathways. Teachers and civil servants needed to possess a qualification in the language. There was generous funding for

---

second language. This area, known as the Pale, never underwent large-scale Gaelicization, and Dublin English developed with distinct features from this early period (Hickey, 2002); English in Ulster was influenced by Ulster Scots; the Presbyterian Scottish settlers maintained their Scots which developed a distinct Ulster form (Hickey, 2002); the new settlers in the south and west of Ireland in the 17th and 18th centuries came from a variety of English and Welsh regions. They may have imported some dialectal differences, but in the long term it is difficult to discern any distinction in these rural elites. There was no maintenance of difference and their language converged with that of the urban elite in Dublin (Hickey, 2002, p. 17). The great landowners, who were often absentee landowners anyway, tended to retain a variety which underlined class distinction rather than Irish locality.

the institutions that functioned in Irish, and for all Irish medium cultural activity.

The ambition to install Irish as the national language of all, to make it the language of power, was, however, never realized. Irish Gaelic survives, but in a state-funded cocoon. The Gaeltacht currently has a population of just under 100,000 but only around 77,000 people use Irish on a daily basis outside the education system (Ó hIfearnáin, 2014). Irish school children continue to have Irish as a school subject, but the number of establishments using Irish as a medium of education peaked in the 1950s (Ó hIfearnáin, 2014) and the level of Irish fluency in the general population has declined.

The reasons for this are partially economic. Top-down government policy never provided enough impetus to counter the bottom-up economic pressure that favoured English. First and foremost, the majority of the elite group in the capital remained English speaking after independence. Social mobility was served by Irish–English bilingualism or English, but not by Irish alone. Second, the pressures for migration continued. In the difficult conditions of the 1950s, 1960s and 1980s large numbers of Irish left Ireland temporarily or definitively to seek work. And even in the good years, there was a tradition of travelling outside Ireland, before settling down. In such circumstances there were pragmatic decisions about English and its use for gaining employment outside Ireland. Third, in the good economic times, the quite spectacular boom years of the 1990s and early 2000s, the utility of being English speaking again became clear. As Ireland became a success story in the global economy, the fact that one of its official languages was becoming the global lingua franca was of significant use.

The second set of reasons is bound up with identity. As Hickey (2007) argues, Hiberno-English developed enough particularity to function as a language of identity. He suggests that Hiberno-English is highly distinctive because so many Gaelic speakers originally learnt English with little input from native speakers. Without strong models, Gaelic features of syntax and lexis were retained. Thus Hiberno-English was and is clearly defined as Irish – and possesses its own literature. It was an Irish language as well as the language of foreign dominion.

The third set of reasons why Irish Gaelic did not reconquer the public space has perhaps to do with the perennial problem of standardization. State language planning in the 20th century abolished the Gaelic script, simplified spelling and created a variety with features from different dialects. The standardization was a top-down process with the linguistic decisions taken mostly by government translators, rather than in consultation with speakers (Ó hIfearnáin, 2014). The need was clear: to rely on mutual comprehension and negotiated interaction within the Gaelic continuum was problematic since the difference among dialects can be significant and mastering one variety does not guarantee full understanding of the others.[33] As in most states there was a desire to reduce imprecision, accommodation and negotiation. However, leaving standardization to civil servants may have loosened some of the emotional, historical attachment to the language.

Thus for many reasons we could suggest that although many Irish have ideological commitment to the standard for reasons of national loyalty (Ó hlfearnáin, 2014), this commitment remains symbolic for the majority, and only a minority translate it into practice.

One can only speculate on how patterns of language loyalty and language practice might have developed if the Irish had not gained independence in the south in 1922. Would Irish Gaelic have become a tool of resistance against a dominant power, the role that Catalan played in Catalonia? Looking at Northern Ireland, the part of Ireland which remained part of the UK and where the Catholic population did not achieve its goals, provides a possible answer. Even after almost a century where feelings have veered between discontent and open confrontation, we have difficulty finding instances where Irish Gaelic has been employed to underscore the strong sectarian divisions. However, acquisition of Irish Gaelic is experiencing a modest rise in Northern Ireland at the present moment. But, interestingly, the motivation for this might have a small economic dimension as well as the usual identity-related reasons. Now that the UK has signed the European Charter for Regional and Minority languages and Irish is recognized as a language of the UK, there is small amount of economic support in a number of areas. Funding for media initiatives, arts programmes and education courses in Irish provides a modest economic reason for learning the language, alongside its symbolic value.

16.4 Conclusion: The role of elites

This comparison of the three states suggests that the relative permeability/impermeability of elites was of immense consequence for group formation – and thus for language choice, use and maintenance.

In France those from the periphery were the object of the centre's attention. The Republic set out to incorporate them linguistically and culturally through the school system, often in a very heavy-handed way. The environment reminded all that they were French; national symbols of the Republic abounded. Geographically, there was an attempt to unify the nation. The tradition of *brassage* meant that all civil servants could be appointed to work in

---

[33] For example, the word *feicfidh* is used only in Connemara Irish; in Leinster, Ulster and Munster the word is *cífidh*. There are two pronunciations: in Leinster/Munster it is *kee-fee*; in Ulster it is *chee-fee*. See www.irishcultureandcustoms.com

regions outside their place of origin. Groups as diverse as *préfets*, teachers, railway workers could expect to be sent anywhere in France. Hierarchically, there were structures to unify the nation. The republican ideology of France emphasized equality in theory, and in practice entry to many posts and functions was by competition. Although elites reproduced themselves by passing cultural capital to their children, it is possible to claim that the French system was (and is) basically meritocratic. There was no systematic exclusion of any regional or hierarchical autochthonous group.

In contrast the majority of the populations of the component parts of the UK were not brought systematically into contact with each other as policy. For example, regiments in the British army were recruited by region[34] and teachers could stay in their locality. There was no equivalent of *brassage* in the UK. Indeed it is difficult to find an adequate translation for the term. Nor were the British as meritocratic as the French. The patrician class preserved its privileges and its belief that men of land and birth are naturally more suited to the exercise of authority than any other social class (Colley, 1992). It was this class that can be seen as the most national. The elites from the periphery were an integral part of the national elite (Colley, 1992).[35] The Irish, Scottish and Welsh nobility intermarried with the English upper class and a patrician elite spent time together in their leisure activities and socializing (the London season, hunting and shooting, etc.). There was one exception to this, the old Anglo-Irish Catholic nobility who were excluded from national political life until a very late date, and even then were subject to prejudice.

In Spain, the centre was not successful in incorporating peripheral groups into a cohesive cultural and linguistic national community. Both traditional and modern groups fought against governance from Madrid. The arch-conservative, highly religious country regions of Aragon and the Basque country sided with the Carlists in the 19th-century civil wars, believing that this would return them to the old world lost in 1714. The innovative business and industrial class in Catalonia saw Madrid as a dead weight that held them back, and continually pressed for devolution/independence. There was neither substantial horizontal nor vertical integration; the continuing power

---

[34] E.g. the Royal Welch Fusiliers, the Royal Regiment of Wales, the Royal Scots Borderers, the Royal Highland Fusiliers, the Black Watch, the Highlanders, the Royal Dublin Fusiliers, the Royal Munster Fusiliers.

[35] Colley (1992) suggests that a *national* upper class resulted from the aristocracy's widespread failure to produce male heirs in the 18th century, which broke the relation of family and region, and from its patterns of association which brought marriage partners together from different regions. The first edition of *Debrett's Peerage* published in 1802 makes no distinction regarding the geographical origin of the family.

of a Castilian speaking hereditary nobility that defended its interests blocked social mobility.

So we have a cline here in elite permeability. France is the state which built social and geographical mobility into its ideology. UK elites accepted geographical mobility but fought to maintain a rigid class structure. Spain practised social closure on both geographical and social axes. This cline of permeability of national elites seems to correlate closely with the maintenance of regional languages (or their revitalization) among periphery groups. We have seen how in Southern France, Ireland and Catalonia the relationship between a centralizing government and groups with distinct history, language and culture played out. Each of the groups incorporated experienced pressure from the centre to assimilate to the national culture and to shift to the national language.

The southern French did so in the majority, responding positively to Renan's 1882 call to his countrymen to forget the past in the service of nation building. The 1789 revolution could be presented as the event that ended the hold of hereditary elites and local loyalties. The break with tradition and a reworking of social structures allowed the spread of French. The relative permeability of the elites and the possibility of social mobility was a powerful element that encouraged language shift to French.

The constituent territories of the United Kingdom did not experience such a break with tradition. In the UK nation building was constructed on the past and hereditary privilege persisted to a far greater extent. The aristocratic network was English speaking. The majority of the rest of the population also moved to standard English, but for a complex mix of reasons including religious practices, industrialization, urbanization and infrastructure – alongside a social mobility that was more constrained. The Irish were a particular case, kept separate by law and left unsupported by central government in times of crisis. In 1922 there were strong reasons to move back to Irish Gaelic, but this did not happen and English maintained its status in an independent Ireland. Its economic utility remains clear and the fact that there is a distinct Hiberno-English variety allows that language to play a role in identity.

In Spain nation building was blocked to an extent by the social closure practised by the hereditary national elite. The usual strategies of nation building were late in coming to Spain because of the role that the Catholic Church played in the state. Regional groups were never successfully incorporated and challenged domination from the centre. The violent conflicts and the repression of the 20th century that opposed different constituencies in Spain are at the heart of regionalism, although economic factors also play a role. The Catalans and Basques maintain their languages and cultures for a complex mix of identity and economic reasons.

We could conclude that shift to the national language seems to have a strong correlation with the amount of access and opportunity it affords. A state where the elite is open to the talented and ambitious from any region correlates with wide acceptance of the language of the state. But where those on the periphery are not easily admitted to the power networks of the centre, the likelihood is that proto-elites will work towards establishing their own power base. Then regional language maintenance has an increased attraction, because its knowledge and use constitutes cultural capital in new political arrangements. However, as the Irish case shows, there is no inevitable cause and effect in any of these phenomena.

References

A. Alarcón and L. Garzón (2011) *Language, Migration and Social Mobility in Catalonia* (Leiden: Brill).

B. Anderson (1991) *Imagined Communities*, 2nd edition (London: Verso).

A. Arenas (2012) *Barcelona and Madrid: Social Networks of the Avant-Garde* (Lanham: Lexington).

J. Álvarez-Junco (2000) *Spanish Identity in the Age of Nations* (London: Hodder Arnold).

G. Baconnier, A. Minet and L. Soler (1985) *La plume au fusil – les poilus du midi à travers leur correspondence* (Toulouse: Privat).

P. Bairoch (1985) *De Jéricho à Mexico: villes et économie dans l'histoire* (Paris: Gallimard).

B. Barère (1794) 'Rapport Barère à la Convention au nom du Comité de Salut Public, 8 pluviose an 2' (www.languefrancaise.net/HLF/RF).

P. Blanchet (2004) 'Provençal as a Distinct Language: Sociolinguistic Patterns Revealed by a Recent Public and Political Debate', *International Journal of the Sociology of Language*, 169, 125–150.

N. Bosch, M. Espasa and A. Solé-Ollé (eds) (2010) *The Political Economy of Inter-regional Fiscal Flows* (Cheltenham: Edward Elgar).

P. Bourdieu (1982) *Ce que parler veut dire* (Paris: Fayard).

P. Bourdieu (2001) *Langage et pouvoir symbolique* (Paris: Le Seuil).

C. Boyd (1997) *Historia Patria: Politics, History, and National Identity in Spain, 1875–1975* (Princeton: Princeton University Press).

F. Braudel (1986) *L'identité de la France* (Paris: Artaud).

R. Carr (1980) *Modern Spain* (Oxford: Oxford University Press).

B. Cerquiglini (n.d.) 'Le français, une religion d'Etat' (www.culture.gouv.fr/culture/.../ article_francais.html, accessed 12 June 2014).

J.-F. Chanet (1988) 'Maîtres d'école et régionalisme en France sous la Troisième République', *Ethnologie française*, 18, 244–256.

L. Colley (1992) *Britons: Forging the Nation 1707–1837* (London and New York: BCA).

Confederacion Occitana de las escòlas laïcas calendretas (2014) 'Lista Escòlas e Collègis' (www.calandreta.org/-Confederacion-.html, accessed 8 May 2014).

D. Conversi (1997) *The Basques, the Catalans and Spain: Alternative Routes to Nationalist Mobilisation* (London: Hurst).

R. Cooper (1989) *Language Planning and Social Change* (Cambridge: Cambridge University Press).

T. Corcoran (1916) *State Policy in Irish Education, A.D. 1536 to 1816* (London: Longmans).

T. Crowley (1989) *Standard English and the Politics of Language* (Basingstoke: Palgrave).

D. Crozes and D. Magne, D. (1993) *Les Aveyronnais* (Rodez: Editions de Rouergue).

P. Dowling (1935/1968) *The Hedge Schools of Ireland* (London: Longmans).

A. Dymond (2012) 'Displaying the Arlésienne: Museums, Folklife and Regional Identity in France' In T. Baycroft and D. Hopkin (eds) *Folklore and Nationalism in Europe During the Long Nineteenth Century* (Leiden: Brill).

V. Ellis, C. Fox and B. Street (2007) *Rethinking English in Schools: Towards a New and Constructive Stage* (London: Continuum).

M. Evans and E. Godin (2004) *France 1815–2003* (London: Arnold).

J. Ferrater Mora (1944/2012) *Les formes de la vida catalana i altres assaigs* (Google e-book).

L. Frader (1991) *Peasants and Protest: Agricultural Workers, Politics and Unions in the Aude. 1850–1914* (Berkeley: University of California Press).

L. Gachon (1970) *La vie rurale en France* (Paris: Presses Universitaires de France).

E. Gellner (1983) *Nations and Nationalism* (Oxford: Blackwell).

R. Gillespie (2005) *Reading Ireland: Print, Reading and Social Change in Early Modern Ireland* (Manchester: Manchester University Press).

H. Grégoire (1794) *Rapport sur la nécessité et les moyens d'anéantir les patois* (Paris: Convention Nationale).

F. Grin, C. Sfreddo and F. Vaillancourt (2010) *The Economics of the Multilingual Workplace* (London: Routledge).

P. Hart (2003) *The IRA at War 1916–1923* (Oxford: Oxford University Press).

R. Hickey (2002) *A Source Book for Irish English, vol. 1* (Amsterdam: John Benjamins).

R. Hickey (2007) *Irish English: History and Present-day Forms* (Cambridge: Cambridge University Press).

E. Hobsbawm (1990) *Nations and Nationalism since 1990* (Cambridge: Cambridge University Press).

C. Hoffmann (1996) 'Twenty Years of Language Planning in Contemporary Spain' In S. Wright (ed.) *Monolingualism and Bilingualism: Lessons from Canada and Spain* (Clevedon: Multilingual Matters), pp. 1–41.

U. Hussey De Burgh (1878) *The Landowners of Ireland* (Dublin: Hodges, Foster and Figgis).

J. Hutchinson (1987) *The Dynamics of Cultural Nationalism: The Gaelic Revival and the Creation of the Irish Nation State* (London: Allen & Unwin).

C. Johnson (1995) *The Life and Death of Industrial Languedoc, 1700–1920: The Politics of Deindustrialization* (Oxford: Oxford University Press).

G. Jourdanne (1897/2000) *Histoire du Félibrige 1854–1896* (Nîmes: Lacour).

J. Leclerc (2007) *Histoire de la langue française (Agence intergouvernementale de la francophonie)* (www.axl.cefan.ulaval.ca/francophonie/histlngfrn.htm, accessed 20 June 2014).

T. Lundén (1979) 'Linguistic Minorities in a World of Communication' In W. Mackay and L. Ornstein (eds) *Sociolinguistic Studies in Language Contact* (Berlin: Mouton de Gruyter), pp. 11–22.

I. Lustick (1985) *State-Building Failure in British Ireland & French Algeria* (Berkeley, CA: University of California).

P. Martel (1988) 'Poètes et paysans: Les écrivains paysans dans le Félibrige 1860–1914' *Ethnologie française*, 18, 233–243.

P. Martel (2001) 'Le petit monde de l'édition en langue d'oc au temps des Félibres', *Bibliothèque de l'Ecole des Chartes*, 159, 153–170.

P. Martel (2007) *L'Ecole française et l'occitan: le sourd et le bègue* (Montpellier: Presses universitaires de la Méditerranée).

P. Martel (2012) 'Une norme pour la langue d'oc? Les débuts d'une histoire sans fin', *Lengas*, 72, 23–50.

P. Mason (2012) 'Unrest Drags Spain towards Buried Unpleasant Truths', BBC Business News, 2 October.

F. Mistral (1868) *Mirèio* (Paris: Charpentier).

T. Nairn (1977/2003) *The Break-up of Britain: Crisis and Neo-nationalism* (Victoria: Common Ground).

F. Napo (1971) *La révolte des vignerons 1907* (Toulouse: Privat).

Nobel (n.d.) Nobel Prize website, www.nobelprize.org/nobel_prizes/literature/laureates/ .../mistral-bio.html, 4 June 2015.

D. Nordman (1998) *Frontières de France* (Paris: Gallimard).

T. Ó hlfearnáin (2014) 'Legitimacy, Ownership and User Participation in Language Standards and Standard Irish', Paper Given at the Workshop 'Language Planning: Theory and Practice in Dialogue', University of Oslo, 14 October.

E. O'Leary (2014) 'Former Catalan President Jordi Pujol to be Stripped of His Titles after Admitting to more than 30 Years of Tax Fraud', *The Independent*, 29 July (www. independent.co.uk/news/world/europe/former-catalan-president-jordi-pujol-to-be-stripped-of-his-titles-after-admitting-to-more-than-30-years-of-tax-fraud-9636343. html, accessed 20 June 2014).

M. Overton (1996) *Agricultural Revolution in England: The Transformation of the Agrarian Economy 1500–1850* (Cambridge: Cambridge University Press).

E. Richards (2013) *The Highland Clearances* (Edinburgh: Birlinn).

F. Romero Salvadó (1999) *Twentieth-Century Spain: Politics and Society in Spain, 1898–1998* (London: Macmillan).

J. Rosés (2003) 'Regional Industrialisation without National Growth: The Catalan Industrialization and the Growth of Spanish Economy (1830–1861)', Economics Working Papers, Barcelona: Universitat Pompeu Fabra.

W. Sabogal (2014) 'Old Spanish Stereotypes Making a Comeback', *El Pais*, 9 July (elpais.com/m/elpais/2014/07/07/inenglish/1404722032_240736.html), 4 June 2015.

F. Schrijver (2006) *Regionalism after Regionalisation: Spain, France and the United Kingdom* (Amsterdam: Amsterdam University Press).

A. Smith (2014) *The Origins of Catalan Nationalism 1770–1898* (Basingstoke: Palgrave).

S. Smith (1990) *W.B. Yeats: A Critical Introduction* (Lanham: Rowman & Littlefield).

M. Strubell (1999) 'Language, Democracy and Devolution in Catalonia' In S. Wright (ed.) *Language, Democracy and Devolution in Catalonia* (Clevedon: Multilingual Matters), pp. 4–39.

M. Tanner (2001) *Ireland's Holy Wars: The Struggle for a Nation's Soul 1500–2000* (New Haven, CT: Yale University Press).

J. Thirsk (1984) *The Rural Economy of England* (London: Hambledon).

M. Tierney (1980) *Eoin MacNeill, Scholar and Man of Action, 1867–1945* (Oxford: Clarendon Press).

A. de Tocqueville (1828/1958) *Journeys to England and Ireland* (New Jersey: Transaction Publishers).

E. Weber (1976) *Peasants into Frenchmen: The Modernization of Rural France 1870–1914* (Stanford: Stanford University Press).

M. Wheatley (2005) *Nationalism and the Irish Party* (Oxford: Oxford University Press).

D. Williams (1967) 'De Valera in Power' In F. MacManus (ed.) *The Years of the Great Test 1926–1939* (Cork: Mercier Press), pp. 170–183.

J. Wormald (1983) 'James VI and I: Two Kings or One?', *History*, 68, 187–209.

S. Wright (2004) *Language Policy and Language Planning: From Nation-building to Globalisation* (Basingstoke: Palgrave).

S. Wright (2007) 'The Right to Speak One's Own Language: Reflections on Theory and Practice', *Language Policy*, 6, 203–224.

R. Wuthnow (2009) *Communities of Discourse: Ideology and Social Structure in the Reformation, the Enlightenment, and European Socialism* (Cambridge, MA: Harvard University Press).

P. Zagorin (1982) *Rebels and Rulers, 1500–1600: Volume 1, Agrarian and Urban Rebellions* (Cambridge: Cambridge University Press).

17
Languages, Regional Conflicts and Economic Development in South Asia

Selma K. Sonntag

17.1 Introduction

The relation between economic development and linguistic diversity has been a topic of inquiry among social scientists, with implications for language planners and policy-makers, for a number of decades. In the aftermath of decolonization, researchers informed by the modernization paradigm of development tended to view ethnic and linguistic diversity within newly independent Third World countries as a hindrance to economic development. Daniel Nettle (2000, p. 336) points to the 'famous studies' by Joshua Fishman (1968) and Jonathan Pool (1972) as the standard bearers of the paradigmatic negative correlation between linguistic diversity and economic development in the field of language policy and planning. Fishman (1968), the doyen of sociolinguistics, gave an impressionistic overview of cross-polity datasets that became available in the mid-1960s and that included a measurement of 'linguistic homogeneity'. Pool (1972) followed up with a statistical analysis, employing techniques that helped fill in gaps in the data.

While noting the problematic definition of 'linguistic homogeneity' in the datasets, Fishman (1968, p. 60) nevertheless summarized his overview as follows:

> One cannot help but come away from this recitation of findings with the decided impression that linguistic homogeneity is currently related to many more of the 'good' and 'desirable' characteristics of polities than is linguistic heterogeneity. Linguistically homogeneous polities are usually economically more developed, educationally more advanced, politically more modernized, and ideologically-politically more tranquil and stable.

Fishman (1968, pp. 61–64) acknowledges political variables as having the most explanatory power for both linguistic and economic variation across polities. He notes, for example, while political stability and political freedom are correlated to a higher degree with economic development than with linguistic homogeneity, 'political enculturation' has a higher correlation with linguistic homogeneity and 'sectionalism' (i.e. 'the presence of significant, politically nonassimilated minorities in extreme opposition') with linguistic heterogeneity than either has with economic development (measured by per capita GNP) (ibid., p. 63). This leads him to conclude that 'the simultaneous pursuit of the advantages of higher economic status coupled with the protection or maintenance of valued cultural-linguistic differences is not a will-o'-the-wisp' (ibid., p. 64). In other words, Fishman takes the position that maintaining linguistic diversity is not at odds with economic development for Third World countries.

Pool (1972, pp. 224–225) contrasts Fishman's prescription with that of Karl Deutsch, a 'modernization' political scientist who predicted increased conflict in a rapidly economically developing country with a high degree of linguistic diversity (Deutsch, 1953). Pool concludes from his analysis of the correlation between linguistic diversity and economic development that the Fishman–Deutsch disagreement is a moot point: in the early 1960s, there were no instances of linguistically diverse countries that were also economically developed, with the possible exception of South Africa and its racialized economic development. He identifies a negative relation between low linguistic 'uniformity' (measured by percentage of population of largest native-language community) and economic development (measured by per capita GNP), although he warns of the 'static' nature of the correlation and the problematic definitions of both variables. He also cautions against making spurious correlations, advising instead to identify 'intervening variables' (Pool, 1972, p. 225).

Although Fishman and Pool were careful in generalizing from their analyses of the data, they both tended to adhere to the modernization assumption that, on face value, linguistic diversity was a problem for developing countries. Coined the Fishman–Pool hypothesis by Nettle (2000), the assumed problematic nature of linguistic diversity for developing countries has been glossed more recently by William Easterly and Ross Levine (1997) as the 'growth tragedy'. Relying primarily on the ethnolinguistic fractionalization index as their measurement of 'ethnolinguistic diversity', Easterly and Levine (1997) suggest that many developing countries, particularly in sub-Saharan Africa, are condemned to low growth given their high degree of 'ethnolinguistic fragmentation'. They take language as the marker of ethnicity; linguistic diversity is their independent variable, presumably 'causing' poor economic performance, which is the dependent variable. The Easterly–Levine update of the Fishman–Pool hypothesis remains the product of the modernization paradigm: linguistic diversity is seen as a problem rather than a resource (Arcand and Grin, 2013).

Easterly and Levine's analysis has generated on-going debate, primarily among economists and political scientists. Daniel Posner (2004) has raised questions about the calculation and relevance of the ethnolinguistic fragmentation index for what Easterly and Levine (1997) are attempting to test. Jean-Louis Arcand and François Grin (2013, p. 245) question the alleged exogeneity of Easterly and Levine's independent variable of ethnolinguistic fragmentation. David Laitin (2000), focusing more on the relation between diversity and conflict, has also called attention to the problem of endogeneity of the independent variable. He and his colleagues have sought to overcome this problem by developing a measurement of linguistic distance, derived from Joseph Greenberg's (1956) work and based on linguistic genealogies or language family trees. While clearly exogenous to the dependent variable, they assume that 'the structural difference between languages' measures 'the degree of cultural difference between ethnic groups' (Laitin, 2000, p.143). They then 'used it [LANGFAM, their measure of linguistic distance] to measure cultural distance' (ibid., p. 148). Posner (2004, p. 852) approves of their 'plausible assumption' that linguistic distance is a proxy for depth of ethnic cleavages which the ethnolinguistic fragmentation index cannot account for, although he opts for developing his own index of politically relevant ethnic groups that, almost by default, jettisons the linguistic proxy.

These critical evaluations of the usefulness of the ethnolinguistic fragmentation index do not raise the issues that would concern linguists and sociolinguists. Laitin (2000, pp. 43–44) offers several possible reasons why Greenberg's 1956 index never caught on, but neglects the most likely and most significant one for linguists: they would disagree with its assumptions about language distance as a proxy for cultural and ethnic distance. The assumption that language genealogies map onto ethnic genealogies is a common misconception among non-linguists (Noonan, 2010, pp. 48–49). While a language's genealogy may be one among many determinants of its grammatical and phonological structure, the notion that a language's structure indexes ethnicity is no more plausible than the now-debunked notion that racial difference can be measured by genetic distance. As Mabry (2011) demonstrates, Laitin and colleagues' measurement of linguistic distance as a proxy for cultural or ethnic distance is highly problematic. Substituting linguistic distance for Easterly and Levine's (1997) linguistic fragmentation as the 'exogenously given datum' (Arcand and Grin 2013, p. 245) may help settle econometric debate, but it does not address, and perhaps even heightens, linguists' concerns.

Easterly and Levine (1997) take linguistic diversity as a pre-existing, 'given' variable independent of economic development. They tend to assume that ethnolinguistic diversity and difference are 'primordial': natural, given 'facts' in existence prior to and independent of economic development or regional conflict or, more generally, the modern nation-state. In contrast, Laitin (2000) successfully identifies an exogenous variable, linguistic distance, but then assumes that it operationalizes cultural diversity, the independent variable in his model. Unsurprisingly for linguists, in the end Laitin (2000) finds his measurement of linguistic distance insufficient in explaining conflict. He reverts to an endogenous typology of 'linguistic communities' and 'linguistic regimes' that implicitly takes political institutions as an intervening variable, similar to Posner's (2004, p. 855) self-admitted endogenous independent variables that offer a 'peek' at the intervening variables of policy mechanisms. Laitin and Posner's more 'instrumentalist' arguments (Brass, 1991) tend to view ethnolinguistic identity not as a 'primordial attachment' (Geertz, 1973, p. 259), but rather as an instrument for elites and ethnic entrepreneurs to manipulate through political and economic incentives and threats. Linguistic diversity, as a measurement of ethnolinguistic identity, is often the dependent variable in instrumentalist analyses or, as Posner (2004) puts it, politically relevant ethnic groups are indeed endogenous to economic policies. Ethnolinguistic conflict and an economy distorted by rent-seeking ethnolinguistic groups are viewed as the outcomes of elites in government and civil society competing, at times violently especially in the Third World, for scarce resources. In a well-governed, economically prosperous country, linguistic homogeneity, or what Pool (1972) calls linguistic uniformity and Laitin (1988) labels linguistic rationalization, would be the most likely outcome, according to instrumentalists.

More recently, constructivists have attempted a reconciliation of sorts between primordialism and instrumentalism (Toffolo, 2003). Constructivists argue that not only ethnolinguistic identity, but language itself, is a social and political construct. Hence linguistic diversity is not a measurable empirical given or outcome, but a fluid and variable reality which can be constructed negatively as 'fragmentation' or positively as 'multilingualism' (Arcand and Grin, 2013, p. 241). Sociolinguists (e.g. Makoni and Pennycook, 2007) contend that concepts such as 'mother tongue', 'native speaker', 'speech', 'standardization', 'linguistic homogeneity', 'linguistic difference', 'linguistic distance' and 'linguistic diversity' are contingent on context. They recognize that most of the people in the world are multilingual despite the Western scholarly bias towards assuming that monolingualism is the norm (Sonntag and Cardinal, 2015). Lisa Mitchell (2009) and James Scott (2009) argue that in South Asia and South East Asia respectively, association of language with a particular people or ethnicity is a late 19th–early 20th century colonial construct. Taking language and ethnolinguistic identity as historical, social and political constructs complicates researching statistical correlations between language diversity, economic development and political stability. Is language standardization the source or the outcome of economic development or both (Nettle, 2000)? Is political stability a prerequisite for or an outcome of linguistic rationalization (Laitin, 2000, p. 149)?[1] With no clearly indicated or stable dependent and independent

---

[1] Ericka Albaugh (2013) has suggested in an analysis of war-torn sub-Saharan West Africa that linguistic homogeneity, in terms of the spread of a lingua franca, and not linguistic

variables, quantitative, econometric data analysis can be irredeemably tricky. Hence, constructivists tend to use the qualitative, case-study methodology of area specialists (Mabry, 2011).

In my examination of the intersection of linguistic diversity, regional conflicts and economic development in South Asia, I adopt the case-study approach. My four cases are India, Sri Lanka, Nepal and Pakistan.[2] While these four cases have similar historical, linguistic and economic circumstances – allowing for 'the most similar design' analysis (George and Bennett, 2005) – they differ in their political circumstances. Historically, all four cases have similar civilizational influences and three out of the four were directly colonized by the British. Linguistic diversity characterizes all four cases.[3] Economically, all four cases are considered 'developing' countries. While economic growth rates have varied among the four, especially in the last decade and a half, with India now considered an emerging market, all four rank towards the bottom of global indices of GDP per capita.[4] Where the four cases diverge is in the political arena. As I will demonstrate below, differing political institutions and policy processes have led to different language regimes (see Sonntag and Cardinal, 2015) and different economic development regimes. Although I am positing that political processes and institutions are important 'intervening variables' in any analysis of the relationship between language, development and conflict, I do not intend to claim any causal relationship between these interacting variables. Rather, by adopting the case-study approach, I can contextualize and temporalize the politics of language, regional conflict and economic development. I begin with the Indian case, followed by Sri Lanka. Nepal and Pakistan are my third and fourth cases respectively, with briefer treatment.

---

distance or diversity, is the outcome of conflict. Furthermore she suggests that there is no state imperative or compulsion for linguistic rationalization. To extrapolate, one could argue that conflict, not stability, is the determinant of linguistic homogeneity.

[2] In addition to these four countries, Bhutan, Maldives and Bangladesh are normally included in 'South Asia'. It is beyond the scope of this chapter to cover these cases, other than the inception of Bangladesh. I have chosen post-World War II political-economic constructs as my units of analysis, although I will make repeated references to colonial constructs in South Asia.

[3] Keeping in mind the highly problematic nature of the ethnolinguistic fractionalization (ELF) index in analyses of the interaction between linguistic diversity, regional conflict and economic development, we can note that India's ELF is above 0.8, the highest of the four cases, while both Nepal and Pakistan are about 0.7. Sri Lanka comes in the lowest, at less than 0.5.

[4] According to World Bank figures for 2013, India, Sri Lanka and Pakistan are all ranked as lower middle income countries, whereas Nepal is ranked as a low income country. See http://data.worldbank.org/region/SAS (accessed 26 July 2014).

17.2   India

The largest and most linguistically diverse country in South Asia, India has developed a complex language regime (Sarangi, 2015).[5] At the time of independence, India's linguistic diversity was assumed to be a liability for the new nation's political and territorial integrity (Harrison, 1960). Jawaharlal Nehru, India's first prime minister, was reportedly deeply troubled by the threat to national unity posed by what were assumed to be primordial linguistic attachments (Geertz, 1973, p. 256; King, 1998). This was in spite of the anti-colonial movement, led by the Indian National Congress, having successfully mobilized the masses under Gandhi's leadership by appealing to them in their own languages: in the 1920s, '[Mohandas K.] Gandhi convinced Congress to organize along regional language lines' (Sonntag, 2003, p. 60). Having unleashed potential 'fissiparous tendencies' in the independence struggle, independent India's new rulers now confronted what they assumed to be the inevitable consequences.

For Nehru in particular, linguistic heterogeneity was considered a setback for a modern India, in which economic development was the primary goal, to be achieved through a centralized state taking the 'commanding heights' of the national economy geared towards industrialization. Nehru perceived English to be the national glue that would hold India together for economic development purposes (Raina, 1991). His vision of India's economic development was in stark contrast to Gandhi's. Gandhi espoused a decentralized system made up of self-sufficient 'village republics' based on cottage industries, supposedly more conducive to accommodating India's linguistic and cultural diversity (Baird, 2003, pp. 30–35). Although Nehru won the economic debate, with India launching an import substitution industrialization development strategy along with centralized five-year plans (Corbridge and Harriss, 2000, p. 60), the prime minister finally conceded to pressure for a linguistic reorganization of state boundaries and the adoption of a federal system based on India's major regional languages.

Most scholars argue that India's linguistic federalism has been a success in terms of political integration (Stuligross and Varshney, 2002, p. 448; Dasgupta, 2003, p. 32; Brass, 2009, p. 213). Some argue that the success is at least partially attributable to linguistic rationalization taking place within the states that make

---

[5] India has recently embarked on a massive linguistic survey. According to the survey's website (http://peopleslinguisticsurvey.org/aboutus.aspx?page=Census), 'the 2001 Census of India lists a total of 122 languages and 234 mother tongues with over 10,000 speakers'. The major regional languages of India are Hindi (reportedly the mother tongue of about 30 to 40 per cent of the population), Telugu, Bengali, Marathi, Tamil and Gujarati (each with mother-tongue speakers ranging between 6 and 10 per cent of the total population), while Gujarati, Kannada, Malayalam, Oriya and Punjabi are above the 2 per cent mark but at or below 5 per cent.

up India's union (Laitin, 1989), often to the detriment of linguistic minorities residing in those states (Dasgupta, 2003). Victor Ginsburgh and Shlomo Weber (forthcoming) define this linguistic rationalization as linguistic standardization, suggesting that India's language regime, in particular its three-language formula component, has resulted in a reduction of India's linguistic diversity. The implication is that India has done the best it could to mitigate the negative impact of linguistic diversity on economic development and political-territorial integrity, as per the Fishman–Pool hypothesis and similar models discussed above. Crucial in this regard is another component of India's language regime: the maintenance of English as an associate official language to Hindi at the national level. English today in India is repeatedly identified as positively correlated with India's recent economic growth and its status as an emerging market and BRIC member (Nilekani, 2008).

A constructivist account of the relative success of India's language regime would emphasize the historical context of the tension between India's linguistic diversity reflected in the multilingualism of its citizenry and the development of its political institutions. During the anti-colonial struggle there was a general consensus that the political outcome would be an independent nation-state based on the Western European model of a liberal bourgeois state (Chatterjee, 1986). At times, however, it seemed that Gandhi might proffer a 'non-derivative' model – particularly when mobilizing the masses during the independence struggle (Chatterjee, 1986). Gandhi's proffering had a linguistic dimension: he championed Hindustani – the colloquial variant of Hindi and Urdu – over Hindi and English as India's official languages. This pitted him against both the traditional, landed elite and Hindu revivalists on the one hand, and against Nehru on the other (Sonntag, 2003, pp. 60–61). Krishna Kumar (1991) has argued that the result was a 'foul contract' in which Nehruvians, preferring English as the language of modernity, allied with the landed elite and political revivalists who preferred a 'purer' Hindi (distinct from Urdu, the language now associated with Muslims). Gandhi's Hindustani alternative lost out. Hindustani was, and is, a colloquial language spoken by both Hindus and Muslims in north India – like India's other colloquial languages, it was not initially associated with a particular people who constituted a nation. It was during the 19th and 20th centuries that Hindustani was politicized: Hindi, written in the Devanagri script with a Sanskrit-derived corpus, was increasingly constructed as different from Urdu, written in the Arabic script with Persian as the lexical source (King, 1994; Rai, 2000). With this distancing, Hindi could be 'imagined' as the language of Hindus and by extension India, whereas Urdu became the language of Muslims pressing for an Islamic nation, Pakistan, separate from India.

The construction of India's multilingualism into distinct separate languages – each associated with a particular people – the prerequisite for linguistic nationalism and the political imagining of modern nation-states (Anderson, 1991) – needs to be placed in the historical context of the late 19th–early 20th centuries. In its 'mania for classificatory order' (Scott, 2009, p. 239), the colonial state constructed typologies in which to categorize what appeared to the British to be a chaotic land of Babel (LaDousa, 2014, p. 17). The 'types' were discrete languages associated with discrete 'peoples' and categorized according to a linguistic genesis based on language 'families'. Crucial in this construction was the codification and standardization of colloquial speech through the writing and development of dictionaries and grammars. This colonial mapping of linguistic activity dovetailed with the spread of newspapers and literacy on the one hand and the diffusion of liberal bourgeois notions of democracy on the other, setting the stage for a perceived threat of ethnolinguistic conflict in Nehru's modern India, committed as it was to centralized economic development.

The first major linguistic challenge that Nehru faced as prime minister of newly independent India was in the Telugu-speaking region of the colonial Madras Presidency. Telugu leaders were demanding separation from the Tamil-speaking region and statehood within a federal India union. A well-respected Gandhian fasted unto death in support of the demand, thus putting insurmountable pressure on Nehru to concede (King, 1998; Mitchell, 2009). The common explanation of this ethnolinguistic conflict, and subsequent challenges by Tamil speakers, is that primordial attachments were activated by the economic consequences of the portending linguistic rationalization of a centralized state with Hindi as the official national language. Mitchell (2009) argues that this is an inadequate explanation. People do not die – by setting themselves on fire or fasting unto death – because their job prospects require the attainment of an additional (linguistic) skill. Rather the economic incentives and associated costs of learning another language need to be placed in the context of an emerging democracy in which political power is dependent on mobilizing the masses. A nascent regional identity based on language can be coupled with charges of economic discrimination for the purpose of challenging the monopoly on political power at the centre. As Narendra Subramanian (1999, p. 129) explains the anti-Hindi riots in Tamil Nadu in the mid-1960s:

> the Dravidianists were assigned the role of champions of the plebeian community, and the state and central governments and Congress, which led them, were cast as alien forces insensitive to the concerns of this community. This completed the populist image of the world – the righteous representatives of the 'people', rooted in local culture, challenging an effete and deracinated elite.

By opposing the centralizing, established Nehruvian elite, emerging populist leaders in south India were able to build a political base.

Nehru's concession was to move forward in constructing a language regime that allowed for oppositional regional power through linguistic federalism and an official language policy at the national level that was not restricted to Hindi. The rise of regional political elites has become India's political and economic story (see e.g. Jaffrelot, 2003). Dipesh Chakrabarty (1998, p. 105) notes that 'the combination of demography, democracy and political growth in India has now ensured' that political power is no longer restricted to a tiny elite. Federalism and democratic processes in India have led to a continuing augmentation and diversification of the Indian elite, almost all of which is committed to the political and territorial integrity of the nation (Mitchell, 2009, p. 21).

India liberalized its economy and abandoned the Nehruvian development strategy of import substitution industrialization in 1991. This change in India's economic development regime, instigated by a debt crisis and the need to stimulate economic growth, has been subjected to democratic debate, including debate and controversy over the increasing saliency of English as a job skill and a class marker (Sonntag, forthcoming). The debate is channelled for the most part in India's democratic and federal institutions and structures, most recently as a stand-off between the courts and state governments (Sonntag, 2015). As D. L. Sheth (1990, p. 66) has claimed, 'the language debate [over English] is an outgrowth of the democratic process of politics' in the institutional context (we might add) of linguistic federalism. By accommodating India's multilingualism at least to some degree through democratic and federal structures and policies, India has averted for the most part regional conflict that could threaten the political and territorial integrity of the state. It seems that this resolution of the tension between linguistic diversity and political integrity bodes well for economic development, although the jury is still out about India's ability to maintain sustained, equitable economic growth. The verdict may only partially depend on the language question. In this regard, language diversity and (lack of) regional conflict provide the context, not the determinant, of India's economic development.[6] India may well be on its way to fulfilling Fishman's hope of a country that can achieve economic growth while maintaining and preserving its linguistic diversity.

17.3 Sri Lanka

Most of the scholarly literature on the conflict in Sri Lanka – indeed a civil war that ended in 2009 with the government's military victory – acknowledges the important role that the language cleavage, between Sinhala and Tamil, has played and gives an instrumentalist account of that role. One

---

[6] I would like to thank François Grin for this formulation of the relationship between diversity, conflict and development implicit in an earlier draft of this chapter.

of the primary reasons given for the manipulation of the language issue by Sinhalese political elites is the economic pay-off for Sinhalese, the majority of the population. As Neil DeVotta (2003, p. 137) has put it, 'Sri Lanka's political elite...reconfigured the socioeconomic opportunity structure' through manipulating the language issue in order to benefit the Sinhalese (who make up about 75 per cent of the population) and 'linguistically disenfranchise' (Dower et al., 2014) the Sri Lankan Tamils (who make up about 12 percent of the population). Increasing the saliency of linguistic difference between the majority Sinhalese and the minority Tamils was the instrument through which Sinhalese political elites sought to enhance the economic opportunities of their constituents. Under these circumstances, linguistic diversity was assumed to be positively correlated with economic development (at least for the Sinhalese), the inverse of the predictions of the standard-bearing models of the modernization paradigm discussed above.

Sri Lanka is a predominantly bilingual, as opposed to a multilingual (such as India), society (DeVotta, 2003, pp. 137–138) in terms of indigenous languages: the two languages are Sinhala – an Indo-Aryan language spoken by the Sinhalese who are almost all Buddhist and live in the south and central highlands part of the island – and Tamil, a Dravidian language spoken by Tamils who mostly identify as Hindu.[7] Sri Lankan Tamils who have not relocated to Colombo live in the north-eastern area and the arid northern part of the island across the Palk Strait from the Indian state of Tamil Nadu (in which Tamil is the official language of the state government; see discussion of India's linguistic federalism above). Tamil is also spoken by what are referred to as Indian Tamils in Sri Lanka: descendants of indentured labour brought over by the British colonizers to work in the highland tea plantations in the centre of the island. These Indian Tamils make up about 6 per cent of the population of Sri Lanka and were not granted citizenship until the late 1970s.[8]

---

[7] Although the two languages in conflict in Sri Lanka belong to different language families, this is not a factor in their distancing or difference. Dravidian and Indo-Aryan languages in South Asia have been in contact for thousands of years, leading linguists to identify South Asia as a single linguistic area (Emeneau, 1956; see also Dasgupta, 2003, p. 29; Schiffman 2010). Lexically, phonologically, morphologically and syntactically, there has been significant congruence between Dravidian and Indo-Aryan languages in South Asia. It is worth noting that Greenberg's (1956) classic paper on linguistic diversity measured on the basis of language families appeared in the same issue of *Language* as Emeneau's equally classic paper. However, the two papers are not theoretically compatible.

[8] The other significant minority population in Sri Lanka are the Moors, who are predominantly Tamil speakers. They are Muslims who came to Sri Lanka probably about a thousand years ago, compared to the Sinhalese and Sri Lankan Tamils who each claim to

Although Sri Lanka can be characterized as a bilingual Sinhala-Tamil society, individuals for the most part are not bilingual in the two languages. According to Robert Kearney (1967, p. 17), 'in 1953, 80 per cent of the population of Ceylon [now called Sri Lanka] spoke only one language. Nearly 60 per cent spoke only Sinhalese [i.e. Sinhala] and more than 20 per cent spoke only Tamil'.[9] English, introduced during British colonial rule, became the link language between the Sinhalese and Tamil elite, who made up approximately 6 per cent of the population. The Sri Lankan Tamils were over-represented among this English-speaking elite. Missionary penetration, land-holding patterns, telluric conditions and caste hierarchy all contributed to the success of a Tamil middle class in the British colonial administration (Kearney, 1967, p. 24). Hence,

> a decade before independence Tamils [held] about twice as great a proportion of pensionable public service posts as their proportion of the population. Sinhalese held less than three times as many of these positions as Tamils, although they were more than six times more numerous in the population (Kearney, 1967, p. 70).

English was a required skill for public service employment, with most of the positions located in the capital, Colombo. In many ways, then, in the first half of the 20th century, the class divide (between the English-speaking upper and rising middle class and the vernacular-speaking lower classes) was more salient than the ethnolinguistic divide between Sinhalese and Tamils (Kearney, 1967, pp. 56–57).

Sri Lankan independence did not involve the type of anti-colonial struggle that took place in India. The co-opted political elite of Sri Lanka, English-speaking and comprised of both Tamils and Sinhalese, negotiated with the colonial rulers rather than mobilizing the masses, as had been the case in India. Nevertheless, as opportunities for upward mobility through English-language education and colonial administrative postings narrowed in the 1930s (Kearney, 1967), those aspiring to the middle class, particularly among the Sinhalese, launched a *swabhasha* ('own language') movement. The thrust of the movement was to demand better educational and employment opportunities for those who had been educated through the vernacular medium (either Sinhala or Tamil) – an education that the British began emphasizing in the

---

have at least a 2,500-year history on the island. DeVotta (2003, p. 111) suggests that most likely the island was inhabited much earlier, probably by pre-Hindu Dravidians.

[9] According to Kearney (1967, p. 7), the demographic breakdown of the island's population in 1953 was 69.4 per cent Sinhalese, 10.9 per cent Sri Lankan Tamils, 12 per cent Indian Tamils and 5.7 per cent Moors. The drastic reduction in the population of Indian Tamils can be attributed to their repatriation to India in the mid-1960s (DeVotta, 2003, p. 107).

late 1800s (Kearney, 1967, p. 55) and which produced a 65 per cent literacy rate by 1953 (DeVotta, 2003, p. 114). The *swabhasha* movement had an anti-colonial element to it, but was predominantly anti-English, catching the co-opted English-speaking Sri Lankan elite in its net of protest and giving the movement a class or anti-elite hue. When democracy was introduced into this context upon independence – and Sri Lanka was 'the first country in Asia to introduce universal adult suffrage' (Kearney, 1967, p. 31) – members of the political elite who had become politicians in the new democracy jumped on the *swabhasha* bandwagon to harness its populist potential for electoral purposes. Exemplary in this regard was S. W. R. D. Bandranaike (DeVotta, 2003, p. 117).

The *swabhasha* movement soon became a Sinhala-only movement as Sinhalese political parties began engaging in 'ethnic outbidding' (Horowitz, 1985). Given the reinforcing cleavages (linguistic, religious and geographical), Sinhalese party leaders found their electoral success enhanced if they appealed exclusively to Sinhalese voters. There was no incentive to accommodate Tamil voters or parties given the logic of electoral politics and its tendency to produce majoritarian governments. The two main Sinhalese parties (the United National Party or UNP and the Sri Lankan Freedom Party or SLFP) traded off forming governments: whichever party was in opposition spouted Sinhalese chauvinist rhetoric in order to 'outbid' the party in government in the next election. The pre-independence *swabhasha* movement facilitated language as the most salient of the cleavages, at least initially, but the religious and geographical cleavages also featured prominently.[10]

In the first instance of ethnic outbidding, in the 1956 election, Bandranaike's newly formed SLFP championed the Sinhala-only movement, the newer incarnation of the *swabasha* movement, and defeated the UNP. The communal passions whipped up spilled over into rioting when the newly elected Bandranaike government passed legislation making Sinhala the sole official language (DeVotta, 2003, p. 124; see also Tambiah, 1996). Bandranaike attempted to pull back, negotiating with the leader of the Tamil Federal Party, S. J. V. Chelvanayakam, to ensure a minimum of accommodation of Tamil speakers at least in the north and north-eastern parts of the country (Kearney, 1967, p. 85; Oberst 2013). Having discovered the pay-off of ethnic outbidding,

---

[10] The SLFP-led United Front government promulgated a new constitution in 1972, privileging Buddhism and explicitly defining Sri Lanka as a unitary state (DeVotta, 2003, p. 131). Although the conflict in Sri Lanka has often been defined as an ethnic conflict, it is important to note that the markers of 'ethnicity' have been language, religion and territory/geography. In other words, there is no biological or genetic basis to the difference between Sinhalese and Tamils: they are not two 'races' (see DeVotta, 2003, p. 111). 'Communal' is often used instead of 'ethnic', given the difficulties of ascribing ethnic difference to the different communities.

the UNP immediately attacked the 1957 Bandranaike–Chelvanayakam Pact. Not to be outbid, Bandranaike reneged on the agreement in 1958, unleashing another wave of rioting (Tambiah, 1996). Yet Bandranaike paid the ultimate price: he was assassinated in 1959 by a Sinhalese extremist (Kearney, 1967, p. 88; DeVotta, 2003, p. 128).

The 1960 election provided an opening for the Tamils. The UNP won the election but fell short of a majority to form the government, leading to negotiations with the Tamil Federal Party for support. Unable or unwilling to meet Tamil demands for fear of appearing too appeasing, the UNP failed a vote of confidence, resulting in new elections which the SLFP, led by Bandranaike's widow, won (Kearney, 1967, pp. 108–109). The first female prime minister in the world, Sirimavo Bandranaike was particularly vitriolic in vilifying Tamils (DeVotta, 2003, p. 128). Once in office, she eschewed even minimal accommodation of Tamil demands, such as issuing implementation regulations to ensure that Tamils in the north and north-east could receive government services and education in Tamil. She 'rigorously implement[ed] the Sinhala-only policy' (ibid., p. 129). For example,

> government officials who did not have proficiency in Sinhala were … denied bonuses and salary increases; public servants … were given three years to learn Sinhala or forfeit their jobs; and … Sinhalese civil servants were transplanted north to ensure that government agencies in the Tamil areas operated in the Sinhala language … . The effects of these policies were dramatic: In 1956, 30 percent of the Ceylon administrative service, 50 percent of the clerical service, 60 percent of engineers and doctors, and 40 percent of the armed forces were Tamil. By 1970 those numbers had plummeted to 5 percent, 5 percent, 10 percent, and 1 percent, respectively (ibid.).

The 1965 election also afforded Tamils a political opportunity, perhaps even more so than the 1960 election. The Tamil Federal Party, along with the Tamil Congress party, joined a coalition government formed by the UNP. The new government finally issued regulations implementing the use of Tamil for administrative and educational purposes in the Tamil regions in the north and north-east, as well as rescinding some of the more draconian anti-Tamil measures of the previous SLFP government (Kearney, 1967, pp. 128–131). The SLFP, now in opposition, immediately attacked the new government on the language issue. By 1970, it was back in power, this time championing a university admissions policy that favoured Sinhalese and discriminated against Tamils. Accordingly, 'Tamil enrollment in universities plummeted … although Tamils were still disproportionately overrepresented in Sri Lanka's universities in 1975' (DeVotta, 2003, p. 131).

Hence, two decades after independence, Sri Lanka's language regime was in full throttle, geared towards economically developing a Sinhalese middle class. Tamil linguistic 'disenfranchisement increased the cost of access to public employment such as civil service jobs and public resources such as higher education' for Tamils, placing them at a serious disadvantage to Sinhalese (Dower et al., 2015, p. 4). This predominantly instrumentalist explanation of the Sri Lanka conflict is not robust enough. Although language politics, as well as the university admissions issue, had paid big dividends to the rising Sinhalese middle class, the majority of Sinhalese were poor and rural. As early as the 1956 riots, low-skilled, manual Sinhalese labourers were rampaging against rural Tamils (Tambiah, 1996, pp. 83–86). Neither the Sinhalese labourers nor the rural Tamils would have been competing for public service or professional jobs or seeking admission to university. In Sri Lanka's post-independence climate of ethnic outbidding, language was being socially and politically constructed, not only as a skill for economic advancement but as the predominant marker of increasingly politicized communal identities. Language policy, which had economic implications for the middle class, became 'interwoven' with economic development policies oriented towards the Sinhalese masses (Tambiah, 1996, p. 86). Most prominent have been rural development projects that entail relocating rural landless Sinhalese to less-populated, predominantly Tamil areas, with government infrastructure such as irrigation schemes being supplied to develop these arid regions. According to Stanley Tambiah (ibid.), as early as 1949 the Tamil leader, Chelvanayakam, claimed that the government's resettlement policy 'was even more dangerous to the Tamil people than the Sinhala-language policy'.

Although both Sinhalese parties championed the resettlement schemes, which continue today with the Mahaweli Development Project, the SLFP had distinguished itself from the UNP by adopting a more socialist, basic-needs approach to economic development. When the UNP returned to power in 1977, 'against the backdrop of a stagnating economy' (Pant, 1986, p. 43) it reoriented the country's economic development strategy from import substitution industrialization to export-oriented industrialization, resulting in the growth of the garment industry in export processing zones clustered around Colombo. By the early 1980s, with recession in most of the developed market economies, and the Third World debt crisis looming, Sri Lanka's new economic development strategy was sputtering (Pant, 1986). Nominally to the benefit of the Sinhalese urban working class, this development strategy was negatively impacting on small shopkeepers. The latter were predominantly Sinhalese and couldn't compete against the flood of imported goods resulting from market liberalization that accompanied the new development strategy.

This change in economic development strategies provides an important context for the 1983 riots that marked the beginning of the civil war. Tambiah

(1996, pp. 96–99) notes that the targets of Sinhalese rioters in the Colombo area included garment factories, Tamil-owned small (petty bourgeoisie) shops that carried imported goods, as well as the big Tamil industrial houses, these all being 'sites of new industrial development stimulated by the economic liberalization initiated by the new government in 1977'. Tambiah (1996, p. 100) asks: 'to what extent [did] the "liberalized open economy" and capitalist, market-oriented policies introduced ... [create] economic dislocations injurious to segments of the Sinhalese population, who might have sponsored, supported, and even participated in varying degrees in the spate of riots against the Tamils?' He answers by claiming that 'Tamils were targeted [because] they were perceived as privileged and a suitable object of redressive action on behalf of the majority Sinhalese population, especially its poorer segments' (ibid.). Tambiah implies that the economic development strategy adopted in 1977 exacerbated the on-going ethnolinguistic conflict. Others suggest that the conflict undermined the success of the new economic development strategy: DeVotta (2003, p. 135) quotes a 1983 article from *The Economist* remarking that 'the majority Sinhalese observed that more than half of "their" new industries were Tamil-owned – and, cutting the nose to spite the face, burnt down the Tamil factories'. According to *The Economist* account, the Sinhalese were not acting in their economic interests. They were reacting on the basis of a socially and politically constructed ethnolinguistic divide, well entrenched despite the UNP government's recognition of Tamil as a national language in the new 1978 constitution.

Nor did the 1978 constitutional provision regarding Tamil have any effect on the alienated Tamil youth who had formed the Liberation Tigers of Tamil Eelam. In 1979, the UNP government passed a draconian Prevention of Terrorism Act, and democratic parliamentary elections were suspended in 1982 in the face of Tamil Tiger violence and the looming civil war. When the electoral process was finally reinstated in 1989 (1988 for presidential elections), the Indian Army had already been invited in to 'deal with' the Tamil insurgency only to find itself in a Vietnam-like quagmire. The Indians exited in 1990 and the following year, while campaigning, Rajiv Gandhi, who was the Indian prime minister at the time of India's intervention in the Sri Lankan civil war, was assassinated by a female Tamil Tiger suicide bomber.

The rest of the story of Sri Lanka's civil war is well known and need not be repeated here (see e.g. Oberst, 2013). After the Tamil Tiger defeat by the Sri Lankan military in May 2009, cosmetic attempts at resurrecting and implementing the guarantees in the 1978 constitution for Tamil have been made. But with (SLFP) President Mahinda Rajapaksa basking in the glory of military victory, consolidating his power (along with his brothers') into what many perceived as an increasingly authoritarian regime, and thumbing his nose at war-crime indictments, there has been little expectation that there will be any genuine post-war reconciliation between Sinhalese and Tamils. Given that many Tamils remained in internal displacement and detention camps waiting for security clearance, the language issue seemed less significant. Although economic development has been negatively impacted on by the civil war, the bigger casualty has been democratic institutions and human rights. The irony is that democratic institutions, in particular electoral democracy, structured a language regime that significantly contributed to the civil war.

17.4   Nepal

Nepal seems to be the quintessential case confirming a negative correlation between linguistic diversity and economic development. An extremely diverse country linguistically, it is one of the poorest in the world. Yet the relation between Nepal's linguistic diversity and its economic performance is unclear and, at best, indirect. One of the reasons for Nepal's linguistic diversity is its topography: the Himalayas and their foothills isolate inhabitants in one valley from their neighbours in the next. This inhospitable terrain undoubtedly has impacted on economic development as well as political integration.

In the late 18th century, Nepali-speaking Gorkhas conquered the Kathmandu Valley, politically 'uniting' Nepal and establishing the political hegemony of the 'caste hill Hindu elite' who make up about 30–40 per cent of the population (Lawoti, 2014). Nepal's current-day borders were established by the early 19th century after a short border war with the British, thus incorporating not only myriad Tibeto-Burman speakers (Magar and Tamang speakers, at approximately 7 and 5 per cent of the population respectively, being among the largest) but also speakers of Indo-Aryan languages in the southern Terai region (making speakers of variants of Hindi the second largest language group in the country, upward of 20 per cent of the population). Hence Nepal was never colonized, although the British kept a British Resident in Kathmandu to 'advise' the Nepalese regime. From the 1850s to the 1950s, the Rana regime kept Nepal in a semi-feudal state, with no attempts at economic development or education (Sonntag, 1980). In these circumstances, Nepal's continuing linguistic diversity was hardly surprising – more likely an outcome of, rather than a barrier to (lack of) economic development.

Decolonization in the rest of South Asia brought about regime change in Nepal. With Indian backing, the Ranas were overthrown, replaced by a nascent parliamentary democracy led by a constitutional monarch, King Tribhuvan. Tribhuvan's son in 1960 replaced the democratic system with a *panchayat raj* – monarchical oligarchic rule 'guiding' the Nepalese from village through district, zonal and national levels. *Bikas* (development) was the gloss justifying a society based on a rigid Hindu caste hierarchy (Pigg, 1993). A monolingual language policy allowing for only the Nepali language to be used in all domains, including education, was tempered only by the limited penetration of the state (Sonntag, 2007). There was no significant resistance to this exclusionary policy because the country was so under-developed (Mukherji, 1986). In other words, attempts at linguistic rationalization – in Nepal's case through mandating Nepali as the sole official and national language – have little impact on linguistic diversity, economic development or conflict if there is no effective state. By the late 1980s, the biggest contributor to Nepal's economy was foreign development aid, accounting for approximately half of the state budget (Parajulee, 2000, p. 223).

Nepal's critical juncture, resulting in not only language regime change but also political regime change, was precipitated by economic issues. As a landlocked country, Nepal is dependent on India for transit of its international trade, not to mention for the little industrialization that Nepal has (Chitrakar, 1994). In 1989 the trade and transit treaty with India was due to expire. Negotiations soon became acrimonious, with India attempting to influence, some would say dictate to, the Nepalese regime. India imposed a blockade, closing Nepal's border crossings and 'spark[ing] off the movement that led to the overthrow of the monarchy in spring 1991' (Wagner, 2005, p. 10) by urbanites in Kathmandu frustrated at the king's kleptomaniac coterie and development policies. This first 'people's movement' (*jan andolan*) 'was relatively unconcerned with the language question ... It was after the democratization process was initiated that the language question was visibly raised' (Sonntag, 2003, p. 99). Requests and appeals to the Constitution Committee, operating on behalf of the new interim democratic government, were made by linguistic minorities, but not seriously entertained, resulting in 'a somewhat ambiguous position on the question of language' in the new constitution (Hutt, 1991, pp. 1028, 1036). Nepal was recognized as a 'multilingual' country, with Nepali as the official or state language (*rashtra bhasa*) and Nepal's other languages as national languages (*rashtriya bhasa*), a 'murky distinction' at best (Sonntag, 2003, p. 94). Furthermore, these constitutional designations did not entail any government obligation to formulate or implement multilingual policies (ibid., pp. 94–95).

By the mid-1990s, promising progress towards a new multilingual language regime entailed identification and standardization of languages to be used in broadcasting and other governmental services (Sonntag, 1995). The process highlighted the social and political construction of linguistic identity, with minorities such as Tharus searching for a common language and others such as Tamangs using their language to forge a common identity (ibid.). Progress was cut short, however, by the Maoist insurgency that erupted in 1996, leading to a ten-year civil war. While the Maoists included minority grievances in their platform, language demands took a backseat to religion and casteism. Mahendra Lawoti (2003) claims that at least initially the Maoists' concern for the Tibeto-Burman low-caste minorities was superficial, an appeal to get willing recruits to serve as cannon fodder in the civil war. The higher echelons of the Maoists remained dominated by upper-caste Nepali speakers. With the success of the Maoist insurgency and the second people's movement (which overthrew the monarchy once again after a new king had usurped power in 2005), a more inclusionary political regime was envisioned. The vision, however, has been thwarted by the inability of the constituent assembly to come up with a new constitution, primarily because of differences over issues of ethnolinguistic-based federalism and the electoral system (Lawoti, 2014). The stalemate reflects the continuing domination of the Nepali-speaking upper-caste hill Hindu elite.

The *panchayat raj* regime, followed by civil war and more recently on-going political instability, has not boded well for Nepal's economic development. If and when a new political regime emerges, it will govern a linguistically diverse country where linguistic identity has been constructed in the context of economic under-development and political conflict.

17.5   Pakistan

Pakistan, like Sri Lanka and Nepal, imposed a monolingual language regime on a linguistically diverse, new and modernizing 'nation-state'. The imposition of Urdu as the sole national and official language in Pakistan was even more artificial than the imposition of a Sinhala-only language regime in Sri Lanka or a Nepali-only language regime in Nepal. Urdu is a stylized version of the colloquial language spoken by both Muslims and Hindus in what is now central north India. In the context of increasingly politicized communalism in north India in the late 19th and early 20th century, Urdu became associated with Muslims and socially constructed as distinct from Hindi spoken by Hindus (King, 1994). When the Muslim League's demand for a separate 'nation' for Muslims was agreed to by the departing British, leading to the partition of British India into two separate and independent states, the leadership of the Muslim League was transplanted, along with Urdu, from north central India to the western wing of the new Islamic Republic of Pakistan. Hence Urdu was not the mother tongue of those residing in the territories of the British Raj that became Pakistan. Instead it was the language spoken by *muhajirs*, the migrants to Pakistan from India during the traumatic partition. *Muhajirs* composed Pakistan's bureaucratic and political elite, and were alienated from local roots, including the local landed aristocracy (Jalal, 1995). This alienation, with its linguistic dimension, contributed to an 'abject failure to institute...democracy' (ibid., p. 48; see also Oldenburg, 2010). In lieu of establishing democratic institutions, Pakistan rapidly drifted into a bureaucratic authoritarian regime upon independence, subsequently morphing into military regimes and what Ayesha Jalal (1995, p. 185) calls an 'aid-inebriated political economy of defence'.

Pakistani governments, whether civilian or military, have had difficulty holding the ethnolinguistic regions of the country together. Pakistan was imagined in the context of the 'two-nation theory': that Muslims and Hindus constituted two separate nations. But religion has not proven to be a strong enough glue. The most blatant disproof of the two-nation theory was the secession of Bangladesh in 1971. Formerly East Pakistan, religion was the only cultural bond that Bangladesh had to Pakistan. East Pakistanis spoke Bengali (also the official language of the state of West Bengal in India's federal union), ate and dressed as Bengalis, lived a thousand miles away from West Pakistan in much greater density, and had an economy based on primary commodities like jute and hence were much poorer than and dependent on West Pakistan. The East Pakistanis constituted a majority of the population of Pakistan: 'according to the 1951 census, 56 percent of Pakistan's population counted Bengali as their mother tongue' (Ayres, 2003, p. 57). When nearly all East Pakistanis voted for the Awami League in the 1970 election, leading to parliamentary victory and the expectation of an Awami League government in Islamabad, Pakistan's capital, the departing military ruler, Yahya Khan, annulled the election results rather than turn over power to an East Pakistani/Bengali government. This unleashed a civil war, with Yahya Khan's military brutally repressing Awami League supporters. Military repression quickly widened into an alleged genocide primarily targeting the minority (Bengali-speaking) Hindus living in East Pakistan (Bass, 2013). Faced with a massive refugee problem, as well as for regional hegemonic purposes, India intervened in the war, defeating the Pakistani army and ensuring Bangladesh's independence (ibid.).

Subsequent ethnolinguistic-based conflicts in what remained Pakistan, among the Sindhis (approximately 12 per cent of the total population), Baluchis (3 per cent of the population in 1981) and Pashtoons (about 13 per cent of the population), have echoes of the Bengali resistance (Ayres, 2003). The Sindhi-Muhajir conflict has taken on sectarian dimensions recently, and the Baluchis' and Pashtoons' identity struggles have become interwoven with the larger regional conflict involving Islamists in Afghanistan, Pakistan and Kashmir. Like the Sri Lankan case, conflict has moved beyond the language issue. With Punjabis dominating the political, bureaucratic and military elite, and Pakistan headed towards 'failed state' status, it is hard to see how economic development, let alone a resolution of regional conflict, can progress. This is despite a relative success of Pakistan's economic development after independence, compared to India (Mukherji, 1986), and implementation of green revolution technology in the 1960s. But Pakistan has rich and powerful friends and allies: the United States continues to supply Pakistan with enormous amounts of aid in return for Pakistan's alleged partnership in America's 'war on terrorism', and China is investing heavily in Pakistan, in particular a deep-water port in Baluchistan for oil shipments.

Jalal (1995, p. 183) claims that Pakistan is a

> vivid illustration of the proposition that...[regional] conflicts have less to do with cultural or 'ethnic' divisions in heterogeneous societies than with the complex and shifting ways in which social identities are forged and refashioned in response or resistance to structures of states and political economies.

In Pakistan's case, state structures and the political-economic regime directed by the state have been militarized. In this political-institutional context, endemic conflict seems inevitable.

17.6 Conclusion

What can we learn from these four South Asian case studies about the relationship between language, economic development and regional conflicts? First and foremost is that the political context of this relationship is imperative for any analysis. While all four cases are marked by linguistic diversity, three of the cases (Sri Lanka, Nepal and Pakistan) opted for monolingual language regimes, with India being the only case of espousing multilingualism through political structures such as linguistic federalism. Although India has witnessed conflict over language, such conflicts have not threatened the national integrity of the country.

India has also sustained democratic institutional structures. The only other prolonged democracy among our case studies was Sri Lanka. Would some kind of federal political structure have circumvented the Sri Lankan civil war? The same question is now posed in Nepal as it embarks on a democratic transition. On the other hand, Pakistan did have a federal structure – although not one that acknowledged regional languages – and its national unity was shattered by civil war. While this suggests that political systems and institutional structures are not the determining variable, any more so than the degree of linguistic diversity or economic development, in ensuring national stability and integrity, their neglect in analysis can lead to faulty causal relationships.

All of the South Asian cases are linguistically heterogeneous, the least being Sri Lanka. If there was a negative relation between linguistic diversity and economic development, as posited originally by Fishman and Pool, then Sri Lanka should be the most economically developed. Yet Sri Lanka's civil war has thwarted any such accomplishment. Furthermore, as we saw above, the Sri Lankan political elite instituted a language regime premised on increasing linguistic difference in order to enhance economic development, the reverse of the Fishman–Pool hypothesis. In Nepal, linguistic diversity and a dismal record of economic development appear to be co-determined – in spite of the state's attempts at linguistic rationalization. Here conflict and civil war stemmed from weak state institutional structures and poor economic performance, rather than threats posed by linguistic diversity.

As suggested above, causal relations between linguistic diversity, economic development and regional conflict emanating from primordialist and instrumentalist approaches are not sufficiently robust. Understanding language difference and diversity as socially and politically constructed through language regimes that are path-dependent on state institutional contexts (Sonntag and Cardinal, 2015) enriches analyses of language, regional conflicts and economic development.

References

E. Albaugh (2013) 'Wars, Schools and Cities: Language Spread in West Africa', paper presented at Congrès AFSP (Association Française de Science Politique) Paris 2013, ST14 Governing Languages, 9–11 July.

B. Anderson (1991) *Imagined Communities* (London: Verso).

J.-L. Arcand and F. Grin (2013) 'Language in Economic Development: Is English Special and Is Linguistic Fragmentation Bad?' In E. Erling and P. Seargeant (eds) *English and Development: Policy, Pedagogy and Globalization* (Bristol: Multilingual Matters), pp. 246–266.

A. Ayres (2003) 'The Politics of Language Policy in Pakistan' In M. Brown and S. Ganguly (eds) *Fighting Words: Language Policy and Ethnic Relations in Asia* (Cambridge, MA: The MIT Press), pp. 51–80.

R. Baird (2003) 'The Convergence of Distinct Worlds: Nehru and Gandhi' In H. Coward (ed.) *Indian Critiques of Gandhi* (Albany, NY: State University Press of New York), pp. 19–39.

G. Bass (2013) *The Blood Telegram: Nixon, Kissinger and a Forgotten Genocide* (New York: Knopf).

P. Brass (1991) *Ethnicity and Nationalism: Theory and Comparison* (Thousand Oaks, CA: Sage).

P. Brass (2009) 'Elite Interests, Popular Passions, and Social Power in the Language Politics of India' In A. Sarangi (ed.) *Language and Politics in India* (New Delhi: Oxford University Press), pp. 183–217.

D. Chakrabarty (1998) 'Modernity and Ethnicity in India' In D. Bennett (ed.) *Multicultural States: Rethinking Difference and Identity* (London and New York: Routledge), pp. 91–110.

P. Chatterjee (1986) *Nationalist Thought and the Colonial World: A Derivative Discourse* (London: Zed Books).

R. Chitrakar (1994) *Foreign Investment and Technology Transfer in Developing Countries* (Brookfield, VT: Avebury).

S. Corbridge and J. Harriss (2000) *Reinventing India* (Cambridge, UK: Polity).

J. Dasgupta (2003) 'Language Policy and National Development in India' In M. Brown and Š. Ganguly (eds) *Fighting Words: Language Policy and Ethnic Relations in Asia* (Cambridge, MA: MIT Press), pp. 21–50.

K. Deutsch (1953) *Nationalism and Social Communication* (New York: Wiley).

N. DeVotta (2003) 'Ethnolinguistic Nationalism and Ethnic Conflict in Sri Lanka' In M. E. Brown and Š. Ganguly (eds) *Fighting Words: Language Policy and Ethnic Relations in Asia* (Cambridge, MA: MIT Press), pp. 105–139.

P. Dower, V. Ginsburgh and S. Weber (2015) 'Colonial Legacy, Linguistic Disenfranchisement and the Civil Conflict in Sri Lanka', unpublished manuscript.

W. Easterly and R. Levine (1997) 'Africa's Growth Tragedy: Policies and Ethnic Divisions', *The Quarterly Journal of Economics*, 112, 1203–1250.

M. Emeneau (1956) 'India as a Linguistic Area', *Language*, 32, 3–16.

J. Fishman (1968) 'Some Contrasts between Linguistically Homogeneous and Linguistically Heterogeneous Polities' In J. Fishman, C. Ferguson and J. Dasgupta (eds) *Language Problems of Developing Nations* (New York: Wiley), pp. 53–68.

C. Geertz (1973) *The Interpretation of Cultures* (New York: Basic Books).

A. George and A. Bennett (2005) *Case Studies and Theory Development in the Social Sciences* (Cambridge, MA: Belfer Center for Science for International Affairs, Harvard University).

V. Ginsburgh and S. Weber (forthcoming) 'Linguistic Diversity, Standardization and Disenfranchisement' In B.-A. Wickström and M. Gazzola (eds) *The Economics of Language Policy* (Cambridge, MA: MIT press).

J. Greenberg (1956) 'The Measurement of Linguistic Diversity', *Language*, 32, 109–115.

S. Harrison (1960) *India: The Most Dangerous Decades* (Princeton, NJ: Princeton University Press).

D. Horowitz (1985) *Ethnic Groups in Conflict* (Berkeley: University of California Press).

M. Hutt (1991) 'Drafting the Nepal Constitution, 1990', *Asian Survey*, 31, 1020–1039.

C. Jaffrelot (2003) *India's Silent Revolution: The Rise of the Low Castes in North Indian Politics* (Delhi: Permanent Black).

A. Jalal (1995) *Democracy and Authoritarianism in South Asia* (Cambridge: Cambridge University Press).

R. Kearney (1967) *Communalism and Language in the Politics of Ceylon* (Durham, NC: Duke University Press).

C. King (1994) *One Language, Two Scripts: The Hindi Movement in Nineteenth Century North India* (Bombay: Oxford University Press).

R. King (1998) *Nehru and the Language Politics of India* (New Delhi: Oxford University Press).

K. Kumar (1991) 'Foul Contract,' *Seminar*, 377, 43–46.

C. LaDousa (2014) *Hindi Is Our Ground, English Is Our Sky* (New York and Oxford: Berghahn).

D. Laitin (1988) 'Language Games', *Comparative Politics*, 20, 289–302.

D. Laitin (1989) 'Language Policy and Political Strategy in India', *Policy Sciences*, 22, 415–436.

D. Laitin (2000) 'What Is a Language Community?', *American Journal of Political Science*, 44, 142–155.

M. Lawoti (2003) 'Maoists and Minorities: Overlap of Interests or the Case of Exploitation?', *Studies in Nepali History and Society*, 8, 67–97.

M. Lawoti (2014) 'Nepal' In R. Oberst et al. *Government and Politics in South Asia*, 7th edn (Boulder: Westview), pp. 397–485.

T. Mabry (2011) 'Language and Conflict', *International Political Science Review*, 32, 189–207.

S. Makoni and A. Pennycook (2007) *Disinventing and Reconstituting Languages* (Clevedon: Multilingual Matters).

L. Mitchell (2009) *Language, Emotion, and Politics in South India* (Ranikhet: Permanent Black).

I. Mukherji (1986) 'Economic Growth and Social Justice in South Asia: Growing Potential for Domestic Conflict' In U. Phadnis, S. Muni and K. Bahadur (eds) *Domestic Conflicts in South Asia, Volume 2: Economic and Ethnic Dimensions* (New Delhi: South Asian Publishers), pp. 1–25.

D. Nettle (2000) 'Linguistic Fragmentation and the Wealth of Nations: The Fishman-Pool Hypothesis Reexamined', *Economic Development and Cultural Change*, 48, 335–348.

N. Nilekani (2008) *Imagining India: The Idea of a Renewed Nation* (New York: Penguin).

M. Noonan (2010) 'Genetic Classification and Language Contact' In R. Hickey (ed.) *The Handbook of Language Contact* (Oxford: Wiley-Blackwell), pp. 48–65.

R. Oberst (2013) 'Ethnic Conflict in Sri Lanka' In S. Wadley (ed.) *South Asia in the World* (Armonk, NY: M.E. Sharpe), pp. 201–214.

P. Oldenburg (2010) *India, Pakistan, and Democracy* (London and New York: Routledge).

G. Pant (1986) ' "New" Economic Policy of Sri Lanka: Conflict and Contradictions' In U. Phadnis, S. D. Muni and K. Bahadur (eds) *Domestic Conflicts in South Asia, Volume 2: Economic and Ethnic Dimensions* (New Delhi: South Asian Publishers), pp. 41–60.

R. Parajulee (2000) *The Democratic Transition in Nepal* (New York: Rowman & Littlefield).

S. Pigg (1993) 'Unintended Consequences: The Ideological Impact of Development in Nepal', *Comparative Studies of South Asia, Africa and the Middle East*, 13, 45–58.

J. Pool (1972) 'National Development and Language Diversity' In J. Fishman (ed.) *Advances in the Sociology of Language*, vol. 2 (The Hague: Mouton), pp. 213–230.

D. Posner (2004) 'Measuring Ethnic Fractionalization in Africa', *American Journal of Political Science*, 48, 849–863.

A. Rai (2000) *Hindi Nationalism* (Hyderabad: Orient Longman).

B. Raina (1991) 'A Note on Language, and the Politics of English in India' In S. Joshi (ed.) *Rethinking English* (New Delhi: Trianka), pp. 264–297.

A. Sarangi (2015) 'India's Language Regime: The Eighth Schedule' In L. Cardinal and S. Sonntag (eds) *State Traditions and Language Regimes* (Montreal: McGill-Queen's University Press), pp. 205–218.

H. Schiffman (2010) 'Language Contact in South Asia' In R. Hickey (ed.) *The Handbook of Language Contact* (Oxford: Wiley-Blackwell), pp. 738–756.

J. Scott (2009) *The Art of Not Being Governed: An Anarchist History of Upland Southeast Asia* (New Haven: Yale University Press).

D. Sheth (1990) 'No English Please, We're Indian', *Illustrated Weekly of India*, 19 August, 34–37.

S. Sonntag (1980) 'Language Policy and Planning in Nepal', *ITL: Review of Applied Linguistics*, 48, 71–92.

S. Sonntag (1995) 'Ethnolinguistic Identity and Language Policy in Nepal', *Nationalism and Ethnic Politics*, 1, 116–128.

S. Sonntag (2003) *The Local Politics of Global English: Case Studies in Linguistic Globalization* (Lanham, MD: Lexington Books).

S. Sonntag (2007) 'Change and Permanence in Language Politics in Nepal' In A. Tsui and J. Tollefson (eds) *Language Policy, Culture, and Identity in Asian Contexts* (Mahwah: Lawrence Erlbaum), pp. 205–217.

S. Sonntag (2015) 'Narratives of Globalization in Language Politics in India' In T. Ricento (ed.) *The Political Economy of Language* (Oxford: Oxford University Press), 209–227.

S. Sonntag (forthcoming) 'Linguistic Diversity in India's Polity and Economy' In B.-A. Wickström and M. Gazzola (eds) *The Economics of Language Policy* (Cambridge, MA: MIT press).

S. Sonntag and L. Cardinal (2015) 'State Traditions and Language Regimes: Conceptualizing Language Policy Choices' In L. Cardinal and S. Sonntag (eds) *State Traditions and Language Regimes* (Montreal: McGill-Queen's University Press), pp. 3–26.

D. Stuligross and A. Varshney (2002) 'Ethnic Diversities, Constitutional Designs, and Public Policies in India' In A. Reynolds (ed.) *The Architecture of Democracy:*

Constitutional Design, Conflict Management, and Democracy (Oxford: Oxford University Press), pp. 429–458.

N. Subramanian (1999) *Ethnicity and Populist Mobilization: Political Parties, Citizens and Democracy in South India* (New York: Oxford University Press).

S. Tambiah (1996) *Leveling Crowds: Ethnonationalist Conflicts and Collective Violence in South Asia* (Berkeley: University of California Press).

C. Toffolo (ed.) (2003) *Emancipating Cultural Pluralism* (Binghamton: SUNY Press).

C. Wagner (2005) 'From Hard Power to Soft Power? Ideas, Interaction, Institutions, and Images in India's South Asia Policy', *Heidelberg Papers in South Asian and Comparative Politics* (May) (www.hpsacp.uni-hd.de/).

18

Is Language Destiny? The Origins and Consequences of Ethnolinguistic Diversity in Sub-Saharan Africa

Brandon de la Cuesta and Leonard Wantchekon

18.1 Introduction

The economic and political effects of linguistic diversity have been the subject of scholarly research in both political science and economics for over a half-century, and many of the literature's seminal entries are case studies of the African continent. Early entries in political science (e.g. Fishman, 1968; Pool, 1972; Bates, 1974; Horowitz, 1985; Horowitz, 1991) and in economics (e.g. Esteban and Ray, 1994; Easterly and Levine, 1997; Sachs and Warner, 1997) set the tone for much of the research that followed, focusing on the ways in which the high levels of both ethnic and linguistic diversity in Africa, aided in part by the arbitrary nature of national boundaries in the wake of colonization, have reduced growth and contributed to political instability. Africa-centric studies of linguistic diversity have also played an integral part in informing broader literatures, particularly those related to the political economy of diversity and ethnic conflict (see e.g. Alesina et al., 1999; Alesina et al., 2003; Ahlerup and Olsson, 2011; Caselli and Coleman II, 2013; Alesina et al., 2015).

That Africa should be the focus of scholarship on the effects of linguistic diversity is no accident: sub-Saharan Africa has the highest regional linguistic diversity in the world, and contains the top 18 most linguistically diverse countries (Alesina et al., 2003, p. 163). The effects of that diversity are, with few exceptions, statistically significant and substantively important predictors of most outcomes of interest for economists and political scientists. Ethnolinguistic diversity – a measure that includes ethnic and linguistic components, and which we will discuss in greater detail below – has been associated, both in Africa and beyond, with greater redistribution (Desmet et al., 2009), lower public goods provision (Habyarimana et al., 2007), poor government policies (Easterly and Levine, 1997; Sachs and Warner, 1997), lower quality of governance (La Porta, 1999), and an increased probability of civil conflict

(Montalvo and Reynal-Querol, 2005). While the mechanisms that account for these relationships are often implicit or only partially theorized, the effects of linguistic diversity on the continent are in line with those in other regions: more diversity appears to be bad for economic performance (broadly defined) and for political stability as well. While modern statistical techniques have allowed for a more precise estimation of the effects of diversity, scholars as far back as Fishman (1968) and Pool (1972) have noted the strong correlation between poor political and economic outcomes and linguistic heterogeneity.[1]

Yet, as we discuss further below, the study of linguistic diversity in the African case has often been subsumed beneath, or conflated with, the studies of ethnic diversity. This blending of two forms of diversity – which, it must be noted, are often highly co-linear (Alesina et al., 2003, p. 162) – has been both a boon and a drawback for our understanding of the economic and political effects of linguistic diversity in Africa. On the one hand, the focus on linguistic diversity has enabled the development of global datasets that have underpinned much of the cross-national work that has come to define the literature (e.g. Alesina et al., 2003; Desmet et al., 2009). On the other hand, linguistic diversity is often taken as a proxy for broader measures of cultural and ethnic diversity rather than understood as possessing an effect in its own right (Desmet et al., 2009, p. 1292).

In this chapter, we examine the literature on ethnic and linguistic diversity together, both as a means of noting the similarity in the ways that each is thought to affect a range of political and economic outcomes, and to draw attention to the ways that linguistic diversity imposes a distinct set of obstacles to Africa's developing states. We discuss several mechanisms that have been proposed by the literature to help understand the effects of language on political and economic outcomes. We then propose a set of policies that would promote ethnic cooperation in spite of a high level of ethnic diversity in Africa. In doing so, we highlight cases in recent history where African governments have taken conscious steps to overcome considerable linguistic diversity, and have succeeded in creating stronger state institutions. Linguistic diversity – or a lack thereof – is not destiny. Rather, the difference between success and failure has often hinged not on how linguistically divided a country is, but on its government's capacity to overcome the obstacles diversity can (but need not) create.

The chapter proceeds as follows. First, we advance a two-part explanation for Africa's relatively high levels of ethnolinguistic diversity, one that emphasizes long-term trends in human settlement as well as the continent's more

---

[1] See Chapter 17 in this volume for a more in-depth discussion of these and other early works.

recent colonial history. We then review the existing literature, drawing attention to important measurement issues as well as outlining key findings, recent additions, and what we feel are fruitful areas for future research. Finally, we conclude by discussing how existing research can inform policies that seek to overcome some of the negative effects of ethnolinguistic diversity.

18.2   Why does Africa have such high levels of linguistic diversity?

There are two primary reasons for Africa's comparatively high levels of linguistic diversity, one rooted in historical patterns of migration and settlement occurring over thousands of years, the other in the way in which state borders were drawn at the eve of colonization on the continent. These two forces are also responsible, to a large extent, for Africa's high levels of ethnic diversity, and for the high correlation between both measures. While these forces have contributed to the poor outcomes often associated with diverse societies, the channels through which they do so may be quite different. In this section, we consider each in isolation, as well as the ways in which they have acted together to produce the poor economic and governance outcomes that have accounted for Africa's dismal growth record in the post-colonial period.

To begin, however, it is useful to note exactly how much more linguistically diverse Africa is with respect to other world regions. As a benchmark, Table 18.1 reports the share of total living languages by region for the world according to the most recent Ethnologue data. Despite having only 12.7 percent of the world's total population, Africa is home to nearly a third of its living languages, with the median number of speakers per language a mere 27,000 compared to Europe's 61,150. Comparing Africa with Asia, we see that while they have a nearly identical share of the world's living languages, Asia's share of the world population is nearly five times as large. As we will see, this means that many

Table 18.1   Africa's share of world languages

	Living languages		Speakers			
	Number	**%**	**Total (Million)**	**%**	**Mean (1,000)**	**Median (1,000)**
Africa	2,138	30.1	815	12.7	381.3	27.5
Americas	1,064	15.0	51	0.8	48.4	1.1
Asia	2,301	32.4	3,779	60.0	1,642.6	12
Europe	286	4.0	1,646	26.4	5,727.2	35.6
Pacific	1,313	18.5	6	0.1	5,166	0.95
Totals	7,102	100.0	6,291	100.0	877,751	7

Source: Ethnologue Global Dataset (2014).

of the welfare-decreasing aspects of linguistic diversity are more present in the African case than in other regions. Table 18.1, because it uses measures of currently spoken languages, also reveals a striking trend that will be discussed in greater detail below: the richest regions of the world are also those that have the fewest languages per capita.

18.2.1   The origins of ethnolinguistic diversity in Africa

The exceptional linguistic diversity of sub-Saharan Africa is rooted in its role as the 'cradle of humankind' (Ashraf and Galor, 2013, p. 2). East Africa is widely regarded as the population centre from which all early migration originated, and Africa has been home to both sedentary-agriculturalist and hunter-gatherer societies for longer than any other place on earth. Empirical evidence suggests that this feature is strongly related to levels of observed diversity today. Migratory distance from the early population centre of Addis Ababa, Ethiopia, for example, is a strong predictor of both genetic and ethnolinguistic diversity (Michalopoulos, 2012, p. 1510). The role of distance from this centre is substantively important, and is as important in explaining differences in diversity as geographic variation. But how does the comparatively longer settlement history of Africa translate into greater diversity? Existing work suggests at least two mechanisms. The first, proposed by Michalopoulos (2012), is that, in addition to being the origin point for early migration, Africa also exhibits high levels of geographic variation. Reviewing biological and anthropological work, Michalopoulos (2012) finds that the importance of geographic variation for linguistic diversity is substantial: examining North America during the time of European colonization, Mace and Pagel (1995) find linguistic diversity to be approximately six times higher at latitudes that support greater ecosystem variation. This effect persists even when latitude is ignored and only habitat variety is considered; more ecological variation is associated with a greater number of linguistically different human populations. Africa, by virtue of having so much of its total landmass in tropical or near-tropical latitudes (a much greater share, in fact, than any other continent), exhibits extremely high levels of ecological diversity. The greater geographical variation induced by Africa's location relative to the equator has thus contributed to a higher level of linguistic diversity than any other place in the world.

The relationship between ecological diversity and species diversity is not, in fact, limited to *Homo sapiens*. Rapaport's Rule, which originated from the observation that the range size of a species increases with latitude, has long been noted in both terrestrial and aquatic species. In the case of linguistic diversity, Mace and Pagel (1995, p. 20) conjecture that the relationship between ecological and linguistic diversity may arise either because the underlying climatic or geographic feature that promotes habitat variety may also encourage linguistic diversity, or because the latter is a function of the former. This connection between linguistic and non-human species diversity also holds in Africa, where studies have found that vertebrate species diversity and cultural diversity are closely related (Moore et al., 2002), and that African countries exhibiting high bird and mammal diversity are also linguistically diverse.

The mechanism that accounts for the relationship between habitat and linguistic diversity, however, has only recently become the focus of rigorous quantitative scholarship. In a recent entry, Michalopoulos (2012) suggests that geographic diversity gives rise to linguistic diversity via the formation of location-specific human capital. Using a novel dataset of agricultural suitability, Michalopoulos (2012) finds that variation in land quality and elevation – which affects both land productivity and rainfall – is statistically and substantively significant predictors of modern linguistic fractionalization. While this finding is supportive but not conclusive evidence of a skill-specificity explanation, an examination of linguistic groups in Africa finds a statistically significant correlation between pairs of subsistence practices of non-adjacent areas whose inhabitants share a common language. Simply put, as humans adapted to their environment by cultivating the skills necessary to succeed, the importance of location-specific knowledge limited the possibility of local migration. Over time, Michalopoulos suggests, this dynamic led to the formation of localized identities, homogenizing populations that lived within similar ecosystems while also accentuating differences between ecosystems.

In an earlier qualitative study, Bates (1990) notes a similar differentiation in the structure of kinship networks and the stock of human capital according to ethnolinguistic group. For Bates (1990, p. 57), variation in the local environment, particularly in rainfall, was a critical determinant of the nature of the agrarian activity that could be sustained there:

> In many portions of Eastern Africa, environmental conditions are a function of altitude. Lower elevations yield semi-arid environments. Rainfall is infrequent; it generates but limited amounts of moisture; and it is unreliable... The result is higher levels of risk. At higher elevations, rainfall is more frequent; it is also greater in quantity and more reliable, enabling the production of standing crops. At such altitudes, people invest in crops of higher value, such as tea bushes and coffee trees, and establish permanent gardens on plots of fixed locations.

The result of this elevation-induced variation in climate, Bates suggests, is that groups inhabiting different elevation zones developed, over time, different risk-sharing institutions, which in turn led them to invest their material wealth in different forms of human capital. For the Luo, who live at lower elevations, the optimal response to more variation in rainfall and less productive land was to spread risk through a lineage system that granted both rights and obligations to even distantly related family members. This allows, among other things, for the transfer of livestock to healthier pastures owned by family members during times of drought. Because rights to use pastures are granted by lineage, rights of access are given to all households that can count themselves as part of the lineage (ibid., p. 158). When individuals die, their assets are distributed broadly across the lineage, and even while alive households are expected to support others in their lineage. Because of the relatively higher risk faced by the low-altitude Luo, households did not accumulate wealth, but rather used that wealth to invest in the lineage structure, increasing their effective insurance against hard times.

In contrast to the Luo, the Kikuyu, who live at a much higher altitude where rain is both more abundant and more reliable, specialized in cash crops that yielded greater economic returns but also were more capital-intensive. Reflecting the relatively lower risk environment, the Kikuyu eschewed the extended kinship of the lineage system for a household-centric family system that allowed for individual families to amass much larger amounts of wealth, contributing both to a higher level of income inequality but also higher levels of literacy, education and urban migration (ibid., p. 154). While Bates does not make explicitly the argument that Michalopoulos (2012) would make two decades later, it represents another channel – social organization – through which variation in geography can induce, over time, the endogenous emergence of diversity. It is also worth noting that the Luo-Kikuyu case, in which language and ethnicity overlap nearly perfectly, is the rule rather than the exception in Africa. Indeed, so strong is this correlation that ethnic diversity and linguistic diversity often produce nearly identical substantive results when used in a cross-country setting. The empirical regularity with which this occurs is most likely due to the fact that the same forces – climatic and geographic variation – drive both forms of differentiation. As we will see in the following sections, this historical process of differentiation has important implications for contemporary patterns of economic prosperity and political conflict. Perhaps nowhere is this more true than in Kenya, the modern home to the Luo and Kikuyu tribes, where political competition is intensely tribalistic and the two most recent presidential elections have seen Kikuyu-led coalitions narrowly defeating their Kalenjin-Luo competitors (see Gibson and Long, 2009, p. 5).

18.2.2 Border assignment and the post-colonial period

While African states were granted sovereignty only in the mid-20th century, most contemporary borders were drawn well before decolonization. In fact, much of the African map was drawn in the late 19th century, starting with the Berlin Conference in 1884 and five additional agreements struck in the following decade. As European powers moved into Africa, they established colonies, trade routes, and spheres of influence on the continent. Yet they had relatively little information of local geography or ethnic composition of the regions they negotiated over (Michalopoulos and Papaioannou, 2011). The result of this lack of knowledge was two-fold. First, the borders themselves were remarkably artificial, often consisting of long stretches of straight, clean lines unbroken or bent by natural barriers such as mountains or waterways. So artificial are these barriers that they are visually apparent on a standard map, even at a cursory glance. Statistics tells a similar story: 80 percent of African borders, according to Alesina et al. (2011, p. 246), are drawn along latitudinal or longitudinal lines. Other estimates are more conservative but nonetheless speak to the arbitrariness of border assignment. Posner (2006), for example, reports that 44 percent of borders in Africa follow meridians or parallels, while an additional 30 percent are drawn along rectilinear or curved lines.

Second, and most importantly, the inattention to existing social and political units was such that borders frequently bisected ethnolinguistic groups, placing pieces of a single ethnolinguistic unit in multiple countries. Previously coherent units, which were governed by the same set of kinship obligations and social norms, were broken apart and subsumed beneath a central government whose boundaries were set not by consensus or the ability to broadcast power, but by (uninformed) European bureaucrats who had limited and often incorrect information about the distribution and size of linguistic groups.

In an early attempt to quantify just how fractionalized African states were as a result of this process, Asiwaju (1985) estimated that the border assignment partitioned 177 ethnic or cultural groups. Even after decolonization and formal independence, the vast majority of these borders remained unchanged. Upon granting formal independence, most European powers were eager to maintain the economic and political partnerships of their now-former colonies, and had little interest in border alterations that might endanger them (Jackson and Rosberg, 1982). African leaders, for their part, were focused on the task of nation building, and believed that this process was more urgent and important than (potentially enormous) changes in their countries' shape (Michalopoulos and Papaioannou, 2011).

The post-colonial state formation process in sub-Saharan Africa was thus highly artificial relative to that of Europe, which took place over centuries and through a succession of armed conflict and political compromise between and among its indigenous peoples (Tilly, 1990; Herbst, 2000). Equally as important, by the time many African states were recognized, the possibility of meaningful changes in state size or shape relative to the status quo was remote; international norms had moved towards a 'juridical' notion of statehood whereby states were defined not by the areas over which they exercised power but by the borders ascribed to them, irrespective of the existence of a coherent or powerful political unit (Jackson and Rosberg, 1982). This criterion was substantially different from that which prevailed during European state formation, where the ability to control and defend a territory were necessary conditions for recognition by other states in the system. Nearly every modern African state would have failed this test at the time of formal independence (Alesina et al., 2011, p. 251).

To get a sense of exactly how poorly post-colonial boundaries matched the existing ethnic and linguistic units, Figure 18.1 shows, on the left, a commonly used map of ethnopolitical units on the eve of African independence (Murdock, 1959), and on the right, the same map overlaid with the juridical borders of modern African states. As is clear from the left panel, boundaries rarely respected existing political boundaries. Many countries bifurcated multiple ethnic groups and included multiple groups in a single country.[2] The level of incongruence is striking and is a major source of the high levels of linguistic diversity we observe on the continent. In attempting to quantify the level of bifurcation, Michalopoulos and Papaioannou (2014) find that more than a quarter of all ethnic groups can be classified as partitioned – that is, as having 10 percent or more of its population residing in a different country than the larger portion. The practical effect of this level of fractionalization on African polities is perhaps best captured by the fact that, in the median African country, between 40 and 43 percent of its population belongs to one of these partitioned groups (Alesina et al., 2011; Michalopoulos and Papaioannou, 2014). Not all ethnic groups, particularly those that are geographically proximate to each other, speak different languages, and many speak dialects of a common language family. As we discuss in greater detail below, however, there is substantial evidence from the cognitive psychology that the strength of boundaries are less important than the existence of the boundaries themselves (Garcia-Montalvo and Reynal-Querol, 2005). Thus, even where dialects are mutually intelligible, the effects of linguistic heterogeneity may nonetheless be felt.

The practical effect of border assignment on the continent was, on balance, to deepen within-country linguistic diversity. The previous section noted that this diversity was already high, due largely to Africa's comparatively long history of human settlement, which interacted with geographic diversity to produce the endogenous formation of distinct human populations whose languages diverged over time. Yet, this spatial diversity was a necessary but not sufficient condition for the high levels of linguistic fractionalization we observe in modern Africa. Had borders followed pre-existing linguistic cleavages – which, it must be noted, were often also political cleavages – the continent would have comprised of many, smaller states rather than the comparatively few, large ones

---

[2] Note also the decrease in the number of groups and increase in their relative range as one moves away from the equator, consistent with Rapaport's Rule.

521

Figure 18.1 Spatial distribution of ethnic groups (left panel) and modern state boundaries (right panel)

that exist today. The size and shape of African countries would resemble the complicated jigsaw puzzle of Western Europe, rather than the straight lines of US states. Instead, the arbitrary assignment of national borders created in Africa resemble a disproportionate number of what Alesina et al. (2011) term 'artificial states'. These boundaries did not respect existing linguistic or political units, and indeed often split such units up, placing them on either side of the new border. It is impossible to understate the importance of the mismatch between political units and state boundaries. Rather than creating linguistically and culturally homogeneous countries where political leaders were seen as representing a single people, Africa's 'artificial states' were ones in which many heterogeneous units were forced to compete for political power.

Just as important as absolute levels of heterogeneity is the form that such heterogeneity takes. In constructing his own measure of ethnic and cultural diversity, Fearon (2003, p. 204) finds Africa housing, by far, the largest number of groups per country at 8.16, nearly doubling the groups per country of the next region. While Africa accounts for only a quarter of total countries, it houses 43 percent of its ethnic groups (ibid., p. 205). More importantly, however, while diversity in the rest of the world often takes the form of a single majority group and several smaller groups, this is not the case in Africa. Instead, African diversity tends to be characterized by several groups whose relative size falls far below the majority threshold. As a result, African politics is, broadly speaking, characterized by unstable, large, and unwieldy coalitions comprised of several small groups. As we will see later, the large number of ethnolinguistic groups has contributed to conflict and poor governance on the continent in a way that is exceptionally rare in more homogeneous societies.

18.2.3 Diversity as both symptom and cause

Linguistic diversity is often thought to activate a series of mechanisms that lead to poor governance. While we will touch on these mechanisms more deeply later in the chapter, it is important to note that linguistic diversity in Africa is both a consequence of its pre-colonial past and a cause of the continent's modern political history. It is a cause insofar as linguistic diversity: imposes transaction costs in the form of linguistic barriers; makes inter-group competition more likely due to the strength of linguistic boundaries; and may also structure democratic political competition such that large linguistic groups come to dominate, and perhaps even exploit, smaller ones. Yet, while there is little doubt that diversity can have negative consequences for a range of economic and political outcomes, Africa's diversity is, at least partially, a by-product of a political process that had a substantial role in producing such outcomes, a role that both reinforced the negative features of diversity and acted independently of it. A good example of the independent effect of this political process can be found in the role of the prevailing social norms that existed at the time of decolonization. While colonial administrators built institutions sufficient for the limited functions required of the colonial state, such as levying taxes and delivering basic services (Sandbrook, 1985), they were able to do so because they were insulated from the social obligations and pressures of the African society over which they ruled.

These institutions, particularly the merit-based civil service, were not compatible with existing social norms, which may emphasize kinship and familial ties over objective performance. After independence, norms of intra-elite redistribution, kinship obligations and the dominance of hierarchical, particularistic forms of provision often referred to as 'patrimonialism' reasserted themselves in many countries. To paraphrase Peter Ekeh, African leaders were forced to cater to 'two publics', with ethnic allegiances much stronger than the civic-minded, careerist goals of colonial administrators. The result was that the modern African state came to have the trappings of well-developed institutions, but the actors who inhabited those institutions were subject to social pressures that may have undermined their efficacy. This dynamic occurred in the context of high linguistic diversity, but was independent of it: even a linguistically homogeneous society would have found itself in a similar circumstance. Thus, while we believe that linguistic diversity can be rightly considered to have a causal effect on political and economic processes, the effects of it should not be confused with the effects of conditions that often accompany that diversity.

Equally as important, the political incentives of colonial administrators also led them, in some cases, to artificially create diversity or to heighten existing ethnolinguistic boundaries. It has long been recognized by Africanists and political scientists more generally that colonial administration, in some cases, led to the creation of new ethnic identities (e.g. Horowitz, 1985). Colonial administration was 'thin' across much of Africa insofar as its reach was limited. As a result, the dominant strategy in several cases was to rely on intermediaries, purchasing their acquiescence with monetary means or by granting some local autonomy (see e.g. the case of Nigeria in Kohli, 2004). In doing so, colonial administrators often drew boundaries and conceptualized groups in ethnic terms.

This had the dual effect of creating identities that may have pre-existed but were less important and, in some cases, privileged certain ethnic groups over others. Where the latter obtained, so-called 'ranked' ethnic groups came into being, with the canonical case being that of Rwanda, where the Tutsis were identified early by the Belgians and came to constitute a large majority of the civil service at the time of independence. As Horowitz (1985) notes, ethnic political competition has a strong equilibrium tendency: once it becomes the dominant mode of political organization, it is very difficult to mobilize along the class cleavages that constitute the major democratizing and development force in much of the broader comparative political economy literature (e.g. Boix, 2003; Acemoglu and Robinson, 2006). Importantly, ethnic salience also makes it much more difficult to negotiate political solutions in a democratic context. To the extent that colonialism encouraged this process, and in some cases created the ethnic categories that would later be the basis for political mobilization, it has a large impact on the subsequent development of African States. That Africa was ethnolinguistically diverse made the divide-and-rule strategy possible, but it is incorrect to conceptualize diversity as the root cause of Africa's governance difficulties in the post-colonial period.

The above discussion highlights two major features of linguistic diversity in Africa. First, Africa's historical role as the cradle of human civilization provided more time, relative to other, and more recently settled regions, for the endogenous formation of groups which acquired highly specialized, location-specific human capital – such as farming practices – that exploited very particular environmental conditions. Over time, this specialization led to the proliferation of small tribes with unique linguistic characteristics and social organization. Second, while this feature of the African continent made possible the extremely high levels of linguistic diversity we observe today, it was a necessary but not sufficient condition. The arbitrary and haphazard nature of African borders, drawn as they were by European colonizers with little local knowledge and no incentive to respect pre-existing political or linguistic units, is ultimately responsible for Africa's linguistic diversity. Had borders drawn with attention to the advantages of ethnic and linguistic homogeneity, Africa's developmental trajectory might have been very different.

In one of the most influential and widely cited articles on the effects of ethnolinguistic diversity, Easterly and Levine (1997) characterized Africa's post-independence experience as a 'growth tragedy'. Even while recognizing that Africa's diversity is, in part, a function of political processes, the existing literature suggests that linguistic diversity, whatever its cause, reduces growth, encourages lower levels of public goods provision, and may encourage group-based rather than class-based political competition. After discussing methodological issues regarding the measurement of diversity, the following section reviews this literature, focusing both on key findings and, critically, on the mechanism – that is, the causal process – put forth to explain them.

18.3   The economic and political effects of linguistic diversity

It is common in reviewing the literature on the effects of ethnolinguistic diversity to focus on their impacts in substantive areas such as conflict, growth or political stability. Yet, this approach tends to obscure what we suggest is a deeper and more important issue: the mechanisms that account for the observed relationships across issue areas. For this reason, we break existing research into two categories: those that demonstrate macro-level relationships between diversity and the outcome of interest, and those that provide micro-level evidence of the causal processes activated by such diversity.[3]

Within this latter category, we propose a further disaggregation by the type of mechanism. We suggest three mechanisms: strategy-based, preference-based and institution-based. Strategy-based mechanisms are those in which linguistic barriers force actors to behave differently when they are dealing with someone of a different language compared to the circumstance in which they are dealing with a co-linguist. Preference-based mechanisms are those that locate the obstacles of diverse societies in divergent preferences for public goods or public policies by group. This heterogeneity, in turn, makes agreement difficult and may result in sub-optimal provision. Finally, institution-based mechanisms are those in which prevailing political or economic institutions – particularly electoral ones – encourage political parties to mobilize along linguistic lines. Beyond heightening group boundaries further, this process also discourages the formation of broad-based, public-goods oriented political parties, which some have suggested are a necessary condition for sustained economic growth (e.g. Keefer and Vlaicu, 2007; Kitschelt and Wilkinson, 2007).

One or a combination of the three mechanisms discussed above can be at play in a given case or a given set of circumstances, but they all lend themselves to one basic implication: an economic policy that lowers the ethnic segregation and inter-regional economic integration will facilitate inter-ethnic cooperation (Wantchekon, 2014). The same can be said about electoral institutions that provide incentives for cross-ethnic campaigning (see e.g. Horowitz, 1985).

18.3.1 How has linguistic diversity been measured in Africa?

Here, we discuss two well-established ways of measuring diversity, and touch briefly on important theoretical points, including the implication of capturing the distance and relationship between two languages. Measurement strategy is not trivial. As we will see, choosing between measures requires the researcher to decide how to operationalize distances between languages, whether to account for that distance at all, what one means by 'diversity', and how to deal with the strategic use of linguistic categories by politicians. These choices are substantively important: some measures of linguistic diversity place African countries as the most diverse in the world, while others suggest it is far less so.

The most common measure of linguistic diversity in Africa, commonly referred to as ethnolinguistic fractionalization (ELF), measures the probability

---

[3] An example of the former is Easterly and Levine (1997), who utilize cross-country regression to demonstrate a negative growth effect of ethnolinguistic diversity, while an example of the latter is Miguel (2004), who examines the effects of diversity on household participation in public goods provision.

that two randomly selected individuals from the country's population will belong to the same ethnolinguistic group (e.g. Alesina et al., 1999, 2003; Desmet et al., 2009). Fractionalization for a given country *i* is computed using Greenberg's (1956) A-index:

$$A_i = 1 - \sum_{j=1}^{N} p_{ji}^2,$$

where p_{ji} is the proportion of the total population representing group *j* in country *i*.[4] This quantity is bounded between 0 and 1, with 0 representing total ethnic homogeneity and 1 representing the case where every individual belongs to a different group. Fractionalization is the most common measurement for indices of ethnolinguistic diversity, though scholars have criticized the underlying source data for earlier indices, the Atlas Narodov Mira (1964), as being highly imperfect (see e.g. Posner, 2004a). Measures of linguistic fractionalization are considered more exogenous and well-defined than their ethnic counterparts, both because language changes relatively slowly and because the possibility of manipulation of linguistic identity by political entrepreneurs is less of a concern than in the case of ethnicity.[5]

The principal disadvantage of the fractionalization A-index is that it does not take into account the distances between languages, both for those within the same family as well as those in separate families. The measure is thus highly sensitive to how one defines what constitutes a unique group. To take an example from eastern Africa, Ethiopia has four major language families: Cushitic, Nilo-Saharan, Omotic, and Semitic. Taking these designations as the dividing line between different languages would yield a modest fractionalization score, since there are only four major groups to which an individual can belong. However, each group hosts many dialects: in south-western Ethiopia alone, there are 87 distinct languages across these four families. Using these languages as the group designation in a fractionalization index would produce a much higher value.

The second most common measure is that of polarization, which measures the extent to which a society is organized into dissimilar groups. The concept of polarization and its measurement was formalized by Esteban and Ray (1994), who sought to measure the degree of antagonism present in a society and, in doing so, developed a measure of potential conflict independent of income inequality. Polarization is both intuitively appealing and relevant for the study of economic and political conflict, since we should expect that polities with

---

[4] While often referred to as ELF, this formula is also given in Greenberg (1956), where it is referred to as the A-index.
[5] For an overview of the difficulties in accurately measuring the number and type of ethnic cleavages, see Scarritt and Mozaffar (1999, p. 85).

fewer, highly dissimilar groups are more likely to experience such conflict than ones with more numerous but more similar groups.

Polarization measures are more commonly calculated using ethnicity rather than language (see e.g. Alesina et al., 2003), but Desmet et al. (2009) use a modified version of the Esteban and Ray measure that takes into account distances between languages. The latter captures Esteban and Ray's concept of 'alienation' by capturing the degree to which two languages are different from each other. Combining these two concepts, Desmet et al. (2009) define linguistic polarization as a combination of these two sources of antagonism, calculated as follows:

$$A(\alpha, d) = \sum_{j=1}^{K} \sum_{k=1}^{K} s_k s_j^{1+\alpha} d_{jk},$$

where the 'effective antagonism' of an individual in group j towards a second group k is the product of group j's share of the population, s_j, and group k's share of the population, s_k, weighted by the distance between the two groups, d_{jk}. The α parameter specifies the extent to which identification is a function of group size. For positive values of α, identification is assumed to be increasing. The ds measure the distance between any two groups in the society, and can be specified flexibly. This formula is a general one that encompasses the fractionalization index presented above, as well as several alternative measures discussed in greater detail in Desmet et al. (2009).

Of course, whether one prefers the conventional fractionalization to measures that include linguistic distance hinges on theories of group identification and on assumptions about the importance of distance itself. In justifying a measure of polarization that does not take into account the distances between groups, Garcia-Montalvo and Reynal-Querol (2005) suggest that the in-group–out-group tension created by boundaries, however thin, is more important than how similar the groups are with respect to the differentiating characteristic. This assertion is supported by experimental work in cognitive psychology, which suggests that even arbitrary group assignment using superficial criteria can induce subjects to favour in-group members and discriminate against out-groups (Tajfel and Turner, 1979; Hewstone et al., 2002).

Moreover, institutional features may make distances less important than they might otherwise be. In his study of Zambia, Posner (2006) notes that the move from single to multi-party rule encouraged politicians to cast aside the ethnic axis along which they had previously mobilized supporters, and to emphasize instead linguistic differences. To the extent that languages came to form the basis for political organization in Zambia, their relative distances are probably less important in explaining subsequent political outcomes. A strong state, by creating a common language, can also neutralize the importance of linguistic diversity. Tanzania's embrace of Swahili as a national bridging language is perhaps the best known of these efforts, and the most successful. By emphasizing Swahili in primary and secondary education, Tanzania was able to achieve better public goods provision than neighbouring Kenya (Miguel, 2004). Nonetheless, and as we will see in subsequent sections, the obstacles posed by linguistic diversity are several and severe. That Tanzania was able to ameliorate these problems is instructive, but its experience is the exception to a narrative of ethnolinguistic conflict that is rife with poor governance, poor growth and, not infrequently, violence conflict.

18.3.2 The effects of diversity: Macroeconomic evidence in Africa and beyond

The seminal paper in the debate over the effects of diversity in Africa is Easterly and Levine (1997), who utilize the traditional fractionalization measure presented above, using the Atlas Narodov Mira data in a series of cross-country regressions. Seeking to explain Africa's slow rate of growth in the second half of the 20th century, particularly with respect to their East Asian counterparts, they focus on the role of ethnolinguistic diversity, which they suggest can lead to poor public goods provision as well as inferior government policies. Noting the role of polarization echoed by Horowitz (1985), Easterly and Levine (1997) suggest that diversity may 'impede agreement about the provision of public goods and create positive incentives for growth-reducing policies ... that create rents for groups in power at the expense of society at large'. Controlling for a range of possible confounders, Easterly and Levine (1997) find that ethnolinguistic diversity reduces real GDP and leads to lower per-worker output. This relationship holds for several alternative measures of diversity and is substantively significant: Easterly and Levine (1997) suggest that approximately 28 percent of the difference in growth outcomes between Africa and fast-growing East Asia can be attributed to Africa's comparatively high diversity.

However, the across-the-board findings reported by Easterly and Levine (1997) using the conventional fractionalization measures have been disputed by Posner (2004a). Suggesting that the quantity of interest is the number of politically relevant groups rather than the absolute number, Posner (2004a) constructs an alternative index of politically relevant ethnic groups. When restricting the sample to African cases only, he finds that the conventional measure is not a statistically significant predictor of (log) schooling, financial depth, the black market premium, or a country's fiscal surplus. Nonetheless, even when African cases are considered in isolation, the negative finding of Easterly and Levine (1997) with respect to growth in real per capita GDP holds.

What is less clear is the mechanism that accounts for this relationship. While Easterly and Levine (1997) suggest that diversity may yield poor government policies, Posner (2004a), noting that the relationship between ELF and growth holds only when controlling for proxies of government policy, argues that the effect of diversity is likely coming through a channel other than government policy. A natural expectation of the mechanism proposed by Easterly and Levine (1997) – that of increased inter-group conflict – is that more diverse countries should be more likely to suffer from violent conflict as well as governance conflict. Yet, examining all violent domestic conflict since 1945, Fearon and Laitin (2003) find that more diverse countries are no more likely than their homogeneous counterparts to experience such events. Horowitz (1985) suggests that this relationship may be non-monotonic, with the greatest probability of diversity-driven conflict in countries with one majority group and one sizable minority group. Controlling for the presence of a large ethnic minority, however, does not produce statistical significance for measures of fractionalization (Fearon and Latin, 2003, p. 1302). In their study of violent conflict, Collier and Hoeffler (2004) also find little support for the importance of diversity. In a reply to Cederman and Girardin (2007), Fearon et al. (2007) likewise find little support for the diversity–violence link.

In a wide-ranging study of linguistic, ethnic, and religious fractionalization, Alesina et al. (2003) reproduce many of the same results as previous studies with respect to ethnolinguistic fractionalization. Interestingly, however, the results on the main dependent variables examined in Easterly and Levine (1997), with the important exception of growth and GDP, are strengthened when using linguistic fractionalization. Indeed, linguistic fractionalization has an especially strong relationship with schooling and the log of telephones per worker, important measures of human capital and technological progress. The interpretation of coefficients in fully specified models with GDP and growth as dependent variables, however, are not straightforward. This is especially true of measures of religious and ethnic diversity. While Easterly and Levine (1997) claim that their measures of ethnolinguistic diversity, being drawn from a dataset created by Russian surveyors in the mid-20th century, are plausibly exogenous with respect to growth and other economic indicators, subsequent work has demonstrated that ethnic categorization was often manipulated by colonial occupiers as well as indigenous politicians. There is also a vast literature on the strategic manipulation of ethnic categories by colonizers and local elites alike (see e.g. Bates, 1983; Fearon, 1999; Chandra, 2004; Posner, 2004b; Chandra, 2006; Posner, 2006), most of which treats ethnicity as an ascriptive category and thus one that is unlikely to be exogenous with respect to prevailing political and economic conditions.[6]

---

[6] Unlike language, where difference is much starker even for languages in the same family, ethnic identity is more easily altered and categorization is likewise more difficult. Classic examples of the flexibility in constructing ethnic identity can be found in the ambiguity over what constitutes 'Yoruba' in Nigeria and 'White' in the United States (Fearon, 1999).

The potential endogeneity between measures of ethnic diversity and economic indicators makes straightforward causal claims about the relationship between diversity and economic performance difficult. As Alesina et al. (2003) demonstrate, ethnic diversity is correlated with several of the determinants of growth and real per capita GDP, as well as with latitude. These correlations manifest themselves as statistically significant relationships when ethnic diversity is used as a predictor of these outcomes in standard regression models. As a result, when these outcomes are used as independent variables to predict GDP and growth, ethnic diversity drops to insignificance. Alesina et al. (2003) suggest that this sensitivity to model specification represents the way in which these outcomes may represent channels through which diversity affects growth. While plausible, such a claim cannot be verified by existing data, and the relationship may be explained by a non-causal correlation between diversity and the determinants of growth. One possible candidate is that newer countries, many of them in sub-Saharan Africa, have simply had less time to develop efficacious, transparent institutions. These countries, because they are also highly diverse, may account for the observed relationship, but that would be spurious: time since independence, rather than diversity, would be the underlying cause.

In contrast to ethnic diversity, linguistic diversity is more plausibly exogenous. In the most basic sense, linguistic differentiation is much less amenable to manipulation because linguistic diversity cannot be manufactured in the short term: the emergence of differentiated languages occurs over thousands of years. Equally as important, while one can acquire a new language, the conventions of that language – its syntax, diction, articulation – are established collectively and cannot be readily altered by a single individual. Perhaps because of these qualities, the strategic manipulation of linguistic difference is far less prevalent than for ethnicity; indeed, to our knowledge there are no existing studies that reveal a strategic manipulation of language in the way that is often seen for ethnicity. As a result, endogeneity between economic indicators and linguistic diversity is less of a concern than for ethnicity.

As discussed above, however, all but one of these studies, Cederman and Girardin (2007), have in common a reliance on measures of fractionalization. While fractionalization is a valid measure of diversity, Garcia-Montalvo and Reynal-Querol (2005) rightly note that it does not adequately capture Horowitz's concept of polarization. The distinction is important, since polarized societies – that is, those in which one large minority faces a majority – are precisely those in which we expect the most conflict. This may be especially true in democratic societies, where the larger group's electoral advantage allows complete control of the state to the exclusion of the large minority. Employing a measure of 'discrete polarization', Garcia-Montalvo and Reynal-Querol (2005) find that, while ethnolinguistic fractionalization does not predict the onset of armed conflict, ethnolinguistic polarization is a powerful predictor of civil war onset. The finding holds both when alternative data sources are used to calculate polarization, as well as when alternative armed conflict data is used.

Further support for the importance of polarization comes from Desmet et al. (2009), who demonstrate that linguistic polarization has statistically significant and substantively large effects on economic performance. Depending on the polarization measure chosen – Desmet et al. (2009) use both the Esteban-Ray and Greenberg indices – a 1 s.d. increase in polarization yields a decrease in redistribution between 0.97 and 1.41 per cent of GDP. It is worth noting, however, that Desmet et al. (2009) recover similar estimates for fractionalization measures. The key, in both cases, is to take into account linguistic distance. Regardless of the particular measure used, Desmet et al. (2009) find that incorporating information about distance improves the statistical performance of the measure when used to predict redistribution as a share of GDP.

It should be noted, however, that many of these studies, while they use data that include linguistic cleavages or, as in the case with Fearon (2003), use linguistic diversity as a proxy for cultural diversity, also turn towards the features of ethnic identity in deriving explanatory mechanisms to account for the observed relationship between diversity and their respective outcomes of interest. Indeed, much of this literature uses the term 'ethnolinguistic' and 'ethnic' interchangeably, and often uses linguistic diversity to proxy for other forms of diversity rather than examining linguistic diversity independently of the ethnic diversity with which it is so highly correlated. In discussing the interpretation of their linguistic diversity measures, Desmet et al. (2009, p. 1292) suggests that 'our measure of linguistic diversity should be viewed as a proxy for the broader notion of ethno-linguistic or cultural diversity'. In discussing the widespread use of the Greenberg A-index (commonly referred to as ELF), Alesina and La Ferrara (2005, p. 763) note that ethnic and linguistic diversities are conflated not only in practice but in theory as well. Thus, while the existing literature provides strong support for the hypothesis that ethnolinguistic diversity, broadly defined, is associated with negative economic and political outcomes, the extent to which this relationship is a function of the dynamics of group membership or a feature of linguistic differences is less clear than it might otherwise be. As such, a fruitful avenue for future research may lie in disentangling what dynamics are purely a function of linguistic heterogeneity, and which are a function of political competition in the presence of many groups which have developed, for reasons mentioned above, strong norms of co-ethnic favouritism.

It may be, for example, that linguistic diversity presents difficulties in the formation of national markets but has a relatively small role to play in explaining why diverse countries appear to perform poorly on broader measures of economic performance. We suspect, in fact, that it is the psychology of group boundaries and the tendency of groups to favour co-members over outsiders that underpins the causal relationship between diversity and most political outcomes. Nonetheless, careful observational work, combined with creative experimental interventions, may help us to identify mechanisms that are unique to linguistic differences, and eventually to theorize more fully what effects are driven by linguistic diversity alone. While the overlap between ethnic and linguistic groups is often substantial, there are many cases where ethnic groups seen as politically distinct speak the same language. Leveraging these cases, either in an experimental or observational context, may allow researchers to vary linguistic diversity while holding ethnic diversity constant. Whether through behavioural games, such as in Habyarimana et al. (2007), or through the micro-level observational work in, for example, Miguel (2004), exploiting the (admittedly few) cases in which linguistic and ethnic boundaries overlap imperfectly may help us to uncover the importance of language in its own right.

18.3.3 Policy implications

In spite of high levels of ethnolinguistic fractionalization, national borders remain relatively stable in Africa. Secessionist movements such as those in Belgium, Spain and Eastern Europe are relatively less common, suggesting African leaders' success in crafting nationalist discourses at the time of independence. Many early African leaders such as Tanzania's Julius Nyerere, Ghana's Kwame Nkrumah and Senegal's Leopold Senghor engaged in a set of nation-building policies to project nationalist, and even pan-African, ideals. The success of these policies may have served to counteract or dampen the salience of ethnolinguistic identities, as suggested by Miguel (2004) in the case of Tanzania. At the very least, African citizens have shown a remarkable ability to hold both localized and national identities as equally salient attachments. Furthermore, Fearon and Laitin (1996) have pointed out that inter-ethnic cooperation is the rule rather than the exception in many cases in Africa. Diversity in and of itself is not problematic in the short term if, for instance, the different groups involved developed norms of inter-ethnic contact, cooperation, bargaining and dispute resolution.

It also remains unclear whether the negative association between ethnic diversity and economic and political outcomes is not instead driven by isolation. For example, Kasara (2013) finds that localities in Kenya with high rates of ethnic segregation are more likely to report low inter-ethnic trust, whereas ethnically diverse localities report high levels of inter-ethnic trust. In this case, it would not be ethnic diversity per se, but rather the spatial concentration and relative distance between ethnic groups that contributes to negative outcomes. The policy implication here would be the promotion of infrastructure that links spatially segregated ethnolinguistic groups together. In addition to the well-documented positive returns to infrastructure for economic development, there may be positive externalities in the form of increased inter-ethnic contact.

The second policy implication is the establishment of additional or alternative national languages. Top-down language policies relying on the universal use of European languages may be less desirable because they are politically charged. On the other hand, instituting the language of the largest ethnolinguistic group as the official language may further aggravate between-group tensions and competition. The use of trading languages, however, may be a promising alternative. Colonial languages may be good to the extent that they connect to the outside world, but traditional trade languages such as Swahili or Hausa have an unrivalled cultural and historical heritage. Not only may they help to facilitate interregional and perhaps cross-national trade across ethnic groups (Osafo-Kwaako and Robinson, 2013), but they would also be a source of cross-cutting cleavages, the development of which are generally regarded as helping to reduce political conflict and promote stability.

Finally, the centrepiece of the nationalist project, as put forth by Gellner (1983), is a national education system. Decentralized, regional schooling systems may reinforce ethnic divisions by perpetuating the formal use of several different languages, limiting each group's ability to partake in the economic and political resources of other groups. In contrast, national schools where leaders and political elites are equally trained in the same language can foster elite cooperation, giving them the basis for a common history and experience. Considering that much ethnic violence can be stoked by intra-elite conflicts, an education system that fosters the development of common elite networks may help to combat this trend. In cases where a single national language may not be available, or where its association with a dominant ethnic group makes it a potentially problematic choice as the national language, states can opt for an inclusive strategy, as South Africa has, by designating the languages of *all* large ethnic groups as national languages. While this is less than desirable from an efficiency perspective, inclusive strategies are also less likely to foster ethnic conflict and thus less likely to politicize ethnic identity.

18.4   Conclusion

In this chapter, we have attempted to explain both the cause and consequences of ethnolinguistic diversity in Africa. In Section 18.2, we focused on what we argued are the two major drivers for contemporary Africa's high diversity: the fact that Africa has seen human settlement for longer than any other continent, and the arbitrary borders drawn by colonial powers that later became the basis for Africa's modern states. In Section 18.3, we turned to the consequences of that diversity, which have, in general, been of the negative variety.

At the heart of the many studies demonstrating this effect, whether it be public goods provision in the case of Miguel (2004) or per capita GDP in Easterly and Levine (1997), is a basic truth of political and economic performance: linguistically diverse societies are also, broadly speaking, those with a greater diversity of preferences, a weaker sense of national identity, and a higher incidence of social conflict. Regardless of the mechanism at work, the negative relationship between diversity and many socially desirable outcomes is perhaps the most robust finding in the African political economy literature.

The natural question for policy-makers is straightforward: what can be done to overcome the obstacles ethnolinguistic diversity presents? We have suggested several policies, some already tried and others more aspirational, that may diminish the extent to which ethnolinguistic differences structure economic and political competition. We also suggest that more attention should be paid to economic policies that would limit ethnic segregation such as infrastructure provision. It may be, for example, that infrastructure is essential not only to economic growth and regional integration, but for nation-building and ethnic cooperation as well (see Wantchekon, 2014). It facilitates social interactions and the transfer of people and ideas. In this sense, the current emphasis by African governments and development agencies on roads and rural infrastructure is heartening. Indeed, the best antidote against the gloomy outlook of much of the literature on ethnolinguistic diversity in Africa will be the cases where African governments themselves, despite all the difficulties presented by their linguistic legacies, are able to transcend ethnic and geographic divisions.

References

D. Acemoglu and J. Robinson (2006) *Economic Origins of Dictatorship and Democracy* (Cambridge, UK: Cambridge University Press).

P. Ahlerup and O. Olsson (2011) 'The Roots of Ethnic Diversity', *Journal of Economic Growth*, 17, 71–102.

A. Alesina, R. Baqir and W. Easterly (1999) 'Public Goods and Ethnic Divisions', *The Quarterly Journal of Economics*, 114, 1243–1284.

A. Alesina, A. Devleeschauwer, W. Easterly, S. Kurlat and R. Wacziarg (2003) 'Fractionalization', *Journal of Economic Growth*, 8, 155–194.

A. Alesina, W. Easterly and J. Matuszeski (2011) 'Artificial States', *Journal of the European Economic Association*, 9, 246–277.

A. Alesina and E. La Ferrara (2005) 'Ethnic Diversity and Economic Performance', *Journal of Economic Literature*, 43, 762–800.

A. Alesina, S. Michalopoulos and E. Papaioannou 'Ethnic Inequality', *Journal of Political Economy*, forthcoming.

Q. Ashraf and O. Galor (2013) 'The "Out of Africa" Hypothesis, Human Genetic Diversity, and Comparative Economic Development', *American Economic Review*, 103, 1–46.

A. Asiwaju (1985) *Partitioned Africans: Ethnic Relations across Africa's International Boundaries, 1884–1984* (New York: St. Martin's Press).

Atlas Narodov Mira (1964) The Miklucho-Maklai Ethnological Institute at the Department of Geodesy and Cartography of the State Geological Committee of the Soviet Union.

R. Bates (1974) 'Ethnic Competition and Modernization in Contemporary Africa', *Comparative Political Studies*, 6, 457–484.

R. Bates (1983) *Essays on the Political Economy of Rural Africa* (Cambridge, UK: Cambridge University Press).

R. Bates (1990) 'Capital, Kinship, and Conflict: The Structuring Influence of Capital in Kinship Societies', *Canadian Journal of African Studies*, 24, 151–164.

C. Boix (2003) *Democracy and Redistribution* (Cambridge, UK: Cambridge University Press).

F. Caselli and W. Coleman II (2013) 'On the Theory of Ethnic Conflict', *Journal of the European Economic Association*, 11, 161–192.

L. Cederman and L. Girardin (2007) 'Beyond Fractionalization: Mapping Ethnicity onto Nationalist Insurgencies', *American Political Science Review*, 101, 73–185.

K. Chandra (2004) *Why Ethnic Parties Succeed: Patronage and Ethnic Head Counts in India* (Cambridge, UK: Cambridge University Press).

K. Chandra (2006) 'What Is Ethnic Identity and Does It Matter?', *Annual Review of Political Science*, 9, 397–424.

P. Collier and A. Hoeffler (2004) 'Greed and Grievance in Civil War', *Oxford Economic Papers*, 56, 563–595.

K. Desmet, I. Ortuño Ortín and S. Weber (2009) 'Linguistic Diversity and Redistribution', *Journal of European Economic Association*, 7, 1291–1318.

W. Easterly and R. Levine (1997) 'Africa's Growth Tragedy: Policies and Ethnic Divisions', *The Quarterly Journal of Economics*, 112, 1203–1250.

J. Esteban and D. Ray (1994) 'On the Measurement of Polarization' *Econometrica*, 62, 819–851.

J. Fearon (1999) 'Why Ethnic Politics and "Pork" Tend to Go Together', Working Paper, University of Chicago.

J. Fearon (2003) 'Ethnic and Cultural Diversity by Country', *Journal of Economic Growth*, 8, 195–222.

J. Fearon, K. Kasara and D. Laitin (2007) 'Ethnic Minority Rule and Civil War Onset', *American Political Science Review*, 101, 187–193.

J. Fearon and D. Laitin (1996) 'Explaining Interethnic Cooperation', *The American Political Science Review*, 90, 715–735.

J. Fearon and D. Laitin (2003) 'Ethnicity, Insurgency, and Civil War', *American Political Science Review*, 97, 75–90.

J. Fishman (1968) 'Some Contrasts between Linguistically Homogeneous and Linguistically Heterogeneous Polities' In J. Fishman, C. Ferguson and J. Dasgupta (eds) *Language Problems of Developing Nations* (New York: Wiley).

J. Garcia-Montalvo and M. Reynal-Querol (2005) 'Ethnic Polarization, Potential Conflict, and Civil Wars', *American Economic Review*, 95, 796–816.

E. Gellner (1983) *Nations and Nationalism* (Ithaca, NY: Cornell University Press).

C. Gibson and J. Long (2009) 'The Presidential and Parliamentary Elections in Kenya, December 2007', *Electoral Studies*, 28, 497–502.

J. Greenberg (1956) 'The Measurement of Linguistic Diversity', *Language* 32, 109–115.

J. Habyarimana, M. Humphreys, D. Posner and J. Weinstein (2007) 'Why Does Ethnic Diversity Undermine Public Goods Provision?', *American Political Science Review*, 101, 709–725.

J. Herbst (2000) *States and Power in Africa: Comparative Lessons in Authority and Control* (Princeton: Princeton University Press).

M. Hewstone, M. Rubin and H. Willis (2002) 'Intergroup Bias', *Annual Review of Psychology*, 53, 575–604.

D. Horowitz, (1985) *Ethnic Groups in Conflict* (Berkeley: Berkeley University Press).

D. Horowitz (1991) *A Democratic South Africa? Constitutional Engineering in a Divided Society* (Berkeley, CA: University of California Press).

R. Jackson and C. G. Rosberg (1982) 'Why Africa's Weak States Persist: The Empirical and the Juridical in Statehood', *World Politics*, 35, 1–24.

K. Kasara (2013) 'Separate and Suspicious: The Social Environment and Inter-Ethnic Trust in Kenya', *Journal of Politics*, 4, 921–936.

P. Keefer and R. Vlaicu (2007) 'Democracy, Credibility, and Clientelism', *Journal of Law, Economics, and Organization*, 24, 371–406.

H. Kitschelt and S. Wilkinson (2007) *Patrons, Clients and Policies: Patterns of Democratic Accountability and Political Competition* (Cambridge, UK: Cambridge University Press).

A. Kohli (2004) *State-Directed Development: Political Power and Industrialization in the Global Periphery* (Cambridge, UK: Cambridge University Press).

R. La Porta, F. Lopez de Silanes, A. Shleifer, and R. Vishny (1999) 'The Quality of Government', *Journal of Law, Economics, and Organization*, 15, 222–279.

R. Mace and M. Pagel (1995) 'A Latitudinal Gradient in the Density of Human Languages in North America', *Biological Sciences*, 261, 117–121.

S. Michalopoulos (2012) 'The Origins of Ethnolinguistic Diversity', *American Economic Review*, 102, 1508–1539.

S. Michalopoulos and E. Papaioannou (2011) 'The Long-Run Effects of the Scramble for Africa', NBER Working Paper 1760.

S. Michalopoulos and E. Papaioannou (2014) 'National Institutions and African Development: Evidence from Partitioned Ethnicities', *The Quarterly Journal of Economics*, 129, 151–213.

E. Miguel (2004) 'Tribe or Nation? Nation Building and Public Goods in Kenya versus Tanzania', *World Politics*, 56, 327–362.

J. Montalvo and M. Reynal-Querol (2005) 'Ethnic Diversity and Economic Development', *Journal of Development Economics*, 76, 293–323.

J. Moore, L. Manne, T. Brooks, N. Burgess, R. Davies, C. Rahbek, P. Williams and A. Balmford (2002) 'The Distribution of Cultural and Biological Diversity in Africa', *Proceedings of The Royal Society: Biological Sciences*, 269, 1645–1653.

G. Murdock (1959) *Africa: Its Peoples and Their Culture History* (New York: McGraw-Hill).

P. Osafo-Kwaako and J. Robinson (2013) 'Political Centralization in Pre-Colonial Africa', *Journal of Comparative Economics*, 41, 6–21.

J. Pool (1972) 'National Development and Language Diversity' In J. Fishman (ed.) *Advances in the Sociology of Language*, vol. 2 (The Hague: Mouton).

D. Posner (2004a) 'Measuring Ethnic Fractionalization in Africa', *American Journal of Political Science*, 48, 849–863.

D. Posner (2004b) 'The Political Salience of Cultural Difference: Why Chewas and Tumbukas Are Allies in Zambia and Adversaries in Malawi', *American Political Science Review*, 98, 529–545.

D. Posner (2006) *Institutions and Ethnic Politics in Africa* (Cambridge, UK: Cambridge University Press).

J. Sachs and A. Warner (1997) 'Sources of Slow Growth in African Economies', *Journal of African Economies*, 6, 335–76.

R. Sandbrook (1985) *The Politics of Africa's Economic Stagnation* (Cambridge, UK: Cambridge University Press).

J. Scarritt and S. Mozaffar (1999) 'The Specification of Ethnic Cleavages and Ethnopolitical Groups for the Analysis of Democratic Competition in Contemporary Africa', *Nationalism and Ethnic Politics*, 5, 82–117.

H. Tajfel and J. Turner (1979) 'An Integrative Theory of Intergroup Conflict' In M. J. Hatch and M. Schultz (eds) *Psychology of Intergroup Relations* (Oxford: Oxford University Press).

C. Tilly (1990) *Coercion, Capital, and European States, AD 990–1990* (Cambridge, MA: Basil Blackwell).

L. Wantchekon (2014) 'Nation-Building in Africa: Challenges and Opportunities' In *Evaluation Matters* (African Development Bank Group).

19
Languages, Regional Conflicts and Economic Development: Russia

Denis V. Kadochnikov

19.1 Introduction

Ever since the 16th century when unified Russia emerged after a long period of feudal fragmentation the state played a key role in the development and standardization of the Russian language and in its spreading among various ethnic groups. Specific tasks and tools of state policy with regard to Russian and other languages varied greatly over time. Nevertheless, for centuries the major trend of Russia's language policy was the standardization both in a narrow sense (aimed at reducing dialectical barriers among ethnic Russians through the development and promotion of a standardized version of Russian) and in a wider sense (aimed at the expansion of the use of Russian in public affairs along with or sometimes instead of other languages).

Russia has certainly not been unique in this respect: standardization policies have historically been a response to the challenges of linguistic and ethnic diversity/fractionalization in many societies throughout the world. Linguistic fractionalization, as Ginsburgh and Weber (2014) note, often leads, among other things, to bureaucratic inefficiency, corruption, and political and economic instability; standardization thus is a natural response to fractionalization.

Ideally, language standardization policy should lead to the removal of linguistic barriers in society by ensuring universal knowledge of a common language (languages); it does not imply deliberate restrictions of using other languages (except for certain cases, when no feasible alternative for one and only one language exists – such as in the military). Language standardization policy is supposedly fundamentally different from the policy of language discrimination that aims instead at creating or preserving language barriers in society, thus disenfranchising some of its members. In practice, however, expanded use of one language may naturally lead to narrower use of other languages. Even in the best-case scenario, the impact of the standardization policy on different people or social groups may be different: expanded opportunities for some may imply a loss of opportunities for others. For instance when members of an ethnic group learn another language (especially if it is used more widely or spoken by a majority of people in the country) while retaining their own language the range of opportunities in all spheres of life for them undoubtedly expands. This implies greater opportunities and greater competition, be it in politics, ideology and culture or in business. However, while some actors gain from that increased competition, others (both from within this group and outside) may lose. To see why, let us turn to the economic interpretation of language barriers – the barriers to communicating or acquiring information due to actual lack of relevant language skills or due to restrictions on using specific languages.

Language barriers may be viewed as a specific kind of market barriers; in this respect they are similar for instance to customs duties or licence requirements. Language barriers allow some actors to extract monopolistic rents in various kinds of markets (markets for political and ideological control, labour markets, markets for goods, markets for literary works and the media, etc.). An elimination of language barriers within a country (through standardization and promotion of a common language) and between the country and the outer world (through ensuring broader command of foreign languages) should presumably have the same overall effect as, for instance, an elimination of internal and external trade restrictions. And similarly to controversies accompanying trade liberalization such language policy is also likely to raise objections from those who fear that their political and economic status is threatened.

In theory language policy should aim at reducing threats to a country's political and economic integrity inherent in its ethno-linguistic diversity (as posited for instance by Laitin, 2000) while preventing large-scale conflicts and antagonism on language grounds. In practice, language policies may be motivated not so much by the considerations of improved well-being for a greater number of people, but by the pursuit of rents and of political and economic power by various actors. The outcome of these policies may or may not enhance the well-being of society at large or its elements.

Russia's case offers numerous examples of how language policy was a matter of struggle between the country's central and local elites in their quest for political and economic control. This overview covers in brief the history of language policies in Russia over the last several centuries – from the late medieval Moscow state to the Russian Empire to the Soviet Union and finally to the modern-day Russian Federation. The chapter ends with a discussion of the socio-economic and political factors and the implications of language policy in Russia in a historical perspective.

19.2   The standardization of the Russian language in late medieval Russia (16–17th centuries)

Various remnants of feudal fragmentation of Russian lands survived through the 16th and early 17th centuries despite the continuing consolidation of political power in the hands of Moscow princes. The relative isolation of individual principalities during and after the Mongol yoke contributed to the fragmentation of the ancient Russian language and led to the divergence of its various dialects. When the process of unification and centralization of Russian lands under the rule of Moscow allowed the restoring of political and trade ties, the dialectical differences came to be seen as a practical challenge for the state bureaucracy. As the centralized system of government evolved and the communications between the centre and the periphery intensified, the task of standardizing the language used in official affairs was becoming more and more pressing.

Addressing this task was predictably not easy. In addition to the remnants of territorial and dialectical fragmentation, the task of standardizing the Russian language was complicated by its essentially secondary status in the highly religious Russian society. In medieval Russia, the predominant type of literature was religious literature and virtually the only type of schooling was that provided at church schools. The language used by the church was not Russian but Church Slavonic. The prevailing position of the latter language in literature and education persisted for centuries, reflecting the role that the church played in medieval Russian society.[1] But the Church Slavonic language was based on Southern Slavic dialects and was too different from Russian and the East Slavic dialects to fill in a niche for the standardized national language for unifying Russia. In terms of its applicability in all sorts of daily transactions, Church Slavonic was too archaic and overcomplicated.

The idea of expanding the use of Russian as opposed to Church Slavonic emerged around the 17th century when it became clear that the latter was ill-suited for use in administration and business affairs. Even earlier than that the Russian language was already occasionally used in some official documents, such as those containing instructions of judicial process. The development of a Russian-language secular literature (oral folklore) during the period also

---

[1] In medieval Russia elements of Church Slavonic and the Russian languages were often simultaneously present in speech and in writings; these languages were essentially intermingled and that complicated the emergence of standard Russian. See Halperin (2007) for an overview of scholarly work on the relationship of the Russian and Church Slavonic languages in the 16th-century Russia; and Matthews (1953) for an overview of the history of the Russian language before 1700.

promoted the use of Russian. The first printed books in Russian were published in the middle of the 17th century, almost a century later than the first book in Church Slavonic was printed in Moscow. These were the Russian translation of the German book on the infantry tactics and drills by Johann Jacobi von Wallhausen in 1647 and the legal code (*Sobornoye Ulozheniye*) of Tsar Alexey Mikhaylovich in 1649.

The basis for the standardization of the Russian language was the so-called Moscow official (or chancery) language, which was itself a product of the long process of convergence of different dialects of ancient Russian.[2] The development of the norms of the official language of Moscow was strongly shaped by the practice of the government chanceries and departments (*prikaz*) and by the steps undertaken in these official bodies to standardize the vocabulary and the orthography of the Russian language. Yakubinskiy (1986) mentions a decree issued by Tsar Alexey Mikhaylovich that determined the orthographic principles to be used in official documents; this may well have been one of the earliest examples of state language policy in Russia.

19.3 Language policy in the context of the reforms of Peter the Great and his successors (18th century)

The standardization and the modernization of the Russian language were given a further strong impulse during the reforms of Peter the Great.[3] The state shaped this process both directly (by regulations regarding the various aspects of Russian language usage) and indirectly (by developing secular education and science).

The importance of standardizing the Russian language was obvious to Peter the Great, no less than it was to his immediate predecessors. It was crucial for the development of a modern system of government, education and science, and thus for the economic development of the country. Peter continued the policy of raising the status of the Russian language and bringing it into official use instead of Church Slavonic. By the early 18th century, the use of the official version of the Russian language became widespread enough to oust completely Church Slavonic from secular affairs. This coincided with and reinforced the general secularization of life in Russia under Peter the Great.

Another important aspect of Peter's language policy concerned the orthography. In order to facilitate the spreading of knowledge throughout Russia, Peter the Great found it necessary in 1708–1710 to reform the alphabet and the fonts to be used in secular books and newspapers. New letters were added

---

[2] See, for instance, Yakubinskiy (1986).
[3] See Cracraft (2004) for an extensive discussion of Peter the Great's cultural revolution and its linguistic implications.

to the alphabet and new so-called civil fonts (civil type) were designed with Peter's active participation. The fonts were simplified compared to the fonts that were and would be used in religious books (historically based on hand-written scripts). The reform of the fonts brought Russian letters closer to the Latin fonts used in Western Europe.

While the promotion of using Russian instead of Church Slavonic in all official secular affairs was a part of Peter's policy and vision, its spreading in the 18th century was also promoted by a new generation of thinkers. They saw the modernization of the Russian language, literature and poetry as an integral part of the overall modernization of the nation. Russia's first native-born 18th-century encyclopaedical scientist Mikhail Lomonosov, whose interests ranged from the exact sciences to poetry, authored the first scientific grammar of the Russian language, developed a theoretical system of styles for the language and wrote on the art of rhetoric among other things. Lomonosov was the first to introduce several new literary genres in Russia using Western European examples. As a major figure of Russian enlightenment, the founder of the first Russian university (the Academic University) and as a member of the Academy of Sciences and Arts, Lomonosov made the greatest contribution to the development and expansion of the use of the Russian language in the middle of the 18th century. In doing so he continued and took further the vision set by Peter the Great.

The re-emergence and standardization of Russian as an official and business language was the most important language-related phenomenon of the 18th and early 19th century. This was when the foundations of the modern Russian language were laid. But no less important from the social and economic points of view was the expanding study and use of foreign languages.

19.4   The role of foreign languages in Russia of the late 18th and early 19th centuries

The study and use of foreign languages in Russia remained very limited until the time of Peter the Great. In previous centuries there were some people in Russia, mostly clergy, as well as some noblemen and officials, who learnt Greek and Latin, sometimes Polish. The interest to contemporary Western European languages developed slowly among the aristocracy in the late 17th century when foreign language study came to be seen as an important element of home education. The situation changed radically during Peter's reign.

The 18th century was the time of major changes in the vocabulary of the Russian language as new ideas and concepts entered Russian life. Some of them were given names derived from original Russian words, but in most cases the new terms were adopted from other European languages. Borrowing foreign terms and the expanding use of foreign languages were not so much a purposeful policy as a natural side effect of the overall policy of Westernization. For a while scientific research in Russia (including scientific study of the Russian language) was mostly done by foreigners and in foreign languages. The dominant position of foreign languages applied to not only the sciences but also to the humanities; many scholars and officials believed that the Russian language was not suited for poetry, literature and science as it lacked an appropriate vocabulary.

From then on, the learning of foreign languages was no longer seen as a personal choice motivated by curiosity but as an obligation on every aristocrat, every official, as an important aspect of Russia's modernization. This requirement was articulated and formalized in various documents issued by Peter the Great and his successors.

While German states and northern Europe were a source of new technical knowledge (broadly defined) as well as of technical experts, France (especially by the late 18th century) became the source of fashions and all things related to a luxurious lifestyle that the imperial court and the aristocracy were eager to absorb. Thus by the time of empresses Elizabeth and Catherine the Great the French language had become the preferred language of the court and aristocracy, although German retained strong positions among scientists and officials.

By the late 18th century the Russian aristocracy had become bilingual – Russian- and French-speaking (other European languages were also widely spoken but these two were the primary ones). In St Petersburg and Moscow as well as in other large cities the position of the French language was very strong with many noblemen learning it before Russian and using it more often and eagerly. This was even more so because more and more members of the imperial family were foreign born and had problems with learning Russian.

In the late 18th century and well into the 19th century, French was the language of the Russian Imperial Court and of senior government officials. While it did not have an official status, the social and protocol pressures ensured that without it no one could succeed at court. This was not a state policy *de jure* (unless one considers the emphasis of foreign languages in the curricula of both home education and of formal education at state schools and universities) but certainly a *de facto* policy of the ruling class which during that period included numerous foreigners. The position that the French language played in Russian life was not damaged even by the war of 1812, although some nobles actually tried to express their patriotism by speaking Russian sporadically (often with a French accent). Emperor Alexander I, the defeater of Napoleon, up until his death addressed his family members and courtiers mostly in French.

The situation began changing gradually when Alexander's brother and successor Nicholas I started regularly using Russian at court and in government affairs. The protocol of the imperial court required responding to the Emperor in the language that he used, which is why the choice of the language by him was of great importance for courtiers and officials. Nevertheless French continued to be the language used in conversations with high-born ladies for a long time. In addition to the French language, German and English were used in high society but to a lesser extent.

Foreign languages, primarily French, played a very important role in the life of Russia's ruling class for almost a century – roughly from the middle of the 18th to the middle of the 19th century, and even after that their positions remained strong up until the Revolution of 1917. This phenomenon had a thorough and controversial impact on Russian society and culture of the 18th–19th centuries. The bilingualism (or multilingualism) of the Russian ruling classes was not an obstacle to the development of the Russian language and culture in the 18th and 19th centuries; instead it was one of the key factors behind the impressive progress in all of these spheres. It ensured that Russian aristocracy and the Russian political, social and intellectual elite had access to the ideas, knowledge and fashions of Western Europe. This had a profound impact on the development of Russian culture, arts and science, as well as social thinking. Being familiar with contemporary literature and the intellectual discourse of Western Europe Russian writers, poets and scientists of the early-to-middle 19th century proved capable of greatly advancing Russia's own literature, poetry and language. Paradoxically as it may seem at first sight, this period, despite the dominance of the French language, was later recognized as the golden age of Russian culture. This was the period when the archaic Russian language of the earlier centuries finally gave way to the modern Russian language, the use of which in literature was pioneered by Russia's greatest poet Alexander Pushkin and his contemporaries.

At the same time an opinion popular among many Russia intellectuals was that the negative effect of the officially promoted bilingualism of the Russian elite was that it deepened the social and cultural divide between them and the common people. Considering that the Russian clergy continued using Church Slavonic not only during services but to some extent in daily life then it becomes obvious that the different social strata of post-Petrine imperial Russia literally spoke and thought to a significant extent in different languages, as noted, for instance, by Okenfuss (1985).

19.5   Language policy in the context of the territorial expansion of the Russian Empire (17–19th centuries)

It was under Peter the Great that the official vision of Russia as an Orthodox Christian (and more or less theocratic) state was transformed into the vision of it as an empire with a multi-ethnic and multi-religious population. This certainly did not imply equal status for all of the ethnic and religious groups and minorities composing this empire, but it did acknowledge most of them as integral elements of its political and economic system. Two key issues in this context were the choice of language (languages) for instruction at schools for non-Russians and the choice of language (languages) for governance and official affairs in areas with a predominantly non-Russian population.

The choice of language for instruction at schools for non-Russians was itself an element of the greater issue of education policy. The early steps towards developing educational institutions for the non-Russian residents of the Russian Empire were mostly made in the context of the missionary activities of the Russian Orthodox Church beginning in the 16th century. Schools established by the church were mostly used for the training of clergy of non-Russian origins with the subsequent goal of proselytizing. This was, however, a very limited practice that involved relatively few people.

In the later part of the 18th century the government began purposefully and systemically organizing schools for non-Russians, where instruction involved learning Russian and Church Slavonic with the aim of preparing bilingual or trilingual Orthodox priests and missionaries of non-Russian origin, as well as of local officials. These attempts, however, were sporadic and most importantly ineffective as they lacked a well-structured methodical system of teaching which accounted for the linguistic and cultural background of pupils.

The first attempts at developing such a pedagogical system were only undertaken in the second half of the 19th century. Nikolai Ilminskiy (1822–1891) developed a system of education for the non-Russian subjects of the empire based on the idea that it was not the Russian language but rather Russian Orthodoxy (or at least sympathy to it) that could unite all subjects regardless of their ethnicity.[4] That Ilminskiy gave priority to the religious education and missionary work was predetermined by his clerical background (he began his pedagogical career at a theological academy but later entered the civil service). Based on his own missionary and teaching experience (as well as on his extensive knowledge of Arab and Turkic languages), he came up with an idea and a method of education which was aimed at promoting the Christian faith but it in a flexible, non-coercive way, trying to motivate and raise interest in it among pupils rather than simply obliging them to learn and perform various religious practices. This implied first and foremost that the key language of instruction at primary schools for non-Russians had to be the native language of the pupils (supplemented by the Russian language later into studies), and that the teachers had to be of the same ethnicity as their students. Ilminskiy's system was first implemented in the city of Kazan at the school for Christian Tatars and proved

---

[4] See Dowler (1995) for a review of Ilminskiy's system, the reactions to it and its application in the official government policy of the Russian Empire.

to be more effective than the traditional approach utilizing solely the Russian language. A number of schools for non-Russians organized according to this model were later established in various parts of the Russian Empire.

The reaction to Ilminskiy's system was mixed. It was generally praised by specialists (especially liberally minded ones) in pedagogy and education, but faced opposition from conservatives who believed that education in native languages would drive non-Russian subjects of the empire away from the Russians and promote nationalistic sentiments among the former. These objections, however, were not based on objective evidence but rather reflected the fears and mindset of a reactionary part of society. It was also opposed by the Islamic clergy, but for the opposite reason – its potential effectiveness with regard to proselytizing. The actual experience with bilingual education proved successful enough to ensure eventually support for this system in government circles.

Ilminskiy's system was not the only approach to education among non-Russians which involved a combination of Russian and other (native) languages in instruction. A somewhat similar approach was used for instance at the so-called New Method (*Jadidist*) schools for Muslims which developed as an alternative to the state-supported Ilminskiy's schools as will be discussed further below.

In 1870 the minister of education of the Russian Empire, Count Dmitry Tolstoy, in his report *On the Measures on Education of the Non-Russian Residents of Russia*[5] to Emperor Alexander II formulated basic principles of state policy regarding the education of non-Russian subjects of the empire in several southern provinces. In the report, which was subsequently developed into official regulations, the minister specifically noted that he was guided by the idea of producing firmer ties between non-Russians and Russians through gradually spreading Russian language skills among the former. In pursuing this goal the government had to adopt a rather flexible approach which accounted for the differences in both the language background (including the knowledge of Russian) of specific ethnic minorities as well as in their religion. The primary and secondary education of the non-Russian Christian (traditionally Orthodox or newly converted) subjects of the empire was to be aimed at both the development of Russian language skills and the strengthening of the authority of the Russian Orthodox Church. In the case of Muslim subjects the religious component was absent (as the government was eager to avoid any suspicions among Muslims about the possibility of religious proselytizing), though the task of ensuring knowledge of the Russian language was still regarded as a crucial one. Tolstoy clearly stated that the ultimate goal of education of non-Russians was bringing them into the Russian civilization.

---

[5] *Vsepoddaneyshiy doklad ministra narodnogo prosvesheniya D.A. Tolstogo 'O merah s obrazovaniyem naselyayushih Rossiyu inorodtsev'* (1870).

The structure of the curriculum at schools for non-Russian subjects was to be designed in a way that would ensure a gradual transition of pupils from early learning in their native language to more advanced learning in Russian. The ministry of education considered that the optimal strategy in this respect was teachers' bilingualism – they had to be proficient in both Russian and in local languages. This called for the establishment of special schools for the training of such bilingual teachers, both ethnic Russians and representatives of other ethnicities. The minister of education also called for adopting measures that would raise the willingness of non-Russian subjects to learn Russian – such as the gradual introduction of the minimal educational requirements (including the knowledge of Russian) for those who wanted to advance in various official and/or religious positions. Such requirements were to be announced several years in advance as the goal was not to prevent non-Russians from making a career but to ensure their full integration into the bureaucracy and clergy.

In the second half of the 19th and the early 20th century, a number of Russian-Native schools (*Russko-Inorodcheskiye shkoly, Russko-Tuzemniye shkoly*) were established in the Volga region, the Caucasus and Central Asia. They provided elementary education in the native language of the local people with the Russian language being an important part of the curriculum. Often they were attended by both ethnic Russians and children of other ethnicities, in which case training was organized along two tracks (one completely in Russian, one in other languages plus Russian). Teachers at these schools were both Russians and locals, and while some elements of state ideology were a part of the training (pupils had to learn about the imperial dynasty, the reigning emperor, etc.) the overall curriculum was not aimed at religious proselytizing; in fact Muslim pupils were taught the basics of their religion at these schools. These schools gradually gained trust among local people in the Muslim regions of the Russian Empire who saw the practical benefits of this education including the study of Russian which was useful in the context of expanding contacts and trade with the core of Russia and Russians. While the Ministry of education approved of this type of school, there was not much financial support for them; they were organized with partial financial support from the local population. For that reason this type of school was only accessible to a small number of pupils.

Nevertheless the knowledge and the use of Russian by people of various ethnic backgrounds within the empire grew during the 19th century slowly but surely, sometimes due to and often despite of the tools and methods chosen by the authorities to advance the language. The specifics of the official policies regarding the use of Russian and other languages in education and in official affairs will now be described further with respect to selected territories of the Russian Empire.

19.5.1   Ukraine and Belarus

As mentioned earlier the standardization of the Russian language in the 18th century was seen by the authorities as an element for forging the unity of the Russian Empire. This policy was aimed at overcoming the divisions inherited from the time of feudal fragmentation and foreign domination in various parts of the empire. It should be remembered, however, that in Russia's political language during the 18th–early 20th centuries the term 'Russian' (both with respect to people and to their language) was a general term encompassing the Great Russians, the Small Russians and the White Russians. Up until the establishment of Soviet power all these peoples were officially regarded as representing one imperial nation and their languages were regarded as versions of the same language. Back in the 18–19th centuries this view was based on the opinions of early Russian philologists, including Mikhail Lomonosov.

In this context the state policy with regard to the standardization of the Russian language also implied that the languages spoken by the Small and White Russians (which eventually came to be recognized as Ukrainian and Belorussian in the 20th century) were dialects which emerged as a result of Polish and Lithuanian domination which lasted up until the late 17th century. From the point of view of the imperial authorities these dialects had to follow the destiny of all other dialects within the Russian language with concrete educational and publishing policies ensuing. The Russian (Great Russian) language (or rather Moscow's official language) was introduced in official affairs in Ukraine and Belarus in the 17th century. Starting from the 18th century Russian was prescribed for the use in education and the publishing of academic and religious books. These policies were generally accepted by local elites in the process of their integration into the imperial elite (which was accompanied by the recognition of old and the granting of new benefits and rights). This policy, however, eventually brought on a linguistic divide between different classes within Ukrainian and Belorussian societies.

The vision of Ukrainian and Belorussian languages as separate from the Russian generally emerged in the 19th century in the context of the sociopolitical changes which brought along nationalist aspirations among the intelligentsia of Ukraine and Belarus. It also was invoked by the opposition to what came to be regarded as the Russification of Ukrainians and Belorussians. By the late 19th century the view of Ukrainian and Belorussian as separate languages was already shared by a significant number of Russian intellectuals, although still rejected by the authorities. The emergence of literary Ukrainian and Belorussian languages was both evolutionary and revolutionary, a process in which writers and poets sought not only to bring the language of the common people onto the pages of their books, textbooks and dictionaries, but also to avoid using what they perceived as words and phrases characteristic of the Russian language, despite the fact that they were commonly used.

19.5.2 Finland

Compared to other territories, the Grand Duchy of Finland enjoyed the highest degree of autonomy within the empire. Since its incorporation in the early 19th century Finland had its own constitution, parliament, citizenship and many other elements of a sovereign state.

The official language of the Grand Duchy was Swedish whose privileged status was guaranteed to the Swedish-born elites of Finland following the secession of Finland from Sweden to Russia in 1809. Throughout much of the 19th century, Swedish remained the language of educated people in Finland. It was the language of business, literature and culture, while Finnish was still mostly the language of commoners and was fragmented into several dialects. The Swedes of Finland were eager to protect the status of the Swedish language along with their privileged economic status and their cultural links with the former metropole. Even though they were a minority they still had enough influence actually to push through a regulation banning publishing books in Finnish with the exception of religious and agricultural books.

Nevertheless the growing national awareness of the Finns by the middle of the 19th century led to calls for a greater role for the Finnish language. These demands were not opposed but rather welcomed by the imperial authorities as the pro-Swedish sentiments and Swedish influence in Finland eventually came to be seen as a threat to Russian interests. After a series of initiatives in the 1850s and 1860s by the Governor-general of Finland, Count von Berg, supported by Emperor Alexander II, the status of the Finnish language was raised and from 1865 it began to be used in official and academic affairs.

As for the Russian language, after some steps aimed at advancing it in Finland in the early 19th century, the Russian government eventually limited its use in Finland to government affairs (and even in this respect it was only semi-official) by the second half of the century. The Russian government on several occasions included the requirement of knowledge of Russian as a prerequisite for holding major state positions in Finland, but these requirements were not strictly enforced, especially considering that there were not enough candidates with a good command of Swedish, Finnish and Russian at the same time.

By the end of the 19th century, the political and economic autonomy of Finland began to be regarded in Russia as an anomaly. This perception which strengthened during the reigns of Alexander III and Nicholas II brought on the policy which is traditionally known in Finland as the 'Russification of Finland'. In essence it was aimed at integrating Finland into the Russian legal, military and economic system and involved limiting its autonomy and bringing its legislation closer to Russian law. Its intended impact on religious, cultural and linguistic spheres was, however, rather limited from the start.

In 1900 Nicholas II issued a manifesto on the introduction of the Russian language for official affairs at selected administrative units of the Grand Duchy of Finland. According to the document the Russian language was to be used in the official affairs of the major governing bodies of Finland (the office of the Governor-general, the State Secretariat of Finland, the Passport Expedition, the Senate and governors) and in their dealings with each other. They were also required to consider appeals in Russian along with Finnish and Swedish. The manifesto did not contain any provisions on expanding the use of Russian in other spheres of life. It still caused protests in Finland because it was regarded as a step towards limiting the nation's autonomy. The implementation of the manifesto did not go very far anyway as the staff of the concerned government units were not sufficiently proficient in Russian.

Overall the language policy of the Russian Empire in Finland rather promoted the use of Finnish rather than Russian up until the 20th century. During the reign of Nicholas II the mood had changed, but World War I and the revolutions of 1905 and 1917 drew attention away from this matter. Finland became independent in 1917 and in 1922 adopted Finnish and Swedish as the state languages.

19.5.3   Poland

A larger part of Poland was united with the Russian Empire as the Kingdom of Poland in 1815 following the Congress of Vienna (parts of Poland had been absorbed into the empire earlier, under Catherine the Great). Initially it was a nominally sovereign state in a personal union with Russia through the person of the Emperor who held the title of the King of Poland. The 1815 Constitutional Charter of the Kingdom of Poland stipulated that the official language for all state, military and judicial affairs was Polish. The knowledge of Polish was also a prerequisite for candidates for official positions (although it could be waived for specific persons by the Emperor). Eventually the Constitutional Charter was replaced with the Organic Statute of 1832 which abolished most of the elements of sovereignty. The Polish language, however, remained the official language in all affairs of the kingdom. At the same time the study of Russian was introduced at secondary schools (gymnasiums), particularly with a view to their graduates either entering state or military service or continuing their education at Russian universities.

The situation only began to change in the 1860s and 1870s. The Russian government under Alexander II faced increased revolutionary and nationalist sentiments in Poland (and pretty much throughout most of the empire). After the Polish uprising of 1863 the policy of complete integration of Poland with the Russian Empire was launched. This policy involved introducing in Poland legal regulations and administrative procedures similar to those applied in core Russian provinces, as well as transferring control of various aspects of local affairs to central authorities.

The Russian language was introduced in official and later judicial affairs, although the use of Polish was still allowed in petitions submitted to local official bodies by citizens. Primary and secondary schools with teaching in Russian were organized for Russians and ethnic and religious minorities (Lithuanians, Jews and others). Since 1869 the study of Russian had been required at all primary schools while at all secondary schools it was initially prescribed for teaching of selected disciplines (such as history, geography, Russian literature and several others); eventually the number of disciplines taught in Russian was expanded so that it became the only language of instruction. All higher educational institutions where the language of instruction was Polish were closed down after the uprising of 1863. They were replaced by the Imperial University of Warsaw in 1869 at which the language of instruction was Russian. The majority of professors and students there, however, were also Russian, while Polish students often chose to go to universities in neighbouring countries for political reasons.

The sphere of the Russian language usage in Poland was expanded further under Alexander III in the 1880s, particularly after it was made the language of instruction at primary schools. According to Corrsin (1990) the Russification policy, including its linguistic aspect, in Poland was aimed at neutralizing the Polish elite and intelligentsia and at minimizing their influence on ethnic minorities (Ukrainians, Jews, Lithuanians, etc.) on the territory of Poland. The attitude to this forceful policy of introducing Russian in official and academic affairs among the Polish public was predictably negative and became an important factor of growing national opposition towards Russian rule.

19.5.4 Baltic provinces

In the Baltic provinces (also known as the Ostsee governorates) of the Russian Empire, which covered the territory of modern-day Latvia, Estonia and a smaller part of Lithuania, the use of the Russian language remained limited up until the late 19th century. After the absorption of these lands by the Russian Empire in the 18th century, the Baltic provinces enjoyed a certain degree of autonomy and self-government which among other things involved official use of German in governance and education (local noble landowners were mostly of German origin).

During the reigns of Alexander III and Nicholas II, the autonomy of these provinces was limited. This reflected the overall trend towards a standardization of the legal system throughout the empire and also to a large extent was a response to the pan-German and separatist feelings of the local German-born nobility stimulated by the establishment of the German Empire. Local laws were gradually abolished and substituted with the Russian laws already applied in other regions.

The introduction of Russian as the official and business language and as the language of instruction at local schools began in the 1880s and was eventually extended to some of the regional universities; Russian schools for the growing number of ethnic Russians were opened even earlier – in the 1860s. These policies predictably were opposed by the privileged minority of local Germans but hardly by the native people of these lands who were given a chance to get rid of the German domination which involved the severe suppression of any signs of ethnic cultural and linguistic revival.

The de-Germanization of the Baltic provinces and the advancement of the Russian language coincided with the resurgence of national culture in the Baltic provinces (mostly Latvia and Estonia) including the development of local languages and literature.

The larger part of Lithuania at the time was located beyond the Baltic provinces in the so-called North-Western region which included much of what is today Belarus and Lithuania. There Russian language was introduced into business and education in the early 19th century and the overall atmosphere was less favourable to all local languages and dialects as well as to Polish, especially after a series of peasant revolts in the second half of the 19th century.

19.5.5   Caucasus

Most of Caucasus was included in the Russian Empire by the early 19th century but it took several more decades before the government began dealing with the task of socio-economic, cultural and linguistic integration of this region. Some elements of Ilminskiy's system of education for non-Russians were introduced in Caucasus in the second half of the century. During the later part of the reign (1855–1881) of Alexander II in Caucasus, not only at primary but also at secondary schools instruction in Russian was often accompanied by the study of native languages. The primary schools' curriculum of 1881 stipulated that the language of instruction during the first year of schooling was to be a local language; and this proved to be very effective and popular among the local people. This system, however, found opposition among the reactionary imperial elite which pushed for greater and faster Russification.

With the ascent of Alexander III (1881–1894) the use of local languages at schools was minimized. This, however, led to the drastic fall of the quality of training as well as to the alienation of non-Russians, who now began to see their native languages as an important part of their identity of which they were being deprived.

In 1907 the Viceroy of Caucasus, Count Vorontsov-Dashkov, summarized his vision of the political, social and economic problems in the region in his *Most Loyal Note on the Governance of the Caucasus Region*.[6] A separate chapter in the *Note* is dedicated to educational issues. Vorontsov-Dashkov starts with citing the results of the 1897 census showing that only 9.6 per cent of men and 3.3 per

---

[6] *Vsepoddaneyshaya zapiska po upravleniyu Kavkazskim krayem general-adyutanta grafa Vorontsova-Dashkova* (1907).

cent of women in Caucasus were literate in any language. He then proceeds to state that the major goal of public schools in Russia was 'the promotion of mental development among people'. An additional goal in Caucasus was the advancement of the Russian language among non-Russian residents which, according to the count, was the major factor in uniting the multi-ethnic population of the region with the empire. In his willingness to advance the Russian language the count, however, was very critical of the existing practice of primary schooling in the region. The language of instruction at the majority of local schools was Russian but, as the count indicated, the pupils usually had very little or no prior knowledge of it; the command of Russian among local teachers was also rather poor. As a result the effectiveness of training was very low: the schooling did not ensure either a solid command of Russian or a deep knowledge of other subjects. Local people came to see these schools as useless or even harmful.

Vorontsov-Dashkov specifically pointed out in his *Note* that the task of bringing all subjects of the empire closer to the Russian civilization through education and the Russian language could be only effectively achieved if it was based on a respect of the national and religious senses of the people involved and if the benefits of education and knowledge of Russian were made the major motivating factor for those being trained. He thus stressed that non-Russian schools required teachers who were either local natives with a good command of Russian or Russians with a good command of local languages and culture. Training such teachers was a separate task that was to be implemented through special pedagogical schools.

19.5.6 Central Asia

In Central Asia just as in Caucasus the authorities saw Russian and Russian-Native schools as the key tool for bringing the new subjects of the empire closer to the Russians and for strengthening the socio-economic ties of these territories with the Russian core. The first Governor-General of Turkestan, Konstantin Petrovich von Kaufman, on numerous occasions and in letters to the emperor stated that the Russian language and education rather than religious proselytizing was the only way to ensure the successful integration of Turkestan into the Russian Empire. The same idea was shared by his successors. With the growth of the Russian population in the newly acquired territories upper secondary and specialized secondary schools (gymnasiums) were opened in the late 19th and early 20th centuries in some cities of Caucasus and Central Asia. The training was conducted in Russian while the students included not only Russians, but also people of other ethnicities (usually graduates of Russian-Native schools). Some native students continued studies in higher educational institutions in Russian cities. Despite the official support, the extent of Russian schooling in Turkestan, however, remained limited.

Nikolai Ostroumov, Ilminskiy's student, Russian ethnographer, translator and researcher of Turkestan, held the position of school director and school inspector in Tashkent and was close to the Governors-General of Turkestan for several decades. He left extensive observations of the Russian governance in Turkestan including the educational/language policies. According to Ostroumov (1910) the implementation of the idea of a joint Russian-Native education in Turkestan was very limited; the number of pupils at Russian-Native schools was 20–30 times smaller than the number attending traditional Muslim schools which the regional imperial administration was hesitant to control. Ostroumov blamed inefficient, corrupt and unmotivated officials for the limited spread and impact of the Russian language and education, despite the fact that this was the official policy.

In Kazakhstan the first Russian-Kazakh (Russian-Native) schools were opened in the first half of the 19th century, while the earliest attempts at organizing training in Russian and various lay disciplines for Kazakhs (with a view to preparing local officials) date back to the end of the 18th century. Their curriculum included the study of the Russian language as opposed to the practice of traditional religious schools established at mosques. Russian was also taught at all other types of educational institutions (military, professional schools and gymnasiums) established in Kazakhstan. In the late 19th century Russian became a required subject in all schools of Kazakhstan; religious schools that did not organize the study of Russian were closed by governors.

The relatively small share of pupils (to the overall number of children) at Russian-Native schools was mainly determined by religious considerations as well as by social pressures. Traditional Muslim education in the Russian Empire evolved on its own to the point where, by the end of the 19th century, the Russian language was often included into the curriculum without any pressure from the authorities. This trend later manifested itself vividly in the so-called New Method Muslim schools (*novometodnye shkoly*), also known as Jadidist schools.[7] They were established in various parts of the Russian Empire with large Muslim populations as well as in some other countries in the late 19th century. The term Jadids was used to denote commonly a group of Muslim modernizers in the Russian Empire who believed that without a reform of traditional educational institutions in Muslim areas of the empire (along with introducing modern approaches in other spheres of life) that Russia's Muslim community would stagnate and remain backward and oppressed. The New Method schools, the first of which was founded by Crimean Tatar intellectual and politician Ismail Gasprinskiy in 1884, implemented a new approach to the elementary and secondary education of Muslims. It was relatively less religion-focused and more oriented towards the practical skills necessary in modern life. The training

---

[7] See Baldauf (2001) for an overview of Jadidist movement in Central Asia.

was carried out in the native language of the pupils. However, the curriculum also included Russian and sometimes other European languages (along with Arabic, which was important from a religious point of view) as the Jadidists considered the proficiency in European languages the key to advanced knowledge and technology. Not only was the Russian language taught at the New Method schools but Russian literature was actively translated by these schools' ideologists and teachers into the native languages of the empire's Muslims. For many Muslims the New Method schools represented a viable and relatively popular alternative to Russian-Native schools. These schools, however, raised the concerns of both the imperial authorities (wary of the supposedly Pan-Turkist and Pan-Islamic ideology of the New Method schools) and, to an even greater extent, of the traditionalist Muslim clergy. The New Method schools also did not become a mass phenomenon in most Muslim areas (with the exception of the Crimea and Volga regions).

The policy of promoting the study and the use of the Russian language among people of Central Asia and Caucasus, while clearly stated and formulated in official documents and in writings of state officials of the Russian Empire, was still rather poorly implemented. The primary obstacle was that, up until the last years of the Russian Empire, accessible government-financed universal education was not among the government priorities in these areas. In fact it was hardly a priority even in the core regions of Russia. By the late 19th century, obligatory universal primary education was introduced in many Western countries and in Japan. In Russia, however, the discussion of legal provisions for this only started at the end of the first decade of the 20th century as this issue was among the ones actively discussed in the newly created parliament of the Russian Empire – the State Duma (first convened in 1906). By 1917 according to Saprykin (2009) even in the European part of the empire the enrolment at primary schools was only universal for boys, while half of school-age girls were not enrolled; in the Asian part of the empire, these indicators were generally worse.

19.6 Language and politics in late imperial Russia

By the end of the 19th century Russia has created an empire whose different parts were separated by both huge geographical distances as well as by significant cultural, political, religious and linguistic differences. According to the imperial census of 1897, native Russian speakers comprised 44.31 per cent of the total population of the empire (without Finland); other major languages spoken each by more than 1 per cent of the population included Ukrainian, Polish, Belorussian, Yiddish and Hebrew, Kazakh, Tatar, German, Latvian and Bashkir.[8]

---

[8] See http://demoscope.ru/weekly/ssp/rus_lan_97.php (retrieved on 22 August 2014).

Rapid urbanization and growth of industry across the empire created a new class of industrial workers, more politically aware and active than the traditional peasantry. The development of science, culture and the mass media led to the emergence of an intelligentsia, including national intelligentsias in various ethnic areas of the empire. Fast economic growth was accompanied by increasing socio-economic inequalities. Meanwhile the political system remained unchanged; by the early 20th century Russia was still an autocratic monarchy with a thoroughly divided society and with no representative political bodies at the national level and with very limited scope for local self-government. But ruling the empire as if it was a conglomerate of different nations with varying legal and administrative systems as it had been in the 18th and early 19th centuries was no longer a viable option, primarily for political and economic reasons. Social and political unrest throughout the country as well as the rise of the German and Japanese Empires, the Pan-Turkist movement and other external factors fuelled separatist feelings in various parts of the empire and posed a challenge to the unity of the Russian state. Central authorities sought greater control over developments in the periphery of the empire and the expanding of the use of Russian in administrative and social affairs was part of this trend.

The introduction of universal conscription in 1874 implied corresponding changes in the language policy as it could not be implemented to full extent before ensuring universal knowledge of Russian throughout the empire (members of selected ethnic groups were initially exempt from conscription and the language issues were among the reasons).

Economically one of the most important aspects of the situation in Russia in the late 19th and early 20th centuries was the formation of an integrated imperial market. This was made possible in particular by the development of a transportation infrastructure which was promoted and assisted by the government from the middle of the 19th century. Newly built railways connected inner industrial and agrarian Russian regions with industrial areas and seaports in Poland, Finland and the Baltic provinces, as well as with oil mining areas in Caucasus and cotton-producing Turkestan. The growing fleet of river and sea vessels allowed increasing transportation via waterways.

This process unfolded along with the development of large-scale capitalist enterprises aiming not just at local but at national and international markets. Eventually most of these enterprises merged into syndicates and cartels, controlled by major Russian banks. The interests of these financial-industrial groups stretched all over the Russian Empire and beyond its borders. The old local bourgeoisie was giving way to the new entrepreneurs and corporate employees who were members of national and international business networks. The growing monopolistic syndicates were closely affiliated with the state bureaucracy and the aristocracy of the empire and were eager to use these ties to strengthen their hold on the existing markets and to conquer new ones. The fact that certain parts of the empire enjoyed even a limited degree of autonomy and were governed according to specific local laws could be an advantage to local businesses and bourgeoisie but was an obstacle to the expansion of monopolistic financial-industrial groups.

Thus by the late 19th century, Russian authorities responding to the needs of the new class of capitalists and in close cooperation with it began what Lenin called *internal colonization* and *the economic conquest which occurred later than the political one.*

In this context, the spreading of the knowledge and use of Russian was regarded as one possible way to ensure greater socio-cultural, economic and legal integration within the Russian Empire. The policy of Russification involved both the standardization of laws and regulations used throughout the empire (and thus the elimination of the remaining bits of political-administrative autonomy in non-Russian parts of the empire) and the forceful and rapid introduction of the Russian language in education and administration in various part of the empire, often regardless of whether there were objective preconditions for the success of such a policy (including the accessibility of education), along with restricting the use of other languages. In many areas this language policy represented a radical turn away from a relatively more flexible and gradual approach that was used during the previous decades, which predictably raised opposition among the ethnic minorities and the new political forces that represented them.

The ineffectiveness of the state language policy aimed at expanding the use of the Russian language eventually became obvious. It had its roots in the limited and inconsistent nature of the state educational policy that did not envision universal and accessible education for all social classes. To spread the Russian language without actually spreading education was a task doomed to fail. The attempts to solve the task of spreading the use and knowledge of it among non-Russian subjects in a fast and radical were not very successful. Instead of integrating people of other ethnicities with the Russians it alienated them, starting from parents of children who were deprived of the opportunity to get primary education in a language which they understood, to national intelligentsia who saw in it a threat to ethnic uniqueness, to local political and business circles who were not willing to surrender their position routed in part in the use of local languages.

At the turn of the century, the Russian Empire faced the escalation of social and political unrest. The discontent with the political and economic realities of late tsarism was growing all over the nation and concentrating in the capitals and major cities. The demands for civil freedom, political reforms and social justice were voiced throughout the empire. In the ethnic periphery they also included demands for national autonomy and/or independence and, at the very least, for greater rights and opportunities to use native languages in administration, publishing and education. The issue of languages was destined to become a recurring theme in the agenda of the emerging nationalistic political movement and parties in the context of the radical language policy of Alexander III and his heir Nicholas II. The authorities made a few concessions in the wake of the revolution of 1905–1907. These included for instance greater opportunities for education in native languages at the primary level (in 1905 the Committee of Ministers of the Russian Empire allowed using local languages in teaching arithmetic). The extent of these concessions was, however, limited.

In 1906 Nicholas II signed Russia's first constitution – the Fundamental Laws of the Russian Empire.[9] The third paragraph of the Fundamental Laws stipulated that the Russian language was the state language required for use in the army, navy and at all state and public establishments. According to the same paragraph the use of local languages at state and public establishments would be regulated by special laws; but the adoption of these was postponed and, due to World War I and the revolutions of 1917, never actually occurred.

Opinions on the issue of the state language policy among Russian politicians diverged. Conservatives and monarchists were proponents of the single state language which in their view had to be used throughout the country and be required for study at schools. More liberal politicians also spoke in favour of Russian being the state language but called for a more flexible policy including allowing the use of native languages in primary education and in other certain cases.

Marxists and Lenin in particular objected to the idea of state language regarding it as a tool of suppression. According to Lenin the economic development of the country would eventually bring various ethnic groups closer (including in the linguistic sense) without any forceful state policy. In his article 'Is there a Need for a Required State Language?' published in 1914 in the Marxist newspaper *Proletarskaya Pravda* he wrote:

> Those who need the Russian language in their life or work will learn it without being forced to. The compulsion will only lead to one thing: it will hinder the acceptance of the great and mighty Russian language within other ethnic groups, and most importantly – it will intensify the antagonism, will create a million new tensions, will strengthen the resentment, mutual distrust, etc.... This is why Russian Marxists say that there must be no compulsory state language while people should have access to schools with teaching in all local languages and that there should be a constitutional provision eliminating any privileges to a single ethnic group and any restrictions of rights of ethnic minorities (Lenin, 1973 [1914], p. 295).

---

[9] *Svod osnovnyh gosudarstvennyh zakonov* (1906).

19.7 The socialist revolution of 1917 and early Soviet language policy (1920–1930)

The views of Lenin and Russian Marxists on language issues and more generally on the issue of nationality and ethnicity reflected their idea that the working classes of different ethnicities and of different countries shared the same class interests and the same class enemies – the capitalists. The early 20th-century Russian Marxists cherished the idea of the world revolution which would get rid of the oppressive bourgeois state starting from Russia and then extending to other countries. Consistent with the idea that in order to make the global revolution possible the proletarians of the world would have to unite the followers of Marx and Lenin called for the removal of all factors that could separate and antagonize the proletarians. This implied the removal of any ethnic privileges including the privileged status of certain languages.

The position of Russian Marxists regarding ethnic and language issues in its original pure and radical form was virtually incompatible with the existence of a unified multi-ethnic state or for that matter of any state, at least in their early 20th century form. Their position made sense mostly in the context of the vision of the communist future in which the phenomenon of state (whether imperial or national) would be extinct. Predictably the implementation of Lenin's ideas (especially after his death) was eventually adapted to reality, although they were still revered in theory.

In November 1917 the Soviet government established the state commission on enlightenment and determined its tasks including that of achieving universal literacy. An important aspect of early Soviet education policy was the promotion of education in native languages. By the end of the 1920s, native language education was made available to most Soviet children. According to Smith (1997) this was a major factor in ensuring that people of various ethnicities recognized that Soviet Russia was no longer a 'prison house of nations'.

Also among the first practical steps of the government in the language sphere was the reform of Russian orthography. The traditional orthography was overly complex, thus causing significant difficulties for those studying Russian. As the task of attaining universal literacy was rising to the top of the official agenda, this issue could no longer be ignored for practical educational reasons. And there was another issue with easily calculable economic implications – the traditional spelling required more letters than was necessary to record the sounding of Russian words.

The discussion of the reform simplifying Russian orthography began long before the revolution – in 1904 at the Imperial Academy of Sciences. The debates and preparation lasted several years before it was ready and published in 1912. It was welcomed by the majority of the academic community and school teachers, although some conservatives opposed it on ideological and aesthetic pretexts. For a number of reasons the reform was not officially adopted until the end of tsarism in May 1917 when the provisional government of Russia approved it, though its actual implementation did not begin until 1918 after the Bolshevik Revolution. The orthographic reform of 1918 had important implications for the campaign for the eradication of illiteracy launched by the Soviet authorities as well for the typographic industry. Russian writer Lev Uspenskiy (1962) calculated that a long literary text (for example the novel *War and Peace* by Tolstoy) using the letter 'ъ' (hard sign) according to the old orthographic rules (where in most cases it was absolutely redundant) contained at least 3.4 per cent more letters than the text in which the use of that letter was limited to the cases where it actually affected pronunciation. Making printed texts several per cent shorter meant commensurable cost and time savings for the printing industry.

At the end of 1922 the First Congress of the Soviets of the Union of the Soviet Socialist Republics declared the establishment of the Union of the Soviet Republics of Russia, Ukraine, Belarus and Transcaucasia (Azerbaijan, Georgia and Armenia). The Constitution of the USSR was adopted in stages in 1923–1924. It confirmed the rights of the peoples of the USSR to self-determination and the federative nature of the new state. The constitution did not contain any mentions of state language or languages.

In 1924 the All-Russian Central Executive Committee issued a decree[10] stipulating that in the national republics and territories of the Russian Federation local languages were to be used in official affairs by the state bodies. This provision applied to these bodies' office work and their dealings with citizens, but not to their dealings with central authorities that had to be carried out in Russian. The decree called for organizing work on translating Soviet laws and government acts into local languages in order to make them known and accessible for those who could not speak Russian. The decree also stipulated preferences for those candidates for official and clerical positions who spoke local languages of the territories concerned. Similar acts were adopted in other constituent republics of the USSR. In 1925 the Council of People's Commissars of Russia issued a decree[11] on organizing at pedagogical institutes and universities the training of teachers for schools at which Russian was not the language of instruction.

---

[10] *Dekret Vserossiyskogo Centralnogo Ispolnitelnogo Komiteta ot 14.04.1924 'O merah k perevodu deloproizvodstva gosudarstvennyh organov v natsionalnyh oblastyah i respublikah na mestnye yazyki'.*
[11] *Dekret Soveta Narodnih Kommisarov RSFSR ot 21.11.1925 'O podgotovke prepodavateley dlya shkol natsionalnostey nerusskogo yazyka'.*

One of the most controversial language policy issues in the early Soviet years was the campaign for Romanization of alphabets. Lunacharskiy, the Soviet commissar of enlightenment in 1917–1929, was among the most ardent supporters of this idea. As early as 1919 he called for the transition of all languages in the territory of Soviet Russia to the Latin alphabet, including the Russian language. Lenin, while against immediate and hasty introduction of the Latin script for the Russian language, was not against it in principle. He called for a thorough investigation of and even preparation for such a step in the future.

The issue of alphabets for the peoples of the USSR was a subject of discussion and conflict even before the revolution. East Slavic people, including Russians, Ukrainians and Belarusians, had used the Cyrillic alphabet for centuries. The Latin alphabet was used by Finns, Poles, Lithuanians, Estonians, Latvians and by other peoples in the western parts of the Russian Empire. Jews, Armenians and Georgians used their own ancient alphabets, and so did the Chinese and Koreans living in the far east of Russia. Muslim peoples of the Russian Empire used the Arabic alphabet. In the 18–19th centuries Russian orthodox missionaries made the first attempts at using the Cyrillic alphabet to record translations of religious books into the languages of non-Christian people. In the early 19th century Nicholas I considered the idea of introducing Cyrillic for the Polish language but this idea was eventually abandoned. In the second half of the 19th century for instance Ilminskiy in cooperation with some of his Tatar students developed an alphabet for the Tatar language based on Cyrillic and used it for the Tatar versions of the Bible and other religious books.

By the early 20th century Cyrillic-derived alphabets were developed for many languages of the Russian Empire. As they usually were introduced in the context of religious proselytizing, the attitude towards them among non-Russian peoples reflected their fears of Russification and Christianization. The quest for national autonomy or independence and the struggle against tsarism often contained calls for abandoning Cyrillic in favour of Latin or Arabic. The justification for using Latin or Arabic scripts was primarily political and ideological, based both on the idea that the Russian language and the Cyrillic alphabet had been a tool of imperial oppression and (in the case of Latin) on the belief that the Latin script was destined to eventually become the standard global alphabet, universal and associated with modernity. The latter idea had in fact emerged much earlier when some Russian scholars suggested using the Latin script for the Russian language as early as the first half of the 19th century. Several versions of a Romanized Russian alphabet were developed then, but the idea did not gain much popularity before the Revolution of 1917.

The Romanization campaign according to its proponents was to eventually involve all languages of the Soviet state. It started in the early 1920s, not with Russian but with the languages of Caucasus and Transcaucasia. In 1923 the Latin alphabet was introduced in Azerbaijan. The Azeri experience gave the momentum to further movement in this direction (not only in the Soviet Union, but also in Turkey where the Latin alphabet was introduced in 1928; at about the same time a discussion of potential Romanization started in Persia). In 1926 the All-Union Congress of Turkologists representing both the academic community and various Turkic nationalities and ethnic groups of Russia met in Baku, the capital of Azerbaijan, to discuss the issue of alphabet reform for Turkic languages. While some candidates argued for the continued use of a reformed Arabic script most of the Congress attendees spoke in favour of Romanization. The Congress's resolution was supported by the Soviet authorities and in 1929 after some preparatory work the Soviet government and the Communist Party decreed that within two years the Latin alphabet was to be introduced for Turkic languages. Soon after that similar decisions were made with respect to a number of other languages. In most cases the Latin alphabet was introduced either in place of Arabic or for languages that had no script at all. There were, however, some cases (such as with the Yakut language) where the Latin alphabet replaced Russian Cyrillic.

By the mid-1930s most languages on the territory of the Soviet Union were provided with Latin-based alphabets. To the supporters of Romanization it seemed an obvious success and indication that soon Russian and other Slavic languages along with Georgian, Armenian and Yiddish would also start using the Latin alphabet. The Commissariat of Enlightenment in 1929 formed a group of experts to discuss and prepare a project of introducing the Latin alphabet for the Russian language. In addition to the earlier arguments in favour of Romanization (such as the overall global trend for greater standardization in all areas) additional economic arguments were raised: using the Latin alphabet would presumably lead to lower costs of publishing as Latin letters were more compact than most of their Cyrillic equivalents.

However, already in 1930, the project of introducing the Latin alphabet for the Russian language was denounced by Stalin who explicitly ordered the cessation of any further work on the Romanization of the Russian alphabet. Not only was the Romanization of Russian language associated with much greater costs than that of most other languages of the USSR (especially considering the literary tradition and the amount of already existing books and publications in Cyrillic) but it also came into conflict with the changing ideological atmosphere in the Soviet Union – during this period it was already very different from the 1920s.

19.8   Late Soviet language policy (1930–1980)

The 1930s were marked by a serious shift in the ethnic and language policy in the Soviet Union. The revolutionary mood of the 1920s along with the hopes of the global communist revolution spreading from Russia to other countries was gone, together with the old Bolsheviks, many of whom became victims of Stalinist purges. What had earlier been known as the internationalism was now classified as the cosmopolitanism and began to be regarded as an ideological threat to the Soviet state. The federative principle that was observed (at least to some extent) in the early years of the Soviet Union gave way to the practice of political centralization with the ensuing implications for ethnic and language policies.

Starting in 1936 the policy of Romanization was reversed and the Russian Cyrillic alphabet was within a few years introduced for most languages of the Soviet Union. In 1940 the Cyrillic alphabet was also adopted in Mongolia in the context of the strengthening links with the Soviet Union.

The transition of most languages in the USSR to the Cyrillic alphabet was a political decision; the earlier Romanization was criticized as detaching ethnic minorities from Russians and driving them closer to the 'imperialist' Western countries (and in the case of Muslim peoples – to Turkey). Nevertheless this step had its own positive consequences. The unification of the alphabets of the peoples of the Soviet Union on the basis of the Cyrillic alphabet facilitated the campaign for universal literacy as well as the study of Russian by non-Russians as students no longer had to learn several alphabets.

Meanwhile the Soviet authorities continued promoting the publishing of literature in the native languages of the peoples of the USSR. Initially the publishing was organized centrally (in Moscow and other major cities) and in 1931 the Presidium of the Central Executive Committee of the USSR ordered[12] that this task was to be carried out by publishing houses established in the national republics and regions of the Union; for those regions and ethnic groups that did not have publishing houses yet the literature in their languages was to be published by central houses that had to establish special departments for each relevant language.

The Soviet Constitution of 1936 reiterated the principle of the federative nature of the Soviet state as the union of autonomous republics. Similarly to the Constitution of 1924, it did not contain any mention of a state language. Interestingly, at the very same time that the constitutions of the Soviet republics of Georgia and Armenia were adopted, in 1937, Georgian and Armenian respectively were declared as the state languages of these republics. The constitutions of other Soviet republics did not contain such provisions, though in 1956 a similar provision was added to the 1937 constitution of Azerbaijan regarding the Azeri language.

---

[12] *Postanovleniye Prezidiuma Centralnogo Isponitelnogo Komiteta SSSR ot 21.09.1931 'Ob izdanii literatury na yazykah natsionalnyh menshinstv'.*

In 1938 the Council of People's Commissars of the USSR and the Central Committee of the Communist Party issued a joint decree[13] making the Russian language a required subject at all schools of the Soviet Union. At the same time it was specifically noted in the decree that making Russian the required subject did not imply that it should become the language of instruction instead of native languages at national schools. The decree instructed state and party bodies of the Soviet republics to undertake steps needed to ensure that graduates of schools where Russian was not the primary language of instruction possessed a sufficient working knowledge of it. Following this decree the national republics and regions of the Soviet Union adopted their own plans and programmes of introducing and/or improving the teaching of the Russian language at national schools.

The making of the Russian language a required subject at schools reflected a major turn in the ethnic and state-building policy of the Communist Party and the Soviet state in the 1930s. By then Stalin and the Soviet authorities had abandoned the naïve post-revolutionary vision of the Soviet Union as a conglomerate of nations that would expand as the revolutionary communist ideas gained popularity among the proletarians of the world. Instead they adopted a goal of consolidating and developing the Soviet Union as a state federation in principle but one which was centralized (especially in economic and ideological spheres) in practice. With regard to the ethnic/national issues the Communist Party declared its adherence to the idea put forth by Lenin about nations and ethnicities being transitory phenomena that would eventually converge due to social and economic progress. While on a global scale this still seemed a distant future in the Soviet Union, this process was to be facilitated and advanced. The natural foundation for the new composite Soviet nation were Russians and the Russian language. As Kirkwood (1991) notes, on the territory of the USSR no other language could compete with Russian in terms of its communicative importance. The elevation of the status of the Russian language in the 1930s was thus inevitable once the need for a common language was recognized.

The most pressing practical reason was the problem of military conscripts without the knowledge of Russian. Although universal conscription existed in the Russian Empire and was after a short break reinstituted in the Soviet Union, in practice up until the late 1930s it was rather selective with numerous exemptions and modifications. These included among others ethnic exemptions: representatives of various ethnic minorities were either not conscripted at all or were drafted into appropriate ethnically homogeneous and/or territorial units of the Red Army. By the late 1930s this practice was officially recognized

---

[13] *Postanovleniye SNK SSSR, CK VKP(b) ot 13.03.1938 No324 'Ob obyazatelnom izuchenii russkogo yazyka v shkolah natsionalnyh respublik i oblastey'.*

to be outdated; starting from 1938, the ethnicity and the territory of the origin of conscripts were no longer considered during the draft. Thus, the command of Russian among conscripts was crucial for the modernization of the Soviet army, and hence it was introduced into schools throughout the country.

In addition, the industrialization of the Soviet Union involved large-scale infrastructure projects and the construction of factories, plants and industrial facilities in previously less developed areas. The construction and exploitation of the new industrial facilities and infrastructure in the centrally planned and administered economy necessitated a broader knowledge and use of Russian. To an extent this shift occurred following the failure of the earlier policy of promoting native cadres in national republics and regions along with the use of national languages (the policy known as *korenizatsiya* (nativization)). This had rather devastating effects in less developed regions with a shortage of local educated and experienced personnel (in Asia and Caucasus) while in more developed European regions it often led to the loss of administrative and ideological control by the central Soviet authorities. The authorities admitted that, ideological considerations aside, there were few and not enough alternatives to Russian-speaking experts and administrators in most regions.

Starting from the late 1930s the use of Russian in official affairs and in education began to expand. This process reflected both the strategy of the Soviet government as well as the growing pragmatic interest of the non-Russian Soviet citizens who saw the professional and career advantages of speaking Russian. During the same period, the practice of denouncing the historical and cultural heritage of Russia as a throwback and an old-regime relic was partially abandoned. The new vision of the Soviet people united around the Russians had predictable implications regarding the common language for this new society.[14] In a way, however, this was not an entirely new vision and policy; according to Smith (1998), it echoed the policies that had already been used by the authorities of the Russian Empire long before that.

At the same time the Soviet government both officially and in practice continued to favour the establishment of schools with teaching in native languages and provided them with textbooks and literature, which was made possible by the parallel campaign of developing the publishing industry in the national republics and regions. Anderson and Silver (1984) in their study of Soviet language policy admit that it was neither absolutely egalitarian nor russificationist, but rather promoted bilingual education.

This applied mostly to secondary education, however; the situation with higher education was different. Higher education in the USSR developed mostly

---

[14] See, for instance, Blitstein (2006) for a discussion of the ideological shift in the Soviet ethnic policy in 1930s.

as highly specialized technical education (as opposed to liberal education). Universities and institutes were to serve the needs of the centrally planned economy and their graduates were assigned to enterprises and organizations throughout the Soviet Union. It was important that the skills of the graduates were standardized and applicable throughout the country. Therefore the language of higher education was predominantly Russian. A few old universities and institutes in the national republics continued using native languages but newly established institutes used mainly Russian.

The Great Patriotic War (1941–1945) and the victory of the Soviet Union and the allies had a thorough and complex impact on all spheres of life in the USSR and Eastern Europe including in the language sphere. In the Soviet Union the fight against the fascist invaders brought together tens of millions of people of different ethnic and linguistic backgrounds; the Russian language firmly established itself as the language of interethnic communication. For those non-Russians who fought side by side with the Russians during the war as well as for their family members, the Russian language was no longer a language associated with oppression or colonialism of the past but the common language of the victors in the Patriotic War.

In the post-war period the newly obtained superpower status and the ambitions of the Soviet Union greatly expanded the study and the use of the Russian language far beyond its borders and made it one of the international languages. It became one of the official languages of the United Nations and the official and/or working language in a number of other international organizations and institutions. The establishment of communist regimes in the countries of Eastern Europe and the increased Soviet influence in Asia brought the Russian language into the academic curricula of many countries as a required subject. The interest in the language also grew in Western countries.

Following the Great Patriotic War, the vision of Soviet society as a new meta-ethnic unity was taken further by Nikita Khrushchev. Further convergence and fusion of the nationalities of the Soviet Union was officially declared to be a step in the building of a communist society in the Third Programme of the Communist Party of the Soviet Union adopted in 1962. The Programme guaranteed the development of all nationalities and languages of the Soviet Union at the same time calling for the study of the Russian language along with native languages.

The reform of the educational system in the 1960s and 1970s aimed at bringing curricula closer to the practical needs of the economy. It provided local authorities with greater flexibility in determining the language of instruction at schools as well as the number of hours dedicated to the study of various languages depending on the ethnic composition of the local population and the parents' opinions. This led to an increase in the number of schools with Russian as the language of instruction and to the increase in the number of academic hours allocated to Russian in the curricula of non-Russian schools. The study of the other languages of the peoples of the USSR was essentially made optional. This policy was finally formalized in the 1970s. Article 20 of the law of 1973 'On the Fundamentals of the Legislations of the USSR and of the Union Republics on Public Education'[15] stipulated that parents had the right to choose the school for their children depending on the language of instruction; the study of other languages of the peoples of the USSR besides the language of instruction was optional. For schools where Russian was not the language of instruction, the conditions for its study to full command were guaranteed. Foreign languages were also to be taught at schools.

The demand for Russian language education was high among the peoples of all nationalities as it was considered necessary for successful further studies and professional activities. This led to the expansion of its study and/or use in schools, especially urban schools; it was introduced as the primary language of instruction, or the number of hours dedicated to it was increased, at many schools in response to parents' demands. In some parts of the Soviet Union (for instance in Kazakhstan and Central Asia) this process also reflected the growing share of Russians and Russian-speakers in the urban population as a result of the mass migration of people from core Russian regions.

In 1977 a new Soviet Constitution was adopted. It confirmed the equal status of all nationalities. Article 36 guaranteed the opportunity to use a native language or any other language of the peoples of the Soviet Union. Article 45 introduced universal free and compulsory secondary education and stipulated the right for school education (secondary) in a native language. Article 116 stipulated that the laws and official acts of the Soviet Union were to be published in the languages of all Soviet republics. Article 159 said that judicial procedures were to be conducted in the language of the republic, autonomous republic or autonomous region; for people without the knowledge of that language a translator was to be provided; citizens had the right to speak in court in their native language.

In 1978 following the adoption of the new Soviet Constitution, new constitutions were adopted in all Soviet republics. The provisions regarding languages to be used to publish legal acts and in judicial affairs were similar to the provisions of the Union Constitution and in most republics implied the use of the local language or languages along with Russian. As before most of the new constitutions of the Union and autonomous republics did not contain any mention of state or official languages and indicated the equal status of languages. The three notable exceptions were the constitutions of Armenia, Georgia and Azerbaijan

---

[15] *Zakon SSSR ot 19.07.1973 No 4536-VIII 'Ob utverzhdenii osnov zakonodatelstva Soyuza SSR I soyuznyh respublik o narodnom obrazovanii'.*

which did mention state languages, thus continuing the legal tradition established in their earlier constitutions. Initially the drafts of the new constitutions prepared by local state and party authorities and published in 1978 for public discussion mentioned Russian as the state language replacing Armenian, Georgian and Azeri in these republics, while guaranteeing the continued use of other languages. It is difficult to say whether this was a local initiative or a response to a request from Central Soviet authorities; more likely it was the former as it represented an obvious deviation from the pre-dominant constitutional and legal practice. In practical terms this provision would not have any effect on the de facto official bilingualism of each of these republics. Whether it reflected local party officials' genuine eagerness to please their superiors in Moscow or was a carefully calculated provocation it did spark public protests, first in Georgia and later in Armenia. In response to these protests the Georgian, Armenian and Azeri languages were made the state languages of the respective republics. About a decade later, in 1989, in the context of political liberalization and growing separatist and nationalist sentiments, most other Soviet republics adopted similar norms in the form of amendments to their constitutions or in the form of new laws.

By the end of the Soviet era the knowledge of Russian among peoples of different ethnicities was high, though it was uneven among urban and rural residents and across ethnicities. The census of 1989 indicated that out of the total population of almost 286 million people more than 232 million (81.4 per cent) declared that Russian was either their native or their second language.

The goal of ensuring a strong command of the Russian language was more or less achieved by the state at the end of the 1980s, at least among the urban population. Whether it was done at the expense of other languages has long been a matter of debate. Some observers during that period would claim that the other languages of the USSR were suppressed and that non-Russian citizens were increasingly deprived of opportunities to study or obtain information in their own languages.[16] The available statistics[17] on languages of instruction at regular secondary schools in the republics of the USSR at the end of the 1980s does not support this view. The use of Russian as the language of instruction at schools varied across Soviet republics while being positively correlated with the share of ethnic Russians in the population. The share of pupils at Russian-language schools was the largest in the Russian Soviet Federative Socialist Republic (98.2 per cent), Belorussian SSR (79.2 per cent), Kazakh SSR (67.4 per cent) and Ukrainian SSR (51.8 per cent). In other republics the share

---

[16] See, for instance, Bilinsky (1981) for a critical (if not rather anti-Soviet) review of Soviet language policy.

[17] *Narodnoye obrazovanie i kultura v SSSR: Statisticheskiy sbornik* (Moscow: Finansy i statistika, 1989), pp. 88–91.

was not dominant: 15 per cent in Uzbek SSR, 23.6 per cent in Georgian SSR, 18.5 per cent in Azerbaijan SSR, 15.8 per cent in Lithuanian SSR, 40.9 per cent in Moldavian SSR, 47.6 per cent in Latvian SSR, 35.7 per cent in Kirgiz SSR, 9.7 per cent in Tadjik SSR, 15.1 per cent in Armenian SSR, 16 per cent in Turkmen SSR and 36.5 per cent in Estonian SSR.

The development of national/ethnic cultures of the peoples of the USSR was one of the declared priorities of cultural and ethnic policy of the Soviet Union and was supported by the central Soviet authorities throughout all the years of the Soviet era. A substantial share of publications in languages other than Russian was published not in the respective national or autonomous republics but in Moscow, Leningrad and the other major centres of the USSR, although as the capacity of publishing houses and typographies elsewhere grew so did their share of printed matter. According to the available statistics,[18] in 1988 in the Soviet Union books were published in 70 languages of the peoples of the USSR and 54 foreign languages; newspapers were published in 56 languages of the peoples of the USSR and ten foreign languages; and magazines and journals were published in 44 languages of the peoples of the USSR and 26 foreign languages.[19]

It should be acknowledged though that despite various measures aimed at supporting and developing the minor languages of the Soviet Union (such as the promotion of publishing in the native languages of the peoples of the USSR) their actual role in peoples' lives was decreasing as the knowledge and the use of the Russian language expanded.

Gorbachev's political liberalization in the second half of the 1980s invoked demands for greater autonomy if not independence of the Soviet republics which among other things involved calls for restoring the role and status of their respective languages, particularly in education. In some of the Soviet republics, this led to the introduction of optional study of native languages at Russian schools and to further calls for the required study of local languages along with Russian. By the end of the 1980s the authorities of many republics of the USSR were considering or had already given official status to native languages. This trend was opposed by the central Soviet authorities who regarded it as a reflection of separatist and nationalistic tendencies.[20]

In April 1990 the Supreme Soviet of the USSR adopted the 'Law on Languages of the Peoples of the USSR'. It was the first law using the term 'official language'

---

[18] *Narodnoye obrazovanie i kultura v SSSR: Statisticheskiy sbornik* (Moscow: Finansy i statistika, 1989), pp. 376–377.

[19] *Narodnoye obrazovanie i kultura v SSSR: Statisticheskiy sbornik* (Moscow: Finansy i statistika, 1989), pp. 387–392.

[20] See Kirkwood (1991) for an overview of the language policies in the USSR in the late 1980s.

(but not 'state language' as that would contradict Lenin's ideas about state language being unnecessary) to be adopted in the Soviet Union. This law pretty much put the earlier existing practice into a legal framework; it did not contain any radical novelties, nor did it give the Russian language some exclusive status. The law stipulated that the Russian language was the official language of the Soviet Union and the language of interethnic communication. Its official status meant that it was the language to be used by Union authorities (the government, the union courts, the deputies of the soviets). The status of the languages of Union republics was to be determined by the republican authorities; the republics were entitled to finance and to carry out measures on the development of their respective languages. The law guaranteed the right of citizens to a primary and secondary education in their native language which meant that parents could choose a specific school with a relevant language. The study of the Russian language as the official language of the Soviet Union was still required at secondary schools where the language of instruction was different. The Russian language was also still the only language to be used in the military forces and in the diplomatic missions of the Soviet Union. Central TV channels and the mass media were to use Russian; the use of other languages in republican mass media was to be determined by republican authorities.

This law continued the earlier Soviet language policy while providing the republics with greater rights in determining local language policies including those aimed at development of local languages. It was not, however, destined to have a lasting impact as the Soviet Union was dissolved in 1991.

19.9   Russian and other languages of the Russian Federation in the post-Soviet period

The first post-Soviet Constitution of the Russian Federation was adopted in 1993. Article 26 of the Constitution stipulates that everyone has the right to use a native language and to choose freely the language of communication, upbringing, study and creativity. Article 29 bans any propaganda of social, racial, ethnic or language superiority. Article 68 stipulates that the state language of the Russian Federation throughout its territory is Russian. The ethnic republics of the Russian Federation may set their own state languages to be used by state and municipal bodies and agencies of these republics on an equal basis with Russian. Article 68 also guarantees all ethnic groups on the territory of Russia the preservation, study and development of their own languages.

The Constitution of 1993 provides a general framework for the language policy in Russia which is regulated in more detail by the law 'On the languages of the peoples of the Russian Federation' (adopted in 1991) and the law 'On the state language of the Russian Federation' (adopted in 2005). Federal language policy is implemented on the basis of a series of federal targeted programmes entitled 'Russian language'. The first two programmes were adopted for the periods 2002–2005 and 2006–2010. The current programme was adopted in 2011 for the period 2011–2015. The goal of the programme is the support, preservation and spreading of the Russian language in Russia and among compatriots residing abroad. The programme envisions such measures as: the state support of the development and publishing of specific audience-targeted dictionaries and textbooks of Russian, both in Russia and abroad; the state support of the training of teachers of Russian; the development and promotion of new technologies and tools of distance education to make academic literature in Russian available and accessible to students worldwide; the research and monitoring of the use of Russian in Russia and abroad in order to mitigate and prevent possible conflicts and to increase the effectiveness of the programme.

The census of 2010 indicated that the total number of residents of Russia with a command of Russian was 137.5 million out of the total population of 142.9 million people (96.2 per cent). Russian was the most widely spread language both among ethnic Russians and among all major ethnic groups.

Despite the dominant role of the Russian language in all spheres of life and particularly in education other languages are also widely used within the ethnic republics of the Russian Federation. While the share of secondary schools with Russian as the language of instruction exceeds 90 per cent for the country as a whole, there are regions (primarily ethnic republics) where a substantial share of schools (and in some cases most secondary schools) either combine instruction in Russian with instruction in native languages or provide training solely in native languages.

In the publishing industry the Russian language also enjoys the dominant position and even more so than in the Soviet period. This is a result of several factors. On the one hand the state support of publishing in different languages which was a part of the Soviet language policy is not as substantial as it used to be. Also the titles and number of copies published in different languages are currently mostly determined by market forces and it is predictably more feasible for publishers to address as wide a market share as possible, which means that the Russian language is the preferred choice without any state interference.

As ethnic republics of Russia are allowed by the Constitution and laws of Russia to set their own state languages in addition to Russian (and other regions may introduce the official use of specific languages in areas with a high concentration of people of particular ethnicities) there are now more than 40 languages with an official status in Russia. In several ethnic republics (Tatarstan, Bashkortostan, Yakutia) the study of the state languages of these republics is required at all schools along with the study of Russian.

In the former Soviet republics the situation around the study and the use of Russian varies greatly. A Gallup poll carried out in 2008 aimed at identifying the actual language preferences of people in the post-Soviet states by registering the respondents' choice of language for the Gallup interview. According to the poll Russian was the preferred language for the majority of people in Ukraine, Belarus and Kazakhstan, as well as for significant shares of the populations of Kyrgyzstan and Moldova.[21] The preference for Russian over national languages in other republics was significantly lower, but as related Gallup research suggests even there the absolute majority of respondents consider knowledge of Russian as a foreign language very important or somewhat important and one of the primary reasons is the importance of the Russian labour market for migrants from the former USSR.[22] It should also be noted that the role and the popularity of the Russian language varies greatly across regions of the post-Soviet countries as well as between the urban and rural population.[23]

According to Arefyev (2012, p. 390) in 2010 the total number of people with at least some knowledge of Russian was 260.3 million people and the number of those for whom Russian was the native language was 146.8 million people worldwide (down from 312 million and 164.6 million respectively in 1990). Arefyev also provides estimates of the number of people with at least some knowledge of Russian in 2009–2012 (depending on the availability of data for specific countries) beyond Russian borders. The countries with the largest number of Russian-speakers include Ukraine (36.8 million), Kazakhstan (13.5 million), Uzbekistan (11.8 million), Belarus (9.3 million), Poland (5.5 million) and Germany (5.4 million), followed mostly by countries of the former Soviet bloc (Arefyev, 2012, pp. 432–433).

19.10 Summary: Socio-economic and political factors and implications of language policy in Russia in historical perspective

It is possible to postulate that the dialectical and linguistic diversity was only seen by the Russian and later the Soviet state as a problem insofar as it complicated the task of governing and controlling such a huge nation. Within the unified Russian state that had emerged by the 16th century, dialectical and linguistic diversity became a practical problem particularly because it limited the effectiveness of communication between central and local officials. It was necessary to standardize the language and the choice of the future standard was

---

[21] S. Gradirovski and N. Esipova. *Russian Language Enjoying a Boost in Post-Soviet States*, www.gallup.com/poll/109228/russian-language-enjoying-boost-postsoviet-states.aspx, retrieved on 22 August 2014.

[22] S. Gradirovski and N. Esipova. *Russia's Language Could Be Ticket in for Migrants*, www.gallup.com/poll/112270/russias-language-could-ticket-migrants.aspx, retrieved on 22 August 2014.

[23] See Pavlenko (2008) for an overview of the Russian language's status in post-Soviet countries.

predetermined by the dominant status of Moscow as the capital of the unifying Russia. Moscow official (or chancery) language which eventually became the foundation of the Russian language of later periods did not come to dominance through solely evolutionary means. This was an outcome of a purposeful state policy that reflected the authorities' understanding of the role of language in state governance.

Similar practical considerations, although understood more broadly, also guided Peter the Great in the early 18th century. His policy with regard to the Russian language was to bring the language used in official affairs and in secular publications closer to the colloquial language, thus ensuring the accessibility of knowledge and information to a wide audience as it was crucial to Russia's modernization. Following his orders, foreign books began to be translated into the Russian language. As many of these books (textbooks, manuals) were of practical importance, translators were ordered to use a language as close to common Russian as possible and to avoid expressions and constructs pertaining to Church Slavonic.

The drive towards the standardization and expansion of the use of the Russian language (combined with favouring the learning of European languages) was initially motivated by the rather practical considerations of administrative efficiency and socio-economic modernization. As such, it concerned primarily state bureaucracy and elites. However, by the second half of the 19th century language issues were brought to the top of the political agenda as they were closely linked to the challenges that Russia faced then. These challenges were of an economic and political nature.

Economically, Russia began transforming into a capitalist economy. This led to the rise of the class of capitalists who were very different in their resources and ambitions from Russian merchants of the previous eras. New capitalist enterprises needed secure access to new markets on the periphery of the Russian Empire to buy commodities and to sell their produce. That also meant that legal regulations, judicial procedures and all other aspects of the business environment had to be as similar as possible throughout the empire. Standardizing the regulation and official procedures without using a common language would be next to impossible.

Politically, the rapid territorial expansion of the Russian Empire by the second half of the 19th century brought on a task of integrating diverse ethnic groups into a single imperial organism. The empire was comprised of territories that were not only very diverse ethnically, culturally, religiously and linguistically, but also were governed differently. Russian law was applied throughout core Russian regions, Siberia and much of modern-day Ukraine, Belarus and Lithuania. Some territories, however, enjoyed a varying degree of autonomy in local governance, religious and judicial affairs. This implied a wide variety of approaches used in state language policy throughout the empire although the core task of promoting the use of Russian was of course present in all its parts although to different extents. The government's policy of advancing the use of the Russian language in most spheres of life was not led so much by the desire to assimilate other peoples or to make them Russian (especially considering that the scale of religious proselytizing by the Russian Church was very limited) as by the task of turning an imperial conglomerate of nations into a unified political and socio-economic space. Weeks (2004) suggests the Russification policy in the late 19th century was to a large extent a defensive policy adopted by imperial authorities in response to the growing influence of separatist and nationalist elites in some parts of the empire.

It is important to realize that in Russia the key socio-economic phenomenon of the second half of the 19th century was the development of capitalism and the formation of the integrated imperial market. The construction of new railways, the development of means of transportation and telecommunications coincided with the emergence of large-scale industrial and trade companies which eventually came under the control of financial-industrial groups. These monopolistic groups led by St Petersburg and Moscow-based banks sought to expand their influence and to secure access to markets all over the empire. While supported in their quest by the imperial court and the government, they naturally faced resistance from local bourgeoisie that relied on legal and/or political advantages entrenched in local laws and governance practices, including those related to languages. The economic resources and the political influence of the rapidly growing Russian cartels and syndicates eventually overpowered those of the old local elites in the ethnic periphery of the empire and brought along the new policies aimed as deeper integration and unification, including in the language sphere. Lenin (1899) noted that Russian capitalism was pulling Caucasus, Central Asia, Siberia and other regions into global trade while creating markets for itself and simultaneously neutralizing local specificity.

The strongest opposition to the expanding use of Russian at the end of the 19th and into the early 20th century was usually found not among common people of a certain ethnicity but among specific social classes whose position and privileges were threatened by the changes in the regulatory environment and by the intensifying economic competition with Russian companies.[24]

The most obvious example is the Baltic provinces (the Ostsee governorates), where up to the late 19th century political and economic power belonged to German barons whose rights and privileges had been affirmed after the conquest of the Baltic region by Peter the Great. While Germans represented a very small part of the population of the Baltic provinces, they did everything to

---

[24] See Thaden (1981).

limit the use of any other language but German. This situation contradicted at once the interests of the imperial authorities and of the native peoples of these lands. The opposition there and the sabotage of the introduction of the Russian language to a significant extent reflected the political and economic interests of the German barons. In the case of the Grand Duchy of Finland, the interests of the dominant Swedish community should not be overlooked when analysing obstacles to the development of the Finnish language and literature for decades after the inclusion of Finland into the Russian Empire and for any attempts to expand the usage of Russian. And in Poland and territories with a substantial Polish population, nationalist sentiments and the opposition to Russification were intermingled with the opposition to the de-Polonization of Ukrainian, Belorussian and Lithuanian territories that had previously been under strong Polish influence.[25]

The ethnic and language issues were high on the agenda of political parties and revolutionary movements up until the revolution of 1917 causing significant controversies and conflicts. Political movements and public figures representing ethnic minorities objected to the idea of Russian being the official state language required for study throughout the empire and called for the greater or exclusive use of native languages in administrative affairs and education in non-Russian territories. The socialist revolution of 1917 brought not only the idea of national and ethnic autonomy and self-governance with ensuing changes in language policy. In the early years of the Soviet regime the Russian language not only lost its privileged status but in some ways was even discriminated against while perceived by some as a tool of former imperial oppression. More importantly, the substitution of Russian with other languages in administration and education at the regional level allowed placing local activists and members of the Communist party into official positions. This process of entrusting regional and local decision-making to the representatives of ethnic groups native to these regions came to be known as the *korenizatsiya* (nativization). It was both supported by and in its turn ensured the raising of the status of native languages and the downgrading of the status of the Russian language. This policy had both positive consequences (such as the fostering of local elites, presumably more aware of the needs of the local people, and promoting the development of ethnic cultures and native-language education) and negative consequences (many if not most of the newly promoted local

---

[25] It is difficult to determine to what extent the opposition to the Russian Empire's language policy (by Baltic Germans, Poles in Ukraine, Belorussia and Lithuania, and Swedes in Finland) was the opposition to Russification and to what extent it was motivated by the fear of losing traditional influence over local ethnically different populations. An attempt to analyse the response to the 19th century Russian ethnic and language policies in the Western borderlands of the Empire can be found in Staliunas (2007).

officials would have never qualified for any position under the old regime not only due to their poor knowledge of Russian but also due to their low level of skills and/or ethics). Both the campaign of the nativization and the policy of promoting linguistic diversity in the Soviet Union took a rather anarchic form so that their negative consequences eventually outweighed the positive ones.

There was a radical change in the ethnic and language policies of the Soviet Union in the 1930s. While many authors are aware of it, they often do not notice the underlying economic factors. Starting from 1928 Soviet economic policy was implemented according to five-year plans aimed at the rapid industrialization of the country. The development of the system of centralized socio-economic planning was contingent upon establishing a firm control by the central authorities over regional affairs. This had profound implications for ethnic and language policies. A major shift in the language policy occurred with the reintroduction of Russian as a required subject at all Soviet schools in 1938. The motivation behind this decision was complex, involving both purely practical and political-ideological reasons.[26]

From the 1960s to the 1980s Central Soviet authorities began actively promoting the knowledge of Russian among the peoples of the other ethnicities as it corresponded to the post-war ideological goal of forging the unity of the peoples of the USSR and more specifically to the goal of guaranteeing equal socio-economic status for them. In this policy context, the knowledge of Russian among non-Russians was regarded not only by central authorities but also by the leadership of ethnic republics as a way to ensure broad access to the best educational, professional and political (party) career opportunities for people of different ethnicities. A series of reforms carried out in the 1960s and 1970s while preserving the required study of Russian at all schools made the study of the other languages of the USSR at Russian-language schools optional (depending on the wishes of parents). As a result, Russian-language instruction expanded rapidly. Eventually growing Russian bilingualism among non-Russians and the increased geographical mobility of both Russians and non-Russians who were increasingly dispersed all over the Soviet Union became mutually reinforcing processes.[27]

By the 1980s, the Russian language became not just a language of inter-ethnic communication but the primary language of communication among the majority of people of the USSR regardless of their ethnic origin. Some external and internal observers in the final decade of the Soviet Union saw it as proof of a deliberate policy aimed at replacing all other languages of the country with

---

[26] See Koutaissoff (1951) and Kirkwood (1991) for an overview of the evolution of Soviet language policy.

[27] See Lewis (1971) for a discussion.

Table 19.1 Historical summary of Russian state language policies and their socio-economic factors and implications from the 15th to the 21st century

Period	Language policy priorities	Potential economic and political motivation
15th–17th centuries	Standardization of the Russian language based on Moscow official (chancery) language.	Dialectical differences complicated communications between central and local authorities, created ambiguities in the interpretation of regulations and thus limited the efficiency of state governance.
18th century	Orthographic/script reform aimed at standardizing and simplifying the scripts used in secular texts.	The task of Russia's socio-economic modernization required publishing more practice-oriented books/textbooks. The old script was complex and archaic thus complicating reading and writing as well as the study of Russian.
18th to the first half of the 19th century	The early attempts at organizing the study of Russian for non-Russian subjects of the empire.	The territorial expansion of the Russian Empire created the demand for bilingual (non-Russian) administrators and clergy. Similarly to the situation from the 16th to the 17th centuries, linguistic differences complicated the governance in areas different ethnically and linguistically from core Russian regions.
	French language enjoys the de facto status of an official language/the language of the elite (along with Russian).	Russia's modernization implied the need for knowledge transfer from the West (both in the form of book knowledge and in the form of experts/scholars/administrators invited from other European countries). Promoting knowledge of French as well as other European languages was thus more than just a fashion, but also a way to create conditions for such import of knowledge and brains.
Middle of the 19th century	Expanding the study of Russian among non-Russian subjects of the empire (official policy at state schools and non-official initiatives/voluntary study).	In addition to the earlier rationale (preparing local bilingual administrators) the motives for this policy included the newly emerging idea of integrating the diverse population of the Russian Empire into a more cohesive social, economic and political organism. The major economic reason was the formation of the common all-Russian market and the development of capitalism which created stimuli for the increased interaction of entrepreneurs from different parts of the empire.
Late 19th to the early 20th century	Russian is introduced as the language of administration and/or education in Poland, Finland and the Baltic Provinces.	The task of ensuring greater socio-economic and political/administrative unity within the empire (to support the formation of the integrated national market) was amended with the task of minimizing the external (German, Turkish, etc.) economic, political and cultural influence in the ethnic periphery of the Russian Empire.

Table 19.1 (Continued)

Period	Language policy priorities	Potential economic and political motivation
1904–1918	The development and (post-revolutionary) implementation by the Soviet authorities of the orthographic reform of the Russian language.	Simplifying the orthography was important in the context of raising the literacy and ensuring universal primary and secondary education, crucial for further industrialization. The modernized orthographic rules required fewer letters and thus also saved typographic costs.
1920s–1930s	The use and study of local languages expand. Most alphabets of ethnic minorities are Latinized. The idea of introducing the Latin script for the Russian language is discussed.	The idea of the global revolution and of the consequent expansion of the Soviet ideology and the Soviet state as a union of nations resonates with the old idea of Lenin that there was no need for a state language in Russia.
1930s–1950s	The Russian language is reintroduced as a required subject at all Soviet schools. The Cyrillic alphabet is readopted for most languages of the USSR.	The forceful industrialization of the country, the introduction of central economic planning along with the introduction of universal military conscription made the universal knowledge of Russian a major practical issue.
1960s–1980s	The study and knowledge of Russian expand further and become nearly universal within most ethnic groups of the USSR.	The knowledge of Russian is regarded by the authorities and the people as a major factor for socio-economic and geographic human mobility in the Soviet Union ensuring the equalization of the opportunities and status of people from different ethnic groups. Ideologically, the expansion of the knowledge and use of Russian is seen as a way to ensure the formation of the composite Soviet nation
1990s–2000s	The Russian language's status as the state language and the language of interethnic communication is uncontested; a number of other languages enjoy official status in ethnic republics of Russia. The focus of the state language policy shifts towards promotion and preservation of Russian in other countries, primarily former Soviet republics.	The study and knowledge of Russian in neighbouring countries create among other things favourable conditions for social and business dealings between Russian-speaking people and businesses, and allow a high level of human trans-border mobility, which is important both for ethnic Russians residing in neighbouring countries and for non-Russian labour migrants coming to Russia.

Russian.[28] Such a view, however, seems to ignore the fact that within the common political and socio-economic space of the Soviet Union the benefits of learning and using Russian were significant enough, even if there had been no state support of Russian bilingualism. Jones and Grupp (1984) note in their overview of the Soviet equalization policy from the 1960s to the early 1980s that the most successful of equalization programmes were those aimed at promoting the Russian language since it was 'an important key to upward social and economic mobility' (Jones and Grupp, 1984, p. 176).

Soviet policies concerning the promotion of the knowledge of Russian turned out far more effective than those of the imperial authorities of the pre-revolutionary Russia. The legacy of the Soviet period language policies is evident in modern Russia, where the knowledge of Russian is close to universal among virtually all ethnic groups.

Table 19.1 summarizes the patterns that can be identified when looking at the centuries of Russian language policies with regard to the motives of the authorities and those who opposed them.

Acknowledgements

I would like to thank Shlomo Weber, Victor Ginsburgh, Danila Raskov, Charles Becker, Edward Tower and Iryna Nasadiuk for their helpful comments that allowed me to improve this chapter.

References

B. Anderson and B. Silver (1984) 'Equality, Efficiency, and Politics in Soviet Bilingual Education Policy, 1934–1980', *The American Political Science Review*, 78, 1019–1039.

A. Arefyev (2012) *Russkiy yazyk na rubezhe XX-XXI vekov [Elektronniy resurs]* (Moscow: Tsentr sotsialnogo prognozirovaniya i marketinga), www.isras.ru/index.php?page_id=1330&id=2503&param=http://www.isras.ru/files/File/Publication/russkij_yazyk.pdf, retrieved 22 August 2014.

I. Baldauf (2001) 'Jadidism in Central Asia within Reformism and Modernism in the Muslim World', *Die Welt des Islams*, New Series, 41, 72–88.

Y. Bilinsky (1981) 'Expanding the Use of Russian or Russification? Some Critical Thoughts on Russian as a Lingua Franca and the "Language of Friendship and Cooperation of the Peoples of the USSR"', *Russian Review*, 40, 317–332.

P. Blitstein (2006) 'Cultural Diversity and the Interwar Conjuncture: Soviet Nationality Policy in Its Comparative Context', *Slavic Review*, 65, 273–293.

M. Bruchis (1984) 'The Language Policy of the CPSU and the Linguistic Situation in Soviet Moldavia', *Soviet Studies*, 36, 108–126.

S. Corrsin (1990) 'Language Use in Cultural and Political Change in Pre-1914 Warsaw: Poles, Jews, and Russification', *The Slavonic and East European Review*, 68, 69–90.

---

[28] See, for instance, Bruchis (1984).

J. Cracraft (2004) *The Petrine Revolution in Russian Culture* (Cambridge, MA: Belknap Press of Harvard University Press).

W. Dowler (1995) 'The Politics of Language in Non-Russian Elementary Schools in the Eastern Empire, 1865–1914', *Russian Review*, 54, 516–538.

V. Ginsburgh and S. Weber (2014) 'Culture, Languages, and Economics' In V. Ginsburgh and D. Throsby (eds) *Handbook of the Economics of Art and Culture*, vol. 2 (Amsterdam and New York: Elsevier), pp. 507–544.

C. Halperin (2007) 'The Russian and Slavonic Languages in Sixteenth-Century Muscovy', *The Slavonic and East European Review*, 85, 1–24.

E. Jones and F. Grupp (1984) 'Modernisation and Ethnic Equalisation in the USSR', *Soviet Studies*, 36, 159–184.

M. Kirkwood (1991) 'Glasnost, "the National Question" and Soviet Language Policy', *Soviet Studies*, 43, 61–81.

E. Koutaissoff (1951) 'Literacy and the Place of Russian in the Non-Slav Republics of the USSR', *Soviet Studies*, 3, 113–130.

D. Laitin (2000) 'What Is a Language Community?', *American Journal of Political Science*, 44, 142–155.

V. Lenin (1973 [1914]) 'Nuzhen li obyazatelniy gosudarstvenniy yazyk?' In K. Ostroukhova (ed.) *Polnoye sobraniye sochineniy V.I. Lenina*, vol. 24 (Moscow: Politizdat), 293–295.

V. Lenin (1899) *Razvitiye Kapitalizma v Rossii* (St. Petersburg: Izdaniye M.I. Vodovozovoy).

E. Lewis (1971) 'Migration and Language in the USSR', *International Migration Review*, 5, 147–179.

W. Matthews (1953) 'The Russian Language before 1700', *The Slavonic and East European Review*, 31, 364–387.

M. Okenfuss (1985) 'From School Class to Social Caste: The Divisiveness of Early-Modern Russian Education', *Jahrbücher für Geschichte Osteuropas, Neue Folge*, 33, 321–344.

N. Ostroumov (1910) 'Kolebaniya vo vzglyadah na obrazovaniye tuzemtsev v Turkestanskom kraye' In *Kaufmanskiy sbornik* (Moscow: Tipo-litografia T-va I.N. Kushnerev i Ko), pp. 139–160.

A. Pavlenko (2008) 'Russian in Post-Soviet Countries', *Russian Linguistics*, 32, 59–80.

D. Saprykin (2009) *Obrazovatelniy potentsial Rossiyskoy Imperii* (Moscow: IIET RAN).

J. Smith (1997) 'The Education of National Minorities: The Early Soviet Experience', *The Slavonic and East European Review*, 75, 281–307.

M. Smith (1998) *Language and Power in the Creation of the USSR, 1917–1953* (Berlin: Mouton de Gruyter).

D. Staliūnas (2007) 'Between Russification and Divide and Rule: Russian Nationality Policy in the Western Borderlands in mid-19th Century', *Jahrbücher für Geschichte Osteuropas, Neue Folge*, 55, 357–373.

E. Thaden (ed.) (1981) *Russification in the Baltic Provinces and Finland, 1855–1914* (Princeton: Princeton University Press).

L. Uspenskiy (1962) *Slovo o slovah* (Leningrad: Lenizdat).

T. Weeks (2004) 'Russification: Word and Practice 1863–1914', *Proceedings of the American Philosophical Society*, 148, 4471–489.

L. Yakubinskiy (1986) 'Kratkiy ocherk zarozhdeniya i pervonachalnogo razvitiya russkogo natsionalnogo literaturnogo yazyka (XV–XVII veka)' In L. Yakubinskiy (ed.) *Izbrannye raboty. Yazyk i yego funktsionirovaniye* (Moscow: Nauka), pp. 128–158.

Part IV

Globalization and Minority Languages

20
English as a Global Language

Jacques Melitz

20.1 Introduction

There has never been in the past a language spoken more widely in the world than English is today. How far has English already spread? How much further can we expect it to go? What are the welfare implications? These are the three central questions in this chapter. The first two are deeply intertwined. We must have a clear idea how far the spread of English has already gone in order to assess how much further it can be expected to go. The role of the language as a lingua franca in some areas is of particular interest. On all these matters, a popular book by the linguist Crystal (2003) with the same title as this chapter is extremely useful. So are two works by the sociologist Graddol (1997, 2006) that were commissioned by the British Council. In dealing with both questions, I will try to move beyond these two authors most of all in connection with publishing, foreign trade and language learning. As regards trade, we know from economic research that common languages promote bilateral trade between countries. We also know from many sources, including survey evidence of exporting firms, that trade stimulates language learning. There is recent econometric support for this. To what extent does the expected growth of world trade in the future imply the further spread of English? To what extent does it instead imply limits to the expected spread of English because of the similar inducement to learn other languages as well? Do other factors besides trade also play an important role? These issues form the subject matter of what follows.

The third central question, regarding the welfare aspect, clearly raises distinct issues. There is much concern today about the welfare impact of the spread of English on native speakers of the other major world languages. One example, of course, is the well-known French support of *'l'exception culturelle'* (the cultural exception) in the field of trade. It is indeed surprising the extent to which English dominates in certain cultural areas, including the song, the film and the best-seller, though not necessarily publishing in general. Is there possibly too much English in some areas for the good of mankind?

20.2   The status of English as a global language

20.2.1   The world distribution of native and spoken languages

We may begin with approximate numbers for the native and total speakers of English and the other principal languages in the world. Table 20.1 provides such figures for the 12 largest languages in terms of total speakers. Turkish/Azerbaijani/Turkmen, Italian and Dutch/Afrikaans are added to these 12 languages even though they are not exactly the next three largest because they enter in a study of language learning on which I shall report prominently later on. The table shows two sets of estimates, one from *Ethnologue* and the other from Melitz and Toubal (2014) (hereafter MT), the source of the data for the relevant study of language learning. The figures from *Ethnologue* (obtained on the internet in May 2013) apply to different dates. To give an idea, they go back to 1998 for Arabic and 2001 for English, and refer to census data for 2000 for Chinese, 2006 for French and data as recent as 2010 for Spanish. The data from MT (which omit 2 of the 12 largest world languages, Hindi/Urdu and Bengali), all collected in 2010, are mainly bunched around 2001–2007. For the moment, it is not possible to produce such a table for a uniform year. All such tables rely on the assumption that language is a slow-moving variable, which is of course more reliable for native than for spoken language.

There are some large discrepancies between *Ethnologue* and MT calling for explanation. Regarding spoken English, the principal cause is that *Ethnologue* draws figures from an incomplete table in Crystal (2003, Table 1) that concerns only 'territories [75 of them] where English has held and continues to hold a special place' (ibid., p. 60), by which Crystal evidently means, almost without exception, territories that were under the administrative control of English-speaking countries at some time in living memory or else where the language is official or both. Consequently, those figures do not include spoken English in places like the Netherlands, Germany and the Scandinavian countries, where the language is widely spoken but has never been either that of the ruling political power in the country or official. The MT data largely replicates the data in Crystal's table for the same 75 territories he mentions (except for the tiny territories that are not in their study), but adds data for spoken English in other parts of the world wherever the authors could find it. MT generally draw no distinction between speakers in countries where the language has 'a special place' and other countries.[1] One important source of their data is an EC 2005 survey of (self-reported) ability to hold a conversation in foreign languages in the 28 current (2014) members of the EU plus Turkey (Eurobarometer, 2006). *Ethnologue* generally tends to collect data for spoken language by non-natives

---

[1] Ostler (2010) does the same. For further detail about the MT data, see Melitz and Toubal (2014). Their data by individual country are available on Toubal's website.

(termed L2) from a selection of territories in Crystal's sense (though without being explicit). This explains the wide discrepancies between *Ethnologue* and MT for spoken French and German as well as for English. In the case of Turkish/Azerbaijani/Turkmen, Italian and Dutch/Afrikaans, *Ethnologue* offers no L2 data. See the note to Table 20.1 about Chinese and Arabic.

There are more native speakers of Chinese than any other language by far. However, based on Table 20.1, English is neck and neck with Chinese as world leader in total speakers. All other languages lag far behind. In fact, it would be

Table 20.1   Worldwide speakers (millions)

Language	*Ethnologue* native speakers (1)	*Ethnologue* total speakers (2)	MT native speakers (3)	MT total speakers (4)
Chinese[1]	1,197	> 1,197	1,161	1,165
English[2]	335	> 765	357	1,123
Spanish	406	466	401	479
Hindi/Urdu[2]	324	> 387	–	–
Arabic[1]	206	246	244	272
Russian	162	272	184	267
French	68	118	69	260
Bengali	193	250	–	–
Portuguese	202	217	209	222
German	84	112	89	168
Malay[2]	23	> 163	22	158
Japanese	122	123	126	126
Turkish/Azerbaijani/ Turkmen[2]	83	> 83	91	102
Italian[2]	61	> 61	64	77
Dutch/Afrikaans[2]	28	> 28	22	37

Source: MT: Melitz and Toubal (2014).

[1] Chinese and Arabic are 'macrolanguages' in *Ethnologue*'s terms, ones that group together native speakers of distinct and often mutually unintelligible dialects. These are single languages only on the basis of custom and the tendency of native speakers to identify themselves with the general label (Mandarin serving as the main reference point for Chinese, standard Arabic for Arabic). The 1,197 figure for Chinese combines Mandarin (population 847.8 million), Gan Chinese, Hakko, Huizhou, Jinyu, Min Bei, Min Dong, Min Nan, Min Zhong, Pu-Xian, Wu (Shanghainese, 77.2 million), Xiang, and Yue (Cantonese, 62.2 million). While *Ethnologue* cites a figure of 178 million L2 speakers for Mandarin, the vast majority of these are native speakers of a separate Chinese dialect and I have no way of knowing how many of these there are as opposed to native speakers of a foreign language (though I believe the number is small). This explains the inscription >1,197 in column 2. As regards Arabic, *Ethnologue* draws upon Wiesenfeld (1999), a world almanac.

[2] The '>' inscriptions in column 2 call for explanation. As regards the >387 for Hindi/Urdu, *Ethnologue* cites a precise figure of 120 million for L2 speakers of Hindi, but this figure includes an uncertain number of the 57 million Urdu speakers. That is why I have added a total of 63 million (120 minus 57) to the 324 million in this column; the 387 figure therefore yields a minimum. As concerns the other five '>' signs, *Ethnologue* explicitly says 'over 430 million' for L2 for English, 'over 140 million' for Malay (cited under the language of Indonesia rather than Malaysia), and does not provide any L2 figures for Turkish/Azerbaijani/Turkmen, Italian, and Dutch/Afrikaans.

easy to propose figures for English speakers far exceeding those for Chinese by extrapolating on the basis of attendance in English classes and/or some ability to understand. On such grounds, one could readily add an extra 300 million speakers of English for India and China alone (see for example Kachru, 2010, pp. 205–11, and for India see also Crystal, 2003, pp. 46–49). The MT data like its basic sources (prominently including *Ethnologue*) is more conservative, and at least in the authors' minds reflects an ability to converse.

Most important of all, English is way ahead of all other languages as a learned language by non-native speakers, and it is the only one to be well represented in all five continents. In terms of geographical dispersion, only French comes anywhere close to English but is still far behind.

20.2.2   Areas where English serves as a lingua franca

There are situations where reliance on interpreters and translations may even be dangerous for safety. Control towers must be able to communicate with air pilots instantly. Captains of modern vessels at sea must be able to communicate with one another rapidly. Accordingly, in recent decades, active steps have been taken toward a single world language in the field of international safety. An English vocabulary named 'airspeak' has been progressively adopted by over 180 countries based on the recommendations of the International Civil Aviation Organization. There is also a limited vocabulary, 'seaspeak', based on English that has been adopted by the International Marine Organization.

In some other cases, multiple languages are not lethal but prohibitively expensive. Meetings of organizations with large international memberships could take place with simultaneous translation or, perhaps in the future, through automatic translation based on voice recognition. For the moment, though, this would be at excessive cost. In many instances, the mere publication of all the information that international organizations generate in the respective native tongues of the members is almost unimaginable. Thus, nearly by necessity, international political organizations tend to choose a limited number of official languages. Under the UN charter, there are five: Chinese, English, French, Russian and Spanish; Arabic was added as a sixth in 1973. The official language of the IMF and the World Bank, both in Washington, is English. French is a second official language of the OECD (located in Paris) besides English, but it is possible to get along in the organization without French but not without English. Unsurprisingly, the only official language of the Francophonie is French. Similarly, the official languages of Mercosur are Spanish and Portuguese, not English. Yet these are exceptions. Generally, English tends to be at least one of the official languages of international political organizations. Interestingly, English is even the *only* official language of a couple of major regional political associations outside of Europe or North America: namely, OPEC and the South Asian Association

for Regional Cooperation. There is only one international political organization that recognizes numerous official languages but at a notoriously high
cost: the European Union (Fidrmuc and Ginsburgh et al., 2007). Even there,
the organization adopts English, French and German as the only 'working
languages'.

In the case of private rather than public international associations, where
the biblical problem of Babel also rears up, information is less readily available.
Based on some sleuth work, Crystal (2003) calculates that in 1995–1996, 85 per
cent of such organizations made some official use of English. French was second
with 49 per cent, and only Arabic, Spanish and German scored over 10 per cent.
Quite tellingly, he also finds that for European associations as such, English is
an 'official or working language' in 99 per cent of cases, and English plus French
plus German is 'the most popular European combination'.

There are other areas where English serves largely as a lingua franca in the
world. The international press and international sports are two (see Graddol,
1997, 2006). People in the business of diffusing international news, or the firms
active in the diffusion process itself, must obtain their information quickly. As a
result, they have veered heavily toward English in data transmission among
themselves. In close connection, there is a heavy concentration of providers of
international news in English-speaking countries, including Reuters, the Associated Press, the BBC, NBC and the *New York Times*. As relevant too, Crystal
(2003, pp. 91–93) traces the early development of the news industry largely
to the English-speaking world. International sports also require a lingua franca
for the minimal communication necessary when competing athletes and an
umpire meet on a playing field.

Perhaps the most intriguing area of English as a lingua franca is science and
scholarship since in this case the basic mechanism at work is the self-interest
of the individual scientist and scholar. There have been studies of publications
in the natural sciences from 1880 to 1996 based on American, French, German
and Russian bibliographies. The results, which are drawn from original work
by Tsunoda (1983) and Ammon (1998), are summarized in Hamel (2007). They
show only 36 per cent of publications in English in 1880, followed by a rise
to around 50 per cent in 1940–1950 to 75 per cent in 1980 and 91 per cent in
1996. The 91 per cent average for 1996 covers a top of 94–95 per cent for physics
and mathematics and a low of 83 per cent for chemistry. The information for
the social sciences and humanities starts in 1974 and goes up to 1995 and the
trend proceeds from 67 per cent in 1974 to around 70 per cent in 1980 and on
to 83 per cent in 1995. Therefore, by 1995 the social sciences and humanities
attained the same level as chemistry in 1996. The decentralized nature of the
incentives to publish scientific work in English is clear. Truchot (1996) spells
out the tendency for natural scientists in France to switch from publishing in
French to English since the mid-1970s in the face of political pressures to stick

to the home language. In addition, all the top journals in sociology, political science and economics are in English and the social scientist confronts the same incentives to publish in English as the natural scientist in much of the world. Even if one publishes occasionally in one's home language, those who seek an international reputation mostly try to publish in English, especially their best work.

20.2.3 Areas of puzzling English supremacy

There are, however, some puzzling areas of English supremacy. The song, the motion picture and the best-seller are three. Native speakers of foreign languages who consume English songs do not even necessarily understand the lyrics. As for the film and the best-seller, the content must be dubbed or translated (subtitled) from the English when it is sold to foreign-language speakers. Thus, it is futile even to try to explain the extraordinary supremacy of English in these three areas on the basis of the benefits of a lingua franca.

The facts are striking. The list of best-selling songs since 1942 includes only four physical singles that are not sung in English out of the 126 that sold over five million copies (one Portuguese, one Japanese, one French, one Italian) and only five not sung in English out of the 98 digital singles that did the same (one Portuguese, two Japanese, two Spanish) (personal count based on web search). As regards Europe, of the current (late 2013) 100 best-selling songs, all of the top 20 are sung in English and only six out of the top 40 are sung in different languages. Only for the rest of the top 100 does the count begin to even up between English and all other languages together. This is not true for Latin American countries where Spanish and Portuguese stand up well to English even over the top 20 or so. There are also some countries in the rest of the world, especially in Asia, such as Japan, where the home language dominates the top ten.

In the case of the all-time top-grossing foreign-language films at the box office, not a single non-English-language film shows up in the top 500 (Box Office Mojo). The non-English-language film that grossed the most (*Crouching Tiger, Hidden Dragon*) earned only 62 per cent of the receipts of the 500th film on the all-time list. For each of the years 2008–2012 not one non-English-language film shows up in the top 20 biggest box-office hits.

In the case of books, the best-sellers of all time include exactly two out of the top 100 that were originally written in a non-English language (web search). One is the Swedish trilogy by Stieg Larsson, published posthumously in English as *The Girl with the Dragon Tattoo*, *The Girl who Played with Fire* and *The Girl who Kicked the Hornets' Nest*. The other is Paulo Coelho's *The Alchemist*, originally written in Portuguese. (Specialists in literature may choke.)

We will come back to the arresting dominance of English in these cultural areas in connection with welfare.

20.3   Areas where English faces sharp limits

It is important, next, to discuss areas where English, though in the lead, faces sharp competition. The relevant areas are wide and cover the daily or weekly press, television, the Web, publishing and trade. When it comes to trade, the spread of English encounters limitations not only for consumption but for investment goods and therefore also in strict communication between firms. These areas of activity serve to underline the exceptional situation for the song, the film and the best-seller, where the goods must also meet the market test of individual consumer satisfaction and where the pressure to meet this market test is not even necessarily weaker.

20.3.1   The press

The English press has a wider international presence than others, but the daily presses of the world plainly reflect native languages well. Japan boasts five or six of the ten newspapers with the top world circulation, all in Japanese; the enormous Chinese press is predominantly in Chinese; the German press is in German; the Italian press in Italian, the Czech press in Czech, etc. The newspaper with the single largest world circulation, published in India, *The Times of India*, is in English. Yet Hindi is also well represented in the Indian press. Admittedly, there are many English-language newspapers that are published outside the major English-speaking countries, like the *China Daily* (published in Hong Kong) and the single major world newspaper essentially intended for international distribution is in English: the *International New York Times* (until recently the *International Herald Tribune*). Still, there can be no claim of English dominance outside of native-English countries as regards the press.

20.3.2   Television

The story for television is more interesting. There had been a scarcity of broadcasting space for transmitting TV signals through the air in the 1960s when technological innovations revolutionized the industry. First, cable TV, then the launching of satellite TV, and most recently digital compression have all led to a wealth of television channels. The US developed TV earlier than the rest of the world, partly because of its huge home market. Therefore the country was able at first to supply viewing content to foreign TV channels, hungry for material, at a lower cost than those channels were able to produce it for themselves. This resulted in an enormous trade surplus in audiovisual material for the US in the 1970s and 1980s (*The Economist*, 1997). A highly influential UNESCO study in 1983, updating a similar study made in 1973, showed that the earlier one-way flow of programming material from the US to the rest of the world (Varis, 1984) had continued. The programming material consisted heavily of entertainment. Overall, a third or more of the total programming time in the rest of the world came from the US in 1983, with important differences by country and region. For example, 75 per cent of the viewing content in Latin America, 44 per cent in Western Europe and 21 per cent in the Arab countries came from the US. The US, in turn, hardly imported from anyone. There was talk at this time of US dominance and 'hegemony' (Tracey, 1985; Biltereyst, 1991). (This was the time of the world success of the US television series *Dallas*.) However, studies soon showed that TV audiences everywhere preferred home-made material, and as TV matured and foreign audiences grew, home-made material progressively replaced that which was imported and several observers correctly predicted that the trend would continue in many parts of the world (Berwanger, 1987; Hoskins and McFadyen, 1991).

Graddol (1997) has extended the narrative following the development of satellite TV. Once again, the early development was largely American and fed fears of a massive spread of English and US culture at the expense of other major languages and cultures. However, the 1980s and 1990s saw the arrival of large non-US participants in satellite TV, like Arte and Euronews (which now broadcasts in 15 languages). More telling still, the English providers started to broadcast in other languages and to adapt the language to local preferences. Thus, after beginning broadcasting from Hong Kong exclusively in English and Chinese, Star TV began to promote local Asian languages. Likewise, CNN International launched a Spanish programme in Latin America. Writing in 1997, Graddol predicted (p. 60): 'national networks in English-speaking countries will continue to establish operations in other parts of the world, but their programming policies will emphasize local languages'. On the other hand, he says (2006, p. 46): 'English, however, remains the preferred language for global reach'. The several efforts under way now to broadcast internationally by non-English channels have adopted the model of the German Deutsche Welle, which decided right from the start to broadcast both in German and English.

20.3.3 The internet

The story of the internet largely follows the same script as for TV. The internet began predominantly in the US and there was a strong sense in its early days in the 1980s that it would spur the learning of English. There is probably some truth to this, but what we have seen mostly since is a progressive tendency to make the internet available in other languages. Until the 1990s the only script available on the internet was ASCII, the American Standard Code for Information Interchange, which allowed only 95 printable characters (plus 33 controls such as plus signs). No foreign accents or diacritical marks were possible. However, Unicode followed, remedying the problem, and by September 1999 it allowed 38 different scripts and a total of 49,259 characters. In its most recent version (6:2), dated 2010, it allows 100 scripts, almost all those in current use, and contains 110,182 characters. Crystal (2006) points out nicely that

Table 20.2   Top nine languages used on the web

Top 9 languages in the internet	Internet users by language (millions) (1)	2000–2011 growth on internet (%) (2)	Internet users (% of total) (3)	MT speakers (% of total) (4)
English	565	301	26.8	22.1
Chinese	510	1,479	24.2	22.9
Spanish	165	807	7.8	9.4
Japanese	99	111	4.7	2.5
Portuguese	83	990	3.9	4.4
German	75	174	3.6	3.3
Arabic	65	2,501	3.6	5.3
French	60	398	3.0	5.1
Russian	60	1,826	3.0	5.2
Top nine languages	1,682	421	80.2	80.2
Remaining languages	418	588	19.8	19.8
World total	2,100	482	100.0	100.0

Source: Internet World Stats.

far from contributing to the death of languages, the internet helps to preserve them by permitting more of them to be stored permanently.

The Internet World Stats website brings together world data about internet usage and population statistics. Table 20.2 summarizes the essential failure of English to crowd out other languages on the internet since the year 2000. Column 1 of the table shows the top nine languages on the internet. Column 2 gives the estimated number of users for those nine languages in 2011. The results show that the top nine languages account for 80.2 per cent of all users. (I counted a total of 163 languages on the internet, including Latin and Esperanto, from one of the original sources, Web Technology Surveys.) Column 3 gives the growth of the number of users of the internet during 2000–2011. There we see the massive catch-up of English by Arabic, Russian and Chinese since 2000. Column 4 reproduces the information in column 1 as a ratio of the world total of users (2.1 billion). Column 5 reproduces the same ratios but instead on the basis of the last column of Table 20.1. This is done by dividing the numbers for the nine languages in the column by their sum, 5,090 million, and then multiplying all of them by 80.2 per cent, so that the percentage total is the same as in the preceding column. The ratios *for the individual languages* in columns 4 and 5 are remarkably close. Therefore the relative order of the nine largest languages on the internet now resembles their position in terms of the relative numbers of speakers, even if Spanish, Arabic, French and Russian trail somewhat and English is disproportionately ahead by 4.7 per cent. Obviously a massive adjustment of relative positions must have taken place in 2000–2011 to create this result (see column 3) but it has already happened.[2]

20.3.4 Publishing

Walk into any book store almost anywhere on earth and you will find before you predominantly titles in the main local language. However, regardless of where you are, there may well be a prominent English section. (Alert: the subject now is the number of titles, not the number of best-sellers, which depends on sales of individual titles.) Since people like to read in their home language for pleasure, just as they like to read newspapers in their home language and to hear their home language on television, the book store will be stacked mostly with titles in the home language. Of particular note, though, is the fact that the clientele for books is also smaller than the one for newspapers, television and the internet; it is also more educated and more likely to read a foreign language in the original, both for profit and pleasure. Since English is the world's most prominent lingua franca, we might therefore expect it to be disproportionately well represented in titles.

In earlier related research, covering data from 1971 to 1991 (Melitz, 2007), I found support for this view, and in a renewed study of the same question, based on the latest information, the support appears even greater. According to the UNESCO annual *Statistical Yearbook*, the principal data source, the ratio of published English titles to total world titles around 1971 was 24 per cent (UNESCO, 1973). The total world population at the time was 3.8 billion, and 24 per cent of this is 900 million, which is far above the-then current English-speaking population. Based on Table 20.1, the world ratio of English speakers was around 17 per cent in the vicinity of 2005 and must have been lower in 1971. Therefore English was disproportionately represented.

An interesting development took place in the next two decades. As English penetrated worldwide, the ratio of English titles to the total fell to 21 per cent around 1981 (UNESCO, 1984) and 20 per cent around 1991 (UNESCO, 1995). This was probably a reflection of an improvement in the education and literacy rates in the non-native-English parts of the world, together with faster population growths in those parts than the native English ones. However, according to the latest results, for around 2009, the forces enhancing English relative to other languages have taken over in publishing since the 1980s. The ratio of publications of English titles to the world total rose to around 30 per cent in 2009, well up from 20 per cent in 1991, and quite high relative to the ratio

---

[2] One source of a possible discrepancy between the last two columns, which is difficult to assess, is that the estimates of internet users assign one language to each user, while the ratios in the last column rest on figures that admit bilingualism so that any speaker may be counted two or more times.

of around 17 per cent for English speakers relative to the total world population around 2005.[3] Therefore, English does indeed now occupy a highly disproportionate place in world titles, though other languages are still well represented.

The prominence of English for translations is more pronounced than for original titles. Already for 1960 to 1987, the UNESCO yearbooks show that the share of English in translations as a source language was 41 per cent in 1960 and then rose to 56 per cent in 1987,[4] even though the percentage of English in total titles fell from 24 to 20–21 percent, as we have seen. Correspondingly, the UK and the US publishing industry took little interest in translation. As the world ratio of translations to total titles went down from 9 to 7 per cent during 1960–1987, the British publishing of translations rose from a bare 2.1 to 3.7 per cent and the US one dropped from 6.6 (an exceptional post-war high) to 3 per cent (see Table 2 in Melitz, 2007). In striking contrast, European countries were and remain unusually interested in translations. A study sponsored by the Commission of European Communities (BIPE, 1993) shows a ratio of 17 per cent for translations for the then members (incorporating a 3 per cent figure for the UK) in 1991 (see Table 3 in Melitz, 2007). For the literature classification of titles, the ratio of translations to total titles was almost twice as high at 32 per cent (including 4 per cent for the UK). Ginsburgh et al. (2011) provide highly confirmatory findings in a study exploiting the UNESCO web source, *Index Translationum*. They report that translations out of English were 22.09 times higher than translations into English for publications in the literature classification covering 19 Indo-European languages in 1979–2002. The

---

[3] The 30 per cent figure for 2009 calls for elucidation since the information from the UNESCO yearbooks started shrinking in the 1990s and no longer permits calculating this ratio for any date later than 1991. Happily, though, Wikipedia currently compiles a table of 'books published per country per year' based on the remaining UNESCO data and an assortment of other well-annotated sources. According to the Wikipedia table, publications by the US and UK alone bring up the total for titles in English to 24 per cent (this can be inferred because these two countries publish little in foreign languages). The main difficulty in assessing how much above 24 per cent the ratio lies comes from the absence of the information that UNESCO used to provide about titles in English published by non-native-English countries. In reaching the 30 per cent figure, I allowed for the publications in English in the Wikipedia table by India, Pakistan, Hong Kong, Canada, Australia, South Africa and New Zealand in addition to the US and the UK. This brought the total up to around 27.4 per cent. I then made an allowance of 2.6 per cent more for published titles in English by the rest of the world. I believe this 2.6 per cent estimate to be a reasonable one since, at the time when detailed information was available in the UNESCO Yearbooks, 3.6 per cent of the publications of the rest of the world were in English in around 1971; 2.1 per cent in around 1981; and 2.6 per cent in around 1991.
[4] The trend continued beyond 1987. Table 1 in Sapiro (2010), based on the UNESCO online source *Index Translationum*, shows a rise in the ratio of English in translations from 45 per cent in 1980–1989 to 59 per cent in 1990–1999.

next highest ratio in their sample, for Swedish, is 1.17:1 (and clearly reflects an unusually high level of translations of Swedish into Danish and Norwegian). Russian and French are the only other two languages besides Swedish for which the ratio is even close to one rather than well below it. See the opening chapter by Allen (2007), in a collective work sponsored by the international literary association PEN, for an interesting and compelling account of the worries of specialists in literature about the low level of translations into English in the literature classification.

Nevertheless, I have included translation as an area where English faces sharp limits. The reason is the visible interest in translations of original works in non-English languages outside of the native-English countries. In the above-mentioned BIPE (1993) study, about 43–49 per cent of the translations in the literature classification in France, Italy, Spain and Greece are from other source languages besides English, and the figures are in the range of one-third for Germany, the Netherlands and Denmark.[5] To all indications, authors who write in non-English languages do not face a general problem of translation so much as one of translations into English.

A partial explanation which is inspired by Ginsburgh et al. (2011) may be offered. Based on familiar reasoning in economics, suppose that all readers like a variety of titles for reading pleasure but exhibit a home preference, which means a preference for reading works that were originally written in their home language. This agrees with the estimate of only 7 per cent for translations relative to total titles for the world as a whole in 1991, 17 per cent for the European countries in the BIPE sample in 1993, and the high of 31 per cent in this last sample for titles belonging to the literature classification. Suppose, in addition, that the degree of home preference rises with the size of a language community. In other words, large language communities are more insular than small ones: the small ones are more interested in different cultures and the outside world. Then the arithmetic goes in the right direction. For example, suppose that home preference is twice as high in a language community that is twice as large as another. Then a 90 per cent home preference in the larger language community would mean only a 45 per cent home preference in the smaller one. That makes for 10 per cent translations relative to total titles in the larger community as opposed to 55 per cent in the smaller one. It is easy to see that this hypothesis will go a long way toward reconciling the data with consumer sovereignty. If so, then in terms of standard economic reasoning, there is no market failure.

---

[5] It is also clear from Sapiro (2010) that French publishers, at least, are particularly concerned with translations of literary works from other source languages besides English.

Notice, though, that the reasoning does not even begin to address the evidence for best-sellers. In the previous example of one language community twice as large as the other, if in both communities home sales are the same on average for all works in the home language that are translated into the foreign language as they are on average on all works in the foreign language that are translated into the home one, then *on average* the total world sales *of a translated work* originally written in the large language and the small language would be *exactly the same*. In both cases, the total of home sales plus foreign sales would be the sum of the same two numbers. To take a numerical example, suppose that the average title that is written in the home language in the large language community sells 1,000 copies at home (and this is true for those that are translated into the foreign language as a group as well) and the average title that is translated into the home language also sells 1,000 copies in this community. Suppose next that the corresponding two numbers are 500 in the small language community. Consequently, world sales of a title that is translated and originally written in the large language would be on average 1,000 at home and 500 abroad, and world sales of a title that is translated but originally written in the small language would be on average 500 at home and 1,000 abroad, for a total of 1,500 in both cases. The issue of the best-seller concerns the distribution of sales of individual works (rather than the number of titles), and more specifically the upper tail of the distribution. The extraordinary dominance of English in best-sellers remains as puzzling as before.[6]

20.3.5   Trade

It is intuitive that a common language boosts trade, especially for goods that are not perfectly homogeneous. A series of questionnaire surveys of investment in language skills by exporting firms in Europe confirms this intuition. The series began in 1996 and culminated in a large study in 2005 commissioned by the European Commission from CILT (a British organization focused on foreign language skills in business). This study, by Hagen et al. (2006), covers a sample of 2,000 small- and medium-sized exporting enterprises (SMEs) in 29 European countries, including Turkey, and 30 large multinationals (MNEs), all home-based in France (see Annex 4 of the study). To the question, 'Has your company undertaken foreign language training in the last three years?',

---

[6] Of course, on average home sales of home-language works that are translated are many times larger than sales of other works that sell at home, and this is indeed likely to lead to larger world sales of translated works that are originally written in the language of the large community. But this raises a distinct consideration which, by itself, has no hope of resolving the puzzle. Translated works that are originally written in the other large languages of the world besides English also sell many more times at home than the rest, and the disproportional sales of translations originally written in English resulting from this factor are unlikely to come close to resembling the data.

35 per cent of the 2,000 SMEs answered yes. The percentage of these 2,000 firms foreseeing a need to acquire additional expertise in foreign languages over the next three years was higher at 42 per cent. If anything, the MNEs are more conscious of the importance of investing in linguistic skills than the SMEs. Of the MNEs, 60 per cent recognized deficiencies. This is below the 75 per cent figure in a previous study with similar aims covering 151 multinationals with a broader international distribution of home bases, including the UK, Germany and a sprinkling of other countries besides France (see Feely and Winslow, 2005; Bel Habib, 2011).

The previous survey evidence, however, does not tell us much about the impact of a common language on bilateral trade. For such further knowledge, the gravity model of international trade is better suited. Somewhere in the early 1990s, researchers at the World Bank began introducing common language into this model – which has since become very popular – as a factor promoting trade in merchandise between country pairs along with the other two prominent factors that reduce trade frictions in the model, namely, geographical proximity and a common border (see Havrylyshyn and Pritchett, 1991; Foroutan and Pritchett, 1993; Frankel, 1997). (Studies of bilateral trade in services remain a serious empirical challenge because of inadequate statistics.) This was done by introducing a binary variable equal to 1 if a country pair possesses a common language and 0 otherwise. The early uses effectively depended on peer acceptance and simply avoided ambiguous cases like France or Switzerland. The variable was highly successful. At first this was interpreted as reflecting the importance of cultural proximity in trade with some acknowledged confusion between language and ex-colonial relationships. But the confusion was soon resolved by introducing these relationships concurrently (through one or two additional binary (0 or 1) variables). Since 2000 the use of the common language variable has become pervasive because of the statistical significance of the variable and the intuitive sense of its importance. Systematic use of the variable was also made possible, almost regardless of country sample, by the adoption of a common official language as the criterion. Prominent estimates of the coefficient of common language based on this criterion are near 0.5. There are already two meta-analyses of results of studies using common language (most of which rest on the preceding index but not all of them): Egger and Lassmann (2012) resting on 81 studies, and Head and Mayer (2013) resting on 159. Both papers come up with estimates of around 0.4–0.5 for common language. Since the dependent variable in the estimates is the log of bilateral trade, 0.4 corresponds to about 50 per cent more trade between a country pair with a common language than a pair without one (exp (0.4) $\cong$ 1.5 – 1). This is a large effect. Yet upon reflection, the estimate could be too low since it depends on a flawed measure of common language, and measurement error tends to bias estimates downward.

Consider, for example, the set of 28 countries covered in the above-mentioned Eurobarometer (2006) survey of language skills. In this sample, English is the official language of a single pair: the UK and Ireland. Therefore, based on the measure, common English boosts bilateral trade strictly for this one pair in the entire sample whereas, of course, knowledge of English is widespread in the sample and is also uneven. A similar problem arises for common German, which, according to the measure (or at least the standard application of it), exists strictly between Germany and Austria, whereas German is widely spoken in Denmark (where it could also be considered official) and the parts of Eastern Europe in the sample. There are other reasons for scepticism. Official languages are about as common across countries as national flags. As nearly inevitable, official languages sometimes arise despite moderate or low levels of speakers if linguistic diversity is high.[7] Thus, French and English are official in a good number of African countries where the percentage levels of speakers of either language are below one-quarter and not infrequently below 10 per cent. Spoken English is also only around 20 per cent in some Pacific Islands where the language is official, like Fiji, Kiribati and Mauritius. Quite apart from statistical bias, the earlier issue I raised, if we consider the many reasons why a common language might promote bilateral trade, ranging from ethnicity, tastes and trust to ease of communication and facility of obtaining written or spoken translations, one can easily question that a measure based on official status alone would cover the subject. A recent study, born of such doubts, uses four separate measures of a common language simultaneously: common native language, common spoken language, linguistic proximity and common official language (Melitz and Toubal, 2014).[8] The resulting estimate of the impact of a common language goes up from around 0.5 to about 1.1. On this last estimate, a common language raises bilateral trade by 200 per cent $(\exp (1.1)-1 \cong 2)$.[9] All four measures are also simultaneously important.

---

[7] For some interesting discussion of the varied motives for choosing an official language or a number of them when no choice is obvious, see De Swaan (2001).

[8] The measures of spoken and common native language concern the probability that two people at random for a country pair will share the same spoken language or the same native language, respectively, as the case may be. The measure of linguistic proximity refers instead to similarities of a limited list of words with identical meanings based on expert judgements, where these judgements come from the Automatic Similarity Judgment Program, an international project by ethnolinguists and ethnostatisticians (see Bakker et al., 2009; Brown et al., 2008). The measure of common official language is the usual binary one.

[9] This is similar to the result in an earlier study with a similar aim based on poorer data by Melitz (2008), which had used only two measures of a common language, one of them mostly based on official status and the other strictly on spoken language.

Table 20.3 Linguistic influences on bilateral trade

	(1)	(2)	(3)
Common official language (0,1)	0.351***		0.405***
	(7.56)		(5.64)
Common spoken language (0–1)	0.396***		1.244***
	(4.91)		(8.55)
Common native language (0–1)	0.284**		−0.379**
	(2.34)		(−2.24)
Linguistic proximity (0–1)	0.078**		0.06***
	(4.26)		(2.89)
Common official language: English (0,1)		0.084	−0.237***
		(1.42)	(−2.66)
Common spoken language: English (0–1)		−0.034	−1.447***
		(−0.35)	(−8.38)
Common native language: English (0–1)		−0.001	0.763***
		(−0.01)	(3.17)
Linguistic proximity to English (0–1)		0.092***	0.083**
		(2.89)	(2.32)
No. of observations	209,276	209,276	209,276
Adjusted R^2	0.757	0.755	0.758

Notes: Student *t*s in parentheses. ***$p < 0.01$, **$p < 0.05$, *$p < 0.1$. Downward correction of standard errors for country pairs that appear twice in the same year, with the opposite country as the exporter (2,850 clusters). 0–1 signifies continuous values between 0 and 1; 0,1 signifies binary values, either 0 or 1. Numerous controls are not reported (see text).
Source: Melitz and Toubal (2014).

The natural question to ask here is whether English promotes bilateral trade more effectively than other languages. Table 20.3 focuses on this question based on the MT study. The relevant gravity equation covers 195 countries over the ten years 1998 through 2007 and the dependent variable is (the log of) bilateral trade. The estimates also employ separate exporter-year and importer-year fixed effects so that the results depend entirely on the cross-sections. There are bilateral controls for distance, common border, ex-colonizer/colony relationship, ex-common-colonizer relationship, common religion, common legal system, and years at war since 1815. All the controls enter at values highly significantly different from zero in the estimates and carry the expected signs. But in the interests of space, Table 20.3 reproduces strictly the coefficients and *t* values of the linguistic variables. As is evident from column 1, all four linguistic influences are highly significantly different from zero, all but common native language at the 99 per cent significance level. In addition, the sum of their effects is approximately 1.1, as mentioned above. One might worry that these estimates are subject to simultaneity bias because of the reciprocal effect of bilateral trade on common spoken language. For this reason, the paper also provides estimates founded strictly on common official language, common native language and linguistic distance (in which case those variables partly reflect common spoken language, with which they are highly correlated). The estimates are about the same.

Columns 2 and 3 concern the separate impact of English. Column 2 does so by dropping all the languages except English from the analysis. To see the interest of taking this step, suppose that the results of column 1 depended on English alone. In that case, the measures of the linguistic variables in column 2 would be superior. They would simply remove errors of measurement and should yield higher and better estimated coefficients. However, if instead the measures of a common language in column 1 are the right ones, then, on the contrary, the measures of linguistic influence in column 2 would be noisy and should yield lower and less well-estimated coefficients than the previous ones. Indeed, in this last case – that is, if the broad measures of a common language are the appropriate ones – there are two reasons why the English-based measures of the linguistic variables might perform particularly badly. In the first place, an English-speaking country has a great many solutions for skirting the language barrier altogether. There are lots of other English-speaking countries with which it could trade. Therefore, common English could be an especially weak spur to trade with any single common-language partner.[10] Alternatively, a country speaking Portuguese, for example, would have far fewer alternative partners with which to trade in order to avoid the language barrier and therefore might exploit those opportunities more intensely.[11] On this ground, the coefficients of the linguistic variables based on English alone might be exceptionally low apart from measurement error. The second problem could be equally serious. Relying on English alone means drawing numerous distinctions between country pairs who share a common language other than English based upon their English, and proposing a quantitative ordering of linguistic ties between these non-English pairs based on their common English alone. Especially large distortions might arise. The results in column 2 confirm the broad suspicion from these considerations that basing common language on common English alone may lead to particularly poor estimates. The effect of common English does not even show up, except curiously for linguistic proximity.

Column 3 proceeds, probably more reasonably, by examining whether adding the linguistic effects of English separately improves the estimate. Once

---

[10] This is, of course, the same point that Anderson and van Wincoop (2003) make in explaining why national trade barriers form a far weaker incentive for bilateral trade between two US states than between two Canadian provinces.

[11] Of course, for that very reason, people in the Portuguese-speaking country would have stronger incentives to become multilingual. This diminishes the weight of the point without denying it altogether.

again, the result is negative. But in this case, we get very confusing outcomes except for linguistic distance. The effects of a common official language, a common spoken language and a common native language for the broad measures go in opposite directions to those for English alone, and in addition the coefficients of the previous three measures are largely implausible, especially for spoken language where the negative effect exceeds the positive one. Furthermore, in the case of official and spoken language the signs for English alone are negative, which would imply a negative correction for English, whereas for native language the sign for English is positive, implying a positive correction for English. None of this makes sense.[12] All in all, the clearest conclusion from column 3 is that the effort to estimate the impact of English separately fails, just as it fails in column 2. Column 1 offers the best estimate.

Of course, this is not to deny that English probably has a larger effect on *multilateral* trade or trade with everyone than common Russian, common Spanish, or any other common language. This is true simply by virtue of the language's size. World trade by native English speakers is around 23 per cent of total world trade.[13] The next highest ratio, for Chinese, is 11 per cent, followed by Spanish at 10 per cent and German at 9 per cent. For this reason alone, English ought to contribute more to the reduction of linguistic trade frictions with the rest of the world than any other language. However, even on this reasoning, English contributes most to multilateral trade only on average. For the Portuguese-speaking Brazil, situated in South America, there may well be a greater incentive to learn Spanish than English to promote multilateral trade. The same goes for Russian in Eastern Europe or around Kazakhstan, and for Chinese or Malay in Southeast Asia, and so on.

---

[12] On the other hand, the result for linguistic proximity is sensible: namely, linguistic proximity between languages, regardless of the pair of languages, boosts trade, with a positive correction for linguistic proximity to English. The strong results for linguistic proximity for English in Table 20.3 (for which I have no basic explanation especially in light of the rest of the results) find an echo in a study by Ku and Zussman (2010) of the impact of a common language on bilateral trade that focuses on English alone. These authors implicitly rest the impact of common English on bilateral trade strictly on linguistic proximity since they rely on bilateral differences of scores in different countries on TOEFL, the Princeton-administered Test of English as a Foreign Language. These international differences in test scores will be correlated with difficulties of learning English for people with different native languages and it is difficult to ascribe the effect of the scores on bilateral trade to anything else.

[13] If we multiply aggregate trade by the percentage of native English speakers, country by country, sum up the products over all countries, and divide by the sum of trade over all countries, we get around 23 per cent. This measure means double-counting but since the double-counting is both in the numerator and the denominator it cancels out.

The earlier survey evidence supports these last inferences. Of the 2,000 small- and medium-sized exporting enterprises (SMEs) in the Hagen et al. (2006) study that report foreign language training in the last three years (constituting 35 per cent of the sample, we may recall), only a quarter provided it in English: 18 per cent provided the training in German and 15 per cent in French. In addition, three small languages figure in the top ten: Czech (5 per cent), Danish (3 per cent) and Estonian (3 per cent). The following quote (ibid., p. 19) is especially noteworthy:

> When companies were asked to identify the languages they used in their major export markets it was apparent there is widespread use of intermediary languages for third markets. For example, English is used to trade in over 20 different markets, including the four Anglophone countries, UK, USA, Canada and Ireland. German is used for exporting to 15 markets (including Germany and Austria), Russian is used to trade in the Baltic States, Poland and Bulgaria and French is used in 8 markets (including France, Belgium and Luxembourg).

Thus, even when it is a question of a third language as an intermediary in trade, English is not necessarily the choice.

Unsurprisingly, the special role of English in international commerce emerges best in the survey evidence of the multinational enterprises (MNEs). These firms do indeed have a striking preference for English in their communication with customers and their own subsidiary companies. Of them 63 per cent prefer English and another 20 per cent a mix of English and a home language, basically French in the particular sample (Hagen et al., 2006, pp. 42–43). This is easy to interpret. These firms have the greatest use for a lingua franca as a coordination device. They face a language problem internally and not only in dealings with customers. In addition, they confront the problem on a world scale and therefore have a broader world view of the multilateral aspects than the SMEs. Because of their world concerns, English is their most common choice. Interestingly, though, the multinationals' other target languages for future learning besides English also reflect their broader international concerns than those of the SMEs. Spanish, Chinese and Arabic figure far more heavily for the MNEs than for the SMEs. French is of lesser interest and German and Italian disappear (ibid., p. 45). (The same shift of orientation toward Asia, Latin America and the Middle East in language learning emerged in earlier questionnaires of MNEs.) Nevertheless, only 29 per cent of the language deficiency that MNEs wish to repair concerns English, close to the 26 per cent figure for SMEs.[14]

---

[14] See also Chapter 11 in this volume.

20.4 Language learning

Suppose we turn next to language learning and consider the subject in the same spirit as trade, that is, first in terms of learning foreign languages in general and later in terms of the difference it makes if the language is English. Economists possess a theoretical model for dealing with language learning that stems from Selten and Pool (1991) and Church and King (1993) and that was recently extended by Gabszewicz et al. (2011) (GGW). The model uses game-theoretical reasoning but can serve to study the learning decision independently of such reasoning. It admits three fundamental influences on the learning decision: (1) total world speakers of the target language; (2) total world speakers of the home-country language; and (3) the cost of learning. A recent econometric study by Ginsburgh et al. (2014) (GMT) extends this model beyond GGW by admitting trade with speakers of the target language as a fourth influence on learning. In this case, the trade variable largely absorbs the commercial induce-ments to learn the target language so that, in its presence, the total number of world speakers of the target language reflects essentially the other inducements to learn it, for example, ease of social interaction with people from different cultures and benefits of access to their cultures and their literary and artistic heritages. GMT also introduce linguistic distance (or the inverse of the previous measure of linguistic proximity) and the literacy rate as indicators of the cost of learning (where trade can be understood as also serving this purpose). All five of the expected signs in the model are intuitive:

(1) a larger world population of speakers of a target language should make the language more attractive to learn;
(2) larger trade with speakers of this language should do the same;
(3) a larger world population of speakers of the home language should reduce the incentive to learn the foreign one;
(4) linguistic distance should tend to raise the cost of learning the language;
(5) literacy should help to learn it.

GMT (2014) apply this model to the learning of 13 important world languages over 193 countries. The 13 languages are, in alphabetical order, Arabic, Chinese, Dutch, English, French, German, Italian, Japanese, Malay, Portuguese, Russian, Spanish and Turkish. The database is an extended version of the one in MT (2014). The study centres on 2005, though the values of the language variables refer to different years over 2001–2007. Importantly, the authors do not study the decision of people to learn the primary language of their country of resi-dence on the ground that those who do not already know this language need to learn it for daily living. There is therefore no concern with the learning of

German in Germany or English in the US. But the study does consider the learning of Turkish in Germany and Spanish in the US, for example, though there are native Turkish speakers in Germany and native Spanish speakers in the US.

In testing the model, simultaneity is a problem. Learning has a reciprocal influence on three of the preceding five influences upon it: namely, the world number of speakers of the target language, the world number of speakers of the home language, and trade with speakers of the target language. As regards the first two of these influences, it is possible to handle the difficulty by using native speakers to measure total speakers (since native and total speakers are strongly correlated). But this remedy will not work for the third influence, or trade with speakers of the target language, since learning a language will affect trade with native speakers as well as other speakers of the language. Thus, in order to estimate the impact of this third influence on learning, the study uses an instrument for trade. The instrument is the percentage of the domestic output of the trade-partner countries that is attributable to the native speakers of the target language. Learning the target language will affect this percentage negligibly if at all,[15] whereas the percentage is likely to affect trade with native speakers of the target language. Therefore, the variable is appropriate as an instrument.

One problematic aspect remains. The database contains 2,125 zeros for differences between spoken and native language, or learned languages, and only 240 positive values. There would be fewer zeros and more positive values if positive values of learning had been recorded below 1 per cent of the population. But 1 per cent is a lower threshold in the database.[16] In light of this feature, the authors offer separate estimates for the complete sample including the zeros and for the positive values alone. In the case of the full sample, they substitute values of one for all the positive values in the database and merely study the decision to learn (a value of one) or not to learn (a value of zero). In the other case, where they focus strictly on the 240 observations of learning and keep those observations as they are (as positive percentages), the authors effectively study the percentage of people who learn a foreign language conditional on the presence of some positive learning. In the first case, they apply probit, while in the second case, they apply ordinary least squares. In both cases, they instrument for trade. Effectively, therefore, they use probit with instrumentation in the first case and two-stage least squares in the other.

Table 20.4 summarizes the main results. The probit estimates are the marginal effects evaluated at the sample means of the variables. The results look quite

---

[15] Some effect of learning on the instrument might come from stimulating trade with countries with which there had been no trade before, though this factor can be expected to be negligible since trade is widespread between countries with no common native language based on third languages, interpreters and translations.

[16] Greater precision might also have been questionable.

Table 20.4 Foreign language learning

	Full sample			Positive sample		
		IV Probit			IV 2SLS	
	Probit (1)	First stage (2)	Second stage (3)	OLS (4)	First stage (5)	Second stage (6)
Speakers of acquired languages (log)	0.014*** (4.348)	0.001 (0.720)	−0.001 (−1.109)	0.024* (1.841)	−0.001 (−0.154)	−0.032 (−1.306)
Speakers of native languages (log)	−0.015*** (−3.992)	−0.000 (−0.720)	−0.003*** (−4.049)	−0.024*** (−4.412)	0.002 (0.754)	−0.029*** (−3.384)
Trade with acquired language countries (0–1)	0.465*** (9.243)		0.263*** (3.828)	0.788*** (4.688)		2.665*** (4.129)
Distance between native and acquired language (0–1)	−0.317*** (−6.966)	−0.079*** (−4.657)	−0.058*** (−5.293)	−0.355** (−2.197)	−0.062 (−1.295)	−0.279 (−1.633)
Literacy rate in learning countries	0.249*** (5.323)	0.010 (1.466)	0.041*** (3.292)	0.064 (0.570)	−0.109* (−1.852)	0.286 (1.536)
Instrument (GDP ratio)		0.524*** (11.570)			0.373*** (4.232)	
No. of observations	2,365	2,365	2,365	240	240	240
R-squared		0.202		0.236	0.156	
No. of countries	193	193	193	94	94	94

Note: Student *t*s in parentheses. These are based on robust standard errors clustered at country level. ***$p < 0.01$, **$p < 0.05$, *$p < 0.1$. Intercepts are not reported.
Source: Ginsburgh et al. (2014).

favourable on the whole. In the absence of any correction for the endogeneity of trade, all five explanatory variables come out significantly with the right signs (columns 1 and 4) except for literacy in the OLS result (column 4). The results after correction for the endogeneity of trade are obviously more important. In this case, columns 2 and 5 show that in the first-stage estimates (for the correction), the output instrument is strong. After the correction (columns 3 and 6), the size of world speakers of the target language ceases to be significant but otherwise the results remain confirmatory, particularly in the full sample estimate (column 3). In the case of the positive-sample estimate (column 6), linguistic distance and literacy cease to be significant at the conventional 90 per cent confidence level but they remain so at the 88 per cent level. Generally, trade is the most powerful influence on learning in the estimates.[17] However, in its presence, it becomes impossible to detect the positive influence of the world population of the target language on learning. This is the only basic problem in the results. The other four explanatory variables enter significantly (with minor qualification for linguistic distance and literacy) with the right sign.

How does the model fare for English? More specifically, do the results call for dealing with English separately as a special case? The best way to answer this question would be to introduce as many of the languages as possible simultaneously or at least a large number of them and to see if English performs differently than the rest.[18] In such tests, English is always insignificant and so are the rest of the languages. Therefore, Table 20.5 displays a different set of results. The table shows the errors in the estimates in columns 3 and 6 of Table 20.4 after correcting for endogenous trade. More specifically, it shows the means and the standard errors (as well as the *t*-statistics) of the residuals for both sets of results, language by language. This gives an idea of the direction of the errors and how statistically significant they are.

The general impression from Table 20.5, in conformity with the broad evidence with the use of controls for individual languages (mentioned above),

---

[17] The quantitative impact of trade is also considerable. Suppose a doubling of the trade share with speakers of the destination language (a 100 percentage point increase). According to the probit result, there is a 26.3 rise in the probability of learning where none exists thus far. In the case of the positive-sample result, which is conditional on some positive learning, a single percentage point rise in the trade share of the destination language will increase learning of the language by 2.66 per cent.

[18] If instead one simply introduces a separate term for the world level of English speakers when English is the destination language (or else a dummy variable with a value of one when English is this particular language and zero otherwise), English turns up with a significant coefficient in one test or the other, the full-sample or the positive-value one. But the same is true for most of the other languages in similar tests. The right tests to perform are those I mention where as many languages as possible enter simultaneously.

Table 20.5   Residuals of IV regressions by language

Language	Full sample			Positive sample		
	Mean[1]	Std. dev.	*t*-stat	Mean[1]	Std. dev.	*t*-stat
Arabic	−0.190	0.652	−0.291	0.140	0.229	0.611
Chinese	−0.244	0.473	−0.515	−0.218	0.011	−19.143
Dutch	−0.209	0.360	−0.580	0.049	0.221	0.220
English	−0.647	1.561	−0.414	0.015	0.434	0.035
French	0.005	0.795	0.007	0.035	0.208	0.168
German	−0.075	0.659	−0.114	−0.101	0.184	−0.550
Italian	−0.062	0.676	−0.092	−0.065	0.139	−0.466
Japanese[2]	−0.214	0.554	−0.387			
Malay	−0.070	0.253	−0.278	0.416	0.297	1.400
Portuguese[2]	−0.170	0.274	−0.618	−0.120		
Russian	0.079	0.597	0.131	0.050	0.252	0.199
Spanish	−0.207	1.196	−0.173	−0.021	0.226	−0.093
Turkish	−0.114	0.326	−0.352	0.045	0.186	0.239

[1] Estimates of the positive sample are based on Pearson residuals from the probit regression in Table 20.4, column 3 and those of the positive sample are based on the IV regression in Table 20.4, column 6.
[2] Japanese is not acquired. Portuguese is acquired only in Spain (no standard deviation).
Source: Ginsburgh et al. (2014).

is that the model performs little differently for the separate languages.[19] Perhaps the model performs worst for English if we judge from the mean error of −0.647 for this language in the probit estimate, which is the highest in the sample in absolute terms. This error is also negative (under-prediction), which can be interpreted to mean that English is a world lingua franca, since there is more learning of the language than the model predicts in-sample. However, the standard deviation for English in this estimate is also the highest and it denotes a significant percentage of cases of predicted positive learning when there is none (the *t*-statistic is low, 0.41). Furthermore, in the positive-sample estimate, the mean error for English is almost zero and the lowest of all. This goes entirely against the idea of its status as a lingua franca.[20] In the final analysis, the study

---

[19] The large *t*-statistic of the mean error for Chinese in the positive-sample estimate is arresting but essentially misleading. This result depends strictly on Malaysia and Singapore, the only two countries where there is any learning of Chinese outside of China (at the 1 per cent threshold in the study). Thus, the standard deviation rests on these two observations alone. The mean of the error for Chinese in the probit estimate, which depends on all the observations, is actually about the same as in the positive-value sample but with a much higher standard deviation.

[20] However, the result is entirely consistent with the evidence of English's status as such in some limited areas like air traffic control, scientific writing and international sports.

says that learning English is subject to the same principles as learning other languages. If so, it is wrong to try to assess the future of English in isolation, without allowing for the similar incentives to learn other major languages.

What about the future of English? According to the model, the evolution of trade will have a profound effect. But the effects of trade are notably symmetric. Growth in Chinese/English trade should promote the learning of Chinese in native-English countries just as it should promote the learning of English in native-Chinese countries. Whether it will raise the importance of English relative to Chinese in the world will therefore depend heavily on the evolution of the share of trade with English speakers on the Chinese side relative to the evolution of the share of trade with Chinese speakers on the English side. That is what the econometric model says.[21] The influence of demographic changes is simpler to analyse. Suppose for example that the Arabic- and Spanish-speaking populations grow fast while numbers in the rest of the world remain constant. Then the Arabic- and Spanish-speaking populations will wish to learn fewer foreign languages while speakers of other languages will not wish to learn either more or less Arabic or Spanish. Thus, Arabic and Spanish will become relatively more important. In theory, of course, these same demographic assumptions should mean more learning of Arabic and Spanish in absolute terms, which would simply reinforce the rise in the relative size of those two languages. According to the results of the tests of the GMT model, however, this reinforcing effect depends entirely on a rise in the share of Arabic and Spanish trade in non-Arabic- and non-Spanish-speaking countries and therefore may not materialize. But in any event, the basic demographic assumptions do not favour English. These remarks lend general support to Graddol (1997, 2006) who predicts a significant growth of Chinese, Arabic and Spanish in the future based on trade and demographic trends. In close connection, he also questions how much further the spread of English relative to other languages can be expected to go.

20.5 Welfare implications

There are areas of international encounter where the welfare benefits of a lingua franca are evident. For example, a lingua franca is of mutual benefit to everyone

---

[21] Of course, a spurt of teaching of English in school is well under way in China (see Yong and Campbell, 1995), whereas the teaching of Chinese in English-speaking countries remains meagre today. It would indeed be helpful to introduce school curricula in foreign languages in the model (with the appropriate lag) if it could be done (if the data was widely enough available). However, it is not a foregone conclusion that major revision would follow: instruction in a foreign language as a child need not mean ability to converse in the language in adult life. The factors present in the model *may* still be the critical ones.

in travel and inside the world industry of news diffusion. The spread of multinational organizations promotes a lingua franca too. The political clout of the US may be important in explaining the convergence on English as the preferred choice of lingua franca in these cases. But by and large, no other choice would bring the world population as much benefit. True, as Van Parijs (2011) stresses, from a welfare perspective, the distribution of the gains raises issues. Those who learn English as their native language obtain a certain rent. On the other hand, they are also more likely to be unilingual than hundreds of millions of other people. Consider the child born in a small Eastern European country who, by virtue of circumstance, by the age of 15 is fluent in Russian and German, two major world languages, as well as the home language, and perhaps a fourth one because of a monolingual grandparent. From the language perspective, perhaps this sort of person should be deemed especially lucky. If so, one could easily argue that native English speakers suffer a liability – a winner's curse. The adoption of their native language as the primary lingua franca in the world only worsens the curse: it reduces their incentives to learn a second language still further. The British Chambers of Commerce (2003–2004) and some other British organizations, like the Nuffield Foundation (see the Nuffield Report, 2000), can be understood to lean toward such a view since they deplore the lower possession of foreign languages and the lower attention to foreign languages in school curricula in the UK than most elsewhere in the EU.[22]

It is indisputable, though, that the advantages of native English speakers receive the most attention. True, if English is adopted as the lingua franca in an international assembly or conference room, native speakers of this language are typically in a better position than those for whom English is an inferior choice. In this respect, considerations of fairness will occasionally suggest improvements in the operating rules of organizations. Pool (1991), for example, shows that it is possible to reconcile efficiency and fairness in the distribution of the costs of translation in international organizations. There could also be derogations to the use of English (or any lingua franca, for that matter) based on axioms of fairness as a function of the circumstances (for example, who the principal interested parties are).

What about the normative aspects of the dominance of English in science and the academic world? In 2006 a group organized by the American Council of Learned Societies (ACLS) to report on the translation of social science texts issued 'A Plea for Social Scientists to Write in Their Own Languages' at the annual meeting of the ACLS (see Tymowski, 2006 and also Allen, 2007, p. 29). The group sees no harm if mathematicians and natural scientists worldwide

---

[22] See also the Dearing Report to the Secretary of State for Languages and Skills in the UK (Dearing, 2006).

write in English, but does if social scientists do the same. The idea, therefore, is that the content of social science investigation can only be fully stated in the investigator's language. If true this would mean that the broad switch to English in social science investigation is indeed a collective drawback and, furthermore, quite unfortunately, that social sciences depend heavily on polyglots and the skills of translators. Yet the only evidence is a reference to the early 19th-century writing of Humboldt about the relation of language to empirical perception. In embracing the same position, Hamel (2007, p. 65) refers to the earlier and related philosophical writing of Herder. Many of us would prefer better evidence that the social sciences are more reliant on the diversity of languages in the world in communicating their work than the natural sciences, and that the strong personal inducements social scientists face to express themselves in English impoverish their contributions to knowledge. In a communication to the same Congress to which Truchot (1996) addressed his paper on the (then-current) political pressures facing French natural scientists to write in French, Walter (1996) notably points out that the tendency of scientists to veer toward a single language in writing traces back more than two millennia with the language of choice shifting from Sumerian to Greek to Arabic to Latin. From this perspective, the turn to English in the course of the 20th century was a return to a longer-term trend and the 19th-century condition where German, English and French shared the top spot as the preferred languages in science was an aberration. Perhaps the return to the longer-time trend is for the better: information travels faster.

This is not to deny the possible uneven impact of the central role of English on the welfare of scientists and scholars in the humanities. How far do native-English scientists and scholars in the humanities have an advantage over the rest (despite their smaller incentives to learn a second language, to their possible regret outside of their professional life and maybe inside of it too)? A study by Sandelin and Sarafoglou (2004) has some indirect bearing on the subject. The authors examine whether native-English countries (namely Australia, Canada, Ireland, New Zealand, the UK and the US in their study) display a larger number of articles in professional publications by resident scientists or scholars per habitant than other countries in a sample of 30 countries, and the authors do so separately for social sciences, arts and the humanities, and the natural sciences. They also control for world size of the principal home language (total world native-Spanish population in the case of Spain, for example) and GDP. The results show that the native-English countries do indeed host a larger number of articles in professional publications by resident scientists and scholars per capita (that is, in relation to the total national population) than other countries. Interestingly, however, this is true for publications in the natural sciences as well as the social sciences and the arts and the humanities. The coefficient for the natural sciences is around a third as high as for the other two areas, but it is still statistically significantly different from zero at the 95 per cent confidence level. On this evidence, the native-English status of a country favours a higher ratio of home-produced publications to the national population in the natural sciences as well as in the social sciences (quite apart from the world population of native speakers of the home language), if only to a lesser extent. This would suggest, without implying it, that the difference in the welfare advantage of the prominence of English to a native-English scientist or scholar in the three different spheres is only a matter of degree.[23] But I know no study bearing directly on the question.

Let us next return to the areas where multilingualism, interpreters and translations are able to overcome the problem of Babel, and English is simply 'the first among equals', so to speak. I have argued that these areas are extremely wide and cover the press, television, the internet, publishing (including translation where I had some difficulty defending the theme) and trade, with three exceptions to which I will return. In these areas, the evidence would show that, broadly speaking, while English is in the lead, it faces sharp limits and all other major languages are safe.[24] The evidence concerning language learning is supportive. If English really threatened to marginalize other major languages in these broad areas of life, we would expect that a model of language learning that treated eight or so of the next ten largest languages exactly the same way as English would perform rather badly. Yet the model does fine. Does any general welfare problem arise from the eminent position of English in these cases? It would seem that the answer is negative. From the standpoint of welfare, there is no clear basis for advocating any special international effort to promote or demote English in the press, television, the internet, publishing and trade.

In defending this view, I would reason that it might perhaps be wise to encourage foreign language learning in general in the world to promote wages, trade and/or culture. But the place of English relative to other languages is a separate topic. Learning English comes at the expense of learning other languages. For example, the hypothetical argument (which does not seem exactly alien) that everyone should learn English as a second language is quite dubious. The argument would imply that some of the time that is currently spent on learning other second languages by people who do not know English would be better spent on learning English. Yet no one has yet made the case. An appeal to coordination failures would not suffice since such failures will often argue for promoting other languages as there are at least half a dozen of them that are internationally as widely spoken as English in large regions of the world.

---

[23] This is not the authors' emphasis.

[24] Of course, thousands of minor languages are endangered. See Dalby (2002), Hagège (2009) and Diamond (2012, ch. 10). However, this is a separate point in my view, quite distinct from the spread of English and its implications.

In addition, the principle of diminishing returns interferes. Even if English is now the most useful language to learn in one's homeland and occupation, once enough others learn it, the best language to acquire may well become another. Ginsburgh and Prieto (2011) offer labour market support. Interpreters and translations should also be kept in mind. Translation renders a lot of learning inefficiently costly (mercifully so), which may argue against some learning of English (as well as other second languages).

The cultural areas of English supremacy provide, in my opinion, the only promising ground for the thesis of too much English. Suppose home preference worldwide in the sense that people everywhere, including those with a second language or a smattering of them, prefer to function in their own language in their private lives. The evidence is overwhelming: it comes from the newspapers people read (even if they know a second language), the television they watch, the internet they use, and many of the facts about edition and trade. Interestingly too, the supporting evidence covers the film and the best-seller as well if only we remember that non-native English people mostly view English-language films that are dubbed or, in the case of the majority, only when there is no choice, subtitled, and they mostly read foreign-language best-sellers in translation. How can it then be welfare-improving for English to dominate the song, the film and the best-seller as much as it does?

The argument that it is welfare-improving must be that, somehow, foreign-language speakers obtain compensation for their sacrifice of home language benefits either through higher quality in other regards or else through lower social costs. As one possibility, the native-English countries are simply better at producing the relevant goods. As another, benefits of market specialization are at work. Because of a mix of comparative advantage and economies of scale, all countries do best to narrow the range of their production activities. As one manifestation, native-English countries specialize in producing the relevant cultural products. In other words, just as Germany specializes in the high-quality end of many consumer durables or France does in some niches in jewelry and perfumes, the native-English countries occupy this particular turf. The argument has merit with respect to film where, in fact, the dominance is specifically American as such, and the British film industry is just as dominated by Hollywood as the French one. Hollywood also rose to world prominence under the silent film, before the 'talkies'. Thus, one can even make a case that Hollywood is the fundamental factor, not English, though some of us will remain sceptical because of the contribution of the French, German, Italian, Japanese, Russian, Spanish and Swedish film in the history of the cinema (see also François and van Ypersele, 2002). But in the case of the song and the best-seller, the argument seems wobbly. Where is the benefit in quality or the reduction in social costs? One particular ground for suspicion is that in other related cultural areas, like music without words, photography, painting, sculpture and architecture, the native-English contribution is closer to what we would expect on the basis of relative population size, income, wealth and tradition. There is something special going on in the cultural market where language is concerned.

I would argue that there is a possible long-term danger. Suppose that the budding author and popular singer of talent feel under the same pressure as the scientist and scholar in the humanities to make his or her name in English. Assume also, as seems to be true in science, that the outstanding talents are especially likely to succumb to this temptation. Their odds of success are higher but the lure is at least the same. In fact, we know of several cases of authors in the hall of literary fame who dropped their native language in favour of others with a larger and more impressive literary tradition (never any opposite examples to my knowledge since the move away from Latin and the printing press): Conrad, Kafka and Ionesco, to mention three. Gogol evidently seriously hesitated between his native Ukrainian and Russian. This is crucially relevant. The threat is not that creative writing will generally dry up in other languages but that the best work will be done in English (a tendency which, if already under way, would help to resolve the paradox I underlined before). In the case of science, where such a tendency is manifest, there is no harm and indeed even a benefit. In literature, however, we cannot reason the same. Literature is an area where language as such is a source of pleasure and enjoyment, an end in itself, rather than a mere instrument for conveying information, or as an outstanding economic contribution by Church and King (1993) has it, a 'communication technology'. True, under the previous scenario, English might continue to evolve and to discover new literary veins. But how much comfort is that? If everyone wrote music for the violin, likewise music might still thrive and we might even hear new echoes of the viola and the guitar and who knows what else issuing from violin strings. Still, what about the keyboard, the winds and the percussion? It does not seem plausible to argue that there would be no loss.

Acknowledgements

This chapter reports on a lot of concurrent work in Melitz and Toubal (2014) and Ginsburgh et al. (2014), and as a result some passages in Subsection 20.3.5 and Section 20.4 occur in these papers and should be considered co-authored.

References

E. Allen (2007) 'Translation, Globalization and English' In E. Allen (ed.) *To Be Translated or Not to Be* (Barcelona: Institut Ramon Llull), pp. 17–33.

U. Ammon (1998) *Ist Deutsch noch Internationale Wissenschaftssprache? Englisch auch für die Lehre an den Deutschsprachigen Hochschulen* (Berlin: de Gruyter).

J. Anderson and E. van Wincoop (2003) 'Gravity with Gravitas: A Solution to the Border Problem', *American Economic Review*, 93, 170–192.

D. Bakker, A. Müller, V. Velupillai, S. Wichmann, C. Brown, P. Brown, D. Egorov, R. Mailhammer, A. Grant and E. Holman (2009) 'Adding Typology to Lexicostatistics: A Combined Approach to Language Classification', *Linguistic Typology*, 13, 167–179.

I. Bel Habib (2011) Multilingual Skills Provide Export Benefits and Better Access to New Emerging Markets, www.SensPublic_Ingela_Bel_Habib_Report_Multilingual_Skills.

D. Berwanger (1987) *Television and the Third World: New Technology and Social Change* (Bonn: Friedrich-Ebert-Stiftung).

D. Biltereyst (1991) 'Resisting American Hegemony: A Comparative Analysis of the Reception of Domestic and US Fiction', *European Journal of Communication*, 6, 469–497.

BIPE (Bureau de l'information et de la prévision économique) Conseil (1993) 'Approche statistique de la production littéraire en Europe', mimeo.

British Chambers of Commerce, The (2003–2004) BBC Language Survey. The Impact of Foreign Languages on British Business – Part 1, 2003; Part 2, 2004 (Online, Web publication).

C. Brown, E. Holman, S. Wichmann and V. Velupillai (2008) 'Automatic Classification of the World's Languages: A Description of the Method and Preliminary Results', *Language Typology and Universals*, 61, 285–308.

J. Church and I. King (1993) 'Bilingualism and Network Externalities', *Canadian Journal of Economics*, 26, 337–345.

D. Crystal (2003) *English as a Global Language*, 2nd edn (Cambridge, UK: Cambridge University Press).

D. Crystal (2006) *Language and the Internet*, 2nd edn (Cambridge, UK: Cambridge University Press).

A. Dalby (2002) *Language in Danger* (London: Allen Lane, The Penguin Press).

R. Dearing (2006) 'The Dearing Report to the Secretary of State for Education & Skills', *The Languages Review*, www.education.gov.uk/consultations/downloadableDocs/6869-DfES-Language%20Review.pdf

A. De Swaan (2001) *Words of the World* (New York: Wiley).

J. Diamond (2012) *The World until Yesterday* (New York: Penguin Group).

Economist, The (1997) 'Schools Brief: A World View', 29 November–5 December, 91–92.

P. Egger and A. Lassmann (2012) 'The Language Effect in International Trade: A Meta-analysis', *Economics Letters*, 116, 221–224.

Ethnologue (2010) *Languages of the World* (Dallas, USA: Summer Institute of Linguistics), www.ethnologue.com

Eurobarometer (2006) 'Europeans and Their Languages', *Special Eurobarometer 243* (Brussels: The European Commission).

A. Feely and D. Winslow (2005) *Talking Sense: A Research Study of Language Skills Management in Major Companies* (London: CILT, The National Center for Languages).

J. Fidrmuc and V. Ginsburgh (2007) 'Languages in the EU: The Quest for Equality and Its Cost', *European Economic Review*, 51, 1351–1369.

F. Foroutan and L. Pritchett (1993) 'Intra-Sub-Saharan African Trade: Is It Too Little?', *Journal of African Economics*, 2, 74–105.

P. François and T. van Ypersele (2002) 'On the Protection of Cultural Goods', *Journal of International Economics*, 56, 359–369.

J. Frankel (1997) *Regional Trading Blocs in the World Trading System* (Washington, DC: Institute for International Economics).

J. Gabszewicz, V. Ginsburgh and S. Weber (2011) 'Bilingualism and Communicative Benefits', *Annals of Economics and Statistics*, 101/102, 271–286.

V. Ginsburgh, J. Melitz and F. Toubal (2014) 'Foreign Language Learning: An Econometric Analysis', CEPR Working Paper 10101.

V. Ginsburgh and J. Prieto (2011) 'Returns to Foreign Languages of Native Workers in the European Union', *Industrial and Labor Relations*, 64, 599–618.

V. Ginsburgh, S. Weber and S. Weyers (2011) 'The Economics of Literary Translation: Some Theory and Evidence', *Poetics*, 39, 228–246.

D. Graddol (1997) *The Future of English* (London: British Council).

D. Graddol (2006) *English Next* (London: British Council).

C. Hagège (2009) *On the Death and Life of Languages* (New Haven: Yale University Press).

S. Hagen with J. Foreman-Peck, S. Davila-Philippon, B. Nordgren and S. Hagen (2006) *ELAN: Effects on the European Economy of Shortages of Foreign Language Skills in Enterprise* (London: CILT, The National Center for Languages).

R. Hamel (2007) 'The Dominance of English in the International Scientific Periodical Literature and the Future of Language Use in Science', *AILA Review*, 20, 53–71.

O. Havrylyshyn and L. Pritchett (1991) 'European Trade Patterns after the Transition', Policy Research Working Paper 748, World Bank, Washington, DC.

K. Head and T. Mayer (2013) 'Gravity Equations: Workhorse, Toolkit and Cookbook', CEPR Discussion Paper No. 9322, London.

C. Hoskins and S. McFadyen (1991) 'The U.S. Competitive Advantage in the Global Television Market: Is It Sustainable in the New Broadcasting Environment?', *Canadian Journal of Communication*, 16, 207–224.

B. Kachru (2010) *Asian Englishes: Beyond the Canon* (Hong Kong: Hong Kong University Press).

H. Ku and A. Zussman (2010) 'Lingua Franca: The Role of English in International Trade', *Journal of Economic Behavior & Organization*, 75, 250–260.

J. Melitz (2007) 'The Impact of English Dominance on Literature and Welfare', *Journal of Economic Behavior & Organization*, 64, 193–215.

J. Melitz (2008) 'Language and Foreign Trade', *European Economic Review*, 52, 667–699.

J. Melitz and F. Toubal (2014) 'Native Language, Spoken Language, Translation and Foreign Trade', *Journal of International Economics*, 93, 351–363.

Nuffield Foundation (2000) Languages: The Next Generation; The Final Report and Recommendations of the Nuffield Languages Inquiry (Online).

N. Ostler (2010) *The Last Lingua Franca. English until the Return of Babel* (London: Allen Lane).

J. Pool (1991) 'The official language problem', *American Political Science Review*, 85, 495–514.

B. Sandelin and N. Sarafoglou (2004) 'Language and Scientific Publication Statistics', *Language Problems and Language Planning*, 28, 1–10.

G. Sapiro (2010) 'Globalization and Cultural Diversity in the Book Market: The Case of Literary Translations in the US and in France', *Poetics*, 38, 419–439.

R. Selten and J. Pool (1991) 'The Distribution of Foreign Language Skills as a Game Equilibrium' In R. Selten (ed.) *Game Equilibrium Models*, vol. 4 (Berlin: Springer Verlag), pp. 64–87.

M. Tracey (1985) 'The Poisoned Chalice? International Television and the Idea of Dominance', *Daedalus*, 114, Fall, 17–56.

C. Truchot (1996) 'La langue française en science. Un cas de figure: la situation linguistique des sciences en France' *Le français et les langues scientifiques de demain* (Québec: Colloque Université du Québec à Montréal 19–21 mars).

M. Tsunoda (1983) 'Les langues internationales dans les publications scientifiques et techniques', *Sophia Linguistica*, 13, 144–155.

A. Tymowski (2006) *Guidelines for the Translation of Social Science Texts* (New York: American Council of Learned Societies, Annual meeting, Appendix I).

UNESCO *Statistical Yearbook*, various years.

P. Van Parijs (2011) *Linguistic Justice for Europe and the World* (Oxford: Oxford University Press).

T. Varis (1984) 'The International Flow of Television Programs', *Journal of Communication*, 34, 143–152.

H. Walter (1996) 'L'évolution des langues de la communication scientifique' *Le français et les langues scientifiques de demain* (Québec: Colloque Université de Québec).

L. Wiesenfeld (1999) *The World Almanac and Book of Facts* (Mahwah, NJ, USA: Primedia Reference).

Z. Yong and K. Campbell (1995) 'English in China', *World Englishes*, 3, 377–390.

21
Challenges of Minority Languages

François Grin

21.1 Introduction

The economics of language can claim different lines of parentage in the discipline of economics. This chapter on the economics of minority languages espouses a specific view, put forward by the late Gary Becker, in his *Economic Approach to Human Behavior* (1976), according to which economics is characterized less by its subject matter than by its approach. Without necessarily endorsing the full range of assumptions and ideological tenets associated with Becker's work, this approach opens the door to the application of economic analysis to a wide range of topics, including language-related ones.

Language economics addresses a vast array of language-related issues that can be arranged in two main categories. The first category includes topics that may be seen as natural extensions of mainstream economic ones. For example, research on the effect of language skills on wage rates on the labour market fits quite comfortably into standard labour economics. Keeping things simple, we could say that, in this category, the dependent variables are economic ones. The second category includes topics that require taking bolder steps towards novel applications of economics – in this case, applications to language matters, in which the dependent variables are predominantly linguistic and are not the usual concerns in economic research. The economics, then, ultimately reside in the reference to the Beckerian criterion just recalled, although it may also be reflected, depending on the issue concerned, in a reference to standard economic constructs and variables like supply and demand, or prices, wages and income.

For the most part, the economics of minority languages belong to the second category. The development of research in this area was made possible, particularly since the 1970s, by economic forays into an expanding range of questions, giving rise to new specialities such as the economics of culture, the economics of religion or environmental economics.

The economics of minority languages occupies a well-defined segment of research in language economics, because the issues it deals with are relatively clearly identifiable: how can we account for the often observed decline of those languages or, in some cases, their revival? Can this decline be stopped by the application of appropriately designed language policies – and if so, how exactly? Can *reverse* language shift be sustainable, particularly in a context of deepening international economic integration?

In this chapter, I begin by clarifying some key notions, starting with the actual meaning of the notion of 'minority' language and the nature of processes of language shift and reverse language shift (Section 21.2). I then review, in Section 21.3, the literature on the economics of minority languages, with an emphasis on its special place in the broader language economics literature. Section 21.4 is devoted to the presentation, in general and strictly non-technical terms, of a model of minority language use, which has been chosen because of its demonstrated usefulness for the understanding of several classical minority language situations. Section 21.5 proposes a closer look at a variant of the model, deriving its comparative statics, in particular with respect to changes that can result from language policy. Section 21.5 is the only one in this chapter that contains equations; readers who prefer to skip the formal modelling can easily do so and move on directly to Section 21.6, which discusses the implications of these comparative statics, highlighting the conditions that should be met, according to the model, for policy interventions to be successful. In Section 21.7, I address related issues in the economics of minority languages, namely the question of policy costs and that of the net value of minority language protection and promotion. Section 21.8 takes a step back and proposes to reposition the question of the value of minority languages in the broader context of the value of linguistic diversity in general. Section 21.9 concludes by summarizing the main results of each section.

21.2   What is a minority language?

This deceptively straightforward question raises a number of difficulties, three of which present particular saliency for the economics of minority languages.

The first problem concerns the very identification of 'languages', before we can call some 'minority' as opposed to *non*-minority. This harks back, in particular, to the eternal question of the distinction between 'language' and 'dialect'. Quite apart from the fact that the very label of 'language' as distinct from 'dialect' is the product of history (to wit, the deliberate elevation of one specific, regional form of speech, anchored in Tuscany, to the position of a standard language called 'Italian'), what degree of difference between two idioms do we require to consider them separate, and not mere variants of each other? Standard European French and some forms of French as spoken in Quebec are different enough, particularly in their phonology, to hamper mutual intel-ligibility, but they are all referred to as 'French'; conversely, Portuguese and Galician, which are arguably closer to each other in morpho-syntax and, above all, phonology, are usually counted as separate languages. Answering such ques-tions raises thorny problems of judgement: is linguistic distance a relevant criterion at all, or should we simply rely on socio-political factors? Consider-ing that interlinguistic distance can in fact be measured in very different ways (Ginsburgh et al., 2011; Chapter 5 in this volume), there is probably no general, one-size-fits-all solution to this problem. The latter is made more intriguing by the fact that some measures of linguistic distance usually developed by lin-guists perform well as independent variables in statistical work carried out by economists, although the reason *why* they do (or whether they actually proxy for something quite different) has only been partly examined in the literature. Further, how do we take account of 'register' – a major determinant of the degree of mutual intelligibility between 'continental' and Québécois forms of French? Clearly, these points matter, since the linguistic difference characteriz-ing 'minority language' speakers can often take the form of a deviation from an accepted, dominant standard.[1]

---

[1] A related, though rather contrived, question is that of whether languages exist *at all*. It is true, of course, that processes of social construction in the broadest sense play a cru-cial role in delineating the forms of speech that will be regarded as languages ('French', 'English', 'Wolof', 'Guaraní', etc.). It is also true that the degree of attention paid to differences between languages is, itself, a product of cultural history (Hüning et al., 2012), and the arguably 'European' tradition of establishing sharp distinctions between languages contrasts with other (and allegedly more widespread elsewhere, for example in western Africa) ways of viewing languages, in which such distinctions are given far less importance (Calvet, 2004). However, such well-taken observations carry some com-mentators too far. In an age of globalization, the notion that hybrid forms of speech trump established languages, making the very notion of 'named' languages obsolete, currently enjoys considerable popularity (Makoni and Pennycook, 2007), and current sociolinguistic research contains abundant references to '(trans-)languaging' (Blommaert and Rampton, 2011). 'Languaging' is, in my view, a somewhat problematic notion emphasizing a mode of communication which is assumed to draw, in a creative and unconstrained manner, on the entirety of speakers' linguistic repertoires. It is claimed that in these repertoires different 'named' languages blend into each other, yielding the conclusion that 'we no longer need to maintain the pernicious myth that languages exist' (Pennycook, 2008, p. 67), and that 'the concept of mother tongue should have no place in the sociolinguistic toolkit' (Blommaert and Rampton, 2011, p. 5). In order to expose the problematic nature of many of these claims, it is usually enough to observe that even the most enthusiastic 'translanguaging', but monoglot, speaker of English or French will be lost if his or her interlocutor, who had initiated a conversation in English or French, abruptly switches to Swedish or Turkish. For a robust critique of the notion that languages do not exist, see Edwards (2012) or Phillipson and Skutnabb-Kangas (2013).

Second, once we have agreed on what a language is and what counts as different languages, we need criteria for identifying *minority* languages. A simple, informal approach, along the lines of 'a minority language is a language spoken by a part of the population that constitutes neither the absolute nor the relative majority', soon proves inadequate, because numerous points must be clarified for the analysis to make sense from a sociological, political or policy perspective. The points that require elaboration include in particular the following. Do we mean a language spoken *as a native language* (e.g. a native-born Catalan in a Catalan-speaking home) or do we include secondary speakers of it – that is, people who have acquired the language *after* another (mother) tongue (e.g. Castilian-speaking Spaniards who have settled in Barcelona and lived there long enough to have become fluent in Catalan)? In this latter case, what is the level of proficiency one needs to have acquired to be considered a *speaker* of the language? In the former case, what assumptions are we making regarding minority language speakers? Are they bilinguals with a perfect command of the majority language (just as practically every native speaker of Welsh also is a fluent speaker of English), or do they mostly have limited proficiency in it (a situation often encountered among Aboriginal communities in Australia)? 'Minority language' can mean many different things.[2]

Third, it is difficult to answer this second set of questions without making definitional choices about the reference area considered, since the very same language can be both a minority and a majority language. German is the majority language in Germany, Austria, Switzerland and Liechtenstein; it is co-official and widely used in Luxembourg; it is a minority language in Belgium, Denmark and Italy, not to mention small, but also long-established German-speaking communities sprinkled across Eastern and Central Europe as well as the Commonwealth of Independent States (CIS) (Cordell and Wolff, 2004). French is the majority language of Quebec, but it is a minority language in Canada and – perhaps more to the point – on the North American continent. A related problem is whether a 'unique' minority language, spoken only in one part of the world where it is known by a numerically small share of the population of the reference area, and a language which is in a minority position in one country but in a majority position in another represent instances of the same or different situations – in plain terms: are the cases of Welsh (spoken only in Wales – abstracting from a small community of speakers in Patagonia) and Hungarian *as a minority language* (in Slovakia, Ukraine, Romania, Serbia, Croatia, Slovenia and Austria – while of course it is the majority language in Hungary) similar or not?[3]

---

[2] For a typology, see for example www.mercator-research.eu/minority-languages/facts-figures/

[3] The foregoing suggests that it is probably useful, when embarking on an exploration of minority languages with the standard tools of economics, to bear in mind the complexity

For the purposes of this chapter, let us adopt the definition found in Article 1a of the European Charter for Regional or Minority Languages, which refers to

> languages that are (i) traditionally used within a given territory of a State by nationals of that State who form a group numerically smaller than the rest of the State's population; and (ii) different from the official language(s) of that State; it does not include either dialects of the official language(s) of the State or the languages of migrants.[4]

From a sociological standpoint, the defining trait of these languages is that they face an uphill battle for their continuing use in different sociolinguistic domains, sometimes for their very survival.

There again, the criterion is not iron-clad: even major international languages see their role called into question in certain domains, such as scientific research, by the increasing use of English (Carli and Ammon, 2007).[5] Nevertheless, and for the purposes of this chapter, I shall adopt a relatively narrow view of 'minority languages' by excluding from the definition languages whose *native* speakers, though they may be in a minority in some cases, *usually* find themselves in a majority – in the context of a state, itself defined as a subject of international law. The fact that anglophones are a minority in the Province of Quebec does not, for the purposes of this chapter, make English a minority language; by the same token, we shall not consider French a minority language, despite the fact that francophones are a minority in Switzerland. The same goes for Russian, spoken by a minority of residents of Estonia. Typical minority

---

of the object itself, as well as of the basic concepts required to talk about it. Discussions in the epistemology of economics (for example Leibenstein, 1976; Mayer, 1993) suggest that the formalized approaches favoured in economic research perform comparatively well when it comes to spelling out rigorously the *relationships* between variables; but this sometimes comes at the cost of such oversimplification of the *variables* connected through these relationships that the resulting models, despite their mathematical savvy, may be of mostly anecdotal interest. This risk, which increases with the complexity of the object, is likely to be significant in the case of language (Grin, 2003a). To mitigate this danger, economists studying language issues will generally benefit from referring to the contributions of the language disciplines; putting it differently, language economics has much to gain from being interdisciplinary.

[4] See http://conventions.coe.int/treaty/en/Treaties/Html/148.htm. Note that Article 3(1) of the Charter is designed with implicit reference to the case of Irish, which enjoys official status in the Republic of Ireland and might therefore be excluded by Article 1a (ii). Article 3(1) extends the coverage of the Charter to any 'official language which is less widely used on the whole or part of [the] territory [of a Contracting State]'.

[5] For example, this very volume, published in English, is co-edited by two scholars whose native language is not English; only a minority of the contributors in it have English as a mother tongue.

languages, therefore, are those that appear in Appendix 1.[6] The fact of the matter is that the users of these languages are confronted with more immediate challenges than most.

These challenges can be subsumed under the notion of 'language shift' (Fishman, 1991): minority language speakers are overwhelmingly bilingual, since they typically have a very good command of the majority language. They can therefore carry out many of their activities (media consumption, for example) through the medium of that language and, for a number of reasons discussed below, they may choose to do it. Their fluency in the majority language may also be used by the authorities as an excuse for *not* providing certain public services through the medium of the minority language, and the corresponding activities, therefore, will be carried out in the majority language only, even by minority language speakers who would have preferred, given a choice, to use their language. Thus, whether for reasons of their own or because of external constraints, minority language speakers are much more likely *not* to use their language than majority language speakers would, even if these are bilingual too, which is proportionately far less frequent. In the aggregate, minority language speakers' practices can result in the progressive marginalization of their language, which may end up being squeezed out of some domains, thus losing usefulness and prestige. This will, in turn, discourage its intergenerational transmission, further contributing to the erosion of the language.

The dynamics of language shift have attracted considerable attention, both as a sociolinguistic phenomenon per se (Haugen, 1981; Fishman, 1989) and as a social problem that deserves to be addressed through appropriate policies (Fishman, 1991, 2001). It is in relation to this latter aspect that economists are presented with a challenge: what can we do, as economists, to contribute to the maintenance of threatened minority languages? I turn to this question in the following section.

21.3   The economics of minority language protection and promotion

Theoretical and empirical work on the protection and promotion of minority languages constitutes one of the significant directions in language economics, particularly since the 1990s. This strand of research may be defined more or less

---

[6] The empirical difference between a 'minority' and a 'non-minority' language, however, is fluid, which probably explains the rising popularity of the notion of CRSSLs – that is, 'constitutional, regional and smaller state languages', since even national/official languages may confront challenges not unlike those observed in classical minority situations. Therefore, despite the restrictions just introduced for the sake of analytical consistency, much of what follows applies to a broader range of small languages.

narrowly, and it is often difficult to separate it from a neighbouring one that is mainly concerned with language dynamics, that is, the processes of language spread and decline over time. Contributions that belong to this latter group are relevant too, because language decline is often particularly manifest in the case of minority languages.

For space reasons, I shall not embark on a fully fledged review of the literature, which is available elsewhere (e.g. Grin, 1996, 2003; Zhang and Grenier, 2012), including in recent downloadable resources (Grin, 2013), but for our purposes, the contributions that have particular relevance can be arranged in three groups:

1. analyses of minority language use with a focus on the speakers' decision to use or not to use a minority language, rather than on the policies that can be put in place in order to induce them do so (e.g. Hočevar, 1975, 1983; Grin, 1990, 1994a; Mateo Aierza, 2004; Alarcón 2007; MacLeod, 2009);
2. analyses of minority language spread and decline over time (e.g. Grin, 1992; Abrams and Strogatz, 2003; Mira and Paredes, 2005; Wickström, 2005; Castelló et al., 2007; Irriberi and Uriarte, 2012; see also chapters 2 and 3 in this volume);
3. analyses of the effectiveness and cost-effectiveness of minority language policies in terms of their actual impact on language use (Grin and Vaillancourt, 1999; Chalmers, 2003; Grin, 2009; Milligan et al., 2013).

Note that by highlighting these three groups of contributions, I am deliberately leaving out those that belong to two other categories:

1. Papers that explore the determinants of language use in various contexts (such as, for example, advertising; see e.g. Krishna and Ahluwalia, 2008), but do not concern *minority* languages. This also explains the absence, among the groups of papers mentioned, of contributions about the determination of language *learning* and the subsequent level of language *skills* because, in the main, studies that explain language learning tend to focus on majority, not minority, languages.[7]
2. Papers in which language-related variables (for example, agents' proficiency in a minority language) are approached as *independent*, as opposed to dependent, variables. This is what explains the absence of papers on the *economic* impacts of minority language promotion (for example in terms of regional

---

[7] They would include, for example, the literature on the determinants of the use of French and English at work in Quebec (e.g. Vaillancourt et al., 1994), immigrants' language skills' development (e.g. Chiswick and Miller, 1995, 2007), or investment in foreign language learning (Ginsburgh and Prieto, 2011; Ginsburgh et al., 2014).

economic development),[8] including papers about the rates of return on competence in minority language skills.[9]

By way of consequence, the well-known literature on the economic value of skills in a dominant language, whether English for immigrants to the United States (e.g. various contributions in Chiswick and Miller, 2007) or the two official languages of Canada (e.g. Vaillancourt et al., 2007) also lies outside the scope of this chapter.

This chapter, therefore, clearly focuses on (i) the economic perspectives on the determination of minority language use, sometimes influenced by deliberate protection and promotion policies, sometimes not, and on (ii) closely related issues of minority language policy evaluation. These questions are at the heart of the model discussed in the following section.

21.4   Capacity, opportunity and desire: An overview of the basic model

Ultimately, the 'challenge of minority languages' is not a matter of raw demolinguistics (for example, the percentage of minority language speakers at a given point in time in the population at large, or by age group) or of language learning (what determines the number or proportion of agents who, in a given environment, will opt to learn the language). Having people who know the language or are learning it is fine and well, but what truly matters is whether the language is actually being *used*. Our problem, therefore, is to come up with a workable model of *minority language use*. Our starting point here will be a variant of a formal model based on earlier work (Grin, 1990, 1992), and later refurbished for the purposes of an evaluation of alternative measures for the promotion of the Maori language in New Zealand (Grin and Vaillancourt, 1998). Since then, the model has been used by others, particularly in European research projects.[10] Let us begin by presenting the core model in general, intuitive terms, keeping a discussion of the more technical aspects for the next section.[11]

Speakers of a minority language as defined in this chapter are overwhelmingly bilingual, albeit with varying degrees of competence in the majority

---

[8] The interested reader may turn to Walsh (2009) or Watt and MacLeòid (2009).

[9] See e.g. Henley and Jones (2005) for Welsh; Patrinos and Hurst (2007) for Aymara; or Borooah et al. (2009) for Irish. The earnings equations used in these estimations are essentially identical to those used in the case of 'big' languages like English, German or French.

[10] See Grin et al. (2002), FIONTAR Programme (2009) or Laakso et al. (2013).

[11] The formal model, however, is available at: www.treasury.govt.nz/publications/research-policy/wp/1998/98-06 (accessed 9 September 2014).

language (*A*) and the minority language (*B*). They have a choice to carry out various activities, such as socializing, in one or the other language. If such activities are to be carried out in the minority language, three conditions must be met.

First, users must have adequate competence in the minority language. At first sight, we might wish to describe this condition in terms of skills, and say that those skills must be sufficiently high; the word 'competence', however (which implies no connection with the meaning of 'competence' in Chomskyan generativist grammar), requires not just testable skills, but also the confidence to use them, along with the pragmatic (possibly unconscious) knowledge of how to use these skills appropriately in interaction. Depending on context, it may or may not be necessary for competences to be not only oral, but also written, therefore encompassing *literacy*. Let us refer to this bundle of competences with the word *capacity*. Capacity is, of course, a complex variable whose operationalization, starting with its measurement, is not as easy as it seems. For practical purposes, it is often acceptable to refer to a self-reported degree of competence. If a model requires an aggregate measure of minority language competence, the percentage of people in a given area (e.g. country or region) who declare having that degree of competence constitutes an acceptable proxy. Clearly, capacity can be influenced by policy through the education system, whether in schools or through continuing education programmes.

Second, even if some people qualify as competent users[12] of the language, they need *opportunities* to use it. Opportunities imply, in practice, the existence of a language community, even a small one, as well as the availability of minority-language services of various kinds. Many are in the purview of the authorities, and thus directly subject to policy. This is the case for the administration and courts of law. Others are embedded in the activity of the private sector, but may nevertheless be regulated by policy. This includes, for example, aspects of everyday consumption, because the state can mandate the use of a given language in the labelling and packaging of consumer goods. Likewise, it includes entertainment, since the state may make the granting of broadcasting licences conditional on the use of the minority language by the media concerned. Moving from regulation to incentives, the state can also subsidize selected minority-language goods, such as books, to reduce their relative price and encourage people to read in the minority language.

Third, we need to add one more condition, namely, *desire*. For although *capacity* and *opportunity* are obviously necessary, they are not (on their own or jointly) *sufficient*. 'Desire' might of course be replaced by 'willingness', and either is correlated with the absence of countervailing pressures, such as repression of

---

[12] To avoid repetition, I shall sometimes use the word 'speaker' (of a language) instead of 'user', it being clear that, depending on context, being recorded as a 'speaker' may also imply the presence of written skills.

minority language use in public, or humiliation for those who speak it. Obvious as this may seem, let us remember that the time is not far off when schoolchildren in Britain were persecuted for speaking Welsh or Scottish Gaelic. Clearly, desire (which we shall later operationalize as a parameter of the user's utility function) can be influenced through policy, though only indirectly. It stands to reason that it will, all other things being equal, tend to respond favourably to the abolition of discrimination or – even better – active promotion of the language.

Thus, in the model discussed here, capacity, opportunity and desire operate as three necessary conditions for minority language use, neither of them sufficient on its own, but jointly sufficient if all three are present (Grin and Vaillancourt, 1998). All three can be influenced through language policy, and it is striking that the measures contained in the European Charter for Regional or Minority Languages (discussed and adopted before this formal model was published) can in fact be mapped onto this model, which was developed fully independently of it (and whose earliest versions pre-date by several years the adoption of the Charter). Article 8 of the Charter, which concerns minority language education, maps onto 'capacity'; Articles 9, 10, 11 and 12, which concern public services (including the media), target 'opportunity'; Article 13, which deals with 'economic and social life', amounts to language promotional measures that all encourage the 'desire' or 'willingness' to use the language (see Grin, 2003b, for a more detailed discussion).

This approach provides a generic template for the selection and design of minority language policies. It also suggests modes of cooperation between language planners, economists and sociolinguists, using a public policy perspective as a federating or integrative approach. The sociolinguists, of course, would be called upon to provide appropriate information about the actual situation of a language in a social context, and to establish to what extent the capacity, opportunity or desire are present – or missing. Applying the recommendations of the economic model, decision-makers can select and prioritize policy measures on this basis.

One important feature of the model is that it uses time units as a dependent variable, instead of raw values on linguistic ability. Thus, language use is measured in time units, and the success of a policy will be measured by the *increase* in time units during which the minority language is being used by the typical agent. For an individual who speaks languages A (majority) and B (minority), the relative use of these languages can be defined as the amount of the total time available devoted to A-language and B-language activities respectively. A simple time constraint is enough to capture scarcity. It can be combined with a Beckerian household production function approach in which activities in either language are carried out using market goods and the agent's own time. These activities are the arguments of an agent's utility function, which is maximized under the full income constraint that combines a limitation on the agent's time and on his or her financial resources. Optimal solutions to the bilingual agent's utility-maximization problem can then be formulated in terms of the amount of time devoted to activities taking place in one or another language.

Let me point out that I do not attempt to treat language *itself* as a commodity with an intrinsically economic nature. Suggestions in this direction rest on analogies between language and human capital (explicitly explored as such in an early paper by Grenier, 1982), or some or other form of transaction costs (Breton and Mieszkowski, 1977; Carr, 1985). Although these are quite natural interpretations, they reduce language to its instrumental dimensions and overlook its pervasiveness in every human activity – that is, a phenomenon that makes economic sense beyond its usefulness for international trade or labour market participation. Analysing language as a characteristic of *all* activities therefore represents a more general perspective on language-related decisions. In addition, focusing on language *use* as opposed to 'language' itself provides more connections with the sociolinguistic and language planning literature, as well as some operational policy guidelines.

Language policies operate in a highly complex environment, and a degree of uncertainty necessarily surrounds the actual impact of any specific set of measures, even when they are aimed at relatively more predictable targets, such as 'capacity', which can be increased by giving the minority language more space in school syllabuses. It is therefore useful to take a closer look at the precise conditions for language policies to deliver the expected results.

21.5   Conditions for effective policies

If our analytical tool is a formal model, a logical step is to examine its comparative statics. Much will depend, then, on the specification of the model, which comes, and has been used, in different variants. In what follows, I propose a discussion of these comparative statics for a variant of the model that enables us to consider a wide range of comparative statics lending themselves to an interpretation in terms of the relative effectiveness of various policy measures.

The model developed here, in essence, formalizes the general principle proposed in the preceding section, namely, that the vitality of a minority language requires the co-presence of three conditions: the capacity, the opportunities and the desire to use this language. Readers who prefer to skip the formal discussion can move on straight to the following section, which derives, in a non-technical fashion, the corresponding implications for the effective selection and design of language policies in favour of minority languages.

Consider an individual who speaks languages *A* and *B*, for example of a Welshman living in a strongly Welsh-speaking town such as Aberystwyth. '*A*' will then stand for English, and '*B*' for Welsh. As long as neither language is banned or forced upon him, he has a choice of conducting many of his everyday activities in either language. In order to formalize this idea, I use Gary Becker's 'household production function approach' (Becker, 1965, 1976). In this approach, agents do not maximize utility directly over the consumption of market goods, but over the consumption of complex commodities, which can, equivalently, be interpreted as the practice of certain activities. Commodities (or activities) require the combination, by the agent himself, of market goods with some of his own time. He will then produce the commodity (or practice the activity) himself, applying a 'technology' that reflects the conditions under which an agent operates. This technology is influenced by an agent's capabilities (Sen, 1985), some of which may be the product of earlier human capital investment, while others are broadly contextual and beyond the agent's control.

The utility function needs to be redefined accordingly. Let us therefore define our bilingual agent's quasi-concave, twice-differentiable utility function as:

$$U = U\left(Z_a\left(x_a, t_a, E_a\right), Z_b\left(x_b, t_b, E_b\right)\right), \tag{1}$$

where Z_a and Z_b represent *A* and *B* language Beckerian commodities (or activities) produced using time inputs t_a and t_b and goods inputs x_a and x_b. In addition to time and goods, which are the standard ingredients of the household production function approach, we include two contextual variables, namely E_a and E_b, which denote exposure to language *A* and language *B* respectively. These exposure variables summarize a number of significant factors that have been studied by sociolinguists and geographers when analysing language use. Such factors include the geographical isolation of speakers of a language, language use in advertising, the availability of *A* and *B* language use, and psychological pressure from family and friends in favour of one or the other language (Giles et al., 1977; Williams, 1988; Grin and Vaillancourt, 1999). In line with the sociolinguistic literature, we would say that exposure to one language is higher if it is often heard on the street or in the media, and if institutional or personal surroundings are favourable to its use.

In this model, 'exposure' goes beyond the 'opportunity' discussed in the preceding section, since we assume that higher exposure to a language will increase the agent's proficiency in it, and make him or her more efficient at pursuing activities in this language. The precise meaning of efficiency in our context is that less time and/or goods will be needed to produce a certain amount of commodities in a given language if the individual enjoys higher exposure to it. The marginal productivity of factors is assumed to be positive and decreasing, and it is enhanced by exposure. For activities carried out in both A and B, we have:[13]

$$Z_{tE} > 0. \tag{2}$$

$$Z_{xE} > 0. \tag{3}$$

Agents face a time constraint of the form:

$$T = t_a + t_b + t_w, \tag{4}$$

where T represents total waking time available per period and t_w stands for time spent at paid work. The associated financial constraint is:

$$wt_w = p_a x_a + p_b x_b, \tag{5}$$

where w represents the wage rate and therefore the opportunity cost of time, and p_a and p_b are the prices of goods used in A and B language activities respectively. The constraints (4) and (5) can be combined into what Becker (1976, p. 135) calls a 'full-income' constraint:[14]

$$wT = S = \sum_i (p_i x_i + wt_i) \qquad i = a, b. \tag{6}$$

Maximizing (1) under (6) yields demand functions for all four inputs. Since we are concerned with patterns of language use, we shall devote our attention to the demand for time to spend on A and B language activities. These demand functions (assuming T is fixed and not relevant for the comparative statics) are:

$$t_i = t_i(p_a, p_b, w, E_a, E_b) \qquad i = a, b. \tag{7}$$

These functions are homogeneous of degree zero in prices and wage rate.[15] By defining the amount of time individuals wish to devote to activities A and

---

[13] Formally, $(\partial Z/\partial t)/\partial E > 0$ and $(\partial Z/\partial x)/\partial E > 0$. A more compact notation is adopted here as shorthand.

[14] As Becker points out, 'full income...embodies both the time and money income constraints and its magnitude is independent of the fraction of time the household chooses to allocate to income-earning activities'.

[15] Note that working time t_w is computed residually from the optimal amounts of time devoted to A and B language activities, t_a^* and t_b^*. It is not attributed *a priori* to either language. This standard Beckerian assumption reflects the fact that language of work usually is not an object of choice to the same extent as other activities. Workers will generally not be able to choose a job that always fits their linguistic preferences, and they are assumed to generally adapt to the standard practice of the employing firm, so that the

B, equation (7) describes language use itself as the direct outcome of a resource allocation process, instead of taking the roundabout way of looking at language skills as the result of an investment in human capital, and then assuming that language use must be positively correlated to language skills.

In this chapter, I mostly focus on the demand side of language use, which will therefore depend on goods prices, the opportunity cost of time, total time available and the degree of exposure to the various languages. Exposure, however, may be interpreted as *reflecting* total supply: when the supply of opportunities to use a minority language is higher, one gets more exposure to it. Exposure-enhancing measures, therefore, can proxy for increases in supply. In this model, we focus on how exposure affects demand, and the comparative statics of exposure will be derived (see Appendix 2) with this concern in mind. This implies that the supply of situations in which language *A* and language *B* can be used is perfectly elastic from the standpoint of the individual agent. This assumption is not particularly radical, in that it expresses the well-known sociolinguistic fact that in the context of languages, demand creates its own supply, since individuals who prefer to use *B* provide opportunities to use it for individuals with similar inclinations.[16]

We assume for simplicity that the production functions for both commodities (Z_a and Z_b) display constant returns to scale. Therefore, the production function $Z_i = z_i (x_i, t_i)$ for $i = a, b$ yields $Z_i/t_i = z_i (x_i/t_i, 1)$ and its inverse $t_i/Z_i = z_i^{-1} (x_i/t_i)$. Factor inputs depend on their marginal productivity, and factors are used in such a way that marginal productivity is aligned to price. It follows that the ratio of input to output is itself a function of the price of inputs w/p_i, for $i = a, b$. This enables us to rewrite the full-income constraint as follows:

$$S = \sum_i \left[p_i \varphi_i \left(\frac{w}{p_i}, E_i \right) + w \tau_i \left(\frac{w}{p_i}, E_i \right) \right] Z_i, \tag{8}$$

where $i = a, b$ and φ_i and τ_i represent marginal input–output ratios in the production of 'commodities' – or, in our case, *activities* carried out in language *A* or language *B*. At given relative prices, these ratios (that is, the amount of time

---

analysis of language on the workplace would be best approached by a different type of model. Optimal values for t_a and t_b, however, will still cover the greater portion of waking life. Recall that the total amount of time not devoted to work represents more than 75 per cent of total waking life, even if the individual works an average of 42 hours a week from age 20 to age 65 without ever taking holidays, and enjoys five years of retirement before his or her death. Time allocation to a language or another in private (i.e. non-working) life ultimately determines the extent to which individuals decide to function in language *A* or in language *B*.

[16] This dovetails with the issue of 'ethnic enclaves'; see Xie and Gough (2011).

and goods required for a certain amount of practice of any given activity in language A or B) can be taken as stable if the production functions display constant returns to scale. For $i = a, b$, optimal time inputs then read:

$$t_i = Z_i \tau_i \left(\frac{w}{p_i}, E_i \right) \qquad i = a, b. \tag{9}$$

Note also that the expression between square brackets in (8) can be interpreted as the shadow price of A and B language activities. This expression includes the expenditure on goods and time, and can be expressed as:

$$\Pi_i = p_i \varphi_i + w \tau_i. \tag{10}$$

As pointed out above, the cost of time is evaluated in terms of forgone earnings, and the earnings-intensiveness (as opposed to goods-intensiveness) of activities conducted in language i is signified by f_i and defined as the share of the time cost in the total unit cost of an activity:

$$f_i = \frac{w \tau_i}{\Pi_i}. \tag{11}$$

Since all activities use both time and goods, $0 < f_i < 1$.

The sensitivity of the use of time spent on activities in language i (where $I = a, b$) when the unit price of the associated good changes can be decomposed into an output effect (stemming from the fact that the activities concerned will be practised more or less) and a substitution effect (because the relative use of both production factors will be affected by the change in the relative prices). Bearing in mind this decomposition and applying standard factor demand analysis, we can compute the elasticity of time used in A and B language activities with respect to goods prices as:

$$\gamma_i^p = (1 - f_i)(\varepsilon_i^p + \sigma_{x,t}^i), \tag{12}$$

where $i = a, b$, and ε_i^p stands for the price elasticity of i language activities when the shadow price changes as a result of a change in the price of goods used in i language activities, and $\sigma_{x,t}^i$ denotes the elasticity of substitution between time and goods in the production of i language activities.[17]

---

[17] For readers unfamiliar with the standard tools of economic analysis, let us recall that an elasticity is a ratio of relative changes. For example, if the price of a good goes up by x per cent (say, 4 per cent) and demand for that good goes down by y per cent (say, 1 per cent) as a result, the (own-) *price elasticity* of demand for that good, often symbolized by the Greek letter ε (epsilon), will be y per cent/x per cent – in this example, 0.25. The

Since the former is positive as any normal own-price elasticity, and the latter is negative, equation (12) can be positive or negative, implying that changes in goods prices are not certain to induce clear shifts in one or the other direction. Suppose for example that in order to foster the use of language *B*, the authorities decide to subsidize *B* language children's books, thereby lowering the cost of an activity such as 'reading bedtime stories', if performed in language *B*. *B* speaking residents, however, will not necessarily increase the amount of *B* language books they buy for their children as a result of this change. For (12) to be negative, factor substitutability must be weak, and *B* language activities must be very responsive to their production costs – recalling that 'production', in this household production function approach, is something that persons (or households) do. If the second term between parentheses on the right-hand side of (12) is indeed negative, the subsidizing measures will prove more effective if *B* language commodities display a low earnings-intensiveness, namely, if they tend to be goods-intensive activities – in plainer terms: if what was preventing *B* speaking parents from reading bedtime stories to their children in language *B* was not the cost of the time thus spent, but the expense on *B* language books.

Turning now to the effect of wage rates, and applying the same procedure as before, we obtain the wage-rate elasticity of time spent on *i* language activities, where ε_i^w denotes the shadow-price elasticity of activities performed in language *i* when this change in shadow price stems from a change in the opportunity cost of time:

$$\gamma_i^w = \varepsilon_i^w f_i - (1 - f_i)\sigma_{x,t}^i. \tag{13}$$

Note that just as in equation (12), the sign in equation (13) may be positive or negative. The sign of ε_i^w is ambiguous, because an increase in wage rates causes both full income and the time cost of any non-work activity to increase. This produces an unambiguous outward shift of the full income constraint,[18] but the positivity of ε_i^w does not follow unless certain conditions are met. The reason is that if *i* language activities are particularly 'earnings-intensive' (that is, time-consuming), their cost would rise considerably. An obvious (though somewhat unappealing) sufficient condition for ε_i^w to be positive

---

concept of elasticity can, in fact, be applied to any pair of causally related quantitative variables in order to measure the sensitivity of a dependent variable to changes in the value of an independent variable. Being expressed as a ratio of percentages, elasticities offer the great advantage of not being dependent on the choice of units of measurement for the variables involved, allowing for comparisons of sensitivity in all kinds of relationships.

[18] This increase in full income makes intuitive sense: since full income is the product of the total time endowment *T* and the wage rate *w*, an increase in the latter causes the total resources available to the agent to increase.

is the first-degree homogeneity of the utility function defined over Z_a and Z_b; alternatively, we may impose an identical average earnings-intensiveness on activities pursued in either language, since these cover an *a priori* identical spectrum.[19] In this case, ε_i^w is positive provided i language activities are non-inferior. For (13) to be positive, however, factor substitutability must be negligible.

Finally, let us consider changes in E_i, which denotes exposure to language i. These are of particular interest here, since such changes may result either from legislative steps taken to promote A or B, or from changes in the relative prestige of the two languages, leading one of them to be more widely used in the streets, in the media or in advertising, for example. In order to derive comparative statics results with respect to E_i, I assume the production functions of commodities to display constant returns to scale. The derivation of these comparative statics is relatively burdensome and, for the sake of brevity, the detailed procedure is not provided here; however, the interested reader is referred to Appendix 2 for a step-by-step derivation of these results. The most relevant of these, for the purposes of our discussion, is the exposure-elasticity of the time devoted to activities in language i, which can be expressed as:

$$\gamma_i^E = \eta_i s_i \hat{Z}_i^E - \hat{Z}_i^E + \varepsilon_i\left(-\hat{Z}_i^E + s_i \hat{Z}_i^E\right) - (1 - f_i)\sigma^i(Z_{x_i}^E - Z_{t_i}^E). \tag{14}$$

This expression, which reflects the complexity of the interaction between the determinants of language use, contains seven important terms, in addition to those that have previously been defined:

- η_i is the elasticity of the demand for i language commodities with respect to real full income;
- ε_i is the elasticity of the demand for i language commodities with respect to their real shadow price;
- s_i is the share of i language activities in total expenditure out of full income;
- Z_{ti}^E is the elasticity of the marginal productivity of time used in the practice of i language activities with respect to exposure to language i;
- Z_{xi}^E is the exposure elasticity of the marginal productivity of goods;
- Z_i^E is the elasticity of the amount produced of commodity Z_i with respect to exposure to language i;
- the same with a hat $\hat{Z}_i^E$ denotes this elasticity with inputs held constant.

Note that the sign of equation (14) is ambiguous, that is, an increase in exposure to a language is not a sufficient condition for the use of this language to

---

[19] A necessary and sufficient condition for the slope of the full income constraint to remain constant is $f_a = f_b$.

increase. This runs counter to the common assumption that agents' use of a language can only benefit from greater exposure to it; the processes at hand are more complex and a combination of conditions will be necessary for such an outcome to obtain.

The actual impact of changes in exposure will depend both on the respective values of the parameters in the model, and on the effect of these changes on the production functions themselves. It is certainly more realistic (though by no means simpler) to assume that factor productivities are not equally affected by exposure. The assumption made here is that the productivity of goods is independent of exposure, and that only the productivity of time, which reflects the effect of personal effort, will be affected. If we consider aggregate activities Z_a and Z_b (namely, 'doing things in language A' and 'doing things in language B'), the exposure elasticity of i language activities ($i = a,b$) at constant factor inputs reduces to:

$$\hat{Z}_i^E = f_i Z_{t_i}^E, \tag{15}$$

which can be substituted into (14) to read:

$$\gamma_i^E = (\eta_i s_i - 1 - \varepsilon_i + \varepsilon_i s_i) f_i Z_{t_i}^E + (1 - f_i)\sigma^i Z_{t_i}^E. \tag{16}$$

Equation (16) is the sum of two terms, the first one describing the effect of a change in E_i if factor ratios are constant (as would be the case with a fixed coefficient production function), while the second term captures the effect of factor substitution.

An increase in exposure to language i, by enhancing individual efficiency in the practice of i language activities (or, in more Beckerian terms, the *production* of i language *commodities*), will positively affect the productivity of time, so that $Z_{t_i}^E$ is unambiguously positive. Since the elasticity of substitution is positive and $0 < f_i < 1$, the second term on the right-hand side of (16) is positive. The sign of the first term, however, is ambiguous, because the full-income elasticity of demand, η_i, is positive (with more overall resources, there is scope for producing more of all commodities), but the shadow-price elasticity, ε_i, is negative (if their cost goes up, there will be an incentive to produce less of them, if activities in language A or in language B are not inferior). Let us take a closer look at the first term of equation (16) and define β as:

$$\beta = (\eta_i s_i - 1 - \varepsilon_i + \varepsilon_i s_i) f_i. \tag{17}$$

For an increase in exposure to lead to an increase in the use of the corresponding language, β must be positive or, at least, have a negligibly negative value so as not to offset the positive impact of factor substitution. We first observe that $\frac{\partial \beta}{\partial \eta_i} > 0$, and η_i, which stands for the full-income elasticity of demand, reflects the desirability or prestige of i language activities. In other words, the better the image of the language concerned (or, in sociolinguistic terms, the higher its status), the more effect increased exposure will have. Second, $\frac{\partial \beta}{\partial \varepsilon_i} < 0$. Greater sensitivity to the relative cost of doing things in the language will make increased exposure to it more effective. Thirdly, $\frac{\partial \beta}{\partial s_i} = [(\eta_i + \varepsilon_i) f_i]$ and has an ambiguous sign. The weight s_i can be interpreted as a proxy for language vitality in a given area. In regions where language i is widely used relative to some other language j, s_i will tend to be higher. On the other hand, in areas where language $j \neq i$ is more widely used, s_i will be lower.[20]

The ambiguity of $\frac{\partial \beta}{\partial s_i}$ points to a perennial question in minority language promotion policies. It regularly resurfaces in contexts such as Wales or Ireland, where language planners seek to create the conditions for long-term minority language survival: should exposure-increasing policies focus on areas where a minority language is most alive or most threatened (Ambrose and Williams, 1981; FIONTAR, 2009)? The model provides some guidance with respect to this question: it indicates that when the status of the target language is high, exposure-increasing policies should focus on areas where it is widely used, and in other areas otherwise.

Finally, $\frac{\partial \beta}{\partial f_i}$ is equal to the whole expression in parentheses in (17) and therefore also has an ambiguous sign: a higher average earnings-intensiveness of i language activities will strengthen the effect of increased exposure only on the condition that relative shadow-price elasticity is high.

Since f_i is positive, the necessary and sufficient condition for β to be positive simplifies to:

$$\eta_i s_i + \varepsilon_i (s_i - 1) > 1, \tag{18}$$

which can be interpreted as follows: the income effect plus the relative price effect ('individuals do more things in language i') must outweigh the production effect ('less time than before is needed to do things in language i'). For the overall impact of an increase in exposure to be positive, the income, relative price and substitution effects must outweigh the production effect.

21.6 Guidelines for language policy

The results in Section 21.5 stress the importance of the substitution (σ), price ($\varepsilon, \varepsilon^p, \varepsilon^w$) and income ($\eta$) elasticities;[21] in addition, they precisely identify the impact of factor intensiveness (f) and expenditure shares (s). With the occasional exception of expenditure shares, these parameters tend to be overlooked

---

[20] In an immigration context, so-called 'ethnic' neighbourhoods are cases of high s_j values, if j stands for the immigrant community's 'heritage language'.
[21] A definition of elasticity is provided in note 17.

in sociolinguistic models of language use as well as in language planning. However, they certainly represent key parameters in language behaviour, and could be powerful levers in the selection and design of incentive-based language policies.

Let us consider policy recommendations in favour of language *B*. The reader may think of *B* as a threatened minority language that the authorities are trying to save from language death.[22] If the use of *B* is to be encouraged, the following conditions should be borne in mind.

21.6.1   Subsidies to *B* language goods

1.1. Subsidies will be more effective if the goods subsidized are used in *B* language activities that have a high shadow-price elasticity, that is, activities whose practice is more responsive to the total cost, in goods and/or time, of practising them. This is less likely to be the case for mundane non-work activities that have to be performed anyway (say, household chores), and more likely, by contrast, for leisure activities.

1.2. Subsidies to goods entering production processes with low factor substitutability should be preferred, in order to avoid substitution away from time, which becomes more costly in relative terms; remember that time is the variable that captures actual language use.

1.3. Goods used in goods-intensive activities can be subsidized, and only disappointing results in terms of language use (measured in time units) can be expected from subsidizing other types of goods.

1.4. If working hours are fixed, the increased spending power must be allocated to the purchase of goods used in language *B* for the use of *B* to increase. Therefore, goods-intensive activities in the language must be available; this generally speaks in favour of ensuring that the promotion of a minority language includes measures targeted at high-prestige activities, since the latter tend to be more goods-intensive.

21.6.2   Wage rate increases

2.1. For a given level of average factor-intensiveness of these activities, wage rate increases are more likely to effectively promote minority language use if the positive effect of the increased spending power outweighs the

---

[22] The promotion of a *majority* language, however, is not necessarily ruled out, but the goal would then be quite a different one, aiming for example at encouraging immigrants to integrate linguistically in the host society by using its dominant language. Examples could be the promotion of French in Quebec among non-francophone immigrant communities, or of German among ethnic Germans from Russia who resettled in Germany in the 1990s. Since our focus here is on minority languages as characterized in Section 21.2, we shall not discuss this type of case further.

negative effect of the increase in the time cost of all non-work activities (in essence, the income effect must exceed the substitution effect).

2.2. A low factor substitutability in *B* language activities would also tend to make wage rate increases more conducive to an increase in the use of *B*, because it reduces the scope for substitution away from relatively costlier time.

2.3. A high goods-intensiveness of *B* language activities will prove favourable to the use of *B* only if their wage-rate elasticity is significantly positive.

2.4. Wage rate increases may encourage the use of language *B* essentially through an induced increase of working hours in a *B* speaking workshop or office. In other words, it is crucially dependent on the availability of *B* medium employment possibilities (and flexibility to do overtime).

2.5. If working hours are fixed, the use of language *B* can increase only if the time devoted to *A* language activities declines, which will be the case on the condition that there are opportunities to spend the increased spending power on goods used in *B* language activities.

21.6.3 Exposure-increasing measures

3.1. By making speakers more proficient in language *B*, exposure-increasing measures will enhance their productivity in *B* language activities, whose unit cost will decline. However, the model calls our attention to the fact that the overall impact on time spent on them is ambiguous, because the productivity increase causes real full income to go up, thereby opening the door to a wide range of factor reallocations. An important condition for such measures to be effective, therefore, is a high full-income elasticity of *B* language activities. As in the case of the decline of the price of *B* language goods through subsidization (see condition 1.4 above), this underscores the crucial importance of a positive image for the minority language.

3.2. A high relative (shadow) price elasticity of *B* language activities will also make increases in exposure more efficient.

3.3. If exposure-increasing policies are primarily geared to areas where *A* speakers are concentrated and *B* speakers are few (that is, neighbourhoods where s_b can be assumed to be closer to zero), the relative shadow-price elasticity must be larger than one in absolute value.

Some of the above may, at first sight, look like stating the obvious, in the sense that there is certainly not much point in subsidizing goods used in activities that do not respond to changes in cost (see condition 1.1), or that higher incomes *may* result in an increase in time spent on *B* language activities *if* there are ways to spend the increased spending power on such activities (condition 2.5). A brief look at existing language policies, however, suggests that these principles can hardly be deemed obvious, because they appear to have been ignored throughout much of the history of minority language protection and promotion. Consider for example the experience of many European governments (national, local or provincial) and language agencies when trying to ensure the long-term survival of minority autochthonous languages such as Irish, Welsh, Breton, Basque, Romanche or Frisian.

The unavailability of operational data on little-explored causal links prevents us from testing these relationships, but many pieces of circumstantial evidence strongly suggest that they deserve further investigation.

21.7 The costs and net value of minority language policies

Minority language protection and promotion have been the object of criticism from various sides as an ill-advised policy carrying unjustifiable costs. The criticism, coming from sociolinguistics (Edwards, 1994), economics (Jones, 2000), political science (Pogge, 2003) or normative political theory (Van Parijs, 2011) may target minority languages as such or, more broadly, linguistic diversity, regarded as an overrated value. Reciprocally, many authors support minority language promotion and more generally diversity, on various grounds, for legal (Dunbar, 2006), sociolinguistic (Fishman, 1991; May, 2012), educational (Skutnabb-Kangas, 2000), political (Phillipson, 2010), normative (Kymlicka, 1995; de Schutter, 2007) or economic (Grin, 1994b, 2003c; Mélitz, 2007) reasons. Frameworks for a systematic measurement of the associated benefits and costs (usually centred, however, on the communicational function of language) have been proposed by Selten and Pool (1990) and by Gabszewicz et al. (2011).

From the perspective of an economically guided discussion, the stance taken in this regard ultimately depends on the relative weight attributed to various arguments in a utility function. The fundamental question is whether we have reasons to believe that linguistic diversity matters and contributes, *in net terms*, to welfare.

This is something about which economists may not have very much to say, at least if they wish to be consistent with the profession's oft-proclaimed (but sometimes unconsciously broken) principle to eschew normative judgements. A few observations, however, can still be made.

21.7.1 The collective dimension of value

First, let us note that when referring to the relative weight of different arguments in individual utility functions, we are necessarily led, if not right away, then after a few steps of reasoning, to allow for some kind of *collective* utility function, because language is not something that can be produced and consumed individually, or even privately – putting aside pure solipsism like personal language play, invention of secret languages and the like (Yaguello, 2006; Okrent, 2009). As we have seen in the preceding sections, the structure of individual utility functions is crucial to the understanding of the challenge of minority languages. The collective dimensions at hand may, up to a point, be captured by the inclusion, in individual utility functions, of a (perhaps normally distributed) taste for diversity for its own sake, or of a concern for the welfare of other minority agents, or consideration for non-use values. However, if we are to consider the value of minority languages to society as a whole, and taking into account the fact that languages are typically regarded as essential to the definition of communities, some *additional* reference to collective decision-making will be needed. This points towards social welfare functions or, barring that, indicators serving as acceptable proxies of social welfare (Wheelan, 2011; for a discussion of the operationalization, in this endeavour, of standard criteria like efficiency and fairness, see Grin and Gazzola, 2013; Gazzola, 2014). To my knowledge, this range of problems has not, with the exception of Wickström (Chapter 22 in this volume), been addressed squarely, and most authors fall back on manifestations of collective will expressed and reflected in political regulations. These concern, for example, the choice between language regimes that make more or less allowance for the official use of different languages, including minority languages.

21.7.2 Diversity and market failure

Linguistic diversity is by definition composed of the languages that make it up. There is no diversity without a plurality of elements, and these elements must differ from one another. This simple fact carries several important implications, the main one being that there are strong reasons for viewing linguistic diversity as a public good and to study it as one would a 'commons'; consequently, the individual languages that make it up ought to be approached in the same way.

A more general way of addressing this question is to ask whether decentralized market decisions result in an optimal level of linguistic diversity, and, more specifically, whether small languages, as components of this diversity, will display an optimal level of use, visibility and intergenerational transmission as a result of the interplay of unconstrained market forces. The answer is 'quite certainly not' – and this is, arguably, the error made by many prominent critics of minority language rights, such as Laitin (2006).[23] Of the six textbook sources of

---

[23] Another critic, Van Parijs, recognizes that the choice between alternative policies raises questions that hark back to social choices, but his unquestioned assumption that people do not care all that much about the status of their native language (let alone that of others) *in relation to* the status of some other – often dominant – language contradicts the overwhelming empirical evidence. It is only in the most rarefied, and quite certainly elitist, circles that such a disembodied view of language as a mere tool for communication is embraced (see Barbier, 2012). Even then, it is difficult to overlook the fact that voices

market failure (insufficient information, high transaction costs, missing markets, imperfect market structure, externalities, and public goods), at least three are arguably present, resulting in an inadequate, rather than excessive, supply of diversity. It follows that language policies are relevant in general, and that minority language protection and promotion is justified in particular. Let us consider these three sources in turn.

1. There is *imperfect information* to the extent that agents, independently of their mother tongue, are likely to have insufficient awareness of the contribution that linguistic diversity makes to their quality of life, just like the negative impact of environmental damage is liable to be underestimated by individual agents. This is linked to the dynamic nature of linguistic diversity. As agents fail to appreciate the negative impact that careless handling of the environment now may have on their quality of life in the future, so they may equally overlook the fact that the demise of small languages foreshadows the marginalization of many more, including their own. Yet linguistic diversity is arguably a condition for cultural diversity and multi-polarity, to which actors typically may not assign value *until* they are explicitly confronted with the stark alternative, namely, generalized monolingualism. Since it takes some analytical effort to connect the demise of a Siberian language, or the progressive marginalization of (even major) national languages in favour of English in higher education, with the cultural and experiential barrenness of uniformity, a strong argument can be made that actors fail to fully grasp the issues at hand, and that they would benefit from information that makes the terms of the alternative plain.[24]

2. Some *markets are missing* in the sense that future generations, who may have a taste for linguistic diversity, cannot bid for it, whether by acquiring goods embodying the languages that make up this diversity, by expressing demand for instruction in them, or by voting in favour of linguistic

---

arguing against minority language protection and promotion – or, relatedly, against linguistic diversity – overwhelmingly come from academics whose native language happens to be a particularly dominant one.

[24] A survey carried out in 2014 with a representative sample of 1,103 teenagers and adults in western Switzerland confirms that respondents have positive attitudes towards the English language, even when used in the context of Switzerland, where English is not an official or a national language. The temptation is great, for the superficial analyst, to jump to the conclusion that people do not care about linguistic diversity. However, when specifically asked about their views regarding the *displacement* of national languages by English, 66 per cent of respondents consider 'rather' or 'completely' inappropriate the use of English instead of German or French for contacts between Switzerland's two main language regions (see http://defensedufrancais.ch/association/?page_id=2371). Previous survey evidence points in the same direction.

diversity-supporting public policies. The reference to unexpressed demand only requires that the existence of a *taste* for linguistic diversity in future generations be a plausible conjecture. Additional arguments to the same effect can be found, however, in the frequently made claim that each language is a repository of knowledge, which is lost when the language drops out of use with the death of its last native (or at least fluent) speaker (see e.g. Abley, 2003). The loss of this knowledge restricts the possibility of future use that may only become relevant at a later point in time.

3. To the extent that some degree of welfare attaches to the very existence of diversity per se, the issue at hand may be split into two separate sub-questions.

First, diversity presents striking similarities with the debate over the value of environmental quality as a *public good*. Let me stress that I am not advocating any kind of biologizing parallel between linguistic and biophysical diversity, even though a connection between the two has often been suggested – if only because of climatic conditions (Diamond, 2012).[25] The convergence, rather, has to do with the rationale and tools with which value can be identified and estimated in both cases. Whether we are referring to use or non-use value (including, without being confined to, existence value), much of what matters in language cannot be inferred directly from market signals such as prices (Grin, 1994b); at this time, the application of evaluation methods imported from environmental economics has only been suggested (Grin, 2003c) but never, to my knowledge, actually applied. Let us simply note that the overwhelming circumstantial evidence suggests that agents are not indifferent to their linguistic environment, and that there is a systematic preference for a linguistic environment in which one's native language can be, and actually *is*, used.[26] There again, the notion that language is merely a tool for information transfer is deeply misguided.

Second, increasing attention devoted to plausible correlations between linguistic diversity on the one hand and creativity and multilingualism on the other hand suggests that uniformization may be detrimental to creativity and innovation, and thus destroy economic value. The existence of market or non-market benefits of multilingualism at the individual level looks ever more likely (Bialystok and Shapero, 2005; Bialystok, 2009; Kharkhurin, 2012). *Group*

---

[25] Thus, the correlation appears plausible, without the need to assume any causal relationship between these two manifestations of diversity.

[26] This is reflected, for example, in survey evidence from Catalonia and Quebec to the effect that agents tend to prefer service in their own language, even if they are fluent in another language or may be perfectly bilingual; see e.g. Vaillancourt (1985); see also notes 22 and 23 above.

multilingualism matters just as much, but is far less well-known: the presence of multilingual skills within a team may offer a broader range of instruments for problem analysis, resolution and control, although at this stage this must be considered as conjectural, since this effect has only been observed in qualitative studies (Berthoud et al., 2013). What is far less conjectural, by contrast, is the psycholinguistic finding that specific languages are associated with specific ways of organizing thought. Recognizing this fact does not require a naïve endorsement of the well-known 'Whorf–Sapir hypothesis', which in its strong form amounts to a claim that the language one speaks actually determines perception. We can however agree that different languages do not organize reality in the same way (Fishman, 1982), particularly when it comes to semantic categories reflected in both lexicon and morphology. Consequently, linguistic uniformity may end up being a trap in which the development and processing of knowledge may be curtailed (Wierzbicka, 2014).

21.7.3 Language as a network

Any individual language does present some of the features of a *network*. Even if it can be claimed that it has certain characteristics of a *club* good, it is unsatisfactory to present it as one because of the non-elective nature of the club concerned. Not only can we *not* choose not to have a language – that is, we cannot but belong to *at least* one club – but we also cannot choose which our native language will be – that is, which club we belong to, at least in our initial and formative years. The notion that a person's native language is a 'choice' (branded by some commentators as a 'nationalistic' one, if one is impudent enough to opt to maintain a *non*-dominant language as an L1) must therefore be recognized as problematic, to say the least. The network analogy makes sense only with respect to L_j, where $j = 2, 3, \ldots, n$.

Nevertheless, the concept of network remains fundamentally relevant to language in the perspective of network externalities (Church and King, 1993), because even if language is not *only* a tool for communication, it obviously *is* one (Gabszewicz et al., 2011). The same intuition inspires work by Van Parijs (2000) on 'probability-sensitive learning' and De Swaan (2001) on 'language constellations'. Interesting models have been developed that capture the complex dynamics of second-language acquisition in the presence not only of such network externalities, but also of interpersonal differences in the effort needed to learn a language (Selten and Pool, 1990; Selten, 1997). In other words, network theory is central in understanding patterns of language dynamics; this also applies to the dynamics of decline that often characterize minority languages (Grin, 1992). However, the establishment and spread of a network in itself does not, however, guarantee optimality (Liebowitz and Margolis, 1994). The fact that people may have a private, decentralized interest in joining a network does not mean that the resulting equilibrium is the best possible one.

There are two reasons for this: first, the features of the network may cause inefficiencies – consider for example the baffling complexity (for no discernible gain) of the imperial system of measurement of weight, distance and surface, as opposed to the sleek simplicity of the metric system; second, the very idea of having *one* network (such as *one* standard) may not be such a good one after all, for reasons discussed just above.

More generally, the application of the network analogy to language all too often mixes up the positive ('languages have many of the key characteristics of networks', which can be regarded as true) and the normative ('converging towards the use of a common network is good'). Yet the former proposition does not logically imply the latter, which must stand or fall on its own merits. Typically, the claim that having a common network is good rests on restrictive assumptions about the functions of language that ignore sociolinguistic realities, whether it be the value that people assign to language or the centripetal forces abetting language spread.

21.7.4   Costs of minority language protection and promotion

Let us finally offer a few considerations regarding the costs of minority language maintenance. These have been investigated in a few, mostly European, cases, and these costs turn out to be much lower than appears to be commonly believed. As for any policy debate, the crucial point is the choice of counterfactual. In some cases, the provision of a minority-language service could conceivably be eschewed altogether. This is the case, say, for minority-language television programming: there *could* be no such programming at all, and the money invested in it could, indeed, be saved; estimations of the per-person cost of 17 such policy measures for specific minority languages in Europe reveal typically low costs (Grin, 2004a; see in particular the summary overview of costs in Table 1, pp. 194–195). The amounts spent are likely to be well below agents' willingness-to-pay for minority language maintenance. The issue then becomes a standard policy analysis problem of comparing costs and benefits; this presupposes an appropriate treatment of the complex questions of identification raised earlier in this section.

However, there are many cases where the choice is not between providing a service in a minority language and providing no service at all. Rather, the choice is between providing it in one language *or* another for *some* part of a constituency (typically, the native speakers of the minority language considered). In such cases, the costs of minority language protection and promotion are minor, and arguably negligible. A very good example can be found in minority-language education. Children have to be schooled anyway, whether through language *X* or through language *Y*; in either case, teachers, textbooks and school buildings will be necessary, and total costs will be roughly equivalent, no matter whether education is provided in one language or another.

Independent assessments of the introduction of a Maya-medium education stream in Guatemala (Patrinos and Velez, 1996) and of the bilingualization of the Basque education system (Grin and Vaillancourt, 1999) converge on the same orders of magnitude: moving from a unilingual to a bilingual education system adds an approximate 3–4 per cent to total educational expenditure. Moreover, this extra cost can be expected to taper off in the long run.

Research on the costs of bilingualism in Canadian federal policies (Vaillancourt and Coche, 2009) has generated a concise method for estimating the costs of language protection and promotion. Assume (using the abbreviations favoured by the famous sociolinguist Fishman in his discussions of language promotion) that X is the minority language and Y is the majority language. Further assume that a particular service is already provided to the whole population (native speakers of X and native speakers of Y) through the medium of Y only. What is the cost of offering the service through the medium of X also? To answer this question, the three-step procedure is as follows:

1. calculate the per-person cost of the service for Y speakers *only* by dividing the part of the total subsidy *used by Y speakers* by the Y speaking population;
2. calculate the per-person cost of the service for X speakers at the same unit cost, which means multiplying the previously estimated per capita cost by the number of X speakers; this generates a notional cost for *all* X speakers;
3. subtract from this notional cost the actual total expenditure for X speakers under the current unilingual (Y language) regime; this yields the 'excess cost' of the X speaking component – and, in marginal terms, the only *relevant* part of the cost of providing the service through the minority language.

Summing up, the issue of cost in minority language protection and promotion tends to be blown up out of proportion; this is an area in which economic analysis can make a valuable contribution to a better-informed debate.

21.8   About contingent and absolute multilingualism

Let us now step back a little and reconsider the question of the 'value' of minority languages in the broader context of the value of linguistic diversity. As has already been pointed out, linguistic diversity at any given time is by definition made up of the variety of languages in use, and minority languages are therefore contributors to this diversity. In this perspective, the contribution that any specific language makes to aggregate diversity is independent of the demographic weight of its speakers, as pointed out by the philosopher Iso Camartin (1989).

It is useful, when examining this point, to distinguish between two fundamentally different issues pertaining to the value of languages and linguistic diversity. Let us call these two perspectives those of 'contingent' and 'absolute' multilingualism respectively (Grin et al., 2010); what distinguishes them is their counterfactual.[27]

In the 'contingent multilingualism' perspective, we start out from the recognition that the world is linguistically diverse and examine, given this contingency, various responses to it. These may include, for example, investing more or less in second/foreign language learning. The assessment of alternative responses regarding this investment provides a rationale for empirical work on the private rates of return to language skills or on the social rates of return to second/foreign language teaching in schools, where the counterfactual of a certain level of private or social investment in language learning and teaching is another (higher or lower) level of investment. For another example, let us think about the subsidization of a television station in language X: if its cost is entirely covered by the subsidy, and if the station could not operate without it, the benefits can be estimated through a contingent valuation approach to agents' willingness-to-pay for the service. This willingness-to-pay reflects the utility they derive from the possibility to enjoy X language television programmes, instead of being confined to broadcasts in another language – such as the local majority language. Thus, in a contingent multilingualism context, the value (whether use or non-use, market or non-market, material or symbolic) of a minority language (or of any language, for that matter) will only be considered through the prism of specific skills or specific uses of the language in a real, observable environment. This extends to the evaluation of language regimes encompassing a plurality of languages.

In the 'absolute multilingualism' perspective, however, we ask a much more radical question, namely, whether the very *existence* of a language has any value at all. If generalized to multilingualism, the implicit (and hypothetical) counterfactual is uniformity. The question, then, becomes whether diversity offers genuine advantages over uniformity.

The distinction between both perspectives matters, because the positive valuation of a language, or even of all languages, in a *contingent* multilingualism perspective, does not necessarily imply that such a positive valuation would obtain in an *absolute* multilingualism perspective. Let us clinch this point with an example, namely, that of the (sometimes considerable) rates of return to fluency in a foreign language. These rates reward investment in a skill made necessary by (existing) linguistic diversity. Value attaches to the skill *because*

---

[27] The adjectives 'contingent' and 'absolute' may not be the best possible ones, also because the former invites a somewhat problematic parallel with 'contingent *valuation*'; and even though contingent *valuation* is a relevant tool in the assessment of diversity, both in a 'contingent' and 'absolute' perspective, the two expressions are used autonomously, without particular reference to each other. At this time, however, I have not come across a more suitable pair of adjectives.

linguistic diversity exists. But this fact is not sufficient for concluding that value attaches to *diversity* as such, just like the fact that investing in tuition at an expensive medical school pays off nicely does not mean that humans would not be better off without illness, accidents and death. By the same token, one might claim (as, implicitly, some commentators quoted above do) that humankind would be better off in a uniform world, not just because communication costs would be spared, but because transnational economic solidarity would enjoy more support (La Ferrara, 2004).

In the context of minority languages, the contingent multilingualism perspective would generally lead to the conclusion that these languages hardly merit economic protection, because they do not generate positive rates of return on the labour market, and because their speakers *apparently* display insufficient willingness-to-pay for services in this language.[28]

Such an interpretation, of course, may be queried on a number of counts. Let us leave aside the few cases where minority language skills have been shown to have value on the labour market (see Henley and Jones, 2005, on Welsh; and Borooah et al., 2009 on Irish). Two significant weaknesses of this interpretation is that they display what May (2003) has called 'presentism' and 'linguistic fait accompli'. 'Presentism' refers to the absence of (or, arguably, downright refusal to countenance) historicity in the assessment of the situation of minority languages. The ahistorical view of the position of various languages may result in a truncated identification of the advantages and drawbacks that can be associated with alternative language policy choices. The 'linguistic fait accompli' is an even more brutal casting of languages in given roles, such that we are encouraged to think that nothing can be done about a certain state of affairs. As May (2003, p. 132) puts it, 'we may well regret the past, but there is nothing we can now do about it so it should not, nor can it, usefully inform our present. What is done is done'.

Although these observations need to be borne in mind, it is difficult to ignore the fact that any investment in minority language learning is difficult to justify on the basis of considerations stemming from a contingent multilingualism perspective. And as we have just noted, even if we did, it would not follow that the protection and promotion of a minority language, as a *component* of aggregate diversity, is worthwhile in the absolute, since such a conclusion reached in the contingent perspective does not necessarily carry over to the absolute perspective.

What about the value, then, of linguistic diversity *in the absolute*, and hence of individual languages as components of this diversity? This question has

---

[28] Willingness to pay may be, in this case particularly, a misnomer, since what is at issue is not so much agents' *willingness* to pay for something as their ability to do so – putting it differently, their *solvability*.

already been addressed above in our brief discussion of the possibility that linguistic diversity might have a positive impact on welfare, in terms of direct enjoyment, in terms of non-use value, or through its consequences for creativity and innovation. Ultimately, the value of linguistic diversity is an empirical question. A positive answer would carry the implication that diversity merits protection and promotion, particularly in the case of small or threatened components of diversity, thus suggesting that the minority languages are deserving of such protection and promotion. This is consistent with the observation that people are not completely indifferent to the language(s) they speak and use; they value some languages more than others, presumably because of their connection to individual and group identity. This returns us once more to the notion that viewing language purely as a tool for communication is a very inadequate basis for the evaluation of alternative language policies.

This recurring question may be approached from a symmetrical perspective – reversing, as it were, the burden of proof. Assume that language is, indeed, purely a matter of communication.[29] There is no reason, then, to devote resources to the maintenance of linguistic diversity in general, or of any given language in particular, and uniformity is optimal. Even if languages would not need to be actively killed off, we could simply allow the centripetal dynamics of (dominant) language spread to do its work, resulting, in the long term, in linguistic uniformity. The question then becomes: uniformity *in what language*? In the assumed absence of any reason other than cost-effectiveness for selecting the common language, the latter should be easy to learn and to use by as many people as possible, and minimize inequality of access. It being a stationary choice, the benefits and costs ought to be discounted on an infinite horizon, meaning that transition costs to whatever solution will definitely be amortized (in other words, the counter-argument of recovering sunk costs is perfectly irrelevant). Even if an optimum in the strict sense may be difficult to identify, we can at least rank-order contenders for the role of 'unique' language. These premises deliver the intriguing result that, of the various languages currently available, English is far from being the best solution. From an allocative standpoint, its syntactic and phonological complexity speak against it (Piron, 1994). By contrast, and owing to the (empirically established) swiftness with which Esperanto can be learned, it is, in terms of cost-effectiveness, a solution far superior to English (Portuese, 2012).[30] Interestingly, commentators who

---

[29] We might emphasize 'of *current* communication', omitting the stock of accumulated texts and the information stored in it, or assuming a fixed cost for the maintenance of some translation capacity in order to allow continued access to texts written in ancient or abandoned languages.
[30] From a distributive standpoint, picking a language which happens to be the mother tongue of some, but not all speakers, is of course a grossly unfair solution (Pool, 1991;

emphasize the purely communicational function of language and speak against diversity typically advocate English, thus laying bare the self-contradictory (and often self-serving) nature of their argument.

21.9 Conclusion

When viewed in economic perspective, the situation of minority languages raises a number of analytical challenges, both theoretical and empirical, as well as complex social and political problems. In this chapter, I have attempted to assess these challenges and problems, showing first (Section 21.2) that the very definition of the object of study itself, 'minority languages', was open to different interpretations, and that depending on which interpretation is adopted, the orientations of an economic examination of the challenges at hand might differ as well.

In Section 21.3, I have provided a brief overview of the main directions in the economic literature on minority languages, stopping short, however, of a fully fledged literature review which could easily have taken up all the space available for this chapter, and referring the interested reader to the many literature reviews already published. Economists, in particular, should bear in mind that because of the marginal status of language economics for most of its existence, much of this literature is encountered not in the standard outlets of the discipline, but in journals or edited volumes normally considered as vehicles for other disciplines (first and foremost sociolinguistics, in which occasional theme issues or specialist books offer a focus on economic aspects, with contributions by economists). Putting it differently, an examination of the economics of minority languages is a useful reminder of the need not to let oneself be trapped inside the tight confines of idiosyncratic disciplinary habits.

In Sections 21.4, 21.5 and 21.6, I have attempted to get to the heart of the 'challenges of minority languages' by developing a formal model of language *use* (as distinct from 'language' or 'language skills', for example), since ultimately use is what matters most in the case of small, threatened languages. This model of minority language use, which focuses on the determinants

---

Grin, 2004b) giving rise to substantial transfers (Grin, 2005). These unfair transfers, acknowledged even by outspoken advocates of linguistic hegemony (e.g. Van Parijs, 2011) would fade away over time. Recall, however, that commentators who recommend the adoption of English typically do so on the basis of allocative considerations, but it is precisely because of these that their preferred solution flounders. An occasional rejoinder is that Esperanto is only easy for native speakers of *Indo-European* languages, but this claim is mitigated by the popularity of Esperanto in the Far East; Umberto Eco (1994) also points out that if speakers of Chinese *have* been able to learn English, then they can far more easily learn Esperanto, and that it is therefore illogical to suggest that speakers of 'Eastern' languages should learn English *rather* than Esperanto.

of – overwhelmingly bilingual – agents' decisions to 'do things through the medium of the majority language' or 'do things through the medium of the minority language', was presented in three steps.

The first step (Section 21.4) provided the conceptual cornerstones: for a minority language to be truly alive, it must be used – the proof of the cake being, as it were, in the eating. It will be used if speakers have the capacity to use it, opportunities to use it, and the desire to use it. None of these conditions is sufficient on its own, but each is necessary; jointly, they constitute a set of sufficient conditions for linguistic vitality. This general view dovetails with the philosophy that underpins the European Charter for Regional or Minority Languages.

In a second step (Section 21.5), I translated this general approach into a formal model contained in 18 equations. Starting out from the objectives pursued by agents and the constraints under which they operate, the model lends enables to us to express language use (measured in time units) as a function of a whole range of variables, many of which can be influenced through language policy. The model therefore shows how policy-induced changes in the value of some variables can impact on language use, since the latter is sensitive to changes in the former; this sensitivity is captured using a standard tool of economic analysis, namely, 'elasticities'.

Whereas Section 21.5 is mainly devoted to the relatively technical presentation of the model and its comparative statics (that is, the computation of how dependent variables like language use by a typical agent responds to changes in the value of independent variables like prices, wage rates or exposure to the language), Section 21.6 does not contain a single equation but uses the formal results in Section 21.5 to spell out the conditions needed for language policy to be effective. This enabled us to identify connections that are crucial for language policies, but which appear to have been frequently overlooked in many real-world cases of minority language protection and promotion.

Section 21.7 considered a selection of important problems that surround the economics of minority languages. We critically discussed (i) how to handle the 'collective' nature of language, and hence of the policy choices that target language use; (ii) the problem of 'market failure', which further establishes the relevance of deliberate intervention by the state in favour of minority languages; (iii) the implications and limitations of the 'network' interpretation of language; and (iv) the issue of costs in minority language protection and promotion, stressing the need to identify a relevant counterfactual to estimate cost. As we have seen, such costs, once properly assessed, often turn out to be much more reasonable than is commonly believed.

In Section 21.8, we took a step back to consider a broader question, namely, that of the value of *linguistic diversity* in general, of which minority languages are legitimate components. By making a distinction between *contingent* and *absolute* multilingualism (that is, assessing the pros and cons of multilingualism in a real-world, linguistically diverse context, as opposed to assessing them in the perspective of a hypothetical, linguistically uniform world), I attempted to show that, even if the value of minority languages in a 'contingent' perspective mainly rests on non-market considerations, they matter in an 'absolute' perspective as contributors to aggregate diversity. More fundamentally, I have tried to expose the inner contradiction that characterizes most of the academic discourse that speaks *against* the preservation of linguistic diversity, including small languages as components of it: if language (as they usually claim) is only a matter of cost-effective communication (thus invalidating minority languages), then the currently dominant languages which such commentators defend also ought to be abandoned – but in favour of a far more efficient planned language.

This chapter certainly does not exhaust the rich topic of the economics of minority languages; but I hope that it has, at least, provided some useful orientation and, perhaps, convinced some readers that a host of intellectually stimulating and politically important questions are awaiting further investigation.

Appendix 1   Minority languages in a strict sense: Selected examples (2014)

Country	Language	Estimated number of L1 speakers
Australia	Pitjantjantjara-Yankunytjantjara	2,660
Brazil	Xerente	1,810
Canada	Inuit	34,100
Chile	Mapuche	250,000
China	Tibetan	1,070,000
Finland	Sámi	300
France	Breton	206,000
Germany	North Frisian	10,000 (1976)
Italy	Friulian	300,000
Morocco	Amazigh	2,340,000
Netherlands	West Frisian	467,000
New Zealand	Maori	148,000
Russian Federation	Kalmyk	80,500
Spain	Basque	468,000
Sweden	Sámi	20 (Pite), 1,500 (Lule), 300 (Southern), 20 (Ume)
Switzerland	Romanche	35,100
Turkey	Laz	20,000
United Kingdom	Welsh	508,000
United States of America	Navajo	171,000

Appendix 2   Comparative statics of changes in exposure (*E*)

The procedure used is here adapted from Michael's (1972) analysis of efficiency in consumption of a complex commodity *Z*, which is produced by the individual agent or by a household combining time *t* and a good *x*. In the case of a bilingual agent, commodity *Z* can be produced and consumed in the majority or in the minority language. More intuitively, *Z* can be thought of as an *activity* which can be performed in either language, but where optimality in the amount of the activity performed in one language and another (and the corresponding optimal factor inputs) will depend on a number of exogenous conditions. The question examined in this appendix is how optimal solutions change if the agent receives more exposure to a language, and such exposure increases his or her efficiency at converting time and/or goods into commodity *Z*.

Assume all production functions to display constant return to scale. Omitting subscripts for simplicity, they can be expressed as:

$$Z = xZ_x + tZ_t, \tag{1}$$

where Z_x and Z_t denote the marginal productivity of goods and time respectively. Derive with respect to *E* to obtain:

$$\frac{\partial Z}{\partial E} = \hat{Z}_E = x\frac{\partial Z_x}{\partial E} + t\frac{\partial Z_t}{\partial E}, \tag{2}$$

where the hat over *Z* denotes constant factor inputs. Multiplying through by $\frac{E}{Z}$ provides the exposure elasticity of *Z* with constant factor inputs. Multiplying the two terms on the right-hand side by 1 and rearranging, this can be expressed as:

$$\hat{Z}^E = \frac{Z_x x}{Z}Z_x^E + \frac{Z_t t}{Z}Z_t^E, \tag{3}$$

where Z_x^E and Z_t^E represent the exposure elasticity of the marginal productivities of (market) goods and time in the production of commodity *Z*. We know from the first-order conditions that the ratio of the marginal productivities of factors must equal the ratio of their prices, so that:

$$\frac{Z_x}{p} = \frac{Z_t}{w} = \frac{1}{\Pi}. \tag{4}$$

Substituting (4) into (3), and recalling the definition of the input provided by (10) and (11) in the text, we get the exposure elasticity of *Z* with constant factor inputs:

$$\hat{Z}^E = (1 - f)Z_x^E + fZ_t^E. \tag{5}$$

The value of Z, however, also changes because of factor reallocation. Deriving the production functions expressed using Euler's theorem with respect to E, we get:

$$\frac{\partial Z}{\partial E}\frac{Z}{E} = \bar{Z}^E = (1-f)x^E + ft^E, \tag{6}$$

where the bar over Z indicates that exposure is being held constant, and x^E and t^E stand for the exposure elasticity of factor inputs. The total change in Z is the sum of (3) and (6), which can be written as:

$$Z^E = \hat{Z}^E + x^E - fx^E + ft^E. \tag{7}$$

Adding and subtracting t^E and rearranging equation (7), we obtain an expression for the own-language exposure elasticity of language use:

$$t^E = Z^E - \hat{Z}^E - (1-f)(x^E - t^E). \tag{8}$$

The last term in parentheses on the right-hand side of (8) can be expressed by means of the elasticity of substitution. Given the first-degree homogeneity of Z, the ratio of marginal productivities at equilibrium can be described as a function of factor intensiveness δ and exposure such as:

$$\frac{Z_x}{Z_t} = \theta\left(\frac{x}{t}, E\right) \equiv (\delta, E). \tag{9}$$

Totally differentiating θ and multiplying through by $\frac{E}{\theta dE}$ yields:

$$\theta^E = \frac{\partial\theta}{\partial\delta}\frac{d\delta}{dE}\frac{E}{\theta} + \frac{\partial\theta}{\partial E}\frac{E}{\theta}, \tag{10}$$

where θ^E represents the exposure elasticity of the ratio of marginal products. Equation (10) can be rewritten using the direct elasticity of substitution, since:

$$\frac{1}{\sigma} = -\frac{\partial\theta}{\partial\delta}\frac{\delta}{\theta}. \tag{11}$$

Multiplying and dividing (10) by δ and substituting (11) into the resulting expression yields:

$$\theta^E = -\frac{1}{\sigma}\left(x^E - t^E\right) + \left(Z_x^E - Z_t^E\right). \tag{12}$$

Recall that the ratio of marginal products at equilibrium must equal the ratio of factor prices, so that (12) can be rearranged to read:

$$\left(x^E - t^E\right) = \left[\left(Z_x^E - Z_t^E\right) - \left(p^E - w^E\right)\right]\sigma. \tag{13}$$

Substitute (13) into (8) to get:

$$t^E = Z^E - \hat{Z}^E - (1-f)[(Z_x^E - Z_t^E) - (p^E - w^E)]\sigma. \tag{14}$$

The change in the unit cost of Z resulting from a change in exposure must be evaluated with output held constant, that is, equation (7) must be set equal to zero (Z does not change), which provides the following expression for the exposure elasticity of the goods input:

$$x^E = (-\hat{Z}^E - ft^E)\frac{1}{(1-f)}. \tag{15}$$

Multiplying through by $\frac{x}{E}$ yields:

$$\frac{dx}{dE} = -\frac{\hat{Z}^E x}{(1-f)E} - \frac{ft^E x}{(1-f)E}. \tag{16}$$

Under constant returns to scale, marginal and average productivities at equilibrium will be identical, so that the shadow price can be expressed as:

$$\Pi = \frac{px}{Z} + \frac{wt}{Z}. \tag{17}$$

Differentiating (17) with respect to E yields:

$$\frac{d\Pi}{dE} = \frac{p}{Z}\frac{dx}{dE} + \frac{w}{Z}\frac{dt}{dE}. \tag{18}$$

Substituting (17) into (18), multiplying and dividing the last term on the right-hand side by t and rearranging, we get an expression for the exposure elasticity of the shadow price that simplifies to:

$$\Pi^E = -\hat{Z}^E. \tag{19}$$

Equation (19) describes the percentage change in the unit cost of Z before factors are reallocated. Let us now define a logarithmic price index for activities as:

$$\Pi_G = \Pi_a^{s_a} \Pi_b^{s_b}, \tag{20}$$

where the weights s_a and s_b are defined as percentages of total expenditure. It follows that the relative change in the value of the price index after exposure changes can be expressed as:

$$\Pi_G^E = \sum_i s_i \Pi_i^E = -\sum_i s_i \hat{Z}_i^E. \tag{21}$$

Thus, $(\Pi_i/\Pi_G)^E = \Pi_i^E - \Pi_G^E$; similarly, the exposure elasticity of real full income is:

$$\left(\frac{S}{\Pi_G}\right)^E = S^E - \Pi_G^E = \sum_i s_i \hat{Z}_i^E = \hat{Z}_i^E s_i, \tag{22}$$

assuming that $dE_j = 0$; full income $S = wT$ is unaffected by changes in E_i, and these changes have no impact on the practice of activities carried out in language j. Recall that we are estimating the total effect on Z_b of a change in E, through the elasticity of the former with respect to the latter. This exposure elasticity of the demand for Z_b can be expressed as a function of real full-income elasticity η_b and relative shadow-price elasticity ε_b; using equations (20) and (21):

$$Z_b^{*E} = \eta_b \left(\frac{S}{\Pi_G}\right)^E + \varepsilon_b \left(\frac{\Pi_i}{\Pi_G}\right)^E. \tag{23}$$

Using our previous results, (23) yields equation (14) in the text.

Acknowledgements

The author thanks Marco Civico for research assistance, and Victor Ginsburgh, Shlomo Weber and Michele Gazzola for highly valuable comments.

References

M. Abley (2003) *Spoken Here: Travels among Threatened Languages* (Boston/New York: Houghton Mifflin Co).

D. Abrams and S. Strogatz (2003) 'Modelling the Dynamics of Language Death', *Nature*, 424, 900.

A. Alarcón (2007) 'Informationalism, Globalisation and Trilingualism: An Analysis of the Statistics of Linguistic Practices in Small and Medium Companies in Catalonia', *Noves SL*, http://www6.gencat.cat/llengcat/noves/hm07tardor-hivern/docs/a_alarcon.pdf

J. Ambrose and C. Williams (1981) 'On the Spatial Definition of Minority: Scale as an Influence on the Geolinguistic Analysis of Welsh' In E. Haugen (ed.) *Minority Languages Today* (Edinburgh: Edinburgh University Press), 53–71.

J.-C. Barbier (2012) 'Une seule bannière linguistique pour une justice globale?', *Revue française de science politique*, 62, 469–472.

G. Becker (1965) 'A Theory of the Allocation of Time', *The Economic Journal*, 75, 493–517.

G. Becker (1976) *The Economic Approach to Human Behaviour* (Chicago: University of Chicago Press).

A.-C. Berthoud, F. Grin and G. Lüdi (eds) (2013) *Exploring the Dynamics of Multilingualism* (Amsterdam/Philadelphia: John Benjamins).

E. Bialystok (2009) 'Bilingualism: The Good, the Bad, and the Indifferent', *Bilingualism: Language and Cognition*, 12, 3–11.

E. Bialystok and D. Shapero (2005) 'Ambiguous Benefits: The Effect of Bilingualism on Reversing Ambiguous Fures', *Developmental Science*, 8, 595–604.

J. Blommaert and B. Rampton (eds) (2011) 'Language and Superdiversities', *Theme Issue of Diversities*, 13, 1–21.

V. Borooah, D. Dineen and N. Lynch (2009) *Language and Occupational Status: Linguistic Elitism in the Irish Labour Market* (Dublin: Economic and Social Research Institute, http://rian.ie/en/item/view/50555.html).

A. Breton and P. Mieszkowski (1977) 'The Economics of Bilingualism' In W. Oates (ed.) *The Political Economy of Fiscal Federalism* (Lexington, MA: Lexington Books), 263–271.

L.-J. Calvet (2004) *Essais de linguistique. La langue est-elle une invention des linguistes?* (Paris: Plon).

I. Camartin (1989) *Rien que des mots? Plaidoyer pour les langues mineures* (Genève: Zoé) (originally published as *Nichts als Worte? Ein Plädoyer für Kleinsprachen*, Zürich: Artemis Verlag).

A. Carli and U. Ammon (eds) (2007) *Linguistic Inequality in Scientific Communication Today*, Theme issue 20 of the *AILA Review*.

J. Carr (1985) 'Le bilinguisme au Canada: l'usage consacre-t-il l'anglais monopole naturel?' In Vaillancourt F. (ed.) *Economie et langue* (Quebec: Conseil de la langue française, 27–37).

X. Castelló, L. Loureiro-Porto, V. Eguíluz and M. San Miguel (2007) 'The Fate of Bilingualism in a Model of Language Competition' In S. Takahashi, J. Sallach, and Rouchier (eds) *Advancing Social Simulation: The First World Congress* (Tokyo: Springer-Verlag, 83–94).

D. Chalmers (2003) 'Economic Impact of Gaelic Arts and Culture', PhD thesis, Glasgow: Caledonian University.

B. Chiswick and P. Miller (1995) 'The Endogeneity between Language and Earnings: International Analyses', *Journal of Labor Economics*, 13, 246–288.

B. Chiswick and P. Miller (2007) *The Economics of Language: International Analyses* (London: Routledge).

J. Church and I. King (1993) 'Bilingualism and Network Externalities', *Canadian Journal of Economics*, 26, 337–345.

K. Cordell and S. Wolff (eds) (2004) *The Ethnopolitical Encyclopaedia of Europe* (London: Palgrave Macmillan).

H. De Schutter (2007) 'Language Policy and Political Philosophy: On the Emerging Linguistic Justice Debate', *Language Problems and Language Planning*, 31, 1–23.

A. De Swaan (2001) *Words of the World, The Global Language System* (Cambridge: Polity Press).

J. Diamond (2012) *The World Until Yesterday* (London: Allen Lane).

R. Dunbar (2006) 'Is there a Duty to Legislate for Linguistic Minorities?', *Journal of Law and Society*, 33, 181–198.

U. Eco (1994) *La recherche de la langue parfaite* (Paris: Folio).

J. Edwards (1994) *Multilingualism* (London: Routledge).

J. Edwards (2012) *Multilingualism: Understanding Linguistic Diversity* (London: Continuum).

FIONTAR Programme (2009) *20-Year Strategy for the Irish Language*. Report prepared for the Department of Community, Rural and Gaeltacht Affairs, Dublin: FIONTAR Programme, Dublin City University, www.ahg.gov.ie/en/20YearStrategyfortheIrishLanguage/Publications/Fiontar%20DCU%20report%20on%20the%2020-Year%20Strategy.pdf

J. Fishman (1982) 'Whorfianism of the Third Kind: Ethnolinguistic Diversity as a Worldwide Societal Asset', *Language and Society*, 11, 1–14.

J. Fishman (1989) *Language and Ethnicity in Minority Sociolinguistic Perspective* (Clevedon: Multilingual Matters).

J. Fishman (1991) *Reversing Language Shift: Theoretical and Empirical Foundations of Assistance to Threatened Languages* (Clevedon: Multilingual Matters).

J. Fishman (ed.) (2001) *Can Threatened Languages Be Saved?* (Clevedon: Multilingual Matters).

J. Gabszewicz, V. Ginsburgh and S. Weber (2011) 'Bilingualism and Communicative Benefits', *Annals of Economics and Statistics*, 101/102, 271–272.

M. Gazzola (2014) *The Evaluation of Language Regimes: Theory and Application to Multilingual Patent Organisations*. Amsterdam: John Benjamins.

H. Giles, R. Bourhis and D. Taylor (1977) 'Towards a Theory of Language in Intergroup Relations' In H. Giles (ed.) *Language, Ethnicity and Intergroup Relations* (London: Academic Press), 307–348.

V. Ginsburgh, J. Melitz and F. Toubal (2014) 'Foreign Language Learning: An Econometric Analysis', CESifo Working Paper Series No. 4923.

V. Ginsburgh and J. Prieto-Rodriguez (2011) 'Returns to Foreign Languages of Native Workers in the European Union', *Industrial and Labor Relations*, 64, 599–618.

V. Ginsburgh, S. Weber and S. Weyers (2011) 'Economics of Literary Translation: A Simple Theory and Evidence', *Poetics*, 39, 228–246.

G. Grenier (1982) 'Language as Human Capital: Theoretical Framework and Application to Spanish-Speaking Americans', PhD Dissertation, University of Princeton.

F. Grin (1990) 'A Beckerian Approach to Language Use: Guidelines for Minority Language Policy', Working Paper 0890, Centre de recherche et développement en économique (CRDE), University of Montreal.

F. Grin (1992) 'Towards a Threshold Theory of Minority Language Survival', *Kyklos*, 45, 69–97 [reprinted in D. Lamberton (ed.) (2002) *The Economics of Language* (Cheltenham: Edward Elgar)].

F. Grin (1994a) 'The Bilingual Advertising Decision', *Journal of Multilingual and Multicultural Development*, 15, 269–292.

F. Grin (1994b) 'L'identification des bénéfices de l'aménagement linguistique: la langue comme actif naturel' In C. Phlipponneau and A. Boudreau (ed.) *Sociolinguistique et aménagement des langues* (Moncton: Centre de Recherche en Linguistique Appliquée).

F. Grin (1996) 'The Economics of Language: Survey, Assessment and Prospects', *International Journal of the Sociology of Language*, 121, 17–44.

F. Grin (2003a) 'Language Planning and Economics', *Current Issues in Language Planning*, 4, 1–66.

F. Grin (2003b) *Language Policy Evaluation and the European Charter for Regional or Minority Languages* (London: Palgrave Macmillan).

F. Grin (2003c) 'Diversity as Paradigm, Analytical Device, and Policy Goal' In W. Kymlicka and A. Patten (eds) *Language Rights and Political Theory* (Oxford: Oxford University Press), 169–188.

F. Grin (2004a) 'On the Costs of Cultural Diversity' In P. Van Parijs (ed.) *Cultural Diversity versus Economic Solidarity: Proceedings of the Seventh Francqui Colloquium* (Brussels: De Boeck), 189–202.

F. Grin (2004b) 'L'anglais comme lingua franca: questions de coût et d'équité. Commentaire sur l'article de Philippe Van Parijs', *Économie publique*, 15, 33–41.

F. Grin (2005) *L'enseignement des langues étrangères comme politique publique*. Rapport au Haut Conseil de l'évaluation de l'école, Ministère de l'éducation nationale, Paris, http://cisad.adc.education.fr/hcee

F. Grin (2009) 'Promoting Language through the Economy: Competing Paradigms' In J. M. Kirk and D. P. Ó Baoill (eds) *Language and Economic Development* (Belfast: Queen's University Press), 1–12.

F. Grin (2013) '50 Years of Economics in Language Policy Critical Assessment and Priorities', élf Working Paper 13, University of Geneva, Observatoire ÉLF, www.unige.ch/traduction-interpretation/recherches/groupes/elf/documents/elfwp13.pdf

F. Grin and M. Gazzola (2013) 'Assessing Efficiency and Fairness in Multilingual Communication' In A.-C. Berthoud, F. Grin and G. Lüdi (eds) *Exploring the Dynamics of Multilingualism* (Amsterdam/Philadelphia: John Benjamins), 365–385.

F. Grin, T. Moring, D. Gorter, J. Hägman, D. Ó Riagáin and M. Strubell (2002) *Support for Minority Languages in Europe* (Brussels: Report to the Directorate General for Education and Culture, European Commission, http://europa.eu.int/comm/education/policies/lang/langmin/support.pdf).

F. Grin, C. Sfreddo and F. Vaillancourt (2010) *The Economics of the Multilingual Workplace* (London/New York: Routledge).

F. Grin and F. Vaillancourt (1998) 'Language Revitalisation Policy: An Analytical Survey. Theoretical Framework, Policy Experience an Application to *Te Reo Māori*', New Zealand Treasury Working Paper 98/06, www.treasury.govt.nz/publications/research-policy/wp/1998/98-06

F. Grin and F. Vaillancourt (1999) *The Cost-Effectiveness Evaluation of Minority Language Policies: Case Studies on Wales, Ireland and The Basque Country*. Monograph No. 2 (Flensburg: European Centre for Minority Issues).

E. Haugen (ed.) (1981) *Minority Languages Today* (Edinburgh: Edinburgh University Press).

A. Henley and R. Jones (2005) 'Earnings and Linguistic Proficiency in a Bilingual Economy', *The Manchester School*, 73, 300–320.

T. Hočevar (1975) 'Equilibria on Linguistic Minority Markets', *Kyklos*, 28, 337–357.

T. Hočevar (1983) 'Les aspects économiques de la dynamique fonctionnelle des langues', *Language Problems and Language Planning*, 7, 135–147.

M. Hüning, U. Vogl and O. Moliner (eds) (2012) *Standard Languages and Multilingualism in European History* (Amsterdam: John Benjamins).

N. Irriberi and J.-R. Uriarte (2012) 'Minority Language and the Stability of Bilingual Equilibria', *Rationality and Society*, 24, 442–462.

E. Jones (2000) 'The Case of a Shared World Language' In M. Casson and A. Godley (eds) *Cultural Factors in Economic Growth* (Berlin: Springer), 210–235.

A. Kharkhurin (2012) *Multilingualism and Creativity* (Bristol: Multilingual Matters).

A. Krishna and R. Ahluwalia (2008) 'Language Choice in Advertising to Bilinguals: Asymmetric Effects for Multinationals versus Local Firms', *Journal of Consumer Research*, 35, 692–705.

W. Kymlicka (1995) *Multicultural Citizenship: A Liberal Theory of Minority Rights* (Oxford: Clarendon Press).

J. Laakso, A. Sarhimaa, S. Spiliopoulou Åkemark and R. Toivanen (2013) *ELDIA. European Language Diversity for All. Summary of the Research Report* (University of Vienna, https://fedora.phaidra.univie.ac.at/fedora/get/o:304813/bdef:Content/get).

E. La Ferrara (2004) 'Solidarity in Heterogeneous Communities' In P. Van Parijs (ed.) *Cultural Diversity versus Economic Solidarity: Proceedings of the Seventh Francqui Colloquium* (Brussels: De Boeck), 69–80.

D. Laitin (2006) 'Linguistic Nationalism as a Consumption Item', paper presented at the ECORE Conference on 'Challenges of Multilingual Societies', Université Libre de Bruxelles, 9–10 June.

H. Leibenstein (1976) *Beyond Economic Man* (Cambridge, MA: Harvard University Press).

S. Liebowitz and S. Margolis (1994) 'Network Externality: An Uncommon Tragedy', *Journal of Economic Perspectives*, 8, 133–150.

M. MacLeod (2009) 'Gaelic Language Skills in the Workplace' In J. Kirk and D. Ó Baoill (eds) *Language and Economic Development: Northern Ireland, the Republic of Ireland, and Scotland* (Belfast: Cló Ollscoil na Banríona, Queen's University Press), 134–152.

S. Makoni and A. Pennycook (eds) (2007) *Disinventing and Reconstituting Languages* (Clevedon: Multilingual Matters).

M. Mateo Aierza (2004) 'L'usage du basque dans les grandes entreprises de la communauté autonome basque', in Secrétariat à la politique linguistique: *Les pratiques linguistiques dans les entreprises à vocation internationale* (Québec: Ministère de la culture et des communications), 55–66.

S. May (2003) 'Misconceiving Minority Language Rights: Implications for Liberal Political Theory' In W. Kymlicka and A. Patten (eds) *Language Rights and Political Theory* (Oxford: Oxford University Press), 123–152.

S. May (2012) *Language and Minority Rights: Ethnicity, Nationalism, and the Politics of Language*, 2nd edn (New York: Routledge).

T. Mayer (1993) *Truth versus Precision in Economics* (Aldershot: Edward Elgar).

J. Mélitz (2007) 'The Impact of English Dominance on Literature and Welfare', *Journal of Economic Behavior and Organization*, 64, 193–215.

R. Michael (1972) *The Effect of Education on Efficiency in Consumption* (New York: Columbia University Press).

L. Milligan, D. Chalmers and H. O'Donnell (2013) 'What Can Gaelic Teach Us about Effective Policy through Planning? Strategies in Gaelic Language Planning' In A.-C. Berthoud, F. Grin and G. Lüdi (eds) *Exploring the Dynamics of Multilingualism* (Amsterdam: John Benjamins), 121–136.

J. Mira and Á. Paredes (2005) 'Interlinguistic Similarity and Language Death Dynamics', *Europhysics Letters*, www.edpsciences.org/articles/epl/abs/2005/06/contents/contents. html

A. Okrent (2009) *In the Land of Invented Languages* (New York: Spiegel & Grau).

H. Patrinos and M. Hurst (2007) 'Indigenous Language Skills and the Labor Market in a Developing Economy: Bolivia' In B. Chiswick and P. Miller (eds) *The Economics of Language: International Analyses* (London: Routledge), 473–489.

H. Patrinos and E. Velez (1996) 'Costs and Benefits of Bilingual Education in Guatemala: A partial Analysis', Human Capital Development Paper No. 74, The World Bank.

A. Pennycook (2008) 'Postmodernism in Language Policy' In Thomas Ricento (ed.) *An Introduction to Language Policy: Theory and Method* (Malden, MA: Blackwell Publishing).

R. Phillipson (2010) *Linguistic Imperialism Continued* (New York: Routledge).

R. Phillipson and T. Skutnabb-Kangas (2013) Book Review of Martin-Jones, Marilyn, Adrian Blackledge and Angela Creese (eds) *The Routledge Handbook of Multilingualism* (London/New York: Routledge) *TESOL Quarterly*, 47, 657–659.

C. Piron (1994) *Le défi des langues. Du gâchis au bon sens* (Paris: L'Harmattan).

T. Pogge (2003) 'Accommodation Rights for Hispanics in the United States' In W. Kymlicka and A. Patten (eds) *Language Rights and Political Theory* (Oxford: Oxford University Press), 105–122.

J. Pool (1991) 'The World Language Problem', *Rationality and Society*, 3, 21–31.

A. Portuese (2012) 'Law and Economics of the European Multilingualism', *European Journal of Law and Economics*, 34, 279–325.

R. Selten (ed.) (1997) *The Cost of European (Non) Communication* (Roma: ERA).

R. Selten and J. Pool (1990) 'The Distribution of Foreign Language Skills as a Game Equilibrium', Language and Society Papers, LD9, University of Washington, Seattle.

A. Sen (1985) *Commodities and Capabilities* (Amsterdam: North Holland).

T. Skutnabb-Kangas (2000) *Linguistic Genocide in Education – Or Worldwide Diversity and Human Rights?* (Mahwah, NJ: Lawrence Erlbaum).

F. Vaillancourt (1985) 'Le choix de la langue de consommation' In F. Vaillancourt (ed.) *Economie et langue* (Quebec: Conseil de la langue française), 209–220.

F. Vaillancourt, R. Champagne and L. Lefebvre (1994) 'L'usage du français au travail par les francophones du Québec: une analyse économique' In P. Martel and J. Maurais (eds) *Langues et sociétés en contact* (Tübingen, Schweiz: Niemeyer), 483–493.

F. Vaillancourt and O. Coche (2009) *Official Language Policies at the Federal Level in Canada: Costs and Benefits in 2006* (Vancouver: Fraser Institute).

F. Vaillancourt, D. Lemay and L. Vaillancourt (2007) 'Laggards No more: The Changed Socioeconomic Status of Francophones in Quebec' C.D. Howe Institute Backgrounder No. 103.

P. Van Parijs (2000) 'The Ground Floor of the World: On the Socio-Economic Consequences of Linguistic Globalization', *International Political Science Review*, 21, 217–233.

P. Van Parijs (2011) *Linguistic Justice for Europe and for the World* (Oxford: Oxford University Press).

J. Walsh (2009) 'Ireland's Socio-Economic Development and the Irish Language: Theoretical and Empirical Perspectives' In J. M. Kirk and D. P. Ó Baoill (eds) *Language and Economic Development* (Belfast: Queen's University Press), 70–81.

J. Watt and A. MacLeòid (2009) 'Gaelic and Development in the Highlands & Islands of Scotland' In J. M. Kirk and D. P. Ó Baoill (eds) *Language and Economic Development* (Belfast: Queen's University Press), 117–129.

C. Wheelan (2011) *Introduction to Public Policy* (New York/London: Norton).

B.-A. Wickström (2005) 'Can Bilingualism Be Dynamically Stable? A Simple Model of Language Choice', *Rationality and Society*, 17, 81–115.

A. Wierzbicka (2014) *Imprisoned in English: The Hazards of English as a Default Language* (Oxford: Oxford University Press).

C. Williams (ed.) (1988) *Language in Geographic Context* (Clevedon: Multilingual Matters).

Y. Xie and M. Gough (2011) 'Ethnic Enclaves and the Earnings of Migrants', *Demography*, 48, 1293–1315.

M. Yaguello (2006) *Les langues imaginaires. Mythes, utopies, fantasmes, chimères et fictions linguistiques* (Paris: Seuil).

W. Zhang and G. Grenier (2012) 'How Can Language Be Linked to Economics? A Survey of Two Strands of Research', *Language Problems and Language Planning*, 37, 203–226.

22

Language Rights: A Welfare-Economics Approach

Bengt-Arne Wickström

22.1 Introduction

Different normative approaches to status and acquisition planning and language rights have been analysed by a number of scholars from the point of view of law, political science, philosophy, sociology and economics.[1] In this essay, though we present a stringent analytic approach based on welfare-economics theory, we do not reject other approaches. On the contrary, language rights is such a multifaceted phenomenon that many approaches are indeed needed, and they can fertilize one another, laying bare the weak points of one or another point of view.

22.1.1 Economics analysis

What distinguishes an economics analysis is first and foremost what is known as methodological individualism. That is, individual preferences and individual behaviours are cornerstones of societal-phenomena analysis. Individual behaviour is taken as the smallest building block of society and can be aggregated to describe collective behaviour. This holds true for both a descriptive, positive analysis and for a prescriptive, normative analysis.

Subjective, individual evaluations serve as the basis for societal evaluations. Applying this, however, we encounter several problems, especially in the discussion of distributional issues. There is a wealth of literature discussing problems of preference aggregation.[2] Although allocation efficiency and Pareto efficiency

---

[1] A good overview of the current discussion can, for instance, be found in the volume *Language Rights and Political Theory* edited by Kymlicka and Patten (2003) or, from a political-science perspective, in a recent special issue of *Language Policy*; see especially the introduction by Peled et al. (2014).

[2] This is not the place to review such literature, which goes back as far as the French Revolution and proceeds through the modern revival associated with the work of scholars like Arrow (1951).

are well-defined, applying them to, for instance, cost–benefit analysis is not without methodological problems. This is especially due to income effects, the so-called Scitovsky paradox, which in many cases leads to path dependencies.[3] Another practical problem is how to observe and measure individual evaluations. In a market, these subjective evaluations will be reflected in observed demand (and supply) behaviour and equilibrium prices.[4] In the absence of a market, the issue becomes much more difficult, and the revelation of individual preferences is associated with many incentive problems. For the purpose of this chapter, we will ignore these latter difficulties.[5]

Efficiency analysis as a rule takes preferences and behavioural patterns as given stationary characteristics defining individuals. When it comes to individual preferences for language use, this is not a simple matter. Even in the short run, one might not be justified in treating the linguistic preferences of individuals as constant and given. The language repertory and, hence, the preferences of young individuals are determined by their surroundings. These surroundings can change over the lifetime of the individual as a result of language policy, among other things. In other words, the changing linguistic environment might affect the individual preferences for language use and individual preferences are not static. Consequently the basis of the evaluation is no longer exogenous. In the treatment of several generations, this problem becomes more important. Even if individual preferences were to be static over the lifetime of the individual, the preferences of new young individuals would be formed at least partially by their surroundings when they enter society. If these surroundings were to change with time, each new cohort would have different preferences, and the distribution of preferences would change over time. This could lead to path dependencies and multiple solutions.[6]

22.1.2   Methodological overview

In this chapter, traditional welfare analysis will be made operational by cost–benefit analysis modified to fit the special character of language rights. We will also discuss distributional implications, taking the normative basis for the comparison of individual welfare to be exogenous in the form of preferences of an imaginary planner; see below.

---

[3] For the original contribution, see Scitovszky (1941).
[4] Individuals with a free choice of what to consume will compare their subjective evaluation of the value of a good with its market price. They will only purchase a good with a price that is lower than the subjective value attributed to the good. Hence, through their behaviour in the market, individuals reveal their preferences for the good in question.
[5] This is an empirical measurement problem without importance for our normative analysis.
[6] This is discussed in Wickström (2013).

There are a number of investigations based on cost–benefit reasoning. Pool (1991) or Lo Jacomo (1989), for instance, address the question of learning or translation costs due to, among other things, status planning. Ginsburgh and Weber and various coauthors compare the disenfranchisement effect on speakers of different unofficial languages under various status-planning regimes in the European Union with associated administrative costs.[7] Generally, these contributions do not attempt to model the value individuals attribute to language rights in any detail, a central point in this essay.

Value of language

Language is certainly the most important means of communication in all human societies. Language is also one of the most important aspects of an individual's personality, as well as of his or her social and cultural identity. These two aspects of language often find themselves in conflict with one another.

The practicality of a language certainly increases with the number of speakers; hence, if only communication counts, it would be efficient to have only one language. Opportunities in the labour market, for example, might be the most important argument for being socialized into the majority language of a country. However, being a speaker of a minority language does not exclude a working knowledge of another dominant one. Hence, this argument might not be as strong as one might think at first.[8]

Balancing this tendency is the desire of many individuals to preserve their language as a marker of identity. In a static perspective, language, like talents and other personal characteristics, can be seen as part of the definition, or initial endowment, of an individual. In a dynamic setting, however, the situation is slightly more complex, as noted above. We can here distinguish between changes within a generation and between generations.

Individuals can over their lifespans alter their language or acquire additional idioms. However, the more important aspect is the change between generations. All new-born individuals are endowed with their own characteristics, defining them as individuals. These characteristics are, at least partially, determined by the preferences of the previous generation as well as the linguistic environment the individual is born into. The normative evaluation of this environment is also determined by the preferences of the individuals of the

---

[7] See, for instance, Fidrmuc and Ginsburgh (2007), Ginsburgh et al. (2005), as well as Ginsburgh and Weber (2005). Gazzola (2006) and Gazzola (2014c) also fit into this tradition.

[8] Drinkwater and O'Leary (1997) and Rendon (2007) provide some evidence that being a minority speaker might not be a disadvantage at all.

previous two generations.[9] The preferences transmitted to the new cohorts have a direct effect on the aggregated distribution of preferences during the lifetime of individuals of the parental generation and, hence, on the determinants of the welfare analysis during their lifetime. But they also influence the composition of preferences of subsequent generations. That is, the language policy at any given time influences the composition of preferences at subsequent times, thereby causing various path dependencies.[10]

Status

The survival of a language – its implantation in the next generation – depends on many factors, one of which is its status in society. This status is influenced by, among other things, the possibility of using the language in various social arenas. Status planning is concerned with the issue of defining the official status of languages. This can be made operational in defining the legal rights of speakers of a certain language in different domains. Such domains typically include various public offices, public education at different levels, and public information such as street names or law and regulation texts.

Whether a language receives official status in any specific domain or not is very often a political issue, and it is an instrument that can be used by those in power – be it a dominant majority or a political elite – to control and exploit those who are weak.[11] An analysis of these aspects is closely related to rent-seeking and political, social and economic power. These are questions analysed in, among other disciplines, positive economics and will not be further treated in this essay.[12]

---

[9] For the sake of simplicity, it is assumed in this essay that only two generations overlap at any one time.

[10] The general structure of our analysis is also supported by the observed fact that drastic changes in language use occur between generations, where language shift typically happens over three consecutive generations: the members of one generation are monolingual, their children grow up bilingual and their grandchildren are monolingual in the second language.

[11] The administrative division can also be used to reduce the influence of an ethnic minority. Compare the situation in Slovakia, where there is a large ethnic and linguistic Hungarian minority living on the north shore of the Danube. The arrangement of the districts (okresy), mostly extending from the Danube far into the north, however, is such that there are only two (of eleven) districts bordering the Danube with a Hungarian majority (Komárno/Komárom and Dunajská Streda/Dunaszerdahely). A minor rearrangement of the eleven districts with five or six southern and five or six northern ones would create southern districts with a clear Hungarian majority and would in no other respect alter the administrative structure. Similarly, a southern region (kraj) with a large ethnic Hungarian majority could be set up. This would be in accordance with the economic theory of federalism (see Boadway and Shah, 2009) and, of course, considerably increase the status of the large Hungarian minority.

[12] See, however, Chapter 23 in this volume for an analysis of language rights from the point of view of positive economics.

Normative basis

Our goal is to search for acceptable allocations of rights according to a certain ethical criterion. The choice of rights for minorities can, for instance, be based on the equivalence principle, where (potential) Pareto improvements on some initial situation are looked for, or the desired allocation of rights may be governed by maximization of some (paternalistic) welfare function. The first approach is basically a cost–benefit analysis. A crucial assumption here is the definition of the point of reference, the status quo. Different choices can lead to different conclusions. We discuss this in some detail in Wickström (2007).

A welfare function is seen as a representation of the preferences of a social planner, which gives the problem a consistent frame within which the analysis can be carried out. Individual utility functions are seen as functions of the incomes of the individuals.[13] The welfare function is in turn an increasing function in these individual utilities.[14] The social planner's preferences for redistribution are represented by the marginal welfare changes due to small (real or implicit) income change for the various individuals.[15]

In the discussion of distributional aspects of language planning, we primarily discuss how the desire to redistribute alters the simple cost–benefit analysis. Although dynamic effects are considered, we do not undertake a dynamic analysis but consider only the long-run steady states of welfare which we compare for different allocations of language rights.

In comparison to a traditional welfare-optimizing analysis, there are, hence, some added considerations that alter the analysis in different ways. First, we deal with discrete changes, which imply that there are discrete jumps in implicit incomes and hence in the marginal evaluations of the social value of income redistribution. Second, individual preferences can be endogenous. Third, there are also long-run endogenous dynamic effects altering the composition and distribution of individual preferences of the population.

22.1.3 A vade mecum through the rest of the chapter

In order to make the analysis tractable, we need to limit the scope of the analysis and introduce a certain amount of formal modelling. This is done in Section 22.2. Here the basic concepts are introduced, and the three main variables in our cost–benefit analysis are formally defined: the individual

---

[13] More precisely, indirect utility functions and implicit incomes.
[14] That is, it is Paretian.
[15] Note that we are not attributing any 'deeper' significance to the welfare function in the sense of social-choice theory. Here it is only a representation of the preferences of a social planner for income (re)distributions. The only axioms implied are that it should respect Pareto efficiency and anonymity (see below). The second axiom simply says that individuals are only characterized by their implicit incomes, and two individuals with the same implicit income are treated identically.

propensities to pay, the costs of different allocations of language rights, and the preferences of the social planner. We set up and analyse a benchmark case, which is used as the reference point in further analysis. One robust result emerging from the benchmark case is that the absolute (and not the relative) size of a minority should be an input into the decision criterion for introducing minority-language rights.

In Sections 22.3 and 22.4, we argue that the benchmark case has to be augmented if the cost–benefit approach should be used as a policy tool and that in some cases the welfare analysis actually fails to produce clear recommendations. Section 22.3 analyses the consequences of individual preferences being endogenous. We show that this leads to different external effects which have to be incorporated into the cost–benefit calculations, and that in many cases these externalities produce contradictory results making the cost–benefit analysis impotent as a tool for policy evaluation. Section 22.4 looks at the distributional effects of the introduction of language rights. There are distributional effects both between and within language communities and the distributional consequences of language rights are strongly dependent on the domain considered.

In the Appendix, the informal verbal discussion in the main part of the chapter is formalized in a more stringent analysis of two language groups and a single language right.

22.2   Basic model

In this section we set up a formal framework and a benchmark model for the analysis of language rights. The basic structure and notation closely follow that of Wickström (2013).

22.2.1   Individuals

Society at time t is made up of a set N_t^0 of all individuals born into society at time t as well as the set N_{t-1}^0 of all individuals born at time $t-1$. That is, an individual lives two periods and the set of individuals alive in period t is given by $N_t := N_t^0 \cup N_{t-1}^0$. At birth an individual is socialized into a certain language l, where the set of all languages under consideration is denoted by L.[16] The number of individuals of cohort t in language group l is written as n_t^{l0}. Since individuals live for two periods, the number of older individuals alive at time t is n_{t-1}^{l0}. The total number of individuals in group l at time t is then $n_t^{l0} + n_{t-1}^{l0} =: n_t^l$.

---

[16] For the purpose of this essay, we ignore the fact that individuals can belong to several language groups at the same time. The assumption that each individual is associated with one language simplifies the notation considerably and does not detract from the principal points of the analysis.

22.2.2 Language rights

The actual use of a language is an individual matter, benefiting the individual using it.[17] Whether a person chooses to use a certain language or not in a given situation will, to a large extent, depend upon the constraints he or she is facing.

One important constraint is, of course, whether one is understood or not and manages to communicate. This can partially be determined by legal rights, forcing, for instance, public offices to accept the use of certain languages in doing official business. Ignoring associated costs, such rights to communication in a certain language can in principle be made available to all individuals to the same extent. Unlike many other rights, like the right to smoke in public places versus the right to enjoy fresh air at the same location, the right to use a certain language in a given setting is a non-exclusive right that does not exclude the right to use another language in the same setting per se: my right to communicate with (and get answers from) a public office in Bislama, say, does not infringe on your right to use Volapük in doing your business with the same office. Here we are focusing on these legal rights and not on the many other possibilities for using a language outside of the public sector. In a comprehensive analysis of language rights and justice, these aspects would have to be taken into account.[18]

Let the set of legally defined domains be D. The set of rights in effect at time t is a matrix r_t of zeroes and ones. The right to use language l in domain d in period t is then written as $r_t^{ld} = 1$ and the denial of that right as $r_t^{ld} = 0$. Such

---

[17] Of course, one person's use of a language might very well affect the well-being of the person he or she is talking to, or might want to communicate with, producing external effects, be it positive or negative ones. The larger the number of speakers of a language, the greater the potential number of contacts and, hence, the benefit of the language to all persons knowing it. This network externality is central in the analysis of the long-term dynamics and equilibria of language usage as a means of communication. This is analysed in Chapter 23 in this volume, among others, as well as in Selten and Pool (1991), Church and King (1993), Gabszewicz et al. (2011), and Güth et al. (1997), who look at the benefits of learning other languages in addition to the mother tongue, and in, for instance, Wickström (2005), Fernando et al. (2010), Patriarca and Leppänen (2004), or Minett and Wang (2008), where the possibilities of the survival of communities of speakers of minority languages are analysed. The present analysis treats this external property of language usage as part of the set of exogenous constraints facing the individual and is, hence, a possible factor influencing its propensity to pay for a certain language right.

[18] For more general analyses in this direction, the reader is referred to Kymlicka and Patten (2003) or Patten (2009) and the references therein. For a more formal analysis, see also Van Parijs (2002), as well as the contribution of the same author in Kymlicka and Patten (2003). A basic discussion can also be found in Wickström (2010).

a matrix defines a language regime, specifying which languages are accorded legal rights in which domains.[19]

Often, for practical or other reasons, not all possible allocations of rights are considered, but only certain subsets. Some domains are combined and different categories are defined. For instance, the category 'official status domains' might include important documents and symbolic uses, such as street names. The category 'working-language domains' would include negotiations and certain meetings. The object of analysis is then the allocation of languages to such categories.[20] The fact that in many cases only one category is used – a language either has an official status or it has no status at all – seems unnecessarily restrictive. An optimal system with several categories would improve welfare. If there were no costs in administering a system with very differentiated language rights, the highest degree of differentiation would be optimal.[21] However, due to the administrative costs, the optimal number of categories would be less, but almost certainly greater than one.

22.2.3 Endogeneity of preferences, language status and propensities to pay

Preferences are endogenous in two ways. First, by giving their mother tongue(s) to their offspring, members of the parental generation influence the preferences for different language regimes in society by influencing the number of speakers. We model this as (among other things) a function of the status the language enjoys when the parents make their decision. The higher the status of a language, the higher the probability that a member of the following generation

---

[19] In the European Union, for instance, at the moment 24 languages l are accorded rights in such domains d as legal documents or the European Parliament. For those languages the r^{ld}'s are equal to one at the moment. For some other big languages spoken in the European Union, notably Catalan and Russian, the corresponding r^{ld}'s are equal to zero. If a four-language regime (English, French, German and Polish, for instance) were to be introduced, for those languages the corresponding r^{ld}'s would remain equal to one, whereas for all other languages they would be equal to zero. This describes the idea of language regimes in Ginsburgh and Weber (2005) and the many subsequent articles by the same authors with various coauthors. The definition of r is, however, more general in that it distinguishes various domains, where Ginsburgh and Weber only consider one domain, see below.

[20] In the EU and in all EU organs, all 24 languages have an official status, but in many organs the number of working languages is drastically reduced. The European Central Bank has only English as its working language, but all 24 languages are official, as can be seen on the euro bank notes, where the abbreviation ECB is given in all official languages. Similarly, the Court of Justice uses only French as its working language. One could, hence, imagine a European Parliament with a high number of official languages and a commission with only a few. This corresponds closely to the current practice.

[21] This is just an application of Le Chatelier's principle.

will adopt it and have preferences for its use in society. The second way preferences are endogenous is also given by the status of the idiom. In this model, the intensity of a given individual's preferences for giving rights to a language depends on the social status of that language.

By relating the status of a language to the formal rights granted to the use of the language, we introduce a feed-back mechanism into the system.[22] The feedback mechanism introduces path dependencies; thus there is no guarantee that the optimal policy is stable. Indeed, cyclical societal preferences are a possibility; see Section 22.3.1.

The propensity of individual i to pay for a certain allocation of rights, r, is written as $b^i(r)$. This propensity to pay is, of course, only well-defined in relation to a status quo. That is, we normalize the propensities to pay to be equal to zero at the status quo. Two possible polar choices are $\bar{r} = \mathbb{O}$, all r^{ld} are zero, and $\bar{r} = \mathbb{I}$, all r^{ld} are equal to one. The first case means that our point of departure is that there are in effect no rights at all and the second signifies that the point of departure is the existence of all possible rights in all domains for all languages.

In the first case, we are born without any individual rights, and all rights have to be bought from society. In the second case, we are all born with all possible rights, and the negation of any right has to be bought from the beneficiaries of that right by the rest of society.[23] For the purposes of this essay, we will assume the former: $b^i(\mathbb{O})$ is set equal to 0 for all i.

A rights allocation – the entitlement to the use of certain languages in certain situations – can for our purposes be looked upon as a non-rival good. The 'demand' or propensity to pay for this good will vary according to the individual. The sum of all individual propensities to pay will then give society's total propensity to pay for this specific rights allocation. A difference from the textbook case is that the rights are not continuous, but discrete non-rival goods. Of course, the individual propensity to pay will depend (directly or indirectly) on a number of exogenous factors such as income and prices. The preferences are defined over bundles of individual rights and the availability of other language rights will enter the demand for any specific right to use a certain language. A Swede's propensity to pay for Swedish as an official language, or that of a Pole might depend on the availability of Danish or Czech, respectively,

---

[22] The structure could easily be adopted to deal with questions related to various forms of education. The members of the parental generation decide on the education given to the members of the next generation, which in turn influences their preferences for educating their children, etc. This process can lead to very different societies in the long-run equilibria.

[23] For a further discussion of the choice of status quo the reader is referred to Wickström (2007). The idea set forth in Van Parijs (2011) uses universal rights as a point of departure and then requires the English speakers to compensate all others for accepting English as lingua franca.

since the corresponding pair of languages are more or less mutually comprehensible.[24] Mutual comprehensibility[25] is not the whole story, however, for the identity-defining function of language pulls in other directions.[26]

22.2.4 Costs of different rights regimes

Let $c(r, n)$ be the costs that the realization of the rights allocation r causes society in comparison to the status quo. The function c is assumed to be concave in n^l if $r^{ld} = 1$ for some d.[27] The concavity implies that the cost per beneficiary is decreasing or constant for the linear case.

22.2.5 Cost–benefit analysis and efficiency

Letting N be the relevant set of individuals and suppressing the time index, we denote the aggregated propensity to pay in society for any given rights allocation r by $b(r)$, which is then given by

$$b(r) = \sum_{i \in N} b^i(r).$$

This has to be compared to the costs to society of providing these rights. The change in language rights from the status quo to r is an improvement according to the compensated-variation criterion if

$$\sum_{i \in N} b^i(r) > c(r, n).$$

---

[24] This point can be partially operationalized as the 'linguistic distance' between languages. See, for instance, the analysis in Ginsburgh et al. (2005), Fidrmuc et al. (2005), or Chapter 5 in this book.

[25] The importance of linguistic distance is not self-evident, however, and depends on language policy. Today young Swedes and Danes tend to interrelate in (American) English, a situation that can only be characterized as absurd by a native Swede getting his basic education in the 1950s. However, this is an externality induced by acquisition planning that almost exclusively concentrates on English, coupled with the strong dominance of a certain popular culture as well as the economic and military power behind the language. A very small effort spent on learning the neighbouring language would have a pay-off that by far exceeds the costs, a case where *ex post* optimality does not enter the *ex ante* calculations, due to the reduced practical distance between Swedish or Danish on the one side, and English on the other side, induced by the educational system.

[26] The importance of emotional attachment to language is reflected in, for example, Wales, where virtually every Welsh-speaker is bilingual in English, too – see, for instance, the statistics cited in Grin (1992) – or in the Basque country, where almost all speakers of Basque are bilingual in French or Spanish. Nevertheless, the propensity to pay for an official status for the respective language seems to be considerable among its speakers.

[27] In the dependency on the number of beneficiaries all possible degrees of economies of scale can occur. Having street signs in a certain language does not depend on the number of speakers at all, involving only fixed costs, whereas the provision of elementary education is more or less proportional to the number of beneficiaries.

By introducing payments (or taxes), θ^i, we can reformulate this slightly differently. The sum of the payments exactly covers the costs of introducing the rights if the following equation holds:

$$\sum_{i \in N} \theta^i = c(r, n). \tag{1}$$

If θ satisfies equation (1), we say that it is in the set $\Theta^F(r, n)$. The net benefit to individual i of the allocation of rights r in comparison to the status quo is given by $\Delta a^i(r, \theta^i) := b^i(r) - \theta^i$. A necessary and sufficient condition that the allocation be a Pareto improvement (or Pareto equivalent) is that all Δa's be non-negative:

$$\Delta a^i(r, \theta^i) \geq 0 \quad \forall i. \tag{2}$$

Ignoring distributional aspects, we can define a potential Pareto improvement by

$$\sum_{i \in N} \Delta a^i(r, \theta^i) > 0 \quad \text{for } \theta \in \Theta^F(r, n).$$

The Pareto-efficient allocations can be found by maximizing the sum of the net benefits over all possible allocations of rights subject to the feasibility constraint (1):

$$\max_r \sum_{i \in N} \Delta a^i(r, \theta^i) \quad \text{for } \theta \in \Theta^F(r, n). \tag{3}$$

The program (3) can also be written as

$$\max_r \left[\sum_{i \in N} b^i(r) - c(r, n) \right]. \tag{4}$$

This is our benchmark case, the 'naive' cost–benefit analysis.

If taxes are flexible, we can find a first-best Pareto-efficient allocation satisfying the solution to (3) which is also a Pareto improvement on the status quo, satisfying (2).

This can be modified in two ways. First, not all tax structures are possible; specifically, the first-best case is not institutionally feasible. This necessitates a second-best analysis of the optimal language rights with $\theta \in \Theta^I(r, n)$, the set of institutionally feasible taxes. Second, the social planner has preferences over distributions of incomes, postulating trade-offs between efficiency and more egalitarian distributions. The welfare function is more general than the (sum of) net individual benefits, and problem (3) becomes a special case of the welfare analysis.

22.2.6 Welfare function

We define the (indirect) utility of an individual as a function of its income stream a^i. In our case, it is given by some exogenous income ω^i plus the net benefit of the language rights Δa^i:

$$U^i = u^i \left(\omega^i + \Delta a^i \right).$$

The welfare function is defined as a function of the individual utilities:

$$W = w \left(U^1, \ldots, U^n \right).$$

We assume the welfare function to be Paretian, that is, increasing in each U^i. The change in welfare, ΔW, due to a (discrete) change in a, Δa, can be written as:

$$\Delta W = \sum_i \frac{\Delta w}{\Delta U^i} \frac{\Delta u^i}{\Delta a^i} \Delta a^i =: \sum_i \beta^i \Delta a^i.$$

The parameter β^i is a function of ω^i and Δa^i and is the evaluation of the planner of a unit increase in income a^i when it changes from ω^i to $\omega^i + \Delta a^i$.[28] If the planner is interested in redistribution in favour of the poor, β^i is decreasing in both arguments. If the planner is only interested in efficiency, all β^i are constant and equal. If the planner treats all individuals anonymously and neutrally, that is, only the implicit income matters, all functions $\beta^i \left(\omega^i, \Delta a^i \right)$ are identical and can be written as $\beta \left(\omega^i, \Delta a^i \right)$. In this chapter, this is the case.

In looking at the long-run changes in W, we can compare steady states and make a comparative-static analysis of two steady states. A truly dynamic analysis, on the other hand, would have to analyse a stream of values and compare the values at different times under some assumptions on discounting.

22.2.7 Optimal language rights

The problem of defining optimal language rights can now be written as:

$$\max_{r,\theta} \Delta W = \max_{r,\theta} \sum_{i \in N} \beta(\omega^i, \Delta a^i) \Delta a^i, \text{ subject to } \theta \in \Theta^I (r, n) \cap \Theta^F (r, n).$$

If the planner is only interested in efficiency, the β's are all equal and constant and the problem is reduced to our benchmark case (4).

---

[28] Of course, in a continuous setting the dependency on Δa disappears and β is just the marginal evaluation of an income increase given a certain income. Because of the discrete nature of the problem analysed, we will have an 'income' effect on the β's, since they, in general, are different before and after the change.

Since the cost function is assumed to be concave in the number of individuals benefiting from a rights allocation, the costs per capita decrease in the number of beneficiaries, as already noted above in Section 22.2.4. Hence, by any rights structure where the average propensities to pay are independent of the number of individuals, we can, independent of the planner's policy preferences, conclude that for every rights allocation there will be a critical number of individuals determining whether the rights should be realized or not. If c is linear in n (for instance, schools), the critical mass goes from zero to infinite, as the per capita propensities for payment increase. Then, a different treatment of different language groups can only be motivated by different per capita propensities to pay in the different groups.

Policy conclusion

For any rights allocation, the welfare-optimal decision criterion is characterized by a critical mass of beneficiaries. If the number of beneficiaries is below the critical mass, the rights should not be realized; if it is above the critical mass, they should be realized.[29]

22.3 Modifications due to endogenous preferences

There are two types of modifications to the 'naive' condition (4) to be considered. In the analysis of efficient rights, there are a number of external effects due to the endogeneity of the preferences, which are treated in this section. Additionally there are distributional considerations, which shall be discussed in Section 22.4.

22.3.1 Changes in individual preferences (status effect)

There is a possible change in the preferences of individual users of a language as a result of status changes. This effect simply says that the propensity to pay

---

[29] In reality, the condition for giving rights to minorities is often given as a fraction of the population. In Romania or Slovakia, for instance, the minority has to make up 20 or 15 per cent, respectively, in order to have a claim on certain rights for their language. In Finland, there is a percentage rule (8 per cent), but also a critical-mass criterion of 3,000 individuals. Rights are granted if either condition is fulfilled. Both criteria are, of course, easily manipulable through changes in the administrative units; by redrawing borders between administrative units, making them larger, one can often easily remove the basis for the minority rights if the percentage criterion is in effect. This is, of course, not possible with a critical-mass criterion. On the other hand, dividing jurisdictions could reduce the rights in local jurisdictions in the case of the critical-mass criterion. With the division of jurisdictions, using the percentage criterion, at least one part will get a higher percentage of the minority than the original jurisdiction. Based on this discussion, using a territorial principle, one could develop a theory of optimal jurisdictions, which goes beyond this chapter, but compare note 11.

for rights for the language might be different after a right has been introduced from what it was before the introduction if the implementation of the right increases the status of the language, making the speakers evaluate the rights more positively.[30]

Policy conclusion

The introduction of a right for a language l in a certain domain carries a positive externality if the introduction of the right increases the status of the language, making the users prouder, thereby increasing their propensity to pay. The policy conclusion is that the 'naive' analysis underestimates the efficient extent of language rights and consequently overestimates the size of the critical mass.

A 'paradox'

The status effect also works in the opposite direction when rights are reduced. A reduction in rights reduces the status of the language and this reduction causes a decline in the propensity to pay for the right. In certain cases, this makes the cost–benefit analysis impotent. We can illustrate this with two simple examples.

Let r be an allocation of rights for a minority language and c the associated costs. The aggregated propensity to pay for this rights allocation is in status quo b_0 and after the rights have been introduced b_1, $b_1 > c > b_0$. The external effect is $b_1 - b_0$. It is clear that since $b_1 > c > b_0$, after the introduction of the rights, the cost–benefit allocation gives a positive result; benefits b_1 exceed costs c. However, we can now ask if it pays to remove this rights allocation. Also here the answer is clear: the cost–benefit analysis concludes that the rights are to be removed. The savings c exceed the benefits b_0 of having the rights.

This corresponds to the Scitovsky paradox,[31] whose cause lies in an income effect that causes a change in the propensity to pay by stationary preferences. Due to a change in the environment, the individual senses a change in implicit income and the *ex post* propensity to pay differs from the *ex ante* one. Here, the effect comes from the presence or absence of certain rights.

The inconclusiveness of the cost–benefit analysis can be more complex, as illustrated in the following. Let there be three possible rights allocations, the status quo r_0 as well as r_I and r_{II} with associated costs c_I and c_{II}, $c_I < c_{II}$. The second allocation is more extensive than the first one. The propensity to pay for the two allocations is in the status quo b_I^0 and b_{II}^0, $c_I < b_I^0 < b_{II}^0 < c_{II}$. If r_I is realized, the propensities to pay are b_I^1 and b_{II}^1 with $c_I < b_I^1 < c_{II} < b_{II}^1$ and $c_{II} - c_I < b_{II}^1 - b_I^1$. A cycle

---

[30] Clots-Figueras and Masella (2013) provide evidence for such an effect in Catalonia.
[31] See Scitovszky (1941).

is also present here since r_0 cannot be compared to r_{II} by the argument above. However, if only gradual comparisons are possible, the cost–benefit analysis gives a clear result. It first tells us to choose r_I, but due to the externality, once r_I has been chosen, it leads us to choose r_{II}.

The basic problem then, is that the cost–benefit analysis cannot handle preference changes in a satisfactory manner. Even without taking the preference externality into account, but evaluating the situation with the preferences at hand, in the first example we have two very different allocations that are both efficient by the given preferences. In the second example, the externality is partially taken into account in a straight-forward manner and we have only one efficient allocation when the evaluation occurs with the preferences at hand.

22.3.2 Changes in the size of language groups

It is assumed that the rights for language l in effect at period t influence the status of that language in that period and, hence, the parent generation's choice of language(s) for the next generation, the size of n_{t+1}^{l0}.[32] In other words, we assume that parents in bringing up their children, decide to socialize them into their own language or another (majority) language depending, on the one hand, on the status of their own language compared to the alternative language(s) – the emotional, cultural aspect – as well as, on the other hand, the number of speakers – the practical, communicative aspect. Hence, the distribution of the individuals on different language groups, as well as the rights given to the speakers of the various languages will determine the size of the groups in the next cohort.[33] The distribution of the next cohort on the language groups is assumed to be given by a function g, such that

$$n_{t+1}^{l0} = g^l \left(r_t, n_t^0 \right),$$

---

[32] The long-run effects of certain allocations of language rights would be part of the 'emotional' aspect of determining the propensity to pay. The designation of certain languages as 'official' in given domains gives them a higher status, which reduces incentives for following generations to use the unofficial ones, reducing the number of their speakers. This can also lead to a situation of diglossia where the domains of the official language are constantly extended at the expense of unofficial languages. This, in turn, would give the speakers of the official language a head start in life. In the long run, it might even lead to the death of unofficial languages. For a further analysis of this possibility, see Abrams and Strogatz (2003), Minett and Wang (2008), or Wickström (2005).

[33] Compare Cenoz (2008) who cites statistics showing the use of the Basque language in Spain and France. The policy in Spain is very supportive of Basque and its number of speakers is increasing. In France Basque enjoys fewer rights and the number of speakers is diminishing.

with g^l non-decreasing in n^{l0} and in a further right to language l.[34] The language-group dynamics of the population is then given by

$$\dot{n}^{l0}_{t+1} := n^{l0}_{t+1} - n^{l0}_t = g^l\left(r_t, n^0_t\right) - n^{l0}_t.$$

Steady state

By setting $\dot{n}^{l0}_{t+1} = 0$ for all l, we (generally) find different steady-state sizes of the language groups for different allocations of rights in society.[35] The introduction of more extensive rights for one community increases the size of that community. If the total size of the population is constant, the size of other communities will decrease. Since the cost function is concave in n, the per capita costs of language rights in the first community will decrease and increase in the other communities. There is a positive externality in the first community and a negative one in the other communities. If the first community is smaller than the others, the net effect will be an increase in overall per capita costs. Hence, in the efficiency analysis the conclusions have to be modified.[36]

Contradictory results similar to those we found in Section 22.3.1 can also occur due to the change in the size of the language communities: let b^0 and b^1, $b^0 \leq b^1$ be the average propensity to pay for a certain right in its absence (State 0) and presence (State 1), respectively. If n^0 and n^1, $n^0 < n^1$, are the steady-state sizes of the community in the two states and c the cost to society of introducing the right, then we cannot exclude that $b^0 n^0 < c < b^1 n^1$. The first part of the inequality tells us not to introduce the right if it is absent and the second part that the right should not be abolished if it is in effect. In this case, the cost–benefit analysis fails to provide us with a policy recommendation.

---

[34] Formally, letting $\bar{r}_t$ and r_t be some allocations of language rights,

$$g^l\left(\bar{r}_t, n^0_t\right) - g^l\left(\mathring{r}_t, n^0_t\right) \geq 0, \text{ if } \begin{cases} \bar{r}^{md}_t - \mathring{r}^{md}_t = 0 \text{ for all } d \text{ and all } m \neq l \\ \bar{r}^{ld}_t - \mathring{r}^{ld}_t = 1 \text{ for some } d \end{cases}$$

$$0 \leq \frac{\partial g^l\left(r_t, n^0_t\right)}{\partial n^{l0}_t} < 1,$$

where n^0_t is the vector of all n^{l0}_t.

[35] Let $\bar{r}$ and r be two such allocations giving the same rights to all languages except l and with $\bar{r}$ providing more extensive rights for l than r in some domain(s). Then:

$$n^{l0}\left(\bar{r}\right) = g^l\left(\bar{r}, n^0(\bar{r})\right) \geq g^l\left(r, n^0(r)\right) = n^{l0}\left(r\right).$$

[36] In general, of course, the concave cost structure is an argument for homogeneous communities, ultimately implying societal unilingualism.

Policy conclusion

The introduction of a right for a language l in a certain domain carries a positive externality, increasing the aggregated propensity to pay for further rights for that language through an increase in the size of its community. The policy conclusion is that the 'naive' analysis underestimates the efficient extent of language rights and overestimates the size of the critical mass. However, the introduction of a right also carries a negative externality, decreasing the size of the community of non-speakers of the language in question, thereby increasing the per capita costs in that community. The 'naive' analysis overestimates the efficiency of language rights and underestimates the size of the critical mass due to this effect.[37] The net cost effect of the communities' size changes is negative if the increasing community is a minority and the decreasing one a majority.

22.3.3   Merit-good arguments

The concept of merit goods was introduced by Richard Musgrave to justify public intervention in cases when the strict basis in individual preferences does not suffice. The reason could reflect the uncertainty of the individuals, their limited access to information, or differences between *ex post* and *ex ante* situations, the latter being the case of education, for instance. After having received an education, I value it more than before receiving it.[38] A similar principle can be applied in the case of language rights. We briefly discuss two examples.

Linguistic diversity

Many linguists argue that there is a value in linguistic diversity per se.[39] One tries to draw parallels to biological diversity, claiming that valuable knowledge is lost to humanity through the demise of linguistic variety. If this is the case, giving rights to minority languages will increase their survival chances and, hence, these rights carry a positive externality.

Language death

As a further illustration of this argument, consider the following example. It is well-known that language death is a process, wherein one domain after another is lost until the language is not used in any domain at all.[40] Now, consider a situation with two domains, elementary education and university education. The variable r for a given language can be $r_0 = (0, 0)$, $r_I = (1, 0)$, or $r_{II} = (1, 1)$

---

[37] In the case of bilingual or multilingual individuals, the argument has to be slightly more differentiated, but the core remains unaffected.

[38] For the original source, see Musgrave (1956/1957).

[39] See, for instance, Nettle and Romaine (2000).

[40] See, for instance, the classic study of Gal (1979).

(the language is not used at all in the educational system, used only in elementary education, or used both in elementary and higher education).[41] The corresponding cost structure is $0 < c_I < c_{II}$ (c_0 is zero by definition). If the propensity to pay is state dependent (states are 0, 1, or 2, the propensity to pay for allocation 0 is, *per definitionem*, zero), $b_I^0 < b_{II}^0$, $b_I^1 < b_{II}^1$ and $b_I^2 < b_{II}^2$, we could easily end up in the following situation:

$$b_{II}^2 > c_{II} > b_{II}^1 > b_{II}^0$$

$$b_I^2 > c_I > b_I^1 > b_I^0$$

$$b_I^2 - c_I > b_{II}^2 - c_{II}.$$

Applying simple cost–benefit analysis, we find via the last expression that higher education should be abolished if one is in State 2. One should keep the elementary education, though. However, due to the negative externality caused by a move from State 2 to State 1 ($b_I^1 - b_I^2$), in State 1, the cost–benefit analysis leads us to abolish primary education as well. That is, neither State 2 nor State 1, which are both sensible rights allocations from the point of view of State 2 and cost–benefit considerations, will survive a gradual cost–benefit analysis. In the long run, the language might perish due to its lack of official status. Under perfect information, one could suggest that the second-best allocation in State 2, r_{II}, should be chosen. This would, measured with the preferences in State 2, lead to a better outcome than choosing the best allocation in State 2 that ultimately leads us to outcome 0.

Policy conclusion

The introduction of a right for a threatened language *l* in a certain domain can imply a positive externality, contributing to the survival of the language, thereby also contributing to linguistic diversity.

22.4   Modifications due to redistribution

One can identify several distribution effects, both direct and fiscal ones, as well as income effects. The distribution effects on the fiscal side are connected with the tax system and its redistributive properties due to the fact that taxes cannot be freely levied on different individuals. This is in no way different than other tax-financed public activities. The direct effect of language rights can be found both between communities and within communities.

---

[41] We ignore the case $r = (0, 1)$ as less realistic.

22.4.1 Fiscal effects

With a fully flexible tax-system – lump-sum taxes levied on an individual basis – the planner can achieve any distribution of implicit income and a first-best maximum of the welfare function with respect to language rights. To find the first-best optimum, one would have to find which language rights are efficient in the sense of Section 22.3 and then through lump-sum transfers make the implicit income of everyone equal, thereby taking into account that the propensities to pay b are influenced by the implicit incomes. This is, of course, an unobtainable *fata morgana* in the real world.[42] In reality, the set of possible tax structures is rather limited. The tax structure is determined by a few observable individual parameters, like income, consumption or wealth. The determination of the tax schedules is the well-known second-best optimal-taxation problem without specific aspects related to language rights and will not be further analysed here. We will generally assume a fixed tax system and only analyse the direct distributional effects of the introduction of language rights.

22.4.2 Distributional properties of language rights

We have to distinguish effects between language groups from effects within language groups.

Between-group effects

In Fidrmuc and Ginsburgh (2007) the per-speaker costs of making a language official in the European Union is calculated. They are by far the lowest for German and by far the highest for Maltese.[43] If both a German speaker and a Maltese speaker have the same propensity to pay b for rights for their respective languages and, taking the costs of the German as the unit of measurement, if $1 < b < 230$, the cost–benefit analysis would tell us to introduce the right for German, but not for Maltese. If the normative point of departure is no right

---

[42] However, in Van Parijs (2011) and his other publications, the introduction of English as the sole official language of the European Union could be both efficient and just if the English speakers compensate the non-English speakers sufficiently. An underlying assumption here is that only the communication aspect of the language is important. In that way, efficiency is achieved if only one language is used. If the emotional aspect and its implications for the preference dynamics are considered, the situation is much more complicated, however.

[43] Letting the per-speaker costs of German be the *numéraire*, the per-speaker costs of English and French are 1.5, and the costs of Maltese are 229.2. That is, if taxes were levied on the users of the language, for a certain level of services a German speaker would have to pay €1, an English speaker would pay €1.50 and a speaker of Maltese almost €230 a year.

for anyone and if the per capita tax rate is the same for everyone, the consequence would be that the German speaker has a gain of $b - t$, and the Maltese speaker a loss of t, the per capita tax rate. If the individuals in the two groups are equal in the eyes of the planner, this would be in line with the welfare analysis, maximizing the differences between benefits and costs. However, if the lower implicit income of the Maltese speaker gives her a higher weight β in the welfare function, in a first-best world the German speakers should compensate her until the implicit incomes are equal (and then also the corresponding β's). In a second-best world with equal division of all costs, the average *ex post* implicit incomes (weighted by the β's) in the two situations with and without rights for Maltese should have to be compared, and if b is above a certain value, the result would be the introduction of the rights for Maltese, although it would not be efficient.[44] This argument can be carried further. If a linguistic minority is poorer than the general population or discriminated against, and tax subsidies or other transfers are not politically possible, then the introduction of language rights beyond the level coming from the cost–benefit efficiency measure would be an indirect way of compensating the members of the group for the disadvantages they face.[45]

If the average propensities to pay are different for the two groups (b_g and b_m, $b_g > 1$), and the costs are divided equally, the choice of status quo shows its importance. If the basic right is no right, $\bar{r} = \mathbb{O}$, then, if no rights are in effect, we have an equal distribution. If the rights are introduced for both languages and financed over the general budget, a German would have a gain of $b_g - t^*$ and a Maltese of $b_m - t^*$, where t^* is the per capita cost of this rights

---

[44] If there are only Maltese and German speakers in the Union, if costs are divided equally, if there are n_m Maltese speakers as well as n_g German speakers, and if the costs per language are c, then the implicit income distribution in the absence of rights for Maltese (0) is $(b - \frac{c}{n_g + n_m}; -\frac{c}{n_g + n_m})$ and in the presence of Maltese rights (1) $(b - \frac{2c}{n_g + n_m}; b - \frac{2c}{n_g + n_m})$. If the rights for the Maltese speakers are present, the German and Maltese speakers would have the same implicit incomes (ignoring other possible differences). In the absence of rights, the implicit income of the Maltese is lower than that of the Germans. Let the weights of the planner be $\beta_m^0 =: \beta^0 > \beta^1 := \beta_g^0 = \beta_g^1 = \beta_m^1$. The comparison is then between $W^0 = \beta_g^0 n_g \left(b - \frac{c}{n_g + n_m}\right) - \beta_m^0 n_m \frac{c}{n_g + n_m}$ and $W^1 = \beta_g^1 n_g \left(b - \frac{2c}{n_g + n_m}\right) + \beta_m^1 n_m \left(b - \frac{2c}{n_g + n_m}\right)$. The difference is $W^1 - W^0 = \beta^1 n_g \left(b - \frac{2c}{n_g + n_m}\right) + \beta^1 n_m \left(b - \frac{2c}{n_g + n_m}\right) - \beta^1 n_g \left(b - \frac{c}{n_g + n_m}\right) + \beta^0 n_m \frac{c}{n_g + n_m} = n_m \beta^1 b + \frac{c}{n_g + n_m}[n_m \beta^0 - 2n_m \beta^1 - \beta^1 n_g]$. Let $\varepsilon = \frac{c - n_m b}{c}$ be the difference between costs and aggregated propensity to pay for the rights for Maltese as a fraction of costs. Substituting for $n_m b$, we find $\frac{W^1 - W^0}{c\beta^1} = \frac{n_m}{n_g + n_m} \frac{\beta^0 - \beta^1}{\beta^1} - \varepsilon$. If the Maltese community is not too small and the planner's redistribution inclination sufficiently high, it is welfare improving to introduce rights for Maltese even though the efficiency criterion fails by a fraction ε.

[45] One could speculate further here. The introduction of minority rights for a community like the Roma in some countries might lead to an increase in the culture's pride and thereby become a means of acceptance and inclusion in the larger society.

allocation. The change in the difference in implicit income would be $b_g - b_m$. If $b_m < 230$, the cost–benefit analysis tells us to introduce the right for German, but not for Maltese. The consequence would be that the German speaker has a gain of $b_g - t$, and the Maltese speaker a loss of t. The change in the difference in implicit income is b_g. If, on the other hand, the status quo is $\bar{r} = \mathbb{I}$ and if $b_m > 230$, the right would be kept for both languages, and we stay in the status quo. There is no change. If $b_m < 230$, the Maltese speakers should, according to the cost–benefit analysis, be deprived of their rights and tax money would be freed. They would have a change in implicit income that is $t^{**} - b_m$ and the German speakers would have an increase in implicit income of t^{**}, the per capita tax money freed. The change in the difference of the implicit incomes would then be $b_m (\neq b_g)$. That is, a given rights allocation has different distributional characteristics dependent on the definition of the status quo.

In conclusion, the distribution analysis in addition to the planner's preferences for redistribution also depends on the assumptions of the rights distribution in the status quo if the propensity to pay differs between the individuals. That is, we have no unique way of introducing equality.[46]

Policy conclusion

In a second-best world, the introduction of rights for a language l spoken by a small or disadvantaged group could contribute to a more equal distribution of implicit income. The policy conclusion is that the 'naive' cost–benefit analysis underestimates the optimal extent of language rights and, hence, overestimates the size of the critical mass necessary to justify minority rights.

Within-group effects

Empirical evidence tells us that language skills are distributed very unevenly over socioeconomic characteristics in the society and are generally seen as positively correlated with income.[47] That is, rights for a minority language are likely to open more doors for the low-income person than for the high-income one. At the same time, the 'need' to contact official institutions might vary strongly between situations.[48]

---

[46] One could call the allocation $\bar{r} = \mathbb{I}$ liberalism and $\bar{r} = \mathbb{O}$ absolutism. For a further discussion, see Wickström (2007).

[47] The knowledge of foreign languages in the European Union is analysed in great detail in Gazzola (2014a, 2014b). He finds, among other things, a strong correlation between income and language skills as well as between educational level and language skills.

[48] If we are at the level of the European Union, the necessity to contact EU institutions is probably positively correlated with income. However, the high-income speaker of a small language is likely to master one of the big languages in Europe. Hence, the propensity to pay for rights for the small language might not be too high. The need to have rights in Finnish, say, might not be too critical, since the high-income Finn is likely

In addition to these rather pragmatic arguments, there is the emotional value of having one's language accepted as an equal with all other ones.[49] This part of the propensity to pay might have the properties of a normal good (income elasticity greater than zero), if not a luxurious good (income elasticity greater than one).[50] In either case, the propensity to pay would be positively correlated with income.

Finally, most tax schedules are such that tax payments are progressive: the marginal tax rate on income increases with income, and the fiscal costs associated with the introduction of rights are strongly and positively correlated with income.[51] One can safely assume that the income elasticity of the tax payments is greater than one. To find the within-group redistribution effects of the introduction of language rights, we need to find the distribution of net benefits, the Δa^i's. Bringing the different arguments together, it is not clear how the net benefits are correlated with income. The communication values discussed above seem to indicate that in that example the language rights in relation to the EU are a luxurious good (income elasticity greater than one), but at the national level rather an inferior good (income elasticity negative). The emotional argument, however, could have the properties of a luxury good. This, taken together with the tax schedule can give us both a negative and a positive correlation of net benefits with income. What we can say, though, is that rights at the EU level are less likely to redistribute in favour of low incomes than rights on the local level.

Policy conclusion

The introduction of a right for a language *l* spoken by a minority would affect the distribution of implicit income. Assuming that the net value of the introduction of language rights is negatively correlated with income, the extent of the right should be beyond that given by the simple cost–benefit analysis; that is, the critical mass needed is lower than in the cost–benefit case. Furthermore, this argument for more extensive rights in comparison to the cost–benefit

---

to master English or German at a sufficiently high level. On the other hand, for the Swedish-speaking farmer in Österbotten, who in his work is forced to have a fair amount of contact with central authorities in Helsinki/Helsingfors, the rights provided to the Swedish language in Finland might be of crucial importance.

[49] In many cases, this would be the principal argument since there are hardly any communication problems. Catalan and Gallego in Spain are close enough to Castillano that with some good will on all sides most communication problems can easily be solved. Also, in many minority communities, like the Welsh, Irish or Basque speakers, virtually all individuals are bilinguals, thereby removing the communication aspects from the propensities to pay.

[50] Anecdotal evidence seems to indicate the latter. Many movements for the preservation of minority languages seem to be dominated by intellectuals.

[51] We remind the reader that we are taking the tax schedule as given.

analysis is stronger the lower the level of government. That is, in the European Union on the local level, the cost–benefit criterion should be modified the most and on the EU level the least.

22.4.3   Income effects

The income effects are the result of the fact that language rights are discrete variables. If certain rights are given to a certain language community, this can be seen as a discrete increase in implicit income. If, in turn, the planner wants to redistribute to 'poorer' communities and, hence, gives them a weight higher than the 'richer' communities, then, due to the increase in the implicit income of the poorer community, their relative weight β in the welfare function has to decrease. Hence, *ex post* the evaluation of the situation is lower than what one *ex ante* might have assumed.

Policy conclusion

The introduction of a right for a language l spoken by a poor minority would make their implicit income higher. The policy conclusion is that the *ex ante* 'naive' analysis overestimates the optimal extent of language rights.

22.5   Conclusion

In this chapter we have tried to examine systematically the factors influencing the normative arguments for the allocation of language rights from a welfare-economics point of view. We have seen that – because of Scitovsky-like 'paradoxes' – the welfare analysis provides contradictory results in some cases. Even when this is not the case the simple cost–benefit analysis should be augmented in various directions. Both types of effects are caused by the assumption that language policies induce changes in individual propensities to pay as well as in the distribution of propensities to pay in the population, the latter effect being caused by changes in the transmission of language use from one generation to the next.

The scope of the study has been limited to rights in formal domains which can be regulated by legal means. The larger – and probably more important – issue of how to deal with linguistic discrimination in the market place, has been ignored.[52] Put in a different way, one could also ask which domains should be regulated by legal means.

Also the question of what constitutes a legitimate minority has not been the topic of this chapter. Should recent immigrants be treated differently from minorities, whose ancestors have lived in a territory for numerous generations, often much longer than the majority population? A related question is: When

---

[52] Some of these issues are touched upon by Grin in Chapter 21 of this volume.

does a newly arrived group become the legitimate majority in a territory and left-over members of the old majority a 'normal' minority?[53] This opens up many interesting, contradictory and important questions, which can be approached and partially resolved by economics methodology.[54]

Appendix: Formal analysis

Introduction

In this appendix we illustrate the discussion in the main body of the chapter with a simplified but stringently analysed model.

Notation and simplifying assumptions

In order to make the analysis tractable, we limit ourselves to two languages, A and B, and two language groups N^A and N^B of initial size n^A and n^B. Further, the propensities to pay are positive only for the proper language.[55] We only consider one domain, and the taxes paid by individual i for financing a right of language L in this domain is denoted by θ^{iL}. We write $\sum_{i \in N^A} (\theta^{iA} + \theta^{iB}) =: \theta^{AA} + \theta^{AB} =: \theta^A$ and correspondingly for community B. We compare the situation with the introduction of a right in this domain for both languages $r^A = r^B = 1$ with a situation where the right is only introduced for language A, $r^A = 1$, $r^B = 0$. The introduction of the right will alter the size of the B community by $\Delta n^B =: \Delta n \geq 0$ and of the A community by $\Delta n^A = -\Delta n \leq 0$. These individuals are found in the set ΔN. For the sake of simplicity, we assume that the characteristics of the individuals in this set are distributed like those of the individuals in the set N^A initially and as those of the individuals in the set N^B after the introduction of the right. Define δ^A as $\frac{\Delta n^A}{n^A}$ and δ^B as $\frac{\Delta n^B}{n^B}$. Note that $-\frac{\delta^A}{\delta^B} = \frac{n^B}{n^A}$ is the initial ratio of the number of minority to majority speakers. The introduction of the right also has a 'status' effect on the B community; this is denoted by σb. Since the right is in effect for A, the 'status' effect on the A community is already incorporated in b^{iA}.

Welfare analysis

If the right is introduced only for language A but not for language B, the welfare change from the status quo (no rights) is given by:

$$\sum_i \beta^i \Delta a_0^i = \sum_{i \in N^A} (b^{iA} - \theta_0^{iA}) \beta_0^i - \sum_{i \in N^B} \theta_0^{iA} \beta_0^i.$$

Here, $\beta_0^i := \beta(\omega^i, b^{iA} - \theta_0^{iA})$.[56]

---

[53] One may think of Native Americans both in North and South America.
[54] For a simple analysis, see Wickström (2014).
[55] That is, the propensity to pay $b^{iL} > 0$ if $i \in N^L$ and $b^{iL} = 0$ if $i \notin N^L$.
[56] That is, if $i \in N^A$, $\beta_0^i := \beta(\omega^i, b^{iA} - \theta_0^{iA})$, and if $i \in N^B$, $\beta_0^i := \beta(\omega^i, -\theta_0^{iA})$.

If the right is introduced for both languages, the change in welfare from the status quo is:

$$\sum_i \beta_1^i \Delta a_1^i = \sum_{i \in N^A \setminus \Delta N^A} \left(b^{iA} - \theta_1^{iA} - \theta_1^{iB} \right) \beta_1^i$$

$$+ \sum_{i \in N^B \cup \Delta N^B} \left(b^{iB} + \sigma b^{iB} - \theta_1^{iA} - \theta_1^{iB} \right) \beta_1^i.$$

Here, $\beta_1^i := \beta \left(\omega^i, b^{iA} + b^{iB} + \sigma b^{iB} - \theta_1^{iA} - \theta_1^{iB} \right)$.[57] We isolate the dynamic effects discussed in Section 22.3.2, defining $\Delta \theta^{iA} := \theta_1^{iA} - \theta_0^{iA}$ and $\Delta \theta^{iB} := \theta_1^{iB} - \theta^{iB}$, where θ^{iB} is the (fictitious) value of θ_1^{iB} when $\Delta n = 0$. In the following, we write θ_0^{iA} as θ^{iA}. Again, let it be noted that we do not claim to carry out a true dynamic analysis, but simply a comparative-static analysis of different steady states.

We find the following expression for the difference in welfare:

$$\Delta W = \sum_{i \in N^A} \left[\left(b^{iA} - \theta^{iA} - \Delta \theta^{iA} - \theta^{iB} - \Delta \theta^{iB} \right) \beta_1^i - \left(b^{iA} - \theta^{iA} \right) \beta_0^i \right]$$

$$- \sum_{i \in \Delta N} \left(b^{iA} - \theta^{iA} - \Delta \theta^{iA} - \theta^{iB} - \Delta \theta^{iB} \right) \beta_1^i$$

$$+ \sum_{i \in \Delta N} \left(b^{iB} + \sigma b^{iB} - \theta^{iA} - \Delta \theta^{iA} - \theta^{iB} - \Delta \theta^{iB} \right) \beta_1^i$$

$$+ \sum_{i \in N^B} \left[\left(b^{iB} + \sigma b^{iB} - \theta^{iA} - \Delta \theta^{iA} - \theta^{iB} - \Delta \theta^{iB} \right) \beta_1^i + \theta^{iA} \beta_0^i \right].$$

This can be written as:

$$\Delta W = \sum_{i \in N^A} \left[\left(b^{iA} - \theta^{iA} - \Delta \theta^{iA} - \theta^{iB} - \Delta \theta^{iB} \right) (1 + \delta^A) \beta_1^i - \left(b^{iA} - \theta^{iA} \right) \beta_0^i \right]$$

$$+ \sum_{i \in N^B} \left[\left(b^{iB} + \sigma b^{iB} - \theta^{iA} - \Delta \theta^{iA} - \theta^{iB} - \Delta \theta^{iB} \right) (1 + \delta^B) \beta_1^i + \theta^{iA} \beta_0^i \right].$$

It is welfare improving to introduce the right for language B if ΔW is positive. This is our decision criterion.

Using the fact that

$$\sum_i x^i \beta^i = \overbrace{x \bar{\beta}}^{\text{inter-group effects}} + \overbrace{x \bar{\beta} V_x}^{\text{intra-group effects}}.$$

---

[57] That is, if $i \in N^A \setminus \Delta N^A$, $\beta_1^i := \beta \left(\omega^i, b^{iA} - \theta_1^{iA} - \theta_1^{iB} \right)$, and if $i \in N^B \cup \Delta N^B$, $\beta_1^i := \beta \left(\omega^i, b^{iB} + \sigma b^{iB} - \theta_1^{iA} - \theta_1^{iB} \right)$.

with $x := \sum_i x^i$, $\bar{\beta} := \sum_i \beta^i / n$, and $V_x := \left[\sum_i (x^i - \bar{x})(\beta^i - \bar{\beta})\right] / (x\bar{\beta})$, the expression can be decomposed into several partial effects:[58]

$$
\Delta W = \overbrace{\bar{\beta}_1^B \left[\left(b^B + \sigma b^B \right) \left(1 + \delta^B \right) - \left(C^B + \Delta C^B \right) \right]}^{\text{direct net benefit for } B}
$$

$$
+ \overbrace{\left[\bar{\beta}_1^A \left(1 + \delta^A \right) - \bar{\beta}_0^A \right] b^A - \bar{\beta}_1^A \left(C^A + \Delta C^A \right) + \bar{\beta}_0^A C^A}^{\text{externality on } A} \qquad \text{(A.1)}
$$

$$
+ \overbrace{\left(\bar{\beta}_1^B - \bar{\beta}_1^A \right) \left[\left(\theta^A + \Delta\theta^A \right) \left(1 + \delta^A \right) - C^A - \Delta C^A \right] + \left(\bar{\beta}_0^B - \bar{\beta}_0^A \right) \theta_0^B}^{\text{fiscal redistribution}}
$$

intra-group distribution effect in communities A and B due to the right given to B

$$
+ \quad \overbrace{V_b^A b^A \left[\bar{\beta}_1^A \left(1 + \delta^A \right) - \bar{\beta}_0^A \right] + V_b^B \left(b^B + \sigma b^B \right) \bar{\beta}_1^B \left(1 + \delta^B \right)}
$$

intra-group distribution effect of taxes in community A

$$
- \quad \overbrace{V_\theta^A \left[\left(\theta^A + \Delta\theta^A \right) \bar{\beta}_1^A \left(1 + \delta^A \right) - \theta_0^A \bar{\beta}_0^A \right]}
$$

intra-group distribution effect of taxes in community B

$$
- \quad \overbrace{V_\theta^B \left[\left(\theta^B + \Delta\theta^B \right) \bar{\beta}_1^B \left(1 + \delta^B \right) - \theta_0^B \bar{\beta}_0^B \right]} \; .
$$

Again, we are assuming that the dynamic effects do not influence the distribution characteristics of taxes and propensities to pay within the communities.

Efficiency

Expression (A.1) consists of several effects. Ignoring the distribution effects, that is, setting all $\beta^i = 1$, the equation reduces to:

$$
\Delta W = \left(b^B + \sigma b^B \right) \left(1 + \delta^B \right) - \left(C^B + \Delta C^B \right) + \left(\delta^A b^A - \Delta C^A \right).
$$

Letting all delta variables equal zero, we obtain the benchmark case. The different external effects discussed in Section 22.3 can also readily be found: the positive status effect due to σb and the dynamic effects, positive on community B and negative on community A. With a concave cost function, welfare is reduced due to the change in costs and the decrease in community A and increased due to the status effect and increase in community B.

Distribution

As in the main text, we have to distinguish between inter-community and intra-community effects.

---

[58] Note that the total taxes in the two groups if the right for B is not introduced are $\theta^{AA} =: \theta_0^A$ and $\theta^{BA} =: \theta_0^B$. Also, tax revenue equals costs: $(1 + \delta^A)(\theta^{AA} + \Delta\theta^{AA}) + (1 + \delta^B)(\theta^{BA} + \Delta\theta^{BA}) = C^A + \Delta C^A$ and $(1 + \delta^A)(\theta^{AB} + \Delta\theta^{AB}) + (1 + \delta^B)(\theta^{BB} + \Delta\theta^{BB}) = C^B + \Delta C^B$.

Distributional effects between the communities

If the communities are unequal in the eyes of the planner, there are, as we noted in Section 22.4, redistribution effects due to income differences, changes in implicit income, and fiscal externalities. These effects are easily identified in the formal model of equation (A.1). If the B community is poorer than the A community, the β^B's are on average greater than the β^A's. If, on the other hand, the B community is richer than the A community in general, that is, if the minority is a small elite, the following argument is, of course, reversed. The introduction of the right for B will in the first case have an additional positive effect on welfare if the B community would pay part of the rights for A in the absence of rights for B and/or the A community pays more in taxes for the rights allocation than the costs of the rights for A. This would, of course, be the case with equal taxes for all individuals. Since, in this case, the introduction of the right increases the implicit income of the members of the B community and decreases implicit income of the A community (due to the increased taxation), the values of the β's will increase for the A's and decrease for the B's, which to some extent reduces the effect.

Distribution effects within the communities

There are distribution effects due to the propensity to pay as well as taxation. The effect due to the propensity to pay is clear. The sign of V_b determines the sign of the effect attributable to the B community. The total effect can be reduced due to the decrease in the size of the A community if the income effect on β^A is small enough. It is not likely to change the sign of the total effect, though, since it is an order of magnitude smaller than the effect coming from the B community. Hence, the effect will be positive if the demand for language rights has a negative income elasticity, that is, if rights are an inferior good, giving us an argument for more extensive rights for the minority. If the income elasticity is positive, the effect is an argument for less extensive minority rights.

If taxes are positively correlated with income, all V_θ are negative if the planner wants to redistribute from the poor to the rich. However, the income effect will make β^A bigger and β^B smaller. At the same time, δ^A is negative and δ^B positive. Hence, we cannot unambiguously determine the sign of the effect of the additional taxes necessary to pay for the introduction of the right for language B. On the other hand, following the public-finance tradition, we could separate the taxation problem from the expenditure side, and refer the optimal taxation to another 'table'.

Conclusions

In the formal analysis as in the main text, we have seen that there are arguments for more extensive language rights for a minority than what comes out of a 'naive' cost–benefit analysis. But there are also arguments for an optimal discrimination.

The property justifying discrimination in this sense is the concave cost structure. Generally, due to concavity, the per capita costs of a certain right increases more for the minority than for the majority by an equal change in the size of the group. On the other hand, in a dynamic setting, the possible increase in the propensities to pay for the right of members of the minority due to the higher status of the minority language works in the opposite direction.

If the minority community is poorer than the majority, the introduction of the right with its associated fiscal externalites on the majority provides arguments for more extensive rights for the minority than implied by the simple cost–benefit analysis. Finally, distributional effects within the communities provide arguments for more rights for the minority if language rights are inferior goods.

Table 22.1 summarizes these effects.

Table 22.1 Direction of different welfare effects in addition to the benchmark case due to the realization of minority rights

Dynamic effect		Positive fiscal externality on A		Income effect		Demand distribution	
σb^B		Minority/majority income difference		Fiscal externality on A		Language rights	
Positive	Zero	Negative	Positive	Negative	Positive	Inferior	Normal
$+/-$	$-$	$+$	$-$	$-/+$	$-$	$+$	$-$

Note: The welfare effects appear in the last row.

Acknowledgements

Part of the research leading to this chapter has received funding from the European Community's Seventh Framework Program under grant agreement No. 613344 (Project MIME) and was carried out during visits as a guest to Humboldt-Universität zu Berlin and its research group on economics and language, which is gratefully acknowledged. I also thank Michele Gazzola and the editors of this volume for their many constructive comments. A special word of thanks goes to the copy editors who greatly helped in approximating my English idiolect to standard English.

References

D. Abrams and S. Strogatz (2003) 'Modelling the Dynamics of Language Death', *Nature*, 424, 900.

K. Arrow (1951) *Social Choice and Individual Values* (New Haven: Yale University Press).

R. Boadway and A. Shah (2009) *Fiscal Federalism: Principles and Practices of Multiorder Governance* (Cambridge: Cambridge University Press).

J. Cenoz (2008) 'Achievements and Challenges in Bilingual and Multilingual Education in the Basque Country', *AILA Review*, 21, 13–30.

J. Church and I. King (1993) 'Bilingualism and Network Externalities', *Canadian Journal of Economics/Revue canadienne d'économique*, 26, 337–345.

I. Clots-Figueras and P. Masella (2013) 'Education, Language and Identity', *The Economic Journal*, 123, F332–F357.

S. Drinkwater and N. O'Leary (1997) 'Unemployment in Wales: Does Language Matter?', *Regional Studies*, 31, 583–591.

C. Fernando, R.-L. Valijärvi, and R. Goldstein (2010) 'A Model of the Mechanisms of Language Extinction and Revitalization Strategies to Save Endangered Languages', *Human Biology*, 82, 47–75.

J. Fidrmuc and V. Ginsburgh (2007) 'Languages in the European Union: The Quest for Equality and Its Cost', *European Economic Review*, 51, 1351–1369.

J. Fidrmuc, V. Ginsburgh, and S. Weber (2005) Economic Challenges of Multilingual Societies, Research Rep.

J. Gabszewicz, V. Ginsburgh, and S. Weber (2011) 'Bilingualism and Communicative Benefits', *Annals of Economics and Statistics/Annales d'Économie et de Statistique*, 101–102, 271–286.

S. Gal (1979) *Language Shift: Social Determinants of Linguistic Change in Bilingual Austria* (New York: Academic Press).

M. Gazzola (2006) 'Managing Multilingualism in the European Union: Language Policy Evaluation for the European Parliament', *Language Policy*, 5, 393–417.

M. Gazzola (2014a) Language Policy and Linguistic Justice in the European Union: The Socio-Economic Effects of Multilingualism, Research Rep. 15 (Genève: Observatoire 'Economics-Languages-Training', Université de Genève).

M. Gazzola (2014b) 'Partecipazione, esclusione linguistica e traduzione: Una valutazione del regime linguistico dell'Unione europea', *Studi Italiani di Linguistica Teorica e Applicata*, 43, 227–264.

M. Gazzola (2014c) *The Evaluation of Language Regimes. Theory and Application to Multilingual Patent Organisations* (Amsterdam: John Benjamins).

V. Ginsburgh, I. Ortuño-Ortín, and S. Weber (2005) 'Disenfranchisement in Linguistically Diverse Societies. The Case of the European Union', *Journal of the European Economic Association*, 3, 946–965.

V. Ginsburgh and S. Weber (2005) 'Language Disenfranchisement in the European Union', *Journal of Common Market Studies*, 43, 273–286.

F. Grin (1992) 'Towards a Threshold Theory of Minority Language Survival', *Kyklos*, 45, 69–97.

W. Güth, M. Strobel, and B.-A. Wickström (1997) 'Equilibrium Selection in Linguistic Games: Kial ni (ne) parolas esperanton?' In W. Albers, W. Güth, P. Hammerstein, B. Moldovanu, and E. Van Damme (eds.) *Understanding Strategic Interaction: Essays in Honor of Reinhard Selten* (Berlin: Springer), pp. 257–269.

W. Kymlicka and A. Patten (eds.) (2003) *Language Rights and Political Theory* (Oxford: Oxford University Press).

F. Lo Jacomo (1989) 'Optimization in Language Planning' In K. Schubert (ed.) *Interlinguistics: Aspects of the Science of Planned Languages* (Berlin: Mouton de Gruyter), pp. 121–128.

J. Minett and W. Wang (2008) 'Modelling Endangered Languages: The Effects of Bilingualism and Social Structure', *Lingua*, 118, 19–45.

R. Musgrave (1956/1957) 'A Multiple Theory of Budget Determination', *Finanzarchiv*, 17, 333–343.

D. Nettle and S. Romaine (2000) *Vanishing Voices: The Extinction of the World's Languages* (Oxford: Oxford University Press).

M. Patriarca and T. Leppänen (2004) 'Modeling Language Competition', *Physica A*, 338, 296–299.

A. Patten (2009) 'Survey Article: The Justification of Minority Language Rights', *Journal of Political Philosophy*, 17, 102–128.

Y. Peled, P. Ives, and T. Ricento (2014) 'Introduction to the Thematic Issue: Language Policy and Political Theory', *Language Policy*, 13, 295–300.

J. Pool (1991) 'The Official Language Problem', *American Political Science Review*, 85, 495–514.

S. Rendon (2007) 'The Catalan Premium: Language and Employment in Catalonia', *Journal of Population Economics*, 20, 669–686.

T. de Scitovszky (1941) 'A Note on Welfare Propositions in Economics', *Review of Economic Studies*, 9, 77–88.

R. Selten and J. Pool (1991) 'The Distribution of Foreign Language Skills as a Game Equilibrium' In R. Selten (ed.) *Game Equilibrium Models IV* (Berlin: Springer), pp. 64–84.

P. Van Parijs (2002) 'Linguistic Justice', *Politics, Philosophy and Economics*, 1, 59–74.

P. Van Parijs (2011) *Linguistic Justice for Europe and for the World* (Oxford: Oxford University Press).

B.-A. Wickström (2005) 'Can Bilingualism Be Dynamically Stable? A Simple Model of Language Choice', *Rationality and Society*, 17, 81–115.

B.-A. Wickström (2007) 'Fairness, Rights, and Language Rights: On the Fair Treatment of Linguistic Minorities' In P. Baake and R. Borck (eds.) *Public Economics and Public Choice* (Berlin: Springer), pp. 81–101.

B.-A. Wickström (2010) 'Lingvaj rajtoj kaj lingva justeco' In D. Blanke and U. Lins (eds.) *La arto labori kune: Festlibro por Humphrey Tonkin* (Rotterdam: Universala Esperanto-Asocio), pp. 97–103.

B.-A. Wickström (2013) 'The Optimal Babel: An Economic Framework for the Analysis of Dynamic Language Rights' In F. Cabrillo and M. Puchades-Navarro (eds.) *Constitutional Economics and Public Institutions: Essays in Honour of José Casas Pardo* (Cheltenham: Edward Elgar), pp. 322–344.

B.-A. Wickström (2014) 'Indigenes, Immigration, and Integration: A Welfare-Economics Approach to Minority Rights' In F. Forte, R. Mudambi, and P. Navarra (eds.) *A Handbook of Alternative Theories of Public Economics* (Cheltenham: Edward Elgar), pp. 227–242.

23

A Game-Theoretic Analysis of Minority Language Use in Multilingual Societies

José-Ramón Uriarte

23.1 Introduction

To put this chapter into context, we begin by outlining the use of game-theoretic tools in the study of the economics of language.

We know that communication and information transmission between human beings is done mainly by means of natural languages. Communication, information sharing and coordination are relevant topics in economics. Economists know that one of the requirements for reaching efficiency in competitive markets is the sharing of all relevant economic information among all participating agents. But this condition is rarely met in real situations. To make matters worse, it is widely accepted in economics that agents do not have a preference for truth-telling. When they believe that lying is to their advantage, they will do so and will misreport their preferences or any private information they might have. The theory examined in this chapter seeks to understand the mechanisms by which information may be shared when such information is private. Game theorists who have been attracted to this problem have identified signalling as one method by which agents choose among various costly actions that reveal private information (Spence, 1974). Farrel and Rabin (1996) conclude that in real situations, most of the information sharing is done, not through complex Spence-style signalling, but through ordinary or 'cheap' talk. Since cheap talk may communicate private information in equilibrium, the

Parts of this chapter are based on Iriberri and Uriarte (2012), Sperlich and Uriarte (2014) and Uriarte (2015). I am grateful to Itziar Idiazabal, Ilaski Barañano, Nagore Iriberri and Jaromir Kovarik for their helpful comments. I am also grateful to the editors of the present volume for many useful comments and discussions. Financial support provided by the Basque Government and the Ministerio de Economía y Competitividad (ECO2012-31626) is gratefully acknowledged.

literature studying these equilibria has expanded and come to be known as *cheap talk games*.

Even though natural languages are the main vehicles of information transmission, research in this subset of games has not thoroughly addressed the economics of the (natural) language area. The main reason is that in cheap talk games, what matters is any type of communication device or language players share: noises, signs, codes or words with meanings that only the players involved know can be the 'language' used in these contexts (see, in particular, Crawford and Sobel, 1982; Farrel and Rabin, 1996; Demichelis and Weibull, 2008; and Heller, 2014). Blume and Board (2013) weaken the assumption of a perfectly shared language by assuming that individuals speak the same language but have different language competence and may therefore disagree about meaning. Individual language competence is then assumed to be private information, and Blume and Board show that in common-interest games efficiency losses can be severe. A domain where language competence may differ would be the natural language-based code developed under efficiency pressure inside a firm; the language is known by the members of the firm but not well known by outsiders. Weber and Camerer (2003) show how different firm-specific languages might affect post-merger performances.

A natural language is thought to be shaped by some sort of behaviour that tends to optimize the benefits of communication minus the cost of memory and articulation of linguistic expression (see, for example, Selten and Warglien, 2007). That is, a natural language maximizes the transmission of information with the minimum amount of effort. Along this line, Rubinstein (1996) uses optimality arguments as a potential explanation for why certain properties of binary relations are relatively common in natural language. As a general explanation, Rubinstein states that evolutionary forces would select human beings equipped with binary relations which are better for communication. In subsequent works on economics and language, Rubinstein and Glazer (2001, 2004, 2006) present game-theoretic models of the pragmatics of debating in which a listener makes a decision after being persuaded by the arguments presented by some of the debaters.

An area of the economics of language where game theory has been applied is language learning. The pioneering work was conducted by Selten and Pool (1991). These authors presented a general model (with $n \geq 2$ countries and $m \geq n$ languages) that offers reasons why the inhabitants of a country choose to learn an additional language. In the model, languages are the strategies that players may choose to learn, and the payoffs consist of gross communication benefits minus the player's learning costs. Selten and Pool showed the existence of an equilibrium in which players do learn non-native (natural and/or auxiliary) languages. The works of Church and King (1993), Ginsburg et al. (2007), Gabszewicz et al. (2011) and Ginsburgh et al. (2014) are all based on Selten and

Pool's model. The former two papers deal with theoretical issues related to the learning equilibrium; the latter two use data to estimate probable learning decisions. A detailed survey of these works can be found in Chapter 5 in the present volume.

It can safely be said that the bulk of the literature on the use of game-theoretic tools in the economics of language is limited to *semantics* (the study of meaning) and *pragmatics* (the study of meaning in context), though the area of language-learning is a notable exception. In the present chapter, I use game theory to deal with neglected issues related to *language status*. More specifically, I study the language choice behaviour of the speakers of a minority language in contact with a majority language. It is hard to understand why this competitive situation, in which languages and their speech communities compete for speakers has been so thoroughly studied by sociolinguists but has not received the attention it deserves from game theorists. We hope the game-theoretic approach will shed more light on the situation of minority languages and promote further inquiry.

The chapter is organized as follows. In Section 23.2 I present a multilingual society with two official languages that are linguistically distant. It is assumed that this society is a democracy with a highly developed economy and high standard of living. The idea here is to create a benchmark for all societies with minority languages. In Section 23.3 I create a reference point for the bilingual agents of such a society. A reference point is used to compute gains and losses. I propose a reference point for bilingual speakers which consists of the following: linguistic rights, the linguistic notion of *face* (which will serve to model bilinguals' emotion-based utilities) and expectations. Section 23.4 describes a frequently used procedure by which bilinguals decide to use the majority language when they know that they are interacting with interlocutors, some of whom are not speakers of the minority language. It is called the maximin language choice. In Section 23.5 I provide justifications for the assumption of imperfect information about linguistic types in modern multilingual societies. Section 23.6 introduces the Ultimatum Language Game, which is based on the well known (Mini) Ultimatum Game (see Binmore et al.,1995), in which the linguistic type of the interactants is private information. In Section 23.7 a game of language use is presented.[1] The purpose of the section is to study the play of the population of bilingual speakers to see how they might build a linguistic convention which will serve to facilitate their language coordination problem. In Section 23.8, I show how players' utility functions account for both the expected material payoffs and the emotions that arise in response

---

[1] Pool (1986) introduced a conversation game between two bilinguals with perfect information, each having a different native language; the context and the issues studied in that work are very different from ours.

to the opponent's choices. A new equilibrium concept derived from linguistic politeness theory is presented, the *politeness equilibrium*. This has produced, in my view, a more realistic result, which says that the bilinguals' linguistic conventions are based on two pure strategy politeness equilibria. Finally, in Section 23.9 some policy suggestions are offered for increasing the use of the minority language. Section 23.10 concludes the chapter.

23.2   Multilingual societies

Let us consider societies with two official languages: A denotes the language spoken by every individual of the society, and B denotes the language spoken by the *bilingual minority* of the society. That A and B have official status means essentially that:

> *Language Equality: A* and *B* are, by law, equal; that is, they have equal status, rights and privileges relative to their use.

Let α denote the proportion of bilingual speakers and $1 - \alpha$ the proportion of monolingual speakers.[2] Notice that since the two languages are being used by the same social group, the bilingual speakers, we say that languages A and B are in *contact* (see Nelde, 1987, 1995; Winford, 2003).[3] Languages A and B satisfy the following assumption:

Assumption 1: *The languages with official status, A and B, are linguistically distant.*

Under this assumption, successful communication is only possible when the interaction takes place in one language. This assumption is important in order to demonstrate that the language choice is not a trivial one. In other words, it is not possible to have a conversation where one individual speaks A and the other one B because a monolingual agent would not be able to understand what is being said when someone uses language B.[4] This also implies that when a monolingual interacts with a bilingual, the interaction will necessarily take place in the majority language A. For instance, in the Basque Country, mixed language conversations are not common because the linguistic distance between A (Spanish or French) and B (Basque) is big enough to make mutual intelligibility impossible (Basque is a pre-Indoeuropean language).

---

[2] In the present chapter, a monolingual speaker does not become bilingual by learning any second language. It should be clear from the outset that we are referring only to bilingual speakers in the two 'internal' official languages A and B.

[3] It is assumed too that B is spoken *only* in the concerned society.

[4] Passive bilinguals – those who understand B but do not speak it – are not allowed.

Chapter 5 in this volume surveys methods for computing the distance between two languages.

Languages with their speech communities compete for speakers very much like firms competing for a market share. Language contact could be said to be the most extreme form of competition between languages.[5] The pressure of the competition is particularly felt by the minority of those who speak both official languages and support the continued existence of language *B*. The contact situation will influence the language choice behaviour of this minority, the actual use they make of *B* in interactions amongst themselves, their demand and supply of language *B* related goods and services, and the role they play in the transmission of *B*.

The survival of language *B* and its related culture depends not on linguistic rights but on the effective use bilinguals make of *B*. The advice of the Council of Europe, in the European Charter for Regional or Minority Languages, is to implement the following policy:

> A minority language will only survive if it is used everywhere and not just at home. Therefore, the Charter obliges States Parties to actively promote the use of these languages in virtually all domains of public life: education, courts, administration, media, culture, economic and social life, and trans-frontier cooperation. The Council of Europe monitors that the Charter is applied in practice.

In the light of this policy advice, we may now introduce the concept of *language B loyalty*. It means quite simply that the bilingual is aware that the survival of language *B* depends on its use, as the Council of Europe advises, in addition to those in charge of the language policy concerning *B*. Note that in the type of societies we are dealing with, adults learn *B*, parents send their children to schools where content is taught in *B*, and university students may choose some of their lectures in *B*, because these people support the policy of cultural recovery, of maintaining cultural diversity, of national pride and, also, the social benefits of bilingualism. Thus, it is mainly through the education system, mostly public, that people learn *B* and not as described by Selten and Pool (1991) where the driving force of the decision to invest in the learning of *B* is the communicative benefit. Thus, leaving aside adult learners, the cost of learning *B* is relatively small, and it will grant access to the language-related markets of a small community. Hence, the learning of *B* is more a cultural and political decision than an economic decision based on cost. Then one finds different levels (a continuum) of language *B* loyalty among bilingual individuals.

---

[5] Of course, language competition and contact do not occur between languages, but between speakers of languages.

We distinguish between two limit cases:

- *Strongly loyal to B* is a bilingual who will always use or intends to use *B* (orally or in writing) for communication.
- *Weakly loyal to B* is a bilingual who does not care much about the language issue, and uses language *A* most of the time.[6]

Thus, what is at stake in this competitive situation is the society's linguistic and cultural diversity. In this chapter we do not want to describe the process of how a minority language and its culture fade away (see Crystal, 2002). On the contrary, what we want is to study the subtleties of language competition. Thus, we shall assume here multilingual societies which may compete economically and linguistically. Hence, we may add in Assumption 1 that we shall deal with *highly developed multilingual democracies*. These are societies with a well-articulated language policy and resources devoted to schools, teachers, textbooks, editing houses, media and institutions that support the teaching and transmission of language *B* and its related culture. They also have markets where language-related goods are traded.

Examples of multilingual societies which are economically developed and satisfy Assumption 1 are the Basque Country, Ireland, Wales and Scotland. In the Basque Country, the official languages are Basque and Spanish in the Spanish part and French in the French part; in Ireland it is Irish and English; in Wales it is Welsh and English; in Scotland it is Gaelic and English.[7] The minority languages of these societies will set a kind of benchmark for the set of all threatened languages contemplated in Fishman (2001)'s question, 'Why is it so hard to save a threatened language?'

One would think that steady increases in α, the proportion of bilingual speakers, would imply similar steady increases in the social use of *B*. Data concerning Basque shows that the proportion of bilinguals in the period 1991–2011 increased dramatically, rising from 22.30 to 27.00 per cent. On the other hand, measures of the street use of Basque have been made since 1989.[8] In that year,

---

[6] In Section 23.7, language loyalties take the form of pure language strategies available to a bilingual.

[7] We do not include the case of French in Quebec because (a) it is obvious that the fate of French and its related culture is not exclusively in the hands of the francophones of Quebec, (b) French is a minority throughout Canada, but not inside Quebec, and (c) within Quebec, some fractions of the anglophones and francophones are monolingual in their respective language.

[8] Using random samples of anonymously registered conversations in the streets at a given time and place (say, a municipality or sociolinguistic zone), the Street Use Measure of Basque shows the number of individuals observed in conversations speaking Basque out of the total number of individuals observed in the place. To our knowledge,

the use of Basque registered at 10.8 per cent. In 2001 its use rose to 13.3 per cent.[9] Ten years later, in 2011, the percentage of use was the same, at 13.3. Data concerning the use of Irish, Scottish Gaelic and Welsh are obtained through census records (and other survey methods; see, for instance, the Beaufort Research, 2013 on the use of Welsh; and West and Graham, 2011 on Gaelic) and not from neutral observers, as in the case of Basque. Thus, truth telling incentives do not exist and those data are not statistically reliable. And yet the predicament for Irish and Scottish Gaelic described in those surveys is very dramatic. In Sperlich and Uriarte (2014) the data on Basque, Irish and Welsh are studied in the light of a model presented in Section 23.7.[10]

People concerned with the fate of all these languages observe that their actual use outside the educational system is rather weak. We could say that in these societies there seems to exist a kind of paradox, which we may formulate as follows.

Why is it that having the political system and the legal instruments to facilitate the use of *B*, the resources and the education system to implement a language policy in favour of *B*, and, most importantly, the people's support and preference for the language, there is such a weak use of *B*?[11]

23.3 The reference point: Linguistic rights, linguistic politeness and expectations

When linguistic rights are under discussion, it is always with reference to the rights of a minority group in a specified social context to use a certain language. Indeed, minority languages may have the right, but majority languages have the power, since their usage covers every conceivable domain, and has the support of the established political power (see Kimlicka and Patten, 2003).[12]

---

the methodology for measuring the street use of a minority language based on anonymous observations has been developed by the group Soziolinguistika Klusterra – the Sociolinguistic Cluster, which operates in the Basque Country (see Altuna and Basurto, 2013).

[9] Notice that the probability of a bilingual random match is α^2 and therefore for a clear increase in the street use of *B* a drastic increase in α is needed. See Sperlich and Uriarte (2014).

[10] Of course, there are more minority languages satisfying Assumption 1 and belonging to *economically developed democracies*; the problem is that it is typically hard to get data which allow for deeper insight into daily language use.

[11] See for example in Scotland, the Gaelic Language Act of 2005; in the Basque Country, the Law of Normalization of *Euskera*'s Use of 1982; in Wales, the Welsh Language Measure of 2011, which gave Welsh official status.

[12] The concept of linguistic disenfranchisement developed by Ginsburgh and Weber (2011) by which some language(s) is (are) selected for, say, official use and as a consequence the individuals who do not speak the selected language(s) are disenfranchised

As with many economic questions, a *reference point* is needed for under-standing bilinguals' language choice behaviour. But note that here we are not dealing with consumption plans nor are we, say, trading with financial assets or in the insurance market. We are dealing with a collective good, language. Thus, we need to understand how bilingual people use the reference point to conceptualize and compute gains and losses.

In linguistic politeness theory (see Brown and Levinson, 1987), *face* is the public self-image that every individual wants to claim for him or herself. It consists of two related aspects:

- *Positive face*: one's self-esteem. Positive face is characterized by the desire to be liked, admired, ratified and related to positively.
- *Negative face*: one's freedom of choice of action and freedom from imposition.

A *face threatening act* is an act that inherently damages the *face* of the addressee or the speaker by acting in opposition to the wants and desires of the other. *Face* can be *lost*, *maintained* or *enhanced* and must be constantly attended to in interaction. This will be used to define (in Section 23.8) a utility function for bilinguals that will capture the emotions derived from acts that damage *face*. In general, people cooperate (and assume each other's cooperation) in maintaining face in interaction; such cooperation is based on the mutual vul-nerability of *face* (Brown and Levinson, 1987). Politeness consists of a set of verbal and non-verbal strategies intended to maintain each other's faces with the purpose of creating a common ground on which the interactants may bar-gain and compete. We shall use the vulnerability of *face* to define the bilingual's utility function (see Section 23.8).

An economist may think of *face* as an element of the reference point that any individual has. I propose a reference point for bilinguals composed of three elements: linguistic rights, the linguistic notion of face and expectations. How do these constituent parts of a bilinguals' reference point interact with one another? To have a more precise view of the nature of bilinguals' reference points, we need to adapt the developments of prospect theory (Kahneman and Tversky, 1979; Tversky and Kahneman, 1992; Köszegi and Rabin, 2006) to the field of minority language economics. We should bear in mind that:

1. We are dealing with a minority language in contact with a language known by all members of the society; thus for its survival, B has to be used in social

---

and their well-being diminished, is related to linguistic rights. In what follows we take the limit case, by which language B has passed from a state of no rights, and completely disenfranchised bilingual individuals, to becoming an official language.

situations to avoid being substituted by language *A*. Only bilinguals can do this job, for better or worse.

2. Since *B* is, by law, equal to *A*, then legal linguistic equality is perceived by bilinguals as the status quo for language *B*.

3. Yet for bilinguals the linguistic equality claimed by the law is in fact an aspiration; it is what they expect to reach, rather than a reality. The European Charter for Regional or Minority Languages shows the language policy bilinguals must implement to convert that aspiration into a reality. As a consequence, bilinguals scrutinize one another's behaviour for conformity to the policy.

4. Given the difficulties derived from competition with language *A*, perceptions about linguistic equality also impact on bilinguals' expectations. Every bilingual has, to differing degrees, expectations about *B* increasing its speech population and not being always a minority language. Those expectations play a significant role in shaping the feelings of gains and losses when it comes to the actual usage of *B*. In Section 23.8, we assume that a bilingual computes gains and losses through the effect that the language actually used in the interaction has on his *face wants*.

23.4   The maximin language choice

We present here a commonly utilized language choice procedure. Let $C_j = \{c_{jA}, c_{jB}\}$ denote the language competence set of individual $j = 1, \ldots, n.$; where c_{jl} denotes individual *j*th's competence in language $l = A, B$. Let c_{jl} be a number in the set $\{0, 5, 10\}$, where 0 stands for no knowledge of language *l*, 5 for regular knowledge (he or she understands but cannot speak) and 10 for perfect knowledge. Let individuals *r* and *s* have the following language competencies: $C_r = \{c_{rA} = 10 \text{ and } c_{rB} = 5\}$ and $C_s = \{c_{sA} = 10 \text{ and } c_{sB} = 0\}$. Let the rest of the group $C_j = \{c_{jA} = 10 \text{ and } c_{jB} = 10\}$, $j \neq r, s$. This collection of individuals could be a group of friends in which everyone knows everyone else's language abilities. Everyone knows who is bilingual, that *r* is a passive bilingual who understands *B* fairly well but cannot speak it, and that *s* is monolingual. Let us assume that the bilinguals form a majority in this group. When the conversation starts, there is a tendency to choose the language of the conversation by using, implicitly, the following rule (based on Van Parijs, 2011): let $V_l = (c_{jl}, c_{rl}, c_{sl})$ denote the vector of every individual competence in language $l = A, B$ and $j \neq r, s$. Let us consider two languages *l′* and *l″*

$$l' \succsim l'' \iff \min V_{l'} \geq \min V_{l''}.$$

That is, language *l′* is at least as good as language *l″* if the minimum individual competence on *l′* is at least equal to the minimum individual competence on

l''. Since $\min V_A = (10, \ldots, 10, 10) = 10$ and $\min V_B = (10, \ldots, 5, 0) = 0$, then the language which this predominantly bilingual group will choose will be A.

Proposition 1: In the type of societies we are dealing with, an interaction in which the number of bilingual participants is greater than the number of monolingual participants, the language of the interaction is frequently chosen by means of the maximin language rule.

Why do the bilinguals use the maximin language rule and not a different language decision procedure? Our view is that the *linguistic politeness norms* developed in a situation of language contact help monolinguals block the use of B in their presence.

23.5 Information in modern multilingual societies

As said in Section 23.2, we want to address the use of minority language B in multilingual societies which are economically highly developed. Since we are dealing with competitive societies both in the economic domain and the linguistic domain, we seek to know the conditions under which B might be used in the dynamic parts of these societies, in the urban areas, by the bilingual population working in the core industries of those economies. We think that the survival of B as more than a museum piece to be admired by scholars depends on how often the bilingual population uses B while participating directly and indirectly in these parts of society.

In modern societies, particularly in the areas mentioned previously, there is great mobility (both social and geographical) in the work force. In this context, bilinguals often participate in anonymous interactions in which the linguistic type (bilingual or monolingual) is private information.

Language contact is also a relevant element affecting information. As noted by Nelde (1995), 'neither contact nor conflict can occur between languages; they are conceivable only between speakers of languages and between the language communities!' That is, contact, competition and conflict occur among the bilingual speakers of B and those who only speak A, the official language of the state. Permanent contact with a majority of speakers of language A eliminates some relevant signals or traits of native speakers of language B; for instance, accents are erased. The accents are signals that could reveal who speaks B and who does not, but the contact situation means that both bilinguals and monolinguals will have a similar accent, shaped by the dominant language. For example, on the Spanish side of the Basque Country people of any linguistic type have a Spanish accent, while on the French side, people have a French accent.

For Nelde (1987), 'contact between languages always involves an element of conflict'. Thus, in a language contact situation, the possibility of conflict is always present. Matching between a bilingual and a monolingual occurs more often than the bilingual–bilingual matching. Furthermore, if a monolingual is addressed in *B*, or observes in the interactive partner a display of markers signalling the desire to speak in *B*, he would be forced to reveal his type and confess his ignorance of the official language *B*; this might create feelings of insecurity. In terms of politeness theory (see Section 23.3), both the *positive face* (i.e. the desire to be liked and admired) and the *negative face* (i.e. the freedom from imposition) of the monolingual would be damaged. Further, forcing the conversation in language *A*, the bilingual's *negative face* would be damaged too. And this injury of each other's *face* could hinder the minimal alignment of interests needed for an interaction to follow its natural path (to a common ground in which the interactants may bargain and compete). Thus, we may say that, in the present context, messages conveying support for *B*, preference for language *B* or the desire to speak in *B* could be harmful for both sides. In other words, *talk is not cheap*. (This is developed in Uriarte, 2015.)

But in face-to-face interactions, people try to avoid conflict and to this end they develop specific strategies. Linguistic politeness-based strategies are just a behaviour built to avoid or minimize confrontation. In our context, this has a disproportionate impact on bilinguals because they may choose between languages. Hence, to complete the gradual process of eliminating informative linguistic signals, which is ongoing in modern societies, the bilinguals themselves develop uninformative linguistic strategies (see Section 23.7 for a formal definition) to avoid any possibility of upsetting the (unknown) monolingual. Essentially, that kind of strategy would be the following: if you are in the role of speaker, then start the conversation in language *A*; if you are in the role of hearer and you are addressed in language *A*, then respond in language *A*. You would use language B only if your (unknown) speech partner speaks to you in *B*. Therefore, if two bilinguals play this strategy, they would fail to coordinate in language *B*.

To conclude, in the type of societies we are dealing with, it could be assumed that, in many relevant domains and interactions, there is asymmetric information about the linguistic type of the interactive partners; see also how Blume and Board (2013) apply this assumption to language competence.

Assumption 2: *The participants in an interaction do not have, ex ante, any information about the linguistic type (bilingual or monolingual) of any individual conversation partner. They only know the proportion of bilingual and monolingual speakers, α and $(1 - α)$ respectively, of the society.*

23.6 The ultimatum language game

Assume a situation in which a representative of firm X located in a certain area of the country is sent to meet a representative of firm Y located in another part of the country to negotiate the price of an input produced by firm Y and used intensively by firm X. The representative of firm X is bilingual and is considering using language *B* in the meeting. The only information both representatives have about each other is their name and rank in the hierarchy of the firm. The average proportion of bilinguals in the country is α. The use of *B* in the meeting would only be possible if the representative of Y is bilingual too. Both representatives have imperfect information about the linguistic type of the other.

Contrary to the opinion of Binmore et al. (1995) that 'in everyday life, we rarely play pure take-it-or-leave-it games', bilinguals participate very often in conversations that might be viewed as a take-it-or-leave-it game. The game we describe in this section is an example of a common situation faced by bilinguals.

Let us suppose that both representatives are bilingual speakers with different levels of loyalty to the minority language; let the representative of X be very loyal to *B* and the representative of Y weakly loyal (see Section 23.2 for the definitions of loyalty). We can model a situation that is likely to happen by means of a simple game whose structure is similar to Selten's Chain Store Paradox, later used by Binmore et al. (1995) as the Ultimatum Minigame. In our context this is a game in which the linguistic type (bilingual or monolingual) is private information (see Figure 23.1). Nature moves first and chooses a bilingual speaker to meet a bilingual hearer with probability α^2; and a monolingual speaker with a bilingual hearer with probability $\alpha(1 - \alpha)$.

Note that the game describes not the economic negotiation itself, that is, how an agreement is reached about the amount and final price of a certain input needed by firm X and produced by firm Y. Rather the game shows a preliminary phase of the negotiation, the phase in which the language to be used in the negotiation is determined.

Let firm Y's representative be the player I, the *speaker*, and let the representative of X be player II, the *hearer*. Players have two actions. Player I's actions are languages *A* and *B*. If player I chooses *B*, it is assumed that player II who is highly loyal to language *B* will agree to negotiate using language *B*, and the game ends. But if player I chooses *A*, then we assume II would think, with few doubts, that player I is monolingual and therefore his available action *B* is superfluous. He thinks that the actual set of actions for him would consist of language *A* and *No (negotiation)*. The latter action means that he would leave the negotiation table and both players would get zero.

Payoffs indicate the differences in the players' preference intensity for *B*. Player I is indifferent about using language *A* or language *B*; in both cases he gets 2. Player II prefers to negotiate in language *B*. If player I chooses *B*, then II will get 3 (because for this player it is a signal of trust and of being well treated by I). If I chooses *A*, then II must choose between following the conversation in language *A* *reluctantly*, which, in terms of payoffs, means he would

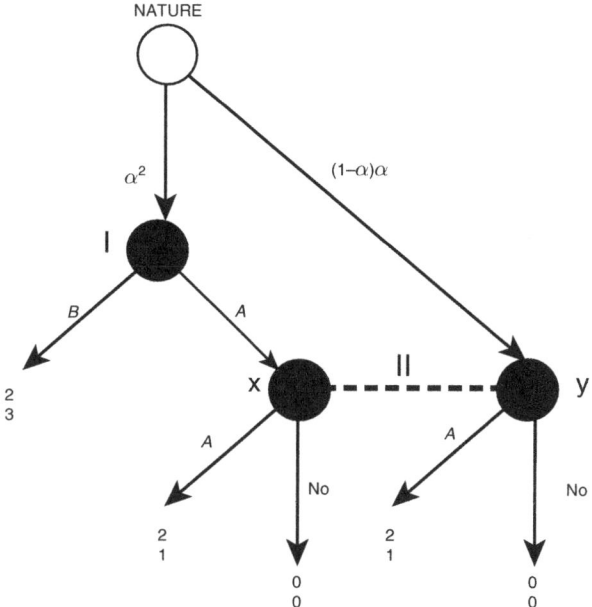

Figure 23.1 The ultimatum language game

get 1, and saying *No*, which would end any possible negotiation, netting zero for both.

Denote the probability that player I chooses language A by p_A; the probabilities assigned to node x and y are denoted by p_x and p_y, respectively. Given player I's choice of A, player II's information set is reached, and, then, regardless of II's belief in his information set, language A is II's optimal choice. Thus, the game has a weak sequential equilibrium in which the strategy profile is (A, A) and II's belief system, if it is consistent with this profile, would be $p_x = \alpha$ and $p_y = 1 - \alpha$, because $p_A = 1$. In this equilibrium, bilinguals speak in language A.

The degree of loyalty of a bilingual speaker to language B will determine the propensity of choosing B, or, more generally, a strategy supporting the use of B, in a given interaction. In general, it is at the beginning of a conversation between bilingual people, unknown to each other, when loyalties condition the language to be used in the conversation. Indeed, it is the speaker, the one who initiates the conversation, who leads the process of choosing the language. But who starts the conversation is a matter of protocol and it seems that, by protocol, the first mover must be the host, player I. Under imperfect information, the weakly loyal player I will choose A with a high probability because he does not care much about the situation of B as a threatened language. It could also happen that player I is not conscious that he is involved in a game and that player II might have a strong preference for using B in the negotiation. The only thing player I is sure of is that the main interest of II, as representative of firm X, is to reach a good agreement.

Proposition 2: Given the propensities of both players to choose B, and how player II perceives the game, the most likely outcome in a one-shot game is the weak sequential equilibrium with profile (A, A) and belief system $(p_x = \alpha,\ p_y = 1 - \alpha)$. Thus, the language that will be used for the negotiation will be A.

One might question why we do not account for the possibility of equilibria that are not weakly sequential and in which B would be spoken, such as (B, No) in which II's beliefs are unrestricted. Note that in the Ultimatum Game you are being offered amounts of, say, money that you, as a responder, may accept or reject. Game theorists were led to reconsider the subgame-perfect prediction of traditional game theory because there was an increasing amount of experimental evidence that positive offers, below a certain amount, were rejected (see Roth and Erev, 1995; Roth et al., 1991). In the present Ultimatum Language Game, actions are languages whose use gives rise to communication benefits as payoffs. There is no empirical evidence of 'rejecting' language A; that is, of player II, the hearer, refusing to speak in the language used by player I, the speaker. Of course, this does not mean that rejection never happens. But, contrary to the detailed study of responders' rejections in the Ultimatum Game, the frequency of language A rejections has not been studied. In fact, social norms encoded in politeness-based strategies coupled with imperfect information reinforce the weak sequential rationality and the use of A by bilinguals. Notice also that the representatives have two different hierarchical roles in this interaction. The representative of X is the potential buyer of a product sold by firm Y. Thus, the representative of firm Y is in a position of relatively greater power and control. This situation determines asymmetric levels of politeness between Player I, the speaker, and Player II, the hearer (see Brown and Levinson, 1987). It is II who has to use a more careful *politeness strategy* in choosing words and language to avoid any confrontation. Thus, II has no choice but to get only a good agreement even if that means his linguistic preferences are not satisfied at all.

One might also ask why II has not contemplated the case that a Player I choosing A could be bilingual too, and include B as an additional action that would allow Player I to code switch from A to B. Code switching is allowed in a game presented in Iriberri and Uriarte (2012). But in the context of the present game, Player II's actual action set seems to be, again, the result of *linguistic politeness norms* grown in a language contact situation, coupled with player II's analysis of the game and the time pressure imposed by a conversation where decision-making (through responses) should be particularly fast.

23.7 The bilinguals as a player population: The building of linguistic conventions

Who is to blame in the Ultimatum Language Game for the bilinguals speaking in language *A*? Is it the weakly loyal player I? Is it the extremely loyal player II whose beliefs led him not to consider replying in language *B*? Did player II misread the game? Is the imperfect information the main source of bilinguals coordinating in *A*? To answer these questions, we are led to study how bilinguals build linguistic conventions to solve their language coordination problem. Let us assume the following:

Assumption 3: *Bilingual players prefer to speak B rather than A.*

A monolingual speaker will always get a sure payoff (or net communication benefit), say, *n*. Since language choices are made under imperfect information, a bilingual may choose *A*; in that case, we will assume that he will get, as a monolingual, the payoff *n*, because this was a voluntary choice. Bilingual speakers will get the maximum payoff, *m*, when they coordinate in *B*. However, $(n - c) > 0$ would be the payoff to a bilingual speaker who, having chosen *B*, is matched to a monolingual and, therefore, is forced to speak *A*. Then *c* denotes the frustration cost felt by this bilingual. In the present context, the payoffs could be interpreted as the net benefits obtained from satisfying the communication needs and, additionally for bilinguals, the degree of language preference satisfaction.[13] The next assumption orders these payoffs.

Assumption 4: *For a given α such that $0 < α < (1 - α)$, the payoff ordering is given by $m > n > c > 0$. Further, $α(m - n) > c(1 - α) > 0$.*

The first inequality, $m > n$, is due to Assumption 2. Since bilinguals prefer *B* to *A*, then they will get a higher utility when they interact in their preferred language *B* than in the case when they choose to use *A*. Further, *c* is smaller than the weighted benefits. In a language contact situation bilinguals face frequent language choice situations. Their linguistic behaviour would then be shaped by repetitive language decision-making. Thus, it is natural for bilinguals to have both language *strategies* and *linguistic conventions* which would serve to minimize the frictions associated with their frequent language coordination decisions and communication problems. We have here a nice real-life example of a one-player population game: a game played by the population,

---

[13] $n =$ communication benefit – speech production cost in language $A = b_1 - c_1$.
$m =$ communication benefit + language *B* preference maximization benefit – speech production cost in language $B = b_2 - c_2$.

N, of bilingual speakers. To facilitate the evolutionary analysis, we now build the Language Use Game (LUG). Under Assumptions 1–4, bilinguals' language behaviour is captured fairly well by the following pure strategies:

s_1: Always use B, whether you know for certain you are speaking to a bilingual individual or not. Use A only when the speech partner reveals he or she is of the monolingual type.

s_2: Use B only when you know for certain that you are speaking to a bilingual individual; use A otherwise.

Notice that in choosing s_1, the bilingual type is revealed. With s_2 the type is hidden; thus, s_2 reinforces the asymmetric information setting, and if both bilinguals play strategy s_2, they will speak A. The agents of the bilingual population play the LUG having $S = \{s_1, s_2\}$ as their *common* strategy set. Let x denote the fraction of bilingual agents playing pure strategy s_1 at any point t in time. We want to build a selection mechanism in continuous time that favours some strategy over the others, the *replicator dynamics*.[14] The replicators are the pure strategies s_i $(i = 1, 2)$ and the *replicator dynamics* will tell us, at each moment of time, the fraction of bilinguals playing s_1 and s_2. The LUG could be easily explained now as follows (see Figure 23.2). There are two possible states of nature: *bilingual* and *monolingual*. Bilingual speakers are unsure of the state when they choose a strategy. A bilingual expects to meet another bilingual with probability α and play the game described by the payoff matrix on the left side

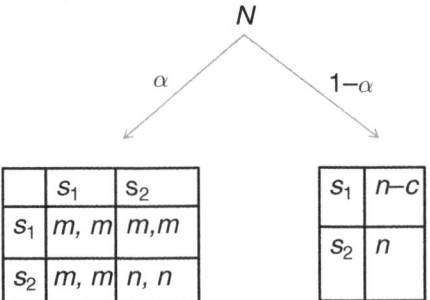

Figure 23.2   The language use game

---

[14] We assume that the bilingual population consists of a large but finite number of individuals who play a certain pure strategy s_i, $(i = 1, 2)$ in the two-player game LUG. The interactions are modelled as pairwise random matching between agents of the bilingual population; that is, no more than two (randomly chosen) individuals interact at a time. To derive the replicator dynamics, it is assumed that the LUG is played continuously in the described manner. For more details, see Weibull (1995).

Table 23.1 Expected payoffs associated with the language use game

	s_1	s_2
s_1	$\alpha(m-n)-c(1-\alpha)$, $\alpha(m-n)-c(1-\alpha)$	$\alpha(m-n)-c(1-\alpha)$, $\alpha(m-n)$
s_2	$\alpha(m-n)$, $\alpha(m-n)-c(1-\alpha)$	0, 0

Note: In each cell, lines 1 and 2 are the payoffs of players 1 and 2 respectively.

of Figure 23.2 (see Assumption 4). With probability $1-\alpha$, the bilingual expects to meet a monolingual and, depending on the strategy chosen, get the corresponding payoff shown in the payoff column on the right side of Figure 23.2 (the monolingual will get, as said above, n). Notice that in choosing s_1, there is the risk of getting the minimum payoff, $n-c$. With s_2 the bilingual would expect to get, at least, n.

Table 23.1 shows the matrix of expected payoffs associated with the game.

Iriberri and Uriarte (2012) prove the following result.

Proposition 3: Under Assumptions 1–4, there exists an interior mixed strategy Nash equilibrium in which the proportion of the bilingual population playing s_1 is $x^* = 1 - \frac{c(1-\alpha)}{\alpha(m-n)}$. This equilibrium is evolutionarily and asymptotically stable in the associated one-population replicator dynamics.[15] There are two additional Nash equilibria (s_1, s_2) and (s_2, s_1) which are unstable.

The mixed strategy equilibrium as a linguistic convention

Evolutionary stability in the present context means that the equilibrium x^* is a *linguistic convention* built by the bilingual speakers.[16] Indeed, the bilingual population is optimally partitioned in two groups, Nx^* and $N(1-x^*)$. Bilinguals of the former group speak B when they interact with any other bilingual; bilinguals of the latter group speak A between them.

Does this evolutionary equilibrium x^* have predictive power? The answer is yes if we redefine x^* by assuming n is the only payoff that does not change with α. Then Sperlich and Uriarte (2014) obtained increasing and convex Nash equilibrium functions $x^* = x^*(\alpha)$ that associate with each α the corresponding mixed

---

[15] It is known that the replicator dynamics could be derived from behaviours observed in social interactive learning settings; for instance, the aspiration-based learning model of Binmore et al. (1995).

[16] For the relation of evolutionary stability equilibrium and conventions, see Weibull (1995).

strategy Nash equilibrium. With data about the use of Basque, Irish and Welsh, they show that the empirical models based on $x^*(\alpha)$ could be good predictors of the fraction of bilingual speakers who, in real-life situations, use language B in their interactions.

23.8   Linguistic politeness equilibrium

This section is based on Uriarte (2015). In the maximin language choice procedure (Section 23.4) and in the Ultimatum Language Game (Section 23.6) we conjectured that the language choice behaviour in those two settings was shaped by linguistic politeness-based social norms developed in a situation in which a minority language comes into contact with a majority language. In particular, bilinguals' uninforming strategies are built to avoid possible conflicts and the difficulties derived from imperfect information (see Section 23.5). The strategy s_2 of hiding the bilingual type does not contradict the interlocutor's language, whether A or B; s_2 is an easy strategy to follow that does not conflict with any linguistic type. Revealing the bilingual type, i.e. playing s_1, makes coordination in B possible, but it is rather risky because you might suffer a frustration cost, and it is more demanding since it requires you to lead the language coordination process, which may conflict with monolinguals. Hence, we may say the following about the relative popularity of s_1 and s_2:

Corollary 1: Based on *politeness theory* (Brown and Levinson, 1987), *dialog theory* (Garrod and Pickering, 2009) and the *principles of communication effectiveness and efficiency* (that is, the maximization of the *benefits* of communication relative to the memory and articulation *costs* of linguistic production, as emphasized by Selten and Warglien 2007), the strategy s_2 may easily become more popular than s_1.

Let us define now a bilingual's utility function in a way that captures the *vulnerability of face* as follows:

$$u_I(s_I, s_{II}) = F_I(s_I, s_{II}) \times \pi_I(s_I, s_{II})$$

$$u_{II}(s_I, s_{II}) = F_{II}(s_I, s_{II}) \times \pi_{II}(s_I, s_{II}).$$

Suppose that two bilinguals play the combination of strategies (s_I, s_{II}), where $s_i \in S = \{s_1, s_2\}$ is player i's strategy, $i = I, II$. The elements $\pi_i(s_I, s_{II})$ denote the expected material payoffs to bilingual I and II derived from the strategy profile (s_I, s_{II}), as shown in Table 23.1; $F_i(s_I, s_{II})$ is the parameter denoting the feelings of player i caused by the strategy profile (s_I, s_{II}). The value of the parameter will capture the vulnerability of *face*. As stated by Brown and Levinson (1987), in an interaction *face can be enhanced* (by a certain factor when both play s_1 and thus talk in B; that is, $F_i(s_1, s_1) = f^* > \alpha(m - n)/[\alpha(m - n) - c(1 - \alpha)])$, *maintained* (so $F_I(s_2, s_1) = F_{II}(s_1, s_2) = 1$) *or lost* (so $F_i(s_2, s_2) = -1, F_I(s_1, s_2) = F_{II}(s_2, s_1) = -1$). *Face* is *lost* because the bilingual choosing the uninforming strategy s_2 is hurting the *face* of the one who chooses s_1, and it is *maintained* because the one choosing the safe s_2 is not bothered by the other's choice. Thus the elements of the new matrix of expected utilities would be: $u_i(s_1, s_1) = f^*[\alpha(m - n) - c(1 - \alpha)]$, $u_i(s_2, s_2) = 0$, $u_I(s_1, s_2) = u_{II}(s_2, s_1) = -\alpha(m - n) + c(1 - \alpha)$ and $u_I(s_2, s_1) = u_{II}(s_1, s_2) = \alpha(m - n)$, $i = I, II$.

Now let us assume, as usual, that each bilingual seeks to maximize his utility function given the emotions he has felt during the course of the interaction. The following result has been proved in Uriarte (2015).

Proposition 4: The LUG has two symmetric politeness equilibria in pure strategies, (s_1, s_1) and (s_2, s_2), which are evolutionarily stable, and an interior mixed strategy equilibrium. In the (s_1, s_1) equilibrium, bilinguals speak their preferred language, B, and in the (s_2, s_2) equilibrium, they speak language A.

Corollary 2: From Corollary 1, the politeness equilibrium (s_2, s_2) seems to be more likely to occur than the (s_1, s_1) equilibrium.

Corollary 2 says that under Assumptions 1–4, in real-life situations bilinguals will coordinate in language A more often than in language B.

Predictions from politeness analysis
The following two predictions can be derived from our analysis:

1. *The best response to s_1 is s_1 and the best response to s_2 is s_2.* These predictions seem to be closer to real bilinguals' behaviour because the stylized facts are that when a bilingual is addressed in language B his or her answer would, very likely, be in B. And when a bilingual is addressed by an unknown speaker (monolingual or bilingual) in language A, it seldom happens that the bilingual would code-switch to B in his or her answer, as stressed by the Ultimatum Language Game (Section 23.6).
2. With imperfect information, bilinguals use the convention (s_2, s_2) amongst themselves, that is, language A, more often than the convention (s_1, s_1), that is, language B.

23.9 Policy suggestions

This section suggests the implementation of policy measures aimed at increasing the *positive signalling of bilinguals*. These signals should be supported by a broad social consensus. The following examples of policy measures could be useful:

- Example 1: Visual signals to reduce imperfect information. The society should accept that bilinguals need to recognize each other by means of (well designed) visual signals (e.g. pins).
- Example 2: Cheap-talk. In the absence of external signals and before starting or at the start of a conversation, bilinguals should have the opportunity to send a message indicating their linguistic type. The content of the message should be constructed thoughtfully, so as to cause no harm and impose no cost on monolinguals (see Section 23.5).
- Example 3: Active bilingual speakers. In situations where the maximin language rule is usually applied, bilinguals should take a more active role; e.g. one bilingual might translate what it is being said to those who do not speak B.
- Example 4: Policy-makers should clarify the implications of language strategies. That is, strategy s_1 has to be related to behaviour in favour of *cultural diversity*. And strategy s_2 should be considered to be the source of bilinguals not speaking B.

23.10　Conclusion

In this chapter, we have assumed modern multilingual societies, such as those found in western Europe: the Basque Country, Ireland, Scotland and Wales. These societies have two official languages which are linguistically distant. We have assumed that in the dynamic parts of these modern economies, bilinguals frequently choose the language to be used in the next interaction under conditions of imperfect information. Thus, we have considered the language contact situation occurring in economically well-endowed societies with well-articulated language policies to promote the minority language and with enough resources to finance an education system capable of satisfying the societies' demands for a bilingual education and language diversity. The reason to proceed this way is to use these societies as a benchmark for a set of multilingual societies with threatened minority languages. Given this setting, the chapter has focused on the study of the language choice behaviour of bilingual speakers.

Bilinguals participate very often in conversations that might be viewed as a take-it-or-leave-it language game. That is, bilinguals, as listeners, are frequently addressed in the majority language. It is possible that the speaker is also bilingual. Then the bilingual listener will, frequently, respond in the majority language, even though he or she would prefer to speak in the minority language. Our view is that this behaviour may be explained by the influence of imperfect information coupled with social norms encoded in politeness strategies grown in a context of language contact. All these elements reinforce the weak sequential equilibrium outcome, in which two bilinguals will be speaking in the majority language (see Figure 23.1).

A more complete strategic analysis shows that bilinguals play, essentially, two pure strategies: s_1 – *reveal your bilingual type* – and s_2 – *hide your bilingual type*. The former is riskier than the latter; further, s_1 might be perceived as a perturbation to the alignment process between interlocutors of a different type. In linguistic politeness theory, s_1 could be labelled as a face threatening act that damages the *face* of the monolingual. Thus, under imperfect information, bilinguals find the strategy of hiding the type (i.e. of keeping information imperfect), s_2, less demanding and could become easily more popular than s_1.

If we redefine the bilingual speakers' utility functions to make them sensitive to *face threatening acts*, then we find that the politeness equilibria (s_1, s_1) and (s_2, s_2) are the linguistic conventions that the bilinguals use to solve their language coordination problem. This result seems to be a more realistic description of when two bilinguals speak B or when they speak A. The politeness model predicts that the relatively low use of B observed in the societies under study (from less to more usage: Irish, Scottish Gaelic, Welsh and Basque) is because, under imperfect information, the convention more frequently used by bilinguals is based on the strategy *hide your bilingual type*; that is, the politeness equilibrium (s_2, s_2). Accordingly, the future research will be on dynamics: the empirical and theoretical reasons why the system gravitates towards the (s_2, s_2) equilibrium.

References

O. Altuna and A. Basurto (2013) *A Guide to Language Use Observation: Survey Methods* (Central Publishing Services of the Basque Government: Vitoria-Gasteiz).

Beaufort Research (2013) Exploring Welsh Speakers' Language Use in Their Daily Lives (http://www.beaufortresearch.co.uk/BBQ01260eng.pdf).

K. Binmore, J. Gale and L. Samuelson (1995) 'Learning to be Imperfect', *Games and Economic Behavior*, 8, 56–90.

A. Blume and O. Board (2013) 'Language Barriers', *Econometrica*, 81, 781–812.

P. Brown and S. Levinson (1987) *Politeness: Some Universals in Language Usage* (Cambridge: Cambridge University Press).

Council of Europe: http://hub.coe.int/what-we-do/culture-and-nature/minority languages

J. Church and I. King (1993) 'Bilingualism and Network Externalities', *Canadian Journal of Economics*, 26, 337–345.

D. Crystal (2002) *Language Death* (Cambridge: Cambridge University Press).

V. Crawford and J. Sobel (1982) 'Strategic Information Transmission', *Econometrica*, 50, 1431–1451.

S. Demichelis and J. Weibull (2008) 'Language, Meaning, and Games: A Model of Communication, Coordination, and Evolution', *American Economic Review*, 98, 1292–1311.

K. Desmet, I. Ortuño-Ortín and R. Wacziarg (2012) 'The Political Economy of Linguistic Cleavages', *Journal of Development Economics*, 97, 322–338.

J. Farrel and M. Rabin (1996) 'Cheap Talk', *Journal of Economic Perspectives*, 10, 103–118.

J. Fishman (2001) 'Why Is It so Hard to Save a Threatened Language?' In J. Fishman (ed.) *Can Threatened Languages Be Saved?* (Clevedon: Multilingual Matters), pp. 1–22.

S. Garrod and M. Pickering (2009) 'Alignment in Dialogue' In G. Gaskell (ed.) *The Oxford Handbook of Psycholinguistics* (Oxford: Oxford University Press), DOI:10.1093/oxfordhb/9780198568971.013.0026.

V. Ginsburgh, I. Ortuño-Ortín and S. Weber (2007) 'Learning foreign Languages. Theoretical and Empirical Implications of the Selten and Pool Model', *Journal of Economic Behavior and Organization*, 64, 337–347.

J. Gabszewicz, V. Ginsburgh and S. Weber (2011) 'Bilingualism and Communicative Benets', *Annals of Economics and Statistics*, 101/102, 271–286.

V. Ginsburgh, J. Melitz and F. Toubal (2014) Foreign Language Learning: An Econometric Analysis, CEPR Discussion Paper 10101.

V. Ginsburgh and S. Weber (2011) *How Many Languages Do We Need? The Economics of Linguistic Diversity* (Princeton and Oxford: Princeton University Press).

Y. Heller (2014) 'Language, Meaning, and Games: A Model of Communication, Coordination, and Evolution: Comment', *American Economic Review*, 104, 1857–1863.

N. Iriberri and J-R. Uriarte (2012) 'Minority Language and the Stability of Bilingual Equilibria', *Rationality and Society*, 2, 442–462.

D. Kahneman and A. Tversky (1979) 'Prospect Theory: An Analysis of Decision under Risk', *Econometrica*, 47, 263–291.

W. Kimlicka and A. Patten (eds.) (2003) *Language Rights and Political Theory* (Oxford: Oxford University Press).

B. Köszegi and M. Rabin (2006) 'A Model of Reference-Dependent Preferences', *Quarterly Journal of Economics*, 121, 1133–1165.

P. Nelde (1987) 'Language Contact Means Language Conict', *Journal of Multilingual and Multicultural Development*, 8, 33–42.

P. Nelde (1995) 'Language Contact and Conict: The Belgian Experience and the European Union' In S. Wright and H. Kelly (eds.) *Languages in Contact and Conict: Experiences in the Netherlands and Belgium* (Clevedon: Multilingual Matters), pp. 65–82.

J. Pool (1986) 'Optimal Strategies in Linguistic Games' In J. Fishman, A. Tabouret-Keller, M. Clyne, B. Krishnamurti and M. Abdulaziz (eds.) *The Fergusonian Impact. In Honor of Charles A. Ferguson. Volume 2. Sociolinguistics and the Sociology of Language* (Berlin: Mouton de Gruyter), pp. 157–171.

A. Roth and I. Erev (1995) 'Learning in Extensive-Form Games: Experimental Data and Simple Dynamic Models in the Intermediate Term', *Games and Economic Behavior*, 8, 164–212.

A. Roth, V. Prasnikar, M. Okuno-Fujiwara and S. Zamir (1991) 'Bargaining and Market Power in Jerusalem, Ljubljana, Pittsburgh, and Tokyo: An Experimental Study', *American Economic Review*, 81, 1068–1095.

A. Rubinstein (1996) 'Why are Certain Properties of Binary Relations Relatively More Common in Natural Language?', *Econometrica*, 64, 343–356.

A. Rubinstein and J. Glazer (2001) 'Debates and Decisions, on a Rationale of Argumentation Rules', *Games and Economic Behavior*, 36, 158–173.

A. Rubinstein and J. Glazer (2004) 'On Optimal Rules of Persuasion', *Econometrica*, 72, 1715–1736.

A. Rubinstein and J. Glazer (2006) 'A Study in the Pragmatics of Persuasion: A Game Theoretical Approach', *Theoretical Economics*, 1, 395–410.

R. Selten and J. Pool (1991) 'The Distribution of Foreign Language Skills as a Game Equilibrium' In R. Selten (ed.) *Game Equilibrium Models*, vol. 4 (Berlin: Springer-Verlag), pp. 64–87.

R. Selten and M. Warglien (2007) 'The Emergence of Simple Languages in an Experimental Coordination Game', *Proceedings of the National Academy of Science*, 104, 7361–7366.

M. Spence (1974) *Market Signaling: Informational Transfer in Hiring and Related Screening Processes* (Cambridge: Harvard University Press)

S. Sperlich and J.-R. Uriarte (2014) 'The Economics of\Why Is It So Difficult to Save a Threatened Language?', Ikerlanak, IL 77/14. University of the Basque Country, Mimeo.

A. Tversky and D. Kahneman (1992) 'Advances in Prospect Theory: Cumulative Representation of Uncertainty', *Journal of Risk and Uncertainty*, 5, 297–323.

J.-R. Uriarte (2015) 'Politeness Equilibrium', Ikerlanak IL 86/15. University of the Basque Country, Mimeo.

P. Van Parijs (2011) *Linguistic Justice for Europe and the World* (Oxford: Oxford University Press).

R. Weber and C. Camerer (2003) 'Cultural Conict and Merger Failure: An Experimental Approach', *Management Science*, 49, 400–415.

J. W. Weibull (1995) *Evolutionary Game Theory* (Cambridge, MA: The MIT Press).

C. West and A. Graham (2011) *Attitudes towards the Gaelic Language* (Scottish Government Social Research).

D. Winford (2003) *An Introduction to Contact Linguistics* (Oxford: Blackwell).

Name Index

Note: locators followed by n refer notes

Subject Index

Note: locators followed by n refer notes

9 781137 325044